Media & Entertainment Law

SECOND EDITION

Ursula Smartt

With a Foreword by Michael Mansfield QC

Routledge
Taylor & Francis Group

LONDON AND NEW YORK

Second edition published 2014
by Routledge
2 Park Square, Milton Park, Abingdon, Oxon OX14 4RN

and by Routledge
711 Third Avenue, New York, NY 10017

Routledge is an imprint of the Taylor & Francis Group, an informa business

© 2014 Ursula Smartt

First edition published by Routledge 2011

British Library Cataloguing in Publication Data
A catalogue record for this book is available from the British Library

Library of Congress Cataloging in Publication Data
A catalog record for this book has been requested.

ISBN: 978–0–415–66270–3 (hbk)
ISBN: 978–0–415–66269–7 (pbk)
ISBN: 978–1–315–81563–3 (ebk)

Typeset in Joanna
by RefineCatch Limited, Bungay, Suffolk

MIX
Paper from
responsible sources
FSC® C013056
www.fsc.org

Printed and bound in Great Britain by
TJ International Ltd, Padstow, Cornwall

Contents

Foreword by Michael Mansfield QC

The importance of this book cannot be overestimated. Its timing alone is impeccable. The book's publication comes at a time of global meltdown in numerous related fields – political, economic and environmental. The forces at work in each of these arenas are underpinned by the dialectic, power, and the needs of instant communications. The demands of state and corporate vested interests on the one hand are desperately seeking to control how we know what we know, whilst on the other hand the awakening of popular conscience is inspired by the transparency and accountability afforded by the possibilities of the information highway. No part of any continent can be untouched by these movements.

We have arrived at the 'global village', a phrase coined by the Canadian philosopher and Professor of English Marshall McLuhan. More than forty years before the development of the World Wide Web, he had foreseen the ramifications of the electronic era. McLuhan popularized the idea that our technologies have a profound effect upon our lives, culture and history.

His works, *Understanding Media* (1964)[1] and *The Gutenberg Galaxy* (1962)[2] explored concepts which are popularly remembered in the well-worn adage 'the medium is the message'. A sequel to this became 'the medium is the massage'. The later book's opening chapter contains these poignantly prophetic words:

> The medium, or process, of our time – electric technology – is reshaping and restructuring patterns of social interdependence and every aspect of our personal life. It is forcing us to reconsider and re-evaluate practically every thought, every action and every institution formerly taken for granted.[3]

McLuhan's central thesis then was the dominance of the 'medium' over its content, which has been rapidly overtaken by the significance of the 'message' which can be conveyed across the globe in a moment – the 'message' has become the means. It has the potential to transcend temporal customs and laws, which struggle to keep up and grapple with the fallout.

With the medium of the internet and social media, we have all become world citizens with responsibilities for what we communicate. This has particular resonance for the weak, the vulnerable, the impoverished and the powerless. Oppression and exploitation are best countered by the universality of knowledge rather than the sword.

A major contribution to that knowledge is provided by the data and discussion in the chapters of this book. Here is a work which all of us, not just the lawyers, would do well to digest in order to assess and analyse the challenges we face at every stage of everyday life. This book is not some esoteric or arcane legal backwater, but the frontline or interface of our social relationships. It charts and pinpoints with alarming accuracy the shape of current dilemmas.

Ursula Smartt's book demonstrates that we are all entwined in a 'screen culture'. This at one time was limited to film and television but now embraces every form of information

---

1 See McLuhan (1964; reprint 2013).
2 See McLuhan (1962).
3 See McLuhan (1964; reprint 2013), Part 1, Chapter 1 at p. 9.

dissemination. Wherever you are, people are locked into their personal iPads, tablets, i-pods and mobile phones. Messaging is instant, social networking is rampant, and twitterspeak is prolific. We now occupy real space and virtual reality at the same time. We are almost more commonly identified by our electronic footprint rather than our physical appearance. Without a second thought we choose to place an enormous quantity of information about ourselves at the disposal of others.

As a result the boundaries of privacy are blurred to non-existence, and the tentacles of surveillance by state and corporate agencies are pervasive. It amounts to two sides of the same coin. It is the same facility which drives our private communication convenience as well as the aspirations of authority: the internet.

The last two years have witnessed an eruption of volcanic proportions whereby the tensions between these disparate and often opposing forces have been laid bare.

Internally the Leveson Inquiry has exposed an unhealthy relationship between three so-called pillars of the state – high-ranking politicians, the tabloid media and the police. Leveson revealed that methods were employed which struck at the very heart of our democracy and revealed a vein of unaccountable governance.

Externally the process has been even more seismic: from the massive WikiLeaks revelations contained in the 400,000 documents compendiously known as the 'Iraq War Logs' to the oppressive prosecution conviction and sentence of 35 years' imprisonment for Bradley Manning in the USA to the relentless pursuit of Edward Snowden on espionage charges. There was the unjustified nine-hour detention and confiscation of property on Sunday 18 August 2013 of David Miranda (friend of *Guardian* journalist Glenn Greenwald) under Schedule 7 of the Terrorism Act 2000; and finally the extraordinary government demand to the *Guardian* for the destruction of the hard drives containing US National Security Agency (NSA) documents, which was then overseen by GCHQ operatives in the UK.

What we have been witnessing is the very eye of the storm. The central thrust is a remarkable inversion in which the whistleblowers are hunted as spies whilst the perpetrators of illegality upon law-abiding citizens go unpunished. The magnitude of this operation implicates the United Kingdom. It should be of concern to us all. What is at stake is the threat to freedom of thought, conscience and expression, and ultimately the essence of truth itself.

This has been echoed by the European human rights watchdog, the Council of Europe, representing its 47 Member States, which moved quickly to question what the UK was up to. The Secretary General of the Council of Europe, Thorbjørn Jagland, observed that the detention of Miranda and the destruction of materials at the *Guardian* 'may have a potentially chilling effect on journalists' freedom of expression as guaranteed by Article 10 of the ECHR'.[4]

What has been uncovered is the capability and capacity to mine, monitor, record and store unlimited quantities of personal data produced by electronic means. This permits the possibility of manipulation, distortion and misconceived assertion.

The NSA in America, through its Prism program, is able to collect data directly from servers operated by companies such as Microsoft, Yahoo, Google and Facebook. There is close collaboration and financial input with GCHQ in the UK, which administers another programme entitled Tempora, which engages in mass tapping of the internet and phone traffic. The ultimate system was revealed on 31 July 2013 by Glenn Greenwald in the *Guardian*. XKeyscore is another NSA tool which can collect nearly everything on the internet, data that is known as digital network intelligence (DNI). Edward Snowden claimed he could accomplish this from his desk. The problem now is merely storage! The pretext for all of this activity is palpably thin: looking after our security and commercial welfare!

---

4 Source: 'Council of Europe asks UK to explain intimidation against the Guardian', by Nicholas Watt and Lisa O'Carroll, The *Guardian*, 22 August 2013.

Successive chapters in this book pinpoint with alarming accuracy the shape of current dilemmas. Clearly and concisely presented for ease of reference, the commentary is constantly accompanied by a historical perspective, citation of the appropriate ECHR articles and a comparative cross-border analysis.

The tensions described above surface in Chapter 1 with the concepts of freedom of expression and open justice confronting the individual right to privacy. The arguments surrounding the Justice and Security Act 2013 and the proposal for Closed Material Procedures (CMP) to 'protect secret service intelligence gathering' are redolent of the justifications put forward for mass secret cable trawls.

Chapter 2 deals with privacy and whether the internet has rendered 'the territorial demarcation of national jurisdictions ineffective'. Is there any aspect of life that can be characterized as private? Similar issues arise over obscenity in Chapter 7, given what is available at the press of a button online.

The culmination of this dialectic comes in Chapter 10, which traverses the Leveson Report (2012) with consummate clarity and precision. The author's perceptive and diligent research has brought to light, buried in the pages of the Report, the opposition of the Director of Liberty to the idea of statutory regulation of the press. On this Shami Chakrabarti was in agreement with Prime Minister David Cameron.

This is understandable when looking at the roles of the *Daily Telegraph*, over the parliamentary expenses scandal, and the *Guardian*, as outlined above. But the problem comes with unscrupulous media moguls, some of whom own more than one print outlet as well as online sites, and whose motivation is plain profit.

The information highway is saturated and it may be that the only real redress is not from the law but from the ability of the individual to control, collate and analyse what is significant and accurate and what can be ignored. Education is the key. Children under the age of five are keyboard and iPad proficient and from that moment need to realize that it is not just entertainment nor a game. There are messages; some obvious, some hidden, some beneficial, some corrosive. Otherwise, the risk is that 'we become what we behold. We shape our tools and thereafter our tools shape us.'[5]

Michael Mansfield QC
London
December 2013

---

5 McLuhan (1967), p. 23.

Preface

The second edition of *Media and Entertainment Law* is a fully revised publication at a time when legislation is fast changing, particularly in the entertainment branch of the law. The chapters (8 and 9) on intellectual property have been completely revised, providing readers and practitioners with the latest case law and details of changes in the duration of copyright in the music industry, both for the original copyright holder and now also protecting performances and recording artists.

Chapters 1 and 2 debate privacy and confidentiality issues, set against freedom of speech and media freedom, which was hard fought for by 'freedom of speech' fighters through the ages, from John Milton (*Areopagitica*, 1644) to Sir Salman Rushdie (*The Satanic Verses*, 1988), or more recently the 'Pussy Riot' members, with Yekaterina Samutsevich set free by a Moscow appeal court, leaving Maria Alyokhina and Nadezhda Tolokonnikova – found guilty of hooliganism and blasphemous religious rioting – serving a two-year prison sentence at a Russian prison labour colony (October 2012).

Wainwright v The Home Office (2003)[1] and **Kaye v Robertson** (1991)[2] confirmed that the UK does not have an established law of privacy. Individuals seeking to protect their private lives from media intrusion have instead brought their grievances to the courts via a number of creative means such as the law of confidence, defamation, Article 8 ECHR, breach of copyright and the Data Protection Act 1998. In the absence of any privacy legislation, the UK courts have been left to develop this area to such an extent that Sedley LJ said in **Douglas v Hello! Ltd** (2001):[3] 'we have reached a point at which it can be said with confidence that the law recognizes and will appropriately protect the right of personal privacy.'

The book reports on fast-moving human rights legislation, in a constant battle between Article 8 ('right to privacy') and Article 10 ('freedom of expression') of the European Convention with a growing body of UK and Strasbourg case law, moving on from Naomi Campbell's and Max Mosley's privacy litigations against British tabloid newspapers to the two *von Hannover* actions at the Strasbourg Human Rights Court (No 1 in 2005 and No 2 in 2012).

In **von Hannover No 1**, Princess Caroline of Monaco (married to German Ernst August von Hannover) was granted her Article 8 right, but not in the second. In each of these cases, the Grand Chamber had to decide whether the publication of private photos in German 'gossip' magazines (e.g. *Frau im Spiegel*, 2002; *Frau aktuell*, 2008) were in the public interest. In **von Hannover No 2**, the European Court of Human Rights (ECtHR) agreed with the German Federal Constructional Court that the magazines and tabloid press were entitled to report on the manner in which Princess Caroline and her family were taking a skiing holiday in St Moritz at a time when her father, Prince Rainier of Monaco, was seriously ill. The ECtHR dismissed Princess Caroline's constitutional complaint, rejecting in particular the allegation that the German courts had disregarded or taken insufficient account of Strasbourg case law as well as Article 8 ECHR.

---

1 [2003] UKHL 53 (HL).
2 [1991] FSR 62.
3 [2001] QB 967.

Chapter 2 discusses and features a number of recent superinjunctions, such as those sought by footballers John Terry, Ryan Giggs and Rio Ferdinand, or TV personalities, such as Jeremy Clarkson and Andrew Marr. Thanks to personalities like these, privacy law is expanding at great speed, though the 'media' judges do not always protect the privacy of celebrities, certainly not when mere reputation is at stake. Social networks are among the biggest challenges that media law currently faces. We can now see that Twitter is more than just a series of fragmented conversations, and it is even permitted to tweet in court during 'live' trials, if the judge has allowed reporting and accredited journalists to do so.

At the same time, libel law is changing and has changed. Without their legal stories, recounted in this book in detail, this book would have been a lot less interesting. And without their willingness to see their names in the law reports, the common law in the area of media law would not be so exciting. Chapter 3 charts the slow progress of the Defamation Bill from 2010 to its final Royal Assent in April 2013. The chapter provides an up-to-date account and full explanation of the Defamation Act 2013, but concludes that London may still remain the libel capital of the world in spite of the new legislation.

Chapters 4 and 5 essentially deal with court reporting. Contempt of court is a British peculiarity and must be adhered to by all journalists who report on 'active' court proceedings. It will be shown how the recent Attorney General, Dominic Grieve QC, has prosecuted those who do not obey strict liability contempt laws in the UK. Some victims have received not only justice for being persecuted but also compensation from the media, such as Christopher Jefferies (wrongly accused by the media of Joanna Yeates's murder, December 2010). Then there was jury foreman, Michael Seckerson, who contravened s 8 Contempt of Court Act 1981 by publishing an article in *The Times* on 29 January 2008, expressing his strong disagreement with the majority jury verdict of 10:2. He believed childminder Keran Henderson had been wrongly convicted of shaking to death 11-month-old Maeve Sheppard from Slough. Nowadays, criminal juries are specifically warned by trial judges that they must not talk to the media about matters discussed and deliberations during jury trials, nor must they tweet or use the internet during a trial.

In July 2010, 19-year-old juror Danielle Robinson was found guilty of contempt of court for sending text messages to another woman sitting in a second trial at Hull Crown Court. She had passed on 'gossip' from her jury room during deliberation to her friend in another jury room. Judge Roger Thorn QC called Robinson's texting a blatant attempt to influence a jury and said that her ignorance was no excuse for such contemptuous behaviour. She received an eight-month suspended sentence.

Chapter 6 discusses the impact of the Freedom of Information Act 2000 (FOIA) on public life. The book moves on from the first disclosures of the parliamentary expenses scandal in 2009 (discussed in the first edition of this book) to revelations in the Westminster Parliament in the **Trafigura** case, to the recent appeals against the Information Commissioner's decisions. Section 6.3 focuses on the row over the publication of letters from Prince Charles, the Prince of Wales to ministers, and the *Guardian* journalist Rob Evans's quest to gain insight into Prince Charles's letters since 2005 under the FOIA. In **Evans v Information Commissioner** (2012),[4] the Upper Tribunal (UT) had to consider the core question: would disclosure of the Prince of Wales's letters be in the public interest? Rob Evans's interest was not to engage in royal gossip but a genuine interest in the continuance of the monarchical system and the opinions and politics of the future reign of Charles III. The Attorney General (AG), Dominic Grieve MP QC, had intervened under s 53 FOIA (statutory veto), barring

---

4 [2012] UKUT 313 (AAC).

access to freedom of information in the Prince Charles case. Many legal and constitutional experts argued that the AG's decision to overrule the UT decision was wrong. The matter is still not fully resolved.

Where the law has not been moving and developing at such an alarming pace is in the UK's obscenity laws. Chapter 7 provides some astonishing case law covering the Obscene Publications Act of 1959, which still provides for prosecutions of theatre productions, art gallery directors and publishers if they provide material which may tend to 'deprave and corrupt' persons who come into contact with, for instance, an 'obscene' play, painting or book. The chapter moves on from the initial banning of D H Lawrence's *Lady Chatterley's Lover* to the play at the National Theatre *The Romans in Britain*, to the question of 'publication' on the internet in the context of the 1959 Act in relation to 'obscene' images which are either uploaded or downloaded by users. The Court of Appeal held in *Waddon*[5] that the content of US websites could come under British jurisdiction when downloaded in the UK. Section 1(3) of the Obscene Publications Act 1959 was duly amended to include electronically stored data or the transmission of such data.

Chapters 8 and 9 deal with new developments in intellectual property law, focusing mainly on the music and publishing industries. Music publishing technology and copyright legislation has moved on from Gilbert and Sullivan during the 1870s (section 8.2.2) to sampling contemporary composers and parodies of well-known artists on YouTube. Where does the law sit on peer-to-peer file-sharing? How long is the duration of copyright in songs and recordings? Thanks to 'Cliff's Law' (championed by Sir Cliff Richard) the EU Parliament finally implemented the long-awaited EU Copyright Term Directive 2011 (Directive 2011/77/EU).[6] The Directive extends the copyright and the related performance right (or 'term of protection') for music performers and sound recordings to 70 years. The implementation of the new Europe-wide legislation means that thousands of music performers, from little-known session musicians to Dame Shirley Bassey, will now receive royalties from songs released in the 1960s for an extra 20 years. Many of the most popular songs recorded in the 1960s were due to come out of copyright, including songs recorded by artists such as Tom Jones, the Beatles and, of course, the man himself, Cliff Richard. Copyright in their hit singles will now not expire until at least 2033.

The final chapter centres on the role of regulators. Some regulators have come and gone, depending on governmental preference and policy issues. When Prime Minister David Cameron set out to overhaul the 'quango' system (quasi-autonomous non-governmental organizations) in May 2010, he particularly declared war on Ofcom (the Office of Communications). Section 10.6 shows that Ofcom is still very much alive, now regulating not only broadcasting (largely the BBC) but also postal services and product placement on TV and radio, being the final enforcement agency for the Advertising Standards Authority (ASA – section 10.8).

The regulation of the film, games and commercial video industry is covered by the British Board of Film Classification (BBFC), a self-regulatory body with some statutory recognition such as the Video Recordings Act 1984. The impact of new media in general, and the internet in particular, continues to dominate the thoughts of those involved in the regulation of online audio-visual material.

The main focus of the last chapter is on the Leveson Inquiry into media practices and the phone-hacking scandal at the (now defunct) *News of the World* and possibly other tabloid newspapers. Leveson essentially recommended statutory regulation of the press, similar to the Irish Press Council model. The newspaper industry considered this an unacceptable violation of the freedom of the

---

5 **R v Waddon** (Graham) (2000) WL 491456 (6 April 2000).
6 Directive 2011/77/EU of the European Parliament and of the Council of 27 September 2011 amending Directive 2006/116/EC on the term of protection of copyright and certain related rights.

press – and if a statutory press regulator were to be set up, they would not join. *The Spectator* magazine's editor, Fraser Nelson, said as much.[7]

The Leveson Report, published in November 2012, resulted in recommendations which led to three different legislative proposals for the future of press regulation, replacing the Press Complaints Commission (PCC). The final question remains: should there be statutory press and online media regulation or should editors be free to self-regulate, therein retaining the freedom of the press which has been had fought for for centuries? Three different draft Royal Charters were presented to the Privy Council at the start of the new Parliament in 2013: one by the phone-hacking victim lobby 'Hacked Off', one by the Coalition Government and one by the newspaper industry, including some of the most powerful proponents, such as Rupert Murdoch's News UK, the *Daily Mail* publishers Associated Newspapers and the Telegraph Media Group. They announced that the new regulator replacing the PCC would be called the Independent Press Standards Organisation (Ipso), with draft constitutional documents published for consideration by some 200 news organizations (section 10.4.4).

The book concludes that the response to the Leveson Report has been plagued with confusion, not only in policy terms, but also in ensuing legislation. Arguably the media are surrounded by a wall of statute and common law, such as contempt of court, libel, surveillance (Regulation of Investigatory Powers Act 2000 (RIPA)), harassment (Harassment Act 1997), data projection, forgery and fraud (Fraud Act 2006). Will a Royal Charter on press regulation stop future malpractice such as intrusion into a person's grief and shock, topless photos of the Duchess of Cambridge and phone-hacking of innocent victims such as the Dowlers and McCanns? No doubt the malpractice of the *News of the World* has had a great impact on the future of journalism and media freedom, but law enforcement officers could have intervened and pursued such malpractice. Instead, we learnt that police and prison offers took bribes and back-handers for supplying information to investigative journalists. The Bribery Act 2010 could have stopped journalists paying police for information; RIPA could have easily been used to pursue and investigate all those journalists and editors who carried out surveillance, illegal phone-tapping or clandestine recordings of celebrities. The question then remains: do we really need statutory press regulation?

Ursula Smartt
Guildford
January 2014

---

7 Source: 'Why The Spectator won't sign the Royal Charter', by Fraser Nelson, *The Spectator*, 23 March 2013.

Acknowledgements

For the second edition of this book, there have been a large number of individuals and professionals who have given their support, time and advice to shape the contents of the book.

First to my husband **Mike Smartt OBE**, for his love, support and patience with me, getting up around 5am every morning for some nine months to write this book. When he reads the book, he will finally understand why I spent so much time in front of the computer 'nerding', as he calls it. I value Mike's encouragement to write 'yet another book', and thank him for delivering copious cups of tea. Above all I value his professional advice as an award-winning journalist with the BBC, which made some of the news sections in the book more realistic against their legal background.

I am indebted to **Michael Mansfield QC** for writing the foreword to this book. He has long been one of my legal heroes, more so after reading his autobiography, *Memoirs of a Radical Lawyer* (2010) and listening to his being a castaway on BBC Radio 4's *Desert Island Discs* (22 October 2010). He is such an eminent barrister and, what is more, some of his music choices, such as Rachmaninov's Second Piano Concerto, would have been mine, had I been invited by Kirsty Young to be a castaway on that programme. He is also an accomplished ballroom dancer, an interest that I share passionately with him, and we are awaiting our turn on *Strictly Come Dancing*.

I tell my students about Michael Mansfield's career as one of the best and most eminent barristers in the UK. 'You too can be like him,' I tell them, but you have to be tenacious and, at times, 'radical' (as he describes himself). I learn from *Desert Island Discs* that there have been threats to his life, as he represented the Birmingham Six, who were released in 1991, nearly 16 years after being wrongly convicted. He also represented the family of Stephen Lawrence, the teenager murdered in 1993; he assisted in both Doreen and Neville Lawrence's private prosecution to find justice for their murdered son, and in the Lawrences' continued fight for justice, such as allegations by a former undercover police officer in June 2013 that Doreen Lawrence's phone was bugged to 'find some dirt' on the Lawrence family during the murder investigation.

The list of high-profile cases Michael has taken on is incredible and so varied, such as acting for the family of Jean Charles de Menezes, the Brazilian man shot dead by the London Metropolitan Police at Stockwell Underground Station on 22 July 2005, after he was misidentified as one of the fugitives involved in the previous day's failed bomb attacks on the London Underground. Michael Mansfield also represented the families and victims of the 'Bloody Sunday Inquiry' in Derry and London. The Saville Inquiry became the longest-running and costliest inquiry in British legal history (1998 to 2010). Thirteen people died in Derry, Northern Ireland, when British soldiers opened fire on civil rights marchers on 30 January 1972.

Michael has represented many families at inquests, including the family of Patrick ('Pat') Finucane, the Belfast solicitor who was shot dead in 1989. His killing was one of the most controversial during the Troubles in Northern Ireland, as 39-year-old Finucane was considered a 'thorn in the side' of the security forces during the Troubles of the 1980s. And more recently, he has helped families of the Hillsborough victims, following the Hillsborough football stadium disaster on 15 April 1989 in Sheffield, during the FA Cup semi-final match between Liverpool and Nottingham Forest football clubs. The High Court had quashed the original inquest verdicts in December 2012, returned on 96 Liverpool football fans who died as a result of the 1989 disaster, ordering a new inquest scheduled for March 2014.

I would also like to take this opportunity to thank those who assisted my research for this book. They helped me gain clarity and more detailed insight into the legal, historical, political and socio-legal field. I want to thank them for their time, assistance and patience with my questions.

Lorna Aizlewood, Music and Intellectual Property Lawyer – Lorna is Managing Director of IMG Artists (Europe) and General Counsel to the Company. Previously she was the Global Vice President of Legal & Business Affairs for EMI/Virgin Classics. As with the first edition of this book, Lorna once again focused my attention on changes to copyright law and the complex layers of intellectual property (IP) law which now exist in UK and EU law. The structure of the IP chapters (Chapters 8 and 9) is largely due to her expertise and vast knowledge in this area of law. She continues to be passionate about protecting artists' copyright and is a tireless campaigner for the protection of performers' and artists' rights.

Cheryl Grant – Having been Vice President at Decca Music and Senior Publishing Executive at EMAP, Cheryl continues to provide me with unmatched knowledge and experience in the music and music publishing industry (as indeed she did for the first edition of this book). She has also shaped Chapters 8 and 9, providing practical examples of copyright and trademark cases which I could then incorporate in the chapters to make the law in the area more accessible. I admire her enormous creative drive and entrepreneurial skills. She founded White Label Productions (WLP) in 2002. As Chief Operating Officer of TargetMCG (of which WLP is a part), Cheryl now has one of the key strategic development roles in the UK's fastest-growing entertainment agencies. She championed the first edition of this book, which is now being used in the entertainment industry as a standard text for practitioners. Above all, she is my best friend, continues to make me laugh and encourages me to keep fit during my long hours of writing the book.

Campbell Cowie – Director of Internet Policy at the Office of Communications (Ofcom). Overlooking the Thames at Ofcom's superb offices on Southwark Bridge Road at the time when the London Olympics 2012 were at their peak in August, and the Royal Marines had just abseiled down the Olympic Rings from Tower Bridge, I met with Campbell to discuss the impact of the Digital Economy Act 2010. Trying to keep up with Campbell's enthusiasm and the speed with which he was describing the complex secondary legislation which was to accompany the 2010 Act, I knew that his legal knowledge and practical thinking would shape Chapter 10 of this book. Section 10.6 was particularly shaped by Campbell, who leads Ofcom's Internet Policy Team. His astute thinking has shaped Ofcom's policy on enforcing copyright breaches as well as educational policy. Campbell firmly believes that educational thinking will harness and shape the way young people in particular will view peer-to-peer file sharing in future. I found his technical and legal advice helpful, as well as his academic specialist advice as an economist, as other sections in Chapter 10 show. Ofcom now has enforcement powers not only in the communications, but also in postal services and advertising (e.g. product placement) fields.

Media lawyer **Mark Stephens CBE**, Partner and Head of International Law at Finers Stephens Innocent LLP, London – Mark also advised and shaped the contents of the first edition of this book. He also launched the book at the journalists' Frontline Club, Paddington, London, in May 2011 at the time when Mark was representing WikiLeaks founder Julian Assange, defending him against extradition to Sweden, where allegations on charges of a sexual nature had been made against Assange. This time, Mark was particularly influential in shaping Chapter 7, specifically with his knowledge of and personal background in 'obscenity and art'. Mark told me that he was inspired by his father, who was a fine artist. Mark is an avid art collector and has undertaken some of the highest profile cases in cultural property and art law. He also alerted me to the new legislation on 'extreme pornography', which made for an interesting afternoon's discussion on how this might be enforced by law enforcement agencies (if at all). Mark was also the founder of the Internet Watch Foundation (IWF) and now chairs the Contemporary Art Society.

Lord Avebury – my dear friend Eric. We met regularly at the House of Lords to discuss recent bills passing through Parliament, such as Lord Lester's Defamation Bill 2010 and the Justice and Security Bill 2012. Eric helped shape Chapter 3 (Defamation) which, during the writing of the text, I had to change three times, trying to keep up with frequent legislative changes as the Defamation Bill slowly progressed, particularly through the House of Lords. He continues to host visits for my law students and helps shape my other publications (e.g. *Optimize Public Law*, Routledge, 2014). Eric also introduced me to Lord Lester's legal team at the time they were drafting the Defamation Bill, and subsequently Lord McNally.

Joanna Dawson – Parliamentary Legal Officer and adviser to Lord Lester at the Odysseus Trust, Fleet Street, London. She pointed me in the right direction of the initial states of the Defamation Bill as it slowly ping-ponged through Parliament.

Paul Norris and Tony (Anthony) Jeeves – Legal Policy Team at the Ministry of Justice (MOJ), 102 Petty France, London SW1H 9AJ, with specific remit to consult on and revise Lord Lester's Defamation Bill, which then became Lord McNally's project in 2011–12. They both assisted with Chapter 3, as the Defamation Bill passed through both Houses of Parliament. In early 2013 we all feared that the Bill would be derailed by suggested amendments following the Leveson Report, as Lord Puttnam proposed an alternative clause to the bill in the House of Lords. At that stage, I feared this book would be published with 'old' defamation law. Fortunately, the Bill received Royal Assent in April 2013 just at the time the parliamentary period was drawing to a close. This means that this book is fully up to date with the Defamation Act 2013 and all the recent cases which have shaped British defamation laws to date.

My editors, **Fiona Briden**, Senior Publisher, and **Damian Mitchell**, Senior Editorial Assistant, who continue to believe in and enthuse about this book. They championed the new layout, cover and attractive overall appearance of the text which have made the book even more marketable and user-friendly. I particularly liked Damian's tenacity and persistence when setting very tight deadlines for the manuscript. It therefore amazes me that I managed to complete the full manuscript in nine months. I am also grateful for Fiona and Damian's understanding and kindness when (thankfully brief) health obstacles stood in my way. My grateful thanks of course also goes to the publishers, Routledge, for getting the book on the shelves in such a short space of time.

There are some people who made enormous contributions to the book, but whose identity I do not know. These are reviewers A, B and C. Their meticulous and at times annoyingly thorough reviews of each chapter of this book made it so up to date and legally precise that I can truly say 'thank you' to all three of you! I hope you are as proud of the book as I am. Unbeknown to you, all three of you provided very different advice: one of you provided detailed legal knowledge, the second paid greater attention to journalistic and media detail and the third created socio-legal awareness, and was pretty sharp on (self-) publication, copyright, providing up-to-date information on P2P file sharing and some rather obscure music choices.

The law in this book is accurate to the best of my knowledge as at 6 January 2014, based on recent case law and legislation. Views and legal opinions expressed are mine, as well as learned legal opinion expressed by academics and lawyers in the specific field of media and entertainment law (where cited). No liability can be accepted by me or the publishers Routledge (Taylor & Francis Books) for anything done in reliance on the matters referred to in this book.

Ursula Smartt
Guildford
January 2014

Glossary of Acronyms and Legal Terms

A

Acte clair (EU Law)	The idea that there is no need to refer a point of law, which is reasonably clear and free from doubt, to the European Court of Justice (ECJ), e.g. this court found the matter *acte clair* and declined to refer the interpretation of Article 5 to the ECJ.
Actio injuriarum (or: iniuriarum)	Scots private law 'injuries to honour'; action covers affront-based delicts such as defamation, wrongful arrest, personal molestation and harassment, breaches of confidentiality and privacy.
Acts of Adjournal	Scots law: regulations as to court procedure made by the High Court of Justiciary in criminal law.
Acts of Sederunt	Scots law: Acts passed by the Lords of Council and Session relating to civil procedure.
Acquis (communautaire)	EU Law; this is a French term meaning, essentially, 'the EU as it is', i.e. the rights and obligations that EU countries share. The acquis includes all EU law, such as treaties, Directives, Regulations, declarations and resolutions, international agreements on EU affairs and the judgments given by the Court of Justice. Accepting the acquis means taking the EU as you find it. Candidate countries have to accept the acquis before they can join the EU, and make EU law part of their own national legislation.
Adduce	Introduce.
Admissible evidence	Evidence allowed in proceedings.
Advocate	Scots law: a member of the Scottish Bar.
Advocate Depute	Scots law: An advocate appointed by the Lord Advocate to prosecute under his/her directions, and paid by salary.
Advocate General (Scotland)	UK Government Minister and the UK Government's chief legal adviser on Scots law.
Advocate General (ECtHR)	The Court of Justice is composed of 27 judges and 8 Advocates General. Advocates General are appointed by Governments of Member States for a term of six years (renewable) (see also: Court of Justice).
Advocate, Lord	Scots law: Senior Scottish Law Officer responsible for the prosecution of crime and investigation of deaths in Scotland, and the principal legal adviser to the Scottish Government.
Affidavit	A written, sworn statement of evidence.

AG	Attorney General. The AG is the Government's principal legal adviser. Usually a Member of Parliament, they provide advice on a range of legal matters. As well as carrying out various civil law functions, the AG has final responsibility for the criminal law. Their deputy is the Solicitor General.
Alternative dispute resolution (ADR)	Collective description of methods of resolving disputes otherwise than through the normal trial process.
A & R (Artists and Repertoire)	The division of a record label that is responsible for talent-scouting and the artistic development of a recording artist. A & R acts as liaison between artist and record label.
Anton Piller order	An *ex parte* court injunction that requires a defendant to allow the claimant to (a) enter the defendant's premises, (b) search for and take away any material evidence, and (c) force the defendant to answer questions (usually in copyright infringement actions). Its primary objective is to prevent destruction or removal of evidence. *Anton Piller* is not a search warrant. The defendant is in contempt of court if he refuses to comply. Named after the case of **Anton Piller KG v Manufacturing** (1976).
Arraign	To put charges to the defendant in open court in the Crown Court.
Arraignment	The formal process of putting charges to the defendant in the Crown Court which consists of three parts: (1) calling him to the bar by name, (2) putting the charges to him by reading from the indictment; and (3) asking him whether he pleads guilty or not guilty.
ASA	Advertising Standards Authority.
Assignment	The transfer of property or rights from one party to another (copyright).
Authorities	Judicial decisions or opinions of authors of repute used as grounds of statements of law.
AVMS	Audio Visual Media Services Directive.

B

BBC	British Broadcasting Corporation.
BBFC	British Board of Film Classification.
Bill of indictment	A written accusation of a crime against one or more persons – a criminal trial in the Crown Court cannot start without a valid indictment.
BitTorrent	BitTorrent tracker is a server that assists in the communication between peers using the BitTorrent protocol for peer-to-peer (P2P) file-sharing. These sites are typically used to upload music files.
BPI	British Phonographic Industry (originally 'The British Recorded Music Industry').

BSI	British Standards Institution.
BTOP	Broadband Technology Opportunities Programme – a US Government project.

C

Case stated	An appeal to the High Court against the decision of a magistrates' court on the basis that the decision was wrong in law or in excess of the magistrates' jurisdiction.
CDPA	Copyright, Designs and Patents Act 1988.
CFA	Conditional fee agreement (also known as 'no win, no fee' agreement) whereby fees and expenses only become payable in certain circumstances (most commonly used in personal injury claims but also in defamation cases). Until 1 April 2013, lawyers entered into CFAs at their own risk, and as a result of this a 'success fee' was usually charged in addition to the lawyer's standard fees if the case was won. If a success fee was also payable it was expressed as a percentage of the standard fee, although it could not be more than 100 per cent of those fees. Part 2 of the Legal Aid Sentencing and Punishment of Offenders Act 2012 (and associated Regulations and changes to the Civil Procedure Rules) abolished the recovery of success fees under CFAs and also abolished the recovery of ATE (after the event) insurance premiums from the losing side, with the exception of clinical negligence cases where some of the ATE premium was likely to be recoverable. From 1 April 2013, claimants are still able to use CFAs but will now have to pay their lawyer's success fee and any ATE insurance.
Champertous	A vexatious claim by a stranger in return for a share of the proceeds.
Community (EU)	In the 1950s, six European countries formed three organizations: the European Coal and Steel Community (ECSC), the European Atomic Energy Community (Euratom) and the European Economic Community (EEC). These three communities – collectively known as the 'European Communities' – formed the basis of what is now the European Union (EU). With the Lisbon Treaty in 2009 the word 'community' disappeared, replaced by the 'European Union'. Many texts still use the word 'community'; it means more or less the same as 'EU'.
Complainant	A person who makes a formal complaint. In relation to an offence of rape or other sexual offences the complainant is the person against whom the offence is alleged to have been committed.
Contempt of Court	Disobedience or wilful disregard of the judicial process (Contempt of Court Act 1981). 'Contempt' can also relate to any attempt to interfere with proceedings or to obstruct or threaten Members of Parliament in the performance of their parliamentary duties.

Convention	This term has various meanings, including (in the EU context) a group of people representing the EU institutions, the national governments and parliaments, who come together to draw up an important document. Conventions of this sort have met to draw up the Charter of Fundamental Rights of the European Union or new EU treaties; the European Convention on Human Rights and Fundamental Freedoms is also meant by this term (see: Convention right).
Convention right	A right under the European Convention on Human Rights (see: ECHR).
Counsel	Barrister. In Scotland a member of the Faculty of Advocates practising at the Bar.
Counterclaim	A claim brought by a defendant in response to the claimant's claim, which is included in the same proceedings as the claimant's claim.
Court of Justice (of the European Union)	[Formerly: European Court of Justice – ECJ] Based in Luxembourg, this court ensures compliance with EU law and rules on the interpretation and application of the treaties establishing the European Union.
CPD	Criminal Practice Direction.
CPR	Civil Procedure Rules or Criminal Procedure Rules.
Contra mundum	An injunction (restraining order) 'against the world'.
Cross-examination	Questioning of a witness by a party other than the party who called the witness.
Cy-près	Scots law: approximation; as near as possible.

D

DAB	Digital Audio Broadcasting.
Damages	A sum of money awarded by the court as compensation to the claimant.
Declaration of incompatibility	A declaration by a court that a piece of UK legislation is incompatible with the provisions of the European Convention on Human Rights (see: ECHR).
De facto	According to the fact; in point of fact.
Defender	Scots law: defendant. A person who disputes the claim of the pursuer and lodges defences (see also: pursuer).
De jure	According to law, or in point of law.
De minimis	*De minimis non curat lex* ('about very little there is no attention to law') means the law has no interest in trivial matters; something which is unworthy of the law's attention.
Deposition	Written record of a witness's written evidence.
Derivative work	A work that is based on (derived from) another work (copyright), e.g. a painting of a photograph. As the adaption of copyright work is a restricted act, unless covered under fair

	dealing rules, the artist will normally require the permission of the copyright owner before making a derivative work.
Devolution	The decentralization of governmental power such as the Scottish Parliament, the National Assembly for Wales and the Northern Ireland Assembly.
Dictum (pl. *dicta*)	'Remark'; refers to a judge's comment in a ruling or decision which is not required to reach the decision, but may state the judge's interpretation of a related legal principle.
Diplock courts	Juryless courts in Northern Ireland from 1973 to 2007.
DMB	A Digital Multimedia Broadcasting – Audio.
DNS	Domain Name System.
DOCSIS	Data Over Cable Service Interface Specification – a technology for next generation broadband services over the cable network.
DPI	Digital Phone Interphase Technology.
DRM	Digital Rights Management.
Draft Bill	A bill that has not yet been formally introduced into Parliament and enables consultation and pre-legislative scrutiny before a bill is issued formally. This process is known as pre-legislative scrutiny.
DS	Developers' System.

E

ECHR	European Convention on Human Rights and Fundamental Freedoms ('The Convention').
ECtHR	European Court of Human Rights: an international court set up in 1959 in Strasbourg; it rules on individual or state applications alleging the violations of civil, political or human rights set out in the European Convention on Human Rights (ECHR) (also known as 'the Strasbourg Court') (see also: Grand Chamber) (see also: HUDOC).
Estoppel	Equitable doctrine that may be used to prevent a person from relying upon certain rights or facts, e.g. words said or actions performed, which differ from an earlier set of facts.
Estreatment (of recognizance)	Forfeiture.
European Arrest Warrant (EAW)	The UK adopted the EAW in 2002, following the terrorism atrocities of 9/11. The EAW is widely used to secure the arrest and surrender of suspected criminals across the European Union. It has a key role to play in the fight against terrorism and in bringing those accused of serious crime to justice, such as Hussain Osman, a suspect in the London bombings in July 2005 who was sent back from Italy to the UK; in June 2005 Viktor Dembovskis, suspected of the rape and murder of Wembley teenager Jeshma Raithatha, was extradited to the UK from Latvia.

Evidence-in-chief	The evidence given by a witness for the party who called him.
Exemplary damages	Damages which go beyond compensating for actual loss and are awarded to show the court's disapproval of the defendant's behaviour.
Ex parte	A hearing where only one party is allowed to attend and make submissions, mainly in judicial review; now cited as, for example, ***R (on the application of Animal Defenders International) v Secretary of State for Culture, Media and Sport*** [2008] 1 AC 1312. Proceedings are *ex parte* when the party against whom they are brought is not heard.

F

Fair dealing (or 'fair use')	Acts which are allowable in relation to copyright works under statutory legislation. What constitutes 'fair use' may differ from country to country, but normally includes educational and private study and news reporting.
FOIA or FOI	Freedom of Information Act 2000.
Footprints	Deliberate mistakes or hidden elements that are only known to the author or creator of a work (copyright), e.g. the software designer who includes redundant subroutines that identify the author in some way.
Forfeiture	A broad term used to describe any loss of property without compensation. In contract law, one party may be required to forfeit specified property if the party fails to fulfil its contractual obligations. In criminal procedures, it is the loss of a defendant's right to his property which has been confiscated by the police when used during the commission of a crime. For example, the seizure by police of a car which was used during a bank robbery; or the forfeiture of illegal narcotics (possession of class A drugs).
Forum conveniens	A discretionary power in common law where a foreign court will accept jurisdiction over matters where there is a more appropriate forum available to the parties.
Forum non conveniens	As applied to a court which, although having jurisdiction, is not the appropriate court for the matter in issue. This doctrine is employed when the court chosen by the plaintiff is inconvenient for witnesses or poses an undue hardship on the defendants, who must petition the court for an order transferring the case to a more convenient court, e.g. a lawsuit arising from an accident involving a foreign resident who files the complaint in his home country when the witnesses and doctors who treated the plaintiff are in the country where the accident occurred, which makes the latter country the most convenient location for trial.
FTT	First Tier Tribunal (formerly: Information Tribunal). Appeals to the First Tier Tribunal are against the decisions from Government departments and other public bodies (see also: FOIA) (see also: Upper Tribunal – UT).

G

General Court	Formerly Court of First Instance as part of the European Court of Justice.
Grand Chamber	(of the European Court of Human Rights – ECtHR) The Grand Chamber is made up of 17 judges: the Court's President and Vice-Presidents, the Section Presidents and the national judge, together with other judges selected by drawing of lots The initiation of proceedings before the Grand Chamber takes two different forms: referral and relinquishment (see also: ECtHR).
Green Paper	A consultation document produced by the Government. The aim of this document is to allow people both inside and outside Parliament to debate the subject and give the department feedback on its suggestions.

H

Hansard	The official report of the proceedings of Parliament, published daily on everything that is said and done in both Houses of Parliament. In the House of Commons the Hansard reporters sit in a gallery above the Speaker and take down every word that is said in the Chamber. In the Westminster Hall Chamber they sit next to the Chairman. The Hansard reporters in the House of Lords sit below the Bar of the House, facing the Lord Speaker. The name Hansard was officially adopted in 1943 after Luke Hansard (1752–1828), who was the printer of the *House of Commons Journal* from 1774. The first detailed official reports were published in 1803 in *William Cobbett's Political Register* by the political journalist of the same name.
Harmonization	This may mean bringing national laws into line with one another; in EU Law this means removing national barriers that obstruct the free movement of workers, goods, services and capital. Harmonization can also mean co-ordinating national technical rules so that products and services can be traded freely throughout the EU (e.g. in copyright and IP law).
HRA	Human Rights Act 1998.
HUDOC	A database which provides access to the case law of the European Court of Human Rights (Grand Chamber, Chamber and Committee judgments, decisions, communicated cases, advisory opinions and legal summaries from the Case Law Information Note), the European Commission of Human Rights (decisions and reports) and the Committee of Ministers (resolutions) (see also: ECtHR).

I

IAB	Internet Advertising Bureau.
IC	Information Commissioner (see also: FOIA).

ICT	Information and Communication Technology.
IFPI	International Federation of the Phonographic Industry; represents the recording industry worldwide. IFPI safeguards the rights of record producers and expands the commercial uses of recorded music (see: BPI).
In camera	Court proceedings in private where the public is not allowed access, though the media may be permitted access by special permission from the legal adviser or judge.
Indemnity	A right of someone to recover from a third party the whole amount which he himself is liable to pay.
Informant	Someone who lays information.
Infringement (copyright)	The act of copying, distributing or adapting a work without permission.
Indictment	The document containing the formal charges against a defendant; a trial in the Crown Court cannot start without this.
Injunction	An injunction is a court order which orders a person to stop (called a 'prohibitory injunction') or to do (a 'mandatory injunction') a particular act or thing. A breach of an injunction is generally punishable as a contempt of court and in some circumstances can lead to imprisonment. Interim injunctions are either obtained 'on notice' or 'without notice'. With an 'on notice' application, the other side is told that the application for an injunction is being made and when and where it will be heard.
Inner House	Scots law: The two appellate divisions of the Court of Session, so called originally on the simple topographical ground that their courts lay further from the entrance to the courthouse than did the Outer House (see also: Outer House).
Intellectual property (IP)	A product of the intellect, including copyright works, trademarks and patents.
Inter alia	Among other things.
Inter partes	A hearing where both parties attend and can make submissions (see: *ex parte*).
Interdict	Scots law: The judicial prohibition issued by the Court of Session or Sheriff Court comparable with the English injunction. It is a court order sought to prevent a particular action being carried out.
Interested party	A person or organization who is not the prosecutor or defendant, but who has some other legal interest in a case.
International Court of Justice (ICTJ)	Judicial organ of the United Nations, based in The Hague. Those who commit crimes on a large or systematic scale such as genocide are tried here. The Court has roots in international legal obligations dating back to the Nuremberg trials, the most recent trials being the International Criminal Tribunals for the former Yugoslavia (ICTY) and Rwanda (ICTR).
IP	Intellectual Property (or Internet Protocol).

IPTV	Internet Protocol Television – television services delivered over the internet.
ISB	Independent Spectrum Broker.
ISDN	Integrated Services Digital Network – a data transfer technology using the copper phone network.
ISP	Internet Service Provider.
IWF	Internet Watch Foundation.

J

Jigsaw identification	The ability to identify someone by using two or more different pieces of information from two or more sources. The media refers to the 'jigsaw effect' in *sub judice* proceedings, where a person's identity is to be kept anonymous for legal reasons (e.g. children and young persons under 18).
Judge Rapporteur	EU law: the Judge Rapporteur draws up the preliminary report of the general meeting of the judges and the Advocates General before the Court of Justice known as 'measures of inquiry' (see also: European Court of Justice).
Judicial review	A remedy used by the Administrative Court (or the Court of Session in Scotland). If a public body (or authority) has made a decision in breach of any public law principle then that decision may be challenged by an individual or group action. Court proceedings can be by judge-alone hearings where the lawfulness of a decision or action made by a public body is reviewed. For example, where the challenge is based on an allegation that the public body has taken a decision unlawfully (*ultra vires*) and usually where there is no adequate alternative remedy.

L

Laches	Equity: A defence to an equitable action that bars recovery by the plaintiff because of the plaintiff's undue delay in seeking relief.
Law Lords	Highly qualified, full-time judges, the Law Lords carried out the judicial work of the House of Lords until 30 July 2009. From 1 October 2009, the UK Supreme Court assumed jurisdiction on points of law for all civil law cases in the UK and all criminal cases in England and Wales and Northern Ireland. The existing 12 Lords of Appeal in Ordinary (Law Lords) were appointed as Justices of the Supreme Court and were thereafter disqualified from sitting or voting in the House of Lords. When they retire from the Supreme Court they can return to the House of Lords as full members, but newly appointed Justices of the Supreme Court will not have seats in the House of Lords (see also: Supreme Court).
Leave to appeal	Permission granted to appeal the decision of a court.

Licence (Copyright)	An agreement in copyright that allows use of a work subject to conditions imposed by the copyright owner.
Limited right	Right by virtue of the HRA 1998 (see: HRA) – so that, within the scope of the limitation, the infringement of a guaranteed right may not contravene the Convention.
Lisbon Treaty	EU law: the current treaty on European union. The treaty was signed on 13 December 2007 in Lisbon, because Portugal held the presidency of the EU Council at that time. It entered into force on 1 December 2009. Technically, the Lisbon Treaty consists of several specific changes of Articles compared to the previous treaties.
Lord Chief Justice (LCJ)	The name given to the judge who presides over the Queen's Bench Division of the High Court (QBD). Since the passing of the Constitutional Reform Act 2005 the LCJ is now Head of the Judiciary of England and Wales, a role previously performed by the Lord Chancellor. In addition, he is President of the Courts of England and Wales and responsible for representing the views of the judiciary to Parliament and the Government.

M

Mandatory order (formerly: mandamus or 'writ of mandate')	Order from the divisional court of the Queen's Bench Division ordering a body (such as a magistrates' court) to do something (such as rehear a case). The writ can order a public agency or governmental body to perform an act required by law when it has neglected or refused to do so. Example: after petitions were filed with sufficient valid signatures to qualify a proposition for a ballot, a town council has refused to call an election, claiming it has a legal opinion that the proposal is unconstitutional.
Mareva order	*Mareva* injunctions (also known as 'asset-freezing orders') are court orders that negate the banker's duty to pay or transfer funds as per the instructions of the customer. A *Mareva* order is an interlocutory order (injunction), granted ancillary to a substantive claim involving money, that seeks to prevent a defendant from rendering a decree against him worthless by removing his assets from the jurisdiction of the court.
Master	Procedural judge for the majority of the civil business in the Chancery (Ch) and Queen's Bench Divisions (QBD). A Master at first instance deals with all aspects of an action, from its issue until it is ready for trial by a trial judge – usually a High Court judge. After the trial the master resumes responsibility for the case.
Master of the Rolls (MR)	Title of an English judge ranking immediately below the Lord Chief Justice. He presides over the Court of Appeal and is responsible for the records or 'rolls' of the Chancery Court (see also: Lord Chief Justice).
MCPS	The Mechanical Copyright Protection Society (now part of the PRS). Collects royalties whenever a piece of music is reproduced for broadcast or online.

Moral rights	Are concerned in copyright with the protection of the reputation of the author, in particular the right to be attributed with the creation of a work, and the right to object to defamatory treatment.

N

NDPB	Non-departmental public body which has a role in the process of national government but is not a government department, or part of one and therefore operates to a greater or lesser extent at arm's length from ministers (see also: Quango).
Nobile officium	Scots law: 'The noble office or duty of the Court of Session' is an equitable jurisdiction in the High Court of Justiciary or the Inner House of the Court of Session which can provide a remedy where none other would be available, or to soften the effect of the law in a particular circumstance.
Nolle prosequi	'Will not prosecute'; formal entry in the records of the case in the court by the prosecutor in a criminal case that they are not willing to go any further in the case. This means that the CPS withdraws the charge(s) against the defendant(s).
Norwich Pharmacal Order (NPO)	A *Norwich Pharmacal* Order requires a respondent to disclose certain documents or information to the applicant. The respondent must be involved in a wrongdoing (whether innocently or not) and is unlikely to be a party to the potential proceedings. An NPO will only be granted where 'necessary' in the interests of justice. Orders are commonly used to identify the proper defendant to an action or to obtain information to plead a claim. An NPO can be obtained pre-action, during the course of an action, and post-judgment. An NPO can be made in one jurisdiction to identify a defendant for the purpose of proceedings in another jurisdiction. For a third party to be liable to present the information requested by the claimant, they must have been involved, innocently or not, in the wrongdoing against the claimant. It must also be clear that justice will be served by the revelation of this information.
Notice of transfer	Procedure used in cases of serious and complex fraud, and in certain cases involving child witnesses, whereby the prosecution can, without seeking judicial approval, have the case sent direct to the Crown Court without the need to have the accused committed for trial.

O

Obiter dictum ('*obiter*')	Opinion given incidentally.
OECD	Organisation for Economic Cooperation and Development.
Ofcom	Office for Communications. Independent regulator and competition authority for the UK communications industries.

Offence triable either way (or 'either-way-offence')	A statutory criminal offence, which may be tried either in the magistrates' or Crown Court.
Offence triable only on indictment	An offence which can be tried only in the Crown Court.
Offence triable only summarily	An offence which can be tried only in a magistrates' court.
OFT	Office of Fair Trading. The organization promotes and protects consumer interests in the UK.
Ombudsman	Now 'Parliamentary and Health Service Ombudsman', which combines the two statutory roles of Parliamentary Commissioner for Administration (the Parliamentary Ombudsman) and Health Service Commissioner for England (Health Service Ombudsman). Investigates complaints from members of the public about government departments; has wide powers to obtain evidence; makes recommendations about cases s/he hears.
Open court	In a courtroom which is open to the public (see also: open justice principle; *in camera*).
Open justice principle	The public (and media) has the statutory right to attend most court proceedings – unless held *in camera* (see: *in camera*; see: open court).
Ordinary, Lords	Scots law: The judges who try cases at first instance in the Court of Session.
Outer House	Scots law: The part of the Court of Session which exercises a first instance jurisdiction (i.e. Inner House). The Supreme Court is split into these two Houses. The Judges in the Outer House deal with 'first instance' (new work) which has not been before a 'Court' but may have been before a tribunal or panel (see also: Inner House).

P

PACT	Producers Alliance of Cinema and Television.
Parliament Acts	The Parliament Act of 1911 was introduced to reform Parliament, and the House of Lords (HL) in particular. It deprived the HL of any power over Money Bills and gave the Speaker the power to decide what was a Money Bill. It allowed Bills that had been passed by the Commons in three successive sessions, but rejected by the Lords in all three, to become law. The Parliament Act 1949 reduced the powers that the HL had to delay a bill from becoming law if the House of Commons approved it. Since the Parliament Act 1911 the HL had been able to delay legislation for two years. The 1949 Act reduced this to one year.
Passing off (Copyright)	Using the work or name of an organization or individual without consent to promote a competing product or service.
Patent	A grant made by a government that confers upon the creator of an invention the sole right to make, use and sell that invention for a set period of time.

PCC	Press Complaints Commission.
Per incuriam	Through negligence, mistake or error.
Perjury	Offence committed by a witness in court proceedings involving the affirmation of a deliberate falsehood on oath or on an affirmation equivalent to an oath.
Petition	A document by which court proceedings are initiated, like a summons but used for specific types of case. Can have various meanings. An indictment is originally called petition until the Crown is in a position to indict the accused on the charges. In civil business the term also relates to certain types of applications to the court.
Phonogram (Copyright)	The symbol 'P' in a circle is a distinct right applied to an individual sound recording, which will operate separately from rights existing in the underlying musical composition.
PII	Public Interest Immunity certificate, where the prosecution contends that it is not in the public interest to disclose any sensitive material (secret courts) (see also *'in camera'*).
PLR	Public Lending Right.
PPL	Phonographic Performance Ltd licenses sound recordings and music videos for use in broadcast, public performance and new media.
Practice direction	Direction relating to the practice and procedure of the courts.
Precedent	The decision of a court regarded as a source of law or authority in the decision of a later case.
Preliminary ruling	EU Law: to ensure effective and uniform application of EU law, national courts can refer to the Court of Justice (or ECJ) and ask it to clarify a point in EU law; reference for a preliminary ruling can also seek the review of the validity of an act of EU law (Treaty provision).
President, Lord	Scots law: The highest civil Judge in Scotland, who presides over the First Division of the Court of Session.
Prima facie case	A prosecution case which is strong enough to require the defendant to answer it.
Primary legislation	Acts of Parliament.
Privilege	The right of a party to refuse to disclose a document or produce a document or to refuse to answer questions on the ground of some special interest recognized by law.
Privy Council	Privy Counsellors are members of the Queen's own Council: the 'Privy Council'. There are about 500 members who have reached high public office. Membership includes all members of the Cabinet, past and present, the Speaker, the leaders of all major political parties, archbishops and various senior judges as well as other senior public figures. Their role is to advise the Queen in carrying out her duties as monarch. Privy Counsellors are referred to as 'The Right Honourable Member'. The Judicial Committee of the Privy Council, situated in the Supreme Court building, is the court of final

appeal for the UK overseas territories and Crown dependencies, and for those Commonwealth countries that have retained the appeal to Her Majesty in Council or, in the case of Republics, to the Judicial Committee.

Procurator Fiscal
Scots law: literally, the procurator for the fiscal or treasury; now the style of the public prosecutor in the sheriff court.

PRS
The Performing Right Society. Body which represents music publishers (see also: MCPS).

PSB
Public Service Broadcasting.

PSN
Public Sector Network.

Pursuer
Scots law: the party initiating a law suit (English law: plaintiff or claimant).

Q

Qualified right
Right by virtue of the HRA 1998 so that, in certain circumstances and under certain conditions, it can be interfered with (see: HRA).

Quango
Quasi-autonomous non-governmental organization; also known as Non-Departmental Public Bodies (NDPBs). Quangos are organizations funded by taxpayers, but not controlled directly by central government. For example, ACAS (Advisory, Conciliation and Arbitration Service); the Big Lottery Fund; the Boundary Commission for Wales; UK Anti Doping (see: NDPB).

R

Remand
A criminal court sends a person away when a case is adjourned until another date; the person may be remanded on bail (when he can leave, subject to conditions) or in custody.

Reporter
Scots law: A person appointed to hold a public inquiry or to whom the court may remit some aspect of a case for investigation or advice (such as the Children's Hearings in Scotland).

Representation order
An order authorizing payment of legal aid for a defendant.

Resident Sheriff
Scots law: The Sheriff who holds the commission to sit at a particular court (as opposed to a Sheriff sitting part time) (see also: Sheriff).

Respondent
The party in a civil action defending on appeal.

Restraining order
Criminal law: A restraining order can be a significant part in managing the risks to a victim in preventing further harassment or harm. Conditions on the perpetrator can include: no contact with the victim; not to go near the victim's address, etc. (under s 12 Domestic Violence, Crime

and Victims Act 2004; or s 2 Protection from Harassment Act 1997).

Restraint order – Civil Restraint Order (CRO)	Civil law: a CRO is an order issued against people who have had more than one court claim or application dismissed or struck out for being totally without merit. The order prevents that person from issuing further claims or making applications in some or all of the county courts in England and Wales and also in the High Court, without first getting the permission of the judge named in the order.
RIPA	Regulation of Investigatory Powers Act 2000.
Royal Assent	The monarch's agreement to make a bill into an Act of Parliament.
Royal Commission	A selected group of people appointed by the Government to investigate a matter of important public concern and to make recommendations on any actions to be taken.
Royalties	A share paid to an author or a composer out of the proceeds resulting from the sale or performance of his or her work (copyright).

S

Security money (also known as 'surety')	Deposited to ensure that the defendant attends court.
Secretary of State	The title held by some of the more important Government ministers, for example the Secretary of State for Foreign Affairs. Usually a member of the Cabinet (the Executive).
Sending for trial	Procedure whereby indictable offences are transferred to the Crown Court (or 'sent') without the need for a committal hearing in the magistrates' court.
Set aside	Cancelling a judgment or order or a step taken by a party in the proceedings.
Sheriff	Scots law: Legally qualified person who sits in judgement at the sheriff court.
SI	Statutory Instrument. SIs are a form of legislation which allow the provisions of an Act of Parliament to be subsequently brought into force or altered without Parliament having to pass a new Act. They are also referred to as secondary, delegated or subordinate legislation.
Sine qua non	Latin for '[a condition] without which it could not be' or 'but for . . .' or 'without which [there is] nothing that can be effectively done'. The term refers to an indispensable and essential action, condition, or ingredient; a necessary condition without which something is not possible.
Skeleton argument	A document prepared by a party or their legal representative setting out the basis of the party's argument, including any arguments based on law; the court may require such

documents to be served on the court and on the other party prior to a trial.

Slander	Defamation: spoken words which have a damaging effect on a person's reputation.
SOCA	Serious Organised Crime Agency. SOCA tackles serious organized crime that affects UK citizens.
Solatium	Scots law: Extra damages allowed in certain delict cases in addition to actual loss – for 'injury to feelings' or 'wounded feelings' (see also: *actio injuriarum*).
Special measures	Measures which can be put in place to provide protection and/ or anonymity to a witness (e.g. a screen separating witness from the accused; or hearing child witnesses on a live link).
SSI	Scots law: Scottish Statutory Instrument. The form in which Scottish orders, rules and instruments, regulations or other subordinate legislation are made.
Stay	A stay imposes a halt on court proceedings, e.g. in contempt of court actions. Proceedings can be continued if a stay is lifted.
Strict liability	Not all offences require proof of *mens rea*. By a crime of strict liability is meant an offence of which a person may be convicted without proof of intention (*mens rea*), recklessness or even negligence. The prosecution is only obliged to prove the commission of the *actus reus* and the absence of any recognized defence (see ***R v Adomako*** (1994)).
Strike out	Striking out means the court ordering written material to be deleted so that it may no longer be relied upon, e.g. a police interview transcript.
Sub judice	A rule that prevents any journalist or Member of Parliament to refer to a current or impending court case (see: Contempt of court).
Subpoena	A summons issued to a person directing their attendance in court to give evidence (see: summons)
Summons	A document signed by a magistrate after information is laid before him/her which sets out the basis of the accusation against the accused and the time and place at which they must appear.
Supreme Court	The Supreme Court of Justice is the final court of appeal in the UK for civil cases. It hears appeals in criminal cases from England, Wales and Northern Ireland.
Surety	A person who guarantees that a defendant will attend court, usually linked to a bail hearing.

T

TEFU	Treaty on European Union (as amended by the Treaty of Lisbon).

Territorial Authority	A national authority which has power to do certain things in connection with co-operation with other countries and international organizations in relation to the collection of the hearing of evidence.
Time-shifting	A person is allowed to make a copy of a broadcast for private and domestic use to watch or listen to at a more convenient time, or for educational purposes, using methods such as video recording or the BBC iPlayer©.
Trademark (™ or ®)	A name, symbol or other device identifying a product or company. Trademarks are registered via national trademark or patent offices and legally restrict the use of the device to the owner; it is illegal to use the ® symbol or state that the trademark is registered until the trademark has in fact been registered.
Tribunal	There are tribunals in England, Wales, Scotland and Northern Ireland covering a wide range of areas affecting day-to-day life. HM Courts & Tribunals administers many of them although some are the responsibility of the devolved governments in Scotland, Wales and Northern Ireland, for example, employment tribunals or immigration and asylum tribunals. Tribunal judges are legally qualified; they usually sit with two tribunal members who are specialist non-legal members of the panel and include doctors, chartered surveyors, ex-service personnel or accountants.
Troll(s)	Internet slang: a 'troll' is someone who posts inflammatory or off-topic messages in an online social networking community, such as a forum, chat room, or blog, with the primary intent of provoking readers into an emotional response.
TSI	Trading Standards Institute.

U

Universal Declaration of Human Rights	Text adopted by the United Nations in 1948 in order to strengthen human rights protection at international level.
Upper Tribunal (UT)	The Upper Tribunal hears appeals from the First Tier Tribunal (FTT) on points of law, i.e. an appeal made over the interpretation of a legal principle or statute. Further appeals may be made, with permission, to the Court of Appeal (see also: FTT).

V

VCS	Video Standards Council – regulator of the video industry.
Venire de novo	A Queen's Bench Division (QBD) order requiring a new trial following a verdict given in an inferior court. In criminal matters the court of trial may, before verdict, discharge the

jury and direct a fresh jury to be summoned; and even after verdict, if the findings are so imperfect as amount to no verdict at all.

W

Warrant of distress (Distress warrant)	Court order to arrest a person.
Wash-up period	Refers to the last few days of a Parliament, after a General Election has been announced but before dissolution. All the unfinished business of the session must be dealt with swiftly and the Government seeks the co-operation of the Opposition in passing legislation that is still in progress. Some Bills might be lost completely; others might be progressed quickly but in a much-shortened form (e.g. Digital Economy Act 2010).
Wasted costs order	An order that a barrister or solicitor is not to be paid fees that they would normally be paid by the Legal Services Commission.
White Paper	A document produced by the Government setting out details of future policy on a particular subject. A White Paper will often be the basis for a bill to be put before Parliament. The White Paper allows the Government an opportunity to gather feedback before it formally presents the policies as a bill.
WIPO	World Intellectual Property Organization.
Without prejudice	Negotiations with a view to a settlement are usually conducted 'without prejudice', which means that the circumstances in which the content of those negotiations may be revealed to the court are very restricted.

Table of Cases

Table of Legislation

Legislation for England, Wales, Northern Ireland and Scotland
Unless otherwise stated, the following statutes cover the jurisdiction of Great Britain. Please note
that certain enactments may not extend to Scotland, Northern Ireland and the Channel Islands
where different legislation may apply.

Statutes

International Instruments

International Legislation

Denmark

France

Table of International Instruments and Treaties

Decisions

Directives

Resolutions

Chapter 1

Media Freedom

> **Key Points**
>
> This chapter will cover the following questions:
>
> ○ How has press freedom developed over time?
> ○ What are the boundaries of media freedom in relation to an individual's right to privacy?
> ○ What does the 'open justice principle' mean for public and media access to the UK courts?
> ○ What is meant by parliamentary privilege?
> ○ How does Scots law differ from English law in terms of personality rights and injury to feelings and reputation? Delicts and the doctrine of *solatium* and *actio injuriarum*.

1.1 Overview

See Chapter 5.3

See case notes below in 1.4.1

This first chapter links the concepts of free speech (or 'freedom of expression' as per Article 10 ECHR) to the open justice principle and therein an individual's right to privacy. Freedom of expression and freedom of the press are of course not identical, though the press (or media) often equate them.[1] The fundamental principle which exists to this very day in all British courts is the open justice principle and therein the right to freely report in the press whatever is heard in courts or tribunals, as long the media adheres to contemporaneous and verbatim reporting rules. This chapter will provide a historical overview by charting the limitations and punishments imposed on many writers over the centuries, many of whom fought for their freedom of expression. Throughout the text we will touch on Scots law and proceedings in Scottish courts, which tend to be different from English or Welsh law, such as different libel proceedings for 'injuries to honour' (*actio injuriarum*). All UK courts have one thing in common: the majority of judicial court proceedings are held in public – unless curtailed by statute (such as reporting on children in court proceedings). Lord Atkinson, as long ago as 1912, warned in **Scott v Scott**[2] that the long-standing doctrine that judicial proceedings must be held in public could be jeopardized by new legislation and that this, in turn, threatens freedom of the press to report court proceedings in a democratic society.

The Justice and Security Act 2013 provides for oversight of the UK Security Services, the Secret Intelligence Service, the Government Communications Headquarters (GCHQ) and other activities relating to intelligence or security matters. The bill, which drew a great deal of criticism from the Parliamentary Human Rights Committee, was introduced by Lord Wallace of Tankerness (Liberal Democrat) in the House of Lords (HL) in 2012, supported by the then Justice Minister, Kenneth Clarke. The 2013 Act provides for 'Closed Material Procedures' (CMPs) – commonly referred to as 'secret courts' – and limits public access in certain high-profile cases where national security is at stake. These CMPs prevent the making of court disclosure orders in civil proceedings of 'sensitive' information. This means that judges do not have complete control over such cases and defendants are not permitted to see all the relevant evidence against them (e.g. in alleged acts of terrorism). Special Advocates (SAs) are appointed by the Government to act in the interests of those whose

---

1   See: **Miami Herald Publishing Co. v Tornillo** (1974) where problems arose in respect of 'the right of reply'. The US Supreme Court overturned a Florida state law requiring newspapers to allow equal space to political candidates, thereby reaffirming the constitutional principle of 'freedom of the press' (First Amendment): state governments were prevented from controlling the content of the press. This case demonstrates the constitutional protection of a free press. See also: **Red Lion Broadcasting Co. v Federal Communications Commission** (1969) which gave protection to media freedom in broadcasting.
2   *Scott (Morgan) and another v Scott* [1913] AC 417 of 5 May 1913 (HL).

appeals are subject to CMP. The SAs are unable to disclose material to the person whose interest they represent, are not allowed to communicate with the person concerned without the permission of the Government and can never communicate with them about the secret evidence. This means that they are often required to contest evidence on the basis of guesswork and estimation.

See below
1.4.1

1.2 Historical development of free speech and press freedom

The history of freedom of expression is filled with struggles against the state and debates over democracy, which includes the rights and privileges of the press. This then provides an essential background to understanding the commitment of a modern democratic society to press (or media) freedom. It also explains the strength of feeling demonstrated by writers and many journalists who fought for freedom of expression. This argument became the focal point during the Leveson Inquiry.[3] Historically, the list of those who have led either public or private crusades for the advancement of free speech is endless and only a few can be mentioned here, such as the English poet and author John Milton in his *Areopagitica*, a speech given to the English Parliament in 1644 in support of the liberty of unlicensed printing.[4]

See Chapter
10.4.3

It was Magna Carta in 1215 – also known as the Great Charter of Freedoms – that first recognized free speech as the cornerstone of liberty in England, albeit in a very limited sense. In it, King John agreed to the right of barons to consult with and advise the king in Great Council. The final chapter of Magna Carta is the most important, confirming the people's right to free speech, a doctrine still relevant today – though for many centuries this was more a theoretical declaration than an actual reality.

See 1.2.2
below

From the advent of the printing press in 1476 until the end of the seventeenth century, state licensing meant that the Government and the Church could control the press, and in particular prevent the printing of seditious or heretical works. In Tudor and Jacobean England, press censorship existed as a means of royal repression and for the suppression of religious dissent. Under Elizabeth I, it was the Crown which, to all intents and purposes, controlled all printing (and therein 'copyright'). The Church also issued edicts of what could and could not be printed and used the Courts of High Commission and Star Chamber to enforce its will.

State control over printing tightened when, in 1538, Henry VIII decreed that all new printed books had to be approved by the Privy Council and registered with the Stationers' Company. This system of state control endured under a series of decrees issued and enforced by the Star Chamber. The licensing regime ended with the abolition of the Star Chamber in 1640. However, in 1643 licensing was reintroduced by Cromwell's Parliament in an effort to suppress the publication of material about Charles I. Clegg (2001: 4ff.) refers to this practice simply as 'censorship' that curtailed free speech.

See Chapter
8.2.1

The 1688 Bill of Rights granted the basic right of 'freedom of speech in Parliament', after James II was overthrown and William and Mary were installed as co-rulers.[5] Whereas Magna Carta can broadly be regarded as a declaration of the rights of the individual, the Bill of Rights is a statement of rights of the subject as represented by Parliament:

> . . . that the Freedome of Speech and Debates or Proceedings in Parlyament ought not to be impeached or questioned in any Court or Place out of Parlyament.

---

3   See: Leveson Report, The (2012).
4   Milton, J. (1644) *Areopagitica: A Speech for the Liberty of Unlicensed Printing to the Parliament of England.*
5   On 4 November 1677 the Protestant Mary Stuart married the Dutch Protestant William of Orange, Charles I's grandson. This marriage strengthened William's claim to the English throne. The Bill of Rights was confirmed by an Act of Parliament on 16 December 1689.

See Chapter 3

The Bill of Rights deals mostly with constitutional matters and 'parliamentary privilege', which guaranteed members of Parliament a certain amount of immunity including slander laws.

Freedom of speech in Parliament significantly related to debates and proceedings in Parliament, and that these ought not to be questioned in any court. In essence, parliamentary privilege was developed as a means of stopping a monarch from interfering with the workings of Parliament. Parliamentary privilege means that – to this day – Parliamentarians have the right to say whatever they like in Parliament without fear of being sued for libel or slander; though they may face parliamentary sanctions for breach of parliamentary conventions in relation to such things as discussing current court proceedings. It also means the media have a right to report what is said in Parliament, later enshrined in the Parliamentary Papers Act 1840. As time has progressed, parliamentary privilege now also covers debates in Parliament, tabled questions and notes.

Other basic rights enshrined in the Bill of Rights 1688 are trial by jury and the presumption of innocence:

> . . . that all Grants and Promises of Fines and Forfeitures of particular persons before Conviction are illegal and void.[6]

The free and fair reporting of proceedings in Parliament is a cornerstone of a democracy. In the UK, publication of fair extracts of reports of proceedings in Parliament made without malice – generally covered by *Hansard* – is protected by the Parliamentary Papers Act 1840. Such publications cannot be fettered by a court order.

The Bill of Rights 1688 was invoked as recently as 1 December 2010, when four members of Parliament tried to claim parliamentary privilege as a defence to charges of false accounting and misappropriation of public funds under the Theft Act 1968, resulting from the parliamentary expenses scandal in 2009. Sitting with nine Lords Justice, the Supreme Court unanimously dismissed three appeals by former MPs Morley, Chaytor and Devine.[7] The three appellants were subsequently committed for trial in the Crown Court on charges of false accounting, contrary to s 17(1)(b) of the Theft Act 1968. The charges related to claims for parliamentary expenses, concerning mortgage payments, IT services, rent for accommodation, cleaning and maintenance services, and the supply of stationery. Lord Hanningfield, member of the House of Lords, faced similar charges. In April 2011, former Labour environment minister Elliot Morley pleaded guilty to dishonestly claiming £32,000 of his parliamentary expenses. Jim Devine was found guilty a month earlier by a judge of falsely claiming £8,385 and was sentenced to 16 months' imprisonment. David Chaytor and Eric Illsley were also imprisoned for falsely claiming £22,000 and £14,500 respectively, and Tory peer Lord Taylor of Warwick was sentenced in May 2012 to 12 months in prison after being found guilty by a jury of defrauding the parliamentary claims system by more than £11,000 for travel and overnight subsistence.

See Chapter 3

Section 3 of the Parliamentary Papers Act 1840 provides that 'any extract from or abstract of' a 'report, paper, votes, or proceedings' of Parliament is immune from civil and criminal liability if published in good faith and 'without malice'. The right of the press to report matters in Parliament is also codified in statute in Schedule 1 of the Defamation Act 1996. This confers 'qualified privilege' of, generally, matters which are in the public interest, such as the Trafigura[8] affair.

See Chapter 6.3.4

---

6   Art 12 Bill of Rights 1688 (from the original).
7   **R v Chaytor and others (Appellants)** [2010] UKSC 52 (on appeal from the Court of Appeal (Criminal Division) [2010] EWCA Crim 1910).
8   Trafigura is the world's third largest independent oil trader and the second largest independent trader in the non-ferrous concentrates market with industrial assets around the world of more than US$3.3 billion. Trafigura controls a shipping fleet of around 100 vessels, and tankers are controlled through offices in Geneva, Houston, London, Dubai and Singapore, carrying around five million tonnes of crude, refined products and chemicals per month. Source: www.trafigura.com.

1.2.1 International law and freedom of speech

The First Amendment of the US Bill of Rights 1791 guarantees freedoms of religion, speech, the press and the right to free assembly.[9] In Europe, after the twentieth-century dictatorships of Adolf Hitler[10] in Germany, Benito Mussolini[11] in Italy and General Franco in Spain,[12] freedom of speech was formally identified as an absolute human right under Article 19 of the Universal Declaration of Human Rights of 1948.[13]

What all these dictatorships had in common was the implementation of severe measures to curtail press freedom and the systematic suppression of dissident views through censorship and coercion. For example, under Goebbels[14] during Germany's Nazi regime, a decree in 1935 banned any foreign press or radio broadcasts, punishing those who disobeyed the law with either imprisonment or the death penalty.[15] Other decrees banned national newspapers issued by the Catholic press (*Der Generalanzeiger*) but permitted the *Frankfurter Zeitung*, *Kölnische Zeitung* and *Deutsche Allgemeine Zeitung* since the regime needed these public organs to 'shape' public opinion abroad.[16] Further decrees paved the way for the National Socialist Press. In 1948, the Universal Declaration of Human Rights was adopted by the UN General Assembly. Its main aim was to promote human, civil, economic and social rights, including freedom of expression and religion, among all its subscribing nations. There followed the European Convention on Human Rights and Fundamental Freedoms ('the Convention' or ECHR), adopted in 1950. The ECHR is a unique reflection of the values of civilization and democracy, and a direct result of rebellion against Nazi excesses and suppression of freedom of expression in literature, music and art. It gives practical form to certain fundamental human rights, such as the right to life (Article 2), the prohibition of torture, slavery and forced labour (Article 3), and the right to private and family life (Article 8) and freedom of expression (Article 10). The subsequent International Covenant on Civil and Political Rights 1966 (ICCPR) recognized the right to freedom of speech as 'the right to hold opinions without interference'.[17]

1.2.2 Freedom of speech fighters

One of the key issues of the English Civil War (1642 to 1649) was freedom of speech and one of the first great proponents of free speech was Cromwell's secretary, the great poet John Milton, who vehemently opposed literary censorship, a view he argued so eloquently in his *Areopagitica* (1644), after Parliament had issued the 'Licensing Order of 16 June 1643' which was designed to bring publishing (and therein copyright) under Crown control by creating a number of official censors. This Act incensed Milton to write:

---

9 The first 10 amendments to the US Constitution are collectively known as the 'Bill of Rights'; there are five freedoms guaranteed by the First Amendment, the fifth being the right 'to petition the government for a redress of grievances'.
10 Chancellor of Nazi Germany 1933–45.
11 Italian Fascist dictator and founder of the Organizzazione per la Vigilanza e la Repressione dell'Antifascismo (OVRA) (Organization for Vigilance and Repression of Anti-Fascism), 1927–45, the Italian equivalent of the German Gestapo.
12 General Francisco Franco, the military head of Spain from 1936 to 1975.
13 The Universal Declaration of Human Rights (UDHR) is a milestone document in the history of human rights. Drafted by representatives with different legal and cultural backgrounds from all regions of the world, the Declaration was proclaimed by the United Nations General Assembly in Paris on 10 December 1948 (Resolution 217 A III).
14 Joseph Goebbels was the German Minister of Propaganda from 1933 to 1945.
15 Decree issued on 24 April 1935 by President Amann of the Reich Press Chamber.
16 Source: *New York Times* (2001) Political Censorship, pp. 119ff.
17 International Covenant on Civil and Political Rights (ICCPR), United Nations Treaty, New York, 16 December 1966. UN Treaty Series, vol. 999, p. 171 and vol. 1057, p. 407 (procès-verbal of rectification of the authentic Spanish text); depositary notification C.N.782.2001.

> The attempt to keep out evil doctrine by licensing is like the exploit of that gallant man who thought to keep out the crows by shutting his park gate . . . Lords and Commons of England, consider what nation it is whereof ye are: a nation not slow and dull, but of a quick, ingenious and piercing spirit. It must not be shackled or restricted. Give me the liberty to know and to utter and to argue freely according to conscience, above all liberties.[18]

No doubt Milton was referring to the writings of the Athenian orator Isocrates (436–338 BC) who published his speeches in his *Areopagiticus*, where he referred to the rule of law which requires that citizens obey the laws. Isocrates argues that democracy established in Athens was designed to be impartial and create better citizens; one of the main principles of a democratic society was freedom of speech.[19]

Milton's plea went unheeded and for the next half century the press was governed under a licensing system which suppressed all but official publications. Licensing eventually ended in 1695 when the House of Commons refused to renew the licensing legislation. Ever since the licensing of the press was abolished, there has existed a general right to publish newspapers, books or magazines without state authorisation. *Areopagitica* remains the most influential and eloquent philosophical work defending the principle of the right to freedom of speech and embodies the cornerstone of press freedom. Pre-publication licensing was abolished in 1695.

See Chapter
7.2.1

There were still a large number of constraints on freedom of the press which remained in place until recent times, such as the offences of criminal and seditious libel, which remained punishable at common law. The outdated offences of criminal libel and sedition were finally abolished under s 73 of the Coroners and Justice Act 2009, thus sweeping away the old common law offences of sedition, seditious libel, obscene libel and defamatory libel.

In 1738, Parliament banned reporting in print of the proceedings of both Houses of Parliament, and the Stamp Act 1712 introduced taxes (a 'stamp duty') on the press. Such 'taxes on knowledge', intended to curb the radical press, created a culture in which journalists and newspapers subsisted through bribes and government subsidies. The Stamp Act 1712 marked a crucial change in government thinking about the press and could be seen as the first press regulation of its time. The Act continued to be in operation until 1885.[20]

One of the causes of the French Revolution of 1789 during the bourgeoisie's struggle for 'liberté, égalité, fraternité' was the egalitarian principle of freedom of speech which led to the *Déclaration des droits de l'homme et du citoyen* ('Declaration of the Rights of Man and Citizen') in 1793. Additionally, the European educated middle classes were inspired by philosophers such as Immanuel Kant, Voltaire, Jean-Jacques Rousseau and John Locke, who had spread the ideas and values of the Age of Enlightenment through the late seventeenth and early eighteenth centuries, when the concepts of equality and freedom of the individual had become paramount.

When Edmund Burke, an intellectual Protestant and Whig in Parliament, published his criticism of the French Revolution in his *Reflections* (1790), he repudiated the belief in divinely appointed monarchic authority and the idea that the people had no right to depose an oppressive government. Burke advocated that citizens should have a stake in their nation's social order which would aid constitutional reform (rather than by revolution, as in France). Burke advocated specific individual rights such as freedom of speech including writing and printing – a form of freedom of expression against oppression by Government. Burke famously detested injustice and abuse of power.

---

18 Milton (1644) at p. 41.
19 Isocrates. *Isocrates with an English Translation in three volumes*, by George Norlin, PhD, LLD. Cambridge, MA, Harvard University Press; London, William Heinemann Ltd. 1980.
20 For further discussion see: Downie (1979).

English philosopher John Stuart Mill fought for freedom of speech in Parliament and in his writings. In his essay *On Liberty* (1859) he argued in favour of tolerance, individuality and freedom of expression:

> . . . if any opinion is compelled to silence, that opinion may, for aught we can certainly know, be true. To deny this is to assume our own infallibility.[21]

Mill argued for a 'liberty of the press' as paramount safeguard against 'corrupt or tyrannical government':[22]

> . . . though the law of England, on the subject of the press, is as servile to this day as it was in the time of the Tudors, there is little danger of its being actually put in force against political discussion, except during some temporary panic, when fear of insurrection drives ministers and judges from their propriety . . . The best government has no more title to it than the worst. It is as noxious, or more noxious, when exerted in accordance with public opinion, than when in opposition to it.

> . . . But the peculiar evil of silencing the expression of an opinion is, that it is robbing the human race; posterity as well as the existing generation; those who dissent from the opinion, still more than those who hold it.[23]

During the Second World War, government censorship returned in the form of the Defence of the Realm Regulations, which was secondary legislation which could be passed without consultation to Parliament under the Defence of the Realm Act 1914 (DORA).[24] Regulation 2D conferred on the Home Secretary the personal power to ban any publication which published 'material calculated to foment opposition' to the war. DORA severely curtailed and censored published information during the wars which was thought to be indirectly or directly of use to the enemy; this became an offence punishable by either a fine or imprisonment. Information forbidden by the legislation in the press included any description of war and any news that was likely to cause any conflict between the public and military authorities. In a memorandum to the Churchill War Cabinet Office on 8 October 1940,[25] the then Home Secretary, Sir John Anderson, explains the purpose of Regulation 2D, namely, to stop any newspaper publications which impede the war effort:

> Under Defence Regulation 2D, 'If the Secretary of State is satisfied that there is in any newspaper a systematic publication of matter which is in his opinion calculated to foment opposition to the prosecution to a successful issue of any war in which His Majesty is engaged, he may by Order apply the provisions of this Regulation to that newspaper'.

Relying on this power, the Government closed down two communist papers and warned the *Daily Mirror* and the *Sunday Pictorial* that the papers should cease publishing anti-Government war

---

21 Mill (1859), Introduction, p. 26.
22 For further discussion see: Wragg (2013b).
23 Mill (1859), Chapter II, 'Of the liberty of thought and discussion', pp. 30ff.
24 On 8 August 1914 the House of Commons passed the Defence of the Realm Act (DORA) without debate. The legislation gave the Government executive powers to suppress published criticism, imprison without trial and to commandeer economic resources for the war effort.
25 Source: Memorandum by the Home Secretary 8 October 1940: 'This document is the property of his Britannic Majesty's Government. Secret Copy No W.P. (40) 402. 8th October 1940. War Cabinet. Subversive Newspaper Propaganda'. The National Archives at: http://ukwarcabinet.s3.amazonaws.com/documents/cab-66-12-32-0001.pdf.

propaganda. The Home Secretary's memorandum quotes a number of leader columns from the papers. Here is an example of 'propaganda' from the *Daily Mirror*, with a leader from 1 October 1940:

> When Parliament is allowed to meet again, will M.Ps. be able openly to ask a few questions concerning the conduct of the war? . . . . . are we to waste our fighting strength in futile clashes at remote strategical points? . . . . . will Dakar be the last of these fumbling fiascos . . . . . will our two oddly selected London Defence dictators cancel the Committee imbroglio and hasten their job of getting London ready for the long winter night raids . . . . . shall we hear less tosh about having already won the war or about winning it in 1950 or later, and get on with the winning of it from day to day.[26]

Following mass rallies in response, the ban was lifted. In general, however, the press response to the unprecedented levels of government censorship which characterized the war period was muted, as expressed by George Orwell:

> Any fair-minded person with journalistic experience will admit that during this war official censorship has not been particularly irksome. We have not been subjected to the kind of totalitarian 'co-ordination' that it might have been reasonable to expect. The press has some justified grievances, but on the whole the Government has behaved well and has been surprisingly tolerant of minority opinions. The sinister fact about literary censorship in England is that it is largely voluntary.[27]

Freedom of expression was then enshrined in Article 10 of the European Convention of Human Rights and Fundamental Freedoms ('the Convention' or 'ECHR') in 1950. Though Article 10 is a protection for individual rather than corporate freedom of expression, and does not expressly refer to the media, journalistic freedom has consistently been recognized in case law (both in common law as well as Strasbourg jurisdiction) as protected speech. In this regard, the European Court of Human Rights (ECtHR) has emphasized the pre-eminent role of the press in a democratic society and its duty to act as a 'public watch-dog', as expressed by the ECtHR in the 'Spycatcher action'.[28]

In both **Spycatcher No 1** and **No 2** actions in the UK courts,[29] temporary injunctions had been imposed in relation to the book *Spycatcher*, the memoirs of former MI5 spy Peter Wright, then living in Australia. The book includes an account of allegedly illegal activities by the British Security Services. Some extracts of Peter Wright's book had previously been published in the UK by the Guardian & Observer and Times newspaper groups, as well as quoted in other books and in television interviews. In September 1985 the Attorney General of England and Wales commenced proceedings in Australia on behalf of the British Government to restrain publication of the *Spycatcher* memoirs. But the UK court could not enforce an injunction against a foreign court, and the Court of Appeal of New South Wales found in favour of Peter Wright and his (Australian) publishers. The book was subsequently also published in Canada and the United States.

On 14 February 1989, Valentine's Day, British Indian author Salman Rushdie was telephoned by a BBC journalist and told that he had been 'sentenced to death' by the Ayatollah Khomeini. For

See Chapter
2.2.5

---

26 Ibid.
27 'The Freedom of the Press', proposed preface to *Animal Farm* (1945), publication of which was delayed until the end of the war to avoid causing offence to the Soviet Union. Source: http://home.iprimus.com.au/korob/Orwell.html.
28 **Observer and Guardian v UK** (1992) 14 EHRR 153, para 59 (ECtHR).
29 See: *AG v Guardian Newspapers Ltd* **(No 1)**; *AG v Observer Ltd*; *AG v Times Newspapers Ltd* [1987] 1 WLR 1248 ('Spycatcher case'); see also: *AG v Guardian Newspapers Ltd* **(No 2)** [1990] 1 AC 109 ('Spycatcher No 2').

the first time he heard the word *fatwa*. His crime? To have written a novel called *The Satanic Verses* (1988)[30] which was accused of being 'against Islam, the Prophet and the Qur'an'. Sir Salman Rushdie became another dissident who had to live in exile for his writings. In his memoirs, *Joseph Anton* (2012),[31] Rushdie describes the extraordinary story of his life in exile, forced underground, living with the constant presence of an armed police protection team. He was asked to choose an alias that the police could call him by. He thought of writers he loved and combinations of their names; then it came to him: Conrad and Chekhov – *Joseph Anton*. His story is of one of the crucial battles for freedom of speech.

In April 1989 two bookshops, Dillons and the left-wing Collets, were firebombed for stocking the Rushdie novel. There followed explosions in High Wycombe and London's King's Road and a bomb in Liberty's department store, which had a Penguin bookshop – because Penguin had published *Satanic Verses*. Rushdie lived in secretly guarded exile for 10 years until 1998 when the *fatwa* was withdrawn.

In November 2002, Nigerian journalist Isioma Daniel incensed Muslims in her country by writing about the Prophet Muhammad in a newspaper article. In her fashion column for a Lagos newspaper she commented about the Miss World pageant which was about to be held in Nigeria:

> . . . the Muslims thought it was immoral to bring 92 women to Nigeria and ask them to revel in vanity. What would Mohammed think? In all honesty, he would probably have chosen a wife from one of them.[32]

A *fatwa* was issued on Isioma Daniel by the deputy governor of Zamfara State because her article had incited major religious riots for being held a 'blasphemous' publication. Information Minister Umar Dangaladima reiterated Zamfara state policy by his public announcement:

> . . . it's a fact that Islam prescribes the death penalty on anybody, no matter his faith, who insults the Prophet.[33]

The killing of film-maker Theo van Gogh on 2 November 2004 shocked the Dutch nation, crystallizing fears about international terrorism and national identity in the Netherlands where 20 per cent of the population is of foreign descent. Van Gogh's killer, 27-year-old Mohammed Bouyeri, an Amsterdam-born Muslim of Moroccan descent, pleaded guilty to murder and was given a life sentence on 27 July 2005. The motive for the killing was van Gogh's film *Submission*, released in 2004. It told the fictional stories of four Muslim women who suffered physical and sexual abuse. Verses from the Qur'an were superimposed on the bodies of the semi-naked women, which many Muslims found deeply offensive. Van Gogh believed that the film would encourage public discourse.[34]

In February 2009, the far-right Dutch politician Geert Wilders, who leads his own 'Freedom party' in the Netherlands, the anti-Islam PVV (*Partij voor de Vrijheid*), was prevented from entering Britain by Labour Home Secretary Jacqui Smith, who argued that his presence was likely to incite racial hatred. Wilders antagonized the Muslim world by calling for a ban on the Qur'an, which he likened to Adolf Hitler's *Mein Kampf*. The 'Freedom Party' went from winning nine seats in the 2006 election to 24 in 2010, taking a bigger share of the vote than the Christian Democrats – the main

---

30 The title refers to a group of Qur'anic verses that allow for prayers of intercession to be made to three pagan goddesses in Mecca. See: Rushdie (1989; new edition 1998).
31 See: Rushdie (2012).
32 Source: *Thisday* press office release, Kaduna, 27 November 2002.
33 Source: 'Fatwa is issued against Nigerian journalist', by James Astill and Owen Bowcott, *Guardian*, 27 November 2002.
34 Source: 'Unrepentant killer of Dutch film-maker jailed for life', by Ian Traynor, *Guardian*, 27 July 2005.

party in the outgoing Dutch Government. Wilders had planned to show a film, called *Fitna* (Arabic for strife), to members of the House of Lords in 2009, which denounces Islam as a 'fascist' religion. The film shows the aftermath of Islamist terror atrocities, including 9/11 and the 7/7 London bombings, intercut with selected verses from the Qur'an. Wilders won his appeal in October 2009 before the Asylum and Immigration Tribunal, arguing successfully his Article 10 rights on grounds of freedom of speech.

In *Centro Europa 7 S.R.L. and Di Stefano v Italy* (2012),[35] the Strasbourg human rights court recognized the importance of pluralism in the media, noting that 'there can be no democracy without pluralism. Democracy thrives on freedom of expression.'

Centro Europa[36] concerned an Italian TV company's inability to broadcast, despite having a broadcasting licence, due to lack of television frequencies allocated to it. The Italian broadcasting authorities had granted the company a licence for national TV broadcasting via Hertzian waves in 1999, but the national frequency allocation plan of 1998 was never implemented. Due to a series of interim legislative schemes, existing TV channels were allowed to extend their use of frequencies that they should in principle have given up. As a result, Centro Europa had no frequency attributed to it and it was unable to broadcast. The applicants complained that this amounted to an unjustified breach of their right to impart information, relying on Article 10 ECHR (freedom of expression and information), and that they had suffered discrimination, relying on Article 14 (prohibition of discrimination) of the Convention.

The ECtHR held by 16 votes to 1 that there had been a violation of Article 10 ECHR and ruled that the respondent state (Italy) was to pay the applicant company €10,000,000 (ten million euros) within three months (plus any tax in respect of pecuniary and non-pecuniary damage). The court held unanimously that Italy was to pay the applicant company a further €100,000 (one hundred thousand euros), plus any tax that may be chargeable to the applicant company, in respect of costs and expenses within three months.[37]

While most European countries, including the former Communist-controlled countries of Eastern Europe, are signatories to the European Convention on Human Rights (ECHR), and thus subscribe to Article 10, liberal democratic notions of 'freedom of expression' accepted in countries such as the UK, France and Germany still struggle for full acceptance, as was illustrated by the recent prosecution in Russia of the Pussy Riot group.

In August 2012 Russian judge Marina Syrova sentenced three members of the punk bank Pussy Riot to two years in a prison-labour camp for staging a 40-second punk feminist 'flash mob' inside Moscow's official church as they performed a 'punk prayer'. One Pussy Riot member, Yekaterina Samutsevich, was set free by a Moscow appeal court in October 2012, leaving Maria Alyokhina and Nadezhda Tolokonnikova – found guilty of hooliganism and blasphemous religious rioting – to serve two years in a Russian labour colony.[38] No doubt the punk band members had offended many Russian Orthodox believers by screaming lyrics such as 'Shit, shit, the Lord's shit' inside the Cathedral of Christ the Saviour, but the trial itself became an old-fashioned Soviet show trial, one of the first criminal crackdowns of President Vladimir Putin's campaign against political activists. It seems that not much has changed since Russian dissident Aleksandr Solzhenitsyn experienced a Siberian labour camp ('the Gulag') during the Stalinist era, for publishing his famous autobiographical account *One Day in the Life of Ivan Denisovich* some fifty years ago.[39] Today, this novel by the

35 (2012) (Application No: 38433/09). [2012] ECHR 974 (ECTHR). Grand Chamber judgment of 7 June 2012.
36 The applicants were Centro Europa 7 S.R.L., an Italian company based in Rome, and Francescantonio Di Stefano, its statutory representative.
37 Ibid., at para 227 (judgment delivered by Françoise Tulkens, President, Grand Chamber, ECtHR).
38 Source: 'One Pussy Riot member walks free as her bandmates wait to be sent to prison camp', by Miriam Elder, *Guardian*, 11 October 2012.
39 Aleksandr Solzhenitsyn, *One Day in the Life of Ivan Denisovich* (first published in the Soviet literary magazine *Noviy Mir* ('New World') in November 1962).

postmodernist writer is seen as a courageous endeavour of freedom of speech, where Solzhenitsyn writes about his own experience of the Gulag, imprisoned for eight years after 1945 for writing derogatory comments about Joseph Stalin, when serving in the Red Army during the Second World War.

1.3 Theoretical foundations of media freedom

Media freedom can be defined as the ability and opportunity for journalists to say and write what they want without restriction or interference from the state and elsewhere. Though the UK prides itself on having a free press, journalistic activities today are restricted by numerous pieces of legislation, the majority of which form the subject matter of this book. As common law has developed, particularly in the area of human rights, it will be demonstrated that the courts have attempted to strike a fine balance between the freedoms and responsibilities of the press, while safeguarding an individual's right to privacy.

See Chapter 2

1.3.1 Censorship and freedom of expression

Every society determines its own position on freedom of expression according to its own history and constitutional make-up. This means that the laws governing such freedoms will change over time. Many constitutions and international treaties now guarantee freedom of speech, such as the German Constitution (*Grundgesetz*), which was certainly not the case during the Third Reich or the Weimar Republic.[40]

See Chapter 1.2.1

The struggle for press freedom in England resulted in a royal proclamation in 1534, requiring pre-publication licensing, particularly in relation to religious matters. The Tudor and Stuart monarchs introduced restrictive measures in the form of censorship, particularly aimed at political and religious criticism. Severe restrictions on the press also existed in seditious libel and blasphemy laws, which made it an offence to criticize the Government or members of Parliament in speech or writing or to challenge the orthodoxy of the Church of England. Not only writers but also printers could be arrested and imprisoned for publishing seditious material. Any criticism of the Government was considered libellous and it was not until the mid-nineteenth century that 'truth' became an admissible defence in the tort of defamation.

See Chapter 1.2.2

See Chapter 3

The idea that citizens can receive free and objective information and engage in free debate and critical reflection was adopted in the twentieth century by the German philosopher Jürgen Habermas, who traced the rise of free speech back to the Age of Enlightenment, made possible by a free press. Habermas believed that the emancipation of the informed citizen could be brought about only by 'critical communication and analysis of modern institutions'. The only way such informed criticism could take shape was through a free and uncensored press, which he included in his 'three normative models of democracy'.[41]

See Section 1.2.2

How much can we trust the media today? While information is abundant in the form of online material and Twitter feeds, it is often misinformation or disinformation. How sure can we be that what we read in the press has been thoroughly checked and verified? After the Leveson Inquiry[42] into media ethics and phone-hacking, how can we judge whether information obtained by journalists has been obtained legally?

See Chapter 10.4

---

40 For further discussion see: Stein (2000), pp. 347ff.
41 See: Habermas (1994).
42 The Inquiry led by Lord Justice Leveson was established under the Inquiries Act 2005. A large number of witnesses were summoned from 13 July 2011 to give evidence in the two-part inquiry investigating the role of the press and police in the phone-hacking scandal.

Yet for daily practical journalistic and investigative purposes we need to place our trust in the media and broadcasting institutions – it is hoped that post-Leveson, this will be done well.[43] Index on Censorship is one of the leading organisations that probes abuses of freedom of expression in the UK and around the world. John Kampfner was the organisation's Chief Executive from 2008 until 2012. Through their campaigns Index have challenged threats to free expression, giving a voice to journalists, writers, artists and activists who have been prevented from speaking out.[44]

1.3.2 Media freedom in the twenty-first century

Today press freedom accepts certain restrictions on providing information, such as war reporting,[45] contempt, blasphemy, the protection of minors, racial discrimination and national security. Frost (2011: 50ff.) argues that it can be rather confusing that many people in Britain and other Western European countries appear to support freedom of speech and a free press on the one hand, while supporting censorship on specific matters on the other, such as the coverage of terrorism or sexually explicit material. Ultimately, there are ethical and moral issues that govern war reporting, for instance, or news-gathering and broadcasting. These are usually left to broadcasting organizations' policy.

 FOR THOUGHT

On 22 February 2012 *Sunday Times* correspondent Marie Colvin and French photographer Remi Ochlik were killed in the besieged Syrian city of Homs after the house where they were staying was shelled. War correspondents are increasingly seen as dangerous subversives. You are the legal adviser to the editorial board of a public broadcaster. Advise the board whether they should continue with their detailed coverage of Middle Eastern conflict.

1.3.3 Press coverage of terrorism

The Prevention of Terrorism (Temporary Provisions) Acts of 1974 and 1989 were a series of acts that conferred emergency powers upon police forces, particularly aimed at the 'Troubles' in Northern Ireland with suspected terrorism from the IRA (Irish Republican Army). It had been Prime Minister Margaret Thatcher's unrelenting aim to stop violence in Northern Ireland. The policies her Government actually did implement from 1979 included a decree whereby members of the Republican political party Sinn Féin and several other paramilitary organizations were banned from speaking about the conflict in media broadcasts. Thatcher claimed this would deny terrorists 'the oxygen of publicity.' In reality, it led to a ludicrous situation in which Sinn Féin members could be seen speaking on British television, but their voices were overdubbed by actors, and elected members of Parliament of Sinn Féin and the SDLP (Social Democratic Labour Party), such as Martin McGuinness, Gerry Adams and Danny Morrison, were banned from entering the Westminster Parliament. The broadcasting bans were introduced by Conservative Home Secretary Douglas Hurd under the Terrorism Act 1989 and affected 11 loyalist and republican organizations (though Sinn Féin, the political wing of the IRA, had been the main target of this legislation).

---

43 For further discussion see: Burchill, White and Morris (2005).
44 Index on Censorship is a registered charity in London: www.indexoncensorship.org/about-index-on-censorship.
45 For further discussion see: Burchill, White and Morris (2005).

Karen Sanders (2003: 71) points out that journalistic coverage of terrorism is particularly difficult in terms of free speech and ethics. She specifically examined broadcast reporting during the Troubles from 1989 to the Belfast (Northern Ireland) Agreement in 1998, looking particularly at interviews with IRA and INLA (Irish National Liberation Army) members, concluding that these were difficult times for press freedom. A BBC documentary by Paul Hamann featuring an extensive interview with Martin McGuinness of Sinn Féin was banned by the Government, and McGuinness's voice was replaced by an actor until the start of the peace talks in 1994. Media restrictions in Northern Ireland were gradually lifted and both Terrorism Acts 1974 and 1989 were repealed. Hamann's documentary – *Real Lives: At the Edge of the Union* – could finally be shown in 1994. There is no doubt that the documentary and subject matter caused immense controversy between the Thatcher Conservative Government and the BBC in the mid-1980s.

1.3.4 Do the rich and famous have a right to privacy? The Lord McAlpine case

Today, personal information about celebrities and people in public life is freely available on the internet and is frequently shared on social networking sites such as Facebook and Twitter, encouraging our obsession with royalty, the rich and the famous, and stimulating uncensored expressions of personal opinion. There is, as yet, no apparent legal censorship on those websites that demand the stoning of gays or the subjugation of women. No censor authorized the taking down of the 'Stop Rod Liddle' blog campaign in January 2010, when a petition gathered over 3,000 signatures protesting against the proposal that the polemical journalist would become the new editor of the *Independent* newspaper. There was no realistic legal avenue that Mr Liddle could have taken to sue the originators for libel other than action against the internet service provider (ISP) (see: **Godfrey v Demon Internet** (2001)[46]). Yet, in July 2012, *The Spectator* magazine was ordered by Judge Howard Riddle to pay £5,625 in fines and compensation (for distress to Stephen Lawrence's parents) for contempt of court for breaching reporting restrictions over a Rod Liddle comment piece in November 2011, published during the trial of Stephen Lawrence's killers.

Between November and December 2012, Conservative politician, former principal adviser to Mrs Thatcher and successful businessman Lord (Alistair) McAlpine spent a horrifying time defending his reputation as he had been libelled on the BBC *Newsnight* programme on 2 November. The broadcast on BBC Two featured a special investigation into child sexual abuse in North Wales care homes in the 1970s and 1980s. The *Newsnight* report claimed that two victims had been abused by 'a leading Conservative politician from the Thatcher years'. The alleged perpetrator was not identified. By the time the *Newsnight* report was broadcast, there had been 12 hours of speculation online regarding the identity of the alleged perpetrator.

This was not the end for Lord McAlpine. Hundreds of tweets started to emerge, even before the programme went out, since the TV producers had written about the child abuse in Wales before the programme was broadcast. The *Newsnight* report itself and its contents immediately became a prominent news story. Between 2 and 4 November, online and traditional media widely reported upon, and repeated, *Newsnight*'s allegations. The coverage included, but was not limited to, the following articles: the *Guardian* on 3 November, www.telegraph.co.uk on 3 November, the *Sunday Telegraph* for 4 November and www.telegraph.co.uk, and *MailOnline* on 4 November. The BBC later admitted that the man anonymously alleged to be the perpetrator in the *Newsnight* report was Lord McAlpine. The then Director-General of the BBC Executive, George Entwistle, commissioned a report by Ken

---

46 [2001] QB 201.

MacQuarrie, Director of the BBC in Scotland, into the complexities of what had happened (the 'MacQuarrie Report').[47]

On 9 November 2012, Newsnight broadcast an unreserved apology, also including a clip of an interview with the abuse victim, Steven Messham, in which he offered his 'humble apologies to Lord McAlpine' for wrongly identifying him as the abuser. Following the findings of the BBC Editorial Standards Committee (in the MacQuarrie Report) the BBC Trust took immediate action. George Entwistle resigned as Director-General on 10 November 2012; he had been in the post for just 54 days. Apart from the apology broadcast on Newsnight, the BBC agreed terms to settle Lord McAlpine's libel claim for £185,000 plus costs (and the apology) out of court. Three further BBC employees were subject to disciplinary action.

One of the most prominent tweets on the subject came from the wife of the Speaker of the House of Commons, Sally Bercow, and Lord McAlpine subsequently sued Mrs Bercow for defamation.[48] The case was heard before Mr Justice Tugendhat in May 2013, who found defamatory the tweet which Mrs Bercow had sent on 4 November, following the Newsnight broadcast. The tweet read: 'Why is Lord McAlpine trending? *Innocent face*.' People who were not familiar with Twitter may not have understood the words 'trending' and 'innocent face'. But users of Twitter would understand: the Twitter website has a screen with a box headed 'Trends'. It lists names of individuals and other topics. Twitter (who had been asked to disclose the names of Twitterers by a High Court order to the US ISP) explained to the court that this list is:

> . . . generated by an algorithm which identifies topics that are immediately popular, rather than topics that have been popular for a while or on a daily basis, to help you discover the hottest emerging topics of discussion on Twitter that matter most to you. You can choose to see Trends that are tailored for you . . .[49]

Tugendhat J explained that 'innocent face' was to be read as a stage direction. Readers were to imagine that they could see an expression of innocence on Sally Bercow's face. She claimed it was a deadpan look. She had, she said, simply noticed in all innocence that McAlpine's name was circulating widely on Twitter – 'trending' – and was hoping someone would tell her why. However, the claimant, Lord McAlpine, argued that Mrs Bercow was using irony – that 'innocent face' was meant to be read as the opposite of its literal meaning. The judge decided the reasonable reader would understand Bercow's words as insincere and ironical.

Tugendhat J found that Mrs Bercow's tweet meant, in its natural and ordinary defamatory meaning, that the claimant was a paedophile who was guilty of sexually abusing boys living in care and that was why Lord McAlpine was 'trending' on 4 November. He also found that the tweet bore an innuendo with a meaning to the same effect. Mrs Bercow did not avail herself of a public interest defence (i.e. Reynolds privilege or reportage). The tweet was seriously defamatory and Bercow was left without a defence to the libel action brought by McAlpine. The judge ruled that the tweet was defamatory not only in its 'natural and ordinary meaning' but also through innuendo to Mrs Bercow's 56,000 followers on Twitter. Mrs Bercow settled out of court with an offer to make amends of £150,000, which Lord McAlpine donated to charity.

The **McAlpine** case demonstrates that Twitter (and other social networking sites) are no different from people chatting in the pub. They are a public platform and tweets can seriously harm people's reputation. The worst of it is that tweets cannot be taken down, and stay for ever on the internet. Just before the Bercow judgment on 25 May 2013, a number of other Twitterers quickly apologized

---

47 See: BBC Trust (2012).
48 See: **Lord McAlpine of West Green v Sally Bercow** [2013] EWHC 1342 (QB).
49 Ibid., at para 3 (Tugendhat J).

to Lord McAlpine, since he had also started legal action against them. This included *Guardian* columnist George Monbiot, who agreed in an out-of-court settlement to undertake three years of charitable work in recompense.[50]

See also Chapters 3 and 4

The interest of the public can be particularly heightened when celebrities go to extensive – and expensive – lengths to stop reporting of various activities. The world of celebrity reporting is complex. Celebrities use social media themselves, sometimes allowing journalists to make stories appear 'unauthorized', so there may be differences between what *appears* to be and what actually *is* an invasion of privacy, based on matters such as previous contacts with the press, off-the-record or unattributable interviews, etc. It may be worth making a quick reference at some point to this complexity.

In January 2010, then England football captain John Terry[51] had asked the High Court for what became known as a 'superinjunction' to cover up his alleged affair with a French lingerie model. This prevented not only reporting of the affair but even reporting of the existence of the injunction itself. After initially granting the injunction, Tugendhat J overturned the decision a few days later after an outcry, particularly in the press, led by the *Guardian* newspaper, against media restrictions by the courts. This had the opposite effect to the one Terry was hoping for, resulting in blanket coverage in the tabloid press for days.

See also Chapter 2.2.4

Formula One motor racing chief Max Mosley sought the right to privacy after the *News of the World* had exposed his alleged penchant for call girls dressed up in Nazi uniform (**Mosley v Newsgroup Newspapers Ltd** (2008)). Mr Mosley was not successful, however, in his Strasbourg action.[52] The human rights court ruled against any pre-notification regime which would require powerful civil or criminal sanctions. Max Mosley's application for 'pre-notification' measures would have had an adverse impact on media freedom beyond the limits of 'responsible journalism'. The court unanimously rejected Mr Mosley's application and rejected 'compulsory pre-notification'. The decision was welcomed by John Kampfner of Index on Censorship. While the careful and balanced Strasbourg judgment acknowledged the privacy concerns of celebrities, it recognized the media's Article 10 right and the public interest in such matters.

 FOR THOUGHT

Should a High Court judge have the right to deny a newspaper the reporting of a married multi-millionaire football player's sexual peccadilloes? Discuss with reference to recent superinjunctions.

The two **von Hannover** actions (nos 1 and 2) demonstrate two conflicting Strasbourg (ECtHR) judgments. The first action granted Princess Caroline of Monaco, married to the German Prince Ernst August von Hannover, privacy with certain conditions, as she had been repeatedly exposed in the German magazine print media in relation to her stormy marriage and other relationships (see: **von Hannover v Germany** (2005)[53]). In the conjoined judgments of **von Hannover (No 2)**[54] and **Axel Springer**,[55] handed down by the Grand Chamber (ECtHR), the human rights court made it clear that

---

50 Source: 'Lord McAlpine row: George Monbiot reaches "unprecedented" settlement', by Josh Halliday, *Guardian*, 12 March 2013.
51 **John Terry (previously referred to as LNS) v Persons Unknown** [2010] EWHC 119 (QB) (*sub nom* 'John Terry Superinjunction').
52 **Mosley v UK** (Application no. 48009/08) ECTHR of 10 May 2011.
53 **Von Hannover v Germany (No 1)** (2005) 40 EHRR 1 (Application no 59320/00); [2004] EMLR 21, of 24 June 2004 (ECTHR)
54 **Von Hannover v Germany (No 2)** (2012) (Application Numbers – 40660/08, 60641/08) Strasbourg judgment of 7 February 2012.
55 **Axel Springer v Germany** (2012) (Application No 39954/08) Strasbourg judgment of 7 February 2012.

See also
Chapter 2.2.3

Article 8 ('right to privacy') had to be carefully balanced against Article 10 ('freedom of expression'), and additionally how the publication in question would contribute to a debate of general and genuine public interest. The ECtHR held (in both cases) that it had taken account of the nature of the individuals involved and the publications – and that the media's right to freedom of expression prevailed over the right to privacy.

Axel Springer concerned the publication of articles about the arrest and conviction of a well-known German TV 'cop' (X) who had been arrested for the possession of class A drugs. The German court (Hamburg) held that the actor's right to protect his personality rights prevailed over the public interest, even though the facts were not disputed. An injunction was granted against the popular tabloid *Bild Zeitung* ('Bild') and a number of gossip magazines. The Grand Chamber (by a majority of 12:5) disagreed with the domestic court and held that there had been violation of Article 10 ECHR since there was a degree of public interest: the actor (X) was well known, had actively sought publicity in the past and the information relating to the criminal drugs charges had been publically disclosed by the German state prosecuting authorities.

Von Hannover (No 2) concerned the publication of photographs in the gossip magazine *Frau im Spiegel* of Princess Caroline of Monaco and her husband, Ernst August von Hannover, during their skiing holiday in St Moritz. The photos were accompanied by an article reporting on the poor health of Caroline's father, Prince Rainier of Monaco. She claimed that the publication was an 'unfavourable' intrusion and breached her Article 8 right, relying on the earlier judgment in 2004.

The Grand Chamber noted that the photographs of the von Hannovers were not in themselves offensive and that the German courts had carefully balanced the Article 10 rights of the publishers against the right of the applicants to respect for their private life. Having regard to the national margin of appreciation as laid down in **von Hannover (No 1)**, it held unanimously that there had been no violation of Article 8.

See also
Chapter 3.4.3

It can be argued that everyone, no matter how famous, has some right to privacy, particularly within the realms of their own home, when they are hospitalized or undergoing rehabilitative treatment (see: **Campbell v Mirror Group Newspapers Ltd** (2004)[56]). It is only when a fine balance has been struck between the competing rights of the personality and the right to free speech that the issue of whether a matter is in the public interest can be decided. Publication at all costs, merely designed to satisfy the public's curiosity and to increase newspaper sales, should be avoided.

See Chapter
10

1.3.5 Unlimited freedom of speech via the internet

Freedom of speech means different things to different societies. There is precious little that can be banned from the internet today, though there are organizations such as the UK Internet Watch Foundation (IWF) and the communications regulator Ofcom that have the power to inform and enforce law.

There is no doubt that the internet has considerably widened public interest in what goes on. Not only national but international newspapers can be read online, and we can also read any exposé on Facebook or Twitter, or view extensive video footage on YouTube of material which was either in the private domain or had been restrained by the courts. This was the case with the 'naked Prince Harry in Las Vegas' photos, published initially only on US and foreign websites, when the *Sun* became the first British newspaper to publish the naked photos on 22 August 2012, with the headline 'Harry grabs the Crown Jewels'. The photo also briefly appeared online before being removed. A News International spokeswoman told the BBC that the photo had been published online 'in error' and was never intended to go online because the real pictures were available on the internet

---

56 [2004] UKHL 22.

from media organisations outside the UK. The case of footballer Ryan Giggs shows the impotence of court orders (in this case a superinjunction[57]) which bind traditional forms of media (in Giggs's case News Group Newspapers) but in effect are totally ignored by the public.[58]

Prior to the Leveson Inquiry, most 'red tops' would undoubtedly have published the blurred images of a naked prince 'cavorting' and 'romping' over their front pages. But post-Leveson, no paper chose (or dared) to publish them. Rupert Murdoch defended the decision of the *Sun* to publish the naked Prince Harry pictures, saying it was necessary to make a point about the lack of 'free press' in Britain and it was right of the editor to publish 'in the public interest'. Murdoch's comments were made on Twitter (26 August 2012) as the row over the pictures continued to escalate with an intervention from the culture secretary, Jeremy Hunt, who said the *Sun* was wrong to publish. Murdoch made his stance public after more than 850 complaints were sent to the (now defunct) Press Complaints Commission (PCC) about an alleged invasion of privacy. Hunt told BBC News he did not believe the *Sun* was acting in the public interest but said it was not his place to tell editors what to do. The *Sun*'s decision to publish was widely seen as a defiant act, coming just 48 hours after Prince Charles's personal solicitors, Harbottle & Lewis, issued a letter to newspapers warning them there was no justification for publication in English law.

There is no doubt that the Leveson Inquiry has had a taming effect on the British media. Had the *News of the World* (*NOW*) still been around, it would have served up as many titillating pictures of Prince Harry as possible for Sunday breakfasts over the August bank holiday weekend. But most British newspapers made the judgement that because the photos were taken in a private room without the knowledge of the subject, then the privacy of that individual should be respected.

See Chapter 10.4

 FOR THOUGHT

Do you think the British newspapers (and online editions) made the right decision not to publish the naked Prince Harry in Las Vegas photos in August 2012? Or do you agree with the *Sun* newspaper that the subject matter was of genuine public interest? Or was it simply 'stuff' the public is interested in? Discuss, using existing case law in your argument.

On 18 July 2013, Russian anti-corruption (and anti-Putin) blogger, lawyer and political activist Alexei Navalny was tried and sentenced at a court in Kirov, some 500 miles east of Moscow, to five years' imprisonment, guilty of four charges of embezzlement. The verdict against him – that he embezzled 16 million roubles (£325,000) from a timber firm while advising the governor of Russia's Kirov region – was widely seen by the Western media as a means of silencing him, for the 37-year-old was President Putin's most vociferous critic.[59] Since the controversial presidential elections in Russia in December 2011, Navalny had openly blogged about allegations of malpractice and corruption at some of Russia's biggest state-controlled corporations on his blog, 'rospil.info'. On 20 July 2013, Alexei Navalny was unexpectedly released from custody on bail, addressing hundreds of supporters at Moscow station, and declared that he was going to win the capital's mayoral election. On 16 October the Russian Court of Appeal in Moscow upheld the Opposition Leader's conviction for embezzlement, but suspended his prison sentence, allowing him to go free. However, his conviction is likely to prevent him from running in the next presidential election.[60]

---

57 See: **CTB v News Group Newspapers** (Ryan Giggs superinjunction) [2011] EWHC 1326 (QB), 23 Mary 2011.
58 For further discussion see: Smartt (2012) at pp. 50–52.
59 See: 'Alexei Navalny jailed: Russia's Mandela moment?' by Daniel Sandford, *Guardian*, 19 July 2013.
60 Source: 'Russia's Alexei Navalny's sentence suspended on appeal', *BBC News Online*, 16 October 2013.

In an unprecedented legal announcement in December 2010, Lord Judge LCJ gave the go-ahead to 'tweeting' in court, during the bail applications by WikiLeaks founder Julian Assange as he began his legal battle to oppose the European Arrest Warrant (EAW)[61] and extradition to Sweden to answer accusations against him on rape charges. The UK Supreme Court had ruled in June 2012 that Assange must be extradited to Sweden to stand trial on charges of rape, which he denied. Assange was granted bail, living electronically tagged on home detention curfew with friends in Suffolk. The decision to grant bail had been appealed by the CPS, and considered on 16 December 2010 by Mr Justice Ouseley in the Administrative Court. The grant of conditional bail was upheld but the conditions were varied: in addition to his electronic tag, nine people were ordered to put up surety for Assange in case he failed to surrender to court.

These sureties, amounting to more than £240,000, were called in on 8 October by Senior District Judge (Chief Magistrate), Mr Justice Riddle, at Westminster Magistrates' Court after Julian Assange had 'skipped bail' and sought political asylum at the Ecuadorian embassy in London on Tuesday 19 June 2012. The WikiLeaks founder feared that if he were sent to Sweden to be charged with the rape of two women, Sweden would, in fact, extradite him to the USA to face potential charges of treason over the release of thousands of confidential US documents on WikiLeaks. Assange relied on the UN Universal Declaration of Human Rights obligation to review all applications for asylum while taking refuge at the Ecuadorian embassy.[62]

Meanwhile the Westminster District Judge had called in the sureties for the 'absconded' Julian Assange, namely £10,000 from Tricia David, £15,000 from Lady Caroline Evans, £3,500 each from Joseph Farrell and Sarah Harrison, £15,000 each from Phillip Knightley and John Sulston, £12,000 each from Sarah Saunders and Vaughan Smith and £7,500 from Tracy Worcester. Those amounts were due to be paid into court in full by 6 November 2012; if there was any amount outstanding thereafter, persons in default were told they could be committed to custody for non-payment. Those who stood surety for Assange were eventually saved by a group of celebrities and activists, including the socialite Jemima Khan, film director Ken Loach and publisher Felix Dennis, who posted cash securities amounting to £200,000 to court. By 15 July 2013 the WikiLeaks Founder had been seeking asylum at the embassy for 390 days, and detained without charge (by Sweden) for 952 days.

Meanwhile, Private Bradley Manning, who had leaked the infamous 'Iraq tapes' to WikiLeaks, had been imprisoned in the USA without sentence for nearly three years. Manning appeared before a court martial in June 2013. Some saw Manning as a heroic whistleblower and fighter for freedom of speech; many army personnel regarded him as a traitor. Private Manning's court martial was heard in secret at the Army Base at Fort Meade in Maryland, where he was charged with 'aiding the enemy' by leaking national secrets to WikiLeaks. The non-jury court martial, presided over by Colonel Denise Lind, was held behind closed doors with no media present on the grounds that testimony from some witnesses may contain classified information. Manning faced 22 charges. The main charge against him was that he had 'knowingly transferred highly sensitive materials to WikiLeaks, including video footage of civilians being mistakenly killed during a US Apache heli-copter attack'. Among the 150 or so witnesses who testified against Manning were members of the US Navy Seal team that carried out the lethal raid against Osama bin Laden.[63]

After the seven-week court martial, Bradley Manning was convicted of 20 charges, including theft and computer fraud. He had admitted leaking the documents to anti-secrecy organisation

61 Council Framework Decision of 13 June 2002 on the European Arrest Warrant and the surrender procedures between Member States (2002/584/JHA) [2002] OJ L 190/1.

62 Source: 'Oh, what a circus! Assange taunts UK from embassy balcony', by Vanessa Allen and Mario Ledwith, *Daily Mail*, 19 August 2012.

63 Source: 'Bradley Manning, WikiLeaks and the secret trial at Fort Meade: proceedings begin for the soldier charged with leaking national secrets', by David Usborne, *Independent*, 2 June 2013.

WikiLeaks but said he did so to spark a debate on US foreign policy. Judge Colonel Denise Lind handed down the 20 guilty verdicts, but importantly acquitted Private Manning of the most serious charge, 'aiding the enemy'.[64] In August 2013, after three years in prison awaiting trial, the 25-year-old soldier and former intelligence analyst was sentenced to 35 years in prison.[65]

Private Manning's court martial raised questions about why the US Army had put Manning in such a sensitive position after testimony revealed he had severe emotional problems, including what a military psychiatrist described as a gender identity disorder for which he did not receive treatment while in Iraq. Manning had sent a photo, showing himself wearing a wig and makeup, to his immediate superior along with an email in which he said his gender problem was causing him pain and problems in his career, following the US military's 2011 repeal of the ban on homosexuals in the military.[66]

See also
Chapter 5.2.2

Some would say that freedom of speech might have got out of hand in that there is, at present, very little legislation which allows control of what is published on the internet. There now exists internet-freedom of expression in form of 'tweets' and blogs which carry enormous privileges but, with them, implied moral and ethical responsibilities not to write anything about people or organizations which may well harm them. Despite contempt-of-court legislation and strict anonymity orders, police suspects and people standing trial are increasingly featured on the US-based video-sharing site YouTube. The purpose of court orders and protective child legislation will be further argued in Chapters 4 and 5.

This leaves us to conclude that just about anything can be shared and written about via the World Wide Web. The internet has become a worldwide collective of free speech, which some say has spiralled out of control. Others defend it strenuously, arguing that the internet is the one place where the essence of free speech lives unmolested.

 FOR THOUGHT

> Should there be regulations or laws to control publication on the internet? Are such laws necessary to prevent Internet Service Providers (ISPs) from restricting content or prioritizing one type of traffic over another? Or would you agree with some proponents of internet free speech that any proposed regulations would choke new innovations and freedom of expression? Discuss.

1.4 The open justice principle

The open justice principle has been recognized by all British courts for hundreds of years. This means that theoretically the public and the press cannot be excluded from *any* court proceedings unless prevented by statute. The general principle behind open justice is that this discourages any abuse of the judicial process and that the media can freely report on judicial proceedings, as expressed by Jeremy Bentham:

See Chapters
4 and 5

> . . . publicity is the very soul of justice. It is the keenest spur to exertion and the surest of all guards against improbity. It keeps the judge himself while trying under trial.[67]

64 Source: 'Wikileaks source Manning convicted on most charges', by Jude Sheering, BBC News Online, 30 July 2013.
65 Source: 'Bradley Manning sentenced to 35 years in prison over leaks', by Stephanie Kirchgaessner, Financial Times, 21 August 2013.
66 Source: 'Bradley Manning sentenced to 35 years for espionage', by Luis Ramirez, Voice of America online, 21 August 2013.
67 Bentham (1843), p. 316.

The American legal theorist John Rawls (1921–2002) developed the concept of open justice in relation to the 'difference principle'. This asserts the notion of inequality and the (unfair) distribution of scarce goods in society, such as power, money and access to justice. In *A Theory of Justice* (1971), Rawls equates 'justice' with 'fairness'. This notion rests on three principles:

(1)   the principle of equal liberty in that each person has an equal right to the most extensive system of equal basic liberties compatible with a similar system of liberty for all;
(2)   the principle of equality of fair opportunity, open to all under conditions in which persons of similar abilities have equal access to office;
(3)   the difference principle, which requires social and economic institutions to be arranged in such a way that they equally benefit the worst-off.

It is generally accepted that there are two systems of criminal trial, the inquisitorial and the accusatorial. The latter is practised in the Anglo-Saxon tradition and the former in continental European jurisdictions and elsewhere. The English accusatorial tradition dates back to the twelfth and thirteenth centuries, which was also the beginning of the common law system. Trials were conducted in *judicium dei*; that is, judgment before God rather than the court. The inquisitorial system involves the judge or magistrate finding out for himself what happened in a case, by asking the parties in court questions. This is commonly practised in France, Germany, Spain and other Roman law-based jurisdictions. The principle of open justice is embedded into the framework of all common law countries and enshrined in the Sixth Amendment of the United States Constitution of 1791.

1.4.1 'Justice should not only be done, but should manifestly and undoubtedly be seen to be done': secret courts and courtroom TV

The words 'open justice' express a fundamental principle at the heart of the British justice system, vital to the rule of law. This is not a new fundamental principle, as cited by Bayley J in **Daubney v Cooper** (1829):

> . . . we are all of the opinion, that it is one of the essential qualities of a Court of Justice that its proceedings should be in public, and that all parties who may be desirous of hearing what is going on, if there be room in the place for that purpose, provided they do not interrupt the proceedings and provided there is no specific reason why they should be removed – have the right to be present for the purpose of hearing what is going on.[68]

All lawyers will recognize the much-cited dictum of Lord Hewart from **Rex v Sussex Justices** of 1924:

> . . . it is not merely of some importance but is of fundamental importance, that justice should not only be done, but should manifestly and undoubtedly be seen to be done.[69]

Lord Atkin said that it is the duty of the press to report court proceedings 'in the public interest', necessary for those in society who cannot attend daily court proceedings, since 'justice is not a cloistered virtue'.[70] In 1913 Lord Atkinson said in **Scott v Scott** (see below):[71]

---

68   [1829] 109 ER 438; 10 B & C 237 at 240.
69   **R v Sussex Justices, Ex parte McCarthy** [1924] 1 KB 256 at 259 (Lord Hewart).
70   **Ambard v Attorney-General for Trinidad and Tobago** [1936] AC 322 at 335 (Lord Atkin).
71   [1913] AC 417.

. . . the hearing of a case in public may be, and often is, no doubt, painful, humiliating, or deterrent both to parties and witnesses, and in many cases, especially those of a criminal nature, the details may be so indecent as to tend to injure public morals.

In *Scott v Scott*, the House of Lords affirmed in the strongest possible terms the long-established *dictum* that all court hearings should be held in public, including messy divorces. As Professor Richard Meredith Jackson so eloquently commented in his first edition of *The Machinery of Justice* (1903), the common law rule of open court should eventually triumph.

❖ KEY CASE   *Scott v Scott* (1913) AC 417 of 5 May 1913 (HL)

Precedent
❖   The English system of administering justice requires that it is done in public.
❖   'Open justice' provides a safeguard against judicial arbitrariness or idiosyncrasy and maintains the public confidence in the administration of justice.

Facts
Mrs Scott filed her petition for divorce against her husband to declare their marriage as null and void because of his impotence. She asked that the petition be heard in private. This was granted by the judge with the decree absolute on 15 January 1912. Mrs Scott objected to the court transcripts being made public, claiming that the proceedings had been *in camera*. Their Lordships considered the Matrimonial Causes Act 1857, which states that divorce petitions must be heard in open court.

Decision
The House of Lords ruled that there was nothing in the 1857 Act which authorized *in camera* proceedings and that there was nothing that 'authorised the exclusion of bona fide representatives of a newspaper or news agency' (at para 485); that the original order of the nullity proceedings should never have been made 'private' by the first judge. This meant that all transcriptions of the proceedings could be made public, including the full names of the parties and all the indelicacies mentioned during the divorce proceedings. Consequently Mrs Scott's appeal was dismissed.

Analysis
Lord Halsbury LC referred to common law on press reporting of proceedings in court as going beyond 'merely enlarging the area of the court, and communicating to all, that which all had the right to know',[72] as a positive duty to report proceedings and to act as the 'eyes and ears' of society and to inform members of the public about issues of public interest in the civil, criminal and administrative courts of justice. It is for this reason that everyone involved in court proceedings can be identified, including the parties and the justices.[73] Lord Diplock explained in ***AG v Leveller Magazine Ltd*** (1979)[74] that proceedings being held in open court meant that not only were the general public permitted to attend court proceedings, but also the press, and that only fair and accurate reporting of proceedings must be published.

---

72   *MacDougall v Knight* [1889] AC at 200 (Lord Halsbury LC).
73   *R v Felixstowe Justices Ex parte Leigh and Another* [1987] 1 All ER 551.
74   [1979] AC 440.

The outcome of the *Scott v Scott* case had the effect that Parliament reversed the decision to a large extent by introducing the Judicial Proceedings (Regulation of Reports) Act 1926. The Act largely regulated proceedings in matrimonial courts and severely restricted the publication of reports of judicial proceedings in such manner as to prevent 'injury to public morals' (section 1). It became unlawful to print or publish in relation to any judicial proceedings any indecent matter or indecent medical, surgical or physiological details mentioned in court (largely divorce proceedings). The 1926 Act also made it unlawful to print or publish in relation to any judicial proceedings for dissolution of marriage, for nullity of marriage, or for judicial separation, or for restitution of conjugal rights, any particulars (other than the names, addresses and occupations of the parties and witnesses).[75]

In summary, there are occasions when statute automatically restricts reporting of court proceedings. The most common example occurs where the circumstances are such that openness would put at risk the achievement of justice, which is the very purpose of the proceedings. Youth justice proceedings are normally closed to the public, with strict reporting restrictions and anonymity orders in place applied to children and young persons under the age of 18 in England and Wales.[76] This differs in Scotland, where if a person under 17 years old is in custody, charged with a criminal offence or involved in the Children's Hearing system, there should be no reporting.[77] The occasions where the public are being excluded, or where anonymity orders are being issued, is widening, such as in terrorism cases, which are increasingly heard *in camera* (see: **Re. Guardian News and Media Ltd** (2010)).[78] These exceptions and restrictions will be further discussed in Chapter 5.

See Chapter 5

That said, the principle of open justice has never been absolute. There are numerous exceptions which have developed in statute, such as reporting of criminal cases involving juveniles. Attempts to limit the principle, however, usually attract great controversy, as is illustrated by the UK Coalition Government's controversial Justice and Security Act 2013.

See Chapter 5.3

In a leading judicial review case involving the request for disclosure by the *Guardian*, the media organization was eventually granted 'open justice' by the courts.[79] In this case the question had arisen whether a district judge, who made two extradition orders on the application of the US Government, had power to allow the *Guardian* to inspect and take copies of affidavits or witness statements, written arguments and correspondence, which were supplied to the judge for the purposes of the extradition hearings. The documents were not read out in open court but they were referred to during the course of the hearings. The *Guardian* had been seeking access to documents used to justify the extradition of two Britons, Jeffrey Tesler and Wojciech Chodan, to the US. After they were sent to Texas, the pair pleaded guilty to taking part in a decade-long conspiracy to channel bribes worth $180m to Nigerian officials and politicians. The newspaper argued that the documents would help explain why the pair were being extradited. The US Government argued that the media had an established right to see documents in civil cases, but there was no such right in criminal hearings.

The original district judge in the Westminster Magistrates' Court case, DJ Tubbs, had refused the *Guardian*'s application to see the extradition documents. She found that she had no power to allow it to do so. Sullivan LJ and Silber J in the administrative court agreed with her and the *Guardian*

---

75 Section 1 Judicial Proceedings (Regulation of Reports) Act 1926 ('Restriction on publication of reports of judicial proceedings').
76 Sections 39 and 49 Children and Young Persons Act 1933.
77 Section 46 Children and Young Persons (Scotland) Act 1937.
78 *Guardian News and Media Ltd and others in Her Majesty's Treasury v Mohammed Jabar Ahmed and others (FC)*; also cited as: *Her Majesty's Treasury v Mohammed al-Ghabra (FC); R (on the application of Hani El Sayed Sabaei Youssef) v Her Majesty's Treasury* [2010] UKSC 1 of 27 January 2010.
79 *The Queen (on the application of Guardian News and Media Ltd) v City of Westminster Magistrates' Court* [2012] EWCA Civ 420.

THE OPEN JUSTICE PRINCIPLE

appealed against the refusal. In the administrate court (judicial review) Lord Neuberger MR, Hooper LJ and Toulson LJ allowed the *Guardian*'s appeal by ordering the US Government to disclose the extradition documents to the newspaper. Toulson LJ said the decision 'breaks new ground in the application of the principle of open justice' and that the courts should 'assist rather than impede' the media when reporters seek copies of documents used in criminal cases. Alan Rusbridger, editor-in-chief of Guardian News and Media, said: 'This is a very significant judgment in favour of open justice and should greatly strengthen the hand of journalists in being able to see documents used in criminal cases.'[80]

Lord Neuberger MR pointed out that 'open justice' is part of human rights law, enshrined in Article 6 ECHR, reaffirming the House of Lords decision in **Scott v Scott** when he said:

> . . . the importance of open justice as a fundamental principle has not only secured its place in our legal system. It has also secured its place in the legal systems of all those countries which are signatories to the European Convention on Human Rights.[81]

There have been high-profile cases since the terrorism atrocities in New York (9/11 – 11 September 2001) and London (7/7 – 7 July 2005) which have led to recent law reforms. The most compelling is that of Binyam Mohamed, the former Guantànamo detainee, who was eventually paid £1m compensation in 2010, over claims he was tortured with the complicity of the British Government and the imposition of control orders.[82] According to the UK security services, it was impossible to fight the allegations without the use of intelligence too dangerous to reveal. Though the Mohamed case was concluded, it was believed that there were another 27 'secret evidence' cases being heard in 2012. Can it then be justified to create a statutory situation, such as the Justice and Security Act 2013, where suspects may not know the full extent of evidence against them, and cannot therefore defend themselves? Though Public Interest Immunity (PII) certificates can achieve the same result for genuinely sensitive material, at least a judge can review the material in such an application and can decide whether such a certificate can be granted.

The Criminal Procedure Rules 2005[83] set out the procedure to be followed when the prosecution makes an application to the court for non-disclosure of material. PII claims are always assessed by the court. When doing so, the court must balance two competing interests:

● the public interest that, in the fair administration of justice, the courts should have the fullest possible access to all relevant material; and
● the need to maintain the confidentiality of information the disclosure of which would cause real damage to the public interest.

How then does court secrecy sit with journalists being allowed to 'tweet' in court?[84] Lord Judge LCJ told journalists in December 2010 that they no longer had to make an application to use Twitter or 'text-based communication' from courts in England and Wales following guidance

---

80 Source: 'Judgment over extradition case is victory for open justice', by Rob Evans, *Guardian*, 3 April 2012.
81 Source: 'Open Justice Unbound', by Lord Neuberger of Abbotsbury MR. Address to the Judicial Studies Board, Annual Lecture, 16 March 2011.
82 Made by the Secretary of State on 5 September 2005 under ss 2 and 3 (1)(a) of the Prevention of Terrorism Act 2005. See: **R (on the application of Binyam Mohamed) v Secretary of State for Foreign and Commonwealth Affairs** [2010] EWCA Civ 65; see also: **Secretary of State for the Home Department v MB**; **Secretary of State for the Home Department v AF** [2007] UKHL 46; see also: **Secretary of State for the Home Department v AF and others** [2009] UKHL 28.
83 S.I.2005 No.384.
84 Source: 'Interim practice guidance: the use of live text-based forms of communication (including Twitter) from court for the purposes of fair and accurate reporting'. Lord Judge The Lord Chief Justice of England and Wales 20 December 2010. The Judiciary of England and Wales.

issued by him. The guidance emphasized that anyone using electronic text is strictly bound by the existing restrictions on reporting court proceedings under the Contempt of Court Act 1925.

In May 2010, Paul Chambers was found guilty by District Judge Bennett at Doncaster Magistrates' Court for 'sending a menacing electronic communication' via the 'public communications network[85] contrary to provisions of the 2003 Communications Act. The judge fined him £385 and ordered him to pay £600 costs. The 27-year-old accountant had tweeted to his 600 followers in a moment of frustration after snow forced the closure of Robin Hood Airport in January 2010. In dismissing his first appeal at Doncaster Crown Court in September 2010, Mrs Justice Jacqueline Davies said the Twitter message was 'menacing in its content and obviously so. It could not be more clear. Any ordinary person reading this would see it in that way and be alarmed.' Chambers' tweet had read: 'Robin Hood Airport is closed. You've got a week and a bit . . . otherwise I'm blowing the airport sky high!' His conviction was upheld and costs increased to £2,600. Mr Chambers subsequently argued before the Appeal Court in February 2012 that he thought no one would ever have taken seriously his joking threat against Robin Hood Airport. The appeal court reserved judgment and in June 2012 the case was scheduled to be heard before Lord Judge LCJ, Owen J and Griffith Williams J. During the two-and-a-half year legal battle, Mr Chambers won the support of Twitter-using comedy stars including Al Murray, Graham Linehan and Stephen Fry in his fight against his conviction; they also helped raise about £30,000 to cover legal costs. The appeal was eventually allowed.

In July 2012, Justice Minister Nick Herbert published the Government's White Paper on criminal justice reform, *Swift and Sure Justice: the Government's Plans for Reform of the Criminal Justice System.*[86] The White Paper set out a programme of reform building on some of the lessons learned from the response to the August riots in 2011 during which the police, prosecutors and courts worked together – offenders were brought to justice within days and the courts were open through the night and at weekends. The White Paper proposed legislation to deliver 'swift', 'sure', 'efficient' and 'open' criminal justice by increasing use of court technology, 'virtual' trials, court video links, prosecutors using iPads and widespread naming of offenders on the judicial internet.

This led to the introduction of 'courtroom TV' in the UK in 2013. The UK Supreme Court had already been streaming its proceedings live on Sky TV since 2009. From October 2013, all Supreme Court judgments were uploaded to YouTube, announced Lord Neuberger, President of the Supreme Court, who said: 'We hope this new service will open up another window on our work and the reasoning behind our decisions, and broaden our audience.'[87]

The first historic televised appeal hearing at the Court of Appeal took place on 31 October 2013. Proceedings concerned Kevin Fisher, of Goffs Oak, Hertfordshire, who was imprisoned in May for his role in what is believed to be the UK's biggest plot to counterfeit pound coins. Lord Justice Pitchford refused Fisher's application to appeal against his sentence after hearing submissions from the appellant's barrister Alex Cameron QC, older brother of the Prime Minister. Safeguards during appeal against convictions include a time-delay system operated by a specialist video journalist to protect normal court restrictions such contempt of court and broadcasting regulations. The High Court in Scotland had already televised the 'Nat Fraser' appeal in July 2013. Fraser, originally found guilty in 2003 of the murder of his wife Arlene, had received a 25 year prison sentence. This was followed by a lengthy appeal and led to his conviction being quashed. At a re-trial in May 2012, Fraser was found guilty by a majority verdict and sentenced to at least 17 years in prison. The second trial was shown in its entirety as a documentary. Lord Bracadale, the Judge, Advocate-Depute Alex Prentice QC, and defence QC John Scott were shown in full together with two security officers.[88]

85 *Chambers (Paul) v R* (unreported) 8 February 2012.
86 Ministry of Justice (2012a) Cm 8388.
87 The UK Supreme Court, YouTube video footage at: www.youtube.com/user/uksupremecourt?feature=watch.
88 Source: 'Revealed: the inside story of Nat Fraser re-trial', by Russell Leadbetter, *The Herald*, Scotland, 9 July 2013.

See above 1.1

Let us return to the Justice and Security Act 2013, mentioned at the beginning of this chapter, which came into force on 25 April 2013. Part 1 of the Act created a new Intelligence and Security Committee of Parliament (the ISC), to replace the Intelligence and Security Committee created by the Intelligence Services Act 1994. The statutory remit of the ISC includes:

(1)   a role in overseeing the wider Government intelligence community beyond the three security and intelligence agencies ('the Agencies'); and

(2)   retrospective oversight of the operational activities of the Agencies on matters of significant national interest.

In addition, the ISC is given powers to require information from the Agencies subject only to a veto by the Secretary of State rather than, as was the case under the Intelligence Services Act 1994, Agency heads. This means that Parliament now has a more substantial role in ISC appointments.

For the purpose of our discussion on secret courts and closed material proceedings, Part 2 of the 2013 Act is the most interesting, providing for Closed Material Procedures (CMP) in civil proceedings before the High Court, the Scottish Court of Session, the Court of Appeal or the Supreme Court. It sets out a framework whereby the judge can allow elements of a case to be heard in closed court, in addition to the open proceedings. The process broadly consists of two stages:

●   The Secretary of State or any party to the case may make an application to the court to make a declaration that the proceedings are ones in which a closed material *application* may be made. The court may grant a declaration following an application or of its own motion provided that certain conditions are met.

●   Once the declaration has been made, a closed material application may then be made by a party to the proceedings not to disclose specific pieces or tranches of material, except to the court, a special advocate and the Secretary of State. An application will be granted where the disclosure of that material would be damaging to the interests of national security.[89]

In summary, Part 2 of the Justice and Security Act 2013 provides for Closed Material Procedures (CMP) in relation to certain civil court proceedings to prevent the making of court disclosure orders in relation to sensitive information closely connected to the purposes of and oversight by UK Security and Secret Intelligence Services (MI5 and MI6) and Her Majesty's Forces. This means the Secretary of State (for Justice) can make a CMP application that the particular proceedings be held in private and that disclosure of sensitive material to the defendant may not take place.[90]

In a letter to the *Daily Mail* in February 2013, some 702 lawyers said that the closed sittings ('secret courts') would 'fatally undermine' the fairness of the open justice system and would 'erode core principles of our civil justice system'.[91] The bill was passed anyway and received Royal Assent on 25 April 2013. While it might not be the (new) Justice Secretary Chris Grayling's intention to undermine the open justice principle, is it right that national security and intelligence sources should be protected by law? Many regard the Justice and Security Act 2013 as being driven by the demands of the US intelligence service, anxious to hide sensitive issues such as extraordinary rendition. Have these law reforms gone a step too far where the status quo of the UK ideal of open justice has been seriously undermined? Does this mean that closed or 'secret' courts in terrorism cases

---

89   Part 2, section 6 ('disclosure of sensitive material') Justice and Security Act 2013.

90   Section 6(1) Justice and Security Act 2013.

91   Source: 'No to secret justice: The letter from 700 legal professionals', *Daily Mail*, 27 February 2013 at: www.dailymail.co.uk/home/article-2285480/No-secret-justice.html#ixzz2Zf7ZNfmE.

come close to non-democratic practices by despots? Or is it a price worth paying to safeguard the nation's security services?

 FOR THOUGHT

How is the rule of law of open justice as suggested in the Government White Paper (2012) *Swift and Sure Justice* to be policed? Study the Justice and Security Act 2013, Part 2 and answer the question: *Quis custodiet ipsos custodies* – who will guard the guardians – in a democracy where the legal process must be preserved as well as providing open justice to the public of the legal process? When, in your opinion, should the public (and media) be excluded from court proceedings? Discuss the legislative proposals to extend 'secret' court hearings.

1.5 Scotland's privacy principle of *actio injuriarum* ('wounded feelings')

In the Roman law tradition, an attack on someone's honour (*injuria*) has historically been regarded as an invasion of privacy and a violation of personality. This concept has been used in Scottish courts of record since 1500.[92] For example, calling someone a liar or cheat amounts to a verbal injury and the private pursuer can seek redress in the criminal courts by way of '*solatium*' for pain and suffering or character 'disfigurement'.

The doctrine of *solatium* in Scots law is an action that deals with the *delict* (tort) of 'wounded' or 'injured feelings' (*injuria* or *iniuria* = injury, insult or affront) and is part of property law.[93] *Solatium* generally arises from an infringement of a non-patrimonial right of personality by *injuria* and is regarded as a subjective wrong. *Injuria* can only be identified as an invasion of the right to peace of mind and human dignity, and an invasion of privacy; it is not calculable as an objective loss and it has to be borne in mind that 'wounded feelings' are not the same as psychiatric injury.[94]

1.5.1 Rights of personality and the action for *solatium* for affront

The Roman law concept of a man's 'injuries to honour' was adopted in Scots law and indeed the tort laws (delicts) of most Western European jurisdictions, such as the Netherlands,[95] Germany and France, where the rights to dignity and honour are still protected in their respective Civil Codes today. The doctrine in its modern form comprises a right of personality, providing for a principled legal framework covering actions such as defamation, privacy and harassment. The right to dignity properly understood in Roman law is a non-patrimonial right of personality, and in Scots law such an infringed right is remedied by a claim for *solatium* for 'wounded feelings' by the *actio injuriarum*; this includes post-mortem cases, the main common law authority being **Pollok v Workman** (1900).[96]

---

92 Source: Zimmermann (1996).
93 See: Duncan, Gordon, Gamble and Reid (1996); also: Reid and Zimmermann (2000), Chapter 31.
94 See: Whitty (2005).
95 See: Neethling, Potgieter and Visser (1996); also: Neethling, Potgieter and Scott (1995).
96 [1900] 2 F 354 (Scottish Inner House). This case concerned the interest in a person's dead body on the part of the surviving spouse.

Today, Scottish delict and property law provides a sophisticated structure of real rights and (as is also the case in German law) of acquiring things – deriving from Roman civil law through the *ius commune*.[97] The tort of defamation is then regarded as 'delictual liability' in Scots law and amounts to an infringement of a personality right. In summary, *actio injuriarum* covers affront-based delicts in a wide jurisprudential field of Scots private law, such as defamation ('verbal injury'), the interference with liberty (such as a wrongful arrest), personal molestation (such as harassment or stalking) and breaches of confidentiality and privacy.[98] It also covers medical law (see: **Stevens v Yorkhill NHS Trust**[99]).

See Chapter 3

 FOR THOUGHT

Should the Scottish doctrine of *actio injuriarum* be introduced into English and Welsh law? Does it conflict with any Article 10 ECHR rights?

1.6 The boundaries of a free press: analysis and discussion

How impartial should the media be? What is the difference between comment, conjecture and fact? Traditionally, in Britain at least, a person's choice of (online) newspaper is seen as a reflection of their views and values. If we buy the *Guardian*, for instance, we are seen as slightly left-wing, whereas the *Daily Telegraph* reader will be seen as more conservative, with the *Daily Mail* often being seen as appealing particularly to a female readership. Some newspaper proprietors pin their political allegiances to one party, though not necessarily the same one all the time, as was seen when Rupert Murdoch changed his historical Conservative allegiance to Labour in 1996–97, supporting Tony Blair in the 1997 General Election. Former Downing Street Director of Communications for Labour Alastair Campbell further claimed in his memoirs that Mr Murdoch pressed Prime Minister Blair over the timing of the war on Iraq, thereby pledging support by News International (e.g. the *News of the World* and the *Sun*). Mr Campbell's book *The Burden of Power: Countdown to Iraq* (2012) further suggests that Rupert Murdoch made moves which would have helped US Republicans the week before a House of Commons vote in 2003 on deploying British troops to Iraq.

One of the few certainties in the world of journalism and editorial policy is that the age-old tension between freedom of expression and the right to robust and occasionally rude debate will, from time to time, come into conflict with the sensibilities of those who feel insulted or abused and minorities who can feel oppressed by the slights, real or imagined, of the majority. When David Cameron gave evidence at the Leveson Inquiry on 14 June 2012, Mr Jay QC, cross-examining the Prime Minister, referred to the 'too close relationship between press and politicians'. But David Cameron repeatedly denied that there was a 'nod and a wink' relationship between the Conservatives and the Murdoch press. Cameron had met with James Murdoch 15 times, with Rupert Murdoch 10 times, and had met with journalists 1,404 times while in opposition government.

When the Danish newspaper *Jyllands-Posten* published cartoons of the Prophet Muhammad in September 2005 (reprinted by Norwegian and French newspapers) it caused outrage in the Muslim

---

97 See: Carey Miller and Irvine (2005), paras 1.17–1.18.
98 Source: Reid (1993), vol. 18 paras 4ff; 539ff.
99 [2006] SLT 889 Outer House, 13 September 2006. This was one of many cases covering the 'organ scandals' at Bristol and Alder Hey (Liverpool) hospitals. In this Scottish case the mother of a child born on 30 June 1995 with a congenital abnormality of the diaphragm raised an action of damages in *actio injuriarum* against the health trust for psychiatric injury allegedly sustained following the defendant's disclosure that her daughter's brain had been removed in the course of a post-mortem.

world, with violent protests erupting across the Middle East. Hundreds of Iranians attacked the Danish embassy in Tehran and Saudi Arabia recalled its ambassador to Denmark, while Libya closed its embassy in Copenhagen and Lebanese demonstrators set the Danish embassy in Beirut on fire. By 2009, 11 Danish newspapers had been contacted by the Saudi lawyer Faisal Yamani, representing eight Muslim organizations claiming to represent in turn 94,923 descendants of Muhammad, demanding that *Jyllands-Posten* and the other newspapers remove the cartoons from their websites and print apologies. On 26 February 2010, Danish newspaper *Politiken* published an apology for reprinting the cartoons. Though this was welcomed by the Danish Prime Minister, he equally stressed the importance of press freedom. The editor of *Jyllands-Posten* said that its sister paper had failed in the fight for freedom of speech and called it a 'sad day' for the Danish press.[100] When examining Strasbourg jurisprudence it could be argued that the ECtHR has, in the past, ruled in favour of Article 9 ECHR ('freedom of religion') as opposed to Article 10 ('freedom of expression') (see: **Otto-Preminger-Institut v Austria** (1995);[101] **Murphy v Ireland** (2000)[102]).

When it comes to balancing the freedom of expression and the right to privacy in human rights law (Article 10 versus Article 8 ECHR), the Strasbourg court has repeatedly stressed the limitation on freedom of expression, but equally the limitations on an individual's right to privacy; that is, Article 8 should not extend to the protection of someone's reputation or commercial interest (**Karakó v Hungary** (2009)).[103]

❖ KEY CASE	*Karakó v Hungary* (2009) European Court of Human Rights

Precedent
❖ Article 8 ECHR does not extend to 'reputation'.
❖ Member states to the Convention have their own legislation to deal with a person's reputation (e.g. defamation laws).

Facts
During the Hungarian Parliamentary elections of 2002, Mr László Karakó (K), Member of Parliament for the Fidesz Party ('the Civic Union') and a candidate in one of the electoral districts of Szabolcs-Szatmár-Bereg County, complained that the respondent state (Hungary) had breached his Article 8 rights. K had pressed criminal charges and brought a private prosecution for libel against 'LH', chairman of the county regional assembly (Szabolcs-Szatmár-Bereg). LH had accused K of regularly voting against the interests of the county. The prosecuting authorities decided not to pursue K's libel charges, also dismissing his private prosecution. K argued before the Strasbourg court that the Hungarian authorities had failed to assist him to pursue his libel actions against his political opponent, claiming that this had violated his right to reputation which he argued breached his Article 8 right.

Decision
As K claimed a violation of Article 8 by way of 'injury to his reputation', the Strasbourg court had to determine whether Article 8 included 'reputation' as part of the privacy right.

100 Source: 'Danish newspaper apologises in Muhammad cartoons row', by Lars Eriksen, *Guardian*, 26 February 2010.
101 (1995) 19 EHRR 34 (Case No 13470/87) (ECtHR).
102 (2000) 38 EHRR 13 (ECtHR).
103 (2009) (Application no. 39311/05) Strasbourg, 28 April 2009 (ECtRH).

The Court found that the impugned statement was a value judgement, dismissing K's complaint on the grounds that the 'right to privacy' under Article 8 did not imply a right to reputation. The judgment referred to the principle established in **von Hannover No 1**,[104] where the ECtHR had extended the protection of private life to the protection of personal integrity which did not extend to 'reputation'.

This meant that the complainant's allegation that his reputation as a politician had been harmed by an allegedly libellous statement was not a sustainable claim regarding the protection of his right to respect for personal integrity under Article 8 ECHR.

Analysis

In **Karakó** the ECtHR held that there was sufficient legislation in several Member States to the Convention (such as the UK), whereby reputation had traditionally been protected by the law of defamation.[105] A limitation on freedom of expression for the sake of Karakó's (K's) reputation would have been disproportionate under Article 10. Consequently, there had been *no* violation of K's Article 8 right.

The Strasbourg court decision in **Karakó** is an important one and impacts on many other cases thereafter (such as **LNS – John Terry**), where the individual – very often a celebrity – claims that Article 8 of the Convention should also protect his reputation (rather than 'just' his right to privacy). The ECtHR reaffirmed its jurisprudence that 'reputation' cannot form part of a personality right under Article 8 ECHR. In this case K had not shown that the publication constituted such a serious interference with his private life as to undermine his personal integrity. Accordingly, it was K's reputation alone which was at stake in the context of an expression made to his alleged detriment.[106]

The ECtHR correctly noted that the Hungarian authorities had taken into account the fact that K was a politician, active in public life, and that the statement was made during an election campaign in which he was a candidate, and constituted a negative opinion regarding his public activities. On those grounds, they found that it was constitutionally protected.

In summary, the Human Rights Court decision in **Karakó** conformed with Convention rights and standards in carefully balancing Articles 8 and 10 ECHR. In the circumstances, K's allegation that his reputation as a politician had been harmed was not a sustainable claim regarding the protection of his right to respect for personal integrity under Article 8. The Court pointed out that national laws of Member States were adequate enough to deal with claims of defamation[107] or other causes of action, such as 'harassment' (see: Protection of Harassment Act 1997).

Conversely, in **Lindon v France** (2007)[108] the ECtHR determined that the right to reputation should always be considered as safeguarded by Article 8. This case arose from a novel published in France

---

104 **Von Hannover v Germany** [2004] EMLR 21.
105 See paras 21–29 of the judgment.
106 For further discussion see: Milo (2008), pp. 15–43 (29).
107 See *Gatley* [on *Libel and Slander* 11th edn], §27.17 and the cases there cited.
108 **Lindon, Otchakovsky-Laurens and July v France** (2007) (Applications nos. 21279/02 and 36448/02) judgment of 22 October 2007 (ECTHR).

entitled 'Jean-Marie Le Pen on Trial' (*Le Procès de Jean-Marie Le Pen*) in respect of which Monsieur Le Pen and his right-wing National Front party brought defamation proceedings in France against the writer and publisher of the book.[109] The serious and murderous allegations against Le Pen and the National Front were found to be factually incorrect, defamatory and unproven and the Paris court upheld the defamation claims. The three applicants (Lindon, Otchakovsky-Laurens and July – respectively, the author, the chairman of the board of directors of the publishing company P.O.L. and the publication director of the newspaper *Libération*) were found guilty of defamation.

See also
Chapter 2.4.6

The three applicants claimed before the Strasbourg Court that their Article 10 right had been breached, that any exceptions to freedom of expression should be 'construed strictly' and that politicians ought to 'display a great degree of tolerance'. The ECtHR ruled that the French appeal court had made a reasonable assessment of the facts in finding that to liken Monsieur Le Pen to a 'chief of a gang of killers' overstepped the permissible limits of freedom of expression. The **Lindon** case was in stark contrast to the UK **Reynolds** jurisprudence, whereby Judge Loucaides in the ECtHR particularly emphasized both the importance of truth and of media organizations being accountable to those against whom they make false or defamatory allegations.

This chapter has discussed freedom of speech as a fundamental human right, protected by a number of international conventions and the open justice system. Some authoritarian regimes were highlighted where writers were unable to freely exercise their power of free expression and had to go into exile. The notion of censorship was highlighted, where governments have tried to suppress or restrict freedom of speech and the press. Strasbourg jurisprudence has shown more recently that Articles 8 and 10 ECHR provide for a balancing of interests, which has led to a more nuanced approach to freedom of expression in Europe compared with the more absolutist approach in the USA, where freedom of expression is a rather dominant right compared with privacy and other rights.

What is and is not allowed on the internet is one of biggest challenges facing many national governments. Governments issuing legislation such as the UK Digital Economy Act 2010 (DEA) have to balance the interests and freedom of internet users and the protection of personal integrity rights with the requirement for commercial and personal security so that the internet is not being misused. The DEA 2010 aims to punish illegal internet file-sharing (unauthorized downloads of films, games, musical works) and make Internet Service Providers (ISPs) responsible for all content posted on their server.[110] Parts of the legislation compel ISPs to hand over user data related to

See Chapter
10

suspected illegal file-sharers at the request of rights holders, such as record labels and film distributors (see: **R (on the application of BT and TalkTalk) v BPI and others** [2012][111]).

Freedom of expression and freedom of the press do not always go hand in hand: there can be abuses by powerful media moguls which threaten media pluralism, as the Leveson Inquiry has shown. There are increasing challenges facing the use of new technologies and there is an urgent need for more stringent compliance with international legislation that protects both freedom of expression and an individual's right to privacy. Certainly, there needs to be clarification as to how human rights are to be protected if there is to be freedom of expression in electronic media.

---

109 See: Lindon (1998).
110 Section 3 Digital Economy Act 2010 'Obligation to notify subscribers of reported infringements' and section 4 'Obligation to provide infringement lists to copyright owners'.
111 **R (on the application of (1) British Telecommunications, (2) TalkTalk Telecom Group plc) v Secretary of State for Culture, Olympics, Media and Sport and (1) BPI (British Recorded Music Industry) Ltd, (2) British Video Association Ltd, (3) Broadcasting Entertainment Cinematograph and Theatre Union, (4) Equity, (5) Film Distributors' Association Ltd, (6) Football Association Premier League Ltd, (7) Motion Picture Association Inc, (8) The Musicians' Union, (9) Producers' Alliance for Cinema and Television Ltd, (10) Unite** [2012] EWCA Civ 232; [2011] EWHC 1021 (Admin).

FOR THOUGHT

In the **BT and TalkTalk** judicial review case the applicants argued that anti-file-sharing legislation (DEA 2010) may have been rushed through Parliament and contravened EU law by being incompatible with provisions of Directive 2000/31/EC of 8 June 2000, the 'Electronic Commerce Directive' (ECD). Do you agree?

 ## 1.7 Further reading

Baden-Powell, E. and Anthony, L. (2012) 'Digital Economy Act 2'. *Entertainment Law Review*, **23(5), 130–133.**
This article discusses recent legislation in relation to intellectual property in EU and UK law in line with ever-changing developments in information technology. The article principally discusses the Digital Economy Act 2010, the duty imposed on Internet Service Providers (ISP) and notification of online copyright infringement.

Carey Miller, D. L. and Irvine, D. (2005) *Corporeal Moveables in Scots Law*. **2nd revised edition. Edinburgh: W. Green Publishers.**
This book deals with litigation liabilities in Scots law, relating to the duties and obligations of barristers and solicitors engaged in and preparing for litigation, covering litigators' statutory, contractual and common law duties. The book deals with the practical impact of the Woolf Reforms and explains the law and practice of claims for professional negligence and applications for wasted costs arising from the mishandling of litigation.

Frost, C. (2011) *Journalism, Ethics and Regulation*. **3rd edition. Harlow: Longman.**
Though this book is principally aimed at working journalists and editors, it is a comprehensive volume addressing ethical considerations, dilemmas and challenges that practising journalists face. The text looks at practical challenges in the digital age, such as news-gathering in line with ethical and regulatory frameworks. The text illustrates the conflicts between the law, ethics and the public's right to be informed from a journalistic perspective.

Jordan, B. (2010) 'Reputation and Article 8: *Karako v Hungary*. **Case Comment'.** *Entertainment Law Review*, **21(3), 109–11.**
The article discusses the *Karakó* human rights court case and the complainant's allegation that his reputation as a politician had been harmed by an allegedly libellous statement and that this should be protected under Article 8 ECHR.

McInnes, R. (2010) *Scots Law for Journalists*. **8th edition. Edinburgh: W Green/ Sweet & Maxwell.**
This is the only book on this subject in Scotland. The book has been completely updated, and is clear and concise in Scots Law, aimed mainly at practising journalists and editors. It provides good comparative coverage of English and Scots law on topics such as 'freedom of information' and human rights legislation, as well as case law in the area of privacy.

Rawls, J. (orig. 1971; 1999) *A Theory of Justice*. **Reprinted and updated edition. Oxford: Oxford University Press.**
This is a twentieth-century classic, discussing John Rawls's highly regarded and compelling theory of social justice. For example, Rawls's political liberalism does not endorse welfare state capitalism.

Sanders, K. (2003) *Ethics and Journalism*. **London: Sage.**
This book provides readers with a summary of philosophical perspectives relevant to the topic in relation to the print press and broadcast journalism. There are also relevant references to film and literature.

Spencer, J. R. (1989) *Jackson's Machinery of Justice*. **8th edition (of the original publication by Professor R. M. Jackson in 1903). Cambridge: Cambridge University Press.**
This is a classic text. First published in 1940, R. M. Jackson's *Machinery of Justice* has long been an established text on the subject of 'justice' in England and Wales. For this edition, J. R. Spencer has undertaken a full-scale revision, incorporating major topical issues such as PACE (Police and Criminal Evidence Act of 1984) and the Prosecution of Offences Act 1985.

Wragg, P. (2013) 'Mill's dead dogma: the value of truth to free speech jurisprudence'. *Public Law*, **April, 363–385.**
The purpose of this article is not so much to articulate fresh insights into John Stuart Mill and his famous work *On Liberty*[112] but to scrutinize the role of Mill's argument in the UK in relation to Article 10 ECHR jurisprudence. Paul Wragg argues that Mill's theory is sometimes misrepresented in the academic literature as chiefly concerned with 'the truth' about uninhibited discussion. The author looks at the complexity of Mill's argument on free speech which, Wragg argues, has at times been oversimplified. The author argues that, given certain societal conditions, absolute freedom of thought and 'almost' absolute freedom of expression represent the optimal conditions by which 'truth' may be discovered. Although truth in philosophical terms is a highly contested concept, Mill uses it simply to indicate knowledge pertinent to Enlightenment pursuits of self-perfection and happiness.

Wylie, A. B. and Crossan, S. J. (2010) *Introductory Scots Law: Theory and practice*. **2nd edition. London: Hodder Gibson.**
Anything a law student needs to know about the subject: both for working practices and exam revision in Scots law.

Zimmermann, R. (1996) *The Law of Obligations: Roman foundations of the civilian tradition*. **Oxford: Clarendon Press.**
This book is widely regarded as one of the classic textbooks on comparative law, discussing Roman law of obligations in Europe, the UK and the USA. The scholarly work traces the transformation of the Roman law (of obligations) into German, French, South African and Scots law, and contrasts the legal systems in depth.

---

112 *See:* J S Mill, 'On Liberty' in *Collected Works of John Stuart Mill* (UTP, 1977), vol. XVIII, pp. 243 and 247.

Chapter 2

Privacy and Confidentiality

Chapter Contents

Key Points

This chapter will cover the following questions:

○ What is the difference between confidentiality and privacy in common law?

○ How should the courts balance Articles 8 ('right to privacy') and 10 ('freedom of expression') of the European Convention?

○ How has privacy law developed since the Human Rights Act 1998?

○ What is the meaning of the 'public interest test'?

○ Can a child claim his own right to privacy – independent of his parents?

○ Should the internet be regulated by stricter legislation?

○ Is there a tort of privacy in the making?

2.1 Overview

In February 2013, St James's Palace commenced legal action for breach of privacy against the Italian magazine Chi, which had put photographs of the pregnant Duchess of Cambridge in a bikini on its front cover with the words 'the belly is growing'. The royal couple, Prince William and his wife Catherine, were on a beach at the private Caribbean island of Mustique during their 'luna di miele in tre' ('honeymoon for three' – a play on words on the title of a 1976 Italian sex comedy, featuring Linda Lovelace's hirsute co-star of *Deep Throat*, Harry Reems). Five months earlier legal action was brought for breach of privacy against the French magazine *Closer* (also owned by the former Italian Prime Minister and media tycoon Silvio Berlusconi) for publishing topless photos of the Duchess sunbathing in the gardens of a private chateau in Provence.[1] Editor Alfonso Signorini of Chi magazine also published the topless photos of Catherine, tweeting that not even a call from the Queen could have stopped him printing the paparazzi shots of the Duchess. The Italian Chi magazine published 18 photographs spread over 19 pages of the royal couple sunbathing at the chateau.

Prince William and his wife Catherine launched a privacy action in the French courts against Laurence Pieau, editor of the French edition of *Closer*,[2] and its Italian-based publisher, Mondadori.[3] The Irish *Daily Star* also published the topless photographs of the Princess. British media tycoon Richard Desmond, who part-owns the Irish tabloid, called the editor's decision to publish the topless photos 'abhorrent', threatening to close the paper down. Desmond, owner of the Northern and Shell group and the Irish-based Independent News and Media, argued that their Royal Highnesses had every expectation of privacy when they had rented Chateau D'Autet, the private chateau in Provence, owned by Viscount Linley, the Queen's nephew.[4] Editor of the Irish *Daily Star*, Michael O'Kane, defended his decision to publish the topless photos of the Duchess, by saying: 'I'm absolutely stunned that Kate Middleton would think, her being the most photographed woman in the world, I think one of the most famous people in the world, that she would expose herself

---

1 Source: 'Magazine publishes bikini snaps of pregnant Duchess on holiday', by Valentine Lowe, *The Times*, 13 February 2013.
2 Source: 'Oh my God! Les photos qui vont faire le tour du monde.' *Closer*, numéro 379, vendredi 14 septembre 2012. Also on the *Closer* website : 'Seulement dans closer: Kate et William, leurs vacances très hot en Provence', 13 September 2012.
3 Source: 'Palace goes to court over "grotesque" invasion of privacy', by Ian Burrell, *Independent*, 15 September 2012.
4 Source: 'New privacy laws for Ireland as *Irish Daily Star* editor is suspended after "indecent" decision to print topless Kate photos', by Martin Robinson and Mark Duell, *Daily Mail*, 17 September 2012.

topless, outdoors, and not expect the world to take notice of it', speaking in an interview with an Irish radio station.[5]

The French court subsequently ordered *Closer* magazine to hand over the original photographs. On 19 September 2012 the editor of Danish gossip magazine *Se og Hør* ('See and Hear') said that he was 'incredibly proud that we have rights to the pictures of Britain's future Queen', featuring a 16-page supplement in spite of the injunction granted in the French courts.[6] The incident was reminiscent of the worst excesses of the media some 15 years earlier when Prince William's mother, Diana, Princess of Wales, died in a car crash, while being chased by paparazzi through Paris.[7]

Former editor of the *News of the World*, Phil Hall, argued that the Duchess may have been a little 'naïve' and her advisers negligent in allowing the ('topless Kate') situation to arise, particularly at the point where the couple were about to visit a Muslim country, Malaysia. Defence lawyers for the French and Italian press outlets argued that the Duchess of Cambridge is in a privileged position which comes with responsibility and that the public interest test had been established as per the **von Hannover (No 1)** ruling in the Strasbourg Court. Therefore, it did not matter whether the photos were taken in private or not.

Only a month earlier, the *Sun* had justified printing naked pictures of Prince Harry on the grounds that they had been distributed on the internet in the USA. Though France has strict privacy laws,[8] these did not stop the sensationalist intrusions of privacy in 'Kate Middleton's' case. The timing of these publications was unfortunate for the British media at the time that Lord Leveson's inquiry into media standards (the Leveson Inquiry) was about to impose tougher regulation on the press.

This chapter follows on from the first chapter by looking at the development of press freedom, with aggressive popular journalism and social networking via the internet coming into conflict with increasing demands for effective protection of personal privacy being strongly argued by groups such as 'Hacked Off' (chaired by film star Hugh Grant). The aim of the chapter is to clarify and distinguish the terms 'confidentiality' and 'privacy' in English common law and European Court of Human Rights (ECtHR) jurisprudence. The main focus will be on the way courts have made use of orders in the form of (super)injunctions, to restrain publication and grant individuals anonymity with a view to keeping confidential information which some celebrities would rather was not published for a whole variety of reasons. But privacy is not just about celebrities; it particularly concerns ordinary people, such as the Dowler family whose 13-year-old daughter Milly disappeared in March 2002. The Leveson Inquiry was told in May 2012 how Milly's phone was hacked into by *News of the World* reporters, and how the police knew about it. Levi Bellfield was convicted of her murder in June 2011, and sentenced to a whole life tariff.

The by now well-known case of **Kaye v Robertson** (1991)[9] highlights the failure of both the English common law and statute to protect in an effective way the personal privacy of individual citizens. This has been the subject of much comment over the years, particularly compared with continental European law, as Professor Markesinis has commented:

> English law, on the whole, compares unfavourably with German law. True, many aspects of the human personality and privacy are protected by a multitude of existing torts but this means fitting the facts of each case in the pigeon-hole of an existing tort and this process may not only involve strained constructions; often it may also leave a deserving plaintiff without a remedy.[10]

---

5 Source: 'Irish Daily Star editor defiant over topless Kate photos', *Daily Telegraph*, 16 September 2012.
6 Source: 'Hertuginde Kate: Fræk fortid. Se det meget afslørende billede af den smukke brunette', Af Lousie Rømer og Peter Bugge, 20. September 2012 at: www.seoghoer.dk/Nyheder/Royalt/Kate%20Middleton%20fraek%20fortid.aspx.
7 Diana, Princess of Wales, died on 31 August 1997. The accident happened after the Princess left the Ritz Hotel in the French capital with her companion Dodi Al Fayed – son of Harrods owner Mohammed Al Fayed.
8 France's privacy laws are based on Article 9 of the Civil Code of 1970.
9 (1991) FSR 62.
10 See: Markesinis (1990) at p. 316.

If ever a person has a right to be left alone by strangers with no public interest to pursue, it must surely be when he lies in hospital, like the *'Allo 'Allo!* actor Gorden Kaye, recovering from brain surgery and in no more than partial command of his faculties. It is this invasion of his privacy by the newspaper at the time which underlay Mr Kaye's complaint. Yet it alone, however gross, does not entitle him to relief in English law.

As Glidewell LJ summarized in **Kaye v Robertson**:

> We do not need a First Amendment to preserve the freedom of the press, but the abuse of that freedom can be ensured only by the enforcement of a right to privacy. This right has so long been disregarded here that it can be recognised now only by the legislature.

The facts of the **Gorden Kaye** and many subsequent cases suggested in this chapter remain a graphic illustration of the desirability of Parliament considering whether and in what circumstances statutory provision can be made to protect the privacy of individuals in English law.

See Chapter 6.5

This chapter will advance the argument as to whether a new tort of privacy has been created in common law and via Strasbourg jurisprudence. Consideration will be given to the correct test for the courts to apply when assessing whether a breach of privacy, and therein confidentiality, has occurred and what the possible remedies might be. It must be borne in mind that there exists an indirect statutory provision, such as the Data Protection Act 1998, which can achieve some degree of protection for 'personal data'. Also worth noting is the contractual relationship which can enshrine express confidentiality, such as an existing (contractual) relationship between two people, where the other party is a personal assistant, nanny or servant, for example; breaching such express confidentiality during the course of employment will lead to a breach of contract. If a newspaper or broadcaster becomes aware of this contract, yet persuades the employee to reveal secrets about the employer, there may be a liability in either contract or tort law.

This was the case in March 2000 when Mrs Cherie Blair, wife of then Prime Minister Tony Blair, successfully blocked the publication and serialization in the *Daily Mail* of memoirs by Rosalind Marks, the Blairs' former nanny from 1994 to 1998. Mrs Blair obtained a High Court injunction for Ms Marks's breaching her confidentiality clause in her employment contract with the Blairs. The *Mail on Sunday* had already distributed early morning copies; after the injunction was in place, all remaining copies were withdrawn that contained the 'nanny tells all' story. Online links to the earlier *Mail* editions had to be withdrawn, including those provided by the BBC, whose editor Mike Smartt received an early morning warning by the Attorney General for contempt of court.[11]

See below 2.4.5

Part of this consideration involves balancing the rights of those who wish to disclose information and exercise their Article 10 rights with those who wish to protect their privacy and exercise their Article 8 rights under the Convention. Some newspaper editors, such as Paul Dacre of the *Daily Mail*, would argue that common law judge-made development has created a privacy law 'via the back door', a view he gave in a lecture to the Society of Editors in November 2008, referring *inter alia* to Eady J's ruling in the **Max Mosley** case.[12]

It is our human craving for stories and gossip that helps keep the newspaper and magazine industries alive. The Twittersphere now cites personal information and gossip about celebrities', sports personalities' and politicians' indiscretions, even if there are superinjunctions in place. The World Wide Web has rendered territorial demarcation lines of national jurisdictions almost ineffective when we can read the most secret and often controversial information on WikiLeaks (published

---

11 Source: 'Blair defends book injunction', *BBC News Online*, 5 March 2000 at: http://news.bbc.co.uk/1/hi/uk/666450.stm.
12 See: 'Society of Editors: Paul Dacre's speech in full', *Press Gazette*, 9 November 2008: www.pressgazette.co.uk/story.asp?storycode=42394.

in the *Guardian*), such as the US secret Guantánamo Bay files. These consisted of 759 'detainee assessments' – prisoner dossiers written between 2002 and 2009 that spelt out the Americans' suspicions about individual detainees' involvement with terrorism, their intelligence value and the threat they posed if released.[13]

Does an individual – even though they might be rich and famous – have a reasonable expectation of privacy? Mr Justice Patten argued in the 'J. K. Rowling case'[14] that there is a clear difference between celebrities' and private individuals' private lives:

> If a simple walk down the street qualifies for protection then it is difficult to see what would not. For most people who are not public figures in the sense of being politicians or the like, there will be virtually no aspect of their life which cannot be characterized as private. Similarly, even celebrities would be able to confine unauthorized photography to the occasions on which they were at a concert, film premiere or some similar occasion. . . . Even after *von Hannover* [no 1] there remains, I believe, an area of routine activity which when conducted in a public place carries no guarantee of privacy.[15]

As the line between public and private blurs on the internet, can the courts truly protect what they regard as 'private' and 'confidential' in an attempt to protect a person's reputation, including personal image and photographs?

See below 2.8

2.2 The 'red carpet' rule: protection of private and confidential information

The modern concept of public opinion emerged with the production of relatively cheap newspapers in the seventeenth century. At the time that the common law of confidentiality developed in England, America borrowed heavily from English court rulings, resulting in the First, Fourth and Fifth Amendments of the US Bill of Rights 1791, which increasingly protected the freedom of individuals to choose whether or not to perform certain acts or subject themselves to certain experiences.[16] Later the 'liberty' clause was added in the Fourteenth Amendment, granting individuals anonymity rights in terms of 'intimacy' and 'solitude'.[17]

The concept of 'privacy' was first mentioned during the late 1880s by two American lawyers and partners in a Boston law firm, Samuel D. Warren (1852–1910) and Louis D. Brandeis (1856–1941 – later a Supreme Court Judge), whose privacy theory was based on natural rights, responding to new technologies and forms of communication in North America, such as the telephone, photography and sensationalist journalism (the emergence of the paparazzi) – also known in America as 'yellow journalism'.[18] In their seminal 1890 article, 'The Right to Privacy' in the *Harvard Law Review*, Warren and Brandeis[19] argued that privacy was the most cherished of freedoms in a democracy and should be reflected in the Constitution, and that:

---

13 Source: 'What are the Guantánamo Bay files? Understanding the prisoner dossiers', by David Leigh, *Guardian*, 25 April 2011.
14 **Murray v Big Pictures** [2008] EWCA Civ 446 (Patten J).
15 Ibid., at 65–66.
16 For further comparative analysis see: Schilling (1991), pp. 169–176.
17 For further discussion see: Strachan and Singh (2002), pp. 129–161.
18 'Yellow Press' or 'yellow journalism' is an American term, akin to 'tabloid' journalism in the UK, meaning 'exaggeration', 'scandal-mongering' and 'sensationalism'. See: Campbell (2001) who defines the 'yellow press' as having daily multi-column front-page headlines covering a variety of topics, such as sports and scandal, using bold layouts, with large illustrations and color. This type of journalism presents little or no legitimate well-researched news and instead uses eye-catching headlines to sell more newspapers. The term was extensively used to describe certain major New York City newspapers around 1900 as they battled for circulation.
19 See: Warren and Brandeis (1890) at pp. 193–220.

the press is overstepping in every direction the obvious bounds of propriety and decency. Gossip is no longer the resource of the idle and of the vicious, but has become a trade, which is pursued with industry as well as effrontery. To satisfy a prurient taste the details of sexual relations are spread broadcast in the columns of the daily papers.[20]

This article gave rise to several strands of privacy protection including a positive 'publicity right' to control the use of images for commercial purposes (see: **Midler (Bette) v Ford Motor Co and Young & Rubicam** (1988)[21]). Warren and Brandeis also argued that information which was previously hidden and private could now be 'shouted from the rooftops'. They urged that making personal privacy matter should become part of US constitutional law, identifying the Government as a potential privacy invader, because the new inventions (such as the telephone or photography) were making it possible for the Government (the Executive) to obtain new evidence for court proceedings. However, the dominance of the First Amendment[22] has meant that personal privacy is rather truncated in the United States, with 'First Amendment' issues often trumping personal privacy rights, which are less protected in European law, where there is a more nuanced (or proportional) approach.

See below
2.2.3

Warren and Brandeis were right: during the 1970s, long after their death, new computing and recording technologies began to raise serious concerns about privacy, resulting in the US Federal Trade Commission's Fair Information Practice Principles (FIPs), guidelines that represented widely accepted concepts concerning fair information practice in an electronic marketplace.

See Chapter
1.2.2

The concept of 'private and public spheres' was further developed during the 1960s by German Philosopher Jürgen Habermas. He defined the 'public sphere' as an area in which social life can take place, where people can get together and freely discuss and identify societal problems. Habermas argued in favour of open public opinion, which should be aired in the press and could thereby influence political opinion and lead to a truly democratic society.[23] Raymond (1998) picked up Warren and Brandeis's argument almost one hundred years later, when he argued that the emergence of newspapers and the mass media brought freedom of expression into the public domain but to the detriment of a person's privacy.[24] Today, we are faced with a new phenomenon escalating the problem of privacy, namely social networking sites via the internet, such as Twitter, YouTube and Facebook, modern versions of Habermas's public sphere.

Strasbourg's message sent out in **von Hannover No 2** and **Axel Springer** (2012)[25] (compared with **von Hannover No 1**[26]) is helpful, making a distinction of what is of genuine public interest and what is not. In **von Hannover No 2**, the article did not centre on Princess Caroline. Instead, its main focus was her father, Prince Rainier of Monaco, and his deteriorating health, which was a matter of public interest given his official role as reigning head of state. The ECtHR therefore did not grant Princess Caroline the right to privacy under Article 8 ECHR, because the picture portrayed the Princess on holiday in St Moritz during her father's illness (in any case, the article discussed how his health was impacting on members of his family).

In **von Hannover No 1** the photographs at issue depicted Princess Caroline's personal relationships and day-to-day life and activities, such as horse riding, skiing and playing tennis, which the ECtHR decided were purely private.

---

20 Ibid., at p. 196.
21 [1988] 849 F 2d 460 Case No: 87–6168) United States Court of Appeal (for the Ninth Circuit) on 22 June 1988. The case centred on the protectability of the voice of the celebrated chanteuse from commercial exploitation without her consent.
22 US Amendment 1: 'Congress shall make no law respecting an establishment of religion, or prohibiting the free exercise thereof; or abridging the freedom of speech, or of the press; or the right of the people peaceably to assemble, and to petition the government for a redress of grievances.'
23 See: Habermas (1962, translation 1989).
24 See: Raymond (1998), pp. 109–136.
25 *Von Hannover v Germany* (*No 2*) (2012) (Application Numbers – 40660/08, 60641/08) (unreported); *Axel Springer v Germany* (2012) (Application No 39954/08) Strasbourg judgment of 7 February 2012 (ECTHR) (Grand Chamber) (unreported).
26 *Von Hannover v Germany* (*No 1*) (2005) 40 EHRR.

What is clear from both judgments is that where an article and accompanying photo can be shown to contribute to a debate of genuine public interest, it can be justified and be published. Let us call this the 'red carpet' rule, where the ECtHR defined what is meant by 'public' and 'private sphere' more clearly. The **Max Mosley**[27] ruling four years earlier had made it clear that matters concerning the 'extramarital bed', 'death bed' or 'hospital bed' are out of bounds as far as freedom of expression and media reporting are concerned.

See below 2.3

2.2.1 The emergence and demise of the print press

The *Daily Universal Register*, launched in January 1785 by John Walter (1793–1812), saw the start of mass publication in Britain and became *The Times* in 1788. Former coal merchant and Lloyd's underwriter Walter turned his hand to printing, and developed and patented the revolutionary logographic printing press, greatly speeding up typesetting. As editor-in-chief, Walter used contributions from significant political and intellectual writers. Because of the accessible reporting and writing style of *Times* reporters, the newspaper gained rapid popularity among the readership, which, in turn, quickly shaped public opinion. Walter also pioneered 'news from the continent', concentrating in the main on news from across the English Channel covering the French Revolution and the fall of the Bastille on 14 July 1789. The Battle of Waterloo in June 1815 received prominent coverage and the *Times* correspondent in France provided extensive coverage of the trial and execution of Queen Marie Antoinette, with a detailed description of her being guillotined at Place de la Révolution at 1pm on 16 October 1793.[28]

More than 190 years later, in 1981, Australian media mogul Rupert Murdoch, bought Times Newspapers from Canadian Lord Thompson of Fleet, who had grown tired of losing money on newspapers as a result of increasing industrial action by printers and journalists which had frequently stopped publication.[29] Murdoch, who already owned the *Sun* and *News of the World* at the time, as well as a string of newspapers and broadcasting stations in the United States and Australia, decided to revolutionize the print press by building a new printing plant in East London. Mr Murdoch agreed with union leaders at the time that he would preserve the editorial integrity of the newspaper which by then had got into financial difficulties. He agreed to grant freedom of expression and freedom from attachment to any political party; although Mr Murdoch drew criticism at the time for the *New York Post*'s dramatic switch from being the voice of the liberal-leaning Democrats to campaigning for Ronald Reagan and right-wing Republicanism (Murdoch also owned the *New York Post* at the time).

Mr Murdoch's taking over *The Times* and *Sunday Times* in 1981 and moving the printing to Wapping resulted in 563 redundancies, following months of bitter protests by the print unions. By 1986 the pivotal transformation had taken place whereby Rupert Murdoch changed from an Australian press baron to a global media mogul. By 1988, all UK newspapers had moved from Fleet Street to Wapping and Docklands with cheaper and more modern printing technology. *Times* editor, William Rees-Mogg, had stepped down to make way for Harold Evans.[30]

See also:
Chapter 4.2.2

Over the years, Mr Murdoch's empire grew into what later became News Corporation ('News Corp'). Part of the company's portfolio included Sky TV and a 39 per cent stake in British Sky Broadcasting Group Plc (BSkyB) – a pay-to-view TV company. When revelations of phone-hacking

---

27 **Mosley (Max) v NGN** [2008] EWHC 1777 (QB).
28 Source: Aubrey (1895), Vol 3, p. 311.
29 See: (Sir) Harold Evans's account of his editorship of the *Sunday Times* and working with Rupert Murdoch in *Good Times, Bad Times* (1983), preface, p. xv.
30 See: Evans (1983) preface at p. xv.

at the (now defunct) News of the World (NOW)[31] broke in early 2011, this overshadowed Murdoch's bid for an outright bid for BSkyB. Accusations that NOW had hacked into the mobile phone of a 13-year-old murder victim, Milly Dowler, in 2002 and the bribing of police and prison officers provoked widespread criticism from politicians over whether the New York-based company was 'fit and proper' to own a UK broadcaster such as BSkyB. Conservative Culture, Media and Sport Secretary, Jeremy Hunt MP, was therefore forced to refer News Corp's bid for BSkyB to the regulator Ofcom and the Office of Fair Trading. They, in turn, would focus on media plurality, whether the deal would reduce the number of voices, and the fit and proper test. Ofcom, which had the power to revoke BSkyB's licence, could then still hold up the deal as it considered the fit and proper criteria.[32] Shares in BSkyB fell dramatically when the Culture, Media and Sport Select Committee claimed in its report in May 2012 that Mr Murdoch was 'not a fit person to exercise stewardship of any international company', and that News Corp was 'corporately' responsible for 'wilful blindness' over the NOW phone-hacking scandal.[33]

In the end Ofcom ruled that no one was unfit and BSkyB remains controlled in effect by the Murdoch family – though other shareholders are demanding better corporate governance and some reduction of the Murdoch influence. It was probably not much of a surprise that soon after the publication of the Parliamentary Select Committee Report, the 81-year-old Rupert Murdoch announced his resignation on 20 July 2012. By July 2013, Mr Murdoch had split his News Corporation into two separately listed companies, the entertainment division (TV, including Sky, and film), renamed '21st Century Fox', and the newspaper-heavy 'new News Corp'.[34] Rupert Murdoch's voluntary resignation from the UK newspaper industry could well be seen as a sign of things to come: the fact that the print press would soon become history. The NOW phone-hacking affair and the fallout from the Leveson Inquiry may well have been a convenient route for Mr Murdoch to restructure his investments so that the loss-making newspaper print divisions could be disposed of more easily (he had already closed down the News of the World a year earlier). It is a fact that journalism has become an increasingly internet-based occupation and the readership is mostly online. After the then chairman of the then PCC, Lord Hunt, had given evidence to the Leveson Inquiry in July 2012, Lord Justice Leveson summarized the state of British newspapers as 'depressing' given the financial situation of most daily newspapers.[35]

The Culture, Media and Sport Committee's Report (May 2012) examined whether or not there was sound evidence to suggest that the Committee and its predecessor Parliamentary Committees had been misled by any witnesses during the course of their work on the phone-hacking scandal, which continued to reverberate around News International and to have major repercussions for the British newspaper industry as a whole. Several times at both the Leveson Inquiry and at the Culture, Media and Sport Select Committee hearings during 2011 and 2012, there appeared to be several contradictions between witnesses, such as Rupert and 'heir apparent' James Murdoch, former executive chairman of News International Les Hinton, former NOW editor Colin Myler, and the former Sun and News of the World editor and ex-News International chief executive Rebekah Brooks

---

31 On 7 July 2011, James Murdoch, Deputy Chief Operating Officer and Chairman and Chief Executive Officer (International), News Corporation, made a public statement announcing the closure of the 168-year-old News of the World, in which he stated that wrongdoing was not confined to one reporter and that both the newspaper and News International had failed to get to the bottom of this affair. Source: News International Press Release, 7 July 2011.

32 House of Commons – Department of Culture, Media and Sport Select Committee (2010c) Press standards, privacy and libel, Session 2009–10, HC 362.

33 See: House of Commons – Department of Culture, Media and Sport Committee (2012a) News International and Phone-hacking. Eleventh Report of Session 2010–12 Volume. 1 May 2012 HC 903-I.

34 Source: 'Murdoch empire readies for big split', by Andrew Edgecliffe-Johnson, Financial Times, 10 June 2013.

35 See: Witness statement and submission to the Leveson Inquiry from the Rt Hon the Lord Hunt of Wirrall MBE, Chairman of the PCC on 9 July 2012.

(aka Rebekah Wade). Sue Akers, Deputy Assistant Commissioner of the Metropolitan Police, revealed at the Leveson Inquiry in February 2012 that evidence examined by her force's 'Operation Elveden' into police corruption even suggested the *Sun* had been paying bribes of tens of thousands of pounds to a 'network of corrupted officials'. Giving evidence to Lord Leveson's inquiry into press standards in March 2012, Jane Furniss, Independent Police Complaints Commission (IPCC) chief executive, said that between 2006 and 2011 the IPCC received 5,179 complaints about improper disclosure of information, ranging from information being sold to organized criminals, to corruption among police and prison officers.[36]

See also Chapter 10.4

With more and more people subscribing to online newspaper editions via their iPads, tablets or smartphones, the writing was perhaps on the 'Murdoch' (pay)wall that printed newspapers would no longer exist in ten years' time. By mid-2012, *The Times* and *Sunday Times* were losing anything between £11m and £60m a year. The Lebedev-owned *Independent* and *London Evening Standard* were losing a combined £27.4m and the *Guardian* and *Observer* were losing around £44.2m between them. Both the *Daily Telegraph* and the *Financial Times* (FT) were still in the black.[37] The ink-stained era of the print press was probably coming to an end, although it is to this fight for what limited sales there are that many ascribe the debasing effect of modern British tabloid journalism and circulation-driven sensationalism leading to extensive incidents of media intrusion.

The demise of the print press was also confirmed by Ofcom's Ninth Annual Communications Market Report of 2012.[38] The regulator's report showed that traditional forms of communications were declining in popularity, with the overall time spent talking on the phone falling by 5 per cent in 2011. Ofcom's research report found that home internet access in the UK rose to 80 per cent by 2012, and the largest increase of 9 per cent (2011–12) was among 'silver surfers' (65- to 74-year-olds). Ofcom's research highlighted that two-fifths of UK adults owned a smartphone, a rise from 27 per cent in 2011 to 39 per cent in 2012.[39]

Since teenagers and young adults are now leading these changes in communication habits, increasingly socializing with friends and family online and through text messages, it follows that fewer newspapers are going to be read in print. With the rapid increase in ownership of internet-connected devices, such as tablets and smartphones, news and current affairs will be read online as tablet ownership increases. In 2012, one in ten UK adults had an e-reader. So how can the internet be legally controlled? This question will be further addressed in Chapter 10.

2.2.2 Common law development in privacy and confidentiality

A privacy right serves to protect a personal and private state of affairs, preventing information that the individual has chosen not to convey from being disclosed. This explanation was first given by John Stuart Mill in his writings 'on liberty', where he argued that privacy allows people to engage in 'experiments in living'.[40]

See Chapter 1.2.2

The protection of someone's privacy is frequently seen as a way of drawing the line as to how far society can intrude into an individual's private affairs. To define 'privacy' is perhaps most difficult, as the notion of privacy differs from country to country and from culture to culture.

---

36 Source: 'Leveson Inquiry: Report into corruption by police and journalists will be published 'imminently'', by Martin Hickman and John Fahey, *Independent*, 28 March 2012.
37 Source: 'News industry struggles with the fear that general interest has had its day', by Peter Preston, *Observer*, 22 July 2012.
38 Source: Office of Communications (Ofcom) (2012b) *Communications Market Report* 2012. Research Document of 18 July 2012: http://stakeholders.ofcom.org.uk/binaries/research/cmr/cmr12/CMR_UK_2012.pdf.
39 Ibid., pp. 4–10. Summary of findings.
40 Mill (1859).

Individual states have defined their constitutional laws and substantive case law as the notion of privacy has developed.[41]

See below
2.2.3

As newspapers became more widespread and readership interest in gossip and tittle-tattle increased, intrusion into people's private and personal lives grew. To this day, there is no UK statute which covers expressly an individual's right to privacy, as the court in *Kaye v Robertson* (1991)[42] famously and uncompromisingly pointed out: there is no tort of privacy known to English law. This can often be to the detriment of the claimant as they have to fit their privacy claim into existing tortious actions. For this reason privacy laws in the UK have been compared rather unfavourably with French and German law.[43]

Privacy prevents others from learning everything about our activities.[44] The lack of a substantive law of privacy in the UK has led to concern that sufficient legal remedies may not be available for invasions of privacy.[45] This may have been negated somewhat by the courts' flexibility in interpreting the equitable action for breach of confidence and in how they assess breaches of privacy, and the fact that it is considered on a case-by-case basis.[46] However, the flexible nature of privacy in English common law has meant that a person's privacy right does not sit comfortably with press freedom, particularly when the opposing rights of confidential information and freedom of expression coincide (see: *Spencer v UK* (1998)[47]).

See Chapter
6.3

To complicate matters even further, the terms 'privacy' and 'confidentiality' have remained flexible in English common law and have been frequently tested and interpreted by the courts. Definitions of the terms vary widely according to context and environment and it is important not to confuse privacy law with the modern notion of data protection, which deals with the management of personal information.

Before we look at the wealth of common law, particularly before the Human Rights Act 1998 (HRA), it might be an idea to consider some definitions of the meaning and common law coverage of 'privacy'. American Sociologist Barrington Moore defines 'privacy' within the following categories:

- Information Privacy involves the establishment of rules governing the collection and handling of personal data such as credit information and medical records.
- Bodily privacy concerns the protection of people's physical selves against invasive procedures such as drug testing.
- Privacy of communications covers the security and privacy of mail, telephones, email and other forms of communication.
- Territorial privacy concerns the setting of limits on intrusion into the domestic environment such as the workplace or public sphere; to control the channels through which one's image is distributed.[48]

Moore provides detailed historical and comparative analyses in his writings, comparing specific societies such as Britain, France, China, Japan and the United States by producing important testable generalizations about societal change, including the notion of privacy and how this notion is threatened in modern civilizations. Rachels (1975) argues that privacy is

41 See: Hixson (1987).
42 (1991) FSR 62.
43 See: Markesinis and Unberath (2002).
44 See: Barber (2003).
45 See: Witzleb (2009).
46 See: Bennett (2010).
47 (1998) (28851/95, 28852/95) 25 EHRR CD 105.
48 Source: Moore (1984), p. 5ff.

valuable in that it allows us to limit the information that others know about us: that there are different sorts of social relationships that bring different levels of intimacy. Some information remains confidential to us.[49]

As privacy law developed by way of common law jurisprudence in the English courts, the notion of 'confidence' developed alongside. Neither concept ever made it into the torts (*delicts*) of privacy in continental European jurisdictions, such as France or Germany, where strict privacy laws prevail. But the current law on privacy was not created by Eady J or by any other judge, but by Parliament when it introduced the Human Rights Act 1998 (HRA) by way of Article 8 ECHR ('right to privacy'). We also know that each court now has to take note of Article 10 ECHR, which affords special protection for freedom of expression, plus creating the right balancing act between the two, demonstrating that the courts have also taken into account whether the publication (or photos) are in the public interest.

See below
2.2.3

Shortly after the **Max Mosley**[50] judgment in 2008, movie actress Sienna Miller launched a legal battle against News International and the photo agency Big Pictures for breach of her privacy. The offending tabloids, *News of the World* (*NOW*) and the *Sun*, had written, accompanied by pictures, about the actress as she was on holiday in Italy with a 'friend', Balthazar Getty, heir to the Getty oil fortune. She argued that the photos were 'intrusive'. In May 2011, Sienna Miller accepted a 'generous offer' of £100,000 from News International together with an apology for hacking into her phone. There followed a number of phone-hacking payouts and out-of-court settlements, including one with actor Jude Law, who reportedly received the highest payout of £130,000 ($200,000), and former Deputy Prime Minister, John Prescott (£40,000). Undisclosed sums were awarded to Sara Payne, mother of murdered schoolgirl Sarah, and Shaun Russell, whose wife and daughter were murdered in 1996. By mid-2012, some 37 phone-hacking cases had been settled out of court.

To date, no government has attempted to introduce privacy legislation into Parliament. In 1973, the Younger Committee advised against enactment of any general tort of invasion of privacy, recommending that the then Press Council should deal with the continued regulation of the print press and that any breaches of privacy be dealt with on a case-by-case basis.[51] In 1990, the Calcutt Committee[52] recommended that a tort of infringement of privacy should not be introduced.[53] This means that the courts continue to iron out deficiencies in existing law with piecemeal common law jurisdiction.

2.2.3 Privacy in European jurisdictions

Sweden's Freedom of the Press Act 1766 is widely regarded as the oldest piece of freedom of information legislation in the world. Article 1 of the Freedom of the Press Act reads:

> . . . the freedom of the press is understood to mean the right of every Swedish citizen to publish written matter, without prior hindrance by a public authority or other public body, and not to be prosecuted thereafter on grounds of its content other than before a lawful court, or punished therefore other than because the content contravenes an express provision of law, enacted to preserve public order without suppressing information to the public.

---

49 See: Rachels (1975), pp. 323ff.
50 *Mosley (Max) v Newsgroup Newspapers Ltd* [2008] EMLR 679.
51 Source: House of Commons (1973) 'Privacy: Younger Committee's Report'. HC Debate, 6 June 1973.
52 House of Commons (1990) 'The Calcutt Report'. HC Debate, 21 June 1990.
53 For further discussion see: Robertson and Nicol (2007), Chapter 14, 'Media Self Regulation', pp. 759–795.

The current version of the 1766 Act is also one of four fundamental laws which make up Sweden's written Constitution, others being:

- The Act of Succession 1810 (*Successionsordningen*)
- The Freedom of the Press Act 1949 (*Tryckfrihetsförordningen*)
- The Instrument of Government 1974 (*Regeringsformen*)
- The Fundamental Law on Freedom of Expression 1991 (*Yttrandefrihetsgrundlagen*)[54]

See also
Chapter 6

The initial purpose of the 1766 Act was to abolish the political censorship of public documents and to ensure the right for everyone to publish written documents. Right of access to public documents was also listed in the first versions of the Act. Today, if a citizen is unhappy with a government decision not to disclose requested information, they can make a request to the Parliamentary Ombudsman (*Justitieombudsmännen*), who will then decide whether public information can be disclosed. This model was used as a basis for the Freedom of Information Act 2000 in the UK.

Sweden is generally seen as a benchmark for openness in government due to its long history of freedom of information. Press freedom is specifically guaranteed under Article 2 *Regeringsformen*[55] as well as the *Tryckfrihetsförordningen*.[56] Chapter 1 ('basic provisions') of the Fundamental Law on Freedom of Expression states under Article 1:

> Every Swedish citizen is guaranteed the right under this Fundamental Law, vis-à-vis the public institutions, publicly to express his or her thoughts, opinions and sentiments, and in general to communicate information on any subject whatsoever on sound radio, television and certain similar transmissions, through public playback of material from a database, and in films, video recordings, sound recordings and other technical recordings.

In July 2010, Sweden passed new legislation to reuse public information.[57] The legislation is based on the EU Directive On the Re-use of Public Sector Information ('the PSI Directive')[58]. The purpose of the law is to give citizens better opportunities to understand how the public sector works, for example how the Executive spends public money, and to give citizens easier access to data-powered enterprises.

The delict of privacy in French law was first identified in Article 2 of the *Déclaration des droits de l'homme et du citoyen* 1789 ('Declaration of the Rights of Man and of the Citizen'), first applied in the 'Rachel affaire' (1858), which made sensational headlines in both London and Paris at the time (see below). The 1789 Declaration, proclaimed by the French National Assembly and comprising 17 Articles, stated that the 'imprescriptible rights of man' were 'liberty, property, security and resistance to oppression'.

The 'Rachel affaire' extended the privacy concept in French law to the protection of the private life of the dead. The (in)famous French actress and courtesan Mademoiselle Rachel (1821–58), daughter of Jewish peasants from the Alsace, had risen to pan-European stardom through determined self-education. Among her many lovers were Napoleon I's illegitimate son, Alexandre Joseph Count Colonna-Walewski, with whom she had a son. While touring in London, Rachel had a brief affair with Louis Napoleon Bonaparte (later Napoleon III). There was considerable public and press interest in 'la Rachel', and when she died the Parisian tabloid press even wanted to show an image

---

54 Source: Swedish Parliament: www.riksdagen.se.
55 *Regeringsformen*, SFS 1974: 152.
56 *Tryckfrihetsförordningen*, SFS 1949: 105.
57 Law No 2010:566 of 3 June 2010 on the reuse of public administration documents.
58 Directive 2003/98/EC of the European Parliament and of the Council of 17 November 2003. All 28 Member States have implemented the PSI Directive in different ways.

of her on her deathbed. The Tribunal civil de la Seine of 1858 ruled that the protection of private life in death was absolute, which included respect for the grieving family.[59] The private life of dead persons has been part of the theoretical framework of French personality rights ever since, a right which cannot be 'seized, given up, transmitted or acquired'.[60] Lord Hoffmann (2009) examined the universal claim by the French 'Declaration – agreeing *inter alia* with Jeremy Bentham on this subject – that the French claim to fundamental human rights rested purely on the country's philosophical foundations rather than actual humanitarian principles.[61]

The French media is still regulated by the Press Law of 1881. The Law on the Freedom of the Press of 29 July 1881 (*Loi sur la liberté de la presse du 29 juillet 1881*)[62] marked the end of censorship and pre-licence authorization in France. But the 1881 statute limited the freedom of speech concerning political opinion. Amended over the years, the 1881 statute still prohibits any one media group from controlling more than 30 per cent of the daily press. It also prohibits, during the preliminary stage of a judicial investigation, the publication of images relating to a crime or offence and information about the identity of the victim of a sexual offence. The law also prohibits photographing, filming and recording court proceedings. There was a national outcry in France in May 2011 when the former head of the International Monetary Fund, Dominique Strauss-Kahn, was being paraded by the American police in front of the cameras, accused of trying to rape a New York City hotel maid. Though those charges were eventually dropped, the US media implicated him in another scandal — that he knowingly partied with prostitutes and paid for them – which put an end to his aspirations to the French Presidency the following year.[63]

The Cour de cassation[64] – the constitutional court and highest appeal court in the French judicial system – frequently refers to the 'right to privacy' under Article 8 ECHR, whereby judges make interim injunctions in the form of a *référé*, if a media organization has breached Article 9 *Code Civil*. Article 9 provides for the 'protection of private life', which inherently includes protection from the media.[65] Though the privacy right was not explicitly included in the French Constitution of 1958, the Cour de cassation ruled in 1994 that the right to privacy was implicit in the Constitution because it had been added to the French Civil Code (of 17 July 1970).

Article 22 *Code Civil* additionally restricts the scope of private life to 'intimate private life' (*intimité de la vie privée*). This permits the courts to order urgent measures in the form of restraint of publication or even seizure of articles and photographs. Though Dupré (2000) notes that there is hardly any French case law which covers breaches of privacy by the media, because the French courts have 'always sought to protect private life in an efficient and appropriate manner',[66] there is one case which tested French privacy laws, that of Marlene Dietrich and the weekly society magazine *Société France-Dimanche*.[67] The case concerned the unauthorized publication of Marlene Dietrich's personal memoirs and photographs in the magazine.

France-Dimanche had published a series of articles on 10, 17 and 23 December 1950, entitled 'My Life, by Marlene Dietrich'. The first article was headlined: 'My Life, by Marlene Dietrich, chevalier

---

59 Tribunal civil de la Seine, 16 juin 1858, D. P. 1858. 3. 62.
60 For further discussion see: Deringer (2003), p. 191.
61 Hoffmann, Lord (2009) 'The universality of human rights', LQR at 421–423.
62 Amended by the *Ordonnance* of August 1944.
63 Source: 'Strauss-Kahn's prostitution scandal taints image of a city's beloved hotel', by Maia de la Baume, *New York Times*, 11 April 2012.
64 The origins of the Court of Cassation can be dated back to the French Revolution where a 'tribunal of cassation' was established by a decree of 27 November 1790 The fundamental change in this law was that judicial power was transferred from the monarch to the courts. The established Court of Cassation harmonizes and interprets laws to this very day and is seen as the final appeal court in civil and criminal matters.
65 Article 9 of the Civil Code, Statute No. 70–643 of 17 July 1970; Décision 94–352 du Conseil Constitutionnel du 18 janvier 1995.
66 See: Dupré (2000), pp. 627–649.
67 Cour d'Appel de Paris D. 1955, **Marlene Dietrich v Société France-Dimanche** (295 Case) 16 March 1955.

of the Légion d'honneur and daughter of a ranking Prussian officer.' The magazine claimed to be the first to have access to the German actress's unpublished memoirs. The claimant, Marlene Dietrich, and the defendant publishers, *Société France-Dimanche*, both appealed from a judgment of the civil tribunal of the Seine on 30 June 1952, which had awarded her damages in the sum of 50,000 francs. Dietrich argued that the damages be increased to $50,000 dollars, while the defendant sought the reversal of the judgment.

In a judgment of 30 June 1994, the Versailles appeal court held that:

> Any person, however famous, has an exclusive right to his picture and to the use which is made of it, by virtue of which he can oppose its reproduction and dissemination without his express and special authorization, subject to the requirements of freedom of information.

The **Marlene Dietrich** case confirmed an individual's right to privacy which includes photographic images and the necessity of that person's express authorization to reproduce the picture or to disclose private and confidential information by the media. This meant that disclosing and reproducing Dietrich's memoirs without her consent in the publication and sharing these with third parties was a fundamental breach of privacy in French law. Dietrich was granted compensation for the breach of confidentiality and invasion of her privacy by way of 1,200,000 francs (approximately €180,000) in damages.

The revelation at President Mitterrand's[68] funeral that he had an illegitimate daughter, Mazarine, came as an enormous surprise to French citizens, since no mention was made of Mitterand's second family during his lifetime, because of France's strict privacy laws; although when it was finally revealed this did little to harm his image. Only some ten years after his death did the media expose allegations that the former president had a hand in the illegal wiretapping of journalists who knew about his illegitimate daughter.

In broadcasting terms, the French state not only directly funds and supervises public broadcasters but also regulates the output of private television by, for instance, implementing legally binding quotas (unlike in Britain where media deregulation has taken place since 2009). This means that the popular commercial station Canal Plus has to invest ever larger sums of money (a fixed percentage of its profits) in French cinema production. On radio stations, 35 per cent of songs must be of Francophone origin, including African–French and Arabic–French. Advertising is also limited to 8 minutes per hour on public TV channels, and 12 minutes on private channels.[69]

German law too has strict codified privacy regulations though the German Constitution – the Basic Law (*Grundgesetz* – GG) of 1949[70] – also guarantees freedom of speech under Article 5 GG. The *Grundgesetz* grants protection to all aspects of human personality ('personality rights' – *allgemeines Persönlichkeitsrecht*). This includes fundamental human rights such as the 'right to human dignity' and the 'right of free development' under Articles 1(1) and 2(1) GG. Article 10 GG also enshrines the protection of privacy in 'letters, post and telecommunications', which 'shall be inviolable'. After the ECtHR ruling in **von Hannover (No 1)**[71] the German courts reviewed their legislation, whereby it was agreed that the German courts had failed to recognize Princess Caroline of Monaco and her family's right to private life under Article 8 ECHR.

See below
2.4.1

When the German Parliament (Bundestag) passed the new 'Registration Laws' in July 2012,[72] there were violent protests by the privacy-conscious Germans. The new legislation (due to come

68 François Mitterrand was socialist president of the Fifth Republic from 1981 to 1995. He died in his eightieth year in 1996.
69 For further detailed information see: Scherer, (2013).
70 *Grundgesetz* (GG) of 23 May 1949; last updated 29.7.2009 I 2248 GG.
71 **von Hannover v Germany** (2005) (Application no. 59320/00) 40 EHRR 1, 24 June 2004.
72 *Bundesdatenschutzgesetz* (BDSG Novelle 2012): Direktmarketing und Datenschutz 2012.

into force in 2014) means that every time a German citizen moves to a new address and gives the new location to the local authorities (as he is legally obliged to do) the authorities are allowed to pass on his personal data to third parties. This means that local councils can sell on private data to marketing companies. More than 120,000 people signed an online petition lobbying the Bundestag not to enforce the new data protection laws.

2.2.4 The 'red carpet rule': what really is in the public interest?

A factor which often dictates whether or not an individual's privacy is protected is the consideration of 'public interest'. Before the Human Rights Act 1998 came into force in October 2000 (1998 in Scotland), English common law recognized that the public interest could justify the publication of information that was known to have been disclosed in breach of confidence. This was initially limited under the 'iniquity rule', whereby confidentiality could not be relied upon to conceal wrongdoing, upheld in **Lion Laboratories v Evans** (1985).[73] As common law has developed, 'public interest' is now the most common justification for publishing information which is either confidential or which has been challenged in the tort of defamation.

See Chapter 3

The public interest consideration is the argument that intrusion into people's private lives should be permitted where it is in the public's interest for them to be made aware of the private information. This may be considered a defence to a breach of privacy (or confidence), now supported by Article 10 ECHR when the courts balance freedom of expression with that of the right to privacy (see below: **Francome v Mirror Group Newspapers Ltd**[74]).

Public interest has also included the consideration of role models and correcting a false impression, and the effect this has upon whether publication should be permitted, as in the cases of footballers John Terry[75] and Ryan Giggs[76], or supermodel Naomi Campbell.[77]

But what about the British university student (known to the courts only as AMP[78]) who used her mobile phone to take explicit naked photos of herself at her home; the mobile was subsequently stolen while she was on a tram in Nottingham in 2008. After the phone was found, her photos were uploaded to the BitTorrent network and circulated under the name 'Sexy Rich Chick Mobile Phone Found By IRC Nerdz'. Her application for an interim (super)injunction to prevent transmission, storage and indexing of any part or parts of these photographic images was granted by Ramsey J in December 2011 to protect the claimant's rights to privacy under Article 8 ECHR and to prevent harassment under s 3 Protection from Harassment Act 1997.

After the Human Rights Act 1998 (HRA) had incorporated Articles 8 and 10 of the Convention into UK law, the courts began to liberally interpret the public interest defence in a number of innovative yet often confusing ways, best illustrated in one of the early cases, that of TV and radio presenter Jamie Theakston.[79] Theakston had been photographed without his consent while in a brothel in Mayfair. He had been drinking with friends that night, and could not remember much of what happened whilst at the brothel. He received various text messages on his mobile telephone over the few weeks following his visit in which he was told that the prostitute would go to the press with photographs of him at the brothel unless he paid her money. The prostitute took her story to

73 [1985] QB 526.
74 [1984] 1 WLR 892.
75 *John Terry (previously referred to as LNS) v Persons Unknown* [2010] EWHC 119 (QB).
76 **CTB v NGN** ('Ryan Giggs superinjunction') [2011] EWHC 1326 (QB); see also: **Giggs v NGN and Imogen Thomas** [2012] EWHC 431 (QB).
77 **Campbell v MGN** [2004] 2 AC 457.
78 **AMP v Persons Unknown** [2012] All ER (D) 178.
79 **Theakston v MGN** [2002] EWHC 137 (QB).

the *Sunday People*, and the injunction sought to prevent publication of both the details of the claimant's activities whilst in the brothel and the photographs which were taken there without his consent. The issue before the court was whether the details of Mr Theakston's acts whilst at the brothel and the information contained in the photographs were then confidential and whether he was entitled to an injunction to prevent publication. It is worth noting that Theakston had previously allowed certain aspects of his love and sex life to be reported in the press.

Mr Justice Ouseley granted an order in January 2002, banning the *Sunday People* from using any photographs of the *Top of the Pops* presenter taken inside the brothel. However, the High Court judge allowed the newspaper to publish an article based on interviews with the prostitute involved. The article was accompanied by a photo, showing a bed set up for sado-masochistic sessions, offered as part of the services at the brothel. Ouseley J said that not all relationships of a sexual nature should be afforded the same quality of confidence, particularly as the claimant did not at the time he entered the brothel stipulate that his activities in the brothel should be kept confidential. Further, there was a public interest in publishing the fact that the popular presenter had behaved in the manner he did, given his public role which had been perceived particularly by young people as a role model and respectable figure. The photographs, however, merited special consideration as the details contained in them were likely to be of an especially intimate, personal and intrusive nature, and consequently the claimant's right to keep the details contained in them private outweighed the paper's and the prostitute's rights of freedom of expression. As part of the **Theakston** judgment Ouseley J stated that the law of confidence should not be judged solely from the point of view of 'one participant'. Mr Theakston's view of confidentiality was clearly different from that of the prostitute.[80]

The **Theakston** case is interesting because the court differentiated between the protection afforded to the claimant in relation to photographs of him taken whilst in the brothel, compared with the details provided by the prostitute of the time Jamie Theakston spent with her at the brothel. Clearly, these photos were taken without Theakston's consent, which was part of the judge's distinctive and important judgment. Ouseley J justified his differentiation (of photos provided by the prostitute to accompany her article and photos taken of Mr Theakston at the brothel without his consent) as a basis for balancing the rights enshrined in Articles 8 and 10 ECHR in that 'the resolution of conflict between Article 10 and Article 8 cannot be dependent on narrowly defined exceptions to the law of confidentiality'.[81] Phillipson (2003) argues that Mr Justice Ouseley appreciated the need for proportionality in his decision in that the photographs taken of the claimant at the brothel (without his consent) had a lower level of public interest than the disclosure of his visit.[82]

If not in statute, how can the term 'public interest' be defined? The (now defunct) Press Complaints Commission's definition probably came closest, to defining 'public interest' as:

- detecting or exposing crime or serious impropriety;
- protecting public health and safety;
- preventing the public from being misled by an action or statement of an individual or organization.[83]

See Chapter
10.3

The definition is deliberately loose, in order to allow the PCC to judge each case fully on its merits.

Until **von Hannover (No 1)**[84] there existed some confusion as to the meaning of 'public' and 'private' domain' as to what would be regarded in the 'public interest' in relation to an indi-

---

80 Ibid., at 69 (Ouseley J).
81 Ibid., at 68 (Ouseley J).
82 See: Phillipson (2003) at 54–57.
83 PCC Editors' Code of Practice of 1 January 2012.
84 **Von Hannover v Germany** [2004] EMLR 21.

vidual's right to privacy. This was perhaps better defined in **Spycatcher (No 2)**,[85] where the ECtHR ruled that the public interest test does not always amount to a justification for publication of confidential information.

2.2.5 What is a breach of confidence?

The common law or, more precisely, the courts of equity, have long afforded protection to the wrongful use of private information by means of the cause of action which became known as breach of confidence. A breach of confidence has been defined in equity as a form of unconscionable conduct, akin to a breach of trust. A breach of confidence goes back to the time when the cause of action was based on improper use of information disclosed by one person to another in confidence. To attract protection the information had to be of a confidential nature. But the gist of the cause of action was that information of this character had been disclosed by one person to another in circumstances 'importing an obligation of confidence' (**Coco v A. N. Clark (Engineers) Ltd** (1969)[86]).

The **Coco** case and others of its time (and earlier) were mainly concerned with the protection of trade secrets and adaptation of these cases to cases concerning personal privacy. Additionally, intellectual property and copyright laws were weak and trade secrets could easily be stolen or copied.[87] In other words, a duty of confidence arose between two parties when information came to the knowledge of a person in circumstances where one party had notice of the other's 'secret'; or the parties agreed to keep the imparted information as 'strictly confidential'. A breach of confidence occurred where there had been an unauthorized use or disclosure of that confidential information. This, in essence, is the basis of the **Coco Engineers** case, still valid in common law today.[88]

See also
Chapter 8.4.1

How then do the courts deal with breach of confidence? First, it must be established that a confidential relationship existed between the two parties. If there has been a breach of confidence, a remedy is possible. The orthodox definition of a 'breach' needs to be made up of three essential elements, as outlined by Megarry J in the **Coco Engineers** case:

> 1. The information itself must have the 'necessary quality of confidence' about it;
> 2. The information 'must have been imparted in circumstances importing an obligation of confidence'; and
> 3. There must have been an 'unauthorized use of that information to the detriment of the party communicating it'.[89]

How then are damages recoverable for breach of confidence? Ten years later, Sir Robert Megarry VC commented in **Malone** on the unsatisfactory state in the law of equity in that:

> . . . the right of confidentiality is an equitable right which is still in the course of development, and is usually protected by the grant of an injunction to prevent disclosure of the confidence. Under Lord Cairns' Act 1858 damages may be granted in substitution for an injunction; yet if there is no case for the grant of an injunction, as when the disclosure has already been made,

85 *AG v Guardian Newspapers Ltd (No 2)* [1990] 1 AC 109.
86 [1969] RPC 41 at 47 (Megarry J).
87 For further discussion see: Richardson and Thomas (2012).
88 For further discussion see: Carty (2008) at pp. 416–455.
89 [1969] RPC 41 at 47 (Megarry J).

the unsatisfactory result seems to be that no damages can be awarded under this head . . . In such a case, where there is no breach of contract or other orthodox foundation for damages at common law, it seems doubtful whether there is any right to damages, as distinct from an account of profits.[90]

During the 1980s, we can see two branches of 'confidentiality' developing in common law, one in relation to trade and business secrets (usually enshrined in express confidentiality clauses in contracts and protected under contract law – as per **Coco Engineers**) and the second in relation to misuse of private information mostly referred to as 'kiss and tell' stories. It is important not to confuse these two branches of law in this respect.

'Kiss and tell stories' which fuel popular tabloid sales are often inextricably linked to breach of confidentiality, and as we learnt much later through the Leveson Inquiry, obtaining information by clandestine means, such as phone-hacking. In **Francome v Mirror Group Newspapers Ltd** [1984][91] the Court of Appeal granted an injunction, based on breach of confidence, restraining the Daily Mirror, its editor and two journalists from publishing information which had been received from unidentified persons, including one who had obtained the information by tapping the claimant's telephone. The case concerned the tapping of the jockey John Francome's private telephone line (Francome was a seven-time Champion Jockey in National Hunt racing during the 1970s and 1980s).The tapes had been offered for sale to the Daily Mirror, whose reporters approached Mr Francome to confirm their authenticity. Mr Francome and his wife brought an action in breach of confidence seeking an interlocutory injunction to stop the publication of the transcripts or extracts. The defendant newspaper denied liability and argued that publication was justified in the public interest as exposing Francome's breaches of racing rules.

See Chapter 10.4.2

However, the Court of Appeal held that the telephone tap was unlawful. Lord Donaldson MR suggested that the Mirror editor or journalists should have brought the information to the notice of the police and/or the Jockey Club first; only if the police had not investigated the matter could the newspaper have reported on it, and possibly the police's inaction. The court noted that the Mirror had first notice of the alleged wrongdoing, and in any case would also be liable as a third party for breach of confidence if it went ahead with its publication, and the public interest did not justify this since the tapes could have been given to the police or Jockey Club to deal with through official channels. This meant that unlawful telephone-tapping by the media amounted to a prima facie breach of confidence. The CA stressed that the public interest would be better served by passing information to the police than publishing it. If it turns out that the suspicions are without foundation, the confidence can then still be protected.

See Chapter 10.4

The Leveson Inquiry heard in November 2011 that an ex-policeman, Derek Webb, had been hired by the News of The World (NOW) for eight years and had engaged in covert surveillance and phone-tapping of celebrities and the royals on a huge scale. They included Prince William, Prince Harry's ex-girlfriend Chelsy Davy, former Attorney General Lord Goldsmith and football manager José Mourinho. Mr Webb had set up his private detective agency in 2003, and continued to work for NOW until it was shut down in July 2011 after a string of allegations emerged about the hacking of phones, including that of murdered schoolgirl Milly Dowler.

As common law developed after the HRA 1998, a breach of confidence was no longer constrained by notions of unconscionable conduct or a breach of trust as established in the **Coco Engineering** case. Additionally, there was no longer the need to prove an initial confidential

90 **Malone v Metropolitan Police Commissioner** [1979] 1 Ch 344 (Sir Robert Megarry VC).
91 [1984] 2 ALL ER 408.

relationship. This development had already been recognized by the House of Lords in their judgment as pronounced by Lord Goff of Chieveley in the **Spycatcher No 2**[92] action, outlining the general principles as regards confidential information, and the corresponding duty not to disclose such information, when he stated:

> . . . a duty of confidence arises when confidential information comes to the knowledge of a person (the confidant) in circumstances where he has notice, or is held to have agreed, that the information is confidential, with the effect that it would be just in all the circumstances that he should be precluded from disclosing the information to others. . . . I have used the word 'notice' advisedly, in order to avoid the (here unnecessary) question of the extent to which actual knowledge is necessary; though I of course understand knowledge to include circumstances where the confidant has deliberately closed his eyes to the obvious. The existence of this broad principle reflects the fact that there is such a public interest in the maintenance of confidences, that the law will provide remedies for their protection.[93]

Since **Spycatcher (No 2)** the law imposes a 'duty of confidence' whenever a person receives information which he knows or ought to know is fairly and reasonably to be regarded as confidential. Nevertheless, the law remains awkward and bewildering, caused partly by confusing case law relating to trade secrets with misuse of private personal information, which may require different parameters and treatment. This has given rise to ever greater legal actions. Arguably, the use of 'duty of confidence' and the definition of information being 'confidential' still has not been adequately defined by the courts; it could even be argued that the courts have skirted around the issue since **Douglas v Hello!** (2001)[94]. Would it not be simpler to say that the information is 'private'?

See also
Chapter 1.2.2

For example, Naomi Campbell's common law claim was initially presented to the courts exclusively on the basis of breach of confidence in 2001;[95] that is, the wrongful publication by the *Daily Mirror* of private information. In **Jameel**,[96] Lord Bingham made the following observations within the context of confidentiality:

> . . . the necessary precondition of reliance on qualified privilege in this context is that the matter published should be one of public interest. In the present case the subject matter of the article complained of was of undoubted public interest. But that is not always, perhaps not usually, so. It has been repeatedly and rightly said that what engages the interest of the public may not be material which engages the public interest.[97]

At a trial for a claim for misuse of private and confidential information, a claimant must first establish that he has a reasonable expectation of privacy in relation to the confidential information of which disclosure is threatened, as established in **Murray v Express Newspapers** (2008)[98]:

> . . . whether a reasonable person of ordinary sensibilities would feel if he or she was placed in the same position as the claimant and faced the same publicity.[99]

---

92 *AG v Guardian Newspapers Ltd (No 2)* ('Spycatcher No 2') [1990] 1 AC 109.
93 Ibid., at 281 (Lord Goff of Chieveley).
94 *Douglas v Hello! Ltd* [2001] QB 967.
95 *Campbell v Mirror Group Newspapers Ltd* [2002] EWHC 499 (QB).
96 *Jameel (Mohammed) v Wall Street Journal* [2007] 1 AC 359.
97 Ibid., at 31–33 (Lord Bingham).
98 [2008] EWCA Civ 446.
99 Ibid., at 24.

See below in
2.5

That case concerned photographs of a young child (David, son of J. K. Rowling) in a public place taken covertly and published without the parents' permission.

2.2.6 Restraining unauthorized publications

When comparing cases involving Prince Charles and his royal ancestor Prince Albert, we note the similarities of breach of confidence and therein breach of trust by a royal servant, albeit some 157 years apart. In *Albert v Strange* (1849)[100] His Royal Highness, the Prince Consort, Prince Albert, had to ask the courts for an order to restrain the printer William Strange and his publishers Jasper Tomsett Judge and Son from reproducing private royal family drawings and etchings for 'mass' publication and to exhibit these 'sketches' in public.

Both Princes of Wales (Albert and Charles) asked the courts to restrain 'mass' publication of their private thoughts. Prince Albert's was in the form of some drawings which he and his wife Queen Victoria had made to amuse themselves about goings-on at the royal household in Windsor and Osborne House on the Isle of Wight. Prince Charles found that his private travel journals had fallen into the wrong hands and were about to be published in the press. Both princes successfully stopped publication by way of court injunctions, on the grounds of breach of confidentiality.

See also
Chapter 6.4

In **HRH Prince of Wales v Associated Newspapers**,[101] Prince Charles's travel journals had fallen into the hands of a servant who had sold the private and locked-up manuscripts to the *Mail on Sunday*, which published extracts of the Prince's first travel journals. Prince Charles successfully gained a court order restraining any further publications of the other seven journals, citing breach of confidence and copyright as well has his right to privacy under Article 8 ECHR. In their defence, the publishers of the *Mail*, Associated Newspapers, counterclaimed by using the public interest test, in that the public had a right to know about the future king's personal and political views, in this case his derisive and mocking remarks on the Chinese hierarchy at the time that Hong Kong was passing to China (see also: **Ashdown v Telegraph Group Ltd** (2001)[102]).

The **Prince Albert** case set the precedent for any subsequent similar actions in privacy and confidentiality (as well as copyright), where the Lord Chancellor ruled that the right and property of an author or composer in his work (published or unpublished), kept under lock and key for his private use or pleasure, entitled the owner to withhold the material completely from the public knowledge of others. It ought to be said, however, that this case caused some degree of jurisprudential confusion at the time, about the basis of a confidence action; that is, whether confidential information was 'property' or not. The nature of the judgment in this case is therefore rather too wide.

One thing is clear in both cases: the courts will interfere by way of injunction with any party who avails themselves of unauthorized material in violation of any right or breach of confidence of contractual nature.

Mindell (2012: 52–58) argues that there are two forms of privacy that are protected in English law: the torts of trespass (to the person and to land) and protection under the Human Rights Act 1998. The author further argues that there exist 'secondary forms of privacy', the first being 'the informational realm' and the other 'territorial information', depicted in **Peck v UK**[103] (personal information).

100 *Albert (Prince) v Strange* [1849] 1 Macnaghten & Gordon 25 (1849) 41 ER 1171.
101 [2006] EWHC 522 (Ch).
102 [2001] Ch 685 (Ch D).
103 (2003) 36 EHRR 719.

2.2.7 A new tort of privacy

Media lawyer Mark Stephens CBE argues that there now exists an independent tort of privacy.[104] In his long-standing legal career, Stephens has successfully defended both individuals' privacy rights and media freedom of expression. In 2006, along with Geoffrey Robertson QC, Stephens successfully defended the *Wall Street Journal* (*WSJ*) in the leading defamation case of **Jameel v Wall Street Journal**.[105] The case centred on an article published in the *WSJ* in 2002, which alleged that the United States were monitoring the bank accounts of a Saudi Arabian businessman to ensure he was not funding terrorists. Mr Jameel, represented by solicitors Carter Ruck, was originally awarded £40,000 in damages but this was overturned in favour of the *WSJ*. Stephens views **Jameel** as one of the landmark cases which brought about a new tort of privacy, thereby redefining **Reynolds'** 'qualified privilege'[106] by upholding the right to publish if it is deemed to be in the public interest. Stephens has represented a number of freedom of speech and privacy cases in the Strasbourg court, including **Mosley v UK**[107] and **Haldimann v Switzerland**;[108] the latter concerned the criminal conviction of two Swiss journalists for the use of hidden recording devices. The prominent media lawyer also secured pre-trial settlements with News International for some eleven phone-hacking victims.

See also 3.1.2 and 3.5.1

How then was breach of confidence established in this and any subsequent cases? The starting point was Megarry J's definition in **Coco v Clarke**,[109] establishing the three qualifying factors (as mentioned above):

1. The information disclosed must have the necessary quality of confidence;
2. The claimant must have disclosed the information to the defendant in circumstances which created an obligation of confidence; and
3. The information must have been used to the detriment of the claimant without authorization.[110]

Once a breach had been established, remedy for breach of confidence came into existence (civil remedies), including:

1. injunction;
2. compensatory damages;
3. exemplary damages;
4. account of profits;
5. delivery-up;
6. proportion of costs.

See below 2.6

Schauer (1991: 699) describes the use of private information as 'injurious truth-telling', and arguably the courts have since explored this development based on the principles from the origins of privacy in the **Coco Engineers** case, which, in turn, have led to the use of superinjunctions. As Strasbourg jurisprudence has developed post HRA 1998, we can see how truth-telling forms part of the media's right to free speech given certain circumstances in which the public interest

104 Interview conducted by the author, Ursula Smartt, with Mark Stephens CBE, partner at the law firm Finers, Stephens, Innocent LLP on 20 July 2012.
105 *Jameel (Mohammed) v Wall Street Journal Europe Sprl (No 3)* [2007] 1 AC 359.
106 *Reynolds v Times Newspapers Ltd* [2001] 2 AC 127.
107 *Mosley v UK* (Application no. 48009/08) Judgment by the Strasbourg European Court of Human Rights of 10 May 2011.
108 *Haldimann v Switzerland and Others* (2011) (unreported) (application no. 21 830/09) March 2011 (ECTHR): www.mediadefence. org/sites/default/files/uploads/Haldimann%20v%20Switzerland_MLDI%20intervention.PDF.
109 *Coco v AN Clarke (Engineers) Ltd* [1969] RPC 41.
110 Ibid., at 47 (Megarry J).

test prevails and when truth-telling infringes privacy rights (see: **von Hannover (No 1)**[111] and **von Hannover (No 2)**[112]). We can then define breach of confidence as the tort that protects private information (particularly following **Campbell** (2002).[113]

However, we also know the famous dictum by Glidewell LJ in **Kaye v Robertson**[114] which stated expressly that there is no right to privacy in English law:

> . . . it is well known that in English law there is no right to privacy, and accordingly there is no right of action for breach of a person's privacy.[115]

In this case the editor and publishers of the *Sunday Sport* had published 'lurid and sensational style' photographs accompanied by an interview with the well-known actor Gorden Kaye, who was lying in hospital on life support. The actor, best known for his role as René in the popular TV series *'Allo 'Allo!* had sustained severe head injuries on 25 January 1990 when, as he was driving in London during a gale, a piece of wood from an advertisement hoarding smashed through his windscreen and struck him on the head. This case established that 'hospital beds' are out of bounds for the media.[116] It is worth noting that subsequent case law demonstrates that Lord Glidewell's *dicta* in **Kaye v Robertson** have been superseded, although courts continue to use and perhaps distort the action for breach of confidence instead of recognizing they have created a tort of 'misuse of private information'.

See below

2.3.5

The grant of an injunction which prohibited the *Sun* from publishing the account of entertainer Michael Barrymore's[117] homosexual relationship re-engaged the original form of breach of confidence established in **Coco**. In **Barrymore**, the doctrine of confidential relationships and breach of confidence applied to 'kiss and tell' stories was extended to 'close relationships', as summarized by Jacob J in the *dictum* 'the fact is that when people kiss and later one of them tells, that second person is almost certainly breaking a "confidential arrangement".'[118] It has to be noted that Michael Barrymore had drawn up an express confidentiality clause in the agreement with his lover Paul Wilcott not to 'kiss and tell' should their relationship break up.

Markesinis and Unberath (2002), citing the **Gorden Kaye** case, have highlighted the failure in English common law to protect an individual's right to privacy compared with German or French law, where a number of aspects of human personality and privacy are protected by a multitude of existing torts. In English law it means fitting the facts of each case into the pigeonhole of an existing tort, a process involving legal constraints often leaving the deserving plaintiff without remedy. Arguably, the English courts have slowly *de facto* developed a tort of privacy under the guise of expanded confidence law, such as the House of Lords in **Campbell** (2004).[119]

There is no doubt that **Spycatcher (No 2)** had a significant impact on breach of confidence actions, diverging from the original concept as defined by Lord Goff, who said that 'there is no need to prove an initial confidential relationship' and that a duty of confidence arises when 'a person

111 *Von Hannover v Germany* (2005) 40 EHRR 1.
112 *Von Hannover v Germany (No 2)* (2012) (Application Numbers – 40660/08, 60641/08) Strasbourg Judgment of 7 February 2012.
113 **Campbell v Mirror Group Newspapers Ltd** [2002] EWHC 499 (QB).
114 (1991) FSR 62.
115 Ibid., at 66 (Glidewell LJ).
116 Ibid., at 66 (Glidewell LJ).
117 **Barrymore v NGN** [1997] FSR 600.
118 Ibid., at 603 (Jacob J).
119 [2004] 2 AC 457.

receives information which he knows or ought to know is fairly and reasonably to be regarded as confidential'. The argument advanced in **Spycatcher** was that the second **Coco** requirement, the need for a confidential relationship, would justify equity's interference with freedom of speech, as it served as the link between the recipient's conscience in not revealing the confidential information and the doctrine itself. This meant that the maintenance of confidential relationships was thereby sidelined.

Goff LJ stated further *obiter* that an obligation of confidence would arise where 'obviously confidential information' was accidentally disclosed. This important step heralded further the detachment of the 'confidential relationship' as separate from the 'duty of confidence'. It not only lessened the importance of the confidential relationship but – as we can see in common law development thereafter – removed it completely. What was (and still is) important is the nature and character of the information itself, which then becomes the definitive factor in assessing whether a situation of confidence has arisen and the need for an express or implied agreement between the parties becomes obsolete. This move from the protection of sensitive relationships to the protection of sensitive information has seen the doctrine of breach of confidence broaden, which has enabled it to be used on increasingly more frequent occasions to protect invasions of privacy and therefore brings it more in line with Strasbourg jurisprudence.

It is debatable whether the law regarding a tort of privacy and the defence of 'public interest' have gone full circle. There now exists a wide interpretation by the courts of the concept of privacy and what amounts to 'confidential information'. The domestic and Strasbourg jurisdictions have taken more restrictive views in certain social situations of press intrusion into an individual's private life, where newspaper articles were purely prurient. In **Campbell**[120] the House of Lords ruled (by a narrow majority) that any person undergoing rehabilitative or hospital treatment is guaranteed a right to privacy under Article 8 ECHR. In **von Hannover (No 1)**[121] the ECtHR ruled that a celebrity has a 'public' and a 'private sphere', the latter being strictly protected by privacy with no invasion by the paparazzi. In the **Beckham** case[122] the ruling was similar, in that famous couples like Victoria and David Beckham and their children have a right to privacy in the comfort and circumference of their own home. This standpoint was challenged by the press in the **Rio Ferdinand** superinjunction case,[123] and subsequently clarified by the Strasbourg court in Princess Caroline's second privacy action, i.e. **von Hannover (No 2)**.[124] Neither Rio Ferdinand nor Princess Caroline von Hannover were awarded privacy in their actions, because the court held that the matters in question were in the public interest (i.e. the fact that she was skiing in St Moritz whilst her father, Prince Rainier of Monaco, was seriously ill, and that the then England football captain was having an extramarital affair, when he had professed to being 'clean living').

More recent jurisprudence has given greater weight to the public interest test, by allowing the media their Article 10 right. Legal uncertainly continues to exist, creating ambiguity for both the claimant in the level of 'tortious' protection in their privacy rights and for the media on the other hand, whose editors have to make decisions on such common law considerations.

---

120 *Campbell v Mirror Group Newspapers Ltd* [2004] 2 AC 457.
121 *Von Hannover v Germany* (2005) 40 EHRR 1.
122 *Beckham v MGN Ltd* (June 28 2001; unreported).
123 *Ferdinand (Rio) v Mirror Group Newspapers Ltd* [2011] EWHC 2454 (QB).
124 *Von Hannover v Germany (No 2)* (2012) (Application Numbers – 40660/08, 60641/08) Judgment of 7 February 2012.

FOR THOUGHT

On 30 July 1998, the House of Lords by a majority of three to two granted an injunction to restrain the newspapers from publishing Peter Wright's *Spycatcher* book.[125] Lord Bridge of Harwich (dissenting) said that 'the maintenance of the ban as more and more copies of the book, *Spycatcher*, enter this country and circulate here will seem more and more ridiculous. If the Government are determined to fight to maintain the ban to the end they will face inevitable condemnation and humiliation by the European Court of Human Rights in Strasbourg . . . Freedom of speech is always the first casualty under a totalitarian regime. This is a significant step down that very dangerous road.' Do you agree?

2.3 Media practices and human rights

See below
2.3.1

The Council of Europe, founded in 1949, recognized that dictatorships did not arrive overnight but arose gradually and that the first step would usually comprise the suppression of individual rights and the restriction of freedom of speech and therein the censorship of the press. It was for this reason that the European Convention on Human Rights and Fundamental Freedoms (the Convention) was drafted in 1948 and ratified in Rome on 4 November 1950.

Article 8(1) of the European Convention makes it clear that the concept of privacy is not limited to isolated individuals, but includes the general 'zone' of the family, the home, correspondence with others, telephone conversations and a person's well-being. Article 8(1), 'Right to respect for private and family life', reads:

> Everyone has the right to respect for his private and family life, his home and his correspondence.

However, a Member State to the Convention may derogate under Article 8(2) ECHR making an Article 8 a qualified right:

> There shall be no interference by a public authority with the exercise of this right *except* such as is in accordance with the law and is necessary in a democratic society in the interests of national security, public safety or the economic well-being of the country, for the prevention of disorder or crime, for the protection of health or morals, or for the protection of the rights and freedoms of others.

This was held by the UK courts in **Malone**,[126] where the phone-tapping action by the police on a Surrey antiques dealer, charged with handling stolen goods, was held to be lawful, and said to be not capable of amounting to 'confidential information'. As confirmed by Megarry VC:

> . . . it seems to me that a person who utters confidential information must accept the risk of any unknown overhearing, that is inherent in the circumstances of communication . . . when this is applied to telephone conversation, it appears to me that the speaker is taking such risks of being overheard as are inherent in the system.[127]

---

125 *AG v Guardian Newspapers (No 1)* [1987] 1 WLR 1248 ('*Spycatcher No 1*').
126 *Malone v Metropolitan Police Commissioner (No 2)* [1979] 1 Ch 344.
127 Ibid., at 405 (Megarry VC).

In the absence of a right to privacy in English law, there exists a general concern as to the limited availability of legal remedies in English law for the invasion of someone's privacy.

However, the Human Rights Court in **Malone v UK**[128] held that the UK had breached Article 8(1) of the Convention because the police had not sought the specific court's permission to intercept the applicant's telephone communications, including the unauthorized release of metering records and telephone numbers dialled. The clandestine recording by the Metropolitan Police amounted to a breach of Mr Malone's right to privacy by the unauthorized interference by the state authorities (namely the Post Office and the Police). At the same time the ECtHR found that the power to tap telephones was not subject to any clearly defined legal instruments and measures and that there were urgent remedies needed.

See above
2.2.7

The ECtHR judgment in **Malone** resulted in the UK Parliament passing the Interception and Communications Act 1985, where s 1 established a statutory offence of the interception of telephone communications.[129] Now, the Regulation of Investigatory Powers Act 2000 (RIPA) grants public authorities additional and far-reaching powers to carry out surveillance and investigations, covering interception of *all* forms of communications, including emails and mobile phones.

Phone-hacking continued to fuel newspaper coverage such as the political scandal which made the headlines in 1992 when Conservative politician and Heritage Minister, David Mellor MP, was forced to resign after his extramarital affair with actress Antonia de Sancha came to light. the *People* and the *Sun* newspapers had obtained the information by recording the minister's phone conversations. Seeking an injunction and criminal charges against the tabloids, the courts did not find any contravention of s 1 Interception and Communications Act 1985 as the recordings were made on another phone extension from the subscriber's telephone. Mellor told the Leveson Inquiry in June 2012 that Prime Minister John Major refused to countenance his resignation at the time when Mellor's affair first emerged in July 1992. He told Leveson LJ that he believed that Prime Minister Major feared the press would expose his own relationship in the 1980s with Edwina Currie MP, which was then still a secret.[130] Mrs Currie later revealed in her own memoirs that she had a four-year affair with John Major between 1984 and 1988.[131] David Mellor told the Leveson Inquiry in relation to his phone being hacked:

> My story included, on the part of *The People*, a recourse to phone tapping that was wholly disproportionate to any public interest in the story. *The Sun* went one better, with a lot of cynically invented trash about Chelsea shirts, that exposed the moral bankruptcy of the whole kiss and tell industry. The story was cooked up for cash by Max Clifford and *Sun* executives, and given front page publicity, even though they all knew it to be totally false. The cynicism was breathtaking, as was the arrogance. What they did to me in 1992 led inexorably to phone hacking etc., because these were people who considered themselves above and beyond the law, over-mighty subjects, unencumbered by any requirement for responsibility. It is surely the plain duty of this Inquiry to cut them down to size.[132]

---

128 (1984) 7 EHRR 14.

129 In order for a civil action to be brought, the party to the intercepted conversation must identify himself, and such identification may also be inevitable in any criminal proceedings. Section 2 of the Act established the exception, essentially giving legislative approval to the old system of ministerial warrants for interception of telecommunications or postal communications, with a quasi-judicial system of review in the form of a tribunal added via s 7. This gives the state the right to intercept telephone conversations in the interests of national security and the purpose of detecting or preventing serious crime under ss 2(2)(a) and (b).

130 Source: The Leveson Inquiry. Official transcript MOD300014662: Witness Statement of David Mellor 26 June 2012, afternoon: www.levesoninquiry.org.uk/wp-content/uploads/2012/06/Witness-Statement-David-Mellor.pdf.

131 See: Currie (2002)

132 The Leveson Inquiry. Official transcript. Witness Statement of David Mellor at MOD300014665.

It is worth noting that David Mellor famously warned in 1991 that the press was 'drinking in the last-chance saloon', when commenting on the publication of the first report by Sir David Calcutt QC, who headed an inquiry into press intrusion and how to protect privacy. Mellor warned against the threat of statutory press regulation then, which would spell the end of freedom of the press. The Calcutt Report concluded that while self-regulation was the ideal way forward, the current system under the toothless Press Council was manifestly failing. This was proved in the **Gorden Kaye** case, when the *Sunday Sport*'s unsolicited call was made to the *'Allo 'Allo!* actor, who was recovering in hospital from brain surgery.

See also
Chapter 10.3

Inquiries into journalistic clandestine practices such as phone-hacking and subterfuge (by the *News of the World* – *NOW*) had been pursued by the *Guardian* since 2007, resulting in a new PCC Code for Editors covering phone-tapping (Clause 10). While the PCC did not find any evidence of malpractice at *NOW* in 2007, the *Guardian* reported on 9 July 2009 that phone-hacking and subterfuge at *NOW* was still going on.

2.3.1 Articles 8 and 10 ECHR: conflict and media impact

It is argued here that Strasbourg jurisprudence, based on the European Convention, has provided the impetus for the development of breach of confidence in English tort law in respect of private life.[133] The ECtHR has acknowledged various meanings of 'privacy', such as the right to live privately and protected from publicity (**X v Iceland** (1976)[134]). The term was extended to 'private life', including the physical and psychological integrity of a person (see: **Peck**[135] and **Pretty**[136]). The right to establish details of an individual's identity as an individual human being was established in **Goodwin**[137] and **von Hannover (No 1)**.[138] It is also important to note that Convention rights have been interpreted as having 'vertical effect' (i.e. they can be used in actions against the state) and 'horizontal effect' (i.e. they can be used in actions against private bodies such as newspapers and broadcasters).

See also
Chapter 10.5

If there is an Article 8 challenge, the courts will now ask two questions:

1.   Has there been an interference with a person's Article 8 (1) right? If so,
2.   Was the interference justified under Article 8(2) ECHR?

This principle is known as 'negative obligation'. Any interference must have been made in accordance with domestic law (**Malone v UK** (1984)[139]). There must have been some form of legal protection provided to the individual by the state and there must not be any arbitrary interference by public authorities (**Segerstedt-Wiberg v Sweden** (2007)[140]). If there has been interference by a public authority with an individual's right to privacy, the Article 8(2) derogation must be justified by legitimate aims specified in the interests of national security, public safety, economic well-being, the prevention of disorder or crime or the protection of health, morals, or the rights and freedoms of others.[141] The measure and derogation must

---

133   For further discussion see: Moreham (2008), pp. 44–79.
134   (1976) 5 D. & R. 86.
135   **Peck v UK** (2003) 36 EHRR 41.
136   **Pretty v UK** (2002) 35 EHRR 1.
137   **Goodwin v UK** (2002) 35 EHRR 18.
138   **Von Hannover v Germany** (2005) 40 EHRR 1.
139   (1984) 7 EHRR 14.
140   (2007) 44 EHRR 2.
141   For further discussion see: Harris *et al.* (2009), pp. 290ff.

be 'necessary in a democratic society'[142] and there must be a 'pressing social need' for the interference.[143]

The ECtHR held in **Jersild v Denmark**[144] that it was not for national courts to substitute their own views for those of the press as to what technique of reporting should be adopted by journalists, for this would amount to censorship of the press by the courts. Furthermore, the court stressed that Article 10 not only protects the substance of ideas and information expressed but also the form in which these are conveyed, such as photographs and broadcast and other media. The Human Rights Court has essentially left it up to each state's media editorial policy and ethical practice as to the revelation of someone's identity, in line with the message an article or broadcast intend to convey (see: **Re S (A Child)**[145]). As Lord Hoffmann opined in **Campbell**,[146] judges are not newspaper or broadcasting editors.

The issue as to where the balance is to be struck between the competing rights of Articles 8 and 10 must be approached on this basis. This means there are numerous ECtHR decisions which contain as a common theme the importance of the role of the media in a democratic society, which is to be interpreted broadly as the support for the freedom of expression, as formulated in **Fressoz and Roire v France** (1999):[147]

> (i) Freedom of expression constitutes one of the essential foundations of a democratic society. Subject to paragraph 2 of article 10, it is applicable not only to 'information' or 'ideas' that are favourably received or regarded as inoffensive or as a matter of indifference, but also to those that offend, shock or disturb. Such are the demands of pluralism, tolerance and broad-mindedness without which there is no 'democratic society'.

> (ii) The press plays an essential role in a democratic society. Although it must not overstep certain bounds, in particular in respect of the reputation and rights of others and the need to prevent the disclosure of confidential information, its duty is nevertheless to impart – in a manner consistent with its obligations and responsibilities – information and ideas on all matters of public interest. In addition, the court is mindful of the fact that journalistic freedom also covers possible recourse to a degree of exaggeration, or even provocation.[148]

The time has come to recognize in UK domestic law that the values enshrined in Articles 8 and 10 of the Convention have become part of the cause of action for breach of confidence and equally in the right to privacy, as Lord Woolf CJ stressed in **A v B plc** (2003).[149] Therefore, we can assume that there now exists an independent tort of privacy in English law.

See below 2.8

2.3.2 Freedom of speech: matters of official secrets and national security

In a democracy freedom of speech is a primary right; without it an effective rule of law is not possible. Article 10 of the European Convention is a fundamental civil and political right which

---

142 See: Clayton and Tomlinson (2009), para 6ff.
143 See: Fenwick and Phillipson (2006), pp. 104–106.
144 (1994) 19 EHRR 1.
145 **Re S (A Child) (Identification: Restriction on Publication)** [2004] UKHL 47.
146 [2004] UKHL 47.
147 (1999) 31 EHRR 28.
148 Ibid., at 45.
149 [2003] QB 195 at 202 (Lord Woolf CJ).

engages the ability of the individual to speak out against the state without fear of undue repression. Nevertheless, freedom of expression is not an absolute right and is thereby qualified in Article 10(2) ECHR. Freedom of speech must at times yield to other cogent social interests, such as national security, recognized in the **Spycatcher**[150] action well before the European Convention entered UK domestic law. In **Derbyshire County Council v Times Newspapers Ltd**[151] Lord Keith of Kinkel, speaking for a unanimous House, observed about Article 10:

> As regards the words 'necessary in a democratic society' in connection with the restrictions on the right to freedom of expression which may properly be prescribed by law, the jurisprudence of the European Court of Human Rights has established that 'necessary' requires the existence of a pressing social need, and that the restrictions should be no more than is proportionate to the legitimate aim pursued.[152]

The British secret services, particularly MI5, have always been the object of conspiracy theories, according to Cambridge professor Christopher Andrew, author of the first official history of MI5.[153] For a long time, what MI5, the domestic part of the British secret service, was up to was generally defined as 'defence of the realm' and they were left to get on with it. MI5 activities were partly exposed by the 'Profumo' affair in 1963. John Dennis Profumo, Tory Secretary of State for War, had a brief and passionate affair with a call girl, Christine Keeler, at the same time as there were reports that she was consorting with a naval attaché at the Soviet Embassy in London. Profumo made a fundamental error: he lied to the House of Commons about his affair with Keeler. In March 1963 he told the chamber that there was 'no impropriety whatever' in his relationship with Miss Keeler. Ten weeks later he appeared before MPs again to say 'with deep remorse' that he had misled the House, and would resign.

The secret services continued to be protected by layers of official secrecy, until the publication *Spycatcher* came onto the (Australian) market, in which former MI5 officer Peter Wright described how 'we bugged and burgled our way across London at the State's behest, while pompous, bowler-hatted civil servants in Whitehall pretended to look the other way'.[154] Secrecy may be essential in the case of a respondent who, if tipped off, is likely to defeat the purposes of an application by publishing the material before he can be shown to have had notice of the injunction, or before it can be granted. There may be compelling reasons why the Crown or the Attorney General apply for an injunction on the grounds of public security and state secrecy. In **Spycatcher (No 2)**[155] Lord Goff of Chieveley expressed the opinion that in the field of freedom of speech there was in principle no difference between English law on the subject and Article 10 of the Convention.

There have been three famous cases in UK legal history which have tested the notion of state secrecy and confidentiality; two were decided prior to the Human Rights Act 1998, namely the **Crossman Diaries**[156] and **Spycatcher**, with the **David Shayler**[157] case decided post the Convention's incorporation into UK law involving, *inter alia*, criminal action. In **Crossman Diaries** and **Spycatcher**, prior restraint orders to stop publication were applied for by the Attorney General on behalf of the respective governments at the time, citing breach of confidence.

---

150 *AG v Guardian Newspapers Ltd (No. 1)* [1987] 1 WLR 1248.
151 [1993] AC 534.
152 Ibid., at 550H–551A (Lord Keith of Kinkel).
153 See: Andrew (2009).
154 See: Wright (1987), pp. 104–106.
155 *AG v Guardian Newspapers Ltd (No 2)* [1990] 1 AC 109, at 283–284 (Lord Goff of Chieveley).
156 See: Crossman (1976–7).
157 *R v Shayler* [2003] 1 AC 247.

The 'Crossman Diaries' case (*AG v Jonathan Cape Ltd* (1976)[158]) presented the first court action that tested the conventions of the paradigm of restraint of a government minister's publication of Cabinet 'secrets'. The Government had applied via the Attorney General to injunct the publication of Cabinet minister Richard Crossman's posthumous diaries. The courts, in turn, had to balance the competing interests, namely the public's right to know about government secrets and indiscretions ('the public interest test'), and Cabinet confidentiality and government secrecy. Lord Widgery CJ's judgment makes this abundantly clear when he lifted the injunction and the publication of the three volumes of diaries could go ahead:

> . . . it is unacceptable in our democratic society that there should be a restraint on the publication of information relating to Government when the only vice of that information is that it enables the public to discuss, review and criticise Government action. Accordingly, the court will determine the Government's claim to confidentiality by reference to the public interest. Unless disclosure is likely to injure the public interest, it will not be protected.[159]

The *Spycatcher* (**No 1**)[160] and (**No 2**)[161] actions followed, arguably best known for their numerous injunctions. Former MI5 spy Peter Wright had entered into a publishing contract with an Australian company in 1985 after he had retired to Tasmania, where he had written his memoirs: *Spycatcher: the Candid Autobiography of a Senior Intelligence Officer.* The first court action ('**Spycatcher No 1**') concerned the application by the Attorney General to restrain prior publication of the book in order to preserve the confidentiality of the Wright material, subject to him signing the contract of employment which inherently included the Official Secrets Act 1911.[162] Once the British Government learnt that *Spycatcher* was going to be published on a large scale in the Antipodes and North America, it became obvious that the British secret services of MI5 and its international counterpart MI6 would never be truly secret and confidential again. The question arose in the UK High Court whether the Crown could injunct a publication outside the United Kingdom.[163]

❖ **KEY CASES**

Attorney-General v Guardian Newspapers Ltd (No 1) [1987] 3 All ER 316 ('*Spycatcher No 1*'); *Attorney-General v Guardian Newspapers Ltd (No 2)* [1990] 1 AC 109 ('*Spycatcher No 2*')

Precedent

❖ A duty of confidence arises when confidential information comes to the knowledge of a person (the confidant) in circumstances where he has notice, or is held to have agreed, that the information is confidential.

❖ Article 10 freedom of expression is a fundamental right, though not an absolute right, qualified by Article 10(2) ECHR.

❖ Freedom of speech can be restricted by law (e.g. Official Secrets Acts 1911 and 1989).

❖ There is a convention that Cabinet 'confidences' should be preserved and protected by the law.

---

158 [1976] QB 752.
159 Ibid., at 735 (Lord Widgery).
160 [1987] 1 WLR 1248.
161 [1990] 1 AC 109.
162 For further discussion see: Barendt (1989), pp. 204ff; also: Bindman (1989), pp. 94ff.
163 See: Lee (1987), pp. 506ff; see also: Leigh (1992), pp. 200ff.

❖ But the public interest may outweigh constitutional conventions if disclosure of
   Government and state secrets are in the public interest.
❖ The 'Spycatcher doctrine': a *contra mundum* (against the world) injunction against
   one news organization binds all other media organizations.

Facts

Former MI5 member of the British secret service, Peter Wright (W), had written his
memoirs of 20 years in the secret service (MI5), during his retirement in Tasmania, under
the title *Spycatcher*. The book alleged unlawful activities carried out by MI5 during
W's period of service, including the intention of destabilizing Harold Wilson's Labour
administration in 1977.

The Crown (via the Attorney General – AG) asked the High Court for an injunction to stop
the book's publication in New South Wales (Australia) and the United States, because the
manuscript had disclosed information that constituted a breach of confidentiality owed to
the Crown, such as MI5 investigations and operations. The *Independent, Guardian* and
Observer newspapers reported on the AG's intended press 'gagging' orders, stating that
this amounted to an interference with the freedom of the press.

On 11 July 1986 Millett J granted injunctions against the newspapers, restraining the
Spycatcher publication. The newspapers' appeal was dismissed on 25 July by the Court of
Appeal (CA). On 27 April 1987, the *Independent* published a summary of allegations
contained in *Spycatcher*, after which the AG commenced 'contempt' proceedings against
the newspaper. On 2 June 1987, Sir Nicolas Browne-Wilkinson VC held that the publication in the *Independent* and two London evening newspapers could *not* amount to
'contempt' because there was no injunction in place restraining publication in the
Independent, only the *Guardian* and *Observer*.

On 12 July 1987, the *Sunday Times* published extracts from the book and on 13 July the AG
commenced 'contempt' proceedings against the Sunday paper for publishing the article
while a restraining order was still in place. On 22 July 1987, Sir Nicolas Browne-Wilkinson
VC discharged all injunctions, allowing a cross-appeal from the AG on 24 July and
thereafter modifying the injunctions by allowing the newspapers to publish a summary
of Peter Wright's book.

Decision in *Spycatcher No 1*

The CA upheld all interim injunctions against the newspapers and agreed with the AG that
they were necessary to maintain the efficiency of the security services upon which the
safety of the realm was dependent. The basic argument by defendant newspapers in
Spycatcher No 1 was that the information contained in Peter Wright's book was public
property and already public knowledge in that the book had already been published in
Australia and the United States. Therefore, the claimant (the AG) had to show not only that
the information was confidential in quality and that it was imparted so as to import
an obligation of confidence, but also that there would be 'an unauthorized use of that
information to the detriment of the party communicating', as per ***Coco v A. N. Clark
(Engineers) Ltd*** (1969).[164]

---

164 [1969] RPC 41.

Decision in *Spycatcher No 2*

In its judgment in ***Spycatcher No 2***, the House of Lords held that the book contained material prejudicial to national security and was in serious breach of confidence. In the end their Lordships had no choice but to lift the injunction because a restraining order could not be applied against Peter Wright and the publishers because they were resident outside the UK, which provided them with a jurisdictional shield. This meant that a UK court order could not bind the High Court of Australia, the New Zealand Court of Appeal or indeed any other foreign jurisdiction. Since the book had already been published in New South Wales, New Zealand and the United States, *Spycatcher* was already in the public domain and an injunction would effectively be worthless.

Lord Griffiths in ***Spycatcher No 2*** referred to the provision of freedom of expression under Article 10 ECHR, commenting that he saw no reason why English law should take a different approach in relation to confidentiality.[165] Lord Goff of Chieveley, in his judgment, identified the following limiting principles where the law would protect the notion of 'confidence':

> . . . although the basis of the law's protection of confidence is that there is a public interest that confidences should be preserved and protected by the law, nevertheless that public interest may be outweighed by some other countervailing public interest which favours disclosure. This limitation may apply . . . to all types of confidential information. It is this limiting principle which may require a court to carry out a balancing operation, weighing the public interest in maintaining confidence against a countervailing public interest favouring disclosure.[166]

Analysis

While the courts condemned Peter Wright's conduct, it was still unavoidable that British citizens had either read reports or reviews of the book, or comments on it in the newspapers, or they had bought a copy of *Spycatcher* in foreign bookshops. In the second ***Spycatcher*** action, the House of Lords was sympathetic to the Attorney General's fear that newspapers might publish the contents of such a book without careful consideration of the public interest and without giving him the opportunity, if he challenged the editors' judgement, to have the issue determined by the court. It was for this reason that the first judge, Scott J, had granted the injunction in ***Spycatcher No 1***. The *Spycatcher* litigation was viewed by some foreign jurisdictions as an authoritarian attempt by the British Government over its former Commonwealth to quash freedom of speech, freedom of access to information and freedom to publish. Unsurprisingly, English judges took a different view.

It is worth mentioning that the *Sunday Times* publishers and its editor Andrew Neil were severely criticized in **Spycatcher No 2**: they were held liable to account to the Crown for profits because they had ignored the existing court injunction. The newspaper had still gone ahead and published extracts from the book in July 1987. The publishers and editor were found guilty of contempt of

---

165 Ibid., at 273 (Lord Griffiths).
166 Ibid., at 282 (Lord Goff of Chieveley).

court and Lord Keith of Kinkel specifically referred to Mr Neil's blatantly ignoring the interim injunction as employing 'peculiarly sneaky methods'.[167]

Breach of confidentiality matters featured rather differently in the *David Shayler* case,[168] involving the criminal action of a former MI5 'whistleblower', who took it upon himself to disclose British secret service information by publishing articles in the press during August 1997. On 24 August, the *Mail on Sunday* ran a front-page story headlined 'MI5 Bugged Mandelson', with the claim that Tony Blair's favourite minister had his phone tapped for three years during the late 1970s. Not only did Mr Shayler not succeed in publishing his memoirs but he was also convicted for unlawfully disclosing official documents to the press, thereby breaching the Official Secrets Act 1989.[169] When a prosecution against Mr Shayler ensued for seriously breaching the 1989 Act, he used the right to freedom of expression under Article 10 ECHR as a defence.[170]

❖ KEY CASE   *R v Shayler* (2003) 1 AC 247 (House of Lords)

Precedent
* ❖ Disclosure of official secrets is not protected by Article 10(1) ECHR.
* ❖ Defences of duress, necessity of circumstances and public interest are not available to a defendant charged under ss 1(1) and 4(1) Official Secrets Act 1989.
* ❖ Official secrets legislation continues to apply even after leaving the service.
* ❖ The Official Secrets Act 1989 is compatible with Article 10(1) ECHR.

Facts
David Shayler was a member of the security service MI5 from November 1991 to October 1996. As part of his contract, he had signed the Official Secrets Act 1989, acknowledging the confidential nature of documents and other information relating to security or intelligence that might come into his possession. On leaving the service he signed a declaration acknowledging that the provisions of the Act continued to apply. In 1997 Mr Shayler disclosed documents relating to security and intelligence matters to a national newspaper, claiming that MI5 held files on more than 500,000 subjects, including two Cabinet ministers. He also alleged that Britain had tried to assassinate the Libyan leader, Colonel Gaddafi. David Shayler escaped to France to avoid prosecution for breaching secrecy laws. In 1999, government lawyers applied for an injunction to block the publication of his memoirs. In August 2000, Mr Shayler returned to the UK, where he was arrested and charged with disclosing documents without lawful authority, contrary to ss 1 and 4 of the 1989 Act.

Moses J ruled that the defence of duress or necessity of circumstances was not available to the defendant, as implied in the 1989 Act. Shayler was also not permitted to invoke Article 10(1) ECHR, claiming that the disclosures were necessary in the public interest to avert damage to life or limb or serious damage to property. The CA dismissed Shayler's appeal invoking his Article 10 right and opined that there was no public interest defence in relation to the offences he was charged with.

167 *AG v Guardian Newspapers (No 2)* [1990] 1 AC 109 at 261 (Lord Keith of Kinkel).
168 *R v Shayler* [2003] 1 AC 247.
169 For further discussion see: Hollingsworth and Fielding (1999).
170 HRA 1998, Sch 1, Pt I.

Decision
The House of Lords dismissed David Shayler's appeal on the grounds that ss 1(1)(a), 3(a) and 4(1) of the 1989 Act made it clear that Parliament did not intend that a defendant prosecuted under those sections should be acquitted if he showed that it was in the public or national interest to make the disclosure in question. The prosecution did not have to prove that the disclosure was damaging or was not in the public interest. For that reason, the defendant was not entitled to argue as a defence that the unauthorized disclosures he had made were made in the public interest.

In view of the special position of members of the security and intelligence services, and the highly confidential nature of information which came into their possession, the interference with their right to freedom of expression prescribed by Article 10(1) ECHR was not greater than was required to achieve the legitimate object of acting in the interests of national security. Accordingly, ss 1 and 4 OSA 1989 came within the qualification in Article 10(2) ECHR as a justified interference with the right to freedom of expression and were not incompatible with Article 10. David Shayler was sentenced to six months in prison.

Analysis
Their Lordships stated *obiter* that in order to 'whistleblow' on irregularities or unlawful practices in the UK security services, Mr Shayler should have sought judicial review as the appropriate recourse of effective action, having exhausted internal procedures of the Civil Service. Instead, Mr Shayler chose to impart highly confidential MI5 information to a national newspaper for financial and professional gain.

2.3.3 Kiss and tell: breach of confidence in the domestic setting

When people kiss and later one of them tells, the person who does so is almost certainly breaking a confidential arrangement. Though it is necessary for the media to report on all proceedings in open court, as was held in the divorce proceedings in **Scott v Scott** (1913),[171] the courts have never given a carte blanche approach to the disclosure of private communication between couples and free distribution to the press of private correspondence. This point was further developed in the '**Duchess and Duke of Argyl**' case relating to confidentiality; see also: **Stephens v Avery** (1988[172]).

See Chapter 1.4.1

The ECtHR has consistently applied its jurisdiction on the subject of Article 8 ECHR when determining what is necessary in a particular state's society where an action is being brought. This is widely acknowledged where the ECtHR has held that it will apply narrower measures with reference to an aspect of a person's private life, such as one's sexuality.[173] A variety of different interferences fall within the category of 'private life' and interest, including unwanted observation and intrusion into one's home and the workplace as well as the unwanted dissemination of CCTV images (**Peck v UK** (2003)[174]).

See below: 2.3.4

Recognition of the need to protect against such interferences is unsurprising. Although English courts have not yet recognized physical intrusion as part of the tort of privacy, there are a number

---

171 [1913] AC 417.
172 [1988] 1 Ch 449.
173 *Norris v Ireland* (1989) 13 EHRR 186.
174 (2003) 36 EHRR 41.

of Strasbourg rulings which could be regarded as persuasive, such as the right to be free from physical assault or bodily searches, surveillance and the dissemination of images (**YF v Turkey** (2004)[175]); or where the ECtHR expressly held that an individual's mental and physical health is part of a person's 'physical or moral integrity' (**Bensaid v UK** (2001)[176]). The next challenge to privacy may well be aerial kite photography, used already for military reconnaissance and during the London Olympics in 2012 (see also: **Bernstein v Skyviews** – below).

> ### ❖ KEY CASE *Bernstein of Leigh v Skyviews & General Ltd* [1978] 1 QB 479
>
> **Precedent**
> - ❖ The rights of a landowner in the airspace above his land are restricted to such a height necessary for the ordinary use and enjoyment of his land and the structures upon it.
> - ❖ Above that height the landowner has no greater rights than the general public.
>
> **Facts**
> Bernstein (B) claimed that Skyviews wrongfully entered his airspace to take an aerial photo of his house. The defendants, Skyviews (S), admitted they took the photo, but said they did not go into B's airspace; they took the aerial shots whilst over the adjoining property. S claimed that when they flew over B's land they had implied permission to do so. The issue before the court was: does flying over a person's private property constitute trespass of airspace?
>
> **Decision**
> The CA held that S's aircraft did not infringe any rights of B's airspace – thus no trespass.
>
> **Analysis**
> Bernstein (B) clearly relied on the old maxim, which – translated from the Latin – was: 'whomsoever the soil belongs, he owns also to the sky and to the depths'. English cases in which this has been used all concern structures attached to adjoining land that hang over a claimant's property (see: *Gifford v Dent* [1926][177] – sign projected 4 feet was trespass; *Kelsen v Imperial Tobacco Co* [1957][178] – sign projected 8 inches – injunction granted). Which means that adjoining land owners have no right to erect structures overhanging their neighbour's land.
>
> The *Bernstein* case concerned aircraft which fly at a height which in no way affect the use of the land. In this case it was held to be no trespass (see also: *Pickering v Rudd* [1815][179] – it is not trespass to pass over a man's property in a balloon). The case established that a property owner does not have unqualified rights over the airspace above their land. Additionally there is no authority stating that a landowner's right in the airspace over land extends to an unlimited height.

---

175 (2004) 39 EHRR 34.
176 (2001) 33 EHRR 10.
177 [1926] WN 336.
178 [1957] 2 QB 334.
179 [1815] 171 ER 70.

2.3.4 *Argyll v Argyll*: the scandal that rocked the nation

Central to the **Argyll v Argyll** (1967)[180] action were sexually explicit photos in the Duke and Duchess of Argyll's divorce proceedings which formed part of the 'confidentiality' action. The eleventh Duke of Argyll had been unlucky in love. Twice divorced, he had met socialite Margaret Whigham, a millionaire's daughter and divorcee, on a blind date in London. They were married in 1951 and the couple lived at the ancestral seat at Inveraray Castle in Scotland. Soon Margaret became bored, spending most of her time in London. In early 1954, the Duke accused his wife of a string of affairs and filed for divorce in 1959. The **Argyll** judgment coincided with the Profumo affair and fed the papers for months with social tittle-tattle and political bile.

❖ KEY CASE — *Argyll v Argyll and Others* [1967] Ch 301

Precedent

- ❖ Confidential communications between husband and wife during marriage are within the protection of breach of confidence.
- ❖ A spouse's immorality does not nullify his or her right to protection against breach of confidence relating to past events.
- ❖ The confidentiality in marriage principle applies even after divorce.

Facts

In 1959, the Duke of Argyll (D) began divorce proceedings against his wife (M). In 1960, M cross-petitioned and in 1963 D was granted a decree of divorce on the ground of his wife's adultery. The main evidence in the 'fault' divorce proceedings amounted to the Duchess's private diaries and explosive Polaroid 'headless' photographs, all of which had been seized in a raid by the Duke at the Duchess's own house at 48 Upper Grosvenor Street, London. The Polaroids, dated on the back 1957, showed the Duchess wearing nothing but a string of pearls performing fellatio on her lover, while revealing a shot of another man in a gilt mirror, performing a sex act on the first naked man. The men's heads had been cropped out of the photograph. The divorce was a three-year-long drawn-out affair with lengthy (super)injunctions and two-way adultery counter-claims.

The divorce was finally heard in an 11-day hearing at the Edinburgh High Court in 1962, where the Duke alleged that his wife had had 88 lovers. The judge granted the divorce on the grounds that Margaret committed adultery 'only' with three men: American businessman John Cohane; former press officer for the Savoy Hotel, Harvey Combe; and German diplomat Sigismund von Braun. Most importantly for the purpose of this case, the 'headless' Polaroid photos were shown in open court. They had even been subject to an investigation by Lord Denning, who had been given the task of establishing the identities of the 'headless' lovers to provide evidence of the Duchess's infidelity. But the identities of the two headless men in the photos could not be revealed in court due to the nature of the photos.

Following the decree of divorce, the Edinburgh court granted an injunction that the subject matter of the action should never be made public despite the fact that the Duchess

---

180 [1967] Ch 301.

(M) had allowed certain articles relating to her infidelities to appear in the *People* newspaper (P). The Duke had also leaked marital secrets to the press, including an American newspaper, and it was at this point that the Duchess sought an injunction to restrain the publication of the same material in England. M argued that the publication in England would be more harmful to her than publication in America. M sought interlocutory injunctions to restrain the editor and publishers of the Sunday newspaper (P) from publishing all statements and secrets about her (including the 'headless' Polaroids), revealing every secret of her private life and communications during her marriage to D. She also sought restraint of all particulars of D's divorce petition.

Decision

Lord Wheatley granted an interlocutory injunction, restraining publication of secrets relating to M and D's private life during marriage. It followed that it was unlawful to publish or make public any offensive material (including the headless photographs) or name any party cited during the infidelity proceedings.[181] Any contravention would constitute a tort and criminal actions could follow if the restraining order were disobeyed. Lord Wheatley's judgment in **Argyll v Argyll** of 8 May 1963 set an important precedent in common law of confidentiality, summarized as follows:

1. A breach of confidence or trust or faith can arise independently of any right in property or contract and the court in the exercise of its equitable jurisdiction will restrain a breach of confidence independently of any right at law;
2. The principle applies even after divorce or after adultery or previous disclosures;
3. The confidential nature of the marital relationship is of its very essence and so obviously and necessarily implicit in it that there is no need for it to be expressed. This would apply not merely to private affairs but business matters and things discovered by one party to the marriage about the other which but for the close relationship they would not have discovered. It also encompasses things done as well as things talked about.[182]

Analysis

One of the most important precedents in the **Argyll** ruling – still applied today – is that confidential communication between husband and wife (e.g. letters, diary entries, photographs etc.) is within the scope of the court's protection against breach of confidence. This also meant that the Duchess's immorality did not nullify her right to protection against breach of confidence relating to past events, prior to the breakdown of the marriage.

The **Argyll** injunction was granted against the revelation of marital confidences. The right to personal 'marital' privacy is clearly one which the law has sought to protect. And if a newspaper has made a profit out of the revelations in breach of confidence of details of a person's private life, it is only appropriate that the profit should be accounted for to that person (this would normally be heard in the Chancery Division). It is then in the public interest that such (marital) confidences should be respected and protected, enforcing the obligation of confidence even where the confider can point to no specific detriment to

---

181 Section 1 Judicial Proceedings (Regulation of Reports) Act 1926.
182 (1967) Ch 301 at 632 (Lord Wheatley).

himself. It a sufficient detriment to the confider that information given in confidence is to be disclosed to persons whom he would prefer not to know of it, even though the disclosure would not be harmful to him in any positive way. The newspaper (the *People*) to which the Duke of Argyll had communicated the information about the Duchess was restrained by injunction from publishing it. There was no doubt but that the publication would cause detriment to the Duchess.

Incidentally, we finally learnt about the identity of the 'headless' photos some 41 years later. On 10 August 2000, a Channel 4 TV documentary named the two men (after their deaths): the actor Douglas Fairbanks Jr and Cabinet minister Duncan Sandys.[183]

Some couples have been able to rely on the **Argyll** judgment, and some have not. Cynthia and John Lennon (of the Beatles) could not rely on **Argyll** when they divorced on 8 November 1968. Cynthia Lennon was granted a decree nisi on the grounds of John's adultery with Yoko Ono. Cynthia retained custody of their son Julian. Ten years later, Cynthia[184] sold her story and memoirs to the *News of the World* and John Lennon[185] sought to injunct the publication. The court ruled that he could not rely on **Argyll** for breaches of marital confidences on the grounds that:

1. He himself had publicized the most intimate details of their marriage; and
2. There was nothing left which was confidential; all the information was already in the public domain.

2.3.5 Breach of confidence in domestic partnerships

On 17 March 1997, the *Sun* released extracts from confidential handwritten letters between TV personality Michael Barrymore and his lover Paul Wincott. Though Mr Barrymore had made it known in August 1995 to his wife and close family members that he was homosexual, the matter was not of general public knowledge at the time.

On the day the *Sun* outed Michael Barrymore as gay, he sought an *ex parte* injunction from the High Court, claiming breach of confidence at common law and in equity and in relation to 'A Trust and Confidence Agreement' made between the second plaintiff, the company owned jointly by Barrymore and his wife, and Paul Wincott.[186] The agreement – made by deed – included the obligation not to disclose or make use of any confidential business or personal information. The High Court granted the injunction to restrain any further publications, citing Lord Wheatley's judgment in **Argyll**, extending the principle of confidentiality in correspondence between married couples to that of 'close relationships'.

It is then only common sense, if people enter into a personal relationship and exchange letters, photographs, emails or text messages, that this is not done for the purpose of publication in the press or any other medium. It would be highly unlikely in close personal relationships that the parties draw up a contract to keep their relationship confidential. If there is a breach of confidentiality, and one party 'kisses and tells' and sells their story to the press, only common law can then provide a remedy to stop the papers from printing such information as outlined in **Scott v Scott**, **Argyll** and **Barrymore**.

---

183 Source: '"Headless men" in sex scandal finally named', by Sarah Hall, *Guardian*, 10 August 2000.
184 See: Lennon, C. (2005).
185 **Lennon v News Group Newspapers** [1978] FSR 573.
186 **Barrymore v News Group Newspapers Limited and Another** [1997] ESR 600.

2.3.6 Remedies for breach of confidence

The media, being fed information by a jilted partner about correspondence exchanged between the couple when they were still in love, will always try to publish a juicy story. When BBC TV and then Radio 1 presenter Jamie Theakston[187] attempted to block a story and photographs in the *Sunday People* and *News of the World* about his visits to a Mayfair brothel, the 'public interest' prevailed when the court ruled that Theakston was a role model for young viewers, being a presenter on *Top of the Pops* and *Live and Kicking*.

In **Barrymore**, however, the High Court did grant the injunction to restrain any further publication in the newspaper of information released by his former lover Paul Wincott. However, the question of compensation was a tricky one, as Jacobs J pointed out:

> . . . the financial consequences will no doubt be a matter for the court to decide in due course. I say no more at this stage other than that newspapers which think that they can pay their way out of breach of confidence may find it more expensive than it is worth to print the material.[188]

See 2.3.7 below

This leaves the concept of breach of confidentiality (and privacy) rather open-ended and perhaps too flexible. In 'privacy' cases it leaves the courts to decide on a case-by-case basis as to the nature of the breach and how (if at all) damages can be awarded in equity. As common law on privacy and confidentiality has advanced and has gradually merged the two concepts, they tend to have a rather uneasy relationship with the right to freedom of expression under Article 10 ECHR, as demonstrated in the **Earl Spencer** case.[189] This tension is particularly acute where people in a relationship share confidential information and one partner discloses it, usually for financial gain, after the relationship has gone sour.

2.3.7 Remedies for breach of confidence prior to the Human Rights Act 1998

The main reason why breach of confidence was not previously able to provide adequate protection of privacy was because a claimant had to prove the three elements in **Coco v Clark**,[190] the second element of which was that the information must have been imparted in circumstances importing an obligation of confidence. Invasions of privacy are often done by those with no relationship with the victim, for instance by a journalist with a telephoto lens. With no relationship between confider and confidant, the obligation of confidence is not established and a claimant would not have succeeded in a confidentiality action.

In his privacy action before the Strasbourg court, the ninth Earl Spencer,[191] brother of the deceased Diana, Princess of Wales, submitted that the United Kingdom had failed to comply with its obligations to protect his and his wife's right to respect for his private life under Article 8 ECHR. The Earl claimed that the state had failed to prohibit the publication and dissemination of information relating to Countess Spencer's private affairs and therein failed to provide a legal remedy. He argued that the UK ought to have prevented the release of private and confidential information concerning the Spencers' private affairs by restraining the newspaper from publishing their stories and photographs, and that the UK courts ought to have provided damages for his wife's

187 **Theakston v MGN** [2002] EWHC 137 (QB).
188 **Barrymore v NGN** [1997] FSR at 602 (Jacobs J).
189 **Earl Spencer and Countess Spencer v UK** (1998) 25 EHRR CD 105.
190 [1969] RPC 41.
191 **Earl Spencer and Countess Spencer v UK** (1998) 25 EHRR CD 105.

distress and the family's harassment by the media. Reasons for the media frenzy were that both Earl Spencer's wife Victoria[192] and his sister, Diana, had been suffering from an eating disorder.

 **KEY CASE**

Earl Spencer and Countess Spencer v United Kingdom (1998) 25 EHRR CD 105 (ECtHR)

Precedent
* There are adequate remedies available in the UK courts for breach of confidence.
* Before an application can be made to the European Court of Human Rights (ECtHR) in Strasbourg the applicant has to exhaust the domestic courts' remedies to the full; otherwise he will not be heard.

Facts
The *News of the World* (*NOW*) published an article on 2 April 1995, entitled 'Di's sister-in-law in booze and bulimia clinic'. This detailed some of the personal problems of Countess Spencer and included a photograph taken with a telephoto lens while she walked in the grounds of a private clinic. Earl Spencer complained to the Press Complaints Commission, which concluded there was a clear breach of Code 3 ('privacy') vis-à-vis his wife. The second publication was an article in the *People* on the same day, referring to the Countess's admission to a private clinic for an eating disorder. The third article was published in the *Sunday Mirror*, on the same day, alleging that the Countess had a drink problem.

Instead of suing the newspapers, the Earl and Countess applied to the European Commission on Human Rights (and therein to the Strasbourg court), complaining that English law had failed to provide adequate respect for their privacy and so violated Article 8. Apart from arguing the breach of confidence action, the Spencers complained that the UK had no effective remedy in common law for the invasion of their privacy by the media. Citing the **Barrymore** judgment, they submitted that it must be shown that the relevant newspapers had been put on notice prior to publication and that the disclosure of confidential information amounted to a breach of a duty of confidence owed by the source to the subject of the information. As to the remedies available for a breach of confidence, the Spencers referred to the impossibility of obtaining an injunction prior to publication in the absence of prior warning. In short, the court would not make a restraining order if the material information has already been published. The *dicta* of Laws J and the ruling of the **Spencer** case did not amount to a right of privacy.

Decision
The ECtHR declared inadmissible an application by Earl and Lady Spencer on the basis that they had not exhausted their domestic remedies, rejecting the Spencers' complaints under Article 8 on the basis that the couple had not completely exhausted the domestic remedies available to them for breach of confidence as outlined in **Spycatcher No 2** and **Barrymore**. The Commission also found their complaint under Article 13 ill-founded within the meaning of Article 27(2) of the Convention.

---

192 Victoria Lockwood had married Earl Spencer in 1989, with Prince Harry as a pageboy.

Analysis

The Strasbourg court found in the **Earl Spencer** case that the UK's common law provisions in the law of confidence were adequate and reasonable to remedy the Spencers' complaint. However, since the Spencers had chosen not to avail themselves of any domestic court action in 'privacy' (not following the hierarchy of the courts) they were not entitled to seek redress in the Human Rights Court.

But the watershed was yet to come with case law building up following the introduction of the Human Rights Act 1998 in the United Kingdom.

2.4 The impact of the Human Rights Act 1998 on UK common law

On 8 January 2001, 50 years after the United Kingdom ratified the European Convention, Sedley LJ in **Douglas v Hello! Ltd**[193] stated:

> We have reached a point at which it can be said with confidence that the law recognises and will appropriately protect a right of personal privacy.[194]

The judge gave two reasons for his comment. First, that equity and the common law had to respond to an increasingly invasive social environment. Secondly, that such recognition was required by the HRA and in particular Article 8 ECHR.

Sedley LJ went on to say that since **Kaye v Robertson** had been decided, 'the legal landscape has altered'[195] and that the right of privacy was grounded in the equitable doctrine of breach of confidence.[196]

Since the Human Rights Act 1998 (HRA) came into effect in October 2000, importing the European Convention on Human Rights into UK law, it is fair to say that the UK has developed into a rights-based society – previously unfamiliar to the English common law tradition. Since this chapter deals mainly with challenges under Articles 8 and 10 of the Convention – the right to privacy and freedom of expression – it is fair to say that not all cases have been reported and many of them have been settled out of court. Some have claimed (super)injunctions under Article 8, many filed against the most popular 'red tops' and their senior editors. More recently, the Strasbourg court confirmed that Articles 8 and 10 ECHR are of equal value, as long as the 'balancing exercise' is genuinely conducted by domestic courts, following the margin of appreciation (see: **Axel Springer** case[197]).

There is now ample case law that has identified infringements of a person's Article 8 rights, particularly where personal identification in the form of photography is at issue. The only permitted exception for publication appears to be where there is a countervailing public interest which – given particular circumstances – is strong enough to outweigh the right to privacy. If there is an Article 8 'privacy' challenge, domestic courts will now ask:

---

193 [2001] EMLR 563 (QB).
194 Ibid., at 234, para 115 (Sedley LJ).
195 Ibid., at 236, para 116.
196 Ibid., at 239, para 125.
197 **Axel Springer v Germany** (2012) (Application No 3995/08) Strasbourg judgment of 7 February 2012 (ECTHR).

1.   Was it necessary and proportionate for the intrusion to take place, for example, in order to expose illegal activity or to prevent the public from being significantly misled by public claims hitherto made by the individual concerned (e.g. Naomi Campbell's public denials of drug-taking); or

2.   Was it necessary because the information would make a contribution to a debate of general public interest (e.g. **von Hannover No 2**)?

2.4.1 When are celebrities in the public interest? The *von Hannover No 1* and *No 2* and *Axel Springer* actions

The German weekly 'gossip' magazines have always been interested in the private lives of European royalty, focusing particularly on Princess Caroline of Monaco[198] during her various marriages. The **von Hannover No 1**[199] action was of particular interest to the German media, because of its ongoing uneasy relationship with Monaco's royal family ever since Prince Rainier married the glamorous American actress Grace Kelly. The couple sold photographs of their newborn child, Princess Caroline, to a French newspaper in 1957, with the German paparazzi intruding into Princess Caroline's private life ever since. The three-times-married Princess has taken French and German newspapers and magazine publishers to court a number of times in privacy actions. Among the many photographic incidents complained about by Princess Caroline was issue No 30 of the *Freizeit Revue* of 22 July 1993, which showed her in the company of the actor Vincent Lindon after the tragic death of her second husband, Stefano Casiraghi. Lindon and the Princess were photographed at the far end of a restaurant courtyard in Saint-Rémy-de-Provence, captioned: 'These photos are evidence of the tenderest romance of our time' – following the dating gossip about the Princess's numerous suitors. Princess Caroline has on numerous occasions applied to the German courts for injunctions to prevent publication of photographs and accompanying articles in magazines, such as *Bunte*, *Freizeit Revue* (published by Burda) and *Neue Post* (published by Heinrich Bauer Verlag). She claimed that the publications infringed her right to protection of her personality rights guaranteed by Articles 1(1) and 2(1) of the German Constitution (*Grundgesetz*) as well as her right to protection of her private life under Article 8 ECHR.

In **von Hannover No 1**, Princess Caroline additionally complained that the offending magazine had used her image without consent, arguing the provisions under Articles 22 and 23 of the *Kunsturhebergesetz* (KUG – 'the German Arts Domain Copyright Act'). This meant that, under Article 22 KUG, pictures could be disseminated or exposed to the public eye only with the express approval of the person represented. In German law, consent is implied where the person has received a fee. Pictures relating to contemporary society are excluded from that rule under Article 23(1) KUG. This means that if a celebrity or politician is photographed in public performing a public office or duty, the publication of these images is allowed. However, that exception does not apply where the dissemination interferes with a legitimate private interest of that person (Art 23(2) KUG).

The Strasbourg court criticized the German courts' decision for making a distinction between figures of contemporary society 'par excellence' and merely 'relative' public figures. For this reason the ECtHR granted Princess Caroline her right to privacy under Article 8. Concurring with the opinion of Judge Cabral Barreto, Judge Zupani stated that the distinctions between the different levels of permitted exposure in German copyright and constitutional jurisprudence were far too complex (*Begriffsjurisprudenz*). But Judge Zupani also observed that the 'balancing test between the

---

198 Her official title is: Princess Caroline Louise Marguerite, Prinzessin von Hannover, Herzogin zu Braunschweig und Lüneburg. She married Ernst August Prinz von Hannover on 23 January 1999, her second marriage, after Caroline of Monaco had married Philippe Junot on 28 June 1978; their marriage was annulled on 9 October 1980.
199 **Von Hannover v Germany** (2005) 40 EHRR 1.

public's right to know on the one hand and the affected person's right to privacy on the other hand must be adequately performed', commenting:

> . . . he who willingly steps upon the public stage cannot claim to be a private person entitled to anonymity. Royalty, actors, academics, politicians etc. perform whatever they perform publicly. They may not seek publicity, yet, by definition, their image is to some extent public property.[200]

The ruling in **von Hannover (No 1)** is significant and impacts on media practices throughout Europe. Whenever a photograph becomes a complaint issue in privacy and confidentiality, the domestic courts now have to weigh up whether the photo was taken in public, whether it was taken secretly or by clandestine means, whether by long-lens paparazzi or close-up, whether the image shows the individual undertaking an official duty or whether the 'public figure' is in a 'private sphere' or setting. If it is found that the picture was of public interest it can be published, irrespective of consent.

The ruling in **von Hannover No 2**[201] was different. The ECtHR did not really reverse the ruling in the **No 1** action (see above) but ruled differently, and did not grant the Article 8 'privacy' right to the applicant, Princess Caroline von Hannover. The action concerned the publication of photographs of the Princess and her husband, Prince Ernst August von Hannover (joint applicants), on a skiing holiday in St Mortiz. The photograph in question was accompanied by an article reporting on the deteriorating health of the Princess's father, Prince Rainier III of Monaco. The German courts had granted an injunction in respect of two of the photographs but dismissed an application in respect of one photograph which had been published in the 'gossip' magazine Frau im Spiegel in 2002. The applicants argued that the failure to prevent the publication of one photo in Frau im Spiegel by the German national courts was inconsistent with the ruling in **von Hannover No 1** and an infringement of their Article 8 rights.

The ECtHR ruled that the 2002 photo in the magazine of the von Hannover couple (Princess Caroline and Prince Ernst August), taking a walk in St Moritz, as part of an article on the poor health of Prince Rainier was a subject of general public interest, since he was the reigning Prince of Monaco. The court also confirmed that the link between the photographs and the subject matter of the accompanying article was sufficiently close so as to render their publication justifiable.

 **KEY CASE**   *von Hannover (No 2)* and *Axel Springer v Germany* (2012) (Joint Application No 3995/08) Strasbourg judgment of 7 February 2012 (ECTHR)

Precedents (in both actions: *Axel Springer* and *von Hannover No 2*)

❖   The domestic courts must strike a balance between Articles 8 and 10 ECHR, depending on the facts and circumstances.

❖   **Contribution to a debate of general interest** – this covers not only political issues or crimes but sporting issues or performing artists.[202]

❖   **How well known the person was and the subject of the report** – a distinction has to be made between private individuals and persons acting in a public context, as political or public figures.[203]

---

200 **Von Hannover No 1** (2005) 40 EHRR 1 at 32 (Judge Zupani).
201 **Von Hannover v Germany (No 2)** (2012) (Application Numbers – 40660/08, 60641/08) (unreported) Judgment of 7 February 2012.
202 *Axel Springer v Germany* (2012) at para 90.
203 Ibid., at para 91.

❖ **Prior conduct of the person concerned: the conduct of the person prior to the publication is a relevant factor** – although the mere fact of having cooperated with the press cannot be an argument for depriving a person of all protection.[204]

❖ **Method of obtaining the information and its veracity** – these are important factors – the protection of Article 10 is subject to the proviso that journalists are acting in good faith, on an accurate factual basis, providing reliable and precise information in accordance with the ethics of journalism.[205]

❖ **Content, form and consequences of the publication** – the way in which the photo or report is obtained and the way in which the individual is represented are factors to take into account.[206]

❖ **Severity of the sanction imposed.**[207]

❖ **Courts have to balance Articles 8 and 10 ECHR equally.**

❖ **Article 8 does not create an 'image right', nor does it create a 'right to reputation'.**

❖ **Individuals who seek the public limelight have their Article 8 right to privacy severely curtailed.**

Facts: *Axel Springer*

The applicant, Axel-Springer-Verlag, is the publisher of the daily German tabloid *Bild-Zeitung* ('*Bild*'), registered in Hamburg since 1952, with a circulation of about 2.6 million per day (in 2004). *Bild* is famous for its salacious gossip and sensational journalistic headlines.

The case concerned two articles about X, a well-known TV actor.[208] X had been the subject of two stories and photos in *Bild* in 2004 and 2005, after he was arrested in a beer tent at the Munich Oktoberfest for possessing cocaine. The story made the headlines: 'Cocaine! Superintendent caught at Munich Beer Festival', with a photo of X. The second article was published some ten months later and reported details of X pleading guilty to the drug possession offence and how he was sentenced to an €18,000 fine. Axel Springer claimed that prior to publication the journalist had confirmed the arrest with the police sergeant present at the scene; the public prosecutor had also verified the charges.

Whilst the Hamburg regional court had granted X an injunction, restraining *Bild* (and other publications) from publishing the story, *Bild* went ahead and published the story and photos. The Hamburg court found Axel Springer guilty of contempt by disobeying the existing court order. The applicant publishers petitioned the ECtHR relying on their Article 10 right.

Decision: *Axel Springer*

The Grand Chamber (of the ECtHR) disagreed with the German courts' reasoning for granting the injunction to the actor. Judges of the Grand Chamber opined that X's arrest and conviction was of general public interest, particularly since the public prosecutor had

---

204 Ibid., at para 92.
205 Ibid., at para 93.
206 Ibid., at para 94.
207 Ibid., at para 95.
208 The German left-wing daily newspaper TAZ (*Tageszeitung*) disclosed X's identity, that of Bruno Eyron, well-known for playing a RTL-TV cop, 'Kommissar Balko'. Source: 'Caroline von Monaco zu Recht geknipst. Ein europäisches Gericht stärkt die deutsche Pressefreiheit: Ein Foto von Caroline von Monaco durfte gedruckt werden. Ebenso das Bild eines koksenden Schauspielers', by Christian Rath, TAZ, 7 February 2012.

confirmed the criminal charges of possession of class A drugs. It was also in the public interest and therefore of importance to uphold the law, since X had been a role model for young people, playing the character of a police superintendent (*der Kommissar*) whose job it was to combat crime. The Court noted that X had regularly contacted the press himself or via his PR company and that he had previously revealed detailed information about his private life in a number of media interviews. The Court reasoned that X's 'legitimate expectation' of protection for his private life was reduced by virtue of the fact that he had 'actively sought the limelight'. Because 'TV cop' X was a well-known actor, known particularly as a law enforcement officer on screen, the ECtHR held:

> . . . he was sufficiently well known to qualify as a public figure. That consideration . . . reinforces the public's interest in being informed of X's arrest and of the criminal proceedings against him.[209]

The Grand Chamber found by 12 votes to 5 that the German courts had violated the publishers' Article 10 rights by their overzealous injunctive sanctions imposed on the tabloid newspaper. The restraining order had been too severe and accordingly there had been a violation of the publishers' Article 10 right. The newspaper publishers were awarded damages and costs in the domestic proceedings and in the Strasbourg action.

Analysis of *Axel Springer* and *von Hannover No 2*

The difficulty with both the conjoined cases was compounded by a series of appeals and cross-appeals by the applicants and various publishers, including complaints in respect of publications and photographs elsewhere. Nevertheless, the ECtHR's decision in both cases is an important win for the media, particularly as media practices were severely criticized at the Leveson Inquiry in London's High Court of Justice. The *Axel Springer – von Hannover No 2* judgments remind us of the important role played by a free and uncensored press in a pluralistic democracy where the human rights court undertook a careful balancing exercise between freedom of expression and the individuals' privacy rights. In both cases the Grand Chamber of the ECtHR explained the criteria, based on existing human rights law, which are to be applied when balancing the competing Article 8 and 10 rights in the public interest. Both the ECtHR decisions in *Axel Springer* and *von Hannover No 2* can be seen as important victories for the media and for press freedom in general. With the Leveson Inquiry into media ethics and phone-hacking dominating the headlines at the same time as the Grand Chamber judgment in 2012, the judgment provides suitable encouragement and support for the media across Europe in relation to the publication of stories and photographs about the private lives of celebrities.[210]

See Chapter 3

The Strasbourg judgment in both conjoined cases is an important development in the consistent application and interplay of Articles 8 and 10 across the jurisprudence of Convention Member States. It strikes one that the **Axel Springer** and **von Hannover No 2** criteria appear rather similar to the **Reynolds**[211] criteria established in qualified privilege in the UK action. These criteria can now be helpfully adopted as a methodology for the domestic courts when considering Article 8 versus

---

209 Ibid., at para 99.
210 See also: Pillans (2012).
211 *Reynolds v Times Newspapers Ltd* [2001] 2 AC 127.

Article 10 criteria in similar privacy actions. What has become clear from the ECtHR reasoning in these two conjoined cases is that both Convention Articles carry the same weight in the balancing process. Most importantly, the ECtHR decision in both cases underlines the importance of freedom of expression in a modern, dynamic democracy.

 FOR THOUGHT

'The original purpose of the Council of Europe's Convention on Human Rights was to enable public attention to be drawn to any revival of totalitarian methods of Government and to provide a forum in which the appropriate action could be discussed and decided' (Simpson 2004: 777). In the light of Professor Simpson's quotation, do you not think it remarkable that the European Convention (ECHR) has one fundamental flaw in the basic concept of having an international court of human rights that deals with the concrete application of those rights in 47 different countries with 800 million citizens? (See also: http://hub.coe.int.)

2.4.2 Restraining publication and the freedom of expression under Section 12 Human Rights Act 1998

A claimant who applies for an interim restraining order (superinjunction) against publishers is obliged to give advance notice of the application under s 12 HRA, especially where the publisher or media organization relies on their Article 10 ECHR right to 'freedom of expression'. The order is then binding on the party against whom injunctive relief is sort by application of the *Spycatcher* principle, *unless*:

1. The claimant has no reason to believe that the non-party has or may have an existing specific interest in the outcome of the application; or
2. The claimant is unable to notify the non-party having taken all practicable steps to do so; or
3. There are compelling reasons why the non-party should not be notified.

Section 12 HRA will only apply at any trial or at the application of a superinjunction or possible life-long anonymity order when the freedom of expression under Article 10 ECHR is challenged. Section 12 HRA reads:

1. This section applies if a court is considering whether to grant any relief which, if granted, might affect the exercise of the Convention right to freedom of expression.
2. If the person against whom the application for relief is made ('the respondent') is neither present nor represented, no such relief is to be granted unless the court is satisfied:

    (a)   that the applicant has taken all practicable steps to notify the respondent; or
    (b)   that there are compelling reasons why the respondent should not be notified.

3. No such relief is to be granted so as to restrain publication before trial unless the court is satisfied that the applicant is likely to establish that publication should not be allowed.
4. The court must have particular regard to the importance of the Convention right to freedom of expression and, where the proceedings relate to material which the respondent claims, or which appears to the court, to be journalistic, literary or artistic material (or to conduct connected with such material), to:

(a)   the extent to which (i) the material has, or is about to, become available to the public; or (ii) it is, or would be, in the public interest for the material to be published;

(b)   any relevant privacy code.[212]

See below
2.6.1

The problem in the **John Terry** superinjunction[213] was that the famous Chelsea footballer claimed not to know the name of the newspaper that had a specific interest in his story. Tugendhat J did not accept that explanation since it had become quite clear that the *News of the World* intended to publish on Sunday 24 January 2010 the story about Terry's affair with the lingerie model, Vanessa Perroncel, then girlfriend of Terry's best friend and fellow England defender Wayne Bridge. The public interest lay in the fact that Terry was England football captain at the time and had portrayed himself as a 'clean-living' family man.

Mr Justice Tugendhat noted that the newspaper should have been given notice by Mr Terry's lawyers under s 12 HRA, confirming the application to have the story injuncted. But this did not happen, or rather – as the judgment states – notification happened too late, pending the handing-down of the judgment of 29 January 2010.

There is then an inherent dilemma when an applicant tries to curtail freedom of expression under notification of s 12 HRA: if he or she gives notice to the media to have the impending story or photograph restrained, the very information upon which an attempt is being made to keep secret is revealed. It is possible that, up until then, the media organization only knew part of the story and the mere attempt to injunct may confirm as fact what is at that stage only rumour.

When the *Guardian* requested sight of the evidence in opposing the **John Terry** superinjunction under s 12 HRA 1998, the newspaper's lawyer, Gillian Phillips, made the following four salient points:

> . . . it appears to me that this latest order is symptomatic of a trend whereby this sort of order is (1) sought against persons unknown, by which I deduce that no one was heard in opposition to the injunction request. No advance notice was given to the media; (2) immediately served on the legal departments of the national media, who are not defendants to the action; (3) dispenses with any obligation to serve evidence in support; (4) protects an anonymous claimant.[214]

In response to the *Guardian's* request for sight of the evidence, solicitors for John Terry asked for an undertaking that the information be kept secure and not disclosed. Because of the limited reporting of such cases, frequently known only by acronyms and randomly selected letters of the alphabet, it is difficult to come to a single and rigid standard conclusion governing all applications for superinjunctions (see: *G and G v Wikimedia Foundation Inc* (2009)[215]).

The effect of s 12(3) HRA is that a court is not to make an interim restraint order unless satisfied that the applicant's prospects of success at trial are sufficiently favourable to justify such an order being made in the particular circumstances of the case and taking into account the relevant jurisprudence under Article 10 ECHR. Looking at the judgment by Tugendhat J in **LNS**, it appears that the general approach by the courts in the granting (or continuation) of superinjunctions tends to be 'exceedingly slow', by making an interim restraint order where the applicant has not satisfied the court that he would probably succeed at trial.[216] However, where the potential adverse

---

212 For example the PCC Code Clause 3 'Privacy'.
213 **LNS v Persons Unknown** [2010] EWHC 119 (QB).
214 Quote by Gillian Phillips, Director of Editorial Legal Services to Guardian News Media Ltd. as cited in **LNS v Persons Unknown** [2010] EWHC 119 (QB) at 116.
215 [2009] EWHC 3148 (QB).
216 Ibid., at 120 (Tugendhat J).

consequences of disclosure are particularly grave – say, in family cases, or where a short-lived injunction is needed to enable the court to hear and give proper consideration to an application for interim relief pending trial or any relevant appeal – the courts have granted such restraining orders under s 12 HRA with great expediency (see: **X (a woman formerly known as Mary Bell) and another v O'Brien and others** (2003)[217]).

See below 2.5 and 2.6

On 29 September 2008, Max Mosley filed an application before the ECtHR and on 11 January 2011 his case was heard in Strasbourg, where Mr Mosley asked the court to rule in favour of 'prior notification', which would compel the British (and EU) press to notify the subject of a story before publication.

See 2.4.5 below

Although we all have a right to privacy, it is entirely up to the editor of a newspaper or media organization whether or not we are able to exercise that right in any effective or meaningful way. The editor of a newspaper (or online edition), acting alone, can take a decision to publish material which may ruin a life or destroy a family, safe in the knowledge that even if publication is later held to be unlawful, there will be no significant consequences for him or his employers. As Eady J in the original **Mosley** judgment observed, the UK media is well aware that most people would not have taken legal action had they been in Mr Mosley's shoes.

Bringing a privacy claim for damages in the High Court is extremely costly and puts the very information the claimant wishes to keep private back in the public domain. Because of the greater chance of an injunction, a newspaper editor will be even less likely to notify an individual with a very strong privacy claim (perhaps concerning particularly intrusive material) because this individual will almost certainly not sue once the material has been published. By placing his claim before the Strasbourg Human Rights Court, Mr Mosley was not seeking any further damages. If the application had been successful, and effective measures were implemented as a result, everyone in the UK could equally share in the right to have an editor's decision to publish reviewed by a judge before irreparable damage could be done.

An injunction will always be refused if there is a strong and legitimate public interest in publication, in which case the editor can continue to publish and recover the newspaper's legal costs from the applicant. Max Mosley's ECtHR ruling has had no 'chilling effect' on investigative journalism where the exposure of private material has a legitimate purpose in the public interest.

◉ FOR THOUGHT

In May 2011, footballer Ryan Giggs's extramarital affair with a lingerie model Imogen Thomas was exposed (initially only referred to as CTB).[218] Despite the court superinjunction being in place, Mr Giggs was widely identified on social networking sites such as Twitter. Would you agree with *Top Gear* presenter and broadcaster Jeremy Clarkson that superinjunctions are now outdated and rather pointless? (see: **AMM v HXW** [2010] EWHC 2457 (QB) ('Jeremy Clarkson superinjunction').)

2.4.3 Balancing the freedom of expression and the right to privacy

Since the HRA 1998 came into force there have been a number of challenges concerning breach of confidence and the right to an individual's privacy under Article 8 ECHR. Central to the argument

---

217 [2003] EWHC 1101 (QB).
218 *Giggs v NGN and Imogen Thomas* [2012] EWHC 431 (QB) (also re. CTB).

See above
2.2.1

in each case has been the interaction of the rights and the qualifications of those rights set out in Articles 8 and 10 of the Convention.[219] It has already been discussed that the press fulfils the function of forming public opinion and that the courts now have to balance two human rights elements: Article 8 and 10 ECHR. Arguably, entertainment literature, such as glossy magazines, and online blogs such as the *Huffington Post*[220] can, at times, stimulate or influence public opinion more than purely factual information, and it can be observed that there is a growing tendency in the media to replace news-type information in favour of 'infotainment'.

Consequently, many readers obtain information they consider to be important or interesting from entertainment coverage and the internet. To some of us, celebrities and the royals embody certain moral values and lifestyles which we then seek to emulate, be it a famous model like Naomi Campbell or the Duchess of Cambridge (aka Kate Middleton). The UK media world was outraged when the *Huffington Post* showed photos of the Duchess 'in jeans and boots' shopping for 'veggies, milk, chicken and Häagen-Dazs ice cream' in a Tesco's store in North Wales. The 'HuffPo' wrote: 'For those wondering, we didn't see any typical pregnancy-craving items in her cart . . . nor did we see her famous sapphire engagement ring.'[221] *Heat* magazine had taken the 'HuffPo' picture and republished it in the UK – for this, *Heat*'s publishers had to apologize to the Duchess, mediated by the Press Complaints Commission (PCC):

> In our issue cover-dated 3–9 December 2011, we published a photograph of the Duchess of Cambridge, taken while she was shopping in a store. We now accept that we should not have done so, and apologise to her for our actions.[222]

The reality is that lawyers can do little to prevent the publication of images – such as a naked Prince Harry – by websites that are not covered by the European Convention and therefore obliged to adhere to the right to privacy. Glossy magazines like *Hello!*, *Grazia* or *OK!* appeal to some members of society, because they can base their choice of lifestyle on role models like Katy Perry or David Beckham. It is this which explains the public interest in entertainment magazines or online versions of gossip magazines. The lives and lifestyles of politicians have always been matters of public interest. It is then a duty and function of the media to show such personalities in situations that are not limited to specific functions or events, which then fall within the sphere of protection of press freedom. It is only when a balancing exercise is struck between competing personality rights and press freedom that an issue arises as to whether matters of essential interest for the public are at issue and treated seriously and objectively or whether private matters, designed merely to satisfy the public's curiosity, are being disseminated.

2.4.4 Exclusivity and privacy in photos of celebrities

In July 2012, the mother of actor Hugh Grant's baby, Ms Ting Lang Hong, received a High Court 'permanent undertaking' from the picture agency Splash News not to pursue, doorstep or harass her or her child.[223] The order was made under s 1(1)(a) of the Protection from Harassment Act, a

---

219 See: Human Rights Act 1998, Schedule 1, Part 1.
220 The *Huffington Post* ('HuffPo') is a progressive liberal American news website and aggregated blog founded by Arianna Huffington in May 2005. The site offers news, blogs and original lifestyle content largely aimed at women.
221 Source: 'Kate Middleton Shops at Tesco in Jeans & Boots', by Ellie Krupnick, *The Huffington Post*, 23 November 2011: www.huffingtonpost.com/2011/11/23/kate-middleton-jeans_n_1109652.html.
222 Source: 'Apology: HRH Duchess of Cambridge', posted by 'Heatworld' on 1 May 2012: http://www.heatworld.com/Celeb-News/2012/05/Apology-HRH-Duchess-of-Cambridge.
223 **Ting Lang Hong and Child KLM v XYZ and Others** [2011] EWHC 2995 (QB).

ruling by Mr Justice Tugendhat which may well be used by celebrities in future actions, providing enhanced measures of protection against paparazzi photographers. Ms Hong claimed that on several occasions as many as 10 journalists had camped outside her house, staying all night even in the rain, in the hope of getting a picture. An illustrated article appeared in the *News of the World*, dated 8 April 2011, headlined 'Hugh's Secret Girl'. At the time of the publication Ms Hong had no idea that she was being followed and photographed.[224]

In the **David and Victoria Beckham** case,[225] Eady J reversed the decision of the duty judge that the claimants gave a cross-undertaking not to publish photographs of their house, holding that this would have prejudiced their basic rights of privacy and freedom of contract. Eady J then upheld the interim injunction in favour of the Beckhams, preventing the *Sunday People* from publishing photographs of their matrimonial home and protecting the claimants from unwarranted intrusions into their privacy under Article 8, 'with regard to material which the law recognises as being confidential'.[226] Although Mr and Mrs Beckham were themselves considering selling the rights to allow publication of certain photographs of their house, they were particularly concerned that the unauthorized photographs might reveal and thereby jeopardize some of the security measures taken to protect them and their home.

Increasingly, however, the courts have been faced with the protection of a famous individual's identity where the single most important element of the information sought by way of photographs was the detection of the future identity of individuals who had committed famous crimes, such as the Bulger killers – Thompson and Venables – or Maxine Carr, who had lied on behalf of her boyfriend Ian Huntley in the Soham killings. In these cases the courts had to decide what type of information ought to be protected under the right to privacy and why the media had sought such information.

The background to **Douglas v Hello! Ltd**[227] is well known, and summarized briefly here. Prior to their wedding on 18 November 2000 at the Plaza Hotel in New York, the famous actor-couple, Michael Douglas and Catherine Zeta-Jones, had contracted OK! magazine to publish their exclusive wedding photographs for £1 million. However, in a 'spoiler', rival magazine Hello! published five photographs ahead of OK! in a special issue, no 639. The photos had been surreptitiously taken by an unauthorized photographer, Rupert Thorpe, pretending to be a waiter at the Plaza Hotel.[228]

On 20 November 2000, OK! obtained an *ex parte* injunction restraining publication of Hello!'s issue 639. Counsel for the Douglases argued that the illicit photos breached their right to privacy under Article 8(1) ECHR. Notably, the HRA 1998 had only just become effective in English law. The Sanchez family, publishers of Hello! (and ¡HOLA! in Spain), advancing their Article 10 right, were successful in persuading the Court of Appeal to discharge the injunction on 23 November and issue 639 could now be back on sale within a few hours.

Reasons for the CA's discharging the injunction were partly because the Douglases had sold most of their privacy rights to OK! and partly because, had the restraining order been wrongly granted, it would have been very difficult to quantify the damage suffered. The claimants had entered into a contract with OK! for profit and all exclusive rights had been granted to OK!, who were able to exploit the commercialization of the wedding in its entirety and attract large amounts of advertising revenue given the special wedding feature. Additionally, the Douglases' wedding did not remain private for long as they were happy for it to be widely

---

224 Ibid., at para 5.
225 **Beckham v MGN Ltd** (28 June 2001; unreported).
226 Ibid., at 9, line C (Eady J).
227 [2001] QB 967.
228 For further discussion see: Moreham (2001), pp. 767ff.

publicized by *OK!*'s special wedding issue. Lord Justice Sedley's observations in this case in respect of balancing the Douglases' right to privacy and the media's freedom of expression are highly relevant when he said:

> . . . the Convention right, when one turns to it, is qualified in favour of the reputation and rights of others and the protection of information received in confidence. In other words you cannot have particular regard to Article 10 without having equally particular regard at the very least to Article 8.[229]

Though the Douglases did not succeed in their 2001 action claiming their Article 8 right to privacy, Lindsay J held that *Hello!* was nevertheless liable for breach of confidence, applying the well-known **Coco** criteria, summarized by Megarry J as:

> . . . first, the information itself . . . must have the necessary quality of confidence about it. Secondly, that information must have been imparted in circumstances importing an obligation of confidence. Thirdly, there must be an unauthorised use of that information to the detriment of the party communicating it.[230]

In **Douglas v Hello!** the claimants had set out to make a profit from the wedding but *Hello!* scooped the exclusive deal. In contrast, **Beckham v MGN** did not have that commercial backdrop and the photographs were taken inside the Beckhams' home, not at a celebrity wedding in the Plaza Hotel. As the Court of Appeal put it in the Douglas follow-up action:[231]

> . . . the photographs published by *Hello!* fell within a generic class of commercially confidential information . . . which *OK!* were entitled to protect.[232]

What followed the 2001 'privacy' action of the Douglases was a seven-year action in the Chancery Division, where *OK!* and the Douglases sued *Hello!* for breach of confidence and for the tort of causing loss by unlawful means. It was held that the obligation of confidence was binding on *Hello!*'s publishers under the third **Coco** requirement. Lindsay J decided (in the **Douglas No 7** litigation) that *Hello!* was liable to *OK!* for the loss caused by the publication, which he assessed at £1,033,156 (the moneys owed by *OK!* to the Douglases). By granting *OK!* magazine damages, by implication this turned valuable private information into property.

 FOR THOUGHT

Discuss the remedies available in the UK courts for breach of confidence for an unauthorized disclosure of personal information, accompanied by unsolicited photographs of a famous claimant.

---

229 [2001] QB 967 at 134 (Sedley LJ).
230 *Coco v AN Clark (Engineers) Ltd* [1969] RPC 41 at 47 (Megarry J).
231 **OBG Ltd. and others v Allan and others; Douglas and another and others v Hello! Ltd and Others; Mainstream Properties Ltd. v Young and others and another** [2007] UKHL 21 (sub nom 'Douglas v Hello! No 7').
232 **Douglas v Hello! Ltd** [2006] QB at para 138.

2.4.5 Privacy in hospital beds and rehabilitation clinics: the Gorden Kaye and Naomi Campbell cases

British tabloid journalism is well known for its intrusion into the private lives of celebrities. The use of long-lens photography has at times been taken to extremes, intruding through the private hospital windows of *'Allo 'Allo!* actor Gorden Kaye, for example, who was photographed in his hospital bed by two *Sunday Sport* journalists while recovering from brain surgery after his car accident on 25 January 1990.[233] The reporter and photographer had disguised themselves as medical staff. Although Mr Kaye could not remember being interviewed by Roger Ordish, or being photographed, he sued the newspaper editor and publishers, with the Court of Appeal stating that his privacy had not been invaded — a low point in UK privacy laws. Eady J noted the lack of legal protection against publication for Mr Kaye, saying that there was 'a serious gap in the jurisprudence of any civilised society, if such a gross intrusion could happen without redress.'

Eady J observed in his speech on 'privacy' to intellectual property lawyers in 2009 that the statutory tort could be less restrictive of the media than the law of privacy as it subsequently developed. For example, it would have excluded anything touching on the conduct of a business, trade or profession, and it would have been directed purely at the protection of personal life. It would also have excluded anything occurring in a public place. He said:

> We were, rather naively perhaps, attempting to achieve certainty and predictability. Anyway, that was not adopted by the legislature. Instead, ministers were heard to say at the time, on more than one occasion, that it was best to trust an independent judiciary to develop the common law by reference to Articles 8 and 10 of the European Convention. That is not a view one hears much about these days, since in certain quarters the process is thought to have gone too far in the wrong direction. It has become fashionable to label judges, not as independent, but rather as 'unaccountable'. Following measured representations from the *Daily Mail*, the Justice Secretary has recently announced that something called a statutory 'nudge' may after all be required.[234]

Photographs are a record of a frozen moment in time and therefore have a permanence and presentational power which the human eye and words alone cannot capture. We have seen in **Douglas v Hello!** (2001) that the mere taking of photographs is not of itself actionable except where the photographing itself represents a misuse of confidential information when protected by contract. Photographs can have a special intrusive effect, as was held in the **Beckham** case (above), conveying visual information which words alone cannot achieve. In determining whether photographs taken in a public place are capable of protection the courts have taken account of the context in which the photographs were taken and published, and whether the person photographed had a reasonable expectation of privacy in relation to their subject matter, and whether the photographs were taken surreptitiously. Additionally, the information conveyed by photographs has to be judged by reference to the captions and surrounding text.

In the first Naomi Campbell action in 2001,[235] a cause of action arose in February 2001 upon the publication of surreptitiously taken photos when the *Daily Mirror* published an image of and extensive articles on the famous supermodel receiving drug rehabilitation treatment at a Narcotics Anonymous clinic in 2001. Miss Campbell sued the newspaper for damages for breach

---

233 *Kaye v Robertson* [1991] FSR 62.
234 Source: Sir David Eady's Speech on Privacy to TIPLO (The Intellectual Property Lawyers' Association), House of Lords, 18 February 2009: www.publications.Parliament.uk/pa/cm200809/cmselect/cmcumeds/memo/press/uc7502.htm.
235 *Campbell v MGN* [2002] EWHC 499 (QB).

of confidentiality. The Mirror carried a number of stories at the time on the supermodel, with headlines such as 'Naomi: I am a drug addict' and 'Pathetic – No hiding Naomi'. The articles in question contained the information that Campbell was a drug addict, and that she was receiving treatment at the Narcotics Anonymous rehabilitation clinic, as well as details of that treatment. The stories were supported by pictures of Miss Campbell leaving a drug therapy clinic. During the first proceedings Miss Campbell claimed damages for breach of confidence and compensation under the Data Protection Act 1998. Morland J did not grant Miss Campbell the right to privacy though he upheld a data protection claim, awarding her £2,500 plus £1,000 aggravated damages.[236]

The newspaper appealed and the CA, allowing the appeal, discharged the injunction. Miss Campbell appealed to the House of Lords on 23 February 2003. Their Lordships Lord Nicholls of Birkenhead, Lord Hoffmann, Lord Hope of Craighead, Baroness Hale of Richmond and Lord Carswell held that the law of confidence does not protect the trivial.[237] Their Lordships stated that Miss Campbell could not complain of the exposure of her drug-taking, especially since she had previously denied that she was a drug addict, but the HL felt that the Court of Appeal had erred in holding that the details of the claimant's treatment and attendance at the clinic plus the photographs were not private and confidential and that the article could not credibly have been written without the inclusion of that material.

Allowing the appeal (Lord Nicholls of Birkenhead and Lord Hoffmann dissenting), the House of Lords set the threshold test as to whether information was private: whether a reasonable person of ordinary sensibilities, placed in the same situation as the subject of the disclosure (rather than its recipient), would find the disclosure offensive. Miss Campbell's details of her drug therapy should have been afforded privacy related to her physical and mental health. The treatment she was receiving amounted to confidential information contained in her medical records and the publication clearly breached that confidentiality and her right to privacy. Their Lordships found the disclosure of the photographs highly offensive, stating that this had caused the claimant a setback in her recovery. The publication of that information went beyond disclosure which was necessary to add credibility to the legitimate story that the claimant had deceived the public and went beyond the journalistic margin of appreciation allowed to a free press. Though the photographs of Miss Campbell were taken in a public place, the context in which they were used and linked to the articles added to the overall intrusion into the claimant's private life.

In summary, looking at the publication as a whole and taking account of all the circumstances, Naomi Campbell's Article 8 right outweighed the newspaper's right to freedom of expression because she was undergoing rehabilitative treatment. Accordingly, the publication of the articles and the accompanying photos in the Mirror constituted an unjustified infringement of Miss Campbell's right to privacy for which she was entitled to damages.

2.4.6 Social utility and the protection of private information: the Max Mosley case

Their Lordships said in **Campbell** (2004) that the law of confidence does not protect useless information or trivia. We have seen in **Mosley** (2008) that the courts protect the individual when the intrusion into a claimant's life has been 'highly offensive' and when the objective 'sober and reasonable man' would agree that intrusion has been unacceptable. In **Mosley**, Eady J extended the confidentiality notion to what amounts to personal conduct and what would be regarded as

236 Ibid., at 502 (Morland J).
237 **Campbell v MGN** [2004] 2 AC 457.

'socially harmful'. He then applied the term 'social utility', first coined in **Francome**[238] by Sir John Donaldson MR, where he explained that:

> . . . the 'media', to use a term which comprises not only the newspapers, but also television and radio, are an essential foundation of any democracy. In exposing crime, anti-social behaviour and hypocrisy and in campaigning for reform and propagating the view of minorities, they perform an invaluable function.[239]

Max Mosley sued the *News of the World* (News Group Newspapers Ltd), complaining about a number of articles.[240] *News of the World* (NOW) journalist, Neville Thurlbeck, headlined the 'exclusive' on 30 March 2008: 'F1 Boss Has Sick Nazi Orgy With 5 Hookers', with the subheading: 'Son of Hitler-loving fascist in sex shame'. Of 'public interest' – the newspaper argued – was that Mr Mosley, son of the right-wing fascist leader Sir Oswald Mosley, had engaged not only in an orgy with call girls, but in a 'Nazi orgy'. Mr Mosley knew nothing of the article before publication nor of the clandestine video footage which had been taken by an undercover reporter posing as a prostitute. The first he knew of the scoop was on the very same Sunday that millions of people were reading the article and watching the accompanying footage on the NOW website.

The cause of action was breach of confidence (not defamation) and the unauthorized disclosure of personal information, said to infringe Max Mosley's right of privacy under Article 8 ECHR. Clearly, it was not alleged that the Formula 1 boss had engaged in unlawful activity, since the matter at trial concerned sexual activities between consenting adults in private. But Eady J referred to the principle of 'social utility', where revealing someone's identity in court and therefore in the media was useful to society and 'of social utility', for the purpose of revealing criminal misconduct and antisocial behaviour (see: **X v Persons Unknown** (2006)[241]). The High Court judge stressed that not all conduct that is socially harmful is unlawful and that the law is rather inconsistent in this area. He drew the analogy between the law on consumption of alcohol with that on other intoxicating substances: was such conduct in private and by consenting adults in the public interest and of social utility? Eady J stated that in our plural society there will be some, such as newspaper editors, who would suggest that what Mr Mosley did ought to be discouraged.

In conclusion, Eady J decided in **Mosley** that the photographs of and articles on the Formula 1 chief's sado-masochistic activities with hired call girls were of no social utility at all. They rather amounted to 'old-fashioned breach of confidence' by way of conduct inconsistent with a pre-existing relationship, rather than simply of the 'purloining of private information'. Eady J ruled that the content of the published material was inherently private in nature, consisting of S & M sexual practices. Moreover, there had been a pre-existing relationship of confidentiality between the participants, who had all known each other for some time and took part in such activities on the understanding that they would be private and that none of them would reveal what had taken place. Clearly 'Woman E' had breached that trust by recording her fellow participants.[242]

Interestingly, Max Mosley did not sue the NOW and its editor for libel but chose to pursue a privacy claim instead, whereafter he was awarded £60,000 plus his court costs. Perhaps it was not the effective remedy that Mr Mosley would have wanted because the UK courts could not prevent the publication in the first place by means of an injunction. This meant that the offending articles and video footage of the 'Nazi Orgy' were already in the public domain and the damage to Mr Mosley's reputation was done.

---

238 **Francome v MGN** [1984] 1 WLR 892.
239 Ibid., at 989 (Sir John Donaldson MR).
240 Mr Mosley had been President of the Fédération Internationale de l'Automobile (motor racing's ruling body) since 1993.
241 [2006] EWHC 2783 (QB).
242 **Mosley v NGN** [2008] EWHC 1777 QB at 2–6 (Eady J).

Mr Mosley subsequently lost his 'pre-notification' claim in the Strasbourg court.[243] The then editor of the *NOW*, Colin Myler, had admitted in the UK court action that the main reason why he did not notify Mr Mosley before deciding to publish this explosive private material was that he knew Mr Mosley would seek an injunction. Mr Myler was quite safe in making this admission in court because in the UK there is no legal or regulatory obligation upon newspaper editors to notify those whose private lives they intend to expose.

During his testimony at the Leveson Inquiry on 24 November 2011, Max Mosley told Lord Justice Leveson that he was suing the Google search engine in France and Germany in a libel action, in an attempt to force the internet company to monitor and censor search results about his alleged sado-masochistic orgy and the *NOW* video. His intention was that Google should have prevented these publications from appearing in the search engine results in the first place. Mr Mosley also told the inquiry he had taken legal action in 22 other countries and ordered the removal of material from 193 websites in Germany.[244]

Whilst it is understood that Google has since removed hundreds of references to the defamatory claims after requests from Mosley's solicitors, a Google spokesman told *Guardian Media*:

> Google's search results reflect the information available on billions of web pages on the internet. We don't, and can't, control what others post online, but when we're told that a specific page is illegal under a court order, then we move quickly to remove it from our search results.[245]

Whether Mr Mosley's attempts in the German, French and Californian courts will be successful in attempting to force the search engine to monitor its search results so that the material never appears is debatable. Presently, Google only removes specific weblinks from its search results when they are ruled unlawful by a court and reported to the company (see: **Godfrey v Demon Internet;**[246] **Tamiz v Google**[247]).

In conclusion, if we accept that there now exists a tort of privacy it follows that we can safely assume that this law now affords protection to information in respect of which there is a reasonable expectation of privacy, even in circumstances where there is no pre-existing relationship. This in itself will then give rise to an enforceable duty of confidence. The law now seems to be concerned with the prevention of the violation of a person's autonomy, dignity and self-esteem taking into account Convention rights as well as common law development since the **Douglas** case in 2001. The law of old-fashioned breach of confidence is now well established in common law jurisprudence, deriving historically from equitable principles. These have now been extended by the HRA 1998 and the content of the European Convention.

When a public figure chooses to make untrue statements about their private life, as was the case with Naomi Campbell's drug addiction, is it not the press who should be entitled to set the record straight? Should disclosure not be justified when it serves to prevent members of the public from being misled? The *Daily Mirror* would argue that the photos and details about Miss Campbell's drug treatment exposed her lies, demonstrating that the newspaper had done an excellent piece of investigative journalism. The courts would argue that it depends how the information was obtained and by what means, such as by covert or surreptitious long-lens photography or phone-hacking,

243 **Mosley v UK** (Application no. 48009/08) Judgment by the Strasbourg European Court of Human Rights of 10 May 2011 (ECTHR).
244 Source: Witness statement by Max Rufus Mosley to the Leveson Inquiry at MOD100023418 and MOD100023425 signed & dated 31 October 2011: www.levesoninquiry.org.uk/wp-content/uploads/2011/11/Witness-Statement-of-Max-Mosley.pdf.
245 Source: 'Max Mosley sues Google in France and Germany over "orgy" search results', by Josh Halliday, *Guardian Media* online, 25 November 2011: www.guardian.co.uk/media/2011/nov/25/max-mosley-google-france-germany.
246 [2001] QB 201.
247 [2012] EWHC 449 (QB).

without the subject's consent or in a private place (see: **Wainwright v Home Office** (2004);[248] **Fressoz and Roire v France** (1999);[249] **Jersild v Denmark** (1994);[250] **Peck v UK** (2003)[251]).

 FOR THOUGHT

Compare the rulings in **Theakston** [2002], **Campbell** [2004] and **Mosley** [2008]. In what circumstances will the courts grant privacy protection in the absence of 'Max Mosley-style' pre-notification legislation to editors?

2.5 A child's right to privacy

Children occupy a very special place in society. Common law recognizes that a child's interests and welfare are paramount.[252] There are international treaties which guarantee the rights of a child, such as the UN Convention on the Rights of the Child 1989 or Article 24(2) of the EU Charter of Fundamental Rights 2000.

When publishing a photograph of a child taken without his or her parents' consent, the courts will expect defendant newspapers or media organizations to put forward an extremely compelling reason as to why the publication (or photograph) is necessary. For example: why will the picture add to the public interest, beyond the text of the article?

In July 2012, the publishers of the *Daily Mail* and the *Mail on Sunday* were ordered to pay £15,000 in privacy damages after one of its papers published unpixelated pictures of a less than one-year-old child whose alleged father was a 'philandering' politician. While the stories did include private information about a child, they were deemed to be in the public interest. This was because they discussed a politician's recklessness in relation to an extramarital affair which had resulted in a woman becoming pregnant. However, the High Court found that the child's Article 8 rights had been infringed by the publication of the unpixelated photograph of her. The judge found that the photograph did not add anything to the discussion and was therefore unnecessary, particularly given the photograph was taken without her parents' consent.

Mrs Justice Nicola Davies made the order to the child, named only as AAA in the High Court, whose father was understood to be an adulterous politician.[253] The girl's mother had not named the father on her daughter's birth certificate, saying she wanted to find the 'right time' to reveal his identity to her. The unnamed Associated Newspaper title had carried a story in 2010, alleging that the politician fathered the child while he was married to somebody else and when the mother was in another relationship and that, shortly after conception, the mother was appointed to a post by the politician, which suggested cronyism. In her ruling handed down on 25 July 2012, Davies J said that the publication breached the child's right to privacy:

> In publishing the photographs, the rights of the claimant have been breached, any award should reflect this fact and serve as notice, both as to the present and the future, as to how seriously

---

248 [2004] 2 AC 406.
249 (1999) 31 EHRR 28.
250 (1994) 19 EHRR 1.
251 (2003) 36 EHRR 719.
252 See Lord Oliver's judgment in **KD (A Minor) (Ward: Termination of Access)** [1988] FCR 657 (HL) ('**Re KD**').
253 **AAA v Associated Newspapers** [2012] EWHC 2224 (QB) of 25 July 2012.

the court regards infringement of a child's rights. This is particularly so in a case when there is such interest in the public persona of the alleged father.[254]

The publication of the photo of the child had resulted in considerable speculation on social networking sites about the identity of her father. However, the judge ruled that it was not reasonable or justified by the paper's arguing 'exceptional public interest'. Davies J said in her judgment:

> It is undisputed there is a public interest in the professional and private life of the claimant's supposed father. His professional position speaks for itself. As to his private life, he is a man who has achieved a level of notoriety as result of extramarital adulterous liaisons. . . . I find that the identified issue of recklessness is one which is relevant to the professional and personal character of the supposed father. Specifically, I find that it goes beyond fame and notoriety.[255]

However, the judge added that so much information about the mother's affair with the supposed father, the child's birth and supposed paternity was now in the public domain, that an injunction to prevent any further publication upon the topic would serve no real purpose. She added:

> I accept the claimant's argument that if the sole issue at trial had been the photograph, this would have entailed evidence and submissions as to the balancing exercise as between the competing Article 8 and Article 10 rights. That said, the sticking point in correspondence was not the photographs but the issue of the claimant's paternity upon which the claimant failed. This was a story which was going to be published. If the defendant had not done it, another newspaper would.[256]

The High Court awarded damages to the infant child for breach of her privacy following the publication of a photograph of her on three occasions. The defendant newspaper, however, succeeded in demonstrating a public interest in publishing the fact of her alleged paternity by a politician. Mrs Justice Nicola Davies accepted that a child's paternity is a matter which engages the child's Article 8 privacy rights. The child's mother accepted in evidence that she had in fact spoken to friends at a party about her daughter's paternity. Davies J rejected the claimant's argument that a man's conduct and character are matters of public interest except insofar as they are within the purely private sphere which even prominent public figures retain. She decided that the issue of recklessness on the part of the supposed father was relevant to both his private and his professional character, in particular his fitness for public office, and that his alleged recklessness was a matter of public interest. The proportionately balanced decision in *AAA* illustrates important points of practical application in child privacy cases, including the potential of conduct to compromise an expectation of privacy, bars to obtaining injunct relief and the likely shortfall in damages.

In **Re Z** (1996)[257] the Court of Appeal granted an injunction preventing Channel 4 TV from broadcasting the identity of a child with special educational needs, in spite of the fact that its mother had given permission to film and identify her child, who attended a special school. The broadcast of *Boys and Girls Alone* did not go ahead after complaints had been received from Cornwall County Council that the programme-makers had 'emotionally abused' the young participants, seeking an injunction. Channel 4 producers had argued the programme was in the public interest by showing the children's learning difficulties. *Boys and Girls Alone* was eventually broadcast on

---

254 Ibid., at para 7 (Davies J).
255 Ibid., at para 10.
256 Ibid., at para 14.
257 **Re Z (A Minor) (Identification: Restrictions on Publication)** [1996] 2 FCR 164.

Channel 4 between 3 and 24 February 2009 at 9pm. Some viewers complained to Ofcom about the four-part documentary that showed 10 boys and 10 girls, aged between 8 and 12 years old, as they apparently experienced life without adults for two weeks. Viewers were concerned that the children appeared to have been left largely to their own devices in a potentially unsafe environment without adequate adult supervision. Ofcom's detailed investigation concluded that this was not the case.[258]

In English and Scots law, there is a general presumption that a child's anonymity is protected under (super)injunctions, usually made by Family Courts; these court orders tend to protect parents and guardians who are participating in court proceedings, as Lord Steyn said in **Re S (A Child) (Identification on Publication)** (2004):[259]

> . . . it is important to bear in mind that from a newspaper's point of view a report of a sensa-
> tional trial without revealing the identity of the defendant would be a very much disembodied
> trial. If the newspapers choose not to contest such an injunction, they are less likely to give
> prominence to reports of the trial. Certainly, readers will be less interested and editors will act
> accordingly. Informed debate about criminal justice will suffer.[260]

There have been times when the courts have interfered in parental responsibility on behalf of children and in the child's interest, for example when parents refuse to consent to a blood transfusion on religious grounds or when it is in the child's interest not to appear on TV in spite of a mother's consent, as in **Re Z**.[261]

2.5.1 Children of famous parents: the J. K. Rowling case

The 'J. K. Rowling' (**David Murray**) case[262] was concerned with the issue of whether parents can validly waive their child's right to privacy. The Court of Appeal ruling stated that they cannot: a child's right to privacy is distinct from that of its parents. The **Murray** case concerned the publication of a photograph of the famous Harry Potter author's son, David Murray, in the Sunday Express magazine in April 2005, accompanied by an article on Joanne Rowling's attitude to motherhood. The child, aged 19 months at the time, was photographed in a buggy as the author was strolling in a public street in Edinburgh. The photo had been taken covertly in November 2004 with a long lens by a photographer from Big Pictures, a celebrity photo agency which licenses its photos in the UK and internationally.

The CA held in the 'J. K. Rowling' case that a child's right to privacy is distinct from that of each of its parents owing to its vulnerability and youth.[263] The CA stated that the circumstances in which a child has a legitimate expectation of privacy are wider than those in which an adult has such expectations: adults can expect a greater degree of intrusion as part of their daily lives whilst a little child may be unaware of media hype. Citing the 'legitimate expectation' test in **Campbell**, Lord Hope asked:

> . . . what a reasonable person of ordinary sensibilities would feel if she was placed in the same
> position as the claimant and faced with the same publicity?[264]

---

258 Source: Ofcom 'Boys and Girls Alone' report 2009: http://consumers.ofcom.org.uk/2009/10/boys-and-girls-alone.
259 [2004] UKHL 47; the case concerned the reporting of a trial of a parent charged with the murder of a son.
260 Ibid., at 34 (Lord Steyn).
261 **Re Z (A Minor) (Identification: Restrictions on Publication)** [1996] 2 FCR 164 CA.
262 **Murray v Express Newspapers and others** [2008] EWCA Civ 446 (CA) (also known as: '**Murray v Big Pictures**')
263 For further discussion see: Carter-Silk and Cartwright-Hignett (2009).
264 **Campbell v MGN Ltd** [2004] 2 AC 457 (HL).

That said, unlike adults, children are very unlikely to derive any benefit from publication of information. This does not mean that children should never be photographed in public, as long as it is not detrimental to the child at the time of publication or in the future. In any case this should be in line with normal parental responsibility and the statutory duty to protect the child's well-being.

Since the 'J. K. Rowling case' there has been a tendency by celebrities to include their children in lifestyle magazines or reality programmes which enhance their celebrity status as 'yummy mummy' or 'superdad'. When we see Madonna's children Rocco and Lourdes, or Katie Holmes and Tom Cruise's Suri or the Beckhams' children Brooklyn, Romeo, Cruz and Harper Seven, we can be sure that the celebrities will have allowed publication of the images for financial gain. Otherwise we would see the children's photographs pixelated.

2.5.2 Protecting the right to life: anonymity orders for child killers

The HRA and ECHR have enabled the law of confidence to develop to protect a citizen's right to life (under Article 2 ECHR) and right not to be subjected to torture or to inhuman or degrading treatment or punishment (under Article 3 ECHR).

The issue of lifelong anonymity orders in respect of children who kill was first raised in the case of **Mary Bell** when, in 1968, 10-year-old Mary was convicted at Newcastle Crown Court of the murder of two little boys, aged three and four, by strangulation. After conviction Mary Bell spent 12 years at Red Bank Approved School near Newton-le-Willows in Lancashire and was released on licence in 1980 with a new identity. There followed a number of applications to the courts for the anonymity order to continue beyond her coming of age. The first application on 25 May 1984 concerned an injunction to conceal the identity of her baby daughter (Y) and the baby's father after the News of theWorld had tracked down Mary Bell and her child (**Re X** (1985)[265]). Mr Justice Balcombe granted a restraining order on Y's eighteenth birthday, preventing identification of Mary's daughter as well as the child's father, and continuing the order on Mary (X) indefinitely. A further injunction was granted in 1988 when the identities of X and Y (then aged four) had been revealed to the press by villagers where the mother and daughter lived at the time.

The third period was in 1998 after the publication of Gitta Sereny's book on the story of Mary Bell, Cries Unheard, whereby Sereny had paid Mary a 'substantial sum of money' to co-author the book.[266] Home Secretary Jack Straw did not succeed in injuncting the publication of the book and condemned the payment to Bell in an open letter to the Sun, stating that by collaboration on the book, Mary Bell should forfeit her right to anonymity. Prime Minister Tony Blair criticized the payments to the former child killer as 'inherently repugnant'.

The fourth period began in December 2002 when Mary's acquitted co-accused 'Norma' demanded in the Sunday Sun on 15 December that it was 'time to unmask Mary Bell'. The Newcastle Evening Chronicle published a lead article on 11 April 2003, 'Still Haunted', in which family members of the two killed boys demanded that Mary Bell's identity be disclosed.[267]

The waiver of a child's privacy may not be permanent, though the (family) court can reimpose privacy at any time even if it has previously been waived. One of the most notorious cases involved two 10-year-old child murderers, Jon(athan) Venables and Robert Thompson, who killed 18-month-old James (Jamie) Bulger in February 1993. In **Venables and Thompson v News Group Newspapers Ltd**[268] the 18-year old claimants applied for injunctions preventing disclosure of their

---

265 Re X (a woman formerly known as Mary Bell) and CC v A [1985] 1 All ER 53.
266 See: Sereny (1998).
267 Re X: A Woman Formerly Known as 'Mary Bell' and another v O'Brien and others [2003] EWHC 1101 (QB).
268 Venables and Thompson v News Group Newspapers Ltd [2001] Fam 430.

new identities, current physical appearance and their time spent in secure units since their conviction at the adult Preston Crown Court in November 1993. The murder of little James Bulger had shocked the nation and Venables and Thompson continued to be the object of death threats. They were given new identities to assist in their reintegration into the community.

Butler-Sloss P held that, as the court was a public authority under s 6(3) of the HRA, she had to act compatibly with the Convention rights and have regard to Strasbourg jurisprudence. She recognized that any restriction on freedom of the press had to fall within one of the exceptions in Article 10(2), which should be construed narrowly and the onus of which was on the claimants.[269] Dame Elizabeth Butler-Sloss, when grating a lifelong anonymity order *contra mundum* on the – by now – 18-year-old Venables and Thompson, cited Article 2 ECHR, 'right to life' as a reason for granting the order.

She referred to the fact that the evolution of the common law, and in particular the law of confidence, had been given considerable impetus by the HRA. Taking into account Articles 2, 3 and 8 ECHR, and the real possibility that the claimants may be the objects of revenge attacks, she stated that:

> the court does have the jurisdiction, in exceptional cases, to extend the protection of confidentiality of information, even to impose restrictions on the press, where not to do so would be likely to lead to serious physical injury, and there is no other way to protect the applicants.[270]

Butler-Sloss P granted the injunctions as they satisfied the requirements of Article 10 (2), namely:[271]

1.   They were in accordance with the law, namely the law of confidence;
2.   They would be imposed to prevent the disclosure of information received in confidence;
3.   There was a very strong possibility, if not probability, that on the release of the claimants there would be serious efforts to find them and if that information became public they would be pursued by those intent on revenge. Their rights under Articles 2 and 3 gave a strong and pressing social need in a democratic society for their confidentiality to be protected; and
4.   The injunctions were proportionate to the legitimate aim pursued, namely protecting the claimants from the real and serious risk of death or physical harm.

The defendant newspapers had argued that the young killers' rehabilitation process and education whilst in youth custody were matters of genuine public interest and for that reason Venables and Thompson's identities should be revealed, citing – *inter alia* – freedom of expression. Butler-Sloss P granted the injunctions against the whole world (*contra mundum*), stating that:

> in the light of the implementation of the Human Rights Act, we are entering a new era, and the requirement that the courts act in a way compatible with the Convention, and have regard to European jurisprudence, adds a new dimension to those principles.[272]

For these reasons the court had a duty of care to grant lifelong anonymity orders on the young men (see also: **Davies v Taylor** (1974);[273] **Re H (Minors) (Sexual Abuse: Standard of Proof)** (1996)[274]).

---

269   Ibid., at 268, para 25.
270   Ibid., at 288, para 82 (Butler-Sloss P)
271   Ibid., at 286–290, paras 77–87.
272   Ibid., at 295, para 101.
273   [1974] AC 207.
274   [1996] AC 563.

2.5.3 Identification of child killers: Jon Venables confesses real identity

In March 2010, the by now 27-year-old Jon Venables – now on life licence – disclosed his identity to prison and probation staff. On 8 March the *Daily Mirror* broke the news that the 'Jamie Bulger killer' was back in prison on suspicion of a 'serious sexual offence'. Justice Minister Jack Straw released a press statement which confirmed the identity of the 'Bulger-killer' in preventive custody, though stating that Venables had not been charged with any sexual offence. This angered the press and the blogosphere was wild with speculation about Venables's identity and the alleged crime. The *Daily Mirror* and the *Sun* demanded that the lifelong anonymity order on Venables and his accomplice Thompson be lifted.

On 9 March 2010, Baroness Butler-Sloss addressed the House of Lords, giving reasons why the *contra mundum* anonymity order must never be lifted, repeating her reasons at the time based on Article 2 ECHR and the state's duty to protect the Bulger killers' individual lives in spite of the heinous crime they committed in 1993. She opined that the risk of harm to Jon Venables in the present case would be too great and the court had a duty of care to protect even the most dangerous offenders (see also: **Osman v UK** (1998)[275]).

On 23 July 2010, Jon Venables pleaded guilty to three offences under the Protection of Children Act 1978. The first involved downloading 57 indecent pictures of children between February 2009 and February 2010. The second involved distributing three indecent photographs of children in February 2010, while a third involved distributing 42 images in February 2008. Mr Justice Bean, sitting at the Old Bailey, said Venables had 'colluded in the harm of children'. However, the judge said it would be 'wrong' for Venables's sentence to be increased because of his previous crime. Jon Venables was sentenced to two years' imprisonment. The judge refused to lift reporting restrictions, and Venables appeared at the Old Bailey via video link from prison to admit downloading and distributing scores of indecent images of children.[276]

There are other occasions when the media demand that reporting restrictions be lifted on children. This was the case with the 'Edlington killers' when the 'red tops' demanded their identity in January 2010 as Mr Justice Keith passed an indeterminate life sentence for public protection on the two brothers, aged 10 and 11. The brothers had executed 'unimaginable' violence against two 11- and 9-year-old boys in Edlington, near Doncaster, South Yorkshire in April 2009. The brothers admitted the torturous killing on 4 September 2009.[277] The Ministry of Justice denied media access to the Doncaster Social Services Report, which described the brutal attacks by the young killers on the children in their neighbourhood. The court subsequently ordered that the Edlington boys' identities be protected for life.

The British media remain fascinated by child-killer stories, but it is also fair to say that the press has provided a valuable public service, uncovering a number of horrendous stories involving children, such as Mark Bridger who was sentenced in May 2013 to life imprisonment for the abduction and subsequent brutal murder of five-year-old April Jones from her home in Machynlleth, Wales. April had disappeared on 1 October 2012 from the Bryn-y-Gog estate. With the help of the media, local police tracked Bridger down and secured his conviction. There followed the Prime Minister's anti-child pornography campaign asking the main internet service providers to block such content on the internet. The media also alerted the public to the tragic death of Victoria Climbié in 2000 as well as the maltreatment and death of 17-month-old Baby P (Peter) in 2007 and the systemic

---

275 (1998) 29 EHRR 245.
276 Source: 'Sordid secret life of Bulger killer exposed as he is jailed for two years over shocking child pornography', by Nicola Boden, *Daily Mail*, 30 July 2010.
277 Source: 'Reign of terror that took them to the brink of murder: The descent of two brothers into depravity', by Arthur Martin, Fay Schlesinger and Paul Harris, *Daily Mail*, 4 September 2009.

failures in child protection by Haringey Social Services in both cases. Eight-year-old Victoria starved to death after prolonged abuse at hands of guardians in London; social workers, police and the NHS had failed to raise alarm. Seventeen-month-old Baby Peter suffered 50 injuries including a broken back, allegedly missed by the local doctor. Peter endured an agonizing death at home inflicted by his mother, her boyfriend and lodger in Haringey, North London. The media campaign in both cases resulted in the sacking of the Head of Children's Services at Haringey Council after a series of damning inquiries revealed 60 missed opportunities to save Baby P's life.

 FOR THOUGHT

Was it 'just' for Dame Elizabeth Butler-Sloss to grant a lifelong anonymity order on the two James Bulger killers, Venables and Thompson, in 2001? Discuss why child-killer anonymity should (or should not) be protected for life.

2.6 Superinjunctions: protection of privacy or freedom of expression?

Before 2000 there was in England and Wales no general right to privacy and therefore no right to an injunction to protect or enforce any general claim to privacy. The development of privacy rights since 2000 was an inevitable consequence of the enactment of the Human Rights Act 1998 (HRA) and the incorporation of the European Court Convention of Human Rights (ECHR), in particular Article 8 ECHR, into domestic law. Although confidential information has long been protected (as per *Coco Engineers* etc.), a general right to respect for privacy was not recognized until 2000 when the HRA came into force. Concerns have since been expressed in some legal quarters about the way in which the law of privacy and confidentiality has developed, particularly in superinjunction (or interim injunction) cases, given Parliament's intention in passing s 12 HRA, which was particularly concerned with maintaining a balance between privacy and freedom of expression.

In October 2011, BBC *Top Gear* presenter Jeremy Clarkson 'outed' his own superinjunction by stating that these 'gagging orders' are 'pointless.' Clarkson told the *Daily Mail*: 'Superinjunctions don't work. You take out an injunction against somebody or some organization and immediately news of that injunction and the people involved and the story behind the injunction is in a legal-free world on Twitter and the internet.'[278] In the aptly named *AMM* ('Aston Martin Man') v *HXW* ('His ex-wife')[279] Clarkson had applied for a 'gagging' order in September 2010 to restrain his former wife, Alex Hall, from publishing a book about their extramarital affair, after the couple had divorced and Clarkson had remarried. Edwards-Stuart J granted the injunction after hearing that Ms Hall (HXW) was trying to blackmail Mr Clarkson by threatening to expose their relationship to the media unless he paid a 'very substantial sum' of hush money. As soon as the order was also served on the *Daily Mail* (Associated Newspapers Ltd) on 30 September 2010, the 'Jeremy Clarkson super-injunction' story reached the 'Twittersphere', with the 'red tops' freely reporting on it.[280]

The debate about privacy laws has intensified over the past decade as more and more superinjunctions have come to light, challenged by the media under Article 10 ECHR. Some, such as Jeremy

278 Source: 'Jeremy Clarkson lifts the gag on his ex-wife: She claims she had an affair with Top Gear star after he remarried', by Michael Seamark, *Daily Mail*, 27 October 2011.
279 [2010] EWHC 2457 (QB); [2010] All ER (D) 48 (Oct) ('Jeremy Clarkson superinjunction').
280 See: Smartt (2011), pp. 135–140.

Clarkson or TV personality Andrew Marr, would argue that superinjunctions are a waste of time and money, spoilt largely by the 'Twitterati'. Andrew Marr – like Jeremy Clarkson – also decided to speak out about his own injunction, thereby technically breaking his own injunction. Mr Marr told the *Daily Mail* in April 2011: 'I did not come into journalism to go around gagging journalists. Am I embarrassed by it? Yes. Am I uneasy about it? Yes.'[281]

There have been a number of high-profile cases where celebrities have sought privacy injunctions and – in turn – were granted so-called 'superinjunctions' by the courts. Superinjunctions (also referred to as 'double gagging orders' by the media) have attracted a great deal of criticism from freedom of speech fighters and pressure groups in that justice is being seen to be done behind closed doors. Superinjunctions can restrain the disclosure of the fact that a privacy injunction has been obtained.

See below
2.6.2

The use of such injunctions to stop reporting of potentially embarrassing revelations has been a growing trend amongst celebrities since about 2009. Superinjunctions that were sought – but not granted or subsequently lifted – involved, for instance, the then Chelsea football captain John Terry, England striker Wayne Rooney and Manchester United and Wales football star Ryan Giggs, all of whom had the financial means to use expensive lawyers to exercise legal rights denied to ordinary members of the public. Nevertheless, many superinjunctions have been exposed on social networking sites such as Twitter and Facebook[282] or via online blogs, making the double gagging orders effectively worthless. None of these were linked to children but involved either famous celebrities or company misdemeanours. The public learnt about the *Guardian*'s successful fight against the 'Trafigura' superinjunction and interim orders on Portsmouth football manager Avram Grant,[283] footballer Ashley Cole[284] and TV presenter Vernon Kay.[285]

2.6.1 Superinjunctions: double gagging orders and restraint on publication

Superinjunctions (also 'super-injunctions') is a term commonly given to an order restraining disclosure of the claimant's identity and the fact the claim has been brought. These are usually interim court orders which prevent news organizations from revealing the identities of those involved in legal disputes, or even reporting the existence of the injunction at all. They were originally used exclusively in the family courts as a result of privacy and *in camera* proceedings, mostly concerning the protection of juveniles and children in care, adoption or divorce proceedings. In their simplest form, superinjunctions prevent the media from reporting what happens in court, usually on the basis that doing so could prejudice a trial or someone's right to privacy. Superinjunctions in their strictest form mean derogation from the *open justice principle* in that they seek:

1. a private hearing (*in camera*);
2. anonymity for the applicant (and other persons involved in the 'relationship');

---

281 'Gagging orders are out of control, says Andrew Marr as he abandons High Court injunction over his extra-marital affair', by Sam Greenhill, *Daily Mail*, 26 April 2011.
282 Social networking site, Facebook, was started at Harvard in 2004 by Mark Zuckerberg, spread to university networks on both sides of the Atlantic, migrated from the universities as its users graduated, and became increasingly popular with older users in the media and television industries. At the end of 2011 the company had 845 million active users. Facebook floated on the stock market in May 2012. By August 2012, CEO Zuckerberg acknowledged that Facebook had taken a 'painful' stock market hammering. Source: 'Mark Zuckerberg admits Facebook stock tumble is "painful" to watch', *Telegraph*, 17 August 2012.
283 Source: 'Get any Rompy Pompey Avram?' by Tom Wells, Jamie Pyatt and Alex Peake, the *Sun*, 5 February 2010.
284 Source: 'Chelsea's Cole is a love cheat', by Richard White and Philip Chase, the *Sun*, 25 January 2010.
285 Source: 'Vernon Kay admits sending racy text and Twitter messages to Page 3 girl behind wife Tess Daly's back', *Daily Mail*, 9 February 2010.

3.   that the entire court file should be sealed;[286] and

4.   that the court order should prohibit publication of the existence of the proceedings, usually until after the conclusion of any trial.[287]

If such an order is disclosed, say by a newspaper, this can amount to contempt of court – but only if the publication is in breach of an express prohibition: for example, where the court order expressly prohibits the publication of certain information relating to the hearing or the proceedings, to third parties with knowledge of such an order. The media organization may well be in contempt if they disclose the information that the court has ordered not to be disclosed.

See Chapter 4.4

In **Re H (a Healthcare Worker)** (2002)[288] the claimant was seeking to prevent the disclosure by N, a health authority, of confidential information that he was HIV positive. Kennedy LJ held that the court could properly make an order in the proceedings, restraining the publication of information made available in the course of the proceedings which, if disclosed, would pre-empt the decision of the court on the issues before it.

What should be borne in mind is that if an individual is properly entitled to a privacy injunction, the whole purpose of that injunction may in some situations be undermined by disclosure of the fact that an injunction has been obtained by that individual. In such circumstances the alternative to justice being done behind closed doors is that justice will not be done at all.

In February 2012 a law firm's letter was leaked to the *Daily Telegraph*, warning Members of Parliament and peers that they would face 'diplomatic repercussions' unless they removed a document detailing aspects of one of Britain's last remaining superinjunctions from the parliamentary records. The 13-page submission from Channel Islands businessman Mark Burby claimed he had been gagged by the ex-spouse of an Asian head of state in a superinjunction in 2009. It was alleged that the 'Asian head of state' was a 'substantial' backer of Al Qaeda who had received advance warning of the suicide bombings on London's transport system in July 2005. Mr Burby alleged the unnamed ex-spouse, whom he described as one of the wealthiest women in the world, had a sexual relationship 'with one of her two solicitors', as well as two other men, one of which resulted in her having an abortion. The firm of solicitors in question, acting for the ex-wife of the 'unnamed Asian head of state', made a series of threats against the joint Parliamentary Committee on Privacy and Injunctions – made up of 26 MPs and peers – requesting an urgent 'takedown notice' from the committee's website. The same law firm also threatened the *Telegraph* with an injunction ahead of its reporting of Mr Burby's submission.[289]

This attempt to gag and undermine the supremacy of Parliament followed widespread existing criticism of the UK courts for injuncting the publication of information such as the Trafigura oil scandal in 2009. MPs have since broken several other injunctions by naming public figures such as Ryan Giggs or former RBS chief, (the then Sir) Fred Goodwin[290] – all of whom had used the courts to suppress information about their personal lives.

When are superinjunctions granted? In the first instance, it is up to the courts to assess whether there is a 'pressing social need' for any restriction by making an injunction after applying the public interest test and a certain margin of appreciation of an individual's right to privacy and the confidentiality of the subject matter. Arguably, it should be in the public interest of our democratic society to ensure that the freedom of the press is maintained. Similarly, courts will weigh up, if they place any reporting restriction or superinjunctions on a publication, whether this measure is

286 Criminal Procedure Rules (CPR) 5. 4C(7).
287 For a detailed discussion how to conduct any privacy action see: Tugendhat and Christie (2011) pp. 706–719.
288 **H (A Healthcare Worker) v Associated Newspapers Ltd** [2002] EMLR 425.
289 Source: 'Exclusive: Lawyers order Parliament to stop publishing super-injunction document', by Christopher Hope and Robert Winnett, *Daily Telegraph*, 28 February 2012.
290 **Goodwin (Sir Fred) v News Group Newspapers** [2011] EWHC 1309 (QB).

proportionate to the legitimate aim pursued. Where the published information invades an individual's right of privacy, as protected by Article 8 ECHR, the courts will give careful consideration as to whether the information is truly of public interest rather than merely of interest to the public. This is a fundamental distinction. As the Strasbourg Court observed in **von Hannover (No 1)**:

> ... the court considers that a fundamental distinction needs to be made between reporting facts – even controversial ones – capable of contributing to a debate in a democratic society relating to politicians in the exercise of their functions, for example, and reporting details of the private life of an individual who, moreover, as in this case, does not exercise official functions. While in the former case the press exercises its vital role of 'watchdog' in a democracy by contributing to 'impart[ing] information and ideas on matters of public interest' it does not do so in the latter case.[291]

In the case where a litigant intends to serve a prohibitory injunction upon a publication, the courts rely on the **Spycatcher** principle, in that the individual author, journalist or publisher should be given a realistic opportunity to be heard on the appropriateness of granting the injunction and the scope of its terms, mirrored closely by the provisions contained in s 12 HRA 1998.

2.6.2 Superinjunctions: John Terry, Ryan Giggs and others

On 22 January 2010, lawyers acting for the then England football captain, John Terry, asked the High Court for a prohibition in the form of an interim superinjunction on publishing details of a 'specific personal relationship' between their client and another person. This became known later as the 'John Terry Superinjunction' (**LNS v Persons Unknown** (2010)[292]). Terry's lawyers argued that the intended publication in the *News of the World* would amount to a breach of confidence and misuse of private information in that £1 million had been promised to an informant to keep the story quiet. The newspaper was about to publish their scoop on the footballer's adulterous affair with French underwear model Vanessa Perroncel, who happened to be the former girlfriend of Terry's friend and team-mate Wayne Bridge. The story was to be the front-page headline on Sunday 24 January 2010.

See above
2.2.6

The John Terry (LNS) 'double gagging order' sought complete privacy, stating that any publication of any information, including photographs, evidencing the extramarital relationship could lead to harming the private family life of the applicant. Opposing the injunction at the hearing on 29 January 2010, News Group Newspapers (NGN) made a strong submission before Mr Justice Tugendhat, supporting freedom of expression under Article 10 and the public's 'right to know' in this case, i.e. that John Terry as England football captain was a role model to many young people and prided himself on being a family man. Tugendhat J considered Articles 6, 8 and 10 of the Convention in turn, giving additional consideration to the open justice principle. Balancing one right against the other, he considered the right to speak freely, the right to private life and reputation and the right to a fair hearing. Tugendhat J applied the 'confidentiality test' as cited in the 'Prince Charles' Diaries' case':[293]

> ... not simply whether the information is a matter of public interest but whether, in all the circumstances, it is in the public interest that the duty of confidence should be breached.[294]

---

291 *Von Hannover v Germany (No 1)* [2005] 40 EHRR 1 at 63.
292 [2010] EWHC 119 (sub nom 'John Terry Superinjunction').
293 *Associated Newspapers Ltd v HRH Prince of Wales* [2006] EWCA Civ 1776; [2008] Ch 57 (sub nom 'The Prince Charles' Diaries' case).
294 Ibid., at 68 (Tugendhat J).

Tugendhat J noted that there was no evidence before the court and no personal representation from the applicant of proof to convince him to apply the right to privacy under Article 8, nor was there proof that any confidentiality had been breached: no photographs were produced, nor was there any confidential or private information disclosed (see: **X v Persons Unknown** (2006)[295]). For this reason Tugendhat J lifted the interim (super)injunction granted initially a few days earlier, stating that privacy law was not there to protect someone's reputation, which in this case meant the footballer's commercial interests.

John Terry did indeed have some very lucrative contracts and sponsorship deals at the time. For example, in 2009 the footballer had been named 'Dad of the Year', landing a sponsorship deal with Daddies Sauce. Other commercial deals included Umbro, Samsung and Nationwide. Most of Terry's lucrative advertising deals were aimed at either children or young family men. After Terry's failed appeal regarding the superinjunction, he may well have gone down badly in the estimation of the public after his sex scandal revelations. Summing up, Mr Justice Tugendhat said:

> . . . that is why sponsors may be sensitive to the public image of those sportspersons whom they pay to promote their products. Freedom to live as one chooses is one of the most valuable freedoms. But so is the freedom to criticise (within the limits of the law) the conduct of other members of society as being socially harmful, or wrong.[296]

The lifting of the 'John Terry superinjunction' was regarded as a victory for press freedom. Thereafter, the tabloid press became increasingly daring and aggressive in their revelations about other infidelities and indiscretions of celebrities, often completely ignoring any superinjunctions which might have been in place at the time.

One of these was the 'Ryan Giggs superinjunction'.[297] Despite the court anonymity order, the extramarital affair of the married Manchester United and Wales football star – referred to only as 'CTB' in the restraining order – with a lingerie model was widely exposed on social networking sites as well as in Parliament in May 2011. Giggs had hired Schillings solicitors to represent him against the *News of the World* and former Miss Wales, Ms Imogen Thomas, whom he had accused of blackmailing him.

On 15 December 2011, Imogen Thomas issued a public statement in which her lawyer said that one of the UK's most famous footballers had finally accepted there was no basis on which to accuse her of blackmail. Ms Thomas categorically stated that she was not the source of the *Sun* article.[298] She also reiterated that she did not wish any private information to be published, and that her conduct in retaining the publicist Max Clifford was not to procure publication, but to prevent it. Ms Thomas even gave an undertaking to the High Court:

> . . . not to disclose or cause or permit another to disclose any confidential information (as defined . . .) to any third party.[299]

This undertaking to the court had the same effect in law as an injunction.

It is now well known that in both the 'Ryan Giggs' and 'Trafigura' cases, the superinjunctions were ruined by both the social networking powers and parliamentary privilege, combining thousands of tweets, information by media organizations on foreign-based ISPs and Parliamentarians

---

295　[2006] EWHC 2783 (QB) at 290.
296　**LNS v Persons Unknown** [2010] EWHC 119 (QB) at 104 (Tugendhat J).
297　**CTB v News Group Newspapers Ltd** [2011] EWHC 1326 (QB) 23 May 2011 ('the Ryan Giggs superinjunction').
298　Imogen Thomas 'vindicated' after footballer drops blackmail claim – video, *Guardian Online*, 15 December 2011: www.guardian.co.uk/uk/video/2011/dec/15/imogen-thomas-footballer-blackmail-video.
299　See: Statement in Open Court read on her behalf on 15 December 2011 (para 39).

mentioning the individuals in both houses of Parliament. The Ryan Giggs 'gagging order' was identified by the Liberal Democrat MP John Hemming, using parliamentary privilege to name him in
the House of Commons. By the time the High Court revisited the anonymized 'Ryan Giggs' injunction in March 2012, it appeared to have blown up in Giggs's lawyers faces. Ultimately, the injunction was compromised between Mr Giggs and Ms Thomas.

The problem with the original 'Ryan Giggs superinjunction' of 14 April 2011 was that it lasted
four months longer than necessary, because his lawyers failed to comply with the court order
arising from the litigation on 2 November 2011 before Tugendhat J. The result was that the order
was immediately struck out, a full six months *after* the world had learnt of Mr Giggs's identity. As
Tugendhat J noted in the first paragraph of the March judgment:

> There can be few people in England and Wales who have not heard of this litigation. The initials
> CTB have been chanted at football matches when Mr Giggs has been playing for Manchester
> United. And Mr Giggs has been named in Parliament, raising questions as to the proper rela-
> tionship between Parliament and the judiciary.[300]

What made the 'Ryan Giggs Part 2' litigation of March 2012 infamous was that the order for the
Manchester United footballer to be anonymized did not achieve its purpose. Had Mr Giggs known
in April 2011, at the time the principal injunction was sought, that Imogen Thomas was not the
source of the *Sun* article, and if he had believed that News Group Newspapers (NGN) had no more
information to publish, and no intention to publish further information, it may well be that the
footballer would not have joined NGN in the action or proceeded any further. But Ryan Giggs's
lawyers thought otherwise. In the March 2012 action there followed a plea of aggravated damages
seemingly directed only against Ms Thomas.[301] Mr Justice Tugendhat threw out the application for
damages, adding that there was 'no purpose' in allowing the case and injunction to continue.

As we have seen from Strasbourg jurisprudence, there is now a basic framework within
Articles 8 and 10 that provides for a social equilibrium between individuals, the media and society.
It is argued that superinjunctions have curtailed the extent to which a newspaper or media organization can report on individuals in the public interest. The Tugendhat rulings in the John Terry and
Ryan Giggs cases have given hope to the media where an individual's right to privacy has been
overridden by freedom of expression granted in the public interest. As common law and ECtHR
jurisprudence have developed the courts have stressed that the 'necessity' for any restriction on
freedom of expression must be convincingly established as a matter of general principle (see: **Fressoz
and Roire v France** (1999)[302]).

Domestic courts have recently deemed personal information as 'private' and 'confidential'
when a reasonable person of ordinary sensibilities who finds themselves in the same position as the
claimant would have had a reasonable expectation of privacy in all the given circumstances. Such
was the case in **AMP**,[303] where the judge granted a superinjunction against 'Persons Unknown' to
prevent the transmission of sensitive, personal photos belonging to the claimant who had lost her
mobile phone. When some of her naked photos were uploaded on to Facebook, the court order not
only protected her and the images (which were subsequently removed) but also stopped the threats
which not only endangered her reputation but also that of her father's business; her father had
allegedly been blackmailed over some of his daughter's images.

300 **Giggs (Ryan Joseph) v News Group Newspaper Ltd and Imogen Thomas** [2012] EWHC 431 (QB) (Tugendhat J) at para 1.
301 **Giggs (Ryan Joseph) v News Group Newspapers Ltd and Imogen Thomas** [2012] EWHC 431 (QB) 2 March 2012.
302 [1999] 31 EHRR 28.
303 **AMP v Persons Unknown** [2012] All ER (D) 178.

In May 2011 a committee chaired by the Master of the Rolls, Lord Neuberger, published its findings on superinjunctions, anonymity injunctions and open justice. Lord Neuberger's Committee was formed in April 2010 following a report of the Culture, Media and Sport Select Committee, and in the light of growing public concerns about the use and effect of superinjunctions and the impact they were having on open justice. The Neuberger Report provides guidance to lawyers and journalists on the steps to be followed before a superinjunction or anonymity order ('anonymized injunction') is applied for. The Report maintains the fundamental principles of open justice and freedom of speech. Where privacy and confidentiality are involved, a degree of secrecy is often necessary to do justice. However, where secrecy is ordered (in the form of a superinjunction or anonymity order) it should only be to the extent strictly necessary to achieve the interests of justice. And, when it is ordered, the facts of the case and the reason for secrecy should be explained (to the media opposing the injunction), as far as possible, in an openly available judgment. A fair balance has to be struck by the courts making such an order between the principles of open justice and freedom of expression for the public and the media, and an individual's right to confidentiality and privacy.[304] The Neuberger Report established the framework in which applications for superinjunctions may be made and should be decided.

2.7 Internet privacy

Much of this chapter has discussed how professional writers, journalists, editors and publishers are dealt with by the courts when it comes to privacy. But there are now literally millions of amateurs who blog or 'tweet' online and who will be less knowledgeable about court restraining orders that exist on reportage, comment, rumour and abuse. The coming years are going to present many challenges for legislators and the courts in dealing with online content.

In the digital age it is normal that most people conduct a significant part of their lives via social networking sites or share their thoughts on blogs. At present domestic and human rights laws are unclear as to the interpretation of an individual's right to privacy on the World Wide Web. In the absence of any privacy laws one could even argue that there exists no restraint or protection for an individual other than resorting to court restraining orders against an ISP, asking for the disclosure of the 'defamer' or 'harasser' via a court order (to the ISP), or relying on confusing case law to ask an ISP directly to take down offending statements visible to all online (see: **Godfrey v Demon Internet**[305]). And what about material that is intended to be shared privately by individuals or groups? There is some technology in place that allows that privacy can be denied to online users as per ss 3 and 4 of the Digital Economy Act (DEA) 2010.

We live in an era where people routinely share extremely personal information online via a whole host of sites including Facebook, Twitter, YouTube and mobile phone messaging. Can the internet be controlled by privacy and censorship legislation? Legal boundaries are blurred between countries, making privacy invasion online less actionable in law. And if information which a site visitor thinks is secure can be harvested by illegal – and sometimes legal – means, what can be done about it, especially if the information-thief or snooper is in a country many thousands of miles away?

How – if at all – can legislation manage the privacy of online users? If people voluntarily post their most intimate details and thoughts online, what protection is there for them, such as Tom Stephens's own blog that he knew the (murdered) prostitutes in the Ipswich 'Ripper' killings in

---

304 See: Master of the Rolls (2011).
305 [2001] QB 201.

See Chapter 4

November 2006? The 37-year-old supermarket worker was arrested on suspicion of murdering five women whose bodies were found at sites around the Ipswich area. Stephens became the prime suspect when he was interviewed on BBC Radio Ipswich; yet the public broadcaster was not charged with 'contempt of court' for its 36-minute interview with Stephens in December 2006.[306] The reason was that he himself had exposed his name and personal habits on his MySpace blog ('call me the Bishop'); under those circumstances – it was argued by the Attorney General – contempt rules did not apply.

See also
Chapter 3

2.7.1 The Facebook case

The question of breach of privacy via an online social network came before the English courts in 2007–08. The case of *Applause Store v Raphael*[307] is an important privacy case whereby the claim for misuse of private information (in addition to 'online libel') was raised.

In *Applause Store* a false group profile was created on Facebook, attributed to the claimant. In relation to the misuse of private information, damages were awarded 'for the hurt feelings' and distress caused by the 'misuse of their information'.[308]

❖ **KEY CASE**   *Applause Store Productions Ltd v Raphael* [2008] EWHC 1781 (QB)

Precedent

❖ If a claimant is a member of a social networking site (e.g. Facebook) the court may not grant 'reasonable privacy' to the claimant.

❖ If the claimant is not a member of a social network and/or the disclosure of his personal information was by someone else, he can claim a 'reasonable expectation of privacy' under Article 8 ECHR.

Facts

This case concerns an unfortunate dispute between two former Brighton school friends, the claimants being Mathew Firsht (F), a successful businessman, and his company, Applause Store Productions Ltd ('Applause Store' – X), which provided audiences for popular television programmes such as *Big Brother*, *The X Factor* and *Top Gear*. The defendant, freelance lighting cameraman Grant Raphael (R), had since fallen out with his former school friend F.

On 4 July 2007, F, his twin brother Simon and his brother's girlfriend discovered a (false) profile of F and a group page on F and his company X on Facebook. The profile, named Mathew Firsht (F), including highly personal information on him, such as F's sexual orientation, his relationship status, his birthday, his political and religious views (neither the profile nor the group was set up by F). The Facebook group was entitled 'Has Mathew Firsht lied to you?' F was shocked and extremely upset: he regarded the material as a gross invasion of his privacy, and he was particularly distressed by the fact that his personal details, including false details as to his sexuality, had been 'laid bare for all to

---

306 Tom Stephens was later cleared of all charges and Stephen Wright was found guilty of the prostitutes' murders in February 2008.
307 *Applause Store Productions Ltd v Raphael* [2008] EWHC 1781 (QB); [2008] Info. T.L.R. 318 (QBD).
308 Ibid., at 81.

see'.[309] He was worried that the defamatory material had the potential to cause serious damage to his professional reputation and that of his company (X).

Counsel for the claimants (F and X) argued that the claim in misuse of private information (by F alone) under Article 8 ECHR arose from the false profile, while the claim in defamation (brought by both F and X) arose from the group page.

It emerged that the profile was set up on R's computer at the premises where R lived. Though there was no dispute that the material was defamatory, R denied responsibility for setting up the profile and the Facebook group and thereby publishing them to those who visited either Facebook address. On 1 August 2007, his solicitors obtained a *'Norwich Pharmacal'* order against Facebook Inc for disclosure of the registration data provided by the user responsible for creating the false material, including email addresses and the IP addresses of all computers used to access Facebook by the owner of those email addresses. Evidence was adduced of an activity log for R's ISP address, showing that R had accessed Facebook during the day the profile was set up. In his defence, R said that that night he had given a party for 12 people, including four strangers who stayed at his flat the following day when he went out. R contended that it must have been someone else who had accessed his computer and set up the profile of F and X on Facebook.

Decision
The court did not accept Grant Raphael's (R) explanation for the Facebook usage and held the evidence as implausible. Richard Parkes QC, sitting as a Deputy Judge of the High Court (QB) on 24 July 2008, called it 'far-fetched' that a complete stranger, visiting R's flat for the first time, would have used R's computer without permission to create a false profile about a man R knew well and had fallen out with. It was also established that R had searched for F's profile via Google, only to discover that F had no profile, and that R had simply made one up by creating a new profile.

In relation to the claim for damages for defamation the judge noted that the profile was only up for 17 days. Whilst the libel was not at the top end of the scale, the words used in the profile suggested that F owed substantial sums of money which he had avoided paying by repeatedly lying, and was not to be trusted in the financial conduct of his business.

Damages for the libel were awarded to F at £15,000 (including aggravated damages); and for X at £5,000. In relation to the claim for misuse of private information, damages were awarded to compensate F for 'hurt feelings and distress caused', at £2,000.

Analysis
The reason why Mr Firsht's (F) privacy claim under Article 8 succeeded was because he was not a member of Facebook, but his profile and that of his company 'Applause Store' (X) was created for him by R, without his knowledge or consent. The entitlement of a company to recover general damages had been affirmed by the House of Lords in the previous year in **Jameel v Wall Street Journal**,[310] where it was held that a company's good

---

309 Ibid., at 69.
310 [2007] 1 AC 359.

See Chapter
3.8

name is a thing of value. In *Applause Store* there was no evidence of actual financial loss and it was held that the information was only 'live' on Facebook for a relatively short time (17 days).

The case set a precedent that people have a 'reasonable expectation of privacy' online, particularly where claimants have not disclosed their own private information. A company may stand in a slightly different position, for it has no feelings to hurt. It then follows that considerations of aggravated damages may not apply to company claims. The determination of damages will depend on the information revealed, the motive behind disclosure, the effect on the claimant and the frequency with which the claimant uses the social medium himself (if at all). The court ruled that there had been a breach of privacy via a social networking site, which makes this an important decision, particularly in realizing the importance of Article 8 ECHR in relation to online social media context. This is also one of the rare cases where Facebook agreed to identify the author of the material in question by way of a court order.[311] With the implementation of secondary legislation coming into force in relation to the Digital Economy Act 2010 (DEA) we will see more such disclosure orders in relation to breach of copyright (e.g. peer-to-peer file-sharing).

See Chapter
9

In deciding whether to grant a privacy claim, the courts will look at the circumstances in which the information 'came into the hands of the publisher' (the ISP) – this appears to be fraught with difficulties when it comes to persuading the ISP or social networking site to reveal the user or registered member of the particular social media community. After all, users of, say, Facebook or Twitter register with the express understanding that their registration enables other members to publish private information about them. This will then limit the standard of 'reasonable expectation' of privacy under Article 8 ECHR and enhance the right to freedom of expression under Article 10.

It is interesting to note that Facebook changed its privacy policy in 2011, now capturing information about the end-user at any time he uses Facebook. The social networking site knows everything about its users, including birthdays and 'likes'. Most of this information is viewable on a user's Facebook timeline and can be accessed indefinitely. Though there are enhanced privacy settings on the website, the vast majority of Facebook users do not use this facility. By 2012, there were 900 million users worldwide, and 59 per cent of users had little or no trust in the company to keep their information private, according an AP-CNBC poll. By using Facebook (and other similar social networks), the onus is being placed on the user to decide the privacy settings for different elements of information revealed via the site.[312]

Bennett (2010: 145–149) notes that due to the instant and widespread nature of publication on Facebook, and the effortless means by which any comment can be published, without any vetting process by ISPs, one might have thought that the courts would be concerned that such a decision would open the floodgates for an uncontrollable number of cases of this nature. Yet this has not occurred. By the time this book went to print, there has been no precedent set on privacy and confidentiality in relation to social media and the internet in general, other than the 'reasonable expectation' context as identified in the **J. K. Rowling** case.[313] This means the courts must consider:

See: 2.5.1
above

---

311 For further discussion see: Mindell (2012) pp. 52–58.
312 See: Denham (2009).
313 **Murray v Express Newspapers Plc** [2008] EWCA Civ 446.

- the attributes of the claimant;
- the activity in which the claimant was engaged;
- the place at which it occurred;
- the nature and purpose of the intrusion;
- consent;
- the effect on the claimant and the circumstances in which the information came into the hands of the publisher.[314]

2.8 A tort of privacy

We have seen that the courts have developed the law of 'confidentiality' and 'privacy' in a very fluid manner, and boundaries and conditions of application have become blurred. Based on some equally confusing Strasbourg judgments the UK courts have applied different privacy conditions in either expansive or perplexing manners on different occasions, depending on the judge who is hearing the case.

Is it not about time that there ought to be a statutory tort of privacy, particularly in the digital age of online blogs and social networking? Mindell (2012: 52–58) argues that 'proper' privacy legislation could acknowledge breaches of privacy 'in both primary and secondary forms and understanding the remedial possibilities of each' so that the law could ultimately protect private information because it is 'private' and undisclosed, rather than because it is 'confidential information'.

Rowbottom (2012: 355–383) argues that there should not be a 'blanket protection of all speech' and that a distinction should be drawn that is reflected in the free speech cases, particularly where internet libel and privacy are concerned. He argues for a specific set of regulations suited to the digital context and that 'procedure and sanctions should be proportionate' not only to the harm, but to the level of responsibility expected from the 'speaker'.

Clearly there are misunderstandings and social differences in what some deem 'private' and some regard or even misuse as 'confidential' information. The law in this area could then provide objective criteria for the courts to apply when misuse of another's private information has taken place. It is hoped that the measures which are being imposed by secondary legislation emerging from the DEA 2010 will encourage greater responsibility and awareness of the consequences among those who exercise communicative freedoms.

2.9 Further reading

Bingham, T. (1996) 'Should there be a law to protect rights of personal privacy?' *European Human Rights Law Review* 1996, 5: 455–462.
This article discusses the protection of breach of confidence and whether there should be law to protect personal privacy following the Kaye case, presumably because Mr Kaye's legal advisers considered that there was not an appropriate remedy for their client in common law. Lord Bingham, who was one of the judges who heard the case, argues (extra-judicially) that it would not have succeeded. Bingham argues that the expansion and distortion of any confidence action cannot serve as an adequate substitute for a full privacy action and a 'proper' privacy law, unless, by either judicial sleight of hand or the bold grasping of the privacy nettle, a free-standing right to privacy emerges fully formed like 'Athena' from the limitations of the confidence action.

---

314 Ibid., at 36.

Carter-Silk, A. and Cartwright-Hignett, C. (2009) 'A child's right to privacy: "out of a parent's hands" '. *Entertainment Law Review* 2009, 20(6), 212–217.
This article discusses whether children have a fundamental right to privacy separate from that of their parents and what happens if the parents 'waive' their children's rights in order to gain financially. Some celebrities use their children to obtain privacy via the back door. The authors ask whether any purported waiver of that privacy right is void unless it is in the child's best interests. The media should not rely on parental consent as a defence to an interference with a child's right to privacy. In any matter where a child's interests are to be considered, whether joined with adult interests or alone, the child's interests are paramount.

Deringer, K.F. (2003) 'Privacy and the press: the convergence of British and French law in accordance with the European Convention of Human Rights'. *Penn State International Law Review*, 22, Summer, 2003. Carlisle, PA: Dickinson School of Law.
The death of Diana, Princess of Wales in 1997 prompted the privacy debate in the UK. This article compares continental (mainly French and German) jurisdictions and privacy laws in the light of the European Convention on Human Rights which was just about to be incorporated in UK law via the Human Rights Act 1998.

Fenwick, H. and Phillipson, G. (2006) *Media Freedom under the Human Rights Act.* **Oxford: Oxford University Press.**
The book provides a comprehensive analysis of the conflict between Articles 8 and 10 ECHR, focusing specifically on the substantive law governing freedom of expression in the media. Key cases include: the privacy action in *von Hannover v Germany (No 1)* and *Campbell v MGN*. Strasbourg case law is critiqued, with full consideration of theoretical approaches to explicit speech and blasphemy as well as a discussion of the offence of incitement to religious hatred. The Communications Act 2003 is emphasized in the light of Prolife Alliance. The authors draw on significant comparative decisions to formulate a coherent and provocative critique of the relationship between media law and freedom of expression, suggesting principles which make a significant contribution to the legal discourse surrounding media freedom in the Human Rights Act era.

Foster, S. (2011) 'The public interest in press intrusion into the private lives of celebrities: the decision in *Ferdinand v MGN Ltd'.* *Communications Law* **16(4), 201, 127–131.**
This article discusses the decision of the High Court in *Ferdinand*, which has reopened the legal and moral debate as to whether there is, or can be, a genuine public interest in the revelation of details of the private lives of celebrities by the press. Foster looks at earlier common law under the HRA 1998 (and before), which suggested that press intrusion into the private lives of public figures and celebrities could be justified on the basis of the inevitable public interest in their activities and the consequential devaluation of their expectation of privacy. However, the House of Lords in *Campbell* thought otherwise. Foster also questions the validity of genuine public interest in the ECtHR decision in the first *von Hannover* action.

Harris, D., O'Boyle, M., Warbrick, C., Bates, E. and Buckley, C. (2009) *Law of the European Convention on Human Rights.* **2nd Edition. Oxford: Oxford University Press**.
This book facilitates an in-depth understanding of human rights law and fully explores the extent of the Convention's influence upon the legal development of the contracting Member States. The book critically examines each Article that constitutes the substantive law and scrutinizes national Parliaments and courts that apply Strasbourg jurisprudence.

Mindell, R. (2012) 'Rewriting privacy: the impact of online social networks'. *Entertainment Law Review*, 23(3), 52–58.
This article discusses the meaning of 'privacy' in English common law as the most important protection in a democratic society. The author examines how technological innovations, namely the internet and social networking sites, may well have put privacy at risk, particularly where members of Twitter and Facebook have frequently waived their right to privacy by openly

disclosing their personal details. The force of social media remains uncontrolled and may well restrain freedom of expression.

Moreham, N A. (2008) 'The right to respect for private life in the European Convention on Human Rights: a re-examination'. *European Human Rights Law Review*, 1: 44–79.
This article comprehensively analyses Strasbourg jurisprudence in interpreting Article 8, the right to private life. The article identifies five sub-categories of private life interest. First, three 'freedoms from': the right to be free from interference with physical and psychological integrity, from unwanted access to and collection of information, and from serious environmental pollution. Then there are the 'freedoms' to: the right to be free to develop one's personality and identity and to live one's life in the manner of one's choosing.

Phillipson, G. (2003) 'Breach of confidence, celebrities, freedom of expression, legal reasoning, newspapers, privacy, public interest, right to respect for private and family life'. *European Human Rights Law Review* (Special Issue on 'Privacy'), 54–72.
The article criticizes the legal reasoning applied by the Court of Appeal in *A v B Plc* in respect of two key issues around the development of a right to privacy under Article 8 ECHR. The author argues that the judgment exposes unwillingness by the court to deal with the complexities of the Convention and explores in detail: (1) the horizontal application of Article 8 in cases concerning media intrusion, and (2) the circumstances in which the public interest justification for publication may outweigh the right to respect for private life in respect of the court's approach to the question of public interest in 'public figures' and the argument about role models and the public's 'right not to be misled'.

Pillans, B. (2012) 'Private lives in St Moritz: *von Hannover v Germany (no 2)*'. *Communications Law*, 17(2), 63–67.
The article discusses both judgments by the Strasbourg Grand Chamber (*Axel Springer* and *von Hannover No 2*) where the Strasbourg court made it clear that the right to privacy has to be carefully balanced against the contribution which a publication makes to a debate of general public interest. In both cases, taking account of the nature of the individuals involved and the publications, the right to freedom of expression prevailed over the right to privacy. The author discusses the need for a careful balancing exercise in privacy cases versus Article 10 freedom of expression and popular journalism.

Smartt, U. (2011) 'Twitter undermines superinjunctions'. *Communications Law*, 16(4), 135–140.
The article discusses common law in respect of personal privacy, grounded in the equitable doctrine of breach of confidence and relevant case law (e.g. *Douglas v Hello! Ltd* (2001)). Superinjunctions are discussed in detail, with specific reference to *CTB v NGN* (2011) and *DFT v TFD* (2010). As the law has developed post the HRA 1998, it has become clear that the law no longer needs to construct an artificial relationship of confidentially between the 'impostor' and the confider. The article examines the remedies available in an action for breach of confidence which, according to common law, can vary considerably, generally left to the court's discretion as to which particular remedy to award, including (super)injunctions. The article furthers examines the way in which the disclosure of private and confidential information applies to social media networks.

Tugendhat and Christie, *The Law of Privacy and The Media* (2011) (Warby, M., Mareham, N. and Christie. I., eds) 2nd edition. Oxford: Oxford University Press.
This is a substantial leading reference work on the rapidly developing law of privacy in England and Wales compiled by a specialist team of barristers from media, entertainment and human rights chambers, many of whom appeared or advised in the leading cases which are shaping the law of privacy. The text considers how the law protects the publication of personal information without undermining the fundamental principle of freedom of expression. The text further argues that there now exists a separate tort of privacy with equitable remedy. The common law continues

to be influenced by the competing rights under Articles 8 and 10 ECHR and its concurrent Strasbourg jurisprudence and, to a lesser extent, by application of the principles established in the Data Protection Act 1998. The case law is highlighted in this text with a useful section on comparative legal and academic sources from Europe.

Warren, S. D. and Brandeis, L. D. (1890) 'The right to privacy'. *Harvard Law Review,* 4(5) (15 December 1890), 193–220.

This is a classic article by the two American lawyers, written at the end of the nineteenth century and still very much appropriate today. Warren and Brandeis developed the concept of an individual's right to privacy at the time when this was absent in (US) law, during a fast-developing technological and information-sharing age, via the telephone, tabloid journalism and photography.

Chapter 3

Defamation

Chapter Contents

Key Points

This chapter will cover the following questions:

○   How do common law and defamation legislation
    interact?
○   What is the difference between the multiple and single
    publication rule?
○   What is the meaning of 'reputation' in defamation
    actions?
○   What is the significance of 'malice' in a defamation action?
○   What are the available defences in defamation?
○   How are damages assessed?
○   Does the Defamation Act 2013 codify all existing defa-
    mation laws?
○   Is there a future for libel juries?
○   Can companies sue in defamation?
○   Do current defamation laws stifle academic and scientific
    criticism?
○   Do UK libel laws interfere with 'freedom of expression'?
○   Has the Defamation Act 2013 made a difference to libel
    tourism in the UK?

3.1 Overview

In essence, defamation law exists to provide a means of redress for someone whose reputation has
suffered unjustifiable harm by the publication of defamatory information. There is still no statutory
definition of what is 'defamatory' in English law and the new Defamation Act 2013 does not
include this in its codification either. Therefore, we are left with a continued abundance of case law
in this area of law. The courts have generally treated a statement as defamatory when it 'lowers a
person in the estimation of right-thinking members of society generally' (see: **Skuse v Granada
Television Ltd** (1996)[1]).

As the Defamation Bill 2010–11[2] progressed at a snail's pace from Lord Lester's first draft in
2010 to that championed by Minister of State for Justice Lord McNally (and his legal team), it
became clear that the Bill was set to be derailed at the last minute. Both peers had made clear that
the Defamation Bill was essential to the well-being of British democracy, that people should be free
to debate issues and challenge authorities in all spheres of public life, whether political, scientific,
academic or any other, and that the Bill should revolve around the right to freedom of speech, a
cornerstone of the UK constitution. As the Bill made its passage through the House of Lords during
the consultation period (2011–12), Lord Lester and Lord McNally ensured that freedom of speech
did not mean that people should be able to ride roughshod over the reputations of others, and that
the new defamation law ought to strike the right balance – between protection of freedom of
speech on the one hand and protection of reputation on the other.[3]

---

1   [1996] EMLR 278 at 286 (Sir Thomas Bingham MR).
2   See: Ministry of Justice (2011a).
3   Ibid., Ministerial Foreword at p. 3.

It took three years to pass the Defamation Act 2013, following an initial promise by the then Labour Justice Minister, Jack Straw, in early 2010, to reform the libel laws after a series of revelations that libel threats had silenced scientists, doctors, biographers, community lawyers, consumer groups and human rights activists. The cases of **Singh**[4] and **Flood**[5] had demonstrated the complexity and difficulties of modern English libel laws with a multifaceted substantive law and a costly procedure.

When Lord Lester of Herne Hill proposed a private member's Defamation Bill in July 2010 in the House of Lords (HL), his main aim was to assist the new Coalition Government (Conservative and Liberal Democrats) in its libel reform to reduce London's reputation as the 'libel capital of the world'; that is, to avoid litigants from other countries being able to sue parties (often also not from the UK) in the High Court in a defamatory action. Equally, he aimed to reduce the 'chilling effect on freedom of expression'[6] that had resulted from some high-profile actions involving academic criticism, such as the **Simon Singh** action. Lord McNally, the Liberal Democrat leader in the Lords and Secretary of State for Justice, continued to champion the bill through Parliament in 2011 and 2012, with an extended remit to provide the free exchange of ideas and information, whilst providing an effective and proportionate remedy to anyone whose reputation had been or could be unfairly damaged. The **Singh** case is a good example of the law of libel in action and why Parliament sought to review and reform English 'libel' laws, particularly with the predicament of claimants who might be in danger of jeopardizing their career and reputation in the name of 'freedom of expression', including academic and scientific debate.

See below 3.9

The Supreme Court (UKSC) ruling in **Flood** (2011) was significant in that the media regained their right to freedom of expression by being allowed the defence of 'qualified privilege' under the **Reynolds**[7] principle, because the report of allegations in *The Times* of police corruption was seen as being of considerable public interest. By overturning the Court of Appeal judgment of 2010, the Supreme Court Justices finally allowed the newspaper to claim the **Reynolds** defence of 'qualified privilege', after reporting that a police officer, DS Gary Flood, might have taken bribes. The **Reynolds** defence protects publications on matters of public concern that result from responsible journalism. On the naming of DS Gary Flood, Lord Dyson said:

See below 3.5.1

> The court should be slow to interfere with an exercise of editorial judgment and would hold on that ground too that the naming of the individual was justified in this case . . .
>
> It is unlawful to publish the details of an accusation of criminal conduct regardless of the public interest in the subject-matter of the article and the other circumstances of the case; this is bound to have a 'chilling' effect on investigative journalism of this type. This is undesirable in a democratic society.[8]

The **Flood** ruling marked the end of a six-year legal battle that began with an article by Michael Gillard on 2 June 2006 in *The Times* (and its online edition) headed 'Detective accused of taking bribes from Russian exiles'. Sergeant Flood sued *The Times* for libel, arguing that the article wrongly alleged that there were strong grounds to believe that Flood had abused his position as a police officer and had accepted bribes from a private security company acting for a Russian oligarch. Tugendhat J had ruled in the High Court in 2009 that the newspaper could use the **Reynolds** defence,

---

4 *British Chiropractic Association (BCA) v Singh* [2010] EWCA Civ 350.
5 *Flood v Times Newspapers Ltd* [2011] UKSC 11.
6 Source: Press release by the Ministry of Justice on 9 July 2010.
7 *Reynolds v Times Newspapers Ltd* [2001] 2 AC 127.
8 *Flood v Times Newspapers Ltd* [2011] UKSC 11 at paras 193–199 (Lord Dyson).

but the Court of Appeal overturned the ruling in 2010. The UKSC ruling crucially meant that the truth of the allegations did not have to be proved as long as the matter was of serious public concern and the journalistic practices had been responsible (the so-called 'responsible journalism test') (see also: *Spiller and another v Joseph and others* [2010][9]).

Academic critics, such as Mullis and Scott (2009), expressed initial concern about the reforms proposed by Lord Lester's 'Libel Bill'. They argued that the draft Defamation Bill was too indiscriminate and remarkably one-sided, stating:

> . . . we are nervous that the important societal functions performed by libel law have been underplayed. Libel reform should be coherent, not piecemeal and un(der)principled.[10]

Milo (2008: 5ff) argued further that the law of defamation was outdated and conflicted with freedom of expression under Article 10 ECHR and possibly a person's right to a fair trial under Article 6 of the Convention.

Following the publication of the Leveson Report in November 2012, legislative fall-out from the Leveson Inquiry with its proposed Royal Charter became inextricably linked with the draft Defamation Bill which had been nearing its completion in February 2013. Lord Justice Leveson had suggested that the Defamation Bill be amended to include a system of press regulation. Leveson further suggested that news organizations that declined to co-operate with a new regulator should be liable for all costs in libel and privacy cases, even when they won, and that politicians and officials should be entitled to curb media reporting, provided 'it is for a legitimate purpose and is necessary in a democratic society'.[11]

Additionally, the 'Hacked Off' pressure group had given a clear indication to Parliament during the consultation stages of the Bill that press regulation should be included in the draft Defamation Bill, spurred by the disclosures during the Leveson Inquiry into the unedifying ethics of segments of the press: the harassment and abuse of Kate and Gerry McCann after the disappearance of their daughter Madeleine, the turmoil suffered by Chris Jefferies after he was wrongly accused of the murder of Joanna Yeates, the tales of celebrities and private individuals whose voicemails were hacked – all of which had revealed a reckless press in which a small section such as the *News of the World* had been out of control, showing an indifference to morality and the rule of law.

The 'Leveson clause' was introduced by Labour Lord and former film producer Lord Puttnam, in early February 2013, and looked set to sabotage the Defamation Bill, with Prime Minister David Cameron arguing that this was press regulation by the back door. For Labour, which favoured statutory regulation of the press, this was a way to kill two 'media' birds with one legislative stone. In fact, for a while it looked as if the Defamation Bill was totally dead. In a last-minute attempt to quell the revolt in the House of Lords[12] Lord McNally promised the much-discussed government proposal for a Royal Charter to oversee press regulation in order to save the long-awaited defamation legislation.

See also
Chapter 10.4

During a House of Lords debate on the Bill on 24 March 2013, Tory peer and Executive Director of the Telegraph Media Group Lord Black of Brentwood condemned proposals to allow courts to impose exemplary damages on newspapers who lost libel cases as 'shotgun legislation' that would create 'a constitutional nightmare'. He called the Puttnam amendment to the bill wrong in principle and fundamentally flawed, and said that the Bill was there to reform Britain's 'libel laws'

---

9   [2010] UKSC 53.
10 See: Mullis and Scott (2009), pp. 173–183.
11 Source: Leveson Report (2012), Volume 4, Part K, 'Regulatory Models for the Future', at para 15.3, pp. 1703–1704. For a full set of recommendations see: ibid., pp. 1584–1594.
12 The rebellion in the House of Lords included prominent Tories such as Lord Fowler, Lord Hurd and Lord Ashcroft, as well as more than 60 crossbenchers including Baroness O'Neill (the chair of the Equalities and Human Rights Commission) and former Speaker of the House of Commons Baroness Boothroyd.

rather than to address the Leveson recommendations on press regulation. The two were completely different matters, dealing with different problems.[13] When the draft Defamation Bill returned to the House of Commons in April 2013, Prime Minister David Cameron challenged the Puttnam clause, which, he argued, placed an immovable obstacle in the path of those who hoped to shepherd the Leveson Report quietly and unremarked into long grass. Just before the end of the Parliamentary session, a compromise was reached between the parties after the Bill had ping-ponged through Parliament and on 25 April 2013 the Defamation Act 2013 finally received Royal Assent. Justice Minister Lord McNally announced to Parliament:

> . . . this Act represents the end of a long and hard fought battle to reform the libel laws in England and Wales. Throughout the process all parties have listened and worked together to produce legislation that delivers the reforms required in the 21st century. Everyone involved can be rightly proud of this Act and the protections and freedoms it offers.[14]

3.1.1 What is defamation?

Defamation cases often 'lift the carpet' on things people want kept out of public view. It is fair to say that the media thrives on gossip stories about celebrities, trying to find any given opportunity to expose the lives of famous people and the royals. Nearly fifty years ago Diplock LJ referred to 'the artificial and archaic character of the tort of libel' in **Slim v Daily Telegraph Ltd**.[15] So, has anything changed with recent updated defamation laws?

In **Brent Walker Group plc v Time Out Ltd**[16] Parker LJ commented on the absurdity of the 'tangled web of the law of defamation'. It is fair to say that until the Defamation Act 2013 there has been little statutory reform other than the Defamation Act 1996, which introduced the out-of-court settlement in the form of the 'offer to make amends', under s 2 of the 1996 Act, intended to speed up the process and keep defamation matters out of court.

There are two types of defamation: libel, when the defamatory statement is in writing (also including broadcasting); and slander, when it is spoken. Material is libellous where it is communicated in a permanent form or broadcast, or forms part of a theatrical performance. If the material is spoken or takes some other transient form, then it is classed as slander. Whether material is defamatory is a matter for the courts to determine. If it is a publication which is in a permanent form, such as a book, magazine or film, then it is libel. Here follows a summary of the definition of defamation as established in common law:

Definition of defamation

- An imputation which is likely to lower the person in the estimation of right-thinking people;
- An imputation which injures a person's reputation, by exposing them to hatred, contempt or ridicule;
- An imputation which intends to make a person be shunned or avoided.

---

13 Source: 'Press regulation: Lord Black attacks exemplary damages plans', by Lisa O'Carroll, *Guardian*, 25 March 2013.
14 Source: Press release 'Defamation Act reforms libel law', Lord McNally, Ministry of Justice, 25 April 2013.
15 [1968] 2 QB 157.
16 [1991] 2 QB 33.

The statement has to lower the claimant in the estimation of right-thinking members of society. If the statement affects only a limited group but not society in general then it would not be defamatory. An insult or vulgar abuse is not considered to be defamatory because generally it is not considered likely to lower the reputation of the claimant in the estimation of right-thinking members of society.

Until recently, defamation claims have been heard in the civil courts (county or High Court) by 'libel' juries. This changed with the Defamation Act 2013. Section 11 of the 2013 Act ('Trial to be without a jury unless the court orders otherwise') removed the presumption in favour of jury trial in defamation cases.

The law of defamation recognizes two types of meaning:

- **Natural and ordinary meaning of the words:** this is not limited to the literal and obvious meaning but includes any inference which the ordinary, reasonable reader would draw from the words.
- **Innuendo meaning:** there are two types of innuendo meaning:

  (a) **false innuendo:** an alternative meaning which the ordinary reasonable person can read between the lines or infer from the words.
  (b) **true innuendo:** where the words appear to be innocent to some people but appear to be defamatory to others because they have special knowledge or extra information. An example of this would be the *Sally Bercow*[17] case.

Publication (libel)

Words need to be published to a third party. Section 5 of the Defamation Act 2013 provides a defence to persons who are not authors, editors or commercial publishers of websites if they take reasonable care in the publication and did not know or had any reason to believe that what they had inadvertently contributed to the publication (online) of a defamatory statement. This covers printers, distributors, online device providers etc. An internet service provider (ISP) who provides news content is not deemed to have behaved in a defamatory manner. If, however, once notified of the offending material the provider fails to remove the defamatory material (words or phrases), then the ISP is deemed not to have acted reasonably and the above defence would then not be available (see: *Godfrey v Demon Internet* (2001);[18] *Tamiz (Payam) v Google Inc, Google UK Ltd* (2012)[19]).

Identification

The claimant must show that the defamatory statement referred to him, which is normally not too difficult. If the claimant is not identified by name, then he has to show that the words complained of are understood by some readers to be referring to him.

Juxtaposition

Although a statement may be quite innocent, it can become defamatory in relation to the article if read as a whole or if placed next to a picture, as was the issue in the *Petters*[20] case, where solicitor Leigh Petters appeared in a Channel 5 Quiz Show called *Brainteaser*, filmed in Bristol. Mr Petters had beaten the other

---

17 *Lord McAlpine of West Green v Sally Bercow* [2013] EWHC 1342 (QB); (Lord Alistair McAlpine of West Green 1942–2014).
18 [2001] QB 201.
19 [2012] EWHC 449 (QB).
20 *Petters (Leigh) v BBC*, 22 October 2007 (unreported).

three contestants to get through to the final round, which he then won together with prize money. On 8 March 2007, Channel 5 disclosed that there had been irregularities in the way in which *Brainteaser* had been run. In particular, it was revealed that on five occasions, when no member of the public had phoned in, the production company had put up the names of fictional winners and in one case a member of the production team went on air pretending to be the winner. Channel 5 suspended the programme and issued a statement apologizing unreservedly to viewers. In June 2009, Ofcom fined Channel 5 £300,000 for the irregularities on *Brainteaser* and the show was axed.

The discovery of these irregularities on *Brainteaser* formed the subject of reports on news bulletins on BBC One News at 6pm and 10pm and BBC News 24 at 6pm, 7pm, 8pm, 9pm, 10pm, 11pm and midnight on 8 March 2007. The story also featured prominently on *Newsnight* on BBC Two that evening and was again referred to in a subsequent edition of *Newsnight* on 14 March. These news reports all featured library footage of *Brainteaser* which showed Mr Petters taking part in the quiz. He was variously shown on his own on several occasions and with other contestants. Mr Petters claimed that the juxtaposition of these pictures of him with the reports of the quiz irregularities were defamatory of him. He sued the BBC in libel, claiming that viewers would have understood that he was in fact involved in the *Brainteaser* scam. This allegation was untrue. Mr Petters had taken part in the *Brainteaser* quiz show in good faith and he had won it fairly. The BBC settled out of court with a published and broadcast apology, stating that there was no question of him having pretended to be a winner or of him having in any way been complicit in any kind of deception or 'scam'.[21] In short, the juxtaposition of pictures with the report including Leigh Petters were deemed defamatory and he won damages of £60,000 from the BBC and Channel 5.

In February 2012 a week-long libel trial between the multi-millionaire financier Nat Rothschild[22] and the *Daily Mail* offered an intimate glimpse into the lives of the politically powerful and super-rich (see below). Journalists reporting on the case revealed a rare insight into 'how the other half lives', involving the then EU Trade Commissioner Lord Mandelson, billionaire Russian industrialist Oleg Deripaska and Rothschild. The paper had reported that Rothschild had taken Lord Mandelson on a trip to Moscow and Siberia to impress a key business contact, exposing Lord Mandelson to allegations of a conflict of interest.

❖ KEY CASE	*Rothschild (the Hon. Nathaniel Philip Victor James) v Associated Newspapers Ltd* [2012] EWHC 177 (QB)

Precedent
❖   It is a complete defence to a defamatory action that the words complained of are true.
❖   The meaning of a defamatory statement must be understood as such by a hypothetical reasonable reader.

Facts
The claimant, Mr Rothschild, sued the defendant newspaper publishers, Associated Newspapers Ltd (ANL), for libel on the article headed: 'EXCLUSIVE: Mandelson, an oligarch and a £500m deal', published on Saturday 22 May 2010. The article was described as a 'special investigation', and extended over the front page and pages 2, 8 and 9 of that

---

21   Source: 'Mr Leigh Petters – An apology', *BBC News Online*, 22 October 2007.
22   [2012] EWHC 177 (QB).

issue. The headline on page 9 read: 'Revealed: the astonishing story of the night Lord Mandelson was flown to Moscow by private jet to join a billionaire friend desperate to strike a deal that cost British jobs'.

Decision

Tugendhat J found that some elements in the *Daily Mail* article were incorrect and that the paper had withdrawn the claim that Mr Rothschild facilitated Lord Mandelson's attendance at a dinner at a Moscow restaurant which sealed a £500m deal involving aluminium plants owned by Mr Deripaska (Lord Mandelson had responsibility at the time for EU metals tariffs). But the judge said Mr Rothschild should have known that Lord Mandelson's travelling from Moscow to Siberia on Deripaska's private jet and staying at the tycoon's chalet would give 'at the very least reasonable grounds' for confusion, as outlined in the EU Commissioners' Code of Conduct. The *Daily Mail* argued that Rothschild's conduct was 'inappropriate in a number of respects'.

In deciding whether the words complained of bore a defamatory meaning, which, read by a reasonable person, would amount to libellous allegations, the court stated that it was not concerned with what the writer or publisher intended, nor with what any actual reader may have understood. Tugendhat J said that there must be a single meaning, 'that is a meaning which the court finds would be understood by the hypothetical reasonable reader' (see also: **Slim v Daily Telegraph** (1968)[23]).

In deciding what meaning that reader would attribute to the words complained of, the court applied the well-known test, cited more recently by Sir Anthony Clarke MR in **Jeynes v News Magazines Ltd** (2008)[24] as:

> The legal principles relevant to meaning . . . may be summarised in this way:
>
> 1. The governing principle is reasonableness.
> 2. The hypothetical reasonable reader is not naïve but he is not unduly suspicious. He can read between the lines. He can read in an implication more readily than a lawyer and may indulge in a certain amount of loose thinking but he must be treated as being a man who is not avid for scandal and someone who does not, and should not, select one bad meaning where other non-defamatory meanings are available.
> 3. Over-elaborate analysis is best avoided.
> 4. The intention of the publisher is irrelevant.
> 5. The article must be read as a whole, and any 'bane and antidote' taken together.
> 6. The hypothetical reader is taken to be representative of those who would read the publication in question.
> 7. . . . the court should rule out any meaning which 'can only emerge as the produce of some strained, or forced, or utterly unreasonable interpretation . . .
> 8. It follows that it is not enough to say that by some person or another the words might be understood in a defamatory sense.

---

23 [1968] 2 QB 157.
24 [2008] EWCA Civ 130 (Sir Anthony Clarke MR)

Tugendhat J concluded:

> In my judgment, that conduct foreseeably brought Lord Mandelson's public office and personal integrity into disrepute and exposed him to accusations of conflict of interest, and it gave rise to the reasonable grounds to suspect that Lord Mandelson had engaged in improper discussions with Mr Deripaska about aluminium.

The court held that ANL had established that the words complained of by Mr Rothschild were substantially true (notwithstanding the admitted inaccuracies); that the allegation – that the purpose of the visit to Moscow was for Lord Mandelson to assist in the closing of the Alcoa deal by discussing tariffs – was so serious that it precluded the finding that the court made, namely that the facts surrounding the trip to Siberia for the joint venture proved that the meaning of the article was substantially true.

Analysis
The general principle is that it is a complete defence to an action for libel that the words complained of are substantially and materially true.[25] Though ANL were able to prove only part of the defamatory allegations made against Mr Rothschild, the law is clear in that a defendant may nevertheless succeed if he can prove, on the balance of probabilities, that what he has alleged is substantially true (see: *Sutherland v Stopes* (1925);[26] *Maisel v Financial Times Ltd* (1915)[27]).

It is important to note that a preliminary ruling can be sought from the judge, who has to decide whether the words are legally capable of being defamatory, to avoid the expense of a full trial. If the judge rules that the words are capable of being defamatory, if there is a jury, the jury will decide as a matter of fact whether in the particular context the words are actually defamatory.

3.1.2 Libel or slander?
We have already established that slander involves the spoken word. The difference between claims for libel and claims for slander is that a claimant must prove some damage (i.e. economic loss) to succeed in a slander action. In a libel claim a claimant does not have to prove that they have suffered loss or damage as a result of the publication, as opposed to a claim in slander where the party must prove actual damage. However, there are exceptions to this: if those spoken words accuse a claimant of committing a crime or being unfit for his job, then in those situations damage is presumed and need not be proved.

In *Westcott v Westcott* (2009)[28] Richard Westcott sought damages for slander and libel as well as an injunction to restrain further publication against his daughter-in-law, the defendant Sarah Westcott, over allegations which she had made about him during an interview with the police. After a heated family argument, Mrs Westcott had telephoned the police and claimed in an oral and written statement that Mr Westcott, her father-in-law, had assaulted her and her baby. But the police decided to take no further action. Mr Westcott then sued Sarah Westcott for defamation. It was held

---

25 See ss 5 ('Justification') and 6 ('Fair Comment') Defamation Act 1952.
26 [1925] AC 47.
27 (1915) 84 LJKB 2145.
28 [2009] QB 407; [2009] 2 WLR 838.

that the police investigation and proceedings were protected by absolute privilege. The Court of Appeal in Westcott relied on *Taylor*,[29] establishing that immunity for out-of-court statements was not confined to persons who were subsequently called as witnesses. The policy of 'absolute privilege' was therefore applied and extended to police investigations, enabling people to speak freely, without inhibition and without fear of being sued.

See below 3.5

A defamatory publication is usually in words, but pictures, gestures and other acts, such as a tweet, a blog or a cartoon, can also be defamatory – as the *Sally Bercow*[30] case proved.

Section 14 of the Defamation Act 2013[31] provides for special damage for slander. Some special damage must be proved to flow from the statement complained of unless the publication falls into certain specific categories. The publication of a statement that conveys the imputation that a person has a contagious or infectious disease no longer gives rise to a cause of action for slander unless the publication causes the person special damage.[32]

See also
Chapter 1.3.4

3.2 History of defamation law

This section is primarily concerned with the common law development of the tort of defamation and the protection of an individual's reputation. It is assumed that most readers will be familiar with the substantive common law in this area and the end of this chapter suggests some wider reading for more in-depth study of the tort law of defamation. Defamation is substantially governed by common law plus statutory intervention, namely the Defamation Acts of 1952, 1996 and 2013. The 'offer of amends' to speed up matters in the courts and to encourage the parties to settle was introduced with the 1996 Act by way of an apology and damages.[33]

3.2.1 General framework of common law

People have been fascinated by high-profile defamation cases for more than three hundred years and the civil law has developed through the common law tradition over hundreds of years, periodically being supplemented by statute, most 'recently' by the Defamation Acts of 1952 and 1996 and finally by the 2013 Act.

Defamation is the collective term for libel and slander, and occurs when a person communicates material to a third party, in words or any other form, containing an untrue imputation against the reputation of a claimant. As Lord Atkin defined it:

> Defamation is a publication of an untrue statement about a person that tends to lower his reputation in the opinion of 'right-thinking members of the community' (*Sim v Stretch* (1936)[34]).

See below
3.2.7

Clement Gatley famously said in his textbook on *Libel and Slander* in the 1930s: everyone has a reputation.[35]

---

29 *Taylor v Director of the Serious Fraud Office* [1999] 2 AC 177 (HL).
30 *Lord McAlpine of West Green v Sally Bercow* [2013] EWHC 1342 (QB).
31 Section 14 (1) repeals the Slander of Women Act 1891 and overturns a common law rule relating to special damage; the provision in the 1891 Act which provides that 'words spoken and published . . . which impute unchastity or adultery to any woman or girl shall not require special damage to render them actionable'.
32 In case law dating from the ninteenth century and earlier, this applied to imputations of leprosy, venereal disease and the plague.
33 For further discussion see: Gibbons (1996).
34 [1936] 2 All ER 1237 (Lord Atkin).
35 Now edited by Rogers and Parkes and in its 12th edition (2013).

3.2.2 Exposure to hatred and ridicule: common law development

The basis of the tort of defamation is injury to reputation, so it must be proved that the statement was communicated to someone other than the person defamed – a third party – because it can reasonably be assumed that a third party may well communicate the information independently of the author of it. If the statement is not obviously defamatory, the claimant must show that it would be understood in a defamatory sense, such as by some innuendo. It is not necessary to prove that the defendant intended to refer to the claimant. The test is whether reasonable people would think the statement referred to him. Professor Winfield gave the widely accepted definition of a defamatory statement:

> . . . [one which] tends to lower a person in the estimation of right thinking members of society generally; or which tends to make them shun or avoid that person.[36]

The main tests established by the courts in deciding whether material is defamatory are whether the words used 'tend to lower the claimant in the estimation of right-thinking members of society generally',[37] 'without justification or lawful excuse [are] calculated to injure the reputation of another, by exposing him to hatred, contempt, or ridicule',[38] or tend to make the claimant 'be shunned and avoided and that without any moral discredit on [the claimant's] part'.[39]

There is an abundance of case law where a claimant has been the subject of a comical or satirical portrayal subjecting him or her to ridicule or contempt (see: Dunlop Rubber Co. Ltd v Dunlop (1921)[40]; Hulton v Jones (1910)[41]). A typical example arose where the claimant Mrs Victoria Gillick asserted that she would be ridiculed, shunned and avoided during her anti-contraceptive campaign throughout the 1980s. A mother of 10, Mrs Gillick later appeared on a live BBC TV chat show and during the programme it was implied that she was morally responsible for the deaths of pregnant girls, following her campaign through the 1980s to prevent doctors from giving contraceptive advice to under-16-year-old girls without their parents' consent (see: **Gillick v BBC** (1996)[42]).

3.2.3 The single publication rule

One historic relic in defamation law was the long-standing principle that each republication of a defamatory statement or broadcast gave rise to a separate cause of action which was subject to its own limitation period. This was known as the 'multiple publication rule', based on a Victorian-era doctrine known as the 'Duke of Brunswick' principle (see: **Brunswick v Harmer** (1849)[43]).

The central character in the **Brunswick** case was an exiled German ruler, Karl II.[44] In 1848, the Duke sent a servant to procure a copy of an article which had been published in 1830, containing an alleged defamatory statement about the Duke. The statement had been known to him since its original publication. Clearly, the then six-year limitation period for bringing an action for defamation had expired, but still, the Duke sent his servant to procure copies of the offending article and brought defamation proceedings for injury to his reputation. After obtaining a fresh copy of the

---

36 Winfield (1937).
37 *Sim v Stretch* [1936] 2 All ER 1237 (Lord Atkin).
38 *Parmiter v Coupland* (1840) 6 M & W 105 at 108 (Lord Wensleydale; then Parke B).
39 *Youssoupoff v MGM Pictures Ltd* (1934) 50 TLR 581 at 587 (Slesser LJ).
40 [1921] 1 AC 367 (HL).
41 *Hulton (E) & Co. v Jones* [1910] AC 20 (HL). [1910] AC 20 (HL).
42 [1996] EMLR 267 (CA); see also: *Gillick v Department of Health and Social Security* [1986] AC 112 (HL).
43 [1849] 14 QB 185.
44 Official title: Herzog zu Braunschweig-Lüneburg-Wolfenbüttel.

said article from the London publishers, the Duke promptly sued on the basis that he had the original copy and a fresh copy of the article, thereby suing for republication. The Queen's Bench held that the act of procuring the 'fresh' article by the Duke amounted to a new publication of a libel, giving rise to a fresh cause of action in respect of each article; and that was in spite of the fact that there was a statute in place which limited the bringing of such a civil action to six years. The court held that publisher Harmer's back issue of the offending publication in 1848 constituted a separate act of publication and was therefore within the statutory time limit. The new action commenced at the point in time when the publication was received, rather than the date of its original printing and distribution 17 years previously.

Astonishingly, the **Brunswick** ruling on re- and multiple publication still governed the UK defamation laws until it was challenged more recently in the courts. Kirby J criticized the doctrine in **Dow Jones & Co Inc v Gutnick**,[45] where he said that the open-ended liability for publishers made the limitation period pointless in the internet (archive) age. Every time the defamatory material was accessed online, the 'stopwatch runs anew from zero'.[46] Jordan (2010a: 41–47) argues that this open-ended liability amounts to a chilling effect on free speech, which goes beyond UK borders. Balin *et al.* (2009) argue that the mere fact that a few English readers access via the internet defamatory material published in the USA is enough for a potential defamatory libel action to be brought to the UK courts.[47]

The old **Duke of Brunswick** principle of republication was upheld in a range of internet cases, such as the HL ruling in **Berezovsky v Michaels** (2000)[48] or the CA ruling in respect of archived online material in **Loutchansky v Times**,[49] although the latter was regarded as a controversial judgment. The effect of the **Brunswick** doctrine was that each individual access to an alleged libellous publication could potentially give rise to a separate cause of action, with a separate limitation period attached to it – particularly acute in actions concerning internet archives (though the limitation period was changed under s 4A of the Limitation Act 1980 to one year in which an action could be brought (see below – s 8(6) Defamation Act 2013).

Each separate publication, however, was subject to the one-year limitation period and running from the time at which the material was accessed. A defendant was also liable if he was a 'secondary publisher' and could not use the defence contained in s 1 of the Defamation Act 1996. **Loutchansky** highlighted the serious restrictions on press freedom under Article 10 ECHR implied in the multiple publication rule, and unsuccessfully claimed the necessity of applying the approach taken in the USA where the single publication rule limitation period runs from the first internet posting.[50]

Section 8 of the Defamation Act 2013[51] introduced a *single publication rule* to prevent an action being brought in relation to publication of the same material by the same publisher after a one-year limitation period from the date of the first publication of that material to the public or a section of the public. This replaces the long-standing **Brunswick** principle that each publication of defamatory material gives rise to a separate cause of action which is subject to its own limitation period (the 'multiple publication rule'). This measure underpins freedom of speech under Article 10 ECHR by providing far greater protection to publishers. It equally safeguards the right to reputation since the court has discretion to extend the one-year time period whenever it is just to do so. The new rule applies only to material that is 'substantially the same' as the original publication.

---

45 [2002] CLR 575.
46 Ibid., at para 92 (Kirby J).
47 Balin, Handman and Reid (2009) at pp. 303–331.
48 [2000] 1 WLR 1004.
49 *Loutchansky v Times Newspapers Ltd (nos 2–5)* [2001] EWCA Civ 1805.
50 [2002] 1 All ER at p. 312.
51 Section 8, clause 6(2)–(5).

Specifically, s 8(1) of the Defamation Act 2013 ('single publication rule') indicates that the provisions apply where a person publishes a statement to the public (defined in subsection (2) as including publication to a section of the public), and subsequently publishes that statement or a statement which is substantially the same. The definition in subsection (2) is intended to ensure that publications to a limited number of people are covered (for example where a blog has a small group of subscribers or followers). Section 8(1) reads:

1.   This section applies if a person—

   (a)   publishes a statement to the public ('the first publication'), and
   (b)   subsequently publishes (whether or not to the public) that statement or a statement which is substantially the same.

The aim of s 8(1) is to ensure that the provisions catch publications which have the same content, or content which has changed very little so that the essence of the defamatory statement is not substantially different from that contained in the earlier publication. Publication to the public has been selected as the trigger point because it is from this point on that problems are generally encountered with internet publications, and in order to stop the new provision catching limited publications leading up to publication to the public at large.

Section 8(3) of the 2013 Act has the effect of ensuring that the limitation period in relation to any cause of action brought in respect of a subsequent publication within the scope of this section is treated as having started to run on the date of the first publication. It specifically will not apply to material that is published in a 'materially different manner', taking into account the level of prominence and extent of the subsequent republication.

Section 8(4) provides that the single publication rule does not apply where the manner of the subsequent publication of the statement is 'materially different' from the manner of the first publication.

Section 8(5) provides that in deciding this issue the matters to which the court may have regard include the level of prominence given to the statement and the extent of the subsequent publication. A possible example of this could be where a story has first appeared relatively obscurely in a section of a website where several clicks need to be gone through to access it, but has subsequently been promoted to a position where it can be directly accessed from the home page of the site, thereby increasing considerably the number of hits it receives (see: **Budu v BBC** (2010)[52]).

Section 8(6) confirms that the section does not affect the court's discretion under s 32A Limitation Act 1980 to allow a defamation action to proceed outside the one-year limitation period where it is equitable to do so. It also ensures that the reference in subsection (1)(a) of s 32A to the operation of s 4A of the 1980 Act[53] is interpreted as a reference to the operation of s 4A together with s 8 of the Defamation Act 2013. Section 32A provides a broad discretion which requires the court to have regard to all the circumstances of the case, and it is envisaged that this will provide a safeguard against injustice in relation to the application of any limitation issue arising under this section.

Arguably, the new *single publication rule* under s 8 of the 2013 Act may have been drafted too narrowly. While it protects the individual who originally published the material once the one-year period has expired, it does not protect anyone else who republishes the same material in a similar manner later. For instance, an online archive that publishes material written by someone else could be sued successfully, even though the original author could no longer be pursued for continuing to

---

52   [2010] EWHC 616 of 23 March 2010 (QB).
53   Section 4A concerns the time limit applicable for defamation actions.

make the material available to readers. A publisher who republishes material previously published by a different person will similarly be exposed. It is argued further that the single publication rule should protect anyone who republishes the same material in a similar manner after it has been in the public domain for more than one year. The law is also not clear on merely transferring a paper-based publication onto the internet, or vice versa; does this amount to republication which is in a 'materially different' manner? Would this undermine the usefulness of the single publication rule? The answer will lie in the courts' interpretation of s 8 of the 2013 Act.

3.2.4 On whom lies the burden of proof?

In 1997, the *Daily Mail* printed a controversial front page referring to the killing of Stephen Lawrence in 1993 in south-east London, and the subsequent campaign in which the original five suspects were not brought to justice. The front page of 14 February 1997 became famous for its 'Murderers' headline, under which the newspaper printed photographs of the five men suspected of Stephen Lawrence's murder, declaring, 'The *Mail* accuses these men of killing. If we are wrong, let them sue us.' In its subsequent campaign over the Stephen Lawrence murder case, the *Daily Mail* reprinted the front page in July 2006 after new evidence emerged in the case. Suffice it to say, the five suspects never sued the paper in defamation, and in January 2012 Gary Dobson and David Norris were convicted of Lawrence's racist murder. Gary Dobson was sentenced at the Old Bailey to a minimum of 15 years and two months' and David Norris to 14 years and three months' imprisonment because both had been under 18 at the time of the killing.

Libel cases are notoriously expensive and – in spite of the Human Rights Court ruling in 'McLibel' in 2005[54] that certain defendants in defamation cases ought to qualify for legal aid – the law in this respect has not changed. Some claimants have thought they warranted higher libel damages than anticipated. It is relatively rare for individuals to defend a libel case successfully against a big corporation as the 'McLibel Two', gardener Helen Steel and postman David Morris, found during their seven-year action against McDonald's. Steel and Morris were found guilty in 1997 of libelling the world's largest hamburger corporation in a leaflet campaign issued by London Greenpeace. The 'McLibel Two' spent 314 days in the High Court defending themselves because defamation actions do not warrant legal aid. McDonald's were awarded £60,000 in damages (later reduced to £40,000 on appeal). The ECtHR ruled that Steel and Morris did not have a fair trial under Article 6 ECHR, because of the lack of legal aid available to libel defendants in the UK, and that their freedom of expression had been violated by the 1997 High Court judgment.[55]

It is common that a claimant in civil law has to prove his case to succeed at trial. Not so in a defamation action: here the claimant claims that a publication is false and the defendant has to prove the statement at the heart of the case is true. It seems ironic that the defendant's burden of proof was originally established to protect a person's honour and that this ancient common law principle has since been used in favour of libel claimants in the British courts. However, the Defamation Act 2013 requires under s 1 that there must be 'serious harm' to the reputation of the claimant as a primary requirement. Otherwise the statement (or 'sting of the libel') is not regarded as defamatory.

In 1998, *Coronation Street* actor William (Bill) Roache – who plays Ken Barlow in the popular soap opera – sued his lawyers Peter Carter-Ruck for negligence over its handling of his libel action against the *Sun* in 1992.[56] Mr Roache won his libel action over a claim in November 1990 that he

---

54 *Steel and Morris v United Kingdom* [2005] (Application no 68416/01); judgment of 15 February 2005 (ECHR).
55 Ibid.
56 *Roache v Newsgroup Newspapers Ltd* [1998] EMLR 161.

was as boring as his screen character and hated by his television colleagues. The defendants (News Group Newspapers Ltd, editor Kelvin Mackenzie and freelance journalist Ken Irwin) pleaded 'fair comment' and, to a limited extent, justification. They paid first £25,000 and then a further £25,000 into court, but Mr Roache did not accept the amount of damages, arguing that £50,000 would not cover his six-figure court costs. He had expected at least £100,000. The appeal judge looked closely at the facts of the 'Bill Roache' case and asked: 'Who, as a matter of substance and reality, has won? Has the plaintiff won anything of value which he could not have won without fighting the action through to the finish? Has the defendant substantially denied the plaintiff the prize which the plaintiff fought the action to win?'

Sir Thomas Bingham MR said that two important principles were relevant here. The first was that costs normally followed the event, the winner recovering his costs from the loser. The second was that where a plaintiff claimed a financial remedy and the defendant paid into a court a sum, not accepted by the plaintiff, equal to or greater than the plaintiff recovered in the action, the plaintiff should pay the defendant's costs from the date of payment in. Consequently, the Court of Appeal allowed the defendant newspaper's appeal. A year later, in 1999, Mr Roache had to declare himself bankrupt with debts of around £300,000 after suing not only the Sun for libel but also his lawyers.

Another litigant who was virtually bankrupted through his libel action was self-professed 'Third Reich' specialist David Irving, who has consistently denied the Holocaust. In **Irving v Penguin Books Ltd and Deborah Lipstadt** (1996),[57] Irving lost his lengthy libel action against American academic Deborah Lipstadt and her publishers Penguin. Lipstadt said in her 1994 book that Irving had misinterpreted historical evidence to minimize Hitler's culpability in the Holocaust.[58] Gray J – sitting without a jury (because the bulk of evidential material produced by Mr Irving was in German) – ruled that Mr Irving was 'an active Holocaust denier, anti-Semitic and racist' who had 'distorted historical data to suit his own ideological agenda'.[59]

Still, not much has changed with the new libel laws: the burden of proving that the material is defamatory still lies with the claimant, though the claimant is not required to show that the material is false.

3.2.5 Truth

Section 2 of the Defamation Act 2013 ('Truth') replaces the common law defence of justification with a new statutory defence of truth. Section 2(1) reads:

> It is a defence to an action for defamation for the defendant to show that the imputation conveyed by the statement complained of is substantially true.

Section 2(1) Defamation Act 2013 provides for the new defence to apply where the defendant can show that the imputation conveyed by the statement complained of is substantially true. This subsection reflects common law as established in the case of **Chase v News Group Newspapers Ltd** (2002),[60] where the Court of Appeal indicated that in order for the defence of justification to be available, 'the defendant does not have to prove that every word he or she published was true. He or she has to establish the "essential" or "substantial" truth of the sting of the libel.'[61] There remains a rebuttable presumption that this is the case and it is for the defendant to prove otherwise.

---

57 (1996) judgment of 11 April 2000 (QBD) (unreported).
58 See: Lipstadt (1994).
59 Lipstadt (2006), quoting Gray J at p. 214.
60 [2002] EWCA Civ 1772.
61 Ibid., at para 34.

Section 2 (1) of the 2013 Act focuses on the imputation conveyed by the defamatory statement and raises two questions:

> 1. What imputation is actually conveyed by the statement; and
> 2. Whether the imputation conveyed is substantially true.

The defence of 'truth' will apply where the imputation is one of fact.

Sections 2(2) and (3) of the 2013 Act replace s 5 of the Defamation Act 1952 (the only significant element of the defence of 'justification'). Their effect is that where the statement complained of contains two or more distinct imputations, the defence does not fail if, having regard to the imputations which are shown to be substantially true, those which are not shown to be substantially true do not seriously harm the claimant's reputation. These provisions are intended to have the same effect as those in s 5 of the 1952 Act, but are expressed in more modern terminology. The phrase 'materially injure' used in the 1952 Act is replaced by 'seriously harm' to ensure consistency with the test in s 1 of the 2013 Act.

For an action to be successful, not only does the meaning of the material complained of have to be defamatory, the statement (or 'imputation') must refer to the claimant and must have been communicated to a third party. This effectively means the claimant does not have to do anything except make an application to the court; the onus is then on the party defending the claim to ensure the statement is substantially true (unlike in 'ordinary' civil or criminal matters where 'he who alleges must prove').

Section 2(4) abolishes the common law defence of 'justification' and repeals s 5 of the 1952 Act. This means that where a defendant wishes to rely on the new statutory defence, the court will be required to apply the words used in the statute (i.e. *not* case law). Only in cases where uncertainty arises will existing case law constitute a helpful but not binding guide to interpreting how the new statutory defence of 'truth' should be applied.

3.2.6 Unintentional libel and the *'Artemus Jones'* rule

At times, journalists have got it wrong when their intention is to be either particularly funny or witty in satirical sketches by using innuendo. This can be to the detriment of their newspapers (or online editions) and can lead to a very expensive libel action. There is nothing particularly funny about the cost of libel actions with damage awards in the region of up to £200,000. Some journalists have learned, to the financial detriment of their newspapers, that a sense of humour or, worse still, a joke, finds no favours in the courts either. The same legal principle applies to photographs, cartoons and waxworks of a person: that an image or statement is considered to be 'defamatory' if it 'lowers a person in the estimation of right-thinking members of society' or holds them up to hatred, contempt or ridicule – though it is rare for a photograph on its own to be defamatory nowadays. The problem arises when the wrong caption has been added.

The common law rule dates back to an early twentieth-century case, that of **Artemus Jones** (see: **Hulton v Jones** (1910)[62]). The case remains the authority for 'lookalike' situations. A seemingly simple joke misfired when, in 1910, the *Sunday Chronicle* published a satirical sketch about a certain 'Artemus Jones', said to be a fictional Peckham church warden, who had gone to France with a woman 'who was not his wife'. A Welsh barrister called Thomas Artemus Jones (who was not from Peckham and

---

62 [1910] AC 20 (HL).

was not a church warden) complained to the defamation courts and received the then enormous sum of £1,750 in libel damages. He satisfied the House of Lords that reasonable people might conclude that the defamatory words referred to him. The newspaper's assertion that its Artemus Jones was completely imaginary was somewhat undermined by the fact that Thomas Artemus Jones had been a subeditor on the paper seven years earlier. The '*Artemus Jones*' case remains the precedent for strict liability in defamation law, placing the burden on the publisher, editor and/or author to ensure – as a matter of principle – that no individual has to put up with a damaged reputation as a result of that publication, even if the person concerned suffers damage wholly independently of any fault on the part of the publisher.

The *Artemus Jones* rule was applied in **Dwek v Macmillan Publishers Ltd** (1999),[63] where a book published a photograph – taken some twenty years earlier – showing the claimant Norman Dwek sitting next to a woman who was (correctly) described as a prostitute. The photo in question showed a young woman sitting between two men on a sofa, published in an unauthorized biography of then Harrods owner Mohammed Al Fayed. It was the caption which dramatically transformed the meaning of the image. It read: 'Fantasies: Louise "Michaels" was a prostitute who befriended Dodi (left in photograph)'. But the man on the left in the photo was not Dodi Al Fayed, but Norman Dwek, a family dentist from Richmond. The same photograph (with the other man cropped out of the picture) was reprinted in both the *Mail on Sunday* and the *Evening Standard*, with the respective captions: 'Shared: Dodi with high-class prostitute Louise Dyrbusz, who also saw his uncle' and 'Louise "Michaels" was a prostitute who befriended Dodi at Tramp'.

Mr Dwek successfully sued the book publishers and the newspapers for defamation. The Court of Appeal agreed with Mr Dwek that readers would look at the photograph in the context of the caption and believe that the man in the photo had sex with prostitutes. Mr Dwek rightly argued that many readers would recognize him as being that man, even though it was said to be a photograph of Dodi Al Fayed. The CA held that the photographic juxtaposition was defamatory.

The addition of a caption to a photograph may render it defamatory, so care should be taken when choosing appropriate captions, particularly when the subject matter is controversial. The media publisher may seek to defend the libel action on the basis that any reader who identified the person in the photograph would know that the allegation was untrue. It used to be a matter for the 'libel' jury to decide on the specific facts of the case, but the Defamation Act 2013 virtually rules out jury trials under s 11 of the Act.

With digital photo-imaging and the ease with which images can now be changed or enhanced, there are additional potential dangers highlighted in the now famous defamation action brought by the *Neighbours* actors Anne Charleston and Ian Smith.[64] The actors, best known as the respectable married couple Harold and Madge Bishop in the television soap, sued the publisher and editor of the *News of the World* over photographs showing their faces on the bodies of pornographic models. The headlines read: 'Strewth! What's Harold up to with our Madge?' and 'Porn Shocker for Neighbours stars'. The accompanying article made clear that the photographs were from a pornographic computer game and produced by superimposing the actors' faces on the bodies without their knowledge. The argument advanced by Ms Charleston and Mr Smith was that many readers simply scan headlines and 'eye-catching' images without bothering to read the whole of the article. However, the House of Lords decreed that, when determining whether the photograph and text were defamatory, the whole of the accompanying article must be taken into account. This means if a photograph is altered or an image is enhanced, the caption ought to state so, or a disclaimer be added to clearly explain that the image has been altered. Then a defamation claim is unlikely.

---

63 *Dwek v Macmillan Publishers Ltd & Others* [1999] EWCA Civ 2002.
64 *Charleston v News Group Newspapers Ltd* [1995] 2 AC 65 (HL).

Another case, involving Harrods owner Mohammed Al Fayed, demonstrates how the '*Artemus Jones*' case is still applied in 'lookalike' situations. On 31 March 2002 Harrods issued a press release headed 'Al Fayed reveals plan to "float" Harrods', inviting the media to contact someone called Loof Lirpa[65] as there was to be an important announcement on the morning of the following day, i.e. 1 April: the launch of a floating shop on a canal boat.[66] The *Wall Street Journal* picked up the story on 5 April under the headline, 'The Enron of Britain?', reporting that 'if Harrods, the British luxury retailer, ever goes public, investors would be wise to question its every disclosure'. Mr Justice Eady determined that the resulting libel action should be heard in the UK, rather than the US, stating that the words could mean that every corporate disclosure of Harrods should be distrusted, and even that 'it is reasonably suspected that if the claimant [Harrods] were to become a public company it would prove itself to be Britain's Enron by deceiving and defrauding its investors on a huge scale'. The case was settled out of court (under the 'offer to make amends') with Harrods demanding an apology and damages to be paid to charity. The journal's defence stated that it was 'meant to be a humorous comment on the bogus press release'.[67] The April fool joke had badly backfired. The history of the 'joke' defence is therefore not a happy one. Words are defamatory and intention is irrelevant.

In **O'Shea v MGN** (2001)[68] Morland J endeavoured to strike a balance between freedom of expression and an individual's right to the protection of his privacy when considering strict liability libel. The judge had to decide whether a photograph (of Miss E) would be recognized by those who knew the claimant and would identify her – albeit wrongly – as being the person in the photograph, which would give her the cause of action in libel. Miss E had appeared in an advertisement for a pornographic internet service provider (the second defendant), who in turn had advertised in the *Sunday Mirror*. In this case the claimant bore a striking resemblance to a 'Miss E', though the photograph in question did not name or identify the claimant, other than by virtue of the strong resemblance between her and Miss E. Referring to **Hulton v Jones**, Morland J concluded:

> The test in law is objective. Would the ordinary reader of the advertisement, having regard to the words complained of and the photograph in the context of the advertisement as a whole and clothed with the special knowledge of the publishers, that is that the photograph was the 'spit and image' of the claimant, have reasonably concluded that the woman speaking into the telephone [in the photograph] was the claimant?[69]

Morland J ruled that the strict liability principle should not cover the 'lookalike' situation in this case, and to allow it to do so would be an unjustifiable interference with the vital right of freedom of expression and the democratic principle of a free press. Consequently, Miss O'Shea may well have suffered some embarrassment, but the court held that she was not protected under Article 8 ECHR, nor did she win her libel action.

To be successful in a libel action, the words complained of must be interpreted in their context and the claimant is not allowed to select passages which are prima facie libellous if the passage taken as a whole is not defamatory, for example just a newspaper headline (see: **Charleston v News Group Newspapers Ltd** (1995)[70]).

---

65 Note: 'April fool' – spelt backwards!
66 The statement was only available until noon on the chairman's personal website, www.alfayed.com.
67 See also: **Dow Jones & Company, Inc v Harrods Ltd, and Mohamed Al Fayed** (2003) (Docket No. 02–9364). United States Court of Appeals, Second Circuit. Argued: 23 September 2003. Decided: 10 October 2003.
68 [2001] EMLR 40 (QBD).
69 **Hulton v Jones** [1910] AC at 84 (Morland J in **O'Shea v MGN**).
70 [1995] 2 AC 65 (HL).

FOR THOUGHT

What happens if a journalist unintentionally refers to a fictitious name which he has made up, and there is such a person 'out there'? Discuss with reference to common law, the new statute (Defamation Act 2013) and Article 10 ECHR.

3.2.7 Malicious falsehood: the role of malice

It is widely understood that the claimant will not receive any legal aid for pursuing an action in defamation. But he is entitled to legal aid if he pursues a 'malicious falsehood' (rather than defamation) claim, but only if he can demonstrate some economic loss rather than purely non-economic damage to his reputation.

The Court of Appeal allowed an appeal by the claimant Linda Joyce[71] against the decision of Gilbert Gray QC, sitting as a deputy High Court judge on 12 December 1990, to strike out, as an abuse of the process of the court, her statement of claim for damages for malicious falsehood against the defendants Kim Sengupta, chief crime correspondent of the *Today* newspaper, and the publishers News (UK) Ltd. Ms Joyce's claim was that the article contained serious untruths about her and that it had been published maliciously: the defendants were recklessly indifferent about the truth or falsity of the allegations. She claimed damages and an injunction against repetition.

The case had attracted considerable public attention at the time since it involved the Princess Royal's maid, Linda Joyce, and intimate love letters written by the Queen's daughter, Princess Anne. The disclosure that Princess Anne had received personal letters from Royal Navy Commander Timothy Lawrence had sparked rumours about the Princess Royal's troubled 15-year marriage to Captain Mark Phillips. Kim Sengupta had published the offending article on 25 April 1989, headlined 'Royal Maid Stole Letters', alleging that Ms Joyce had stolen the love letters from her employer, Princess Anne. Though the article appeared grossly defamatory, Ms Joyce did not have the money 'up front' to sue in libel and legal aid was clearly not available in 'ordinary' libel actions. Ms Joyce argued 'injurious falsehood' (also referred to as 'trade libel') and that the article had caused her financial loss by loss of reputation, loss of employment and future references.

What is the difference between ordinary libel (defamation) and malicious (injurious) falsehood? An essential feature of both torts is injury to reputation, of one kind or another. The ordinary tort of defamation is the publication of words or matter to a third person injurious to the reputation of another.[72] It is not necessary for the claimant to prove 'special damage', that is, that he has suffered real damage to his reputation as a result of the statement. The importance of *Joyce v Sengupta* lies in the fact that it established the precedent of actions in malicious falsehood which attract legal aid – though this is now somewhat restricted under the Jackson Reforms post April 2013.

The burden of proving or disproving malice will vary from case to case, and from claimant to claimant, according to the nature of the action and the nature of the malice as well as the notion of express and implied malice, which therefore leaves the matter totally open to the courts. Part of the difficulty lies in the fact that the law distinguishes between actual (or express) malice and presumed malice. Actual malice is referred to as 'malice in fact', as opposed to presumed malice which is 'malice in law'. Actual malice amounts to maliciousness including ill-feeling and a desire to cause harm. Presumed malice can simply be a publication without lawful excuse,

---

71 *Joyce v Sengupta* [1993] 1 WLR 337.
72 See: Milmo *et al.* (2010), p. 4.

inferred malice either from the words used or from evidence of the circumstances which prompted the words. The courts have attempted to define actions of 'malice,' though 'express malice' is still difficult to define in certain circumstances. What is important is that damages need to be quantified and the claimant has to prove economic (financial) loss, as was proved in the '*Stéphane Grappelli*'[73] case.

In this case the claimants were internationally famous jazz violinist Stéphane Grappelli (1908–97) and professional guitarist William Charles Disley ('Diz' Disley, 1931–2010). The defendants, concert promoters Derek Block (Holdings) Ltd, had purported to arrange concerts for the claimants, amongst these 'gigs' of the Grappelli Jazz Trio at Tameside on 26 November 1976 and Milton Keynes on 4 December 1976. On 21 September 1976 Derek Block cancelled the Tameside and Milton Keynes concerts, with the explanation that Mr Grappelli was 'very seriously ill in Paris', adding that it would be surprising 'if he ever toured again'. Lord Denning MR dismissed the original defamation action on the grounds that the statement itself was not defamatory. The claimants filed a new action relying on injurious falsehood and maliciousness, since the announcement was clearly damaging to Mr Grappelli's and the Trio's future success. The claimants were successful in their malicious falsehood action after they had provided the court with evidence of financial loss by way of a statement of quantum of damages and evidence of express malice.[74] (See also: **Tolley v JS Fry & Sons Ltd** (1931)[75]).

The controversy in the meaning of express or implied malice led Professor Loveland (1998) to observe that malice 'has become an horrendously imprecise facet of English defamation law'.[76] Loveland (2000) went on to criticize the application of the test for malice in English political libel cases because it failed to emphasize the electorate's entitlement to know the truth about its elected representatives, contrasting English law unfavourably with the US position.[77]

In summary, an action in malicious falsehood for a publication or statement in fact must be injurious to the character of another and must require proof of economic loss. It is only then that the law will consider the publication 'malicious', and the courts will interpret the meaning of 'malice' narrowly.[78]

In **Tse Wai Chun Paul v Albert Cheng**[79] Lord Nicholls of Birkenhead was concerned with the ingredients of 'malice' which could defeat the defence of fair comment, when he said:

> First, the comment must be on a matter of public interest. Public interest is not to be confined within narrow limits today. Second, the comment must be recognisable as comment, as distinct from an imputation of fact. If the imputation is one of fact, a ground of defence must be sought elsewhere, for example, justification or privilege. . . . Third, the comment must be based on facts which are true or protected by privilege . . .
>
> If the facts on which the comment purports to be founded are not proved to be true or published on a privilege occasion, the defence of fair comment is not available. Next, the comment must explicitly or implicitly indicate, at least in general terms, what are the facts on which the comment is being made. The reader or hearer should be in a position to judge for himself how far the comment was well founded . . .

73 *Grappelli v Derek Block (Holdings) Ltd.* [1981] 1 WLR 822.
74 Referring *inter alia* to **Wright v Woodgate** (1835) 2 CR M & R 573 at 577.
75 [1931] AC 333 (HL).
76 See: Loveland (1998), p. 637.
77 See: Loveland (2000).
78 For further discussion see: Mitchell (1999).
79 [2001] EMLR 777 (Lord Nicholls of Birkenhead, sitting in the Court of Final Appeal of Hong Kong).

Finally, the comment must be one which could have been made by an honest person, however prejudiced he might be, and however exaggerated or obstinate his views[80]

(see also: *Turner v Metro-Goldwyn-Mayer Pictures Ltd* (1950)[81])

See Defences
3.5 below

This meant that a defendant was in the past not entitled to rely on the defence of fair comment if the comment was made maliciously (the onus of proving 'malice' lay on the claimant). Libel lawyers have had great difficulty in defining the difference between a statement of fact and a comment in the context of the defence of 'fair comment'.

One recent case in 'malicious falsehood' was the **Tesla Motors** case which first began its action against the BBC and its popular programme *Top Gear* in 2008. Electric sports car maker Tesla Motors, based in Palo Alto, California, claimed that *Top Gear* had faked a scene that appeared to show a Tesla Roadster running out of power, which Tesla claimed led to lower sales. The company first sued in defamation against the BBC after the show's presenter Jeremy Clarkson said in the programme that the Roadster ran out of battery power after 55 miles on its track – far short of the 200 miles that Tesla claimed it could achieve. Tesla claimed $171,000 of lost sales revenue at the time.

In 2011, Mr Justice Tugendhat ruled that no *Top Gear* viewer would have reasonably compared the car's performance on the show's airfield track to its likely performance on a public road. Though the initial defamation action was lost, the company still sued for malicious falsehood over the episode that showed the Roadster model running out of battery in a race. In its ruling in 2013,[82] the CA finally dismissed the Tesla Motors malicious falsehood claim over the allegedly false statements made by Jeremy Clarkson in relation to the electric Roadster sports car.

Moore-Bick LJ agreed with the first instance judge that the comments made by Clarkson regarding the car's range and reliability whilst testing them on the *Top Gear* test track could not bear the defamatory meaning Tesla attributed to them, specifically that Tesla had intentionally and significantly misled potential customers. With respect to the malicious falsehood claim, the judge also agreed that Tesla had failed sufficiently to particularize any damage the allegedly false statements were calculated to cause. While the court did not go so far as to say Tesla's claim was an abuse of process, it did not consider Tesla's prospect of recovering a substantial sum by way of damages sufficient to justify continuing the proceedings. Moore-Bick LJ found it difficult to believe that Tesla claimed to have suffered the loss of almost $4 million by that time, since the company was not able to show any 'special damage' right from the outset of its claim in 2008.

While a claimant is entitled to rely on probable rather than actual damage under s 3(1)(a) of the Defamation Act 1952 ('malicious falsehood'), and indeed does not have to identify the *exact* amount of pecuniary loss, claimants still have to identify 'the nature of the loss and the mechanism by which it is likely to be sustained'; that is, a claimant has to fully particularize the relevant facts and account properly to the court in a malicious falsehood claim.

3.3 Libel tourism

There have been growing concerns in recent years that defamation law in Britain has come to be more protective of reputation than elsewhere in the world, to such an extent that London has become the preferred location for defamation actions involving foreign parties with only a tenuous

---

80 Ibid., paras 16–21.
81 [1950] 1 All ER 449 (Lord Porter).
82 **Tesla Motors Ltd v British Broadcasting Corporation** [2013] EWCA 152 (CA Civ Div).

link to one of the UK jurisdictions. Most disconcerting have been cases where both the claimant and defendant have come from outside the EU, making London the 'libel capital of the world'.

One of the main reasons why foreign nationals prefer the English courts in defamation actions is that the present law is perceived as loaded against the defendant. The simple fact remains that claimants from anywhere in the world can come to the London courts to defend their reputation by way of a defamation action by making use of the UK's archaic laws (see: **GKR Karate (UK) Ltd v Yorkshire Post Newspapers Ltd** (2000)[83]). British libel laws have been seen as more favourable to pursuing a defamation action than those in the United States, for instance, where libel laws are not only less generous to claimants but there is also the single publication rule, which now also exists in English law.[84]

See above
3.2.3

It is for these reasons that claimants choose to seek redress in the London courts (see: **Lewis v King** (2004)[85]; **Richardson v Schwarzenegger** (2004)[86]; **New York Times v Sullivan** (1964)[87]).

One example was that of a Russian businessman, Boris Berezovsky (1946–2013), who became a frequent litigant in the London courts. The powerful Russian oligarch moved to the UK in 2000 and began to sue *Forbes* magazine the same year in the High Court.[88] The political background is important in this case and may shine some light on the untimely death of one of the most powerful businessmen in the world in March 2013 at his home in Ascot, Berkshire.

In the wake of the collapse of the Soviet Union, the transition of Russia from communism to a market-orientated economy, Russian society was accompanied by a dramatic upsurge in organized crime and corruption. The media became increasingly interested in the transformation of Russian society and published many reports on the criminalization of Russian oligarchs. *Forbes*, an influential American fortnightly magazine, devoted considerable resources to the investigation and reporting of the situation in the post-Soviet phase in Russia. In its issue of 30 December 1996 *Forbes* described two men as 'criminals on an outrageous scale'. The first was Nikolai Glouchkov, Managing Director of Aeroflot; the second businessman and politician, Boris Berezovsky, who was described as follows:

> Is he the Godfather of the Kremlin? Power, Politics, Murder. Boris Berezovsky can teach the guys in Sicily a thing or two.

The flavour of the article, which together with a prominent photograph of Mr Berezovsky was spread over seven pages, captured in an editorial published by James W. Michaels, the editor of *Forbes*. It stated:

> . . . this is the true story of the brilliant, unscrupulous Boris Berezovsky, a close associate of President Boris Yeltsin and a man who parlayed an auto dealership into Russia's most formidable business empire. Berezovsky stands tall as one of the most powerful men in Russia. Behind him lies a trail of corpses, uncollectible debts and competitors terrified for their lives.

---

83 [2000] (No 1) 1 WLR 2571.
84 For further discussion and comparison with US law, see: Klazmer (2012) at pp. 164–168.
85 [2004] EWCA Civ 1329. The case concerned Don King, the US boxing promoter, who was suing Judd Burstein for remarks he made about him on a couple of boxing websites. The High Court and Court of Appeal held that England was an appropriate forum for the case.
86 [2004] EWHC 2422. The claimant was a British TV host who accused actor-turned-politician Arnold Schwarzenegger of touching her breast during the course of his election campaign. Mr Schwarzenegger's publicist alleged that it was Ms Richardson who had behaved provocatively and that Ms Richardson had concocted her story. This allegation was reported in the *Los Angeles Times*. Hard copies of this paper were published in England and the article was also posted on the internet. The High Court refused to set aside the Master's order giving permission to serve the second defendant outside the jurisdiction.
87 376 US 254.
88 *Berezovsky v Forbes Inc (No 2)* [2001] EWCA 1251.

Boris Berezovsky had been Deputy Secretary of the Security Council of the Russian Federation, but in November 1997 President Yeltsin dismissed him. In April 1998 Mr Berezovsky was appointed as Secretary of the Commonwealth of Independent States, with responsibility for co-operation between the various parts of the Russian Federation. Both Mr Berezovsky and Mr Glouchkov sued *Forbes* in England for defamation (rather than in Russia or the United States). On 12 February 1997 they issued separate proceedings for damages for libel and injunctions against Forbes Inc. (the publisher of the magazine) and Mr Michaels (the editor). The plaintiffs confined their claims for damages to the publication of *Forbes* within the jurisdiction through distribution of copies of the magazine and through publication on the internet. Though both cases would have been more suited to an action in either the United States or Russia, the House of Lords gave leave to Mr Berezovsky to sue in London, based on his reputation in the UK, applying the **Duke of Brunswick** principle of the multiple publication rule (see: **Berezovsky v Michaels** (2000)[89]).

There followed a second action by the Russian oligarch and the whole action took six years before being resolved in the magazine's favour (see: **Berezovsky v Forbes Inc (No 2)** (2001)[90]). The ruling in **Berezovsky No 2** was followed in other common law countries, such as by the High Court of Australia in **Dow Jones v Gutnick** (2002).[91] In response to this, legislation was introduced in the United States in 2010, specifically to prevent foreign libel judgments from being enforceable there.[92]

Research by publishers Sweet & Maxwell in 2012[93] found that celebrities were increasingly turning their backs on libel suits in the UK as a way to defend their reputation and curb negative stories in favour of privacy claims and superinjunctions. The number of reported defamation cases fell 15 per cent in 2011, from 84 to 71 (year ending 31 May 2012). Those who sued for libel included *Big Brother* contestant Imogen Thomas, the singers Charlotte Church and Morrissey, and socialite Nancy Dell'Olio. The research attributed the reduction in part to recent changes in the law and better press behaviour after the phone-hacking scandal and the Leveson Inquiry.

Whilst defamation actions declined, privacy injunctions became increasingly fashionable as they could prevent damaging articles from ever seeing the light of day, whereas an action in defamation cannot generally be used to prevent allegations being published, but only to set the record straight through an action for damages *after* the event. That said, the **Ryan Giggs** and **John Terry** superinjunctions demonstrated that it became increasingly difficult to obtain anonymity orders keeping the identities of celebrities out of the media spotlight.[94]

See Chapter 2.6

Wacks (2013) argues that the line between a privacy claim and an action for defamation has become somewhat 'fuzzy' – with the overriding obstacle in defamation being 'truth' as a complete defence, thereby providing a valuable safeguard for the media for freedom of expression.[95] Warren and Brandeis (1890) regarded the principles of the law of defamation as 'radically different' from those underlying the protection of 'privacy'.[96]

Section 2 of the Defamation Act 2013 now deals with the statutory defence of 'truth', which has replaced the common law defence of 'justification', providing the defendant with a defence if he can show that the imputation conveyed by the alleged defamatory statement complained of is substantially true.

See above 3.2.5

89 [2000] UKHL 25
90 [2001] EWCA 1251.
91 [2002] CLR 575.
92 The SPEECH Act (Seeking the Protection of [US] Enduring and Established Constitutional Heritage) was passed in the United States in 2010.
93 Source: 'Defamation cases plummet 15%', research findings by Sweet & Maxwell. Thomson – Reuters. London, UK, September 2012 at: www.sweetandmaxwell.co.uk/downloads/defamation_cases_plummet_15_per_cent.pdf.
94 For further discussion see: Smartt (2011) at pp. 135–140.
95 See: Wacks (2013) at pp. 180–181.
96 See: Warren and Brandeis (1890) at pp. 193–220.

Section 9 of the Defamation Act 2013 deals with persons not domiciled in the UK or a Member State of the EU. Section 9(1) specifically addresses the issue of 'libel tourism' and focuses the provision on cases where an action is brought against a person who is not domiciled in the UK, an EU Member State or a state which is a party to the Lugano Conventions of 1988 and 2007.[97] This is in order to avoid conflict with European jurisdictional rules (in particular the Brussels Regulation on jurisdictional matters[98]). Section 9(2) of the Defamation Act 2013 states:

> A court does not have jurisdiction to hear and determine an action to which this section applies unless the court is satisfied that, of all the places in which the statement complained of has been published, England and Wales is clearly the most appropriate place in which to bring an action in respect of the statement.

This means that in cases where a statement has been published in the jurisdiction of England and Wales and also abroad, the court will be required to consider the overall global picture to consider where it would be most appropriate for a claim to be heard.

Parliament clearly intended that this would overcome the problem of courts readily accepting jurisdiction simply because a claimant frames their claim so as to focus on damage which has occurred in one of the UK jurisdictions only. For example, if a statement was published 100,000 times in Australia and only 5,000 times in England, that would be a good basis on which to conclude that the most appropriate jurisdiction in which to bring an action in respect of the statement was Australia rather than England.

There are, however, a range of factors which the court may still wish to take into account including, for example, the amount of damage to the claimant's reputation in this jurisdiction compared to elsewhere, and the extent to which the new legislation seeks to prevent claims against defendants who are not domiciled in the UK or in another EU Member State without a strong link existing to the jurisdiction of England and Wales.

What is clear is that the new law prevents a court from hearing an action in defamation in England and Wales unless it is satisfied that the UK jurisdiction is the 'most appropriate place for a defamation action to be brought'.

Section 9(3) provides that the references in subsection (2) to the statement complained of include references to any statement which conveys the same, or substantially the same, imputation as the statement complained of. This addresses the situation where a statement is published in a number of countries but is not exactly the same in all of them, and will ensure that a court is not impeded in deciding whether England and Wales is the most appropriate place to bring the claim by arguments that statements elsewhere should be regarded as different publications even when they are substantially the same.

It remains to be seen whether libel tourists in the UK will decrease with the new Defamation Act 2013 now well in place. But nothing has changed in the respect that a libel defendant is guilty until proven innocent.

---

97 The Lugano Convention on Jurisdiction and the Enforcement of Judgments in Civil and Commercial Matters was concluded in Lugano on 16 September 1988. The following countries have acceded to it: the old Member States of the European Union, Poland and the members of the European Free-Trade Association (EFTA). It is a parallel convention to the Brussels Convention of the same name of 27 September 1969 on the jurisdiction and the enforcement of judgments in civil and commercial matters. The Lugano Convention 2007 entered into force for the EU, Denmark and Norway on 1 January 2010, but it has only applied for Switzerland since 1 January 2011. For Iceland it entered into force on 1 May 2011. Under Article 3 para 3 of Protocol 2 to the Lugano Convention 2007, the Court of Justice of the European Communities remains responsible for the exchange of information on decisions taken in application of both Lugano Conventions of 1988 and 2007 (as well as the legal instruments named in Article 64).

98 Council Regulation 44/2001/C on jurisdiction and the recognition and enforcement of judgments in civil and commercial matters.

 **FOR THOUGHT**

Should anyone be able to benefit from the claimant-friendly libel laws in the UK? Discuss the common law tradition and the new defamation laws in relation to an action for defamation against a person who is not domiciled in the UK or the EU.

3.4 Defamation Act 2013

Defamation law is one of the most criticized areas of English law and it is its complexity which often confuses students (and journalists) studying English 'libel' laws. Over recent times a sustained campaign spearheaded by the *Guardian* newspaper among others has vigorously argued for reform of what is seen as a complex law which thwarts media freedom but does not provide genuine redress for those libelled, particularly if they are not wealthy – thus failing both claimants and defendants.

For this reasons it is important to note that the Defamation Act 2013 reforms aspects of the law of defamation which means that common law continues to co-exist alongside statute (i.e. the Defamation Acts of 1952 and 1996 and now the 2013 Act). It is for this reason that this chapter explains the historic origins of common law, the vast body of case law which still exists (unless put on a statutory footing) and the co-existence of the 1996 and the 2013 statutes.

3.4.1 Reform of defamation laws in England and Wales

The Defamation Act 2013 was enacted on 25 April 2013. Though this chapter has already covered some of the major sections of the Act and their meaning, this section will summarize the Act and discuss some likely practical implications.

The aim of the 2013 Act was to reform the law of defamation to ensure that a fair balance is struck between the right to freedom of expression and the protection of reputation. The Act makes a number of substantive changes to the law of defamation, but it does not codify existing law into a single statute. For this reason, as mentioned before, common law co-exists alongside the three main statutes, namely the Defamation Acts of 1952, 1996, and 2013.

Defamation Act 2013: key areas

- includes a requirement for claimants to show that they have suffered serious harm before suing for defamation;
- removes the presumption in favour of a jury trial;
- introduces a defence of 'responsible publication on matters of public interest;'
- provides increased protection to operators of websites (ISPs) that host user-generated content, providing they comply with the procedure to enable the complainant to resolve disputes directly with the author of the material concerned;
- introduces new statutory defences of 'truth' and 'honest opinion' to replace the common law defences of justification and fair comment.

3.4.2 Summary of contents

Section 1: Requirement of serious harm

Section 1: Serious harm

> (1) A statement is not defamatory unless its publication has caused or is likely to cause serious harm to the reputation of the claimant.

Section 1(1) Defamation Act 2013 provides that a statement is not defamatory unless its publication has caused or is likely to cause *serious harm* to the reputation of the claimant. The provision extends to situations where publication is likely to cause serious harm in order to cover situations where the harm has not yet occurred at the time the action for defamation is commenced. The section builds on the consideration given by the courts in a series of cases to the question of what is sufficient to establish that a statement is defamatory.

The Court of Appeal affirmed the 1936 HL decision in **Sim v Stretch**[99] in the **Sarah Thornton** case,[100] where the threshold for 'seriousness' had been set for what is defamatory. The CA in the **Yousef Jameel v Dow Jones** case (2005)[101] established that there needs to be a real and substantial tort.

Section 1 has certainly raised the bar for bringing a claim so that only cases involving serious harm to the claimant's reputation can be brought. It is therefore expected that potentially trivial cases will be struck out at first hearing on the basis that they are an abuse of process because they do not meet the s 1 threshold test.

Section 2: The defence of 'truth'

Section 2: Truth

> (1) It is a defence to an action for defamation for the defendant to show that the imputation conveyed by the statement complained of is substantially true.

Section 2(1) replaces the common law defence of 'justification' with a new statutory defence of truth. The section is intended broadly to reflect the current law while simplifying and clarifying certain elements.

The new defence of truth applies where the defendant can show that the imputation conveyed by the defamatory statement complained of is substantially true. The new defence was established in the case of **Chase v News Group Newspapers Ltd** (2002),[102] where the CA indicated that in order for the defence of justification to be available the defendant does not have to prove that every word he published was true. All he has to establish is the 'essential' or 'substantial' truth of the sting of the libel.

Section 3: The defence of 'honest opinion'

Section 3: Honest opinion

> (1)   It is a defence to an action for defamation for the defendant to show that the following conditions are met.
>
> (2)   The first condition is that the statement complained of was a statement of opinion.

---

99 [1936] 2 All ER 1237.
100 **Thornton (Sarah) v Telegraph Media Group Ltd** [2011] EWHC 1884 (QB).
101 **Jameel (Yousef) v Dow Jones & Co Inc** [2005] EWCA Civ 75.
102 [2002] EWCA Civ 1772.

(3) The second condition is that the statement complained of indicated, whether in general or specific terms, the basis of the opinion.

(4) The third condition is that an honest person could have held the opinion on the basis of –

(a) any fact which existed at the time the statement complained of was published;

(b) anything asserted to be a fact in a privileged statement published before the statement complained of.

Section 3 replaces the common law defence of 'fair comment' with a new defence of honest opinion. This section broadly simplifies and clarifies certain defence elements, but does not include the previous requirement for the opinion to be on a matter of public interest. Subsections (1) to (4) provide for the defence to apply where the defendant can show that three conditions are met. These are:

- **Condition 1**: that the statement complained of was a statement of opinion;
- **Condition 2**: that the statement complained of indicated, whether in general or specific terms, the basis of the opinion; and
- **Condition 3**: that an honest person could have held the opinion on the basis of any fact which existed at the time the statement complained of was published or anything asserted to be a fact in a privileged statement published before the statement complained of.

Section 4: The defence of publication on matter of public interest

Section 4: Publication on matter of public interest

(1) It is a defence to an action for defamation for the defendant to show that –

(a) the statement complained of was, or formed part of, a statement on a matter of public interest; and

(b) the defendant reasonably believed that publishing the statement complained of was in the public interest.

Section 4 creates a new defence to an action for defamation of publication on a matter of public interest. The section was established in common law in **Reynolds v Times Newspapers**.[103] Section 4(1) provides for the defence to be available in circumstances where the defendant can show that the statement complained of was, or formed part of, a statement on a *matter of public interest* and that he reasonably believed that publishing the statement complained of was in the public interest (see also: **Flood v Times Newspapers Ltd**[104]). The public interest at the time of publication is an objective test.

Section 5: Operators of websites

Section 5: Operators of websites

(1) This section applies where an action for defamation is brought against the operator of a website in respect of a statement posted on the website.

(2) It is a defence for the operator to show that it was not the operator who posted the statement on the website.

(3) The defence is defeated if the claimant shows that –

---

103 [2001] 2 AC 127 (HL).
104 [2011] UKSC 11 (Supreme Court).

(a) it was not possible for the claimant to identify the person who posted the statement,
(b) the claimant gave the operator a notice of complaint in relation to the statement, and
(c) the operator failed to respond to the notice of complaint in accordance with any provision contained in regulations.

Section 5 creates a new defence for the operators of websites (ISPs) where a defamation action is brought against them in respect of a statement posted on the website. Section 5(2) provides for the defence to apply if the ISP can show that they did not post the statement on the website. Section 5(3) provides for the defence to be defeated if the claimant can show that it was not possible for him or her to identify the person who posted the statement; that they gave the operator a notice of complaint in relation to the statement; and that the operator failed to respond to that notice in accordance with provision contained in regulations to be made by the Secretary of State.

Section 6: Defence of qualified privilege for peer-reviewed statements in scientific or academic journals

Section 6: Peer-reviewed statement in scientific or academic journal etc.

(1) The publication of a statement in a scientific or academic journal (whether published in electronic form or otherwise) is privileged if the following conditions are met.
(2) The first condition is that the statement relates to a scientific or academic matter.
(3) The second condition is that before the statement was published in the journal an independent review of the statement's scientific or academic merit was carried out by –

    (a) the editor of the journal, and
    (b) one or more persons with expertise in the scientific or academic matter concerned.

Section 6 creates a new defence of qualified privilege relating to peer-reviewed material in scientific or academic journals (whether published in electronic form or otherwise). The term 'scientific journal' includes medical and engineering journals. Subsections (1) to (3) provide for the defence to apply where two conditions are met.

- **Condition 1**: that the statement relates to a scientific or academic matter; and
- **Condition 2**: that before the statement was published in the journal an independent review of the statement's scientific or academic merit was carried out by the editor of the journal and one or more persons with expertise in the scientific or academic matter concerned.

The requirements in condition 2 are intended to reflect the core aspects of a responsible peer-review process.

Section 7: Reports etc. protected by privilege

Section 7 amends the provisions contained in the Defamation Act 1996 relating to the defences of 'absolute' and 'qualified privilege' to extend the circumstances in which these defences can be used.

Section 7(1) of the 2013 Act replaces s 14(3) of the 1996 Act, which concerns the absolute privilege applying to fair and accurate contemporaneous reports of court proceedings.

Section 7(1) extends the scope of the defence so that it also covers proceedings in any court established under the law of a country or territory *outside* the United Kingdom, and any international court or tribunal established by the Security Council of the United Nations or by an international agreement.

Section 7(2) of the 2013 Act amends s 15(3) of the 1996 Act by substituting the phrase 'public interest' for 'public concern', so that the subsection reads:

This section does not apply to the publication to the public, or a section of the public, of matter which is not of public interest and the publication of which is not for the public benefit.

Section 7(6)(b) of the 2013 Act makes the same amendment to paragraph 12(2) of Schedule 1 to the 1996 Act in relation to the privilege extended to fair and accurate reports etc. of public meetings.

Sections 7(3) to (10) make amendments to Part 2 of Schedule 1 to the 1996 Act in a number of areas so as to extend the circumstances in which the defence of qualified privilege is available. Section 15 of and Schedule 1 to the 1996 Act currently provide for qualified privilege to apply to various types of report or statement, provided the report or statement is fair and accurate, on a matter of public concern, and that publication is for the public benefit and made without malice. Part 1 of Schedule 1 sets out categories of publication which attract qualified privilege without explanation or contradiction. These include fair and accurate reports of proceedings in public, anywhere in the world, of legislatures (both national and local), courts, public inquiries and international organisations or conferences, and documents, notices and other matter published by these bodies.

Section 8: The single publication rule

Section 8: Single publication rule

(1) This section applies if a person –

(a) publishes a statement to the public ('the first publication'), and

(b) subsequently publishes (whether or not to the public) that statement or a statement which is substantially the same.

Section 8 introduces a single publication rule to prevent an action being brought in relation to publication of the same material by the same publisher after a one-year limitation period from the date of the first publication of that material to the public or a section of the public. This replaces the long-standing principle that each publication of defamatory material gives rise to a separate cause of action which is subject to its own limitation period (the **Duke of Brunswick** rule or 'multiple publication rule').

Section 9: Jurisdiction: action against a person not domiciled in the UK or a Member State

Section 9: Action against a person not domiciled in the UK or a Member State etc.

This section applies to an action for defamation against a person who is not domiciled –

(a) in the United Kingdom;

(b) in another Member State; or

(c) in a state which is for the time being a contracting party to the Lugano Convention.

Section 9 addresses the issue of 'libel tourism' and focuses the provision on cases where an action is brought against a person who is not domiciled in the UK, an EU Member State or a state which is a party to the Lugano Convention. Subsection (2) provides that a court does not have jurisdiction to hear and determine an action to which the section applies unless it is satisfied that, of all the places in which the statement complained of has been published, England and Wales is clearly the most appropriate place in which to bring an action in respect of the statement. This means that in cases where a statement has been published in this jurisdiction and also abroad, the court will be required to consider the overall global picture to consider where it would be most appropriate for a claim to be heard. It is intended that this will overcome the problem of courts readily accepting jurisdiction simply because a claimant frames their claim so as to focus on damage which has occurred in this jurisdiction only.

Section 9 then limits the circumstances in which an action for defamation can be brought against someone who is not the primary publisher of an allegedly defamatory statement.

Section 10: Action against a person who was not the author, editor etc.

Section 10: Action against a person who was not the author, editor etc.

> (1) A court does not have jurisdiction to hear and determine an action for defamation brought against a person who was not the author, editor or publisher of the statement complained of unless the court is satisfied that it is not reasonably practicable for an action to be brought against the author, editor or publisher.

Section 10 limits the circumstances in which an action for defamation can be brought against someone who is not the primary publisher of an allegedly defamatory statement. It provides that a court does not have jurisdiction to hear and determine an action for defamation brought against a person who was not the author, editor or publisher of the statement complained of unless it is satisfied that it is not reasonably practicable for an action to be brought against the author, editor or publisher.

Section 11: Trial without a jury

Section 11: Trial to be without a jury unless the court orders otherwise

> (1) In section 69(1) of the Senior Courts Act 1981 (certain actions in the Queen's Bench Division to be tried with a jury unless the trial requires prolonged examination of documents etc.) in paragraph (b) omit 'libel, slander'.
> (2) In section 66(3) of the County Courts Act 1984 (certain actions in the county court to be tried with a jury unless the trial requires prolonged examination of documents etc.) in paragraph (b) omit 'libel, slander'.

Section 11 removes the presumption in favour of jury trial in defamation cases (this was provided under s 69 Senior Courts Act 1981 and s 66 County Courts Act 1984 in certain civil proceedings, such as malicious prosecution, false imprisonment, fraud, libel and slander). Subsections (1) and (2) of the 2013 Act amended the 1981 and 1984 Acts to remove libel and slander from the list of proceedings where a right to jury trial exists.

The reality is that defamation cases are now tried without a jury unless a court orders otherwise.

Section 12: Summary of court judgment

Section 12: Power of court to order a summary of its judgment to be published

> (1) Where a court gives judgment for the claimant in an action for defamation the court may order the defendant to publish a summary of the judgment.
> (2) The wording of any summary and the time, manner, form and place of its publication are to be for the parties to agree.
> (3) If the parties cannot agree on the wording, the wording is to be settled by the court.
> (4) If the parties cannot agree on the time, manner, form or place of publication, the court may give such directions as to those matters as it considers reasonable and practicable in the circumstances.

(5) This section does not apply where the court gives judgment for the claimant under section 8(3) of the Defamation Act 1996 (summary disposal of claims).

Section 12 gives the court power to order a summary of its judgment to be published in defamation proceedings more generally. Subsection (2) provides that the wording of any summary and the time, manner, form and place of its publication are matters for the parties to agree. Where the parties are unable to agree, subsections (3) and (4) respectively provide for the court to settle the wording, and enable it to give such directions in relation to the time, manner, form or place of publication as it considers reasonable and practicable. Under s 8 Defamation Act 1996 the court still has power to order an unsuccessful defendant to publish a summary of its judgment where the parties cannot agree the content of any correction or apology. The section gives the court power to order a summary of its judgment to be published in defamation proceedings more generally.

Section 13: Removal of statements

Section 13: Order to remove statement or cease distribution etc.

(1) Where a court gives judgment for the claimant in an action for defamation the court may order –

(a) the operator of a website on which the defamatory statement is posted to remove the statement, or

(b) any person who was not the author, editor or publisher of the defamatory statement to stop distributing, selling or exhibiting material containing the statement.

(2) In this section 'author', 'editor' and 'publisher' have the same meaning as in section 1 of the Defamation Act 1996.

Section 13 relates to situations where an author may not always be in a position to remove or prevent further dissemination of material which has been found to be defamatory. Section 13(1) provides that where a court gives judgment for the claimant in an action for defamation, it may order the operator of a website (ISP) on which a defamatory statement is posted to remove the statement, or require any person who was not the author, editor or publisher of the statement but is distributing, selling or exhibiting the material to cease disseminating it. This will enable an order for removal of the material to be made during or shortly after the conclusion of proceedings.

Section 14: Special damage in actions for slander

Section 14 repeals the Slander of Women Act 1891 and overturns a common law rule relating to special damage. In relation to slander, some special damage must be proved to flow from the statement complained of unless the publication falls into certain specific categories. These include a provision in the Slander of Women Act 1891 which provides that 'words spoken and published . . . which impute unchastity or adultery to any woman or girl shall not require special damage to render them actionable'.

Section 15: General provisions: the meaning of 'publish' and 'statement'

Section 15: Meaning of 'publish' and 'statement'

In this Act –

'publish' and 'publication', in relation to a statement, have the meaning they have for the purposes of the law of defamation generally;

'statement' means words, pictures, visual images, gestures or any other method of signifying meaning.

Section 15 sets out definitions of the terms 'publish', 'publication' and 'statement' for the purposes of the 2013 Act. Broad definitions are used to ensure that the provisions of the Act cover a wide range of publications in any medium, reflecting the current law.

Section 16: Amendments to existing law

Sections 16(1) to (3) ('Consequential amendments and savings etc.') make consequential amendments to s 8 of the Rehabilitation of Offenders Act 1974 to reflect the new defences of truth and honest opinion. Section 8 of the 1974 Act applies to actions for libel or slander brought by a rehabilitated person based on statements made about offences which were the subject of a spent conviction.

Section 17: Title and commencement

Section 17: Short title, extent and commencement

(1)   This Act may be cited as the Defamation Act 2013.

(2)   Subject to subsection (3), this Act extends to England and Wales only.

(3)   The following provisions also extend to Scotland –

   (a)   section 6;
   (b)   section 7(9);
   (c)   section 15;
   (d)   section 16(5) (in so far as it relates to sections 6 and 7(9));
   (e)   this section.

(4)   Subject to subsections (5) and (6), the provisions of this Act come into force on such day as the Secretary of State may by order made by statutory instrument appoint.

Section 17 sets out the territorial extent of the provisions and makes provision for commencement. Section 15, the savings-related provisions in subsections (4) to (8) of s 16 and s 17 (short title, commencement and extent) came into force on 25 April 2013.

See below 3.7

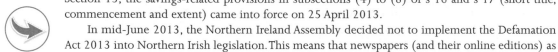

In mid-June 2013, the Northern Ireland Assembly decided not to implement the Defamation Act 2013 into Northern Irish legislation. This means that newspapers (and their online editions) as well as Twitterers and bloggers could potentially still face libel tourism claims and threats of legal action by big companies trying to stifle free speech in Northern Ireland.

In a subsequent House of Lords debate, Lord Lester said it would be 'a stain on the reputation of Northern Ireland if it were to replace London as the libel tourist capital by clinging to archaic and uncertain common law – great for the vested interests of wealthy claimants and their lawyers in Belfast but wholly against the public'.[105]

This could mean that the High Court in Belfast would replace the London High Court as the forum of choice, as libel tourists could seek regress in the Northern Irish Court. It is worth noting though that the UK (Westminster) Parliament can still impose the legislation on Northern Ireland due to its supremacy, whether Northern Ireland is devolved or not.

---

105 Source: 'Northern Ireland decides not to follow English and Welsh libel reforms', by Lisa O'Carroll, *Guardian*, 27 June 2013.

3.4.3 The essence of the Defamation Act 2013

Under s 1 of the 2013 Act, 'a statement is not defamatory unless its publication has caused or is likely to cause serious harm to the reputation of the claimant'.

Section 1 then provides a new 'definition' of what is meant by 'defamatory', setting out an additional requirement for a claimant to prove that he has been defamed. This must amount to 'serious harm' over and above the existing common law definitions of a defamatory meaning. In any new action for defamation, a claimant now has to show that the words complained of:

> (a) caused or are likely to cause serious harm to the claimant's reputation; and
>
> (b) tend, for example, to lower the claimant in the estimation of right-thinking or reasonable members of society; or
>
> (c) substantially affect in an adverse manner the attitude of others towards the claimant (. . . to be 'shunned and avoided').

It is anticipated that most claimants are unlikely to be affected by the 'serious harm' threshold, because most defamatory statements (which are disputed) are clearly likely to cause serious damage to a person's reputation. Can the defendant then prove the 'truth' or another defence? Here are some scenarios:

- The claimant has a bad reputation anyway and it is in doubt whether the claimant's reputation would be seriously harmed over and above his existing (suspect) reputation.
- The claimant needs to prove an innuendo identification and the people (with the special knowledge) who would identify the claimant would not believe the words would seriously harm the claimant's reputation (under the previous law, this would generally not prevent the meaning being defamatory).
- There is limited publication in the jurisdiction and/or the claimant is not known in the jurisdiction.
- The meaning is borderline vulgar abuse, 'pub talk' or a mere criticism of goods or services.
- Any damage was transient or short-lived due to a quick retraction, clarification or apology from the publisher.

See above
3.4.2

There might also be a **Jameel** abuse-type argument being deployed by the defendant and a 'serious harm' requirement could lead to early strike-out applications by defendants on both grounds.

The 2013 Act shifts the balance, between free speech and the right to reputation, in favour of free speech. In some areas this shift is likely to be significant, particularly where companies who wish to sue for libel are concerned. In terms of defences, there is one new area of practice, namely the 'honest truth' defence (s 3 Defamation Act 2013).

See below
3.4.4

3.4.4 Corporate defamation: can a company sue for libel?

The tort of defamation exists to afford redress for unjustified injury to reputation. By a successful action the injured reputation is vindicated. The ordinary means of vindication is by the verdict of a judge or jury (though juries are now no longer in use) and an award of damages. Most claimants are individuals, who are not required to prove that they have suffered financial loss or even that any particular person has thought the worse of them as a result of the publication complained of. The question arises whether a corporation with a commercial reputation should be subject to a different rule in the UK.

It was held in **Jameel**[106] that a corporation can generally sue for defamation on its reputation and may recover damages without proof of special damage (i.e. economic loss). By a majority of three to two, the Law Lords agreed that reputation is a thing of value and applies equally to companies as to individuals.

There are of course many defamatory things which can be said about individuals (for example, about their sexual appetite) which could not be said about corporations. But some statements may well be seriously injurious to the general commercial reputation of trading and charitable corporations. For example, that an arms company has routinely bribed officials of foreign governments to secure contracts; that an oil company has wilfully and unnecessarily damaged the environment; that an international humanitarian agency has wrongfully succumbed to government pressure; that a retailer has knowingly exploited child labour; and so on. Should the corporation be entitled to sue in its own right only if it can prove financial loss? The House of Lords in **Jameel** did not think so.

The concept that a company can sue for libel was first developed in the **Derbyshire**[107] case. The claimant was a county council constituted as a non-trading corporation. The defendant newspapers questioned the propriety of investments made in the claimant's superannuation funds. The HL clearly established that a trading corporation is entitled to sue in respect of defamatory matters which can be seen as having a tendency to damage it in the way of its business. This became known as the '**Derbyshire** Principle'.

The **Derbyshire** Principle was applied three years later in **Shevill v Presse Alliance SA** (1996),[108] where a differently constituted committee of the HL decided that a trading company with a trading reputation in the UK may recover general damages without pleading or proving special damage if the publication complained of had a tendency to damage it in the way of its business.

The *Wall Street Journal* in **Jameel No 3**[109] argued that, in accordance with the trend towards enhanced recognition of freedom of expression, the **Derbyshire** Principle should be abrogated. Lord Hoffmann (dissenting) agreed, stating:

> In the case of an individual, his reputation is a part of his personality, the 'immortal part' of himself and it is right that he should be entitled to vindicate his reputation and receive compensation for a slur upon it without proof of financial loss. But a commercial company has no soul and its reputation is no more than a commercial asset, something attached to its trading name which brings in customers. I see no reason why the rule which requires proof of damage to commercial assets in other torts, such as malicious falsehood, should not also apply to defamation.[110]

Baroness Hale (also dissenting) quoted the constitutional writer Weir, stating that a 'company had no feelings which "might have been hurt and no social relations which might have been impaired"'.[111]

A damaging libel may lower the company's standing in the eyes of the public and even its own staff, and make people less ready to deal with it or less willing and less proud to work for it. If this were not so, corporations would not go to the lengths they do to protect and burnish their corporate images. In his leading judgment in **Jameel**, Lord Bingham found nothing repugnant in the notion that this is a value which the law should protect. He did not accept that a publication, if truly damaging to a corporation's commercial reputation, would result in provable financial loss, since

---

106 *Jameel (Mohammed) v Wall Street Journal Europe Sprl (No 3)* [2007] 1 AC 359.
107 *Derbyshire County Council v Times Newspapers Ltd and Others* [1993] AC 534.
108 [1996] AC 959.
109 *Jameel (Mohammed) v Wall Street Journal Europe Sprl (No 3)* [2007] 1 AC 359.
110 Ibid., at para 91.
111 Ibid., at para 154.

the more prompt and public a company's issue of proceedings, and the more diligent its pursuit of a claim, the less the chance that financial loss would actually accrue.

Herzfeld (2005) argued that trading corporations should be allowed to sue in defamation only in respect of an attack on their business reputation and not any other reputation (e.g. performing charitable duties). He argued that this would simply be an indirect way to protect the company's business reputation. An example would be a company accused of exaggerating the amount of money it donated to charity. Herzfeld further contended that a company would have to show *actual* loss and be able to prove special damage.[112]

Section 2(1) of the 2013 Defamation Act sought to address this area of 'corporate' law in respect of defamation claims. Section 2(1) states:

> For the purposes of this section, harm to the reputation of a body that trades for profit is not 'serious harm' unless it has caused or is likely to cause the body serious financial loss.

This means that a for-profit company is likely to need to specify in its letter of defamation claim its 'Particulars of Claim', including that the defamatory statement:

(a)   has caused or is likely to cause the body financial loss; and
(b)   specify the type of loss; and
(c)   that the loss is serious.

The serious financial loss requirement may be difficult for some companies to show when suing for defamation, which may well reduce such claims in future.

3.4.5 No win, no fee?

Legal aid is not generally available for defamation cases, so the cost of proceedings will generally have to be paid personally by the defendant – as in the case of Dr Simon Singh.[113] Prior to the Jackson[114] reforms, firms of solicitors would offer Conditional Fee Agreements (or 'CFAs' – commonly known as 'no win no fee'). Before CFAs were permitted, libel claims were the preserve of the wealthy. There was no legal aid available. This meant that the media could pretty much say whatever they wanted about those less well off, without fear of a libel claim.

Prior to the introduction of CFAs with recoverable success fees and recoverable ATE (after the event) insurance premiums, claimants could not realistically bring defamation claims, however meritorious, against newspapers because they could not afford the legal fees. Newspapers and media organizations would regularly and deliberately outspend claimants in order to force them into submission. Raphael (1989) cites a lawyer for the *Daily Express*, as he researched the Jeffrey Archer libel action (and others):[115]

> If a newspaper were honest I suspect they would admit to drawing actions out in the hope that a [claimant] runs up large legal bills, loses heart and settles.[116]

---

112 See: Herzfeld (2005) at pp. 135ff.
113 **BCA v Singh** [2010] EWCA Civ 350.
114 See: Ministry of Justice (2010b) *Review of Civil Litigation Costs.* Final Report by Rupert Jackson J, December 2009 ('The Jackson Report').
115 See: Raphael (1989); the book was written prior to the introduction of CFAs.
116 Ibid., quoting Justin Walford, a lawyer employed at that time by the *Daily Express*.

Conditional fee agreements were first made enforceable under the Courts and Legal Services Act 1990, brought into effect in 1995. Initially, CFAs mainly related to personal injury cases, and the maximum success fee was set at 100 per cent of base cost. As Lord Justice Jackson pointed out in his extensive review,[117] lawyers could typically charge an uplift of up to 100 per cent in 'success fees', which encouraged them to accept cases with a 50/50 chance of success. Increasingly CFAs were used for defamation cases. This meant that newspapers and other media groups were increasingly subjected to numerous 'libel' claims from individuals who had until then been unable to enforce their legal rights against them. This had a chilling effect on freedom of speech, particularly academic comments in refereed and scientific journals. A CFA agreement then enabled a defamation litigant to engage a lawyer on a total or partial 'no win no fee' basis with an agreement that the lawyer would be paid up to twice their fee if they were successful.

Supermodel Naomi Campbell sued Mirror Group Newspapers, publishers of the *Daily Mirror*, for breach of confidence, defamation and misuse of private information after the newspaper published pictures of her leaving a drug addiction clinic in February 2001. The High Court found that the newspaper had invaded Ms Campbell's privacy and she was awarded £3,500 in compensation. The newspaper appealed to the Court of Appeal and won. Ms Campbell then appealed to the House of Lords in 2004, who found in her favour, and in addition to the compensation, awarded her legal costs of just over £1 million. Nearly £600,000 of this related to the appeal to the House of Lords where Ms Campbell's solicitors and counsel were acting under a CFA with success fees of 95 and 100 per cent respectively.

Though many 'ordinary' people availed themselves of CFAs it is true to say that some more wealthy litigants also used CFAs, such as Naomi Campbell in her action against the *Daily Mirror*. For this reason, there were a number of complaints, particularly from publishers and the media, as it left defendant publishers often facing disproportionately high costs on losing, meaning that cases were often settled early, to avoid the risk of paying these costs. On 18 January 2011, the European Court of Human Rights (ECtHR) unanimously ruled in **MGN v UK** (see below) that recovery of success fees by lawyers under CFAs in defamation and privacy cases was unlawful and represented a significant violation of the right to freedom of expression under Article 10 ECHR.

 **KEY CASE**   *Mirror Group Newspapers (MGN) v United Kingdom (Application no. 39401/04) 18 April 2011 (ECtHR)*

Precedent
❖   100 per cent success fees in CFA agreements for privacy and defamation cases violates freedom of expression.

Facts
The case related to the supermodel Naomi Campbell's suing MGN (publishers of the *Daily Mirror*) for breach of confidence, misuse of private information and defamation in her action in 2001, for publishing pictures and articles about her leaving a drug addiction clinic. The House of Lords had found in her favour and she was awarded just over £1 million in compensation and damages. A CFA enabled Ms Campbell to bring her action.

---

117 See: 'The Jackson Report', 2010.

MGN took its case to the ECtHR on the basis that the award of damages to Ms Campbell for invasion of her privacy and the award of costs, including the success fee, constituted a disproportionate interference with the newspaper's Article 10 right.

Decision

Though the ECtHR rejected MGN's privacy argument and upheld the HL's privacy ruling (Article 8 ECHR) due to Ms Campbell's physical and mental health and rehabilitative treatment, the Strasbourg Court decided that the requirement for MGN to pay a success fee was a disproportionate interference with MGN's right of freedom of expression and thus a violation of Article 10. The ECtHR concluded that although CFAs were based on a 'legitimate aim' by the Government to ensure access to justice, they were not a proportionate vehicle through which to achieve this aim in defamation and privacy claims and, as such, had violated MGN's right to freedom of expression under Article 10.

Analysis

The decision highlighted a number of conclusions. In particular, the ECtHR placed great emphasis on justification for CFAs, particularly that there appeared to be no qualifying requirements to enter into a CFA, which meant that they could be used by wealthy litigants who could well afford to pay for legal representation. Furthermore, the overwhelming cost burden of CFAs meant that defendants were forced to settle – even when they had a good defence – leading to a denial of justice. The ECtHR highlighted this particularly in the *Naomi Campbell* case, which showed up the flaws of CFAs and how wealthy litigants like Ms Campbell could run up excessive legal costs, placing pressure on a defendant newspaper with reasonable prospects of success. The effect was particularly chilling and damaging in media cases which, in turn, stifled freedom of expression.

The decision in *Mirror v UK* is binding on the UK Government but not necessarily on other domestic courts subscribing to the Convention. Furthermore, the ECtHR failed to determine whether only 100 per cent recoverable success fees are in breach of Article 10 ECHR, or whether any level of success fee under the 100 per cent mark might be acceptable.

In January 2010, Lord Justice Jackson had condemned the system of recoverable success fees (under CFAs), which could force a losing party to pay fees that could be double the winning side's initial costs. In his review, Jackson LJ commented that, specifically in relation to defamation and related claims, the CFA system as it stood was 'the most bizarre and expensive system that it is possible to devise', citing the **Naomi Campbell** case.[118] These problems were exacerbated in cases where the claimant was represented under a CFA with a success fee. The outcome was that claimants worthy of censure were succeeding with claims simply because the media could not afford to defend themselves.

The Bar Council's response to Lord Jackson's reforms (to do away with recoverable success fees and recoverable ATE insurance premiums) stated that the reforms in the Legal Aid, Sentencing and Punishment of Offenders Act 2012[119] (LASPO) would lead to unjustifiable unfairness.[120] Chairman of the Bar Council, Peter Lodder QC further argued that LASPO had taken no account of the fact that

---

118 See: The Jackson Report at para 5.11. Ministry of Justice (2010b)
119 Part 1: Civil Legal Aid.
120 Source: Bar Council, The (2011). Peter Lodder QC, Chairman's Report. May 2011.

defendants had in the past also been aided by CFAs in defending their actions. Section 8 LASPO deals specifically with civil legal services, namely services comprising advice and assistance provided in relation to the law as it applies to a particular case, legal proceedings and the resolution of legal disputes.[121]

The ramifications of the decision in **Mirror v UK**[122] are far-reaching when it comes to implementation of the Jackson reforms for the future of civil legal aid. One thing is clear: the ECtHR decision came as a huge relief for the media and publishers. Now that LASPO is in force, the defects of CFAs in relation to defamation and privacy cases are slowly being addressed. Following the Jackson reform of civil legal aid, the Government announced in January 2012 that it would establish a Supplementary Legal Aid Scheme (SLAS), which would take 25 per cent of the damages of anyone bringing a civil claim with legal aid. From March 2013 this limited solicitors from taking more than 25 per cent of a claimant's damages as their success fee.

3.5 Defences

See above 3.4

A person who publishes a defamatory statement may be able to rely on the defences of 'absolute' and 'qualified' privilege in a wide variety of circumstances. The defence of absolute privilege, as its name suggests, protects the publisher whatever their motive for publication. The defence of qualified privilege is defeated if the publisher was malicious in the sense that the dominant motive for publication was improper. There are other defences available in statute.

3.5.1 Summary of defences available

The defences available in a defamation action cut across a number of statutes:

See below
Reynolds
privilege' –
3.5.2

- **Justification** that the material is true (s 5 Defamation Act 1952).
- **Fair comment (now repealed)**[123] – this in the past protected statements of opinion or comment on matters of public interest (with no malice) (s 6 Defamation Act 1952).
- **Absolute privilege** which guarantees immunity from liability in certain situations such as in parliamentary and court proceedings (s 14 Defamation Act 1996).
- **Qualified privilege** which grants limited protection on public policy grounds to statements in the media provided that certain requirements are met (s 15 Defamation Act 1996).
- **Honest opinion** replaces common law defence of 'fair comment' (see above) (s 3 Defamation Act 2013).
- **Publication on matter of public interest** (s 4 Defamation Act 2013).
- **Peer-reviewed statement in scientific or academic journal etc.** (s 6 Defamation Act 2013).

The defence of *absolute privilege* gives the author of a 'defamatory' statement utter freedom in the communication of views and information. This privilege of free speech, dating back to Article 9 of

---

121 Civil legal services are all legal services other than those services that are required to be made available under the provisions about criminal legal aid. This is in order to avoid any overlap between civil and criminal legal aid.
122 *Mirror Group Newspapers v United Kingdom* (Application no. 39401/04) 18 April 2011 (ECtHR).
123 Section 3(8) Defamation Act 2013 abolishes the common law defence of 'fair comment' and also repeals s 6 Defamation Act 1952.

the Bill of Rights 1688, is extended to all Members of Parliament and to statements made during judicial or tribunal proceedings. However, absolute privilege does not protect ministers or peers *outside* the Houses of Parliament (such as on College Green) or outside the courthouse (see: **Church of Scientology of California v Johnson-Smith** (1972)[124]).

Examples of absolute privilege include testimony by a witness in court and contemporaneous reports of proceedings in open court. Although often classified as 'Parliamentary Privilege', Members of Parliament participating in parliamentary proceedings are similarly protected. This category of privilege reflects a particularly strong public interest in there being no inhibition on being able to speak or write freely even if there is an adverse impact on the other person's reputation. The defence is central to the proper functioning of an orderly and democratic society.[125]

In addition, s 2 of the Defamation Act 1996 provides a procedure by which a defendant can make an offer of amends to enable valid claims to be settled without the need for court proceedings. Section 2(2) Defamation Act 1996 reads:

> . . . the offer may be in relation to the statement generally or in relation to a specific defamatory meaning which the person making the offer accepts that the statement conveys ('a qualified offer').

In the offer to make amends, under s 4 of the 1996 Act: the defendant must:

(a) make a suitable correction of the statement complained of and a sufficient apology to the aggrieved party;
(b) publish the correction and apology in a manner that is' reasonable'; and
(c) pay to the aggrieved party (the claimant) compensation (if any) and costs.

Johnson (2008b) argues that the substantive defences in a defamatory action, such as absolute and qualified privilege, are going 'quite strongly in favour of the publisher of the material' and that the courts and human rights court rulings have been in favour of freedom of expression.[126] But if the basic elements of responsible journalism, such as accuracy and reliable sources, are ignored, the courts will take a dim view of journalists if they put basic economics to sell newspapers or promote their websites before truthful reporting.

While print media may eventually fade in people's memories, online publications and news archives will potentially remain in cyberspace indefinitely. As Mr Justice Tugendhat remarked in **Clarke (t/a Elumina Iberica UK) v Bain & Another** (2008): 'what is to be found on the Internet may become like a tattoo.'[127]

3.5.2 Qualified privilege

The defence of qualified privilege can protect private communications that contain defamatory material where there is a shared duty and interest between the publisher and the recipient. Qualified privilege also applies by statute[128] to a wide range of reports of public proceedings and notices, provided the relevant material is on a matter of public concern and for the public good. This

---

124 [1972] 1 QB 522.
125 See: Smartt (2013).
126 See: Johnson (2008b), pp. 126–131.
127 [2008] EWHC 2636 para 55 (Tugendhat J) (QB).
128 Originally contained in the Defamation Act 1952, now part of the Defamation Act 1996, section 15 and Schedule 1.

defence arises where media freedom warrants some additional protection from the threat of litigation, particularly relevant to newspaper reports of public meetings or court proceedings. 'Qualified'
means it is not 'absolute' and there will be certain conditions put on the author of the statement. A
statement made in the performance of a duty may attract the defence of qualified privilege under
common law,[129] provided that the person making the statement has a legal, moral or social duty to
make the statement and the person receiving it has an interest in doing so in that it allows such
person to make a quality decision.

Section 15 Defamation Act 1996 unfortunately does not define 'qualified privilege'; it just
states that the publication must not be made with malice. Otherwise 'there is no defence'. There are
a number of situations defined in Schedule 1 of the 1996 Act which detail 'qualified privilege'
scenarios. The prima facie defence of qualified privilege is lost if the claimant can prove that the
defendant was motivated by 'actual' or 'express malice', though there is no sufficient definition in
common law as to the meaning of 'malice'. A defendant establishes a prima facie defence of qualified privilege in common law if he can show that the publication was made by him in pursuance
of a duty or in protection of an interest to a person who had a duty or interest in having the matter
published.[130]

The qualified privilege common law defence was extended by way of the 'circumstantial' test
established by the Court of Appeal in *Reynolds*: 'Were the nature, status and source of the material,
and the circumstances of the publication, such that the publication should in the public interest be
protected in the absence of proof of express malice'[131] (though this was rejected in the House of
Lords). In his 'libel' action against *The Times*, the former Irish Taoiseach (Prime Minister) Albert
Reynolds, found himself embroiled in a political crisis in 1994. The Irish section of *The Times* had
alleged that Mr Reynolds had misled the Irish Parliament (Dáil Éireann), with the UK version of the
paper omitting the Taoiseach's 'right of reply'. After a number of cross appeals, the House of Lords
set the precedent for the now famous *Reynolds* qualified privilege defence, which set the tone for
future media cases in defamation.

In the *Reynolds* action, a series of allegations emerged about Taoiseach Reynolds appointing a
new President of the High Court, Harry Whelehan, whom Mr Reynolds had elevated to that post
from Attorney General. As AG Whelehan had delayed the extradition of a couple of Irish priests who
were wanted in the Belfast court for alleged child sex abuse, and the newspaper alleged that both
Reynolds and Whelehan had deliberately procrastinated in signing the extradition warrants. This
caused great political embarrassment for Mr Reynolds as the extradition of the priests to the
Northern Ireland court was delayed. His Government fell shortly afterwards, resulting partly from
the controversial piece in *The Times*.

During the ensuing defamation action with a jury, Lord Nicholls gave the leading judgment,
providing the now legendary 10-point list of factors to take into account when deciding whether
the qualified privilege defence ('in the public interest') should be available to journalists. The
House of Lords' *10-point-Reynolds* test comprises:

1. **The seriousness of the allegation**. The more serious the charge, the more the public
    is misinformed and the individual harmed, if the allegation is not true.
2. **The nature of the information**, and the extent to which the subject matter is a matter
    of public concern.

---

129 Common law is recognized by s 15(4) Defamation Act 1996.
130 *Hebditch v MacIlwaine* [1894] 2 QB 54.
131 *Reynolds v Times Newspapers Ltd* [1998] 3 All ER 961 at 995a (CA).

3. **The source of the information**. Some informants have no direct knowledge of the events. Some have their own axes to grind, or are being paid for their stories.
4. **The steps taken to verify the information**.
5. **The status of the information**. The allegation may have already been the subject of an investigation which commands respect.
6. **The urgency of the matter**. News is often a perishable commodity.
7. **Whether comment was sought from the claimant**. He may have information others do not possess or have not disclosed. An approach to the claimant will not always be necessary.
8. **Whether the article contained the gist of the claimant's side of the story**.
9. **The tone of the article**. A newspaper can raise queries or call for an investigation. It need not adopt allegations as statements of fact.
10. **The circumstances of the publication**, including the timing.[132]

The **Reynolds** qualified privilege defence can now be raised where it is clear that a journalist (or 'author' generally), accused of defamation, has a duty to meet the '10-point' criteria test in order to claim the defence, as affirmed in *Jameel v Wall Street Journal* (2007).[133]

The result of the strict 10-point **Reynolds** criteria has meant that journalists, editors and broadcasters have had to take steps – particularly in investigative stories and publishing 'in the public interest' – to verify the truth of what is being reported and follow the 10 criteria to the letter. Fairness to those whose names appear in the media has had to give the 'right to reply' or opportunity to give their side of the story.

The **Reynolds** 10-point test was applied in the *'George Galloway'* case,[134] where the former Glasgow MP sued the *Daily Telegraph* for publishing libellous articles during April 2003, which claimed that Mr Galloway had 'received money from the Iraqi ruler Saddam Hussein's regime, taking a slice of oil earnings worth £375,000 a year', and that the Scottish MP had asked for 'a greater cut of Iraq's exports' and 'was profiting from food contracts'. A further article had stated that, according to the claimant's Iraqi intelligence profile, the claimant 'had a family history of loyalty to Saddam Hussein's Ba'ath Party', and referred to him as a 'sympathiser with Iraq'. The High Court (affirmed by the CA) ruled in **Galloway** that the defendant newspaper could not rely on **Reynolds** qualified privilege, because not all of the 10-point criteria had been satisfied. Though the court said that the subject matter was 'undoubtedly of public concern', the sources of information could not be regarded as 'inherently reliable', and the *Telegraph*'s publishers, the editor and journalist had not taken sufficient steps to verify the information. The court, presiding without a jury, ruled in favour of Mr Galloway, who was awarded £150,000 in damages.

What can be concluded from **Galloway** is that a newspaper which obtains critical material from an anonymous or slightly dubious source will not be able to rely on the qualified privilege defence unless the source material passes the **Reynolds** – qualified privilege – test. George Galloway's success against the *Telegraph* effectively meant that breaking any one of the 10-point Reynolds criteria means the defence may be lost.

The '**Reynolds** defence' has since been regarded as a divisive and controversial issue. Clayton and Tomlinson (2009) argued that **Reynolds** qualified privilege left the law of defamation in a state of uncertainty in relation to media discussion of matters of public interest, stating:

---

132 [2001] 2 AC at para 205 (Lord Nicholls of Birkenhead).
133 [2007] 1 AC 359.
134 *Galloway v Telegraph* [2004] EWHC 2786 (QB).

> . . . in the absence of a developed body of case law, a responsible media organisation publishing material relating to matters of 'public interest' will be unable to determine whether a defence is available. It seems that the full background to the publication will have to be investigated in each case in order to satisfy the court that there is a 'right to know'. It is arguable that this uncertainty, of itself, constitutes an unacceptable restriction on freedom of expression.[135]

Clayton and Tomlinson further criticized the **Reynolds** 10-point criteria in that they did not support journalistic practice and free speech under Article 10 ECHR as a defence of qualified privilege in 'matters of legitimate public concern'.[136]

Generally speaking, the **Reynolds** 10-point test has had a 'chilling effect' on journalistic practice with the defence of qualified privilege being a very tall order to meet. Once any one of the 10-point criteria is not met, the whole defence is effectively lost, as **Galloway** proved. But, as **Jameel** demonstrated, the House of Lords provided a fresh impetus to 'responsible journalism' which lessened the importance of the **Reynolds** 10-point test to a certain extent (see also: **Hughes v Rusbridger** (2010)[137]).

The Supreme Court (UKSC) ruling in **Flood** (2011)[138] was seen as an important victory for investigative journalism for which newspapers such as the *Independent* and *Guardian* had fought for for many years. At last *The Times* was granted the **Reynolds** qualified privilege defence because the Gary Flood 'police corruption' story was of genuine public interest. As Lord Nicholls said in **Reynolds**: 'A newspaper can raise queries or call for an investigation.'[139] West Sussex Detective Sergeant Gary Flood had argued that a story published in *The Times* (and its online edition) on 6 June 2006, headlined 'Detective Accused of Taking Bribes from Russian Exiles', was defamatory. *The Times* had alleged that DS Flood had abused his position when he was working with the Metropolitan Police's extradition unit by corruptly accepting £20,000 in bribes from Russian criminals.

Lord Phillips and Lord Mance in **Flood** addressed the seriousness of the allegation, striking a balance between the public interest to receive such important information and the potential harm caused if the individual was being defamed.[140] Lord Phillips and Lord Brown opined that a journalist must have regard to the full range of information before deciding whether to publish a story, and when it is important to verify a story and its source.[141] The UKSC held that the DS Gary Flood story was of 'high public importance' and the allegations against the police officer were 'the whole story'.[142] The public interest in this case lay in the content of the allegations and the fact that they might be true. The **Reynolds** qualified privilege defence would only be allowed if *The Times* journalist honestly and reasonably believed the published facts to be true.[143] Their Lordships found that naming the respondent DS Flood was also justified as he would be identified in any event by his fellow officers and suspicion should not fall on other members of the Extradition Unit.[144] In respect of 'responsible journalism', Lord Mance held that journalistic judgement and editorial freedom were entitled to weight when considering how much detail should be published, but any journalist must consider carefully the public interest in doing so when allegations have not been investigated or their accuracy determined.[145]

---

135 Clayton and Tomlinson (2009) at para15.249.
136 Ibid.
137 [2010] EWHC 491 (QB).
138 *Flood v Times Newspapers Ltd* [2011] UKSC 11 (on appeal from: [2010] EWCA Civ 804).
139 *Reynolds v Times Newspapers Ltd* [2001] 2 AC 127 at para 205C (Lord Nicholls).
140 *Flood* at para 48.
141 Ibid., at paras 51 and 111.
142 Ibid., at paras 68 and 119.
143 Ibid., at para 78.
144 Ibid., at paras 75 and 169.
145 Ibid., at para 177.

FOR THOUGHT

Should the reason of the public interest defence not be enough in allowing a high-profile news story to be published without fear that a particular error of fact will restrict the willingness of the press to work in a certain fashion? Discuss with reference to the Defamation Act 2013 and existing common law defences.

3.5.3 Honest opinion

Section 3 of the Defamation Act 2013 introduced the defence of 'honest opinion' and thereby replaced the common law defence of 'fair comment'. This section reads:

(1) It is a defence to an action for defamation for the defendant to show that the following conditions are met.

(2) The first condition is that the statement complained of was a statement of opinion.

(3) The second condition is that the statement complained of indicated, whether in general or specific terms, the basis of the opinion.

(4) The third condition is that an honest person could have held the opinion on the basis of –

(a) any fact which existed at the time the statement complained of was published;

(b) anything asserted to be a fact in a privileged statement published before the statement complained of.

Section 3 of the 2013 Act broadly reflects and simplifies elements of the recent common law, but no longer includes the requirement for the opinion to be on a matter of public interest. Subsections (1) to (4) provide for the defence to apply where the defendant can show that three conditions are met. These are:

- **Condition 1: that the statement complained of was a statement of opinion**. This condition is intended to reflect the current law and embraces the requirement established in **Cheng v Tse Wai Chun Paul** (2000)[146] that the statement must be recognizable as comment as distinct from an imputation of fact. It is implicit in Condition 1 that the assessment is on the basis of how the ordinary person would understand it. As an inference of fact is a form of opinion, this would be encompassed by the defence.

- **Condition 2: that the statement complained of indicated, whether in general or specific terms, the basis of the opinion**. This reflects the test approved by the Supreme Court in **Spiller v Joseph** (2010)[147] that 'the comment must explicitly or implicitly indicate, at least in general terms, the facts on which it is based'.

- **Condition 3: that an honest person could have held the opinion on the basis of any fact which existed at the time the statement complained of was published or anything asserted to be a fact in a privileged statement published before the statement complained of**. This condition is an *objective* test and consists of two elements. It is enough for one to be satisfied.

  (i) The first is whether an honest person could have held the opinion on the basis of any fact which existed at the time the statement was published (as expressed in s (4)(a) of

146 [2000] 10 BHRC 525.
147 [2010] UKSC 53.

the 2013 Act 'the statement complained of was, or formed part of, a statement on a matter of public interest'). The existing case law on the sufficiency of the factual basis is covered by the requirement that an 'honest person' must have been able to hold the opinion. If the fact was not a sufficient basis for the opinion, an honest person would not have been able to hold it.

(ii) The second element of Condition 3 (as expressed in s (4)(b): 'the defendant reasonably believed that publishing the statement complained of was in the public interest') is whether an honest person could have formed the opinion on the basis of anything asserted to be a fact in a 'privileged statement' which was published before the statement complained of. For this purpose, a statement is a 'privileged statement' if the person responsible for its publication would have one of the defences listed in subsection (7) ('Reports etc. protected by privilege') if an action was brought in respect of that statement.

Conditions 2 and 3 have simplified the law by providing a clear and straightforward test (the conditions test). By providing these conditions, Parliament intended to retain the broad principles of the current common law defence of 'fair comment' as to the necessary basis for the opinion expressed but avoid the complexities which had arisen in case law, in particular over the extent to which the opinion must be based on facts which are sufficiently true and as to the extent to which the statement must explicitly or implicitly indicate the facts on which the opinion is based.

When drafting the legislation it was felt that existing areas of the common law of defamation had become increasingly complicated and technical. It had become clear that case law had become antiquated and had at times struggled to articulate with clarity how the law should apply in particular circumstances. For example, the facts that may need to be demonstrated in relation to an article expressing an opinion on a political issue, comments made on a social network, a view about a contractual dispute, or a review of a restaurant or play – all would differ substantially.[148]

Section 3(5) Defamation Act 2013 provides for the defence to be defeated if the claimant shows that the defendant did not hold the opinion. This is a *subjective* test which means the defence of 'fair comment' will fail if the claimant can show that the statement was actuated by malice.

Section 3(6) makes provision for situations where the defendant is not the author of the statement. For example, where an action is brought against a newspaper editor in respect of a comment piece rather than against the person who wrote it. In these circumstances the defence is defeated if the claimant can show that the defendant knew or ought to have known that the author did not hold the opinion.

Section 3(8) abolishes the common law defence of 'fair comment'. Although this means that the defendant can no longer rely on the common law defence, in cases where uncertainty arises in the interpretation of s 3, case law continues to provide a helpful but not binding guide to interpreting how the new statutory defence should be applied. Section 3(8) also repeals s 6 of the 1952 Act. Section 6 of the 1952 Act provided that in an action for libel or slander in respect of words consisting partly of allegations of fact and partly of expression of opinion, a defence of fair comment would not fail by reason only that the truth of every allegation of fact was not proved if the expression of opinion was fair comment having regard to such of the facts alleged or referred to in the words complained of as are proved. This provision is no longer necessary in light of the new approach set out in s 4(4) of the 2013 Act. A defendant will be able to show that conditions 1, 2 and 3 are met without needing to prove the truth of every single allegation of fact relevant to the statement complained of.

---

148 Based on an interview with Lord McNally's legal advisers at the Ministry of Justice, Paul Norris and Tony (Anthony) Jeeves in August 2013.

3.6 Defamation law in Scotland

Defamation law also exists in Scots law, but there are differences compared with English/Welsh jurisprudence. The two main distinctions are award of damages and the almost total absence of a jury in defamation cases. The purpose of this section is to provide a basic background outline of Scots law on the subject. The more detailed practical scope can be found in legal textbooks listed at the end of this chapter.

3.6.1 Roman law tradition

Scots civil law on defamation has developed through common law over hundreds of years, periodically being supplemented by statute – similar to what has happened in England – such as the Defamation Acts of 1952 and 1996.

While some areas of Scottish jurisprudence clearly derived from the civil Roman law tradition (or Canon law), the delict (i.e. wrongdoing) of defamation cannot be readily attributed to the differences in the sources of the two systems.[149] As far as the delict of defamation is concerned, Scots law is not substantially different from English (and Welsh) law. Nor can it be said that the seventeenth-century institutional writer Viscount Stair contributed much information in this area of Scots law.[150] In a short passage in his *Institutions of the Law of Scotland* (1681) on 'defamation', Stair notes that English law is identical to the law of Scotland in so far as claims for damages for defamation are concerned with some minor procedural differences. He writes that such actions:

> . . . upon injurious words, as they relate to damage in means, are frequent and curious among the English, but with us there is little of it accustomed to be pursued, though we own the same grounds, and would proceed to the same effects with them, if questioned.[151]

3.6.2 Definition of 'defamation' in Scots law

The definition of a 'defamatory statement' or communication is the same in Scots as it is in English law, being essentially harmful to the character, honour or reputation of the affected person (the pursuer) because it is 'derogatory' or 'disparaging' or 'demeaning' or 'calumnious' in the eyes of the reasonable person (see: **Sim v Stretch** (1936)[152]). Material can be defamatory regardless of the form in which it is communicated, i.e. whether in words or any other form, and whether in a permanent or transient form – in publications (whether sold, or distributed freely), on the internet, in TV or radio broadcasts, in recordings, as part of a theatrical performance, written or spoken in other arenas. For a successful defamation action in the Scottish courts, it must be shown that there was a disparaging statement made by one person about another, which is communicated, and for which there is no defence.

Communication includes traditional methods such as through oral dissemination or via the newspapers (and their online editions) as well as internet posts via blogs or other social media channels such as Facebook or Twitter.

There are some distinctive features which differ between English and Scottish jurisprudence. Most importantly, in contrast to other jurisdictions, in Scotland a communication need not be to a third party in order to be actionable: communication solely to the victim of a defamatory statement

---

149 For a historical overview, see: Normand (1938), pp. 327–338.
150 See: Smartt (2006), pp. 231–271.
151 See: Stair, Viscount – The Stair Society (1981), Chapter I, ix, p. 4.
152 [1936] 2 All ER 1237 (Lord Atkin).

may result in that person suffering relevant insult or affront. Whether material is defamatory (i.e. harmful to reputation) is a matter for the courts to determine, based on established principles of Scots law. The burden of proof in this regard rests with the pursuer. However, the pursuer is not required to show that the material is false; there is a rebuttable presumption that defamatory material is also false material, and it is for the defender to prove otherwise. Most importantly, there is a reverse onus (the same as in England): that it is up to the defender to prove his case if the defence is based on *veritas* (justification). The pursuer in a Scottish defamation action enjoys the same advantage as his English counterpart (the claimant).

In English law, a distinction is made between defamation in permanent form (libel) and not in permanent form (slander). This distinction is not made in Scotland. In Scots law, 'defamation' is a separate delict amounting to 'verbal injury' or *convicium*. The pursuer's claim is largely of the nature of *solatium* for hurt feelings or an award of damages for the loss proved or presumed from a reputation unjustly attacked. Since there has been little precedent set to put a precise figure on 'injured reputation' or 'hurt feelings', Scottish judges can at times find it problematic to assess the seriousness of an account for damages in relation to the defender. Allegations of drunkenness made about a minister or of dishonesty made about a solicitor would be treated more seriously than if the same statement was made about an ordinary member of the public.

There is also a separate delict of 'invasion of privacy' linked to Article 8 ECHR, in which the making of a statement may give rise to liability to an attack on someone's reputation.[153] Neither of these delicts comes under the general heading of 'defamation'.

Professor Norrie (1995) states that the delict of defamation occurs when a person makes a communication which contains a damaging and untrue imputation against the reputation of another person. He further describes Scots law as 'peculiar' in this area and defines the delict as follows:

> . . . it is an intentional delict in which the intent to injure is usually irrebuttably presumed;

> . . . it is a delict only if the statement or communication upon which it is based is false, but with which falsity is rebuttably presumed;

> . . . the pursuer does . . . always have the onus of proving that the statement or communication complained about is 'defamatory' and that it has been 'communicated'.[154]

Defences to defamation under Scots law include *veritas*, i.e. that the statement was in fact true (similar to the 'truth' defence under s 2 Defamation Act 2013 in England and Wales) or that the statement was 'fair comment'. Remedies can take the form of *interdict* to prevent further publication of the defamatory statement, or damages, which seek to compensate the pursuer for injury to feelings or to reputation. The wider the audience which receives the defamatory statement, the greater damages are likely to be.

3.6.3 Judge-alone trials

Jury trials in Scottish defamation cases have been extremely rare (compared with England), brought about by changes made by the Evidence (Scotland) Act of 1866 (still in force today), which makes judge-alone trials possible if 'special cause' can be shown. Though 'special cause' is not defined in

---

153 Sections 29 and 57 Scotland Act 1998 also provide that the Scottish Parliament and Scottish Ministers must not contravene certain Convention Rights, as defined in the Human Rights Act 1998, including Article 10 of the ECHR.
154 Ibid.

either common law or statute, it is generally assumed that it means 'special circumstances' depending on each individual case. Once a Scottish court holds the words to be capable of bearing a defamatory meaning, the following are presumed:

1. that the words are false;
2. that the words are spoken with intent to injure; and
3. that the pursuer has suffered some form of material injury which must result in financial compensation being due from the defender.

Although Scottish judges have largely followed English precedent in the law of defamation, there are certain procedural differences. The main one is that there is no jury, which many Scottish lawyers regard as an advantage compared with 'libel' juries south of the border, who have repeatedly allowed substantial punitive awards of damages, as in the '**Elton John**'[155] or '**Esther Rantzen**'[156] cases. Contrary to English and Welsh jurisdiction, conditional fee arrangements (CFA – 'no win, no fee') are not available in Scotland (though this is changing in England with Lord Jackson's reforms of civil 'legal aid' from March 2013). Neither is summary disposal. The remedies which can be sought usually amount to damages and injunction.

In terms of general defences, Scots law follows the English law tradition (i.e. justification; fair comment; absolute privilege, qualified privilege). There is also the 'offer to make amends' under s 2 of the Defamation Act 1996.

In cases where publication has been with malice, aggravated damages will be awarded if the case is proved. Even if the statement is truthful but designed to injure the claimant out of malice, an action can be brought when a statement is communicated; but only to the person defamed. This action includes injury to the feelings of the person defamed as well as injury to reputation. The pursuer of such a 'personal injury' claim cannot take advantage of the Court of Session procedure afforded to accident cases, for example.[157] The Scottish courts regard money damages as the remedy for a wrong done. Damages are always to compensate, never to punish. In 1908, Lord President Dunedin reviewed the question of punitive or exemplary damages and could find no authority for them in the law of Scotland. In fact, he felt that the heading of 'reparation' under which the matter is treated in the textbooks excluded the very idea of exemplary damages. When the argument was again raised in a defamation case 60 years later, Lord Justice Clerk Grant held that the fact that a libel was actuated by malice was not enough to entitle the pursuer to greater damages.

In **Baigent v BBC** (1999),[158] temporary Judge Coutts QC awarded exceptionally high damages. The case concerned a television programme which alleged that the owners of a nursing home were operating 'a callous and uncaring regime'. Mrs Baigent was awarded £60,000, Mr Baigent £50,000 and each of the three Baigent children £20,000 (upheld on appeal). The Baigent case probably marked the turning point when the Scottish courts began to award similarly high damages to the English courts. Coutts J stressed that damages in Scottish libel actions are compensatory rather than punitive. Similarly high awards, each of £60,000, were made in **Clinton v News Group Newspapers Ltd** (1999)[159] and **Wray v Associated Newspapers Ltd** (2000).[160]

Another major difference is the limitation period afforded to a pursuer, which makes litigation in the Scottish courts more attractive to litigants. Section 17 of the Prescription and Limitation Act (Scotland) 1973 grants a litigant three years in which to raise proceedings (compared to the

---

155 **John v Mirror Group Newspapers Ltd** [1997] QB 586.
156 **Rantzen v Mirror Group Newspapers** (1986) Ltd. [1994] QB 670.
157 Practice Note No 2 of 2003 explaining rule 43.1 of the Rules of the Court of Session 1994.
158 [1999] SCLR 787.
159 [1999] SC 367.
160 [2000] SLT 869.

one-year time limit in England and Wales). While Article 6 ECHR permits access to a court, that right is not absolute and the granting of an award of caution is a permissible limitation to that right (see: **Monarch Energy Ltd v Powergen Retail Ltd** (2006)[161]).

'Serial litigant' Terence Patrick Ewing took advantage of Scottish legislation when he sued in both the delicts of 'personal injury' and 'injury to privacy'. However, judging that Mr Ewing was a 'vexatious litigant', the Edinburgh High Court of Sessions took the unprecedented step of merely granting the pursuer a motion for caution in the sum of £15,000. In **Ewing v Times Newspapers Ltd** (2008),[162] Lord Brodie additionally refused leave to reclaim any damages at a later hearing (though it is understood that Mr Ewing marked an appeal at the time). Pursuer Mr Ewing, co-founder of the Euston Trust, whose members travel around the UK to make objections to planning applications, filed a 'defamation' claim against the Scottish edition of the Sunday Times in respect of an online article of 11 February 2007, entitled 'Heritage Fakers Hold Builders to Ransom', in which investigative journalists Daniel Foggo and Robert Booth had claimed to have exposed Mr Ewing as a fraudster; and also of having considerable debts from statutory demands for payment of fines. The publication in question had been downloaded by Mr Ewing's companion at the Edinburgh City Library.[163]

Mr Ewing sued for defamation, claiming, inter alia, breach of data protection, invasion of his privacy and harassment as well as breach of confidence. The court held that there was a 'stateable case' on his pleadings, and confined the pursuer's damages to a claim that would not be 'substantial' because his case did not have 'serious merits' and was an 'artificial litigation',[164] based on Lord Donaldson's ruling in **Henry J Garratt & Co v Ewing** (1991).[165] One crucial factor for the court's decision was that the pursuer had made 'at least 25 vexatious claims . . . none of this bodes well for the manner in which he is likely to conduct this action in a jurisdiction'[166] (see also: **Rush v Fife Regional Council** (1985)[167]).

Henderson (2009) argues that it would be wrong to presume that the finding in the **Ewing** claim (including privacy) was not stateable, as disclosing any emerging principle of the approach that the Scots courts will take to such actions. First there was an absence of any expectation of privacy on the part of the pursuer and second the context of the libel complaint had to be taken into account in that Mr Ewing had simply supplied a photocopy of the cases cited, where the court held that the pursuer 'did not set out in any comprehensive way in his pleadings the basis upon which he avers that delictual liability has been incurred'.[168]

3.6.4 The deceased cannot sue in defamation: developments in Scots law

See below
3.7.2

Internet 'trolls' used social networking sites like Twitter and Facebook to post sickening messages supporting the person responsible for the shooting of WPCs Fiona Bone (32) and Nicola Hughes (23) in September 2012. The two unarmed police constables were killed attending a 'routine burglary incident' in Tameside, Greater Manchester, on 18 September, when they were ambushed by one-eyed fugitive Dale Cregan (29), who was said to have been wielding a gun and a grenade. The Chairman of the Metropolitan Police Federation, John Tully, said he believed online comments praising the alleged murderer for his actions should be investigated as a public order offence. Tully

---

161 [2006] SLT 743.
162 [2008] CSOH 169, Outer House, Court of Session, Edinburgh.
163 Ibid., at paras 3 and 21.
164 Ibid., at para 25.
165 [1991] 1 WLR 1356 at 1357E (Lord Donaldson MR).
166 [2008] CSOH at para 29 (Lord Brodie).
167 [1985] SLT 451 (Lord Wheatley).
168 [2008] CSOH 169 at para 28 (Lord Brodie).

formally complained to Metropolitan Police Commissioner Bernard Hogan-Howe, asking him to investigate whether any criminal offences may have been committed by persons using internet sites and thereby defaming the deceased women. He wrote: 'I believe offences may have been committed under Section 5 of the Public Order Act 1986.[169] The last time we saw people investigated over matters such as these was during the Olympic Games when the diver Tom Daley received online abuse.'[170]

Concern for posthumous good name and reputation is not new and dates back at least to William Shakespeare, who wrote: 'The evil that men do lives after them; the good is oft interred with their bones.' [171] A remedy for injury to reputation or honour of a deceased relative exists in the jurisdictions of France, Germany and Quebec.[172]

In English and Scots law, relatives of the deceased have no right of action in the law of defamation because reputation is personal.[173] Essentially, the law on defamation proceeds on the basis that when people die, they are beyond harm and beyond help. Therefore, a defamatory statement about a deceased person in the UK does not give rise to a civil action in the tort (or delict) of defamation on behalf of the deceased's estate. Taking into account this key legal principle – that a right to redress should be predicated on *damnum injuria datum* (i.e. loss wrongfully caused) – the absence of loss seems inevitably to suggest an absence of a right to redress.[174] This then reflects the central principle in UK civil proceedings generally, that a claim for damages can only be brought by the person who has suffered the injury, loss or harm to his reputation as a result of the act or omission of another person.[175]

Victim Support Scotland has described this as 'a clear gap in the legislative protection of victims and the bereaved family's right to privacy and family life'.[176] The victim pressure group has argued before the Scottish Parliament that the death of a loved one can be a source of significant pain and grief, especially when it occurred in sudden or traumatic circumstances. If the death is then followed by unfounded allegations which denigrate the character or activities of the deceased, that pain and grief is likely to be made even more acute. Under present Scots (and English) law, relatives of the deceased cannot challenge such stories effectively in the tort of defamation. In 2011 the Civil Law Division of the Scottish Government published a consultation paper, *Death of a Good Name: Defamation and the Deceased*,[177] which looked at possible changes in the law.

In November 2006, the Home Office, Scottish Executive and Northern Ireland Office published a joint consultation paper on criminal memoirs, *Making Sure That Crime Doesn't Pay*.[178] The paper referred to the views of the families of victims of homicide, and their concern not just about preventing criminals profiting from publications about their crimes, but about the fact that they may paint a defamatory picture of the victim. Legislation on criminal memoirs has subsequently been enacted, with Part 7 of the Coroners and Justice Act 2009. This introduced a new civil scheme through which courts can order offenders to pay amounts in respect of profits or other proceeds derived by them from the exploitation of accounts about their crimes, for example by selling their memoirs,

---

169 Causing 'harassment, alarm or distress'.
170 Source: 'Calls for "sick" internet trolls to be prosecuted', *Daily Telegraph*, 19 September 2012.
171 Mark Antony, in William Shakespeare's *Julius Caesar*.
172 Hannes Rösler compares the different approaches taken in countries such as Germany, where the concept of *postmortales Persönlichkeitrecht* is illustrated by the 'Mephisto Decision' of 1971, and suggests that the 'the German posthumous personality right has some potential to inspire a common law equivalent'. See: Rösler (2008) at pp. 153–205.
173 If an action for defamation has been raised by the claimant prior to his death, an executor may continue the action. Similarly, liability in defamation does not die with the defamer (i.e. a defamation action may be raised against a deceased defamer's executor).
174 For further discussion see: Reid (2010).
175 See also: Whitty (2005) at pp. 194–237.
176 Source: 'No Going Back'. Victim Support Scotland Manifesto 2011–15: www.victimsupportsco.org.uk/lib/liDownload/749/13109%20VSS%20Manifesto.pdf.
177 Scottish Government (2011).
178 See: Scottish Executive; Northern Ireland Office; Home Office (2006).

or receiving payments for public speaking or media interviews. The scheme is restricted to cases where the memoirs, etc., pertain to the most serious offences.

The Scottish Parliament has made it clear, during its consultation exercise for the Defamation (Scotland) Bill 2011, that the law must not limit freedom of expression under Article 10 ECHR, which is essential for the proper protection of countervailing rights, such as the law on defamation, where the limitation applies only to the living.[179] When a person dies, the protection offered by the law on defamation dies too.[180]

If a right to protect the deceased from defamatory material were to be introduced into Scots law (by way of a new defamation act), it could then be made possible for actions to be brought either against the alleged defamer or against the publisher of the allegedly defamatory material (by the deceased's estate). Extending the law in this way would be welcomed by victim support organizations. It is also important to consider the potential disadvantages, as the Global Campaign for Free Expression 'Article 19' Report points out:

> . . . any interest surviving relatives may have in the reputation of a deceased person is fundamentally different from that of a living person in their own reputation. Furthermore, a right to sue in defamation for the reputation of deceased persons could easily be abused and might prevent free and open debate about historical events.[181]

These arguments have also been considered by the Scottish Parliament. Significant concern has been raised during the consultation period of the Defamation (Scotland) Bill that there would be disquiet about any potentially detrimental impact on journalism, the media and publishing industries, through the creation of the possibility of additional litigation and associated costs.

FOR THOUGHT – CASE STUDY

Discuss the following scenario:

In private conversations with Ms Jones, Mr Smith confesses that he owes some money. Shortly afterwards Mr Smith dies. Ms Jones subsequently publishes statements on Twitter which are clearly defamatory about Mr Smith, calling him a 'thief'. Mr Smith's widow, Mrs Smith, wishes to protect her late husband's memory and to take legal action in relation to the tweets by Ms Jones. The tweets are clearly defamatory in that they tend to lower the late Mr Smith in the estimation of right-thinking members of Scottish society. Since she cannot question and cross-examine Mr Smith in court, how is Ms Jones to prove (as required by standard defamation law) that her claims are indeed truthful? Advise both Mrs Smith and Ms Jones. Draft a skeleton argument.

---

179 Although the case of **Walker v Robertson** (1821) appeared to suggest that it was competent in Scotland to sue for *solatium* as regards distress arising from the post-mortem defamation of a relative, that approach appeared to have been overruled by the case of **Broom v Ritchie & Co.** (1904) (see: **Walker v Robertson** (1821) 2 Murray 516 (jury court, Scotland)).

180 As with physical injuries (see the Damages (Scotland) Act 1976), certain rights may persist post mortem and transfer to an executor, but only where the wrongdoing occurred prior to death.

181 Source: 'Defining Defamation: Principles on freedom of expression and protection of reputation.' International Standard Series. Global Campaign for Free Expression 'Article 19' at p. 6: www.article19.org/data/files/pdfs/standards/definingdefamation.pdf.

3.6.5 Developments in the law of defamation in Scotland

Similarly to its English counterpart, Scots common law development in defamation, coupled with 'privacy' challenges, is in a state of flux in that even relatively recent decisions can soon become out of date, best illustrated with reference to cases involving photographs, as was highlighted in the '**Frances Curran**' case (below). Scottish courts have frequently referred to the **von Hannover (No 1)**[182] decision in relation to the invasion of someone's privacy when defamatory actions are being considered. When the court considered privacy in the **Ewing** action it referred, *inter alia*, to **Reklos v Greece** (2009).[183]

In **Reklos** a Greek couple, Dimitrios Reklos and Vassiliki Davourli, complained to the ECtHR that the taking of a photograph of their newborn child, Anastasios, in a private clinic, violated Article 8 ECHR. The parents objected to this intrusion by the clinic's professional photographer, especially since the photos were taken in the sterile environment of the birthing unit without their prior consent. The Athens Court of Cassation[184] had dismissed their action as unfounded, but the Strasbourg court upheld their claim. In a chamber judgment, President Nina Vaji held that the taking of clandestine photographs and the keeping of negatives of a newborn child, without parental consent, was an infringement of their Article 8 right (see also: **Egeland and Hanseid v Norway** (2009)[185]).

Conversely (applying **Reklos**), the Scottish '**Frances Curran**'[186] case was seen as a major victory for press freedom, ensuring that the Scottish media could continue to report fearlessly on a matter of great public interest, thereby succeeding in the **Reynolds** qualified privilege defence.

 KEY CASE
Curran (Frances) v Scottish Daily Record and Sunday Mail Ltd [2011] CSIH 86 (A952/08). Extra Division, Inner House, Court of Session, 29 December 2011.

Facts

The pursuer was Frances Curran;[187] the defenders the publishers of the *Daily Record*. On 7 August 2006 the defenders published a four-page article based on an interview with Tommy Sheridan,[188] in which certain remarks were made about the pursuer and three other MSPs, Colin Fox, Rosie Kane and Carolyn Leckie, accompanied by photographs. The front page headline read: 'I'll destroy the scabs who tried to ruin me: Tommy vows to win back leadership of Scottish Socialists.' The defenders sought dismissal of the action on the basis that no relevant case of defamation was made out in the pursuer's pleadings and an *esto* position that, were the action to proceed to proof before answer, deletions would be required to be made.

---

182 **Von Hannover v Germany (No 1)** (2005) 40 EHRR 1 (ECHR).
183 (2009) (Application No. 1234/05) ECtHR of 15 January 2009.
184 Supreme Court (Άρειος Πάγος).
185 (2009) (Application no. 34438/04) Strasbourg, 16 April 2009 (ECtHR).
186 **Curran (Frances) v Scottish Daily Record, Sunday Mail Ltd** [2010] (A 952/08) CSOH 44 (2010 WL 902938) Outer House, Court of Session of 26 March 2010.
187 Frances Curran (born 21 May 1961, Glasgow) is a leading activist in the Scottish Socialist Party (SSP). She was a member of the Scottish Parliament (MSP) for West of Scotland during 2003–07, and an unsuccessful candidate in the July 2008 Glasgow East by-election.
188 Tommy Sheridan MSP, member of the SSP at the time, won a libel action against the *News of the World* on 4 August 2006 when the jury returned their verdict, finding in favour of Mr Sheridan, awarding him damages of £200,000.

The defenders submitted that criticism by an MSP of another MSP did not amount to defamation because of the permitted latitude in criticizing those who hold public office. Further, it was submitted that the comments made in the article were protected by the *Reynolds* qualified privilege defence. The pursuer would have to prove malice for the defence to fail. This she had not done. The defenders further submitted that the article be looked at as a whole, representing an attack on the public as well as the political activities of the pursuer(s), and that the term 'scab' in the article referred to her being a 'political scab'. Counsel for Ms Curran submitted that the case should be sent to proof and submitted that the tenor of the article was that she was guilty of dishonest conduct with base motives, and that it went beyond fair criticism of a holder of a public office.

Opinion

Temporary Judge Mrs Morag Wise QC dismissed the action. She considered whether the article, taken as a whole, would tend to lower the pursuer in the estimation of right-thinking members of society generally, or be likely to affect her adversely in the estimation of reasonable people generally. She ruled:

> I do not consider that it would have that effect. Right-thinking members of society are well able to read an article of this sort and see it as no more than a robust criticism of the pursuer as a former colleague and ally of Mr Sheridan. The reference to the pursuer as a 'scab' simply has no context without the detail given of the political plot alleged by Mr Sheridan and the references to collaboration with 'the enemy' namely Newsgroup Newspapers Limited.[189] In relation to the photograph this should not be seen in isolation but as part of the whole article, as demonstrated in *Charleston v News Group Newspapers Ltd* (1995).[190]

Analysis

The Edinburgh court felt that the photo of the Scottish MPs amounted to neither defamation nor an infringement of their privacy under Article 8 ECHR, citing the *Reklos* judgment. Mrs Justice Wise QC's opinion focused on the 'eye-catching' photograph in particular and stated that the matter was in the public interest, thereby allowing the qualified privilege defence under *Reynolds* (where all the 10-point criteria had been met by the newspaper). She stated that it was of particular public interest – and therein protected by Article 10 ECHR – that the leadership of a political party was explained and the (in this case) inability of some of its members to work with each other. Accordingly she did not consider that this was an attack on the private character of the main pursuer, Frances Curran, but rather on her political decisions and political loyalties (also applied: *McLeod v News Quest (Sunday Herald) Ltd* (2007)[191]).

3.7 Internet libel

The rise in defamation cases linked to the internet has been inevitable, where blogs or tweets have failed to put in place the same kind of pre-publication controls that traditional media use. As a

---

189 [2010] CSOH 44 at para 29 (Judge Morag Wise QC).
190 [1995] 2 AC 65 (HL).
191 [2007] SCLR 555.

result, there exists an ongoing battle between individuals trying to protect their privacy and the media trying to publish ostensibly private material.

3.7.1 When is an ISP a publisher?

The term 'ISP' (internet service provider) is mostly used to describe an internet access or service provider such as BT or Sky Broadband, but it is also used loosely to describe other types of internet intermediaries such as 'hosts' (or 'hosting providers'), for example, Demon Internet, social networking platforms such as Facebook and Blogger, and even search engines such as Google. How does the law of defamation view these intermediaries? It appears they do not always fulfil the same functions in UK, European and US jurisdictions, and cannot therefore be 'lumped' together under one legislation.

United Kingdom law currently classifies internet access providers and other so-called 'mere conduits' as non-publishers, but in certain circumstances recognizes that other internet intermediaries (including website operators) can be classified as publishers if they are notified of defamatory material being published via their servers or websites but fail to do anything about it. Although discussion forums and social networking sites are often full of robust, forthright and even offensive opinions posted by individuals, the case **Godfrey v Demon Internet** (2001)[192] hinged on whether the British ISP Demon could be treated as publisher of the material.

In 2000, Demon Internet was held liable for defamatory statements on a discussion forum which it hosted after it was notified of the material but failed to remove it for 12 days (although it was liable only for the damage caused in the 12-day period). Dr Laurence Godfrey's action against Demon related to a message posted in 1997 on soc.culture.thai, purportedly coming from him and containing damaging allegations of a personal nature. Dr Godfrey then asked Demon to remove the message but the ISP refused. The message was copied to its servers around the world, and to many others containing newsgroup messages. The UK-based ISP Demon Internet settled the first UK internet libel case out of court, after Dr Godfrey alleged that the ISP failed to remove defamatory material from a newsgroup it hosted. Godfrey was paid £15,000 plus legal costs, totalling £200,000, by Demon Internet. Godfrey said after the case was settled:

> I am happy with the settlement. I don't think there is a right, in fact I'm quite sure there's no right, to libel other people on the internet, to concoct fabricated allegations and try to destroy people's reputations.[193]

Godfrey affected other ISPs – all of which host newsgroups – who feared they could become liable for offensive material which millions of their users might write. **Godfrey** gave rise to the unwelcome practice of ISPs simply removing material upon complaint without a great deal of scrutiny, causing a chilling effect on freedom of expression.

In March 2011, Carmarthenshire political blogger Jacqui Thompson sued the Chief Executive of the local council of Llanwrda, Mark James, for libel (see: **Thompson (Jacqueline) v James (Mark) and Carmarthenshire County Council** (2013)[194]). Ms Thompson had posted a series of defamatory internet posts (blogs), falsely accusing Carmarthenshire Council officers of corruption. She had also secretly filmed council hearings in April 2011 and was subsequently arrested. Mr James counter-sued and Ms Thompson lost. In March 2013, after a six-day trial without a jury, the High Court ordered Ms Thompson to pay the Chief Executive £25,000 in damages. Mr Justice Tugendhat concluded that

---

192 [2001] QB 201.
193 Source: 'Demon settles net libel case', BBC News Online, 30 March 2000.
194 [2013] EWHC 515 (QB) 15 March 2013.

she had acted irresponsibly and described her blog as an 'unlawful campaign of harassment, defamation and intimidation'.[195] Tugendhat J concluded:

> The strongest point in favour of Mrs Thompson is the fact that the publications on which Mr James has succeeded were to a small number of readers of her blog.[196]

The Directive 2000/31/EC ('E-Commerce Directive')[197] and the implementing Regulations, the Electronic Commerce Regulations 2002,[198] provide immunities for ISPs who are regarded as mere conduits, caches and hosts in EU law. This means that EU law recognizes 'internet intermediaries' as 'information society service providers' under the 'E-Commerce Directive'. The Directive considers that some, but not all, internet intermediaries deserved immunity from legal action in respect of third-party content. Examples of services covered by the Directive include online information services (such as online newspapers), online selling of products and services (books, financial services and travel services), online advertising, professional services (lawyers, doctors, estate agents), entertainment services and basic intermediary services (access to the internet and transmission and hosting of information). These services also include services provided free of charge to the recipient and funded, for example, by advertising or sponsorship.

Furthermore, there is the existing (secondary) defence under s 1 Defamation Act 1996 for publishers who are exempt from defamation actions if a defamatory statement was published without their knowledge and they took reasonable care. This was followed in **Tamiz v Google Inc** (2012)[199] by Eady J. He noted that none of the cases involving ISPs so far had settled how ISPs fitted with common law principles on publication, but that if Google was not a publisher before notification, it was then difficult to see how it could become one thereafter given it took a neutral stance despite its technical ability to take down content (see below) (see also: **Bunt v Tilley** (2006)[200]).[201]

In the United States things are different. Virtually all ISPs are regarded as 'hosts' – that is, these internet intermediaries are immune from being sued for damages for defamation. The anonymity of bloggers or those using fake identities on Twitter or Facebook can make life intolerable for those individuals who wish to object to what is written about them or seek regress through the courts because naming the abusive individuals in a defamation action is often impossible. For this reason, Mr Justice Eady's decision in **Tamiz** is an important one in this respect.

❖ **KEY CASE**   *Tamiz (Payam) v Google Inc, Google UK Ltd* [2012] EWHC 449 (QB)

Precedent

❖ An ISP is only a 'host' and is granted immunity in defamation actions under Regulation 19 of the Electronic Commerce (EC Directive) Regulations 2002.

❖ The Internet Service Provider (ISP) 'Google Inc' is not a publisher according to common law principles.

---

195 Source: 'Carmarthenshire blogger Jacqui Thompson loses libel claim – must pay £25k to council chief executive', *The Llanelli Star*, 15 March 2013.
196 [2013] EWHC 515 at para 420.
197 Directive 2000/31/EC On 'Liability of Intermediary Service Providers' on Electronic Commerce of 8 June 2000 ('E-Commerce Directive').
198 Electronic Commerce (EC) Regulations 2002 (SI 2002/2013).
199 [2012] EWHC 449 (QB).
200 [2006] EWHC 407 (QB).
201 For further discussion see: McEvedy (2013) at pp. 108–112.

Facts

The Claimant in this libel action, Mr Payam Tamiz (T), sued both Google Inc and Google UK Ltd in relation to eight comments which were said to be defamatory of him and which were posted on a blog bearing the name 'London Muslim' at various times between 28 and 30 April 2011. T had been in the news in 2011, following allegations that his resignation as Conservative Party candidate for local elections in Thanet had come about after he had made inappropriate remarks online. The blog posts on the 'London Muslim' website appeared under a photograph of Mr Tamiz, saying:

> . . . Payam Tamiz a Tory Muslim council candidate with a 5 o'clock shadow has resigned from the party after calling Thanet girls 'sluts'.

> . . . Tamiz who on his Twitter page describes himself as an 'ambitious British Muslim' is bizarrely studying law so one would have though (sic) this Tory prat with Star Trek Spock ears might have engaged the odd brain cell before making these offensive remarks.[202]

There were other serious and abusive allegations, and T used the 'report abuse' function on the website to complain immediately about these messages in April. In June he sent a letter of claim to Google UK, who passed it on to Google Inc. They asked his permission to contact the author of the blog, and the claimant subsequently complained about five further comments. The comments were eventually removed by the blogger himself in August. A claim was issued shortly afterwards, and T was granted permission to serve the claim form on Google Inc in California on a without notice application on 22 September.

Catrin Evans, acting for the first defendant (Google Inc), submitted that the Claimant had not pleaded that a 'real and substantial tort' had been committed in 'this jurisdiction' (i.e. the UK) because it could not be proved that a substantial number of readers had downloaded or accessed the words complained of (see: *Jameel (Yousef) v Dow Jones & Co Inc* (2005)[203]). Ms Evans also argued that the content of the words complained of did not reach the necessary 'threshold of seriousness required to establish a cause of action in libel'.[204] The defence further submitted that Google Inc is not a publisher for the purposes of the English law of defamation. And even if Google Inc were to be regarded as a publisher of the words complained of, Ms Evans argued that it would be protected against liability by Regulation 19 of the Electronic Commerce (EC Directive) Regulations 2002.[205]

Decision

Eady J considered the defence submission that there was a lack of evidence of a 'real and substantial' tort in British defamation law. The judge examined some witness statements which the claimant had adduced and found that at least three of them were relevant to potential damage to reputation.

Eady J then addressed the more problematic question of whether Google Inc is a publisher according to common law principles, finding that there is as yet no common law decision

---

202 Ibid., at para 6 (Eady J).
203 [2005] QB 946.
204 [2012] EWHC 449 at paras 11–13.
205 These implement in the law of the UK the provisions of Article 14 of Directive 2000/31/EC relating to electronic commerce.

establishing how web publishers fit into the traditional framework of defamation law. Referring to the judgment by HHJ Parkes QC in **Davison v Habeeb** (2011),[206] where it was said that Google was a publisher and was liable post-notification, Eady J suggested that the position 'may well be fact sensitive', pointing to the differences between the position in law of the ISPs in **Godfrey v Demon Internet** (2011)[207] (see also: **Bunt v Tilley** (2006);[208] **Metropolitan International Schools Ltd (t/a SkillsTrain and/or Train2Game) v Designtechnica Corpn (t/a Digital Trends)** (2009)[209]).

On the question of whether Google Inc could be liable after notification, the judge referred to the Blogger.com platform which contained more than half a trillion words, with 250,000 new words added every minute. He held that accepting the responsibility to notify the offending bloggers did not necessarily change Google's status:

> The fact that an entity in Google Inc's position may have been notified of a complaint does not immediately convert its status or role into that of a publisher. It is not easy to see that its role, if confined to that of a provider or facilitator beforehand, should be automatically expanded thereafter into that of a person who authorises or acquiesces in publication.[210]

Finally, the judge turned to the statutory 'hosting' defence, found under Regulation 19 of the Electronic Commerce (EC Directive) Regulations 2002, which succeeded in **Davison**.[211] The provision protects the provider of an 'information society service', which consists of the storage of information, where that service is provided 'for remuneration, at a distance, by means of electronic equipment for the processing (including digital compression) and storage of data, and at the individual request of a recipient of a service.[212]

On the evidence, Google Inc was the provider of the service and the 'London Muslim' blogger its recipient. For the defence to succeed there must be 'no actual knowledge of unlawful information', and with trillions of pieces of unsubstantiated information posted every second on the web, the ISP host cannot possibly have actual knowledge of every alleged illegality posted on the World Wide Web. This point was reinforced by Regulation 22 of the e-Commerce Directive, which concerns the notice by means of which knowledge is imputed, and requires it to include details of the unlawful nature of the activity or information in question (see also: **L'Oréal SA v eBay International AG** (2012)[213]).

In reaching his conclusion, Eady J ruled that Google Inc should not be regarded as a publisher of the offending words, in accordance with common law principles; and that, in any event, the ISP was exempted from liability in accordance with Regulation 19 of the Electronic Commerce (EC Directive) Regulations 2002.[214]

---

206 [2011] EWHC 3031 QB (HHJ Parkes QC).
207 [2001] EWHC QB 201 (Morland J at paras 205–207).
208 [2006] EWHC 407 (QB).
209 [2009] EWHC 1765 (QB).
210 [2012] EWHC 449 at para 38 (Eady J).
211 *Davison v Habeeb* [2011] EWHC 3031 (QB) (HHJ Parkes QC).
212 [2012] EWHC 449 at paras 51–54 (Eady J).
213 *L'Oréal SA and Others v eBay International AG and Others* (2012) (Case C–324/09). Judgment of the Court of Justice. Grand Chamber, 12 July 2011.
214 Ibid., at para 61.

Analysis

Mr Justice Eady's decision in March 2012 in the **Payam Tamiz** case is an important one. He found against the former Conservative council candidate, about whom some outrageously defamatory falsehoods had been posted on Google's blogger.com platform. The court held that the ISP's role was purely passive, that of a host or 'wall' on which any graffiti could be freely posted. Google Inc was not held to be a 'publisher' and was not capable of having 'authorized' the defamatory publications. Matthew Parris, commenting on the case in *The Spectator* magazine, wrote:

> May this not mean that bloggers and tweeters can scoop professional journalists and journals with material that the latter dare not risk publishing? . . . Aren't court judgments like these going to lead in the end to the death of the civil tort of defamation, and of privacy too?[215]

Google Inc availed itself of the 'hosting' defence provided by Regulation 19 of the Electronic Commerce Regulations 2002 in respect of bloggers and similar social networking services. *Tamiz* confirms the broad protection under EU law, confirmed by the European Court of Justice in relation to notification in *L'Oréal SA v eBay* (2012).[216]

The case sends a message of positive inaction taken by the UK courts towards those individuals who are being defamed online. Judge Eady made the position of ISPs abundantly clear in that they are purely passive hosts.

Similarly to **Davison v Habeeb** (2011),[217] **Tamiz** points to the potential conflict between the s 1 Defamation Act 1996 defence and EU law (i.e. the E-Commerce Regulations 2002). The judge granted the ISP immunity under Regulation 19, affirming that internet publishers are merely hosts concerning any defamatory material on their servers. This means that courts will in future invariably say that they are in no position to adjudicate on the merits of any libel complaint. The decisions in **Davison** and **Tamiz** set the precedent for liability under the E-Commerce Regulations materially higher than s 1 Defamation Act 1996. The burden of proof is then on the complainant to substantiate his claim – which in most cases is an impossible task.

3.7.2 Internet trolls

An increasing threat to a person's reputation comes from internet trolls.[218] The feminist activist Caroline Criado-Perez had to endure thousands of trolls in July 2013 as a response to her successful campaign to put Jane Austen on the new £10 note. The trolls even threatened her with rape.

In August 2013, internet troll Oliver Rawlings was made to apologize to academic classicist Professor Mary Beard, after sending hundreds of abusive messages to her. Rawlings (20) used his Twitter account to call the Cambridge University professor a 'filthy old slut', making highly offensive sexual comments about her online. But Professor Beard re-tweeted the remarks to all her

---

215 Source: 'The writing is on the wall for restrictions on free speech', by Matthew Parris, *The Spectator*, 10 March 2012 at p. 26.
216 *L'Oréal SA and Others v eBay International AG and Others* (2012) (Case C–324/09). Judgment of the Court of Justice. Grand Chamber, 12 July 2011.
217 [2011] EWHC 3031 (QB).
218 A 'troll' is a person who sows discord on the internet by starting arguments or upsetting people by posting inflammatory messages. See Glossary for full explanation.

followers, saying she would not be 'terrorized' by online abuse. It was by this method that Rawlings was 'outed' and Professor Beard could therefore discover the troll's identity.[219]

Another example was Nicola Brookes (45), a single mother suffering from Crohn's disease, who faced 'vicious and depraved' abuse on Facebook after she posted a comment supporting former X Factor contestant Frankie Cocozza when he left the show in 2011. Her anonymous tormentors set up a fake Facebook profile in her name using her picture to post explicit comments. Her local Sussex Police Force was unable to help her track the perpetrators since there is no adequate law to protect her. She took her case to the High Court, where a Norwich Pharmacal Order[220] was granted in June 2012 ordering the US social network provider Facebook to reveal the IP addresses and other information of the people who had abused her.[221] By having the names of the anonymous internet perpetrators disclosed to her, Ms Brookes was then able to bring a private prosecution against her abusers in form of a defamation action similar to the one actioned by Lord McAlpine against Sally Bercow and others.[222]

In June 2012 Frank Zimmerman (60) from Gloucester was given a 26-week prison sentence, suspended for two years, after telling the then Conservative MP for Corby, Louise Mensch, she faced a 'Sophie's choice' via setting up as an internet troll. She was also threatened by him that she would have to pick which of her three children to save and which would die. Zimmerman had targeted Mensch after the August riots in 2011 when the Corby MP had suggested that sites such as Twitter ought to be closed down if the police thought it necessary.[223] Mensch had been in the public eye as a member of the Commons Culture, Media and Sport Committee, when she was admired for her robust questioning of Rupert and James Murdoch over the News of the World phone-hacking affair in Spring 2012.

In July 2013, Reece Elliott (24) was given a two-year prison sentence at Newcastle Crown Court for posting internet threats on Facebook to kill 200 US children. Elliott had left abusive comments on tribute pages set up for two teenagers who died in car accidents in Warren County, Tennessee, in February 2013. A Deputy Sheriff from Tennessee Police Department began investigating, along with the FBI and Homeland Security, asking Facebook to disclose Elliott's identity, tracing him to South Shields, South Tyneside. Elliott admitted one count of making threats to kill and eight Communications Act 2003 offences.

In September 2012, the then Director of Public Prosecutions (DPP) Keir Starmer QC clarified the law in respect of the (mis)use of 'public electronic communications networks' (such as Twitter, Facebook etc.) where communications were said to be 'grossly offensive'. In his statement the DPP said that the Communications Act 2003 was sufficient to deal with situations of harassment and threats via the internet. The policy statement followed the case of Daniel Thomas, a semi-professional footballer, who had posted a homophobic message on Twitter on 30 July 2012, relating to Olympic divers Tom Daley and Peter Waterfield. The troll attack became available to their 'followers' and was widely re-tweeted. Mr Thomas's case was referred to CPS Wales to consider whether he should be charged with a criminal offence. The Chief Crown Prosecutor for Wales, Jim Brisbane, concluded that on a full analysis of the context and circumstances in which this single message was sent, it was not so grossly offensive that criminal charges needed to be brought.[224]

There is no doubt that the messages posted by Mr Thomas or Mr Zimmermann (above) are offensive and would be regarded as such by reasonable members of society. Even if the identity of

---

219 Source: 'Internet troll who abused Mary Beard apologises after threat to tell his mother', Daily Telegraph, 1 August 2013.
220 See: Glossary for full explanation.
221 Source: 'Facebook to release trolls' IP addresses', Daily Telegraph, 8 June 2012.
222 **Lord McAlpine of West Green v Sally Bercow** [2013] EWHC 1342 (QB).
223 Source: 'Louise Mensch "troll" sentenced over threatening email', by Steven Morris, Guardian, 11 June 2012.
224 Source: 'DPP statement on Tom Daley case and social media prosecutions', Press Release, CPS on 20 September 2012 at: www.cps.gov.uk/news/latest_news/dpp_statement_on_tom_daley_case_and_social_media_prosecutions/index.html.

the 'offenders' is being disclosed by an order to the ISP, it would be extremely difficult to pursue a defamatory action against the 'persons unknown'. The DPP has made it clear that criminal charges will be brought only if these types of grossly offensive messages amount to repeated harassment. The distinction is an important one and not easily made. Context and circumstances are highly relevant and, as the ECtHR observed in **Handyside v UK** (1976),[225] the right to freedom of expression includes the right to say things or express opinions 'that offend, shock or disturb the state or any sector of the population'.

The CPS estimated that on Twitter alone there were 340 million messages sent daily in late 2012. DPP Starmer noted that the context in which this interactive social media dialogue takes place is quite different to the context in which other communications take place, whereby access to social media is ubiquitous and instantaneous. He noted: '. . . banter, jokes and offensive comment are commonplace and often spontaneous. Communications intended for a few may reach millions.'[226]

 FOR THOUGHT

Do you think there will ever be a global legal regime that can be applied to the World Wide Web that ISP 'publishers' must obey? Or will the international jurisdiction in this respect be open to permanent anarchy and internet trolls? Discuss.

3.7.3 Online archives and republication

In the past, before the development of online publications, such as newspaper archives and social networking sites, even if someone was made aware of a reference to him and a possible defamatory statement in print, it would have required a trip to a newspaper's offices or a local library to search archives to confirm what had been written – just as the servant to the **Duke of Brunswick**[227] had done over 160 years ago. And then a relevant piece might be missing from the record anyway – local newspaper archives, in particular, were sometimes incomplete. As already mentioned, issues in relation to the multiple publication rule and online publications and archives have become increasingly disconcerting to news websites and online editors. It is now common for media organizations to make previously published material available to everyone through online archives, such as those maintained by newspapers or the BBC. Blogs, online diaries and other discussion forums also fall within this category.

See above 3.2.3

One of the early concerns of the internet was the possibility of defamation published via the World Wide Web. Potentially – taking the **Duke of Brunswick** rule literally – each time a person accesses a particular web page, that page creates a new publication and therefore falls within the multiple publication rule, potentially giving rise to a separate cause of action should it contain defamatory material. Each cause of action has its own limitation period of one year, running from the time at which the material was accessed.

Case law has done little to diminish those fears and there have been some high-profile cases highlighting the dangers of the internet in this context. The arrival of the Google search engine changed things for journalists and editors on newspapers and websites when it came to defamation. Mike Smartt, former editor-in-chief of BBC News Interactive, explains:

---

225 1 EHRR 737 (ECTHR).
226 Source: Keir Starmer QC. 'DPP statement on Tom Daley case and social media prosecutions', CPS 20 September 2012 (see above).
227 **Brunswick v Harmer** (1849) 14 QB 185.

> ... before the internet, people were often unaware of material written about them. Unless they read an article themselves or a friend or relative pointed it out, they could easily be ignorant of what a publication had said about them. And because newspapers were all tomorrow's fish and chip wrapping, inaccuracies frequently went uncorrected.[228]

With the emergence of internet search engines, people began to type in their own names – and up came everything written about them. This meant that for the first time material that was incorrect – or in some cases possibly defamatory – was easy to find. Those unhappy about what had been written contemporaneously, on the day itself or the previous week or so, were relatively easy to deal with. Most media publishers make mistakes from time to time, the majority of which are not particularly serious. One big advantage of the internet is that inaccuracies can be changed almost instantly and an apology provided if necessary. But there were a handful of cases where people read something in the online archive which dated back some years previously and they then might challenge the publications. Mike Smartt concludes:

> The problem was that the journalist who had written the piece may have left, be unavailable or could not remember how the report was compiled. He or she would almost certainly have discarded their notes or wiped the recording device; therefore there was no record of what was said at the time or details of sources, and investigating whether a complaint was indeed justi-fied was very difficult. It very soon dawned on writers and editors, though, that this new way of accessing archives online meant that accuracy and impartiality were even more important than they had been before.

The landmark ruling in **Loutchansky**[229] (see below) centred on the findings that *The Times* had libelled Tashkent-born international businessman Dr Grigori Loutchansky in articles accusing him of being the boss of a major Russian criminal organization involved in money laundering. This case raised a number of issues relating to republication on the internet. The Russian businessman brought two actions against the newspaper. The first related to articles published in October 1999, which were subsequently placed on the *Times Online* archive. The claimant brought a second action more than one year after the original publication in December 2000.

The Court of Appeal was asked to consider two issues in respect of the second action: the limitation period applicable to archives; and the nature of any privilege that should attach to them. On the issue of limitation, the court held that 'it is a well-established principle of English law that each individual publication of a libel gives rise to a separate cause of action, subject to its own limitation period', referring to the **Duke of Brunswick** multiple publication rule. The second issue concerned the defence of 'privilege' and whether this could be attached to an online edition of a publication. The court dismissed *The Times*' defence of 'archive privilege'.

❖ KEY CASE	*Loutchansky v Times Newspapers Ltd (Nos 2–5)* [2001] EWCA Civ 1805; [2002] QB 783.

Precedent

❖   A 'publication' takes place every time material is made available (including online archives).

❖   There is no 'internet archive' privilege defence.

---

228 Source: interview with Mike Smartt on 22 April 2013.
229 **Loutchansky v Times Newspapers Ltd (No 2)** [2002] QB 783.

❖ The standard applicable for determining whether a defendant had a duty to publish defamatory words to the world at large is that of 'responsible journalism' in accordance with the **Reynolds** principle.[230]

Facts

The claimant was an international businessman, Dr Grigori Loutchansky (of Russian and Israeli dual nationality). The defendants were the publisher and editor of *The Times* and two of its journalists. The claimant sued for libel in respect of three *Times* articles (8 September 1999 and 14 October 1999, and 23 December 2000 and the same articles on *The Times* website), which accused him of being involved in serious international criminal activities including money laundering and the smuggling of nuclear weapons. The defendants pleaded **Reynolds** qualified privilege in the first action in 2001, but not justification. In the second action, *The Times* pleaded 'online' qualified privilege, arguing that the limitation period began to run as soon as the allegedly defamatory article was first posted on the website and that subsequent occasions upon which the website was accessed did not give rise to separate causes of action. They also argued that if defamation actions were permitted more than one year after the initial publication, this amounted to a restriction of freedom of expression.

The issues for the Court of Appeal to consider were: (1) Whether the judge was correct in ruling that the articles were not covered by qualified privilege ('The Internet Qualified Privilege appeal'). (2) Whether the single publication rule applied to online archived material. (3) Whether the Judge was correct to order summary disposal of the damages claim even though the issue of liability had been decided by a jury.

Decision

The Court of Appeal held that as soon as *The Times* had become aware of the criticisms of the (online) articles, and had not made any attempt to justify them, it should have drawn readers' attention to the fact that their truth was disputed. Its failure to do so meant that it was not entitled to rely on any protection by way of privilege attaching to the original articles. However, the appeal was allowed as the court decided that the initial High Court ruling misapplied the test in relation to qualified privilege for determining whether *The Times* was under a duty to publish the articles.

The CA held that *The Times* had not made out the **Reynolds** defence of qualified privilege and found in the claimant's favour. The CA observed, *inter alia*, that the two libel actions related to the same articles and both had been commenced within 15 months of the initial publication of the articles. *The Times'* ability to defend itself effectively was not therefore hindered by the passage of time and the problems linked to ceaseless liability did not arise. The CA emphasized that, while individuals who are defamed must have a real opportunity to defend their reputation, libel proceedings brought against a media publication after too long a period might well give rise to a disproportionate interference with Article 10.[231] The court held that there is a duty upon the journalist to behave as a 'responsible journalist'. This means that he can have no duty to publish unless he is acting responsibly and that there is a public interest in the subject matter. Only when the journalist, editor and/or publisher have acted and behaved responsibly is the defence of qualified privilege permissible.

---

230 The 10-point test set out in **Reynolds v Times Newspapers Ltd** [2001] 2 AC 127.
231 **Loutchansky (No 2)** [2002] QB 783 at para 76.

The second issue related to the continued publication of the editions online. The court ruled that the continued publication of the unqualified article on the internet after a complaint had been made and after it was known that no attempt to justify it would be made, led to the summary striking out of the defendant's defence claiming qualified privilege. Lord Justice Simon Brown MR summarized:

> We do not accept that the rule in the **Duke of Brunswick** imposes a restriction on the readiness to maintain and provide access to archives that amounts to a disproportionate restriction on freedom of expression. We accept that the maintenance of archives, whether in hard copy or on the internet, has a social utility, but consider that the maintenance of archives is a comparatively insignificant aspect of freedom of expression. Archive material is stale news and its publication cannot rank in importance with the dissemination of contemporary material. Nor do we believe that the law of defamation need inhibit the responsible maintenance of archives. Where it is known that archive material is or may be defamatory, the attachment of an appropriate notice warning against treating it as the truth will normally remove any sting from the material.[232]

Analysis

This is an important application and development of the defence of **Reynolds** qualified privilege, clarifying the test of 'responsible journalism'. *The Times* sought unsuccessfully to challenge the meaning of 'publication' in the context of archived material online. The traditional **Brunswick** rule was upheld: a 'publication' takes place *every time* material is made available, and there is no exception for materials kept on the internet.

The ruling in **Loutchansky** remains controversial, outraging not only British but also American journalists and publishers; the Scottish courts have also since applied the **Loutchansky** principle (see: **Ewing v Times** (2008)[233]). In **Loutchansky**, the CA acknowledged that online archives were of 'social utility' but they also commented, *obiter*, that it was a 'comparatively insignificant aspect of freedom of expression'.[234]

In relation to republication, the court accepted that the notion of permitting actions based on fresh disseminations was 'at odds with some of the reasons for the introduction of a twelve months limitation period' and stated that any resulting damages were 'likely to be modest'.[235]

The CA ruling in **Loutchansky** was considered in relation to a US website publication in **Firth v State of New York** (2002).[236] That case concerned a report published at a press conference which was then placed on the internet the same day, but the claim was not filed for over a year. It was held that the limitation period ran from the time that the article was placed on the website, and that each 'hit' on the website did not amount to a new publication. It was also held that unrelated modifications made to other parts of the site were irrelevant and did not create a new publication. The **Loutchansky**

---

232 Ibid., at 74.
233 [2008] CSOH 169.
234 **Loutchansky (No 2)** [2002] QB 783 at 676.
235 Ibid.
236 [2002] NY int 88.

judgment meant that publishers and online editors could be potentially liable for *any* defamatory material published by them, no matter how old, stored in the online archives of a news and media organization or broadcaster. Each 'view' on an internet search engine would effectively mean a new or republication of a libellous statement.[237]

On 30 April 2002 the House of Lords refused leave to appeal in **Loutchansky**, the main reason being that *The Times* had repeatedly republished defamatory material regarding the claimant on their internet website and had kept the publications in their online archives without qualifying the allegations or seeking a response from the claimant, which had been prescribed under the 10-point **Reynolds** criteria.

After *The Times* failed in the House of Lords, the newspaper publishers took their case to the ECtHR in March 2009, where they subsequently also lost.[238] The Strasbourg Court unanimously held that *The Times* had libelled Dr Loutchansky by its continued online archived publications. The court also ruled that there had not been a breach of Article 10. The ECtHR noted that, while internet archives were an important source for education and historical research, the press had a duty to act in accordance with the principles of responsible journalism, which included accuracy and reliable sources of information. The Strasbourg court further noted that limitation periods in defamation proceedings were there to ensure that those who had to defend their actions were able to defend themselves effectively. In any case, it was for all contracting states to the Convention to set their appropriate limitation periods in domestic law. The ECtHR commented *obiter* that should a 'Duke of Brunswick' type action arise, it might well be contrary to Article 10 even in a fresh publication.

 FOR THOUGHT

The **Loutchansky** case illustrates the dangers for those who host websites. What is the effect of the traditional **Duke of Brunswick** principle – that a publication takes place every time the statement is issued to a third party, including the author, editor, publisher – even the vendor of a newspaper on the high street? Discuss with reference to s 8 Defamation Act 2013.

3.7.4 There are no legal borders in cyberspace

Cyberspace has no territorially based boundaries, and messages or information can be instantaneously transmitted from one physical location to another. There are no physical or legal barriers to prevent access of information from geographically remote places, and in many cases we do not know the physical location of either an internet service provider (ISP) or the server or indeed the author of a defamatory message on Twitter. For example, a server that hosts a '.uk' domain name may or may not be located in the United Kingdom; a server with a '.com' domain name could well be anywhere. It is for these reasons that we can access pictures of a naked Prince Harry from August 2012 on the US celebrity gossip site TMZ[239] or topless images of the Duchess of Cambridge in the Italian Chi, [240] French *Closer*[241] or Danish *Seoghoer* [242] magazines.

237 For further discussion see: Dunlop (2006).
238 See: **Times Newspapers Ltd (Nos 1 and 2) v UK** (2009) (Applications 3002/03 and 23676/03, 10 March 2009, ECHR. Source: *Times Online* 11 March 2009, available at http://business.timesonline.co.uk/tol/business/law/reports/article5883783.ece.
239 Source: 'Prince Harry put the crown jewels on display in Vegas this weekend . . . getting BARE ASS NAKED during a game of strip billiards with a room full of friends in his VIP suite.' TMZ.com 21 August 2012: www.tmz.com/2012/08/21/prince-harry-naked-photos-nude-vegas-hotel-party/#ixzz266EgJeoy.
240 Source: 'Grande esclusiva: Kate Middleton. Scandalo Corte. La Regina e Nuda!', Chi, 16 Settembre 2012.
241 *Closer* at: www.closermag.fr.
242 *Seoghoer* at: www.seoghoer.dk.

How relevant is the judgment in **Godfrey v Demon Internet Limited** (2001)[243] following the **Tamiz** [244] ruling? It was noted in the latter case by Eady J that an ISP, such as Google, is merely a host – similar to the laws in the USA. So, who is responsible for defamatory postings on the internet? In **Godfrey**, the respondent ISP (Demon Internet) had received and stored on its news server an article defamatory of the respondent. The High Court held that whenever an ISP transmitted a defamatory posting, this amounted to a new publication of that posting to any subscriber who accessed the material containing that posting on that server, consistent with the old law established in the **Duke of Brunswick** case. This meant that every time one of Demon's customers accessed soc.culture.thai (in the present case) and saw the posting defaming the university lecturer, there was a publication to that customer.

Because of Demon's refusal to remove the offending material from its bulletin board as soon as the ISP had been alerted by lecturer Mr Godfrey, the court held that the second and third requirements (above) had not been satisfied. As an argument in court, Demon referred to US case law on electronic commerce in relation to defamation and pointed out that US law clearly states that an ISP is only 'hosting' information on its server. But the English court rejected this argument.[245]

In contrast, the US court in **Prodigy**[246] ruled that an ISP cannot be held liable for any material posted on its server since it was merely a host. In this case an unknown imposter had opened a number of accounts with the ISP, Prodigy Services Company, by assuming and usurping the (real) name of Alexander Lunney, a teenage Boy Scout claimant in this appeal. The imposter posted two vulgar messages in Lunney's name on a Prodigy bulletin board and sent a threatening, profane email message in Lunney's name to a third person, with the subject line: 'HOW I'M GONNA'KILL U'. Lunney sued Prodigy (through his father), asserting that he had been stigmatized by being falsely cast as the author of these messages. Regarding the defamatory message in question, the court accepted Prodigy's argument that the ISP had not 'participated in preparing the message, exercised any discretion or control over its communication, or in any way assumed responsibility'. Even if Prodigy were a publisher (which the court held it was not), it was entitled to qualified privilege in the same way that telephone companies are protected from claims for defamation under the US law.

The United States has undeniably taken the lead in the regulation of the internet and its efforts have been closely observed by the international community. Following the **Tamiz** ruling it could even be argued that the UK courts have adopted the US model based on the Digital Millennium Copyright Act 1998 (DMCA),[247] which in turn is very similar to the EU E-Commerce Directive 2000/31.[248] The main aim of the DMCA is to provide ISPs with certain protection from liability without requiring them to determine the merits of rightholders' claims. This legislation has provided the US courts with a common-sense, fact-based approach, although McEvedy (2002) argues that this seeming advantage of a 'safe harbour' means that the conditions for ISPs are large and that the servers must comply with a 'myriad of minute circumstances'.[249] The author also states

---

243 [2001] QB 201.
244 **Tamiz (Payam) v Google Inc, Google UK Ltd** [2012] EWHC 449 (QB).
245 For further discussion see: Macmillan (2009) at pp. 80–82.
246 **Lunney (Alexander G.) & c. v Prodigy Services Company et al** (1999) 99 NY Int 0165.
247 The relevant statute is the Online Copyright Infringement Liability Limitation Act, which was incorporated as Title II of the DMCA, Pub. L. No. 105–304. It amends Chapter 5 of Title 17 USC, signed into law on 28 October 1998. The DMCA was enacted to bring US law into compliance with private international law and in particular with the WIPO Copyright Treaty 1996 and the WIPO Performances and Phonograms Treaty of 2006, which also introduced the 'black box' measures to protect authors against the circumvention of technology used in protecting copyright management information. These measures were enacted in Title I of the DMCA.
248 EU Directive 2000/31/EC on 'Liability of Intermediary Service Providers' on electronic commerce of 8 June 2000. Directive 2000/31 EC deals with certain legal aspects of Information Society Services, in particular Electronic Commerce (e-Commerce) in the Internet Market. (2000/31) [2000] OJ L178/1.
249 See: McEvedy (2002) at pp. 65–73

that DMCA application in the US courts has been 'disappointing' – citing the clearest example in the Court of Appeals for the Ninth Circuit and their refusal to apply the DMCA in the **Napster** case.[250]

Article 15(1) of the E-Commerce Directive[251] obliges electronic service providers to 'police' the content of archives for defamatory material. All 28 EU Member States are obliged under this legislation to monitor content on 'information society service providers'. Still, it is difficult to see how the multiple publication rule could effectively impose a monitoring obligation on ISPs by virtue of Regulations 17 to 19 of the E-Commerce Regulations 2013.[252]

Most protective schemes and attempts to restrict the flow of information based on geographical locations have proved futile so far. The French courts ruled, for example, that Yahoo! Inc. must block French users from its sites auctioning Nazi artefacts. Yahoo! argued that it could not possibly limit access to certain geographical regions; alternatively, it could comply with French legislation and block everyone from bidding for the artefacts. The other difficulty is that policing any such legislation across cyber borders is very difficult to impossible.

Can a Google function such as 'autocomplete' be libellous? This question was asked in the German courts after former first lady Bettina Wulff took legal action against Google Deutschland to suppress rumours about her past. For years the rumour had floated around Berlin's political dinner circles that Bettina Wulff, the second wife of ex-president Christian Wulff,[253] was a former prostitute. Internet search engines attempt to guess what users are looking for and offer them suggested words. But can these terms constitute defamation? Bettina Wulff argued that they do by suing Google over searches that pair her name with terms like 'prostitute' or 'escort'. Google maintains it is an automatic mechanism, generated by its users, based on 'algorithmic results', based on objective calculations and popular usage.

In September 2012, the German daily *Süddeutsche Zeitung* reported that Frau Wulff had submitted an affidavit stating that all claims about her having worked as an 'escort' in her younger years were false.[254] The report said that 34 German and foreign bloggers as well as Austrian media outlets (*Mediengruppe Österreich*) had signed declarations pledging to cease and desist from citing such allegations, otherwise they were asked to pay. *Süddeutsche* reported that, apart from the action against Google (Germany), Frau Wulff had also filed a separate lawsuit with the Hamburg district court against well-known German TV personality Günther Jauch, who had quoted the newspaper article regarding the rumours in Berlin in his talk show on 9 September 2012. Jauch had refused to sign a cease-and-desist declaration after being requested to do so by Wulff's lawyers in May 2012. Reports in the tabloid *Bild Zeitung* argued that PR agent Bettina Wulff was only trying to promote her own book *Jenseits des Protokolls* ('Beyond Protocol'),[255] which was about to be published (ghost-written by Nicole Maibaum).[256] But the court injunction did little to gag the search engine. If one enters the words 'Bettina Wulff' into the German (or English) Google search engine, words are still automatically formed, such as 'Bettina Wulff Escort' ('call girl') or 'Bettina Wulff Prostituierte' ('prostitute'). It remains debatable what did more harm: the nasty rumours about Bettina's past in prostitution, or her disastrous efforts to set the record straight through the courts.

---

250 *A&M Records, Inc. v Napster, Inc.*, No. 99–05183, 2000 WL 573136 (ND Cal. 12 May 2000) (motion for summary judgment); *A&M Records, Inc. v Napster, Inc.*, 114 F. Supp. 2d 896 (ND Cal. 2000) (motion for preliminary injunction); *A&M Records, Inc. v Napster, Inc.*, 7 ILR (P & F) 3004 (appeal against preliminary injunction).

251 EU Directive 2000/31/EC.

252 EU Regulations 2002/2013 EC on Electronic Commerce.

253 Christian Wulff, of the German Christian Democratic Union (CDU) and close ally of Chancellor Angela Merkel, became President of Germany (*Bundespräsident*) in 2010. He was forced to resign from his office after increasing pressure over a home loan and an apparent attempt to block reports in *Bild Zeitung* regarding his wife's private life in February 2012.

254 Source: 'Bettina Wulff wehrt sich gegen Verleumdungen' von Hans Leyendecker und Ralf Wiegand, *Süddeutsche Zeitung*, 7 September 2012.

255 See: Wulff and Maibaum (2012). The ghost-written book gallops through Bettina's early life until she arrived as the second Mrs Wulff at Bellevue Palace, seat of the German presidency. Here she feels overwhelmed and isolated by the demands of diplomatic protocol and the tight corset of security.

256 Source: 'Google beharrt auf "Bettina Wulff Escort"', Die Zeit, 9 September 2012.

The Google autocomplete function undeniably helps spread rumours and can lead to defamation and harm to someone's reputation. Unsubstantiated rumours can reach the top of the search list by merely surfacing on some obscure websites on an unregulated server (e.g. in Ukraine). It may well have been the politicians and journalists who spread the false rumours about Bettina Wulff's 'red light past' – a rumour she has vehemently denied. Google have denied that a combination of terms the algorithm generates as a suggestion constitutes an allegation. Google also denies that they are responsible for the word combinations created by such an algorithm. They argue that the displayed content is generated by others – in this case, by other users of the search engine.

Bettina Wulff's legal action against Google resembles the legal battle between Max Mosley and Google. The former president of Formula 1 also asked Google to stop making it possible to locate illegal photos of him online. He wanted them to be automatically filtered out of the search results.

Should the search engine be ordered by the (national) courts to monitor its search results for the good of society, or for the good of a particular individual or company? Interestingly, Google's subsidiary YouTube decided to block links in Egypt and Libya to the Islamophobic video 'Innocence of Muslims',[257] which sparked outrage and violence in the Islamic world. It is presently impossible to imagine a law or legal decision that would provide a fair and practicable solution to these conflicts.

 FOR THOUGHT

> What legal action should be taken against an internet search engine when it morphs into an active suggestion generator, such as Google's 'autocomplete'? Discuss this complex and controversial function of a medium which we all enjoy and many of us perceive as determining reality.

3.7.5 Defences for operators of websites

The Defamation Act 2013 seeks to prevent actions in relation to publications online outside the one-year limitation period for the initial publication, unless the publisher refuses or neglects to update the electronic version, on request, with a reasonable letter or statement by the claimant by way of explanation or contradiction. This would reflect the Strasbourg ruling in **Times Newspapers v UK** (2009),[258] which recognized the important role played by online archives in preserving and making available news and information as a public service and as a important educational research tool in our information society.

Section 5 Defamation Act 2013 ('Operators of websites') creates a new defence for the operators of websites where a defamation action is brought against them in respect of a statement posted on the website. Section 5(2) provides for the defence to apply if the operator can show that they did not post the statement on the website.

Section 5(3) provides for the defence to be defeated if the claimant can show that it was not possible for him to identify the person who posted the statement; that he gave the operator a notice

---

257 'Innocence of Muslims' (also known as 'Muhammad Movie Trailer' and 'The Real Life of Muhammad') by 'Sam Bacile' (not his real name) is an anti-Islam video originally uploaded to YouTube in July 2012. The film claims Islam is a lie and Mohammed was a paedophile. It is thought that the response to the video resulted in the death of US Ambassador J. Christopher Stevens and three other Americans on 11 September 2012.
258 **Times Newspapers Ltd (Nos 1 and 2) v United Kingdom** (2009); [2009] EMLR 14 (Applications 3002/03 and 23676/03, 10 March 2009 (ECTHR).

of complaint in relation to the statement; and that the operator failed to respond to that notice in accordance with provisions contained in regulations to be made by the Secretary of State.

Section 5(4) interprets subsection (3)(a) ('... the defence is defeated if the claimant shows that – (a) it was not possible for the claimant to identify the person who posted the statement') and explains that it is possible for a claimant to 'identify' a person for the purposes of that subsection only if the claimant has sufficient information to bring proceedings against the person.

Section 5(5) provides details of provisions that may be included in regulations. This includes provision as to the action which an operator (or ISP) must take in response to a notice (which in particular may include action relating to the identity or contact details of the person who posted the statement and action relating to the removal of the post); provision specifying a time limit for the taking of any such action and for conferring a discretion on the court to treat action taken after the expiry of a time limit as having been taken before that expiry. This would allow for provision to be made enabling a court to waive or retrospectively extend a time limit as appropriate. The subsection also permits regulations to make any other provision for the purposes of this section.

Section 5(6) sets out certain specific information which must be included in a notice of complaint. The notice must:

(a)   specify the complainant's name;
(b)   explain why the statement is defamatory of the complainant;
(c)   specify where on the website the statement was posted; and
(d)   contain other information as may be specified in regulations. Regulations may specify what other information must be included in a notice of complaint.

Section 5(7) of the 2013 Act permits regulations to make provision about the circumstances in which a notice which is not a notice of complaint is to be treated as a notice of complaint for the purpose of the section or any provision made under it.

Section 5(8) permits regulations under this section to make different provision for different circumstances.[259]

Section 5(11) provides for the defence to be defeated if the claimant shows that the website operator (ISP) has acted with malice in relation to the posting of the statement concerned. This might arise where, for example, the ISP had incited the poster to make the posting or had otherwise colluded with the poster of the statement.

Section 5(12) explains that the defence available to a website operator is not defeated by reason only of the fact that the operator moderates the statements posted on it by others.

3.8 Juries or no juries?

Unlike most other civil claims, defamation claims have in the past generally been heard by a jury (also known as 'libel juries') in a county or High Court (depending on the amount claimed). The judge decides if the words possibly have a meaning which is damaging to the claimant's reputation and the jury's role was generally to:

(a)   determine what the words mean in their rational sense; and
(b)   decide if that meaning is defamatory.

---

259 No specific regulations were in place at the time of going to print.

When deciding what the words mean, the intentions and knowledge of the person who published the words are irrelevant.

Section 11 of the Defamation Act 2013 removed the presumption in favour of jury trial in defamation cases ('trial to be without a jury unless the court orders otherwise'). This means that s 69 Senior Courts Act 1981 and s 66 County Courts Act 1984 still provide for a right to trial with a jury in the Queen's Bench Division (QBD) in certain civil proceedings, such as malicious falsehood (criminal prosecution), false imprisonment and allegations of fraud on the application of any party, 'unless the court considers that the trial requires any prolonged examination of documents or accounts or any scientific or local investigation which cannot conveniently be made with a jury'.[260]

The fact that defamation cases are now generally heard without a jury caused great debate in Parliament, where it was argued during the passing of the Defamation Bill by some proponents that 'libel juries' are a constitutional right, as expressed by Nourse LJ in the **Sonia Sutcliffe**[261] case:

> . . . whether someone's reputation has or has not been falsely discredited ought to be tried by other ordinary men and women and, as Lord Camden said, it is the jury who are the people of England.[262]

See above 3.6

During the initial reading of the Bill in the House of Lords in 2010, Lord Lester recommended judge-alone trials in defamation actions, based on common practice in Scotland. Human rights lawyers, on the other hand, vehemently argued the continued presence of a jury in defamation cases as a significant factor and long-established constitutional principle of English law: when a man's life, liberty or honour is in jeopardy, he should have the right to be judged by his fellow men. As has been established in criminal trials, juries are one of the most democratic aspects of constitutional Britain, an institution which is open to the public, where ordinary people participate in decisions of such immediate importance and wield real power.

As already stated in section 3.6 above, jury trials in defamation cases in Scotland are exceptionally rare and civil jury trials virtually died out in Scotland at the end of the fifteenth century (only momentarily reappearing in the early twentieth century).[263] The Strachan Committee Report (1959) into civil jury trials undertook a comprehensive review and decided to retain civil juries. One of the arguments advanced by the committee was that they award more realistic awards of damages than judges.[264] In spite of Strachan's recommendations, civil jury trials declined in Scotland. In 1988, the Scottish Courts Administration issued a consultation paper, inviting views as to whether the right to a civil jury trial should be abolished. On Lord Advocate Lord Fraser of Carmyllie's suggestion, the matter was dropped and civil jury trials were retained in theory but have practically never been used in modern times.[265] Criminal jury trials remain in Scottish courts.[266]

In England and Wales, 'libel' juries have traditionally determined the damages a claimant may receive in a defamation action, unless the case required a lengthy examination of documents or a complex scientific investigation or language – as was the case in the David Irving trial, held partly in German.[267] It was then the (libel) jury who decided whether the words complained of were actually defamatory, though the judge ruled initially whether as a matter of law the words were capable of being defamatory.

---

260 Section 11(2) Defamation Act 2013.
261 **Sutcliffe v Pressdram Ltd** [1991] 1 QB 153.
262 Ibid., at 182 (Nourse LJ).
263 See: Smith (1964), pp. 1076ff.
264 See: Strachan (1959).
265 Source: 'Lord Advocate plans review of civil juries', *Glasgow Herald*, 12 May 1989.
266 See: Scottish Government (2009) 'The Modern Scottish Jury in Criminal Trials – Next Steps'.
267 **Irving (David John Caldwell) v Penguin Books Ltd and Deborah Lipstadt** (1996), judgment of 11 April 2000 (QBD) (unreported).

Libel juries were popular with claimants because of the at times extremely high awards of damages exercised by juries such as in the **Elton John**[268] or **Esther Rantzen**[269] cases. In both cases the judges took the unprecedented step of reducing the damages awarded by the respective juries, stating that damages in defamatory actions should be interpreted in a manner consistent with the fundamental freedom of expression of the Convention (though Article 10 ECHR was at that time not part of UK law). In **Rantzen**, the jury had awarded £250,000 to the popular TV presenter when the *Daily Mirror* appealed, seeking a reduction in the level of damages. Under the provisions of s 8 of the Courts and Legal Services Act 1990, the Court of Appeal allowed the appeal and reduced the award to £110,000. At the same time a jury awarded pop legend (Sir) Elton John £350,000. John's claim against the *Sunday Mirror* arose over false allegations that he suffered from a bizarre eating disorder, headlined on 27 December 1992: 'Elton's Diet of Death'. Drake J reduced the amount of damages to £75,000 (see also: **Tolstoy-Miloslavsky v Aldington** (1995)[270]).

In July 2009 *Express* newspaper proprietor Richard Desmond lost a libel battle against the author and journalist Tom Bower. A jury at the High Court in London returned a majority verdict rejecting Desmond's claim that he was defamed by Bower in a biography of the former *Daily Telegraph* boss (Lord) Conrad Black. The trial centred on a passing reference to Mr Desmond in Bower's book: *Conrad and Lady Black: Dancing on the Edge* (2006). Bower's book said that Desmond had been 'ground into the dust' by business tycoon Conrad Black. Desmond denied a claim that he had told *Express* journalists to run critical stories about Black, with whom he was locked in a joint venture business dispute at the time. In his libel action, Mr Desmond claimed the book had damaged his business reputation ('business libel'). The jury found no defamation in favour of Bower. Mr Desmond's total legal bill for the trial amounted to nearly £1.25m. Lord Conrad Black, detained at a US prison at the time after his conviction for fraud in 2007, had provided support to Desmond in the form of a witness statement dictated from his cell.[271]

Juries' accessing the internet has become a big problem, particularly in cases involving disputed expert evidence, or, in the case of libel trials involving famous personalities where previous sensational media coverage may have a prejudicial effect on juries, such as Morrissey's[272] libel battle against the NME (*New Musical Express*). The former Smiths frontman began his defamation action in October 2011 in order to clear his name over alleged racism accusations. Mr Justice Tugendhat allowed the action to proceed against the former NME editor, Conor McNicholas, and the magazine's publisher IPC Media, after balancing the music magazine's Article 10 right of freedom of expression and Mr Morrissey's right to the protection of his individual reputation. The NME had viciously attacked the singer in 2007, labelling him a racist and a hypocrite.[273] In June 2012 Morrissey and NME agreed to settle their libel action out of court with an apology and an 'undisclosed' settlement.

See Chapter 4.8

The practical result of the Defamation Act 2013 is now that most libel and slander cases will be tried without a jury unless a court orders otherwise.

3.9 Academic and scientific debate

There have been a number of high-profile libel actions over the past decade involving scientists who have commented on and criticized medical practices in public. The US manufacturer NMT

268 **John (Elton) v Mirror Group Newspapers Ltd** [1997] QB 586.
269 **Rantzen (Esther) v Mirror Group Newspapers Ltd** [1994] QB 670.
270 **Tolstoy-Miloslavsky v Aldington** [1996] Court of Appeal (Lord Justice Rose, Lord Justice Roch and Lord Justice Ward) 13 December 1995 (unreported).
271 Source: 'Richard Desmond loses libel case against Tom Bower,' by Helen Pidd and Chris Tryhorn, *Guardian*, 23 July 2009.
272 Steven Patrick Morrissey (born 22 May 1959), the singer known as Morrissey.
273 Source: 'Morrissey's libel battle against NME to be heard next year', by Josh Halliday, *Guardian*, 26 October 2011.

Medical Inc, based in Boston, sued British cardiologist Dr Peter Wilmshurst for libel after he criticized its research at a US cardiology conference in 2007. Wilmshurst's remarks concerned a medical trial which he himself designed, called MIST, to find out whether closing small holes in the heart with one of NMT's medical devices could stop migraines. The trial did not succeed. One of Dr Wilmshurst's allegations was that doctors in the medical trials were paid large consultancy fees by NMT and even owned shares in the company.[274] The company argued that the payment of such fees was normal and acceptable, and the shareholdings were below the 'significant' $50,000 (£30,000) level that would have caused concern.

However, NMT did not sue the American specialist online cardiology journal, *Heartwire*, which had published a version of Dr Wilmshurst's remarks; instead, the company sued Wilmshurst personally in the English High Court in 2009. Additionally, NMT claimed that by discussing the details of the case on national radio (BBC Radio 4's *Today* programme in 2011), Dr Wilmshurst defamed their reputation further. Wilmshurst paid in excess of £100,000 of his own money to defend himself against NMT in three defamation claims, each time for both libel and slander. In defending the actions he was in danger – similar to Dr Simon Singh (below) – of losing his home. In January 2011, NMT Medical was ordered by the High Court to pay £200,000 into court as security for costs in its case against Dr Wilmshurst. The libel case against the cardiologist appeared to come to an end in April 2011 after NMT Medical went into liquidation.[275] The doctor vowed to take the case to trial in order to defend scientists' rights to free academic debate.

3.9.1 Publications of statements in scientific or academic journals

Academic science writer Dr Simon Singh[276] won his long-drawn-out 'libel' action in the Court of Appeal, relying on the defence of 'fair comment' after he had criticized British Chiropractors' claim that they could successfully treat children and babies for conditions such as asthma, colic and ear infections. Dr Singh had suggested there was a lack of evidence in a *Guardian* article in April 2008. The British Chiropractic Association (BCA) sued Simon Singh personally in defamation, rather than bringing an action against the Guardian newspaper group. Dr Singh eventually won an appeal that allowed him to use the 'fair comment' defence, which led to the case against him being dropped.

Many of their fellow scientists have been put off by the **Wilmshurst** and **Singh** actions from voicing their concerns about medical research and reviewing such results in scientific or medical journals. Such fears of the medical, scientific and academic community are well founded, also expressed in a report on 'Press standards, privacy and libel' (2010) by the House of Commons Culture, Media and Sport Committee. The report expressed strong concerns about the country's present libel laws in the internet age, in particular the defence of fair comment when challenged in the libel courts over academic and peer-reviewed publications.[277] The **Simon Singh** case eventually influenced Lord Lester's Defamation Bill in 2010.[278]

The '**Sarah Thornton**' case[279] (see below) arose out of a book review by well-known journalist Lynn Barber of Thornton's book *Seven Days in the Art World*.[280] Mr Justice Tugendhat granted summary judgment to the defendant in respect of libel claims, where Dr Thornton was successful after a number of cross-appeals. The case also made headlines, being the first where a defendant's 'offer of

---

274 See: Wilmshurst (2011) at pp. 1093–1094.
275 Source: 'NMT Medical, Inc. Assigns All of Its Assets for the Benefit of Creditors', Press Release by NMT Medical, Finance Yahoo online news 19 April 2011 at: http://finance.yahoo.com/news/NMT-Medical-Inc-Assigns-All-iw–3913728736.html.
276 **British Chiropractic Association v Singh** [2010] EWCA Civ 350.
277 See: House of Commons (2010a) at para 142.
278 See: 'Reform of libel laws will protect freedom of expression', Ministry of Justice, 23 March 2010, op. cit., fn. 75.
279 **Thornton (Sarah) v Telegraph Media Group Ltd** [2011] EWHC 1884 (QB).
280 See: Thornton (2009).

amends' was overturned by a finding of malice (on the journalist's behalf) and the court awarded general damages for malicious falsehood.

 KEY CASE | *Thornton (Sarah) v Telegraph Media Group Ltd* [2011] EWHC 1884 (QB)

Precedent

❖ There must be a 'threshold of seriousness' in what constitutes a 'defamatory' imputation.

❖ There must be 'substantial harm' suffered (and not trivial) by the claimant in potential loss of reputation (including 'business libel').

❖ 'Substantial harm' to the claimant has to be balanced with Article 10 ECHR relating to freedom of the press.

❖ A statement is not defamatory unless its publication has caused or is likely to cause serious harm to the reputation of the claimant.

Facts

The claimant, an author and academic Dr Sarah Thornton, sued for libel and malicious falsehood in respect of a book review published by the defendant newspaper, the *Daily Telegraph*. Part of the words complained of said that Dr Thornton's academic approach 'means that her interviewees have the right to read what she says about them and alter it ("copy approval")'. Thornton claimed that those words meant that she engaged in the reprehensible practice of 'copy approval' and was thereby lacking integrity as a writer. Her primary case was that the article reflected upon her professional reputation ('business libel'), but, from the context of the entire article, it was also a personal libel.[281] The review on page 28 of the newspaper on 1 November 2008 ('*Seven Days in the Art World* by Sarah Thornton') had the following words complained of:

> Sarah Thornton is a decorative Canadian with a BA in art history and a PhD in sociology and a seemingly limitless capacity to write pompous nonsense. She describes her book as a piece of 'ethnographic research', which she defines as 'a genre of writing with roots in anthropology that aims to generate holistic descriptions of social and cultural worlds'. She also claims that she practices [*sic*] 'reflexive ethnography', which means that her interviewees have the right to read what she says about them and alter it. In journalism we call this 'copy approval' and disapprove. . . .

> Thornton claims her book is based on hour-long interviews with more than 250 people. I would have taken this on trust, except that my eye flicked down the list of her 250 interviewees and practically fell out of its socket when it hit the name Lynn Barber. I gave her an interview? Surely I would have noticed? I remember that she asked to talk to me, but I said I had already published an account of my experiences as a Turner Prize juror which she was welcome to quote, but I didn't want to add to.

After Ms Thornton's first libel action, the defendants made an offer of amends in relation to parts of the review, relying otherwise on the defence of fair comment. This was struck

281 [2011] EWHC 1884 at paras 21–22.

out by Sir Charles Gray[282] and the defendant newspaper sought permission to appeal. At
the first appeal hearing, Tugendhat J conducted a comprehensive analysis of what the
term 'defamatory' actually meant, suggesting a 'systematic ordering' by applying the
following distinction between two varieties:

> (A) personal defamation, where there are imputations as to the character or attributes
> of an individual and (B) business or professional defamation, where the imputation is
> as to an attribute of an individual, a corporation, a trade union, a charity, or similar
> body, and that imputation is as to the way the profession or business is conducted.
> These varieties are not mutually exclusive: the same words may carry both varieties
> of imputation.[283]

Decision

On 26 July 2011 Mr Justice Tugendhat handed down a reserved judgment after the trial in
Thornton, reversing the previous judgment at trial by judge and jury. The crucial evidence
was that of journalist Lynn Barber concerning her state of mind when she wrote the words
complained of. Tugendhat J found that 'Ms Barber had in fact been interviewed by Dr
Thornton' and that Ms Barber had 'lied in the course of giving her oral evidence'.[284] The
fact that Barber knew she had been interviewed and conveniently forgotten amounted to
a 'reckless' and thereby malicious action. The judge also allowed the claimant's contention that there had been 'business libel', relying on the principle in **Drummond-Jackson v
BMA** (1970)[285] to the effect that a person, business or organization can sue for libel in
respect of imputations which imply a lack of skill, qualification or efficacy even if they do
not imply any moral fault.

On the question of damages, the judge took into account the circulation of the *Telegraph*
and the 'serious aggravating factor' of Ms Barber's malice. Taking some mitigation into
account, resulting from the newspaper's apology – albeit some ten months after the
first publication – the judge held that the least award of damages necessary in this case
would be one of £65,000. He attributed £50,000 to the libel and £15,000 to the malicious
falsehood.[286]

Analysis

The somewhat controversial judgment in **Thornton** introduced the 'substantial harm' test
as part of the definition of what constitutes a defamatory allegation.[287] The judgment
further advanced the requirement of 'non-triviality' in what amounts to 'substantial harm'
in a defamatory action. The judge also balanced the 'substantial harm' with Article 10
ECHR; that is, if harm is not 'substantial' then it is unlikely that the Article 8 right to reputation will apply in favour of the claimant. After reviewing the various definitions of the
test for what is defamatory found in the authorities, Tugendhat J held that they require a
claimant (whether pursuing a 'business libel' or 'personal libel') to satisfy a threshold test
that the allegation is sufficiently serious. He also held that the 'threshold of seriousness'

282 [2009] EWHC 2863 (QB) (Sir Charles Gray).
283 **Thornton (Sarah) v Telegraph Media Group Ltd.** [2010] EWHC 1414 at 33(i) (Tugendhat J).
284 [2011] EWHC 1884 at para 82.
285 [1970] 1 All ER 1094.
286 [2011] EWHC 1884 at 189.
287 Now in section 1 Defamation Act 2013, which defines 'serious harm', whereby 'a statement is not defamatory unless its
publication has caused or is likely to cause serious harm to the reputation of the claimant'.

had to be consistent with the obligations under Article 10 ECHR, the right to freedom of expression, citing *Jameel v Dow Jones* (2005).[288]

The case illustrates the fundamental point that whatever comments a reviewer makes, he will be liable for defamation if the review includes false defamatory allegations of fact. The false statement that the claimant had not interviewed Ms Barber was a particularly clear case of such an allegation. In an ordinary case the offer of amends might have been accepted but the claimant chose to challenge this defence because she believed Ms Barber was malicious. Though a risky strategy, it was vindicated by Dr Thornton's success at the final Court of Appeal hearing.

In his ruling, Mr Justice Tugendhat made clear that the case was not about a bad review or a critic's liberty to loathe a book. *Thornton* was not about opinions, but facts. The judgment sent a 'chill' towards the journalistic and book reviewer profession which simply states that one ought to make sure one gets one's facts right, even in the context of a book review. If newspapers (and online editions) have made a factual mistake they must publish a correction with immediate effect to put the record straight. These are the essential responsibilities that ought to underpin press freedom.

The case was a decisive victory for the claimant, who wrote in the *Guardian* after her victory that that this was a 'matter of journalistic integrity . . . At a time when the ethics of the tabloids are under scrutiny, here is an example of a "quality" journalist's abuse of power.'[289] The case set the precedent for the 'threshold of seriousness' into the legal definition of what constitutes a 'defamatory' imputation, the consequences of which were potentially far-reaching.

Interestingly, Sarah Thornton financed her final appeal action by way of a CFA, agreeing that her lawyers – barristers Ronald Thwaites QC and Justin Rushbrooke and solicitors Taylor Hampton – would receive no pay unless they won. She also signed an after the event (ATE) insurance contract so she would be covered if she lost her case and had to pay the *Telegraph*'s legal costs. Daniel Taylor, of Taylor Hampton solicitors, said: 'Critics are rightly valued for their opinions but the judge has made clear that they must not misrepresent the underlying facts deliberately or recklessly. We believe that this is the first ruling in decades to find malice against a reviewer.'[290]

3.9.2 Qualified privilege defence for peer-reviewed statements and scientific journals

Section 6 of the 2013 Act has created a new defence of 'qualified privilege' relating to peer-reviewed material in scientific or academic journals (whether published in electronic form or otherwise).[291] This is welcome news for all academics who review books or voice their opinion in academic journals.

288 [2005] QB 946 at paras 60–62, 89(ii), 94.
289 Source: 'Telegraph in £65k payout over "spiteful" Barber review', *Press Gazette*, 26 July 2011 at: www.pressgazette.co.uk/node/47586.
290 Ibid.
291 The term 'scientific journal' includes medical and engineering journals.

Sections 6(1) to (3) provide for the defence to apply where two conditions are met. These are:

- **Condition 1** – that the statement relates to a scientific or academic matter.
- **Condition 2** – that before the statement was published in the journal an independent review of the statement's scientific or academic merit was carried out by:
  - (a)   the editor of the journal, and
  - (b)   one or more persons with expertise in the scientific or academic matter concerned.

Section 6(8) provides that the reference to 'the editor of the journal' is to be read, in the case of a journal with more than one editor, as a reference to the editor or editors who were responsible for deciding to publish the statement concerned. This may be relevant where a board of editors is responsible for decision-making (such as the Entertainment Law Review or the Communications Law Review).

Section 6(4) extends the protection offered by the defence to publications in the same journal of any assessment of the scientific or academic merit of a peer-reviewed statement, provided the assessment was written by one or more of the persons who carried out the independent review of the statement, and the assessment was written in the course of that review. This is intended to ensure that the privilege is available not only to the author of the peer-reviewed statement, but also to those who have conducted the independent review who will need to assess, for example, the papers originally submitted by the author and may need to comment.

Section 6(5) provides that the privilege given by the section to peer-reviewed statements and related assessments also extends to the publication of a fair and accurate copy of, extract from or summary of the statement or assessment concerned.

Section 6(6) states that the privilege given by the section is lost if the publication is shown to be made with malice. This reflects the condition attaching to other forms of qualified privilege.

Section 6(7)(b) has been included to ensure that the new section is not read as preventing a person who publishes a statement in a scientific or academic journal from relying on other forms of privilege, such as the privilege conferred under s 7(9) to fair and accurate reports etc. of proceedings at a scientific or academic conference.

3.9.3 The responsible journalism test: *Reynolds* revisited

Running a **Reynolds** defence is not always successful. It is for this reason that the House of Lords judgment in **Jameel** (below) was particularly welcome in that it tested the scope and application of the qualified privilege defence, emphasizing the need for flexibility of the defence so that it appropriately protects the media's freedom of expression. What remains of concern is that the defence remains costly and therefore inaccessible to many publishers and media outlets with poor financial resources.

The last notable occasion in which the **Reynolds** privilege defence was advanced was in **Loutchansky v Times Newspapers Ltd**,[292] when The Times invoked the defence to demonstrate the exercise of responsible journalism. This meant that the published allegations were based on reports from reliable, responsible and authoritative' sources. The Court of Appeal held:

> At the end of the day the court has to ask itself the single question whether in all the circumstances the 'duty-interest test or the right to know test' has been satisfied so that qualified privilege attaches.[293]

---

292 (Nos 2–5) [2001] EWCA Civ 1805, [2002] QB 783.
293 Ibid., at para 23.

Reynolds privilege arises not simply because of the circumstances in which the publication is made, although these can bear on the test of responsible journalism. *Reynolds* privilege arises because of the subject matter of the publication itself. Furthermore, it arises only where the test of responsible journalism is satisfied, and this requirement leaves little or no room for separate consideration of malice.

In this light and in view of the ruling in *Loutchansky*, it is important to see how the responsible journalist test and *Reynolds* privilege were applied in the *Jameel* case. The background to *Jameel* was the destruction of the World Trade Center in New York on 11 September 2001 by terrorists, 15 of whom had been financed by Saudi Arabia. On 28 September 2001 the UN Security Council had passed Resolution 1373, which required all states to prevent and suppress the financing of terrorist acts, with the United States making diplomatic efforts to secure the co-operation of the Saudi Arabian Monetary Authority (SAMA).

❖ **KEY CASE**   *Jameel (Mohammed) v Wall Street Journal* (2007) (HL)

Precedent

The *Reynolds* qualified privilege defence will only be allowed if:

* ❖ the publication as a whole is of genuine public interest;
* ❖ the publication passes the 'fairness test';
* ❖ the publication complies with the 'responsible journalism test';
* ❖ all the journalistic sources are reliable.

Facts

On 6 February 2002 the *Wall Street Journal* (W) published an article headlined 'Saudi Officials Monitor Certain Bank Accounts', claiming that SAMA, at the request of the US Treasury, was monitoring the accounts of certain named Saudi companies, including those of Mr Jameel (J),[294] principal director of the holding company named in the article, to trace whether any payments were finding their way to terrorist organizations. The article was written by James Dorsey, W's special correspondent in Riyadh, and checked by financial journalist Glenn R. Simpson. The claimants brought their proceedings in the UK against the publishers of the European edition of the *Wall Street Journal*, where the article also appeared.

The judge rejected the newspaper's claim to *Reynolds* privilege and the jury found that the article was defamatory of both claimants, J and the Jameel Group, culminating in awards of £30,000 and £10,000 respectively. The Court of Appeal refused W leave to raise a new ground of misdirection, and thought that the jury had 'almost certainly' based their answers on the impression made by witnesses in court.[295] The principal question before the House of Lords was whether the journal was entitled to the *Reynolds* defence of publication in the public interest.

---

294 The Abdul Latif Jameel Company Ltd, the second claimant, was known as a substantial Saudi Arabian trading company with interests in a number of businesses, including the distribution of Toyota vehicles, and was part of an international group owned by the Jameel family, including Hartwell plc, a company which distributes vehicles in the United Kingdom. Mr Mohammed Abdul Latif Jameel, the first claimant, was general manager and president at the time.

295 [2003] EWHC 2322 (Eady J).

Decision

Summarizing their Lordships; decision, Lord Scott of Foscote stated that the original judge was wrong to withdraw from the jury the possibility that the author could reasonably have been intending to convey some lesser defamatory meaning than that of 'reasonable grounds to suspect' the conduct alleged. Their Lordships ruled that the story was of international interest, not only because of the identity of the names on the list, but also that there was such a list, evidencing the highly important and significant co-operation between the US and the Saudi authorities in the fight against terrorism. For this reason the *Reynolds* privilege defence was allowed. Above all, the journalists had a professional duty to disclose the vital information amounting to the main criterion of responsible journalism.[296]

The House of Lords set the following criteria when considering the meaning of 'responsible journalism' – thereby qualifying the *Reynolds* defence:

1. Is the publication in the public interest in the context of the work as a whole?
2. Will the work or article pass the 'fairness test'?
3. How much weight is attached to the professional judgment of the journalist and his reliable sources?

Analysis

Since *Jameel* – and more recently *Flood*[297] – we can see a shift towards the (libel) courts' accepting that responsible investigative journalism is embraced by Article 10(1) ECHR as well as covered by the *Reynolds* qualified privilege defence, particularly where a story is of genuine public interest. *Reynolds* privilege is not exclusively reserved for the media, but it is the media who are most likely to take advantage of it, for it is usually the media that publish to the world at large. The privilege has enlarged the protection enjoyed by the media against liability in defamation (see also: *AB Ltd v Facebook Ireland Ltd* (2013).[298]

Investigative journalism was also given a major boost in *Charman v Orion* (2007),[299] where the CA found in favour of BBC reporter Graeme McLagan, whose book *Bent Coppers* was previously judged to have defamed a former Flying Squad officer, Michael Charman.[300] Applying the *Jameel* test and *Reynolds* privilege, Ward LJ allowed the appeal against the ruling of Gray J about allegedly defamatory passages in the book.

In its response to the Culture, Media and Sport Select Committee Report on 'Press Standards, Privacy and Libel' (2010),[301] the Government Libel Working Group recognized the difficulties with present libel laws where the burden of proof lies on the defendant. The response document concluded that 'in the interests of natural justice, defendants should be required to prove the truth of their

---

296 [2007] 1 AC at 113ff (Lord Scott of Foscote).
297 *Flood v Times Newspapers Ltd* [2011] UKSC 11.
298 [2013] NIQB 14 (QB (Northern Ireland)).
299 [2007] EWCA Civ 972 (CA Civ Div).
300 See: McLagan (2004).
301 Source: The Government's Response to the Culture, Media and Sport Select Committee on Press Standards, Privacy and Libel. Presented to Parliament by the Secretary of State for Culture, Media and Sport by Command of Her Majesty April 2010. Cm 7851. London: HM Stationery Office.

allegations'.[302] The report by the Libel Working Group expressed concern, however, to see cases where that burden becomes overly onerous, referring *inter alia* to the **Simon Singh** and **Wilmshurst** cases. Recommendations in the report were then made, regarding the defence of 'responsible journalism' and the burden of proof on companies suing for defamation, which, it was hoped, the new legislation would address and thus 'level the playing field and assist publication in the public interest'.[303]

Furthermore, the report urged legislators drafting the Defamation Bill to examine the operation of UK libel laws and how the courts might better require claimants to make reasonable disclosures of evidence, without increasing costs even further through expensive appeals. The Committee's conclusion included that defendants should be required to prove the truth of the allegations, though the burden of proof in this area of law should not be changed.

3.10 Defamation and human rights

There is a constant conflict between Articles 10 and 8 ECHR, and the Strasbourg jurisdiction has sent mixed messages in respect of whether 'reputation' falls within the ambit of the protection afforded by Article 8 or not (see **Cumpana and Mazare v Romania** (2004)[304] and **Pfeifer v Austria** (2007)[305]). In **Reynolds**, Lord Nicholls described adjudicating on a reputation claim to qualified privilege as 'a balancing operation'.[306] The importance of the public interest in receiving the relevant information has to be weighed against the public interest in preventing the dissemination of defamatory allegations, with the injury that this causes to the reputation of the person defamed.

3.10.1 Freedom of expression or right to reputation?

One of the core principles of the Defamation Act 2013 revolved around making it easier for the ordinary citizen to understand and use defamation law where the existing defamation laws had largely developed in common law and through many – often archaic – judicial decisions, dating back to the late nineteenth and early twentieth centuries.

The law governing defamation is crucial to the proper functioning of any democratic society. As already discussed in the previous chapter, there is a fine line which the courts need to balance: the right to freedom of expression (protected by Article 10 ECHR) and the right to reputation. The latter right is a more contentious issue and Strasbourg jurisprudence has not made this point clear. It remains debatable whether 'reputation' is encompassed within the right to a private and family life under Article 8. The ECtHR ruled in **Karakó v Hungary**[307] that it was not.

Defamation law can then at times conflict with human rights legislation where reputation of individuals becomes an issue – including more recently the good name of companies and organizations. This was argued in the case of **Jameel v Wall Street Journal**.[308] In this case the journal had published an article that asserted that at the request of the United States the central bank of Saudi Arabia was monitoring certain bank accounts to prevent them from being used, wittingly or unwittingly, for channelling funds to terrorist organisations. The article included a number of names that were alleged to be on the 'blacklist', including that of Mr Jameel's trading group. The claimants succeeded

---

302 Ibid., at para 3.5.
303 Ibid., at para 3.7.
304 (2004) 41 EHRR 200 (GC) at para 91.
305 (2007) 48 EHRR 175 at paras 33 and 35.
306 **Reynolds v Times Newspapers Ltd** [2001] 2 AC at para 205 (Lord Nicholls).
307 (2009) (Application no 39311/05) Strasbourg, 28 April 2009 (unreported).
308 (No 3) [2007] 1 AC 359.

at first instance where the (libel) jury found that the article defamed the Jameels (i.e. that the article suggested that there were some grounds for suspecting that the claimants might be involved in funnelling funds to terrorists). The Wall Street Journal's claim of **Reynolds** privilege was rejected by both the trial judge and the Court of Appeal. The House of Lords reversed those decisions by reasoning that knowledge of the existence of the blacklist and the names on it was in the public interest.[309] Publication of the names on the blacklist was justified because this 'gave credibility to the story, per Lord Scott, or because without the names the impact of the story would have been much reduced, per Lady Hale.

When the Defamation Bill was debated in the House of Lords in April 2013, having ping-ponged with a number of controversial proposals from the Labour peers, such as Lord Puttnam, one of the obstacles was whether companies should be able to bring libel actions at all. One (Labour) amendment was then proposed that companies should evidence actual financial loss before they could sue in defamation. Company lawyers were outraged, arguing that companies and businesses operate largely on goodwill, which equates to a company's reputation as well as value. And, just like individuals, who can take steps to protect their reputation by way of court action, the same legal path should be available to companies like the Jameel group. Why should the law draw a distinction regarding a company that is bullied by the press just because it has wealthy individuals at its helm?

See above
3.4.4

British courts have developed the defence of public interest privilege under the influence of principles laid down by the ECtHR in Strasbourg. There is now a wealth of case law which empha-sizes the importance of the role of the media as public or social watchdogs (see: **Jersild v Denmark** (1994);[310] **Goodwin v UK** (1996);[311] **Affaire Vides Aizsardzības Klubs v Lettonie** (2004);[312] **Társaság A Szabadságjogokért v Hungary** (2009);[313] **Riolo v Italy** (2008);[314] **Flux (No 7) v Moldova** (2004);[315] **Axel Springer AG v Germany** (2012);[316] **von Hannover v Germany (No 2)** (2012)[317]).

The idea that loss of reputation has such a high perceived monetary effect on the person or company libelled is regarded as a difficult notion to accept in the modern age. After all, reputations are formed and reformed by the near-constant barrage of information available to us every day. But the basic principle remains: the tort of defamation exists to protect against blatantly untrue damaging statements which can potentially ruin someone's reputation or a company's business acumen. As John Disley said when he and Chris Brasher won their libel action in 1995, 'Take away my good name and you take away my life.'[318]

The basis of the tort is injury to reputation and it is important that the claimant will be presumed to have a good reputation in most cases, so it must be proved that the statement was communicated to someone other than the person defamed – a third party – because it can reason-ably be assumed that a third party may well communicate the information independently of the author of it. If the statement is not obviously defamatory, the claimant must show that it would be understood in a defamatory sense, such as by some innuendo. It is not necessary to prove that the defendant intended to refer to the claimant. The test is whether reasonable people would think the

---

309 Ibid., most clearly seen in the speeches of Lord Hoffmann at para 49, Lord Scott of Foscote at para 142 and Baroness Hale of Richmond at para 148.
310 (1994) 19 EHRR 1 at para 35.
311 (1996) 22 EHRR 123 at para 39.
312 (2004) (Application No 57829/00) at para 42.
313 (2009) (Application No 37374/05) at paras 27, 36 and 38.
314 (2008) (Application No 42211/07) at para 55 and 62.
315 (2004) (Application No 25367/05) at para 40.
316 (2012) (Application No 39954/08) at paras 79 and 91.
317 (2012) (Applications Nos 40660/08 and 60641/08) at paras 102 and 110.
318 Source: *The Reunion: The First London Marathon*, BBC Radio 4, 4 April 2010. Brasher and Disley, original founders and organizers of the London Marathon, accepted more than £380,000 in libel damages in an out-of-court settlement on 23 May 1995 over magazine and TV allegations that they used the London Marathon to enrich themselves.

statement referred to him, but the defendant may escape liability for unintentional defamation by making an out-of-court settlement by way of an apology and damages ('an offer to make amends').[319]

Descheemaeker (2009) argues that the tort of negligence ought to deal with 'reputation' – rather than defamation law. He calls the conflict between defamation and reputation 'bijection' in that 'defamation only protects reputation, while reputation is only protected by defamation' and that there exists a concurrent liability or fusion of the two.[320] The author looks at 'reputation' in the sense that it is 'goods' and the way German law deals with loss of reputation (German for 'goods' is *Rechtsgüter*[321]).

3.10.2 Freedom of expression and operators of websites

The Wall Street Journal in **Jameel** [322] had relied on Article 10 of the Convention. The case proved that 'freedom of expression' is not a guaranteed and absolute right in that it may be restricted by prescribed law such as the tort of defamation (see also: **Derbyshire County Council v Times Newspapers Ltd** (1993)[323]).

In a groundbreaking judgment Mrs Justice Sharp, in **Budu v BBC** (2010),[324] ruled that publishers cannot be held liable for libellous material republished out of context on internet search engines. Revolving around the dispute between the BBC and Sam Budu, the High Court deemed that neither a search engine nor a publisher should face libel claims, even if articles contain clearly libellous material, and that such contentious articles should only be read in context when filing a libel action.

The case of **Budu** concerned three BBC online articles which Ghanaian-born Mr Sam Budu found via the Google search engine when he entered his own name. The first article, which did not refer to the claimant by name, reported that Cambridgeshire police had been compelled to withdraw a job offer from 'an applicant' when it transpired that he was an illegal immigrant. The second and third article, giving Mr Budu's name, reported in June 2004 that Sam Budu, Ipswich and Suffolk Council's racial equality director, was later rejected as diversity manager after security vetting. Although the two later articles put the claimant's side of the story, Mr Budu alleged that they conveyed the defamatory meaning that he had failed a vetting process and posed a security risk.[325]

Following the **Loutchansky** judgment, the BBC had posted updating notices in respect of the **Budu** articles complained of; they had not apologized for publishing the articles. In view of this, Sharp J ruled that the BBC was not liable for the Google snippets.[326] She also held that the case on publication of the first article must be limited to persons who had also seen the later article, because it was only by searching and finding those that it was reasonable for a reader to have found the first article and understood it to refer to the claimant. Any reader who saw the first article would have also read the authoritative rejection of the allegation that the claimant was an illegal immigrant.[327]

In relation to press freedom, Sharp J focused on **Jameel**, stating that – irrespective of whether the claimant had a potential case or not – she would have struck out Mr Budu's claim because the articles were old and only available via the BBC online archive. Because of the passage of time it would have been difficult for the BBC to advance a **Reynolds** defence since the journalist concerned

---

319 Section 2 Defamation Act 1996.
320 See: Descheemaeker (2009) at pp. 603–641.
321 In German law of negligence meaning: physical integrity, personal reputation, self-esteem, autonomy, dignity.
322 **Jameel (Mohammed) v Wall Street Journal Europe Sprl (No 3)** [2007] 1 AC 359.
323 [1993] AC 534.
324 [2010] EWHC 616 (Sharp J) (QB).
325 Ibid., at paras 18, 23 and 25 (Sharp J).
326 Ibid., at para 70.
327 Ibid., at para 44.

had already disposed of her notes in the normal course of events. Permitting Mr Budu's action to continue would have constituted a disproportionate interference with the BBC's Article 10 rights.[328]

3.11 Will the Defamation Act 2013 make a difference to academics and libel tourists?

The law of defamation is at times concerned with conflicting issues of great sensitivity, involving both the protection of good reputation and the maintenance of the principles of free expression. In defending a libel action the difference between a statement of verifiable fact and one of opinion can be crucial.

As the law stands at present, a defendant who has to justify a statement of fact, as in the case of Dr Simon Singh,[329] has to prove that the defamatory statement is true. This fact has not changed with the 2013 Act. This means that the burden of proof still lies on the defendant, which can involve calling vast amounts of evidence at huge personal cost with no legal aid available. The unique problems in relation to defamation conducted on the internet have already been explored in detail and leading to the discussion and analysis of the concept of self-governance in cyberspace as opposed to governmental territorial legislation.

Arguably, the existing definition of what is defamatory has not changed with the 2013 Act, and there is still no clear definition of what is meant by defamatory. However, it has become more challenging to bring an action in defamation, since the bar has been raised before such an action can be brought, this being the threshold from 'substantial harm' to 'serious harm' under s 1 of the 2013 Act. This had already been mention by the courts in the **Sarah Thornton** case[330] and the **Jameel v Dow Jones**[331] cases with the requirement of a 'real and substantial tort'. This means that courts have already dismissed trivial libel case applications which potentially failed the 'serious harm' test for abusing the court process, for example, a complaint made about an article headlined 'The return of the man eater' in the **Nancy Dell'Olio**[332] case. Her application was struck out on the basis that it did not cross the threshold of seriousness, i.e. the words complained of were not capable of being defamatory.

In **Dell'Olio v Associated Newspapers Ltd** (2011),[333] Tugendhat J struck out Nancy Dell'Olio's libel action against the *Daily Mail* because the 'words complained of were not capable of bearing the meaning attributed to them by the claimant in her particulars of claim or any other defamatory meaning of which she might complain'.[334] The *Strictly Come Dancing* star claimed that an article of 20 April 2011 ('Return of the man eater') about her affair with Sir Trevor Nunn was defamatory, with an innuendo that Miss Dell'Olio was a serial gold-digger who had 'deliberately set out to snare herself a wealthy man by making their adulterous affair public thereby destroying his marriage for her own personal gain'. Tugendhat J ruled in **Dell'Olio** that the words complained of were not capable of bearing the meaning attributed to them by the claimant in her particulars of claim, or any other defamatory meaning of which she might complain. It followed that her claim was dismissed.

Hooper *et al.* (2013)[335] argue that the Defamation Act 2013 has not made enough changes, and still favours claimants. However, the authors also state that the sections of the 2013 Act relating to 'serious harm', operators of websites and the 'single publication rule' will ultimately restrict libel

---

328 Ibid., at para 128.
329 **BCA v Singh** [2010] EWCA Civ 350.
330 **Thornton (Sarah) v Telegraph Media Group Ltd** [2011] EWHC 1884 (QB).
331 **Jameel (Yousef) v Dow Jones & Co Inc** [2005] EWCA Civ 75.
332 Annunziata Dell'Olio (born 1961), better known as Nancy Dell'Olio, is an Italian-American lawyer who first came to public notice as the girlfriend of Sven-Göran Eriksson, then manager of the England national football team.
333 [2011] EWHC 3472 (QB).
334 Ibid., see paras 26–34 of judgment (Tugendhat J).
335 Hooper, Waite and Murphy (2013) at pp. 199–206.

tourism, combined with the abolition of jury trials, which may well assist the defence of actions in defamation.

The law of defamation remains complex and arguably lacks clarity in some areas, remaining inaccessible to the layman. As a consequence, the high degree of uncertainty in the outcome of defamation claims has undoubtedly increased costs of such proceedings in the High Court – often described in law reports as the 'chilling effect'. Though most lawyers and academics agree that there is a need for greater clarity in the law, there were strong differences of opinion during the consultation period of the Defamation Bill on the benefits of seeking to enshrine existing common law in statute by 'codification'. Furthermore, there was considerable disagreement on what reforms were required and the extent to which existing principles could be refined or codified, such as the *Reynolds* qualified privilege approach in defending a libel challenge.

It remains to be seen what the results of the Leveson Inquiry and the Royal Charter on press regulation will bring with them.

See Chapter 10.4

 FOR THOUGHT

If a defendant newspaper has archived materials that are or may be defamatory, would an appropriate notice warning against treating it as the truth remove the sting of the libel from the material or will the courts regard this publication as equally important to the dissemination of contemporary material? Discuss.

 3.12 Further Reading

Crossan, S.J. and Wylie, A.B. (2010) *Introduction to Scots Law: Theory and practice.* **2nd Edition. London: Hodder Gibson.**
Chapters 1 ('The Scottish Legal Framework') and 3 ('Introduction to the Law of Delict') are particularly useful in this standard practitioners' textbook for those lawyers who wish to practise in Scotland. The text is user-friendly in respect of theory and practice in Scots law, offering straightforward and accessible coverage of the key areas of Scots Law and the most recent developments within it.

Descheemaeker, E. (2009) 'Protecting reputation: defamation and negligence'. *Oxford Journal of Legal Studies,* **29(4), 603–641.**
The article concerns itself with the relationship between defamation and negligence in the protection of the interest in reputation. There is a constant debate between defamation and reputation: defamation only protects reputation. This article shows that there is no reason why the tort of negligence could not prima facie extend the scope of its protection to reputation. It might seem that the fact that negligence, as a tort, requires by construction culpa, whereas defamation appears to rely on either more or less than that as a standard of liability, would prove an insuperable stumbling block in the way of this suggestion. The hurdle, however, is not nearly as formidable as it might appear at first, because, as this article documents, negligence has for more than a century been acting as a magnet on the law of defamation, surreptitiously bringing its standard of liability increasingly close to negligence-culpa.

Gatley on Libel and Slander **(2008) (Milmo, P., Rogers, W.V.H., Parkes, R., Walker, C. and Busuttil, G., eds); 11th revised edition. London: Sweet & Maxwell.**
This pivotal work, now in its 11th edition, has a high reputation in a number of countries. There are more than 130 pages of cited cases, including references to the decisions in *Mosley, Jameel,*

Charman v Orion Publishing, *Buckley v Dalziel*, *Wescott v Westcott* etc. This book, originally written by Clement Gatley, is specifically for the legal practitioner. The text discusses libel and slander in detail, the torts with which this book is primarily concerned and which protect the reputation of the individual. The in-depth coverage contained in this reference text includes examination of substantive and procedural law and gives guidance on recent case law, developments in legal principles and relevant legislation and any changes to procedural aspects of practice.

Haig, S. (2013) 'The Defamation Act 2013 and what it means for the Internet'. *E-Commerce Law & Policy*, **15(6), 14–15.**
Samantha Haig assesses the impact of key provisions of the Defamation Act 2013 on website operators. She focuses on: (1) the defence available to a website operator where it was not responsible for posting a statement under s 5(2) of the 2013 Act; (2) the powers of the courts to hear an action against a person who was not the author, editor or publisher under s10; (3) the limitation period for claims under s 8, introducing a single publication rule; and (4) orders to remove statements or cease distribution under s13.

Hooper, D., Waite, K. and Murphy, O. (2013) 'Defamation Act 2013 – what difference will it really make?' *Entertainment Law Review*, **24(6), 199–206.**
The authors examine the Defamation Bill as it passed through Parliament and ask how much difference the Defamation Act 2013 will really make to practitioners and publishers. They discuss how the Bill was nearly derailed in the House of Lords at the last minute following the Leveson Report and Lord Puttnam's attempt to include the Lord Justice Leveson recommendations in the defamation legislation.

Johnson, H. (2008) 'Defamation: the media on the defensive?' *Communications Law*, **13(4), 126–131.**
This article discusses practical differences between absolute and qualified privilege, the limitation period in which an action can be brought in defamation and the offer of amends as the parties are encouraged under the Defamation Act 1996 to settle matters out of court.

Mullis, A. and Scott, A (2009) 'Something rotten in the state of English Libel Law? A rejoinder to the clamour for reform of defamation'. *Communications Law*, **14(6), 173–183.**
This article discusses the various campaigns seeking reform of English 'libel' laws, principally freedom of speech. The authors then examine Lord Lester's libel reform Bill, and the House of Commons Select Committee on Culture, Media and Sport' response. This academic discourse seeks to provide an accurate and nuanced view of the existing state of the law of defamation which sets the agenda for changes in legislation as the Defamation Bill took its passage through Parliament to reform certain aspects of the libel regime in the UK.

Whitty, N.R. and Zimmermann, R. (eds) (2009) *Rights of Personality in Scots Law: A comparative perspective*. **Dundee: Dundee University Press.**
This book considers, in a comparative perspective, important trends and issues affecting the law on rights of personality in jurisdictions drawn from the families of common law civil law and mixed legal systems. The main focus is on the private law of personality rights (including defamation – delict) taking into account the impact of human rights law under the European Convention on constitutional legislation and Scots law conventions.

Chapter 4

Contempt of Court

Chapter Contents

Key Points

This chapter will cover the following questions:

- ○ What is the common law development of contempt of court?
- ○ What is the purpose of the Contempt of Court Act 1981?
- ○ What is meant by active and *sub judice* proceedings?
- ○ Why does the Attorney General not always prosecute for contempt?
- ○ What are the general defences for the media when 'contempt' is alleged?
- ○ Are the punishments for contempt fit for the digital age?
- ○ How should UK contempt laws be reformed?
- ○ Who still observes the law of contempt?

4.1 Overview

At the end of July 2013, two jurors were sentenced to two months' imprisonment after being found guilty of contempt of court for misusing the internet during crown court trials. Kasim Davey (21) from Palmers Green, north London, had posted a message on Facebook about a sex offences prosecution at Wood Green Crown Court declaring that he wanted to 'fuck up a paedophile'. In his defence, Davey told the court that there had been 'a lot of Jimmy Savile news at the time' and that he sent the Facebook message as a result of 'spontaneous surprise at the kind of case I was on'. His post – 'Woooow I wasn't expecting to be in a jury deciding a paedophile's fate, I've always wanted to Fuck up a paedophile & now I'm within the law!' – amounted to contempt.

Joseph Beard (29) of Esher, Surrey, used Google to research the fraud case he was sitting on at Kingston Crown Court in order to find extra information about victims, which he was said to have shared with fellow jurors. The trial of two men accused of conspiracy to defraud and money laundering in 2012 collapsed and the defendants, Ian Macdonald and David Downes, had to go through a retrial and were eventually convicted in March 2013 and jailed. The total cost of the case amounted to £300,000.

See below 4.8

Both cases were sent to the High Court by the Attorney General, Dominic Grieve QC, on the grounds that the men's actions interfered with the administration of justice, under the Contempt of Court Act 1981. Sir John Thomas, the then president of the Queen's Bench Division (Lord Chief Justice of England and Wales from 1 October 2013), explained that the cases sent out a warning to prospective jurors generally that immediate custodial sentences for up to two years were almost inevitable in cases of this kind.

Contempt of court ('contempt') is improper interference with the administration of justice. British contempt laws ensure that the court is free to decide on the matters before it, without undue influence from the media. The concept of contempt was established at common law as 'an act or omission calculated to interfere with the administration of justice'. The common law is still the starting point for determining what constitutes 'contempt', and case law has established the powers of courts to deal with contempt. Common law and statutory provision (in the form of the Contempt of Court Act 1981) ensure that *any* court – be it civil or criminal jurisdiction and certain tribunals, such as employment tribunals[1] – is free to decide on the matters before it, without undue influence from the media.

---

1   See: ***Peach Grey and Co v Sommers*** [1995] 2 All ER 513 where the High Court ruled that an employment tribunal is a form of court.

Section 1 of the Contempt of Court Act 1981 (CCA) creates a strict liability offence in form of the 'strict liability rule'. This means the rule of law applies, whereby conduct may be treated as 'a contempt of court' as tending to interfere with the course of justice in particular legal proceedings regardless of intent to do so.

Sections 2(1) and (2) CCA limit the scope of the strict liability rule, stating that it only applies to 'publications' including 'speech, writing and other communication in whatever form' which is addressed to the public at large; and only to publication which creates a 'substantial risk that the course of justice in the proceedings in question will be seriously impeded or prejudiced'. This chapter will examine whether the UK contempt laws are still fit for the digital age.

In July 2011, the *Daily Mirror* was fined £50,000 and the *Sun* £18,000 for contempt of court for articles published about a suspect arrested on suspicion of murdering Joanna Yeates.[2] Three senior judges — the Lord Chief Justice, Lord Judge, Lord Justice Thomas and Mr Justice Owen — ruled that the tabloid newspapers breached contempt laws with their reporting of the arrest of Christopher Jefferies, Yeates's landlord, who was later released without charge and was entirely innocent of any involvement.

The disappearance and tragic death of Miss Yeates during the Christmas period in 2010 had commanded enormous public interest and concern. Her body was discovered on 25 December and much of the initial criminal investigation had focused on Mr Jefferies, who lived in the same building. He was arrested on suspicion of her murder on 30 December. The front page of the *Mirror* of 31 December was headlined: 'Jo suspect is peeping Tom: Arrested landlord spied on flat couple', positively asserting that Mr Jefferies was a voyeur.[3] The *Sun* of 1 January 2011 carried the front-page headline 'Obsessed by death', alleging that Mr Jefferies 'scared kids' by a macabre fascination with Victorian murder novels. There were more allegations on pages 4 and 5, with interviews of neighbours and 'former acquaintances' describing how Mr Jefferies liked blondes — and Miss Yeates, too, was blonde. Someone portrayed him as 'quite a dominant personality', a 'control freak' who made her feel 'very uncomfortable'. There was then a report of speculation among neighbours that Mr Jefferies was gay, although the blonde woman believed that he was 'bi-sexual'. Another couple living in the building were said to have described Mr Jefferies as 'Hannibal Lecter' and 'posh and a little creepy'.[4] Both papers alleged that Mr Jefferies may be a paedophile.

Attorney General, Dominic Grieve QC, sought contempt action against the newspapers in May 2011, arguing that reports about Jefferies were 'so exceptional, so memorable' that it presented a 'risk of serious prejudice' to any potential future trial of Yeates's killer and therefore amounted to statutory 'strict liability' contempt under s 2(2) of the Contempt of Court Act 1981.

In *AG v Mirror Group Newspapers Ltd and News Group Newspapers Ltd* (2011), the court held that the material in the two tabloid publications was extreme and prejudicial. Had Mr Jefferies been charged with Ms Yeates's murder, these articles would have provided Mr Jefferies with a serious argument that a fair trial would have been impossible. If he had been convicted, he would have argued on appeal that the trial was unfair because of the adverse publicity.[5] To that extent the criminal justice process would have been held up and delayed.

The court also held that the impact of the tabloid articles on potential defence witnesses would have been extremely damaging to Mr Jefferies, since reluctant witnesses would have been even more reluctant to come forward, and witnesses who might have been prepared to come forward may very well have assumed that anything helpful or supportive they might have said about Mr Jefferies could not be right. Vincent Tabak, a 33-year-old Dutch engineer, was convicted of

---

2 See: *AG v Mirror Group Newspapers Ltd and News Group Newspapers Ltd* [2011] EWHC 2074 (Admin) 29 July 2011.
3 Ibid., paras 5 and 6.
4 Ibid., at para 8.
5 Though Lord Judge LCJ anticipated that any such appeal would have failed on the 'fade factor'. Ibid., at para 34.

murdering his next-door neighbour Joanna Yeates and jailed for a minimum of 20 years in October 2011 at Bristol Crown Court.

In July 2012 the Mirror Group and Associated Newspapers were found guilty of contempt of court for publishing potentially prejudicial material whilst the jury was considering its verdict in relation to Rachel Cowles's alleged abduction by Levi Bellfield. After a prosecution brought by the Attorney General, Dominic Grieve, Sir John Thomas and Mr Justice Tugendhat, at the High Court, ruled that the allegations published by the *Daily Mirror* and *Daily Mail* that Levi Bellfield had a sexual interest in young girls was highly prejudicial to his continuing trial on a charge of the attempted abduction of Rachel Cowles.[6]

See below
4.3.1

See below 4.9

We can find parallels with the Joanna Yeates murder coverage where trial by media has taken place, such as in the cases of Peter Sutcliffe (the 'Yorkshire Ripper' trial), Tom Stephens (the 'Suffolk Ripper' story), Colin Stagg,[7] Robert Murat[8] and Barry George[9]. In each case there were either contempt warnings by the Attorney General (or Solicitor General) to the media, or the newspapers were found guilty of contempt.

The CCA 1981 provides that the proceedings must be 'active' within the meaning of the Act. It is accepted on behalf of both newspapers that the proceedings were active and the reports complained of amounted to a publication. The newspaper coverage went 'way beyond' what the jury had been told or what had been broadcast by the television networks following the conviction of Levi Bellfield for the murder of Milly Dowler. If the jury had not been discharged there would have been a seriously arguable point that any conviction was unsafe, the judges ruled.[10]

The trial of Levi Bellfield began before Wilkie J at the Central Criminal Court on 6 May 2011. He was charged on Count 1 with the attempted kidnap of Rachel Cowles, aged 11, on 20 March 2002 and the kidnapping and murder of Milly Dowler, 13, on 21 March 2002. The trial judge made rulings about pre-trial publicity and as to the bad character evidence which was admissible; he gave the jury, as would be usual, clear directions at the outset of the trial and in his summing up as to deciding the case on the evidence and ignoring anything that was published outside the court-room.[11] Although the attempted kidnapping of Rachel Cowles and the murder of Milly Dowler had occurred in March 2002, Bellfield had been convicted on 25 February 2008 of:

(i)   The murder of Marsha McDonnell on 4 February 2003.
(ii)   The murder of Amelie Delagrange on 19 August 2004.
(iii)   The attempted murder of Kate Sheedy on 28 May 2004.

The judge ruled on 20 April 2011 that these convictions could be placed before the jury as evidence of bad character.[12]

---

6   Source: 'Attorney General welcomes Bellfield contempt judgment', Attorney General's Office Press Release, 18 July 2012, Ministry of Justice.
7   Detectives wrongly pursued Colin Stagg in 1992 for the killing of Rachel Nickell, using an undercover policewoman in a honeytrap operation to try to entice a confession from him. Stagg spent 13 months in prison on remand. He was saved from a potential life sentence for a crime he did not commit when a judge dismissed the case before it reached a jury, condemning the police actions and the use of a forensic profiler. Robert Napper, a paranoid schizophrenic, confessed to Rachel Nickell's killing in December 2008.
8   A group of British newspapers settled with Murat for a £600,000 payout in July 2008. Eleven daily and Sunday titles published by the four groups (News International, Mirror Group Newspapers, Express Newspapers and Associated Newspapers) were also ordered by the High Court to issue a full high-profile public apology for falsely accusing him of involvement in Madeleine McCann's disappearance in Portugal. Madeleine was nearly four when she vanished from her family's holiday apartment in Praia da Luz in the Algarve on 3 May 2007 as her parents dined at a tapas restaurant with friends nearby.
9   In November 2007, Lord Phillips LCJ issued a press warning not to publish anything that might prejudice the new trial of Barry George over the murder of TV presenter Jill Dando, after his successful appeal against his 2001 murder conviction.
10 *AG v Associated Newspapers Ltd and Mirror Group Newspapers Ltd* [2012] EWHC 2029 (Admin) of 18 July 2012.
11 Ibid., at para 1 (Sir John Thomas).
12 Ibid., at para 16.

The contemptuous articles concerning Levi Bellfield were published in the *Daily Mirror* and the *Daily Mail* on 24 June 2011 after the jury had returned a guilty verdict in relation to Milly Dowler's kidnap and murder but before it had reached a verdict in relation to the attempted kidnap of Rachel Cowles. Even though the jury was already aware of Levi Bellfield's previous convictions for murder and there had already been earlier adverse publicity, this prosecution illustrated that the strict liability test under the Contempt of Court Act 1981 applied to coverage which nevertheless created an additional risk of prejudice or exacerbated an existing risk of prejudice.

The articles published by the *Daily Mail* and *Daily Mirror* contained bad character evidence which had been *excluded* from the trial and there was a clear risk that the effect of the publicity on the jury could not be cured by directions. The President of the Queen's Bench division concluded:

> The material in each newspaper was in my view highly prejudicial to Bellfield in that it set out material in relation to his sexual perversion in relation to his partners and his perverted interest in and rape of girls. I accept that some of the evidence given was highly prejudicial, but this material went way beyond what the jury had been told about Bellfield, murderer though they knew him to be and had again found him to be. There was a real risk that the jury would have thought that the additional material was relevant to the remaining count where he was charged with attempting to abduct a schoolgirl. I am quite satisfied that both the *Daily Mail* and the *Daily Mirror* by publishing the further material, particularly that relating to his rape of girls, created a quite separate and distinct risk of serious prejudice.[13]

It is doubtful that members of the media have short memories and simply do not remember the strict liability rule which is inherent in contempt of court legislation.[14] It is probably fair to say that many of the 'red tops' have taken the risk in order to increase their newspaper sales by printing popular background stories when the subject matter was *sub judice*, writing off possible legal costs against the benefit of extra sales.

This chapter first charts the common law development of contempt of court, a criminal offence, which some foreign jurisdictions regard as a rather peculiar piece of UK law. 'Contempt' today exists in common as well as statutory law in the form of the Contempt of Court Act 1981.

See below 4.3.3

The meaning of 'active' court proceedings will be discussed, along with what is meant by *sub judice* proceedings. The chapter further deals with the confidentiality of jury deliberations and problems connected to jury behaviour and social networking in the digital age. This will be linked to the coverage of courtroom TV and practices already in place in the United States. Since the law of contempt covers the whole of the United Kingdom, Scottish and Northern Irish authorities will be referred to. Available defences are discussed and human rights legislation in this area of law will be highlighted.

See below 4.7.1

The chapter concludes with the question 'who still observes the law of contempt?' and looks at potentially prejudicial media coverage where the respective Attorney Generals did not take any action against publishers or editors who openly published during *sub judice* periods in high-profile criminal cases.

4.2 Contempt at common law

Contempt is closely linked to the Anglo-Saxon concept of trial by jury examined by the late Senior Master of the Supreme Court Chancery Division, Sir John C. Fox, who described contempt of court

---

13 Ibid., at para 33.
14 Section 1 of the Contempt of Court Act 1981 imposes a strict liability rule whereby conduct may be treated as a contempt of court on the basis of its tendency to interfere with the course of justice, regardless of any intention to do so.

See below
4.6.1

(*contemptus curiae*) as an 'eccentricity' of the English legal system and as a necessary regulatory evil to preserve the discipline of the courts and the defendant's right to a fair trial.[15] Penalties for breach can be by way of a fine or imprisonment (or both). Proceedings for serious breaches are commenced by the Attorney General (AG).

There are three types of contempt under common law which continue to exist alongside the statutory provision. These are:

See below
4.2.1 and 4.10

1. Interfering with 'pending or imminent' court proceedings; that is, conduct tending to interfere with a trial which is under way or just about to begin;[16]
2. Contempt 'in the face of the court'; and
3. Scandalizing the courts.

Contempt covers both civil and criminal jurisdiction, meaning that *anything* which generally interferes with the course of justice may potentially amount to a contempt of court. Forms of contempt then include:

- the strict liability rule;
- common law contempt;
- breach of publication bans (i.e. court injunctions).

The branch of contempt known as 'scandalizing the court' was described by Lord Diplock as 'virtually obsolescent,'[17] and the last recorded successful prosecutions were in 1930[18] and 1931. **Colsey** concerned a criticism of Lord Justice Slesser's interpretation of legislation which he had steered through Parliament when he was Attorney General:

> Lord Justice Slesser, who can hardly be altogether unbiased about legislation of this type, maintained that really it was a very nice provisional order or as good a one as can be expected in this vale of tears.[19]

The leading authority is **Gray**,[20] where a journalist was found to be in contempt by scandalizing the court for describing Mr Justice Darling as an 'impudent little man in horsehair, a microcosm of conceit and empty-headedness'. In **Gray**, the offence of scandalizing the court was described by Lord Russell of Killowen CJ as follows:

> Any act done or writing published calculated to bring a court or a judge of the court into contempt, or to lower his authority, is a contempt of court. That is one class of contempt. Further, any act done or writing published calculated to obstruct or interfere with the due course of justice or the lawful process of the courts is a contempt of court. The former class belongs to the category which Lord Hardwicke LC characterised as 'scandalising a court or a judge'.[21]

---

15 See: Fox (1927), pp. 394ff.
16 *AG v NGN* [1987] QB 1 ('Cricketer Ian Botham' case). The court took a robust view of the ability of jurors to decide cases uninfluenced by outside pressures, especially if the trial takes place many months after any potentially prejudicial publicity has occurred. This approach has generally prevailed in more recent years.
17 See: *Secretary of State for Defence v Guardian Newspapers Ltd* [1985] AC 339, 347 (Lord Diplock).
18 R v Wilkinson, The Times 16 July 1930.
19 R v Colsey, The Times 9 May 1931.
20 R v Gray [1900] 2 QB 36.
21 Ibid., at 40 (Lord Russell of Killowen CJ).

There have been unsuccessful prosecutions since,[22] but most of the cases reported since the 1930s have been appeals to the Privy Council from Commonwealth countries.[23] Allen (2002) argues that the offence of scandalizing the court has been used more frequently in Asia and the Pacific Rim than in England and Wales. This offence of 'scandalizing the courts' was under review by the Law Commission in December 2013.

See below
4.10

The first published opinion on criminal contempt 'in the face of the court' was that of Wilmot J in **Rex v Almon** (1765)[24] He said:

> . . . it is a necessary incident to every court of justice to fine and imprison for a contempt to the court, acted in the face of it.[25]

The case concerned bookseller John Almon, who was tried on a charge of criminal libel (*scandalum magnatum*) for selling Junius's 'Letter to the King' in 1770, itself a breach of a court order. Almon was found guilty of contempt and criminal libel because he had refused to obey a court injunction to stop selling the letter.

Blackstone wrote in his *Commentaries* (1765) about contempt 'in the face of the court':

> If the contempt be committed in the face of the court, the offender may be instantly appre-
> hended and imprisoned, at the discretion of the judges.[26]

The practical function of the law of contempt has the purpose of preserving the integrity of the legal process in order to provide a fair trial to all parties in court. It is particularly relevant in criminal proceedings, where 'the court is under a duty to ensure the accused a fair trial', also covered by Article 6 ECHR.[27]

A judge may stay a trial if he feels the outcome would be deemed unfair or impossible for a jury to decide, the main issue being unfair publicity shortly before or during the trial, known as 'active' proceedings. In the **Poulson**[28] and **Kray**[29] cases, for example, there were widespread

---

22 **R v Metropolitan Police Commissioner ex parte Blackburn (No 2)** [1968] 2 QB 150.
23 **Ambard v AG for Trinidad and Tobago** [1936] AC 322; **Perera v R** [1951] AC 482 (PC); **Maharaj v AG for Trinidad and Tobago** [1977] 1 All ER 411; **Badry v DPP of Mauritius** [1983] 2 AC 297 (PC); **Ahnee v DPP** [1999] 2 AC 294 (PC). On **Ahnee**, see Coutts (1999) at 472.
24 (1765) Wilm. 243.
25 Ibid., at 254 (Wilmot J).
26 See: Blackstone (1765 – revised in 1825 – 16th edn), Book IV, p. 286.
27 See: **R v Sang** [1980] AC 402.
28 See: **R v Poulson and Pottinger** [1974] Crim LR 141 where the trial judge said that he did not see how the press could report the evidence in the case without running the risk of being in contempt of other criminal proceedings which had already begun against John Poulson and other defendants in respect of similar offences. The 'Poulson' trials through the 1970s were the most high-profile tax evasion cases brought by the Inland Revenue at that time, resulting, *inter alia*, in the resignation of the Conservative Home Secretary Reginald Maudling, who had formerly been chairman of two of Poulson's companies. John Poulson had taken advantage of the post-war depression, using his political contacts to obtain large-scale civic building work. He used bribes as his main weapon. In the 1960s he built a series of public hospitals and grandiose new shopping centres, including the Arndale Centre in Leeds. By 1966 his turnover was £1.16m, with a net profit of £112,500. The Poulson case of 1972–76 was the largest case of public corruption brought in Britain in the twentieth century, but was played down politically because both major parties were involved; as the Salmon Committee on 'Standards in Public Life' put it: 'We doubt if Mr Poulson would ever have been prosecuted but for his bankruptcy and his habit of meticulously preserving copies of everything he wrote or that was written to him.' Poulson's first conviction, for which he was sentenced to five years' imprisonment in February 1974, related to the development of a winter sports centre at Aviemore – the papers reported on the background during the case. The following month Poulson received a further sentence of seven years, to run concurrently, on further charges of conspiracy. The papers reported his previous conviction during the trial. John Poulson was released from prison in 1977 and died in February 1993. A book on the subject (Tomkinson and Gillard, 1980) suggests that the bankruptcy proceedings instituted in 1972 were much hindered by unusual pressure put on Muir Hunter QC and the rest of the legal team representing the trustee in bankruptcy, and all involved in the case found themselves both lamed and discriminated against in their careers.
29 **R v Kray** (1969) 53 Cr App R 412.

See Chapter
5.3

See Chapter
5.2.2

reports of proceedings against persons who were likely to be tried on other charges in the near future.[30]

There are other statutory restrictions known as 'quasi contempt'; if breached these are not 'contempts' but substantive statutory offences, including:

- ss 39 and 49 Children and Young Persons Act 1933 – prohibition on publication of a name, address or school calculated to identify a child under 18;
- s 8 Magistrates' Courts Act 1980 – restrictions on reports of committal proceedings;
- s 5 Sexual Offences (Amendment) Act 1992 – prohibits publication of details that identify a victim of rape or other serious sexual offence who has anonymity.

4.2.1 Contempt in the face of the court

This can arise before, during or after criminal proceedings being prosecuted at either the Crown Court or the magistrates' court. Described at times as 'criminal contempt' – irrespective of the court in which the proceedings are heard – a court may deal with contempt 'in the face of court' when the contempt is committed either:

- in the courtroom itself (for example, interrupting or interfering with the proceedings); or
- in the court building where it has been reported to the judge (for example, threatening a witness waiting to give evidence); or
- in breach of an undertaking to the court (**DPP v Channel Four Television Co. Ltd** (1993)[31]); or
- beyond the courtroom and the court's precincts,[32] when it is reported to the judge and it relates to proceedings whether in progress or pending (for example, improper approaches to witnesses or jurors).[33]

The powers of magistrates to deal with contempt in the face of the court are contained in s 12 Contempt of Court Act 1981 (CCA). Section 12 creates two contempts:

- wilfully interrupting the proceedings; and
- otherwise misbehaving in court.

'Insults' does not include threats. It could be argued that this is a defect which needs to be remedied. Another problem has been inconsistency between the powers of the magistrates' courts and those of the Crown Court. The Crown Court can issue proceedings for contempt 'in the face of the court' in the following circumstances:

- *any* contempt seen by the judge; or
- disobedience of a court order; or
- breach of an undertaking to the court.[34]

---

30 Ibid., at para 1348.
31 [1993] 2 All ER 517.
32 Section 41 Criminal Justice Act 1925 creates a contempt to take any photograph, make or attempt to make any portrait or sketch of a justice or a witness in, or a party to, any proceedings before the court, either in the courtroom or its precinct, such as the waiting room outside the courtroom or in the immediate circumference of the courthouse.
33 Part 62 of the Criminal Procedure (Amendment No. 2) Rules 2010 deals with contempt by obstructive, disruptive, insulting or intimidating conduct in or near the courtroom.
34 See: **DPP v Channel Four Television Co. Ltd** [1993] 2 All ER 517.

The Law Commission proposed new statutory powers,[35] applicable to both magistrates' and Crown Courts, to deal with:

(i)   intentional threats of insults to people in the court or its immediate precincts; and
(ii)   misconduct in the court or its immediate precincts committed with the intention that proceedings will or might be disrupted.

This would replace the existing powers in s 12 CCA, provide a clearer definition of contempt and bring consistency across the courts.

Photographs can be a particularly big problem when newspapers or broadcasters reveal a police suspect and identification at trial is an evidential issue. As the Court of Appeal indicated in **R v Bieber** (2006),[36] the publication of a photo can have an enormous prejudicial effect on a jury trial where visual identification is an issue and relied on. The closer the publication to a trial, the greater the risk of jury prejudice.

When a Crown Court judge indicates that he wishes to deal with someone for contempt, prosecutors must ensure that prosecuting counsel is in a position to assist the court with as much information as possible, including relevant authorities. When contempt is not admitted, the trial should take place at the earliest opportunity. In **R v McLeod** (2000),[37] the Court of Appeal held there was no reason why a trial judge could not be considered to be an independent and impartial tribunal for proceedings for contempt of court. The CA further stated that Article 6 ECHR does not add to, or alter, the normal requirement that proceedings should be conducted fairly before an independent and impartial tribunal. Therefore, the trial judge in **McLeod** was entitled to deal with the intimidation of a witness, which had occurred in a corridor outside the courtroom.

Sometimes the contempt may be sufficiently serious to justify proceedings for a criminal offence (for example perverting the course of justice or witness interference); however, the court may prefer to deal with the conduct as part of its inherent jurisdiction to administer justice in a speedy and orderly manner. This power should be exercised only when it is urgent and it is important to act immediately. In the absence of urgency, the matter should be referred to the Attorney General to consider bringing proceedings in the Queen's Bench Division.[38]

Criminal contempt is usually raised by the court itself or by the AG. A contempt involving a Crown Court that does not fall into any of the above categories is to be dealt with by the Administrative Court.[39]

Contempt in the face of court remains an offence of summary jurisdiction, whereby magistrates have the power to order the offender 'to the cells' in the courthouse with immediate effect until the end of the day's sitting.[40]

Quasi contempt

There are other statutory restrictions on the reporting of proceedings which, if breached, are not contempts but substantive offences, known as 'quasi contempt'. Examples include:

---

35   See: Law Commission Consultation Paper No 209 'Contempt of Court', Chapter 5, November 2012.
36   [2006] EWCA Crim 2776.
37   **R v McLeod (Callum Iain)** 29 November 2000 (CA) (unreported).
38   See: **Balogh v St Albans Crown Court** [1975] 1 QB 73.
39   In accordance with CPR Schedule 1, RSC Order 52.
40   Section 108 Magistrates' Courts Act 1980 applies by virtue of subsection 12 Contempt of Court Act 1981.

- Section 39 Children and Young Persons Act 1933 – prohibition on publication in a newspaper, sound and television broadcast only of a name, address or school calculated to identify a child or a picture of a child concerned in the proceedings, as a victim, witness or defendant. Identification through other means, e.g. social media, is not covered by s 39 (confirmed by Tugendhat J in *MXB v East Sussex Hospitals NHS Trust* (2012)[41]).
- Section 49 Children and Young Persons Act 1933 – automatic restriction on publication in a newspaper report and programme service (as defined in s 101 Broadcasting Act 1990) only of a name, address or school or any particulars likely to identify a child or a picture of a child concerned in the proceedings as a victim, witness or defendant.
- Section 8 Magistrates' Courts Act 1980 – restrictions on reports of committal proceedings.
- Section 5 Sexual Offences (Amendment) Act 1992 – prohibits publication of details that identify a victim of rape or other serious sexual offence who has anonymity.

4.2.2 'Thalidomide' and the permanent injunction 'against the world' (*contra mundum*)

Before 'contempt' existed under statute, one of the leading authorities could be found in Lord Diplock's characterization of the term in the 'thalidomide' case,[42] when he said:

> . . . [contempt covers] particular conduct in court proceedings which tends to undermine that system or to inhibit citizens from availing themselves of it for the settlement of their disputes.[43]

In this case, involving decades of lengthy action by victims of the drug thalidomide, five Law Lords overruled the Court of Appeal and directed the Divisional Court to grant an injunction to the Attorney General against the publishers of *The Times* '*contra mundum*', restraining the *Sunday Times* (and therefore all other media outlets) from publishing any matter which might prejudice present and future court proceedings involving Distillers Co. (Biochemicals) Ltd in respect of the manufacture, distribution and use of thalidomide. On 23 December 2009, some fifty years after one of the worst disasters in medical history, hundreds of survivors of the thalidomide scandal finally received an apology from the Government with a new £20 million compensation package.[44]

The case concerned some 466 'Thalidomiders', born between 1958 and 1961 to mothers who unwittingly took the drug 'Distaval' ('Contergan' in Germany[45]) for morning sickness in the early months of pregnancy. The babies suffered a variety of deformities. Thalidomiders and their parents began legal action against the drugs company Distillers from 1961 onwards. Some cases were settled out of court, but parents found that the *ex gratia* payments were not sufficient and not flexible enough to meet the young people's changing needs. Former *Sunday Times* editor Sir Harold (Harry)

---

41 [2012] EWHC 3279.
42 *AG v Times Newspapers* [1974] AC 273.
43 Ibid., at para 298 (Lord Diplock).
44 Source: '50 years on, an apology to thalidomide scandal survivors', by Sarah Boseley, *Guardian*, 15 January 2010.
45 Contergan, the brand name of a sleeping pill manufactured by Chemie Grünenthal GmbH, caused the greatest tragedy in the history of the German pharmaceutical industry. In the late 1950s and early 1960s, approximately 5,000 children in West Germany were born with deformities. The active drug substance in Contergan was thalidomide. Grünenthal obtained a patent for thalidomide in West Germany in 1954. At that time, the standards required for the development of a medicine were very different to the way they are today. Approximately 2,800 thalidomide victims live in Germany today.

Evans championed the cause through the early 1970s, publishing his first editorial article on 24 September 1972. In the article Evans criticized Distillers for not offering parents of thalidomide-affected children more generous compensation; the editor had planned six further editorials on this subject, but was 'gagged' by the courts. The 'thalidomide' case is known for its injunctions and cross-appeals by the Attorney General between October 1972 and March 1973. A heated parliamentary debate concerning press freedom also ensued.[46]

The House of Lords heard the final application and – allowing the Attorney General's appeal – granted a permanent injunction *contra mundum* ('against the world') on 1 March 1973 for the duration of all future thalidomide actions. This meant that nothing relating to *any* thalidomide actions could be published until all cases had been settled.[47] The case set the precedent for contempt of court, with Lord Reid summing up:

> . . . there has long been and there still is in this country a strong and generally held feeling that trial by newspaper is wrong and should be prevented . . . What I think is regarded as most objectionable is that a newspaper or television programme should seek to persuade the public, by discussing the issues and evidence in a case before the court, where civil or criminal, that one side is right and the other wrong.

After the *Times* publishers lost their case in the House of Lords, they filed an application with the European Commission of Human Rights in 1978, claiming that the injunction infringed their right to freedom of expression guaranteed by Article 10 of the Convention.[48] The ECtHR held – by 11 votes to 9 – that the interference with the applicants' freedom of expression was not justified under Article 10(2) as a 'pressing social need' and could not therefore be regarded as 'necessary'.

Reform of the law of contempt had been in the air since Lord Hailsham set up the Contempt of Court Committee in 1974. Lord Justice Phillimore had presented his report on the law of contempt of court to Parliament in December 1974 and the topic had been briefly discussed in Parliament at that time.[49] The conclusions of the Phillimore Report revealed certain difficulties and deficiencies in the operation of the law of contempt, particularly in criminal contempt matters, and that the freedom of the press, while paramount, involved a measure of restraint.

Legislation was eventually hastened following the House of Lords (1974) and the Strasbourg (1980) judgments in the 'thalidomide' action. A Green Paper followed, leading to the Contempt of Court Bill dealing specifically with criminal contempt.[50] It was the intention of Parliament at the time to liberalize the law by more clearly defining what could constitute 'contempt', in particular in relation to the question of when the proceedings were deemed to be active.

4.3 The Contempt of Court Act 1981

The Contempt of Court Act 1981 (CCA) redefined the strict liability offence of contempt of court, which now requires court proceedings to be 'active'. Section 1 CCA creates the strict liability rule, meaning that a journalist or editor's conduct may be treated as a contempt of court by interfering with the course of justice in particular legal proceedings regardless of intent to do so. The 'strict liability rule', contained within s 1 CCA, provides that 'conduct may be treated as a contempt of

---

46 See: Hansard, 29 November 1972.
47 For further comment on the court action, see the foreword by Sir Harold Evans in Smartt (2006) at pp. ix–xi.
48 See: **Sunday Times v UK** (1980) 2 EHRR 245 (ECHR).
49 See: Hansard, The Phillimore Report on 'Contempt', HC Deb 25 April 1978 vol 948 cc1340–1350.
50 See: Young (1981).

court, as tending to interfere with the course of justice in particular legal proceedings, regardless of intent to do so'.

This can be particularly pertinent in criminal proceedings during the *sub judice* ('active') period. For example, ss 7 and 8(3) CCA relate to breach proceedings for contempt under the strict liability rule. Section 8 relates specifically to proceedings for contempt regarding breaches of confidentiality of jury deliberations. The main areas of the Contempt of Court Act 1981 are summarised below:

See below
4.3.3

Contempt of Court Act 1981

See below 4.8

- Limits liability for contempt under the 'strict liability rule' (ss 1–7).
- Deems jury interference as contempt (s 8).
- Prohibits the use of tape recorders in court or bringing sound recording equipment into court without leave of the court and deems publication of a sound recording as a contempt (s 9).
- Provides limited protection against contempt for a person refusing to disclose the source of information contained in a publication for which he is responsible (s 10).
- Empowers magistrates' courts to deal with contempt in the face of the court by imposition of a fine of £2,500 or committal to custody for a maximum of one month or both (s 12).
- Restricts the period of committal to prison for contempt where there is no express limitation to two years for a superior court and one month for an inferior court (s 14).

4.3.1 The Contempt of Court Act 1981 comes into force: the Yorkshire Ripper trial

Contempt risk may start before a suspect has been charged with a criminal offence at the point of arrest – particularly in a high-profile case – which means the case becomes 'active' at the point where someone is a key suspect. Following the fatal shooting of WPCs Nicola Hughes, 23, and Fiona Bone, 32, when they were answering a routine burglary call in Mottram, Greater Manchester on 18 September 2012, the Attorney General, Dominic Grieve QC (via Nazir Afzal, Chief Crown Prosecutor for the CPS North West) issued a general press warning, telling the media to be careful in their reporting in the wake of the arrest and charge of 29-year-old Dale Cregan:[51]

> May I remind all concerned that as Dale Cregan has now been charged with criminal offences, it is very important that nothing is said or reported, which could prejudice that trial and jeopardise the course of justice in this case.[52]

In spite of the AG's press warning, there were several broadcasters and newspapers reporting emotional allegations made by the Greater Manchester Chief Constable about the alleged circumstances of the two officers' deaths, and similar remarks were made by Prime Minister David Cameron. The newspapers carried the quotes in their print editions following the arrest and charge

---

51 Dale Cregan was charged with the policewomen's murders and with the murders of Mark Short, who was killed at the Cotton Tree Inn in Droylsden on 25 May 2012, and David Short, who was killed at his home in Clayton on 10 August 2012. Cregan was also charged with the attempted murders of Michael Belcher, Ryan Pridding and John Short on 25 May and Sharon Hark on 10 August.

52 Source: 'Dale Cregan charged with four murders and four attempted murders', CPS press notice, 20 September 2012 at: www. cps.gov.uk/news/latest_news/dale_cregan_charged_with_four_murders_and_four_attempted_murders/index.html.

of Cregan. This, in turn, put AG Dominic Grieve in an awkward position when the most potentially prejudicial material appeared to have emanated from Greater Manchester Police and the Prime Minister's statements following the killings. The Sun, the Daily Mirror, the Guardian and the Daily Mail were among those printing verbatim comments made by the Greater Manchester Chief Constable, Sir Peter Fahy, and David Cameron. Should the newspapers and broadcasters be held in contempt for reporting information that had come from the police and Prime Minister?

What the above situation shows is that the Contempt of Court Act 1981, created by Parliament before the existence of the internet, rolling TV news, social media networks and smartphones, is possibly no longer fit for purpose.

Around the time the Contempt of Court Act became law in 1981, the 'Yorkshire Ripper' – Peter Sutcliffe – was arrested on 2 January 1981 by West Yorkshire police. This marked the sub judice period and no reporting other than his name, address and charge was allowed.[53] On 5 January, 35-year-old Sutcliffe of 6 Garden Lane, Bradford, was charged at Dewsbury Magistrates' Court with the murder of Jacqueline Hill.[54] Later, in total, Sutcliffe was charged with the murder of 13 women over a five-year period, most of them prostitutes.

In spite of the CCA 1981 coming into force, there followed extensive 'red top' newspaper coverage, alleging that the Ripper's last murder victim, Jacqueline Hill, could have been saved, and implying total police incompetence during the five-year 'Ripper' investigation.[55]

The papers reported that around 300,000 persons had been questioned in the hunt for the 'Yorkshire Ripper', one of them being Peter Sutcliffe in 1977. Following Sutcliffe's arrest, West Yorkshire Assistant Chief Constable George Oldfield gave every indication 'off the record' to the press that the 'Yorkshire Ripper' and prime suspect, long-distance lorry driver Peter Sutcliffe, were one and the same person, stating that the police were 'scaling down' their search for the 'Ripper'.

The government's Solicitor General, Sir Ian Percival, had issued a press warning in line with the new contempt legislation, intimating that the media would be liable to prosecution if their stories impeded a fair trial for Sutcliffe. Nevertheless, long before any trial, there was sensational news coverage that the 'Yorkshire Ripper' had finally been arrested, including full background coverage of the accused. The tabloid press relied heavily on police-supported leaks. Journalists held their breath to discover whether the Attorney General, Sir Michael Havers QC, would prosecute for contempt. But he did no so such thing.[56] After a two-week trial at the Old Bailey, Peter Sutcliffe was found guilty of 13 counts of murder and sentenced on Friday 22 May 1981 to 30 years behind bars.

Following Sutcliffe's arrest, Private Eye magazine accused his wife, Mrs Sonia Sutcliffe, of doing a deal with the Daily Mail worth £250,000, for telling her story, 'My life with the Yorkshire Ripper'. The satirical magazine alleged there had been a squalid race to buy her story and claimed she had negotiated with the press to profit from her fame as the wife of a serial killer. On 24 May 1989, Mrs Sutcliffe won a libel action against the 'Eye' and its editor, Ian Hislop. A jury at the High Court in London awarded £600,000 damages to Sonia Sutcliffe (the award being £100,000 more than any

---

53 Section 8 Magistrates' Court Act 1980 ('Restrictions on reports of committal proceedings').
54 Jacqueline Hill, from Middlesbrough, a 20-year-old student, was found battered to death on 17 November 1980, on waste ground in Leeds. She was Yorkshire-born killer Peter Sutcliffe's final victim.
55 In connection with this allegation see: **Hill v Chief Constable of West Yorkshire Police** [1989] AC 53 where the plaintiff, Mrs Hill, mother of the deceased Jacqueline Hill, the last of the 'Yorkshire Ripper' victims, sued the police in negligence alleging that the police conduct and investigations relating to the earlier 'Ripper' murders in West Yorkshire could have prevented her daughter's killing. Mrs Hill claimed that the West Yorkshire Police had failed to apprehend Sutcliffe on a number of occasions. But the trial judge struck out Mrs Hill's claim, a decision upheld by the Court of Appeal and affirmed by the House of Lords on the grounds that there was no proximity between the parties. The police were granted the 'immunity' effect in respect of crime investigations and prevention.
56 Source: Press Council Report, House of Lords Debate; HL Deb 20 July 1983 vol 443 cc 1159–1170.

See Chapter
3.8

previous libel sum in the UK at the time[57]). Mr Hislop commented afterwards: 'If this is justice, I'm a banana.' The sum was reduced to £60,000 on appeal. To date, about a quarter of the magazine's turnover is still set aside each year for possible libel and contempt settlements.

The Byford Report of 1981, released under the Freedom of Information Act 2000 on 1 June 2006, exposed details of 'systematic failure' by the West Yorkshire Police in the 'Ripper' inquiry and the handling of the press. The report included a letter from Hillsborough MP, Martin Flannery, to the Home Secretary William Whitelaw, warning that police 'off the record' comments to the media about the prime suspect amounted to a 'presumption of guilt' and contempt of court, and that Peter Sutcliffe would never stand a chance of a fair trial.[58] Sir Lawrence Byford summarized:

> Since the Sutcliffe press conference, the Contempt of Court Act 1981 has become law, neither the police nor the media can escape blame for the limitations clearly exposed in the 'Ripper' case and both agencies should recognise their duty to act in furtherance of the public weal.[59]

In 1983, the Press Council (a pre-runner to the Press Complaints Commission – PCC) had also conducted an inquiry, inviting views from the Attorney General, the police and the editors involved in the 'Ripper' investigation and trial proceedings.[60] The report stated that there was a considerable degree of co-operation, but:

> . . . regrettably the same cannot be said of the reaction of all the editors. While some editors were forthcoming, it required a prolonged and detailed correspondence to obtain from others information, often given unwillingly, about their own newspaper's attempts to buy the stories of people connected with the case.[61]

See Chapter
10.3

The Press Council had already expressed strong views about 'cheque book journalism' 17 years earlier after the trial judge in the 'Moors Murder' case (involving Myra Hindley and Ian Brady), Mr Justice Fenton Atkinson, had made his anxieties known to the then Attorney General (Lord Elwyn-Jones). The Press Council had issued a statement that no payment or offer of payment should be made by a newspaper to any person known or reasonably expected to be a witness in criminal proceedings already begun, in exchange for any story or information in connection with the proceedings, until they have been concluded.

This rule was deliberately breached by the *Sunday Telegraph* in 1979 when it entered into a contract with a prosecution witness in the 'Jeremy Thorpe' trial and the Norman Scott affair. Scott had claimed to be the former homosexual lover of Liberal Party politician Jeremy Thorpe. Thorpe was charged with the attempted murder of Scott and stood trial at the Old Bailey on 8 May 1979. Chief prosecution witness, former Liberal MP Peter Bessell, claimed to have been present while the murder plot was discussed within the Liberal Party. His credibility was damaged because he sold his story to the *Sunday Telegraph* for a reported fee of £50,000. George Carman QC, counsel for Mr Thorpe, claimed that Scott had sought to blackmail Thorpe and that there was a serious contempt of court in the key witness being paid by the newspaper. The jury reached a verdict of not guilty, acquitting all four defendants on 22 June 1979.

Whether lessons were learnt from the 'Ripper' inquiry by the Press Council or the recommendations in the Byford Report is unclear. It will never be known whether the published material in the 'Ripper' trial ultimately prejudiced the considerations by the Old Bailey jury, but arguably it was

---

57 See: **Sutcliffe v Pressdram Ltd** [1991] 1 QB 153.
58 Source: Home Office (1987), paras 466–482.
59 Ibid., at paras 518–519; 667–668.
60 See: Press Council (1983).
61 Ibid., at para 2.12.

potentially highly prejudicial and did not grant Mr Sutcliffe a fair trial. The Attorney General at the time, Sir Michael Havers QC, could have issued contempt proceedings under the new 1981 Act against a number of newspapers and their editors after the verdict, but he did not.[62] Payments to witnesses by the media and those actually convicted remains an unresolved issue.

4.3.2 Contempt by publication

Contempt covers media reporting by 'publication' which asserts or assumes, expressly or implicitly, the guilt of the defendant or possible negligence on behalf of the respondent in civil cases. In newspaper reporting terms (and online editions) this can be just a single headline or in broadcasting terms it can be a biased commentary or news item before or during a trial. In criminal proceedings, extraneous information – such as background material on a defendant – might sway a juror's mind and prejudice a final verdict. In the case of an offending publication or broadcast, defence lawyers may well ask a trial judge to stay trial proceedings if they feel that their client has been adversely treated by the media.

The strict liability rule may render the publication a 'contempt', regardless of any intent to interfere with the course of justice in the proceedings. 'Publication' refers to:

- broadcasts, websites and other online or text-based communication (including Twitter, Facebook etc.) addressed to the public at large or any section of the public; which
- creates a substantial risk that the course of public justice will be seriously impeded or prejudiced.

The element of 'risk' is judged at the time of publication and applies only to legal proceedings that are 'active' at the time of the publication. The longer the gap between publication and the trial (known as the 'fade factor'), the less the substantial risk of serious prejudice is likely to be. See below 4.3.3

In the **Geoffrey Knights** case at Harrow Crown Court in October 1995,[63] eight newspapers were referred to the Attorney General, Sir Nicholas Lyell, by trial judge Roger Sanders for publishing various stories about Mr Knights after the case had started. Sanders J ruled that the pre-trial coverage of Knights' charges of wounding with intent against *EastEnders* actress and girlfriend Gillian Taylforth amounted to a 'hate' campaign. The Solicitor General, Sir Derek Spencer, Sir Nicholas's deputy, ordered a police investigation into claims of 'improper collusion' between journalists and some witnesses. The judge stayed the trial because of adverse pre-trial and 'active' trial stories in newspapers, stating that there was a 'substantial risk of serious prejudice' to the trial proceedings. One of the tabloids, the *Daily Mirror*, had published interviews with Mr Knights and the man he had been charged with attacking. Further stories emerged about Geoff Knights's relationship with the then *EastEnders* star Gillian Taylforth.[64]

The standard of proof of whether a publication amounts to strict liability contempt is the criminal 'heightened' standard – beyond reasonable doubt – that the publication may cause a

62 Press Council (1983) at paras 10.16 and 10.24.
63 **R v Knights (Geoffrey)** (unreported, 1995) Harrow Crown Court 6 October 1995.
64 Source: 'Trial by media: watching for prejudice. After the Geoff Knights fiasco, can we trust the press to allow the accused a fair hearing?', by Grania Langdon-Down, *Independent*, 11 October 1995.

substantial risk that the course of justice in the proceedings in question may be seriously impeded or prejudiced. If a trial is stayed – due to adverse media reporting for contempt of court – the accused will – in certain cases – never stand trial. This effectively means that justice will not be seen to be done in the public interest. Paradoxically, the more publicity there is in a high-profile case, the less likely it is that any one individual publication will have had a substantial affect on the reader.

4.3.3 Active proceedings: *sub judice*

'Active' proceedings are defined in Schedule 1 CCA 1981. Proceedings are active if a summons has been issued or a defendant arrested without warrant. Where a warrant has been issued, proceedings cease to be active once 12 months have elapsed without the suspect's arrest, and where there has been an arrest when the suspect is released without charge otherwise than on bail. Proceedings cease to be active where they conclude by, *inter alia*, acquittal or sentence, or by any other order bringing proceedings to an end, or by discontinuance or operation of law. The CCA 1981 provides for strict liability from the point a case becomes 'active'. This is known as the period of *sub judice*, as set out in s 1 CCA:

> . . . the strict liability rule means the rule of law whereby conduct may be treated as a contempt of court as tending to interfere with the course of justice in particular legal proceedings regardless of intent to do so.

The publication or broadcast can mention the following when reporting on criminal proceedings:

- the name of the accused;
- his or her address;
- the offence he or she is charged with.

see Chapter
5.3

The law does not generally allow for any identification of children or young persons under 18 (England, Wales and Northern Ireland) appearing in a Youth Court.[65] In Scotland the anonymity can be lifted as soon as the young person has reached the age of 16.[66]

The limitation of the scope of strict liability in relation to a publication is defined by s 2 CCA, 'Limitation of scope of strict liability':

> (1) The strict liability rule applies only in relation to publications, and for this purpose 'publication' includes any speech, writing, programme included in a cable programme service, or other communication in whatever form, which is addressed to the public at large or any section of the public;[67]
>
> (2) The strict liability rule applies only to a publication which creates a substantial risk that the course of justice in the proceedings in question will be seriously impeded or prejudiced;
>
> (3) The strict liability rule applies to a publication only if the proceedings in question are active within the meaning of this section at the time of the publication.

---

65 Automatic reporting restrictions and anonymity orders under ss 39 and 49 Children and Young Persons Act 1933.
66 Section 47 Criminal Procedure (Scotland) Act 1995.
67 In this section 'programme service' has the same meaning as in the Broadcasting Act 1990: s 2(5) inserted by Broadcasting Act 1990 (c. 42, SIF 96), s 203(1), Sch. 20, para 31(1)(b).

Criminal proceedings are concluded by:

> (a) an acquittal or sentence;
> (b) any other verdict, finding, order or decision which puts an end to the proceedings;
> (c) discontinuance of the charge.[68]

How should the media react when there is an appeal? Criminal appellate proceedings are active from the time when arraignments for the hearing are made.[69] Once the 'active' (*sub judice*) period has started, a journalist, broadcaster or publisher must adhere to the contempt legislation in the usual way.[70] Civil appellate proceedings are active from the time when arraignments for the hearing are made or – if no such arraignments are previously made – from the time the hearing begins, until the proceedings are disposed of or discontinued or withdrawn.[71]

It is important to note that a contempt action is treated as a criminal matter and the burden of proof is the heightened standard ('beyond all reasonable doubt'). In addition each paper or media outlet is judged on its contribution to any risk or prejudice alone and not as part of the whole media circus – so paradoxically it can be argued that the greater the media circus the less likely a single outlet will have contributed to any risk or prejudice. Here are some examples of cases which are likely to attract national media interest. Reasons can include:

- **The defendant is famous** (e.g. when BBC broadcaster Stuart Hall admitted in May 2013 that he had indecently assaulted 13 girls during the 1960s, 70s and 80s; or the serial child abuse carried out by BBC broadcaster Jimmy Savile (deceased)).
- **The complainant is famous** (e.g. when ex-TV 'weathergirl' and TV presenter, Ulrika Jonsson, accused an ex *Blue Peter* presenter of rape in 1988 in her autobiography, serialised in the *Daily Mail*).
- **The case is one of a serial rapist** (e.g. black cab driver John Worboys, who was convicted as a serial rapist in March 2009 for attacks on 12 women).
- **A high-profile cold case solved because of DNA advances** (e.g. the murder of BBC newsreader and presenter, Jill Dando, by gunshot outside her home in Fulham, West London, on 26 April 1999 has not been solved and her killer has not been identified; Barry George was wrongly convicted of Dando's murder and spent eight years in prison; he lost his legal battle for compensation as a 'victim of a miscarriage of justice' in July 2013).
- **Criminal appeal cases** (e.g. 'the Airline Bombers case' – see: *R v Abdulla Ahmed Ali and Others*) (2011).[72]

One high-profile cold case was that of the murdered schoolgirl Milly Dowler. Dowler went missing on 21 March 2002 and Levi Bellfield was found guilty of abducting and murdering the 13-year-old in June 2011. At the end of the trial, the *Daily Mail* and the *Daily Mirror* were found guilty of contempt

68 Schedule 1 (6) CCA; s1 Powers of Criminal Courts (Sentencing) Act 2000; s 219 or 432 Criminal Procedure (Scotland) Act 1975; Article 14 Treatment of Offenders (Northern Ireland) Order 1976.
69 Schedule 1(12) CCA 1981.
70 Remand proceedings in the magistrates' court prior to committal are covered by s 8 Magistrates' Court Act 1980; during the trial proceedings reporting is covered by s 4 CCA 1981 ('contemporary reports of proceedings').
71 Schedule 1(11) and 1(15) CCA 1981.
72 [2011] EWCA Crim 1260 (CA Crim Div).

of court over their coverage of Levi Bellfield's trial and conviction.[73] The extensive media coverage before and during the trial had resulted in the trial judge dismissing the Old Bailey jury before they could reach a verdict on a second charge, that he had also allegedly attempted to abduct schoolgirl Rachel Cowles.

In a judgment handed down at the High Court in London on 18 July 2012, Sir John Thomas, President of the Queen's Bench Division, and Mr Justice Tugendhat said coverage in the two newspapers did 'significantly exacerbate' the risk of serious prejudice to the high-profile jury trial under s 2 CCA 1981. Sir John Thomas said:

> I am sure that each publication did create such a substantial risk of serious prejudice. The allegations of his sexual interest in and depraved conduct to young girls was highly prejudicial to the count that the jury were then still considering. What was set out went way beyond what the jury had been told or what had been broadcast on the preceding evening. . . . I have little doubt that if the jury had not been discharged, there would have been a seriously arguable point that the conviction was unsafe.[74]

The *Daily Mail* and *Daily Mirror* were each fined £10,000 by the two High Court judges in the contempt case brought by the Attorney General, Dominic Grieve QC.

4.3.4 Strict liability and substantial risk
Section 1 CCA creates the strict liability rule, whereby conduct may be treated as a 'contempt of court' if it tends to interfere with the course of justice in particular legal proceedings, regardless of intent to do so. This means even the most experienced journalist can fall foul of the law of contempt, even if he just wants to write a background piece to a forthcoming trial – it may well be that the publication is deemed to interfere with the course of justice. It is for this reason that every journalist, editor and publisher ought to be familiar with current contempt legislation.

4.4 Reporting on court proceedings

If covering active court proceedings, a court reporter is allowed to report verbatim and contemporaneously what was said in court. This is covered by s 4(1) CCA, which states that:

> . . . a person is not guilty of contempt of court under the strict liability rule in respect of a fair and accurate report of legal proceedings held in public, published contemporaneously and in good faith.

So a reporter or publisher is not guilty of strict liability contempt if the publication amounts to fair and accurate reporting of legal proceedings held in public and published 'in good faith'.

On 24 September 2012, a s 4(2) CCA 1981 order was made in Manchester Crown Court preventing reporting of any pre-trial proceedings in the **Dale Cregan** case until after the conclusion of the trial. One-eyed Cregan (30) was accused of murdering police officers Fiona Bone (32) and Nicola Hughes (23) on 18 September 2012 by luring them to their deaths by dialing 999 to report

---

73 ***AG v Associated Newspapers Ltd and Mirror Group Newspapers Ltd*** [2012] EWHC 2029 (Admin) of 18 July 2012 ('Levi Bellfield contempt case').
74 Ibid. (President of the Queen's Bench Division).

a bogus burglary, then using a Glock handgun and a military grenade to murder the two women in Hattersley, Greater Manchester. Section 4(2) CCA reads:

> In any such proceedings the court may, where it appears to be necessary for avoiding a substantial risk of prejudice to the administration of justice in those proceedings, or in any other proceedings pending or imminent, order that the publication of any report of the proceedings, or any part of the proceedings, be postponed for such period as the court thinks necessary for that purpose.

In the **Dale Cregan** case, His Honour Judge Gilbart QC imposed additional reporting restrictions under s 4(2) CCA 1981 on the ground of 'very real risk of prejudice' because the case had attracted high-profile media and public attention. He was not concerned about the 'very proper expressions of loss' from the Chief Constable of Greater Manchester Police, but about other information including press conference answers and 'accounts', which had been 'widely disseminated on the internet, in broadcasts, and in newspapers.' Talking about the 'extensive material' published, which may be relevant to cases against other defendants, the judge said: 'the time has come for that flow of material and comment to cease.' In May 2013 at Preston Crown Court, Dale Cregan admitted the murders of the two policewomen as well as admitting causing an explosion at a property in Luke Road, Droylsden, shortly after murdering father and son David and Mark Short. He also admitted the attempted murders of John Collins, Michael Belcher and Ryan Pridding during the attack on Mark Short at a Droylsden pub in May 2012.[75] Cregan was sentenced to a whole-life tariff by Mr Justice Holroyde QC at the end of the four-month trial that laid bare the brutality of Manchester's underworld.

The practicalities of a blanket reporting ban order – as in the case of Dale Cregan – mean that there is no further reporting until the jury is sworn in. Any reports of preparatory hearings are limited to basic facts such as the name of the accused and the offences he is charged with. Pre-trial hearings cannot be reported until the conclusion of the trial, and anything likely to cause a substantial risk of serious prejudice to the proceedings in the forthcoming trial is prohibited by the CCA 1981. The s 4(2) CCA order excludes the trial from its scope, which means that, unless further restrictions are imposed, once the jury is sworn in, it would be business as usual for any court reporter as long as he complies with s 4(1) CCA: 'fair and accurate report of legal proceedings held in public, published contemporaneously and in good faith'.

 FOR THOUGHT

> In criminal cases such as Dale Cregan (murder of two female police officers and others in Greater Manchester) or Vincent Tabak (murder of Joanna Yeates), where there is intense public and media interest, and the suspect is awaiting trial, is it right that a judge can impose total reporting restrictions under s 4(2) CCA 1981? Do these restrictions not interfere with the open justice principle and Article 10 ECHR? Is newsworthiness and public interest sufficient reason to impose reporting restrictions? Discuss.

---

75 Source: 'Police killer Dale Cregan pleads guilty to murders of father and son in gun and grenade attacks', by Rob Cooper, *Daily Mail*, 22 May 2013.

4.4.1 Contemporaneous court reporting

As we have seen above, a court may postpone reporting until the completion of the trial or may make a complete anonymity order, banning any reporting until the proceedings are concluded under s 4(2) CCA.[76] This practice has been increasingly used by the courts in pending terrorism cases where the court deems it necessary for public security reasons and the protection of jury members to make such an order. Permanent anonymity from reporting is covered by s 11 CCA 1981 ('Publication of matters exempted from disclosure in court'), and in certain delicate high-profile cases the trial judge can postpone reporting until post-conviction and/or sentence, as illustrated in the 'Baby P' case.

Seventeen-month-old Baby Peter died in Haringey, North London, on 3 August 2007, suffering from more than 50 injuries over an eight-month period, in the care of his mother Tracey Connelly (28) and her partner Steven Barker (33). There were total reporting restrictions in place because – as we learnt later – there were other children involved who were still alive at the time of the trial(s) and there was a significant risk of identifying those children. But the seminal reason for the s 4(2) CCA order was that Barker was, at the conclusion of the 'Baby P' trial, additionally to stand trial for the rape of a two-year-old child and might not otherwise have been able to have a fair trial (Article 6 ECHR). By naming Tracy Connelly there would be jigsaw identification.[77] It was for these reasons that the total anonymity order was in place on all the defendants until after conclusion of the rape trial. Only then was the order lifted.

However, those who really wanted to know the identity of Baby P's mother, her boyfriend and other associates could have easily found their identities freely available on the internet via YouTube. After the individual and joint trials and sentences in August 2009, the surname of Baby Peter, Connelly, was released, as well as the name of the third defendant in the case, Jason Owen, 37, identified as Barker's brother. In May 2009, Tracey Connelly and Steven Barker were sentenced to a minimum of 5 and 12 years' imprisonment respectively for causing or allowing the death of Peter. In a separate trial, Steven Barker was given a life sentence for raping a two-year-old girl; this also contributed to the delay in naming all three defendants. It emerged that Owen had changed his name to avoid being connected to the killing of Baby P; Owen was sentenced to three years' custody. It also emerged that Peter had four siblings.

See also
Chapter 5.2.3

Before a court makes an anonymity order, or orders (total) reporting restrictions, it has to abide by the general rule in favour of open justice and the fair and accurate reporting of public court proceedings. Article 10 ECHR (the right to freedom of expression) – a qualified right – should also be borne in mind, and interference of it in the form of restrictions may be appropriate where this is necessary and proportionate in pursuit of a legitimate aim such as the protection of the rights of others to a fair trial (Article 6 ECHR) or to privacy (Article 8 ECHR). Interference with the freedom of the press under Article 10 is appropriate only to the extent to which it is truly necessary, and there should be no interference (or a lesser degree of interference) where the result might be achieved by other means.

The Crown Prosecution Service encourages its prosecutors to oppose reporting restrictions if they do not consider these necessary for a 'fair trial'.[78] Media representatives will also seek to oppose reporting restrictions in the interest of open justice.

---

76 In Scotland a s 4(2) CCA 1981 order is made in either the High Court of Justiciary, the Court of Session or the Sheriff Court, depending on the type and seriousness of the offence and charge. Persons found guilty of contempt in Scotland will be sentenced under the Criminal Procedure (Scotland) Act 1995.

77 Jigsaw identification can occur when the media reveal several pieces of information in words or images about an individual (usually during *sub judice* proceedings) which, when pieced together, could lead to revealing the identity of that individual. See also: Glossary.

78 Source: The Consolidated Criminal Practice Direction, Part 1, paragraph 1.3, CPS October 2012.

4.5 Problems of identification

See below
4.5.2

The Attorney General's office issues frequent media warnings in high-profile cases that editors should not be complacent and rely on the 'fade factor' It is agreed, however, that common law development in this respect has not been very helpful. Besides, the AG has not issued any hard and fast rules as to when he may commence contempt proceedings in relation to publication and active trial proceedings.[79]

In **Re B** (2006),[80] the BBC and other media organizations appealed against a High Court ruling that had ordered a complete reporting ban under s 4(2) CCA until the conclusion of the trial proceedings. In this case, B and his co-defendant D had been arrested as part of an extensive police anti-terrorism operation which had been widely reported by the media. B and D were indicted for 23 offences, including conspiracy to commit murder and acts of terrorism. B had already pleaded guilty to some offences. B and D contended that the extraneous comments made by the media on B's previous sentencing hearing were potentially disastrous to a fair hearing in the present case and D's trial. The defendants argued that the media coverage would seriously prejudice a (yet unselected) jury, arguing, *inter alia*, Article 6 ECHR and their right to a fair trial.

Allowing the appeal, Sir Igor Judge ruled that media editors ought to be trusted to fulfil their responsibilities and exercise sensible judgment in the publication of such information – reasoning that the media would be familiar with contempt legislation. Balancing the principles enshrined in human rights legislation, the Court of Appeal ruled in favour of 'freedom of expression' and that the media should act as the 'eyes and ears of the public'. At the time, the CA sent a stern warning to the press that they should observe the contemporaneous reporting rules as ordered in statute.

When the (now retired) Assistant Commissioner of the Metropolitan Police (the Met), Andy Hayman, was about to publish the book (co-written with Margaret Gilmore[81]) *The Terrorist Hunters* in 2009,[82] the Attorney General sought an injunction to stop the book being published because he found that the subject matter, concerning national counter-terrorism operations, would seriously contravene confidentiality law in respect of safeguarding national security. The book was initially injuncted until all terrorists in the (ongoing) trial proceedings had been tried.

The Terrorist Hunters charts Hayman's personal involvement in major terrorist investigations – overt and covert – and the Met's response to the 7/7 London bombings (7 July 2005), as well as the intelligence operation concerning the murder of the Russian dissident Alexander Litvinenko. Copies of the book had been sent two months in advance of publication to the Crown Prosecution Service, the Cabinet Office, MI5 and MI6 and the Metropolitan Police Authority.

Thousands of copies of the 372-page book had already been distributed to bookshops nation-wide to go on sale on 2 July 2009.[83] The 'liquid bomb' trial was at that time 'live', with closing speeches on 29 June 2009. Attorney General Baroness Scotland stepped in at the last minute to obtain an injunction preventing the book from going on sale on 9 July 2009 (see below). The book was reissued in March 2010.

---

79 Though the AG issued guidelines in 2008 on 'The Prosecutor's role in applications for witness anonymity orders' under the Criminal Evidence (Witness Anonymity) Act 2008. Source: Attorney General's Office, London, 21 July 2008.
80 **R v B** [2006] EWCA Crim 2692 ('Re B').
81 Margaret Gilmore is a Senior Research Fellow with the Royal United Services Institute. She specialises in homeland security. Before taking that position she was a BBC Home Affairs Correspondent.
82 See: Hayman and Gilmore (2009).
83 About 800 copies of the book had already been sold by retailers, 10,461 had been sent to retailers in preparation for the publication date of 2 July, and 3,430 had been sent to export markets.

❖ **KEY CASE** *Attorney-General v Random House Group Ltd*
[2009] EWHC 1727 (QB) 15 July 2009

Precedent

❖ A publication can amount to 'serious prejudice' if the subject matter of the publication and the nature of the 'expression' represent different types of 'speech' which can
impede the course of justice (e.g. political speech, speech on public affairs or national
security).

❖ It is in the public interest (represented by the AG) for the publication to be injuncted.

Facts

The Attorney General applied for an injunction to restrain the sale of the book *The Terrorist
Hunters* on the ground that such publication would create a substantial risk that the
course of justice in a current criminal trial would be seriously impeded or prejudiced,
within the meaning of s 2(2) CCA 1981. The defendants (in the 'liquid bomb trial') were
Abdulla Ahmed Ali and seven co-accused before Henriques J and a jury at Woolwich
Crown Court. The publishers, Random House, argued that the injunction would dispro-
portionately interfere with the right of freedom of expression of the authors under
Article 10 ECHR.

The 'liquid bomb' trial was in fact a retrial[84] and the accused were part of a large police
investigation called 'Operation Overt' – as part of the 'airline plot', allegedly to use on
aircraft improvised explosive devices, some concealed in soft drink bottles. The main
charge was conspiracy to murder by detonation of improvised explosive devices on board
transatlantic passenger aircraft. After the earlier acquittal of Mohammed Gulzar and the
unsatisfactory outcome of the 2008 trial, the 'liquid bomber' case attracted vast publicity
at the time, much of which was easily accessible on the internet, including BBC online. On
that basis the (present) accused sought a stay of proceedings on the ground that they
could not have a fair trial.

The AG took exception to five pages of the book in Chapter 9, which described events which
were part of 'Operation Overt', though none of the accused were expressly identified. With
the book going on sale during the closing speeches of the trial (29 June 2009 with jury
deliberation expected at the end of July) the AG asked for a short injunction, restraining
the sale of the book for the duration of the trial until all verdicts had been delivered.

Decision

In delivering his decision, Tugendhat J considered whether a careful direction to the jury
would suffice in the present 'liquid bomb' trial (rather than injuncting the book).[85]
However, he stated that the terrorist (re)trial was of 'the highest importance' and that the
judicial proceedings must not be impeded by any form of prejudice.

The judge noted that in the present case seven accused had been in custody for three
years already, and there were three further accused (two in custody) whose trial was

---

84 The first trial lasted from April to September 2008. On 8 September 2008 the jury acquitted Mohammed Gulzar. Ali, Sarwar and
Tanvir Hussain were convicted of conspiracy to murder. The jury failed to agree on the other charges.
85 [2009] EWHC 1727 at para 104 (Tugendhat J).

about to follow the trial of these present accused. If there was going to be (another) retrial, they would have to wait for many more months before there could be a verdict. Tugendhat J also reminded the defendant publishers that there had been two juries (to that date) who had sat for many months in two separate trials. The publication of the book would put even greater strain on the administration of justice by fear of seriously prejudicing the present and any future trials. For this reason the proportionate injunction was granted for eight weeks.[86]

Analysis

When the courts 'injunct' a publication this is always a major step and the costs incurred can be large following a committal for contempt, which will also incur court costs and a fine. For this reason, the court in *AG v Random House* had to weigh up the consequences, as well as balance the AG's application 'in the public interest' (i.e. in this case to apply to commit for contempt of court and the publisher's and authors' right to freedom of expression.

4.5.1 Photographs

Photographs are a major source of contempt by publication, particularly in criminal cases where a police suspect has not been positively identified by a witness, for example in an ID parade. At first hearing at the magistrates' court, the defendant may argue that he was not at the scene of the crime and plead not guilty. It is then not particularly helpful when a newspaper publishes a photo of the suspect.

Section 41 Criminal Justice Act 1925 creates a contempt to take any photograph, make or attempt to make any portrait or sketch of a justice or a witness in, or a party to, any proceedings before the court, either in the courtroom or its precincts. Section 9 CCA 1981 prohibits the use of tape recorders and other recording devices in court and deems publication of a sound recording as a contempt, although this section was partly amended by s 31 Crime and Courts Act 2013 ('Making, and use, of recordings of Supreme Court proceedings') allowing for filming in the Supreme Court and future 'courtroom TV' of Court of Appeal proceedings.[87]

The *Daily Mail* and the *Sun* were found guilty of contempt in November 2009 for publishing a picture of a murder trial defendant posing with a gun on their websites (see below). The papers' online editions published a photograph of Ryan Ward – albeit for only a few hours before being ordered to take down the image – who was about to stand trial for the murder of car mechanic Craig Wass at Sheffield Crown Court. Neither paper published the picture in print.[88] In the landmark ruling for internet publishing, the High Court found that the publication of the photograph created a 'substantial risk' of prejudicing the defendant's forthcoming trial. Angus McCullough QC, acting for the Attorney General, said both newspapers had breached the strict liability rule under s 1 CCA 1981.

---

86 Ibid., at para 110.
87 Section 31(2) Crime and Courts Act 2013 inserts new subsection (1A) into s 9 Contempt of Court Act 1981. Subsection (1A) disapplies the prohibition laid out in s 9(1)(b) of the 1981 Act (which prohibits the broadcast of sound recordings of legal proceedings) where a recording of UK Supreme Court proceedings is broadcast or disposed of with the leave of the court. Section 31(3) of the 2013 Act provides that the UK Supreme Court is able to grant leave to use in court, or to bring into court for use, any tape recorder or other instrument for the purpose of recording sound, subject to any conditions the UK Supreme Court considers appropriate relating to the subsequent publication or disposal of any recording. Section 31(4) of the 2013 Act makes it a contempt of court to publish or dispose of any sound recording which is made in contravention of any conditions of leave granted under new subsection (1A).
88 *AG v Associated Newspapers Ltd and Newsgroup Newspapers Ltd* [2011] EWHC 418 (Admin).

> ❖ **KEY CASE**
>
> *Attorney-General v Associated Newspapers Ltd and Newsgroup Newspapers Ltd* [2011] EWHC 418 (Admin) ('the Ryan Ward' case).

Precedent

❖ The Contempt of Court Act 1981 imposes a strict liability under s 1, including the publication of the image of an accused.

❖ The publication of a photograph during the *sub judice* period of an accused amounts to serious risk of prejudicing the impeding trial and interfering with the course of justice.

Facts

On Tuesday 3 November 2009 at Sheffield Crown Court a jury was sworn in to hear the trial of Ryan Ward for murder. The nature of the case was relevant to the issues in the application by the Attorney General for a committal of the defendants (the *Daily Mail* and the *Sun*) newspapers for contempt. It was alleged that the victim, a 39-year-old father, Craig Wass, had intervened after Ward had head-butted a young woman. Mr Wass was merely trying to keep the peace. Ward took hold of a brick and struck him on the head, fracturing his skull and causing other head injuries from which he died. Ward's defence was self-defence and lack of a murderous intent. The case had received considerable publicity.

After the jury was empanelled, the judge, His Honour Judge Murphy QC, gave conventional warnings that the jury should not speak to anyone and that they must ignore any reports they may have read in the press. The judge also warned the jury that they may not get 'outside' information by consulting the internet. Following the prosecution opening, the jury were sent home.

At 5.04pm on the same day, an article was published on *Mail Online* (Associated Newspapers Ltd) accompanied by a picture which showed Ward holding a pistol in his right hand with his index finger on the trigger while he indicated firing a handgun with his left hand. The caption read: 'DRINK-FUELLED ATTACK: Ryan Ward was seen boasting about the incident on CCTV.' The picture remained online for 4 hours and 54 minutes, until it was removed at 9.58pm.

Publication in the *Sun Online* (News Group Newspapers Ltd) occurred at 1.22am on Wednesday 4 November 2009. The photograph had been supplied to the second defendants by a photographic agency from a social networking site, on the 'page' of a co-defendant. The picture was the same as that intended for use in the newspaper version on 4 November. Though the picture had been cropped, it still showed Ward's hand and the top part of the gun barrel. The picture remained online until the officer in the case contacted the *Sun*'s news desk and requested its removal. It was removed 10 minutes after the request at 8.50pm. There were some 4,766 unique visitors to the online article on 4 November 2009, with 3,078 in England and 78 located in Sheffield.

The defendant newspapers were charged with strict liability contempt under s 1 CCA 1981. Both defendants argued that there was no substantial risk of any juror seeing or choosing to look at the offending photograph, also relying on the 'comparatively brief' period the photograph remained online.[89]

Decision

Lord Justice Moses and Mr Justice Owen held in the High Court that both newspapers were guilty of contempt by publication, concluding that there was a substantial risk that a juror would see the photograph of the accused (Ward) and that that photograph would have made a serious impact. The justices explained that visual images in the media were designed for impact and that was the reason why the editor would be keen to use them to add to the impact of the news story. Since Ward was running the defence of 'self-defence', the image of the accused brandishing the pistol in an apparently brazen manner may well have given the impression that Ward had a propensity for violence. Therefore, the online publication of the photograph was regarded as prejudicial in a manner directly relevant to the issues in the case.

In making the costs judgement on 19 July 2010, the judges said that both newspapers had now taken steps to avoid repetition and apologized to the Attorney General. They accepted that the publications were the result of a genuine mistake. The publishers were also required to pay the AG's costs of £28,117.23.

Analysis

The criminal courts have been troubled by the dangers to the integrity and fairness of a criminal trial, where juries can obtain easy access to the internet and to other forms of instant communication. Once information is published on the internet, it is difficult if not impossible to remove it completely.

Though the jury in the Ward case was warned not to use the internet, the court could not be completely satisfied that a juror might not have accessed Ward's 'gun' photograph either via the internet or through Twitter.

There will be jurors who disobey the judge's directions regarding the prohibition not to search the internet. This case demonstrates the need to recognize that instant news requires instant and effective protection for the integrity of a criminal trial.

Photographs of police suspects in newspapers or on TV can be problematical, particularly where there are identification issues during primary disclosure. If the complainant has not managed to identify an aggressor – say, in an ID parade – but suddenly sees an image of the individual in a newspaper or on TV, how can a court be sure that the complainant did not identify the accused from the publication rather than from memory? (see: *AG v Express Newspapers* (2004) – the 'footballer rape case'[90]).

In *Re S (A Child)*,[91] a child's nine-year-old older brother, DS, died of acute salt poisoning in the Great Ormond Street Hospital. At a hearing in July 2002, Hedley J found that the salt poisoning had been administered by the child's mother. As a result of this finding, the mother was charged with murder, with a trial set for November 2004.

---

89 Ibid., at para 34. See also Sir Igor judge's argument in **R v Barot** [2006] EWCA Crim 2692 at para 31.
90 [2004] All ER (D) 394.
91 **Re S (FC) (A Child) (Identification: Restrictions on Publication)** [2005] 1 AC 593.

In the pre-trial proceedings, the trial judge was asked in the interests of the child (a five-year-old boy) to ban normal reporting of the trial of his mother for the murder of his nine-year-old brother. Since this terrible situation was going to be known to the boy's school, his neighbours and friends, his guardian applied to the High Court for an injunction to prevent publication of any information which might lead to the child's identification under s 39 Children and Young Persons Act 1933, including his name, address, school or any picture of him and his parents. Hedley J declined to do so.

Balancing Articles 8 and 10 of the Convention, Hedley J decided that the order should contain a proviso such that the newspapers were not prevented from publishing the identity of the defendant mother or the deceased child DS or photographs of them in reports of the criminal trial. The appeal to the Court of Appeal was dismissed and the child's guardian appealed to the House of Lords. Both the CA and the HL upheld the trial judge's decision.

See Chapters 2.6 and 5.3

The decision in *Re S* underlines the considerable difficulties confronting a court when carrying out a balancing exercise between a child's right to private life under Article 8 and the right of the press to freedom under Article 10.

What about taking photographs in court? After all, journalists are now permitted to 'tweet' in court and take in mobile phone and handheld devices. The Lord Chief Justice, Lord Judge first allowed the use of 'live text-based communication' (e.g. Twitter) in court on 20 December 2010. This meant that reporters gained permission to tweet from extradition proceedings against WikiLeaks founder Julian Assange, at City of Westminster Magistrates' Court.

On 14 December 2011, Lord Judge further relaxed the rules on 'live text-based communications in court', which meant that journalists no longer had to ask for permission to tweet in court, paving the way for more live coverage of trials.[92] Until then, reporters had to seek permission from the trial judge to tweet on a case-by-case basis. The trial of Vincent Tabak in October 2011, who murdered the landscape architect Jo Yeates, was closely followed by users of the microblogging service Twitter; and so was the (new) Stephen Lawrence murder trial in December 2011, of Gary Dobson, 36, and David Norris, 35, who were convicted of the 18-year-old student's murder by stabbing him to death in a racist gang attack in Eltham, south-east London in 1993. Dobson and Norris were found guilty by an Old Bailey jury in January 2012.

See also Chapter 5.2.1

In September 2011, 19-year-old Paul Thompson was sentenced to two months' imprisonment for taking a photograph in the courtroom of Luton Crown Court with his Blackberry.[93] He was watching a friend being sentenced for robbing an off-duty police officer when he took a snap of the courtroom on his mobile phone. Her Honour Judge Mensah dealt with the matter under the Contempt of Court Act 1981 (not s 41 of the Criminal Justice Act 1925). In sentencing, she considered the totality of Mr Thompson's behaviour in court: he had been disruptive throughout the sentencing hearing and had been warned twice by the court usher to keep quiet in court before being finally asked to leave the court; Mr Thompson had also taken a photograph in court of the victim in the case, who had suffered a violent robbery. Upon hearing his sentence, Thompson said 'that's stupid, man', though his lawyer encouraged him to show remorse.[94]

---

92 Source: Practice Guidance: The use of live text-based forms of communication (including Twitter) from court for the purposes of fair and accurate reporting. Lord Judge The Lord Chief Justice of England and Wales, 14 December 2011 at: www.judiciary.gov.uk/Resources/JCO/Documents/Guidance/ltbc-guidance-dec–2011.pdf.

93 **R v Thompson** (**Paul**) 26 September 2011, Crown Court Luton (unreported). Source: 'Teenager jailed for taking photo at Luton Crown Court', BBC *News Online*, 26 September 2011 at: www.bbc.co.uk/news/uk-england-beds-bucks-herts–15057842.

94 Ibid.

4.5.2 The fade factor

Substantial risk does not mean a 'large' or 'great' risk but a risk which is not remote,[95] and the risk must be a practical rather than a theoretical risk.[96] The publication of noticeable prejudicial material during a trial is likely to create a much more substantial risk than the same publication which takes place a year before. If strict liability contempt is alleged, either the Divisional Court or the Attorney General will assess the 'fade factor' in the light of a particular publication. That is, whether the offending publication appeared shortly before an impending trial and whether this may have influenced the decision-making of that trial. If the publication was a long time previously – common law stipulates that this usually amounts to six to nine months prior to the trial – the court will say that the jurors' recollection of adverse publication in the media may well have faded (see: *AG v ITN* (1995)[97]).

See below
4.7.1

If the court then decides on the 'fade factor', this would make otherwise prejudicial reporting no longer contemptuous, especially when combined with appropriate jury direction by the presiding judge at the trial. Still, some facts may be so prejudicial that they are unlikely to fade from public consciousness following their publication by the media. For example, if a newspaper publishes the previous criminal convictions of an accused (otherwise inadmissible at trial), this is particularly dangerous. Whether a publication amounts to a contempt is essentially a value judgment for the court (see: *AG v BBC and Hat Trick Productions Ltd* (1997);[98] *AG v News Group Newspapers* (1987)[99]).

Equally, the court may decide that the publication of seemingly very seriously prejudicial matter may not amount to a 'substantial risk' if there is likely to be a substantial elapse of time between publication and the trial, as a result of the 'fade factor'.[100] The Divisional Court held in *AG v ITN*[101] that the publication of highly relevant and prejudicial previous convictions in conjunction with background information of the most serious nature may not amount to contempt: 'when the long odds against the potential juror reading any of the publication is multiplied by the long odds against any reader remembering it, the risk of prejudice is . . . remote.'[102]

The risk of prejudice will depend on the nature and weight of the publication, the identity of the accused and the facts of the case. Sensational reporting of high-profile cases is likely to stay in the mind of potential jurors for much longer than more mundane events. Equally, local newspaper reports or broadcasts are likely to impact more on a local jury than on a randomly selected jury at the Old Bailey. It is worth noting that a contempt action may still be actioned by the Attorney General against a media organization even if the defendant is found not guilty or even not tried because of death or health reasons: it is not the occurrence of 'serious prejudice' but the *risk* of it that is significant here.

4.6 Administration of justice

The worst outcome for trial proceedings and interference with fair justice takes place when a trial judge stays the entire court proceedings. Defence lawyers will frequently apply for proceedings to be stayed if there has been undue and adverse media coverage in a prominent case, arguing

---

95 *AG v English* [1983] AC 116 at 141–142.
96 *AG v Guardian Newspapers (No 3)* [1992] 1 WLR 784 at 881.
97 [1995] 2 All ER 370.
98 [1997] EMLR 76 at para 81 (Auld LJ).
99 [1987] QB 1 ('Cricketer Ian Botham' case).
100 *AG v Unger* [1998] 1 Cr. App. R.308 (Simon Brown LJ).
101 *AG v ITN Ltd* [1995] 2 All ER 370.
102 Ibid., at 383G (Legatt LJ).

that the accused will not be granted a fair trial before the jury which, *inter alia*, will also be argued under the Article 6 ECHR provision (see: *AG v Express Newspapers* (2004) – the 'footballer rape' case[103]).

4.6.1 The role of the Attorney General in contempt proceedings

The Attorney General (AG) is the government's chief legal adviser on domestic and international law and the Solicitor General is his or her deputy. They also have public interest roles, for example in relation to criminal cases and contempt of court proceedings. The AG's main responsibilities are:

● chief legal adviser to the Government and Parliament;
● guardian of the rule of law and the public interest;
● superintendent of the prosecuting departments.[104]

The AG has certain public interest functions: for example, in taking action to appeal unduly lenient sentences; giving consents for prosecutions; issuing a *nolle prosequi* ('will not prosecute'); referring to the Court of Appeal on a point of law; protecting charities; and bringing proceedings under the Contempt of Court Act 1981.

Contempt proceedings are public law proceedings brought by the Attorney General (AG) for England and Wales in the public interest. Section 14 CCA states that mode of trial in contempt proceedings does not apply and that the maximum punishment for strict liability contempt is two years' imprisonment, taking into account any relevant mitigating factors. Recent case law decisions generally fall into the following 'contempt' categories:

● media publication of material which is prejudicial to trial proceedings;
● abusing a judge, magistrate or other officer of court 'in the face of the court';
● attempting to influence or intimidate witnesses or jurors;
● witnesses refusing to give evidence;
● giving false statements (affidavit) before the court.

If the Attorney General believes that the strict liability contempt has been an issue, he (or she) will commence separate criminal proceedings against an offending publication or broadcaster, publisher and/or editor, usually after the (original) trial has concluded.[105]

4.6.2 When court proceedings are stayed

During the (first) *sub judice* period in **R v Bowyer and Woodgate** (2000),[106] the BBC's *Match of the Day* coverage on 26 November 2000 broadcast a cup match between Leeds United and Arsenal with the Leeds United footballers Jonathan Woodgate and Lee Bowyer as pixelated (headless) players for fear of contravening contempt legislation. Woodgate and Bowyer had been remanded on bail at the time, having been charged with serious wounding offences for an alleged assault on a young Asian student, Sarfraz Najeib, in a Leeds city centre nightclub in January 2000. The Leeds footballers' trial (No 1) took place at Hull Crown Court in 2001. At the start of the trial proceedings Poole J had

---

103 [2004] EWHC 2859 (Ch).
104 The AG has a statutory duty to superintend the discharge of the duties of the Director of Public Prosecutions (DPP), the Director of the Serious Fraud Office (SFO) and the Director of the Revenue and Customs Prosecution Office (RCPO).
105 Rules of the Supreme Court Order 52 (RSC Ord 52); see: **Regina v M** [2008] EWCA Crim 1901.
106 **R v Bowyer (Lee) and Woodgate (Jonathan) (No 1)** (2000) (unreported).

emphasized to the jury that the accused were not charged with racism offences and that the jury should ignore such thoughts.

During the jury's deliberation in April 2001, the *Sunday Mirror* published an interview with the victim's father, Muhammed Najeib, alleging a racist attack. On application by the defence, Mr Justice Poole stayed the proceedings, citing contempt of court, and ordered a retrial. He made it clear that the newspaper had seriously prejudiced the jury verdict by its publication, stating that the editor should have known better, and ordering costs against the Trinity Mirror Group newspaper organization.[107]

At their retrial a year later in 2002, Woodgate and Bowyer were acquitted of ss 18 and 20 wounding charges (Offences Against the Person Act 1861). Woodgate pleaded guilty to affray and was sentenced to 100 hours' 'community service' and ordered to pay eight weeks' wages as a fine. Bowyer also pleaded guilty to affray and was fined four weeks' wages. After the conclusion of the second trial, the Attorney General issued contempt proceedings against the Trinity Mirror Group and the *Sunday Mirror*'s editor, Colin Myler. They were found guilty of contempt and subsequently fined a total of £175,000. Colin Myler resigned. Kennedy LJ and Rafferty J contended that the offending article had seriously impeded justice during a lengthy, expensive, high-profile case at a crucially difficult time. (See also: **R v West (Rosemary)** (1996) 2 Cr App 374.[108])

❖ KEY CASE *Attorney General v ITV Central Ltd* [2008] EWHC 1984 (Admin)

Precedent

❖ A broadcaster (or other media organization) is guilty of strict liability contempt if he broadcasts or 'publishes' information during 'active' court proceedings or broadcasts any other extraneous information about the case.

❖ Where the contemnor has offered an immediate apology and offered to pay third-party costs the court must take this into account in assessing the appropriate amount that the broadcaster should be fined.

Facts
A regional television breakfast news bulletin of 23 seconds by Central TV (ITV) in relation to the trial of five men for murder later that day referred to the fact that one of the men had been convicted of, and was currently serving, a sentence for murder. Defence counsel brought the ITV broadcast to the attention of the trial judge and the trial was stayed. The broadcaster offered an immediate and unreserved apology to the court, agreeing to pay all third-party costs to cover the postponement of the trial. Subsequently, all five defendants were convicted with court costs amounting to £37,014, which ITV paid.

After the trial, the Attorney General applied for an order for committal for contempt of court against the broadcaster ITV Central.

Decision
The Divisional Court took the view that the ITV Central news broadcast was a 'serious and basic error' which had caused disturbance to the court, and delays and further distress to

---

107 A 'wasted costs' order can be made against third parties—here the media – by the magistrates or presiding judge under the Courts Act 2003, for wasting the court's time in a 'cracked' trial (where a trial had to be abandoned).

108 [1996] 2 Cr App 374.

third parties. However, in mitigation wasted costs had been voluntarily paid, and allowing for that it would be appropriate to impose a fine of £25,000.

Analysis
The case is a harsh reminder to media editors that there is no scope for honest error in contempt of court offences. The judgment in *AG v ITV* suggests that the courts take the strict liability offence under s 1 CCA 1981 seriously. The AG's application was granted for the reasons that the 'publication' (the broadcast) had amounted to a 'serious and basic error', creating a substantial risk of prejudice that the news bulletin might be seen by members of the jury due to hear the impending trial.

A murder charge is serious and the simplicity of the editorial error by the broadcaster could not detract from the seriousness of the publication. ITV should have known that where a person was convicted of murder and was due to be tried on another charge of murder, his previous conviction should not be disclosed. The court upheld the contempt and additionally pointed out that this had resulted in a disturbance of the court, causing additional delay and distress to all parties.

It is worth mentioning that if a trial is stayed or collapses because of a finding of contempt (on behalf of the newspaper or media organization) the court can issue a 'wasted costs' order, which is aimed at the causing of loss and expenses to litigants by the unjustifiable conduct of litigation by either side's lawyers.[109]

4.6.3 Impertinent courtroom behaviour

'Contempt' also covers courtroom behaviour, such as being disrespectful to a bench of magistrates, wearing inappropriate clothing in the public gallery or the use of mobile phones in the courtroom.

On 11 May 2003, Judge Huw Daniel, sitting at Mold Crown Court, dismissed a potential juror for 'contempt in the face of the court'. The male juror was wearing a top with a 'misspelt Anglo Saxon word' (a French Connection 'FCUK' T-shirt). The judge said that this was not only a distraction but was disrespectful of court proceedings. The juror had to stand down and was asked to leave the court.[110]

The issue of taking photos in a courtroom was addressed in **R v D (Vincent)** (2004).[111] The law in this area is very old, covered by s 41 Criminal Justice Act 1925 ('Prohibition on taking photographs, &c., in court') and reads:

(1) No person shall –

  (a) take or attempt to take in any court any photograph, or with a view to publication make or attempt to make in any court any portrait or sketch, of any person, being a judge of the court or a juror or a witness in or a party to any proceedings before the court, whether civil or criminal; or

  (b) publish any photograph, portrait or sketch taken or made in contravention of the foregoing provisions of this section or any reproduction thereof;

109 Wasted costs in criminal cases come under s 19A of the Prosecution of Offences Act 1985 (as amended by s 93 Courts Act 2003). The applicable regulations are the Costs in Criminal Cases (General) Regulations 1986 (SI 1986 No 1335), and in particular Part II A of those Regulations. The applicable practice direction is the Practice Direction (Costs in Criminal Proceedings) and in particular Part VIII of that practice direction.
110 Source: 'Judge bars four-letter word T-shirt', *BBC News Online*, 11 May 2003.
111 [2004] EWCA Crim 1271.

and if any person acts in contravention of this section he shall, on summary conviction, be liable in respect of each offence to a fine.

R v D addressed the illegal use of mobile phone cameras in court. The juvenile appellant had taken three photographs with his mobile phone camera at Liverpool Crown Court: one in the court canteen; one from the public gallery towards the witness box; and the third of his brother in the secure dock. The last picture also revealed one of the security officers. The trial judge seized the appellant's mobile phone and charged him with the summary offence of criminal contempt.[112]

The accused 'photographer' was convicted and sentenced to 12 months' imprisonment, whereupon he appealed against that sentence. The Court of Appeal had to decide whether the contemnor's sentence for contempt of court by using a mobile phone camera in the court room was manifestly excessive. Their Lordships expressed concern about the ease with which photos could now be passed on to third parties by electronic means and could easily fall into the wrong hands. Lord Aikens noted:

> . . . intimidation of juries and witnesses is a growing problem generally in criminal cases. Recently there have even been physical attacks on prosecuting counsel in a case. A person could use photographs of members of the jury or a witness or advocates or even a Judge in order to try to intimidate them or to take other reprisals. Witnesses who are only seen on a screen or who are meant to be known only by an initial could possibly be identified. The anonymity of dock officers or policemen who are involved in a case could be compromised if a photograph is taken and is used to identify them.[113]

Though the young appellant in **R v D** had argued that he had taken the photos in a 'spirit of fun', explaining that the photos of his brother in the dock were meant as a text message for his niece on her eighteenth birthday, the Court of Appeal upheld his sentence on the grounds that taking photos in a courthouse was illegal and gravely prejudiced the administration of justice because taking photos of witnesses or jury members could lead to their intimidation. The principle of fair justice and the right to a fair trial could be severely impeded.

4.7 Procedure and punishment

The courts' jurisdiction to deal with contempt is divided into two broad categories: criminal contempt and civil contempt. In essence, a criminal contempt, such as contempt in the face of the court, is an act which threatens the administration of justice. Courts are empowered to protect the administration of justice by acting on their own initiative, punishing those guilty of such contempt with detention in custody or a fine.

Civil contempt involves disobedience of a court order or undertaking by a party who is bound by it. The court's sanction in civil contempt has been seen primarily as coercive or remedial. Civil contempt has largely arisen in respect of an order or undertaking made in civil litigation. However, as some civil orders are now made in criminal cases, for example a restraint order considered in **R v M**,[114] a civil contempt may occur in the course of proceedings in a criminal court.

---

112 Section 41(1) Criminal Justice Act 1925 ('Prohibition on taking photographs, &c., in court').
113 (2004) EWCA Crim 1271 para 15 (Lord Aikens).
114 [2008] EWCA Crim 1901.

4.7.1 General defences and exceptions

See above
4.2.2

Following the Human Rights Court ruling in **Sunday Times v UK** (1980),[115] the Strasbourg Court opined that the overriding importance of a free press had to be maintained in order to keep the public informed, thereby upholding Article 10.[116] This case followed on from the domestic court action in the thalidomide action and concerned a long-drawn-out action in damages and compensation. The Contempt of Court Act 1981 was enacted, following the *Sunday Times* case,[117] though the creation of such legislation had already been discussed much earlier by a House of Commons Committee on 'Contempt of Court' (1974).[118]

General defences can be found under Schedule 1, s 3 CCA 1981:

(1) A person is not guilty of contempt of court under the strict liability rule as the publisher of any matter to which that rule applies if at the time of publication (having taken all reasonable care) he does not know and has no reason to suspect that relevant proceedings are active;

(2) A person is not guilty of contempt of court under the strict liability rule as the distributor of a publication containing any such matter if at the time of distribution (having taken all reasonable care) he does not know that it contains such matter and has no reason to suspect that it is likely to do so;

(3) The burden of proof of any fact tending to establish a defence afforded by this section to any person lies upon that person.

If faced with contempt allegations by the Attorney General (or a Sheriff Court in Scotland), the burden of proof lies on the journalist, editor, publisher or contemnor to convince the court that they were not in contempt when publishing offending material. This will be advanced under s 5 CCA 1981. A strong argument would be that the publication was made as part of a discussion, in good faith, of public affairs or as a matter of general public interest. It is up to the Attorney General to decide whether the strict liability contempt rules apply and whether there was a risk of impediment or prejudice to particular legal proceedings or whether the publication amounted to a mere incidental discussion.

Section 5 CCA 1981 provides a statutory defence concerning 'discussion of public affairs':

. . . a publication made as or as part of a discussion in good faith of public affairs or other matters of general public interest is not to be treated as a contempt of court under the strict liability rule if the risk of impediment or prejudice to particular legal proceedings is merely incidental to the discussion.

See above
4.3.2

Section 5 CCA can save a publication that would otherwise fall foul of the strict liability rule (as defined in s 1 CCA) if it is made a 'discussion of public affairs' and generally passes the public interest test (which is not defined by statute). This means that the s 5 defence is not altogether satisfactory, particularly where the restraint imposed would interfere with the journalist or publisher's freedom of expression as being 'necessary in a democratic society'. How do we know whether a publication or online report is crucial to the public interest aspect in a particular case?

As already stated above, the principal aim of the 1981 'contempt' statute was to introduce the 'strict liability rule', which applies only if a publication creates a 'substantial risk' of prejudicing forthcoming court proceedings or seriously impeding the course of justice under s 2(2) CCA.

---

115 (1980) 2 EHRR 245 (ECHR).
116 Ibid., at para 66.
117 Source: House of Commons (1980).
118 Source: House of Commons (1974).

The test of whether the s 5 defence can be successfully applied is left to the Attorney General or the Divisional Court and usually comprises:

1. the size of the risk (of serious prejudice), and
2. the severity of impact of the publication.

Neither a remote risk of serious impediment nor a substantial risk of minor impediment will suffice.

Section 5 puts the public interest element secondary to the objectivity principle of assuring the unprejudiced administration of justice. But it is ultimately up to the Attorney General to decide whether a publication could have the potential of creating such a 'substantial risk' of serious prejudice to a trial. Since jury research is not permitted under s 8 CCA, there is no evidence whether a publication did create the liability for contempt or whether it was merely incidental to a particular trial.

See below
4.8.1

In **AG v English** (1982),[119] the House of Lords ruled that the s 5 defence was available to the publishers of the *Daily Mail* and columnist Malcolm Muggeridge, because his comment piece had been written in 'good faith' and the piece was held to be 'in the public interest'. The opinion piece had been written by Muggeridge in support of a pro-life candidate running for Parliament. Though no actual mention was made of the 'Dr Arthur Trial'[120] at the time, the journalist made reference in general to medical practices of failing to keep deformed children alive after birth. Lord Diplock opined that s 5 CCA provided the exception to the strict liability rule.[121]

A case where the 'public interest defence' under s 5 CCA did not succeed involved the popular BBC TV news quiz *Have I Got News For You* ('HIGNFY'; see below).[122] In 1996, the BBC and Hat Trick Productions were fined £20,000 for contempt of court after chairman Angus Deayton said on the show: 'The BBC are cracking down on references to Ian and Kevin Maxwell, in case programme-makers appear biased in their treatment of these two heartless, scheming bastards.'

❖ **KEY CASE**

Attorney-General v BBC and Hat Trick Productions Ltd [1997] EMLR 76 (sub nom 'Have I Got News For You case')

Precedent

❖ The mention of an active court case (or charge) on a TV or radio programme amounts to a contempt of court.

❖ There is no s 5 CCA 1981 defence, despite the humorous context given to the remarks in the broadcast.

❖ The 'fade factor' is not a permissible defence if the trial is imminent (usually amounting to six months).

Facts

Have I Got News For You was screened on BBC Two on Friday 29 April 1994 between 22.00 and 22.30 hours. One main topic of the news quiz was the forthcoming fraud trial of the Maxwell brothers, Kevin and Ian, sons of the deceased *Mirror* newspaper tycoon Robert

---

119 [1982] 2 All ER 903 (HL).
120 Sheffield paediatrician, Dr Arthur, was standing trial at the time for murdering a prematurely born, severely disabled baby boy, by not operating on the child or giving life-sustaining treatment. Dr Arthur was later acquitted by the jury.
121 [1982] 2 All ER 903 at paras 918 f–g (Lord Diplock).
122 *AG v BBC and Hat Trick Productions* [1997] EMLR 76.

Maxwell. The trial was scheduled for 31 October 1994. At the time of the broadcast the Maxwell brothers were charged with two counts of conspiracy to defraud the trustees and beneficiaries of the Mirror Group Pension Fund. The news quiz was chaired by Angus Deayton.

When team leaders Ian Hislop, editor of *Private Eye*, and actor-comedian Paul Merton played the 'odd one out' round, the fourth photo showed some *Mirror* pensioners. The team members' repeated banter centred on the pensioners being 'allegedly' defrauded by Robert Maxwell, implying the 'guilt' of the Maxwell brothers. The programme was repeated the following night unedited.

At the start of the Maxwell sons' trial, their lawyers applied for proceedings to be stayed, arguing that the BBC news quiz had contravened contempt legislation and that Kevin and Ian Maxwell would not stand a fair trial due to adverse media coverage. Though the trial went ahead, and the Maxwell brothers were acquitted, the AG commenced contempt proceedings against the programme makers Hat Trick Productions and the BBC immediately after the conclusion of the fraud trial.

Decision

The court found both parties guilty of strict liability contempt for the reasons that the programme makers and the BBC should not have broadcast any material in connection with the forthcoming Maxwell trial during the *sub judice* period. The court further held that the public broadcaster had made no attempt to edit out the 'irrelevant' and 'rude' comments, particularly in its repeat programme. Auld LJ said:

> The degree of risk of impact of a publication on a trial and the extent of that impact may both be affected, in differing degrees according to the circumstances, by the nature and form of the publication and how long it occurred before trial. Much depends on the combination of circumstances in the case in question and the court's own assessment of their likely effect at the time of publication. This is essentially a value judgment for the court, albeit that it must be sure of its judgment before it can find that there has been contempt. There is little value in making detailed comparisons with the facts of other cases.

Hat Trick and the BBC were each fined £10,000.

Analysis

In the *Have I Got News For You* case, it was clear that the 'publication' (broadcast) alluding to the possible 'guilt' of the Maxwell brothers, who were standing trial at the time, amounted to strict liability contempt. It did not matter that the panel members of the satirical TV show did not intend the broadcast to interfere with the impending fraud trial. The court clearly held that the broadcast created a substantial risk that the course of justice would be seriously impeded and the jury in the case might well have been prejudiced. The 'fade factor' was not allowed, since the trial was imminent; neither was there a s 5 CCA defence available to the public broadcaster or the independent company making the programme. Criminal proceedings were clearly 'active' at the time of the 'publication'.

Arguably the terms used in s 5 CCA may well form part of the *actus reus* of contempt. But the terms are separately defined in s 2(2) CCA ('limitation of scope of strict liability') in the interests, presumably, of clarity and emphasis. This then is the confusing part of the 1981 Act: to judge whether an element forms part of the *actus reus* of the strict liability crime or is a defence as strictly defined has of course a bearing on who carries the burden of proof. The statute is unclear on the matter of whether s 5 implies an exception to the 'strict liability' rule outlined in s 2 CCA (see also: **R v Hunt** (1987);[123] **R v Lambert** (2001)[124]).

Who then has to prove strict liability contempt? Clearly, the Attorney General will avail himself of the conditions set out in s 2(2) CCA, in which case the onus must lie with the defendant to prove that it met the conditions set out under s 5 CCA. Or should the burden of proof lie on the Attorney General to prove that s 5 will not apply in certain circumstances? This ultimately means that it is a question of law rather than of fact.

More recently the courts have made exceptions and have allowed for a s 5 defence in the discussion of public affairs relating to permitting publication and even photographs during *sub judice* proceedings in terrorism-related cases. Following the atrocities of the 7/7 London bombings in 2005, and the attempted terrorism attacks of 21 July of the same year, the CPS issued new practice guidelines allowing the media to make more extensive use of publishing police intelligence during active proceedings (following pre-trial proceedings), such as photos, CCTV footage and previous convictions of suspects — in this case Hussain Osman (27), Ibrahim Muktar Said (27), Yassin Hussan Omar (26) and Ramzi Mohamed (23). Their trial took two years to come to Woolwich Crown Court. Each accused received a life sentence in July 2007.

FOR THOUGHT

You are representing a terrorist suspect accused of plotting a pressure-cooker-bomb attack on a famous London nightclub. She is standing trial at the Old Bailey. The 'red tops' (and their online editions) continue with their sensational and inflammatory press coverage during the trial and as the jury is deliberating its verdict. Media coverage includes the accused's family and schooling background in Yorkshire, a slur on her faith and reporting on her previous convictions. How would you argue strict liability contempt and Article 6 ECHR in your application to the trial judge to stay the whole proceedings? Produce a skeleton argument for the court.

4.7.2 Sentencing contemnors

The penalties for contempt offences can be substantial, ranging from two years' imprisonment if committed (by the AG) to the Crown Court and one month if committed by magistrates. Fines can be unlimited at the Crown Court[125] (see: **R v Bolam, ex parte Haigh** (1949)[126]).

R v Montgomery (1995)[127] is a contempt case involving an unco-operative witness. The contemnor (witness) had given evidence in court relating to a confession made by the defendant,

---

123 [1987] AC 352 (HL).
124 [2001] UKHL 37 (HL).
125 Section 14 CCA 1981. If proceedings are brought by the AG for Northern Ireland under s 18 CCA 1981; s 35 Criminal Justice Act (Northern Ireland) 1945 applies to fines imposed for contempt of court by any superior court other than the Crown Court as it applies to fines imposed by the Crown Court.
126 (1949) 93 SJ 220.
127 [1995] 16 Cr App R (S) 274.

who was charged with conspiracy to defraud. The contemnor's statement turned out to be false and he was subsequently charged with contempt of court. The Court of Appeal held that the question of sentencing the contemnor should best be left until the end of the original trial (i.e. the outcome of the **Montgomery** hearing). At that point the CA made the following sentencing recommendations to be taken into account when sentencing unco-operative witness-contemnors:

- the gravity of the offence being tried;
- the effect upon the (original) trial;
- the contemnor's reasons for failing to give evidence (or being unco-operative);
- whether the contempt is aggravated by impertinent defiance to the judge;
- the antecedents, personal circumstances and characteristics of the contemnor.[128]

In sentencing contemnors, the general principles and guidelines are as follows:

1. An immediate custodial sentence is the only appropriate sentence to impose upon a person who interferes with the administration of justice, unless the circumstances are wholly exceptional.
2. Whilst review of the authorities suggests that interference with, or threats made to, jurors are usually visited with higher sentences than the case of a witness who refuses to give evidence, there is no rule or established practice to that effect; the circumstances of each case are all important.
3. Although the maximum sentence for failing to comply with a witness order is three months, this should not inhibit a substantially longer sentence for a blatant contempt in the face of the court by a witness who has refused to testify.
4. The principle matters affecting sentence are the gravity of the offence being tried; the effect upon the trial; the contemnor's reasons for failing to give evidence; whether the contempt is aggravated by impertinence or defiance rather than a simple and stubborn refusal to answer; the scale of sentences in similar cases; the antecedents; personal circumstances and characteristics of the contemnor; whether a special deterrent is needed.[129]

4.7.3 Contempt proceedings in Scotland

On 17 September 2007, in a broadcast outside the High Court in Edinburgh, solicitor Aamer Anwar launched a bitter attack on the trial process, after his client Mohammed Atif Siddique had been found guilty of terrorism offences. Nine months later, trial judge Lord Carloway referred Mr Anwar to the High Court for contempt of court, as a result of those comments.[130] Mr Anwar was acquitted (see key case below).

The Contempt of Court Act 1981 covers the whole jurisdiction of the United Kingdom. Scottish contempt proceedings are dealt with by either the Sheriff or the District Court and are known as a breach of interdict.[131] Depending on the severity of the contempt, the penalty can range from a maximum Level 4 fine to two years' imprisonment (or both) (see: **Johnson v Grant**

---

128 See: Part 62 Criminal Procedure Rules 2005 of 5 October 2009.
129 See: **R v Richardson** [2004] EWCA Crim 758.
130 See: **Anwar (Aamer) (Respondent)** [2008] HCJAC (case no. 36 IN932/06).
131 Section 15 CCA 1981 (incorporated by Criminal Procedure (Scotland) Act 1995).

(1923);[132] *Johnston v Johnston* (1996)[133]). Active civil proceedings in the Scottish courts are covered by Schedule 1(14) CCA 1981; active appellate criminal proceedings are covered by Schedule 1(16) CCA.

As is the case in English and Welsh courts, Scottish jurisdiction also remains very strict where photographs and identifications are an issue; in this case contempt proceedings will usually ensue.[134]

Scottish courts have traditionally punished contempt more harshly than English courts. This changed with the case of '**Cox and Griffiths**',[135] when Peter Cox, a former *Sun* newspaper executive 'south of the border', became editor of the Glasgow-based *Daily Record* in 1998. In this landmark case, Peter Cox challenged the Scottish courts in contempt proceedings, arguing that the 1981 Contempt of Court Act contravened human rights legislation and press freedom under Article 10 ECHR. Lord Prosser allowed the petition by stating that 'juries are healthy bodies' and that they do not need a 'germ-free' media atmosphere. The finding of contempt was quashed.

The ruling by the Scottish Court of Appeal in '**Cox and Griffiths**' was seen as rather liberal at the time, demonstrating a more tolerant attitude towards contempt and *sub judice* in the Scottish press. Some Scottish editors have interpreted Lord Prosser's approach in the case as too liberal, worried that '**Cox and Griffiths**' may be misinterpreted, leading to greater liberties when reporting during a *sub judice* period. McInnes (2009b) undertook a research study whereby she examined court reporting and possible contempt situations. She concluded that there is a discrepancy between the Scottish and the English courts' contempt proceedings, arguing that contempt proceedings by the Attorney General 'south of the border' have become increasingly rare.[136]

 **KEY CASE** | *Aamer Anwar (Respondent in contempt proceedings)* [2008] HCJAC (case no. 36 IN932/06)

Precedent

❖ Members of the public will not be deterred from performing their public duty as jurors, when called upon to do so, even though they may have heard a potentially contemptuous comment.

❖ Comments and opinions expressed post trial outside the court do not amount to contempt.

Facts

The background to this (contempt) case was that on 17 September 2007, at the High Court in Glasgow, Mohammed Atif Siddique was found guilty after trial on several charges under the Terrorism Acts 2000 and 2006. He was sentenced to a total of eight years' imprisonment. Mr Siddique's solicitor was Aamer Anwar.

On the day when the jury's verdict was delivered, Mr Anwar read a statement outside the court building in the presence of members of the public and journalists, which was

---

132 [1923] SC 789.
133 [1996] SLT 499.
134 See: *Haney v HM Advocate* [2003] Appeal Court, High Court of Justiciary; also: *HM Advocate v McGee* [2005] High Court of Justiciary of 12 October 2005 (Lord Abernethy) (unreported); also: *HM Advocate v Cowan* [2007], 27 February 2007 (Sheriff Sinclair) (unreported).
135 *Cox (Petitioner) and another* [1998] SCCR 561.
136 See: McInnes (2009b).

televised. The statement included the observation that Mr Siddique 'was found guilty of doing what millions of young people do every day, looking for answers on the internet . . . It is farcical that part of the evidence against Atif was that he grew a beard, had documents in Arabic which he could not even read and downloaded material from a legitimate Israeli website run by Dr Reuven Paz, ex Mossad . . .'[137]

During the evening of 17 September 2007, Aamer Anwar gave an interview on BBC *Newsnight Scotland*, expressing an opinion as to the sentence which he considered might be imposed upon the Mohammed Atif Siddique. As a result the (original) trial judge, Lord Carloway, instructed the High Court that Mr Anwar's remarks might constitute a contempt of court. On 23 October 2007 the respondent, Aamer Anwar, was charged with contempt of court, by the Advocate Depute, on behalf of the Crown.

Opinion

The opinion was delivered by The Right Honourable Lord Osborne.[138] The Court concluded that, while the statements made by Mr Anwar contained 'angry and petulant criticism of the outcome of the trial process' and 'a range of political comments concerning the position of Muslims in our society', no contempt of court was committed by the respondent Aamer Anwar.[139] Lord Osborne opined:

> . . . while the jurors in this case may have been annoyed, or even hurt, to hear or to read the comments of the respondent, their personal participation in this particular trial will never be disclosed; their anonymity is protected . . . we have no reason to suppose that members of the public will be likely to be deterred, in any way, by what has been said, from performing their public duty as jurors, when called upon to do so, although it should be appreciated by all that that duty requires them to reach a verdict in accordance with the evidence and with the law, as it is, whatever others may think of it. In all these circumstances, we conclude that no contempt of court has been committed by the respondent.[140]

But the court added a postscript to the non-contempt finding, commenting that Mr Anwar was a professional solicitor and an 'officer of the court'. In this respect Lord Osborne said: 'Any solicitor practising in the High Court of Justiciary owes a duty to the court, a fact recognised in paragraph (I) of the Preamble to the Code of Conduct for Scottish Solicitors of 2002. The court then left it to the Law Society of Scotland to deal with the matter of professional standards in the face of the court. The court expressed the view that the standards expected from a solicitor in exercising his public duty were not met and 'that a court is entitled to expect better of those who practice before it'.[141]

Analysis

Though solicitor Mr Anwar was acquitted of contempt of court, it is worth noting the *obiter* opinion of Lord Osborne, expressed on behalf of the High Court Justiciary, Scotland's

---

137 Source: 'Press Release – Monday 17 September 2007 – *HMA v Mohammed Atif Siddique* – Guilty Verdict', statement read on the steps of the High Court by Mr Siddique's Solicitor – Aamer Anwar.
138 Sitting with Lord Kingarth and Lord Wheatley on 1 July 2008. The full opinion can be studied at: http://www.scotcourts.gov.uk/opinions/2008HCJAC36.html.
139 Aamer Anwar (Respondent in contempt proceedings) [2008] HCJAC at para 44 (The Right Honourable Lord Osborne).
140 Ibid. at para 44.
141 Ibid. at para 45.

supreme criminal court, in relation to the duty and implied obligations upon solicitors who appear before it. Whilst the court accepted that Mr Anwar's comments outside the courthouse and on TV did not amount to contempt, their Lordships made it clear that his actions fell short of what they would expect from a solicitor, thereby 'directing' the Law Society of Scotland towards reviewing the guidelines on media contact. Lord Osborne opined that 'officers of the court' have a duty to ensure that their public utterances, whether critical or not, are based upon an accurate appreciation of the facts of those proceedings, and that their comments are not misleading. It was for this reason that the court mentioned *obiter* that those professional standards were not met in this case.

4.8 Juries and contempt of court

Approximately 800,000 jurors sit each year and yet this practice is still shrouded in secrecy because contempt legislation forbids any jury research under s 8 CCA 1981. The examples of jurors tweeting during trials or researching cases online whilst deliberating a verdict is becoming an increasing problem. From 2010 onwards, the Attorney General, Dominic Grieve QC, demonstrated his determination to prosecute any juror who would interfere with the course of justice by taking these individuals to court, which sent a stern warning to prospective jurors not to use the internet or social networking media; otherwise they would be prosecuted for contempt.

There have been numerous debates in Parliament on whether jury trials should be abolished. The 'Morris Committee on Jury Service' (1965) observed that 'in general [there is] an acceptance of the desirability of maintaining the jury system in criminal cases'.[142] The Runciman Royal Commission (1993) urged research into the workings and deliberations of juries, principally with a view to improving the system of jury trials; the report summarized:

> . . . we are conscious that the jury system is widely and firmly believed to be one of the corner-stones of our system of justice. We have received no evidence which would lead us to argue that an alternative method of arriving at a verdict in criminal trials would make the risk of a mistake significantly less.[143]

See also Chapter 3.8

Former (Labour) Attorney General Lord Goldsmith had begun to review contempt legislation in 2006 when Baroness Scotland took over as Attorney General. She did not pursue any reform of contempt legislation.

It is fair to say that since the new Conservative/Liberal Democrat Coalition Government took over in May 2010, Attorney General Dominic Grieve QC has resurrected contempt legislation, prosecuting a number of cases (as mentioned above), including Christopher Jefferies, who was vilified by the 'red-tops' in the Joanna Yeates murder case in July 2011 (including libel damages), and Rod Liddle for his article in *The Spectator* magazine during the Stephen Lawrence trial.[144] The article was published at a critical time in November 2011, when Gary Dobson and David Norris were standing trial for murdering the 18-year-old A-Level student. In his article, Mr Liddle, an associate editor of *The Spectator*, had raised concerns about how Dobson and Norris could receive a fair trial when the

---

142 Ministry of justice (Home Office), *Report of the Departmental Committee on Jury Service* (The Morris Report) (1965), paras 3 and 6.
143 Royal Commission, *Report of the Royal Commission on Criminal Justice* (1993), Chapter 1, para 8.
144 CPS London Chief Crown Prosecutor Alison Saunders said: 'On 24 November 2011 the Attorney General referred an article published in *The Spectator* magazine to the Crown Prosecution Service for consideration of whether a reporting restrictions Order in place at the time had been breached.' Source: CPS Press Statement, 24 November 2011.

public had been assured over the previous 18 years that the men were 'absolutely guilty and bang to rights'.[145] The judge in the historic Stephen Lawrence murder trial had ordered the jury not to read the article by Rod Liddle, which clearly breached strict reporting restrictions and could have potentially led to the collapse of the case in December 2011.

Though he had originally considered contempt charges against The Spectator and Rod Liddle, the Attorney General, Dominic Grieve, eventually decided to prosecute the magazine's proprietors, the Barclay brothers, and editor, Fraser Nelson, under s 83 Criminal Justice Act 2003 in May 2012, for breaching reporting restrictions imposed during the case.[146] The trial against **The Spectator (1828) Ltd** began at the City of Westminster Magistrates' Court on 7 June 2012. The maximum penalty for this offence is a £5,000 fine. Interestingly, the author of the opinion piece, Rod Liddle, did not face any such charges.

On 7 June 2012, Mr Justice Riddle sentenced the publishers of The Spectator to a fine of £3,000, with an additional £2,000 in compensation for the distress caused to Stephen Lawrence's parents. The Spectator had pleaded guilty to breaching a court order with the Rod Liddle article. Riddle J commented that the magazine would have faced the maximum fine of £5,000, but accepted in mitigation that the magazine had apologized and removed the offending article from the online edition swiftly after notice from the Attorney General.[147]

Section 8 CCA was enacted after the New Statesman magazine was acquitted of 'contempt' by Lord Chief Justice Widgery in 1980,[148] against the background of publishing an interview with one of the witnesses in the sensational 1979 Old Bailey trial in which Jeremy Thorpe, the Liberal politician, and other defendants were acquitted of conspiracy to murder. In relation to the contempt charge, the Attorney General had applied for an order at common law following the publication in the magazine of a juror's account of significant parts of the jury deliberations in the course of arriving at their verdict in the trial of Thorpe. The AG's application failed on the ground that the contents of the article did not justify the title of contempt in relation to jury verdicts. The court held that there were 'no special circumstances', other than publication of some of the secrets of the jury room, that called for condemnation. Section 8 Contempt of Court Act 1981 (CCA) creates an offence:

> . . . to obtain, disclose or solicit any particulars of statements made, opinions expressed, argu-
> ments advanced or votes cast by members of a jury in the course of their deliberations in any
> legal proceedings.

It would be unrealistic to assume that jurors always adhere to a judge's warning, especially when extraneous material is easily accessible online. What is even more disconcerting is that, increasingly, jurors have been known to talk to the press 'off the record' after the completion of a trial.

In April 2009, the Attorney General instigated legal proceedings against The Times and a jury foreman, Michael Seckerson, for breaching s 8 CCA 1981. Following the manslaughter conviction of childminder Keran Henderson at Reading Crown Court in November 2007, jury foreman Michael Seckerson published an article in The Times on 29 January 2008, expressing his strong disagreement with the majority jury verdict of 10:2. He believed Mrs Henderson had been wrongly convicted of shaking 11-month-old Maeve Sheppard from Slough to death.[149]

---

145 The Rod Liddle comment article was published on 7 November, three days after the trial of Dobson and Norris began.
146 Due to the intense media interest in the Stephen Lawrence murder trial, an order under s 82 Criminal Justice Act 2003, was made prohibiting publication of certain assertions about the defendants, imposed by the Court of Appeal on 18 May 2011 and was continued at the commencement of the trial on 14 November 2011.
147 Source: 'Spectator to pay out £5,625 over Rod Liddle's Stephen Lawrence article', by Josh Halliday, Guardian, 7 June 2012.
148 *AG v New Statesman and Nation Publishing Co Ltd* [1981] QB 1.
149 Source: 'Juror speaks out' by Mike Seckerson, The Times, 29 January 2008.

Criminal contempt charges were brought by Attorney General, Baroness Scotland QC against the newspaper and Mr Seckerson under s 8 CCA. Both The Times and Mr Seckerson argued 'freedom of expression', stating in their defence that Article 10 ECHR provided them with the right to reveal what went on in judicial proceedings, as long as it did not prejudice or jeopardize the authority and impartiality of the judiciary. The jury foreman and The Times were found guilty of contempt on 13 May 2009. The newspaper publishers were fined £15,000 and Michael Seckerson £500. The AG was awarded £27,426 costs, which had to be paid by The Times due to Mr Seckerson's limited financial means.

Section 8 CCA does not permit the public interest defence. Otherwise The Times might have had a strong basis for arguing that alleged child cruelty (in the Keran Henderson case) was in the public interest.

Barsby and Ashworth (2004)[150] argue that the s 5 CCA 1981 defence does not sit comfortably with s 8 of the 1981 Act, because s 5 states that a person is not guilty of the strict liability contempt if they can show that publication is part of a discussion in good faith and is a matter of public interest; and that the risk of impediment or prejudice is merely incidental to that discussion. The authors further state that the rules of evidence, developed over hundreds of years of jurisprudence, are there to ensure that the facts that go before a jury have been subjected to scrutiny and can be challenged from both sides. Jurors are not supposed to seek information outside of the courtroom. They are required to reach a verdict based only on the facts in the case and they are not supposed to see evidence that has been excluded as prejudicial.

One of the main reasons for abolishing jury trials in defamation cases has been the influence of the internet. This has been particularly acute in criminal cases, where there have been instances of jurors using internet search engines at home during an active trial or using their mobile phones to 'tweet' their friends about an ongoing trial. This has compromised some verdicts and resulted in some contempt of court prosecutions. In July 2010, 19-year-old juror Danielle Robinson was found guilty of contempt of court for sending text messages to another woman sitting in a second trial at Hull Crown Court. She had passed on 'gossip' from the jury room, such as: 'Hi, it's Danielle from court. Are you doing the kid's case?' and 'He's been in prison before and is a paedo, and when he broke into the pub he took all the kids underwear xx.' Though both women were subsequently dismissed from sitting on the juries, it was touch and go whether the cases would be allowed to continue. Judge Roger Thorn QC called Robinson's texts a blatant attempt to influence a jury and said that her ignorance was no excuse for such contemptuous behaviour. She received an eight-month suspended sentence.[151]

See Chapter 3.8

The introduction of extraneous material into jury deliberations via online material is probably inevitable, though each judge will nowadays direct a jury not to look at the internet in connection with the trial. If the internet is used for 'research purposes' during a trial, it can just as easily influence the juror's mind as a discussion with a friend or neighbour – which, of course, no juror is permitted to have during a trial.

 **FOR THOUGHT**

Would you suggest to Parliament that s 8 Contempt of Court Act 1981 should be repealed because it does not sit comfortably with the s 5 defence under the 1981 Act?

---

150 See: Barsby and Ashworth (2004) at pp. 1041–1044.
151 Source: 'Teenager who jeopardised trials with texts to juror escapes jail', by Jo Adetunji, Guardian, 14 July 2010.

4.8.1 Contempt laws and the digital age

In June 2011, juror Joanne Fraill,[152] 40, from Blackley, Manchester revealed highly sensitive details about jury room discussions when she swapped online messages with Jamie Sewart, 34, who had been acquitted at the trial. Fraill had used Facebook to contact the defendant in a multi-million-pound drugs trial when the jury was still considering charges against the other defendants. Fraill admitted breaching the Contempt of Court Act 1981 by using Facebook and also conducting an internet search into Sewart's boyfriend, Gary Knox, a co-defendant, while the jury was still deliberating in his case. Fraill's contemptuous actions led to the collapse of that trial, contributing to a £6 million legal bill. The Lord Chief Justice, Lord Judge, and two other senior judges sentenced Ms Fraill to eight months' imprisonment for contempt of court.

Can jurors be trusted nowadays to obey the judge's instructions to abandon their normal online habits during trial proceedings? It would be unrealistic to expect judges or lawyers to police jurors' accessing the World Wide Web. There will always be jurors who will seek information on Google about the people they have heard about in court.

Since jury research is not permitted under s 8 CCA 1981, we do not know how many jurors in today's digital society are obeying the judge's orders at a trial. By using mobile phones or hand-held devices they can look up the name of a defendant on the Web or examine a crime's location by using Google Maps, thereby violating the legal system's complex rules of evidence. They can potentially also tweet their friends outside the court or jury room about jury deliberations in spite of the trial judge's warnings in advance of the hearing to keep their opinions and deliberations secret.

Following the Joanne Fraill contempt conviction in 2011, the Lord Chief Justice, Lord Judge, issued a general warning over the need to preserve the integrity of jury trial and the jury system.[153] Lord Judge LCJ said in his press statement:

> I remain concerned at the ease with which a member of the jury can, by disobeying the judge's instructions, discover material which purports to contain accurate information relevant to an individual case or an individual defendant. I am also concerned that the use of technology enables those who are not members of the jury to communicate, in both directions. In the context of current technology, we must be astute to preserve the integrity of jury trial and the jury system.

Lord Judge further cited three separate appeals (in 2010–11) in the Criminal Court of Appeal where convictions were found to be unsafe in the light of jury irregularities. Retrials were ordered in two of those cases, and in two other cases the CA endorsed decisions made in Crown Courts that the trials should proceed without a jury where there had been a danger of jury tampering (**R v Twomey**[154]) and where jury tampering had occurred (**R v G & Others**[155]).[156]

In **Re G** (2011) Riccardo Guthrie and the other three defendants were standing trial in a complex conspiracy to defraud and proceeds of crime case in February and March 2011 at Wood Green Crown Court before Miss Recorder English and a jury. The jury retired on 11 March to reach its verdict. During the course of their retirement they acquitted one defendant. It was brought to

---

152 See: *AG v Fraill and another; R v. Knox* [2011] All ER (D) 103 (Jun) (unreported).
153 The warning was part of the Court of Appeal Criminal Division's 'Annual Review of the Legal Year 2010/11'. Source: Press Release by the Judiciary of England and Wales on 9 December 2011: 'The Lord Chief Justice Issues Warning over Jurors Judicial Office news release'.
154 **R v Twomey (John) & Blake (Peter) & Hibberd (Barry) & Cameron (Glen)** [2011] EWCA Crim 8.
155 **R v Guthrie (Riccardo) & Guthrie (Bianca) & Guthrie (Cosimo) & Campbell (Courtney)** [2011] EWCA Crim 1338.
156 Source: The Court of Appeal Criminal Division Review of the Legal Year 2010 – 11 at www.judiciary.gov.uk/Resources/JCO/Documents/Reports/cop-crim-div-review-legal-year–2011.pdf.

the judge's attention by one juror that one of the defendants, Cosima Guthrie, had improperly engaged with that juror near the public canteen on 15 February. There was a further allegation of improper conduct between Cosima and another juror on 3 March, when the defendant had asked the juror for her telephone number. This caused the jurors great concern and distress. Given that the jury was already deliberating its verdicts, it was impossible to cure the problems arising from jury tampering by discharging a single juror. For this reason, the Recorder decided that the entire jury should be discharged. She later continued the trial without a jury and delivered the remaining verdicts.[157] The four defendants appealed.

Delivering the CA's judgment, The Lord Chief Justice, Lord Judge[158] dismissed the appeal, reasoning that the court could not find any unfairness in the Recorder's decision to continue the trial without a jury and that the verdicts delivered were to stand.

Present-day jury direction at the start of a trial now includes a warning by the judge not to consult the internet or any other form of communication (including social networking sites) until the full conclusion of the trial. It is therefore generally assumed that the judge's directions are accepted and obeyed.

On 13 July 2012, former England football captain John Terry was found not guilty by a District Judge at Westminster Magistrates' Court of racially abusing the Queens Park Rangers defender Anton Ferdinand during a vigorous exchange of insults in a match in 2011.

In advance of the John Terry trial in February 2012, Newcastle United footballer Joey Barton sent some robust tweets with plain views on Terry and his opinion about the alleged racism charge: that on 23 October 2011, at Queens Park Rangers' Loftus Road ground, the Chelsea captain John Terry used 'threatening, abusive or insulting words or behaviour or disorderly behaviour' which were likely to cause 'harassment, alarm or distress' and that the alleged offence was racially aggravated against QPR defender Anton Ferdinand. The prosecution said that had responded to Mr Ferdinand with a string of swear words, curses and other insults which included the word 'black'. Terry was cleared of the charge in July 2012. Senior District Judge Riddle ruled that while John Terry had used language that could amount to an offence, the player was not guilty because the crucial phrase may not have been said as part of an insult.

In respect of Joey Barton's tweets, the Attorney General, Dominic Grieve, decided to take no action, which was good news for Barton as he escaped contempt of court proceedings. Seemingly, the AG took the view that the tweets did not cause a serious impediment to John Terry's case by influencing any witnesses or the magistrate who heard the case. Barton unfortunately failed to recognize the competing right to a fair trial and the presumption of innocence central to the British criminal justice system.

Social media undoubtedly poses a challenge for enforcement of British contempt laws. The Joey Barton 'tweets' are only one example of recurring situations where celebrities express their views during high-profile cases via social networking sites and blogs. Can the Attorney General allow this practice to continue, thereby risking trials being stayed at the cost of the taxpayer? Prejudicial conversations about ongoing trials which were once confined to the dinner table, pub or dressing room are now conducted with an online audience of millions. How stringently should the contempt laws be applied to new media?

Following several prejudicial tweets and blogs in relation to the 'monstered' Christopher Jefferies (landlord of murder victim Joanna Yeates) and the impending trial of the real murderer, Vincent Tabak, and equally contemptuous online opinions expressed in their thousands during the trial of Levi Bellfield, the man who murdered Milly Dowler, the Attorney General, Dominic Grieve

---

157 Under s 46(3) Criminal Justice Act 2003.
158 Sitting with Mr Justice Beatson and Mr Justice Bean on 26 April 2011.

QC, speaking on BBC Radio 4's *Unreliable Evidence*,[159] drew a clear distinction between traditional media and social media when it comes to contempt risk:

> The contempt of court laws have never existed to stop tittle-tattle. It is easy to exaggerate the power of the tweeter. There may be lots of people tweeting and saying things they shouldn't be saying and some of those people may be outside the jurisdiction and it may be impossible to do anything about it. I still think for the most part we can maintain a much greater degree of certainty that jurors are not being exposed to information which they shouldn't have if main-stream media which publish in the United Kingdom, whether online or in print, respect the law ... The fact that someone is tweeting, for example, in England and Wales, doesn't mean they are exempt from the law and if they are tweeting in a way that is a flagrant contempt of court, at some point one of these individuals is going to find that they're in court.

Writing in the *Guardian* in February 2012, the Attorney General continued the contempt debate:

> It is not always easy to balance freedom of expression with the needs of the justice system. As Attorney General I see my role as defender both of press freedom and of the fair administration of justice. And it is as guardian of the public interest, not a government minister, that I act in cases of contempt: protecting the right of a defendant to a fair trial is clearly and compellingly in the public interest. . . . In the UK system, the Contempt of Court Act is part of the apparatus that protects this right, by limiting what can be published about a case while it is live, so that allegations that are not relevant or not tested in court do not form part of a juror's considera-tion. Other jurisdictions have different ways of endeavouring to protect this right (for example, some – including many in the US – practise jury selection) . . . There is no doubt that the char-acteristics of the internet, and of social media in particular, pose challenges for enforcement. Comment and information – or misinformation – posted from outside the UK jurisdiction can only be addressed with great effort and international co-operation. In the democracy of the internet, what is published by one individual can 'go viral' within hours, with obvious implica-tions. Comments on the web can soon be published far beyond their original, limited audience. And I use the word published advisedly, as publication is, of course, the phrase used within the Contempt of Court Act – an online article that breaches the strict liability rule runs the risk of running foul of the law of contempt.[160]

But how can we judge the impact of a prejudicial press report on a potential juror? Can a juror draw a distinction between new media and traditional print media, as the Attorney General suggests? Some jurors will read the daily newspapers (or their online editions) and it may well be that a prejudicial article or photograph will have a great impact on the juror's opinion when deciding the verdict in a case. Increasingly, jurors will be accessing material via their smartphones, tablets, laptops or PCs. Whilst they will be confiscated in the jury room, there is nothing to stop a juror going home every day during deliberations and accessing background resources on the World Wide Web.

Could the Barton tweets, with thousands of followers and re-tweets, have influenced a poten-tial bench of (lay) magistrates or possible jurors? Why did the Attorney General not commence contempt proceedings, when he had taken action against a number of weekly newspapers with circulations of millions in other cases? Arguably, AG Dominic Grieve QC had been ignoring the

---

159 BBC Radio 4, 29 October 2011 at: www.bbc.co.uk/programmes/b01684k6.
160 Source: 'Contempt laws are still valid in the internet age', by Dominic Grieve QC, *Guardian*, 8 February 2012.

overwhelming, global power of the internet search engines, such as Google, and social networking sites, such as Twitter and Facebook, which shape public opinion, delivering information straight to a juror's or judge's eye.

 FOR THOUGHT

In our global world of the World Wide Web, do you think that jurors really are prejudiced by what they have seen or heard in the media? Can courts still rely on the 'fade factor', assuming that the risk of prejudice is greater the nearer the reporting is to the trial, and fades over time? Discuss.

The Attorney General issued guidelines to prosecutors in December 2012[161] on how they should make decisions in relation to cases where it is alleged that criminal offences have been committed by the sending of a communication via social media. The guidelines are designed to give clear advice to prosecutors who have been asked either for a charging decision or for early advice to the police, as well as in reviewing those cases which have been charged by the police. The guidelines cover the offences that are likely to be most commonly committed by the sending of communications via social media. These guidelines equally apply to the resending (or re-tweeting) of communications.

Communications which may constitute a contempt of court fall under s 8 Contempt of Court Act 1981 in relation to jurors' texting or tweeting messages or researching a case on the internet whilst a trial is active, or by using credible threats of violence to a person via social networking (e.g. internet blogs, using Facebook or Twitter), may well fall under s 16 Offences Against the Person Act 1861 if the intimation amounts to a 'threat to kill'. Other credible threats of violence to a person may fall to be considered under s 4 Protection from Harassment Act 1997 if they amount to a course of conduct within the meaning of that provision and there is sufficient evidence to establish the necessary state of knowledge. Other threats can also be considered under s 1 Malicious Communications Act 1988, which prohibits the sending of an electronic communication which conveys a threat, or s 127 Communications Act 2003, which prohibits the sending of messages of a menacing character by means of a public telecommunications network (see: *Chambers v DPP* (2012)[162]).

 FOR THOUGHT

There is increased openness regarding freedom and access to public information via the Freedom of Information Act 2000. Should there not be similar increased openness in the justice system? Does the public not have a right to know how a jury decides its verdict or how it reaches an award for damages in defamation actions? Discuss whether s 8 CCA should be repealed.

---

161 See: CPS Guidelines on prosecuting cases involving communications sent via social media at www.cps.gov.uk/legal/a_to_c/communications_sent_via_social_media.
162 [2012] EWH2 2157 (Admin).

4.8.2 Technology in the courtroom

In September 2011, Prime Minister David Cameron used his 'crime speech' to announce the government's go-ahead to the televising of judicial verdicts. The shift towards courtroom TV has been hampered in the past partly by prime time TV trials in the United States, such as the O. J. Simpson trial in 1995 or the trial of Michael Jackson's personal physician, Dr Conrad Murray, who was found guilty of involuntary manslaughter of the King of Pop in November 2011.[163]

The world witnessed how 'Madam Foreperson' handed the jury's 'not guilty' verdict (on both counts of murder) to the court clerk, Mrs Robertson, on 3 October 1995 in the O. J. Simpson trial, as TV cameras zoomed in on the visible grief and shock of the family victims of murdered Nicole Brown Simpson (O. J.'s former wife) and her murdered gym friend Ronald Goldman.[164]

Millions watched the live coverage of Dr Conrad Murray's trial, as he sat stone-faced as the verdict was read on 7 November in a Los Angeles courtroom. Michael Jackson's sister, LaToya, screamed out upon hearing the verdict, while his crying mother, Katherine, was consoled by her son, Jermaine. The trial was televised live and streamed on the internet.[165]

The decision to allow TV cameras to film the sentencing of serious criminals was announced in the Queen's Speech in May 2012. This government decision is part of a move towards transparency in public services and 'open justice'. Cameras have been allowed in some Scottish courts – under tight restrictions – since 1992, including the 2002 appeal of Abdelbaset al-Megrahi against his conviction for the Lockerbie bombing.[166]

Further TV courtroom history was made in the Criminal Division of the Court of Appeal in November 2004, when TV cameras were allowed to film and record the 'Speechley Appeal'.[167] The recording took place at the Royal Courts of Justice from 16 to 18 November 2004, when robotic cameras focused mainly on the judges and barristers, but not on the dock or the witness box.

The appeal concerned former Lincolnshire County Council Leader Jim Speechley after he had been convicted at Sheffield Crown Court in April 2003 of 'misconduct in public office' and sentenced to 18 months' imprisonment. The councillor, who was released pending his appeal, was found to have tried to influence the route of the Crowland bypass to increase the value of a pocket of land he owned.

During the appeal hearing, the cameras were focused on the lawyers and appeal judges, Lord Justice Kennedy (presiding), Mr Justice Bell and Mr Justice Hughes. William Harbage QC and Catarina Sjolin appeared for the appellant. Though the case was never broadcast, the pilot project was the first step towards the introduction of courtroom TV in England and Wales, approved by the Lord Chancellor, the Lord Chief Justice and the Master of the Rolls. Both the conviction and sentence were upheld, though Lord Justice Kennedy reduced £25,000 court costs to £10,000.

The televised 'Speechley Appeal' was regarded as a resounding success and the panel commented that there should be no reason why such appeals should not be shown on public TV as part of bringing the 'open justice principle' to people who had otherwise no time or inclination to attend court.

---

163 Michael Jackson died on 25 June 2009.
164 Nicole Brown Simpson and Ronald Goldman were found stabbed to death at Nicole's house in Brentwood, Los Angeles on 12 June 1994.
165 Source: 'Dr. Conrad Murray Found Guilty of Involuntary Manslaughter of Michael Jackson', Fox News, 7 November 2011.
166 On 22 December 1988, at 19.03 hours, Pan Am Flight 103 fell out of the sky over the Scottish town of Lockerbie. All 259 passengers and crew members and 11 residents of Lockerbie were killed. As a result, two men – Abdelbaset Ali Mohmed al-Megrahi and Al-Amin Khalifa Fhimah – were arrested and their trial began on 2 February 2000 in the Netherlands, tried by the Scottish court. The Lockerbie trial proceedings were broadcast live (in both English and Arabic) over the internet by the BBC and streamed across the world. See: **HM Advocate v Abdelbaset Ali Mohmed Al Megrahi and Al Amin Khalifa Fhimah (Prisoners in the Prison of Camp Zeist [Kamp van Zeist] v the Netherlands** [2000] Case No: 1475/99, in the High Court of Justiciary at Camp Zeist (sub nom 'The Lockerbie Trial').
167 **R v Speechley** [2004] (unreported) (CA).

When Britain's most senior court – the Supreme Court – was opened in September 2009 it was fitted with cameras. Live streamed footage is routinely available. It allows visitors to watch appeals and judgments on televisions around the building without sitting in the courtrooms, but it is seen to be a different case since Supreme Court hearings do not involve witnesses being cross-examined or juries.

Television companies have been pressing for greater access to the highlights of court cases, and a consultation on courtroom TV was undertaken by the previous Labour Government but was eventually discarded. The present Coalition Government believes transparency would aid public understanding of the court process, and the idea has gained momentum in the aftermath of the August 2011 riots.

In April 2012, permission was granted by Lord Hamilton, the Lord President and Lord Justice General for Scotland, to record judge Lord Bracadale's sentencing of David Gilroy, 49, at the High Court in Edinburgh for the murder of (missing) bookkeeper Suzanne Pilley.[168] Gilroy, from Edinburgh, was found guilty on 15 March 2012 of murdering 38-year-old Miss Pilley. This was a legal first in Scotland's legal history. Broadcaster Scottish Television (STV) focused only on the judge as the sentence of life imprisonment (with a minimum custodial part of 18 years) was read out. Gilroy was not filmed, and neither was anyone else in the courtroom TV footage (except for the macer (mace bearer) and the legal clerk).[169]

The Nat Fraser trial, filmed in the Edinburgh High Court in 2012, was shown on British TV in full in July 2013. The documentary *The Murder Trial* was made by Windfall Films as a Channel 4 production, following the full trial for six weeks as the jury returned a guilty verdict against Fraser on the charge of murdering his wife. The programme provided a rare insight into proceedings in Scottish courts. Television viewers heard and saw the same evidence as the jury of the retrial of a man who was found guilty, in 2003, of the murder of his wife Arlene in 1998, but whose conviction had been quashed. They heard the opening statement by prosecutor Alex Prentice QC, and his introductory description of the case as 'tricky', since neither Arlene Fraser's body nor a murder weapon were ever found. Additionally, Fraser had accounted for his movements on the day of the murder.

The two-hour edited version of the six-week trial made for utterly addictive viewing, illustrating both the minutiae of court proceedings and the extraordinary complexity of a case being prosecuted (and defended) on entirely circumstantial evidence. It proved that courtroom TV serves as a valuable source of open justice, since very few citizens have the time or opportunity to see the judicial process at work in such detail. Furthermore, by seeing witnesses and family members in close-up and how they were affected by the crime, the cross-examination and the process of giving evidence in court, the documentary fully captured the formalities and procedures of the (Scottish) court process. What was important was the confirmation that the judicial process is impartial and that the rule of law prevails. Ultimately, Fraser was found guilty by a majority verdict and the film's biggest shock emerged – a history of domestic abuse that had been inadmissible at the trial.

The Crime and Courts Act 2013 (Part 2) has permitted the introduction of courtroom broadcasting (in limited circumstances) to help demystify the justice system. Section 31 of the 2013 Act ('Making, and use, of recordings of Supreme Court proceedings') has partly amended s 9 of the Contempt of Court Act 1981 (which prohibits recording, in addition to s 41 Criminal Justice Act 1925 in respect of photography) to allow for filming and recording in the UK Supreme Court. This – in turn – has paved the way to courtroom TV, which started in the Court of Appeal in England and

168 Source: 'TV cameras in front row as Gilroy faces jail for murder', by David Brown, *The Times*, 11 April 2012.
169 Source TV footage: 'David Gilroy jailed for life for the murder of missing bookkeeper Suzanne Pilley', STV, 18 April 2012: http://local.stv.tv/edinburgh/303870-david-gilroy-jailed-for-life-for-the-murder-of-missing-bookkeeper-suzanne-pilley.

Wales in October 2013. As the law stands, broadcasting images of the witness box would not comply with victim protection legislation such as the Crime and Disorder Act 1998, the Protection from Harassment Act 1997 or the Vulnerable Witness (Scotland) Act 2004.[170] However, there could be a public interest in allowing filming of a prosecution or defence opening to a jury and of mitigation and sentence; judicial discretion should then allow or disallow filming built into contempt of court legislation.[171]

Television broadcasting started in the UK Court of Appeal in October 2013 and there are plans to expand 'courtroom TV' to the Crown Court. Filming only concentrates on judges' (sentencing) remarks. The announcement was made by the then Justice Secretary, Ken Clarke, who confirmed in September 2011 that victims, witness, offenders and jurors would not be filmed. The idea was that the Government and Judiciary were jointly determined to improve transparency and public understanding of court proceedings by allowing court broadcasting. Additionally, the Ministry of Justice (MOJ) will include statistics and case details as part of the broadcasts. The UK Supreme Court has been broadcasting live since 2009 with all rulings and pronouncements now available on YouTube.

One danger of courtroom TV is that it might be seen as sensationalist and have a potential effect in high-profile trials, as already witnessed in the media circus which surrounded the 'Soham trial' of Ian Huntley in December 2003. Huntley was the school caretaker accused of killing 10-year-old schoolgirls Holly Wells and Jessica Chapman in August 2002. The argument against courtroom TV rests on the belief that the camera's presence might intimidate witnesses and affect their testimony, thereby creating an O.J. Simpson-style media circus. But equally, as the Lockerbie trial and Speechley Appeal have shown, there is a strong case for courtroom broadcasting, not just for public interest concerns but also for educational reasons, such as law school training and introducing the open justice principle to schools and colleges.

The argument in favour of courtroom broadcasts is that television has long been the principal source of information for the majority of people. Just as parliamentary broadcasts are freely accessible, public broadcasting should now cover all aspects of public life, including the justice system. With the advancement of technology and the inclusion of internet video transmission on most public media websites, the administration of justice ought to be publically accessible.

It remains to be seen whether British courtroom TV will catch on and, if so, whether it will change public opinion towards the justice system by granting greater access to the open court system. However, it may be that courtroom TV could become primarily entertainment like the *Jeremy Kyle Show* or *Judge Judy*.

4.9 Who still observes the law of contempt? Analysis and discussion

One story dominated the British 'red tops' from the beginning of December 2006, culminating in a *Sunday Mirror* 'scoop' on 17 December about someone dubbed the 'Suffolk Ripper', who had killed five prostitutes near Ipswich, Suffolk. The story featured Tom Stephens, a former Special Constable and supermarket worker. At that time, Stephens was merely a police suspect. Relentlessly, the story

170 The Vulnerable Witness (Scotland) Act 2004 is aimed at making it easier for child and adult vulnerable witnesses to give their best evidence by formalizing existing special measures for giving evidence and introducing new measures, such as locations outside the court house known as 'remote sites'.
171 Sections 4(2) and 11 CCA 1981 would still be available to the court should it be felt necessary.

ran for days – including the full *sub judice* period – well into the run-up to Christmas – increasing the sales of the Mirror.

See above
4.3.1

Identification was clearly an issue and police were still appealing for call girl witnesses to come forward. The story was likened to the Yorkshire Ripper story. Tom Stephens was linked to the prostitutes by the *Sunday Mirror* because he had said on his social networking MySpace page that he knew and had befriended the girls. The Mirror used Stephens's own online blog title with its sensational headline – ' "Call Me The Bishop": Ripper Exclusive' – on 19 December 2006.

This became problematic for the Attorney General, Lord Goldsmith, and media editors at the time, because, in the newspapers' defence, prime suspect Stephens had 'outed' himself via his own blog – and had further stated on BBC local radio that he knew the murdered women' intimately'. BBC Radio Suffolk broadcast a live 36-minute interview conducted by Trudi Barber with Tom Stephens on 12 December during the *sub judice* period when he had been formally arrested by Suffolk police. Was this not clearly contempt of court by the public broadcaster? Adrian Van-Klaveren, Deputy Director of BBC News at the time, thought not and defended the BBC's decision to broadcast the Stephens interview on his editor's blog on 21 December 2006.

Why did the then Attorney General, Lord Goldsmith, not intervene in the 'Suffolk Ripper' story? Why did contempt laws not defend a subsequently innocent Tom Stephens? Interestingly, AG Dominic Grieve did intervene in a similar action, in the Christopher Jefferies case, when the *Daily Mirror* and the *Sun* were found guilty of contempt of court in July 2011.[172] Had Tom Stephens been tried for their murder instead, it would have been open to the Attorney General to commence contempt proceedings against the media, because, arguably, Stephens would not have stood a chance of a fair trial, particularly since the 'Suffolk murder' trial was eventually held locally at the Crown Court in Ipswich with a local jury who would almost certainly have remembered the extensive adverse media coverage at the time. Forklift truck driver Stephen Wright was found guilty of murder of the five prostitutes by a majority verdict by an Ipswich jury of nine men and three women on 21 February 2008.

4.9.1 Do UK contempt laws interfere with the freedom of expression?

By its very nature, the law of contempt places restrictions on the freedom of expression and press freedom in general. In **Gregory v United Kingdom** (1997),[173] the ECtHR drew attention to its decision in **Remli v France** (1996),[174] commenting that Article 6(1) ECHR imposes an obligation on every national court to check whether it is 'an impartial tribunal' within the meaning of that provision, which was considered in relation to admissible (hearsay) evidence before a jury and whether such evidence adduced would jeopardize a fair trial. What if jurors 'research' the background to the trial via the internet? Would that amount to jury bias? In **Remli** the trial judges had failed to react to an allegation that an identifiable juror had been overheard to say that he was a racist. In the circumstances, the court established within the meaning of Article 6(1) ECHR that sufficient guarantees were put in place to dispel any doubts.

In **Sander v United Kingdom** (2000),[175] an Asian accused was on trial with two others for conspiracy to defraud. The judge had almost completed his summing up when a juror handed a letter to the court usher in which he alleged that at least two of the jurors had been making openly racist remarks during the jury's deliberation; the said juror had expressed his concern that the defendants would not receive a fair trial verdict. The judge, having discussed the complaint with

---

172 See: *AG v Mirror Group Newspapers Ltd and News Group Newspapers Ltd* [2011] EWHC 2074 (Admin) 29 July 2011.
173 (1997) 25 EHRR 577.
174 (1996) 22 EHRR 253, 271–272, paras 47 and 48.
175 (2000) 31 EHRR 1003.

counsel in chambers, decided not to discharge the jury immediately or to conduct an inquiry. He told the jury to search their consciences overnight and to let the court know if they felt that they were not able to try the case solely on the evidence. Having received their assurances by letter the next morning that the jury had reached its verdict without racial bias, the judge allowed the trial to proceed and the accused were duly convicted.

In **Sander**, the ECtHR held that there had been a violation of Article 6(1) ECHR on the ground that the trial judge should have acted in a more robust manner; that he had failed to provide sufficient guarantees to exclude any objectively justified or legitimate doubts about the impartiality of the court. **Sander** is important because the Strasbourg Court took the opportunity to review its decision in **Gregory** (1997),[176] regarding the fundamental importance of public confidence in the courts and the rule governing the secrecy of jury deliberations.

The same question was addressed by the House of Lords in the two parallel appeals in **Mirza** and **Connor** (2004):[177] whether evidence about jury deliberations that revealed a lack of impartiality was always inadmissible under the common law secrecy rule. The issue in **Mirza** concerned a juror who had revealed after the verdict that some jury members were associated with a neo-Nazi group, and that, during jury deliberations, they strongly influenced the conviction of the accused because he was a black immigrant. In **Connor**, a juror had revealed after the verdict that a majority of the jury refused to deliberate at all and had made up its mind virtually at the start of the trial; that jury ultimately arrived at a guilty verdict by spinning a coin.

Dismissing appeals in both **Mirza** and **Connor**, the House of Lords stated that common and statutory provision of contempt of court was well established in the area of jury deliberations. However, their Lordships commented *obiter* that this law may not be altogether well suited towards the 'modern' jury member today and that the courts may have attached undue weight to the confidentiality of jury deliberations in the past. It was for these reasons that their Lordships did not admit the evidence and allegations in the letters by the jurors in both **Mirza** and **Connor**, stating that this was not a sound basis on which one could base an unsafe jury verdict. The appeals were dismissed. Their Lordships commented *inter alia* that the Court of Appeal could not be held in contempt of itself when exercising the jurisdiction to hear evidence about what happened in the jury room. For this reason s 8 CCA would not impinge on the jurisdiction of the Court of Appeal to receive evidence which it regards as relevant to the disposal of an appeal.

4.10 Proposals for law reform of the law on contempt

Following a number of media reports during *sub judice* proceedings in high-profile cases the Law Commission[178] began a review and consultation process of UK contempt laws. The Consultation Paper on Contempt of Court (2012)[179] included, *inter alia*, consulting on how the law surrounding jury trials may need to be changed to protect secret trials fairly and how to tackle the increasing use of social media and web-based devices by trial juries.

The Commission suggested that jurors who conduct online research on cases they are trying may need to be prosecuted under a new criminal offence. Furthermore, courts should also be given additional powers compelling media organizations to take down old stories from electronic

---

176 (1997) 25 EHRR 577.
177 **R v Connor and another; R v Mirza** [2004] (conjoined appeals) UKHL 2 (HL).
178 The Law Commission was set up by s 1 of the Law Commissions Act 1965 for the purpose of promoting the reform of the law. For the purpose of the Law Commission Report 2012 on 'Contempt', the Law Commissioners were: The Hon Mr Justice Lloyd Jones (Chairman), Professor Elizabeth Cooke, Mr David Hertzell, Professor David Ormerod and Frances Patterson QC.
179 See: Law Commission (2012) at: http://lawcommission.justice.gov.uk/areas/contempt.htm.

archives in order to remove potentially prejudicial material, particularly in retrials and appeal cases. The Law Commission's suggestions, involving stricter controls over the use of the internet and introducing ambitious efforts to police online content, are intended to reduce the risk of contempt of court and protect a defendant's right to a fair trial under Article 6 ECHR. The Commission also considered the confiscation of jurors' mobile phones and internet-enabled devices when they attend court.

The Law Commission acknowledged that recent well-publicised cases, such as Christopher Jefferies or Dale Cregan, have highlighted shortcomings in the current law on contempt committed by way of publication of information about imminent or active proceedings and the impact of social networking sites. In spite of a number of initiatives, including the Lord Chief Justice's guidance on the use of social media and 'text-based communications' in court proceedings (2011), many aspects of the law have failed to keep pace with cultural and technological advances that mean information about trials can be easily published on the internet. This poses particular problems since, once material gets onto the internet, the original publisher can very easily lose control of it and any precautions he takes to minimize impact on a trial may be ineffective. In addition, the growth in the use of blogs and social networking sites means that members of the public have the opportunity to publish opinions and information about imminent and ongoing criminal proceedings that can reach a global audience.

The permanence and ability to search online news archives also raises the worrying prospect of the media being expected to purge their archives of prejudicial material once someone has been arrested. At the moment the guidance from previous Attorney Generals has been that archive material can be left untouched, but the media should not actively link to it. It would be a huge task if media organizations had to vet archives for potentially prejudicial material.

The law in this area is further complicated by the fact that there are a number of offences scattered across different statutes relating to publication of specific information in criminal proceedings. The number of and the variations between these offences make the law in this area unnecessarily complex. Although the Criminal Procedure Rule Committee has made important progress in clarifying the position, the substantive law remains unclear (already discussed by the Law Commission in its Eleventh Programme).[180] During the 2012 consultation, the Commission identified the following areas of difficulty:

- the uncertainty whether the Crown Court and Court of Appeal have the power to detain or bail a person pending determination of an allegation of contempt;
- the restrictive power of the magistrates' courts, who presently do not have the power to deal sufficiently with contempt 'in the face of the court';
- while the Crown Court and Court of Appeal have the power to suspend a committal to custody, it is uncertain whether the magistrates' courts have the same power.[181]

It is argued here that British contempt laws have failed to keep pace with the way people access information. Current contempt laws as they are enforced come down unduly harshly on UK-based print media and their websites, while leaving live TV relatively untouched, and the internet entirely untamed. It is further submitted that the powers of the criminal courts to deal with contempt committed in the face of the court or by way of breach of court order are unsatisfactory. While the powers of the magistrates' courts are found in statute, those of the Crown Court and Court of Appeal derive mainly from common law. There is uncertainty as to the scope of the common law powers, gaps in the statutory provisions and unjustifiable inconsistency between them.

---

180 Source: The Law Commission (2011) at p. 6ff at: http://lawcommission.justice.gov.uk/docs/lc330_eleventh_programme.pdf.
181 See: Law Commission (2012).

The Law Commission further consulted on the offence of 'scandalizing the court' (also known as 'scandalizing judges' or 'scandalizing the judiciary'), another form of contempt of court (see above). The scope and purpose of the consultation was to ascertain whether this offence should be abolished, retained in its current form or replaced by a modified offence, and, if so, what form that offence might take.[182]

The rationale for an offence of 'scandalizing the court', derived from the need to uphold public confidence in the administration of justice, is particularly acute in a democracy, where the power and legitimacy of the judicial branch of government derives from the willingness of the people to be subject to the rule of law. Current contempt law maintains and supports public faith in the judicial system. As human rights law has developed, stressing under Article 10 ECHR that the media has a right to express itself freely in a democracy, it could be argued that contempt laws including an archaic 'scandalizing the courts' offence is outdated.

Is the scandalizing the courts offence fit for the twenty-first century as a necessary means of preserving the dignity of and respect for the courts?[183] The interest in the offence in the UK was revived in March 2012 when the Attorney General for Northern Ireland obtained leave to prosecute Peter Hain MP for statements in his book *Outside In*, in which he criticised Lord Justice Girvan's handling of a judicial review application.[184]

The Law Commission's consultation document argues that in a democracy, where the judicial system enjoys high levels of public confidence, there might be greater room for criticism because displacing that confidence by such criticism is less likely. Balancing this right to freedom of expression with the importance of upholding public confidence in the administration of justice is at the heart of this particular debate about the offence of scandalizing the court. Is there still a need for special rules to control the judiciary's role in society?

 FOR THOUGHT

The permanence of and ability to search online news archives which may contain prejudicial material before someone's trial is a worrying prospect for courts and media organizations alike. Would you agree that current contempt law has failed to keep pace with the way people access information?

 4.11 Further reading

Barendt, E. (2009) *Media Freedom and Contempt of Court: Library of essays in media law.* **London: Ashgate.**
The essays discuss the restrictions imposed by contempt of court and other laws on media freedom to attend and report legal proceedings. Part I contains leading articles on the open justice principle, examining the extent to which departures from that principle should be allowed to protect the rights of parties. The essays in Part II examine the open justice principle in legal broadcast proceedings. Part III looks at the application of contempt of court to prejudicial media publicity. Part IV asks whether journalists should enjoy a privilege not to reveal their sources of information. This is a particularly interesting section.

---

182 Ibid.
183 For further reading see: Iyer (2009) at p. 245.
184 See: Hain (2012).

Brooks, T. (2004) 'A defence of jury nullification'. *Res Publica*, **10(4), 401–423.**
In both Great Britain and the United States there has been a growing debate about the modern acceptability of jury nullification. Properly understood, juries do not have any constitutional right to ignore the law, but they do have the power to do so nevertheless. The journal article argues that to nullify may be motivated by a variety of concerns: overly harsh sentences, improper government action, racism, etc. In this article, Thom Brooks defends jury nullification on a number of grounds: the use of general verdicts; verdicts based upon mistakes and racial prejudice, perverse verdicts; and the question of whether or not juries are guilty of legislating when nullifying the law. Finally, Brooks examines the awarding of excessive damages by juries. The article provides a sound theoretical defence of the practice of jury nullification.

Callery, C. (2010) 'John Terry: reflections on public image, sponsorship, and employment'. *International Sports Law Review*, **2, 48–52.**
The article comments on the 'John Terry superinjunction' case[185] and discusses the maxim that 'the price of greatness is responsibility'. Callery stresses the importance of accountability where power or success is bestowed upon a famous individual, such as leading athletes or professional footballers. These leading sporting celebrities are lavished with immense wealth and fame, where, in Tiger Woods's words, 'normal rules don't apply'. Callery discusses the presumption that celebrities are morally 'untouchable' in their private lives, resulting in numerous indiscretions on their part. Leading broadsheets have sought to rely on the Article10 ECHR right to freedom of expression in reporting and condemning this behaviour, thereby contributing to public debate.

Jaconelli, J. (2002) *Open Justice: A critique of the public trial*. **Oxford: Oxford University Press.**
In this topical study, Joseph Jaconelli explores the issues of open justice and the rise of modern media in the context of English law, particularly important in criminal cases where the accused is traditionally viewed as possessing the right to a public trial. He discusses the global media audience in high-profile cases which may lead to prejudicial values. He also discusses the privacy of parties, rehabilitative considerations, national security, commercial secrecy and the need to safeguard witnesses and jurors from intimidation.

MacQueen, H. (2012) *Studying Scots Law* **(4th edn). Edinburgh: Bloomsbury Professional.**
This standard textbook, in its fourth revised edition, provides a highly readable account of the Scottish legal profession and offers essential information on Scots law.

Matthews, R., Hancock, L. and Briggs, D. (2004) *Jurors' Perceptions, Understanding, Confidence and Satisfaction in the Jury System: A study in six courts*. **Research Development and Statistics Directorate. Home Office Report No. 05/04/2004, at: http://library.npia.police.uk/docs/hordsolr/rdsolr0504.pdf**
This Home Office report is a rare insight into (permitted and controlled) jury research. It also highlights the growing concerns about public confidence in the criminal justice system. The report provides a well-grounded approach by focusing on those sections of the population who had direct experience and involvement in the court process as jurors. The authors took as a starting point Lord Auld's review of the criminal justice process and his recommendations in 2001[186] The research specifically focused on s 8 CCA 1981: that jurors are not permitted to discuss cases or their deliberations in the jury room with the media (or indeed anyone else).

---

185 **LNS v Persons Unknown** [2010] EWHC 119 (QB).
186 See: Ministry of Justice (2001).

Smartt, U. (2007) 'Who still observes the law of contempt?' *Justice of the Peace Journal*, 3 February 2007, 171, 76–83.

This article looks at media coverage in the UK and 'contempt' legislation, providing examples when action was not taken by the Attorney General to punish editors and journalists for contempt. Smartt focuses on the extensive tabloid coverage of the 'Suffolk Ripper' story and finding the (wrong) killer of five prostitutes in December 2006. She examines how supermarket worker Tom Stephens was branded the 'Ipswich Strangler', and compares the coverage with the 'Yorkshire Ripper' story in 1981 when the Contempt of Court Act 1981 first came into force.See below 4.10

Chapter 5

Reporting Legal Proceedings

Chapter Contents

> **Key Points**
>
> This chapter will cover the following questions:
>
> ○ What can and cannot be reported in a UK court of law?
> ○ How are children protected in the court process in English and Scots law?
> ○ When does a court order reporting restrictions?
> ○ Why are anonymity orders necessary in sexual offence cases?
> ○ How does the public interest test apply in family court proceedings?
> ○ How are court martial proceedings reported?
> ○ Should court proceedings ever be held in 'secret'?

5.1 Overview

See Chapter 1.1

The open justice principle, as clearly recognized by Parliament and the courts, grants the public and media statutory and common law rights to attend all court proceedings in UK courts and tribunals, as was held by Lord Atkinson in **Scott v Scott**.[1] The openness of judicial proceedings is also enshrined in Article 6(1) of the European Convention (ECHR – 'right to a fair trial') as a fundamental principle of open justice. In criminal proceedings, this underpins the requirement for a prosecution witness to be identifiable not only to the defendant but also to the open court and this can therefore be reported fully in the media. The vast majority of legal proceedings are in fact held in private for reasons of administrative convenience (e.g. civil cases in judges' chambers; *locus standi* (standing) decisions in judicial review cases). But 'private' does not mean 'secret' and if a particular case arouses interest, provision must be made to admit the public and the media, of if necessary, move to a larger venue (such as the **Hillsborough Inquiry**[2]). It is also important to determine in relation to any restriction whether it applies equally to the 'public' and to members of the media.

There are circumstances when the court may justify hearing a case *in camera* (in private or 'in secret'), for instance where the open justice principle can hinder successful prosecutions, particularly in cases that threaten national security and acts of terrorism. Witnesses may fear that if their identity is revealed to the defendant, his associates or the public generally, they or their friends and family may well be at risk of serious harm.[3] The test is one of 'necessity' and an application to proceed *in camera* should be supported by relevant evidence. When informed that a witness is fearful of giving evidence, prosecutors will liaise closely with the police to consider the range of options available to them both at common law and by virtue of statute.[4]

---

1   *Scott (Morgan) and another v Scott* [1913] AC 417 of 5 May 1913 (HL). See also: *MacDougall v Knight* [1889] AC 200 (Lord Halsbury LC).
2   Referring to the tragic football disaster on 15 April 1989 when over 50,000 people travelled to the Hillsborough Stadium, home of Sheffield Wednesday Football Club, to watch the FA Cup Semi-Final between Liverpool and Nottingham Forest. Ninety-six people died as a consequence of a crush in the stands and hundreds more were injured and thousands traumatized. An inquiry was led by Lord Justice Taylor. There were civil litigations, criminal and disciplinary investigations, and inquests into the deaths of the victims, judicial reviews, a judicial scrutiny of new evidence conducted by Lord Justice Stuart-Smith, and the private prosecution of the two most senior police officers in command on the day. In July 2009 the 'Hillsborough Family Support Group' presented to the Home Secretary a case for disclosure based on increasing public awareness of the circumstances of the disaster and the appropriateness of the investigations and inquiries that followed. A new inquest was scheduled for the end of March 2014, to be held before a jury. Lord Justice Goldring announced the decision at a pre-inquest hearing in London on 5 June 2013.
3   A direction of special measure can be made under s 19 Youth Justice and Criminal Evidence Act 1999; a witness anonymity order can be made under s 86 Coroners and Justice Act 2009.
4   Section 17 Youth Justice and Criminal Evidence Act 1999 deals with intimidated witnesses and provides that special measures may be provided where the quality of evidence given by a witness is likely to be diminished by reason of fear or distress on the part of the witness in connection with testifying in the proceedings.

To restrain the freedom of the press there should be a pressing social need for the restriction, convincingly established by proper, concrete evidence, and the restrictions must be proportionate to the legitimate aim pursued. The need for any reporting restriction must be convincingly established and the terms of any order ought to be proportionate, going no further than is necessary to meet the relevant objective, as was held in *A-G v Leveller Magazine Ltd* (1979).[5] One example could be if one report refers to an unnamed defendant having been convicted of rape of his daughter and another report names the defendant but does not identify the relationship between the defendant and the witness. This is referred to as 'jigsaw identification'.

There may also be occasions when the open justice principle and the right of the media to report are restricted in order to ensure fair trials for, and the protection of, those who are vulnerable such as children and victims of sexual offences. This chapter discusses youth justice legislation in particular with some reference to 'special measures' in court proceedings for vulnerable adult witnesses.[6] The Court of Appeal held in *Murray v Big Pictures (UK) Ltd*,[7] for instance, that a child has a civil right to privacy distinctly separate from that of each of its parents.

See chapter 2.5

It is important where any automatic restriction applies or a discretionary order is made that it is made clear in the judgment of the court so that journalists understand the issue of such a discretionary order. This chapter examines such proceedings and orders.

In high-profile cases where media interest is particularly acute it may well be that journalistic reporting has taken place even before a particular case reaches the court, such as allegations of paedophilia following the Jimmy Savile allegations in 2012–13. In the month following allegations that (deceased) BBC presenter Jimmy Savile was accused of 31 rapes and suspected of at least 200 sex crimes against children in 17 areas of the UK during his working lifetime at the corporation, the police warned of more child abuse arrests in December 2013. Revealing the scale of the police investigation in co-operation with the NSPCC,[8] Commander Peter Spindler (interviewed by the *Guardian*) reported that 450 individuals had made allegations against the former BBC celebrity, mostly of sexual assault. The police investigation also included allegations against other (still living) child sex abusers. Spindler said that 82 per cent of the alleged victims who had come forward were women. Seven men – including singer Gary Glitter (real name Paul Gadd), comedian Freddie Starr, BBC Radio 5 Live reporter Stuart Hall, DJ Dave Lee Travis, BBC producer Wilfred De'ath and publicist Max Clifford – had all been questioned by the Savile inquiry team, Operation Yewtree. In August 2013, Dave Lee Travis (68) (real name David Patrick Griffin) had been charged with 11 counts of indecent assault and one of sexual assault against alleged victims aged between 15 and 29. The former Radio 1 DJ was charged with offences spanning three decades, from 1977 to 2007, and relating to nine alleged victims. All of those named denied wrongdoing.[9]

See Chapter 4

Courts will then have to weigh proportionately whether open reporting is in the public interest under Article 10 ECHR or whether a (temporary) anonymity order in the form of an interim injunction may be put in place in addition to statutory contempt legislation. In any case, the court should be very slow to interfere with the principle of open justice, particularly in family court proceedings (see: *R v Southwark Crown Court Ex parte Godwin and Others* (1992)[10] – below).

It is of course important to distinguish between reporting the facts and contents of a case and applying names to the participants. Increasingly questions are being asked by media organizations,

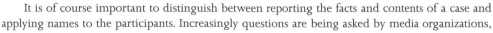

5   [1979] AC 440 at 450.
6   Section 46 Youth Justice and Criminal Evidence Act 1999 enables courts to make a reporting direction in relation to adult witnesses which prohibits any matter relating to the witness to be included in any publication during the lifetime of the witness if it is likely to lead members of the public to identify the individual as a witness in criminal proceedings.
7   See: *Murray v Express Newspapers and others* [2008] EWCA Civ 446.
8   The National Association for People Abused in Childhood and the Child Exploitation and Online Protection Centre had also received complaints from former child abuse victims and were adding to the NSPCC scoping study.
9   Source: 'Dave Lee Travis charged with 12 sexual offences', by Josh Halliday, *Guardian*, 16 August 2013.
10 [1992] QB 190.

particularly where children are involved, if it is sufficient if the content of the case is published without the need to provide specific identities. The courts will then ask whether the subject matter (if reported) merely feeds a prurient public curiosity or whether open reporting is justifying a wider public interest. It is not always easy to distinguish between bona fide arguments about open justice and a genuine public interest in knowledge as opposed to self-serving press arguments to help boost circulation sales in an ever-decreasing newspaper industry. As Eady J ruled in the **Max Mosley** case:[11]

> I cannot believe that a journalist's sincere view on public interest, however irrationally arrived at, should be a complete answer. A decision on public interest must be capable of being tested by objectively recognised criteria. But it could be argued as a matter of policy that allowance should be made for a decision reached which falls within a range of reasonably possible conclusions.[12]

5.2 Hearings from which the public are excluded

The democratic principles of a free and open society contain a number of essential features: the rule of law, accountable political institutions, an independent and impartial judiciary upholding the law, and a free press whose journalistic investigations and ability to publish the results provide an essential part of a free and open society. As the nineteenth-century philosopher and jurist, Jeremy Bentham, put it:

> . . . publicity is the very soul of justice. It is the keenest spur to exertion, and the surest of all guards against improbity. It keeps the judge himself, while trying, under trial.[13]

Section 12 of the Administration of Justice Act 1960 defines a number of specific situations where publication of information about proceedings in private (whether in *camera* or in chambers) constitutes a contempt of court. Those relevant are:

● where the court sits in private for reasons of national security; and
● where the court, having power to do so, expressly prohibits the publication of all or any information relating to the proceedings.

Like 'without notice' (formerly *ex parte*) hearings, hearings in *camera* raise concerns about fairness, particularly in light of the principle that justice should not only be done but should appear to be done.[14] Generally, court proceedings attract reporting restrictions or anonymity orders only where publicity would defeat the object of the hearing; for example, a trial concerned with protecting commercial secrets or where privacy is needed to protect the interests of a mental patient.

5.2.1 Statutory automatic reporting restrictions

There are a number of automatic reporting restrictions (anonymity orders), which are statutory exceptions to the open justice principle. These apply to:

---

11 **Mosley (Max) v News Group Newspapers Ltd** [2008] EWHC 1777 (QB).
12 Ibid., at para 138 (Eady J).
13 Bentham cited in **Home Office v Harman** [1983] 1 AC at 303 (Lord Diplock).
14 See: **Hobbs v Tinling and Company Limited** [1929] 2 KB 1 at 33 per Lord Sankey LC; see also: **R v Sussex Justices; Ex parte McCarthy** [1924].

- reporting restrictions on proceedings in the Youth Court;[15]
- children and young persons (under 18 in England and Wales) in general court proceedings;[16]
- victims of sexual offences (lifetime ban);[17]
- discretionary exceptions: judicial imposition of media reporting restrictions on identification of victims, defendants or witnesses aged under 18:[18]
- vulnerable adult witnesses;[19]
- withholding personal details from open court;[20]
- reporting restrictions during trial (postponement of fair and accurate reporting);[21]
- appeals and preparatory appeal hearings;[22]
- prosecution appeals.[23]

5.2.2 Reporting sexual offences and rape

Current law provides anonymity for rape victims, ensuring that their names cannot be made public from the time they make an allegation through the rest of their lives. Anonymity is not available to rape defendants. Courts have powers under s 2 of the Sexual Offences (Amendment) Act 1992 to make provision for anonymity in relation to a full range of sexual offences including rape (though a complainant may waive this entitlement). This section applies only to a victim of a sexual offence but not the perpetrator. Once an allegation of one of the relevant offences has been made, nothing can be published[24] which is likely to lead members of the public to identify the alleged victim. The following *cannot* be published for the victim's lifetime:

> (a) her or his name;
> (b) her or his address;
> (c) the identity of any school or other educational establishment attended by them;
> (d) the identity of any place of work;
> (e) any still or moving picture of them.[25]

The Heilbron[26] Committee,[27] a Home Office Advisory Committee on the law of rape in 1975, had recommend anonymity for rape defendants.[28] The Committee's subsequent report recommended that the identity of rape complainants should be kept secret, and that the defence should be limited in its ability to cross-examine the complainant about their sexual history in an effort to attack their character. The Heilbron Committee did not recommend anonymity for rape defendants because it

---

15 Section 49 Children and Young Persons Act 1933.
16 Sections 39 ('Power to prohibit publication of certain matter in newspapers') and 49 ('Restrictions on reports of proceedings in which children or young persons are concerned') Children and Young Persons Act 1933.
17 Section 2 Sexual Offences (Amendment) Act 1992 (as amended by Schedule 2 of the Youth Justice and Criminal Evidence Act 1999).
18 Section 39 Children and Young Person's Act 1933.
19 Section 46 Youth Justice and Criminal Evidence Act 1999.
20 Section 11 Contempt of Court Act 1981.
21 Section 4(2) Contempt of Court Act 1981.
22 Section 35 Criminal Procedure and Investigations Act 1996; s 9(11) Criminal Justice Act 1987.
23 Sections 58 and 82 Criminal Justice Act 2003.
24 'Publication' includes any speech, writing, relevant programme or other communication in whatever form, which is addressed to the public at large or any section of the public, and does not include an indictment or other document prepared for use in particular legal proceedings.
25 See: Youth Justice and Criminal Evidence Act 1999 Schedule 2 'Reporting Restrictions'.
26 Dame Rose Heilbron DBE QC (1914–2005) was a barrister and the first woman to win a scholarship to Gray's Inn, the first woman to be appointed King's Counsel and first female judge to sit at the Old Bailey. She chaired the committee on rape laws in 1975.
27 See: Home Office (1975).
28 Ibid., at pp. 27–31.

felt complainants and defendants were not comparable in principle, and that in cases of other serious crimes where the complainant was often anonymous (such as blackmail) defendants were not granted anonymity. However, during the subsequent passage of the Sexual Offences (Amendment) Act in 1976, which introduced anonymity for rape victims for life, a concessionary amendment was adopted providing anonymity for rape defendants as well. The main reason for this was to guard against the possibility of reputation damage for those acquitted of rape and to provide equality between complainants and defendants in rape cases.[29]

In 1984, the Criminal Law Revision Committee revisited the issue of anonymity in rape cases. It endorsed the reasoning of the Heilbron Committee that underpinned the granting of anonymity to rape complainants and agreed with its original arguments against extending it to defendants.[30]

The issue of rape defendants' anonymity arose again in Parliament in 2003 during the passage of the Sexual Offences Bill in 2002–03. The Parliamentary Home Affairs Select Committee supported an amendment to the Sexual Offences Act 2003 to reinstate anonymity for those accused of rape up to the point of charge.[31] However, concern was expressed by members of the committee over unintended, adverse effects of media reporting restrictions relating to rape defendants. For example, if a rape defendant escaped custody before conviction, the police could not automatically warn the public that a suspected rapist was on the loose due to the anonymity of the alleged assailants. Professor Liz Kelly, giving evidence to the inquiry, argued that persons accused of sexual crimes should not be treated any differently to those accused of other crimes. She told the Committee:

> The idea that those accused of sexual crimes should be privileged can only be sustained if one takes a position that either these crimes are of an entirely different order than any other and/or that there is a far higher rate of 'false accusations'.[32]

But still, the Parliamentary Home Affairs Committee recommended extending anonymity to the accused, by stating:

> We believe that sex crimes do fall within an entirely different order to most other crimes. In our view, the stigma that attaches to sexual offences – particularly those involving children – is enormous and the accusation alone can be devastating. If the accused is never charged, there is no possibility of the individual being publicly vindicated by an acquittal.[33]

However, this amendment was not accepted in the final passage of the Bill. The current position is that anonymity is legally granted to all rape complainants but not to defendants. Anonymity is not granted for rape defendants in any other common law country, with the exception of the Republic of Ireland where a rape defendant's identity can be made public only if they are convicted of rape.

Following the conviction of BBC celebrity presenter Stuart Hall (aged 83) in June 2013, after admitting 14 sexual offences involving girls between 1967 and 1985 – one girl being as young as nine at the time – there followed a public and media debate about the granting of anonymity to alleged sexual perpetrators before conviction. The Met Police's 'Operation Yewtree' followed the revelations that DJ and TV personality Sir Jimmy Savile had been a 'prolific, predatory sex offender' who had abused more than 200 children and young people over a 60-year period.[34] Savile died on 21 October 2011, aged 84. Operation Yewtree subsequently exposed more well-known public

---

29 See: Ministry of Justice (2010c) at p. 2
30 See: Criminal Law Revision Committee (1984).
31 See: House of Commons (2003) at paras 72–80.
32 Ibid., at para 72.
33 Ibid., at paras 76–77.
34 Source: 'Operation Yewtree', *BBC News Online*, 11 January 2013.

figures alleged to have committed sexual offences against children during their lifetime. Suspects included Australian entertainer and painter Rolf Harris[35] and *Coronation Street* actor Michael Le Vell[36] (48), who plays garage boss Kevin Webster in the ITV soap. Le Vell appeared at Manchester Crown Court in March 2013, charged with six counts of raping a girl under 16, six counts of indecent assault of a girl under 16 and seven counts of non-penetrative sexual touching of a girl under 13, relating to complaints between 2001 and 2010.[37] *Coronation Street*'s Bill Roache (81), who plays Ken Barlow, was charged with raping a 15-year-old in 1967. He was arrested by Cheshire Police on suspicion of two counts of rape involving the girl in 1967.[38]

The proposal to grant anonymity to rape and sexual offence suspects before conviction was supported by Neil and Christine Hamilton, who stood accused of raping Nadine Milroy-Sloan in 2005. Her preposterous story had been disseminated, via an exclusive in the *News of the World*, by the publicist Max Clifford. Ms Milroy-Sloan was later sentenced to three years' imprisonment for making false accusations of rape against the famous media couple. Clifford later paid the Hamiltons undisclosed damages for related disobliging remarks in a separate defamation law suit. Clifford has also been exposed by Operation Yewtree and was facing 11 charges of indecent assault against teenage girls between 1966 and 1985.[39]

As the present law stands, the media are free to make public the names, addresses and charges of those accused of rape. This reflects the fundamental principle of open justice in operation in England and Wales.

Section 5 of the Sexual Offences (Amendment) Act 1992 provides for prosecution (in addition to contempt of court legislation under the Contempt of Court Act 1981) for anyone publishing any details of sexual offence or rape victims during their lifetime. There are other legal avenues available to punish Tweeters and bloggers, such as s 127 Communications Act 2003, if the tweets can be deemed to be grossly offensive or of an indecent, obscene or menacing character. Section 4A Public Order Act 1986 can also be used by prosecutors if the tweets or other social networking messages or text messages can be deemed to contain threatening, abusive or insulting words. Both have previously been used in successful prosecutions of Tweeters, and can carry more significant sentences than the anonymity provision, which is limited to a fine.

In April 2012, a number of people on Twitter identified and named the 19-year-old rape victim of Ched Evans, a Sheffield United footballer, convicted for rape on 20 April 2012. Evans had been sentenced to five years' imprisonment for the rape. Almost immediately, the hashtag '#ChedEvans' appeared on Twitter, and later, #JusticeForChed. Some tweets questioned why one defendant was found guilty and the other not (Evans's co-accused, Port Vale footballer Clayton McDonald, was found not guilty). Others blamed the victim, particularly focusing on her being drunk. The 'Tweetmob' posed a legal first for the Attorney General, Dominic Grieve QC, as to whether to commence criminal proceedings under contempt legislation or for contravening s 5 of the Sexual Offences (Amendment) Act 1992 within the realm of social media networking.[40]

See also Chapter 4

The AG's decision was of particular interest to the traditional print press, who had broken this law in the past. The law in this area is particularly rigorous, because it is believed rape victims are often deterred from coming forward by a fear of being identified. Dominic Grieve had issued

---

35 Source: 'Scotland Yard detectives interview woman "witness" after travelling to Australia to pursue investigation into sex abuse claims against Rolf Harris', by Richard Shears, *Daily Mail*, 2 May 2013.
36 Real name: Michael Robert Turner.
37 Source: 'Michael Le Vell: Coronation Street Kevin Webster actor in court accused of 19 child sex offences', by Michael Cockerton, *Daily Mirror*, 21 March 2013. Le Vell was later acquitted of all charges.
38 Source: 'Coronation Street's William Roache in court on sex charges', *BBC News Online*, 10 June 2013.
39 Source: 'Max Clifford to face trial over indecent assault charges in March', Josh Halliday, *Guardian*, 12 June 2013.
40 Source: 'How do you prosecute a Twittermob? What if, instead of 40 people accused of breaking the law, it is 400, or 4,000?' by David Banks, *Independent*, 26 April 2012.

earlier warnings to bloggers and Tweeters that they are bound by the Contempt of Court Act 1981. In November 2012, nine people – mostly from Wales – pleaded guilty to naming the 'Ched Evans Rape Victim' on Twitter and Facebook; they were each fined £624 at Prestatyn Magistrates' Court. Among the accused were Evans's cousin Gemma Thomas from Rhyl, the footballer's friend Craig McDonald, 26, from Prestatyn and 25-year-old biology schoolteacher Holly Price from Prestatyn. They were all charged with publishing material likely to lead members of the public to identify the complainant in a rape case, contrary to s 5 of the Sexual Offences (Amendment) Act 1992.[41]

The decision to prosecute may well have complicated implications for future charging decisions in social networking cases. The scale of potential prosecutions as a result of unwise tweeting could be potentially very large. What if the Tweetmob breaches a superinjunction and names a company accused of pollution – as happened in the case of *Trafigura*?[42] If a defendant in a criminal action requests an order for anonymity (including an allegation of internet child paedophilia), the court has to be satisfied either that the administration of justice would be seriously affected or that there is a real and immediate risk to the life of a defendant if anonymity were not granted (e.g. a police informer). However, even a significant interference with the rights of the accused under Article 8 ECHR might be proportionate when account is taken of the weight that must be given to the competing right to freedom of expression under Article 10.[43] When a party makes such an application, the court must be satisfied that the quality of evidence or level of co-operation by the witness is likely to be diminished by reason of fear or distress in being identified by the public.[44] On appeal, automatic reporting restrictions apply from the moment the prosecution indicates its intention to appeal to prevent the publication of anything other than certain specified factual information.[45]

5.2.3 Other reporting restrictions

In December 2012, the Director of Public Projections (DPP), Keir Starmer QC, released a set of interim guidelines outlining regulations for communications sent via social media, such as Twitter, and when prosecutions are likely to take place.[46] Mr Starmer said in a CPS press release:

> These interim guidelines are intended to strike the right balance between freedom of expression and the need to uphold the criminal law. They make a clear distinction between communications which amount to credible threats of violence, a targeted campaign of harassment against an individual or which breach court orders on the one hand, and other communications sent by social media, e.g. those that are grossly offensive, on the other. The first group will be prosecuted robustly whereas the second group will only be prosecuted if they cross a high threshold; a prosecution is unlikely to be in the public interest if the communication is swiftly removed, blocked, not intended for a wide audience or not obviously beyond what could conceivably be tolerable or acceptable in a diverse society which upholds and respects freedom of expression. The interim guidelines thus protect the individual from threats or targeted harassment while protecting the expression of unpopular or unfashionable opinion about serious or trivial matters, or banter or humour, even if distasteful to some and painful to those subjected to it.[47]

---

41 Source: 'Ched Evans: Nine admit naming rape victim on social media', BBC *News Online*, 5 November 2012.
42 *Trafigura Ltd v BBC* (2009) High Court of Justice, Queen's Bench Division of 15 May 2009 (Claim No: HQ09X02050) (unreported).
43 See: *AG's Ref (No. 3 of 1999)* concerning the BBC's application to set aside or vary reporting restrictions order [2009] UKHL 34 at para 28.
44 Part 16 Criminal Procedure Rules 2012 ('reporting and access restrictions').
45 Sections 71 and 82 Criminal Justice Act 2003.
46 See: Crown Prosecution Service (2012) 'Interim guidelines on prosecuting cases involving communications sent via social media', issued by the Director of Public Prosecutions on 19 December 2012.
47 Source: 'DPP launches public consultation on prosecutions involving social media communications', CPS Press Release, 19 December 2012, www.cps.gov.uk/news/latest_news/dpp_launches_public_consultation_on_prosecutions_involving_social_media_communications/index.html.

The Contempt of Court Act 1981 provides further guidance. Section 4(2) of the 1981 Act provides:

> In any such proceedings [i.e. legal proceedings held in public] the court may, where it appears necessary for avoiding a substantial risk of prejudice to the administration of justice in those proceedings, or in any other proceedings pending or imminent, order that the publication of any report of the proceedings, or any part of the proceedings, be postponed for such period as the court thinks necessary for that purpose.

Section 11 CCA 1981 provides:

> In any case where a court (having the power to do so) allows a name or other matter to be withheld from the public in proceedings before the court, the court may give such directions prohibiting the publication of that name or matter in connection with the proceedings as appear to the court to be necessary for the purpose for which it was so withheld.[48]

Consistent with the requirement to protect the open justice principle and freedom of expression, an order under s 11 Contempt of Court Act 1981 ('section 11 order') should only be made where the nature or circumstances of the proceedings are such that a hearing in open court would frustrate or render impracticable the administration of justice and the court has power to do so (see: *A-G v Leveller Magazine* (1979)[49]). The court may order the postponement of publication of a fair, accurate and contemporaneous report of its proceedings where that is necessary to avoid a substantial risk of prejudice to the administration of justice in those or other proceedings.[50]

See also
Chapter 4

These above CCA 1981 orders are intended to avoid 'a substantial risk of prejudice' to the proceedings to which they are made, or to linked or related proceedings, such as a subsequent trial involving the same defendants or witnesses. Other examples of the use of the power in s 4(2) CCA 1981 can be found in prohibitions against the publication of evidence or argument before the judge in the absence of the jury and, after a successful appeal against conviction, when a new trial is ordered and, to avoid prejudice to any retrial, an appropriate order is made.

An order under s 4(2) CCA should, however, be made only when it is *necessary* to do so and as a last resort. Essentially, s 4(2), as its wording suggests, is aimed at the *postponement* of publication rather than a permanent ban. An order prohibiting publication for an indefinite period carries with it the natural inference not merely that the publication has simply been postponed, but that a permanent ban has been imposed.

This became the issue in **R (Press Association) v Cambridge Crown Court** (2012),[51] whereby the Press Association (PA) appealed against a lifelong 'rape' anonymity order on the defendant, imposed by His Honour Judge Hawksworth at Cambridge Crown Court on 16 April 2012, following the defendant's conviction of five counts of rape and four counts of breaching a restraining order in February 2012. The trial had taken place in open court, listed under the defendant's full name. Upon sentencing him to imprisonment for public protection (IPP), with a minimum term of eight years, the judge also imposed a lifelong anonymity order preventing any future disclosure about the victim's name or personal details as well as the defendant's in this case, which might lead to jigsaw identification:

48 See: **R v Arundel Justices ex parte Westminster Press Limited** [1985] 1 WLR 708 and in **Re Trinity Mirror plc** [2008] QB 770.
49 [1979] AC 440.
50 Section 4(2) Contempt of Court Act 1981.
51 [2012] EWCA Crim 2434, 21 November 2012 ('**Re Press Association**').

> ... an order superseding the initial order under s 1(2) of the Sexual Offences (Amendment) Act
> 1992, again imposing a prohibition, unlimited in time, on the publication of 'anything relating to
> the name of the defendant which could lead to the identification of the complainant which could
> have serious consequences for the course of justice'.[52]

On making the order, Hawksworth HHJ informed the media that the ambit of s 1 of the 1992 Act
was not limited to the press alone – encompassing publication of prohibited material in the
media – but extended to anyone and whatever means by which publication occurs, including
bloggers and 'Twitterers' or any other social networking commentators.[53] The judge also warned
that any contravention of the order would amount to serious contempt of court and would be
prosecuted under s 5 Sexual Offences (Amendment) Act 1992.

The Press Association's ground of appeal was that the judge had no power to make an order
anonymizing the defendant, whether under ss 4(2) or 11 of the Contempt of Court Act 1981. The
PA argued that the issue was of major importance to open media reporting (here: on convicted
rapists), expressing considerable concern at the apparent willingness of the court to make such an
'unnecessary' order, arguing that the judge had acted beyond his powers. It was further submitted
that s 1 of the Sexual Offences (Amendment) Act 1992 conferred automatic anonymity on rape
victims (and victims of sexual offences generally) and that there was no reason for the court to
continue with the s 4(2) CCA 1981 order; not least because there had been no reporting restrictions during the trial itself.

The CA in **Re Press Association** (2012) stated that legislative provision made it clear that the
responsibility for decisions relating to publication and protecting the identity of a complainant in
a sexual case was paramount and had to be strictly obeyed by the press, as cited in **Re B** (2006):[54]

> The responsibility for avoiding the publication of material which may prejudice the outcome of
> a trial rests fairly and squarely on those responsible for the publication. In our view, broad-
> casting authorities and newspaper editors should be trusted to fulfil their responsibilities accu-
> rately to inform the public of court proceedings, and to exercise sensible judgement about the
> publication of comment which may interfere with the administration of justice. They have
> access to the best legal advice; they have their own personal judgements to make. The risk of
> being in contempt of court for damaging the interests of justice is not one which any respon-
> sible editor would wish to take. In itself that is an important safeguard, and it should not be
> overlooked simply because there are occasions when there is widespread and ill-judged
> publicity in some parts of the media.[55]

In **Re B** the issue was similar to that in the **Press Association** case, i.e. whether the media could be
trusted with fair and accurate reporting on the defendant's (in this case Dhiren Barot[56]) sentencing.
Furthermore, would the publication create a risk of substantial prejudice to the fair trials of his

---

52 Ibid., at para 2.(ii).
53 Ibid., at para 9.
54 **R v B** [2006] EWCA Crim 2692 (sub nom 'Re B'). This case concerned reporting restrictions post conviction on Dhiren Barot on
    12 October 2006, after he had pleaded guilty to conspiracy to murder. Reporting restrictions were in place until the conclusion
    of the trial of his co-defendants. The judge was concerned that reports of Barot's sentencing would cause a risk of substantial
    prejudice to the trial of the co-defendants, as his reasons for sentence would give rise to a great deal of legitimate public interest
    and discussion.
55 Ibid., at para 25.
56 Indian-born Barot admitted in November 2006 at Woolwich Crown Court that he had planned to detonate a radioactive 'dirty
    bomb' and launch an attack on London's Underground and the Heathrow Express. After Barot was given a life sentence, Peter
    Clarke, Head of the Metropolitan Police's Anti-Terrorist Branch, said there was a 'wealth of evidence' that he was a 'very
    important figure' within Al Qaeda. Source: 'Muslim convert who plotted terror', BBC News, 7 November 2006.

remaining co-defendants if they were not postponed until after trial? The Court of Appeal held that the media could be trusted, which was then applied in the **Re Press Association** appeal. In both cases the CA lifted the anonymity orders. Unsurprisingly this was seen by the media as a triumph.

The existence of an automatic restriction may render some discretionary restrictions unnecessary, such as in respect of child or young offender proceedings. In such cases the judge or magistrate will usually remind the media of any automatic restriction under s 39 of the Children and Young Persons Act 1933. The court has power to restrict reporting about certain adult witnesses (other than the accused) in criminal proceedings on the application of any party to those proceedings for a 'reporting direction' under s 46 Youth Justice and Criminal Evidence Act (YJCEA) 1999.

See below 5.3.1

When a discretionary restriction order is made, it is clearly desirable that the media is given every assistance to comply with it. The judge usually makes an oral direction, stating that if there are any particular problems arising from the making of the order, the media should make representations in writing to the court, highlighting the specific issues. Typically, every court will ensure, given human rights challenges in line with Article 10 ECHR, that adequate steps are taken to draw any discretionary restriction order to the attention of media representatives who may not have been in court when the order was made. Because factors known to the media in advance of a court hearing may not be apparent from the case papers in a criminal trial, for instance, neither the prosecution nor the defence may be aware of them or have any particular interest in advancing them. The court will usually invite representations from the media and encourage open debate in advance of a court hearing (see the Divisional Court ruling in **R v Teesdale and Wear Valley Justices ex parte M** (2000)[57]).

5.2.4 The court martial

As more and more members of the armed forces have faced court martial charges of desertion and other offences after the war in Iraq and actions in Afghanistan, we are reminded that such proceedings are also held in open court unless there is a compelling reason for the judge to direct otherwise. A court martial is a public court with similar powers to a Crown Court. It can impose prison sentences, fines or other forms of justice depending upon the nature of the crime. A court martial hearing is presided over by a Judge Advocate and a board of up to seven military members, individuals with no legal training much like a jury in civilian courts. In line with the Government's 'transparency and open data initiative', the Military Court Service now publishes all court martial results in respect of the military court centres.[58]

Charges are brought by the Service Prosecuting Authority (SPA),[59] an independent prosecuting authority dealing with all criminal cases and offences contrary to military discipline. The SPA fulfils its functions in support of the operational effectiveness of the British Armed Forces throughout the world. The role of the SPA is to review cases referred to it by the Service Police or Chain of Command and prosecute that case at court martial or Service Civilian Court where appropriate. The SPA will also act as respondent in the Summary Appeal Court and represent the Crown at the Court Martial Appeal Court.

Section 158 of the Armed Forces Act 2006 specifies that the court martial must sit in open court, subject to any provision made by court martial rules. Rule 153 of the Armed Forces (Court

---

57 (2000) of 7 February 2000 (unreported).
58 See: Court Martial Results from the military court centres at: https://www.gov.uk/government/publications/court-martial-results-from-the-military-court-centres.
59 The SPA was formed on 1 January 2009 and at the time of publication its head was Bruce Houlder QC as Director Service Prosecutions (DSP). The SPA was formed with the incorporation of the Navy Prosecution Authority, Army Prosecuting Authority and Royal Air Force Prosecuting Authority and has its headquarters at Royal Air Force Northolt, North West London; there is also a service branch based in Bielefeld, Germany.

Martial) Rules 2009 states that the court may give leave for any name or other matter given in evidence in proceedings to be withheld from the public and therein from media reporting.

On 13 October 2012 the SPA directed that five Royal Marines be charged with the offence of murder. The charge read:

MURDER CHARGES IN RESPECT OF 5 ROYAL MARINES

Committing a criminal offence contrary to section 42 of the Armed Forces Act 2006, namely murder. PARTICULARS OF OFFENCE (A, B, C, D and E): on or about the 15th day of September 2011, murdered an unknown captured person.[60]

The background to this high-profile case was that five Royal Marines had been charged by the SPA with the murder of an injured Taliban fighter in Afghanistan in 2011, when Royal Marine 3 Commando Brigade was based in Helmand. There had initially been nine marines arrested by the Service Police after video footage was found on a marine's laptop that allegedly showed members of 3 Commando Brigade discussing what to do with a wounded gunman caught inside a compound in Helmand. The images were said to have been discovered after one of the soldiers was arrested by civilian police who were investigating an unrelated crime in the UK. Four marines were later released without charge. Details of the incident were not revealed but the Ministry of Defence (MOD) described it as 'an engagement with an insurgent' with no civilians involved. It was also claimed that the injured Taliban fighter did not pose a threat to the marines.[61] The charges followed the Baha Mousa atrocity when an innocent 26-year-old father had been arrested and killed in Iraq in 2003 by British troops who inflicted 93 injuries.[62]

See Chapter
4.4

In November 2012 the five Royal Marines appeared before the court martial in respect of their joint murder charge. They were subject to the *sub judice* process under the Contempt of Court Act 1981 (CCA), whereby nothing extraneous could be reported to prejudice the prosecution case or the fair trial of these accused or the administration of justice generally. However, as contempt legislation permits, their names, ranks, station and charge could be revealed in the press.

This was the first time UK servicemen had been arrested and charged with murder in modern military history. His Honour Judge Blackett ordered a complete reporting ban, with the five marines only being mentioned as 'Marines A–E' in the first hearing.[63] The Press Association appealed against the complete reporting ban (see: **R v Marines A–E** (2012)[64]), where the Judge Advocate ruled that the five defendant marines should remain anonymous until the full conclusion of the proceedings. The order included that there was to be no publication of the names and addresses of the defendants or any kind of image of the soldiers published on the indictment for murder of the Afghan civilian. The anonymity order was also to protect the identity of the four marines who had been released without charge.

In its application for the total anonymity order for the five marines, the MOD had asked security expert Mr Tucker-Jones to give expert witness evidence in court. He told the court martial that there would be a high risk to the defendant marines and their friends and families if their names were released. By naming the defendants and their background, Tucker-Jones argued, their whereabouts could be found on the internet, their names could be posted on jihadist websites and the marines could become the focus of a *cause célèbre*. As one would expect, the application was opposed by the PA, submitting that the anonymity order on the marines should be removed. Counsel for the media submitted that 'good news' stories were frequently reported about armed service personnel

---

60 Source: Military Court Centres Court Listings: www.mod.uk/DefenceInternet/AboutDefence/CorporatePublications/ LegalPublications/MilitaryCourtService/MilitaryCourtCentresCourtListings.htm.
61 Source: 'Five Royal Marines are charged with murder after video emerges showing patrol discussing if injured Taliban insurgent should be given aid', by Ian Drury, *Daily Mail*, 14 October 2012.
62 See also: Williams (2012).
63 The order was made under Rule 153 Armed Forces (Court Martial) Rules and s 11 Contempt of Court Act 1981.
64 Case Number 2012 CM 00442. In the Court Martial before the Judge Advocate General on 6 November 2012.

who were going to, or returning from, active service in Afghanistan, often for engagement with the enemy which led to the award of gallantry medals.

Blackett HHJ ordered complete anonymity on all five marines, citing Latham LJ in the **Times Newspapers** case of 2009:

> In order therefore for us to be entitled to make any order for anonymity for all or any of the soldiers we must be satisfied that either the administration of justice would be seriously affected were we not to grant anonymity or that there would be a real and immediate risk to the life of the soldiers were anonymity not granted. The only other route would be by statute.[65]

The 'Marines' anonymity order of 6 November 2012 remained in place until the conclusion of the court martial murder trial in November 2013.

The MOD's main concern in this case was how the Afghan authorities would respond to the killing of one of their people and how the Taliban would use the court martial 'Marines' story for their own purposes. Another concern was the impact on the wider mission: why British troops needed to remain in Afghanistan for another two years. This incident would only add fuel to that debate. British military forces had hoped to leave Afghanistan with their heads held high and yet these serious murder allegations threatened to undermine the British Armed Forces' reputation, not just for the Royal Marines on trial for murder of an Afghani citizen but for everyone in uniform.

In October 2012, hundreds of people marched through Plymouth, Devon, in support of the marines, holding placards with the words 'Justice For The Five'. At a plea and case management hearing held on Friday 8 March 2013, three marines (A, B and C) were arraigned and pleaded not guilty to a joint charge of murder[66] of an unknown captured person while on patrol in Afghanistan in September 2011. All three marines were granted bail. Two further marines, known as D and E, were told at the hearing that the murder charges against them had been dropped.[67] The timeline for proceedings was set as follows:

- A pre-trial REVIEW to be held on 5 and 6 August 2013 to deal with any legal submissions or arguments;
- the trial itself was provisionally scheduled for 21 October to 15 November 2013 at Bulford Military Court Centre.[68]

The anonymity order, granted on 10 December 2012 by Judge Advocate General Jeff Blackett to protect the identities of all five marines, remained in force until sentencing of Marine A in December 2013. This included a complete reporting ban on any previous statements to the effect that nothing was to be said, written or broadcast that may prejudice the trial of the accused. Of the final three marines charged, Marine A was found guilty of murdering a Taliban prisoner in Helmand province, Afghanistan on 15 September 2011. On conviction, on 5 December 2013, he was named as Sergeant Alexander Wayne Blackman (39), member of 42 Commando. Judge Advocate General, Jeff Blackett HHJ, sentenced Blackman to serve at least ten years in a civilian prison. Blackman was also dismissed with disgrace from the Royal Marines. The other two Marines, found not guilty, were also named as Corporal Christopher Watson and Marine Jack Hammond, who had found the insurgent seriously injured by helicopter gunfire. The murder was inadvertently filmed by Cpl Watson on his helmet-mounted camera and the footage was shown in court during the two-week trial. Blackman had lodged an appeal against his conviction and sentence at the time of publication.

65 **Re Times Newspapers Ltd and another** [2009] 1 WLR 1015 at 1021F (Latham LJ).
66 Under s 42 Armed Forces Act 2006.
67 Source: 'Royal Marines deny murder of Afghan national', *Plymouth Herald*, 8 March 2013.
68 Source: Press Statement by the Service Prosecuting Authority (SPA) of 13 March 2013. RAF Northolt, Ruislip.

5.2.5 Vulnerable witnesses and special measures

In criminal proceedings particularly, witnesses can experience stress and fear during the police investigation of a crime and the process of attending and giving evidence to a court. Stress affects the quantity and quality of communication with witnesses of all ages. Also, certain witnesses have particular difficulties attending court and giving evidence due to their age or personal circumstances, or because of their particular needs or their fear of intimidation.[69]

See below 5.3

Special measures for most vulnerable or intimidated witnesses can be authorized by the court only if they are likely to improve the quality of a witness's evidence. The single exception to this general rule is that this requirement is not applicable to children 'in need of special protection'. For children, victims of sexual offences and people with learning difficulties the process of giving evidence in court can be particularly difficult.[70]

There are, however, times when the judge in a juvenile trial decides to lift the automatic reporting restrictions on the youth if he feels that the matter is of genuine public interest. This was the case – post conviction – with Joshua Davies, aged 16 at the time, who was found guilty of murdering his former girlfriend Rebecca Aylward (15) in July 2011. Mr Justice Lloyd Jones named the boy after the guilty verdict had been announced on 27 July, by saying, 'this is a crime in a small and closely knit community and it is right that the public should know there has been a conviction and who has been convicted.' Davies had denied murder when the charge was read that on 23 October 2010 Davies had killed 'Becca' in Aberkenfig Woods in Maesteg, near Bridgend, Wales. The jury at Swansea Crown Court heard how Davies had later boasted to his friends that he had attacked Rebecca from behind with a heavy rock.[71]

Part II of the Youth Justice and Criminal Evidence Act 1999 (YJCEA) deals with 'special measures' designed to protect 'vulnerable' or intimidated adult witnesses and *inter alia* the practices and procedures which are particularly relevant to the prosecution of rape and serious sexual offences. The YJCEA introduced a wide range of measures to facilitate the gathering and giving of evidence by vulnerable and intimidated witnesses. These are subject to the discretion of the court and have to be applied for at least 14 days in advance of proceedings. Different presumptions apply to different categories of witness. Special measures include:

- screens around the witness box (or sometimes the dock) to prevent the witness from having to see the defendant (known as 'eyeballing the victim') (s 23 YJCEA);
- 'live link': giving evidence through a TV link where the witness can sit in a room outside the courtroom and give evidence via a live television link to the courtroom (s 24 YJCEA);
- video-recorded evidence: the witness's evidence is videotaped and played to the court (mostly used for complainants in serious sexual offences) (s 27 YJCEA);
- video-recorded cross-examination is admissible if the witness has already been permitted to give their evidence-in-chief on video prior to the court case (s 28 YJCEA);
- 'communication aids' to enable the witness to give evidence through a 'communicator', intermediary or interpreter, provided that the communication can be independently verified and understood by the court (only available to vulnerable witnesses and often used with children) (s 30 YJCEA).

---

69 Intimidated witnesses are defined by s 17(1) YJCEA 1999, as those suffering from fear or distress in relation to testifying in the case.

70 Sections 16 and 17 YJCEA 1999 define the witnesses who are eligible for special measures such as vulnerable witnesses. Children are defined as vulnerable by reason of their age; s 16(1)(a) YJCEA.

71 Source: 'Rebecca Aylward: A shocking teenage murder with no apparent motive', by Steven Morris, *Guardian*, 28 July 2011.

In cases affecting the media where freedom of expression and the right to receive and impart information are an issue, prosecutors are required to apply a number of specific principles in addition to the general principles set out above. Therefore, in such cases, prosecutors must follow the CPS Code of Practice, including that they distinguish between:

(a) The public interest served by freedom of expression under Article 10 ECHR and the right to receive and impart information; and
(b) The separate question of whether a prosecution is in the public interest (the second stage of the CPS Code test).

A complete reporting ban was ordered on all parties involved in the tragic death of 'Baby P'.[72] The 17-month-old toddler had died on 3 August 2007 after enduring months of abuse in Haringey, North London. At the time of death, the toddler had a large number of injuries, including eight fractured ribs, a missing tooth which he was found to have swallowed, missing parts to two of his fingernails and tips of fingers, a missing toenail, ulcerated lesions on his scalp and both his ears, a tear between the upper lip and gum, extensive bruising and a broken spine which would have caused paralysis.[73]

Initially it was not clear why his mother could not be named (after charge), though anyone with an internet connection could have circumvented the court anonymity orders to find out that her name was Tracey Connelly and her boyfriend was Steven Barker. By simply typing 'Baby P Mother' into Google or YouTube all names and pictures connected to Baby P could be revealed in seconds, while the media continued to adhere to contempt of court rules for the best part of two years. All of this raises the question: is there any point in reporting restriction laws in the digital age?

The complete reporting ban surrounding the Baby P case only became clear in the spring of 2009, following a nine-week trial where three people were convicted at the Central Criminal Court, the Old Bailey, over the death of the 17-month-old child, known until then only as 'Baby P' or 'Baby Peter'. When the s 4(2) CCA reporting ban was lifted, we learned that his name was Peter Connelly. The s 4 order had been in place to prevent the naming of his assailants – his mother Tracey Connelly, her boyfriend Steven Barker and his brother Jason Owen – all of whom had tortured and abused Baby Peter. There was about to be a second trial for the rape of a two-year-old.

Jason Owen (37), Baby Peter's 'stepfather', was subsequently found guilty of raping a two-year-old girl (one of the main reasons for the reporting ban during the Baby P trial). The allegation of anal rape of the little girl had come to light after Baby P's mother Tracey and Jason Owen had been arrested over Baby Peter's death. Both Tracey Connelly and Jason Owen were tried at the Old Bailey in relation to the girl under false names amid fears that an internet hate campaign would try to influence jurors, and to assure a fair trial for the accused. The jury of eight men and four women had no idea of the defendants' true identities. With the additional sentence for rape of the little girl and for allowing Baby Peter's death, Jason Owen received a life sentence with an additional indefinite sentence for public protection (IPP) as a real and future danger to the public.

The Head of CPS London's Homicide Team, Judith Reed, said that her landmark decision to allow a four-year-old rape victim to give evidence in the Jason Owen case was the toughest of her career. She said, 'It was quite clear that she was raped by this man and I felt it was important for her that we went to trial. In the years to come she will know that the prosecution took her account seriously and worked hard to ensure that a jury were able to consider her evidence.' The girl, who was two years old when she was raped, was interviewed by police some twelve months after her ordeal. Judith Reed continued:

See also Chapter 4.4.1

---

72 The order was made under s 4(2) Contempt of Court Act 1981.
73 Source: 'Three convicted over protracted death of toddler', CPS Press release post conviction and sentence, 11 November 2008.

... having viewed the video of her interview I have to say she was really quite remarkable. I'd never seen a child so young give as clear and consistent an account. The problem was we had very little corroborative evidence to draw on ... I have never made a decision around a case of a child so young. Having said that, she was one of the best child witnesses of any age I've seen giving evidence on video.[74]

Judges and magistrates have to strike a balance between protecting the defendant's rights to a fair trial under Article 6 ECHR and Article 10 ECHR, ensuring that trials and court hearings are openly reported to the public. While the YJCEA 1999 created an expectation that the court ought to be concerned that witnesses are enabled to give their best evidence, the court also imposes an obligation on judges and magistrates to raise the question of whether special measures should be used.[75] This is an example of the increasing inquisitorial nature of the justice system.

5.2.6 Inquests and Coroner's Courts

An inquest is a formal legal inquiry into the medical cause and circumstances of a sudden or unexplained death. It is held in public – sometimes with a jury – by a Coroner, in cases where:

- death was violent or unnatural;
- death took place in prison or police custody;
- the cause of death is still uncertain after a post-mortem;
- a person dies abroad and the body is brought back to the UK.

Coroners have a vital role to play in giving certainty and reassurance to bereaved people, meeting the public interest by determining the facts of deaths that are reported to them and protecting public health by making recommendations to prevent future deaths.

Recent reviews and inquiries about the Coroner system have identified some fundamental problems, including a lack of consistency across England and Wales, an absence of national supervision or leadership and, most importantly, a lack of clear rights for bereaved families to participate in the process, and of standards for the treatment and support of all those who come into contact with Coroners.

In the past, Coroners were generally judicial officers responsible for investigating violent, unnatural or sudden deaths where the cause is unknown. They were drawn largely from medical practitioners and legal practitioners who would investigate unexplained deaths in particular situations; they would also arrange for a post-mortem examination of the body and arrange inquests.[76]

A new legal framework was introduced with the Coroners and Justice Act 2009 for all 96 Coroners in England and Wales. The main aim of the Act was to ensure the same consistent standards across all Coroners' Courts, thereby ending the past inconsistencies which led to criticisms of a postcode lottery – with bereaved people in some areas facing long waits for inquests.[77] The Coroner Services are now overseen by the first Chief Coroner of England and Wales, His Honour Judge Peter Thornton QC; the work of Coroners is now locally delivered within national standards designed to lead to a more efficient system of investigations and inquests. The 2009 Act came into force on 25 July 2013. This means that the Coroners are:

---

74 Source: 'Why I let four-year-old rape victim give evidence in court – prosecutor', CPS Press Release, 1 May 2009.
75 Section 19(1) YJCEA 1999.
76 Section 5 Coroners and Justice Act 2009.
77 See also: Ministry of Justice (2013).

- able to speed up the release of bodies after post-mortem;
- required to notify the deceased's next of kin or personal representative if the body cannot be released within 28 days;
- able to permit less invasive post-mortem examinations;
- required to complete inquests within six months of the date on which they are made aware of the death, unless there are good reasons not to;
- required to notify those who are bereaved within a week of setting the date for the inquest;
- required to report any cases that last more than a year to the Chief Coroner, and give reasons for any delays;
- required to provide greater access to documents and evidence, such as post-mortem reports, before the inquest takes place, to enable bereaved families to prepare for the hearing.

The announcement was made by Justice Minister Helen Grant, who said:

> We are making absolutely sure that the needs of bereaved people are put first and foremost – and that this is done consistently around the country. I want to see all Coroners delivering the same, efficient service across the board, and we have put these changes in law so people can be assured inquests are being conducted quickly, with adequate care and the right support available for those who lose loved ones.[78]

Under the new legislation and implementation, the Chief Coroner now oversees the work of all national Coroners for England and Wales, providing oversight and national leadership of the whole 'unified' system. His main responsibilities are to:

- provide support, leadership, guidance and national training for Coroners;
- approve all future Coroner appointments;
- keep a register of Coroner investigations lasting more than 12 months and take steps to reduce unnecessary delays;
- monitor investigations into deaths of service personnel overseas;
- oversee transfers of cases between Coroners;
- direct Coroners to conduct investigations;
- provide an Annual Report on the Coroner System to the Lord Chancellor, to be laid before Parliament;[79]
- collate, monitor and publish Coroners' Reports to authorities to prevent other deaths.

In January 2012, Cheshire Coroner, Nicholas Rheinberg, ruled in a narrative verdict that the cause of death of the Wales football manager Gary Speed was hanging and that there was not enough evidence to suggest that Speed had intended to take his own life on 27 November 2011 at his home in Huntington, Cheshire.[80] The Coroner's narrative verdict meant that it was not clear whether Mr Speed had taken his own life, only fuelling totally unfounded rumours on Twitter, which had been started by Gary Speed's brother-in-law, Anthony Haylock, in the wake of the Welsh manager's death. Open reporting of the Coroner's verdict was important since Speed had been a well-known

---

78 Source: Press release by the Ministry of Justice 'Implementing the Coroner reforms in Part 1 of the Coroners and Justice Act 2009', 25 July 2013.

79 Section 43 Coroners and Justice Act 2009 enables the Lord Chancellor, with the agreement of the Lord Chief Justice, to make Regulations about the investigation process (excluding inquests, which are dealt with by Coroner Rules), including post-mortem examinations, exhumations and disclosure of information.

80 Source: 'Gary Speed may not have meant to kill himself, Coroner rules. Inquest hears there is not enough evidence to determine whether the Wales football manager's death was intentional', Helen Carter, *Guardian*, 30 January 2012.

public figure and the public had a legitimate interest in knowing the reasons behind what, at first sight, appeared to be a suicide.

All inquests must be held in public in accordance with the principle of open justice, and members of the public and journalists have the right to attend. Whether journalists attend a particular inquest – and whether they report on it – is a matter for them. If any such report is fair and accurate it cannot be used to sue for defamation. The only exception is made with inquests where issues of national security are involved; here the Coroner can exclude the public and the media.[81]

An inquest into a death can be held with or without a jury, but *must* be held with a jury if the senior Coroner has reason to suspect that:

(a)   the deceased died while in custody (police or prison);
(b)   the death was a violent or unnatural one;
(c)   the cause of death is unknown;
(d)   the death was caused by a notifiable accident, poisoning or disease.[82]

See below
5.3.1

Coroners' Courts and inquests sometimes make orders banning the identification of dead children, even though the name of the deceased child may have already been published in the newspaper.[83]

Normally Coroners will not impose anonymity since it is one of the principal functions of a Coroners' court to establish the identity of a person who has died. The media frequently tries to persuade courts against imposing or renewing child anonymity orders, particularly where small children have been victims of domestic violence and abuse, such as in the Victoria Climbié case in 2005 or that of Baby P in 2009. Media representatives will argue that a child of such tender years would not suffer any ill effects from being named. The only anonymity awarded in the Coroners and Justice Act 2009 is to families of UK Special Forces and deceased servicemen and women abroad. Sections 10 and 12 of the 2009 Act guarantee confidentiality for soldiers and their families if they so wish.[84]

5.3 Reporting on children and young persons

See also 5.3.2
below

see below 5.5

The freedom of a child to grow up and make mistakes, to act badly and not to have this permanently recorded, is an essential human right recorded in the UN Convention on the Rights of the Child 1989.[85] The 1989 Convention was the first legally binding international instrument to incorporate the full range of human rights – civil, cultural, economic, political and social. Article 40 of the UN Convention guarantees the right of a child defendant 'to have his or her privacy fully respected at all stages of the proceedings'. Spencer (2000) argues that many countries have interpreted the Convention differently, but that the UK courts have adopted the role of 'naming and shaming' young offenders as a sanction in the legal system as an additional form of punishment (see: **McKerry v Teesdale and Wear Valley Justices** (2000)).[86] Spencer argues further that in countries like Holland and Germany it would be standard practice for the media to suppress the names of young offenders even when they have turned 18.[87]

---

81   Rule 17 of the Coroners Rules 1984.
82   Section 7 Coroners and Justice Act 2009 ('where jury required').
83   Section 39 Children and Young Persons Act 1933 does not apply to protect the identity of dead children; and if such an order has been in force, it may be challenged.
84   Subject to service law by virtue of s 367 Armed Forces Act 2006; s 50 Coroners and Justice Act 2009 amends the Fatal Accidents and Sudden Deaths Inquiry (Scotland) Act 1976.
85   Document A/RES/44/25 of 12 December 1989.
86   [2000] 164 JP 355 (DC).
87   Source: Spencer (2000), p. 468.

Where the welfare and interest of a child is concerned, the Strasbourg human rights court has sought to protect the privacy of a child under Article 8, and any court can now make an order prohibiting the identification of the child. However, human rights jurisprudence equally states that this power must be used carefully, balancing other interests protected by Articles 6 and 10 of the Convention.

See Chapters 2.4.2 and 2.6.1

It is then regarded as a fundamental human right not to disseminate public information concerning a child – such as family court or youth justice proceedings – which may impact on the future behaviour and development of a child. It is for this reason that 'public' proceedings are usually held in private where children are concerned and that the media are prevented from commercializing childhood or child offences. It was held in **V v UK and T v UK** (1999)[88] that a Youth Court is best designed to meet the specific needs of children and young persons, even when charged with very serious offences. A trial in the Crown Court with greater formality and an increased number of people involved (including a jury and the public) should be reserved for the most serious adult cases.

Following the incorporation of the Human Rights Convention into UK law by way of the Human Rights Act 1998, it can be argued that S's daughter in **Godwin**[89] would also have had the right to respect for her own private life under Article 8, in addition to the terms prescribed by s 39 Children and Young Persons Act 1933. The relationship between Articles 8 and 10 ECHR was considered by the House of Lords in **Re S (A Child) (Identification: Restrictions on Publication)** (2004),[90] where the court did not consider that there was scope for extending the restrictions on freedom of expression beyond what was provided by statute as construed in **Godwin**. It is fair to say that there has been considerable criticism of the use of the 'open justice' principle to justify the naming of the parties in the **Re S (A Child)** case, where it is worth noting that all the facts could have been reported except for the identity of the parties.

Although there was no opposition to the granting of a lifelong anonymity order in the **Mary Bell** case (**Re X** (2003)), the Attorney General has not advanced any public interest argument against the granting of protective lifelong injunctions, as Lord Woolf CJ said in **A v B (a company)** (2002).[91] This means that any interference with the freedom of expression, and therein press freedom, has to be justified. In the case of 'naming and shaming' a youth, are the media simply pursuing and pandering to the prurient interests of the public?

see 5.4.1 below

Where children and young persons under the age of 18 are involved in Youth Court proceedings these are automatically held in private (*in camera*).[92] Parents, guardians and close relatives are also permitted in the Youth Court. Accredited reporters can attend and report, provided they adhere to the legislation that covers the non-identification of the youngster when evidence is given.[93] It is entirely legitimate to report that 'a 13-year-old Cardiff boy was today accused of causing criminal damage'. An adult criminal court can prohibit publication of the name, address, school or any information calculated to lead to the identification of any child or young person (under 18) concerned in criminal proceedings before that court. The power also extends to images of the child or young person (s 39 Children and Young Persons Act 1933).

The Children and Young Persons Act 1933 (CYPA) is still a very practical statute, with the principal aim of protecting the welfare of the child, particularly in court proceedings – enshrined in s 44 of the 1933 Act. If a child or young person under 18 is found guilty of an offence, proper

---

88 (1999) 30 EHRR 121 (ECtHR); see also: *R v Secretary of State for the Home Department, ex parte Venables; R v Secretary of State for the Home Department, ex parte Thompson* [1998] AC 407 (HL).
89 *R v Southwark Crown Court ex parte Godwin and Others* [1992] QB 190.
90 [2004] UKHL 47 (HL).
91 *A v B plc (a company)* [2002] EWCA Civ 337.
92 Section 49 Children and Young Persons Act 1933 (CYPA) ('Restrictions on reports of proceedings in which children or young persons are concerned').
93 Section 47 CYPA ('Procedure in Youth Courts').

provisions are put in place to secure his or her education and training until school-leaving age (age 16).

The Youth Justice and Criminal Evidence Act 1999 (YJCEA) makes additional provisions for youth justice proceedings, such as the referral of offenders under 18 to Youth Offender Panels. Sections 21 and 22 YJCEA detail some special provisions for child witnesses under the age of 17. These provisions create presumptions that apply to different categories of child witnesses and concern how they will give their evidence. The provisions state:

- Where there is a child witness in a sexual case involving violence, abduction or neglect, the child witness is deemed to be 'in need of special protection'.
- All child witnesses in need of special protection will have the video recording of their evidence admitted as evidence-in-chief, unless this is excluded by the court on the basis that to admit the video recording would not be in the interests of justice.
- Child witnesses in cases of violence will normally be cross-examined via the live link.
- For all other child witnesses, there will be a presumption that evidence-in-chief will be given by video recording, if one has been made, and that cross-examination will be via the live link. However, the court must be satisfied that this will improve the quality of the evidence.

In such cases, the court does not have to consider whether the special measure(s) will improve the quality of the evidence; this will be assumed to be the case.

Sections 21 and 22 YJCEA 1999 also concern witnesses *over* 17 years of age. The following must be noted:

- If a court makes a special measures direction in respect of a child witness who is eligible on grounds of youth only and the witness turns 17 before beginning to give evidence, the direction no longer has effect. If such a witness turns 17 after beginning to give evidence, the special measures direction continues to apply.[94]
- If a witness is under 17 when evidence-in-chief or cross-examination (when available) is video recorded before the trial but has since turned 17, the video recording is still capable of being used as evidence.
- A witness who is over 17 at the beginning of the trial but who made a video recording as their evidence-in-chief when they were under 17 is eligible for special measures in the same way that they would be if they were under 17, and the same presumptions apply to them.

The House of Lords held in **R v Camberwell Youth Court ex p D & others** (2005)[95] that the presumption for children in need of special protection did not breach Articles 6 ('right to a fair trial') or 14 ('discrimination') of the European Convention. The HL stated that the norm for child witnesses giving evidence for either the prosecution or defence was by video evidence-in-chief (recorded) and live link for cross-examination. Where a court exercises its statutory powers to allow any name (including an adult) or any other matter to be withheld from the public in criminal proceedings, the court may make a direction as is necessary prohibiting publication of that name or matter in connection with the proceedings.[96]

---

94 Section 21(9) YJCEA 1999.
95 [2005] UKHL 4.
96 Section 11 Contempt of Court Act 1981.

5.3.1 Identification of young persons in court

Section 39 of the Children and Young Persons Act 1933 was intended to be complementary to s 49 of the 1933 Act, which imposes an automatic restriction on news reports identifying children and young persons involved in youth proceedings.[97] This means that the media cannot simply argue that the public have a right to know if such an order has been properly made. Any journalist who publishes any matter in contravention of a s 39 court order is liable on summary conviction under s 39(2) of the 1933 Act, to a maximum Level 5 fine.[98]

Normally, if a child or young person (under 18) has committed a criminal offence, he will be tried summarily by magistrates in a Youth Court. In more serious cases ('grave crimes') a youth may be sent to be tried at a Crown Court. If the young person is charged in conjunction with an adult offender, youth magistrates may consider it necessary in the interests of justice to commit them both for trial to the Crown Court. But the line has to be drawn somewhere. If children are not being included in a prosecution, a s 39 order will not be permitted to protect them from media reporting, despite the strong evidence that any revelation of their family history might seriously damage their well-being. For example, if the prosecution is for manslaughter, only the accused child or young person can be protected when giving evidence. Anonymity should not be extended to others who do not fall into any of the statutory categories (e.g. s 39 order).

See below 5.3.3

In **ex p. Crook** (1995),[99] the appellant journalists challenged a s 39 order which stated that nothing should be published which would lead to the identification of children who were alive and named on the indictment. The indictment included a count of manslaughter of another child of the defendant, whose surviving children were in local authority care. The three young children in this case, for whom the protective order was made, were the alleged victims of cruelty by both parents, charges which were heard together with the allegation of manslaughter in respect of their sibling. The CA, dismissing the appeal, stated that a judge (or magistrate), in making the s 39 order, has complete discretion to allow representatives from the media – who have a legitimate interest – to make representations before the order is made. The CA ruled that the original judge had been completely correct in making the s 39 order on receipt of the borough council's report and that any publication would have had an otherwise damaging effect on the surviving children. In making the order, the judge had correctly weighed the children's interest against the freedom of the press to report and had reached the conclusion that the likely harm to the children outweighed the restriction of freedom to publish.

In **R v Central Independent Television** (1994),[100] a wife failed to secure an injunction preventing the broadcasting of a programme identifying her husband as a convicted molester of small boys. She argued that a broadcast would be prejudicial to the welfare of her five-year-old daughter. The identity of the boys was covered by a s 39 order, but the girl was regarded as too remote from the proceedings and the programme had nothing to do with her care or upbringing. More precisely, the little girl was not within the specific categories covered by s 39.

It was held in **ex p Godwin** (1992)[101] that a s 39 order – originally imposed by Judge Laurie at Southwark Crown Court – was only available where the terms of s 39(1) Children and Young Persons Act 1933 relate to a relevant child. In this case the newspapers had previously reported the abusing stepfather's (S) name, referring to the victim as 'an 11-year-old schoolgirl'. There was a serious risk of jigsaw identification in that the composite picture would present the identification of that child.

---

97 The 1933 Act consolidated the Children and Young Persons Act 1932. In the latter Act the equivalent provisions to ss 39 and 49 of the Act of 1933 were all contained in s 81.
98 Upper limits for a Level 5 fine were abolished under s 85 Legal Aid, Sentencing and Punishment of Offenders Act 2012 (£5,000 or more) ('Removal of limit on certain fines on conviction by magistrates' court').
99 **R v Central Criminal Court ex parte Crook** [1995] 1 WLR 139 (CA (Crim Div)).
100 (1994) 9 February 1994, (CA) (unreported).
101 **R v Southwark Crown Court ex parte Godwin and Others** [1992] QB 190 (CA (Civ Div); [1991] 3 WLR 689 at p.196.

The appellants, Caroline Godwin, the *Daily Telegraph*, Mirror Group Newspapers and Associated Newspapers Ltd, appealed against the s 39 order under s 159 Criminal Justice Act 1988.[102] The appellants argued that the judge had wrongly interpreted s 39. They further argued that there was no evidence that the naming of the defendant (S) would lead to the identification of the child.

The CA in **Godwin** quashed the original s 39 order in its entirety and substituted a new order with an express restriction on the identification of S, as well as 'the nature of the case against him'. S's daughter was therefore protected during the proceedings and after the conclusion of the trial by way of a lifelong anonymity order provided additionally by s 1 Sexual Offences (Amendment) Act 1992 ('Anonymity of victims in certain offences'). Glidewell LJ allowed the appeal in **Godwin**, stating that it could not have been Parliament's intention to allow greater reporting restrictions in an adult court than in a juvenile court. This means that a s 39 order does not empower a court to prevent the naming of adult defendants in general; s 39 orders are, by their very nature, specifically related to children and young persons under 18. The Court of Appeal made it quite clear in **Godwin** that adult courts do not have greater powers to restrict publicity than juvenile courts.

In **R v Winchester Crown Court ex p. B (A Minor)** (1999),[103] B, aged 14, applied for judicial review of the trial judge's decision to discharge reporting restrictions after sentence and to lift the s 39 order, which had prohibited B's identification.[104] The judge had reasoned that reporting restrictions were no longer necessary on the basis that open justice was essential in a civilized society. Judges Simon Brown LJ and Astill J in the Administrative Court dismissed B's application and reiterated that it was well within the Crown Court's powers to discharge a s 39 order in relation to proceedings on indictment after conviction (see also: **R v Central Criminal Court ex parte Crook** (1995)[105]).

In **Re Gazette Media Co Ltd** (2005),[106] the CA considered the scope of a s 39 order where two men, S and L, were being prosecuted (and eventually convicted) for offences contrary to s 1 of the Protection of Children Act 1978 and for conspiracy to rape. S was charged with offences of making or distributing indecent photographs of his daughter and with the offence of conspiracy to rape. L was charged with conspiracy to rape and also with offences of making and distributing indecent photographs of a child. In this case, the Middlesbrough Recorder had made the s 39 order by stating:

> . . . no reporting of any proceedings in respect of R v S and L. No identification of the defendant S by name or otherwise the nature of the case against him, the identification of the alleged victim [S's daughter], her age place of abode or any circumstances that may lead to her identification in connection with these proceedings.[107]

Solicitors acting for *Gazette Media* wrote to the Recorder complaining about the wording of the s 39 order, citing **Godwin**: that – as a matter of law – the order did not empower a court to prevent the names of (adult) defendants from being published. Maurice Kay LJ in **Re Gazette** remarked that it was clear beyond doubt that the order made by the Recorder 'flew in the face of *Godwin*' in that a s 39 order could not add specifics beyond the words of s 39(1). Therefore, a departure from **Godwin** could not be justified. It was not enough to delete the restriction against the reporting of any proceedings in relation to the defendants and the victim; it was also necessary to delete the express restriction on the identification of S and L and the nature of the case against them.

---

102 That section permits a person aggrieved to appeal to the Court of Appeal against 'any order restricting the publication of any report of the whole or any part of a trial on indictment or any such ancillary proceedings'.
103 [1999] 1 WLR 788.
104 B had been sentenced to three years' detention for an offence contrary to s 1 Criminal Attempts Act 1981.
105 [1995] 1 WLR 139 (CA (Crim Div)).
106 **Gazette Media Company Ltd. & Ors, R (on the application of) v Teeside Crown Court** [2005] EWCA Crim 1983 (CA (Crim Div)).
107 Ibid., at 138.

The additional problem in **Re Gazette** was that the restriction provided by s 1 of the 1992 Act ('Anonymity of victims in certain offences' – see above) was not sufficient to protect the identity of the victim during the proceedings and could be interpreted by the media as 'freedom to report'. While conspiracy to rape was an offence to which s 1 of the 1992 Act applied, other linked offences were not. The order was quashed in its entirety and a new order in conventional **Godwin** terms was substituted. Additionally, it was submitted by the Attorney General that, while a total embargo on the reporting of the proceedings remained unlawful, the prohibition of the naming of a defendant – so as to protect the interests of a child – was now possible within the remits of the human rights provision of Article 8 ECHR and s 3 Human Rights Act 1998, which requires primary legislation to be compatible with Convention rights.

5.3.2 When anonymity orders may be lifted on children and young persons

As already mentioned, proceedings in the Youth Court are 'in private' and no reporting takes place on children and young persons (either as accused or victim) if they are aged 18 and under. However, a s 39 order under the Children and Young Persons Act 1933 may be lifted by the applying court at any time if the magistrates or the presiding judge feel the matter is in the public interest. This was the case post-conviction in the 'Bulger killers' trial of Robert Thompson and Jon(athan) Venables, when the judge lifted reporting restrictions in November 1993 (see below).

Section 49 of the 1933 Act allows the media to publish the name and other full details of a young offender (under age 18) when anonymity can be lifted by the court 'in the public interest'. This principle was established in **Lee**.[108] Generally, where young defendants are tried for 'grave crimes' at the Crown Court, the media are free to identity them unless the court rules otherwise by making a s 39 order.

In **Lee**, a s 39 order was made at the Crown Court trial of L, a boy then aged 14, restricting publication of his identity. On sentencing, the judge lifted the restriction. An emergency order prohibiting identification was made by another judge but was too late to prevent publication in some newspapers. L's lawyers made an application to the sentencing judge to reimpose the order. The CA upheld the refusal of the judge to ban the media from identifying the 14-year-old, convicted of robbery and rape, because it would involve 'no real harm to the applicant, and [have] a powerful deterrent effect on his contemporaries if the applicant's name and photograph were published'. This was the first case where the 'naming and shaming' of a young offender was made possible while court proceedings were still active, although Lord Bingham stressed that publicity should not be used as an 'additional punishment' – contrary to the views of successive Home Secretaries and ministers of justice.

The ruling in **Lee** means that 'any proceedings' for the purposes of a s 39 order does not mean any proceedings anywhere but rather any proceedings in the court making the order.

In April 2012, the presiding judge lifted the anonymity order on 14-year-old Daniel Bartlam, naming the young killer for murdering his mother Jacqueline Bartlam (47). Nottingham Crown Court heard Bartlam was 'obsessed' with *Coronation Street*'s killer character John Stape, who had battered a woman with a hammer before leaving her body in the wreckage of a tram crash to cover up his crime. The court also heard how the teenager had possibly copied the TV crime by hitting his mother seven times with a claw hammer at their home, then padded her body with paper, doused it in petrol and set fire to it in a bid to destroy evidence and commit the 'perfect murder'. It was only after the boy's sentencing that Mr Justice Flaux lifted reporting restrictions which prevented

---

108 **R v Lee (Anthony William) (a Minor)** [1993] 1 WLR 103 (CA (Crim Div)).

him from being named. Sentencing Bartlam to life imprisonment under Her Majesty's Pleasure with a minimum of 16 years for the 'senseless and grotesque killing', the judge said the murder involved a high degree of planning, and Bartlam remained 'extremely dangerous' – one of the main reasons given for the lifting or the (youth) anonymity s 39 order.[109]

The most notorious case of open court reporting concerning child killers is still that of Jon Venables and Robert Thompson, the then 10-year-old boys who killed 18-month-old James ('Jamie') Bulger in 1993. Venables and Thompson had snatched the toddler during a shopping trip with his mother at the Strand shopping centre in Bootle on 12 February 1993 and had brutally tortured him, leaving the toddler's battered body on a freight railway line, where he died. The boys were found guilty of James's murder on 24 November 1993 by the jury at Preston Crown Court and, immediately after, Mr Justice Morland lifted the s 39 Children and Young Persons Act 1933 reporting restrictions 'in the public interest'. A media frenzy ensued, resulting in shocking and distressing facts being published about the boys' dysfunctional family backgrounds. Aged 11, the two boys were sentenced to be detained at 'Her Majesty's Pleasure' (HMP)[110] with an initial maximum tariff of eight years. Subsequently Lord Chief Justice Taylor of Gosforth raised their minimum sentence to 10 years.

Following public outrage over the 'short' youth custody tariff, the editor of the *Sun* handed a petition bearing nearly 280,000 signatures to the then Conservative Home Secretary, Michael Howard, in a bid to increase the time spent by both boys in custody. This campaign was successful, and in July 1994 Mr Howard announced that the boys would be kept in custody for a minimum of 15 years, meaning that they would not be considered for release until February 2008, by which time they would be 25 years old. The boys challenged this decision under judicial review, arguing the Home Secretary had acted *ultra vires*.[111]

Lord Donaldson criticized Howard's intervention, describing the increased tariff as 'institutionalized vengeance . . . [by] a politician playing to the gallery'.[112] The increased minimum term was overturned by the House of Lords, ruling that it was 'unlawful' for the Home Secretary to decide on minimum sentences for young offenders. The increase of the sentencing term was further criticized by the European Court of Human Rights in *V v UK; T v UK* (1999);[113] though the Strasbourg court also ruled that national parliaments may set minimum and maximum terms for individual categories of crime within their legislation. It is the responsibility of the trial judge, with the benefit of all the evidence and argument from both prosecution and defence counsel, to determine the minimum term in individual criminal cases, particularly where youths are concerned.

In *McKerry v Teesdale and Wear Valley Justices* (2000),[114] a 16-year-old boy, with a long record of offending, pleaded guilty at the Youth Court to a 'TWOCing' offence.[115] Upon request by a local newspaper, the magistrates lifted the reporting restrictions and permitted his identity to be revealed under s 49 of the 1933 Act, giving as reasons that the young offender posed a serious danger to the public and had shown a complete disregard for the law. The Divisional Court held that the magistrates' reasons were completely acceptable because 'no doubt the justices had in mind that members of the public, if they knew the appellant's name, would enjoy a measure of protection if they had cause to encounter him'. The court further added that the power to dispense with anonymity 'must be exercised with very great circumspection' and that the public interest criterion must be met.[116]

---

109 Source: 'Coronation Street killer was "fascinated by horror DVDs and violent games from age eight and it was all too easy for him to get hold of them", says victim's former partner', by Andy Dolan and Jill Reilly, *Daily Mail*, 2 April 2012.
110 Section 53(1) Children and Young Persons Act 1933.
111 **Secretary of State for the Home Department, ex parte Venables; R v Secretary of State for the Home Department, ex parte Thompson** [1998] AC 407.
112 Source: *The Times*, 10 October 1995.
113 (1999) 30 EHRR 121 (ECtHR).
114 [2000] 164 JP 355 (DC).
115 Section 12 Theft Act 1968 ('taking a vehicle without the owner's consent').
116 See also: Spencer (2000), p. 468.

In the conjoined cases of **R (on the application of T) v St Albans Crown Court; Chief Constable of Surrey v JHG** (2002),[117] it was held that antisocial behaviour orders (ASBOs) were very much in the general public interest and that reporting restrictions would not be granted. In the first case, the court had refused to grant anonymity under s 39 Children and Young Persons' Act 1933 to an 11-year-old boy (T) in respect of whom an ASBO[118] had been made. T sought a judicial review of that decision. In the second case, the court had granted anonymity to 17-year-old twins (J and D) when making an ASBO, with the Chief Constable of Surrey appealing against that decision. The allegations against T included abuse, minor criminal damage and two assaults, and those against J and D included assault, nuisance, trespass, criminal damage, threatening behaviour and intimidation. T, J and D submitted that, given that ASBOs were civil in character, they were less serious than many of the offences in respect of which s 39 applications were commonly refused in Crown Court proceedings.[119]

T submitted that the court had failed to consider relevant matters, including his age and improvement in his behaviour, and in J and D's case the chief constable submitted that the court had considered irrelevant matters, including the impact on members of J and D's families. Reaffirming the ruling in **Lee**, the court applied the principle (of open reporting) in **R v Winchester Crown Court Ex p. B (A Minor)** (1999).[120] The court applied the **Lee**-balancing exercise: that of the public interest test in disclosure of the name versus the welfare of the young person in question. While the court did not have to refer to every factor that might weigh in favour of a s 39 direction, it was necessary for it to briefly summarize the principal factors weighing in favour, even if its decision was that those factors were outweighed by the public interest. The public interest test weighed in favour of disclosure in **T** and **JHG**, where it could be reported that the individuals were on an ASBO and the neighbourhood could learn about the orders, assisting the police in making the orders effective to prevent future antisocial behaviour.

Newspapers are permitted to report freely on 'young thugs' who 'terrorize suburbia', because no reporting restrictions apply directly to ASBOs. This became the Labour Government's policy from 1997 onwards, geared to 'naming and shaming' young offenders with the introduction of the Crime and Disorder Act 1998 (which introduced ASBOs under s 1 of the Act[121]). Anything on a young person with an ASBO can be published, such as his or her full name, together with addresses and pictures, as well as details of the ASBO, particularly where youths are linked to more serious offending in the neighbourhood.

One example was the *Daily Mail*'s reporting on Stephen Paul Sorton, 17, Jordan Cunlifffe, 16, and Adam Swellings, 19, who were subsequently found guilty of the murder of Garry Newlove in January 2008.[122]

Following on from the Strasbourg ruling in **V & T v UK**, Parliament enacted the Youth Justice and Criminal Evidence Act 1999 (YJCEA) so that young defendants should not be exposed to intimidation, humiliation or distress in court proceedings.[123] Lord Woolf LCJ reinforced the new legislation by a Practice Direction, stating that:

---

117 [2002] EWHC 1129 (Admin) of 20 May 2002 (QBD (Admin).
118 Section 1 Crime and Disorder Act 1998.
119 See: Ministry of Justice (2012b) White Paper, *Putting Victims First: More effective responses to anti-social behaviour* of 22 May 2012. The White Paper proposes to abolish ASBOs and replace these by two new tools: the Criminal Behaviour Order (CBO), which could be attached to a criminal conviction, and the Crime Prevention Injunction (CPI) for other cases.
120 [1999] 1 WLR 788.
121 See: Jack Straw's White Paper 'No More Excuses: A new approach to tackling youth crime in England and Wales'. Home Office (1997) November 1997. CM 3809.
122 Source: 'The three young thugs brought fear to suburbia', by Liz Hull and Rebecca Camber, *Daily Mail*, 17 January 2008.
123 Section 48 and Schedule 2 of the 1999 Act amend the Children and Young Persons Act 1933 by allowing a judge or magistrate to lift or amend reporting restrictions. Schedule 2 contains amendments relating to reporting restrictions under the following: Children and Young Persons Act 1933; Sexual Offences (Amendment) Act 1976; S.I. 1978/460 Sexual Offences (Northern Ireland) Order 1978; Sexual Offences (Amendment) Act 1992; S.I. 1994/2795 Criminal Justice (Northern Ireland) Order 1994.

. . . all possible steps should be taken to assist the young defendant to understand and participate in the proceedings. The ordinary trial process should, so far as necessary, be adapted to
meet those ends.[124]

How then should the media interpret ss 39 and 49 of the 1933 Act, common law development in
child anonymity orders and provisions under the 1999 Act? The question remains whether open
disclosure on juvenile offenders is always in the interest of justice (rather than the public interest)?
Following the lifelong anonymity order by way of a permanent injunction on Jon Venables and
Robert Thompson in 2001, this was never going to appease those who believed the public had an
absolute right to know the whereabouts of the James Bulger killers (see: *Venables v NGN* (2001)[125]).
Even in 2010, Justice Secretary Jack Straw refused to reveal Venables's identity after he had been
returned to prison in spite of rampant speculation in the media, encouraged by an emotive
campaign involving James Bulger's mother.

It is then absolutely right and in the interest of justice that in certain special cases, usually
involving child killers, courts uphold s 39 reporting restriction orders, as well as post-release lifelong anonymity orders usually granted by the Family Court Division of the High Court. The decision by Dame Elizabeth Butler-Sloss to grant anonymity to the Bulger killers on their release from
prison under licence in 2001 was right and humane in the same way as such an order was granted
to 'Mary Bell' and her child. Given that all young murderers have served their sentence, they require
new identities and lifelong injunctive relief from the courts to protect them from media intrusion
and for their own protection. The raw public and media outrage that followed each of their murder
trials was proof enough that their lives might be in danger.

Appearing at the Old Bailey by way of live video link, the then 27-year-old Jon Venables
pleaded guilty on 23 July 2010, after admitting downloading and distributing indecent images of
children. Venables, living in Cheshire at the time when the images were found on his computer by
a probation officer, was sentenced to two years' imprisonment. James Bulger's mother, Denise
Fergus, was at the hearing and said 'justice had not been done'. Mr Justice Bean, sitting at the Old
Bailey, said Venables had 'colluded in the harm of children'. However, the judge said it would be
'wrong' for Venables's sentence to be increased because of his previous crime. The judge partially
lifted reporting restrictions to reveal Venables had been living in Cheshire at the time of the offences
and that the case was dealt with by Cheshire police and the Cheshire probation service.[126]

 FOR THOUGHT

Is it a breach of human rights that children are tried in adult courts for serious indictable
offences? Discuss in the light of the ruling in *V v UK; T v UK* (1999) (ECtHR).

5.3.3 Sexual offences and other grave crimes: venue for trial

If an allegation of any sexual abuse committed by a youth offender has been fully investigated and
there is sufficient evidence to justify commencing proceedings, the CPS stresses in its guidelines that
the balance of the public interest must always be carefully considered before any prosecution is
commenced. However, police and prosecuting authorities have been encouraged by new legislation

---

124 Source: Practice Direction by the Lord Chief Justice of England and Wales (Woolf LCJ): Trial of Children and Young Persons in
  the Crown Court of 16 February 2000.
125 [2001] Fam 430.
126 Source: 'Bulger killer Venables jailed over child abuse images', BBC News Online, 23 July 2010.

to issue reprimands and cautions when 'perpetrator' and 'victim' involve youngsters.[127] Social Services will usually be involved when the decision to prosecute is made, taking into account the consequences for the victim and the victim's family.

All sexual offences are covered by the Sexual Offences Act 2003.[128] Historically, Youth Courts could never accept jurisdiction in a rape case (see: **R v Billam (Keith)** (1986)[129]). However, recent developments in common law and the wider definition of rape under s 1 Sexual Offences Act 2003, including sex by penetration other than by penis, and other sexual assaults under the 2003 Act now mean that certain sexual offence cases do not fall within the 'grave crime'[130] exception and can therefore be tried in the Youth Court by a specialist District Judge (see: **AG's Reference (No 92 of 2009)** (2010)[131]). Juvenile rape cases and other serious sexual offences involving a young offender under 18 are now regularly heard by a circuit judge sitting as a district judge in the Youth Court. This protocol does not alter the test for youth magistrates when determining whether a case is a 'grave crime'.[132] In all cases involving a grave crime, the magistrates will be invited to consider the question of venue before a plea is taken.[133]

Those accused of child rape can no longer argue that the child consented. Any sexual intercourse with a child under 13 will be treated as rape. Other non-consensual offences against children under 13 are sexual assault by penetration, sexual assault, and causing or inciting a child to engage in sexual activity. There are also offences of sexual activity with a child under 16. These cover a range of behaviour, involving both physical and non-physical contact. As children and young persons commit sexual crimes on other children, these offences apply also to persons under 18.

Rape of a child under 13,[134] assault of a child under 13 by penetration[135] and causing or inciting a child under 13 to engage in sexual activity that involves penetration[136] are indictable-only offences with a maximum sentence of life imprisonment. The offences of sexual assault of a child under 13[137] and causing or inciting a child under 13 to engage in sexual activity where there has been no penetration[138] are punishable on indictment with imprisonment for a term not exceeding 14 years. They are all 'grave crimes' for the purposes of s 24 Magistrates' Courts Act (MCA) 1980 and s 91 Powers of Criminal Courts (Sentencing) Act 2000.

The age of consent is 16. Because children can and do abuse and exploit other children, the 2003 Act makes it an offence for children under 16 to engage in sexual activity, to protect children who are victims. However, the CPS states in its guidelines ('Prosecuting of persons under the age of 18 in sexual offences') that children of the same or similar age are highly unlikely to be prosecuted for engaging in sexual activity, where the activity is mutually agreed and there is no abuse or exploitation.[139] Lady Justice Smith in **R (on the application of B & others) v The Richmond on Thames Youth Court**

---

127 Under Schedule 24 ('Youth Cautions') of the Legal Aid, Sentencing and Punishment of Offenders Act 2012 (LAPSO) police can give repeated cautions to a young offender (under 18) (this amends s 66 (A) (1) of the Crime and Disorder Act 1998). Sections 135–138 LAPSO deal with 'out of court disposals'. LAPSO abolished reprimands and final warnings for young offenders, replacing these with 'youth cautions'. Fixed penalties (PNDs) for under 18-year olds were also abolished.
128 The first part of the 2003 Act covers sexual offences. The second part covers offenders with an emphasis on the protection of vulnerable individuals. It gives a comprehensive list of sex offences to protect individuals from abuse and exploitation.
129 [1986] 1 All ER 985.
130 A 'grave crime' is defined in s 91(1) Powers of Criminal Courts (Sentencing) Act 2000.
131 [2010] EWCA Crim 524 (sub nom '**R v Brett (Stephen Lawrence)**' of 3 March 2010) (CA Crim Div).
132 The determination of venue in the Youth Court is governed by s 24(1)(a) Magistrates' Courts Act 1980, which provides that the youth must be tried summarily unless charged with such a grave crime that long-term detention is a realistic possibility or that one of the other exceptions to this presumption arises.
133 The 'allocation' provisions can be found in Schedule 13 Criminal Justice and Immigration Act 2008 to introduce to the youth court plea before venue and committal for sentence. See also: Archbold 5–286.
134 Section 5 Sexual Offences Act 2003 (SOA).
135 Section 6 SOA.
136 Section 8 SOA.
137 Section 7 SOA.
138 Section 8 SOA.
139 The Crown Prosecution Service issued guidance to prosecutors, which sets out the criteria they should consider when deciding whether or not it is in the public interest to bring a prosecution at: www.cps.gov.uk/news/fact_sheets/sexual_offences.

(2006)[140] contended that magistrates would still have the power to commit a juvenile rape case to the Crown Court but that they could equally accept jurisdiction for such indictable and related sexual offences.[141]

In August 2013, the Head of the Judiciary for England and Wales, the Rt Hon The Lord Judge, announced that a select pool of judges with specialist training would be created to handle complex child abuse cases, amid concerns at the way some child witnesses were treated in court by lawyers.

At the same time, in August, Neil Wilson (41) admitted to sexually abusing a 13-year-old schoolgirl at his home in Romford, Essex. During a police search of Wilson's home, officers had also uncovered a stash of images and videos on his computer, depicting child abuse and bestiality. Wilson admitted two counts of making extreme pornographic images and one count of sexual activity with a child.

What caused media outrage was not only the seemingly lenient suspended prison sentence handed down by Judge Nigel Peters QC at Snaresbrook Crown Court on 5 August 2013, but the accompanying remarks made by prosecutor Robert Colover at the time. Mr Colover, employed by the CPS at Wilson's sentencing hearing, said: 'The girl is predatory in all her actions and she is sexually experienced.' Judge Nigel Peters QC took those words into account, along with the fact the girl looked older than she was; he told Wilson: 'On these facts (that were put before the court), the girl was predatory and was egging you on.' The judge suspended Wilson's eight-month prison term for two years. The Attorney General's Office said the sentence and the prosecutor's remarks had been drawn to his attention as 'possibly unduly lenient'.[142]

After child protection groups such as the NSPCC and Barnado's complained about Mr Colover's remarks, a CPS spokesperson announced on 7 August 2013, as the story made every headline:

> The word 'predatory' in this context should not have been used and is of real concern to the CPS. It is not consistent with the work that we have undertaken alongside the judiciary and others in the past year to improve attitudes towards victims of abuse. We expect all of our prosecutors, including self-employed barristers who act on our behalf, to follow our guidance in these very difficult cases. The DPP will be undertaking a review of this case to determine what happened and to decide what action needs to be taken. We are now considering the involvement of this barrister in sexual offence prosecutions and have advised his chambers that we will not instruct him in any on-going or future cases involving sexual offences in the meantime.[143]

Keir Starmer, the then Director of Public Prosecutions, announced that he would carry out a review of the Neil Wilson case to determine what had happened and decide what action should be taken.

When the venue is decided (whether Youth or Crown Court), the prosecutor usually consults the principles set out by Leveson J in **Re R**:[144]

1. The general policy of the legislature is that those who are under 18 years of age and in particular children of under 15 years of age should, wherever possible, be tried in the Youth Court. It is the court which is best designed to meet their specific needs. A trial in the Crown Court with the inevitably greater formality and greatly increased number of people involved (including a jury and the public) should be reserved for the most serious cases.

---

140 [2006] EWHC 95 (Admin) (QBD) (full citation: **R (on the Application of W), R (on the Application of S), R (on the Application of B) v The Brent Youth Court, The Enfield Crown Court, The Richmond on Thames Youth Court** [2006] of 13 January 2006).
141 Section 24 Magistrates Court Act 1980.
142 Source: 'Barrister suspended from sex cases after court comments', BBC News Online, 7 August 2013.
143 Source: Press Release by the CPS on 7 August 2013: Statement from CPS on case of Neil Wilson.
144 **R (on the application of H, A and O) v Southampton Youth Court** [2005] 2 Cr App R 30 (Admin).

2. It is a further policy of the legislature that, generally speaking, first-time offenders aged 12 to 14 and all offenders under 12 should not be detained in custody and decisions as to jurisdiction should have regard to the fact that the exceptional power to detain for grave offences should not be used to water down the general principle. Those under 15 will rarely attract a period of detention and, even more rarely, those who are under 12.

3. In each case the court should ask itself whether there is a real prospect, having regard to his or her age, that this defendant whose case they are considering might require a sentence of, or in excess of, two years or, alternatively, whether although the sentence might be less than two years, there is some unusual feature of the case which justifies declining jurisdiction, bearing in mind that the absence of a power to impose a detention and training order because the defendant is under 15 is not an unusual feature.

In *W v Warrington Magistrates' Court* (2009),[145] W (aged 13 at the time of the offences) applied for judicial review of the decision by the district judge at Warrington Youth Court not to commit him for trial to the Crown Court on charges of attempted rape of an 8-year-old and sexual assault of a 5-year-old and a 13-year-old. It was held that the district judge had correctly exercised his discretion under s 24 Magistrates' Court Act (MCA) to summarily try the (by then) 14-year-old youth at the Youth Court, where both the attempted rape and sexual assault cases were tried. W was found guilty of all four offences and was subsequently sentenced in the Crown Court to imprisonment for public protection (IPP) with a minimum term of two years for the attempted rape, and 12 months' imprisonment to run concurrently for each sexual assault. Accordingly, the district judge had been entitled to hear all four charges.

The conviction of two boys aged 10 and 11 for the attempted rape of an eight-year-old girl in May 2010 must rank among the most depressing legal events involving sexual offences by children. Given the new guidelines established in *Re W* (see above) for Youth Courts, it was even more astonishing that the youngest ever defendants tried for rape appeared before a judge and jury at the Old Bailey. The case involving two unnamed boys provoked intense legal debate over whether juveniles should appear in a Crown Court for sexual offences, either as defendants or as witnesses, or whether they were too immature to understand the allegations involved. Philip Johnston, commenting in the *Daily Telegraph*, stated that 'as a nation, we have lost our marbles'.[146]

Saunders J, passing sentence and placing these youngest ever sex offenders on the sex offenders register, conceded that the Old Bailey case would have been dropped if the victim had been an adult, because the evidence the girl gave via videolink was so contradictory. The eight-year-old had told her mother and police that the boys had 'done sex' with her in a field near her home in Hayes, West London, in October 2009. Under cross-examination, she had denied that either boy had raped her, agreeing that they had just been playing a game.[147]

Having discussed the venue of trials of juvenile offenders above, there is no reason why youths charged with grave crimes should not, where appropriate, be tried in the Magistrates' court. This was also the ruling by the ECtHR in *V & T v UK* (Venables and Thompson) (1999),[148] when the Strasbourg court ruled that the Bulger killers had not received a fair trial in contravention of Article 6 ECHR. The ECtHR mentioned *inter alia* that the particular procedures adopted at the Preston Crown Court trial of Thompson and Venables at the time did not cause suffering beyond that inevitably engendered by any attempt to deal with the defendants for the offence in question and therefore Article 3 ECHR was not contravened.

---

145 [2009] EWHC 1538 (Admin) (sub nom 'Re. W')
146 Source: 'Boys branded criminals for attempted rape: what are we doing to our children?', by Philip Johnston, *Daily Telegraph*, 25 May 2010.
147 Source: CPS Press Release, 24 May 2010.
148 (1999) 30 EHRR 121.

However, the ECtHR held that the young defendants had not received a fair trial in contravention of Article 6 because of the intense media and public interest prior to the trial, the obvious media and public presence in court during the trial and because insufficient adjustments had been made to the Crown Court trial procedure to enable the defendants to participate fully in the trial bearing in mind their ages, level of maturity and intellectual and emotional capacity. The ECtHR did not rule that youth trials in the UK in the Crown Court were unfair per se. As a consequence of the decision, Lord Bingham LCJ issued a Practice Direction addressing the arrangements which should be made for the trial of children in the Crown Court.[149]

In practice, it is then for the Crown Court judge to determine whether to conduct the trial in private and to what extent the media should be allowed to attend the proceedings (see: **R v Devizes Youth Court ex parte A and others** (2000);[150] **R (on the application of C and Another) v Sheffield Youth Court & Another** (2003[151]).

In **CPS v Newcastle-Upon-Tyne Youth Court** (2010),[152] the High Court in Leeds was asked to decide whether the decision by District Judge Earle – made on 21 April 2010 before the Newcastle-upon-Tyne Youth Court – to retain jurisdiction in the Youth Court in respect of rape charges of a young defendant known only as MP was correct. MP was nearly 18 at the time of the offence of rape (on 25 March 2010). MP had had a relationship with the victim during the course of which she fell pregnant. She then commenced a relationship with another young man. In due course she came to give birth but the child was prematurely born at 16 weeks. The child subsequently died. MP visited the victim in hospital in order – so he said – to keep a vigil at the cotside of his dying child. Though the victim said that she was tired, he pulled her out of bed and made her sit beside her child. She went to sleep and when she woke up she had been the victim of intercourse to which she had not consented. The only obvious person who might have done that was MP, who denied having had anything to do with such an event. He did not claim that the sex had been consensual. Forensic examination resulted in a vaginal swab showing that it was his DNA in semen within the victim.

The District Judge was faced not only with the rape allegation but also that MP had attempted to intimidate the new partner of the victim, and so was facing a charge of witness intimidation too. District Judge Earle had to decide whether to keep the trial in the Youth Court or to commit the offender to the Crown Court.[153] Consulting the sentencing guidelines and s 91 Children and Young Persons Act 1933,[154] Earle J considered whether the Youth Court sentencing provisions were adequate enough for the grave crime of rape.[155] The district judge decided to accept the s 91 provisions, accepting the summary judgment of Leveson J in the Divisional Court in **Re R**[156] (see above). Agreeing with the original District Judge (Earle J) in the **Newcastle-Upon-Tyne Youth Court** case, Lord Justice Munby dismissed the application for judicial review, ordering the immediate sentencing of the convicted young rapist.

5.3.4 Youth proceedings in Scotland

Unlike in England – where the age of criminal responsibility is 10 – Scotland raised the age to 12 in 2009.[157] Young persons under the age of 16 concerned in criminal or Children's Hearing

See below 5.3.5 proceedings, or linked adults, will normally never be named or identified in the Scottish media.

---

149 See: Practice Direction: Crown Court: Trial of Children and Young Persons (2000); see also: Archbold 4-96a.
150 (2000) 164 JP 330 (unreported).
151 [2003] EWHC 35 (Admin) 23 January 2003.
152 [2010] EWHC 2773 (Admin) 23 July 2010.
153 Pursuant to s 24(1) Magistrates' Courts Act 1980.
154 Section 91 reads: 'Offenders under 18 convicted of certain serious offences: power to detain for specified period'.
155 Subsection (1) provides for a person aged under 18, convicted on indictment (including rape) with imprisonment for 14 years or more.
156 [2005] 2 Cr App R 30.
157 See: s 52 Criminal Justice and Licensing (Scotland Act) 2010. In March 2009, Scottish Justice Secretary Kenny MacAskill announced to the Holyrood Parliament in Edinburgh that the age of criminal responsibility would be raised from 8 to 12.

Since the establishment of the Children's Hearing System (CHS) in Scotland in 1971, following the publication of the Kilbrandon Report, the welfare of the child has been central to the operation of Scotland's youth justice system (see below). The Children's Hearings (Scotland) Act 2011 continues this principle. The CHS provides for panels of volunteers to meet with children who have committed offences, or who have been victims of neglect or abuse, to attempt to find solutions.

With regard to reporting restrictions, Scots law differs from English law in that there are generally no reporting restrictions for young persons over the age of 16.[158] Similar to the s 39 order in English and Welsh courts, a s 47 order is made in Scotland, prohibiting the media from naming the child and any persons or information leading to the identification of that child. The Aberdeen-based *Press and Journal* was acquitted of contempt of court for reporting on (then) 15-year-old Luke Mitchell, who had been arrested by the police, suspected of the murder of his 14-year-old girlfriend Jodi Jones in April 2003. Mitchell was jailed for life and ordered to serve at least 20 years for the killing of Jodi in Dalkeith, Midlothian. Mitchell (now 23) continued to protest his innocence, with his original appeal against the murder conviction rejected by senior judges in Scotland in 2008.[159] Mitchell's UK Supreme Court application was overturned in 2011,[160] with the case declared to be 'closed'.

Reporting restrictions for young persons under the age of 16 can be lifted under s 47 Criminal Procedure (Scotland) Act 1995 if a judge believes that the matter is in the public interest; in certain high-profile cases this has to be confirmed by the First Minister. The Sudden Deaths Inquiry (Scotland) Act 1976 states that no one under the age of 17 can be named in fatal accident inquiries. In Scotland the Procurator Fiscal is the public official responsible for the investigation of all sudden suspicious and unexplained deaths. Deaths are usually reported to the Procurator Fiscal by the police, a doctor or the Registrar of Births, Deaths and Marriages. Such inquiries are overseen by the Procurator Fiscal, who also decides whether there is a need for a criminal prosecution, or if a Fatal Accident Inquiry should be held under the 1976 Act.

5.3.5 The Scottish Children's Hearing system

The Social Work (Scotland) Act 1968 abolished youth courts following the recommendations of the Kilbrandon Report of 1961.[161] Lord Kilbrandon wrote that the then Secretary of State for Scotland ought to 'consider the provisions of the law of Scotland relating to the treatment of juvenile delinquents and juveniles in need of care or protection or beyond parental control'.[162] It had been the primary conclusion of the Kilbrandon Committee that children who appeared before the criminal courts needed attention from local authorities, rather than the courts, to address their deviant behaviour and that they needed protection rather than state punishment. What followed was the Children's Hearing System (CHS), which has been admired across the world.

The aim of the CHS is to reach consensus about what should happen to stop the child reoffending (or truanting etc.).[163] The child and parent or guardian have to agree to a specific order

---

158 Section 46 Children and Young Persons (Scotland) Act 1937.

159 Source: 'Killer Luke Mitchell in latest bid to overturn Jodi Jones murder conviction', TV Documentary by STV, Edinburgh, 20 July 2012.

160 The Scotland Act 1998 creates a limited right of review for the Supreme Court in relation to criminal cases in which a devolution issue arises because it is said that an act which is or would be incompatible with Community law or any of the Convention rights is proposed or is alleged to have occurred, or that legislation which the court is asked to apply is outside the legislative competence of the Scottish Parliament. See also: *AXA General Insurance Limited and others v The Lord Advocate and others* [2011] UKSC 46.

161 See: Kilbrandon (1964).

162 Kilbrandon (1971), p. 128.

163 For a proposed reform of the Scottish Children's Hearing system see: Scottish Children's Reporter Administration (2012) Reforming Scots Criminal Law and Practice: The Carloway Report.

and this has to be done by way of a 'voluntary disposal'. The Hearing may decide that no compulsory measures of care are required but they may place the child under a supervision or non-residential or residential supervision order. There is the right of appeal against the CHS decision to a Sheriff within 21 days. Where a young person is involved in incest or a sexual offences case, probably involving one or more adults, the media must follow the same rules that apply for children under the age of 16 in that no identification must take place. It is common practice for the Scottish media to report that 'a serious offence against a child' has been committed, rather than mentioning anything about 'incest'.

The CHS began operating fully in 1971. The ethos of the Social Work (Scotland) Act 1968 had been that a child could be prosecuted for an offence only on the instructions of the Lord Advocate, and that no court, other than the High Court of Justiciary and possibly a Sheriff Court, would have jurisdiction over a child for an offence. The Children (Scotland) Act 1995 represented the first major reform of Scottish childcare law but largely preserved the Children's Hearing System set up under the 1968 Act; the 1995 Act merely made some procedural alterations and specified the grounds of referral for a deviant child to a 'Hearing' via a local authority Children's Panel.[164] This meant that each local authority became responsible for Children's Hearings and Children's Panels, staffed largely by volunteers and appointed by the First Minister on the advice of the area's Children's Panel Advisory Committee. The Children (Scotland) Act 1995 also specified the grounds for referral to a Children's Reporter.[165]

Reporters are independent local officials who act as 'gatekeepers' to the CHS. The Reporter works for the Scottish Children's Reporter's Administration (SCRA) and it is his or her duty to look into the child's background, with information mainly from social workers, before taking any action. Anyone, including parents, teachers and social workers, can refer a deviant child to a Reporter if they think that the child may be in need of 'compulsory measures' of care. Grounds for referral may include that the child may have been abused physically or sexually, played truant from school, offended, been a victim of an offence or bullying, misused drugs or alcohol or been outside parental control.

In early 2012, Aileen Campbell MSP, Minister for Children and Young People, announced in the Scottish Parliament that she intended to modernize the CHS; that it should be 'fit for purpose' for the future and that children's welfare should remain at the heart of Scottish justice policy. However, major changes to the running of the CHS system were delayed until late 2013, promised under the Children's Hearings (Scotland) Act 2011.[166]

The number of children and young people referred to Children's Hearings in 2011/12 was 31,593 compared to 39,217 in 2010/11. Despite this drop, this is still 3.5 per cent of the Scottish child population. The vast majority of children and young people who are referred to the Reporter have concerns about their welfare. In 2011/12, 28,017 children were referred on care and protection grounds, while 5,604 were referred on offence grounds (these figures include 2,028 children who were referred on both grounds). The two most common grounds for referral to a CHS are that the child was a 'victim of a Schedule 1 offence'[167] (13,151 children) and lack of parental care (11,194 children). In 2011/12, 40,708 Hearings were held for 18,836 children. This is a drop of 2.7 per cent from 2010/11 (41,825 Hearings). The most common age for children referred on

---

164 Section 44(1) Criminal Procedure (Scotland) Act 1995 states that if a child who is under the supervision of the Children's Hearing System is found guilty of, or pleads guilty to, an offence in the High Court, then the court has the option of asking for a hearing to advise them as to disposal. If this occurs in the Sheriff Court then a Hearing must advise on disposal.

165 Sections 52(2)(a) to (l) and ss 52(2)(i) are concerned with a child who 'has committed an offence' while (j) and (k) are concerned with children involved in alcohol, drugs or substance abuse.

166 Source: 'Children's Hearings reforms delayed to next summer', by Stephen Naysmith, The Herald Scotland, 27 April 2012.

167 Schedule 1 Criminal Procedure (Scotland) Act 1995, 'offences against children under the age of 17 to which special provisions apply'. For example s 18 Sexual Offences (Scotland) Act 2009 (rape of a young child) or s 28 (having intercourse with an older child).

care and protection grounds, was 14 years, followed by those aged under one year. The most common age for children referred on offence grounds was 15 years.[168]

Today the CHS has an annual budget of around £4.5 million and it is expected that new arrangements for managing Scotland's 2,700 volunteer children's panel members will be reformed to shape new national standards for the Children's Panel System, quasi-legal hearings which look to find solutions to problems faced by troubled and vulnerable children. The 2011 Act was intended to improve training and communication within the system and bring it into line with European law.

5.3.6 Open justice in family courts

The family justice system deals with the failure of families, of parenting and of relationships, often involving anger, violence, abuse, drugs and alcohol. The decisions taken by local authorities and courts have fundamental long-term consequences for children, parents and for society generally. Proceedings in family courts have long been under close scrutiny and have presented heated debates regarding in in camera proceedings. Family lawyers and (mainly fathers') pressure groups have argued about whether this type of jurisdiction, such as wardship proceedings, should not be held in open court.[169] However, the Children, Schools and Families Act 2010 poses continued problems with its large number of exceptions and restrictions, often too complex for media editors to challenge. The 2010 Act provides magistrates and judges with extensive powers, preventing or limiting open family court access and limiting reporting in such cases in order to protect the 'welfare of the child'.

Family courts make far-reaching decisions, such as whether children should be taken into care or put up for adoption or given contact with parents who are divorcing. They also decide on custody and how finances should be split. Under youth court rules, it is unlawful to publish anything that would identify a minor (under 18) involved in a case, but it is possible to identify adults such as social workers and doctors. Dame Elizabeth Butler-Sloss P summarized in **Clibbery v Allan** (2002)[170] the effect of general procedures in family proceedings:

> . . . with the exception of wardship and certain declarations in medical cases heard in the High Court, the jurisdiction of the High Court Family Division and of the County Courts and Family Court jurisdiction, whether public or private, remains based on statute and regulated by the statutory framework. The hearing of cases is divided into those which are heard in open court and those heard in chambers. The way in which those cases are heard are regulated by rules and not by custom. In all cases, except adoption which has its separate Adoption Rules 1984, the Family Proceedings Rules 1991 direct the court and the parties to the procedure to be adopted and the way in which the case is to be heard.[171]

As far as publicity and disclosure are concerned, s 12(1) of the Administration of Justice Act 1960[172] treats children's cases as an exception to the general rule relating to the publication of court proceedings. Breach of the strict reporting restrictions is a contempt of court.

With the 2010 Act there has been greater public access to family courts, though it is fair to say that the procedure to decide whether a court can be held in public with free media access still

---

168 Source: Scottish Children's Reporter Administration, Official Statistics 2011/12, 5 July 2012 at: www.scra.gov.uk/home/official_statistics_2011_12.cfm.
169 For further discussion see: Herring (2011).
170 [2002] Fam 261.
171 Ibid., at para 43 (Dame Elizabeth Butler-Sloss P).
172 As substituted by s 108(5) of, and Schedule 13 paragraph 14.2, of the Children Act 1989.

remains under the discretion of the presiding magistrate or judge. Divorce proceedings remain generally open to the public as established in **Scott v Scott** (1913)[173] (upheld in **Argyll v Argyll** (1967)[174]).

When Heather Mills applied for her and Sir Paul McCartney's divorce proceedings to be heard in private, Mr Justice Bennett ruled against the application (citing **Scott v Scott**), making the full divorce settlement available online. The Mills v McCartney divorce judgment of 18 March 2008 revealed that Sir Paul had been ordered to pay his former wife a lump sum settlement of £16.5 million.[175] However, the custody and ward proceedings concerning their child Beatrice were subsequently held in private, in spite of the media's application for open reporting.

See Chapters
2.5 and 2.8

The continuing absence of any general right to privacy in English law has already been discussed and, likewise, the outer limits of freedom of expression. So that leaves us with an assortment of statutory, common law and equitable rules and ongoing disputes between media pressure and an individual's claim to his or her privacy, particularly acute in family courts.

See above 5.3.1

The privacy of minors has already been discussed in that s 39 of the Children and Young Persons Act 1933 prioritizes and supports the welfare principle.[176] Coupled with parental responsibility under ss 1 and 3 of the Children Act 1989, and the common law duty of confidentiality regarding children and young persons (under 18), courts can still determine questions relating to the welfare of a minor arising from a proposed exercise of parental responsibility[177] and the minor's welfare by virtue of s 1(1) Children Act 1989.[178]

See also
Chapter 2.5

The court recognized the strict limitations of a parent's right to waive a child's right to privacy in **Re Z** (1996).[179] This case concerned a child who was attending a special educational institution; a TV company wanted to broadcast the child's treatment with the permission of the mother. The decision of Z's mother to waive her daughter's right to confidentiality and seek publicity for Z's treatment and education was an example of 'parental responsibility' under s 3(1) of the Children Act 1989. But the family court made a s 8 'prohibited steps order',[180] which enabled the court to act under the welfare principle, preventing the exercise of parental responsibility.

The Court of Appeal unanimously held in **Re Z** that the publicity and TV broadcast would damage Z's well-being and future progress, justifying the s 8 order. The court also refused to allow the TV broadcast to go ahead, thereby recognizing the child's own right to privacy under Article 8 ECHR in spite of the fact that her mother had argued that the broadcast was 'in the public interest' (see also: **Re KD (A Minor) (Ward: Termination of Access)** (1988);[181] **Re W (A Minor) (Wardship: Restrictions on Publication)** (1992);[182] **Re M & N (Minors) (Wardship: Publication of Information)** (1990)[183]).

Changes brought about by Part 2 of the Children, Schools and Families Act 2010 have created a more open and visible justice system in the previously closed family courts by allowing the media

---

173 As per Viscount Haldane: 'There it may well be that justice could not be done at all if it had to be done in public. As the paramount object must always be to do justice, the general rule as to publicity, after all only the means to an end, must accordingly yield.' (**Scott v Scott** [1913] AC 417 at 35).

174 [1967] Ch 301.

175 Source: 'Sir Paul McCartney and Heather Mills divorce: Judge's full ruling to be made public', by Caroline Gammell and Matthew Moore, *Daily Telegraph*, 18 March 2008.

176 For further discussion see: Johnson (2006).

177 'Responsibility' under s 3(1) Children Act 1989; under s 10(1)(b) of the 1989 Act, the court can make a 'section 8' order even though no application for such an order has been made to the court.

178 For further discussion see: Ormerod (1995).

179 **Re Z (A Minor) (Identification: Restrictions on Publication)** [1996] 2 FCR 164 (CA).

180 Under s 8(1) Children Act 1989.

181 [1988] FCR 657 (Lord Oliver).

182 [1992] 1 WLR 100.

183 [1990] Fam 211, in which a local newspaper intended to publish a story concerning the removal by a local authority of two wards from a long-term foster home without explanation. The Court of Appeal accepted that there was a clear public interest in knowing more of why the decision to remove had been taken and implemented in this manner. But the welfare of the children dictated that the identity of the children, their previous foster parents, the new foster parents, the parents, the schools and any relevant addresses should not be published.

access to ensure accountability through professional and public scrutiny of court decisions and thereby increase public confidence in the way the family courts work. Part 2, s 13 ('Authorised news publication') of the 2010 Act states:

(1)   A publication of information is an authorised news publication if the following conditions are met.
(2)   Condition 1 is that the information was obtained by an accredited news representative by observing or listening to the proceedings when attending them in exercise of a right conferred on accredited news representatives by rules of court.
(3)   Condition 2 is that the publisher of the information –

    (a)   is the accredited news representative,
    (b)   publishes the information with the consent of, or pursuant to a contract or other agreement entered into with, that representative, or
    (c)   has obtained the information from a publication of information which is an authorised news publication.

In addition, the ruling in **Clayton v Clayton**[184] (see below) was reversed. This enabled anonymity to be waived at the end of a case, replacing it by lifelong anonymity – for both parents and children, not just the child alone as before.

Simon Clayton, at the time of this landmark family court case, was a 47-year-old bookseller from Hay-on-Wye. In 2003, he astonished locals in the Welsh border town by abducting his seven-year-old daughter, days ahead of his divorce hearing, fearing he would lose custody to his wife. He was tracked down to Portugal and brought home under arrest, after which he fought a lengthy custody battle. When his case was concluded, Mr Clayton found he was legally barred from offering a public explanation for what he had done. In 2006 the CA reached a landmark ruling that a parent should be allowed to identify himself and his child and tell his story to the press or in his own publication. The court ruled that a parent's right to freedom of expression was greater than the child's right to privacy.

❖ **KEY CASE** *Clayton v Clayton* **[2006] EWCA Civ 878 (CA Civ Div)**

Precedent

❖ When making a 'Prohibited Steps Order' under s 8 of the Children Act 1989, the court must balance the child's welfare and privacy right under Article 8 ECHR and the freedom of expression under Article 10 ECHR of the applicant parent/guardian and the media organization in their application for a restraining order to be lifted.
❖ The child's ECHR rights need to be protected against disproportionate interference from inappropriate parental action; but
❖ A parent's right to freedom of expression may be greater than a child's right to privacy.

Facts

Mr and Mrs Clayton were married in 1997 but separated in 2000. They shared custody of their child, C. The father abducted the child and took her to Portugal. Ultimately the child

---

184 [2006] EWCA Civ 878 (CA (Civ Div)).

was returned to the mother, and the father served nine months' imprisonment for illegal child abduction. He was permitted to resume contact with his child on release. The parents eventually reached an amicable 'share care' agreement, approved by the family court.

Mr Clayton ('the father') wanted to publish a book about his experiences and to promote the idea of non-court-based 'shared-care' arrangements between the parents. Controversially he also wanted to take his daughter back to Portugal to make a video-diary about the abduction for a TV programme. His wider agenda was to alert the public as to how the courts dealt with the issues relating to family court proceedings and children when parents separated or divorced. Hedley J granted an injunction preventing the father until his child was 18 'from discussing or otherwise communicating any matter relating to the education, maintenance, financial circumstances or family circumstances of C'. The father sought to discharge the injunction to enable him to identify his daughter ('the child') as part of his publicity plans.

Mr Clayton had campaigned for better and more open family justice and for several organizations hoping to bring about change to the family law. But because of the injunction in place he could not refer to his own experiences in the family justice system. For example, he wanted to take issue with the President's opinion published in *The Times* of 31 January 2006 that a 50:50 contact regime for a child is 'simply not practicable', and could only cogently do so by reference to his own experience. In particular Mr Clayton wanted to campaign for equal sharing of tax credits and child benefit where there is shared parenting.

Decision
The Court of Appeal held in *Clayton* that s 97 Children Act 1989 posed a restriction on the right of free expression under Article 10 ECHR in that s 97(2) prohibits publication of material likely to identify 'any child as being involved in any proceedings'. In short, the injunction prevented the father being as politically active as he wanted to because he believed that the most effective lobbying, comments or campaigning involved discussion of the human aspects of his individual case, both positive (the outcome) and negative (the delay, and what he sees as a systemic tendency for parties to fight for court orders, instead of drawing up their own solutions).

The CA ruled that the criminal offence inherent in s 97 of the Children Act 1989 applied only to the naming of the child while the proceedings were active and did not apply once they had been concluded. The court took the view that as a penal provision which restricted freedom of speech and bearing in mind the strictures of s 3 Human Rights Act 1998, the provision should be interpreted narrowly and only apply while the proceedings were active.

The father's appeal against the injunction, preventing him from publishing matters concerning his daughter, was allowed and the injunction quashed, replaced by a s 8 'Prohibited Steps Order', to protect C's welfare in this context as well as her Article 8 rights – which outweighed the appellant's right to freedom of speech and expression.

Analysis
The issue before the court in *Clayton* was to what extent the father could put in the public domain information about the marital dispute and the custody proceedings concerning

their child covered by s 97(2) Children Act 1989, which had been held in the family court in private. Another hurdle was s12 Administration of Justice Act 1960, which prohibited the publication of information relating to court proceedings and, if published, would amount to contempt of court.

The case raises in acute form the purpose and function of long-term injunctions under s 8 of the Children Act 1989 and the circumstances in which a litigant finds himself when restrained by such an injunction ('a section 8 order'). The order states precisely what they can and cannot say and to whom. A s 8 order seeks to ensure that (1) that freedom of expression is not unnecessarily or inappropriately restricted; and (2) that the important issues raised by individual cases both enjoy the widest possible dissemination and are the subject of fully informed public debate.

Clayton is a good example of a major dilemma which often faces family court judges and magistrates, namely when is it 'necessary' to make a s 8 order? When should a court restrict certain aspects of parental behaviour? This then challenges the parents' freedom of expression. Lord Justice Wall opined in this case that open justice in family jurisdiction ought to be promoted for three most compelling reasons;[185] these were:

(1) to enable informed and proper public scrutiny of the administration of (family) justice;
(2) to facilitate informed public knowledge, understanding and discussion of the important social, medical and ethical issues which are litigated in the family justice system;
(3) ... to facilitate the dissemination of information useful to other professions and organizations in the multi-disciplinary working of family law.[186]

The media were rightly interested in this case, more so because Mr Clayton had proved to be a potentially excellent spokesperson for the cause; he had a particularly clear-cut case for a share in benefits (tax credits) and a good case for greater open access to family courts and his own child.

Clayton is an important case as it clarifies the issues surrounding privacy in family court proceedings under the Children Act 1989, Administration of Justice Act 1960 and the Human Rights Act 1998. The President of the Family Division, Sir Mark Potter P, set out new guidance on the restriction that can be placed on reporting after the conclusion of proceedings.[187]

So, have the family court reforms gone far enough? Changes in legislation were regarded as a great victory by fathers' pressure groups, such as 'Fathers for Justice', who had campaigned for years to open up the closed, secretive world of the family courts. However, journalists would argue that the opening up of the family courts is pointless unless changes to allow the identification of all adults in such proceedings are made. The family justice system still faces immense stresses and difficulties. Some apply only in public law; others are more systemic. The motivation for the opening of the family courts was a call for greater transparency and to counter accusations of secret justice,

185 Also expressed in: Wall (1995).
186 [2006] EWCA Civ 878 at para 85 (Wall LJ).
187 Ibid., at paras 77–78.

particularly in care proceedings, which are often seen as demonstrating the state's power to remove children from their parents' care.

Following the **Clayton** ruling in 2006, the Ministry of Justice issued a consultation document to address issues such as the speeding up of the family courts system, ensuring that the voices of children and young people were heard, and to improve judicial leadership by changing the judicial culture in family court proceedings.[188] The outcome was increased open access to the family courts and a parent's right to freedom of expression. There followed the case of **Re Child X**.

❖ **KEY CASE**   *Re Child X* (2009)[189]

Precedent

❖ A party applying for the exclusion of accredited media representatives from family proceedings held in private has to satisfy the court that exclusion is *necessary* in the interests of the child involved.

❖ It is incumbent on an applicant applying for exclusion *ab initio* to raise the matter with the court *prior* to the hearing for consideration of the need to notify the media in advance of the proposed application.

❖ Where temporary exclusion of the public (and media) during proceedings is sought, it is for the hearing judge to balance the competing rights under Articles 8 and 10 ECHR, inviting media representations as necessary.

Facts

The matter concerned ongoing proceedings about residence and contact in relation to X, the young daughter of the applicant celebrity father. The proceedings began in 2007 in the county court and, throughout, the parties gave an undertaking not to disclose information about the proceedings to the press. There were concerns about the impact on the child expressed at directions hearing in December 2008. Up to then the proceedings had been heard in private, but the media applied to attend and report on future hearings in the case.[190]

Decision

In his judgment, the President, Sir Mark Potter, reviewed the history and substance of new rule 10.28 (4) of the Family Proceedings (Amendment No 2) Rules 2009, together with the interaction of s 12 of the Administration of Justice Act 1960 and the ECHR. He concluded that the exclusion of the media was appropriate for this and any future hearing. Potter P made several observations about the procedure for making applications and informing the press and the basis of the *contra mundum* order; he observed that:

> . . . private law family cases concerning the children of celebrities are no different in principle from those involving the children of anyone else. An application by a celeb-rity who happens also to be a parent who is unable to agree with a former spouse or partner over the appropriate arrangements for their child(ren) is not governed by any

---

188 See: Ministry of Justice (2011b) *Family Justice Review*. Final Report. November 2011. www.justice.gov.uk/downloads/ publications/moj/2011/family-justice-review-final-report.pdf.

189 **Re Child X (Residence and Contact – Rights of media attendance)** [2009] EWHC 1728 of 14 Jul 2009 (Fam).

190 Pursuant to amendments to the Family Proceedings Rules 1991 by The Family Proceedings (Amendment No 2) Rules 2009. See: Rule 10.28(4) Family Proceedings (Amendment No 2) Rules 2009.

principle or assumption more favourable to the privacy of the celebrity than that applied to any other parent caught up in the court process.[191]

Granting the *contra mundum* application, Sir Mark Potter stated that cases involving children of celebrities are no different from those involving any other children. But the need for the child's protection under Article 8 ECHR would undeniably be more intense. The President gave important guidance about the procedure to be adopted in cases where parties know that they are to apply for exclusion of the media:

> . . . I consider that para 6.4 of the Practice Direction of 20 April 2009 should be read as if there were added at the end of the final sentence in that paragraph the words 'and should do so by means of the Press Association Copy Direct service, following the procedure set out in the Official Solicitor/CAFCASS Practice Note dated 18 March 2005'.[192]

Sir Mark Potter also said that such proceedings should follow the general principles mentioned by Lord Mustill in *Re D* (1996).[193] The total anonymity order under s 97(2) Children Act 1989 was upheld.

Analysis

The Family Court's decision to exclude the media in *Re Child X* was based on a number of unusual features and therefore possibly unlikely to apply to most other cases involving children. Crucial here was the medical and psychiatric evidence relating to the vulnerability of that child and the likely adverse impact of a media presence on Child X's welfare. There was said to be considerable foreign media interest in the case, which gave rise to a real concern as to how reporting of the details of the case could be prevented. Also significant was the question of duties of confidence on the part of medical and other experts who had not warned the parties and witnesses that their evidence was likely to be heard in the presence of media representatives.

Re Child X concerned a judgment by the President of the Family Court Division about media access to residence and contact proceedings involving celebrities. The Court decided that the existing *contra mundum* order (excluding all the media) should be upheld and that the s 97 order under the Children Act 1989 should continue until the end of the proceedings. However, at the closure of the proceedings the President made an *obiter* comment that family courts should always reconsider the discontinuation of a s 97 (lifelong anonymity) order, balancing this against an order on Article 8 ECHR grounds instead.

The precedent set in this case was for family courts to decide when the media should be excluded from such proceedings. It was held by the President that a court should always consider the grounds for exclusion carefully and whether they should override the media's presumptive right to be present. Furthermore, it was held that the court must have regard to whether the press's interests lie in reporting on matters which may well be the object of interest and curiosity but which are confidential or private and do not involve matters of public concern.

---

191 **Re Child X (Residence and Contact – Rights of media attendance)** [2009] EWHC 1728 at para 11 (Sir Mark Potter P).
192 Ibid. at paras 78–81 (Sir Mark Potter P).
193 **Re D (Minors) (Adoption Reports: Confidentiality)** [1996] AC 593 (Lord Mustill).

The outcome of **Re Child X** was that the media were deprived of the opportunity to see any informative material upon which to base any decision about seeking an application to vary or discharge the order – which, in reporting terms, would not make good copy.

Since the changes were brought in under the Children, Schools and Families Act 2010, it appears that the media has not widely used the new access to family court hearings because so many different layers of legislation have left reporters and editors unclear about what they can and cannot report. Reporting restrictions – particularly under existing youth justice legislation coupled with provisions under the Children Act 1989 – appear more complex than before and guidance from the courts remains unclear.

For these reasons, the media has adopted a cautious approach to reporting on family proceedings and matters involving children. Journalists appear not to be interested in regularly attending family hearings, given the complex reporting restrictions inherent in the 2010 Act (already complicated by virtue of s12 Administration of Justice Act 1960). Family matters, such as divorce or wardship proceedings, take many months and sometimes years to conclude and the press is often unable to attend the many hearings that take place. Additionally, the media is often unaware which hearings are of particular interest. For example, which hearings are likely to unveil details of financial arrangements? Which are simply directional hearings, where open access to documents in a case is restricted anyway?

The only group that has so far benefited from the 2010 legislation appears to be lawyers, instructed to deal with the complex (media) applications and their appeals against *contra mundum* (restraining) orders. That said, there is no doubt that family courts have granted greater access to the media. A judge is now required to engage in a 'proportionality' balancing exercise between the Article 10 rights of the press (and parental applicants) and the Article 8 rights of the child. The factors are then to be weighed in the balance as applicable to particular circumstances of each case. The judge can invite media representations before giving brief reasons for his/her decision.

 FOR THOUGHT

The Children, Schools and Families Act 2010 aimed to clarify what the media can and cannot report on in family cases. Has this law reform increased public confidence in the family court system by making it more visible?

5.4 Special anonymity orders and restrictions

Many witnesses of all ages experience stress and fear during the police and CPS investigatory process. In order to reduce worries and difficulties about giving evidence at court because of possible witness intimidation, the Youth Justice and Criminal Evidence Act 1999 (YJCEA) introduced a range of measures that can be used to facilitate the gathering and giving of evidence by vulnerable and intimidated witnesses. These measures are known as 'special measures', and are subject to the discretion of the court. Different presumptions apply to different categories of witnesses.

See above 5.2.3

There is a long-established principle that, subject to certain exceptions and statutory qualifications, the defendant in a criminal trial is entitled to be confronted by his accuser in court. Courts should only grant an application for an anonymity order (for either the defendant or the witness in a case) after full consideration of all the available alternatives.[194] Some cases may be at an early stage of investigation; in others, the question of anonymity may first come to the attention of the Crown Prosecution Service after the charge. Crown prosecutors must ensure that proper consideration is given to the questions of witness anonymity at the most appropriate time and in a way that does not inhibit the effective progress of the case.

When an application is made to protect the defendant's anonymity, magistrates and judges have to strike a balance under Article 6 ECHR between protecting the defendant's rights to a fair trial and ensuring that his life and safety is protected and that justice will be seen to be done in open court by virtue of Article 10 ECHR.

5.4.1 Lifelong anonymity orders

The possibility of lifelong anonymity orders for child killers has already been highlighted above but warrants further discussion. The issue was first raised in the 'Mary Bell' case (**Re X** (1985)[195]), where a lifelong injunction was sought on behalf of the claimant and her daughter. Mary Bell was convicted of manslaughter by diminished responsibility on 17 December 1968 at Newcastle Assizes for killing two boys aged three and four. Her accomplice, known as 'Norma', aged 13, was acquitted. Mr Justice Cusack described Mary as 'dangerous' and sentenced her to be detained in secure accommodation at Her Majesty's Pleasure. After conviction, her name was released to the public, resulting in permanent media interest and applications to lift reporting restrictions.

After conviction Mary ('X') spent 12 years in secure units, young offender institutions and subsequently prison, during which time her mother repeatedly sold stories about her to the press. Mary Bell was released in 1980 and given a new identity.

There were three major periods when X's identity and whereabouts were either discovered or at risk of discovery by the media. The first was after she formed a settled relationship with a man (the second defendant in **Re X**), and gave birth to Y on 25 May 1984. Child Y was made a ward of court five days later, granted anonymity until her 18th birthday. In July 1984, the *News of the World* became aware of the birth and an injunction was granted by Balcombe J in **Re X** (1985).[196] It is believed that Bell's daughter did not know her mother's identity until it was revealed by reporters.

When Y reached 18, X and Y applied for a lifelong anonymity order at the family court.[197] Granting the lifelong anonymity order on 21 May 2003, Dame Elizabeth Butler-Sloss P made an injunctive order preventing the disclosure of their identities, addresses and other information that might identify them for life (see: **Re X (a woman formerly known as Mary Bell) and others v O'Brien and others** (2003)[198]). Claimants X and Y had argued, *inter alia*, that there was a serious risk that their Article 8 rights would be breached if the *contra mundum* injunctions were not granted. The President opined that there had been exceptional circumstances in young Mary Bell's case, including her age at the time (10), the length of time that had elapsed since the offences were committed, the need to support Mary's rehabilitation, the adverse affect of publicity on rehabilitation and X's mental state. Dame Elizabeth said that Y's life and future well-being was inextricably linked with that of her mother (X) and that it was not possible to treat them separately. The defendants, who were Y's father and two newspaper publishers, did not oppose the applications. The President of the Family Division said that the relief sought by X and Y was not to be taken as a broadening of the principles of the

---

194 Section 88 Coroners and Justice Act 2009 provides guidelines in such cases.
195 **X CC v A** [1985] 1 All ER 53 (sub nom '**Re X (a minor) (wardship injunction – a woman formerly known as Mary Bell**').
196 [1985] All ER 53.
197 For further insight into the original trial and Mary's development see: Sereny (1998).
198 [2003] EWHC 1101 (Dame Elizabeth Butler-Sloss P).

law of confidence nor an increase in the pool of those who might in the future be granted protection against potential breaches of confidence – and that such cases would remain 'exceptional'.[199]

Following Dame Elizabeth Butler-Sloss's judgment in both the **Venables and Thompson**[200] and **Mary Bell (Re X)** rulings, it was then somewhat surprising that Mr Justice Eady granted a lifelong injunction (contra mundum) to protect Maxine Carr – then aged 27 – on 24 February 2005.[201] Carr had served 21 months in prison, being convicted in December 2003 of conspiring to pervert the course of justice. She had provided school caretaker Ian Huntley with a false alibi after he murdered Holly Wells and Jessica Chapman, both aged 10, in 2002 ('the Soham killings'). On her release Carr became one of just four former UK prisoners to be given secret identities, along with child killer Mary Bell and James Bulger's murderers Robert Thompson and Jon Venables.

The '**Maxine Carr**' order banned publication of any details that could reveal Ms Carr's new identity, including any description of where she resided or the nature of her work. Eady J ruled that the contra mundum order was 'necessary' in order to protect Carr's 'life and limb and psychological health'. Eady J said:

> There is a good deal of evidence before me which shows that there has been a continuing interest in the subject of the applicant and the circumstances in which she is now living. If the injunction were to be refused, the task of the police and the probation service would become much more difficult, if not impossible. There is evidence from the claimant herself, from her solicitor, from a senior police officer, from a senior officer of the probation service and from a psychiatrist. For what, I hope, are obvious reasons, I do not propose to go into that evidence. To do so would jeopardise the very object of this application.[202]

The contra mundum order in '**Maxine Carr**' is unusual among those given new identities, as she was not a convicted killer. However, her association with the notorious killer Ian Huntley caused such public revulsion that she too was granted an indefinite anonymity order for her own protection. Responsibility for protecting Maxine Carr remains with the police and the probation service, a costly and challenging task.

It can at times be extraordinarily difficult for a journalist who wants to write a story about, say, Mary Bell, Jon Venables or Maxine Carr, some two decades after their crimes made headlines. How can he check up that a lifelong injunction exists? The legal answer is: if he does publish anything about these persons (who will no doubt have new identities provided by the police) he will be in contempt of court. Editors of newspapers or online editions and broadcasters must therefore be well informed before they allow any photographs or news stories to be published.

There is no doubt that the number of lifelong anonymity orders and superinjunctions is increasing. By their very nature they are unknown and remain difficult for journalists and media editors to check. Some local courts publish statistics, such as the Northern Ireland Court Service, which provided information in respect of the following for the period 1 September 2012 to 30 June 2013:[203]

---

199 **Re X** (2003) EWHC 1101 (QB) at 64 (Dame Elizabeth Butler-Sloss P).
200 **Venables and Thompson v News Group Newspapers Ltd** [2001] Fam 430 (Dame Elizabeth Butler-Sloss P).
201 See: **Carr (Maxine) v News Group Newspapers Ltd and Others** [2005] EWHC 971 (QB).
202 Ibid., at para 5 (Eady J).
203 Source: Northern Ireland Court Service: Integrated Court Operation System (ICOS).

County Court Division	Number of cases in which at least one reporting restriction order was granted[204]	Number of cases in which at least one anonymity order was granted[205]
Belfast	78	1
Londonderry	58	30
Antrim	82	1
Fermanagh and Tyrone	42	0
Armagh and South Down	34	0
Ards	75	0
Craigavon	7	0
High Court[206]	14	26
Total	**390**	**58**

While the statistics are informative they are of limited value to the question: how do we know which reporting restrictions are in place and which anonymity orders relate solely to past criminals or to interim superinjunctions? It is therefore an important reminder that it is necessary for journalists to attend court hearings in order to fulfil their function as public watchdog.

 FOR THOUGHT

Do lifelong anonymity orders (*contra mundum* injunctions) contravene the media's right to freedom of expression? Discuss.

5.4.2 Trials behind courtroom doors: public interest immunity, secret courts and closed material procedures

The openness of judicial proceedings is a fundamental principle enshrined in Article 6(1) ECHR ('right to a fair trial'). In criminal trials the open justice principle underpins the requirement for a prosecution witness to be identified not only to the defendant, but also to the open court. It supports the ability of the defendant to present his case and to test the prosecution case by cross-examination of prosecution witnesses. In some cases it may also encourage other witnesses to come forward, which is often the responsibility of the media to report.

Closed, or in *camera* hearings are not unprecedented. Cases in the family division of the High Court relating to child custody and divorce issues are regularly held in private.

See above 5.3.6

Circumstances may arise in which material held by the prosecution in criminal cases cannot be disclosed to the defence, fully or even at all, without the risk of serious prejudice to an important public interest. The public interest most regularly engaged is that involving the effective investigation and prosecution of serious crime, which may involve resort to informers and undercover

204 Relates to the court order, a Reporting Restrictions Order (REPR), which includes restrictions placed upon the reporting of details relating to a number of matters. The main restrictions are in relation to the identification of a defendant; identification of an injured party; identification of a witness; the address of any party; and reporting restrictions on a court ruling.
205 Relates to the court order, an Anonymity Order Granted (AOG), which includes restrictions placed upon the reporting of details in relation to either the identification of a defendant or a witness.
206 Relates to civil cases with a Special Attention of either (i) Reporting Restriction or (ii) Participant anonymized (for example a minor in a judicial review) and reporting restrictions on criminal appeals to the High Court.

agents, or the use of scientific or operational techniques (such as surveillance) which cannot be disclosed without exposing individuals to the risk of personal injury or jeopardising the success of future operations. In such circumstances some derogation from the golden rule of full disclosure may be justified but such derogation must always be the minimum derogation necessary to protect the public interest in question and must never imperil the overall fairness of the trial.

In such exceptional cases, the courts may adopt total reporting restrictions and hold proceedings in secret to protect vulnerable witnesses such as police informers or the workings and investigations of the UK security services (MI5/MI6). It is a long-established principle that the prosecution should not be required to disclose material which would reveal the identity of an intelligence source unless not to do so might give rise to a miscarriage of justice by denying the defence a legitimate opportunity to cast doubt on the case against them.

The English law of Crown Privilege – which later became Public Interest Immunity (or PII) – was largely developed in civil cases (see: **Duncan v Cammel, Laird & Co.** (1942);[207] **Conway v Rimmer** (1968);[208] **Burmah Oil v Bank of England** (1980);[209] **Air Canada v Secretary of State for Trade (No 2)** (1983)[210]). Public Interest Immunity is a common law rule which has been developed by the courts over a number of years.

Public Interest Immunity is a rule of the law of evidence under which documents may be withheld from parties to legal proceedings when their disclosure would be injurious to the public interest. Certificates or affidavits are made and authorized by a Minster of State (e.g. Home Office or Ministry of Justice), claiming PII. They are generally referred to by the media as 'gagging orders'.

These PII certificates date back to the mid-twentieth century and empower courts to make an order, usually at the request of the Government, preventing disclosure of secrets if their release is deemed damaging to the public interest. Neither side in such cases can rely on the withheld information. In **Duncan v Cammell Laird and Co.**[211] – a wartime case following the *Thetis* submarine disaster in which the documents sought included blueprints of the submarine – the House of Lords unanimously agreed that a court could never question a claim of 'Crown privilege' made in the proper form regardless of the nature of the documents to which it referred. This applied both to the contents of documents and to classes of documents. Ministers of the Crown were to be the sole arbiters of the public interest, and if objection to the production of a document were taken in the proper manner and form by a minister after personal scrutiny, or by the permanent head of the department in the minister's absence, the certificate or affidavit stating that its production would be against the public interest had to be accepted by the court as conclusive. While the House of Lords' decision in **Duncan v Cammell Laird** was not questioned, the legal principles and administrative practices which were sanctioned by the decision in the case attracted considerable criticism in Parliament at the time.

In **Conway v Rimmer**,[212] the HL used the power to depart from its own precedents, which it had granted to itself only in 1966, to override the broader statements in **Duncan v Cammell Laird**. It held that a minister's certificate claiming Public Interest Immunity was not to be regarded as conclusive and that it was for the court to decide where the balance of public interest lies (see also the Scottish case of **Glasgow Corporation v Central Land Board** (1956)[213]).

---

207 [1942] AC 624.
208 [1968] AC 910.
209 [1980] AC 1090.
210 [1983] 2 AC 394.
211 [1942] AC 624.
212 [1968] AC 910.
213 [1956] SC 1 (HL) – when the HL held that the Scottish courts could go behind a minister's certificate and, after weighing private interests against public ones, decide for themselves whether or not a particular item of evidence should attract immunity on public interest grounds.

In the **Burmah Oil** case,[214] Lord Wilberforce observed that even where a claim for immunity from production was based on a level of public interest of the highest importance, that fact by itself was not necessarily conclusive, and the public interest might on occasion prevail against it. This has even been applied where the documents concerned are Cabinet documents, although generally speaking it is likely that the more sensitive the class of document concerned, the greater the degree of respect that is likely to be shown by a court in assessing a claim that it should be withheld.

After the *Attorney General's Guidelines* 1981, disclosure was left largely to the judgment of the prosecuting authorities and the prosecution and only exceptionally did the court make any ruling. Thus the defence were commonly unaware of what had not been disclosed and there was no judicial decision against which a defendant could appeal. In highly sensitive cases the prosecution will apply for a PII certificate where the prosecution contends that it is not in the public interest to disclose any sensitive material. The PII application must state why the material should be withheld, i.e. why the public interest in withholding it outweighs the public interest in disclosure.

The courts' current view of class PII claims remains complex. Ministers have claimed on a number of occasions that where disclosure is imperative in the interests of justice, claims that documents be withheld on the ground that their disclosure would inhibit candour of communication are unlikely to succeed. Well-supported claims for immunity on class grounds are likely to be respected, but no class of document is automatically immune from disclosure.

The shortcomings of this unsatisfactory regime were vividly exposed by the Court of Appeal's ground-breaking decision in the **Judith Ward** case.[215] Ward (25) was convicted to life imprisonment for killing 12 people aboard an army coach which exploded on the M62 motorway in February 1973. Judith Ward spent 18 years in prison before her conviction was quashed in 1992. At her trial she had denied being a member of the IRA, but photographs of her in the outlawed organization's uniform were shown to the jury at Wakefield Crown Court. Three Appeal Court judges concluded Ms Ward's conviction had been 'secured by ambush'. They said government forensic scientists had withheld information that could have changed the course of Ward's trial. Her case was one of a spate of miscarriages of justices revealed in the early 1990s.[216]

The effect of the **Judith Ward** judgment was to require the prosecution, if it sought to claim PII for documents helpful to the defence, to give notice of the claim to the defence so that, if necessary, the court could be asked to rule on the legitimacy of the prosecution's asserted claim.[217] The procedural implications of this judgment were refined by the Court of Appeal six months later in **R v Davis** (1993).[218] In **Davis** the CA distinguished between three classes of case. In the first, comprising most of the cases in which a PII issue arises, the prosecution must give notice to the defence that they are applying for a ruling of the court, and must indicate to the defence at least the category of the material they hold (that is, the broad ground upon which PII is claimed), and the defence must have the opportunity to make representations to the court.

The second class comprises cases in which the prosecution contend that the public interest would be injured if disclosure were made even of the category of the material. In such cases the prosecution must still notify the defence that an application to the court is to be made, but the category of the material need not be specified: the defence will still have an opportunity to address the court on the procedure to be adopted but the application will be made to the court in the absence of the defendant or anyone representing him. If the court considers that the application falls within the first class, it will order that procedure to be followed. Otherwise it will rule.

---

214 [1980] AC 1090.
215 **R v Ward** [1993] 1 WLR 619.
216 See also: Walker and Starmer (1999); Mansfield (2010).
217 See: **R v Ward** [1993] at paras 680–681.
218 [1993] 1 WLR 613.

The third class, described as 'highly exceptional', comprises cases where the public interest would be injured even by disclosure that an *ex parte* application is to be made. In such cases application to the court would be made without notice to the defence.[219]

The court thus modified to a limited extent the ruling in **Ward** that notice of the making of a PII application should always be given to the defence. The test laid down in **Davis**[220] was applied in **Keane** (1994),[221] where the court stressed:

> ... that *ex parte* applications are contrary to the general principle of open justice in criminal trials. They were sanctioned in **Davis** [1993] solely to enable the court to discharge its function in testing a claim that public interest immunity or sensitivity justifies non-disclosure of material in the possession of the Crown. Accordingly, the *ex parte* procedure should not be adopted, save on the application of the Crown and only for that specific purpose.[222]

In **R v H** (2004)[223] the House of Lords signalled its recognition of the importance and topicality of balancing a defendant's right to a fair trial under Article 6 ECHR (and the full disclosure of evidence) and the prosecution's application under PII. The court certified that two points of law of general public importance were involved in its decision, namely:

1. Are the procedures for dealing with claims for public interest immunity made on behalf of the prosecution in criminal proceedings compliant with Article 6 of the European Convention for the Protection of Human Rights and Fundamental Freedoms?

2. If not, in what way are the procedures deficient and how might the deficiency be remedied?[224]

In **Re H**, both appellants had been charged, with others, with conspiracy to supply a class A drug, namely heroin, contrary to s 1 of the Criminal Law Act 1977. The street value of the heroin in question was said to be some £1.8 million. It was alleged that H was the wholesaler of heroin. C was alleged to be an associate of H and to have been involved in the distribution of heroin. Another defendant (who had pleaded guilty to the indictment and was not involved in the appeals) was said to have stored and delivered heroin on behalf of H. Both H and C denied that they had committed any offence. Undercover police had found two kilos of heroin in H's timber-yard. The appellants asked for full prosecution disclosure under the Criminal Procedure and Investigations Act 1996, which gave statutory force to the prosecution duty of disclosure.[225]

In **Re H** the HL held that a trial judge should give detailed consideration to the information in question, noting the nature of the public interest claimed and ensuring that any departure from full disclosure is no more than is necessary in the context of the case. This may require the trial court to modify some of its procedures to guarantee that the requisite scrutiny is given to the claim, for example by inviting submissions from special counsel for the defendant where the prosecution

---

219 Ibid. at para 617.
220 **R v Davis** [1993] 1 WLR 613.
221 **R v Keane** [1994] 1 WLR 746.
222 Ibid., at para 750.
223 [2004] UKHL 3.
224 Ibid. at para 2.
225 Primary disclosure must be made under s 3(1)(a) of any prosecution material which has not previously been disclosed to the accused and which in the prosecutor's opinion might undermine the case for the prosecution against the accused. Secondary disclosure under s 7(2)(a) is to be made, following delivery of a defence statement, of previously undisclosed material which might be reasonably expected to assist the accused's defence. Section 32 of the Criminal Justice Act 2003 amended section 3(1) (a) of the 1996 Act so as to require primary disclosure of any previously undisclosed material 'which might reasonably be considered capable of undermining the case for the prosecution against the accused or of assisting the case for the accused'.

makes an application for PII in the absence of the defendant. However, if such scrutiny is achieved, the House of Lords was of the view that claims for PII can accord with Article 6 ECHR.

Terrorism cases are increasingly heard in private, especially where there is 'secret evidence'.[226] In these hearings the defendant never sees the evidence against him. The main reason given for hearings held in secret is 'national security', though that term has never really been defined in legislation. Both domestic and European courts have considered that the assessment of the threat to national security is essentially a matter for the Executive. In addition, when considering safeguarding national security the courts have accepted that it is proper to take a precautionary approach.[227]

It is possible to infer certain statements about the meaning of the term from statutes.[228] Taken together, case law and statements about national security form the basis for identified legislation, and information laid by security services will form the basis for secret courts.

Under s 15 of the Immigration Act 1971, the Home Secretary has a very broad power to deport any foreign national whose removal from the UK he or she believes would be 'conducive to the public good'. In *Secretary of State for the Home Department v Rehman* (2001),[229] Lord Slynn said that 'there is no definition or limitation of what can be "conducive to the public good" and the matter is plainly in the first instance and primarily one for the discretion of the Secretary of State'.[230] Although the Home Secretary enjoys a very broad ground to deport foreign nationals, this power is traditionally exercised in two kinds of cases:

● where a foreign national is engaged in criminal activity;
● where a foreign national is deemed to be a threat to the national security of the UK.

The case of **Chahal** (1996)[231] (see below) involved an order for the deportation to India of a Sikh separatist for national security reasons. Though there was no question of secret evidence being used against him, the High Court simply could not look at the material that the Home Secretary had used as the basis for his deportation order.[232]

❖ KEY CASE *Chahal v United Kingdom* [1996] ECHR 54

Precedent
- ❖ Article 3 ECHR cannot be derogated from by domestic courts, even in times of emergency.
- ❖ The ruling in *Chahal* prevents national governments from deporting foreign nationals, suspected of involvement in (Al Qaeda-related) terrorism back to countries where they face a real risk of torture.
- ❖ National governments must not derogate from the right to liberty under Article 5(1)(f) ECHR, in order to detain indefinitely a suspect (in this case detention in the UK under Part 4 of the Anti-Terrorism Crime and Security Act 2001).

---

226 Section 1 Prevention of Terrorism Act 2005.
227 See: HL judgment in the appeal of Shafiq Ur Rehman against deportation (*Secretary of State for the Home Department v Rehman* [2001] UKHL 47).
228 For example: Security Service Act 1989; Intelligence Services Act 1994; Radioactive Substances Act 1993; Water Industry Act 1991; Control of Pollution Act 1974; Offshore Safety Act 1992; Town and Country Planning Act 1990.
229 [2001] UKHL 47.
230 Ibid., at para 8 (Lord Slynn).
231 *Chahal v UK* (1996) 23 EHRR 413.
232 Section 15 of the Immigration Act 1971.

❖ Derogation from Article 5 ECHR is unlawful and discriminatory because UK nationals who are suspects are not subject to any restrictions.

Facts

The applicant, a Sikh, illegally entered the United Kingdom but his stay in the UK was later regularized under a general amnesty for illegal entrants. He had been politically active in the Sikh community in the UK and played an important role in the foundation and organization of the International Sikh Youth Federation. Chahal was arrested for but not charged with conspiracy to kill the then Indian Prime Minister. He was later convicted of assault and affray, though the conviction was set aside. A deportation order was issued because of his political activities and was detained until the ECtHR ruling.

Mr Chahal complained to the court that, if he was sent back to India, he would face torture at the hands of the Indian authorities (in violation of Article 3 ECHR). Chahal also argued that the procedures governing his appeal against deportation on national security grounds were unfair: in particular, he had had no opportunity to view or challenge the evidence against him. Instead, his only avenue for appeal against deportation was to an internal Home Office review committee, known informally as the 'Three Wise Men'. The committee had the power to examine the secret evidence upon which the Home Secretary had based his decision. It could also make recommendations to the Home Secretary. However, the committee did not operate like a court and the Home Secretary was under no obligation to follow its recommendations.

Chahal's complaint before the Strasbourg court (ECtHR) concerned violations of Articles 3 and 5 ECHR, claiming that his deportation to India would result in a real risk of torture, inhuman or degrading treatment, amounting to a violation of his right to freedom of liberty guaranteed by Article 5.

Decision

The ECtHR unanimously upheld Mr Chahal's complaint on both grounds. First, it affirmed that the prohibition against torture under Article 3 ECHR prohibited returning any person to a country where they faced a real risk of torture, even if that person was deemed to pose a threat to national security.

Second, the court held that the lack of procedures allowing Mr Chahal to challenge the (secret) evidence breached his right to liberty under Article 5(4) ECHR (because he had been detained for six years pending his deportation) and his right to an effective remedy under Article 13 ECHR. The court said, 'there are techniques which can be employed which both accommodate legitimate security concerns about the nature and sources of intelligence information and yet accord the individual a substantial measure of procedural justice'.[233]

Analysis

The *Chahal* decision by the Human Rights Court in Strasbourg has been controversial, impacting on the use of Home Office deportation orders in terrorism cases (led by the Special Immigration Appeals Commission or 'SIAC'). The Special Immigration Appeals

---

233 *Chahal v UK* (1996) 23 EHRR 413 at paras 130–131.

Commission Act 1997 had introduced the use of Special Advocates, special, security-cleared lawyers appointed to represent an appellant in 'closed' hearings, involving intelligence material which the Home Secretary was unwilling to disclose to the appellant and his lawyers. Special Advocates acted on behalf of appellants in closed hearings but were forbidden from discussing the closed evidence with them, which meant that they effectively acted for the most part without proper instructions from their client.

Because Article 3 ECHR cannot be derogated from, even in times of emergency, the ruling in **Chahal** prevented the Government from deporting foreign nationals it suspected of involvement in any subsequent Al Qaeda-related terrorism back to countries where they faced a real risk of torture. This resulted in the UK Government derogating from the right to liberty under Article 5(1)(f) ECHR instead, in order to detain indefinitely the suspects in the UK under Part 4 of the Anti-Terrorism Crime and Security Act 2001. However, the House of Lords held in **A and others v Secretary of State for the Home Department** (2004)[234] that the Government's derogation from Article 5 ECHR was unlawful, because there were less restrictive measures that could be taken in respect of foreign terrorist suspects, and because the use of indefinite detention against foreign nationals was discriminatory.

The judgment in **Chahal** led the UK Government to introduce the use of control orders (which applied to UK nationals and foreign nationals alike) under the Prevention of Terrorism Act 2005.

With the introduction of the Prevention of Terrorism Act 2005, most terrorism-related court hearings were held in secret ('closed hearings'), which arguably goes against the open justice principle (see also: **R v Keane** (1994)[235] – see above).

In May 2007, the first big terrorism trial following the 7/7 London terrorist bombings in July 2005 was held in secret. Five were convicted in the 'Fertilizer bomb plot' trial (also known as 'Operation Crevice'). Following the 9/11 attacks on the United States and the 7/7 bombings in London, this was one of the most complex trials in legal history, where the accused had been charged with conspiracy to build a substantial home-made bomb from fertilizer but were stopped before they could carry out the plan. Only after the conviction of all five defendants was the trial made public. The media was then permitted to report detailed evidence of how Islamist extremism and jihad ideology had developed among the five men, who had been taken overseas to train with the Taliban, mujahideen fighters and members of the Al Qaeda network and how the ringleader of the plot, Omar Khyam, had organized the purchase and storage of 600kg of fertilizer, the key component of a bomb that he had learned to build while at a paramilitary training camp in Pakistan. The public also learned that the security services and police had spent thousands of man hours of surveillance to smash the conspiracy and bring the men to court.[236]

Closed hearings are now widespread. They are both *ex parte* and *in camera*, where the court considers closed or secret evidence laid by the security services. Closed (or *in camera*) hearings involve the exclusion of one party, as well as members of the public and the press. It is known that defendants in terrorism trials have been convicted on the basis of 'secret evidence'; that is, evidence from anonymous witnesses. Secret evidence can now be used in a wide range of cases, including

---

234 [2004] UKHL 56.
235 [1994] 1 WLR 746 at 750 (Lord Taylor of Gosforth CJ).
236 See: House of Commons (2009), Part B, pp. 15ff.

deportation hearings, control orders proceedings, parole board cases, asset-freezing applications, pre-charge detention hearings in terrorism cases, employment tribunals and even planning tribunals. The essential test of whether a case involves secret evidence or not is whether both parties have seen and had an equal opportunity to challenge all the evidence that is considered by the court in making its decision.[237] So long as the defendant has disclosure of all the evidence that is used by the court, then no question of the use of secret evidence arises.[238]

In **Re. Guardian News and Media Ltd** (2010)[239] the substantive appeals involved five individuals. Four of them, A, K, M and G, were appellants; the fifth, HAY, was the respondent and cross-appellant in an appeal by the Treasury. When the appeals were lodged before the Supreme Court, the individuals' names were concealed by the use of letters, resulting from anonymity orders first made at the outset of the proceedings involving terrorist suspects A, K, M and G. Guardian News and Media Ltd and other members of the press made an application to have the orders set aside to allow for open reporting on these important cases. At that stage, the Supreme Court decided to set aside the order in the case of G, since information concerning his identity was already in the public domain, naming him as Mohammed al-Ghabra. A, K and M, all brothers, had been informed on 2 August 2007 that they were all subject to an asset-freezing order under Article 4 Terrorism (United Nations Measures) Order 2006, on the basis that the Treasury had reasonable grounds for suspecting that they might be facilitating the commission of acts of terrorism. HAY's name was added to the list and on 10 October 2005 the Bank of England issued a press release naming HAY as someone who fell within the financial sanctions regime under the Al-Qaida and Taliban (United Nations Measures) Order 2006.

HAY was concerned that his identification would lead to the jigsaw identification of his wife and children, who would suffer adverse consequences. He also feared that the Egyptian authorities would take retributive action against his family members in Egypt. But it was argued by media representatives that press articles about him, his wife and children had appeared since 1999 (see also: **Youssef v Home Office** (2004),[240] which contained details about him). There had also been Al Jazeera broadcasts about him; yet there was no evidence that any members of his family had been adversely affected in any way. Lord Rodger, in delivering the Supreme Court judgment, concluded that there was no justification for making an anonymity order in HAY's case and he was duly named as Mr Hani El Sayed Sabaei Youssef (or Hani al-Seba'i).

In relation to M's case, M feared that, if his designation as a suspected terrorist was revealed, this might lead to loss of contact, for himself and his children, with the local Muslim community. He also feared that publication of his name would cause serious damage to his reputation. M argued that an anonymity order was needed to protect his privacy rights under Article 8 ECHR. The court considered the impact of publication of M's name in relation to Article 8 and also his reputation as a member of the community in which he lived. As the press were founding their case for setting aside the anonymity order on their Article 10 right, the court had to weigh both human rights articles and examine relevant case law. The question before the court was whether there was sufficient general public interest in publishing a report which identified M to justify any resulting curtailment of his Article 8 right and that of his family to respect for their right to privacy. It was

---

237 See: s 3(1)(a) Criminal Procedure and Investigations Act 1996 (as amended by s 32 Criminal Justice Act 2003): the prosecution must disclose any material 'which might reasonably be considered capable of undermining the case for the prosecution against the accused or of assisting the case for the accused'.

238 See: **Secretary of State for the Home Department v AHK and others** [2009] EWCA Civ 287 per Clarke MR: 'It follows that the CPR contemplate the court looking at documents produced by only one side, although it is fair to say that this is only in the context of disclosure and not in the context of a document upon which reliance is placed. It may also be added that a judge who looks at particular documents for interlocutory purposes may think it right not to take part in a determination of the merits.'

239 **Guardian News and Media Ltd and others in Her Majesty's Treasury v Mohammed Jabar Ahmed and others** (FC); also cited as: **HM Treasury v Mohammed al-Ghabra** (FC); **R (on the application of Hani El Sayed Sabaei Youssef) v HM Treasury** [2010] UKSC 1 of 27 January 2010.

240 [2004] EWHC 1884 (QB).

argued that in M's situation, the right to respect his and his family's private life should outweigh the public interest because M would not have an opportunity to challenge the Treasury's allegation, in making the freezing order, that M was facilitating terrorism. An order was made which kept M's identity confidential but otherwise allowed a full report of the proceedings to be published.

The arguments advanced in favour of press freedom and Article 10 were that stories about particular individuals were always more attractive to readers than stories about unidentified people. Applying the 'responsible journalism test', the judges recognized that editors knew best how to present material in a way that would interest the readers of their particular publication and so help them to absorb the information. A requirement to report it in some austere, abstract form, devoid of much of its human interest, could well mean that the report would not be read and the information would not be passed on.

The approach in **Re Guardian News and Media Ltd** was welcomed by the media. It encouraged open reporting in sensitive terrorism trials, with possible subsequent control and freezing orders, which was ultimately going to attract a wider readership and inform the public. By concealing the identities of the individuals it might be argued that the courts were helping to foster an impression that the mere making of the orders justified sinister conclusions about these individuals. The public also had to learn about the complexity of control and freezing orders and, by allowing anonymity orders to exist, the courts were effectively denying the public information which was relevant to a wider debate about how the state was tackling the funding of terrorism.

Both M and HAY wanted anonymity in respect of their private and family life on the one hand, while simultaneously inviting the press to report their version of the impact of the freezing orders on them and members of their family. This meant that the public could hardly be expected to make an informed assessment of freezing orders and ancillary orders if they were prevented from knowing who was making these points. The court came to the conclusion that there was a powerful general public interest in identifying all those appearing in court, including M, who was named as Mr Michael Marteen (formerly known as Mohammed Tunveer Ahmed).

In its sixteenth report on 'Counter-Terrorism Policy and Human Rights: Annual Renewal of Control Orders' (2010),[241] the House of Lords and House of Commons Human Rights Joint Committee found the system of control orders to be no longer sustainable in the light of important court judgments[242] (see: **A v UK** (2009);[243] see also: **Secretary of State for the Home Department v AF and others** (2009);[244] **Secretary of State for the Home Department v AHK** (2009)[245]).

In February 2011 the Government introduced a new regime called 'Terrorism Prevention and Investigation Measures' (or TPIMs), replacing control order curfews with overnight residents' requirements.

Part 2 of the Justice and Security Act 2013 (known commonly as the 'the Secret Courts Act') came into force on 25 June 2013. The Act provides for oversight of the Security Service, the Secret Intelligence Service, the Government Communications Headquarters (GCHQ) and other activities relating to intelligence or security matters.

The most controversial part of the bill was the provision for Closed Material Procedures (CMP) – known commonly as 'secret courts' — in relation to certain civil proceedings. Applications are made under s 6 of the Justice and Security Act 2013 ('Declaration permitting closed material applications in proceedings'). CMP prevents the making of certain court orders for the disclosure of sensitive information. Secret intelligence can be introduced by the Government but will only be

---

241 House of Lords and House of Commons (2010).
242 Ibid., at para 112.
243 (2009) Application No. 3455/05 [GC], judgment of 19 February 2009 (ECHR).
244 [2009] UKHL 28.
245 [2009] EWCA Civ 287.

seen by the judge and security-cleared 'Special Advocates' allocated to the 'defendant' (claimant). The Special Advocate who represents the interest of the individual claimant cannot reveal precise details of the evidence and may only provide a 'gist' or loose summary to the claimant. This means the claimant may not be aware of all the allegations made against him. Critics have said that this will result in parties no longer being on an equal footing, tilting the advantage in the Government's favour.[246]

When the Justice and Security Bill made its passage through the House of Lords, it suffered a crushing defeat in November 2012, resulting in a significant narrowing of the scope of the Bill. Former Director of Public Prosecutions, Lord Macdonald QC, accused the Government of breaking its promises when it said judges would have the last say on whether or not there should be a secret court hearing:

> ... these amendments would give judges appropriate discretion to balance the interests of national security with justice .... [they] secure a situation where CMPs [closed material procedures] will genuinely be a measure of last resort.[247]

CMPs operate only in civil proceedings where, for example, an individual brings a case against the Government alleging complicity in torture. In defending its case the Government is now able to place evidence before a judge in the absence of the claimant and his lawyers, invoking a claim that disclosure would 'cause harm to national security'. This then prevents the claimant from rebutting the evidence. This is followed by the court's 'open' judgment, which in turn is usually supplemented by a 'closed' judgment, hidden from public hearings as well as from the applicant claimant, who will then know the reasons why he had won or lost the case.

In forcing the bill through Parliament, the Government insisted that it needed this legislation because it had been forced to settle claims of allegations of torturing suspected terrorists. It pointed to litigation involving former Guantánamo Bay detainees which – the Government claimed – had to be settled for substantial sums with at least twenty more such cases to be settled in future.

One of the first cases heard by the Supreme Court, held in closed session, was the judgment in the case of **Bank Mellat**.[248] The Supreme Court Justices heard secret evidence about the Tehran finance house, which was challenging a Treasury-imposed trading ban, and its alleged involvement in transactions relating to Iran's nuclear programme.

The **Bank Mellat** appeal concerned the use of a Closed Material Procedure (CMP) – the production of material which was so confidential and sensitive that it required the court not only to sit in private, but to sit in a closed hearing. Pursuant to various provisions of the Counter-Terrorism Act 2008, the Treasury made the Financial Restrictions (Iran) Order 2009, which Parliament subsequently approved. The 2009 Order effectively shut down the United Kingdom operations of Bank Mellat and its subsidiary. Section 63 of the 2008 Act gives any party affected by such an order the right to apply to the High Court to set it aside. The Bank made such an application. The Government took the view that some of the evidence relied on by the Treasury to justify the 2009 Order was of such sensitivity that it could not be shown to the Bank or its representatives. The UK Treasury had alleged since 2009 that the Tehran-based bank financed firms involved in Iran's nuclear programme.

---

246 See letter to the *Guardian*, 'Secret courts act comes into force', 26 June 2013, signed *inter alia* by: Shami Chakrabarti (Director, Liberty), Andrea Coomber (Director, Justice), Professor Helen Fenwick (Durham University), Allan Hogarth (Head of Policy and Government Affairs, Amnesty International), Katy Vaughan (Swansea University) and Prof. Adrian Zuckerman (Oxford University).

247 Source: 'Lords defeats on secret courts plans exposes coalition splits', by Owen Bowcott, *Guardian*, 22 November 2012.

248 *Bank Mellat v Her Majesty's Treasury (No 1)* [2013] UKSC 38 (On appeal from: [2011] EWCA Civ 1).

Before the Supreme Court, the Bank's appeal was divided into two issues. The first issue concerned the use of a CMP in the Supreme Court. The second issue concerned the Bank's appeal against the Court of Appeal's decision to approve Mitting J's upholding of the 2009 Order. The Supreme Court allowed the Bank's appeal, and thereby quashed the Iran bank sanctions, criticizing secret hearings, and ordering the Treasury to lift sanctions against Bank Mellat. The President of the Supreme Court, Lord Neuberger, read the judgment:

> Having held a closed hearing, it turned out that there had been no point in the Supreme Court seeing the closed judgment [which related to the secret intelligence], because there was nothing in it which could have affected [our] reasoning in relation to the substantive appeal . . . . A [closed hearing] should be resorted to only where it has been convincingly demonstrated to be genuinely necessary in the interests of justice. If the court strongly suspects that nothing in the closed material is likely to affect the outcome of the appeal, it should not order a closed hearing . . . . Appellate courts should be robust about acceding to applications to go into closed session or even to look at closed material.[249]

This meant that the Government's enthusiasm for secret courts suffered a setback with the UK Supreme Court Justice's decision in the **Bank Mellat** case.

FOR THOUGHT

Do Closed Material Procedures (CMPs or 'secret courts') contravene human rights law? If so, in what circumstances should reporting injunctions, CMPs and anonymity orders be permitted to derogate from human rights principles? Discuss with reference to the **Bank Mellat** judgment by the Supreme Court.[250]

5.5 Sensitive court reporting and human rights: analysis and discussion

As has been argued in previous chapters, Article 8 ECHR co-exists with Article 10 ECHR in that the media have a right to freedom of expression. The right to open justice is a fundamental principle applicable equally to claimants and defendants. How is this principle justified and how does it interact with the rights of third parties, particularly when no named individual is before the court, or named as a respondent, as was the case in the 'John Terry superinjunction'?[251] John Terry's application was made without notice; that is, individuals who might have information or who might have been considering publishing it were not cited as respondents to the application and, as a consequence, were given no notice of it. The application was simply made against 'persons unknown'. Mr Terry asserted that any publication of the information would amount to an actionable breach of confidence and that publication would be a misuse of private information. The judge, while accepting that there was a real risk that some information about the footballer's illicit relationship would be published, did not think that there was a real threat that intrusive details or photographs would be published.

See Chapter 2.6.1

249 Ibid., judgment at paras 119, 126, 133, 173.
250 **Bank Mellat v Her Majesty's Treasury (No. 1)** [2013] UKSC 38 (On appeal from: [2011] EWCA Civ 1).
251 **John Terry (previously referred to as LNS) v Persons Unknown** [2010] EWHC 119 (QB).

So what happens in a case where the applicant does not know who the respondent is but has in mind a number of other individuals whom they intend to serve with the order? Should they be required to ensure that those individuals are given a proper opportunity to make submissions to the court – and, if so, how? Should it be at the time the initial 'without notice' application is made? Or at a later 'on notice' hearing after the order has been made? These are important and difficult issues and not new, because they were commented on by Sir William Blackstone in relation to press freedom during the early part of the nineteenth century, when he said:

> The liberty of the press is indeed essential to the nature of a free state; but this consists in laying no previous restraints upon publications, and not in freedom from censure for criminal matter when published. Every freeman has an undoubted right to lay what sentiments he pleases before the public; to forbid this, is to destroy the freedom of the press.[252]

See Chapter 10

Arguably, the present situation of court reporting works well in that there is adequate legislation in place, enhanced by press and broadcasting codes of practice, such as the Ofcom regulations, which protect youths, victims of sexual offences and the bereaved.

A condition of democracy is the free flow of information, which contributes to informed debate about the use and abuse of power. The media's ability to inform the public depends in part on the maintenance of source anonymity.[253] If sources cannot be confident that their identities will be protected, many would not come forward with information. Compelling journalists to reveal their sources undermines their ability to fulfil their democratic role[254] (see: **Goodwin v UK** (2002)[255]).

Freedom of speech and open access to the UK court system belongs indiscriminately to all of us, including those working in the media. It is a journalist's duty and occupation to provide us with the opportunity to take a part in the courtroom as the 'eyes and ears' of the proceedings by way of his reporting or broadcasts and to exercise his right of free speech.

To conclude, here are the words spoken by the then Master of the Rolls, Sir John Donaldson, in the **Spycatcher** case in 1988 when he described:

> [A]n affirmation that newspapers have a special status and special rights in relation to the disclosure of confidential information, which is not enjoyed by the public as a whole. This is not the case. I yield to no one in my belief that the existence of a free press . . . is an essential element in maintaining parliamentary democracy and the British way of life as we know it. But it is important to remember why the press occupies this crucial position. It is not because of any special wisdom, interest or status enjoyed by proprietors, editors or journalists. It is because the media are the eyes and ears of the general public. They act on behalf of the general public. Their right to know and their right to publish is neither more nor less than that of the general public.[256]

The imposition of reporting restrictions on court proceedings or inquests amounts to a fundamental breach of the principle of freedom of expression (Article 10 ECHR), while also contravening the open justice principle. In an age when press freedom and freedom of information

---

252 Blackstone (1765 [1825]), Vol. 2 at p. 152.
253 Where the source is an employee who 'blows the whistle', the Public Interest Disclosure Act 1998 might, depending on the circumstances, provide protection from dismissal. But this is unlikely to be sufficient reassurance for most such sources, who will prefer to remain unidentified.
254 For detailed discussion see: Costigan (2007).
255 (2002) 35 EHRR 18 (ECTHR).
256 *AG v Guardian Newspapers (No 2)* [1990] 1 AC 109 at 183 (Sir John Donaldson MR) ('*Spycatcher No 2*').

are well enshrined in human rights law, there are many who say that any future legislation ought to push for even more openness in the court process, and anything that is done which fetters that freedom should be resisted. In the words of Lord Bingham:

See Chapter 6

> . . . it is elementary that our constitution provides no entrenched guarantee of freedom of speech or of the press, and neither the press nor any other medium of public communication enjoys (save for exceptions immaterial for present purposes) any special position or privileges.[257]

FOR THOUGHT

Howard Johnson (2006) argues that – from a media point of view – there needs to be a major reform of the 'chaotic reporting restriction regime in respect of both civil and criminal proceedings'. Do you agree?

5.6 Further reading

Barendt, E. (1990) 'Broadcasting censorship'. *Law Quarterly Review* **106 (Jul), 354–361.**
Eric Barendt discusses the decision of the Court of Appeal in *R v Secretary of State for the Home Department, ex p. Brind* (1990),[258] raising general and important issues about broadcasting freedom and the effect of the European Convention on Human Rights on UK domestic law. The case concerned the banning of words spoken 'on air' or TV by 'any person representing a prescribed organisation' (namely the IRA); from October 1988 onwards, any time an IRA, Sinn Féin or Ulster Defence Association (UDA) spokesperson uttered a word on the BBC or independent broadcasting channel or radio, their words were spoken by actors. Barendt discusses this famous judicial review case in the light of Article 10 ECHR and whether the Home Secretary's powers were *ultra vires* in that the measure was unreasonable and disproportionate, amounting to open justice and broadcasting censorship.

Blom-Cooper, L. (2008) 'Press freedom: constitutional right or cultural assumption?' *Public Law,* **Sum, 260–276.**
Louis Blom-Cooper explores the notion of press freedom by stating that the open justice system should prevail and that it is a citizen's right to freely and publicly criticize the executive, legislature or judiciary. The article looks back over historic developments of press freedom and court reporting, and then focuses on family courts in the UK, whereby media representatives have a right under s 69(2)(c) Magistrates' Courts Act 1980 to attend family court hearings in the magistrates' court but not the High Court or the county court (pursuant to the Children Act 1989). Blom-Cooper then develops the argument whether it is right that such proceedings should be kept secret, wondering whether it is not the journalist's careful reporting on such proceedings which would open up this justice system to – for instance – fathers who are often excluded from such hearings. The author discusses – *inter alia* – his recommendation for a new press regulator; rather apt in the times of the Leveson Report.

Costigan, R. (2007) 'Protection of journalists' sources'. *Public Law,* **Aut, 464–487.**
This article critiques the jurisprudence of s 10 Contempt of Court Act 1981 (CCA), which affords journalists a qualified immunity from compulsory revelation of sources. Ruth Costigan provides a

---

257 Ibid., at 190 (Bingham LJ).
258 [1990] 2 WLR 787.

fascinating insight into journalists' immunity cases. Such immunity ceases to operate where the court deems it necessary to order disclosure in the interests of justice, for the protection of national security, or for the prevention of crime or disorder. Costigan argues that the courts have failed to appreciate sufficiently the change, from the common law process, in the nature of the decision-making exercise required by s 10 CCA. She also discusses changes brought about under the Human Rights Act 1998. The article contrasts the decision-making process at common law – pre and post the HRA – and highlights problems in judicial conception of these processes. There follows a critique of public perception and what is meant by 'publication in the public interest'. The piece ends with the argument that the Convention requirement of proportionality is not implemented in an appropriate and sufficiently demanding manner.

Herring, J. (2011) *Family Law*. 5th Edn. Harlow: Longman.

Like all other Jonathan Herring textbooks, the text manages to convey some of the most difficult areas of law in an approachable tone and style, making the subject matter insightful and engaging, yet thought provoking. The book captures the zeitgeist, with brilliant analysis of the theories, policies and societal influences underpinning the legal principles that have shaped family law in recent times, providing an in-depth appreciation of the wider social, economic and political tensions which surround family life enabling further study for those who wish to specialize in this area of law.

Johnson, H. (2006) 'Family justice: open justice'. *Communications Law* 11(5), 171–174.

This article – commenting on the case of *Clayton v Clayton* (2006)[259] – discusses family court procedure, essentially still carried out *'in camera'* although (since this article was written by Howard Johnson) the situation has opened up with greater access to justice for both family members and the media. There is no doubt that the pressure group 'Fathers for Justice' has contributed to recent changes in the law. The article reports on the acrimonious proceedings and leaks of confidential information, reflecting on the welfare of their child: will their child really want to look back or have her attention drawn to these reports in later life? Johnson wonders whether behind the high-minded facade of open justice and increased court transparency 'lurks a desire simply to publish some of the more prurient aspects of the domestic disputes of the well-known'.

Mansfield, M. (2010) *Memoirs of a Radical Lawyer*. London: Bloomsbury Publishing.

Michael Mansfield QC is one of Britain's most high-profile defence lawyers, whose unparalleled commitment to his clients and radical approach to forensics, evidence and disclosure have made him a champion of individuals in many miscarriages of justice cases.[260] He is regarded as a left-wing maverick by many members of the Bar, but his record in miscarriage of justice cases is impeccable – for he takes every opportunity to represent defendants in criminal trials and appeals where issues of civil liberty have arisen. His autobiography describes his early life as the son of a station controller at King's Cross and how he worked his own way to a first in philosophy at Keele University before studying law, attracted to the profession from the moment that his mother successfully defended herself against a charge of illegal parking.

The book describes in passionate and readable style how Mansfield unveiled corruption and challenged disclosure from the prosecution when often evidence was withheld. His first big success was the Angry-Brigade trial in 1972. His name became known during the miners' strike of 1984 when he moved to South Yorkshire to defend miners accused of riot and unlawful assembly. He is best known for controversial miscarriage of justice cases, including the Cardiff Three, Judith Ward, Frank Critchlow, the Tottenham Three, the Birmingham Six, the Winchester Three, Prisoners at Risley and involved in the Strangeways Riots, and the Bridgewater Four. More recently he made headlines when representing the family of Stephen Lawrence both in private

---

259 [2006] EWCA Civ 878.
260 Michael Mansfield has had his own chambers since December 2013.

prosecutions for murder and at the Public Inquiry. Other controversial cases have included the Bloody Sunday Inquiry, Angela Cannings, Jill Dando and Barry George, Dodi Fayed and Princess Diana, and the tragic death of Jean Charles de Menezes.

Roberts, A. and Guelff, R. (2000) *Documents on the Laws of War*. **3rd edn. Oxford: Oxford University Press.**

For anyone interested in military law and courts martial, this book is widely accepted internationally as a standard work on international and humanitarian law. The book contains authoritative texts of the main treaties and other key documents covering a wide variety of issues: the rights and duties of both belligerents and neutrals; prohibitions or restrictions on the use of particular weapons; the protection of victims of war, including the wounded and sick, prisoners of war and civilians; the application of the law to forces operating under UN auspices; the attempts to apply the laws of war in civil wars; the prosecution of war crimes and genocide; the legality of the threat or use of nuclear weapons; and many other matters. The book contains key extracts from the statutes of the international criminal tribunals for the former Yugoslavia and Rwanda, and the International Criminal Court. Each treaty is followed by a complete list of all states parties, along with the dates of adherence and details of any reservations or declarations which states have made.

Spencer, J.R. (2000) 'Naming and shaming young offenders'. *Cambridge Law Journal*, **59(3), 466–468.**

The author discusses the basic rules under s 39 Children and Young Persons Act 1933, which provides guidance to the courts as to when they should not name juveniles in court (anonymity orders) and when, in contrast – by way of s 49 – the youth court *may* name (and shame) a young offender. The case of **McKerry v Teesdale and Wear Valley Justices** (2000)[261] is also discussed, where the Divisional Court contemplated the basic rules contained in ss 39 and 49 of the 1933 Act. Spencer contemplates the meaning of 'in the public interest' and whether the naming of a young person – particularly in criminal proceedings – may mean extra punishment incurred by being 'named and shamed'. Looking at the practice in the Netherlands and Germany – where the media normally suppress the names of those whom the courts have convicted – and the proclamation of Article 40 of the UN Convention, Spencer wonders whether the UK has become too punitive towards its juvenile offenders (see also: Spencer, J. R. (2006) 'Can juvenile offenders be "named and shamed" when they are adults?' *Justice of the Peace and Local Government Law*, 170(34), 644–647).

Walker, C. and Starmer, K. (1999) *Miscarriages of Justice: A review of justice in error*. **London: Blackstone Press.**

The 1990s saw a number of miscarriages of justice and subsequent releases from prison including the 'Guildford Four', the 'Birmingham Six', Judith Ward and the 'Tottenham Three'. The 'Maguire Seven' were subsequently cleared of all charges, and the discredited West Midlands Crime Squad was disbanded. The book highlights these events and the serious failures in the criminal justice system which contributed to miscarriages of justice. The authors chart in detail many disturbing features of how the police obtained confessions by unacceptable means, how evidence was fabricated or withheld and how serious failures of disclosure of police evidence led to adverse prosecutions. This book examines the various steps within the criminal justice system which have resulted in the conviction of the innocent, and looks at remedies as to how miscarriages might be avoided in the future that have been suggested, leading eventually to more open disclosure in the criminal procedure. Contributors to this excellent book comprise academics, campaigners and practitioners, some of whom have been involved in the cases mentioned.

---

261 (2000) 164 JP 355.

Ward, Judith (1993) *Ambushed*. **London: Vermillion.**

In 1972, aged 25, Judith Ward was imprisoned for life for killing 12 people in the bombing of an army coach on the M62 motorway. It was 18 years before the evidence which proved her innocence – yet was suppressed at her trial – came to light. This is her own autobiography, in which she describes her long appeal case and how evidence was withheld by the prosecution at her original trial at Wakefield Crown Court. Ward was finally released on appeal in 1992, aged 43. Justice Glidewell concluded her appeal with the phrase: 'Our law does not allow a conviction to be secured by ambush.' After five days and nights of relentless police interrogation, it was just such an arrest and conviction which was to keep Judith Ward for 15 years in the High Security Wing of Durham Prison, a Category A prisoner, allowed only occasional visits, few letters, and locked in her cell for long hours at a stretch. Judith tells the story of her arrest, her several attempted suicides, and her fight to keep sane during one of the harshest of prison lives.

Chapter 6

Freedom of Public Information

> **Key Points**
>
> This chapter will cover the following questions:
>
> - What constitutes freedom of information?
> - What is the role of the Information Commissioner?
> - What type of information can be released under the Freedom of Information Act 2000 (FOIA)?
> - Who can request information under FOIA?
> - What are the exemptions under FOIA?
> - How can decisions by the Information Commissioner be appealed?
> - What is the true meaning of 'for the purposes of journalism, art or literature' under Schedule 1, Part VI FOIA?
> - How do the courts interpret FOIA legislation when it comes to exemptions under the Act?
> - What is the difference between data protection and freedom of information laws?
> - Has FOIA made a difference to access of public authorities' information and improvement of public life?

6.1 Overview

Do we have any idea of how many police and community support officers have criminal records? How can we find out how many fake pound coins are in circulation? Or how much MPs had spent on the 'John Lewis' list as part of their parliamentary expenses? The answers to those and many other questions were revealed in response to freedom of information requests made between 2009 and 2013 to the Information Commissioner's Office (ICO).

This chapter will examine the Freedom of Information Act 2000 (FOIA) in detail and how it gives individuals the right to ask a public authority for any official documents – for example, minutes of council meetings and details of public spending. The authority must then provide the information or explain why the information should not be disclosed. If a public authority refuses to release the information, individuals can complain to the ICO.

However, the FOIA has many exemptions to what information can be disclosed. Some legal experts such as Grant and Round (2012) have argued that these exemptions are too numerous and too generally specified.[1] That said, the legislation has facilitated increasing insights into the workings of Government, the Executive and the workings of public authorities. Ministry of Justice figures revealed, for instance, that 37,313 information requests were made to central government offices in the first three-quarters of 2012, with many more made to local councils, NHS bodies, police forces and other public authorities. We learnt that Roald Dahl and Lucian Freud both turned down the Queen's honours, that there were 900 police officers with criminal records and that there were 43,586,400 fake pound coins in circulation.[2]

---

1 Grant and Round (2012) at pp. 8–12.
2 Source: 'What did we learn in 2012. ICO highlights information revealed by FOI in your area'. Available on the ICO website at: www.ico.gov.uk/news/latest_news/2012/ico-highlights-information-revealed-by-foi-in-your-area-20122012.aspx.

Had it not been for the FOIA, journalists like Heather Brooke would never have been able to disclose the parliamentary expenses scandals which were also disclosed by the *Daily Telegraph* from 2009 onwards, leading to some high-profile prosecutions. Heather Brooke had filed repeated requests for details of MPs' expenses as soon as the Freedom of Information Act 2000 had come into force on 1 January 2005; so did *Sunday Times* reporter Jonathan Ungoed-Thomas and the *Sunday Telegraph*'s Ben Leapman.[3] The *Daily Telegraph* then published extensive coverage of the parliamentary 'expenses and allowances' scandal from mid-2009 onwards, after a secret dossier of MPs' allowances and expenses was leaked to the newspaper. Shortly afterwards most of that information was also made available by Parliament to the public under the FOIA, although certain MPs and peers had fought hard to prevent disclosure. Following months of relentless exposure of Parliamentarians' expenses, many had to pay back money which had been wrongly claimed, running into many thousands of pounds in a number of cases. Many MPs resigned before the General Election in May 2010 and some were found guilty of defrauding Parliament and served prison sentences.

See below 6.3.3

In advance of the FOIA legislation coming into force, the Hutton Report (2004)[4] was published, severely criticizing the reporting of BBC journalist Andrew Gilligan, saying that allegations he made against the 'Blair' Government were 'unfounded'.[5] It cost the corporation its Chairman, Gavyn Davies, and Director General, Greg Dyke, and ushered in an age of self-doubt and caution, reshaping the BBC. Arguably, the full truths have still not been disclosed, despite journalists' FOIA requests. In his book *Stumbling over Truth* (2012[6]), former editor of BBC Radio 4's *World at One* and *Today* programmes Kevin Marsh writes critically about the most extraordinary experiment in news and PR management in Britain at the time, namely the decade of Alastair Campbell, Prime Minister Tony Blair's spin doctor, who delivered New Labour's mission to 'create the truth'. Lord Hutton had condemned the BBC and its journalistic practices in his report, and in his book Marsh criticizes the Hutton Inquiry for not further investigating the allegations that the dossiers had been 'sexed up' in March 2003, when Tony Blair had given US President George Bush his support to commence the 'war on terror' in Iraq.

Marsh reminds readers how (long before the war on Iraq) the Labour Government would stop at nothing to control the news and media agenda. The book was published at the time when Chris Patten had become chairman of the BBC Trust. Marsh, who has since left the BBC, explains his version as editor of the infamous 6.07am broadcast on the *Today* programme on 29 May 2003, where Andrew Gilligan said that claims made in Tony Blair's intelligence dossier on Iraq (that Saddam Hussein could launch attacks with weapons of mass destruction within 45 minutes) were probably known to be wrong by the Government before they were placed in the dossier. Lord Hutton severely criticized the management of the BBC in his report, saying it failed to check the details of Mr Gilligan's story as soon as the Government complained that it had raised grave charges against them. Marsh explains how he was certain the story was true, but also how Gilligan's 'flawed reporting' fatally damaged the BBC's case. And he tells of his growing disillusion with the British media's ability and appetite for holding power to account – or even telling the truth. It can be said that Marsh has provided freedom of information for anyone who wants to understand the confrontations between Tony Blair's Government and the BBC at the time and the fight to maintain journalistic independence in the face of unprecedented government pressure.

Freedom of information is inextricably linked to the right of freedom of expression (Art 10 ECHR) and the right to privacy (Art 8 ECHR). In this chapter the Freedom of Information Act 2000

---

3   See: Brooke (2010); see also: *The Heather Brooke Story*, BBC TV drama, first shown on BBC4, 30 October 2009.

4   House of Commons (2004) *Report of the Inquiry into the Circumstances Surrounding the Death of Dr David Kelly C.M.G. by Lord Hutton* ('The Hutton Report').

5   Ibid., Chapter 2 'Summary of conclusions' paras 466ff.

6   See: Marsh (2012).

will be discussed in detail, looking at the complexity of the legislation and court action which emerged after appeals to the Information Commissioner (IC) and Tribunal had been exhausted.[7] Legal challenges have largely centred on whether an organization is a public authority and whether such an authority may derogate from the freedom of information principle inherent in the legislation under s 32 FOIA. Reference will be made to the Data Protection Act 1998 later in this chapter and how the two statutes interact or differ. The question central to this chapter will be whether the FOIA has made a difference to public life.

See below 6.5

6.2 Historical overview

See Chapters 1 and 2

The legislative struggle in Britain for freedom of information is inextricably linked to freedom of speech and media freedom. Until it was reformed in 1989, s 2 of the Official Secrets Act 1911 made it an offence for any civil servant or public contractor to reveal any information he had obtained in the course of his work; an offence which successive governments continued to prosecute well into the 1990s, despite recommendations published in 1972 by the Franks Committee calling for reform.[8] The 'Press Act' of 1662[9] represented the last occasion on which the censorship of the press was formally and strategically linked to the protection of the economic interests of the Stationers' Company.

See Chapter 2.3.2

The 1662 Press Act revived the system of censorship for books of all kinds as well as for newspapers. It prohibited the publication of any literary work without prior licence, as drawn up by the Star Chamber as a decree in 1637. The 1662 Act set out a comprehensive set of provisions for the licensing of the press and the regulation and management of the book trade. The duty of supervision was assigned to the Secretary of State, the Archbishop of Canterbury and the Bishop of London. In addition, it confirmed the rights of those holding printing privileges (or printing patents) granted in accordance with the Royal Prerogative. The licensing regime was abolished in 1694 and with it the printing monopoly of the Stationers' Company, which led to problems over unofficial or pirate copies, leading, in turn, to the first copyright regime in 1710, the Statute of Anne 1710.

See Chapters 2.2.1 and 8.2.1

The Labour Party first pledged itself to a Freedom of Information Bill in its 1974 election manifesto, but the uncertain positions of the Wilson and Callaghan Governments made progress impossible. In 1978, Liberal MP, journalist and humorist Clement Freud (1924–2009) introduced an Official Information Bill as a Private Member's Bill. The Bill would have repealed the controversial catch-all s 2 of the Official Secrets Act 1911, and would have established the right of freedom of information two decades before the FOIA 2000. Freud secured a second reading of the Bill despite entrenched opposition in Whitehall; it was some way through its committee stage when the Callaghan Government collapsed in 1979. Two years later, Sheffield Labour MP Frank Hooley introduced another Freedom of Information Bill, which was opposed by the Conservative Government and defeated at second reading. Another attempt was introduced by Liberal Leader David Steel MP, which was eventually converted into the Data Protection Act passed in 1984. At the same time, Conservative MP Robin Squire promoted the 'Community Rights Project', which led to the Local Government (Access to Information) Act 1985; this Act granted the public wider rights in respect of public authorities, such as public access to council meetings, reports and papers. The Access to Personal Files Act 1987, introduced by Liberal MP Archy Kirkwood (now Lord Kirkwood of

---

7   For further discussion see: Klang and Murray (2004), Chapter 15; see also: Weber (2010).
8   See: Official Secrets Act debate in Parliament between Prime Minister Edward Heath and opposition leader Harold Wilson, Hansard, HC Deb 12 December 1972 vol 848 cc 231–234.
9   Printing Presses (the Licensing) Act 1662 (13 & 14 Car.II, c.33) ('The Press Act').

Kirkhope), gave citizens the right to see manually held social work and housing records about themselves as well as providing public access to school records.

The Access to Medical Reports Act 1988[10] resulted from another private member's bill by Archy Kirkwood MP. The Act gave people the right to see any report produced by their own doctor for an employer or insurance company. In the same year, the Environment and Safety Information Act 1988 was passed, introduced as a Private Member's Bill by Chris Smith MP, which granted individuals the right to request information from a large number of organizations who had responsibilities for the environment. The Act includes public as well as private authorities, and defines these as bodies that are 'under the control of' a public authority'.

In 1991–92 an amended version of the Freedom of Information Bill was reintroduced by Archy Kirkwood and backed by shadow Home Secretary Roy Hattersley MP, promising a 'Freedom of Information Act' should Labour win the 1992 General Election. The bill lasted only 45 minutes in Parliament and did not receive a second reading. At the same time, the Labour front bench published the Right to Information Bill, which was partly based on the Kirkwood Bill, but also included proposals to reform the Official Secrets Act. But the Conservatives won their fourth general election on 9 April that year, defeating Neil Kinnock and his Labour Party.

Though the Conservative Government under Prime Minister John Major did not support any freedom of information legislation, Cabinet minister William Waldegrave was given responsibility for implementing a more open-style government policy. John Major introduced the White Paper on 'Open Government' and the 'Right to Know Bill' in July 1993, which proposed two new legal rights to information: public access to manually held personal files and to health and safety information. The Bill also proposed to reform the Official Secrets Act 1989.[11] The 'Code of Practice' which was subsequently introduced relating to government openness and access to public official information was established in April 1994, supervised by the new office of the Parliamentary Ombudsman (The Parliamentary Commissioner for Administration), who, when publishing his first report in 1996, recommended the introduction of a Freedom of Information Act. Though the Government rejected this proposal, it accepted that the Code of Practice needed amendment and it introduced an amended Code in February 1997.

When New Labour won the General Election in 1997, they were immediately reminded of their earlier party manifesto promise to introduce freedom of information legislation. However, Home Secretary Jack Straw made it clear that their priority lay in bringing European human rights legislation into UK law, resulting promptly in the Human Rights Act 1998. The Labour Government's White Paper 'Your Right to Know' had been drafted in 1997, proposing wider public access to information from public bodies such as law enforcement agencies.[12]

In May 1998, the Select Committee on Public Administration published its report findings on the White Paper and called on the Government to introduce freedom of information legislation during its next parliamentary session. The Freedom of Information Bill was drafted and introduced into the House by Labour MP Andrew Mackinlay under the 10-minute rule. It was backed by a slightly amended version in the House of Lords in November of that year by the Conservative peer Lord Lucas of Crudwell, receiving its second reading in February 1999. The Macpherson Report of 1999 into the Stephen Lawrence police inquiry, which made the damning declaration that the Metropolitan Police was institutionally racist, recommended inter alia that the police should be fully and openly accountable to public scrutiny; and the only way this could succeed would be by way of freedom of information legislation.

---

10 As amended by the Access to Health Records Act 1990.
11 See debates in Parliament, Mr William Waldegrave and Mrs Marjorie (Mo) Mowlam, Labour MP for Redcar, Hansard, HC Deb 15 July 1993 vol 228 cc 1113–26.
12 See: White Paper, 'Your Right to Know' (Crn 38 18). January 1998.

When the Freedom of Information Act 2000 was ultimately passed, many saw it as a disappointment, with great curtailment of the original proposals in the 'Your Right to Know' White Paper. The range of exemptions and the breadth of grounds on which information can legally be withheld has remained controversial. Tony Blair famously said in his memoirs that he regretted introducing the Freedom of Information Act at all:

> Freedom of Information. Three harmless words. I look at those words as I write them, and feel like shaking my head till it drops off my shoulders. You idiot. You naive, foolish, irresponsible nincompoop. There is really no description of stupidity, no matter how vivid, that is adequate. I quake at the imbecility of it. Once I appreciated the full enormity of the blunder, I used to say – more than a little unfairly – to any civil servant who would listen: Where was Sir Humphrey when I needed him? We had legislated in the first throes of power. How could you, knowing what you know, have allowed us to do such a thing so utterly undermining of sensible government?[13]

See below
6.3.5 – Chilcot
Inquiry

The former Labour prime minister claimed that the FOIA is not used, for the most part, by 'the people', but by journalists. He called freedom of information legislation 'dangerous' because it is important for governments to be able to discuss issues 'with a reasonable level of confidentiality'. FOIA was later used to address the invasion of Iraq by UK forces in 2003.

6.2.1 Lessons from abroad

A government's commitment to freedom of and access to public information is a political principle which asserts that all citizens have a right to know what the Executive is doing and what it knows about individuals by the state in certain circumstances. This usually means a statutory right, where members of the public may inspect their own records held by public authorities as well as examine certain information held by public bodies. This 'right to know' has existed in Sweden since the eighteenth century, in the USA since 1966, in France since 1978, in Canada, Australia and New Zealand since 1982, and in the Netherlands since 1991. In the UK, freedom of information was given statutory force by the Freedom of Information Act 2000 and came into force on 1 January 2005. The FOIA gives UK citizens the right of access to information held by public authorities, similar to practices in Sweden and France.[14]

In June 2010, the Icelandic Parliament in Reykjavik passed 'freedom of information' legislation which also permitted a high level of protection for journalistic sources and whistleblowers, outlawing *inter alia* 'libel tourism'. The new legislation created a framework which permits and indeed encourages investigative journalism, access to free information and the promotion of free speech. The initial Icelandic parliamentary resolution had been drafted by the 'Modern Media Initiative' led by Julian Assange, founder of WikiLeaks.[15]

Today there are still many countries that do not allow the free flow of information or freedom of speech. On 20 June 2010, a Hong Kong publisher announced that he had scrapped plans to publish an insider account of the decision-making behind Beijing's 1989 Tiananmen Square crackdown on pro-democracy student protesters. Bao Pu had planned to release the memoirs of China's

---

13 See: Blair (2010).
14 Two pieces of French legislation provide the right to access government records: (1) Loi no. 78–753 du 17 juillet 1978 de la liberté d'accès au documents administratifs and (2) Loi no 79–587 du juillet 1979 relative à la motivation des actes administratifs et à l'amélioration des relations entre l'administration et le public.
15 The until then rather elusive founder of the electronic whistleblowers' platform WikiLeaks, Julian Assange, surfaced from years of hiding, giving press interviews in Brussels at the EU Parliament in relation to 'freedom of information', supporting the Icelandic campaign. Assange had been a renowned Australian internet hacker, wanted by the US intelligence services.

former Premier Li Peng, providing details on events immediately before and after the killing of workers and students in Beijing in June 1989. But the print run of 20,000 copies of Li's biography was stopped by the publishers, who stated that 'relevant institutions have produced new information about the copyright-holder. We have no choice but to stop right now.' In the purported memoirs, Li claims armed rioters opened fire first at Chinese troops, forcing them to return fire in self-defence. Li also quotes late Chinese leader Deng Xiaoping as advocating martial law, saying his Government would try to minimize casualties, but 'we have to prepare for some bloodshed'.[16] The manuscript would have been one of the few accounts of high-level discussions on how China handled the demonstrations in 1989.

6.3 The Freedom of Information Act 2000 (FOIA)

The media has made extensive use of the FOIA since it came into force on 1 January 2005; most notably the *Daily Telegraph's* exposure of parliamentary expenses and the scandal which followed. Within two months of the statute taking effect, government departments were forced to release over 50,000 files including Cabinet minutes, documents from the Prime Minister's Office and accounts of world history from the Foreign and Commonwealth Office. Due to the large volume of requests, many local authorities had to appoint their own information request officer.

The FOIA covers more than 100,000 public bodies including local councils, police forces, primary schools and GP surgeries. The Act grants general rights of access in relation to recorded information held by public authorities. Part 1 FOIA deals with a person's right of access to information held by public authorities and states in s 1 that:

(1) Any person making a request for information to a public authority is entitled –

   (a) to be informed in writing by the public authority whether it holds information of the description specified in the request, and

   (b) if that is the case, to have that information communicated to him.

Responsibility for freedom of information rests with the Ministry of Justice (MOJ).[17] The FOIA requires each public authority to adopt a publication scheme which contains information routinely made available to all citizens without charge. However, the act does not specify what type of information should be included in such publication schemes. Any person making a request in writing to a public authority for information must, first, be told whether the authority holds that information, and, second, be provided with that information unless it is excluded from the right's scope under one of a number of exemptions.

See below 6.4.1 and 6.4.3

Most public authorities are also covered by the Environmental Information Regulations 2004,[18] which make a number of companies subject to the same obligations. Special 'right to know' rules apply to environmental information which came into force on 1 January 2005 (at the same time as the 'right to know' provisions under FOIA). These Regulations – based on EU legislation – are more generous and the exemptions much narrower than those contained in the main statute of the FOIA 2000. For example, a number of private companies bound by the Regulations are required to release environmental information to the requesting individual and none of the exemptions are 'absolute'. This means that an exemption – that is a lawful reason for withholding information

---

16 Source: 'Tiananmen Square memoir axed by Hong Kong publisher', *Guardian*, 20 June 2010.
17 Initially responsibility lay with the (now defunct) Department of Constitutional Affairs.
18 Replacing the Environmental Information Regulations 1992.

(derogation) – may only be relied on where 'in all the circumstances of the case, the public interest in maintaining the exemption outweighs the public interest in disclosing the information'. This puts the applicant in a very strong position when requesting information on, for instance, emissions, substances, energy, noise, radiation or waste released into the environment.

See Below 6.4.1

The FOIA is generally regarded as a complex yet extremely useful piece of legislation, particularly by investigative journalists. Yet its many complex exemptions and qualifications have led to a controversial area of jurisprudence, resulting in a body of decisions handed down by the courts and the First Tier Tribunal (FTT). Since the Act has been in force, there are now sufficient decisions at appellate level for some definitive rulings and greater clarity in relation to the protection of confidential information and the exemption of material held in relation to the media.

6.3.1 FOIA and Prince Charles's letters

The FOIA was amended in 2010 so that communications between the Prince of Wales and government ministers were 'confidential' in all circumstances. Well in advance of this proposed legislative change, *Guardian* journalist Rob Evans had requested insight into Prince Charles's correspondence in 2005, arguing, *inter alia*, that this proposed statutory amendment was an unjustifiable change in the law. Evans, who had worked for the *Guardian* since 1999, contended that disclosure of the Prince of Wales's correspondence would be in the public interest, at least to the extent that the correspondence involved 'advocacy' on the part of Prince Charles. In due course, Mr Evans requested letters sent to seven government departments. The request was eventually refused by the Information Commissioner and Mr Evans appealed to the Upper Tribunal (Administrative Appeals Chamber – AAC).[19]

In **Evans v Information Commissioner** (2012)[20] the Upper Tribunal (UT) had to consider the core question: would disclosure of the Prince of Wales's letters be in the public interest? Furthermore, would the disclosure amount to a breach of confidence or privacy? One of the main reasons for Rob Evans's initiative was not to engage in Royal gossip but a genuine interest in the continuance of the monarchical system and the opinions and politics of the future reign of Charles III. At the heart of Mr Evans's original FOIA application lay the political opinion of a future monarch which could potentially undermine his position of political neutrality.

On 18 September 2012, the UT ordered the release of the Prince's letters. Reasons for the ordering of disclosure were given by Mr Justice Walker:

> . . . our task is simply to determine whether the law requires the [seven government] Departments to provide Mr Evans with the 'advocacy correspondence' falling within his requests. In the United Kingdom strong views are held by many people for and against the monarchy and for and against the approach which Prince Charles has taken to his role. Some will be horrified at any suggestion that correspondence between government and the heir to the throne should be published. They fear, among other things, that disclosure would damage our constitutional structures. Others may welcome such disclosure, fearing among other things that without it there will be no real ability to understand the role played by Prince Charles in government decision-making. We approach the matter with no pre-conception. Our law requires us to weigh the public interest in disclosure and in refusing disclosure. We seek to do so dispassionately – in the words of the judicial oath, 'without fear or favour, affection or ill-will'.[21]

---

19 Before Mr Justice Walker, Judge John Angel and Ms Suzanne Cosgrave.
20 [2012] UKUT 313 (AAC).
21 Ibid., at para 3 (Walker J).

The tribunal had recognized that there was strong public interest as a reason to disclose the letters. The Upper Tribunal found that the 'Prince Charles letters' contained 'deeply held personal views and beliefs', particularly in relation to public policy. The UT did not order the release of genuinely private correspondence by the Prince; it only wanted the public to know about the Prince's lobbying, such as of the British Bankers' Association or trade unions such as UNISON; how the Prince had frequently availed himself of access to ministers in order to 'drive forward charities and promote views' – as the judgment explained.[22]

It was well known that the Prince of Wales was regularly lobbying ministers advocating his environmental policies. Letters had been leaked to the press in the past, for example in June 2001 when the Prince had sent a letter to Lord Chancellor Lord Irvine on the subject of the Human Rights Act 1998. The Prince had complained that the UK was 'sliding inexorably down the slope of ever-increasing petty-minded litigiousness' and that 'too little is being done to stem the remorseless obsession with rights'. Both Tony Blair's diaries and those of former Labour spin doctor Alastair Campbell's diaries, and their subsequently published memoirs, had commented on Prince Charles's leaked letters to the *Mail on Sunday*, from his objection to the government's 'absurd' Hunting Bill in 2004 to his allegiance with the farming lobby.[23]

It was for this reason that the public interest, expressed by journalist Rob Evans, was intense. The Upper Tribunal found that the Prince was engaged in a 'massive extension' of lobbying that went far beyond precedent and convention. From the judgment by Mr Justice Walker we learn that the Prince was not sending these letters because of a desire to prepare for his future role as king but in order to push forward his own public policy agenda. Walker J noted that 'Prince Charles himself accepts, and government acknowledges, that his role as king would be very different from sending such advocacy correspondence.' The tribunal concluded that the Information Commissioner (IC) had erred in his view that the Prince's correspondence with a number of government departments was not in the public interest:

> Those who seek to influence government policy must understand that the public has a legitimate interest in knowing what they have been doing and what government has been doing in response, and thus being in a position to hold government to account. That public interest is, in our view, a very strong one, and in relation to the activities of charities established or supported by Prince Charles it is particularly strong.[24]

The UT allowed seven appeals by Rob Evans of the *Guardian*, who had challenged a number of decision notices of the IC for more than six years, ordering the full disclosure of correspondence between Prince Charles and ministers in the requested departments. The tribunal further upheld Mr Evans's contentions that the IC had applied the wrong principles, by giving insufficient weight to the public interest in disclosure, and gave too much weight to public interest factors in favour of non-disclosure.

It was then much to the disappointment of journalists and lawyers alike when – in October 2012 – the Attorney General (AG), Dominic Grieve MP QC, intervened under s 53 FOIA (statutory veto), barring access to freedom of information. The AG decided that the Prince of Wales letters must remain confidential because they were part of the Prince's preparation for kingship. According to the AG, the Prince's 'particularly frank remarks' about public affairs could well make politicians

---

22 Ibid., at paras 156–158.
23 Source: 'Too much information: Charles's letters wouldn't tell us anything we didn't already know,' by Steve Richards, The 'i', 18 October 2012.
24 [2012] UKUT 313 at para 60 (Walker J).

unwilling to 'engage' with the future monarch. Reasons given for the s 53 order which warranted 'exceptionality' in this case were:

- the fact that the information in question consisted of private and confidential letters between the Prince of Wales and ministers;
- the fact that the request in this case was for recent correspondence;
- the fact that the letters in this case formed part of the Prince of Wales's preparation for kingship;
- the potential damage that disclosure would do to the principle of the Prince of Wales's political neutrality, which could seriously undermine the Prince's ability to fulfil his duties when he becomes king;
- the ability of the monarch to engage with the government of the day, whatever its political colour, and maintain political neutrality is a cornerstone of the UK's constitutional framework.[25]

Many legal experts, such as Lord Pannick,[26] argued that the AG's decision to overrule the UT decision was wrong. Commenting in *The Times*, Pannick wrote that the AG had 'created a novel constitutional convention: that the heir to the throne may seek to persuade ministers to adopt particular policies'.[27] By overruling the tribunal's decision it could be argued that the AG had broken with FOIA legislation and its tradition of free access to public information.

Arguably, the AG's *Evans* direction amounted to a new constitutional convention, allowing the (future) heir to the throne to meet politicians and freely correspond with them, in order to understand the workings of the state as part of his preparation to be king. Reading between the lines of the Upper Tribunal decision we learnt that the next monarch may well not be neutral, and the AG's choice to overrule the tribunal now means that the public is not able to learn about this uncomfortable fact.

The case did not end here. In May 2013, Rob Evans and the *Guardian* sought judicial review, still seeking disclosure of Prince Charles's letters and also asking the Administrative Court whether the principle enshrined in s 53 of the Freedom of Information Act 2000 could be applied by the Attorney General to the (future) monarch. In July 2013, the Administrative Court granted leave for Mr Evans and the *Guardian* for an appeal against the AG's decision to veto any disclosure of the Royal Letters.[28] The Lord Chief Justice, Lord Judge, and two other High Court Judges, Lord Justice Davis and Mr Justice Globe, allowed the newspaper to appeal.

The Attorney General, Dominic Grieve QC, maintained his stance that if the letters were published, there was a risk that the heir to the throne would be 'viewed by others as disagreeing with government policy'. The 27 letters which had been requested by the Mr Evans were said to be 'particularly frank' and contained the Prince's 'most deeply held personal views and beliefs'.

The Lord Chief Justice said in his judgment that Prince Charles's correspondence had a constitutional function and significance and that – for this reason – a right to appeal was allowed. Judge LCJ also considered the extensive public interest which had originally been identified by the Information Tribunal and that the Tribunal had made the assumption that the Prince of Wales was in no different position from any other lobbyist, when making representations to ministers.[29]

---

25 Source: Rt Hon Dominic Grieve QC MP Attorney General, 16 October 2012.
26 David Pannick QC is a practising barrister at Blackstone Chambers, a fellow of All Souls College, Oxford and a crossbench peer in the House of Lords.
27 Source: 'Why the Prince has no right to secrecy over letters sent to ministers', by David Pannick QC, *The Times*, 1 November 2012.
28 *Evans (Rob) v Attorney General and the Information Commissioner* [2013] EWHC 1960 (Admin).
29 Ibid., at paras 4–6, 21–22.

Rob Evans's and the *Guardian*'s appeal became the latest stage in the eight-year battle by the newspaper to view the Prince of Wales's letters which he had written to ministers in seven government departments over a nine-month period. The appeal was to be heard in late 2013.

6.3.2 The Information Commissioner

Following the appointment of Christopher Graham as Information Commissioner (IC) in 2009,[30] the Government extended his remit within the purposes of the FOIA to include four further public organizations, namely academy schools, the Association of Chief Police Officers (ACPO), the Financial Ombudsman Service and the Universities and Colleges Admissions Service (UCAS).

The Information Commissioner's Office (ICO) is the UK's independent authority under the FOIA to uphold information rights in the 'public interest' and promote openness by public bodies and data privacy for individuals. From data protection and electronic communications to freedom of information and environmental regulations, the ICO is the UK's independent public body set up to uphold information rights in the public interest, promoting openness by public bodies and data privacy for individuals.

What type of information can be obtained is ultimately the decision of the Information Commissioner, who also decides whether the information requested might be exempt because of the risk – for instance – of prejudicing international relations.[31] One of the main challenges for the current IC is to tackle the lengthy backlog of cases that his office (the ICO) is struggling with, especially since the office also deals with breaches of data protection and law enforcement. The IC can override a refusal to publish information in the public interest by issuing an enforcement notice following an appeal by the party whose request was refused.

See below 6.5

 FOR THOUGHT

Your request to the Information Commissioner requiring information on a hospital failure in the Midlands has been refused. Study the Freedom of Information Act 2000 and request the relevant exemption grounds on which your application may have been refused; ask the IC's office for further explanation. Draft a letter to the First Tier Tribunal challenging the decision. You may find the government's data website, data.gov.uk, useful, as it covers health, transport, crime and justice data.

6.3.3 The Parliamentary expenses scandal

In July 2009, following the *Daily Telegraph*'s first revelations about MPs' expenses, the House of Commons also duly published its version of the expenses documents. Publication was brought forward following pressure from journalists for full disclosure of all Parliamentarians' expenses under the FOIA. The leaked documents (via an anonymous source) covered three financial years from 2004 to 2005. By the time the MPs' expenses were in the public domain, some Members of Parliament had announced that they would stand down at the next General Election in May 2010.

---

30 Richard Thomas – appointed CBE in 2009 – was the UK's first Information Commissioner, soon after the organization was first created in 2002; he was followed by Christopher Graham, who took up his post as IC in June 2009.
31 The Data Protection Registrar referred to in the Data Protection Act 1984 became the Data Protection Commissioner by virtue of the Data Protection Act 1998. With the coming into force of certain provisions of the Freedom of Information Act 2000, the Data Protection Commissioner became the Information Commissioner.

On 17 June 2010, Labour MP Eric Illsley[32] appeared before the City of London Magistrates' Court accused of deliberately overclaiming second home allowances for his home in London between 2005 and 2008, totalling £14,500. Other defendants were Elliot Morley, a fisheries minister under the last Labour Government, former Bury North Labour MP, David Chaytor, and former Livingstone Labour MP Jim Devine, plus Lord Hanningfield and Lord Taylor of Warwick – both Conservative peers in the House of Lords.

In advance of the plea and directions hearing at the Old Bailey on 11 June 2010, Mr Justice Saunders refused the defendant MPs' applications for reporting restrictions, citing the open justice principle. More importantly, Saunders J also refused the Parliamentarians' argument claiming Parliamentary Privilege. The judge confirmed that Parliamentary Privilege belongs to Parliament and not to its members individually, citing Article 9 of the Bill of Rights 1688, and that this privilege could not be waived. Saunders J further cited the 'exclusive jurisdiction' of the Diceyan fundamental doctrine of separation of powers. Mr Pannick QC for the prosecution stated that the parliamentary expenses scheme and its administration could not be covered by Article 9 of the Bill of Rights 1688, to which Saunders J responded:

> . . . the fact that it is the submission of the claim form that sets the machinery of Parliament in motion does not make it part of that machinery just as putting a coin in a slot machine does not make the coin part of the mechanism of the slot machine.[33]

David Chaytor, Elliot Morley and Jim Devine, who had attempted to use the 300-year-old law of Parliamentary Privilege to argue that any case against them should be dealt with by Parliament rather than the courts, all lost their appeals when nine Justices of the Supreme Court dismissed the former MPs' claims of privilege. Their Lordships ruled that the defendant MPs were not covered by Parliamentary Privilege and that they were therefore subject to the criminal law just like everyone else.

In January 2011 both Mr Chaytor and Mr Illsley pleaded guilty to defrauding Parliament. Saunders J sentenced Mr Chaytor to three months' imprisonment. Mr Illsley received a 12-month prison sentence and was suspended from the Labour Party. Subsequently, a jury at Southwark Crown Court found Tory peer Lord Taylor guilty of falsely claiming parliamentary expenses. In May 2011, Lord Taylor of Warwick was sentenced to 12 months in prison for falsely claiming more than £11,000 in travel expenses and overnight subsistence allowances. The 58-year-old former barrister was the first Parliamentarian to stand trial over expenses and was found to have pursued a 'protracted course of dishonesty' and to have lied to the jury on oath, said the sentencing judge, Mr Justice Saunders, at Southwark Crown Court.

6.3.4 The *Trafigura* case: Parliamentary Privilege

The United Nations 'Minton Report',[34] commissioned in September 2006, based on 'limited' information, had exposed that a toxic waste-dumping incident had taken place at locations around Abidjan in Ivory Coast in August 2006, involving the multinational Dutch oil company Trafigura.[35]

---

32 The MP for Barnsley Central had been returned to Parliament with an 11,000 majority at the general election on 7 May 2010.
33 Source: 'Jurisprudence', by Joshua Rozenberg, *Standpoint Magazine*, July/ August 2010 at p. 14.
34 The United Nations 'Minton Report' (September 2009) had exposed a toxic waste dumping incident in August 2006 in Ivory Coast, involving the multinational Dutch oil company Trafigura.
35 The author of this initial draft study, John Minton, of consultants Minton, Treharne and Davies, said dumping the waste would have been illegal in Europe and the proper method of disposal should have been a specialist chemical treatment called wet air oxidation. Source: 'Minton Report: Carter-Ruck give up bid to keep Trafigura study secret', by David Leigh, *Guardian*, 17 October 2009.

The Minton Report revealed that truck- and shiploads of chemical toxic waste from a Trafigura cargo ship, the *Probo Koala*, had been illegally fly-tipping toxic waste. The Ivorian authorities claimed that tens of thousands of people in Abidjan had been affected by fumes, reporting serious breathing problems, sickness and diarrhoea, and that 15 people had died.

On 12 October 2009, Labour MP Paul Farrelly tabled a question in the House of Commons (HC), for the then Justice Secretary, Jack Straw, to answer questions in relation to Trafigura's alleged dumping of toxic oil and the UN Minton Report. The second part of Mr Farrelly's question was of greater interest to freedom of speech in Parliament, as it concerned the superinjunction obtained by solicitors Carter-Ruck, acting on behalf of Trafigura at the time. Strictly speaking the 'Trafigura' *contra mundum* superinjunction of 11 September 2009 had prevented the *Guardian* (and therefore all other UK media outlets) from identifying the MP, what the question in Parliament was, which minister might answer it and where the question was to be found. All that could be reported was that the case involved the London libel lawyers Carter-Ruck.[36] The *Guardian* had requested disclosure of the Minton Report under 'freedom of information' legislation (i.e. FOIA) in December 2009, but all matters concerning the report and the spilling of toxic waste off Ivory Coast had been 'gagged' under a superinjunction against the newspaper. The Twitterati revealed that Trafigura lawyers Carter-Ruck had attempted to prevent the issue being raised in Parliament, relying on the *sub judice* rule.

Nevertheless, Mr Farrelly still referred to the 'Trafigura' superinjunction in Parliament, thereby breaching the *sub judice* rule of the injunction, relying on his defence of Parliamentary Privilege.

The **Trafigura** case raised questions about separation of powers; that is, the relationship between the Legislature (Parliament) and the Judiciary (the courts). The Parliamentarian had invoked his Parliamentary Privilege under the Bill of Rights Act 1688, under which he was free to say anything in the House of Commons that he wished to address and would not be found in contempt of court for going against a court injunction. Thousands of tweets called into question the privilege which guarantees free speech in Parliament. The High Court privacy 'Trafigura' superinjunction was then lifted and senior managers at Trafigura and their lawyers admitted that their approach may have been a little 'heavy-handed', insisting it had not been their intention to try to silence Parliament. Trafigura agreed to pay out more than £30m to some 30,000 Abidjan inhabitants who had been affected by the toxic waste.

But all was not over. Trafigura subsequently sued the BBC's *Newsnight* for libel after the company was criticized on the programme on 13 May 2009.[37] Trafigura's lawyers claimed that the oil traders had been wrongly accused of causing deaths and not just sickness in Ivory Coast. The BBC's defence was that it had merely focused on the gasoline waste dumped by Trafigura in Abidjan in August 2006, with *Newsnight* reporting that Trafigura's actions had caused deaths, miscarriages, serious injuries and sickness with long-term chronic effects. After lengthy negotiations with Trafigura's director, Eric de Turckheim, the BBC eventually agreed to settle on 17 December 2009, by apologizing for the investigatory programme and paying £25,000 to a charity. As part of the 'offer of amends' the public broadcaster had to withdraw any allegation that Trafigura's toxic waste dumped in West Africa had caused deaths. The BBC still issued a separate combative statement, pointing out that the dumping of Trafigura's hazardous waste had led to the British-based oil trader being forced to pay out £30m in compensation to victims. The BBC's decision to settle caused dismay in journalistic circles because the public broadcaster was penalized for trying to report what had been factually raised in Parliament and by the United Nations.

---

36 Source: 'Guardian gagged from reporting Parliament', *Guardian*, 12 October 2009.
37 **Trafigura Limited v British Broadcasting Corporation** (2009) QBD 15 May 2009. Claim No: HQ09X02050. Unreported.

6.3.5 The Chilcot Inquiry and freedom of information: the war on Iraq

As soon as the Freedom of Information Act 2000 had come into force in January 2005, there were some 40 requests to various government departments about the process leading up to the Iraq War. The *Daily Telegraph* pursued the Attorney General at the time, Lord Goldsmith, as to the legality of the Iraq War. The newspaper revealed that Lord Goldsmith had initially believed that invading Iraq without a second United Nations resolution was illegal. The Ministry of Justice (MOJ) had relied on class exemptions of the FOIA – such as s 24 (national security), s 26 (defence) and s 27 (international relations) – to hold that the Cabinet minutes on the issue could not be released. The media reported that Elizabeth Wilmshurst, who had resigned as deputy legal adviser to the Foreign Office because she thought the invasion contravened international law, revealed Lord Goldsmith's thinking in a section of her resignation letter. She suggested that the AG had changed his mind twice before advising the then Prime Minister, Tony Blair, that the original UN Security Council Resolution 1441[38] could justify war. Elizabeth Wilmshurst resigned her position on 18 March 2003. Many international lawyers agreed with Mrs Wilmshurst, insisting that UN Resolution 1441 did not provide satisfactory legal justification for the UK's military involvement in Iraq.

See below 6.4.1

Following public pressure and repeated requests by the media under the FOIA, the Labour Prime Minister, Gordon Brown, announced on 15 June 2009 that an inquiry would be set up to identify lessons that could be learned from the Iraq conflict (also known as 'the war on terror') – that is, the invasion by British forces of Iraq in March 2003. The Iraq Inquiry (or 'Chilcot Inquiry')[39] was officially launched on 30 July 2009, chaired by Sir John Chilcot.[40] The inquiry held its final round of public hearings between 18 January and 2 February 2011.

The purpose of the inquiry was to examine the UK's involvement in Iraq, including the way decisions were made and actions taken, and to establish as accurately and reliably as possible what happened and to identify lessons that could be learned. Up until then, the Labour Government had repeatedly said that an inquiry should be held only after combat troops had left Iraq so as not to undermine their role there. In the meantime, Tony Blair had resigned as Prime Minister and Gordon Brown had taken over.

All committee members of the Chilcot Inquiry had long and distinguished careers, such as Professor Sir Lawrence Freedman,[41] Sir Martin Gilbert,[42] Sir Roderic Lyne[43] and Baroness Usha Prashar of Runnymede.[44]

38 UN Security Council Resolution 1441 (2002) of 8 November 2002 offered Iraq, under its leader Saddam Hussein, a 'final opportunity to comply with its disarmament obligations' that had been set out in several previous resolutions. Resolution 1441 stated that Iraq was in material breach of the ceasefire terms presented under the terms of Resolution 687 (1991). Iraq's breaches related not only to weapons of mass destruction (WMD), but also the known construction of prohibited types of missiles, the purchase and import of prohibited armaments, and the continuing refusal of Iraq to compensate Kuwait for the widespread looting conducted by its troops during the 1991 invasion and occupation.

39 See: Iraq Inquiry ('The Chilcot Inquiry into the Iraq War') available at: www.iraqinquiry.org.uk,

40 Permanent Secretary at the Northern Ireland Office from 1990 before retiring from a career as a senior civil servant at the end of 1997. For further information see: www.iraqinquiry.org.uk/people/johnchilcott.aspx.

41 Lawrence Freedman has been Professor of War Studies at King's College London since 1982. For further information see: www.iraqinquiry.org.uk/people/lawrencefreedman.aspx.

42 Sir Martin Gilbert was in the Army's National Service (Intelligence Corps) before going to Oxford University. He taught history at Oxford for 10 years. He is the official biographer of Sir Winston Churchill. For further information see: www.iraqinquiry.org.uk/people/martingilbert.aspx.

43 Sir Roderic Lyne was the Deputy Chairman of the Royal Institute of International Affairs (Chatham House); a member of the Board of Governors of Kingston University; and a non-executive director of Peter Hambro Mining. He was a member of HM Diplomatic Service from 1970 to 2004. For further information see: www.iraqinquiry.org.uk/people/rodericlyne.aspx.

44 Baroness Usha Prashar held the post of Chairman of the Judicial Appointments Commission from 2005 to 2010. She is President of the Royal Commonwealth Society, having previously served as the Society's chairman. From 2000 to 2005 she was the First Civil Service Commissioner. Before that she was Chairman of the Parole Board for England and Wales (1997–2000). For further information see: www.iraqinquiry.org.uk/people/ushaprashar.aspx.

In nearly six hours of testimony, former Attorney General Lord Goldsmith told the inquiry that he was first convinced by his American counterparts in February 2003 that military action might possibly be 'legal' and that a second UN resolution would not be necessary. He then clarified his advice days before war broke out in March after senior commanders convinced him that the armed forces 'deserved' a 'yes or no answer'. As AG at the time of the Iraq War, Lord Goldsmith, presented a picture of someone kept out of the loop of key decision-making. He acknowledged that he changed his advice on the legality of the invasion twice in the five weeks leading up to the start of the conflict.[45]

Former Prime Minister Tony Blair gave evidence to the Inquiry between 21 and 29 January 2010.[46] He was asked how strategy towards Iraq had evolved from September 2002, including key meetings with US President George W. Bush as well as the diplomatic processes at the United Nations which preceded the invasions in March and April 2003.[47] Tony Blair's testimony concluded on 29 January 2011 with the deterioration of the security situation in Iraq, the high levels of violence in 2006 and 2007 and how the United Kingdom had responded to this, followed, finally, by how the British Government had provided strategic direction. Sir John asked the fundamental questions which had been raised by most FOIA inquiries: why did Britain invade Iraq, why was Saddam targeted, and was it legal? Tony Blair replied:

> I think it is unavoidable in a situation where it is that controversial and divisive and it is that – you know, that open to challenge. You see, there actually could have been a major debate about Kosovo and legality; there could have been. There wasn't – because in the end most people went along with the action; they agreed with what we were doing. The truth is that the law and the politics follow each other quite closely, and I think, necessarily in this situation, where we were setting our strategic objectives. You know, we had this strong belief and, as I say, this is my belief now too, that this threat had to be dealt with with a certain amount of urgency. We had our alliance with the United States of America and so on and all the issues to do with Saddam, and then obviously, at the same time, as you are proceeding and strategy is evolving, diplomacy is evolving, you are looking at the issues to do with legality.[48]

The fundamental question raised by the Chilcot Inquiry was whether the war on Iraq was 'legal', questioning the legitimacy of UN Resolution 1441. According to Elizabeth Wilmshurst,[49] Deputy Legal Adviser in the Foreign Office until 2003, the invasion of Iraq lacked legitimacy, and accordingly lacked support from legal advisers in the Foreign Office.[50] She told the inquiry that until 7 March 2003, there appeared to be no difference in opinion between the legal advisers and the Attorney General. Mrs Wilmshurst firmly believed the war on Iraq was illegal. She further stated that the AG, Lord Goldsmith, appeared to change his mind after that date. When Sir John Chilcot asked Mrs Wilmshurst whether it made a difference that the then Justice Secretary Jack Straw was a qualified lawyer, and understood the legality of the UN resolution in this respect, Mrs Wilmshurst answered, 'He is not an international lawyer.'[51] She made it clear that the

---

45 See: Iraq Inquiry: Witness Lord Goldsmith, 27 January 2010.
46 Tony Blair gave further evidence in January 2011.
47 See: Iraq Inquiry: Witness Tony Blair, 29 January 2010 at paras. 14–18, available at www.iraqinquiry.org.uk/media/45139/20100129-blair-final.pdf.
48 Ibid., paras 7–24.
49 Mrs Wilmshurst gave evidence at the Chilcot Inquiry on 26 January 2010, together with Sir Michael Wood, then legal counsel until March 2003. Source: Iraq Inquiry, witness statement by Elizabeth Wilmshurst, 26 January 2010 at paras 3–17, available at www.iraqinquiry.org.uk/media/44211/20100126pm-wilmshurst-final.pdf.
50 Ibid., at paras 15–19.
51 Ibid., at paras 8–10.

Attorney General was not going to stand in the way of the Government going into conflict.[52] Mrs Wilmshurst told the inquiry:

> So far as I was concerned, I mean, I could see that the UK reputation as an upholder of the rule of law and as an upholder of the United Nations would be seriously damaged, at least that's what I foresaw.[53]

The Chilcot Report is expected to be published in late 2014. There appear to be ongoing difficulties in the negotiations between the inquiry team and the Cabinet Office over how much disclosed material can be made public in the report. The long-awaited publication is to offer insight into covert political policies and events, such as the UK's pre-9/11 Iraq strategy in 2003. The seemingly close relationship between President Bush and Prime Minister Tony Blair is regarded as the key to unlocking and challenging the official verdict of the run-up to and aftermath of the Iraq conflict. More recently, new material supplied by (then) Prime Minister Gordon Brown and US President Obama has also been examined by the inquiry.[54]

 FOR THOUGHT

From studying the Chilcot Inquiry website,[55] how far has the Freedom of Information Act 2000 (FOIA) played a part in the 'war on Iraq' revelations? What was the outcome? Discuss with reference to international law.

6.4 Legal challenges under freedom of information legislation

The Freedom of Information Act 2000 created a statutory right to information held by public authorities. The right of access to information is a right that is applicable to everybody, and not merely those who have an interest in the information, such as the media. The duties imposed on public authorities are set out in s 1(1) FOIA and are essentially twofold:

- a duty to 'confirm or deny' that the requested information exists;[56] and
- a duty to communicate that information.

6.4.1 Exemptions under the FOIA: when is information not released?

The exemption sections of the Freedom of Information Act 2000 generally fall within two categories or 'class exemptions': 'absolute exemptions' and 'public interest exemptions'.[57] All exemptions are time-limited, expiring after 30 years when documents containing previously exempt information become historical records, unless the information was specifically exempted from the 30-year

---

52 Ibid., at p. 18, paras 1–18.
53 Ibid., at p. 21, paras 18–21.
54 Source: 'Exclusive: Chilcot report into Iraq conflict will not be released until 2014 as David Cameron echoes Tony Blair with "moral case" for war', by James Cusick, *Independent*, 28 August 2013.
55 Iraq (Chilcot) Inquiry at: www.iraqinquiry.org.uk.
56 Section 1(6) FOIA.
57 Part II s 21 FOIA 'Exempt Information accessible to applicant by other means'.

disclosure rule, such as sensitive information relating to correspondence by members of the Royal family; for example the abdication of Edward VIII in 1936 to marry American divorcee Mrs Simpson, which was sealed for 100 years.

Absolute exemptions disqualify all information of a certain type from the disclosure regime. The second category of public interest exemptions states that information may be exempt subject to a 'prejudice' test.[58] Absolute exemptions include:

- bodies dealing with security matters and government intelligence (s 23 FOIA)[59];
- national security (s 24 FOIA);
- Parliamentary Privilege (s 34 FOIA);
- information provided in confidence (s 41 FOIA);
- information whose disclosure is prohibited by law (s 44 FOIA).

These exemptions covered by the Act are absolute, meaning that if a request is received for information covered by the sections above, there is neither a duty to disclose it nor to confirm or deny that it is held. Moreover there is no need to consider whether there might be a stronger public interest in making the disclosure despite the existence of an exemption. In other words, information is either exempt or it is not.

Class exemptions include court records (s 32 FOIA) and any material relating to actual or potential criminal investigations (s 31 FOIA). More controversially, they also cover material relating to government policy formulation, including background information on which decisions were based. Furthermore, anything else which 'would in the reasonable opinion of a qualified person be likely to prejudice the effective conduct of public affairs' – something again left undefined in the Act and an increasing cause for appeals to the First Tier Tribunal (FTT – see below) and the courts. Exempt information need not be disclosed by the authority. The rights conferred under the FOIA are subject to 'procedural' and 'substantive limitations'. Where access is denied, the public authority has a duty to give reasons. Some *qualified information* that would be in the public interest includes:

- defence (s 26 FOIA);
- international relations (s 27 FOIA);
- the economy (s 29 FOIA);
- law enforcement (s 31 FOIA);
- formulation of government policy (s 35 FOIA);
- communications with the monarch (s 37 FOIA);
- health and safety (s 38 FOIA);
- legal professional privilege (s 42 FOIA);
- commercial interests (s 43 FOIA).

Here follows a brief summary of *standard class exemptions*[60] of procedural access to 'public interest information':

---

58 The rights contained in s 1(1) FOIA are subject to exemptions contained in ss 1 (3), 2, 9, 12, and 14 FOIA.
59 Section 23 FOIA 'Information supplied by, or relating to, bodies dealing with security matters'.
60 Section 2 FOIA explains the effect of the exemptions in Part II of the Act.

- **Section 1(3) FOIA** provides that a public authority may refuse to provide information if it is unable to understand what is being asked for. For example, if an inadequately particularized request is made, where the public authority reasonably requires further particulars in order to identify and locate the information requested. The public authority is then not obliged to provide the information until 'further particulars' have been received.
- **Section 9 FOIA** ('fees') allows the public authority to charge a fee before s 1 (1) FOIA is complied with; the fees notice must be in writing and, once served, the public authority is not obliged to comply with the request for a period of three months.[61]
- **Section 12 FOIA** allows a public authority not to comply with a request for information if the cost of compliance exceeds the 'appropriate' limit.
- **Section 14 FOIA** provides an exemption if the request for information is vexatious.

Increasing concern has been expressed by human rights lawyers about the charging of fees for access to public information, where the standard FOIA legislation states that access to public information is free of charge.

 FOR THOUGHT

You are applying under the FOIA for disclosure of toll charges levied on tunnels and bridges from your local authority in order to establish the profit accounted for by your local authority. Your local authority then duly provides you with this information, but you notice that information provided is more than 10 years old. The explanation given is that the information sought falls under one of the exemptions. Formulate a request for proper disclosure to the Information Commissioner, stating your grounds for disclosure based on the relevant exemption sections of the FOIA (see also: the 'Merseytravel' case: ***Mersey Tunnel Users Association v Information Commissioner***. Tribunal decision of 15 February 2008[62]).

6.4.2 Appeals before the First Tier Tribunal (FTT)

Perhaps rather confusingly, the Information Tribunal has changed its name a number of times. Up until 17 January 2010 the Information Rights Tribunal was called the Information Tribunal (previously called the Data Protection Tribunal) and was originally set up to hear appeals under the Data Protection Act 1984. The tribunal continued to hear appeals after the Data Protection Act 1998 (DPA) came into effect, but was renamed the Information Tribunal when its responsibilities were expanded and it began hearing other information appeals under the Freedom of Information Act 2000, the Privacy and Electronic Communications Regulations 2003 (PECR) and the Environmental Information Regulations 2004 (EIR).The Information Rights Tribunal is now part of the First Tier Tribunal in the General Regulatory Chamber, which is part of the Ministry of Justice Tribunal Service. The FTT is also at times still referred to as the Information Rights Tribunal.

---

61 There are outstanding regulations whereby the Government is proposing to tighten cost rules and fee schedules which will potentially require payment for further disclosure. The proposals include that an organization or public authority can take into account the costs attributable to the time that persons (both the authority's staff and external contractors) are expected to spend on these activities. Such costs were calculated at £25 per hour per person for all authorities regardless of the actual cost or rate of pay (as at August 2011). Source: Information Commissioners Office – 'Freedom of Information Act 2000: Using the Fees Regulations'. Version 2.1. August 2011.

62 Information Tribunal Appeal Number: EA/2007/0052; Information Commissioner's Ref: FS501 36587.

All Information Rights Tribunal judges are solicitors or barristers with at least seven years' professional experience; the principal judge of the Information Rights Tribunal jurisdiction in the FTT is Professor John Angel and there are 15 other judges. In addition there are 36 non-legal tribunal members.

The FTT hears appeals on information rights from appeal notices issued by the Information Commissioner under the following legislation:

- Data Protection Act 1998;
- Freedom of Information Act 2000;
- Privacy and Electronic Communications Regulations 2003;
- Environmental Information Regulations 2004 (see: **Ofcom v The Information Commissioner** (2010)[63]).

A panel composed of a tribunal judge and two other non-legal members – all appointed by the Lord Chancellor – hears appeals at venues across the United Kingdom. These oral hearings are open to the public. When a Minister of the Crown issues a certificate on grounds of national security exemption grounds (i.e. a PII notice), the appeal must be transferred to the Administrative Appeals Chamber of the Upper Tribunal (AAC – UT) once the application is received by the FTT (as was the case with the AG's ruling in the 'Prince Charles letters' case).

See above 6.3.1

The FTT will often require to see information which must be kept confidential from one or more of the other parties to the appeal. Among other things, this can mean that during the hearing the party requesting the information is asked to leave the room. For instance, there will be cases where a person who made a request for information under s 1(1) FOIA is a party to an appeal which examines the application of exemptions to the obligation to supply information.

In many cases, the tribunal will need to see the information which has been withheld in order to reach its decision. However, in cases where disclosure has been refused, it would in most cases undermine the very object of the exemption if the information in question were to be disclosed, during the tribunal proceedings, to the person who made the request. Such evidence will often also reveal something of the nature of the requested information in a way which would undermine the objectives of the exemption. Equally, it may reveal other information which the tribunal requires in order to determine the case, but which would be exempt under the FOIA; for example, commercially sensitive information that is revealed in documents recording a public authority in consultation with third parties. The legal basis for the FTT dealing with confidential information in proceedings was considered in the ruling in the **BBC v Sugar** case.[64]

See below 6.4.4

The Information Commissioner takes a rather restrictive view of commercial interests when it comes to applying the s 43 exemption of the 2000 Act ('commercial interests'). This approach was called into question in the FTT decision in **Student Loans Company (SLC) v Information Commissioner** (2008).[65] The SLC had challenged a decision of the IC that it must disclose a training manual used by staff who dealt with defaulting borrowers. The SLC argued that disclosure of the manual would harm its commercial interests under s 43(2) FOIA, in that it would help borrowers to delay or avoid complying with their obligations. The IC contended that the SLC was not participating competitively in the purchase and sale of goods or services and that a detrimental financial effect of the kind feared by the SLC would not constitute prejudice to the commercial interests of the SLC.

63 [2010] UKSC 3; on appeal from: [2009] EWCA Civ 90.
64 **BBC v Sugar (deceased) (No 2)** [2012] UKSC 4.
65 IC Application EA/2008/0092.

When the matter was appealed before the tribunal, it ruled that the IC's approach to s 43 was too restrictive. The tribunal did not consider it appropriate to tie its meaning directly or indirectly to competitive participation in buying and selling goods or services and to exclude all other possibilities. It held that the word 'commercial' includes debt collection as a commercial activity, even when carried on by a company supported by public funds. The tribunal ruled that a better approach was to ask itself whether a detriment to the SLC, from the delay and reduction of debt collections and increasing the costs of collections, could fairly be described as prejudicing the SLC's commercial interests. For these reasons, the tribunal ordered some parts of the manual to be redacted before disclosure.[66]

6.4.3 Exemptions under the FOIA: *Kennedy v Information Commissioner*

In **Dominic Kennedy v IC & Charity Commissioners** (2010),[67] *Times* journalist Dominic Kennedy challenged the s 32 FOIA exemption ('court records') before the First Tier Tribunal (then Information Tribunal). Mr Kennedy had requested information concerning the Charity Commission's 2007 inquiry into the 'Mariam Appeal', a controversial fund set up by former Labour MP for Glasgow Kelvinside George Galloway. Mr Galloway had set up the 'Mariam Appeal' to help an Iraqi girl suffering from leukaemia. He said that the charitable activities had been well known to the fund's three main backers: Saudi Arabia, the United Arab Emirates and Jordanian businessman Fawaz Zureikat, the appeal's chairman. Mr Galloway had also declared his own travel arrangements on behalf of the appeal to the House of Commons Register of Members' Interests. He described the accusation that he received hundreds of thousands of pounds from Saddam Hussein as a 'lie of fantastic proportions'.[68]

Following the publication of articles by Dominic Kennedy in *The Times* where allegations were made in respect of George Galloway's involvement in the 'Mariam Appeal', the Charity Commission opened an inquiry as to whether the appeal fund had been properly registered as a charity. In total there were three investigative inquiries, one of which established that the objects of the 'Mariam Appeal' were stated to be charitable objects, but that the appeal was not registered as a charity. Its known income was nearly £1.5 million until its closure in 2003. The results of the first two inquiries were published in June 2004 in a 'Statement of Results of the Inquiry' (SORI). But further information requests by Mr Kennedy fell within the terms to be held exempt under s 32 FOIA.

See Chapter 3.2.6

At the time the Charity Commission was investigating the charitable status of the appeal, Mr Galloway had already started his libel action against the *Daily Telegraph* over similar allegations that he had received money from the Iraqi regime involving the 'Mariam Appeal' and that such funds were used for non-charitable purposes. *Telegraph* journalists had found documents in Iraq where it was suggested that the Glasgow MP had been given a percentage of Iraqi oil sales through the oil-for-food programme, allegedly worth about £375,000 a year. Mr Galloway strenuously denied the allegations and won his libel action against the *Telegraph* (see: **Galloway v Daily Telegraph** (2004).[69]

Despite repeated requests to the Information Commissioner by Mr Kennedy, the three inquiries' reports and information were not released and were withheld under s 32 FOIA, this decision

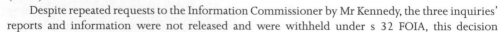

66 Redaction is the process of editing requested information to remove exempt or excepted material. When a public authority decides to redact part of the requested information, it must justify each individual redaction by reference to a specific exemption or exemption, explaining why it applies. The Information Commissioner has applied this principle when investigating complaints made under the FOIA.

67 [2010] EWHC 475 (Admin) of 19 January 2010 (QBD) (IC application EA/2008/0083).

68 Source: 'Britain: Antiwar MP George Galloway suspended from Parliament', *Asian Tribune*, 27 July 2007.

69 [2004] EWHC 2786 (QB).

subsequently upheld by the Information Tribunal. Though Mr Kennedy had argued that the Charity Commission's inquiry into George Galloway's involvement in the 'Mariam Appeal' was of acute public concern, his appeal was dismissed.

In the Court of Appeal, Calvert-Smith J held that the Information Tribunal had been correct in holding that the wording of s 32(2) FOIA had a very wide scope. There was no absolute right under the FOIA to disclosure of documents held by public authorities which had been placed in the custody of or created by a person conducting an inquiry; the documents (of the Charity Commission) fell under these absolute exemptions set out under s 32 FOIA, regardless of their content and the consequences of their disclosure, and notwithstanding the public interest in their disclosure. Maybe we will find out in 30 years' time what the Charity Commission's findings were regarding the 'Mariam Appeal'.

Section 32 FOIA exemptions remain the most legally challenged and subject to appeals before the First Tier Tribunal in the administrative courts. Section 32 covers the following *absolute exemptions* on public information:

- court or tribunal reports of proceedings;
- inquests and post-mortem examinations and records;
- prison custody records.

In **Kennedy v IC** (2010),[70] Calvert-Smith J further ruled that s 32(2) FOIA creates two exemptions from disclosure of information held by a public authority:

(1) any document *placed* in the custody of a person conducting an inquiry or arbitration, for the purposes of the inquiry or arbitration, or

(2) any document *created* by a person conducting an inquiry or arbitration, for the purposes of the inquiry or arbitration.

6.4.4 What is the true meaning of 'for purposes of journalism, art or literature' under exemptions of the FOIA? *BBC v Sugar*

The complex nature of the FOIA and its numerous exemptions[71] was demonstrated by the **BBC v Sugar** (2012) case.[72] This case acutely illustrates the complexities involved in challenging FOIA disclosure and FTT decisions (see also: **Sugar v BBC** (2009)[73]).

The background to the **Sugar**[74] case involved a BBC inquiry into news coverage of the Israeli–Palestinian conflict, resulting in the 'Balen Report', compiled by senior BBC journalist Malcolm Balen in 2004. The inquiry had been commissioned by the BBC's former director of news, Richard Sambrook, following allegations of bias from both sides. Hundreds of viewers and listeners had complained to the Corporation in 2003–04, when the Middle East correspondent Barbara Plett revealed that she had cried at the death of Yasser Arafat. There were also allegations of pro-Jewish bias. The Balen Report was then presented to the BBC's Journalism Board for consideration in 2004.

---

70 See: **Dominic Kennedy v Information Commissioner & Charity Commissioners** EA/2008/0083.
71 Under Schedule I, Part VI FOIA.
72 **BBC v Sugar (deceased) (No 2)** [2012] UK Supreme Court, *The Times*, 28 February 2012.
73 [2009] EWHC 2348 (Admin).
74 Mr Steven Sugar died in January 2011.

Following the Hutton Report[75] in early 2004, the Balen Inquiry was obviously of an equally sensitive nature and the BBC's Board of Governors set up a panel in late 2004, chaired by Sir Quentin Thomas, to provide an external independent review of reporting of Middle East affairs. The 'Thomas Report' was published in April 2006 and concluded there was 'no deliberate or systematic bias' in the BBC's reporting, but said its approach had at times been 'inconsistent' and was 'not always providing a complete picture', which had meant that it was sometimes 'misleading'. The BBC Governors signed off the Thomas Report as a further independent review of the Israeli–Palestinian broadcasting coverage by the BBC. This meant that the Balen Report was never published.

On 8 January 2005, a commercial lawyer, Steven Sugar, asked to see the Balen Report and made a request to the BBC under the Freedom of Information Act 2000. The BBC Governors refused, reasoning that the Balen Report was an internal document aimed at checking its own standards of journalism. This meant that information held by the BBC for the purposes of journalism was effectively exempt from production under the FOIA, even if it was held for other, possibly more important, purposes.[76]

Mr Sugar complained to the Information Commissioner, stating that the BBC – as a public body – was under a duty to disclose the requested information. On 24 October 2005, the IC ruled in favour of the BBC. Mr Sugar subsequently appealed to the Information Tribunal, which ruled in favour of Mr Sugar on 29 August 2006. This meant the BBC should disclose the report and could not derogate under the FOIA.[77]

The BBC appealed against the tribunal's decision. The grounds of appeal before the High Court were as follows: that the tribunal did not have jurisdiction to hear an appeal from the IC; and, even if it did, the IC's decision had been flawed as a matter of law. On 27 April 2007, High Court judge Davies J backed the IC's decision and held that the Balen Report was 'for the purpose of journalism'. Additionally, the judge imposed restrictions on potential appeals to the Information Tribunal in the future, stating, *inter alia*, that the tribunal lacked jurisdiction.[78]

Steven Sugar appealed the High Court decision and on 25 January 2008 the Court of Appeal[79] rejected Mr Sugar's appeal, ruling that the Balen Report was to be prohibited and exempt under s 44 FOIA.[80] Importantly, the CA rejected the view that the BBC was a public body, which meant the Corporation did not have to disclose information relating to its journalistic practices.[81]

Eventually the case reached the UK Supreme Court with a judgment in February 2012.[82] The court had to determine whether, in a situation in which information was held for such dual and opposite purposes, the information fell within the designation under Schedule 1 Part VI FOIA. It was argued on behalf of Mr Sugar's estate that his request for disclosure had engaged his right to receive information under Article 10(1) ECHR. This appeal was dismissed and the Supreme Court held that the BBC could withhold the Balen Report under FOIA exemption since the report was predominantly for the purposes of journalism, meaning that the UK Supreme Court constructed the relevant

75 On 21 December 2006, former Director General of the BBC, Greg Dyke, told the Information Tribunal that he supported an application by the *Guardian* and 'open government' campaigner, Heather Brooke, for the publication of minutes of the special meeting of BBC Governors which took place hours after the Hutton Report had criticized the BBC. Within 24 hours of the report, the BBC governors sacked Mr Dyke and apologized to the Government. Gavyn Davies, the BBC's chairman, also resigned. See also: 'Report of the Inquiry into the Circumstances Surrounding the Death of Dr David Kelly C.M.G.', by Lord Hutton, House of Commons, 28 January 2004, available at http://news.bbc.co.uk/1/shared/spl/hi/uk/03/hutton_inquiry/hutton_report/html/contents.stm.

76 'For the purposes of journalism, art or literature' within the meaning of Schedule 1, Part VI FOIA.

77 *Sugar v BBC* [2007] EWHC 905.

78 [2009] EWHC 2348 (Admin).

79 Lord Buxton J, Lord Lloyd J and Sir Paul Kennedy.

80 Schedule 1, Part VI FOIA.

81 For further discussion see: Johnson (2008a).

82 **BBC and Another v Sugar (deceased) (No 2)** [2012] UKSC 4.

legislation (Schedule1 Part VI FOIA) literally: 'information held for purposes other than those of journalism, art or literature', even if the information was held for other purposes as well. Therefore, the BBC was under no duty to disclose the report. That was sufficient to dispose of the appeal.

It is worth noting that the judgments of Lord Walker and Lord Wilson revealed an academic issue, namely whether the definition meant information held solely for the purposes other than journalism, art or literature or information held *predominantly* 'for purposes other than journalism, art or literature'.[83] The issue centred on the word and the construction of 'predominantly' and whether this should in effect be inserted into Schedule 1 Part VI before the phrase 'for purposes other than those of journalism, art or literature'.

The Supreme Court Justices held that the Court of Appeal in this case had been correct in stating that once it is established that the information sought is held by the BBC for the purposes of journalism, it is effectively exempt from production under the FOIA, even if the information is also held by the BBC for other purposes. That conclusion followed from the Act's legislative purpose and its language. Their Lordships found that the purpose of the FOIA was to promote an important public interest in access to information about public bodies. However, in relation to the BBC, there was a powerful public interest in public service broadcasters being free to gather, edit and publish news and comment on current affairs without the inhibition of an obligation to make public disclosure of or about their work. That warranted the protection granted by the Act for the purposes of the BBC's journalistic, artistic and literary output.

That being the purpose of the immunity, the exemptions available under Schedule 1, Part VI would have failed to achieve its purpose if the co-existence of other non-journalistic purposes resulted in the loss of immunity. That was confirmed by the language of Schedule 1, Part VI. The disclosable material was defined in terms which were positive in form but negative in substance. The real emphasis was on what was not disclosable, which was material held for the purposes of the BBC's broadcasting output. It was the most natural construction, which did not depend on reading in any words. Accordingly, as Lord Wilson put it, the correct approach was to have some regard to the directness of the purpose. It was not weighing one purpose against another, but considering the proximity between the subject matter of the request and the BBC's journalistic activities and end product.[84]

Lord Brown opined that, had Parliament actively considered the situation of information held by the BBC for *dual* purposes, it would expressly have provided that the information was within the scope of the Act if it was held *predominantly* for the other purposes. The fact that the words which in the event Parliament favoured in drafting the FOIA, namely the words of the designation, were in themselves apt to permit such a construction meant that the court should proceed to endorse it. In the instant case, the Balen Report was held for purposes of journalism. On the premise that it was also held for purposes other than those of journalism, it was not *predominantly* so held. Accordingly, the report lay beyond the scope of the Act.[85]

Their Lordships also commented that Article 10 of the Convention created no general right to freedom of information and where, as in the **BBC v Sugar** case, the legislation expressly limited such a right to information held otherwise than for the purposes of journalism, it was not interfered with when access was refused to documents which were held for journalistic purposes. Even if that were wrong, it was open to the state to legislate a blanket exclusion of any requirement to disclose information held, whether predominantly or not, for the purposes of journalism.[86]

---

83 Ibid., at para 61 (as per Lord Walker with Lord Phillips, Lord Brown, Lord Mance agreeing).
84 Ibid., at paras 72, 75–76, 78–79, 83 (as per Lord Wilson).
85 Ibid., at paras 57, 60 (as per Lord Brown).
86 Ibid., at paras 94 and 98.

The Supreme Court decision disappointed the Jewish community, which would have wanted to know whether the Balen inquiry found any evidence of anti-Israeli bias in news programming and reporting. It had taken seven years from Steven Sugar's first submission of his request to the BBC under the FOIA in January 2005 to the final decision by the UK Supreme Court in 2012, with Mr Sugar dying in the meantime and his wife Fiona Paveley continuing the legal battle on his behalf. We will therefore never know whether the BBC's coverage of the Middle East conflict – in particular the news coverage of Israel and Palestine – as investigated by the Balen inquiry was biased either way.

6.5 Data protection and freedom of information

The Data Protection Act 1998 (DPA) established a framework of rights and duties which are designed to safeguard personal data.[87] The 1998 Act is concerned only with living individuals and so if the subject of the information is dead, then the information cannot be personal data. The DPA 1998 applies to a particular activity, namely the processing of personal data, rather than to particular people or organizations. This means that, if an organization processes personal data, they must comply with the 1998 Act and they must handle the personal data in accordance with the data protection principles. Broadly speaking, if any organization collects or holds information about an identifiable living individual, then it is processing personal data. The DPA 1998 requires every data controller (i.e. organization or sole trader) who is processing personal information to register with the Information Commissioner's Office (ICO) unless they are exempt. More than 370,000 organizations were registered with the ICO in 2013.

There is a complex interconnection between two statutes – FOIA 2000 and DPA 1998. The *Independent* ascertained under the FOIA, for example, that NHS hospital trusts in England and Wales had spent £2 million on more than 50 'gagging orders' since 2008, preventing some 600 staff from speaking out. In March 2013, the Health Secretary, Jeremy Hunt MP, banned the use of gagging clauses in compromise agreements for staff.[88]

6.5.1 The scope of the Data Protection Act 1998

The scope of the DPA 1998 is very wide as it applies to just about everything concerned with individuals' personal details; the legislation applies to both manual and electronic systems.[89] Under the DPA, anyone has the right to find out what information an organization (or the 'data controller' of an organization) holds about them by making a subject access request. This right allows individuals to find out important information ranging from details recorded on their credit history to data included in their health record. Once received, a data controller normally has 40 days to reply to the request. The data protection framework balances the legitimate needs of organizations to collect and use personal data for business and other purposes against the right of individuals to respect for the privacy of their personal details. The legislation itself is complex, but essentially the 1998 Act gives an individual the right to see personal data held on them by public authorities and other organizations. 'Data' means information which:

---

87 The Data Protection Act 1998 gave effect in UK law to EC Directive 95/46/EC ('on the protection of individuals with regards to the processing of personal data and on the free movement of such data'). The 1998 Act replaced the Data Protection Act 1984 and was brought into force on 1 March 2000.

88 Source: 'NHS hospitals spend £2m on gagging orders preventing staff speaking out', by David Hughes, *Independent*, 12 June 2013.

89 Privacy and Electronic Communications (EC Directive) (Amendment) Regulations 2011 inserted ss 55A to 55E DPA 1998 into the Privacy and Electronic Communications (EC Directive) Regulations 2003, enabling the Information Commissioner to serve a monetary penalty notice on a person who breaches the 2003 Regulations.

(a) is being processed by means of equipment operating automatically in response to instructions given for that purpose;

(b) is recorded with the intention that it should be processed by means of such equipment;

(c) is recorded as part (or with the intention that it should form part) of a relevant filing system (i.e. any set of information relating to individuals to the extent that, although not processed as in (a) above, the set is structured either by reference to individuals or by reference to criteria relating to individuals, in such a way that specific information relating to a particular individual is readily accessible); or

(d) does not fall within paragraph (a), (b) or (c) but forms part of an 'accessible record' (such as an office filing system of a freelance journalist).[90]

What is the interplay between the DPA 1998 and the Freedom of Information Act 2000? Since the coming into force of the FOIA in 2005, it has become evident that problems have arisen regarding some of the complex exemptions under the FOIA and the interaction between the different sections of the DPA 1998.

See above
6.4.1

The Information Commissioner's Office is now handling both data protection and freedom of information requests, and is therefore covered by both data protection and FOIA legislation. The DPA 1998 sets out rules to make sure that personal information is handled properly by 'data controllers', whereas the FOIA covers the 'right to know' about public authorities. If an organization or business is processing personal data, it usually has to notify the Information Commissioner (IC) about this activity. Failure to notify is a criminal offence. The Information Commissioner's Office is required to keep a register on prescribed data, and the register is available to the public for inspection via the ICO's website. The main purpose of notification and the public register is transparency and openness. It is a basic principle of data protection that the public should know (or be able to find out) who is processing personal data, plus other details about the processing (such as why it is being carried out). So notification serves the interests of individuals by helping them understand how organizations process personal data and for what purpose.

See above
6.4.3

See above
6.4.2

What are the enforcement powers the Information Commissioner may have? There are a number of measures available to the ICO for taking action to change the behaviour of organizations and individuals that collect, use and keep personal information.[91] These include criminal prosecution, non-criminal enforcement and audit. The IC also has the power to serve a 'Monetary Penalty Notice' on a data controller.[92] The main enforcement options for the IC are to:

● Serve information notices requiring organizations to provide the ICO with specified information within a certain time period;

● Issue undertakings committing an organization to a particular course of action in order to improve its compliance;

90 An 'accessible record' is defined in s 68 of the Act and can be summarized here as a health record, educational record (local education authority schools and special schools only), local authority housing record or local authority social services record.

91 Under ss 55A to 55E of the Data Protection Act 1998, introduced by the Criminal Justice and Immigration Act 2008, the Information Commissioner may, in certain circumstances, serve a monetary penalty notice on a data controller.

92 The ICO publishes a public register of data controllers, its main purpose being that of transparency and openness. The register includes the name and address of data controllers and a description of the kind of processing they do. Notification is a statutory requirement and every organization that processes personal information must notify the ICO, unless they are exempt. Failure to notify is a criminal offence.

- Serve enforcement notices and 'stop now' orders where there has been a breach, requiring organizations to take (or refrain from taking) specified steps in order to ensure they comply with the law;
- Conduct consensual assessments (audits) to check organizations are complying;
- Serve assessment notices to conduct compulsory audits to assess whether organizations' processing of personal data follows good practice (data protection only);
- Issue monetary penalty notices,[93] requiring organizations to pay up to £500,000 for serious breaches of the Data Protection Act 1998[94] (see: **Central London Community Healthcare NHS Trust v Information Commissioner** (2013);[95]
- Prosecute those who commit criminal offences under the DPA 1998;
- Report to Parliament on data protection issues of concern.

See also
'Leveson' –
Chapter 10.4

In December 2012, Christopher Niebel and Gary McNeish, joint owners of Tetrus Telecoms, were prosecuted by the ICO for failing to notify under s 17 of the Data Protection Act 1998. The defendants pleaded guilty at two separate hearings and were fined £3,000, which was reduced to £2,000 in both cases due to an early guilty plea. Niebel and McNeish were each ordered to pay prosecution costs of £482.50 and a £15 victims surcharge. The conviction came after Niebel and McNeish were served with monetary penalties totalling £440,000 for a serious breach of the Privacy and Electronic Communications Regulations after the company they owned sent millions of spam texts to members of the public without their consent.

In November 2012, a London barrister was prosecuted by the ICO for failing to notify under s 17 DPA 1998. Jeanette Hayne pleaded guilty at the hearing on 28 November 2012 but Westminster Magistrates decided to dispose of the case by way of an absolute discharge owing to particular mitigating circumstances. Concluding the hearing, the presiding magistrate warned that those whose profession is to prosecute people for failing to comply with the law must meet their legal obligations.[96]

There are very often 'grey areas', where data controllers (and therein the ICO) may find it difficult to determine whether or not certain information is subject to the requirements of the DPA 1998. The ICO has suggested that in those cases where data controllers are unsure whether or not information comes within the definition of data relevant for the filing system of notification, they should evaluate how accessible the data are by making reasoned judgements. Data controllers should then consider the extent to which a decision not to treat the information as being covered by the 1998 Act will prejudice the individual concerned. Where the risk of prejudice is reasonably likely, then data controllers would be expected to err on the side of caution and take steps to ensure compliance.

For example, if information about a particular web-user is built up over a period of time – perhaps through the use of tracking technology – with the intention that it may later be linked to a name and address, that information is personal data. Information may be compiled about a particular web-user but without the intention of linking it to a name, address or email address. There might merely be an intention to target that particular user with advertising or to offer discounts when they revisit a particular website without the intention to actually locate that user in

---

93 Monetary penalties are issued under s 55C(1) of the Data Protection Act 1998.
94 Occurring on or after 6 April 2010, or serious breaches of the Privacy and Electronic Communications Regulations occurring on or after 26 May 2011.
95 (2013) 130 BMLR 135 (FTT) (unreported 15 January 2013). The First Tier Tribunal refused the NHS Trust permission to appeal to the Upper Tribunal after it had earlier rejected its challenge to a £90,000 monetary penalty notice issued by the Information Commissioner. For detailed case commentary see: Johnson (2013b) at pp. 25–28.
96 Source: Information Commissioner's Office website at: www.ico.gov.uk/news/latest_news/2012/spam-texters-fined-nearly-half-a-million-pounds-28112012.aspx.

the physical world. The IC takes the view that such information is, nevertheless, personal data.[97] Should an individual feel that they are being denied access to personal information, they are entitled to contact the ICO for help, such as breaches of data protection (known as a 'compliance assessment').[98]

The ICO has wide discretion to decide how to undertake a compliance assessment and usually takes the following criteria into account:

- whether the request appears to raise a matter of substance;
- any undue delay in making the request;
- whether the person making the request is entitled to make a subject access request.

The Freedom of Information (Scotland) Act 2002 contains much the same terms as its English and Welsh equivalent – though it is much broader in scope. The case of **Common Services Agency v Scottish Information Commissioner** (2008)[99] concerned the attempts to secure statistics about childhood incidents of leukaemia in the Scottish border area of Dumfries and Galloway in relation to public fear about nuclear processing operations at Chapelcross near Annan and Sellafield in neighbouring Cumbria. Section 38 of the Scottish Act (which is much the same as s 40 FOIA 'personal information') decided that this was not available.

Here follow some common data protection myths and realities which are in the form of 'for thought' boxes with the answers supplied in the relevant footnotes.

 FOR THOUGHT NO. 1

The Data Protection Act 1998 stops parents from taking photos in schools. Is this correct?[100]

 FOR THOUGHT NO. 2

A company is never allowed to give a customer's details to a third party. True?[101]

---

97 Source: Information Commissioner's Legal Guidance, March 2007, p. 12.
98 See for example: The ICO's Report on the Surveillance Society (2006) compiled by the Surveillance Studies Network. September 2006. Online report available at www.ico.gov.uk/upload/documents/library/data_protection/practical_application/surveillance_society_full_report_2006.pdf.
99 [2008] UKHL of 9 July 2008.
100 This is not correct. Photographs taken purely for personal use are exempt from the Data Protection Act 1998. This means that parents, friends and family members can take photographs of their children and friends participating in school activities and can film events at school. The DPA 1998 does apply where photographs are taken for official use by schools and colleges, such as for identity passes, and these images are stored with personal details such as names. It will usually be enough for the photographer to ask for permission to ensure compliance with the 1998 Act.
101 Not true. Where an organization is satisfied that someone asking for information about another person's account is authorized to access it, the DPA 1998 does not prevent this. However, organizations should be cautious about releasing customers' details. There is a market in personal information and unscrupulous individuals try to obtain information about others by deception. Therefore, organizations must have appropriate safeguards in place to ensure that, if staff decide to reveal a customer's personal details, such as bank account information, they are sure that the person they are speaking to is either their customer or someone acting on their behalf; for example, evidence that the account-holder has given authority.

FOR THOUGHT NO. 3

The *Daily Telegraph* reported on 30 September 2005 the case of an 11-year-old girl who sat her flute exam but was unable to find out her result. The exam board cited the Data Protection Act 1998 and said that only the person who made the application, the flute teacher, could see the results. Was this correct?[102]

 FOR THOUGHT NO. 4

The case of a car owner trying to find out who damaged his car gained some coverage in the national and local press, including a letter written by Ann Widdecombe for the *Daily Express* in August 2005. It was reported that the car, which was uninsured as it was off the road and out of use, was vandalized on the owner's driveway by a youth. Police apprehended the culprit but refused to release the youth's details to the owner, who wanted to bring civil proceedings against him to repair the damage to his car. The police cited the Data Protection Act 1998 as the reason. Was this correct?[103]

6.5.2 EU data protection legislation: the *Bavarian Lager* case

In the **Bavarian Lager** case[104] (see below), Advocate General Eleanor Sharpston QC opined in the European Court of Justice (ECJ)[105] on the conflicting Regulations concerning the protection of and freedom of access to personal data and information. The Advocate General noted that the two existing Regulations, the 'Access Regulation' 1049/2001 and the 'Data Protection Regulation' 45/2001, contradicted each other. The Advocate General therefore recommended that the Commission revise its legislation in this respect to provide individuals (and companies) with clear, legally enforceable rights; furthermore, that the principles of data protection should apply to *any* information concerning an identifiable person. These rules should then be homogeneously applied in all Member States to safeguard the protection of individuals' fundamental rights and freedoms with regard to the processing of their personal data within the Community.

---

102 Not true. The DPA 1998 does not prevent an exam board from giving results to the students or their parents. The decision by this particular exam board was clearly unfair and unnecessary given that the student's mother in this case had to make a subject access request to discover her daughter's exam result – but at least data protection access rights made sure she got the information to which she was entitled.
103 The claim that the DPA 1998 stops the police from disclosing details of cautioned offenders to the victims of their crime is incorrect. The Act is not a barrier to disclosing relevant details where civil proceedings by the victim are contemplated.
104 **Commission v The Bavarian Lager Co. Ltd** [2009] EUECJ of 15 October 2009 (see also: **Bavarian Lager v Commission** [1999]).
105 Now simply The Court of Justice.

> ❖ **KEY CASE**
> ### The *Bavarian Lager* Case before the European Court of Justice[106]

Preliminary Rulings (ECJ)

❖ Under the Access to Documents Regulation,[107] EU institutions can refuse freedom of access to personal information where disclosure may put at risk the protection of the private life of an individual.

❖ Under the Data Protection Regulation,[108] personal data cannot be transferred to recipients other than Community institutions, unless the recipient organization establishes that the data is necessary for the performance of a specific task, carried out in the public interest or subject to the exercise of a public authority.

❖ Where a request based on the Access to Documents Regulation seeks to obtain access to documents including personal data, the provisions of the Data Protection Regulation become applicable in their entirety, including the provision requiring the recipient of personal data to establish the need for their disclosure (the 'necessity test').

❖ A person requesting access to data information is not required to justify his request and therefore does not have to demonstrate any 'public interest' in having access to the documents requested.

❖ A proper system of personal data protection in each Member State not only requires the establishment of rights for data subjects and obligations for those who process personal data, but also appropriate sanctions for 'offenders' and a proper monitoring by an independent supervisory body (such as the Information Commissioner in the UK).

Facts

The *Bavarian Lager Co. Ltd* ('Bavarian Lager') was established in Clitheroe, Lancashire, in 1992 to import bottled German beer into the UK for pubs. British breweries holding rights in more than 2,000 pubs were required to allow the pub managers the possibility of buying beer from another brewery, on condition that the beer was conditioned in casks with an alcohol content exceeding 1.2 per cent by volume, known as Guest Beer Provision (GBP).[109] Bavarian Lager could not sell its bottled lager because most of the 2,000 pubs were 'tied' into GBP in exclusive purchasing contracts with breweries. Bavarian Lager lodged a complaint with the Commission in April 1993, arguing that this constituted a measure having an effect equivalent to a quantitative restriction on imports and was therefore incompatible with Article 28 EC Treaty.

During the administrative procedure before the Commission, a meeting was held on 11 October 1996 between representatives of the Community and UK administrative authorities and the Confédération des Brasseurs du Marché Commun. Bavarian Lager wanted to take part in that meeting, but the Commission refused. On 15 March 1997, the

106 **Commission v The Bavarian Lager Co. Ltd** [2009] EUECJ of 15 October 2009.
107 Regulation 1049/2001 of the European Parliament and of the Council of 30 May 2001 regarding public access to European Parliament, Council and Commission documents (OJ 2001 L 145, p. 43).
108 Regulation 45/2001 of the European Parliament and of the Council of 18 December 2000 on the protection of individuals with regard to the processing of personal data by the Community institutions and bodies and on the free movement of such data (OJ 2001 L 8, p. 1).
109 Under Article 7(2)(a) of the Supply of Beer (Tied Estate) Order 1989 (SI 1989/2390).

Department of Trade and Industry announced that the GBP provision was to be amended in order for bottled beer to be sold as GBP. The Commission suspended all Treaty infringement proceedings against the UK. By fax of 21 March 1997, Bavarian Lager asked the Director General of the Commission (Internal Market and Financial Services) for a copy of the 'reasoned opinion', and access to the Commission documents concerning the meeting of 11 October 1996. That request was refused. Reasons given included that the related documents were 'data protected' because five individuals wished to remain anonymous.[110]

Bavarian Lager, relying on Article 8(1) and (2) of the Charter, and the Access to Documents Regulation 1049/2001 ('the Access Regulation'), argued for administrative transparency'. The Commission, in turn, relied on Regulation 45/2001 on 'Data Protection' ('DP', the 'Personal Data' Regulation'). The DP requires the person to whom personal data is to be transferred to demonstrate that the transfer is necessary. Bavarian Lager applied to the Court of First Instance[111] for clarification.

When the case reached the European Court of Justice, the Commission, supported by the UK, argued that the Court of First Instance had made errors of law in its findings concerning the application of the exemption in Article 4(1)(b) of Regulation No 1049/2001 and thereby rendered certain provisions of Regulation No 45/2001 ineffective.

Decision by the European Court of Justice (ECJ)

In her judgment, the Advocate General ruled that the Access to Documents Regulation[112] established the general rule that the public may have access to documents of public institutions of Member States (MS). But the ECJ equally laid down exemptions by reason of certain public and private interests, particularly in relation to the right of access to a document where the disclosure would undermine the privacy and integrity of an individual or even put that individual at risk. In certain circumstances, however, an individual's personal data may be communicated to the public. Where a request based on the Access to Documents Regulation seeks to obtain access to documents including personal data, the provisions of the Data Protection Regulation[113] become applicable in their entirety, including the provision requiring the recipient of personal data to establish the need for their disclosure (the 'necessity test').

The ECJ set aside the judgment by the Court of First Instance (CFI), meaning that Bavarian Lager lost its appeal; the ECJ reached the following conclusions:

1. The CFI had erred in law because it failed to correctly interpret Article 6 of the Access Regulation 1049/2001, i.e. processing personal data by EU institutions;[114] a person requesting access is not required to justify his request and therefore does not have to demonstrate any interest in having access to the documents requested.

---

110 See: **Bavarian Lager v Commission** [1999] ECR II-3217(ECJ).
111 Now known as the The General Court. As from 1 December 2009, the date on which the Treaty of Lisbon entered into force, the EU has legal personality and has acquired the competences previously conferred on the European Community (EC). Community law has therefore become European Union law. The term 'Community law' will still be used where the earlier case-law of the General Court is being cited. The General Court is made up of at least one judge from each Member State.
112 Regulation 1049/2001, op. cit.
113 Regulation 45/2001, op. cit.
114 See: **Bavarian Lager v Commission** [1999] op. cit.

2. The DP Regulation 45/2001 requires consideration of whether the applicant has a legitimate ('necessary') interest in receiving the particular personal data. Accordingly;

3. The Commission had not erred when it decided that Bavarian Lager had not established a legitimate interest in receiving the personal data contained in the documents.

4. The ECJ dismissed the action of Bavarian Lager against the Commission's decision of 18 March 2004, rejecting an application for access to the full minutes of the meeting of 11 October 1996, including all the names, i.e. the data had been lawfully withheld by the Commission. In the absence of the consent of the five participants at the meeting of October 1996, the Commission sufficiently complied with its duty of openness by releasing a version of the document in question with their names blanked out.

5. Since Bavarian Lager was unsuccessful in the appeal, the court ordered Bavarian Lager to pay the full costs relating to the appeal, i.e. all Commission appeal proceedings including the CFI.[115]

Analysis

Though the **Bavarian Lager** case originally concerned the 'free movement of goods' principle, the main issue before the Court of Justice centred on freedom of information and access to personal (or in this case company) data. The ECJ made it clear that a fully fledged system of personal data protection not only requires the establishment of rights for data subjects and obligations for those who process personal data, but also appropriate sanctions for offenders and monitoring by an independent supervisory body.

The Advocate General's opinion appears to favour freedom of information principles but at the same time she warned that personal data needs to be safeguarded – relying on the fundamental principles of Article 6 EU Treaty and the Charter of Fundamental Rights of the European Union ('the Charter'). The Charter recognizes the primary importance of both the protection of personal data and the right of access to documents. Article 8(1) and (2) of the Charter provide as follows:

1. Everyone has the right to the protection of personal data concerning him or her.

2. Such data must be processed fairly for specified purposes and on the basis of the consent of the person concerned or some other legitimate basis laid down by law. Everyone has the right of access to data which has been collected concerning him or her, and the right to have it rectified.

The AG then recommended that measures should be adopted which are binding on the Community institutions and bodies. These measures should apply to all processing of personal data by all Community institutions and bodies insofar as such processing is carried out in the exercise of activities all or part of which fall within the scope of Community law, according to Article 6 of the EU Treaty. Access to documents, including conditions for access to documents containing personal data, is governed by the rules in Article 255 EC Treaty.

---

115 Other cases cited and dealt with at the time by the ECJ were: **Council v Hautala** [2001] ECR I – 9565; **Sweden v Commission** [2007] ECR I – 11389; **Netherlands v Council** [1996] ECR I – 2169 (Case C-58/94). The ECJ ordered the Kingdom of Denmark, the Republic of Finland, the Kingdom of Sweden and the UK to bear their own costs.

> The **Bavarian Lager** case demonstrates that under the Access to Documents Regulation,[116] EU institutions may refuse freedom of access to information where disclosure would risk undermining the protection of the private life of an individual. The Data Protection Regulation[117] states that personal data cannot be transferred to recipients other than Community institutions, unless the recipient organization establishes that the data is necessary for the performance of a specific task, carried out in the public interest or subject to the exercise of public authority.

Article 12 of the Council Directive 95/46[118] (the 'Data Protection Directive') defines the individual's (or 'data subject's') right to access data. The Directive states that:

> ... member states shall guarantee every data subject the right to obtain from the controller: (a) without constraint at reasonable intervals and without excessive delay or expense: [abbreviated] ... communication to him in an intelligible form of the data undergoing processing and of any available information as to their source [abbreviated].

This means that every EU Member State's public authority ('the controller') must provide access to requested information within reasonable time intervals (usually interpreted as once a year), without charge and 'without excessive delay', meaning usually within three months. In the UK all 'data controllers' as part of a national organization are now required under the Data Protection Act 1998 to register with the Information Commissioner's Office. The 1998 Act has been strengthened by EU data protection legislation (see also: **Gillberg v Sweden** (2012)[119]).

6.5.3 Developments in EU law: 'the right to be forgotten'

Every day, businesses, public authorities and individuals transfer vast amounts of personal data across borders. There is currently conflicting data protection legislation in different countries, which can disrupt international exchanges. Individuals can still be reluctant or unwilling to transfer personal data abroad if they are uncertain about the level of protection in other countries. Some common EU rules have been established to ensure that personal data enjoys a high standard of protection, at least within the EU. The Data Protection Directive[120] ensures that individuals have the right to complain and seek redress if their data is being misused within the EU.

In November 2012, the Information Commissioner, Christopher Graham, announced the publication of a Code of Practice for anonymized data. The Code advises on how to protect the privacy rights of individuals while dealing with large and rich databases. The Code focuses on the legal framework of the DPA 1998 and incorporates the EU Data Protection Directive, which states that the principles of data protection do not apply to data anonymized in such a way that its subject is no longer identifiable, essentially placing the onus on ensuring that this guarantee of anonymity is met. The IC commissioned a further study to establish the meaning of 'personal data' and how far EU law provision actually provided protection for the individual citizen in the 28 Member States.

---

116 Regulation 1049/2001, op. cit.
117 Regulation 45/2001, op. cit.
118 Council Directive 95/46 on the protection of individuals with regard to the processing of personal data and on the free movement of such data (the Data Protection Directive).
119 (2012) (App. No. 41723/06) of 3 April 2012 (ECTHR).
120 Directive 95/46/EC on the protection of individuals with regard to the processing of personal data and on the free movement of such data. On 25 January 2012, the European Commission unveiled a draft European Data Protection Regulation that will supersede the Data Protection Directive in due course.

The ICO Report *Implications of the European Commission's proposal for a general data protection regulation for business* (2013) found that there was a general lack of understanding about the provisions in the EC's general data protection regulations which existed across businesses in the UK. The report concluded that there is a key role for the ICO to play in educating and supporting businesses to increase awareness and understanding of future changes in EU legisltation on data protection.[121]

On 25 January 2012, the European Commission announced a full review and overhaul of the EU's data protection legislation. The Commission proposed a new Regulation on the processing of personal data in both public and private sectors, to replace the existing Data Protection Directive (95/46/EC). One of the main features of the draft Directive is the 'right to be forgotten', enabling citizens to request that their personal information be totally and permanently removed from the internet or other data collectors. Furthermore, national data protection authorities (like the Information Commissioner) will be given extensive powers to impose financial sanctions against any organizations violating EU Regulations.[122] The draft regulation specifies:

- principles relating to personal data processing;
- rights of data subjects to access their personal data, have it rectified or erased, object to its processing and not be subject to profiling;
- obligations of data controllers and data processors to provide information to individuals, report breaches of data security and put in place technical and organizational measures;
- rules on transfer of personal data to countries outside the European Economic Area (EEA) and to international organizations;
- rules relating to national 'independent supervisory authorities' and how they should co-operate with each other and the European Commission; and
- remedies available to data subjects and administrative sanctions available to supervisory authorities.[123]

Under the Data Protection Directive, personal data can only be gathered legally under strict conditions, for a legitimate purpose. Furthermore, persons or organizations which collect and manage personal information must protect it from misuse and must respect certain rights of the data owners which are guaranteed by EU law. The Directive also defines specific rules for the transfer of personal data outside the EU to ensure the best possible protection of data when it is exported abroad.[124]

The key consideration is then not whether it is possible for an individual to be identified, but rather the likelihood of such identification taking place. The IC Code sets out a framework for an organization to follow when establishing this level of probability, and thus whether or not the DPA legislation applies to the databases it is handling. In addition to the initial anonymization process, those organizations holding such data must account for the likelihood of reidentification, the process by which someone in possession of one data-set could combine it with one or more additional databases to establish an individual's identity.

In January 2012 the EU Commission in Brussels proposed a comprehensive reform of the EU's data protection rules to strengthen online privacy rights and boost Europe's digital economy. Technological progress and globalization have profoundly changed the way data is collected, accessed and used. There are different rules and regulations in place in the 28 EU Member States, resulting in divergences in enforcement. A single law in the form of a new data protection regulation

---

121 See: Information Commissioner's Office (2013).
122 For further discussion see: De Waele (2012) at pp. 3–5.
123 Ibid., at pp. 14–15. See also: European Commission (2012), 11 final, Article 4.
124 See also: Brimsted (2003) at pp. 22–23.

is proposed to abolish such fragmentation and costly administrative burdens. The Commission hopes that this new legislative initiative will help reinforce consumer confidence in online services, providing a much needed boost to growth, jobs and innovation in Europe.[125]

6.6 Has the freedom of information legislation made a difference to public life? Analysis and discussion

Has the Freedom of Information Act 2000 made a difference to public life? Arguably yes. For many supporters, the FOIA and the office of the Information Commissioner have radically altered Britain's climate of secrecy for the better and improved openness within national and local government.

The revelations about MPs' expenses would not have been available to the *Daily Telegraph* had the parliamentary authorities not been preparing a heavily redacted document for FOIA release. Some have criticized the act as a bureaucratic waste of time and money, with requesters complaining that important information is often redacted or withheld by authorities who are only too aware of the complex rules and exemptions of FOIA legislation. Arguably, too much information is being withheld by authorities who try to hide behind the complex exemption clauses. At times, the Information Commissioner has taken years to release information and appeals can take up to four years to process because the ICO is swamped with cases.

6.6.1 Should the free flow of information via WikiLeaks be prohibited?

On 28 December 2007, the whistleblower website WikiLeaks released graphic video footage of the slaughter of Iraqi civilians by US helicopter gunships. The incident was filmed from a military Apache helicopter and showed an attack carried out in the Iraqi suburb of New Baghdad in July 2007, when two Reuters journalists, Saeed Chmagh and Namir Noor-Eldeen, were killed. Reuters had been trying unsuccessfully to obtain the video via the FOIA. WikiLeaks obtained and then decrypted the video via anonymous sources within the military.

The film prompted an instant uproar and confrontation between the Pentagon and its defenders, who argued that the rules of engagement had been followed, and critics, who decried the brutality of killing unsuspecting people from the air and the perverse glee of some of the soldiers. In one exchange on the 38-minute video, soldiers in the helicopter watch a US tank on the ground below and one says, 'I think they just drove over a body.' Another chuckles and says, 'Really?' The two can be heard laughing. When a soldier on the ground reports that a small girl in a van on the scene was seriously wounded, a helicopter gunner says, 'Well, it's their fault for bringing their kids into a battle.' The other responds, 'That's right.' After they blow up a building killing people inside, the gunners can be heard saying 'Sweet' and 'Nice missile'.[126] Following the controversial release of the film by WikiLeaks, the International Federation of Journalists (IFJ) called on US President Barack Obama to open a fresh investigation into the actions of the US army, which was implicated in killings of journalists in Iraq.[127]

---

125 Source: Press release by EU Commission 'Commission proposes a comprehensive reform of data protection rules to increase users' control of their data and to cut costs for businesses'. Reference: IP/12/46 Event Date: 25/01/2012, at: http://europa.eu/rapid/press-release_IP-12-46_en.htm?locale=en.

126 Source: 'Crimes without punishment', by J. Patrice McSherry, *Guardian*, 14 April 2010.

127 The IFJ works for press freedom by trade union development, working for journalists' rights and social conditions. The organization believes that there can be no press freedom where journalists exist in conditions of corruption, poverty or fear. The IFJ is also a founder of the International News Safety Institute, founded in 2003, which promotes practical action worldwide to increase the safety and protection of journalists and media staff. Source: www.ifj.org/en/pages/press-freedom-safety.

WikiLeaks acts as an electronic dead-drop for highly sensitive or secret information, which is then published in a pure and original form. No rewriting is allowed. Created by an online network of dissidents, journalists, academics, lawyers, technology experts and mathematicians from various countries, the website also uses technology that makes the original sources of the leaks untraceable. Within a year of its launch, the site claimed that its database had grown to 1.2 million documents and that by June 2010 some ten thousand secret documents and pieces of information were flooding in daily. The website allows anyone in the world to upload documents that are 'secret'. WikiLeaks' webservers have mostly been located in Sweden, Belgium, the Netherlands and Iceland, countries that have generous legislation on freedom of expression and information. Furthermore, the website never reveals its sources of information, backed by these countries' supportive legislation. WikiLeaks founder Julian Assange describes this process as 'principled leaking', and all material is vetted by a team of experts for authenticity. WikiLeaks is essentially an outlaw operation, creating a viral or word-of-mouth buzz with arresting secret intelligence. It has forced itself to the forefront of journalism in the digital age. The website has become a conduit for publishing material under its premise that every person has a right to freedom of information. It was WikiLeaks that exposed the full Trafigura scandal by releasing the (super)injuncted documents.[128]

See above
6.3.4

On 19 June 2009, Assange released the full report on the corruption that had led to the UK government's taking control of the British overseas territories, the Turks and Caicos Islands (TCI), a popular Caribbean tourist destination and tax haven.[129] Subsequently, following the corruption allegations made against the Islands' political elite, the British Foreign and Commonwealth Office commissioned Sir Robin Auld to head up a Turks and Caicos Islands Commission of Inquiry. The Report by the Parliamentary Commission inquiry found that foreign property developers had given millions of US dollars in secret loans and payments to senior Islander politicians, including the TCI's former Premier, Michael Misick. A lawsuit in the UK High Court ensued, initially resulting in a *contra mundum* injunction against all media reporting. This injunction was overturned, permitting free reporting on the Commission's findings. The UK Government has been in control of the TCI since April 2010.[130]

WikiLeaks was also instrumental in bringing about the resignation of the Prime Minister of Tanzania, Edward Lowassa, by releasing the (secret) Richmond Parliamentary Committee Report that exposed gross corruption at the highest level of Tanzania's Government on 7 February 2008. The website also released the full British National Party (BNP) membership list for 2007–08 and claimed to have swung the Kenyan presidential election in 2007 by exposing corruption at the highest levels.

Should the legal system have prevented publication on free internet websites like WikiLeaks, which pride themselves on releasing secret government information supplied by international bona fide sources? Julian Assange would argue 'no'. On the BBC Radio Four *Media Show* in June 2010, Assange argued strongly in favour of a totally free flow of information. He claimed that the whistle-blower website had released more classified documents than the rest of the world's press combined. Assange said: 'That's not something I say as a way of saying how successful we are – rather, that shows you the powerless state of the rest of the media. How is it that a team of five people has managed to release to the public more suppressed information, at that level, than the rest of the world press combined?'[131]

---

128 Source: 'Ivory Coast toxic dumping report behind secret Guardian gag', WikiLeaks, 13 October 2009, available at http://mirror.
    wikileaks.info/wiki/Ivory_Coast_toxic_dumping_report_behind_secret_Guardian_gag.
129 Source: 'Big Trouble in Little Paradise: the Turks and Caicos Islands takeover', by Julian Assange, WikiLeaks, 19 June 2009.
130 For further discussion see: Smartt (2010b); also: Smartt (2008), pp. 200–203.
131 Source: Interview with Julian Assange from WikiLeaks on the BBC Radio 4's *The Media Show*, 16 June 2010. Assange is a former
    physics and pure maths student; as a former computer hacker he has made it his personal quest to reveal governmental
    corruption around the world.

By December 2013, WikiLeaks founder Assange had spent 18 months in the Ecuadorian Embassy in London to avoid arrest and extradition to Sweden on suspicion of sexual offence charges. In a special video he told the media that he was preparing to publish one million new secret government documents on WikiLeaks.[132]

With the existence of social networking sites such as Facebook, YouTube and Twitter, this raises important issues as to whether privacy and personal data can be realistically protected in the twenty-first century. Websites such as WikiLeaks put the whole area of 'freedom of information' and the complex regime of the FOIA 2000 into question, with its complex applications and class exemptions, where the Information Commissioner has to balance state, individual, corporate and media interests when making an effective decision as to whether to disclose sensitive information or not. In the meantime, someone may well leak the relevant information in any case, either via a social networking site or via a 'whistleblower' site such as WikiLeaks. The MPs' expenses scandal demonstrates this. Most would agree that this was significant and important information which the public had to know. The *Daily Telegraph*'s revelations about the parliamentary expenses 'abuses' were of genuine public interest, and without the FOIA legislation we may never have found out about them.

6.7 Further reading

De Waele, H. (2012) 'Implications of replacing the Data Protection Directive with a Regulation – a legal perspective'. *Privacy & Data Protection,* **12(4), 3–5.**
Henri De Waele examines the legal differences between existing EU Regulations and Directives on data protection and the way such legislation is and will be directly applicable to EU Member States. De Waele concludes that the replacement of the Data Protection Directive 95/46/EC with a Regulation will result in a uniform, transparent and accessible set of rules, which can be effectively enforced across the EU.

Goldsmith, J. and Wu, T. (2008) *Who Controls the Internet? Illusions of a borderless world.* **London/New York: Oxford University Press.**
In this insightful book, Jack Goldsmith and Tim Wu examine the past and future of the internet revolution and the erosion of legal national borders. The authors tell the fascinating story of the internet's challenge to governmental rule in the 1990s, and the ensuing battles with governments around the world. We learn of Google's legal struggles with the French Government and Yahoo's capitulation to the Chinese regime; of how the EU sets privacy standards on the internet seemingly for the entire world; and of eBay's struggles with online fraud. Goldsmith and Wu describe the new legal order that has been created through the internet. While territorial governments have unavoidable problems, it has proven hard to replace what legitimacy governments have, and harder yet to replace the system of rule of law that controls the unchecked evils of anarchy. The book is well written and filled with fascinating examples, including colourful portraits of many key players in internet history.

Grant, H. and Round, N. (2012) 'Recent decisions of the Commissioner and Tribunal'. *Freedom of Information,* **9(2), 8–12.**
Hazel Grant and Nicholas Round analyze decisions from the Information Commissioner and First Tier Tribunal in 2012. The following cases are discussed in detail: *Evans v Information Commissioner* [2012] UKUT 313 (UT (AAC)); *Montford v IC* (unreported August 14, 2012 (FTT)); *Chagos Refugees Group in Mauritius v IC* (unreported September 4, 2012 (FTT));

---

132 Source: 'Julian Assange: expect more from WikiLeaks', by Conal Urquart, *Guardian,* 20 December 2012.

IC v Magherafelt DC [2012] UKUT 263 (UT). The authors examine specifically challenges under s 38 FOIA and s 40(2) FOIA concerning personal information exemptions. The main argument centres on the dispute whether the IC and the FTT have made errors in law.

Kleinwachter, W. (2012) 'Internet governance outlook 2012: cold war or constructive dialogue?' *Communications Law,* **17(1), 14–18.**
The author discusses the potential dangers of freedom and access of information in cyberspace. With two billion people now online, Kleinwachter discusses two options: 'either we continue with a free and open internet which has enabled historically unknown innovation, economic growth, social development and free communication, or we will make a U-turn towards a more regulated, restricted, censored and fragmented internet where national policies of governments and commercial interests of corporations will reduce or strangulate individual rights and freedoms.'

Spurrier, M. (2012) *'Gillberg v Sweden:* **towards a right of access to information under Article 10?'** *European Human Rights Law Review,* **5, 551–558.**
The author comments on and analyses the ECtHR (Grand Chamber) judgment in *Gillberg v Sweden* (App. No. 41723/06) of 3 April 2012 and its implications for locating a right of access to information under Article 10 ECHR. Spurrier discusses this Strasbourg case where the human rights court recognized and developed a positive right of access to information, also closely protected in international law. She suggests that a tension has been created between the rights to information in domestic legislation and the developing standalone right of access to information under Article 10. The author argues that the Strasbourg Court should take a more principled approach to the development of this right and observes that the changing landscape is provoking much debate in the domestic courts.

Weber, R.H. (2010) *Shaping Internet Governance: Regulatory challenges* **(in collaboration with Mirina Grosz and Romana Weber). Zürich: Springer.**
The joint authors discuss legal aspects of internet governance and the manifold aspects of possible regulatory regimes. Weber *et al.* note that at present an international treaty structure is missing and self-regulation as a normative model does not suffice in all respects. This is a thorough and systematic study of the main topics of internet governance, such as legitimacy, transparency, accountability and participation. The authors also address key regulatory issues, for example critical internet resources, access to freedom of information, protection of civil liberties and human rights, realization of security, safety and privacy standards, as well as the overcoming of the digital divide from a legal perspective.

Chapter 7

Obscenity Laws, Extreme Pornography and Censorship

> **Key Points**
>
> This chapter will cover the following questions:
>
> ○ What is the law relating to attacks on religious beliefs?
> ○ What are the common law offences of contravening public decency?
> ○ Does the 'innocent schoolgirl test' still apply to a publication which is considered 'obscene'?
> ○ What constitutes 'obscene publication' in UK legislation today?
> ○ What are the punishments for contravening UK obscenity laws?
> ○ What amounts to possession of extreme pornographic images?
> ○ What are the available defences?
> ○ Are British obscenity laws outdated?

7.1 Overview

American publisher Barney Rosset died in February 2012 aged 89. His obituary read that he was one of the most influential avant-garde publishers of the twentieth century and one of the boldest for his willingness to challenge the laws governing censorship. As head of Grove Press at the time he challenged the ban on D. H. Lawrence's *Lady Chatterley's Lover* in 1959, just at the point when the Obscene Publications Act 1959 had come into force. The novel had been published legally in the USA, one year before the British (Penguin) edition, and published earlier in Italy in 1928. Like the French publisher Maurice Girodias, whose Olympia Press was an abundant supplier to Grove (Miller, Beckett, Genet, Trocchi and Burroughs were all first published there), Rosset liked the risqué element of literature; the Grove titles were those that were artistically daring at the same time.

This chapter concerns itself with what might be described as 'grey area speech', where even societies that guarantee the protection of freedom of expression have felt it necessary for a variety of reasons to ban or restrict such speech for the public good. We will look at legal challenges to art and literature under the UK and EU obscenity laws. Such challenges are set against human rights legislation which, *inter alia*, supports freedom of expression (Article 10 ECHR) and the cultural independence of the artist or those who exhibit works of art (Article 8 ECHR). There have been a number of legal challenges under UK obscenity laws, against either an author, a playwright, a poet, a photographer or an artist. The fact that some successfully fought off challenges to publication or performance of their works in court is evidenced by the fact that we can read books such as D. H. Lawrence's *Lady Chatterley's Lover* or see plays such as Michael Bogdanov's production of Howard Brenton's *The Romans in Britain*. This can be seen as a triumph for freedom of expression, or at least a reflection of the changing nature of cultural and sexual morals and norms in society.

This chapter also briefly charts the history and abolition of blasphemy laws, eventually abolished by s 79 of the Criminal Justice and Immigration Act 2008.[1]

See below
7.2.1

---

1 Section 79 of the Criminal Justice and Immigration Act 2008, 'abolition of common law offences of blasphemy and blasphemous libel'. Previous legislation included under s 1 Criminal Libel Act 1819 the 'orders for seizure of copies of blasphemous or seditious libel' and ss 3 and 4 Law of Libel Amendment Act 1888 'blasphemy and privileged matters'.

While attacks on someone's reputation cannot generally be justified under the right to free speech – nor words which advocate violence or hatred – different laws have emerged over time in different countries which have struck the balance between what would amount to acceptable speech or artistic limitations on the one hand or a claim to freedom of speech in a democratic and liberal society on the other.

7.2 Abolition of blasphemy laws in the UK and new religious hate speech provision: a legal historical perspective

The issue of blasphemy or unjustified attacks or denigration of religious beliefs is a major concern internationally and also in the UK, despite the increasing secularization of the country. Countries such as Saudi Arabia, Pakistan and Iran maintain severe laws on blasphemy that make any discussion of the tenets of Islamic beliefs and statements in the Qur'an a very risky subject matter. This hard-line approach is also reflected in some sections of ethnic minority communities in the UK and leads to demands for more restrictive laws in this area. The balancing of these concerns with a more liberal approach to freedom of speech has the potential to cause tension and also to legal challenges based on Article 9 ECHR ('right to religious freedom and respect for religious beliefs').

Blasphemy laws in the UK were last fully tested in the 'Salman Rushdie' case (**R v Chief Metropolitan Stipendiary Magistrate, ex parte Choudhury** (1991)[2]). The courts confirmed that blasphemy laws did not protect Muslims from anti-Islam blasphemy, when a summons was sought against Salman Rushdie and his publishers for an alleged blasphemous libel by the publication of his novel The Satanic Verses. The summons was refused, and both the court at first instance and the Divisional Court stated that blasphemy law only applied to the protection of the Christian religion, as expressed in the tenets and beliefs of the established Church of England, i.e. Anglican beliefs, and could not be extended to protect Islam, or any other religion or Christian sect adopting different tenets to those of Anglicanism.

See also
Chapter 1.2.2

In **Choudhury v UK** (1991),[3] the applicant contended that English law was prejudicial against Islam, which the European Commission held as manifestly ill-founded and inadmissible because there was no positive obligation on Member States under the European Convention to protect all religious sensibilities. By using its margin of appreciation, the ECtHR allowed the contracting states to apply their own blasphemy (and obscenity) laws.

English blasphemy laws singularly protected the beliefs of the established churches in the UK (Church of England and Church of Scotland), and since the complete abolition in 2008, potentially 'blasphemous' acts are now largely covered by public order legislation, in particular against inciting religious hatred, which does have the potential to cover non-Christian beliefs or indeed no beliefs at all, e.g. attacks on 'militant atheists'. This was the case in **R v Shepperd and Whittle** (2010),[4] where the offenders had produced racially inflammatory material and posted it on a website hosted by a remote server in the USA. It was held that they could be charged and tried in the UK under ss 19 and 29 Public Order Act 1986.

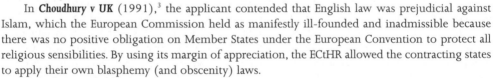

---

2   [1991] 1 QB 429; [1990] 3 WLR 986.
3   (1991) 12 HRLJ 172 (ECTHR).
4   [2010] EWCA Crim 65 (CA Crim Div).

7.2.1 Blasphemy in English law

Blasphemy and heresy laws were used in England from medieval times to protect the official religion of the state – religious orthodoxy was regarded as fundamental to political order, as today illustrated in theocratic states such as Iran. Jurisdiction over 'blasphemous libel' and 'seditious, obscene and defamatory libel' was exercised by the Star Chamber established by the Statute of Westminster 1275 which 'regarded with the deepest suspicion the printed word in general, and anything which looked like criticism of the established institutions of the Church or State in particular'.[5]

Once the Star Chamber was abolished in 1641, the Court of King's Bench inherited its criminal jurisdiction, thereby completing the transfer of jurisdiction over the offences into the courts of the common law. The common law courts then took over the jurisdiction of blasphemy and seditious libel with great enthusiasm. Residual jurisdiction developed to control public morals and public decency – though not necessarily directly connected with any religious connotations.

See Chapter 1.2

The common law offence of blasphemy included the malicious or wanton reproach of God (either written or oral), Jesus Christ, the Bible and the Book of Common Prayer, with the intent to undermine religious beliefs and promote contempt and hatred for the Church as well as general immorality. Blasphemy and blasphemous libel were common law offences triable on indictment and punishable by fine or imprisonment. Blasphemy consisted in speaking and blasphemous libel in otherwise publishing blasphemous matter. Libel involved a publication in a permanent form.[6]

See Chapter 3

The crime of blasphemy did not require an intent in the utterer to blaspheme (see below 'Key Case': **R v Lemon** (1979) ('the *Gay News* case')[7]), or to cause a breach of the peace or fear of violence, or even objective likelihood of such happening as a result of the utterance. Nor did it need proof of shock or distress in the person addressed, since the crime could be committed even though that person shared or welcomed the views expressed.

In 1675 dramatist Sir Charles Sedley was the first person to be tried at common law for blasphemy and 'outraging public decency' ('**Sedley's case**'[8]). Famous for his wit, Sir Charles was a member of the intimate circle of young rakes at the court of Charles II. He had shown himself naked on the balcony of a house in Covent Garden and, in the presence of several people, had urinated on them. He was indicted at common law. *Sedley's case* was cited in **R v Hamilton** (2007),[9] where the defendant appealed his conviction for 'outraging public decency'. Hamilton had surreptitiously filmed up the skirts of women in a supermarket. The offence was only discovered after the films were found during a search of his home for other material. The defendant contended that the offence was not committed since nobody had witnessed the offence. His appeal failed. (See also: **Knuller (Publishing, Printing and Promotions) Ltd v DPP** (1973)[10]).

Hamilton and **Knuller** are good examples showing how the common law of blasphemy became akin to a public order type offence, relating to 'indecent behaviour'. Long before the European Convention entered into UK law, Elliott (1993) canvassed that the common law of blasphemy should be abolished since it interfered with freedom of speech (Article 10 ECHR) and religion (Article 9 ECHR).

For more than fifty years before the prosecution in the '**Gay News** case'[11] (see below), the offence of blasphemy appeared to have become obsolete. In his Hamlyn Lecture in 1949, Lord Denning MR portrayed 'blasphemy' as a 'dead letter', explaining that the law had not been successfully invoked

---

5   See: van Vechten (1904).
6   For further discussion see: Burns Coleman and White (2006).
7   [1979] AC 617 (the decision was by a majority, with Lords Diplock and Edmund Davies dissenting).
8   (1675) Strange 168; (1675) 1 Sid 168.
9   [2007] EWCA Crim 2062 (CA Crim Div).
10   [1973] AC 435.
11   **R v Lemon; R v Gay News Ltd** [1979] 1 All ER 898 (sub nom 'Gay News case').

since John W. Gott satirized the biblical story of the entry of Jesus into Jerusalem in a 1921 pamphlet entitled *Rib Ticklers or Questions for Parsons and God and Gott*.[12] Gott and his supporters promoted active and public attacks on Christianity. Gott, a trouser salesman from Bradford, already had three previous convictions for blasphemy at the time when he was prosecuted for publishing the pamphlet, which satirized the biblical story of Jesus entering Jerusalem (Matthew 21: 2–7), comparing Jesus to a circus clown. Giving the judgment at the Court of Appeal, Lord Trevethin CJ said:

> It does not require a person of strong religious feelings to be outraged by a description of Jesus Christ entering Jerusalem 'like a circus clown on the back of two donkeys'.

The offending leaflet was based on a literal interpretation of the prophecy that the King of Zion would come 'riding upon an ass, and upon a colt the foal of an ass'.[13] Gott was sentenced to nine months' hard labour in prison, despite suffering from an incurable illness, and died shortly after he was released.[14] The case became the subject of public outrage.

Lord Scarman declared in the '*Gay News* case', the first prosecution for blasphemy in England since **Gott** in 1922, brought privately by Mrs Mary Whitehouse,[15] that the modern law of blasphemy was correctly formulated in an article of Stephen's *Digest of the Criminal Law*, which stated that:

> . . . every publication is said to be blasphemous which contains any contemptuous, reviling, scurrilous or ludicrous matter relating to God, Jesus Christ, or the Bible, or the formularies of the Church of England as by law established. . . . The test to be applied is as to the manner in which the doctrines are advocated and not as to the substance of the doctrines themselves. Everyone who publishes any blasphemous document is guilty of the [offence] of publishing a blasphemous libel.[16]

The Criminal Law Act 1967 repealed the Blasphemy Act 1697·, and the Sexual Offences Act 1967 began to decriminalize gay sex. But the '*Gay News* case' confirmed that the apparently obsolete common law offence of blasphemy was still very much alive in the late 1970s.

 KEY CASE   The *Gay News* case (*R v Lemon (Denis); R v Gay News Ltd* [1979] AC 617 (HL)

Precedent
(Note: the offence of 'blasphemy' has since been abolished)

❖   To secure a conviction for the offence of publishing a blasphemous libel, it was sufficient for the prosecution to prove an *intention* to publish material which was blasphemous.

❖   It was not necessary to prove that the accused intended to blaspheme (for the purposes of *mens rea*).

---

12 **R v Gott (John William)** (1922) 16 Cr App R 87 (CCA).
13 Zechariah 9: 9.
14 Cited by Denning (1949), p. 46ff.
15 Mary Whitehouse CBE (1910–2001), was a campaigner for Christian beliefs, societal values and morality. She focused her efforts on the broadcast media, and later on publications and theatrical productions, where she increasingly became involved in litigation. She was the founder and first president of the National Viewers' and Listeners' Association (NVLA) which later became mediawatch-uk. In her famous speech at Birmingham Town Hall on 5 May 1964, she said: 'If violence is shown as normal on the television screen it will help to create a violent society.' See also: Thompson (2012).
16 [1979] All ER 898 at 924 (Lord Scarman).

Facts

In June 1976, Denis Lemon, editor of *Gay News*, decided to include a homoerotic poem by James Kirkup, 'The Love That Dares To Speak Its Name', in issue 96 of the newspaper.[17] The poem, a necrophilic fantasy about the death of Jesus of Nazareth, provoked considerable protest from gay Christians decrying it as 'blasphemous'. Mary Whitehouse expressed her outrage in a letter to *The Times*: 'Although broadcasting is exempt from the Obscene Publications Act 1959, we are advised that broadcast blasphemy is a common law offence and that, though dormant, the relevant law is still operative.'[18] Mrs Whitehouse took out a private prosecution against Gay News Ltd and its editor Denis Lemon on 30 November 1976.[19] The indictment read: 'For publishing and distributing a blasphemous libel concerning the Christian religion, namely an obscene poem and illustration vilifying Christ in his life and in his crucifixion.'[20]

The trial opened at the Old Bailey before Judge Alan King-Hamilton QC on Monday 4 July 1977, with John Mortimer QC and Geoffrey Robertson as counsel for the defence and John Smyth representing Mary Whitehouse. The trial judge disallowed expert literary and theological witnesses for the defence and refused to let Mr Lemon explain his intention in publishing the poem. This left two defence witnesses, novelist Margaret Drabble and journalist Bernard Levin, who testified to the good character of the paper's editor. The only witness for the prosecution was Probation Officer Kenneth Kavanagh, an activist against gay rights and head of the 'Parents Advisory Group' concerned with sex education.

On Monday 11 July the jury returned a guilty verdict by a majority of 10 to 2 on both defendants. Gay News Ltd was fined £1,000 and ordered to pay four-fifths of Mary Whitehouse's costs. Denis Lemon was ordered to pay £500 court costs and sentenced to 9 months' imprisonment, suspended for 18 months; he was also ordered to pay the remaining fifth of Mrs Whitehouse's costs (totalling £7,763). Gay News and Denis Lemon appealed against both conviction and sentence on points of law (including misdirection).

Decision

On 17 March 1978 the Court of Appeal quashed Denis Lemon's suspended prison sentence, but otherwise unanimously rejected all grounds of appeal (Lord Justice Roskill, Lord Justice Eveleigh and Mr Justice Stocker). Mary Whitehouse's appeal costs were ordered to be paid out of public funds. Gay News Ltd and Denis Lemon accordingly lodged a petition for leave to appeal at the House of Lords. The appeal was lost at the House of Lords in November 1978.

Analysis

Their Lordships considered the narrow issue of *mens rea* in relation to publishing a blasphemous statement. Denis Lemon and *Gay News* had contended that intention to do wrong was an essential ingredient of the crime of blasphemy. Five Law Lords could not agree on 'intention' (Lord Diplock said yes; Viscount Dilhorne said no; Lord

---

17 Source: *Gay News*, 3 June 1976, issue 96, p. 26.
18 Source: 'Letters to the editor', *The Times*, 3 November 1976.
19 The charge against the distributor Moore Harness Ltd was subsequently dropped.
20 Under s 8 Law of Libel Amendment Act 1888.

Edmund-Davies said yes; Lord Russell of Killowen said no). The final decision was left to the newest appointee, Lord Scarman, who said that his approach to the appeal was determined by his desire to see blasphemy laws extended. Additionally, Lords Edmund-Davies and Scarman both contended that it was not an essential ingredient of the offence of blasphemy that the publication must tend to lead to a breach of the peace. Their Lordships accepted that the offence of blasphemy could not by its very nature lend itself to any precise legal definition; therefore, national authorities were urged to exercise a degree of flexibility in assessing whether the facts of a particular case fell within the accepted definition of the offence.[21] The *Gay News* appeal was lost.

In a final attempt to obtain redress, Gay News Ltd and editor Denis Lemon lodged a complaint with the ECtHR on 7 August 1979, alleging breaches of Article 7 ('no punishment without law'), Article 9 ('freedom of thought, conscience and religion'), Article 10 ('freedom of expression') and Article 14 ('prohibition of discrimination') of the European Convention. Announcing their decision on 7 May 1982, the Commission agreed that there had been some interference with freedom of expression, but found that Mary Whitehouse's human rights had been infringed by the blasphemous content of the published poem. Consequently, the Commission declared the case inadmissible to be heard by the full plenum of the Strasbourg court.

See Chapter
10.7.1

By April 1983, *Gay News* had ceased to exist, due to financial problems linked to the lengthy court action defending the case against Mrs Whitehouse. She, in turn, regarded the prosecution as one of her greatest victories, upholding public morals and resurrecting the blasphemy laws. (See also: **Tolstoy-Miloslavsky v UK** (1996);[22] also: **Bowman v Secular Society Ltd** (1917)[23]).

The Law Commission had recommended in 1981 and 1985 respectively to abolish the common law of blasphemy, wholeheartedly supported in Parliament by abolitionists such as Tony Benn (1989), Bob Cryer (1990) and Frank Dobson (2001) and Liberal peer Lord Avebury, who argued in his blog during the third reading of the Criminal Justice and Immigration Bill in 2008 that:

> . . . in a free society we must be allowed to criticise religious doctrines and practices, even if that offends some people. While it may be offensive to some Christian believers to hear their beliefs mocked or denied that is equally true of people of other faiths, and of unbelievers, who repeatedly hear atheism equated with a lack of values or immorality. In an open and pluralist society there should be no inhibition to free speech without the very strongest justification, and robust debate should be expected and accepted in religious as in political and other spheres.[24]

Most of the statutory blasphemy offences were repealed by the Indecent Displays (Control) Act 1981, which replaced them with an offence of publicly displaying indecent matter. The 1981 Act, intended to reduce the public display of sexually explicit 'top shelf' magazines, permitted shopkeepers to protect themselves from prosecution by limiting access to indecent material to adults

---

21 [1979] AC 617 at para 42.
22 [1996] EMLR 152 (A/323) at para 41.
23 [1917] AC 406 at 454 (Lord Sumner).
24 Source: with kind permission of Lord Avebury from his blog of Tuesday 11 March 2008: 'At 18.15, meeting with (Baroness) Kay Andrews to discuss my amendment to the Criminal Justice and Immigration Bill abolishing blasphemy and the remaining statutory religious offences, dealt with by the Law Commission in 1985 and covered by my Bills of 1995 and 2002, followed by the Select Committee on Religious Offences which reported in 2003. The Government had tabled their own amendment falling a bit short of mine, in that they retained a couple of obsolete Acts I wanted to repeal'; available at http://ericavebury.blogspot.com/search?q=blasphemy+criminal+justice+and+immigration+bill.

only and either charging for access or displaying a warning notice.[25] The 1981 Act was also repeatedly used to remove 'sexy' postcards advertising prostitution from telephone booths.

Section 73 of the Coroners and Justice Act 2009 abolished the common law offences of 'sedition' ('seditious libel'), 'defamatory libel' and 'obscene libel' in England, Wales and Northern Ireland, leaving 'obscenity' laws intact. The archaic offence of sedition essentially meant an attack on the sovereign or institutions of government, including exciting disaffection against the institutions of government with an intention to incite violence or create public disorder.

Seditious libel was publishing seditious material in a written or permanent form. As common law offences, both sedition and seditious libel were punishable with unlimited fines or imprisonment. Defamatory libel (in effect a criminal counterpart to the civil tort of defamation) consisted of publishing defamatory matter calculated to expose a person to public hatred, contempt or ridicule, in a permanent form. To warrant criminal proceedings, the alleged libel had to be serious enough to justify a prosecution in the public interest. Criminal libel originally covered four distinct categories of libel: obscenity, blasphemous, defamatory and seditious. But obscene material is now covered by the Obscene Publications Acts of 1959 and 1964.

See below
7.3.2

The law has now been refocused on inciting religious hatred as a public order offence.[26] Incitement to racial hatred was established as an offence by the provisions of s 17 Public Order Act 1986, which defined the meaning of 'racial hatred' as 'hatred against a group of persons defined by reference to colour, race, nationality (including citizenship) or ethnic or national origins'. Racial hatred first became a criminal offence under s 1 Race Relations Act 1976 ('Racial discrimination') (as amended by the Race Relations (Amendment) Act 2000. Section 155 of the Criminal Justice and Public Order Act 1994 ('Offence of racially inflammatory publication etc. to be arrestable') made publication of material that incited racial hatred an arrestable offence.

Though Holocaust denial is not covered in the UK by specific legislation, ss 1 to 3 of the Racial and Religious Hatred Act 2006 make provision about offences involving stirring up of hatred against persons on racial or religious grounds. Powers of arrest for these kinds of offences are granted under s 24A Police and Criminal Evidence Act 1984 (PACE) ('arrest without warrant').

7.3 Art or obscenity: obscene publication laws in the UK

Scholars debate exactly when 'pornography' emerged in Europe as a recognizable discourse. Kendrick (1997) insists that its emergence is relatively late in the cultural scheme of things: the word 'pornography', he argues, dates only from the 1820s. Darnton (1990), on the other hand, points to French works of the 1740s and emphasizes the crucial influence of materialist philosophy. Traditional bibliographers, represented by Foxon (1965), go back even further and point to Aretino's postures and the Italian 'whore dialogues' of the mid-sixteenth century. The British Library hosts a private case collection on 'Sex and Sexuality', 1640–1940 ('Literary, Medical and Sociological Perspectives') and 'Erotica', 1650–1900, including contributions from some of the first British pornography publishers such as William Dugdale.[27] Dugdale became notorious for publishing

---

25 Art galleries are specifically exempted from the Indecent Displays (Control) Act 1981 under s 1(4)(b). The repeal of the previous statutory offences, combined with the exemption of art galleries from the Act's coverage, means that the charge most likely to arise out of an allegedly offensive art show is that of outraging public decency.

26 See: Part III ('racial hatred') Public Order Act 1986; specifically s 19 'publishing or distributing written material' and s 20 'public performance of play'.

27 William Dugdale (1800–68) was a publisher, printer and bookseller of politically subversive publications and pornographic literature. His 'Antiquities of Warwickshire' can be used as an authority and reference work on Victorian history whereby 'pornography' was cited as 'the writings of prostitutes', see: Broadway (2008).

'pseudo-medical manuals', such as *An Essay on Onanism* (1772) by M. Tissot, *La Masturbomanie* (1830), *The Secret Companion: A Medical Work on Onanism and Self-Pollution* (1845) and *On the Use of Night-Caps* (1845) by R. J. Brodie.[28]

7.3.1 The 'innocent schoolgirl test' for obscene publications

'Obscenity' is a rather modern notion, first referred to in the Herculaneum exhibition in 1795.[29] Excavations of the ancient Roman town, buried by the eruption of Vesuvius in AD 79, found a large number of erotic frescoes and pornographic symbols indicative of Roman culture at the time. This resulted in an exhibition about Herculaneum which included a special room for 'obscene' antiquities, including a figure of the god Pan in a zoophilic relationship with a she-goat.

Before the Obscene Publications Act 1857, the only law against sexually explicit material in Britain was King George III's Royal Proclamation for the Encouragement of Piety and Virtue, and for the Preventing and Punishing of Vice, Profaneness and Immorality of 1787. This was the first regulation in England against sexually explicit material and included the suppression of all 'Loose and Licentious Prints, Books, and Publications, dispersing Poison to the minds of the Young and Unwary and to Punish the Publishers and Vendors thereof'.

Statutory control of offensive or indecent material tended to be treated as a means of controlling a public nuisance under the Vagrancy Acts of 1824 and 1838 and the Indecent Advertisements Act 1889. The 1889 Act – essentially a public order act – covered advertisements and public displays, which were deemed to be 'obscene' and 'offensive' if they cause a disruption to passers-by.

'Obscenity' had only been tested at common law in the '**Hicklin**' – or 'innocent schoolgirl' – test (see: **R v Hicklin** (1868)[30]), establishing that the words 'obscene' and 'immoral' were exclusively applied to sex. The test was whether the publication had a tendency to deprave and corrupt 'upright' members of society, particularly 'innocent schoolgirls', should the publication fall into their hands. As Lord Chief Justice Cockburn articulated:

> . . . the test of obscenity is this: whether the tendency of the matter charged as obscenity is to deprave and corrupt those whose minds are open to such immoral influences and into whose hands a publication of this sort may fall.[31]

Arguably, the '**Hicklin**' (or 'innocent schoolgirl') test did not constitute sufficient safeguards to reputable publishers and authors, as distinct from mere purveyors of pornography. On strict interpretation, it left the publisher to prove that his publications were suitable reading matter for an innocent schoolgirl.

As soon as the Obscene Publications Act 1857 (also known as 'Lord Campbell's Act') had come into force in September that year, the first arrests were made, including the pornographic publisher William Dugdale (see above). Where works were seized under the Obscene Publications Act 1857, the onus was on the occupier or owner of the premises to give reasons why the works complained of should not be forfeited and destroyed. The author and publisher had no right to be heard and there was also no time limit between the date of the publication of the work complained of and subsequent legal action.

By the mid-1950s, lawyers were becoming increasingly puzzled by the apparent anomalies of the '**Hicklin** test', and the inconsistencies of prescribed law such as 'obscene libel' prescribed by the

---

28 For further discussion see: Colligan (2003); see also: Manchester (1988); Palmer (1997).
29 Herculaneum ('Ercolano' in the Italian region of Campania) was an ancient Roman town destroyed by volcanic pyroclastic flows in AD 79.
30 (1868) LR 3 QB 360.
31 Ibid., at 452 (Cockburn LCJ).

Obscene Publications Act 1857. During a parliamentary debate in the House of Commons in 1954, Lieutenant-Colonel H. M. Hyde (MP for Belfast North) speculated, for example, on why foreign and objectionable material known as 'crime comics or horror comics' were allowed to enter the country unchecked, yet the law permitted a bench of magistrates to order the forfeiture and destruction of other foreign 'obscene' publications such as Boccaccio's *Decameron*, a work which had been regarded as a literary masterpiece throughout the civilized world for more than 500 years.[32]

The MP for Belfast North drew a parallel to German-born Psychiatrist, Dr Frederic Wertham's *Seduction of the Innocent* (1954), a publication concerned with the negative psychological impact of violent comics in the USA that called for more censorship of comics, which Wertham argued could lead to serious juvenile delinquency (Dr Wertham was also known as the 'comic book villain').[33] The US Senate Subcommittee of Juvenile Delinquency debated this very same subject matter in 1954, as did the Westminster Parliament. Subsequently, the Comics Code Authority was founded in the USA in September 1954. This was a self-regulating industry body that was loosely modelled on the 'Hays Code' used in the film industry at the time.

The trial of the 'saucy seaside postcard' artist Donald McGill (1875–1962) in 1954 had a major impact on popular culture. McGill had fallen foul of Britain's obscenity laws, namely the Obscene Publications Act 1857. McGill had produced an estimated 12,000 postcard designs between 1904 and 1962, of which an estimated 200 million were printed and sold. But in 1951 McGill's post-cards came under the scrutiny of the newly elected Conservative Government, who had decided to crack down on public indecency and what they saw as a decline in public morals after the Second World War.

A 'Select Committee on Censorship' was set up to reinforce judgment on public decency and taste by applying the near obsolete Obscene Publications Act 1857. Local policing groups were set up, such as the 'Proclamation Society' (later 'The Society for the Suppression of Vice'), to judge public performances, literature and artworks. Such busybodies took it upon themselves to check the spread of 'open vice, immorality and obscene publications' which were allegedly contaminating the minds of the young. These 'friendship societies' would inform the police about local bookshops, which would then be raided and prosecuted together with publishers and printers while authors would habitually escape prosecution. During the 1950s, some 167,000 bookshops were censored for the sale of 'saucy seaside postcards', from Cleethorpes to Bournemouth, Blackpool to Brighton.

Donald McGill's trial commenced at Lincoln Crown Court before a jury on 15 July 1954. McGill's defence essentially posed the question of whether his seaside postcards were capable of corrupting the minds and morals of an innocent schoolgirl ('the **Hicklin** test'). The jury found him guilty of contravening the 1857 Act, and McGill was fined £50 with an additional £25 in court costs. Together with the forfeiture and destruction of his postcards and templates, and the financial burden imposed by the court sentence, McGill soon went bankrupt.[34] He was hailed by author George Orwell as a unique British artist, famous for the modern cartoon and seaside comic strip. Orwell wrote in his essay 'The Art of Donald McGill' in 1941:

> Who does not know the 'comics' of the cheap stationers' windows, the penny or two penny coloured post cards with their endless succession of fat women in tight bathing-dresses and

---

32 Source: Debate on 'obscene publications'. Hansard, 22 November 1954, Vol 533 cc 1012–1020.
33 Source: Obituary – 'Frederic Wertham, 86, dies; foe of violent TV and Comics', by Bayard Webster, *New York Times*, 1 December 1981.
34 Source: 'Naughty but nice. Jolly seaside smut – or should we be taking Donald McGill's postcards more seriously?', by John Russell Taylor, *The Times*, 11 March 2006.

their crude drawing and unbearable colours, chiefly hedge-sparrow's-egg tint and Post Office red? . . . In general, however, they are not witty, but humorous, and it must be said for McGill's postcards, in particular, that the drawing is often a good deal funnier than the joke beneath it. Obviously the outstanding characteristic of comic cards is their obscenity . . . More than half, perhaps three-quarters, of the jokes are sex jokes, ranging from the harmless to the all but unprintable.[35]

In 1957 McGill gave evidence before the House of Commons Select Committee, which was considering amendments to the Obscene Publications Act 1857. McGill told the Committee that a national system of censorship was open to the vagaries of individual interpretation. As a result Parliament passed the Obscene Publications Act 1959, which ironically eased the ban on the saucy seaside postcard. McGill died, aged 87, in 1962. His collectors' fan base is vast, including members of the Beatles and film director Michael Winner (1935–2013).

7.3.2 The Obscene Publications Acts of 1959 and 1964

When the Obscene Publications Act 1959 (OPA) came into force, it modified the law on obscene publications 'to provide for the protection of literature; and to strengthen the law concerning pornography'.[36] Section 1(1) OPA 1959 provides the 'obscenity' test, in that:

. . . an article shall be deemed to be obscene if its effect or (where the article comprises two or more distinct items) the effect of any one of its items is, if taken as a whole, such as to tend to deprave and corrupt persons who are likely, having regard to all relevant circumstances, to read, see or hear the matter contained or embodied in it.

The OPA 1959 provides for:

● prosecution (by judge and jury); and
● forfeiture.[37]

A prosecution could not be commenced more than two years after the commission of the offence. The 1959 Act punishes publication per se and the 1964 Act makes the possession of publication 'for gain' a criminal offence.[38] The Obscene Publications Act 1964 was designed to:

● penalize purveyors of obscene material by making it an offence under s 2 either to publish an obscene article or to have an obscene article for publication for gain; and
● prevent such articles from reaching the market by way of seizure and forfeiture proceedings under s 3.[39]

The issue of whether a publication, play, picture or film is 'obscene or not' must be tried by a jury without the assistance of expert evidence.

Section 2 OPA 1959 defines the meaning of 'article', which implies any description of a piece of writing containing or embodying matter to be read or looked at or both. This was later

35 Orwell (1941).
36 The Obscene Publications Acts 1959: Archbold: *Criminal Pleading Evidence and Practice* (2013 edn): 31-63, amended 1964: Archbold: 37-76.
37 See: Prosecution of Offences Act 1985, s 3(d); see also Archbold, Chapter 1, 'The Indictment' at para 1-326.
38 Section 1 Obscene Publications Act 1964, 'Obscene articles intended for publication for gain'.
39 Section 3(A) OPA 1964, where the article in question is a moving picture film of a width of not less than 16 millimetres, requires the DPP's consent; see: *Archbold*: 31-74.

extended and amended to include any sound recording, film or other record such as a video recording or DVD (see: **R v Lamb** (1998)[40]; also: **R v Snowden** (2010)[41]). An amendment in 1977 added erotic films, with the Criminal Justice and Public Order Act 1994 amending the Obscene Publications Act 1857, which thereafter included computer images. It became illegal to transmit electronically stored data which was 'obscene on resolution into a viewable form'. This was mainly to protect children, and covered photographs and pseudo-photographs linked to paedophilic activity.

In summary, the 1959 Act relates to publication of an obscene article and the 1964 Act strengthened the previous act by introducing the 'possession' element of an obscene publication for gain, covering 'any person having an obscene article for publication for gain', including wholesalers.

7.3.3 Defences available under the Obscene Publications Act 1959

The Obscene Publications Act 1959 created two defences under s 4:

(1)   The defence of 'innocent dissemination'; and
(2)   The 'defence of public good'.

Section 4 of the 1959 Act reads:

> . . . a person shall not be convicted of an offence against section two of this Act, and an order for forfeiture shall not be made under the foregoing section, if it is proved that publication of the article in question is justified as being for the public good on the ground that it is in the interests of science, literature, art or learning, or of other objects of general concern.

Subsection 2(1)(A) added:

> . . . a moving picture film or soundtrack . . . is justified as being for the public good on the ground that it is in the interests of drama, opera, ballet or any other art, or of literature or learning.

The 'defence of public good' means that a person who publishes any such 'obscene' article, recording or photograph etc. ('the publication') will not be charged with a criminal offence if he can prove that the publication is justified for the public good, such as in the interests of science, literature, art or learning, or is an object of general public concern.

 FOR THOUGHT

Do you not think that the combined effect of ss 1, 2 and 4 of the Obscene Publications Act 1959 generate an absurd paradox? How can something be justified as being for the 'public good' if its tendency is also to 'deprave and corrupt'?

---

40 [1998] 1 Cr App R (S) 77 (CA Crim Div), where the appellant was found in possession of video tapes which he supplied by mail order under s 2(1) OPA 1959. The recordings showed sadomasochistic scenes, some scenes involving animals. His sentence of five years' imprisonment (to be served consecutively) was upheld. The appeal centred on count 1 of the indictment where Lamb had argued that the content of the video was not obscene.

41 [2010] 1 Cr App R (S) 39 (CA Crim Div), where the appellant pleaded guilty to seven counts of publishing an obscene article and for copying DVDs and 2,840 pornographic DVDs, contrary to s 2(1) Obscene Publications Act 1959. Fifty-five of the DVDs were categorized as 'obscene', involving activity with animals and other activities involving defecation, vomiting and urination. The DVDs and videos had been sent to 293 customers. His two-and-a-half-year prison sentence was upheld.

7.3.4 Corrupting public morals and outraging public decency: common law conspiracies

In **Knuller v DPP** (1973),[42] the appellants were directors of a company which published a fortnightly magazine. On an inside page under a column headed 'Males', advertisements were inserted inviting readers to meet the advertisers for the purpose of homosexual practices. The appellants were convicted on counts of conspiracy to corrupt public morals and conspiracy to outrage public decency. The appellants appealed on the grounds that an agreement by two or more persons to insert advertisements in a magazine for the purpose of homosexual acts taking place between consenting adult males in private did not constitute the offence of conspiracy to corrupt public morals. They also contended that the judge had misdirected the jury as to the effect of the Sexual Offences Act 1967[43] on the charge of conspiracy to corrupt public morals, that such an agreement did not constitute the offence of conspiracy to outrage public decency and that the trial judge failed to direct the jury that for that offence the agreement must envisage something in the nature of a public exhibition which was indecent. The Court of Appeal, applying **Shaw v DPP** (1962),[44] dismissed the appeal.

The background to the **Shaw** case was that the Street Offences Act 1959 had made it impossible for prostitutes to ply their trade by soliciting in the streets. It therefore became necessary for them to find some other means of advertising the services that they were prepared to render. It then occurred to the appellant, Frederick Charles Shaw, that he could assist them to this end (with some financial advantage to himself). He published a weekly booklet, called *Ladies Directory*, which contained the names, addresses and telephone numbers of prostitutes with photographs of nude female figures and in some cases details which conveyed to initiates willingness to indulge not only in ordinary sexual intercourse but also in various perverse practices. Shaw charged the prostitutes a fee for inclusion and then sold the directory for a fee. He was convicted of conspiracy to corrupt public morals, by living on the earnings of prostitution under s 1 Obscene Publications Act 1959. Shaw appealed on the grounds that no such offence of 'conspiracy to corrupt public morals' existed. His appeal was dismissed and the House of Lords effectively created a new criminal offence with their precedent. Lord Hobson concluded in **Shaw**:

> In the field of public morals it will thus be the morality of the man in the jury box that will determine the fate of the accused, but this should hardly disturb the equanimity of anyone brought up in the traditions of our common law.[45]

The HL in **Knuller** dismissed the appeal, stating that **Shaw** had been rightly decided (Lord Diplock dissenting)[46] and that even if **Shaw** was wrongly decided it must stand until the offence of 'obscene publication' was altered by Parliament. Their Lordships further ruled that the law relating to the offence of 'conspiracy to corrupt public morals' had not been altered by virtue of s 1(1) of the Sexual Offences Act 1967; that the offence could be committed by encouraging conduct which although not itself illegal might be calculated to corrupt public morals and that, accordingly, it was for the jury to decide whether or not the advertisements were, by present-day standards, corrupting of public morals.[47]

---

42 **Knuller (Publishing, Printing and Promotions) Ltd v DPP** [1973] AC 435 (also cited as: **R v Knuller** [1973] AC 435).
43 An Act to amend the law of England and Wales relating to homosexual acts.
44 [1962] AC 220.
45 Ibid., at para 20 (Lord Hobson).
46 **Knuller** at paras 463A, 495G–496C (as per Lord Reid, Lord Morris of Borth-y-Gest and Lord Simon of Glaisdale). The appeal in **Knuller** rested on the ground that **Shaw v DPP** had been wrongly decided and should be overruled.
47 Ibid., at paras 457B–E, 460D–H, 484F.

According to the HL in **Knuller**, for the common law offence to be made out, the material must be so 'lewd, disgusting and offensive' that the 'sense of decency of members of the public would be outraged'. 'Outrage' was held to be a 'strong word' going beyond offending the susceptibilities of or even shocking and disgusting reasonable people. However, their Lordships also stressed that what would outrage public decency would vary from one generation to the next, and that the jury should be told to remember that they live in a plural society, with a tradition of tolerance towards minorities, and that this atmosphere of toleration is itself part of public decency. Some doubt persisted even after **Knuller** on the question of whether the substantive common law offence existed independent of conspiracy. Only Lord Simon and Lord Kilbrandon positively held that it did.

The law on conspiracy was subsequently changed by Parliament. Section 1(1) Criminal Law Act 1977 created and defined the offence of statutory conspiracy. This offence is triable only on indictment, even if the parties agreed to commit a criminal offence triable only summarily. It is an offence triable only on indictment to agree to do an act which tends to corrupt public morals or outrage public decency, whether or not the act amounts to a crime.[48]

7.3.5 Obscene publications and the digital age

How then is the Obscene Publications Act of 1959 applied to publication on the internet? There are difficult jurisdictional issues when obscene material is hosted on the internet with most such servers (ISPs) hosted overseas, usually outside the European Union and therefore outside EU and UK (criminal) jurisdiction. If a website is hosted abroad and is downloaded in the UK, the case of **R v Perrin** (2002)[49] applies (see below).

Perrin concerned 'publishing' electronic data under the Obscene Publications Act 1959 and states that the mere transmission of data constitutes publication. It confirmed the decision in the earlier case of **R v Waddon** (2000)[50] that there is publication both when images are uploaded and when they are downloaded. Here too the court considered the question of 'publication' on the internet in the context of the 1959 Act and held that this could occur more than once. Publication occurs when images are uploaded on to websites by contributors and when the images are subsequently downloaded by users. The Court of Appeal held in **Waddon** that the content of US websites could come under British jurisdiction when downloaded in the UK. Section 1(3) Obscene Publication Act 1959 was duly amended to include electronically stored data or the transmission of such data.

❖ KEY CASE	*R v Stephane Laurent Perrin* [2002] EWCA Crim 747 (CA)

Precedent
❖ Publication on the internet takes place when images are accessed in the United Kingdom.
❖ It does not matter that the obscene material (e.g. pornographic videos) is made and uploaded abroad.

Facts
On 25 October 1999, Stephane Laurent Perrin published an obscene article, namely the web page on the internet at www.MetropoleNewsGroup.com/Preview.HTML. During the

---

48 See: Archbold 33–34.
49 **R v Perrin (Stephane Laurent)** [2002] EWCA Crim 747 (22 March 2002).
50 **R v Waddon (Graham)** (2000) WL 491456 (6 April 2000).

course of police investigation, a police officer had accessed the relevant web page. The video-recorded trailer revealed coprophilia (people covered in faeces) and men involved in fellatio. The video preview was available free of charge to anyone with access to the internet with a link marked 'subscription to our best filthy sites'. With a search warrant police visited Mr Perrin's home at Millennium Harbour, London, E14, searched the premises and seized computer equipment with the assistance of a French interpreter. Mr Perrin said he was a director of Piazza Financial Services and registered owner of website URL www.sewersex.com. That website was registered to a company called Metropole News Group. He argued at the police interview that some competitor might have put something onto his website. He was charged under s 1(1) Obscene Publications Act 1959. At trial before a jury (which was shown the video trailers) he gave no evidence and called no witnesses. The judge directed the jury in accordance with the statute:

> . . . the law says an article shall be deemed to be obscene if its effect or (where the article comprises two or more distinct items) – and here of course you have different images, haven't you – the effect of any one of its items is, if taken as a whole, such as to tend to deprave and corrupt persons who are likely, having regard to all relevant circumstances, to read, see or hear the matter contained or embodied in it.

The judge then went on to say:

> . . . all relevant circumstances, members of the jury, since we are talking about modern times, includes the sort of people who these days have personal computers and who have modems and who have access to surf the internet. I suppose ten years ago it would have been very few people, wouldn't it, but now, it is a matter for you, you may think there are many people of all ages who sit possibly in their bedrooms at home surfing the internet. Therefore, it is a question for you to decide, having regard for all the relevant circumstances, who might read, see or hear of course does not apply, really does it, the matter contained or embodied in this material which you are considering.

A little later the judge said:

> . . . the definition of obscenity, members of the jury, contains no requirement as to the number of persons which the articles might corrupt or deprave, but if the seller of pornographic material has a large number of customers who are not likely to be corrupted by such material, he does not thereby acquire a licence to expose for sale, or sell such material to a small number of customers who are likely to be corrupted by them.[51]

The jury at Southwark Crown Court convicted Mr Perrin on 16 October 2000 of publishing an obscene article (Count 1 in the indictment). He was sentenced to 30 months' imprisonment on 6 November 2000.

Mr Perrin appealed his conviction on the grounds that the conviction violated his Article 10 rights ('freedom of expression'). He further contended that the conviction violated his

---

51 Ibid., at para 10 (Lord Justice Kennedy).

Article 7 right under the Convention ('no punishment without the law'), in that his conduct was not prescribed by law; he argued that the material was prepared and uploaded abroad (namely in his home country, France). The third ground of appeal was that the judge was wrong to reject the submission that the only relevant publication of the web page was to the officer who downloaded it, and therefore it is wrong to test obscenity by reference to others who might have access to the preview page. Finally, he argued that the trial judge misdirected the jury, arguing it was necessary for a significant proportion of those visiting the web page to be affected by it. Mr Perrin also appealed his sentence on the ground that the offence was acceptable in his country (France).

Decision

The CA held that s 1(1) of the 1959 act could be relied upon and fell within the scope of Article 10 (2) ECHR, namely that a state authority can derogate from freedom of expression provision for the protection of public morals and health, in which case the police and court intervention was justified. There was also no violation of Article 7, since the offence was prescribed by law (the Obscene Publications Act 1959). The court stressed that such a law was still current and necessary in a democratic society and applicable even in the internet age. The justices rejected the appellant's suggestion that it is always necessary for the Crown to show where the major steps in relation to publication should be taken. The appeal against conviction was therefore dismissed.

The appeal against sentence was also rejected on the grounds that the appellant lived in the UK and should have known what he was doing was illegal, and the justices found it difficult to accept that what Mr Perrin was publishing on the internet could have been acceptable in the UK and his own country. As to the (over) harshness of his sentence, Lord Justice Kennedy said that there is a great danger that this kind of material be accessed by the young and vulnerable on the internet, and that the statutory maximum for this kind of offence is three years. The appeal against sentence was also dismissed.

Analysis

The approach taken by the Court of Appeal in **Perrin** was that 'publication' for the purposes of s 1 of the 1959 Act takes place when images are accessed on the internet in the UK. Mr Perrin had clearly published an 'obscene article' (the video trailers), although the material was prepared and uploaded abroad. This meant the CA rejected the appellant's claim that his actions fell outside UK jurisdiction.[52] The approach taken by the CA has been criticized on the grounds that it subjects foreign publications to UK law. Rowbottom (2006)[53] argues that international co-operation would be a more appropriate strategy. What is important to note is that the supplier of the material uploaded online and thereby put on the World Wide Web is liable for prosecution under UK obscenity laws. The reason Mr Perrin could be prosecuted was because he was based in the UK. We know that many websites hosting pornographic and obscene material originate abroad (49 per cent in North America, 43 per cent in Europe (including Russia), the rest in Africa and Asia, in 2011).[54] Though the publisher may well be outside the UK, what matters (according to the

---

52 Ibid at paras 51–52.
53 See: Rowbottom (2006), pp. 97–109; see also: Hirst (2002).
54 See: Internet Watch Foundation (2011) Annual Report at p. 14: www.iwf.org.uk/assets/media/annual-reports/annual%20med%20res.pdf.

See below
7.4.3

Perrin judgment) is that the material will still be accessible to a UK audience.[55] It is for this reason that the Home Office in its 2005 consultation proposed the specific 'possession' offence, which then shifts attention away from those who supply such material to those based within the United Kingdom that create the demand. It was for this reason that Parliament created the separate offence under s 63 of the Criminal Justice and Immigration Act 2008.

7.3.6 Filth or literature? *Lady Chatterley's Lover* and other 'obscene' creative works

There have been a large number of prosecutions under British obscenity laws involving works of literature and art; not all of them can be mentioned here. Gustave Flaubert's *Madame Bovary* and James Joyce's *Ulysses* were just two classic examples where legislative censorship tried to suppress the novels on 'obscenity' grounds (see also: **R v Calder & Boyars Ltd** (1969)[56]). James Joyce's *Ulysses*, published in 1918, was banned on sexual grounds in 1922.

Vladimir Nabokov's *Lolita* first appeared in Paris in 1955,[57] and has been seen by literary academics in American Studies, such as Giles (2000), as symbiotically intertwined with other American literary classic texts during the Truman and Eisenhower years. Giles reports on the cultural reception of *Lolita* in Britain, which focused on delicate and troublesome questions such as the love of a middle-aged European, Humbert Humbert, for an American nymphet, 12-year-old Dolores Haze. Giles states that the book is more than just a lusty publication of lascivious reputation and provides literary pleasures focusing on the relationship between formal aesthetics, public morality and social power; a comic satire of sex and eroticism in post-war America.[58]

Lolita was the second publishing hit for the Frenchman Maurice Girodias, innovative founder of the Olympia Press in Paris. He had found a gap in the market by publishing erotic and pornographic literature written in foreign languages, such as D. H. Lawrence's *Lady Chatterley's Lover*. Olympia was a radical publishing house with the advanced marketing concept of putting into circulation works of literature that 'establishment' publishers would not dare to print or even accept. It published controversial works largely in English, which attracted little attention from the French censors, such as William S. Burroughs' *Naked Lunch*, Samuel Beckett's *Molloy* and *Watt*, works by the Marquis de Sade and John Cleland's *Fanny Hill*. Apart from Olympia's greatest hit *Lolita*, Girodias found similar publishing success with *Candy*, a 1958 reworking of Voltaire's *Candide*, and the *Story of O* by Pauline Réage (the pseudonym of Dominique Aury), one of the earliest works of sadomasochistic erotic fiction to be written by a woman. As the educated British middle classes travelled across to France, the first editions of Olympia Press with their distinctive green covers found their way to UK and American destinations. Olympia Press and Penguin Classics were the forerunners of avant-garde publishing houses whose 'gentleman-pornographer' editors pushed the boundaries of freedom of expression to the limit long before human rights legislation became fashionable.

Once the Obscene Publications Act 1959 had come into force, customs officials had been instructed to seize all copies of *Lolita* entering the United Kingdom. George (later Lord) Weidenfeld, Nabokov's publisher, turned to the most famous libel lawyer at the time, the late Peter Carter-Ruck, whose *Memoirs of a Libel Lawyer* reveal that while he regarded *Lolita* as a 'beautifully written, poignant

55 See: Home Office and The Scottish Executive (2005) Consultation at pp. 21–22.
56 [1969] 1 QB 151.
57 Nabokov (1955); the book was made into a film by Stanley Kubrick in 1962, starring James Mason and Sue Lyon.
58 For further discussion see: Giles (2000).

and tragic' work, he was well aware of its legal risks: 'Obscenity was well to the fore in the minds of the authorities at that time.'[59] Carter-Ruck advised the British publishers and Lolita's author that the book was a fair business risk for publication, subject to the amendment of four sentences.[60]

But Nabokov categorically rejected this advice, stating that Lolita was a work of art which must not be mutilated. In the event, Carter-Ruck devised a scheme of remarkable cunning in order to circumvent the obscenity laws. He advised George Weidenfeld to inform the Government by letter of the intention to publish and distribute the book in the UK, but not to post the letter until just before the dissolution of Parliament on 18 September 1959, before the General Election. This had the desired effect that neither the outgoing Conservative Home Secretary Rab Butler[61] nor Prime Minister Harold Macmillan[62] could take any action over Lolita. When Parliament reassembled on 27 October 1959, the publication of the book was well in place with its distribution beginning on 6 November. Even though the Conservatives had been returned to power, neither the publishers nor the author ever stood trial for obscenity. However, D. H. Lawrence's Lady Chatterley's Lover was prose-cuted the following year and so was Hubert Selby's Last Exit to Brooklyn in 1968. Both books were eventually cleared for publication, with the Court of Appeal in Last Exit to Brooklyn establishing that writers could explore depravity and corruption without necessarily encouraging it.

The most high-profile prosecution arising from the Obscene Publications Act 1959 was undoubtedly the unexpurgated Penguin paperback edition of Lady Chatterley's Lover by D. H. Lawrence. 'Lady Chatterley' was first published in 1928 in Italy and France. The short novel was immediately banned in Britain on account of the rather descriptive steamy bravura love-making scenes between Lady Constance (Connie) Chatterley of Wragby Hall and her gamekeeper Mellors. Perhaps coinci-dentally, at the same time as the Obscene Publications Bill was making its passage through Parliament, Penguin publishers decided to publish Lady Chatterley's Lover in the UK, marking 30 years since D. H. Lawrence's death. What followed was the most significant literary obscenity trial of the twentieth century, where the publishers were charged under s 1(1) Obscene Publications Act 1959. The indictment was based on the premise that the novel put promiscuity on a pedestal, and that the majority of the book was merely 'padding' between graphic scenes of sexual intercourse and filthy language.

'Lady C's trial' – as it became known – took place as Britain was on the cusp of late modernity (or the start of counter-culture): the first Beatles LP had been released, and the contraceptive pill had gone on sale, against the backdrop of 'free love' and flower power emerging from America. Penguin called upon a string of expert witnesses to defend the book's literary merit, including several members of the clergy, one of whom remarked that the work 'was a novel and novels deal with life as it is'. On 10 November 1960, the jury acquitted Penguin of all charges.[63]

As soon as the verdict was pronounced, London's largest bookstore, W&G Foyle Ltd, reported a run on their bookshop with 300 copies sold in just 15 minutes and orders for 3,000 more copies. The next morning, Foyle's reported a queue of some 400 people – mostly men – wanting to buy 'Lady C', available in paperback for 3s 6d (16p). Lady Chatterley's Lover made legal history, highlighting the fact that the rigid British establishment was becoming increasingly out of touch with public opinion on matters of obscenity. The case marked a famous turning point, with a victory for more liberal publishing houses, making prosecutions more difficult and increasingly rare.

---

59 Source: Carter-Ruck (1990), pp. 98ff.
60 See also: Doley et al. (2009).
61 Richard Austen Butler (1902–82).
62 Maurice Harold Macmillan, 1st Earl of Stockton (1894–1986) and grandson of a Scottish crofter, Daniel Macmillan, who founded Macmillan Publishing. Harold Macmillan was Prime Minister from 10 January 1957 to 18 October 1963.
63 See: **R v Penguin Books Ltd** [1961] Crim LR 176.

The **Trial of Oz** in 1971 became the longest obscenity trial in English legal history, held at the Old Bailey under the auspices of Judge Michael Argyle QC. Oz was first published as a satirical humour magazine between 1963 and 1969 in Sydney, Australia, and was known as a 'psychedelic hippy' magazine. The controversial underground magazine was published in London from 1967 to 1973. Central editor of Oz was Richard Neville, with co-editors of the Sydney version Richard Walsh and Martin Sharp. Co-editors in London were Jim Anderson and Felix Dennis. Neville, Sharp and Walsh were twice convicted for obscene publications in New South Wales in 1964 (the 'obscenity' related to several items including a picture of public urination and was prompted by the magazine's satirical criticism of the Sydney police for their anti-homosexual activities).

The London edition of Oz was short-lived. The underground magazine had sprung up in the aftermath of the 'Lady C' trial. Oz was not only alternative but openly permissive, advocating sex and drugs as forms of liberation. The magazine's editors aimed to be satirically subversive in their campaigns against the establishment, particularly the police and the judiciary, by using four-letter words in a provocative fashion. Issue 28 of May 1970, 'Schoolkids' Oz, led to the convictions of Neville, Anderson and Dennis (later overturned on appeal).

The Oz obscenity trial became legendary. Of particular significance was the notoriously explicit cartoon by Robert Crumb, depicting Rupert Bear in a sexual position ravishing a gypsy granny. What made it worse was that the editors – Richard Neville, Felix Dennis and Jim Anderson – had invited young readers, aged between 15 and 18, to edit Issue 28. The 'Schoolkids' issue, with its French erotic cover design ('Desseins Erotiques'), contained 48 pages of content on homosexuality, lesbianism and sadism.

John Mortimer QC (later author of the famous 'Rumpole of the Bailey' series of novels) acted for the defence. Amongst the defence witnesses was DJ John Peel, musician George Melly (who at one point explained a Latin sexual term in detail to the jury) and comedy writer Marty Feldman, who called the judge a 'boring old fart'. At one point in the trial the defendants turned up to court dressed as schoolgirls (possibly hinting at the **Hicklin** 'innocent schoolgirl' test). But the jury at the Old Bailey found the three young editor defendants guilty of publishing an obscene magazine under the 1959 Act in 1971. The sentences were severe: Judge Argyle set out a prison term of 15 months for the editor, Richard Neville, and 12 months and 9 months respectively for his associates. Moral crusader Mary Whitehouse applauded the verdict and the sentence.[64]

The Court of Appeal subsequently revoked the sentences with a judgment by Lord Widgery LCJ, where the court recognized 14 errors of law and a large number of errors of fact in the trial judge's summing-up to the jury. Oz ceased publication not long after the trial. Williams (1972) argues that the trial's significance was political rather than literary and linguistic.

In 1976, *Inside Linda Lovelace* ('ILL')[65] became a bestseller; not so much for its literary merit but because of the Director of Public Prosecutions' action against the publishers in respect of obscenity. The jury decided that ILL's steamy descriptions of sexual orgies would not 'deprave and corrupt' the sort of people likely to buy the book and the publishers of ILL were duly acquitted.[66] The book was made into a notorious 1970s porn film, *Deep Throat*, about a sexually rapacious young woman who swallowed all her suitors.

Everyone thought this would be the last prosecution under UK obscenity laws in respect of written published material. In 1979 a House of Commons Select Committee, chaired by Bernard Williams, recommended that 'the written word' should be excluded altogether from the 1959

---

64 See also: Palmer (1971), which contains court transcripts of the actual trial.
65 Linda Susan Boreman (1949–2002), better known by her stage name, Linda Lovelace, was an American pornographic actress who was famous for her performance of deep throat fellatio in the enormously successful 1972 hardcore porn film *Deep Throat*. Lovelace died in 2002, following a car accident.
66 Source: 'Ex-porn star Lovelace dies after car crash', by Leo Standora, *New York Daily News*, 23 April 2002.

Act, as the prosecution of such cases was expensive and rarely successful; not least because of the absurd spectacle of professors of English in court, trying to find literary merit in works when they clearly contained very little. The report was ignored by the new Conservative Government under Mrs Thatcher.

Four decades after *Deep Throat*, the film *Lovelace*[67] opened in London's West End in late August 2013. The film tells the story of abused porn star Linda Lovelace (aka Linda Susan Boreman) as she tries to take control of her life, with Amanda Seyfried in the lead role as the tragic frontierswoman of 1970s hardcore porn. The film was backed by Harvey Weinstein. *Lovelace* nearly did not make it to the movie stage, because Arrow Productions, which owns the rights to *Deep Throat*, took legal action against Harvey Weinstein Productions[68] to block the release of the new film. Arrow claimed that the film used more than five minutes of unlicensed footage from *Deep Throat*, seeking an injunction against the distribution and marketing of *Lovelace*, together with damages of $10m (£6.4m).[69]

The last novel banned under the 1959 Act was *Lord Horror* by David Britton (1989). The controversial author had founded a series of small press magazines in the 1970s specializing in horror fiction, with titles like *Weird Fantasy* and *Crucified Toad*. In 1976, Britton co-founded a small publishing house, Savoy Books, with Michael Butterworth. Lord Horror (and its sequels) depicted fascism in carnivalesque fashion in comic-book format, offering a historical fantasy based on the life of the pre-war fascist and wartime traitor William Joyce, better known as 'Lord Haw Haw', who broadcast Nazi propaganda from Germany. Britton himself described *Lord Horror* as 'so unique and radical, I expected to go to prison for it. I always thought that if you wrote a truly dangerous book, something dangerous would happen to you. Which is one reason there are so few really dangerous books around.'[70] Manchester magistrate Derrick Fairclough ordered the forfeiture and destruction of all copies of *Lord Horror* under s 3(2) of the 1959 Act. The order was overturned by the Court of Appeal in 1992.

 FOR THOUGHT

The law on obscenity in the UK centres on the notion that a publication – a book, magazine, or photograph – has to have a tendency to 'deprave and corrupt' those who are likely to view it. The Obscene Publications Act 1959 provides a defence if it can be shown that the publication is in the public interest – for example, because of the article's literary value. Find out which books (and films) have been banned in the UK under the 1959 act and on what grounds.

7.3.7 Caricatures and satires

In January 2013, Rupert Murdoch (head of News International) apologized for a *Sunday Times* cartoon depicting the Israeli leader Benjamin Netanyahu building a wall using blood-red mortar, an image Jewish leaders said was reminiscent of anti-Semitic propaganda. What exacerbated matters was that the cartoon by Gerald Scarfe, depicting Netanyahu wielding a long, sharp trowel and

---

67 Directors: Jeffrey Friedman, Rob Epstein. Cast: Amanda Seyfried, Juno Temple, Peter Sarsgaard.
68 *Lovelace* was produced by Millennium Films, while the Weinstein Company is in charge of distribution.
69 Source: 'Deep Throat lawsuit threatens to swallow Lovelace biopic whole', by Xan Brooks, *Guardian*, 7 August 2013.
70 Source: David Britton in an interview with the Savoy publishing house, available at www.savoy.abel.co.uk/HTML/dave.html.

showing agonized Palestinians bricked into the wall's structure, was published on Holocaust Memorial Day. It was meant as a comment on recent elections in which Netanyahu's party narrowly won the most seats in the Israeli parliamentary elections. The caption read, 'Will cementing the peace continue?', a reference both to the stalled peace process and Israel's separation barrier, a complex of fences and concrete walls which Israel portrays as a defence against suicide bombers but which Palestinians say is a land grab under the guise of security. Mick Davis on behalf of the Jewish Leadership Council reacted to this cartoon with a visceral disgust that was unprecedented, due to the gratuitous and offensive nature of the image.

Media mogul Murdoch wrote on Twitter that the cartoonist, Gerald Scarfe, did not reflect the paper's editorial line. 'Nevertheless, we owe major apology for grotesque, offensive cartoon,' Murdoch tweeted. Jewish community leaders called the drawing a 'blood libel' and the Board of Deputies of British Jews, representing the UK's approximately 265,000-strong Jewish community, told the Guardian it had lodged a complaint with the Press Complaints Commission.[71] The Israeli paper Haaretz argued, however, that the cartoon was not offensive, stating that 'Netanyahu's depiction is grossly offensive and unfair but that is only par for the course for any politician when cartoonist Scarfe is at his drawing board'.[72]

Acting editor of the Sunday Times, Martin Ivens, responded to the Jewish organizations' concerns at the ensuing press conference:

> I'm grateful so many community leaders could come together at such short notice. You will know that the Sunday Times abhors antisemitism and would never set out to cause offence to the Jewish people – or any other ethnic or religious group. That was not the intention last Sunday. Everyone knows that Gerald Scarfe is consistently brutal and bloody in his depictions, but last weekend – by his own admission – he crossed a line. The timing – on Holocaust Memorial Day – was inexcusable. The associations on this occasion were grotesque and on behalf of the paper I'd like to apologise unreservedly for the offence we clearly caused. This was a terrible mistake.[73]

In Britain, caricatures and satires are generally dealt with by the tort law of defamation.[74] In **Charleston v News Group Newspapers Ltd** (1995),[75] the House of Lords considered the digitally enhanced photomontage that showed the faces of two famous Australian actors, Anne Charleston ('Madge') and Ian Smith ('Harold'), of the popular TV series Neighbours, superimposed on the nearly naked bodies of others in pornographic poses and agreed with Mr Justice Blofeld's order to strike out the libel action against the publishers of the News of the World. Their Lordships, applying the 'bane and antidote' defence, declined to find defamation in **Charleston** because if the readers who did not take 'the trouble to discover what the article was all about, carried away the impression that two well-known actors in legitimate television were also involved in making pornographic films, they could hardly be described as ordinary, reasonable, fair-minded readers'.[76]

As the law of defamation has clarified, hard-hitting satire cannot be defended as honest comment when it is malicious. Satire can be regarded as being libellous if the insults cannot be anyone's honest opinion and if it merely heaps insults on someone. Generally, the satirist or carica-turist ought to employ this genre to criticize a matter of general relevance, which will then afford

---

71 Source: 'Murdoch apologises for Sunday Times' cartoon depicting Binyamin Netanyahu', Guardian, 28 January 2013.
72 Source: 'Four reasons why U.K. cartoon of Netanyahu isn't anti-Semitic in any way', by Anshel Pfeffer, Haaretz, 15 February 2013.
73 Source: 'Sunday Times statement on Gerald Scarfe cartoon', Guardian, 29 January 2013.
74 See: Rogers, W. V. H. and Parkes, R. (2010) Gatley on Libel and Slander, first supplement to the eleventh edition, para 3.4. For further detail see Gatley on Libel and Slander (2013).
75 [1995] 2 AC 65 (HL).
76 Ibid., at 76 (Lord Bridge of Harwich).

See Chapter 3

him the freedom of expression defence in human rights law. This does not defend him if extreme blasphemy or obscenity has been used or where someone's reputation, honour and human dignity has been infringed.

The provocative power of caricatures was illustrated by the Muhammad cartoons controversy, which originated from the publication of 12 editorial cartoons by the Danish newspaper *Jyllands-Posten* in September 2005. Newspapers and magazines around the world reprinted the cartoons, leading to a global wave of protests and riots by Muslims who claimed that the caricatures were just another expression of Western colonialism.[77] Questions about the use of archaic blasphemy laws emerged in Denmark.

At the same time, it has to be remembered that in many Islamic countries blasphemy laws remain stringent and are strictly enforced, often with severe penalties; even potentially death. This demonstrates that the extent and scope of national laws protecting religious beliefs remain very culture-specific.

 FOR THOUGHT

Was Rupert Murdoch's apology on Twitter for the *Sunday Times* Gerald Scarfe cartoon an attack on the artist's freedom of expression?[78] The (acting) editor of the newspaper had obviously given the go-ahead for the cartoon to be published. Cartoonists, through the visual medium, can often say a great deal more than a journalist can. Was Murdoch's attack and Twitter apology justified?

7.3.8 Censorship of stage productions

In September 1968 Britain abandoned theatre censorship, when the Theatres Act 1968 came into force. The new act repealed the Theatres Act of 1843, which meant that censorship of theatre productions and plays by the Lord Chamberlain's office was finally abolished.[79] Furthermore, the sovereign could no longer exercise his or her powers by virtue of Royal Prerogative in respect of either granting a theatre licence or halting performances. With the 1968 Theatres Act, local authorities became the official licensing authorities of plays, exhibitions and demonstrations.

Section 2 of the Theatres Act 1968 ('Provisions with respect to performances of plays') states that:

(1) For the purposes of this section a performance of a play shall be deemed to be obscene if, taken as a whole, its effect was such as to tend to deprave and corrupt persons who were likely, having regard to all relevant circumstances, to attend it.

(2) Subject to sections 3 and 7 of this Act, if an obscene performance of a play is given, whether in public or private, any person who (whether for gain or not) presented or directed that performance shall be liable –

---

77 The Criminal Code of Denmark (§140 Straffeloven) and of some other European states contains blasphemy provisions. See also: *Otto-Preminger-Institute v Austria* (1995) 19 EHRR 34.

78 Rupert Murdoch @rupertmurdoch: 'Gerald Scarfe has never reflected the opinions of the Sunday Times. Nevertheless, we owe major apology for grotesque, offensive cartoon' 28 January 2013 at: https://twitter.com/rupertmurdoch/status/295964833394851840.

79 Including performances of hypnotism within the meaning of the Hypnotism Act 1952.

(a)   on summary conviction, to a fine not exceeding £400 or to imprisonment for a term not exceeding six months;

(b)   on conviction on indictment, to a fine or to imprisonment for a term not exceeding three years, or both.

Section 3 of the 1968 Act provides the 'defence of public good', which means a person, such as a playwright, producer or artist, charged under s 2 of the Act shall not be convicted of an offence if he can prove that the performance in question could be justified as being 'for the public good' on the ground that it was in the interests of drama, opera, ballet or any other art, or of literature or learning.

Shortly after the 1968 act came into force, London saw the first production of the Broadway musical *Hair*. With its rock anthems and nude hippies, no show could have better illustrated that a new theatrical era had arrived. In 1980, Howard Brenton's play *The Romans in Britain* was staged at the National Theatre (NT); Sir Peter Hall was the NT's Director at the time. The play depicted a male rape and nudity scene and ran at the Olivier Theatre during the autumn and winter of 1980. On 18 March 1982, Mrs Mary Whitehouse appeared on the verge of winning a private prosecution against the play's director, Michael Bogdanov, for allowing the homosexual rape scene, which centred on a young Celt and Druid priest who was subjected to attempted buggery by a Roman soldier.

See above 7.2.1

Charges of gross indecency under s 12 of the Sexual Offences Act 1956 ('unnatural offences' and 'buggery') which had been brought against Mr Bogdanov were suddenly withdrawn, after a senior Treasury counsel, representing Attorney General Sir Michael Havers, appeared in court to end the case immediately after the prosecution withdrew its evidence.[80] Mr Bogdanov, who faced up to two years in prison if convicted under the 1956 Act, claimed that the case had been withdrawn because Mrs Whitehouse knew a jury would not rule in her favour. *Romans in Britain* was a landmark case and alleviated fears in arts circles that a victory for Mrs Whitehouse could have led to a return to severe censorship of theatre productions and subsequent prosecution of performers and directors. In 1998 there was the first performance of Mark Ravenhill's *Shopping and Fucking* with its explicit portrayal of the life of a teenage rentboy and uncompromisingly explicit depiction of anal, oral and violent sex.

One of the last attempts to use censorship and prosecute using blasphemy laws was in 2007 by way of a private prosecution in **R (on the Application of Green) v The City of Westminster Magistrates' Court** (2007),[81] concerning the theatrical work, *Jerry Springer: The Opera*. The aggrieved party in the judicial review legal action was Stephen Green, National Director of an evangelical group, Christian Voice. Mr Green brought his private prosecution against the BBC for its broadcast of *Jerry Springer*, alleging blasphemous libel. Mr Green's action was backed by the human rights group Liberty; together they challenged the producer of the stage musical, Jonathan Thoday, along with Mark Thompson, Director-General of the BBC, for broadcasting the show in January 2005.[82]

Jerry Springer was a parody of the TV chat show, hosted by Jerry Springer, presenting, as entertainment, dysfunctional people who had lurid – and largely sexual – stories to tell. The second act revolved around the host imagining his descent into hell with characters appearing as Satan, Christ, God, Mary and Adam and Eve, who were treated as chat show guests. Their behaviour and language exhibited considerable excesses. The stage version of the musical had been previously performed at London's National Theatre and across the UK between April 2003 and July 2006; a recorded

---

80 Source: Correspondence between the Director of Media Watch UK, John C. Beyer and Mark Thompson, Director General of the BBC, 21 February 2005, re. 'Romans in Britain'.

81 [2007] EWHC 2785 (Admin).

82 Source: 'Sense prevailed over Springer "blasphemy"', by Mark Thompson, BBC Director General, *Daily Telegraph*, 6 December 2007.

performance of the play was broadcast by the BBC on 8 January 2005. The show and television broadcast were regarded by many as sacrilegious and the BBC received 63,000 complaints (55,000 before the broadcast).[83] In addition, the broadcasting regulator, Ofcom, received over 16,000 complaints.

Summonses against both defendants had been sought at Westminster Magistrates' Court. But the district judge refused to issue the summonses and held that the prosecution was prevented by the Theatres Act 1968 (the Act had been passed to abolish censorship of the theatre). Section 2(4)(a) Theatres Act 1968 meant that the ancient offence of blasphemous libel was to be distinguished from criminal defamatory libel, which was preserved by the Theatres Act. In any case, the district judge held that the target of criminal defamation had to be a living person, and Christ could not be regarded as a living human being for these purposes. The gist of defamatory libel was that it exposed the victim to hatred, ridicule or contempt amongst other people or damaged him in his trade. What's more, given the long delay and the circumstances in which this archaic offence had been invoked, the district judge held that this application by Mr Green bordered on the vexatious – though this was not a reason for her decision. It was a fact that Jerry Springer: The Opera had been performed in public for two years without any violence or even demonstrations which would have formed an essential element of the blasphemy offence.

After his unsuccessful attempt in the magistrates' court, Mr Green applied to the Administrative Court for judicial review, seeking a mandatory order requiring the issue of the two summonses refused by the district judge. The applicant relied on the common law of blasphemy principles, alleging that the gist of the blasphemous crime element of Jerry Springer was material relating to the Christian religion and that the material was so scurrilous and offensive that it would undermine society generally, by endangering the peace, depraving public morality, shaking the fabric of society and – particularly in this case – it could be a potential cause of civil strife. Mr Green further claimed that no matter what the merits and artistic qualities of this work were, the musical play contained material which was contemptuous and reviling of the Christian religion and thereby constituted the offence of criminal blasphemous libel.

See also
Chapter 10.7

The High Court held that the Theatres Act 1968 did not apply to the broadcasts by the BBC, because the broadcast was not a live performance given to the viewer by persons present and performing. The Broadcasting Act 1990 brings television and radio programmes within the purview of the Obscene Publications Act 1959, but provides a slightly different 'public good' defence.[84]

Agreeing with the district judge, the court held that it was plainly relevant to examine the context in which the words in Jerry Springer were spoken. If a blasphemer were shown to be roundly condemned, then that would lessen and eliminate any offence and any danger to the public. This meant that the play as a whole was not and could not reasonably be regarded as aimed at, or an attack on, Christianity or what Christians held sacred. In any case, there had not been any occasion of 'civil strife' or unrest over the musical's performances for nearly two years. Accordingly, the application for judicial review was refused (see also: **R v Gibson and Sylveire** (1990)[85] below); **DPP v Schildkamp** (1971);[86] **Knuller (Publishing, Printing and Promotions) Ltd v DPP** (1973);[87] **Shaw v DPP** (1962)[88]).

83 Source: BBC Press Release, Governors' Programme Complaints Committee finding on complaints against Jerry Springer: The Opera, 30 March 2005, available at www.bbc.co.uk/pressoffice/pressreleases/stories/2005/03_march/30/springer.shtml.

84 Para 6 of s 15 Broadcasting Act 1990 contains provisions applicable to broadcasts which are identical to the terms in s 2(4) Theatres Act 1968 (which applies to plays and musicals).

85 [1990] 3 WLR 595.

86 [1971] AC 1.

87 [1973] AC 435.

88 [1962] AC 220.

The High Court, citing the '*Gay News*' case (**R v Lemon**), not only rejected the charge that *Jerry Springer: The Opera* itself was blasphemous but set out a series of legal arguments which made it hard to see how any future prosecution for blasphemous libel could succeed, at least against a theatrical producer or a broadcaster. This was a landmark decision. Since then there has been an unstoppable pushing back of the boundaries (and of course now the offence of 'blasphemy' no longer exists). To be found guilty of racially aggravated hatred, any play would now have to show actual incitement to religious hatred, not merely engage in parody or satire.

In December 2004, a play by Sikh playwright Gurpreet Kaur Bhatti had to be closed down in a Birmingham community centre, for the protection of the playwright herself. Threats of abduction and murder by a mob of some 400 protesters forced Ms Bhatti into hiding, hours after her contro-versial drama opened to violent protests by members of the Sikh community. Protesters argued that her play *Behzti* (*Dishonour*) demeaned Sikhism by showing rape and murder within a gurdwara (temple). The Birmingham Theatre Company then offered to stage the play, just hours after officials at the Birmingham Repertory Theatre had scrapped it over public safety fears.[89]

7.3.9 Art or obscenity?

In 1997 the *Sensation* exhibition[90] of the collection of contemporary works by young British artists at the Royal Academy (RA) in London caused considerable protest with over seventy letters in the newspapers.[91] Reaction to the show was extreme, though the RA said afterwards that *Sensation* had been the most successful contemporary show ever, with visitors 'voting with their feet' to see the controversial exhibits, and more than 25,000 visitors were recorded in the first week of the exhibi-tion. Mindful of the controversy, the RA had given out questionnaires to visitors to gauge their reaction. Of 463 questionnaires returned in the first week, 450 said the RA 'had been right to present art even if it shocks or causes offence'. Against reports of high-level resignations, more than 400 people had applied to become 'Friends of the Royal Academy' – compared with a usual weekly total of 120.[92]

One of the controversial art pieces was the 11ft by 9ft portrait of Moors Murderer Myra Hindley,[93] created with children's handprints, by Marcus Harvey. Part of the controversy in this case was about the fact that a painting of serial child killer Hindley was exhibited at all. It aroused strong feelings amongst art critics and those who saw the 'iconic' image, due to its creation via children's handprints, literally a case of 'the medium is the message'. The artist was no doubt thrilled that his picture of Myra Hindley was not withdrawn by the police under the 'obscene publication' charge of the 1959 Obscene Publications Act. The RA selectors had obviously thought it worthy to be recognized as representing artistic brilliance, since they had no intention of having the picture removed. The Myra Hindley portrait only had to be removed for a short while for restoration after protesters had thrown Indian ink and eggs at it. Inside the Royal Academy there was a genuine sensation. A man was apprehended after two canisters of ink were thrown at the much-publicized painting of the Moors Murderer.[94]

---

89 Source: 'Writer in hiding as violence closes Sikh play', by Tania Branigan and Vikram Dodd, *Guardian*, 21 December 2004.
90 The *Sensation* works are owned by Charles Saatchi and can be viewed online at: www.saatchi-gallery.co.uk/aipe/sensation_royal_academy.htm.
91 See for example: *Daily Telegraph*, 1 December 1999, at p.17.
92 Source: 'RA's 'Sensation' show proves a hit', by Jojo Moyes, *Independent*, 27 September 1997.
93 The 'Moors murders' were carried out by Ian Brady and Myra Hindley between July 1963 and October 1965 in the Greater Manchester area. The victims were five children aged between 10 and 17: Pauline Reade, John Kilbride, Keith Bennett, Lesley Ann Downey and Edward Evans, at least four of whom were sexually assaulted. The murders are so named because two of the victims were discovered in graves dug on Saddleworth Moor.
94 Source: 'Arts: Sensation as ink and egg are thrown at Hindley portrait', by Tamsin Blanchard, *Independent*, 19 September 1997.

In August 2008, the London 2012 Olympic organizers (LOCOG) were embroiled in an embarrassing gaffe after Harvey's image of Myra Hindley was used to promote the Games by LOCOG in its 'Visit London' promotion video. The controversial picture was shown on a three-minute video loop at London House, attended by the then Prime Minister Gordon Brown, London Mayor Boris Johnson, then Olympics Minister Tessa Jowell and Chairman of the London 2012 Olympics Lord Coe. The face of the notorious serial killer also flashed up in the background at the official celebration of the Olympic handover in Beijing.[95]

Another controversial work in the *Sensation* exhibition was *The Holy Virgin Mary* by Chris Ofili (winner of the Turner Prize in 1998). The work upset many Roman Catholics and was called not only 'obscene' but also 'blasphemous' because it incorporates elephant dung and images of explicit sexual naked bottoms from hardcore pornographic magazines. Kearns (2000) thought it significant at the time that this 'holy work' escaped criminal prosecution under UK under the 1959 legislation. He further argues that the fact that parents exercised their judgement in bringing children to the exhibition must have contributed to satisfying the police that adequate protection of public morality had been accommodated so as to preclude the need for any prosecutions.

Sensation can be seen as one of the most successful triumphs for the British art lobby in preventing legal censorship under existing obscenity laws. The way the police and CPS handled the *Sensation* exhibition stands in stark contrast to the treatment of **Gibson and Sylveire** in the 'foetus earrings' case.[96] The appellant, artist Richard Norman (Rick) Gibson, had created a work entitled *Human Earrings*, consisting of a model's head adorned with a pair of earrings. Each earring was made out of a freeze-dried human foetus of three or four months' gestation, with a ring fitting tapped into its skull and attached at the other end to the model's earlobe. The earrings were displayed along with 40 other items, at the Young Unknown's Gallery in The Cut, London, managed by the appellant, Peter Sebastian Sylveire. Unbeknown to Sylveire, Gibson had advertised his exhibit with the result that the police and press were on the scene not long after the exhibition. The appellants were convicted of the common law offence of 'outraging public decency' as per **Knuller**.[97]

Gibson and Sylveire appealed on the grounds, *inter alia*, that the prosecution was barred by s 2(4) of the Obscene Publications Act 1959, which precluded prosecutions for a common law offence where its essence was that the matter was obscene, and that the prosecution could not succeed in the absence of proof of an intent to outrage public decency. Gibson and Sylveire's appeals were dismissed.

7.3.10 Indecent images of children

The removal of a photograph of 10-year-old actress Brooke Shields – fully made-up and naked – from Tate Modern's *Pop Life: Art in a Material World* exhibition in September 2009 reopened the debate about how far art should be allowed to go. It raised questions not only about the validity of freedom of expression and perceived morals but most importantly about the social function of art. Richard Prince's image *Spiritual America*[98] risked breaking obscenity laws, so the display at Tate Modern was closed and its catalogue withdrawn from sale.[99]

---

95 Source: 'Myra Hindley painting taints London 2012 celebrations', by Ashling O'Connor, *The Times*, 25 August 2008.
96 **R v Gibson and Sylveire** [1991] 1 All ER 441.
97 **R v Knuller** [1973] AC 435 at 495 as per Lord Simon.
98 *Spiritual America* depicts Brooke Shields in a photograph of a photograph, originally authorized by Shields's mother for a $450 fee, taken by commercial photographer, Gary Gross, for the Playboy publication *Sugar 'n' Spice* in 1976. Prince used the image as the source material for his own 1983 piece, which he displayed in a shop front in a rundown street in Lower East Side, New York, borrowing the title from a 1923 photograph by Alfred Stieglitz of a gelded horse. Shields later attempted, unsuccessfully, to suppress her picture.
99 Source: 'Tate Modern removes naked Brooke Shields picture after police visit', by Charlotte Higgins and Vikram Dodd, *Guardian*, 30 September 2009.

The police had raised concerns about the *Pop Life* exhibition and its likely 'indecent and obscene' content of child images, covered by legislation, such as s 1 of the Protection of Children Act 1978, the Obscene Publications Act 1959 and s160 of the Criminal Justice Act 1988. The Protection of Children Act 1978 addresses certain aspects of the sexual exploitation of children by penalizing the making, distribution, showing and advertisement of indecent photographs of them.[100] 'Advertising' or displaying indecent photographs of children is covered by s 1(1)(d) Protection of Children Act 1978.[101] The test to be applied in respect of indecent images of children is whether or not they are indecent; rather unhelpfully, however, the word 'indecent' has not been defined by the 1978 Act. Case law has said that it is for the jury to decide based on the recognized standards of propriety.

Richard Prince's work *Spiritual America* had already been shown at a similar exhibition at the Guggenheim in New York in 2007, without attracting major controversy. The *Pop Life* exhibition at Tate Modern also included works from Jeff Koons's series 'Made in Heaven' including large-scale photographic images of Koons and the porn model (and Koons's then wife) La Cicciolina having sexual intercourse. There were also works by Cosey Fanni Tutti, who, as part of her artistic practice, worked as a porn and glamour model in the 1970s and then displayed some of the resulting images at the exhibition. None of these works were either criticized or withdrawn.

Arguments for the Brooke Shields piece's removal centred on the promotion of sexualization of children. It might have been coincidental, but the removal of the *Spiritual America* image coincided with the conviction of nursery worker Vanessa George, who was found guilty in December 2009 of child abuse and sharing child and baby images on Facebook with the convicted sex offender Colin Blanchard and with Angela Allen – both of whom she had never met.[102] George was trusted for three years by parents and staff at Little Ted's nursery in Plymouth, Devon and had been employed as a classroom assistant in a primary school since 1998, having passed all Criminal Records Bureau (CRB) checks.

Was it scaremongering by Metropolitan Police officers in the light of the paedophilic activity of Vanessa George? On one hand, one could defend Prince's provocative image of young Brooke Shields as a comment on the merciless pursuit of celebrity and the commercialization of minors. On the other, one might find a sexually provocative image of the young girl obscene. Some art critics regarded the image as a profound artistic critique of the sexualization of a child star and the dominant 'sex sells' mentality of the American media market. Was the image of Brooke Shields as a seductress art or obscenity? Prince argued that by using the title *Spiritual America* it would conjure up a sense of unease in a country like the USA that prides itself on its democratic principles and Christian values; yet its consumer market revolves around the over-sexualization of individuals, even if they are teenage girls.

Freedom of expression carries with it an obligation to protect minors, covered by the Obscene Publications Act 1959 and embracing plays, books, photographs, magazines as well as, *inter alia*, films displaying or describing sexual activities and controversial contemporary art. Additionally, the Coroners and Justice Act 2009 created a new offence of 'possession of a prohibited image of a child'.[103] The definition of 'pornographic' (in relation to child images) is set out in subsection 62(3):

---

100 The definition of a child was altered from a person under 16 to 18 years of age by section 45(1) of the Sexual Offences Act 2003 (in force from 1 May 2004); see: Archbold: 31-107a and 31-116.
101 Section 1 Protection of Children Act 1978 covers a wide range of offences concerning indecent photographs and images of children, including the making of 'pseudo-photographs'.
102 Source: 'Vanessa George jailed for child sex abuse', by Stephen Morris, *Guardian*, 15 December 2009.
103 Chapter 2 of the Coroners and Justice Act 2009, ss 62–69 (England, Wales and Northern Ireland); ss 62(2) to (8) set out the definition of a 'prohibited image of a child' in that 'an image must be pornographic and must be grossly offensive, disgusting or otherwise of an obscene character'.

. . . an image is 'pornographic' if it is of such a nature that it must reasonably be assumed to have been produced solely or principally for the purpose of sexual arousal.

It is for the jury to determine whether this threshold has been met. Arguably, art and literature should be timeless in their ability to stimulate comment and reflect social morale. The media may be obsessed with paedophilia but it does not necessarily mean that art is.[104]

 FOR THOUGHT

What makes a piece of art like Richard Prince's image of a young, naked Brooke Shields 'obscene' compared with the image of Moors Murderer Myra Hindley by Royal Academician Marcus Harvey? Discuss current legislation in the light of definitions such as 'indecent and obscene'.

7.4 Extreme pornography and human rights: the 'margin of appreciation'

Current legislation in England and Wales prohibits obscene publications, performances and photographs by way of the Obscene Publications Acts 1959. But how does this arguably archaic law sit with freedom of expression under Article 10 of the European Convention? Is there a conflict of interest? Any restriction of freedom of expression that is imposed by national law must be capable of objective justification as being necessary in a democratic society for one of the purposes set out.

Additionally, s 63 of the Criminal Justice and Immigration Act 2008 created the offence of possessing extreme pornographic images. Section 63(10) of the Act defines such acts as 'life-threatening acts' or those which would cause serious injury, such as depictions of necrophilia and bestiality.[105]

7.4.1 What is the test for indecency?

The Perfect Moment by the late Robert Mapplethorpe (1946–89) triggered large-scale controversy about art, indecency and obscenity at the time. American photographer Mapplethorpe was one of the most controversial photographers of his time, known for his large-scale, highly stylized black and white portraits of frank homosexual eroticism. Much of his work depicts male nudes with erections engaged in sadomasochistic sex.

The Mapplethorpe retrospective exhibition Robert Mapplethorpe: The Perfect Moment first appeared in Philadelphia shortly after his death from AIDS in 1989, under the curatorship of Janet Kardon, and resulted in a public outcry of this publically funded exhibition. The Perfect Moment was then about to be exhibited at the Corcoran Gallery of Art in Washington, DC in July 1989 when 7 of the 175 photographs were deemed 'obscene' by the police, resulting in the arrest of Dennis Barrie, the Cincinnati Contemporary Arts Centre director, on 7 April 1990, because he had been publicly

---

104 For further discussion see: Kearns (2000).
105 Under s 63(10) Criminal Justice and Immigration Act 2008, proceedings must be commenced by the Director of Public Prosecutions (England and Wales). The maximum penalty on conviction on indictment is three years' imprisonment for possession of extreme pornographic images or six months if offences are deemed of a summary nature (s 67 Criminal Justice and Immigration Act 2008).

displaying these images for some twelve years in museums and galleries. The Protestant Reverend Donald E. Wildmon had seen a museum catalogue featuring *Piss Christ*, a photograph of the crucifixion immersed in a yellow liquid, which had subsequently resulted in Barrie's arrest. The charges were only withdrawn after the exhibition was cancelled.

The Mapplethorpe controversy even spilt over to the UK, when – 10 years later, in 1998 – the University of Central England was involved in obscenity charges over a Mapplethorpe photographic catalogue, housed in its university library. The book on Mapplethorpe with his typical photographic images had been published by Jonathan Cape in 1992. A postgraduate art student had borrowed the book from the university library for her thesis on 'obscenity and art'. She had taken a photo of two Mapplethorpe images in the book, one of them featuring two males in 'S & M' outfits, with one male urinating into the mouth of the other. The student had then taken the film to Boots the Chemist to be developed, and the shop had informed West Midlands Police because of the seemingly offensive and unusual nature of the images.

On 21 October 1997, West Midlands police officers from the paedophile and pornography unit seized the book – the only copy in the library. The university's Vice Chancellor, Dr Peter Knight, was then interviewed under caution with a view to prosecution, alleging that the book's contents and material were likely to 'deprave' and 'corrupt' under the Obscene Publications Act 1959. The university was informed that the book would be returned only if two images illustrating homosexual and sadomasochistic sex acts were removed. In March 1998, the University Senate voted to support the Vice Chancellor's position of refusing to comply. Nearly a year after the Mapplethorpe book had been seized by police officers, the Crown Prosecution Service announced on 30 September 1998 that they would not prosecute the university's Vice Chancellor. The CPS concluded that the book would not tend to 'deprave or corrupt a significant number of those who are likely to read it'. Robert Mapplethorpe's controversial book was returned, in a slightly tattered state, and restored to the university library.[106]

Fritscher (2002) argues, that in the HIV-AIDS driven times of the late 1980s and early 1990s, gay art was censored and silenced particularly harshly during the Reagan years (1980–88) and also during the Republican presidency of George Bush (1988–92) in the USA, thus advocating 'family values'. By 1990, Senator Jesse Helms had proposed a 'National Endowment for the Arts' (NEA) Appropriations Bill which affected future NEA grant-making procedures. The NEA Act subsequently prohibited funding for projects that were deemed 'obscene'. Senator Helms objected most specifically to aestheticizing Mapplethorpe's 1970s images of ancient uncloseted homoeroticism which revealed a culture of homomasculinity rather than a straight American pop culture.[107] Had the Mapplethorpe photos, depicting leather-clad male-on-male sadomasochism, been shot by a woman or a heterosexual male, the photographs may well never have been censored. Mapplethorpe's homosexuality was therefore a keystone of his work's vulnerability.

Another controversy arose in 1995, when ITN newsreader Julia Somerville (then 48) and her architect boyfriend Jeremy Dixon (then 56) were questioned by Scotland Yard's child-pornography unit, after Boots the Chemist had alerted the police over allegedly indecent photographs of her seven-year-old daughter, opening a debate on the law relating to child pornography. Both Ms Somerville and Mr Dixon strenuously denied the allegations. They said the pictures, which reportedly included a picture of Ms Somerville's daughter naked in the bath, were innocent. As we saw with the Mapplethorpe controversy above, the chemist chain Boots had a policy during the 1990s of reporting any photographs that staff believed may be obscene or pornographic. Shortly afterwards, the CPS dropped the action.[108]

106 Sources: 'Porn Wars', *Panorama*, BBC1, 2 November 1998; BBC World Service, *Witness*, 10 December 2009; BBC Radio 4, *In Living Memory: The Mapplethorpe Affair*, 9 December 2009, broadcast at 11am.
107 See: Fritscher (2002).
108 Source: 'Julia Somerville defends "innocent family photos"', by Rebecca Fowler, *Independent*, 5 November 1995.

In March 2001, the Saatchi Gallery in London was accused by Scotland Yard of exhibiting 'pornographic' photographs of children. These were part of an exhibon, *I am a Camera*, by American photographer Tierney Gearon. The pictures included two naked poses, one of her sons urinating in the snow and a couple of naked child pictures. There were three complaints by members of the public, and the police visited the gallery twice, causing a great deal of media coverage and leading to a debate on the rights and wrongs of such work. Ms Gearon defended her exhibition in the *Guardian* at the time, when she wrote:

> I looked at my pictures today and tried to see the bad things in them that other people have seen. But I can't. Some are describing them as pornographic, others are accusing me of exploiting my children's innocence. I don't understand how you can see anything but the purity of childhood. When the exhibition opened eight weeks ago, the *Observer*'s art critic, Laura Cumming, wrote that I had succeeded in capturing the way that a child would look at the world, almost as though I was a child myself. The exhibition got great press, and the whole experience has been positive – until last Thursday, when I went to the gallery to do an interview and found the police waiting for me. I was completely blown away. I even started joking around with the officers because I simply couldn't believe it was happening. I don't see sex in any of those prints, and if someone else reads that into them, then surely that is their issue, not mine.[109]

The police subsequently took no further action against either the photographer or the gallery owner, Charles Saatchi.

7.4.2 'Europorn' and free movement of pornographic goods

There have been some 'entrepreneurs' who have tried to manipulate EU law on 'freedom of movement of goods', such as the 'movement' of pornographic commodities, including 'top shelf' publications, which flooded the UK market after the country's entry into the 'common market' in 1973. While British customs authorities tried to stop 'continental filth' entering British shores, decisions by the European Court of Justice held otherwise. The overarching question is: can the state censor art or literature and deem it 'obscene' or should citizens be able to make up their own minds?

The relevance of this topic relates to the importing and subsequent distribution of publications of alleged indecent and obscene content. Scholars of European Union (Community) law are well aware of the rules relating to the abolition of 'measures having equivalent effect to quantitative restrictions' (MEQR), which have been central to the development of the single European (common) market for decades. Articles 28 and 29 EC Treaty (ex 30–34 EC Treaty) were designed to eliminate barriers such as the abolition of customs duties, pecuniary restrictions, MEQRs and trade discriminatory practices, which might be capable of hindering the flow of goods from Member State to Member State. This was challenged in two UK cases which involved obscene publications and indecent articles: **Henn and Darby**[110] and **Conegate**.[111] The principal provision for derogation from Articles 28 and 29 (ex 30–34) EC Treaty is Article 30 (ex 36) EC Treaty, which provides that a Member State can impose restrictions or prohibitions on imports and exports on grounds of public morality, public policy and public security.

Criminal 'entrepreneurs' Maurice Donald Henn and John Frederick Ernest Darby tried to take advantage of recent EEC law soon after the UK had joined the Common Market during the mid–1970s, in order to import top-shelf magazines and other pornographic goods from continental

109 Source: 'Where is the sex?', by Tierney Gearon, *Guardian*, 13 March 2001.
110 **R v Henn; R v Derby** (Case 34/79) [1979] ECR 3795 (ECJ).
111 **Conegate v Customs and Excise Commissioners** [1985] (C–121/85) ECR 1007 (ECJ – 4th Chamber).

Europe.[112] In the first criminal action challenging EU law and the UK's derogation from the 'free movement' principle, defendants Henn and Darby argued they were entitled to bring in such merchandise from the European mainland for their personal use and that of their 'friends', and that domestic laws were not only outdated but also contravened the spirit of the Treaty of Rome.[113]

❖ KEY CASE

R v Henn (Maurice Donald); R v Derby (John Frederick Ernest) (Case 34/79) [1979] ECR 3795 (ECJ)

Precedent

- ❖ Article 30 EEC (now Article 34 TFEU) applies to prohibitions on imports in as much as they are the most extreme form of restriction; hence:
- ❖ A law of a Member State prohibiting any importation of pornographic articles into that state constitutes a quantitative restriction on imports within the meaning of Article 30 of the Treaty (now Article 34 TFEU).
- ❖ Under Article 36 TFEU it is for each Member State to determine in accordance with its own values as to the meaning of 'public morality'.
- ❖ Each Member State is entitled to impose lawful prohibitions on imports justified on grounds of 'public morality' (Article 227 EEC; now Article 349 TFEU).
- ❖ Articles which are deemed 'indecent' or 'obscene' must be defined and understood by domestic laws.

Facts

Maurice Henn and John Darby were operating a pornographic films and 'top shelf' magazine mail order business in the UK with imports from Denmark, Germany and Sweden. On 14 October 1975, a truckload arrived at the port of Felixstowe from Rotterdam containing a large consignment of a 'sexually explicit nature'. HM Customs and Excise officers had monitored previous operations. Both Henn and Darby were subsequently indicted for importing 'indecent and obscene' goods contrary to s 42 Customs Consolidation Act 1876, s 304 Customs and Excise Act 1952 and the Obscene Publications Act 1959. Their trial started at Ipswich Crown Court on 17 May 1977. The court heard about the detailed and explicit sexual activities of the films and referred to the magazines as containing photographs of naked under-age girls engaged in adult sexual activities. One magazine advertised for models for acts of buggery. Both men pleaded 'not guilty', arguing that the 1952 Act contravened EU law under Article 28 EEC.[114] The UK invoked Article 36 EEC[115] to justify the seizure of pornographic goods because they would 'deprave and corrupt' UK citizens, on the grounds that they were 'indecent and obscene'. Henn was sentenced to 18 months' and Darby to two years' imprisonment.

Both appeals were rejected by the Court of Appeal Criminal Division on 9 November 1978. The House of Lords referred the case to the European Court of Justice (ECJ) on 29 January 1979 for a preliminary ruling, to seek clarification on the conflict of UK

---

112 For further discussion see: Bernard (1996).
113 The Customs Consolidation Act 1876 prohibited importation of indecent and obscene materials and the Customs and Excise Act 1952 established the criminal offence for evading the prohibition.
114 Post Amsterdam numbering Article 27 EC; now Article 32 TFEU (Treaty on the Functioning of the European Union – as amended by the Treaty of Lisbon).
115 Article 30 EC; now Article 36 TFEU.

customs laws with the 'free movement' principle in respect of obscene publications and pornographic goods. The HL referred several questions to the Court of Justice for a preliminary ruling.

Decision (Preliminary Ruling)

Advocate General Lord Warner opined that the UK had contravened Article 28 EEC. He stated that a Member State should apply the same criteria to 'home-produced' goods – including pornographic publications – as to foreign imports. The UK appeared to tolerate 'home-produced' 'top shelf' literature and prohibited foreign imports from EU Member States, which amounted to a 'quantitative restriction' on imports. Unless there was a valuable reason to derogate from the free movement principle, the UK was duty bound to change its laws in line with EU law. But the ECJ added that if it felt that the goods were deemed 'indecent and obscene' under domestic legislation, the UK could derogate from the 'free movement' principle. However, the UK should then apply this principle to its own nationally published goods of the same (pornographic) nature. For this reason, Henn and Darby's appeals were dismissed and their convictions upheld.

Analysis

Under EU law, if a statute of a Member State prohibits any importation of pornographic articles into that state – such as was the case in *Henn and Darby* – (e.g. the Customs Consolidation Act 1876; the Customs and Excise Act 1952) then this constitutes a quantitative restriction on imports within the meaning of Article 30 of the Treaty (now Article 34 TFEU). The ECJ ruled that this means a Member State may, in principle, lawfully impose prohibitions on the importation from any other Member State (say pornographic goods from Sweden or Germany) which are of an 'indecent' or 'obscene' character as understood by its domestic laws (e.g. Obscene Publications Act 1959) and that such prohibitions may lawfully be applied to the whole of its national territory even if variations exist between the laws in force in the different constituent parts of the Member State concerned. If a prohibition on the importation of goods is justifiable on grounds of public morality and if it is imposed with that purpose the enforcement of that prohibition cannot, in the absence within the Member State concerned of a lawful trade in the same goods, constitute a means of arbitrary discrimination or a disguised restriction on trade contrary to Article 36 EEC (now Article 36 TFEU).

The test is then that of proportionality. As the Advocate General said, there is a clear difference in application of domestic legislation on the prohibition of the importation into the UK of a single book that was lawfully on sale in English bookshops, compared with bulk imports of indecent and obscene articles 'of a kind so obscene and unmeritorious that they may not be published or distributed in any way in any part of the United Kingdom without a criminal offence being committed'. Essentially the problem lies in distinguishing between the kind of situation in which discrimination is 'arbitrary' and the kind of situation in which it is 'justified'. Clearly it would be unreasonable and disproportionate to forbid the importation of such a book just because of the risk that it might be displayed in an English high street bookshop or put on sale in Scotland or the Isle of Man. But in Henn and Darby's case, this was concerned with bulk importation of obscene articles. The HL referred to the *Van Duyn* case,[116] where the ECJ held that, where the competent authorities of a Member State had clearly defined their standpoint as to the socially harmful

---

116 *Van Duyn v Home Office* [1975] Ch 358 ECJ (Case 41/74).

character of certain activities and had taken administrative measures to counteract them, that Member State need not make those activities unlawful before it could rely on the 'public policy' derogation.

Henn and Darby lost their appeal but similar questions concerning free movement of (pornographic) goods were asked a few years later of the House of Lords in **Conegate**, when a number of life-size inflatable dolls were seized and confiscated on import at Heathrow Airport from Germany in October 1982.

The two **Conegate** consignments were described on the import documentation as 'window display models', though it was hard to imagine that the 'Love Love dolls,' 'Miss World Specials' and 'Rubber Ladies' could really be used for this purpose. The consignment was accompanied by some 'sexy vacuum flasks'. Customs inspection officers took the view that these goods were indecent and obscene within the meaning of s 42 of the Customs Consolidation Act 1876. Uxbridge magistrates duly ordered the forfeiture of the goods, upheld on appeal by Southwark Crown Court. Importers Conegate argued that any law prohibiting the importation of such products was an infringement of Article 28 EEC (now Article 32 TFEU), while the UK invoked Article 36 EEC (now Article 36 TFEU), justifying the seizure and forfeiture of the articles within the scope of 'public morality'.[117]

Similarly to the ruling in **Henn and Darby**, the ECJ reiterated in **Conegate** that it was for Member States to determine what laws should be enacted to protect public morality within their jurisdiction. In this case the UK had been unable to satisfy this requirement, because similar pornographic articles were already lawfully sold within its territory, so the UK's restriction on importation could not be justified under Article 36 EEC (TFEU). The Advocate General noted that the Obscene Publications Act 1959 was not at issue in this case and formed the view that a prohibition of imports could not be justified in Community law on the ground of public morality *unless* a broadly comparable standard was accepted for imports and domestic production of similar such articles (see also: **Adoui and Cornuaille v Belgian State and City of Liège** (1982)[118]). This meant that a Member State would have to show that the national measure (to stop the importation of pornographic articles) really did have the effect of protecting public morality.

The conflicting ECJ decisions in **Henn and Darby** and **Conegate** have been the subject of severe criticism in that they do not assist standards of control in European Member States, nor do they clarify the varied and different measures in parts of the UK, such as the Isle of Man or Scotland, which have applied different prohibitions on imports of obscene goods under the ancient 1876 Act. In England and Wales, for instance, there are controls on displays and prohibited goods such as 'blow-up dolls' though – following the **Conegate** ruling – they could have easily been sold in Boots the Chemist.[119]

Conegate is an important decision because the ECJ took a different approach in respect of public morality from that taken in **Henn and Darby**. We see a progressive approach on public morality in **Conegate** where the ECJ held that the domestic courts' decision to ban imported German pornographic goods was unacceptable because the UK court was clearly giving different (discriminatory) treatment to 'domestically produced' pornographic articles – which was held irrational, disproportionate and discriminatory.

---

117 The High Court posed its questions in the light of the conclusion in **R v Henn and Darby** [1979] ECR 3795 (ECJ) that a prohibition on imports justifiable on the ground of public morality and imposed for that purpose could not, in the absence of lawful trade in the same goods within the Member State concerned, constitute a means of arbitrary discrimination or a disguised restriction on trade between Member States within the meaning of the second sentence of Article 36 EEC.
118 [1982] ECR 1665 (ECJ).
119 Under the Indecent Displays (Control) Act 1981. Under the Local Government (Miscellaneous Provisions) Act 1982, if a local authority decided to adopt Schedule 3 to the Act, then premises could not be used as a sex shop unless a licence had been granted; even then the use is subject to compliance with the conditions laid down by the local authority. In fact the definition of a sex shop meant the use of premises for a business which consisted to a significant degree of selling, hiring, exchanging, lending, displaying or demonstrating sex articles or the like. The result was that someone such as an ordinary newsagent, whose business largely consisted of selling ordinary newspapers, books and so on, was not subjected to the licensing requirement when Schedule 3 was adopted.

7.4.3 Criminalizing the possession and making of 'extreme pornography': s 63 Criminal Justice and Immigration Act 2008

What is different between the two statutory provisions, namely s 1 of the Obscene Publications Act 1959 and the new provision under s 63 of the Criminal Justice and Immigration Act 2008? Section 63 of the 2008 Act relates to mere *possession* rather than publication. This means that the new offence of possessing extreme pornographic images impacts on private life (Article 8 ECHR) and freedom of expression (Article 10 ECHR). The offence was created based on the recommendations of the Home and Scottish Offices' Consultation 'On the Possession of Extreme Pornographic Material' (2005).

The reason for the Home and Scottish Offices' examination of current UK obscenity laws was the concern by the Government about the range of extreme pornography available via the internet, which cannot, in practice, be controlled by existing UK laws.[120] The consultation paper refers to 'extreme pornography' as featuring violent rape, sexual torture and other abusive non-consensual acts. These acts were depicted in various forms before the internet but the publication and supply could be controlled by the Obscene Publications Act 1959 and by customs legislation, such as the Customs Consolidation Act 1876 and the Customs and Excise Management Act 1979. Closing down sources of supply and distribution obviated the need for a possession offence. However, the global nature of the internet makes this approach much more difficult.[121]

A new offence of 'possession of extreme pornographic images' was then created by s 63 of the Criminal Justice and Immigration Act 2008. The offence came into force on 26 January 2009 and is not retrospective.[122] Section 63 ('Possession of extreme pornographic images') makes it an offence to possess a limited range of extreme pornographic material. Section 71 of the Act amends the Obscene Publication Act 1959 by increasing the maximum penalty for offences under that Act from three years' imprisonment to five years' imprisonment.

There are three elements to a s 63 offence;[123] an image must come within the terms of *all three elements* before it will fall foul of the offence. Those elements are:

1. that the image is pornographic;
2. that the image is grossly offensive, disgusting, or otherwise of an obscene character; and
3. that the image portrays in an explicit and realistic way, one of the following:

   a. an act which threatens a person's life; this could include depictions of hanging, suffocation, or sexual assault involving a threat with a weapon.
   b. an act which results in or is likely to result in serious injury to a person's anus, breast or genitals; this could include the insertion of sharp objects or the mutilation of breasts or genitals.
   c. an act involving sexual interference with a human corpse; or
   d. a person performing an act of intercourse or oral sex with an animal, and a reasonable person looking at the image would think that the animals and people portrayed were real.[124]

---

120 Ministers at the time of the consultation were the Parliamentary Under Secretary of State, Paul Goggins MP, and Scottish Executive Minister for Justice, Cathy Jamieson MSP.
121 For further discussion see: McGlynn and Rackley (2007).
122 Part 5, ss 63 to 67 Criminal Justice and Immigration Act 2008.
123 Section 63 subsections (2) to (8).
124 See also: Ministry of Justice (2009c).

Section 63 defines such material as 'graphic', 'sexually explicit' and *inter alia* 'grossly offensive'. The section is clearly aimed at material on the internet which tends to contain serious violence towards women and men; it generally depicts activities which are illegal in themselves and in which the participants may in some cases have been the victims of criminal offences. The 2008 Act defines an 'extreme' image as one which is grossly offensive, disgusting or otherwise of an obscene character, and portrays the activity in an *explicit and realistic way*.[125]

Section 63(7) Criminal Justice and Immigration Act 2008 further defines an 'extreme' image as:

> An image falls within this subsection if it portrays, in an explicit and realistic way, any of the following –
>
> (a) an act which threatens a person's life,
> (b) an act which results, or is likely to result, in serious injury to a person's anus, breasts or genitals,
> (c) an act which involves sexual interference with a human corpse, or
> (d) a person performing an act of intercourse or oral sex with an animal (whether dead or alive), and a reasonable person looking at the image would think that any such person or animal was real.

See Chapter 10.7

Section 63 material goes far beyond what is classified for mainstream cinema by the British Board of Film Classification (BBFC) and beyond the material classified by the BBFC for sale only in licensed sex shops (classified as R18). Section 64(3) of the 2008 Act exempts films that have received a classification from the BBFC, who will have already made a determination that the film is not obscene under the Obscene Publications legislation.[126]

Section 63 of the Criminal Justice and Immigration Act 2008 does not replace the existing offence contained in the Obscene Publications Act 1959 of *publishing* or having in one's possession for publication an obscene article – although one of its primary purposes is to identify the type of obscene image that might cause the greatest harm and which thus should be subject to prosecution policies. But the principle of moral corruption inherent in the 1959 Act has been retained in s 63 of the 2008 Act. Rowbottom (2006) argues that the mainstream entertainment industry, working within current obscenity laws (i.e. the 1959 Act) will not be affected by the s 63 offence.[127]

7.4.4 The practicalities of prosecuting a section 63 offence

See 7.4.3 above

The practicalities of prosecuting a s 63 offence may not be that easy. There needs to be evidence of a clear link between possession and harm, exacerbated by the fact that the wording and purpose of the legislation is not articulated clearly and convincingly. The key to accurately assessing what amounts a s 63 offence is to apply all three elements to any example of (online) material under consideration. To focus on just one element in isolation inevitably leads to false conclusions about what is caught. The words 'grossly offensive' and 'disgusting' are not alternatives to 'obscene character' but are examples of it. They are drawn from the ordinary dictionary definition of 'obscene' and reflect different aspects of that concept. They are intended to convey a non-technical definition of that concept. It is a definition which is distinct from the technical definition contained in the Obscene Publications Act 1959, that definition being specifically geared

---

125 Section 63(6) Criminal Justice and Immigration Act 2008.
126 For further discussion see: Munro (2006).
127 For further discussion see: Rowbottom (2006).

to the concept of publication. For possession of an 'extreme pornographic' image to be proved, it is necessary to establish some knowledge of its existence (see: **Atkins v DPP; Goodland v DPP** (2000)[128] – below).

This element of the offence must be read in conjunction with the other two elements. The test as to whether an image comes within the terms of the offence is not simply whether it is grossly offensive, disgusting or otherwise of an obscene character; rather it is a test of whether all elements of the offence are met. It is all three elements working together which should ensure that the only images which are caught are those which would also fall foul of the Obscene Publications Act 1959.

The image then has to be both pornographic and constitute an *extreme* image.[129] An extreme act is one which threatens a person's life, which results or is likely to result in serious injury to a person's anus, breasts or genitals, which involves sexual interference with a human corpse, or which involves a person performing intercourse or oral sex with an animal. But 'life-threatening' is not defined in the 2008 Act.[130]

Serious injury is also not defined in the act and this will be a question of fact for the magistrates or jury. The intention is that 'serious injury' should be given its ordinary English meaning. The reference to 'serious injury' was not intended to expressly link into the case law with respect to 'grievous bodily harm' under ss 18 and 20 of the Offences Against the Person Act 1861, which has been interpreted as being capable of including psychological harm. Taking an example which was raised during parliamentary debates on the Criminal Justice and Immigration Bill, the anal sex scene in *Last Tango in Paris*, even if it were to be considered pornographic and of an obscene nature, would not be caught by the offence, because it is not explicit and does not portray an act resulting or likely to result in serious injury to a person's anus.

Only these specific acts will be caught, and only in conjunction with the other two elements of the offence. It will therefore take its ordinary English meaning and will be a question of fact for the magistrates or jury. The image is then of such nature that it must be *reasonably assumed* to have been produced solely or principally for the purpose of sexual arousal. This provision then employs the objective test in the same way as the Obscene Publications Act 1959 – to determine the purpose of the image. This then means that the actual intention of the producer of the image is not really relevant unless that intention points to the presumed intention. A further requirement in respect of an extreme act is that a reasonable person looking at the image would think that the people and animals portrayed were real. The practical effect of that requirement is that only photographs and films, and images which are indistinguishable from photographs and films, will be caught by the offence.

Finally, the prosecution has to prove 'possession' (similar to s 160 Criminal Justice Act (CJA) 1988, which covers the offence of possession of an indecent photograph of a child). The CA held in **Atkins and Goodland** (see below) that images stored without the defendant's knowledge by browser software in a hidden cache, of which he was also unaware, did not amount to knowledge of possession. The situation was akin to a person having a hold-all in which, unknown to him, was a gun. Knowledge of the bag was enough, but ignorance of the bag itself made it no crime. Though both cases concerned internet child pornography prosecutions (pseudo-photographs of child images) the ruling can be applied to the s 63 offence of the 2008 Act (see also: **R v Bowden** (1999)[131]).

128 [2000] 2 Cr App R 248.
129 Section 63(2) Criminal Justice and Immigration Act 2008.
130 Section 63(3).
131 [1999] EWCA Crim 2270.

7.4.5 Defences

There are three general defences set out in s 65 of the Criminal Justice and Immigration Act 2008. These are the same as for the possession of indecent images of children under s 160 (2) of the Criminal Justice Act 1988.[132] These are:

● that the person had a legitimate reason for being in possession of the image.

This will cover those who can demonstrate that they have a reason for possessing the image/s. This would include, for example, the police and the prosecuting authorities, those involved in the classification of films (such as the British Board of Film Classification – BBFC[133]), those dealing with complaints from the public about content in the mobile and internet industries and those creating security software to block such images.

● that the person was in possession of an extreme image but had not looked at it and therefore neither knew, nor had reason to suspect that it was an extreme pornographic image.

This will cover those who are in possession of offending images but are unaware of the nature of the images – for example, where a person is sent an electronic copy of an image which he saves without looking at it and which gave rise to no suspicion that it might be extreme pornography.

● that the person had been sent the image without having asked for it, on their own behalf or through someone else, and, having looked at it had not kept it for an unreasonable length of time.[134]

This will cover those who are sent unsolicited material by any means and who act quickly to delete it or otherwise get rid of it.

What constitutes an unreasonable amount of time spent looking at the downloaded images depends on all the circumstances of the case. It is a defence to prove that that the person charged with a s 63 offence had a legitimate reason for being in possession of such an 'extreme' image, had not seen the image concerned and did not know, nor had any cause to suspect, it to be an 'extreme pornographic' image; or that that person was sent the image without any prior request, and did not keep it for an unreasonable time.

Unlike the Obscene Publications Act 1959, a charge under s 63 of the 2008 Act does not provide a public interest defence. Once an image has been seen as both 'extreme' and 'pornographic' no argument can be advanced by the defence that the detrimental effect of the publication could advance the contribution to art or literature or a subject of general concern. For a s 63 offence to be proved it must reasonably be assumed to have been produced *solely or principally* for the purpose of sexual arousal.

What about deleting the images on one's computer? Case law suggests that deleting images held on a computer is sufficient to get rid of them, i.e. this would get rid of the 'possession' element of the offence. An exception would be where a person is shown to have intended to remain in

---

132 Section 160 CJA 1988 covers the offence of possession of an indecent photograph of a child. There are four defences to this offence: three are listed in s 160(2) CJA 1988, Archbold 31–115, and one is listed in s 160A.
133 The intention of s 64 Criminal Justice and Immigration Act 2008 is to give certainty to members of the public that they will not be at risk of prosecution if they possess a video recording of a film which has been classified by the BBFC, even if the film contains an image or images, considered by the Board to be justified by the context of the work as a whole, which nevertheless fall foul of the offence in s 63. The fact that the images are held as part of a BBFC classified film takes them outside the scope of the offence.
134 Section 65(2).

control of an image even though he has deleted it – that will entail him having the capacity (through skill or software) to retrieve the image.

In **R v Porter (Ross Warwick)** (2006),[135] the Court of Appeal held that an image (of child pornography) will only be considered to be in *possession* if the defendant had custody or control of the image at that time. If at the time of possession the image is beyond his control, then he will not possess it. Walker had been convicted at Snaresbrook Crown Court in April 2005 (by a majority jury verdict of 10 to 2) on 15 counts of making an indecent photograph of a child contrary to s 1(1)(a) Protection of Children Act 1978, and 2 counts (counts 16 and 17) of possessing indecent photographs of children contrary to s 160(1) of the Criminal Justice Act 1988. Police forensic experts had recovered 3,575 still images and 40 movie files of child pornography from the hard disk drives of the two computers seized. Of the remaining 3,573 found on the first PC's hard drive, 873 had been deleted in the sense that they had been placed in the 'recycle bin' of the computer, which had then been emptied. The remaining 2,700 still images were saved in a database of a programme called ACDSee.[136] All of the larger images had, however, been deleted. The effect of deleting the larger images was that the thumbnail could no longer be viewed in the gallery view. But a trace of each thumbnail (the metadata) remained in the database of the programme. Of the 40 movie files, 7 were recovered from the PC; all of these had been placed in the recycle bin, which had then been emptied. The remaining 33 files were recovered: they had not been saved, but were recovered from the cache (temporary internet files) record of the two hard disk drives.

Mr Porter's appeal rested on the notion of the judge's direction on 'possession'. The trial judge had summed up in the following way:

> . . . possession, as a matter of law . . . means having something under your custody or control with the knowledge that you have such a thing in your custody and control and for practical purposes there is little difference in that definition and the definition of making . . . if a person deliberately and intentionally downloads an image, he makes that image and if that action is done with the knowledge that the downloaded image is or likely to be indecent, the offence is made out . . .

> . . . members of the jury, the direction in relation to deleting the files . . . applies in the same way . . . because you have heard the experts tell you that the nature of a computer is that on the hard disk there are a number of files, data files. Such files may be active or deleted, recovered, lost or unallocated and the mere fact that an image is on a deleted file, rather than an active file, does not mean that the user is not in possession, because the file, deleted or not, is one of the files he had on a hard disk which was in his possession, was his computer and his hard disk. The issue in this case, is whether he knew that the images were indecent, or likely to be indecent.[137]

But the CA held that the judge's summing-up to the jury was flawed in that he directed them that the only issue for them to decide was whether the defendant knew that the images were indecent or likely to be indecent. He did not direct them about the factual state of affairs necessary to constitute possession, and the result was that a vital issue was wrongly removed from the jury. Nor did he direct them about the mental element required to constitute possession. Dyson LJ on behalf of

---

135 [2006] EWCA Crim 560 (16 March 2006).
136 This programme is designed for viewing graphical images and is used by photographers. When opened in the 'gallery view', the programme creates 'thumbnail' images of the pictures viewed. These would originally have been larger images associated with each thumbnail.
137 Ibid., at para 8 (Lord Justice Dyson).

the CA stated that in principle this would require proof that the defendant did not believe that the image in question was beyond his control. For these reasons, Ross Porter's appeal was allowed and his convictions were quashed.

The **Porter** case has implications for the use of forensic computer examinations if an image has been deleted. 'Possession; will depend on whether the defendant had the know-how and or the software to allow him to retrieve the image. Where, however, the offender admits that he down-loaded the image or accessed it on the internet then a charge of 'making' will be laid.[138]

Prosecuting the offence is even more complicated where computers have been seized by the police and the household contains computer equipment with multiple users, where there is no forensic evidence as to which user accessed a site. Additionally, where the possession of material stored within automatically generated areas of the hard drive is concerned, forensic examination of the hard drive can usually identify what material is held within the temporary internet file. Assuming the identity of the user is known, such material may equally attract a charge of 'making' each such image without the need to prove knowledge of the automatic cache. If a user is demon-strated (e.g. by admission, or by proof that he has accessed the temporary internet file offline) to have known of the existence and effect of automatic operating software, the offence of possession may arise. The court in **R v Oliver** (2002)[139] divided indecent images of children into five categories, and gave sentencing guidelines based on the categories. The sentencing guidelines have been amended by guidance from the Sentencing Council. In **R (on behalf of O'Shea) v Coventry Magistrates' Court** (2004),[140] the Divisional Court accepted that it was possible to incite another to distribute indecent images of children even where the 'purchase' of images was a fully automated process.

The cases of **Atkins** and **Goodlands**[141] are significant here again in dealing with the issue of 'possession' and 'making' indecent images (of children). Dr Antony Rowan Atkins was convicted at the Bristol Magistrates' Court on 27 May 1999 of 10 offences of having in his possession indecent photographs of children contrary to s 160(1) CJA 1988.[142]

Dr Atkins had held a lectureship in the Department of English at Bristol University since October 1997. He had available to him there both a Viglen computer set up in his office and also a departmental computer mostly used by others in the department's main office. On 16 October 1997 another member of the department logged into the departmental computer and was imme-diately concerned by the menu of internet addresses recently called up. The IT department checked the computer's cache files and found there pictures of naked young girls in crude postures with the PC's history pointing to Dr Atkins. Similar pictures were found in the Viglen cache. The court found that Dr Atkins had deliberately chosen to store the material on the hard drives of the computers, which amounted to 'possession'.

Dr Atkins raised the defence under s 160(2) of the 1988 Act, namely that he had a legitimate reason for having the photographs in his possession, for the purpose of legitimate academic research. Dr Atkins appealed against his conviction on the 10 possession counts; the prosecutor appealed against Dr Atkins's acquittal on 21 of the 'making' counts. In addressing the issue of 'making' contrary to s 1(1)(a) of the Protection of Children Act 1978, Simon Brown LJ on behalf of the Court of Appeal found that Dr Atkins had made a directory (named 'J') for the specific purpose of storing the material, thereby agreeing with the prosecution that this would 'call for a conviction'. For possession of an indecent image (of a child) to be proved, it is necessary to establish some knowledge of its existence.

---

138 This is covered by s 1 Protection of Children Act 1978 if this concerns child images; see: Archbold 31-118.
139 **R v Oliver, Hartrey and Baldwin** (2002), judgment of 21 November 2002, (2002) The Times, 6 December (unreported).
140 [2004] EWHC Admin 905.
141 **Atkins v DPP; Goodlands v DPP** [2000] 2 Cr App R 248 (CA).
142 See: Archbold 31-118.

It was by sheer coincidence that both cases of **Atkins** and **Goodland** appeared before the Bristol District Judge (a stipendiary magistrate at the time). Mr Peter John Goodland was also convicted at Bristol Magistrates' Court (on 21 April 1999) on one count of having in his possession an indecent pseudo-photograph of a 10-year-old girl. The cross-appeal by the Director of Public Prosecutions was allowed, and Mr Goodland was duly convicted. Since the 'sellotaped' copied images of the little girl were so 'pitifully crude' – according to Blofeld J's summing-up in the Court of Appeal – Mr Goodland was sentenced to a two-year conditional discharge with an order to pay £50 costs. He was, however, placed on the Sex Offenders Register (Sex Offenders Act 1997) for a period of five years.

Section 69 Criminal Justice and Immigration Act 2008 extends the remit of the indecent photographs legislation by amending the meaning of 'photograph' within s 7(4)(a) Protection of Children Act 1978 (PCA) to include 'derivatives of photographs', such as data (or tracings) stored on a computer disc or by other electronic means, capable of conversion. Prosecutors have to prove that the image is derived (either in whole or in part) from a photograph or pseudo-photograph. The police will have to gather sufficient evidence recovered at the scene and/or use computer facial recognition packages to identify whether an image is a known photograph. It is important there is evidence that it is a tracing and not, for example, a freehand drawing, which would be outside of the scope of this provision. This is known as 'indecent tracings'. This means the offender takes a photograph and traces the outline of that photograph onto tracing paper and from there to a piece of paper. They then colour in the tracing and destroy the photograph. Tracings are not restricted to the old-fashioned technique, however, and technology has altered the way that a tracing could be produced. A scanner and appropriate software can 'trace' a photograph and digitally produce the results. This can then be coloured in or manipulated in the same way as a photograph. Some mobile telephones have effects built into them so that when they take a photograph it produces a tracing rather than a full photograph. If the phone is seized with the image it produced, it can then legitimately be said to be a photograph (because it was taken on a camera) and charged as a s 1 PCA (or s 160 CJA 1988) offence. If the image was sent to someone else or printed out, it would be technically difficult to prove that this was a photograph.[143] In **R v Stephen Neal** (2011)[144] the Court of Appeal held that it was unfair for an individual purchaser of a book to be prosecuted for possession of indecent photographs in that book, and neither the publisher nor the retailer was prosecuted.

7.4.6 Cyber rights and human rights

Foster (2010) argues that the new offence created under s 63 of the Criminal Justice and Immigration Act 2008 ('possession of extreme pornographic images') may well conflict with human rights legislation by restricting free speech under Article 10 ECHR and intruding into adult individual's private lives under Article 8. He purports that s 63 fails both in regulating truly harmful images that glorify sexual violence and in imposing necessary and proportionate restrictions on free speech and the right to access those images in private.[145]

And what about the public interest defence which still exists under s 4 of the Obscene Publications Act 1959 ('defence of public good'). In **R v Gibson and Sylveire** (1991)[146] the public interest defence was invoked under s 2(4) OPA 1959. Lord Lane CJ said that the offence existed at common law and the proper interpretation of 'obscene' for the purposes of the 1959 Act was not

---

143 Source: CPS Guidelines to Prosecutors: 'Indecent images of children', 7 November 2011.
144 [2011] EWCA Crim 461.
145 For further discussion see: Akdeniz (2008).
146 [1991] 1 All ER 441.

See above
7.3.8

the broad meaning of 'tending to engender revulsion or disgust and to outrage' but was deemed to be the restricted meaning set out in s 1(1) OPA 1959. As to *mens rea*, it should be the same as for the cognate common law offence of obscene libel, and there was no requirement for the prosecution to prove an intention to outrage or recklessness. Gibson and Sylveire's appeals were dismissed.

In **S and G v UK** (1991)[147] the Strasbourg court held that the Obscene Publications Act 1959 did not breach Article 10 Convention rights. The ECtHR stated that:

> . . . the difference between the common law offence of outraging public decency and the statutory offence of obscenity [is] a qualitative one of fact and morals, the former being concerned with more offensive material which engenders such revulsion, disgust and outrage that it is irrelevant whether its consequence is actually to undermine public morals. This distinction . . . meets the applicants' objection that they could not have foreseen a prosecution for that offence, rather than a prosecution under section 2 of the OPA 1959.

Lewis (2002) submits that that this vastly overstates the degree of foreseeability possible and the degree to which it is possible to discern a distinction between the multiple notions of obscenity and indecency. The Commission in **S and G** seemed to accept that it is not necessarily 'public morals' that the offence may be trying to protect. The Commission found that the interference was prescribed by UK law, reiterating its principles in **Handyside**,[148] and held that the relevant domestic law was sufficiently clear, had a legitimate aim and was not disproportionate, even though there was no defence based on artistic merit.

Does the Human Rights Act 1998 assist artists, authors and film-makers when their works are controversial and possibly obscene (or blasphemous) by applying ECtHR jurisprudence under Article 10 and the 'margin of appreciation? Possibly not always.

Both **Gibson and Sylveire** (and **S and G**) could have argued that the exhibition and works were not an outrage to public decency (as per **Knuller**) and thereby raised the Article 10 issue of freedom of expression, but the prosecution was held to be within the margin of appreciation and could derogate under Article 10(2) ECHR for reasons of a legitimate aim to protect public morals. This means the 'margin of appreciation' developed under Strasbourg jurisprudence enables Member States to have a degree of latitude to decide obscenity and (in some countries) blasphemy laws in line with social policy, cultural and religious values.

Though some might think that the application of blasphemy and obscenity laws is archaic, they can nevertheless be justified and considered necessary in democratic societies of EU Member States where Christianity is the main religion, though it ought to be stressed that their application is increasingly rare in Europe. In spite of human rights legislation, such as freedom of expression (Article 10 ECHR) and religion (Article 9 ECHR), some Member States will have a wider margin of appreciation in making restrictions against items concerning matters of religion, morals or personal beliefs than others. National authorities, rather than the courts, may well decide in the appropriate forum what protection is necessary.[149]

Various obscenity and blasphemy laws in Europe also prohibit film and video releases. Most laws are quite vague in this area and generally apply only to anything which might encourage criminal activity by those watching the films, especially if it encourages violence or sexual violence. This was the case with film releases by the famous Austro-Hungarian film director (living mostly in the USA) Otto Ludwig Preminger (1905–86). He directed over 35 Hollywood movies, mostly of the 'film noir' and intentionally blasphemous genre. Amongst these were titles like *Fallen Angel*

147 [1991] (Application No 17634) (ECtHR).
148 *Handyside v United Kingdom* (1976) 1 EHRR 737 (ECTHR).
149 For a more detailed discussion see: Brems (1996).

(1945) and *The Moon is Blue* (1953). Several of his films pushed the boundaries of censorship by dealing with taboo topics such as drug addiction (*The Man with the Golden Arm*, 1955), rape (*Anatomy of a Murder*, 1959) and homosexuality (*Advise and Consent*, 1962). The case of **Otto-Preminger-Institut v Austria** (1994)[150] concerned the forfeiture of the film *Council of Love* (*das Liebeskonzil*) due to be screened at a private film club before an informed adult audience.[151] *Das Liebeskonzil* was based on a nineteenth-century play in which the Eucharist is ridiculed and God the Father is presented as a senile, impotent idiot, the Virgin Mary as a wanton woman who displays erotic interest in the devil and Jesus Christ as a low-grade mental defective given to fondling his mother's breasts.

The Austrian Constitutional Court in Vienna held the film to be blasphemous because it contained provocative and offensive portrayals of the objects of veneration of the Roman Catholic religion, and therefore the withdrawal of the film was not held to be in violation of Article 10 ECHR. This was confirmed by the Strasbourg court, which ruled that the Austrian authorities had not overstepped their 'margin of appreciation'.[152] For this reason the film was never allowed to be publically shown in predominantly Roman Catholic Austria.

Examining the ECtHR judgment in **Jersild v Denmark** (1994)[153] (see below), the Strasbourg court made no reference to the doctrine of 'margin of appreciation' and found that the repressive measures taken under the Danish criminal law against the applicant journalist violated his right to freedom of expression.

❖ KEY CASE   *Jersild v Denmark* (1994) 19 EHHR 1

Precedent

- ❖ A journalist's publication and remarks are not racist if the aim of the publication is to protect the rights and reputation of others;
- ❖ The publication is justified under Article 10 ECHR if (given the margin of appreciation) the article (or broadcast) contributes discussions of matters of public interest; and
- ❖ It should not be banned under Article 10(2) ECHR.

Facts

On 31 May 1985 the Danish Sunday News Magazine (*Søndagsavisen*) published an article describing the racist attitudes of members of a group of young people, calling themselves 'The Greenjackets' (*grønjakkerne*), at Østerbro in Copenhagen. In the light of this article, the editors of the Sunday News Magazine decided to produce a documentary on the Greenjackets. The applicant, Mr Jens Olaf Jersild, a Danish journalist, contacted representatives of the group, inviting three of them, together with Mr Per Axholt, a social worker, to take part in a TV interview. During the interview, the three Greenjackets made abusive and derogatory remarks about immigrants and ethnic groups in Denmark. The edited film – lasting only a few minutes – was broadcast by Danmarks Radio on 21 July 1985 as part of the Sunday news magazine programme. The documentary feature included avowed racist views.

---

150 [1994] ECHR 26 (Case No 13470/87) 20 September 1994 (ECtHR).
151 [1994] ECHR 26 judgment at para 56.
152 Judgment by the ECtHR of 20 September 1994 with the result of the immediate withdrawal of the movie by the Austrian Constitutional Court (Urteil vom 20. September 1994, A/295-A EGMR Einziehung des Films Das 'Liebeskonzil', verstößt nicht gegen Art 10 EMRK).
153 (1994) 19 EHRR 1.

In their statements the youths described black people as belonging to an inferior subhuman race ('. . . the niggers . . . are not human beings. . . . Just take a picture of a gorilla . . . and then look at a nigger, it's the same body structure. . . . A nigger is not a human being, it's an animal, that goes for all the other foreign workers as well, Turks, Yugoslavs and whatever they are called').

Following the programme, no complaints were made to the Radio Council or to Danmarks Radio, but the Bishop of Ålborg complained to the Minister of Justice. Subsequently, the three youths were convicted for making racist statements and Mr Jersild for aiding and abetting them in making racist comments in a public place.[154] Mr Jersild, but not the three Greenjackets, appealed against the City Court's judgment to the High Court of Eastern Denmark (østre Landsret), but his appeal was rejected and his conviction was upheld by the Danish Supreme Court.

Decision

The ECtHR jointly dissented with the opinion and judgment of the Danish Supreme Court. Judges Gölcüklü, Russo and Valticos stated, 'We cannot share the opinion of the majority of the Court in the Jersild case.' The ECtHR held that Mr Jersild's Article 10 right to freedom of expression had been violated and that he was not a racist. He had a valid defence in the making the programme. The reasons given by the Danish court in support of Jersild's conviction and sentence (and derogation under Article 10(2) ECHR) were not sufficient to justify interference with a journalist's right of free expression in a democratic society.

Analysis

It is interesting that the Strasbourg court in *Jersild* did not show any concern or sensibility towards vulnerable groups in the face of racial abuse compared with its judgment in the *Otto Preminger* case, where the Catholic population of the tiny Tyrol region was very much taken into consideration over the offending film. Were the religious sensibilities so fundamentally different in character in the satirical film by Otto Preminger to the 'nigger' quote in the Danish documentary by Jersild? Why did the ECtHR not apply the 'margin of appreciation' in the *Jersild* case?[155] The Strasbourg court found it particularly important in *Jersild* to send a message to combat racial discrimination. This, in fact, had been Mr Jersild's intention when making the Danish news programme. The ECtHR stressed that freedom of expression at times constitutes publications (or broadcasts) which may shock or offend, but that this is one of the essential underpinnings of a democracy and the media plays an important role in the duty to inform.

7.5 Indecency or freedom of expression? Analysis and discussion

There appears to be a general theme in UK obscenity law that everything in art or literature that sufficiently adversely affects certain moral scruples and the sensibilities of the ordinary decent

---

154 Under Article 266 (b) of the Danish Penal Code.
155 For a detailed discussion see: Mahoney (1997).

citizen would traditionally be prosecuted under the two most prominent offences concerning blasphemy and obscenity. Immediately on the coming into force of the Obscene Publications Act 1959, the publishers of D. H. Lawrence's *Lady Chatterley's Lover* were prosecuted – though at trial found not guilty – for the 'unacceptable' erotic portrayals. Nearly twenty years later, Denis Lemon, editor of *Gay News*, was successfully prosecuted for the violation of blasphemy laws which centred on a poem by James Kirkup, complete with an illustration that evoked images of homosexual behaviour with the body of Christ.

One can safely assume that works of literary merit such as *Lolita* or *Lady Chatterley's Lover* would hardly be prosecuted today. Truly obscene material is easily peddled via the internet on a daily basis and societal attitudes and values have changed over time. One man's literary genius is another's excuse for hatred, such as witnessing Muslim anger at the Danish cartoons in *Jyllands-Posten* about the Prophet Muhammad. It is one of literary history's abiding curiosities that *Lolita*'s publication can be accredited to a man whose tactical adroitness later made him one of the most famous libel lawyers, namely Peter Carter-Ruck.[156]

7.5.1 Contemporary tastes and standards

Looking back at the history of culture wars, concerning censorship under blasphemy and obscenity laws, one can find some of the bravest standard-bearers for freedom of expression. John Milton's 1644 *Areopagitica* remains one of the most forceful English publications supporting the freedom to publish. It claims that killing a book is as bad as killing a man, for 'who kills a man kills a reasonable creature, God's image; but he who destroys a good book kills reason itself, kills the image of God, as it were, in the eye'. We then move forward to the late 1950s, when the British authorities tried to ban the Penguin publication of 'Lady Chatterley' under the Obscene Publications Act 1959.

Some people have suffered for their artistic free expression. On 7 October 2006, Anna Politkovskaya was shot in the lift of her Moscow apartment block. The Russian journalist and author had won international recognition for her passionate reporting work on the conflict in Chechnya, in which she sought to expose human rights abuses. Detained on occasion by the Russian military, the *Novaya Gazeta* special correspondent was famous for her book *A Dirty War*, a collection of articles mainly about the second Chechen conflict which began in 1999.[157] Her last article, published on 28 September 2006, was a condemnation of pro-Kremlin militias operating in Chechnya as part of Moscow's so-called Chechenization policy.

Then there was the public poisoning and killing of Alexander Litvinenko in London in November 2006, who was about to publish his book denouncing the alleged terror tactics of the KGB in provoking the second Chechen war. That book, *Blowing Up Russia: Terror from Within* was promptly and permanently banned in his native land. Litvinenko (then 43) had been a former officer with the Federal Security Service (FSB) in Russia and had become a useful source for Western journalists interested in the machinations of Vladimir Putin's regime. A post-mortem examination suggested Mr Litvinenko had died from radioactive poisoning by a substance called polonium–210. An inquest on Alexander Litvinenko's death was set for 19 June 2013. On 4 June 2013 Sir Robert Owen, Assistant Deputy Coroner for the Inner North London District of Greater London, received a letter from the Home Secretary, Teresa May, in which she explained the rationale behind the government's decision not to establish a public inquiry into the death of Mr Litvinenko.[158] The public inquiry began on 12 July 2013 in courtroom 73 of the Royal Courts of Justice.[159]

---

156 See the obituary of Peter Carter-Ruck, *Daily Telegraph*, 22 December 2003.
157 See: Politkovskaya (2001).
158 Source: Press notice by HM Coroner's Office, 19 July 2013.
159 For further updates see: https://litvinenkoinquest.org.

Modern politicians in fragile multicultural societies often seek control over material that 'offends' by organizing parliamentary lobbies to change the laws. Many liberal-minded people feel glad that British laws passed over recent decades forbid inflammatory racist speech, writing and images, such as the glorification of the Second World War by Holocaust-denier David Irving, who was imprisoned under Austrian law for his inflammatory speech and publications in 2006.[160]

Given the freedom of the internet, it is becoming increasingly difficult to determine what may realistically corrupt public morals or would be deemed 'indecent' and 'obscene'. There is now a vast network of hi-tech censorship that all but violent criminals support, such as Operation Ore, which aimed to eradicate child pornography on the internet. The extension of police and online surveillance powers is ever increasing.

Censorship is at its most dangerous if those who orchestrate it cannot clearly explain the reasons for the decisions they make. When a piece of art or literature is withdrawn under obscenity laws by the authorities, it can be argued that at that stage censorship becomes repression and a curtailment of freedom of expression. When pictures like that of young Brooke Shields by Richard Prince are withdrawn, the public no longer have the option of judging for themselves whether the image is indecent or obscene. It might therefore be a good initiative to abolish the nearly redundant Obscene Publications Act 1959.

Edwards (2000) examined the contemporary application of obscenity laws by police, prosecutors and the courts by presenting her findings of the first national study into pornography trials in English Crown Courts in an international psychological journal. Her findings demonstrated that only five cases in a six-month period were fully considered by a jury during the 1997–98 study. Only one conviction resulted in a six-month prison sentence, from which Edwards concluded that the 'obscenity' offence was virtually obsolete.[161]

So when does art become child porn? Why was the image of a naked 10-year-old Brooke Shields removed from the Tate Modern exhibition in October 2009, when Met police officers warned that the gallery director would face almost certain prosecution unless the Richard Prince photograph was removed from display? Yet we can see Jean-Honoré Fragonard's painting of a young girl masturbating with the aid of her pet spaniel's tail in the Munich Alte Pinakothek; or Jean-Baptiste Greuze's *The Broken Pitcher*, with its pubescent girl holding the cracked vessel with one breast bared? Art historians will explain these paintings as an expression of French society at that period of Louis XV. Why is the Protection of Children Act of 1978 not cited here – as this could clearly be interpreted as the exploitation of a minor, or the indecent image of a child under the age of 18? Maybe it is a combination of the medium (painting), the age of the works (e.g. Etruscan erotic art) and the fact the works have been known to the public for at least two centuries and received critical acclaim which gives these works a protective aura.

And what about policing extreme pornography under the relatively new provision of s 63 of the Criminal Justice and Immigration Act 2008? McGlynn and Rackley (2009) argue that the parliamentary failure to specify exactly where the harm lies in extreme pornography resulted from assumed paternalistic ideas of harm and Christian standards of morality.[162] The authors further contend that Parliament failed to consider the broader arguments of harm, extreme pornography and sexual violence and to specify exactly where the harm lies in extreme pornography. As a result, the Criminal Justice and Immigration Act 2008 provisions on extreme pornography are both over- and under-inclusive.

---

160 See also the defamation case of **Irving (David John Caldwell) v Penguin Books Ltd and Deborah Lipstadt** (1996), judgment of 11 April 2000 (QBD) (unreported).
161 See: Edwards (2000).
162 For further discussion see also: Munro (2007) pp.12–13.

While the Obscene Publications Act 1959 is justified on moralistic and disgust-based justifications, s 63 of the 2008 Act fails to truly recognize the harm that can be done to the victims in society who feature in extreme pornographic and sexually violent material on the internet.

 FOR THOUGHT

Would you agree with Susan Edwards (1998) that s 1(1) of the Obscene Publications Act 1959 is archaic and that the 'deprave and corrupt' test is no longer realistic and workable for determining whether art, literature or films are 'obscene'? What should be the alternative?

 7.6 Further reading

Edwards, S. M. (1998) 'On the contemporary application of the Obscene Publications Act 1959'. *Criminal Law Review*, **Dec, 843–853.**
Susan Edwards examines the contemporary application of the Obscene Publications Act 1959 by police, prosecutors and the courts and presents the key findings of the first national study into pornography trials in the Crown Court in England and Wales. Her research findings demonstrate that only five cases in a six-month period studied were fully considered by a jury. The author concludes that the 'deprave and corrupt' test is an inappropriate and blunt measure by which to determine whether the publishers of pornography are guilty of 'publishing an obscene article', and that since only one conviction in her current study resulted in a sentence of more than six months' imprisonment, the Crown Court jurisdiction, at least for this type of offence, is virtually obsolete.

Foster, S. (2010) 'Possession of extreme pornographic images, public protection and human rights'. *Coventry Law Journal*, **15(1), 21–27.**
This article examines s 63 of the Criminal Justice and Immigration Act 2008 ('possession of extreme pornographic images') and asks whether the new law impacts and conflicts with individual liberty and free speech, thus contravening Articles 8 and 10 of the Convention.

Kearns, P. (2000) 'Obscene and blasphemous libel: Misunderstanding art'. *Criminal Law Review*, **August: 652–660.**
Paul Kearns examines the legal approach to art in the context of UK obscenity (and related public morality offences). The article highlights the cultural independence of art as a special value separate from other facts on which the law operates, and the law's neglect of the special ontology of art. Kearns discusses relevant cases that have affected the relationship between art and law, as demonstrated, for example, by the ethically controversial *Sensation* exhibition at the Royal Academy (1997) and subsequent provocative artwork.

McGlynn, C. and Rackley, E. (2009) 'Criminalising extreme pornography: a lost opportunity'. *Criminal Law Review*, **4, 245–260.**
This article by Clare McGlynn and Erika Rackley considers provisions criminalizing the possession of 'extreme pornography' under s 63 of the Criminal Justice and Immigration Act 2008 ('possession of extreme pornographic images'). The authors highlight the areas of confusion (between the 2008 and the 1959 acts) and where the most likely challenges may arise. They explain that beyond images of life-threatening acts, s 63 also includes images of acts resulting or likely to result in 'serious injury to a person's anus, breasts or genitals'. The article concludes that a legislative opportunity was lost in that 'possession' of extreme pornography was not fully recognized by Parliament.

Samuels, A. (2009) 'Obscenity and pornography'. *Criminal Law and Justice Weekly*, 173(12): 187–189.
The article explores historical and current interpretations of the Obscene Publications Act 1959 regime, including those aspects relating to criminal intent, publication, the prohibition of expert evidence, parts of a publication, corruption, the aversion defence, judicial directions, contemporary standards, police indifference, the public good, search and seizure, sentencing, sex shops, and the possession of extreme pornographic images.

Thompson, B. (ed.) (2012) *Ban This Filth! Letters from the Mary Whitehouse Archive*. **London: Faber & Faber (Kindle edition).**
In 1964, Mary Whitehouse launched a campaign to fight what she called the 'propaganda of disbelief, doubt and dirt' being poured into homes through the nation's radio and television sets. Whitehouse, senior mistress at a Shropshire secondary school, became an unlikely figurehead of a mass movement: the National Viewers' and Listeners' Association. Ben Thompson tells the inside story of Mary Whitehouse's anti-TV campaign through her archived letters. He uncovers Mrs Whitehouse's stand against swearing and sexual licence, and asks whether she was the harbinger of change in the tide of cultural history.

Chapter 8

Copyright I: Intellectual Property Law

Chapter Contents

> **Key Points**
>
> This chapter will cover the following questions:
>
> ○ What constitutes copyright under the Copyright, Designs and Patents Act 1988 (CDPA)?
> ○ What is the purpose and function of the Berne Convention and the WIPO Copyright Treaties in relation to the promotion of creative works across the world?
> ○ How do various durations of copyright differ?
> ○ What is meant by the EU copyright acquis?
> ○ How does EU copyright legislation affect the harmonization of intellectual property in the information society of EU Member States?
> ○ How will the Unitary Patent and Unified Patent Court (UPC) work?

8.1 Overview

Copyright is the means by which an author, lyricist, sculptor, artist or *inter alia* film director makes a living from their creativity. This means that a person who creates, produces or invests in an original creative work should be the one who receives the rewards in the form of accreditation, payment or royalties; in other words, that this person be recognized as the original rights or copyright owner. Copyright provides that the rights holder determines whether and how copying, distributing, broadcasting and other uses of their works take place. For instance, copyright legislation encourages talented composers and performing artists to create musical works, and record companies and music producers to invest in that talent. Both this chapter and Chapter 9 outline the basic social objectives of copyright protection where artists and the media are heavily dependent on the use of copyrighted works, such as in the radio industry in relation to recently issued recordings.

See below 8.4.4 Obtaining appropriate authorization to broadcast such works is therefore crucial.

Copyright law has two basic functions, a property function and an authenticity function, both seeking to establish who is the author of a work. As the history of copyright shows, the property function is now widely accepted in international copyright law – though this was not always the case. The author is then regarded as the single source and is held responsible for this work.

Related moral rights, which developed much later, were introduced with the Copyright, Designs and Patents Act 1988 (CDPA), amended by The Copyright and Related Rights Regulations 2003,[1] establishing that the work must be attributed to the author (the economic owner of copyright)[2] and must generally not be changed or altered in any way. For example, a manuscript can

See below 8.10 only be amended, deleted or modified by contract. This chapter covers statutory provision, reme-
and 8.11 dies and defences.

An intellectual property right is a collective term that covers – *inter alia* – copyright. Intellectual property (IP) or 'copyright' law exists to protect the creator or author of an original piece of work and the ultimate owner of the exploitation rights such as a record or publishing company, so that

---

1 SI 2003/ 2498.
2 Though this can be changed by way of contract or a non-contractual gift waiver, where copyright can be assigned or licensed to another person, such as a publisher or record label. See Chapter 9.7.

others can be prevented from copying or 'pirating' it. Some IP rights are automatic; some have to be registered such as patents[3] and trademarks.[4]

The basic idea behind IP is to ensure that a work is not copied or used without permission and to protect the economic rewards (known as 'royalties') of the creators and authors of the works. The meaning of 'property' can vary and includes designs, films, photos, literature, inventions, etc. Generally, 'property' must be in a fixed or concrete format. The next chapter deals with the recording of material such as music or speech.

See below 8.7

The basic rights of copyright include: the right to copy the work; the right to issue copies of it to the public; the right to rent or lend copies to the public; the right to perform, show or play the work in public; the right to communicate the work to the public, which includes the broadcasting right; the right to make an adaptation, which includes the translation right, of the work.

See Chapter 9

It is an established principle that copyright is territorial in nature; that is, that protection under a given copyright law is available only in the country where that law applies; in the UK it is the Copyright, Designs and Patents Act 1988 (CDPA, also known as the 'UK Copyright Act'). It is important, though, to note that because of the impact of the international treaty in the form of the Berne Copyright Convention, foreign authors are given 'national treatment' in the UK and have the same rights before a UK court as a domestic author does. For example, a French author can sue for an unauthorized translation into English and the sale of that translated work if sold without authorization in the UK.

See below 8.4

This chapter briefly looks at the historical development of UK copyright law, such as the Statute of Anne 1710 and the Copyright Acts of 1911 and 1956. The chapter then moves on to international conventions governing IP legislation, specifically copyright covered by the Paris[5] and Berne Conventions[6] and the World Intellectual Property Treaty (WIPO) and the World Trade Organization Trade Related Intellectual Property Agreement (TRIPS). The main principle established by the Paris (1883) and Berne (1886) Conventions was reciprocity of authors' intellectual property rights and the notion that IP rights were the same as any property right (in the same sense that land or chattels were); in contrast with the typical common law perception that the author's right is merely a polite description of a commercial monopoly.

See below 8.3.

See below 8.2 and 8.3

This chapter importantly analyses new European copyright legislation (known collectively as the 'EU copyright acquis') in the form of Copyright Term Directives (Directive 2011/77/EU).[7] The amending EU Copyright Directive has been welcomed by recording labels and artists alike, following their pleas to extend the life of sound recordings from the late 1950s and early 1960s, many of which had already come out of copyright and had fallen into the public domain. Artists including Sir Cliff Richard and Sir Paul McCartney had long argued they would lose royalties, but will now gain protection until at least 2033. The legislation – known as 'Cliff's law' after its most high-profile campaigner – extends copyright on music recordings from 50 years to 70 years. Copyright on many of the most popular 1960s tunes, including many Dame Shirley Bassey hits, had been due to expire within two years but will now last until at least 2033. All 28 EU Member States have been required to implement the EU copyright acquis by 2014.

---

3   The World Intellectual Property Organization (WIPO) maintains the International Patent Classification (IPC). The IPC is presented as a hierarchical collection of alphanumeric symbols, which represent approximately 70,000 subdivisions or 'groups'. Each group refers to a different type of technical information. Each patent document published will have at least one IPC symbol applied to it. The European Patent Office (EPO) and other patent offices worldwide also use it to classify their own patent documents. In addition to IPC symbols, the UK Intellectual Property Office (IPO) previously applied their own UK Patent Classification (UKC) terms to all UK patent applications considered prior to 1 July 2007. Whilst the UKC terms are no longer applied, it is still possible to search UK patent applications published prior to July 2007 using the UKC terms.

4   A trademark is a sign which can distinguish goods and services from those of their competitors (often referred to as 'brands'). It can be, for example words, logos or a combination of both. The only way to register a UK trademark is to apply to the IPO in London.

5   The Paris Convention essentially deals with industrial property rights, such as patents and trademarks.

6   The Berne Convention and WIPO also protect related rights such as sound recordings, broadcasts, translations of works and adaptations.

7   Directive 2011/77/EU of the European Parliament and of the Council of 27 September 2011 amending Directive 2006/116/EC on the term of protection of copyright and certain related rights.

It is worth noting that this new legislation applies only to *performers* and *sound recordings* of music (i.e. the Directive refers specifically to 'music' and 'musical composition', 'phonograms' and 'performances'). The implication is that other types of audio material are not so protected. This means that, for example, audiobooks, samples (e.g. eight bars of an instrument solo, which can be sold as part of a library of samples for use in computer programmes such as 'GarageBand') and sound effect recordings are not really protected under the Copyright Term Directives. And yet, samples are big business and the same considerations cited in the Directives about the length of musicians' careers also apply here. The Directive also does not specifically cover video performances of songs, because the audio content can be stripped from these and marketed separately. Arguably the law (including EU law) is at least 10 if not 20 years behind what is actually happening in the music industry, which is advancing with ever-increasing technology (such as YouTube) quicker than the legislators are able to keep up. There is no 'future-proof' Directive.

See also
Chapter 9.7

While this chapter and the next concentrate with their examples mainly on the music industry, general principles of copyright will be highlighted, applicable to literary or other artistic works. Case law from English, Scots and European jurisdictions will demonstrate the intricate legal challenges in this area of law, demonstrating the complexities which are involved when representing an international recording artist – such as Bob Dylan – who may well be recording with different labels during his lifetime, in different countries and with the added complications of the varying degrees of copyright duration.

This chapter also looks at music licensing and the statutory assignment of copyright (i.e. temporary passing of ownership), which nowadays is seen as supplementary to contract law. Intellectual property law essentially covers the intangible property rights, such as an assignment of copyright, the exclusivity of a recording contract to record primarily with one record company and the transfer of such rights. Other IP rights, such as industrial rights, patents[8] and trademarks, will be covered in brief.

See below
8.9.2

The chapter concludes with equitable and criminal remedies available to the courts for breach of copyright – although it is fair to say that common law practice in this area has not generally deterred music piracy, illegal (peer-to-peer/P2P) file-sharing, or the copying of films and DVDs. The UK Government and the European Commission face constant demands for IP legislation to be strengthened. Possible defences or 'permitted acts' – as they are known in the CDPA 1988 – include fair dealing (reviews, news reporting, criticism, etc.), research and private study.

See below
8.11

8.2 The origins of copyright: historical overview

During the sixteenth century, the printers, known as 'stationers', formed a collective, called the Stationers' Company. It was provided with the power to require all lawfully printed books to be entered into its register, and only members of the Stationers' Company could enter books into the register under the Licensing Act 1662. The Stationers' Company Register (1556–1695), granted under Royal Charter, provided a monopoly, including the right to search for and seize illicit or 'pirated' copies and to prevent publication of *any* book which had not been licensed. The Company was granted a Royal Patent in 1603 to form a joint stock publishing company funded by shares held by members of the company. Its most profitable patent was for almanacks in the English language,

---

8 The European Patent Convention 2000 (EPC) covers this area of law as a treaty agreement. The 14th edition of the EPC of 2009 contains the texts of the 'Convention on the Grant of European Patents and its Implementing Regulations', the 'Protocol on the Interpretation of Article 69 EPC', the 'Protocol on Centralisation', the 'Protocol on Recognition', the 'Protocol on Privileges and Immunities', the 'Protocol on the Staff Complement and the Rules relating to Fees', together with an extract from the 'Revision Act of 29 November 2000' and the decision of the Administrative Council of 28 June 2001, on the transitional provisions under Article 7 of the Revision Act. The World Trade Organization (WTO) in Geneva largely looks after legislation on and registration of trademarks under the 'Uruguay Round Agreement'.

including the famous (or notorious) *Old Moore*.[9] Enforcement was by a Warden of the company. Any registered books were entered in the Stationers' Company Register (known as the 'entry book of copies'). The Stationers' Register remained in force until 1695, and was replaced by the first Copyright Act in 1709.[10]

When the 1911 Copyright Act was passed there had already been two centuries of legislative history, starting with the Copyright Act 1709, and for most of that time it was the protection of printed words — published literary works — that was the law's principal concern. Moreover, the original legislative purpose of laws on literary copyright was the protection of the commercial interests of stationers (the early publishers) and booksellers, and the control of unlicensed (and possibly subversive) publications, rather than the vindication of the legal and moral rights of authors.

See Chapter 7.2

The 1709 Act protected literary works, books and other writings. During the eighteenth century protection was extended (by statute) to engravings and (by a liberal interpretation of the 1709 Act) to musical and dramatic compositions. Three-dimensional works of art were brought within the scope of copyright by a statute enacted in 1798,[11] but it was very badly drafted and offered little practical protection.[12] This Act was replaced by the Sculpture Copyright Act 1814. What constituted a sculpture became an issue in the '**Star Wars** case' before the UK Supreme Court in 2011.[13]

See below 8.6.4

8.2.1 Publishing history

Following the abolition of state licensing and the ending of the monopoly of the Stationers' Company, the question soon arose as to the rights of the author and who could be defined as an author. In general terms — but also for copyright purposes and all terms of recognition — a named author was seen to be the central organizer, writer and promoter of his own literary or musical works. Authorship meant that he would be allowed to engage in contractual terms with promoters and publishers of his original material. But this was a problem since intellectual property was, by its very nature, an intangible right. How could a work's originality be protected from being copied?

The 'right to copy' introduced by the Statute of Anne 1710[14] came after nearly three centuries of print technology, during which time monarchs and the Stationers' Company had the right to censor radical literature. The statute introduced the principle of a fixed term of protection. When this ran out booksellers would generally argue that once the copyright protection had expired, this gave them a new and perpetual right and inherent monopoly with a 'licence to print' with everlasting effect.[15]

See Chapter 1.2

This principle was eventually clarified and rejected at common law by the House of Lords in their decision in **Donaldson v Becket** (1774).[16] Their Lordships ruled that copyright ('the right to copy') was purely statutory which, in turn, also gave rise to damages. Chancery would grant

---

9 *Old Moore's Almanack* is an astrological almanac, written and published by Francis Moore, a self-taught physician and astrologer who served at the court of Charles II. *Old Moore* contained weather forecasts and astrological observations. It was a best-seller throughout the eighteenth and nineteenth centuries, selling as many as 107,000 copies in 1768. The almanac is still published annually by W. Foulsham & Company Ltd, giving predictions of world and sporting events, as well as more conventional data such as tide tables. In 2014, *Old Moore's Almanack* will be 318 years old and deserves its world record-beating inclusion in the *Guinness Book of Records*. Source: The Stationers' Company at: www.stationers.org/the-hall-a-heritage.html.

10 For further discussion see: Pfeifer (2008).

11 38 Geo III c 71.

12 Lord Ellenborough said in *Gahagan v Cooper* (1811) 3 Camp 111 at 113 that 'The statute seems to have been framed with a view to defeat its own object.'

13 **Lucasfilm Ltd and Another v Ainsworth and Another** [2011] UKSC 39 (sub nom 'The *Star Wars* case').

14 8 Anne (c. 19), with the full title as 'An Act for the Encouragement of Learning, by vesting the Copies of Printed Books in the Authors or purchasers of such Copies, during the Times therein mentioned.'

15 For further discussion see: Baloch (2007).

16 (1774) 2 Bro PC 129 (HL).

equitable injunctions protecting 'out-of-time' books against illegal copying (see: **Millar v Taylor** (1769)[17]). It was affirmed by Lord Kames in **Hinton v Donaldson** (1773)[18] that there was no foundation for literary copyright in either natural law or the law of nations. Nor was any vestige of such a right to be found in the law of Scotland, which only complicated matters in relation to intellectual property 'across the border'.

In **Donaldson v Becket** (1774),[19] the House of Lords had to decide on the question of whether an author, after the expiration of the statutory protection given by the Statute of Anne, had a perpetual right of literary property at common law. This question was decided in the negative. The Scottish case of **Caird v Sime** (1887)[20] established the right of a professor to restrain the publication of lectures orally delivered in his classroom. This case established that the law of property exists in intangible works, such as literature, songs or lectures, irrespective of implied contract or breach of duty. The decision in **Caird v Sime** affirmed the ruling in **Albert v Strange** (1849),[21] that whoever copies or publishes an unpublished work without consent is stealing the author's copyright – a proprietary right. The motive or intention on the part of the defendant was then wholly irrelevant. The Statute of Anne provided the conceptual skeleton for copyright law for centuries to come with economic consequences, affirmed in **Donaldson v Becket**.[22]

See Chapter
2.2.6

The issue in the landmark case of **Walter v Lane** (1900)[23] was as follows: in 1893 the Earl of Rosebery[24] – a Liberal Prime Minister – became well known for giving rousing speeches in Parliament. These speeches were then reported in The Times, and The Times, in turn, claimed copyright on the reported speeches. The newspaper editor argued that the reporters were, in fact, creating 'new works', that is the stenographed (shorthand) notes of Rosebery's speeches, later transcribed into full reports, with added punctuation and corrections of the verbatim-produced-speeches.

Their Lordships held in **Walter v Lane** that copyright subsisted in reports prepared by shorthand writers of public speeches as 'original literary' works. The speeches were made by the Earl of Rosebery in public when reporters were present. A speech and a report of a speech were therefore held to be two different things. Lord Rosebery was the author of his speeches. The shorthand writers were the authors of their reports of his speeches, because they spent effort, skill and time in writing up their reports of speeches that they themselves had not written. Even though the reporters had intended only to reproduce the speeches as accurately as they could, the works they prepared remained original works. It is worth noting, however, that the Times reporters may still have infringed literary copyright in Lord Rosebery's book of his speeches, in spite of the fact they had copyright in their derivative work. This shows that a work can be both a protected work and an infringing work at same time.

See below
8.4.4

That said, **Walter v Lane** is still good law and was confirmed in **Express Newspapers v News (UK)** (1990)[25] and **Sawkins v Hyperion Records Ltd** (2005).[26]

The Copyright Act 1956 introduced no substantive amendments to the 1911 Act, but was significant for the development of the phonogram (record) industry.[27] The 1956 Act extended copyright to related and 'neighbouring rights' in sound recordings (phonograms) and who would

17 (1769) 4 Burr 2303.
18 (1773) Mor 8307 (Lord Kames).
19 (1774) 2 Bro PC 129.
20 (1887) LR 12 App Cas 326 (HL).
21 (1849) 64 ER 293.
22 See also: Deazley (2008).
23 [1900] AC 539 (HL).
24 Archibald Philip Primrose, 5th Earl of Rosebery (1847–1929), was a Liberal statesman and prime minister, also known as Lord Dalmeny.
25 [1990] 1 WLR 1320 (Sir Nicolas Browne-Wilkinson VC).
26 [2005] EWCA Civ 565.
27 The established definition of 'phonogram' is provided by Article 3(b) Rome Convention as 'any exclusively aural fixation of sounds of a performance or of other sounds'.

qualify for these rights. The Copyright Act of 1956 extended copyright to sound recordings, cinematographic works (films) and broadcasts. As well as record producers, there were other entrepreneur investors in the phonogram, entertainment and film industry who were now going to be protected under the 1956 Act.

In **Robertson v Lewis** (1976),[28] the House of Lords applied the principle established in **Walter v Lane**. The claimants had published a song, based on an arrangement of two Scottish airs and a Gaelic song. The court found that the claimants were not entitled to copyright in the underlying musical work. The court placed considerable weight on the fact that published copies of the song stated that the music was 'arranged' by the claimant, and it was said that the arrangement involved insufficient originality to attract copyright in its own right. The claimants, relying on **Walter v Lane**, argued that they had copyright in the printed record of the music that they had published. But Mr Justice Cross found that they had failed to establish infringement. Cross J expressed the view that, following the introduction in the 1911 Act of the express requirement of originality, it was arguable that **Walter v Lane** was no longer good law.[29] The Copyright Act of 1911 had brought provisions on copyright into effect which, for the first time, revised and repealed earlier statutes. The Copyright Act of 1956 acknowledged further amendments to the Berne Convention and the UK's accession to the Universal Copyright Convention (UCC).[30]

See below 8.3.1

8.2.2 Gilbert and Sullivan and music copyright in the nineteenth century

Prior to the Berne Convention of 1886 (and to a lesser degree the Universal Copyright Convention of 1952), copyright law only applied at national level, meaning that outside the author's home country there was very little protection for his original or artistic work. For works to be protected outside the country of origin, it was necessary for the country to conclude bilateral agreements with countries where the works were used. By the mid-nineteenth century, there existed only some bilateral agreements among some European nations. But they were neither consistent nor comprehensive and it is fair to say that the English concept of copyright mainly protected economic concerns.

The famous British lyricist W. S. Gilbert and composer Arthur Sullivan[31] (known better as 'Gilbert and Sullivan') were particularly hard hit by the lack of statutory copyright and performance right protection. Their operettas were regularly performed throughout the United States during the 1870s, but they were never paid any royalties at the time for their operatic productions of, for example, HMS Pinafore (1877). A Boston musician and composer, George Lowell Tracey, would regularly travel to London in order to see a performance of another of Gilbert and Sullivan's works, Princess Ida. Tracey subsequently created his own 'pirate' copy of the piano score. Tracey then owned the legal copyright in the piano 'arrangement' in the United States as an American citizen, which meant that Gilbert and Sullivan had no protection against any unauthorized performance whatsoever.

In 1879, Gilbert and Sullivan assigned the Iolanthe performance rights to Richard D'Oyly Carte,[32] who arranged the operetta's opening performance at London's Savoy Theatre.[33] Carte, in turn, tried to stop the unauthorized simultaneous performances of Iolanthe in America's North East

28 [1976] RPC 169; a case decided in 1960 but not reported until 1976.
29 Ibid., at 171–172 (Cross J).
30 The Universal Copyright Convention (UCC), Law (Approval) revised at Uruguay on 6 November 1992, No. 16.321.
31 Librettist and lyricist William Schwenck Gilbert (1836–1911) and composer Arthur Seymour Sullivan (1842–1900).
32 Representing the vision of British impresario Richard D'Oyly Carte (1844–1901), the D'Oyly Carte Opera Company was launched after Carte split from the Comedy Opera Company in July 1879.
33 For further discussion, see: Ainger (2002).

by taking legal action against some of the theatre producers. But the circuit court in Maryland found that the performances of Iolanthe were not copyright-protected in American law. The producer at the Standard Theatre in New York had hired John Philip Sousa, leader of the Marine band in Washington, to arrange his own orchestral accompaniment to Iolanthe (see: 'The Iolanthe case', 1883[34]).

The court in the Iolanthe case decided that the work's score was not an integral part of the dramatic work. This was in spite of the fact that the Iolanthe libretto was a published work and therefore copyright-protected. But the piano score and performances in the form of the full orchestra version could not be protected, with the conclusion that in order to retain common law copyright, one could not publish any part of an opera. This was an unsatisfactory result for Gilbert and Sullivan, who never received a single dime for their operatic performances in America. The unsuccessful outcome of the Iolanthe case finally ended Gilbert and Sullivan's hopes of protecting the right of public performance in common law.

See also
Chapter 9.3.2

The reason for the lack of copyright protection for the light operatic duo was that the US was not party to the Berne Convention at the time. It was not until 1989 that the USA finally signed up to the Berne Convention (though it was already party to the 'weaker' Universal Copyright Convention).

See Chapter 9.5

Sound recordings gained protection under the Copyright Act of 1911; the Act introduced a new arrangement for calculating the term of copyright, thereby introducing economic rights. The 1911 Act abolished common law copyright protection in unpublished works, apart from unpublished paintings, drawings and photographs.

Iolanthe was not recorded until 1951, when Decca Records took up the challenge under the musical direction of Isidore Godfrey.[35] HMV (His Master's Voice) had already made nine acoustical recording 'samples' of HMS Pinafore, The Mikado and The Yeomen of the Guard in 1907–08, and the subsequent invention of electronic recordings allowed far higher fidelity, which then prompted D'Oyly Carte and HMV to re-record all the operettas.[36] Incidentally, 'Nipper' the dog, used by HMV on their record label since 1899, became one of the most famous trademarks in history.

There was no equivalent copyright arrangement for Scotland. How could the works of Sir Walter Scott (1771–1832), the Scottish historical novelist and poet, who was also popular throughout Europe, be safeguarded if his works could not be protected under registration?[37] This anomaly in the law was only really solved in common law after the decision in Walter v Lane (1900),[38] and with the Copyright Act of 1911.

8.3 Development of international copyright legislation

Though the Copyright Acts of 1911 and 1956 generally safeguarded the artist's rights in the UK, international law did not grant automatic copyright to the author in another country, such as America. Above all, there were no statutes in the late nineteenth century that governed public performances; and therefore there were no penalties for infringement. This led to widespread copying and passing off of creative works, particularly those originating in English-speaking countries.

34 **Carte v Ford and another** (1883) Circuit Court, District of Maryland, 21 February 1883 (sub nom 'the Iolanthe case') 'Dedication of opera by publication of uncopyrighted score and libretto'.
35 Isidore Godfrey (1900–1977) was musical director of the D'Oyle Care Opera Company for 39 years, from 1929 to 1968. He conducted most of the company's performances during that period.
36 Source: Marc Shepherd has compiled an excellent online discography covering all recordings of Gilbert and Sullivan's Mikado at: http://gasdisc.oakapplepress.com/mik.htm.
37 For detailed discussion of copyright and Scottish literature and folk traditions see: Cornish (2009).
38 [1900] AC 539 (HL).

The Paris Convention for the Protection of Industrial Property of 20 March 1883 ('the Paris Convention')[39] established basic levels of protection and reciprocal recognition for so-called 'industrial property', which excluded the predominantly aesthetic works covered by the Berne Convention.[40] The Paris Convention increased foreign patenting opportunities and established the national priority approach whereby national treatment was granted to all subscribing nations. The Paris Convention covers all types of industrial property, such as patents, trademarks and unfair competition.

See below 8.9.2

8.3.1 The Berne Convention and WIPO Treaties

The Berne Convention,[41] based on the principles of the Paris Convention, became the first international agreement to unify a system of copyright protection. The principal aim of the Berne Convention was to help creators gain protection for their works. The Berne Convention created automatic copyright in works as soon as they were created, asserted and declared (without having to register that right). The minimum term of protection was the lifetime of the author and 50 years after his death.[42]

Though the 'public interest' defence is commonly used in the UK in breaches of copyright challenges, the Berne Convention does not explicitly permit this defence when someone's copyright has been infringed, so it would not necessarily be justifiable if an author's copyright has been infringed to argue that the copying was 'for the greater good of society' (see: *Gartside v Outram* (1856);[43] also: *Beloff v Pressdram Ltd* (1973)[44]). In other words, the Berne Convention does not expressly permit the public interest defence to copyright infringement, whereas UK copyright law will take the public interest defence into account (see: *Ashdown v Telegraph Group Ltd* (2001)[45]).

The Universal Copyright Convention of 1952, first created in Geneva, was an alternative to the Berne Convention 1886, because some countries disagreed with certain aspects of the Berne Convention, most notably the United States, who at the time only provided protection on a fixed-term registration basis via the Library of Congress and required that copyright works must always show the copyright symbol ©. The UCC ensures that international protection is available to authors even in countries that would not become parties to the Berne Convention. Berne Convention countries also became signatories of the UCC to ensure that the work of citizens in Berne Convention countries would be protected in non-Berne Convention countries.

The US finally signed up to the Berne Convention on 1 March 1989. Whilst a registration processes still exists in the USA, there is no formal registration *requirement* to establish copyright, and with the US signing the Berne Convention, copyright inherently exists in the work as soon as it is 'recorded' (e.g. written down), although it is advisable when ensuring 'provable' authorship that the author sends a copy of the manuscript (or recording) to himself by recorded delivery, keeping the packet or envelope unopened (with its postmark for dating purposes), which is the same as in the UK by way of the 'postal rule'.[46]

---

39 See: Paris Convention; Stockholm text 1967, Articles 1(2) and 1(3) Paris Convention. The Paris Convention was revised at Brussels on 14 December 1900, at Washington on 2 June 1911, at The Hague on 6 November 1925, at London on 2 June 1934, at Lisbon on 31 October 1958 and at Stockholm on 14 July 1967, and amended on 28 September 1979.

40 See: The Berne Convention of 9 September 1886, completed at Paris on 4 May 1896, revised at Berlin on 13 November 1908, completed at Berne on 20 March 1914, revised at Rome on 2 June 1928, at Brussels on 26 June 1948, at Stockholm on 14 July 1967, and at Paris on 24 July 1971, and amended on 28 September 1979.

41 The original signatory countries comprised: Belgium, France, Germany, Italy, United Kingdom, Switzerland and Tunisia, further joined by Luxembourg in 1887, Monaco in 1889, Norway in 1896, Morocco in 1917, Portugal in 1911, the Netherlands in 1912 and Romania in 1927.

42 Article 7(1) Berne Convention.

43 (1856) 26 LJ Ch 113.

44 [1973] 1 All ER 241.

45 [2001] Ch 685 (Ch D).

46 Historical ruling in contract law (offer and acceptance). The general rule in law states that acceptance is communicated, and has been received by the offeror. The ruling applies where the means of communication are deemed instantaneous (see: *Entores Ltd v Miles Far East Corporation* [1955] 2 QB 327(CA)).

The Berne Convention and the UCC impose general rules and formalities for UK copyright protection in addition to the UK 'Copyright Act' (Copyright, Designs and Patents Act 1988 – CDPA). While the CDPA does not acknowledge the © copyright symbol, the UCC does, though it is fair to say that the UCC is of limited importance today since most countries are now part of the union of the Berne Convention. Today, the Berne Convention is administered by the World Intellectual Property Organization (WIPO). WIPO had 186 contracting member states in 2013.[47]

For the 'three steps test' see below 8.10.3

In summary, the Berne Convention requires member states to offer the same protection to authors from other member countries that it provides to its own nationals – so-called 'national treatment'. It also sets out a common framework of protection and specifies minimum protection levels that are required.

Cynics may argue, however, that in practice law enforcement under the Berne Convention with nearly 190 signatory states may be difficult in practice. Some countries simply do not have the law enforcement capacity (or political willingness) to ensure protection is in place. Some recent discussions have pointed a finger at India as an example.[48]

The World Intellectual Property Organization was established in Stockholm by the WIPO Convention on 14 July 1967 (amended on 28 September 1979). WIPO's main purpose is to encourage creative activity, with a mandate from its member states to promote the protection of intellectual property throughout the world. WIPO's International Bureau is based in Geneva. Membership is open to any state that:

(i)   is a member of the Paris Union ('the Paris Convention') for the Protection of Industrial Property, or of the Berne Union ('the Berne Convention') for the Protection of Literary and Artistic Works; or

(ii) is a member of the United Nations, or of any of the United Nations' specialized agencies, or of the International Atomic Energy Agency, or that is a party to the statute of the International Court of Justice; or

(iii) is invited by the WIPO General Assembly to become a member state of the organization.

See below 8.10.3

Today, WIPO actively promotes the WIPO Copyright Treaty (WCT) and the WIPO Performances and Phonograms Treaty (WPPT), known together as the 'WIPO Internet Treaties'. Together, these treaties must be considered as updates and supplements of the protection granted by the Berne Convention (for the Protection of Literary and Artistic Works) and the International Convention for the Protection of Performers, Producers of Phonograms and Broadcasting Organizations (Rome Convention). They address the challenges posed by the digital technologies advancements, in particular the dissemination of protected material over digital networks such as the internet. Most developing countries have now ratified the WIPO Internet Treaties, which means that copyright holders' expressions, their economic and moral rights, should be protected from abuses of their rights. This in turn is governed internationally by the 'three-step test', originating from the Berne Convention.

The WIPO organization in Geneva provides a range of services for owners and users of intellectual property, including international registration services, which enable applicants to seek protection for their patents, trademarks or designs in multiple countries by filing a single application. WIPO maintains an IP classification system and database. WIPO's Arbitration and Mediation Center offers alternative dispute resolution services for private parties involved in international IP

47 See: WIPO contracting states at: www.wipo.int/members/en.
48 India has been a member of the World Trade Organization (WTO) since 1995 and therein party to the Berne Convention. India's Patents Act of 1970 and 2003 Patent Rules set out the law concerning patents. As in the UK, there is no provision for utility model patents. Source: Intellectual Property Office (IPO) (2013a) *Intellectual Property Rights in India*. April 2013 at: www.ipo.gov.uk/ipindia.pdf.

disputes, including so-called 'cybersquatting', where an internet domain name is in dispute. WIPO has cultivated international 'multi-voiced consultations', which effectively means the introduction of EU Community musical rights in cultural material.

Confusingly there is now an abundance of global IP legislation and conventions that protect musical works. In addition, performers and producers of phonograms enjoy protection under the WIPO Performers and Phonograms Treaty.[49] The WIPO Treaty harmonized the exchange of the music trade at international level, even though some conflicts still exist at World Trade Organization (WTO) level, regarding international copyright law which relates to musical works in particular.[50]

See Chapters 9.5 and 9.6

8.4 The Copyright, Designs and Patents Act 1988 (CDPA)

The Copyright, Designs and Patents Act 1988 (CDPA or 'the UK Copyright Act'), as amended by The Copyright and Related Rights Regulations 2003, introduced an immediate copyright which exists automatically in original literary, dramatic, musical or artistic works. 'Literary work' means any work, other than a dramatic or musical work, which is written, spoken or sung, and accordingly includes tables, compilations, computer programs and databases.[51] 'Dramatic work' includes dance or mime and 'musical work' means a work consisting of music, exclusive of any words or action intended to be sung, spoken or performed with the music.[52]

Copyright does not subsist in a literary, dramatic or musical work *unless* and until it is recorded, in writing or otherwise,[53] though not necessarily by the author – a recording of an extempore jazz performance at a pub if taped by a drinker would vest musical copyright in members of the jazz band.

See Chapter 9.5

The expression of general or common ideas cannot be protected – for example, no one could lay claim to the generic concept of battles in outer space. Similarly, character names cannot usually be copyrighted, although they can be registered as trademarks to distinguish them as a separate brand, such as 'James Bond'. Illustrations or original images of those characters can also be protected. Copyright also applies to the World Wide Web, which is regarded as a publishing medium ('the publisher'), where copyright will be created automatically once an item or photo is published and thereby put into the public domain.

See Below 8.9.2

There have been several attempts to undertake 'generic copyrighting', particularly with computer and video games. In early 2013 the games company Games Workshop's publishing arm, the Black Library, attempted to assert copyright on the concept of 'space marines'[54] – used generally in their book publications – but the term has also existed across a range of science fiction for several decades. Games Workshop sells a popular game *Warhammer 40,000: Space Marine*, and has registered trademarks in the term 'space marine' in connection with games. In December 2012, online retailer Amazon.com removed the e-book *Spots the Space Marine* by M. C. A. Hogarth at the request of Games Workshop, who claimed the use of the phrase 'space marine' infringed on their trademark of the term. In February 2013, the row received some publicity, with authors such as Cory Doctorow, Charles Stross and John Scalzi supporting Hogarth, and Amazon.com then restored the e-book for sale.[55]

---

49 Adopted in Geneva in December 1996; the WPPT came into force on 20 May 2002.
50 For example the dispute between the US and China in which Japan joined as a third party (among other countries) which was initiated on 10 April 2007.
51 Section 3(1) CDPA.
52 Ibid.
53 Section 3(2) CDPA.
54 The 'space marine' is a kind of soldier that operates in outer space or on alien worlds. The earliest known use of the term 'space marine' was by Bob Olsen in his *Captain Brink of the Space Marines* (1932), in which the protagonists were marines of the 'Earth Republic Space Navy' on a mission to rescue celebrity twins from aliens on Titan.
55 Source: 'In the Future, All Space Marines Will Be Warhammer 40K Space Marines', The Art and Writing of M. C. A. Hogarth', 5 February 2013 – online at: http://mcahogarth.org/?p=10593.

Software (i.e. computer programs) and games for games consoles are protected on the same basis as literary works under UK and EU copyright legislation. Many games developers and companies have tried to establish generic copyrights for their games, some of which have succeeded.

8.4.1 General provisions under the UK Copyright Act

The purpose of the Copyright Act (CDPA 1988 as amended)[56] is to protect the rights of creators to be paid for, and to control the use of, their works and to address the needs of users who want access to material protected by copyright. The balance is achieved by providing the creator with statutory rights. These are limited by 'exceptions' for the benefit of certain users (e.g. educational establishments). The categories covered by the Copyright, Designs and Patents Act 1988 are:

- **Literary works**, including novels, instruction manuals, computer programs (see below), song lyrics, newspaper articles.
- **Dramatic works**, including theatrical performance such as plays, pantomimes, musical scores used, scripts, stage directions, set design and ballet. In ballet, for instance, if the choreography of the dance has been recorded in writing or filmed, the dramatic performance of the dance itself can be entitled to copyright.

See Chapters 9.4, 9.5 and 8.5.2 below

- **Musical works**, including compositions, opera, musicals. With a song there will usually be more than one copyright associated with it, i.e. the composer of the music is the 'author of the musical work' and has copyright in that music. The lyrics of a song are protected separately by copyright as a literary work. The person who writes the lyrics will own the copyright in the words. If the work is subsequently recorded the sound recording will also have copyright protection. The producer of the recording will own the copyright in the sound recording. Composers of music may also have moral rights in their work.
- **Artistic works**, including paintings, engravings, photographs, sculptures, cartoons, collages, architecture, technical drawings, diagrams and maps.
- **Typographical arrangements** or **layouts** used to publish a work, such as a book.
- **Recordings** of a work, including sound and film.
- **Broadcasts, TV and films**, including the original screenplay, the music score of a film, and cable, wireless and satellite broadcasts. Films do not have to be original but they will not be new copyright works if they have been copied from existing films. Broadcasts do not have to be original, but there will be no copyright, if, or to the extent that, they infringe copyright in another broadcast.
- **Databases and software**, e.g. computer programs and games; computer languages and codes; databases are usually collections of copyright works, such as a database of poetry from the last 50 years where each poem will also be protected by copyright.
- **Websites** – copyright applies to the internet in the same way as material in other media; e.g. any photographs posted on the internet are protected in the same way as other artistic works; any original written work will be protected as a 'literary' work.

See below 8.6.2

Copyright applies to any medium. This means that a copyrighted work cannot be copied or reproduced in another medium without the permission of the author (i.e. copyright owner). This includes publishing photographs on the internet, making a sound recording of a book, a painting of a photograph and so on.

---

56 The CDPA was amended in May 2007 in order to implement EC Directives, the Copyright (Visually Impaired Persons) Act and Copyright, etc. 2002, the Copyright etc. Trademarks (Offences and Enforcement) Act 2002 and the Statutory Instrument Performances (Moral Rights, etc.) Regulations 2006 (SI 2006/18).

Under the CDPA, copyright arises automatically when an original literary, dramatic, musical or artistic work etc. is created, provided it is either written down or otherwise recorded in some material form. 'Recorded' also includes the digital medium, storage on a computer hard drive or memory stick, as well as digital music recordings. Copyright does not protect ideas for a work. It is only when the work itself is fixed, for example in writing, that copyright automatically protects it. This means there is no form of official registration of copyright in the UK.

Copyright, then, protects form or expression, but the courts have drawn a limit when it comes to protection of ideas. This was highlighted in **Fraser v Thames TV** (1983),[57] where the court held that ideas must be sufficiently developed and must have some element of originality not already in the public domain.

In **Fraser** (also known as the '**Rock Follies** case'), three female claimants, who had formed a rock group, together with their composer and manager, developed an idea for a TV series (later called 'Rock Follies'[58]) based on their experiences, focusing both on their individual lives and on their collective character. One of the group, with the consent of the other two, communicated this idea for a television series in confidence to a defendant scriptwriter. The scriptwriter approached the prospective Head of Drama for Thames Television and negotiations ensued for a possible television series based on the claimants' idea. The group wanted to appear as themselves if the series was commissioned by Thames Television. Thames Television paid £500 for the rights provided by this option agreement. When Thames Television wanted to start filming, one of the group was unavailable. Thames Television produced the highly successful series, Rock Follies, with other actresses incorporating episodes based on the lives and experiences of the real pop group, whose claimants sued in breach of contract, copyright and confidence.

See also
Chapter 2.2

Hirst J held that the claimants' idea as well as their services as actresses did form part of the agreement entered into by Thames Television and that there was an implied agreement by Thames Television not to employ other actresses than the group. For these reasons the claimants succeeded in their breach of contract claim (Hirst J also referred to the **Coco Engineers** case[59]).[60]

Hirst's J ruling is significant and distinguishes actions in breach of confidence with the meaning of protecting ideas in copyright. He identified four points in **Fraser v Thames TV** in relation to ideas. The idea must:

(1)   contain some significant element of originality;
(2)   be clearly identifiable (as an idea of the confider);
(3)   be of potential commercial attractiveness;
(4)   be sufficiently well developed to be capable of actual realization.

In other words, it is not essential for confidential information to be in writing or other permanent form, but for copyright purposes, 'the idea must have some significant element of originality not already in the realm of public knowledge.'[61]

The Court of Appeal held in the **Rock Follies** case (**Fraser**) that, on the facts, there had been an implied option (i.e. a negative covenant) in the contract between the three group members and

---

57 [1983] 1 QB 44 ('The **Rock Follies** case').
58 Rock Follies became a 1970s TV hit and cult programme, written by Howard Schuman, with music from Andy Mackay, starring Charlotte Cornwell, Julie Covington and Rula Lenska in the title rolls. The storyline spread over 12 episodes and two series, following the ups and downs of the fictional female rock band called the Little Ladies as they struggled for recognition and success.
59 **Coco v AN Clarke (Engineers) Ltd** [1969] RPC 41: 'there must be some product of the human brain which suffices to confer a confidential nature upon the information' (claim failed).
60 See also: Colston and Galloway (2010).
61 **Fraser v Thames TV** [1983] 1 QB 44 at paras 65 ff.

Thames TV not to make use of the idea without also casting the three original members of the group (unless they were unwilling to take part). Failure on behalf of Thames TV to offer them the parts amounted to a breach of contract. There was also a breach of confidence in relation to the idea. On that basis Fraser and the other claimants had brought themselves within the requirements of 'breach of confidence' (but not copyright) and were entitled to damages for breach of confidence.

Hirst J's ruling in **Fraser v Thames TV** was applied in **De Maudsley v Palumbo** (1996).[62] This case concerned the idea for a new style all-night nightclub. James (now Lord) Palumbo had offered funding and the idea was subsequently developed by him into what became 'The Ministry of Sound' with a 24-hour licence amid the new wave of dance music. The nightclub opened without the involvement of De Maudsley (the claimant), either as shareholder or as part-owner of the company. De Maudsley claimed breach of contract and breach of confidence.[63] The CA dismissed the action, applying Hirst J's points made in the **Rock Follies** (**Fraser**) case, that:

(1)   there was no agreement of sufficient certainty to be enforceable, and no intention to create legal relations; i.e. no contract existed between the parties;

(2)   it was not essential for the alleged confidential material to be in writing or other permanent form;

(3)   there was no considerable degree of particularity in the definite product; the idea was not sufficiently developed to show some degree of attractiveness to the end user;

(4)   there was no significant element of originality, and the idea was not clearly identifiable.

De Maudsley's idea for a new concept in nightclubs contained vague elements such as 'all night', 'big', 'high-tec décor' and 'high-quality DJs'. Knox J did not hold that these ideas had gone far enough beyond identifying a 'desirable goal' or a commercial aspiration, meaning that the nightclub idea was not sufficiently 'well formed' even though it had sown the seed for the idea of the defendant's successful club.[64]

A copyright-protected work can have more than one copyright, or another intellectual property right, connected to it. For example, an album of music can have separate copyrights for individual songs, sound recordings, artwork, and so on. While copyright can protect the artwork of the album's logo, it could also be registered as a trademark.

A copyrighted work under UK copyright legislation is relatively easy to prove within the CDPA and does not need to meet such stringent standards of novelty and rigours as an invention needs in order to satisfy patent laws or trademarks. Section 4(1)(a) CDPA even provides that artistic works, including photographs, are protected as copyright works 'irrespective of artistic quality'.

The production of the work may involve the exercise of genuine intellectual skill, labour and effort by the creator, in which he may well be excluded from copyright breach, as the House of Lords held in **Walter v Lane** (1900). An author of a work also has the right not to have a work which he has not created falsely attributed to him.[65]

See above 8.2.1

8.4.2 Fundamental principles of the UK Copyright Act

Copyright law is concerned primarily with authorship, ownership and originality. The fundamental principles underlying the UK Copyright Act are summarized in the following sections of the CDPA:

---

62 [1996] FSR 447.
63 For further discussion see: Carty (2007).
64 Knox J in **De Maudsley** [1996] FSR 447, stated that the idea in **Fraser v Thames TV** was 'well formed'.
65 Section 80(7) CDPA.

Section 1(1): Copyright is a property right which subsists in accordance with this Part in the following descriptions of work –

(a)   original literary, dramatic, musical or artistic works . . .

Section 2(1): The owner of a copyright in a work of any description has the exclusive right to do the acts specified in Chapter II as the acts restricted by the copyright in a work of that description.

Section 4(1): In this part 'Artistic work' means (a) graphic work, photograph, sculpture or collage, irrespective of artistic quality.

Section 9(1): In this part 'author' in relation to a work means the person who creates it.

It is important to note that the UK Copyright Act was amended by the Statutory Instrument, The Copyright and Related Rights Regulations 2003.[66] These have to be read in conjunction with the CDPA. This means that the 2003 Regulations updated UK copyright law in line with EU law and measures relating to the prevention of unauthorized extraction of the contents of a databases and the use of the internet.

Under **s 16 CDPA**, the copyright owner has the exclusive right to copy the work, issue copies to the public, rent or lend the work to the public, perform the work in public, communicate the work to the public and make an adaptation of the work. 'Performance' includes a dramatic performance (including dance and mime), a musical performance, a reading or recitation of a literary work, or a performance of a variety act or any similar presentation.[67]

Section 20 CDPA has been amended by the Copyright and Related Rights Regulations 2003, Regulation 6(1). The essence of s 20 CDPA makes the communication to the public an act restricted by the copyright. Section 20 therefore prohibits communication 'to the public' via the internet and safeguards copyrighted work that is made available online without the author's consent, for example, offering a film for download via a website, transmitting a film via cable or wireless technology or streaming a film via the web or emailing a digital file. The exact interpretation of the meaning 'to the public' is left to be interpreted by the courts. The amended version under Regulation 6(1) of the Statutory Instrument, Copyright and Related Rights Regulation 2003, now reads:

Restricted act: communication to the public of the work

6.(1) For section 20 there shall be substituted—

"Infringement by communication to the public

20(1) The communication to the public of the work is an act restricted by the copyright in –

(a)   a literary, dramatic, musical or artistic work,
(b)   a sound recording or film, or
(c)   a broadcast.

---

66 SI 2003/2498.
67 Section 180(2) (a)–(d) CDPA.

(2)   References in this Part to communication to the public are to communication to the public by electronic transmission, and in relation to a work include –

(a)   the broadcasting of the work;

(b)   the making available to the public of the work by electronic transmission in such a way that members of the public may access it from a place and at a time individually chosen by them.

(2)   For section 16(1)(d) there shall be substituted –

"(d) to communicate the work to the public (see section 20 CDPA);".

This means that **s 20(1) CDPA** (as amended) makes it a 'restricted' act if the work (literary, dramatic, sound recording, broadcast etc.) is communicated to the public.

Section 20(2) CDPA (as amended) refers to communication to the public by 'electronic transmission', which now includes the internet. This section also covers 'related rights', which include performers', producers' and broadcasting organizations' rights.[68]

The right to be identified as the author of dramatic, musical or artistic work is defined in **ss 77 and 78 CDPA**. The right has to be asserted by the author in order to have effect. Section 77(4) states that:

The author of an artistic work has the right to be identified whenever –

(a)   the work is published commercially or exhibited in public, or a visual image of it is broadcast or included in a cable programme service;

(b)   a film including a visual image of the work is shown in public or copies of such a film are issued to the public; or

(c)   in the case of a work of architecture in the form of a building or a model for a building, a sculpture or a work of artistic craftsmanship, copies of a graphic work representing it, or of a photograph of it, are issued to the public.

8.4.3 The protection of literary, dramatic, musical and artistic works and internet ownership

Under the CDPA 1988, a literary work is defined as 'any work, other than a dramatic or musical work, which is written, spoken or sung'.[69] This means that copyright cannot subsist in a literary work which is merely spoken or sung, unless and until it is recorded, for example in writing or in other form.[70] On that basis, the 1988 Act introduced a change which impacted significantly on the principle established in *Walter v Lane*.[71]

'Artistic works' can mean graphic work, a painting, drawing, map, engraving, etching, lithograph, woodcut or similar work, a photograph, sculpture or collage, a work of architecture, such as either a building or a model of a building, or a work of artistic craftsmanship – irrespective of artistic quality.[72]

Can a recording artist or publishing author protect his name, a song or title by copyright? It depends. Copyright may or may not be available for titles, slogans or logos, depending on whether

---

68 Part II CDPA 'Rights in Performances', amended by The Performances (Moral Rights, etc.) Regulations 2006.
69 Section 3(1) CDPA.
70 Section 3(2) CDPA.
71 For further discussion of copyright in the spoken word and the origins of authorship, see Gravells (2007).
72 Section 4 CDPA.

they contain sufficient authorship. In most circumstances copyright does not protect names. Does an artist or performer need to register his work or sound recording to be protected? Not really, because copyright protection is formality-free in countries party to the Berne Convention, which means that protection does not depend on compliance with any formalities such as registration or deposit of copies.

Copyright applies to the internet in the same way as material in other media. For example, any photographs you place on the internet will be protected in the same way as other artistic works; any original written work will be protected as a literary work, and so on. The same goes for internet downloads; it is important if one wants to distribute or put material on the internet that belongs to another to ensure that the copyright owner's permission is granted, unless any of the exceptions apply. These include:

- non-commercial research and private study;
- reviews (such as book reviews) or criticism, and reporting of current events (such as news coverage[73]);
- teaching in educational establishments;
- helping visually impaired persons;
- time-shifting (a recording of a broadcast, made on domestic premises for private and domestic use to enable it to be viewed or listened to at a more convenient time).[74]

It is not an infringement of the copyright in a work to draw, take a photograph or make a film of, buildings or sculptures or works of artistic craftsmanship which are located in a public place or in premises open to the public. Copyright is not infringed in any material when it is used in legal proceedings.

8.4.4 Economic rights

In December 2008, Warner Music Group ('Warners') ordered the video-sharing site YouTube (owned by Google) to remove its exclusive recording artists James Blunt, Madonna and Led Zeppelin because of a disagreement over royalties. Warners argued that YouTube had not been willing to accept contractual terms which would fairly and appropriately compensate the recording artists, songwriters, labels and publishers for their copyrighted works.

Intellectual property rights underpin the economic theory by which the owner of a copyright can make money from his published work, song or picture by way of royalty payments or 'royalties'. Royalties are usage-based payments made by one party (usually the licensee) to another (the licensor) for ongoing use of an asset, such as an intellectual property right. Such 'permissions' (licence) are usually by way of a detailed written contract. Royalties are typically a percentage of gross or net sales derived from the sale of a book, music score, music CD or music or film download. A royalty interest is the right of the author or creator of the work to collect a stream of future royalty payments, used in the publishing and music industries to describe a percentage ownership of future production or revenues from a given licence agreement.[75]

See also
Chapter 9.7

---

73 The exception relating to news reporting does not apply to the use of photographs.
74 This time-shifting exception does not, however, cover the making of recordings for placing in a collection for repeated viewing or listening. The making of a recording for purposes other than to time-shift a programme for others is illegal.
75 For further detailed authority on the publishing industry see: Owen (2007); and for music publishing see: Harrison (2011).

See Chapter 9.5

A composer can grant a recording label the rights to his compositions;[76] if recordings are made without the consent of the recording company or that of the performer, this creates a new action relating to the use of illicit recordings.[77] Rights are also conferred on a performer ('performers' rights') by the provisions of Chapter 3 of Part II CDPA.[78] Performers' moral rights include the right to object to derogatory treatment of their performance.[79]

A 'performance' is defined by the CDPA as a:

> (a) **dramatic** performance (which includes dance and mime);
> (b) **musical** performance;
> (c) **reading** or recitation of a literary work; or
> (d) **variety act** performance (or any similar presentation).[80]

A copyright owner or performer's rights are infringed by a person who, without his consent:

(a) makes a copy or recording of the whole or any substantial part of a qualifying work or performance (directly from the live performance);

(b) broadcasts live the whole or any substantial part of a qualifying performance; or

(c) makes a copy or recording of the whole or any substantial part of a qualifying work or performance (e.g. directly from a broadcast of the live performance).[81]

The Court of Appeal's judgment in the **Sawkins** case[82] caused great concern in the music industry. The case centred on musical scholar, Dr Lionel Sawkins,[83] the world's leading authority on Lalande's musical works.[84] One question before the court in **Sawkins** was what actually constituted 'music' in copyright terms. Was it the sound or the scores from which music was played? The problem is that the CDPA does not specifically define 'music'.

The crucial question in **Sawkins** was whether copyright can subsist in modern performing editions, such as those produced by Dr Sawkins. At the same time, concern was raised that relatively small recording labels, such as Hyperion Records, would be deterred in future from recording rare or obscure music only listened to by niche markets if they were faced with an additional financial burden. Furthermore, would the editor of a published (music) edition be granted the elevated status of 'original' composer by overly generous copyright rules?

In 2001, Dr Sawkins had completed three modern performance editions of Lalande's works after spending hundreds of hours making changes and corrections to the existing musical records and notations of Lalande's original works. The editions covered *Te Deum Laudamus* (1684),

76 Sections 181–184 CDPA.
77 Sections 185–188 CDPA.
78 Sections 205 A–F CDPA ('rights in performances' and 'moral rights').
79 Section 205F CDPA.
80 Section 205 F CDPA.
81 Section 182 CDPA.
82 See: *Sawkins v Hyperion Records* [2005] EWCA Civ 565 (CA Civ Div).
83 Dr Lionel Sawkins, a Principal Lecturer in music at the Roehampton Institute in London prior to retirement in 1985, is acknowledged to be a world authority on the music of the French composer Michel-Richard de Lalande. In 2001 the French Government made him an Officier de L'Ordre des Arts et des Lettres. He was twice invited to act as Conseiller Artistique for festivals of music by Lalande in Versailles in conjunction with the Centre de Musique Baroque. Dr Sawkins devoted much of his retirement to preparing editions of Lalande's compositions and of the 22 currently on sale or hire, he has prepared 19. His editions of Lalande (and other Baroque composers such as Lully, Rameau and Royer) have been performed all over the world, and recorded on several different labels.
84 Michel-Richard de Lalande (1657–1726) was the principal court composer of two French kings during the seventeenth and eighteenth centuries. Lalande composed a number of *grands motets* – sacred music written for performance by single voices, choirs and orchestral groups. Few of Lalande's original manuscripts have survived.

La Grande Piece Royale (1695) and *Venite Exultemus* (1701). The Sawkins editions contained information in conventional modern musical notation with indications and directions for performers which affected the sounds they produced while playing their instruments, as well as the combination of sounds heard by listeners hearing the performance. Dr Sawkins had sought to reproduce faithfully Lalande's music in the form of an accurate edition close to the composer's original intentions.

Hyperion Records then produced a CD of early French music, including recordings of performances of Lalande's compositions using the Sawkins scores. The record label had paid Dr Sawkins a one-off ('killer') fee for providing the performing editions, but refused to pay him any subsequent royalties on the basis that an editor was not entitled to copyright in a performing edition of non-copyright music. Dr Sawkins claimed that his performance editions were original musical works with a separate copyright under s 3 CDPA. Hyperion's counter-argument was that Sawkins' works were merely transcriptions of Lalande's music, and the company continued to deny Dr Sawkins any royalties because they claimed that he had not created original musical works within the meaning of the UK Copyright Act.

Discussions in the Court of Appeal revolved around possible commercial results of this case, especially as to who actually obtains money from the licence fee. Would the royalties go to the scholar who prepared the performing edition? **Sawkins** ultimately defined 'music' as 'combining sounds for listening to' as opposed to mere noise; a landmark case for composers and musical scholars.

The CA held that there had been a breach of s 77 CDPA, because the Hyperion CD did not identify Dr Sawkins as the author of the performing editions. Dr Sawkins had clearly spent hundreds of hours making the performing editions, which therefore satisfied the requirement of an 'original' work in the copyright sense. The subsistence of copyright involved an assessment of the whole work in which copyright was claimed (see also: **Ladbroke v William Hill** (1964)[85]). Lord Justice Mummery rejected Hyperion's argument that musical copyright could be secured only by composition in the form of notes on the score, stating that 'Hyperion's arguments ignored the fact that the totality of the sounds produced by the musicians are affected, or potentially affected, by the information inserted in the performing editions produced by Dr Sawkins'.[86]

This meant that the sound on the CD was not just that of the musicians playing music composed by Lalande; on the contrary, in order to make that sound, the musicians had to play from Dr Sawkins's scores in order to 'make music'. Mummery LJ summarized his reasons why Dr Sawkins's editions were original musical works and therefore entitled to copyright protection in their own right:

(a)   Dr Sawkins originated the performing editions by his own expert and scholarly exertions;
(b)   The editions did not previously exist in that form;
(c)   The contents of his editions affected the combination of sounds produced by the performers; and
(d)   The resulting combination of sounds embodied in the CD was music.

The court awarded damages to Dr Sawkins both for infringement of his copyright and for infringement of his 'moral rights', i.e. the right to be identified as the author of the edition. Furthermore, Hyperion Records were ordered to notify Dr Sawkins and seek his permission before any future exploitation of his work could take place.[87]

---

85 [1964] 1 WLR 273.
86 **Sawkins** [2005] EWCA Civ 565 (CA Civ Div) at 32 (Mummery LJ).
87 The trial took place in May 2004 and lasted six days. Mr Justice Patten gave judgment in favour of Dr Sawkins on 2 July 2004. That judgment was unanimously upheld by the Court of Appeal (Lords Justice Mummery, Mance and Jacob) following a two-day hearing in March 2005. Dr Sawkins was represented by Carter-Ruck and Counsel Richard Arnold QC (in the Court of Appeal only) and Andrew Norris. Carter-Ruck and Andrew Norris acted under conditional fee agreements backed by after-the-event insurance. Source: Press release by Carter-Ruck, 19 May 2005.

See also
Chapter 9.6

In addition to receiving royalties for songwriting and CD sales, performing rights royalties are paid to a songwriter, composer or publisher whenever their music is played or performed in any public space. These royalties are collected on behalf of the record label and/or the producer by the Performing Right Society (PRS).[88]

In March 2010, the record label EMI was sued in the US for alleged non-payment of royalties in an action brought against the British label by a company in Tennessee that oversees payments to music writers, namely Bluewater Music Services. The music copyright administrator filed a lawsuit against EMI Music (North America) involving dozens of songs by artists including Chris Le Doux and the Doobie Brothers. The songs were used in compilations and sold as mobile telephone ring-tones. Disclosure of the action came just a few weeks after rock group Pink Floyd won a court claim against EMI (UK) that prevented the record company from selling single downloads of the band's albums on the internet. Pink Floyd had gone to the High Court in London to seek clarification of its contract with EMI, which was last negotiated in 1998–99, before the expansion of music downloads online. The ruling was an additional blow for EMI, owned by Guy Hands's Terra Firma at the time, a private equity group, which lost £1.7bn in 2009.[89]

By the time EMI was broken up in November 2011, the value of its music catalogues amounted to £3 billion, including the Beatles' entire recorded catalogue. For three decades, EMI had taken on the world in record sales. It was eventually sold to arch-rivals Sony and Universal, which marked the end of a major British record label that had looked after Tom Jones, Kylie Minogue and new talents such as Emeli Sandé. EMI's recorded music arm was taken up by Universal Music (giving that company a global market share of over 40 per cent), while EMI Music Publishing was absorbed by Sony/ATV to create a new publishing powerhouse.

In February 2013, the historic British record label Parlophone became part of Warner Music (Warners) in an estimated £487m deal. Parlophone was behind Coldplay and Blur, and was the original label that signed Pink Floyd and the Beatles. Parlophone had been the jewel in the EMI crown. The deal was a personal victory for Warner's billionaire owner Len Blavatnik, also part-owner of the Russian oil conglomerate TNK-BP. Having outbid Roman Abramovich on a £41m house in Kensington Palace Gardens in 2004, Blavatnik is known for his deep pockets and his paying cash for Parlophone.

8.4.5 Exclusive rights

A granting of an 'exclusive licence' means the copyright owner grants a person, recording company or (book) publisher permission to exercise a particular right exclusively (even to the exclusion of the copyright owner themselves). An exclusive licence can be limited in the rights given and the time period and firmly falls within the realms of contract law.[90] It is of course possible to grant non-exclusive licences, though these would be economically less valuable to an individual exploiter – but any action for breach of copyright by a non-exclusive licensee might require the copyright owner to be joined as party to the action.[91]

An exclusive licence must be made in writing. For its correct form, this contract must be signed by or on behalf of the copyright owner, who in turn authorizes the licence – to the exclusion of all other persons, including the person granting the licence – to exercise a right which would otherwise be exercisable exclusively by the copyright owner.[92]

---

88 PRS for Music is the home of PRS and MCPS, representing the rights of over 100,000 members in the UK. They license organizations to play, perform or make available copyright music on behalf of their members and those of overseas societies, distributing the royalties to them fairly and efficiently, and promote and protect the value of copyright. See: www.prsformusic.com.
89 Source: 'EMI sued over failure to pay royalties on songs by Doobie Brothers', *Observer*, 28 March 2010.
90 Section 92(1) CDPA.
91 Sections 101–101A and 102 CDPA.
92 Section 92(1) CDPA.

The recording right in relation to performers is covered by ss 185 to 188 CDPA. Here the Copyright Act deals with the exclusive recording rights of a performer and the record company, where the label is entitled to the exclusion of all other persons (including the performer) to make recordings of one or more of his performances with a view to their commercial exploitation.[93] This section of the CDPA essentially deals with the problem of 'bootlegging', which is the making of unofficial or unauthorized taped recordings of live performances and the making of pirate copies which, in turn, would breach the record company's sound recording copyright.[94]

Exclusive recording rights are then 'assigned' to one label ('the qualifying party') by way of an assignment or licence (contract law). Both parties then have the benefit of an exclusive recording contract and all recordings and performances will then be subject to exclusive commercial exploitation; this means with a view to the recordings being sold or let for hire, or shown or played in public.[95]

It is worth noting that an exclusive licensee has the same right in title (to sue in their own name) as the copyright owner in this respect (such as Warners, Universal or Sony). Therefore, the exclusive licence holder, like a record label, can take action for copyright infringement without joining the copyright owner to the action – which is what some of the famous labels regularly do against samplers and online file-sharers. An exclusive licence holder has the same rights against a successor in title who is bound by the licence as he has against the person granting the licence.[96]

8.4.6 Copyright infringements

The CDPA expresses the economic rights of a copyright owner as a series of 'restricted acts' that only the copyright owner can do or authorize, such as granting consent to a performer to perform his music,[97] or permission to a publisher to 'exploit' a book by way of a publication licence. These restricted acts are set out as follows:

Restricted Acts

(1) Copying or reproduction rights (s 17 CDPA)
(2) Issuing or distribution rights (s 18 CDPA)
(3) Lending and rental rights (s 18A CDPA)
(4) Public performance rights (s 19 CDPA)
(5) Communication rights (including broadcasting rights) (s 20 CDPA)
(6) Adaptation rights (including translation rights) (s 21 CDPA).

Breaches of these rights are called primary infringements, a strict liability action, where the claimant does not have to prove intention, recklessness or carelessness. This means that purely innocent breaches may be actionable. A further group of 'secondary infringements' such as selling, importing, providing premises for infringing performances or equipment to produce infringing items is set out in ss 22 to 27 CDPA. In such instances, the claimant must prove actual or constructive knowledge on the part of the defendant that they either knew or ought to have known that they were committing an infringing act.

---

93 Section 182D(8) CDPA, added by SI 2006/18.
94 Under s 5 CDPA.
95 Section 185 CDPA.
96 Section 92(2) CDPA.
97 Part II CDPA 'Rights in Performances'; Chapter 1, ss 180ff: 'Rights conferred on performers and persons having recording rights'.

The landmark case of **Grisbrook v MGN Ltd** (2009)[98] (see below) examined how far licence terms can be implied when technology has moved on beyond what the legislators of the UK Copyright Act initially intended or even imagined. When freelance photographer Alan Grisbrook began working for the *Daily Mirror*, the internet did not exist and there were certainly no online editions of newspapers. There was little time or need for written commission agreements and his celebrity photos were simply verbally commissioned by editors. It was then understood that if Mr Grisbrook's photos were not used for a particular edition, they would go into the *Mirror's* photo library of back copies. Little did Alan Grisbrook know that some twenty years later, his 'exclusive' photos of celebrities would appear on the newspaper's website, easily and publically accessible to the world at large via the internet.

Alan Grisbrook's work was first commissioned in 1981 to provide photographs for the *Daily Mirror's* 'Diary' page. For the next 16 years he supplied the *Mirror's* publishers, Mirror Group Newspapers (MGN), with hundreds of photographs, many of which made the front page, featuring subjects such as Ali MacGraw, Alan Bates and Sarah Miles. Most of the photos were of celebrities or other well-known individuals, and many of the photographs were taken late at night, showing the person concerned emerging from a restaurant or nightclub.

 **KEY CASE** — *Grisbrook v Mirror Group Newspapers Ltd* [2009] EWHC 2520 (Ch D)

Precedent

- ❖ Whether a licence agreement extends to subsequent forms of (new) technology (such as the internet) depends on the form of words used in the contract.
- ❖ A copyright licence should be limited to what is in the joint contemplation of the parties at the time the agreement was made.
- ❖ A licence does not extend to enable one party to take advantage of a new, unexpected profitable opportunity.

Facts

Between 1981 and 1997 photojournalist Alan Grisbrook supplied hundreds of photographs of celebrities to MGN, publisher of the *Daily Mirror* newspaper. There was no written contract between Grisbrook and MGN; all the pictures had been commissioned verbally by editors. All used and unused photos went into MGN's archives and Mr Grisbrook was paid whenever a photograph was used. It was acknowledged that Mr Grisbrook had retained copyright in the photos and had licensed MGN to use the material in this way. MGN had a hard-copy picture library of more than 30 million photographs, transparencies and negatives. If the picture appeared as part of a reproduction of a newspaper page ('rag-out'), the photographer would not be due a further fee. MGN subsequently developed a digital picture library called 'FastFoto', containing more than a million images. Mr Grisbrook's complaint centred on the online FastFoto library.

In 1998, Mr Grisbrook commenced proceedings to recover unpaid licence fees amounting to £161,000.[99] In 1999, he complained that 191 of his images were included on the website. In a 2002 consent order, following the earlier legal action taken by Grisbrook against MGN over unpaid licence fees, MGN agreed to delete all electronic copies of his photos from its systems.

---

98 [2009] EWHC 2520 (Ch D).
99 Mr Grisbrook's counsel cited **Ray v Classic FM**, where Mr Justice Lightman had taken the 'minimalist' approach following decisions of the HL in **Liverpool CC v Irwin** [1977], and the CA in **Philips Electronique v BSB** [1995].

In 2008, Mr Grisbrook discovered that MGN were making available back copies of their titles to paying customers through websites, and that these contained some of his images. He believed MGN were infringing his copyright and breaching the previous consent order. He found 6,000 original photographs, negatives and transparencies and 2,000 images on the 'FastFoto' system website. Though MGN removed some of the material, the newspaper publishers refused to remove the images from websites that offered complete back issues of the publications.[100]

Alan Grisbrook commenced proceedings for breach of copyright, arguing that the publication of his photographic material on the newspaper's (archive) website amounted to a copyright infringement and was, therefore, in breach of the undertaking that MGN had given. He sought an order for imprisonment of the officers of MGN, and sequestration of MGN's assets. MGN argued that the licence originally granted by Grisbrook permitting publication in the newspaper also extended to subsequent reproduction of the published material, including archiving on the internet. MGN relied on the defence of public interest under s 171(3) CDPA.

Decision
The CA found that the implied licence did not extend to the exploitation of Mr Grisbrook's photos on back-issue websites; this, therefore, amounted to an infringement of copyright. Nevertheless, because it was a difficult question, and one not contemplated at the time the licence was granted (i.e. before the internet), MGN was entitled to take a different view. There had been no deliberate breach of the undertaking. Patten LJ said that though permission to store pictures for possible future use or for archiving could be an 'implied term' of the oral contract, the same could not be said for the presentation of the archived material to the public for a fee. For these reasons, the court held, Mr Grisbrook's copyright in his photographs had been infringed by the operation of the back-number (archive) websites.

Analysis
Mr Grisbrook and other freelance photographers were obviously aware that MGN, like any other newspaper publisher at the time, would retain an archive of published editions. But this was the time before the World Wide Web, and photographs were stored in the form of hard copies and microfiche. Grisbrook's (oral) licence agreement extended to *any* forms of new technology available at the time, and the Mirror Group argued in its defence that this now included the internet. Arguably it would therefore have been an implied term of the dealings with the newspaper publishers that storage, whether on microfiche or in electronic form, was permitted.

The only real issue in this case was whether the licence also extended to making the back numbers database more widely available to members of the public via the internet. The CA held that Mr Grisbrook's photographs on the newspaper's websites were 'a different kind of operation' (at para 65). In effect the exploitation of the photographs of Mr Grisbrook by inclusion in the websites, from which copies could be downloaded and printed at will, was a new method of exploitation which, by reference to the conditions prevailing in the

---

100 The MGN websites included: mydailymirror.com, launched in June 2006 enabling users to buy *Daily Mirror* front pages in the form of posters, T-shirts or greetings cards; arcitext.com, launched in February 2006 allowing subscribers to access the *Mirror's* archives as pdf documents which reproduce part of the newspaper as it was printed; and mirrorarchive.co.uk, launched as a test site in April 2007 but intended to be the commercial equivalent of arcitext.com.

period from 1981 to 1997, was wholly outside anything the parties could have contemplated at the time the photographs were first submitted to MGN.

In the light of the **Grisbrook** judgment, authors of creative works ought to study their licence agreements with media publishers carefully. If they have granted licensed images to a newspaper, which, like MGN, is making back copies of their editions available online to paid subscribers, they may well have a claim in copyright infringement if their licence agreement does not clearly allow such 'extended' use.

 FOR THOUGHT

How would you advise a celebrity photographer when she is asked by a commissioning editor of a news organization (which also has an online archive edition) whether he can use her photo of a celebrity footballer with his three children to accompany a front-page story? Formulate the standard terms for the photographer. You may wish to consult the website for the Association of Photographers at: www.the-aop.org.

8.5 Duration of copyright

More than half a century ago, the Beatles' first single, 'Love Me Do', was released in October 1962, The Beach Boys' 'Surfin' USA' reached No 14 in the US charts in June of the same year, and Bob Dylan's first album was released in March 1962, when he had arrived as a 20-year-old in Manhattan by a freight train. All these sound recordings would by now be out of copyright, had the EU Commission not changed the law on copyright, extending such recordings (most of which were on German and UK labels at the time) to 70 years.

In September 2011, the EU Parliament finally implemented the long-awaited EU Copyright Term Directive 2011 (Directive 2011/77/EU).[101] The Directive extends the copyright and the related performance right (or 'term of protection') for music *performers* and *sound recordings* to 70 years. Composers already own copyright over their music until 70 years after their death. Sir Paul McCartney and Sir Cliff Richard were among the artists who had campaigned and had lobbied the EU Commission to extend copyright on sound recordings.[102]

The implementation of the new Europe-wide legislation (which became known as 'Cliff's law') means that thousands of music performers, from little-known session musicians to Dame Shirley Bassey, will now receive royalties from songs released in the 1960s for an extra 20 years. Many of the most popular songs recorded in the 1960s were due to come out of copyright, including songs recorded by artists such as Tom Jones and the Beatles. Copyright in their hit singles will now not expire until at least 2033.

The EU Copyright Term Directive 2011 benefits particularly lesser known artists and session musicians who have worked all their lives but never really benefited much from royalties. Up to now, session players only received insignificant royalties from public performances of their work, such as radio, but not from record sales. According to Sir Cliff, performers' economic rights needed

101 Directive 2011/77/EU of the European Parliament and of the Council of 27 September 2011 amending Directive 2006/116/EC on the term of protection of copyright and certain related rights.
102 Source: 'Sir Cliff backs royalty campaign', 18 April 2006, BBC News Online, http://news.bbc.co.uk/1/hi/entertainment/4917550.stm.

protection so that they too would have an income for their retirement. He correctly argued that the (previous) 50-year duration of copyright was no longer adequate in these days of increasing life expectancy.

The income from copyright remuneration is important for performers, as they often do not have other regular salaried income. The extended term under Directive 2011/77/EU also benefits record producers, who can now generate additional revenue from the sale of records in shops and on the internet. The Directive allows producers to adapt to the rapidly changing business environment and helps them maintain their investment levels in new talent.

See Chapter 9.5.1

8.5.1 General terms of protection

The original UK copyright legislation in the form of the Copyright, Designs and Patents Act 1988 provided for copyright protection of musical, literary, dramatic and artistic works only for 50 years from the death of the author. This was superseded by EU legislation which now states that all have a 70-year duration of copyright after the author's death.[103]

The CDPA (and related extended EU legislation) cannot be retrospective; that is, it only covers works that have been created since 1 August 1989 when the Act came into force. For works created before that date, one has to refer to the previous copyright legislation. However, the EC 'Duration of Copyright and Rights in Performances Regulations 1995' was retrospective and harmonized the situation regarding the length of copyright protection for existing works irrespective of when they were created. There are several different categories under which different materials are classified in the 1988 Copyright Act and subsequent amendments and additions by way of EU legislation. The box below shows a summary of duration of copyrights.

Duration of copyrights

---

i. Literary, dramatic, musical or artistic works

Seventy years from the end of the calendar year in which the last remaining author of the work dies. If the author is unknown, copyright will last for 70 years from the end of the calendar year in which the work was created, although if it is made available to the public during that time (by publication, authorized performance, broadcast, exhibition, etc.), then the duration will be 70 years from the end of the year that the work was first made available.

ii. Sound recordings

The copyright term for sound recordings has been extended from 50 years to 70 years by the EU Copyright Term Directive.[104] The 70-year period runs from the date of first lawful publication or (if none) first lawful communication to the public (if the publication or, as the case may be, communication occurs within 50 years of the date of recording). If neither occurs within 50 years of the date of recording, the term of copyright will expire at that point. The extension will have prospective and retrospective effect. For existing copyrights, the new legislation applies only to sound recordings that are less than 50 years old

---

103 Section 12 CDPA, as amended by the Duration of Copyright and Rights in Performances Regulations 1995 (SI 1995 No. 3297).
104 Directive 2006/116/EC.

as at the date falling two years after the date of force of the amending Directive (2011). In other words, no copyrights will be 'revived' under the new law.

iii. Films

Seventy years from the end of the calendar year in which the last principal director, producer, author or composer dies. If the work is of unknown authorship: 70 years from the end of the calendar year of creation, or if made available to the public in that time, 70 years from the end of the year the film was first made available.

iv. Typographical arrangement of published editions

Twenty-five years from the end of the calendar year in which the work was first published.[105]

v. Broadcasts and cable programmes

Fifty years from the end of the calendar year in which the broadcast was made.[106]

vi. Crown copyright

Crown copyright will exist in works made by an officer of the Crown. This includes items such as legislation and documents and reports produced by government bodies. Crown copyright will last for a period of 125 years from the end of the calendar year in which the work was made. If the work was commercially published within 75 years of the end of the calendar year in which it was made, Crown copyright will last for 50 years from the end of the calendar year in which it was published.

vii. Parliamentary copyright

Parliamentary copyright applies to work that is made by or under the direction or control of the House of Commons or the House of Lords and lasts until 50 years from the end of the calendar year in which the work was made (e.g. the printing of Acts of Parliament or copies of Hansard).

How does one establish which authors are still in copyright, since there is no national register for copyright works in the UK? Certain interest groups have been formed to look after common interests, negotiate licences and collect fees – so-called 'collecting agencies'.

The Authors' Licensing and Collecting Society (ALCS) promotes and protects authors' rights. The ALCS collects money due to authors for secondary uses of their work (such as photocopying of journal articles or book chapters, cable retransmission in the UK and overseas, digital reproduction and educational recordings). The MCPS-PRS for music is the collection agency for songwriters, composers and music publishers. Music publishers, songwriters and composers usually join MCPS to earn royalties when musical works from their catalogue are reproduced, such as for CDs and digital downloads.

See also
Chapter 9.6

---

105 Section 15 CDPA.
106 Section 14 CDPA.

Identifying the copyright holder may be straightforward or may require some detective work, and particular care must be taken when obtaining an image from a website or search engine such as 'Google Images' (they only cache a copy and the thumbnail page does not display any copyright warning). Copyright lawyers have started to serve notices on people who use the original image without giving ownership details and some people have incurred large bills by assuming 'Google Image' thumbnails may be freely used. Usually, work displayed on most websites will be associated with a user or domain owner, who can be approached via metadata which identifies the rights owner and gives contact details.

Even if a photo appears to be an 'orphan work', it is still someone's copyright and is unsafe to use since copyright persists for 70 years after the death of the photographer. Though it might be all right to use very old photos, some of these, such as portraits of famous composers, may still be owned by agencies or trusts who hold the image under licence. Equally, sometimes the credited author will not be the copyright owner because they have assigned copyright to someone else but retained their moral right to be identified as the author. The table below outlines the major categories and their copyright lifetimes.

Copyright lifetimes

Literary works	Written works. Includes lyrics, tables, compilations, computer programs, letters, memoranda, email and web pages.	Author's life plus 70 years after death. Anonymous corporation authors: 70 years from year of publication (see above for special rules for unpublished works).
Dramatic works	Plays, works of dance and mime, and also the libretto of an opera.	Author's life plus 70 years after death.
Crown copyright	All works made by Her Majesty or by an officer or servant of the Crown in the course of his or her duties.	Published by HM Stationery Office: 50 years from the end of the year when first published. Unpublished work: 125 years beyond the year it was created.
Parliamentary copyright	All works made by or under the direction or control of the House of Commons or House of Lords.	Mostly 50 years beyond year it was created. Exceptions include Bills of Parliament.
Musical compositions and lyrics	Musical composition (music scores) and the lyrics.	This term of protection will (as long as the music and lyrics were specifically created for the relevant work) expire 70 years after the death of the last of the composers of the musical composition and the author of the lyrics (whether or not those persons are designated as co-authors).

Artistic works	Graphic works (painting, drawing, diagram, map, chart, plan, engraving, etching, lithograph, woodcut), photographs (not part of a moving film), sculpture, collage, works of architecture (buildings and models for buildings) and artistic craftsmanship (e.g. jewellery).	Author's/creator's life plus 70 years after death.
Computer-generated works	Literary, dramatic and musical works.	50 years from first creation or 50 years from creation if unpublished during that time.
Databases	Collections of independent works, data or other materials which (a) are arranged in a systematic or methodical way, or (b) are individually accessible by electronic or other means.	Full term of other relevant copyrights in the material protected. Also, there is a database right for 15 years (this can roll forward).
Performers and sound recordings	Regardless of medium or the device on which they are played.	The copyright term for live performances and sound recordings is 70 years. The 70-year period runs from the date of first lawful recording or live performance or (if none) first lawful communication to the public.
Films	Any medium from which a moving image may be reproduced.	70 years from death of whoever is the last to survive from: principal director, producer, author of dialogue, composer of film music.
Broadcasts	Transmissions via wireless telegraphy through the air (not via cable or wires), includes satellite transmissions.	50 years from when broadcast first made.
Cable programmes	Services via cable.	50 years from when broadcast first made.
Published editions	The typography and layout of a literary, dramatic or musical work.	25 years from first publication.
Orphan works	Copyrighted works for which the owner of the copyright is unknown or cannot be found.	70 years from the year in which the work was created or first made available or until 2039.

8.5.2 Moral rights and related rights

Linked to UK copyright legislation are 'moral' rights, covered by Chapter IV of the CDPA 1988, which protect non-economic interests, for example the right to claim authorship of a work, to protect the work from harm and distortion and ultimately to protect the creator's reputation. Section 80 CDPA deals with the author's right to object to derogatory treatment of his work. Moral rights normally exist for as long as copyright exists in the work. Importantly, the author retains these rights even after assigning any economic rights in the work to a publisher, film or recording company. As a property right, with economic value, it can be transferred to a third party (e.g. spouse or heirs). Moral rights may be waived but cannot be assigned or passed on after the author's death.[107]

As already stated, the CDPA 1988, EU legislation and international treaties such as the Berne Convention give the creators of literary, dramatic, musical and artistic works, sound recordings, broadcasts, films and typographical arrangements of published editions special moral rights to control the ways in which their material may be used. The rights cover broadcast and public performance, copying, adapting, issuing, renting and lending copies to the public. This means the creator has the right to be identified as the author and to object to distortions of his work.

Section 79 CDPA makes some interesting exceptions. Moral rights do not extend to computer programs, the design of a typeface or any computer-generated work. Furthermore, the right does not apply to publications in a newspaper, magazine or periodical, or an encyclopedia, dictionary, yearbook or other collective work of reference, or a work in which Crown copyright or parliamentary copyright subsists (such as Hansard).[108]

Related rights are a term in copyright law and have developed alongside copyright. They include those of performing artists in their performances, producers of phonograms in their recordings and those of broadcasters in their radio and television programmes. Related rights tend to be of a more limited nature. They are usually of shorter duration and are used in opposition to the term 'author's rights'. Related rights are primarily a result of technological development and generally concern the exploitation of works. The first organized support for the protection of related rights came from the phonogram industry, which sought (and gained, at least in countries following the common law tradition) protection under copyright law against unauthorized copying of phonograms (i.e. records, CDs etc.) under copyright.

Section 103 CDPA deals with remedies for infringement of moral rights, actionable as a breach of statutory duty owed to the person entitled to the right. In such infringement proceedings of the right conferred by s 80 ('right to object to derogatory treatment of work'), the court may, if it thinks it is an adequate remedy in the circumstances, grant an injunction on terms prohibiting the doing of any act unless a disclaimer is made, in such terms and in such manner as may be approved by the court, dissociating the author or director from the treatment of the work.

8.5.3 Paternity and integrity rights

An author's right of paternity is to be identified in his work when it is published commercially, as defined by s 175 CDPA. In order for the right to be exercised, it must be asserted, arguably weakening the value and strength of the paternity right. A paternity right arises in the music business, for instance, where a third party produces or puts on a live qualifying performance. Simon (2006b) explains that a paternity right cannot be infringed via a live performance per se, because it would be impossible to modify a live performance since, at the point of modification, the performance would have already occurred, and so would no longer be live.

---

107 Section 86 CDPA.
108 Sections 79(6) and (7) CDPA.

Assertion of a paternity right is a statement in writing by the author that he wishes to be named on all copies of the work. The signing of a manuscript would not be construed as assertion because it merely identifies the author and does not explicitly state his intentions to be identified. A letter, though not a legal document, is sufficient, as long as the author makes his desire to assert his right of paternity clear to the recipient. Anyone who has notice of the written paternity statement will be bound by it. In the case of an assignment or licence, a statement must be attached to it stating that the author wishes to assert his right and thus be named on all copies of the work. The right may also be asserted in relation to the public exhibition of an artistic work by securing that when the author or other first owner of copyright parts with possession of the original, the author is identified on the original or copy (or the frame or mount of that picture).[109] The right may be asserted at any time. Infringements are covered by s 78(5) CDPA, which provides court action and remedies.

Paternity rights – as with moral rights – do not apply to computer programs, computer-generated works or the design of typefaces. These rights also do not extend to works where copyright was originally vested in the author's employer because an employer, having paid for the creation of the work, should have total freedom to exploit the work; a controversial topic for university lecturers who like to have their academic publications attributed only to them, rather than jointly (or solely) to the higher education institution.

In September 2012, 'universities minister' David Willetts MP announced plans to make publicly funded research immediately available for anyone to read for free on the internet by 2014. In his 'Open Access' speech[110] at Keele University, the Minister for the Department of Business, Innovation and Skills announced that the Government was planning to shift to 'open access for publicly funded research' published in peer-reviewed journals, following the recommendations by Janet Finch, former Vice Chancellor of Keele University. He talked about the 'removal of pay walls', arguing that this would have 'real economic and social benefits'. This marked the most comprehensive shake-up of academic publishing since the innovation of the internet. It meant that research papers are now freely available online.

As expected there was strong opposition to the Minister's proposals, not only from academic circles but also from the Royal Historical Society, whose fellows include Professors David Starkey and Ian Kershaw, the Political Studies Association and the Council for the Defence of British Universities, whose members include Sir David Attenborough, Richard Dawkins and Alan Bennett. These bodies warned of dire consequences for academic creativity and intellectual freedom. Academic publishers (including journal publications) announced that this would have cost implications in that author processing charges would increase. The new system proposed to extend paternity rights of academic publications to university managements and therein give them unprecedented control over their academics' ability to publish their work.

8.5.4 False attribution and passing off

Section 84 CDPA deals with passing off and the false attribution of a work. In order to satisfy the originality criterion for the purposes of copyright subsistence, the author of the work must first establish that the work originated from him or her. Therefore, 'originality' must be distinguished from 'novelty'. The work must be an independent creation, but it need not be an invention in the sense of striking uniqueness, ingeniousness or novelty. In other words, the author must show that the work and its underlying ideas, facts or information expressed therein originate from him.

---

109 Section 78(3)(a) CDPA.
110 Source: UK Conference on Open Access at Keele University, Staffordshire, 13 September 2012, the Rt Hon David Willetts MP 'Making the Higher Education System More Efficient and Diverse', speech at: https://www.gov.uk/government/speeches/uuk-conference-a-world-without-boundaries.

In **Clark v Associated Newspapers Ltd** (1998),[111] the claimant, maverick Conservative MP and established author Alan Clark (1928–99), invoked two rights to protection from false attribution of authorship: his statutory right under s 84 CDPA 1988 and his common law right of passing off. It was for the judge – Mr Justice Lightman – to exercise his discretion whether a substantial body of readers of the *Evening Standard* had been or were likely to be misled 'more than momentarily and inconsequentially' into believing that the claimant was the author of the articles and whether the claimant, as an author with an established goodwill, had suffered or was likely to suffer damage in consequence.

During and after the General Election in 1997, articles had appeared as a weekly column in the *Evening Standard* (written by Peter Bradshaw), headed 'Alan Clark's Secret Election Diary' and 'Alan Clark's Secret Political Diary', next to a photograph of the claimant. The articles were parodies[112] of Mr Clark's well-known diaries, published in 1993.[113] The format of the parodies was such as to deceive a substantial number of readers into attributing their authorship to Mr Clark. The court granted an injunction to Mr Clark to restrain the defendant from publishing any further such 'diaries' in the *Evening Standard*.

The court was assisted by the evidence of witnesses who had seen or read the articles, and of experts as to the features of the market for newspapers and other published works. The test was that rational men had been deceived and the question before the court was whether by the adoption of the format chosen the defendant had succeeded too well in making the articles look real, and Lightman J reached the conclusion that it had. The judge found that the claimant had a substantial reputation as a diarist and his identity as author of the articles would plainly be of importance to readers of the *Evening Standard* in deciding whether to read the articles. That was reflected in the choice of format adopted and most particularly in the design of the heading, which was calculated to exploit the public recognition enjoyed by the claimant and the public interest which any diary written by him could be expected to generate. The consequent identification of the claimant as author was not sufficiently neutralized to prevent a substantial number of readers being deceived. The problem in this case lay in the format adopted by the 'diarist' Peter Bradshaw, who was in clear breach of s 84 CDPA in that the (headings) articles contained a clear and unequivocal false statement attributing their authorship to the claimant, and Mr Clark was accordingly entitled to relief in respect of the commission of the statutory tort.

The court made it clear that the judgment was no bar to publication of parodies. But the 'vice' in this case lay in the format of the articles. Lightman J concluded that the defendants, Associated Newspapers, the editor Max Hastings and Peter Bradshaw had committed the common law tort of passing off and the statutory tort of false attribution of authorship.

Section 74 Enterprise and Regulatory Reform Act 2013 (ERRA) ('Exploitation of design derived from artistic work') repeals s 52 CDPA, which means that articles to which the section applies will have full copyright protection for the period of the life of the author or creator plus 70 years.[114] An example for s 74 would be where a jeweller makes a ring which qualifies for copyright protection as a work of artistic craftsmanship. The ring is then manufactured, with more than fifty copies being made, and it is marketed throughout the world. Seventy years after the jeweller's (or designer's) death, third parties can make their own copies without infringing copyright in the original ring.

See also
Chapter 9.2.7

---

111 [1998] All ER 6 (Ch D).

112 Normally, parodies are attempts to ridicule an author but not in this case. In this case 'parody' meant an imitation of the style of a particular writer or artist with deliberate exaggeration for comic effect.

113 See: Clark (1993). Alan Clark's published diaries cover the period 1983 to 1992 after he left the House of Commons, describing the government (and downfall) of Prime Minister Margaret Thatcher.

114 The Copyright (Industrial Process and Excluded Articles) (No. 2) Order 1989 No. 1070 made under s 52 would therefore cease to have effect.

8.6 EU copyright acquis

The internet has become the primary portal through which knowledge is disseminated, accessed, distributed and shared. We can now access libraries and newspaper archives instantaneously and receive artistic, literary or musical works in digital form. This has implications for copying, counterfeiting and piracy and can mean that these practices provide a source of revenue for organized crime. Counterfeiting practices impact on the sustainable development of the world economy, causing significant financial loss for holders of intellectual property rights and for legitimate businesses by distributing infringing material and therefore undermining legitimate trade.

Yet libraries and archives want to preserve Europe's rich cultural heritage and make it available online to the public. Persons with disabilities want to benefit from new technologies to enable them to have better access to Europe's collective knowledge. Research and teaching establishments want more flexibility to disseminate teaching materials. At the same time, it is necessary to reconcile these needs with the legitimate expectations of creators, authors and publishers to be adequately rewarded for their works. The creation of mega digital libraries as spearheaded by Google ('the Google Book Library Project'[115]) has only reinforced the urgency for Europe to ensure that its rich cultural heritage and intellectual creation is made available to researchers, scholars, consumers and the public at large.

The EU Commission has acknowledged these implications by addressing legislation to counteract these illegal practices and by encouraging Member States to include measures which include the digital environment. The Commission is also responsible for conducting negotiations on industrial and intellectual property within WIPO – such as audiovisual, broadcasting, resale rights, IP on databases, etc. Furthermore, the Commission has addressed the issue of 'orphan works': works whose authors are unknown or unlocatable or both. Their copyright status is unclear, which means orphan works cannot necessarily be utilized, depriving citizens of an important source of IP.

The result has been the so-called EU copyright acquis, a French term (*acquis communautaire*) meaning 'the EU as it is'. Accepting the acquis on copyright means taking legislation as you find it. All Member States have to accept the acquis, making EU copyright law part of their own national legislation.

8.6.1 Copyright Directives

There has been significant harmonization of the substantive copyright law in Europe to reduce barriers to trade and to adjust the framework to new forms of exploitation. The European Commission has seen it as a primary task to enforce the acquis on copyright and related rights; to advance it further and to modernize and adapt it to new developments in technology or the markets concerned as this is ever evolving.

A considerable number of changes have been made to protect copyright across Europe; this has impacted on UK copyright law (the CDPA). The Copyright, Designs and Patents Act 1988 now incorporates a number of EU Directives. The box below shows the main EU copyright legislation.

---

115 In 1996, Google co-founders Sergey Brin and Larry Page were graduate computer science students working on a research project supported by the Stanford Digital Library Technologies Project. Their goal was to make digital libraries of millions of books available to everyone in the world via the internet. In 2004 the 'Google Print Library Project' was made possible by partnerships with Harvard, the University of Michigan, the New York Public Library, the Bodleian Library at Oxford University and Stanford. By 2007, the Library Project had 28 partners, including 7 international library partners: Oxford University (UK), University of Complutense of Madrid (Spain), the National Library of Catalonia (Spain), University Library of Lausanne (Switzerland), Ghent University (Belgium) and Keio University (Japan). The combined collections at these libraries are estimated to exceed 15 million volumes.

EU copyright legislation

- **Directive 91/250/EEC:** on the legal protection of computer programs.
- **Directive 92/100/EEC:** on rental and lending rights and on certain rights related to copyright in the field of intellectual property.
- **Directive 93/83/EEC:** on the coordination of certain rules concerning copyright and rights related to copyright applicable to satellite broadcasting and cable retransmission.
- **Directive 93/98/EEC:** on harmonizing the term of protection of copyright and certain related rights.[116]
- **Directive 96/9/EC:** on the legal protection of databases.
- **Directive 98/84/EC:** on the legal protection of services based on, or consisting of, conditional access.
- **Directive 2001/29/EC:** on the harmonization of certain aspects of copyright and related rights in the information society ('Information Society Directive')

The objective of this Directive is to adapt legislation on copyright and related rights to reflect technological developments and to transpose into Community law the main international obligations arising from the existing treaties on copyright and related rights adopted within the framework of the World Intellectual Property Organization in December 1996. It is an essential building block for the Information Society.

- **Directive 2006/11/EC:** on the Term of Protection of Copyright and Certain Related Rights Enforcement Directive[117]

This Directive is concerned with the rights of an author of a literary or artistic work which runs for the life of the author and for 70 years after his death, irrespective of the date when the work was lawfully made available to the public.

- **Directive 2006/116/EC:** on the term of protection of copyright and certain related rights (see below: Directive 2011/77/EU)

This Directive established a total harmonization of the period of protection for each type of work and each related right in the Member States – e.g. 70 years after the death of the author for works and 50 years after the event setting the time running for neighbouring rights. Furthermore, it deals with other issues, such as the protection of previously unpublished works, of critical and scientific publications and of photographic works.

- **Directive 2011/77/EU** (amending Directive 2006/116/EC – above): on the term of protection of copyright and certain related rights

This Directive extended the term of protection for performers and sound recordings to 70 years (adopted on 12 September 2011). The aim of the Directive is to bring performers' protection more in line with that already given to authors – 70 years after their death.

- **Directive 2012/28/EU:** On certain permitted uses of orphan works

The Directive sets out common rules on the digitization and online display of orphan works.

---

116 This Directive was repealed and replaced by Directive 2006/116/EC, without prejudice to the obligations of the Member States relating to the time limits for transposition into national law of the Directives, and their application.
117 Incorporates the same meaning of Article 2 of the Berne Convention.

Other changes have arisen from the Copyright (Visually Impaired Persons) Act 2002[118] and the Copyright, etc. and Trademarks (Offences and Enforcement) Act 2002,[119] and from various legislation since 1988 in areas outside copyright. EC legislation has also led to the introduction of 'publication right' and 'database right' in UK law. These changes necessitated a considerable number of consequential amendments throughout the legislation, too numerous to be indicated by footnotes in this text.

8.6.2 Orphan works

Orphan works are copyrighted works for which the owner of the copyright is unknown or cannot be found. Part 6 ('Copyright and rights in performances') of the Enterprise and Regulatory Reform Act 2013 modernized the UK's copyright regime to promote innovation in the design industry, encouraging investment in new products while strengthening copyright protections. Sections 74–78 ERRA create a new level playing field for collecting societies and the thousands of small businesses and organizations that deal with them by strengthening the existing regulatory regime. For the first time orphan works can be licensed for use. There is also a system for extended collective licensing of copyright works.

Section 76 ERRA ('Power to reduce duration of copyright in transitional cases') deals specifically with orphan works.[120] The section allows for regulations to provide for different provisions for different types of work and of different ages. This means that recent works can be treated differently to centuries-old and orphan works under existing copyright legislation (CDPA as amended). Under s 76 ERRA, no works will receive a shorter term of copyright protection than set out in Directive 2006/116/EC ('The EU Term Directive'). For example, for literary works by a known author, the standard term is life of the author plus 70 years.

Where an author is unknown (orphan works), the standard term is 70 years from the year in which the work was created or first made available. Currently, some works caught by the existing transitional provisions enjoy copyright protection until 2039 if this date falls after the standard terms set out in the EU Term Directive. This means that works such as centuries-old unpublished manuscripts in archives, libraries and museums are still in copyright. Also, recent unpublished works that were in existence when the CDPA came into force such as unpublished minutes of meetings from the twentieth century, where the author died before 1 January 1969, remain in copyright until 2039. These unpublished works enjoy a period of copyright protection longer than the standard terms set out in the EU Term Directive.

Many of these unpublished works are orphan works because it is not possible to contact the rights holder, who may be a long-lost historical figure or a beneficiary who cannot be located, to ask permission to use them. By reducing the term of copyright protection to the standard terms, many of these works will fall into the public domain and could be made accessible to the public by archiving institutions. Unpublished films and unpublished photographs are *excluded* from

---

118 This came into force on 31 October 2003; this statute removes barriers to equal access to information for people with sight loss; the UK Copyright Act (CDPA) has to be applied equally to the creation of 'accessible' copies required by a person with a visual impairment as much as to anything else, particularly in areas of activity such as education and public libraries.

119 This Act amends the criminal provisions in intellectual property law, more specifically the law relating to copyright, rights in performances, and fraudulent reception of conditional access transmissions by use of unauthorized decoders and trademarks. The Act brings about some rationalization of these criminal provisions by removing some of the differences. The three areas in which rationalization is provided by the Act are maximum penalties for certain offences in intellectual property law, police search and seizure powers relating to offences, and court orders on forfeiture of illegal material that may have been seized during investigation of offences. The Act does not make any changes to the scope of criminal offences in intellectual property law so that the type of behaviour that can give rise to an offence remains the same.

120 Section 76 amends s170 CDPA 1988 ('transitional provisions and savings') and gives the Secretary of State a power to reduce the duration of copyright in certain unpublished works which are currently subject to the transitional provisions (set out in Schedule 1 CDPA).

s 76 ERRA because of the possibility of their being exploited commercially without having been published.

As long as the use of the orphan work is licensed by an authorized scheme there is no question of any liability in the event of the copyright owner coming forward, as the use of the work will have been authorized by the licence, in the same way that it would have been under a licence from the copyright owner themselves. Similarly, the copyright owner who turns up to find that their work has been used in the belief that it was orphan would have no claim for infringement as long as the use was licensed.

Directive 2012/28/EU 'on certain permitted uses of orphan works' has been designed by the EU Commission to address specific solutions for EU Member States to deal with larger mass digitization issues, such as in the case of so-called 'out-of-commerce' works. The Directive takes into account the specifics of different types of content and different users and builds on the consensus of the relevant copyright stakeholders. The Directive calls on Member States to ensure that voluntary agreements concluded between users, rights holders and collective rights management organizations to licence the use of out-of-commerce works on the basis of the principles contained therein benefit from the requisite legal certainty in a national and cross-border context.[121]

In the case of unpublished works where the identity of the author is unknown, but where there is every ground to presume that he is a national of a country of the Berne Convention, it becomes a matter for legislation in that country to designate the competent authority which shall represent the author and shall be entitled to protect and enforce his rights in the countries of the Union.[122] For older unpublished works, the situation is more complicated, but for any literary, dramatic or musical work that was still unpublished at 1 August 1989, or which was created from 1 August 1989 to 31 December 2005, the term of protection lasts at least until the end of 2039.[123]

8.6.3 Derivative works

A derivative work is a work that is based on (derived from) another work; for example a painting based on a photograph, a collage, a musical work based on an existing piece or samples, or a screenplay based on a book. Sound recordings of, for instance, films, are known as 'derivative works', that is they derive from works which themselves are copyrighted (film soundtracks). Legally only the copyright owner has the right to authorize adaptations and reproductions of their work – this includes the making of a derivative work. The copyright owner is generally the creator of the original work, or it may be someone the creator has given copyright to (e.g. next of kin). Generally, one needs the permission of the copyright owner before making a derivative work. If copyright has expired (i.e. under present legislation this means the author died over 70 years ago), the work will be in the public domain, and may be used as a basis for a derivative work without permission.

Derivative works are covered by s 5 CDPA, meaning:

(a) a recording of sounds, from which the sounds may be reproduced; or
(b) a recording of the whole or any part of a literary, dramatic or musical work, from which sounds reproducing the work or part may be produced, regardless of the medium on which the recording is made or the method by which the sounds are reproduced or produced.[124]

---

121 A Memorandum of Understanding on key principles on the digitization and making available of out-of-commerce works was signed on 20 September 2011 by representatives of European libraries, authors, publishers and collecting societies and witnessed by the Commission.
122 Article 15(4) Berne Convention.
123 See also: s 93 CDPA for copyright to pass 'under will' with unpublished work; see also s 169 CDPA 'anonymous unpublished works'.
124 Section 5(1) CDPA.

A higher standard is applied by the courts where derivative works are concerned, particularly in the digital age of so-called 'recreative' works. These are works that have been derived from, and which purport to be perfectly accurate copies of, antecedent works that were created at an earlier point in history. They can comprise, for example, ancient religious scholarly works, old compositions or music scores and paintings. The recreative author engages in reproducing the work and it is this process which may or may not be defined as 'copying'. This will depend on what raw materials he has to copy from, what sources of information are available to him to help him accurately identify all the expressive contents of the antecedent work that need to be faithfully reproduced, and what tools and resources are at his disposal to facilitate the execution of his recreative enterprise. In what form that copying takes place will vary significantly in each case. Recreative derivative works are then identical to the antecedent works from which they were copied. The test for breach of copyright will depend on whether there is a material difference between the original works and the derivative work.[125]

8.6.4 Film

See also
Chapter 9.2.2

Since the launch of Napster, the first widely adopted file-sharing service in 1999, the sources of unauthorized music to download for free from the internet have proliferated. The advent of broadband has facilitated not only music but also film file-sharing on a much wider scale. It is now easier than ever before to download a film without paying for it or to burn music on to a CD or transfer it to a portable digital music device.

Film piracy cost the UK economy about £700 million in lost revenues from fake DVD sales and illegal downloads in 2013 (though this is a disputed figure since it assumes every sale of a fake or illegal download is a direct loss of one legal sale. Empirical studies in this area indicate this is not the case).[126] Since the film industry is a significant contributor to the UK's economy such a drain on growth is clear copyright theft, making copyright enforcement one of the most challenging areas for police and other law enforcement agencies.

As has already been pointed out, copyright is an unregistered right and arises automatically on the creation of the material, provided that the material is original and that the work must be recorded in permanent form. The copyright in a film lasts for 70 years from the end of the calendar year in which the last principal director, producer or author of the screenplay dies (or composer in the case of the film's soundtrack or recording). If the work is of unknown authorship, copyright is 70 years from the end of the calendar year of creation, or if made available to the public in that time, 70 years from the end of the year the film was first made available. Copyright does not subsist in a film (or sound recording) which is a copy taken from a previous film (or sound recording).[127]

Copyright in the film sector is particularly complex because of the many layers involved and the fact that there is no single creator of a film. The following box shows that copyright exists in each of the 'strata' of a film.

Copyrights existing in film

- **Artistic** – i.e. the set designs used in the film;
- **Dramatic** – if the film is based on a dramatic work, dance or mime material;
- **Literary** – within the source material and the original screenplay;
- **Musical** – the soundtrack of the film, including both musical score and any lyrics;

---

125 For further discussion see: Pila (2010).
126 See: Oberholzer-Gee and Strumpf (2005); see also: Fohl (2009).
127 Section 5(2) CDPA.

- **Film** – the images in the 'first fixation' of the film;
- **Sound recordings** – the physical recording of the soundtrack (now extended to 70 years;
- **Broadcasts** – for sale of the underlying material and film for other exploitation;
- **Performance** – any live interpretation of the film (now extended to 70 years);
- **Published editions** – within the typographical layout of the page for any published versions of the screenplay.

In **Norowzian v Arks Ltd and Others** (1998),[128] film-maker Mehdi Norowzian launched an unsuccessful lawsuit in the High Court Chancery Division in 1998, seeking remuneration for the use of techniques and style from his short film which he made in 1992, called Joy. Mr Justice Rattee had to first decide whether the Joy sequence constituted a 'dramatic work' within the meaning of s 1(1) CDPA in order to decide whether an advertising clip for Guinness stout breached Mr Norowzian's copyright. Mr Norowzian further claimed that his film clip of Joy fell under s 3 CDPA, as a 'work of dance or mime', which entitled him to be regarded as the maker of it and therefore the 'author' within the meaning of ss 9 and 11 of the 1988 Act.

In 1994, drinks giant Diageo had launched a successful Guinness advertising campaign on TV and cinema screens, promoting the stout with a film clip called Anticipation. Mr Norowzian claimed that Anticipation was a copy of his Joy dance sequence clip and that the makers of the Guinness advert had breached his copyright. Anticipation portrayed a man who, having been served by a barman with a pint of Guinness, waits for the frothing liquid in his glass to settle, and, while he waits, carries out a series of dance movements. Was Anticipation a copy of Joy under s 17(2) CDPA? Rattee J concluded that Joy was neither a dramatic work nor a recording of a dramatic work; therefore Anticipation did not infringe copyright.

The Court of Appeal in **Norowzian No 2** (1999)[129] clarified the earlier judgment in the first **Norowzian** action (1998) and held that a film might be purely protected as a film (i.e. a dramatic work) and be subject to copyright law, but not the artistic techniques demonstrated in the film, somewhat similar to the French idea of treating the director as 'the author' (l'auteur). While their Lordships did not criticize the original trial judge, they stated that the standards applied by the law in different contexts vary a great deal in precision, and by applying different standards and factors when weighing up what constitutes a 'dramatic' work in a film.[130] In any case s 5 CDPA did not specifically define 'film' – it merely stated that it is a 'recording on any medium from which a moving image may by any means be produced'.[131]

Copyright law makes the producer and the principal director of film joint first-owners of copyright, although in practice the director will often assign his interest in the copyright to the production company or financiers. The producer must ensure that all underlying rights in the film, including in the screenplay itself, have been acquired by assignment before they will be able to raise finance for the film. Assignments of rights must be in writing, signed by both parties (although technically they only have to be signed by the assignor) and should include rights to exploit the film (or underlying material) in every imaginable manner, including in ways that have not yet been invented at the time of the assignment.

While an idea for a film cannot be protected by copyright, the title of a film might be protected in limited circumstances. Titles most certainly qualify for trademark registration and may therefore

---

128 [1998] EWHC 315 (Ch).
129 See: **Norowzian (Mehdi) v Arks Ltd and Guinness Brewing Worldwide Limited (No 2)** [1999] EWCA Civ 3014 (CA).
130 Ibid. (Buxton LJ, Nourse LJ, Brooke LJ).
131 Section 5(1) CDPA.

be protected. It is worth mentioning that not all films are commercial productions; home movies, mobile phone pictures, camcorder images and so on can also constitute 'film', but have a shorter period of protection of 50 years from when they are made.[132] For instance, if a party films an important or traumatic event – such as the assassination of US President John F. Kennedy in Dallas in 1963 – and a news agency wants to use that film footage, they may not be able simply to use the whole film without consent.

Before a film producer seeks financial backing for his film, he must acquire the following rights, which determine the producer's right to exploit the work as a film, to:

● adapt the work in the form of a screenplay;
● reproduce the work in the form of a film;
● exhibit the work;
● broadcast the work or include it in a cable service programme;
● issue copies of the work in the form of a film to the public;
● rent or lend copies of the work in the form of a film to the public.

When commissioning an original work, the producer will need to acquire similar rights but must be aware of the agreement between PACT[133] and the Writers' Guild,[134] which sets out standard terms for such contracts.

Concerns have been raised when dealing with adaptations of plays or books in the making of a film. With either original or adapted works, the film producer needs to ensure that all *ancillary rights* are acquired;[135] these are to:

● adapt the work for television, radio or live performance on stage;
● publish the screenplay in the form of a book of the film;
● adapt the work in the form of a synopsis or treatment for promotional purposes;
● copy the work in the form of a remake, sequel or prequel to the film;
● produce a soundtrack album;
● use the copyright owner's name and likeness;
● obtain merchandizing rights.

When dealing with character merchandizing and image rights, the law regarding the protection of an individual's image is not as well developed in the UK as in the USA. English law does not recognize an explicit express personality or character right, thus protections are indirect. Where image rights (or 'rights of publicity') exist, they generally establish an individual's right to control and benefit from the commercial use of their image. In Europe, image rights might be limited by overriding human rights law, such as Article 10 ECHR, the right to freedom of expression and free speech. Image protection is available only where the image is being exploited commercially rather than for purposes of artistic expression. Since films are both artistic and commercial endeavours, there is a significant amount of grey area here. This may well change with the Intellectual Property Bill.

See below
8.12.2

The exploitation of artistic works used in films was addressed in **Lucasfilm Ltd v Ainsworth** (2011).[136] The case goes back to artistic drawings and a clay model made in 1976 of a 'military style stormtrooper helmet' by designer Ralph McQuarrie. The first *Star Wars* film (later renamed *Star Wars*

---

132 Section 13 CDPA.
133 PACT is the UK trade association representing and promoting the commercial interests of independent feature film, television, digital, children's and animation media companies: see www.pact.co.uk.
134 The Writers' Guild of Great Britain was established in 1958. Its mission is to ensure that writers of all media are properly represented. see www.writersguild.org.uk.
135 Section 21 CDPA.
136 [2011] UKSC 39 ('the *Star Wars* case').

Episode IV – A New Hope in order to provide for 'prequels' as well as sequels) was released in the United States in 1977. It was an enormous commercial success. It won an Oscar for best costume design.

The 'StarWars' appeal at the UK Supreme Court was concerned with intellectual property rights in various artefacts made for use in the film. The most important of these was the 'Imperial Stormtrooper Helmet' to which the original trial judge, Mister Justice Mann, had referred in his judgment:

> . . . one of the most abiding images in the film was that of the Imperial Stormtroopers. These were soldiers clad in white armour, including a white helmet which left no part of the face uncovered . . . The purpose of the helmet was that it was to be worn as an item of costume in a film, to identify a character, but in addition to portray something about that character – its allegiance, force, menace, purpose and, to some extent, probably its anonymity. It was a mixture of costume and prop.[137]

Andrew Ainsworth had produced over 50 stormtrooper helmets for the film in 1977, having applied 'two-dimensional sculpturing techniques' to the original design. Under UK copyright law, it was argued that under s 4(2) CDPA 1988, 'sculpture' includes a cast or model made for purposes of sculpture. The appeal in the Supreme Court raised two distinct legal issues:

(1) The definition of 'sculpture' in CDPA 1988, and, in particular, the correct approach to three-dimensional objects that have both an artistic purpose and a utilitarian function;

(2) Whether an English court may exercise jurisdiction in a claim against persons domiciled in England for infringement of copyright committed outside the European Union in breach of the copyright law of that country.

Mr Ainsworth had been selling replicas of the helmet in both Europe and the USA. Lucasfilm claimed, *inter alia*, that Mr Ainsworth had breached US copyright and trademark laws, obtaining a default judgment in California with a US$ 20m fine against him. Mr Ainsworth counterclaimed to enforce his own copyright in the helmet. The complex case did not only centre on whether the three-dimensional object was a 'sculpture' for the purposes of s 4 (2) CPDA, but also on the conflict between the UK, the US and EU law. Lucasfilm sued for $20m in 2004, arguing Mr Ainsworth did not hold the intellectual property rights and had no right to sell them – a point upheld by a US court.

Lucasfilm contended that the helmet was 'sculpture' as it had no practical function at all. Its purpose was wholly artistic, to make a visual impression on the filmgoer. That was not, however, how the trial judge and the Court of Appeal had viewed matters. Mann J found the stormtrooper helmet to be a mixture of costume and prop and that its primary function was utilitarian, namely to express an idea as part of character portrayal in the film. He held that this lacked the necessary quality of artistic creation required of a sculpture. The Supreme Court then reviewed the legislative history of the current statutory provisions in UK copyright law as to the meaning of 'sculpture'. The court held that the *StarWars* film itself was the work of art and that the helmet was utilitarian in the sense that it was an element in the process of production of the film. The Supreme Court thus held that the helmet was not a sculpture. The Supreme Court Justices also concluded that, provided there is a basis for *in personam* jurisdiction over the defendant, an English court *does* have jurisdiction to try a claim for infringement of copyright of the kind involved in the 'StarWars' action. This meant that US copyright claims were justiciable in English proceedings.[138]

---

137 [2008] EWHC 1878 (Ch) at para 121 (Mann J).
138 Lord Walker and Lord Collins gave a joint opinion, with which the other members of the court agreed.

The ruling by the UK Supreme Court in July 2011 meant that prop designer Andrew Ainsworth finally won his copyright battle against movie director George Lucas and his company over his right to sell replicas in the UK and Europe. The five-year saga, ending in the new Supreme Court, was witnessed by dozens of fans dressed in *Star Wars* costumes.

 FOR THOUGHT

> Where should a case be decided – as in the *'Star Wars'* case (above) – when intellectual property is protected in the UK but infringed in another country? Can *forum conveniens* solve problems of overlapping jurisdictions? Or would this lead to inconsistent judgments in the international sphere of copyright?

8.6.5 Broadcasts

Copyright can now subsist in terrestrial, satellite or digital transmission,[139] and, as has already been explained, one usually needs to obtain permission from the rights owners of copyright in the content of a broadcast (and the broadcast itself) to make recordings and rebroadcast these to the public. There are exceptions:

- time-shifting (the process of recording and storing data for later viewing, listening, or reading);
- fair dealing for reporting current events (such as news);
- playing or showing in public broadcasts which may include music or film.

The Educational Recording Agency (ERA) operates a licensing scheme for educational use of copyright material (i.e. recording off-air by educational establishments for non-commercial educational purposes). The ERA is also a collecting society, which helps copyright owners and performers derive royalties from the licensed use of their literary, dramatic, musical and artistic works. The Open University Worldwide licences the recording off-air by educational establishments for non-commercial educational purposes of Open University programmes.

Copyright in broadcasts exists for 50 years from the end of the calendar year in which the broadcast was made. Additionally, the Broadcasting Act 1990 states that there is a duty to provide advance information about programmes by the service provider, who, for the purposes of the Act, is 'the publisher' in relation to programming schedules.[140]

A 'broadcast' is defined by the CDPA 1988 as 'a transmission by wireless telegraphy of visual images, sounds or other information' which:

(a)   is capable of being lawfully received by members of the public; or
(b)   is transmitted for presentation to members of the public;
(c)   and references to broadcasting shall be construed accordingly.[141]

Originally the CDPA 1988 divided broadcasting into two categories: broadcasts (s 6) and cable programmes (s 7). Copyright in cable programmes was the same as in general broadcasts: 50 years from the end of the calendar year in which the cable broadcast was made.[142] As a result of changes

---

139 Sections 6(2)–(4) CDPA.
140 Section 176, Schedule 17 Broadcasting Act 1990.
141 Section 6(1) CDPA.
142 Section 14 CDPA.

in EU law this distinction no longer exists, repealing s 7 CDPA: cable programmes are no longer treated as a separate category but subsumed under the general concept of broadcasting.

8.6.6 The use of hypertext links on websites

There has been much controversy regarding whether hypertext links between websites on the internet, which allow users to surf from one site to another, are infringing copyright. In March 2000 Federal Judge Harry L. Hupp for the Central District of California issued a first ruling in favour of Tickets.com.[143] The **Ticketmaster** case[144] involved alleged copyright infringement for hypertext linking. From March 1998 to early 2000, the claimant was the only seller of tickets to certain events. The defendant provided a 'deep link' via its website by which the customer could click and link, stating 'buy this ticket from another online ticketing company' and be transferred to the claimant's website. From there, the customer could purchase tickets from the claimant. Ticketmaster sued Tickets.com claiming such hyperlinks constituted copyright infringement. In his ruling, Judge Hupp concluded that 'hypertext linking does not itself involve a violation of the US Copyright Act 1976[145] since no copying is involved'.

In the second **Ticketmaster** action in 2003,[146] the US court further dismissed several copyright infringement claims brought by Ticketmaster. These included infringement claims arising out of the temporary copying into the RAM of the defendant's computers of data from the claimant's website, including materials in which the claimant held a copyright. These materials were copied as an intermediate step to obtaining, and displaying on Tickets.com's own site, factual information contained therein. The court held that such copying was a protectable fair use given the only materials retained at the end of the process were the facts, such as concert locations, dates and times, contained in the website; as had already been ruled in the 2000 action, these facts could not be protected by copyright. Infringement claims arising out of deep linking to interior pages of the claimant's website were dismissed because, by deep linking into the claimant's site, Tickets.com was not showing or displaying the claimant's copyrighted materials (which instead were being displayed by the claimant himself). Additionally, the copyright infringement claims arising out of copying the URLs from such interior pages were dismissed because such URLs did not have sufficient originality to be copyrightable. The result was that all copyright claims were dismissed including deep linking and the copying and pasting of URLs.

For further discussion on hyperlinks see below 8.7.4

One of the first British cases involved two Scottish newspapers and the legal effect of hypertext links. In **Shetland Times v Wills** (1997),[147] both the online editors were based in the Shetland Islands. Former student rector of Edinburgh University, Dr Jonathan Wills, former editor of the *Shetland Times*, began to publish the *Shetland News* after falling out with Robert Wishart, owner of the *Shetland Times*. Dr Wills also operated a website for his newspaper, *Shetland News*, using news headlines as the means of access to its stories. From 14 October 1996, *Shetland News* incorporated in its website certain news headlines copied verbatim from the *Shetland Times* site. The *Shetland News* page included *Shetland Times* headlines as hypertext links, and by clicking on these a person would be directed to the relevant stories on the *Shetland Times* website, bypassing the front page of that site altogether.

The *Shetland Times* 'online editor' objected primarily because the links enabled browsers to bypass the front pages which contained advertising. The *Shetland Times* editor feared that the paper's advertising revenue would accordingly be reduced. The *Shetland Times* alleged copyright infringement in two separate acts:

143 Tickets.com is an online provider of entertainment, sports and travel tickets and provided hypertext links to Ticketmaster web pages for tickets not available at Tickets.com.
144 **Ticketmaster Corp. v Tickets.com, Inc.** 2000 U. Dist. Lexis 4553 (CD Ca, 27 March 2000).
145 Copyright Act 1976, Title 17 s 106.
146 **Ticketmaster Corp. v Tickets.com, Inc.**, 2003 WL 21406289 (CD Cal 7 March 2003).
147 [1997] SLT 669.

(1) Their website was a 'cable programme service' in terms of s 7 CDPA, and the use of the *Shetland Times*' headlines in the *Shetland News* site constituted an infringement of copyright under s 20 CDPA.

(2) The headlines attracted copyright protection as original literary works and by storing the headlines by electronic means the *Shetland News* had infringed copyright in them subject to s17 CDPA.

The Scottish Court of Session accepted that linking to another website does not involve copying material but simply providing a means of access to the other site. The only material which had been copied was the text of the various headlines. The court held that there was an arguable case for the subsistence of both copyrights. Its decision that a website is a 'cable programme service' was to have far-reaching consequences (beyond copyright law) for the regulation and development of the internet. But the court also ruled that the headlines could in fact attract copyright protection despite the *de minimis* rules. On these findings Lord Hamilton granted an interim interdict.[148]

The case was settled before a full proof could be heard on the facts and for the moment there is no authority to determine whether or not hypertext links constitute a restricted act for the purposes of UK copyright law. The implications of the **Shetland Times** case for website requirements are of some significance. Much of the information gathered on websites will fall into the category of compilation, either as anthologies of material or as expressions of raw data. Since most (news) websites now use hyperlinks to other sites, copyright protection is therefore doubtful. But headlines in hyperlink texts might attract copyright, as Lord Hamilton stated in the **Shetland Times** case.

That said, the **Shetland Times** case is now purely of historical value as a result of the introduction of the 'communication right' under s 20 CDPA, which protects works distributed on the World Wide Web without the need for the complexities involved in the **Shetland Times** case. On the other hand this view may contradict general copyright law, which denies copyright to titles and slogans. But the creation of a headline does involve skill and labour, particularly in 'red tops', where the reader's attention is often drawn to the story by the headline, which will thus provide entertainment and ultimately sales. The *Sun*'s famous headline, 'Freddie Starr Ate My Hamster' (13 March 1996) must have been one of the most perfect headlines and would no doubt have been classed as an 'original literary work' and thereby would have attracted copyright protection.

 FOR THOUGHT

What if the **Shetland Times** case had decided that hyperlinks did infringe copyright? How could this have affected the intrinsic nature of news online websites and the World Wide Web in general? Does the abolition of the separate concept of the cable programme and the introduction of the new communication right under s 20 CDPA (as amended) mean the *Shetland Times* case is of only historic importance?

8.6.7 Copyright in typographical arrangement

In a typical publication, copyright subsists both in the content of a work and also in the typographical arrangement and design elements of the work. Typographical arrangement covers the style,

---

148 An 'interdict' is a Scottish Court order similar to an injunction, which prohibits the person named in the order from taking any action specified in the order. An interdict can be obtained quickly on an interim basis (known as 'interim interdict'). A person who breaches an interdict is liable to be held in contempt of court. This could bring a penalty of up to two years in prison. A fine can also be imposed.

composition, layout and general appearance of a page of a published work. A 'published edition' of the whole or part of one or more literary, dramatic or musical works and the exclusive right to reproduce the typographical arrangement of the published edition is owned by the publisher.[149]

In **Newspaper Licensing Agency Ltd v Marks and Spencer Plc** (2001),[150] Lord Hoffmann traced the history of typographical copyright. He attributed it to two developments in the publishing industry, one artistic and the other technological. One of the issues in this case was whether copyright in a typographical arrangement subsisted in the arrangement of each and every item in a newspaper or other publication or in the publication as a whole. The House of Lords determined that it subsisted in the latter.

Protection for typographical arrangements was introduced after the invention of photolithography in the early twentieth century. The process of photolithography enabled commercial printing based on photographic images of a published edition of a work. The artistic development was a great improvement in typographical design, associated with the arts and crafts movement between 1880 and 1920. A new font could be registered as a design but the typographic layout of a book could not be protected, even though it may have involved considerable skill and effort. Publishers at the turn of the twentieth century were concerned that the skill and labour which had gone into the typographical design of fine editions of classical works could be appropriated by other publishers who used photolithography to make facsimile copies. At the time, publishers reproduced classic literary works that had fallen out of copyright as the duration for protection had elapsed, as for example with Gilbert and Sullivan's music scores. It is worth noting that even if the work reproduced is out of copyright – such as Shakespeare's works – a new edition with an original typographical layout will have its own new and separate copyright. Other publishers were readily able to directly and exactly copy the works and sell those copies in competition with the original publisher. Due to the state of the law at the time, the publisher had no right of recourse against the competitor who had copied their typographical arrangement.

After the Second World War, the Publishers Association[151] was instrumental in amending the Berne Convention to include copyright in typography arrangements. The UK Copyright Act of 1956 first introduced typographical copyright arrangements in s 15, which was later transposed into s 8 CDPA 1988 (s 8 defines these as 'published editions'). The legislative intention was to protect high-quality editions of classic works such as Jane Austen's novels or Beethoven's symphonies.

Before the privatisation of Her Majesty's Stationery Office (HMSO) in October 1996, the vast majority of government material was published by the Crown ('Crown Copyright'). HMSO had acted as the government publisher. When the private company, The Stationery Office Ltd (TSO), took over, still publishing the majority of all government material (such as legislation), situations arose where the copyright in the typographical arrangement of official works would rest with the publisher and the copyright in the content with the Crown. The precise layout and the look and feel of the material is often part of the intrinsic quality that gives it official status, i.e. making legislation instantly recognizable. The 'edition' is the product between the covers which a publisher offers to the public. The edition is treated as the whole of what is published for the purposes of assessing whether infringement has taken place. If a user wishes to reproduce Crown material in the above circumstances and the copyright in the typographical arrangement is held by a third party, the user will require two separate licences: first, one from the Crown covering the content; second, a licence in respect of the typographical arrangement from the Stationery Office. This additional administrative stage, with the risk that permission could be refused, could limit access to the material.

---

149 Section 9(2)(d) CDPA.
150 [2001] UKHL 38 (HL).
151 Today, the Publishers Association (PA) is the leading trade organisation serving book, journal, audio and electronic publishers in the UK. The PA assists publishers with online piracy and copyright infringement. The PA is an authoritative source of statistics on the book publishing industry.

What then is meant by a 'published edition' of a newspaper, for example? Does each typographical arrangement of an article carry its own copyright? 'Typographical arrangement of published editions' is covered under s 1(1)(c) CDPA 1988. The courts have held that the statutory definition of 'published edition' means that copyright can subsist only in the typographical arrangement of the newspaper or book edition *as a whole* and that there is no separate or additional copyright in the typographical arrangement of the individual articles (see: **Newspaper Licensing Agency Ltd v Marks and Spencer Plc**). Published editions do not have to be original but they will not be new copyright works if the typographical arrangement has been copied from existing published editions. The same goes for a book: the product usually embodies more than one copyright in the work. A book will have copyright as a literary work, but there will also be a separate copyright in its typographical arrangement, as would also be the case with printed dramatic scripts and musical scores. Copyright in the typographical arrangement of a published edition expires 25 years from the end of the year in which the edition was first published.

With the advent of digital technology, multimedia products have developed, such as *Second Life* or MMORPG (massively multiplayer online role-playing games) – new online genres in a 3D world, involving role playing, video games or web browser-based games in which a very large number of players interact with one another within a virtual game world. All players assume the role of a character and take control over many of that character's actions. This has raised difficult questions about the mixtures of copyrights and trademarks (brands) inherent in such new products. *Second Life* users enjoy almost completely unfettered freedom to create and market anything they can dream up. Current *Second Life* client software includes editing and scripting tools (e.g. to create colour, add texture, animate three-dimensional objects, introduce lighting effects etc.).[152] A database, for example, has copyright in the selection and arrangement of its contents, but this does not affect any copyright those items of content may have in their own right.

How do we know if a database is original? It is held 'original' only if, by reason of the selection or arrangement of the contents of the database, the database constitutes the author's own intellectual creation. An alphabetical listing of names would not in itself be an original structure for a database, since the author did not create the alphabet. The standard is generally taken as slightly more demanding than ordinary 'originality'. The copyright period for databases is tied first to the lifetime of the author, with the 70-year period added on after the end of the year of his death.

 FOR THOUGHT

Today, many businesses in the publishing world employ press cuttings agencies to scan international, national and regional newspapers which then provide their clients with cuttings of articles that would be of interest to them. The cuttings supplied by the agency are facsimile copies of parts of the typographical arrangement of the newspapers. Have the agencies copied the whole or a substantial part of the typographical arrangement of the published edition (the newspaper)?

8.7 Patents and trademarks

It is important to remember that media industries are affected by other IP rights in addition to copyright and performers' rights. These include so-called industrial property rights, covering

---

152 See: *Second Life* at: http://secondlife.com.

inventions or brand names, which can be patented, or product logos, which can be registered as trademarks (or if not registered, protected by the common law tort of passing off). Governments and parliaments have given creators these rights as an incentive to produce ideas that will benefit society as a whole.[153]

Under the TRIPS Agreement, industrial designs must be protected for at least 10 years to a maximum of 20 years (in the case of patents), so that owners of protected designs are able to prevent the manufacture, sale or importation of articles bearing or embodying a design which is a copy of the protected design. In fact, in the UK registered designs can be protected for a maximum period of 25 years and unregistered designs for a period of 15 years.[154] The box below shows that industrial property can be divided into two main areas.

Industrial property rights

1. **The protection of distinctive signs**; in particular trademarks (which distinguish the goods or services of one undertaking from those of other undertakings) and geographical indications (which identify a good as originating in a place where a given characteristic of the good is essentially attributable to its geographical origin). The protection of such distinctive signs aims to stimulate and ensure fair competition and to protect consumers, by enabling them to make informed choices between various goods and services. The protection may last indefinitely, provided the design in question continues to be distinctive.

2. **Types of industrial property that protect and stimulate innovation, design and the creation of technology**. In this category fall inventions, protected by patents, and industrial trade secrets. The social purpose is to provide protection for the results of investment in the development of new technology, thus giving the incentive and means to finance research and development activities. The extent of protection and enforcement of these industrial property rights varies widely around the world as IP and industrial designs are vitally important in trade and international economic relations. The World Trade Organization's TRIPS Agreement covers a series of internationally agreed trade rules for IP rights which attempt to narrow the gaps in the way these rights are protected around the world and to bring them under common international rules.

8.7.1 Definition and legislation

A patent is a title granted by the state to the creator or owner of an invention, which entitles the inventor to prevent others from manufacturing, using, selling and, in some cases, importing the technology without his permission for a specified period of years (TRIPS states 20 years for inventions). Patent protection must be available for both products and processes, in almost all fields of technology. Plant varieties must be protectable by patents or by a special system, such as the breeder's rights provided by the convention of the International Union for the Protection of New Varieties of Plants (UPOV).

To stop a patent owner from abusing his rights – for example by failing to supply the product on the market – governments can issue 'compulsory licences', allowing a competitor to produce

---

153 For further discussion see: Sterling (2008), p. 779.
154 See: Registered Designs Act 1949 (as amended) and Part III CDPA 1988.

See below
8.12.2 and
8.12.3

the product or use the process under licence. If a patent is issued for a production process, then the rights must extend to the product directly obtained from the process. Under certain conditions, alleged infringers may be ordered by a court to prove that they have not used the patented process.

Trademarks are signs that distinguish goods or services from one business from those of other businesses. Trademarks are registered to ensure that no one else has registered a mark which is the same or similar to the one which is proposed for goods or services. This is usually done by searching the Trademark Register of each country. Section 1 of the Trademarks Act 1994 defines trademarks as:

> any sign capable of being represented graphically which is capable of distinguishing goods or services of one undertaking from those of other undertakings.

A trademark may, in particular, consist of words (including personal names), designs, letters, numerals or the shape of goods or their packaging.

Section 2 of the 1994 Act defines a 'registered trademark' as:

> a property right obtained by the registration of the trademark under this Act and the proprietor of a registered trademark has the rights and remedies provided by this Act.

One can obtain a Community Trademark via the Office for Harmonization in the Internal Market (OHIM) (the 'EU Trademark Office'), which is an EU agency responsible for registering trademarks and designs that are valid in all 28 Member States (subject to some substantive requirements).[155] In trademark disputes, OHIM examines for absolute grounds of objection, for example whether a sign is capable of constituting a mark. It does not examine for existence of third-party rights, such as identical or similar earlier trademarks.

In addition, TRIPS defines what types of signs can be eligible for protection as trademarks and what the minimum rights conferred on their owners must be. Service marks must be protected in the same way as trademarks used for goods, and marks that have become well known in a particular country enjoy additional protection. A place name is sometimes used to identify a product. This 'geographical indication' identifies the product's special characteristics, such as 'Champagne, 'Scotch' or 'Roquefort', and the TRIPS Agreement contains special provisions for such (food) products. But the Agreement also states that place names must not be misused so that the public are not misled, nor should this practice lead to unfair competition by way of registration of geographical indications, such as for wines.

In relation to EU legislation, signs and trademarks may be invoked only if they are of more than 'mere local significance'.[156] 'Local' in the context of EU standards covers a wider scope than it might have under national law. An individual assessment must be made on the particularities of each case and cannot be based on geographical criteria alone. An important element is the intensity of the marketing and the volume of sales made. The amount of population concerned is also a criterion to be taken into account. The basis for protecting integrated circuit designs (or 'topographies') in the TRIPS Agreement is the Washington Treaty on Intellectual Property in Respect of Integrated Circuits (also part of WIPO). In respect of topographies the protection is available for at least 10 years.

8.7.2 Passing off

In addition to registered rights there is also in English law the possibility of bringing a common law action for passing off. Passing off is a common law tort and available remedies include injunctive

---

155 OHIM website: http://oami.europa.eu.
156 Article 8(4) of the EC Regulation 2868/95 of 13 December 1995 implementing Council Regulation 40/94 on the Community trademark (CTMR).

relief, delivery up of the offensive goods and damages to the owner of the rights or an accounting of profits by the offender. This action is most used in unfair competition claims made by rights holders in unregistered trademark cases to stop or prevent others from copying the mark, packaging or brand name and presenting the copied (or counterfeited) goods and services as if they were theirs. There is also 'reverse passing off', where a third party without authorization takes your trademark or brand name and presents it as theirs.

To establish this right of action, the claimant must show three elements, sometimes referred to as the 'classic trinity', first established by Lord Oliver of Aylmerton in the House of Lords' decision of **Reckitt & Colman Products Ltd v Borden Inc.** (1990) ('the Jif Lemon case').[157]

In the **Reckitt & Colman** ('Jif Lemon') case, the HL issued a permanent injunction preventing Borden from marketing a lemon-shaped container to sell 'squeezy' lemon juice, which the US firm had done since 1985. Reckitt & Colman had been selling 'squeezy Jif Lemon' juice since 1956. Reckitt sued Borden for passing off their product as Jif Lemon juice. Reckitt was successful in the lower courts and Borden appealed to the House of Lords. Had the Jif Lemon been a registered trademark, the case would have been much simpler to prove. For this reason Reckitt & Colman could only resort to a passing off claim in their fight against competition from the US brand 'ReaLemon'. Reckitt succeeded in the HL, and Lord Oliver spelt out the 'classic trinity' test as a starting point for all passing off actions:

(1) The claimant supplies his goods or services under a distinctive 'get-up' (e.g. brand or packaging); these goods or services have acquired goodwill or reputation in the marketplace that distinguishes the claimant's goods or services from its competitors;

(2) The defendant misrepresents his goods or services, either intentionally or unintentionally, so that the public believe or are led to believe that the offered goods or services are those of the claimant; and

(3) The claimant may suffer damage because of the misrepresentation.[158]

Choosing a name for a rock or pop band can be difficult and there are a number of cases where band members (who have since left the band) have claimed the rights in the name. Often – especially during the early stages of a band or pop group's early career – their name has not been registered as a trademark. Yet a band's name is a valuable asset and it is crucial to ensure that the name is both free to be used and agreed by all band members so that expensive legal actions can be avoided. Once a name has been decided, it is advisable to obtain protection for that name on the relevant trademarks register. This will provide the artists with the reassurance that they have the rights to that name in a particular territory, which can be used to stop infringing use and to underpin their commercial exploitation of the brand.

In 1998, UK girl band Sugababes was formed. The band members were Siobhán Donaghy, Mutya Buena and Keisha Buchanan. Over the next 12 years the band members changed several times, so much so that none of the most recent line-up, Heidi Range, Amelle Berrabah and Jade Ewen, were in the original band. On 19 November 2009 one of the original Sugababes, Mutya Buena, applied to the Office for Harmonization in the Internal Market for the right to the trademark 'Sugababes' in the European Community.[159] Buena's trademark application was opposed on 7 May 2010 by the Sugababes partnership and on 10 May by the record label, Universal-Island Records Limited. The OHIM decided that the trading name 'Sugababes' belongs to the partnership and not the individual.

A similar situation arose 10 years later when Holly Johnson of the 1980s band Frankie Goes to Hollywood attempted to register the mark 'Frankie Goes to Hollywood' as a Community Trademark

157 [1990] 1 WLR 491.
158 Ibid., at para 880.
159 CTM Application No 8698854 'Sugababes' in the name of Mutya Buena.

(see below). The application was successfully opposed by the four other members of the band on the basis of earlier propriety rights arising from their use of the name in the UK. Relying on Lord Oliver's classic trinity test to establish passing off, the UK Intellectual Property Office (UK-IPO)[160] and OHIM[161] (parallel UK and European actions) decided the rights to the name were owned equally by all original band members and no one band member had the right to claim exclusivity to that name.

❖ KEY CASE | *Gill v Frankie Goes To Hollywood Ltd* [2008] ETMR 4[162]

Precedent

To succeed in a 'passing off action' the proprietor of a non-registered trademark must demonstrate the classic trinity test (as established in the HL action of the 'Jif Lemon' case (see above):

- ❖ the claimant supplies his goods or services under a distinctive 'get-up' (e.g. brand or packaging); these goods or services have acquired goodwill or reputation in the marketplace that distinguishes the claimant's goods or services from its competitors;
- ❖ the defendant misrepresents his goods or services, either intentionally or unintentionally, so that the public believe or are led to believe that the offered goods or services are those of the claimant; and
- ❖ the claimant may suffer damage because of the misrepresentation.

Facts

Frankie Goes to Hollywood (FGTH) was a band formed in Liverpool in the early 1980s, consisting originally of band members Holly Johnson (vocals), Paul Rutherford (vocals; keyboard), Peter Gill (drums), Mark O'Toole (bass guitar) and Gerard (Jed) O'Toole (guitar). The group's debut single 'Relax' was banned by the BBC in November 1983 as 'obscene' and topped the singles charts for five weeks. T-shirts bearing the slogan 'Frankie says . . .' became very popular. In 1984, Jed O'Toole left the band and was replaced by Brian Nash. After a gig at Wembley Arena in 1987 Holly Johnson left the group, citing musical estrangement. The band split up and the name FGTH was not in use until 2003 when the five members were approached by a TV show, *Bands Reunited*, with a view to reforming in order to perform on the programme for a charity concert for the Prince's Trust in 2004. Holly Johnson refused to take part or rejoin the band. He had embarked on a solo career.

In January 2004, Holly Johnson registered a company under the name Frankie Goes To Hollywood Ltd ('Frankie') and sought to register the words as an EU Community trademark[163] in respect of goods and services in Classes 9, 16, 25 and 41.[164]

---

160 UK-IPO 'Frankie Goes to Hollywood', O/140/07 dated 25 May 2007.
161 OHIM Opposition No B849 069 **Gill v Frankie Goes to Hollywood Ltd** [2008] ETMR 4.
162 [2008] ETMR 4 (Case B 849 069). Office for Harmonisation in the Internal Market (OHIM) (Opposition Division) 27 July 2007.
163 The application claims priority from UK trademark application no.2359948 filed on 2 April 2004.
164 The classifications included, *inter alia*, in class 9: apparatus for recording & transmission; CDs; CD-ROMs; DVDs; computer software; mouse mats; mobile phone accessories; sunglasses; in class 16: printed publications; periodicals; books; magazines etc.; calendars; in class 25: clothing; footwear; headgear; belts etc. and in class 41: the provision of online publications and digital music (not downloadable) from the internet; audio and video recording services; live concerts; TV & radio; photography; interactive information provided online from computer databases or the internet.

The opponents (Peter Gill, Mark O'Toole, Jed O'Toole and Paul Rutherford) filed an opposition to this application, which was based on earlier rights resulting from their previous use of the name Frankie Goes to Hollywood in relation to goods listed in the application. It was the contention of the opponents that, by virtue of the identity of the applied-for trademark with the opponents' earlier unregistered name, they were entitled to common law protection under the law of passing off. Additionally, the opponents noted a great similarity of the goods and services in respect of which registration was sought and the appearance of the original FGTH goods, and that there was likelihood of confusion between the new trademark applied for and the earlier mark.

The application to oppose the new trademark registration was filed under s 5(4) Trademarks Act 1994, which states that a trademark shall not be registered if its use is liable to be prevented by the law of passing off. The Trademark Registry upheld the opposition and the hearing officer gave the following reasons:

(1) While the director of the applicant company (Holly Johnson) was credited as being the originator of the name, this in itself did not confer upon him, as inventor of the name, any rights in respect of its use as a trademark.

(2) The band was seen as a partnership at will, in respect of which any goodwill generated by the five members of the band during the 1980s in connection with commercial activities would vest in the partnership itself, rather than giving each member, or any individual member, a discrete right of ownership over the partnership assets in order to enforce that right against other members. This position was maintained when the band dissolved in 1987 as there were no formal arrangements made as to the distribution of partnership assets at that time.

(3) The reformed band, performing without the director of the applicant company (Holly Johnson) in 2004, constituted a new partnership.[165]

Decision
The Opposition Division of the OHIM ruled that the opposition would be upheld. Under Article 8(4) of Regulation 40/94, the opponents' mark must be used in the course of trade. Even though Johnson had invented the name, the UK Intellectual Property Office and OHIM decided (in the parallel actions) the rights to the name were owned equally by all original band members and no one band member had the right to claim exclusivity to that name.

This meant that Holly Johnson could not use the original band name for his new company (cited authorities: *SAXON Trademark* (2003);[166] *Harrods Ltd v Harrodian School* (1996);[167] *Barlow Clowes International Ltd (In Liquidation) v Eurotrust International Ltd* (2005)[168]).

Analysis
The main issue in *Frankie Goes to Hollywood* centred on the law of passing off – particularly of a non-registered trademark. Though Holly Johnson had invented the name, the OHIM ruled that the mere act of inventing a name does not, in itself, bring

---

165 For further discussion see: Keeling, Llewelyn and Mellor (2010).
166 [2003] EWHC 295 (Ch).
167 [1996] RPC 697.
168 [2005] UKPC 37.

the inventor any rights. It then followed that the use of the non-registered trademark Frankie Goes to Hollywood was 'of more than mere local significance', in that the original band members could show that the original band name Frankie Goes to Hollywood was very successful both in the UK and in other European countries between 1984 and 1987; moreover, that the band's music continues to be very popular. It was for this reason that the OHIM prevented the registration of a new trademark in the very same name.[169]

The UK-IPO reviewed its practice in 2004 and allowed partnerships to be recorded as owners of trademarks on the register. This change of practice came about after a High Court dispute over rights to the trademark SAXON, the name of a 1970's heavy metal group. In **Byford v Oliver & Dawson** (2003),[170] an agreement over ownership of the band name SAXON was not in place and the court held that a 'partnership at will' arose with the name being an asset of the partnership to be split equally amongst the band members.

The original band members of Saxon, Graham Oliver, Steven Dawson and Peter 'Biff' Byford, formed the band in the 1970s. Steven Dawson left the band in 1985. Graham Oliver left in 1995. Biff Byford continued as a member throughout its various manifestations. Subsequently Steven Dawson and Graham Oliver played in other heavy metal bands using a variety of names which included one or both of their names as well as the word 'Saxon'. In 1999 Oliver and Dawson registered 'SAXON' as a trademark, maintaining they had exclusive rights in the name. They tried to prevent Biff Byford from using the name. Byford then applied to the Trademark Registry to have the mark declared invalid, due to 'bad faith' under s 3(6) Trade Marks Act 1994. He brought a passing off action to stop the other two from misrepresenting themselves as Saxon under s 5(4) of the 1994 Act.

The Court of Chancery held that the application had been made in bad faith by Oliver and Dawson. The court further established the principle that the name and goodwill of a partnership are owned 'by the partnership' and not the individual partners or band members. This set a new precedent. This means if a band member leaves, and the remaining band members continue in the group, they cannot continue using the band name in the absence of an agreement in contract. The judge concluded that a band would be properly advised to enter into a partnership agreement and register the band name as a trademark in the event of a band member leaving the group.

8.7.3 Criminal provisions for IP and trademark infringement

As has already been discussed above, the owner of a copyright, patent or other form of intellectual property right can issue a licence for someone else to produce or copy the protected trademark, work, invention or design. At the same time, the TRIPS Agreement recognizes that the terms of a licensing contract could restrict competition or impede technology transfer. It says that, under certain conditions, governments have the right to take action to prevent anti-competitive licensing that abuses intellectual property rights. It also says that governments must be prepared to consult each other on controlling anti-competitive licensing.

One such lawsuit involving unfair competition and trademark infringement[171] concerned the famous American-born Greek opera soprano Maria Callas, who died on 16 September 1977. Her surviving estate wanted to register her name as a trademark posthumously for her special jewellery,

---

169 [2008] ETMR 4 at 97–99.
170 [2003] EWHC 295 ('the Saxon trademark case') (Ch).
171 **Re. MC MC S.r.l**, Application No. 79022561 (26 September 2008), US Trademark Office.

which she wore for her performances of *Tosca* in 1956 at the New York Metropolitan Opera. Made of nearly 200 tear-shaped Swarovski crystals, worth approximately $85,000, the original jewellery set – tiara, earrings and necklace – was created specifically for Callas by the Atelier Marangoni in Milan, Italy. The Italian company wanted to register their jewellery as the 'Maria Callas' collection but her surviving estate opposed the trademark application. The US Trademark Office found – following a ruling in the highest Italian court – that anyone could now use the trademark label 'Maria Callas'.

In general, intellectual property – including industrial property – laws give private rights that can be enforced by the owners of the rights using civil remedies. Part 3 of the TRIPS Agreement states that governments have to ensure that IP rights can be enforced under their laws and that the penalties for infringement are robust enough to deter further violations. Procedures must be fair and equitable, and not unnecessarily complicated or costly. They should not entail unreasonable time limits or unwarranted delays. Applicants involved should be able to ask a court to review an administrative decision or to appeal a lower court's ruling.

The TRIPS Agreement describes in some detail how enforcement should be handled, including rules for obtaining evidence, provisional measures, injunctions, damages and other penalties. It states that courts have the right, under certain conditions, to order the disposal or destruction of pirated or counterfeit goods, covering wilful trademark counterfeiting or copyright piracy on a commercial level. All governments that have signed up to TRIPS have agreed to ensure that owners' IP rights must receive the assistance of police, trading standards and customs authorities to prevent imports of counterfeit and pirated goods.

Increasingly, states are resorting to criminal law to enforce civil rights. This means that imprisonment is more likely in repeat offence cases. But this also means that public enforcement bodies, such as local authority trading standards, will have to bear the costs of enforcement. The key issue in a criminal action (unlike in civil cases) is that *mens rea* will be required in that the prosecution will have to show that the defendant knew or ought to have known he was committing an infringing act beyond all reasonable doubt.

The main objective of the Copyright, etc. and Trademarks (Offences and Enforcement) Act 2002 is to remove some of the discrepancies between the nature of IP offences. Maximum penalties under the 2002 Act include an unlimited fine and/or up to 10 years' imprisonment to reflect the seriousness of these crimes and to bring the penalties into line with existing ones for similar trademark offences.[172]

The following four areas of IP law are covered by the Copyright, etc. and Trademarks (Offences and Enforcement) Act 2002 concerning criminal offences in relation to the making for sale or hire or dealing with the following types of illegal material:

- Copies of material that is protected by copyright, such as music, films and computer software that have been made without the authorization of the copyright owner, i.e. infringing or pirate copies, and articles that are specifically designed or adapted for making infringing copies of copyright material.[173]
- Copies of recordings of performances that have been made without the authorization of the performer(s) or a person having recording rights in the performance, i.e. illicit or bootleg recordings.[174]
- Devices or other apparatus, including software, that allow people to access encrypted transmissions without paying the normal fee for their reception, i.e. unauthorized decoders for conditional

---

172 Section 1 of the 2002 Act increased the penalties for criminal offences of ss 107(4)(b), s 198(5)(b) and 297A(2) of the *Copyright, Designs and Patents Act 1988*.
173 See the offences in s 107(1) and (2) in Part I CDPA.
174 See the offences in s 198(1) in Part II CDPA.

access transmissions where the transmissions can be either broadcasts, including satellite broadcasts, cable programme services or information society services.[175]

● Goods, packaging or labels bearing a trademark that has been applied without the consent of the trademark owner, i.e. counterfeit goods, and articles that are specifically designed or adapted for making unauthorized copies of a trademark for use on such goods and other material.[176]

The 2002 Act provides maximum penalties for the above-named offences and grants additional police search and seizure powers relating to these offences; the act also makes provision for court orders on forfeiture of illegal material that may need to be seized during investigation of offences. Section 2 of the 2002 Act allows the police to obtain search warrants for all the offences in s 107(1) and (2) CDPA, including those only triable in the magistrates' courts.[177] These provisions are in addition to any powers available to the police as a result of the Police and Criminal Evidence Act 1984 (PACE).[178]

Section 3 reproduces in Part I of the Copyright, Designs and Patents Act 1988 provisions corresponding to those in ss 97 and 98 Trademarks Act 1994, allowing forfeiture of infringing goods. Section 3 provides forfeiture provisions for goods infringing copyright, i.e. infringing copies and articles specifically designed or adapted for making such copies. Section 97 relates to forfeiture in England, Wales and Northern Ireland; s 98 is a modified version relating to forfeiture in Scotland.

Section 4 of the 2002 Act introduced forfeiture provisions, very similar to those in s 3, into Part II CDPA in respect of goods that infringe rights in performances, i.e. illicit recordings. Section 5 of the 2002 Act introduced forfeiture provisions, very similar to those in s 3, into Part VII CDPA in respect of devices that permit fraudulent reception of conditional access transmissions, i.e. unauthorized decoders used to access transmissions such as satellite television without payment. Section 6 provides for search warrant and seizure provisions corresponding to those that are introduced or amended by s 2 for Parts I, II and VII CDPA 1988 for the offences in s 92 Trademarks Act 1994 relating to counterfeit goods and articles for making them.[179]

See Below
8.12.2

In Scotland, the forfeiture provisions apply where a person has been convicted of one of these offences or on application by the Procurator Fiscal. The court can order destruction of goods or release to another person with conditions. Broadly similar provision is introduced by s 3 into Part I of the 1988 Act. The Act does not make any changes to the scope of criminal offences in IP law, so that the type of behaviour that can give rise to an offence remains the same.

The proprietor of a registered trademark can only succeed in a claim for trademark infringement under Article 5(1) of EU Directive 89/104 if he satisfies six conditions:

(1) There must have been the use of a mark or sign by a third party.
(2) That use must have been in the course of trade.
(3) Such use must have been without the consent of the trademark proprietor.
(4) The allegedly infringing use involved the use of a mark or sign which was identical to the trademark.
(5) That mark was used in relation to goods or services which were identical to those for which the trademark was registered.
(6) That use affected, or was liable to affect, the functions of the trademark, in particular its essential function of guaranteeing to consumers the origin of the goods or services.

---

175 See the offences in s 297A in Part VII CDPA.
176 See the offences in s 92 Trademarks Act 1994.
177 The equivalent provision in s 200 of Part II of the 1988 Act is applied to all the offences in s 198(1) by this section. Equivalent search warrant provisions are introduced by s 2 for the offences in s 297A of Part VII of the 1988 Act.
178 The existing search warrant provisions under Part II of PACE (Powers of Entry, Search and Seizure, ss 9–19) allow a Magistrate (or in Scotland, a Sheriff) to grant a warrant where information/evidence on oath leaves him satisfied that there are reasonable grounds for believing that an offence has been or is about to be committed and there is evidence of this on the premises.
179 This section also extends to the Isle of Man, since the Trademarks Act 1994 also does.

In summary, the Trade Marks Act 1994 (as amended) takes account of the current needs of industry and commerce and has aligned UK law with that of other countries, both in the European Union and internationally. Sections 9 ('Rights conferred by registered trade mark') and 10 ('Infringement of registered trade mark') Trade Marks Act 1994 are the most relevant sections, dealing with the processing of trademark applications and infringement. The Copyright, Designs and Patents Act 1988 made the forgery of a trademark a criminal offence.

8.7.4 E-commerce and online auction providers

Are online providers and auction 'houses' such as eBay liable for IP infringements committed by their users? This was the question raised by the Chancery Court with reference to the European Court of Justice (ECJ) in the landmark case of **L'Oréal v eBay** (2009).[180] The central questions in this case were: did eBay (Europe) itself commit infringements by using trademarks in relation to infringing goods? Or was eBay simply a 'hosting' ISP and therefore not liable for copyright infringement as a mere auction site?

What does the E-commerce Directive[181] say about the legal aspects of hosting (auction) websites and their liability towards either counterfeited or IP-infringing goods? Key provisions of the E-commerce Directive are summarized in Article 14 ('Hosting'), which states:

> . . . where an information society service is provided that consists of the storage of information provided by a recipient of the service, member states shall ensure that the service provider is not liable for the information stored at the request of a recipient of the service, on condition that:
>
> (a) the provider does not have actual knowledge of illegal activity or information and, as regards claims for damages, is not aware of facts or circumstances from which the illegal activity or information is apparent; or
>
> (b) the provider, upon obtaining such knowledge or awareness, acts expeditiously to remove or to disable access to the information.

The auction website eBay is an 'online marketplace', operating some 21 websites in eight languages, which display listings of goods for sale posted by users and which enable buyers to purchase such goods from sellers.[182] The databases on which live listings are stored are not divided by country, but are housed in four locations in the United States. eBay's software platform comprises about 30 million lines of code divided into some 237 sub-systems. Most of the software is bespoke. eBay Europe was launched in October 1999, and today can count around 16 million active listings on the site at any one time. An average of around 1.3 million listings is posted each day, rising to a peak of over 4.5 million at Christmas. eBay operates both auction-style and fixed-price listings.

The largest online auction provider in the world, eBay has appeared as a defendant five times before four different national courts for its role in facilitating the sale of counterfeit products on its site. In the French court, eBay was held liable in three different lawsuits for 'committing gross negligence' by not fulfilling its obligation to make sure that its activity did not generate illegal acts.

---

180 [2009] EWHC 1094; [2009] ETMR 53 (Ch) 22 May 2009.
181 EC Council Directive 2000/31.
182 eBay Inc was founded in 1995 under the name AuctionWeb. It changed its name in 1997. It was listed on the NASDAQ stock exchange in 1998. In 2008 eBay Inc's revenue was $8.54 billion and its income was $1.78 billion. At the time of the L'Oréal court case in 2009, eBay had over 300 million registered users, of which about 84 million were active. More than 125 million active listings appear on eBay's websites at any given time. On average about 7.3 million new listings are posted each day, although this can rise to 12 million new listings a day.

The Paris Grand Tribunal imposed an obligation on eBay because it was held to not merely provide a hosting service but also to be acting as a broker and was therefore subject to the common regime of civil liability (see: *L'Oréal SA v eBay France SA* (2009)[183]).

The French judgment stands in marked contrast to that of the Belgian court. In the Lancôme case, the role of eBay was seen as being a mere 'host', with no obligation to monitor the information hosted on its website and therefore no liability for any IP infringement or any other form of illegal nature that the online auction house was not aware of. If it did become aware of any illegal acts, the duty was to promptly remove the information from the site (see: **Lancôme parfums et beauté et Cie S.N.C. v eBay International AG, eBay Europe SARL and SPRL** (2008)[184]).

In a similar action, the US court, applying the Digital Millennium Copyright Act of 1998 (DMCA)[185] legislation, limited eBay's responsibility, and made the site liable only if eBay had specific knowledge of any trademark infringements. If the site did have knowledge of any infringement, its responsibility was confined to taking down the objectionable items. The court did not say that eBay was under a general obligation to pre-emptively remove items based on generalized knowledge that they might host counterfeit goods (see: **Tiffany (NJ) v eBay Inc** (2008)[186]).

The decision by the German Bundesgerichtshof in 2008 is probably the most interesting one; it sits between the French, Belgian and US extremes. In the **Rolex Counterfeit Watches** case, the Bundesgerichtshof classified an online auction provider as an 'interferer' and therefore subject to the duty to examine, thereby preventing infringements. This means the online auction house must, once it is informed of a clear trademark infringement, promptly remove the infringing item from its website and ensure that similar trademark infringements will not reoccur (including repetitions of infringement of the same brand name) (see: Bundesgerichtshof judgments in the Rolex cases against ricardo.de AG in: **Internet Auction III** (2008); **Internet Auction II** (2007); **Re Internet Auctions of Counterfeit Watches** (2005)[187]).

It could be said the German ruling is the fairest in allocating responsibilities between the trademark owners and online auction providers. The Belgian and US decisions place all the responsibilities of combating IP infringement on the trademark owner whereas the German decision imposes on the online auction provider a duty, upon notification of a clear trademark infringement, to use reasonable measures to remove the infringements and to employ subsequent filtering checks.

L'Oréal v eBay (2009) became the test case in the UK (see below), where the Chancery Court referred the 'e-commerce' harmonization questions to the European Court of Justice with no clear satisfactory solution. The English High Court held that eBay was not liable, which was generally reported in the UK media as a victory for eBay. As the ECJ ruling in the case has been inconclusive, there is no answer to third-party liability in relation to trademark infringement relating to linked sites and link marks online. Given that the key aspects of European trademark law are supposed to have been harmonized by an EC Directive,[188] and that there is also an EC Directive harmonizing the liability of ISPs,[189] European courts ought to be in a position to give the same answers to the questions raised. To date they have not.

---

183 (2009) (RG 07/11365) Tribunal de grande instance, Paris, judgment of 13 May 2009) (unreported).

184 (2008) (A/07/06032) Belgium, Comm. Bruxelles, 28 May 2008.

185 The Digital Millennium Copyright Act 1998 (DMCA – Pub. L. No. 105–304, 112 Stat. 2860) was signed into law by President Clinton on 28 October 1998. The legislation implements two 1996 World Intellectual Property Organization Treaties: the WIPO Copyright Treaty and the WIPO Performances and Phonograms Treaty.

186 (2008) (No.04 Civ. 4607) Southern District of New York, 14 July 2008; **Tiffany (NJ) Inc v eBay Inc** 576 F Supp 2d 463 (SDNY 2008).

187 The Bundesgerichtshof held that, assuming they had used the signs in the course of trade, the sellers had infringed Rolex's trademarks; but that Ricardo had neither infringed the trademarks nor participated in infringement by the users. Accordingly, Rolex's claim for damages was dismissed.

188 EC Directive 2006/116 on the 'Term of Protection of Copyright and Certain Related Rights Enforcement Directive' of 12 December 2006 ('the harmonization Directive').

189 Directive 2000/31 on certain legal aspects of information society services, in particular electronic commerce, in the Internal Market Arts 13, 14, 15 [2000] OJ L178/1.

FOR THOUGHT

Which legal position should be adopted? The German Bundesgerichtshof decision in the Rolex cases, which limits the liability of an online auction provider by exempting it from trademark infringements which cannot be detected by reasonable means? Or the French Tribunal de grande instance ruling, which places the entire responsibly on the online auction house and requires the provider to filter out items based on mere suspicion of an IP infringement?

8.7.5 The *L'Oréal v eBay* case[190]

In this action the Chancery Court (with reference to the European Court of Justice) had to determine whether the sellers had sold goods which infringed the claimants' trademarks in that they were:

(i)   counterfeit;
(ii)   non-European Economic Area (EEA) goods;
(iii) tester products that were not intended for resale; or
(iv)   products which, being unboxed, would have damaged the reputation of claimants' trademarks.

The UK court asked the ECJ to determine whether the defendants (eBay) and linked companies were jointly liable for the infringements committed by their users in selling infringing goods (i.e. joint tortfeasors). The claimants were all cosmetics companies bringing claims for trademark infringement against three defendant companies which facilitated the online auction and sale of goods, as well as seven individual sellers of cosmetic products which, the claimants maintained, infringed a number of Community trademarks and UK trademarks of which they were the proprietors.[191]

L'Oréal made three principal claims against eBay Europe. The first was that eBay Europe was jointly liable for the infringements allegedly committed by the fourth to tenth defendants (companies which traded in L'Oréal and Lancôme products online). L'Oréal's second claim was that eBay Europe was primarily liable for use of the link marks (a) in sponsored links on third-party search engines and (b) on the site, in both cases insofar as such use was in relation to infringing goods. The third claim was that of the products purchased via eBay, 17 were adduced in evidence, with L'Oréal claiming that two of them were counterfeit and that the remaining 15 had not been marketed in the European Economic Area by them (they were consignments for the American market). L'Oréal further argued that the products were unboxed and simply 'testers'; further that the defendants had employed copyright-protected images and text in their listings of goods for sale on the eBay sites without their permission.

L'Oréal also argued that hyperlinks (link marks) at the top of the sponsored link led to a page from the eBay Express site showing a search for 'matrix hair' and 'magie noire' which brought up 48 items from international sellers and that all of these were to infringing goods.

See above 8.6.6

The basis of this allegation was that the country or region stated was the United States in all cases and the items were priced in sterling. L'Oréal contended that, so far as the auction-style listings were concerned, eBay did in fact conduct an auction. eBay disputed this and L'Oréal accepted

---

190 *L'Oréal SA v eBay International AG* [2009] EWHC 1094 (Ch).
191 L'Oréal divided the trademarks into two groups for the purposes of their claims. The first group, referred to as 'the Lancôme Marks', consisted of Lancôme, Renergie, Definicils and Amor Amor. The second group, referred to as 'the Link Marks', consisted of Definicils together with the remaining trademarks not included in the first group.

at least that eBay's activities differ from those of traditional auctioneers. L'Oréal claimed that each of the fourth to tenth defendants infringed one or more of the trademarks by using signs identical to the trademarks of goods to those for which the trademarks are registered. These claims all concerned the Lancôme marks.[192]

Providing the online facility for sellers to sell infringing products would make eBay and the other defendants joint tortfeasors. In their defence, eBay argued that they had set up systems and policies which discouraged the sale of infringing products and which enabled trademark owners, by notifying them, to have the webpages on which allegedly infringing products were sold taken down.[193]

eBay also argued that they were merely fulfilling the function of an ISP ('hosting site') and were not involved in the sale of infringing goods, relying on Article 14 of Directive 2000/1 (the E-commerce Directive). eBay submitted that, as a matter of law, eBay Europe was under no duty or obligation to prevent third parties from infringing L'Oréal's (or anyone else's) registered trademarks. The online trading house also argued that it attempts to prevent or at least minimize infringements, in particular through the VeRO programme which filters infringing goods, such as counterfeit watches by Rolex. eBay further submitted that the companies procuring the (allegedly counterfeited) goods (the fourth to tenth defendants) had sold a large proportion of items previously via eBay without complaint from the cosmetic companies. Counsel for eBay Europe submitted that in reality L'Oréal's claim of joint tortfeasorship was a thinly disguised attack on eBay's business model.

In summary, Mr Justice Arnold's judgment in the **L'Oréal v eBay** case simply means that eBay was not a joint tortfeasor for the sale of counterfeit products online. The judge's reasoning was that under English common law, a defendant would only be a joint tortfeasor if he intentionally procures and shares a common design. Mere knowledge and involvement, including facilitating the infringement, was insufficient to render one liable as a joint tortfeasor.[194]

An important point raised in **L'Oréal v eBay** was that of sponsored links and 'link marks'. If a user clicks on a search engine such as Google using one of the link marks, this will cause a sponsored link to the site to be displayed. The user will then be taken to a display of search results on the site for products by reference to the link mark. eBay Europe, for example, chooses the keywords based on the activity on the site. The sponsored link (to a business) pays a certain amount for each click-through of each keyword, and in turn, receives revenue via eBay.

It was this aspect which was referred to the ECJ by the UK Chancery Court for a preliminary ruling. The question centred on the scope of infringement of Article 5(1) of EC Directive 89/104, which approximates the laws of the Member States relating to trademarks. The problem is that the Directive does not specifically define the use of a trademark by third parties; it only covers the use of a trademark sign in relation to the proprietor's goods.

In this respect, the ECJ did not come to a conclusive decision. It held that EU trademark law had not been completely harmonized in respect of copyright and trademark infringement via hyperlinks and link marks. Since there has been no pronouncement by the ECJ on this issue to date, there is no clear answer about sponsored links, including the main third-party search engines such as Google, MSN and Yahoo and purchased keywords link marks triggered by eBay.

What was really at the heart of the **L'Oréal** case? Was it not – as counsel for eBay Europe argued – an attack on eBay's business model? Mr Justice Arnold agreed with counsel on this, stating that this claim came close to the heart of the issue. It is a fact that eBay (and other online auction houses)

---

192 The complaint against the fourth defendant concerns advertisements and offers for sale for 'Lancôme Maquicomplet Concealer Light Buff RRP £18.50', sold on 23 November 2006; 'Lancôme Renergie Microlift Active Redefining Treatment', sold on 23 November 2006; and 'Lancôme Definicils Full Size Black Mascara Waterproof', sold on 5 December 2006.
193 eBay Europe pleaded defences under ss 10(6) and 11(2) Trademarks Act 1994 (though these were not pursued at trial).
194 **L'Oréal** [2009] EWHC 1094 (Ch) at 381–382 (Arnold J).

have created a new form of trade and a business model which is highly successful. But it also carries with it a higher risk of infringement than more traditional methods of trade. That said, copyright and industrial property rights are at increased risk and it could be argued that the high profits which eBay (and others) make from their sites oblige them to ensure that IP rights are not infringed.

The UK court ruling was that, as a matter of common law, eBay Europe was under no legal duty or obligation to prevent infringement of third parties' registered trademarks. Since Article 11 of the EC Enforcement Directive is not clear on third-party duty obligation with regard to future infringements as a result of online auction site operation, there is, as yet, no liability for past infringements on the ground of joint tortfeasorship. In view of the current uncertainty over this area of law, the ECJ's response to the **L'Oréal** case does not provide *acte clair*.

 FOR THOUGHT

Are eBay (or similar online auction websites) and search engines like Google under a duty to prevent third parties from infringing IP because they are under a duty not to participate in a common design to infringe? Should eBay and Google – having participated in hyper-linked sites (link marks) – prevent third parties from infringement? Discuss with reference to EU and UK law.

8.8 Cross-border measures for copyright infringement

What are the cross-border measures that now exist within and outside the EU? HM Revenue and Customs (HMRC) monitors and prosecutes misuse of intellectual property rights where goods are entering the UK from outside the European Union. Since November 2012 HMRC has used effective enforcement methods in co-operation with Trading Standards[195] to confiscate (and destroy) infringing items at the point of entry into the UK.[196] Most of the IP-infringing commodities consist of counterfeit and pirated goods, patent-infringing goods and national or EU plant variety rights-infringing goods. Most custom-related actions are in relation to goods infringing trademarks ('Grey Market goods').[197]

Though the original author of a piece of work is protected by the UK Copyright Act (CDPA), some would argue that the copyright legislation remains essentially weak in spite of additional European 'harmonization' laws because there are enforcement problems, particularly with digital reproduction. Some major commercial firms may argue, however, that the EU harmonization laws are now too strong.[198] It is essential that all parties seek proper legal advice prior to entering into contract negotiations involving intellectual property rights. Naturally, each party will respectively seek to acquire the ownership rights that will often be the central focus of negotiations (known as the 'deal-breaker').[199]

How has the European Court of Justice (now also Court of Justice of the European Union – CJEU) dealt with cases when considering copyright infringement in other Member States with differing jurisdictions? The German Federal Supreme Court (Bundesgerichtshof) referred this question in the **HI HOTEL HCF** case (Case C-387-12 of 19 October 2012) and asked the CJEU to

---

195 Under ss 107 and 198 CDPA.
196 Regulation 1383/2003/EC; Regulation 1891/2004/EC as amended by Commission Regulation (EC) No 1172/2007.
197 Trademarks Act 1994; Trademarks (Customs) Regulations 1994 (no. 2625).
198 For further details see: Cornish (2013).
199 For further discussion see: Miller, Vandome and McBrewster (2009).

consider whether a court in one Member State has jurisdiction to rule both on a copyright infringement that occurred in its Member State, and also on the 'contributing act' to that copyright infringement which took place in the territory of a second Member State by a person who assisted in the principal infringement on the domestic territory. The Bundesgerichtshof specifically asked for interpretation of Article 5(3) of Regulation 44/2001, which sets out that, for matters relating to tort, a person domiciled in a Member State may be sued in another Member State if that is where the 'harmful event' (in this case the copyright infringement) occurred. The key question in the context of a cross-border copyright infringement is therefore where the 'harmful event' occurs.

A similar reference occurred from the French appellate court (Cour de cassation)[200] in **Peter Pinckney v KDG Mediatech AG** (Case C-170/12)[201] as to the question of where the 'harmful event' occurs. Peter Pinckney, living in Toulouse (France), claimed to be the author, composer and performer of 12 songs recorded by the group Aubrey Small on a vinyl record. When he discovered that those songs had been reproduced without his authority on a compact disc (CD), pressed in Austria by Mediatech, then marketed by UK companies Crusoe or Elegy through various internet sites, accessible from his residence in Toulouse, Mr Pinckney brought an action, on 12 October 2006, against Mediatech before the Tribunal de grande instance de Toulouse (Regional Court, Toulouse) seeking compensation for damage sustained on account of the infringement of his copyrights. Mediatech challenged the jurisdiction of the French courts, arguing that the CDs had been pressed in Austria, where its headquarters is situated, at the request of a UK company which marketed the CDs via an internet site. Thus, it claimed, the only courts having jurisdiction were the courts of the place of the defendant's domicile, which is in Austria, or the courts of the place where the damage was caused, that is the place where the alleged infringement was committed, in the United Kingdom.

By a judgment of 21 January 2009, the Cour d'appel de Toulouse (Court of Appeal, Toulouse) held that the Tribunal de grande instance de Toulouse lacked jurisdiction on the ground that the defendant was domiciled in Austria and the place where the damage occurred could not be situated in France, and that there was no need to examine the liability of Mediatech and Crusoe or Elegy in the absence of any allegation of collusion between them and Mediatech. Eventually, the Cour de cassation (Court of Cassation) decided to stay its proceedings and to refer the following questions to the CJEU for a preliminary ruling: it asked the CJEU whether Article 5(3) of the Brussels Regulation meant that, in a case of online copyright infringement, the claimant can issue proceedings in *any* country where the site can be viewed, or whether the content of the website had to be targeted at that jurisdiction or have some other connection with the jurisdiction; and furthermore, whether it made any difference if the infringing content was in a physical medium.

Specifically, the questions referred to the CJEU were:

(1)   ... Is Article 5(3) of Regulation 44/2001[202] on jurisdiction and the recognition and enforcement of judgments in civil and commercial matters to be interpreted as meaning that, in the event of an alleged infringement of copyright committed by means of content placed online on a website,

–   the person who considers that his rights have been infringed has the option of bringing an action to establish liability before the courts of each Member State in the territory of which content placed online is or has been accessible, in order to obtain compensation

---

200 Original judgment: Cour de cassation, chambre civile 1, Audience publique du Thursday 5 April 2012. No. de pourvoi: 10–15890.

201 **Peter Pinckney v KDG Mediatech AG** (Case C–170/12) (Court of Justice of the European Union). Judgment of the Court (Fourth Chamber) 3 October 2013 (CJEU).

202 Council Regulation (EC) No 44/2001 of 22 December 2000.

solely in respect of the damage suffered on the territory of the Member State before which the action is brought,

or

(2)   does that content also have to be, or to have been, directed at the public located in the territory of that Member State, or must some other clear connecting factor be present?

Is the answer to Question 1 the same if the alleged infringement of copyright results, not from the placing of dematerialised content online, but, as in the present case, from the online sale of a material carrier medium which reproduces that content?

The CJEU held in October 2013 that Article 5(3) of the Regulation must be interpreted as meaning that, in the event of alleged copyright infringement protected by the *Member State of the court seized* (in the **Pinckney** case, France) the latter has jurisdiction to hear an action to establish liability brought by the author of a work against a company established in another Member State (here: Austria) and which has, in the latter State, reproduced that work on a material support which is subsequently sold by companies established in a third Member State (here: the UK) through an internet site also accessible with the jurisdiction of the court seized.

The **Pinckney** ruling demonstrates the complexities and conflict of intellectual property laws within the EU Community. It appears that a court only has jurisdiction to determine and adjudicate on the damage caused in that particular Member State. Since there is as yet no unified EU copyright (or indeed global harmonization of IP) such IP infringements remain a challenge.

8.8.1 Exploitation of copyrighted work: licensing agreements and assignments

Licensing schemes and assignments of copyright are stated to be within the scope of the UK Copyright Act, namely Chapter V of the CDPA 1988. Assignments tend to be more popular in the United States, whereby artists will assign their copyright to a publishing company. An assignment is an outright transfer of ownership of rights by the copyright owner (e.g. the songwriter) to someone else, which usually covers the life of the copyright: 70 years from the end of the year in which the original author and owner of copyright dies. Section 90(1) CDPA states that copyright is transmissible by assignment, by 'testamentary disposition' or by operation of law, as personal or moveable property.

The requirements for a valid express assignment are set out in s 90 CDPA; but fortunately for many the law recognizes in addition to express statutory assignments equitable implied assignments based on the circumstances or conduct of the parties; for example, in university research collaboration agreements where the contracted sponsor may wish to own the IP created by the university research assistants or professors. Then the IP needs to be formally transferred, i.e. assigned to the sponsor. The assignment will then give 'full title guarantee' to the sponsor in the 'research collaboration agreement'. If indeed the university agrees to such an assignment, this will have to be formalised in a contract with guarantees and warranties (e.g. promising that it has the right to dispose of the IP; the IP is free from all charges and encumbrances (such as a mortgage) and rights of third parties; licensing back the IP etc.).

It is important to note that an IP owner can assign rights to future works yet to be created, for example J. K. Rowling assigning rights to her entire Harry Potter series at the start of her enterprise. The CDPA and EU legislation allow the copyright owner to agree to assign the copyright in works that he will create in the future. When such works come into existence they will automatically transfer to the assignee in the agreement. Where insertions into the contract are required to establish rights over the copyright work, only the grant of licensing will be implied. Otherwise an appropriate assignment will be required. The same goes for literary and dramatic works.

The following circumstances may give rise to the need for assignment:

(i)   the right to use the material;
(ii)   the right to exclude the author from using the material;
(iii)   the right to enforce copyright against third parties.

Factors to be considered when determining the likelihood of assignment should include:

(a)   the fee (e.g. lump sum or royalties or combination including any advance payments prior to creation of work);
(b)   the uses assigned (e.g. hardback book copy rights assigned to A, paperback rights to B, film rights to C, etc.);
(c)   the geographical areas of assignment (e.g. US rights to A, European Union rights to B, etc.)
(d)   duration of assignment;
(e)   the impact of assignment upon the author/creator;
(f)   was there an intention for the author to retain first ownership?

It is possible to license a right instead of assigning it. In granting a licence, the copyright owner merely gives another person permission to use that right for the particular purpose as agreed in the licence terms, such as publishing the book from a given manuscript or to make a CD from a particular sound recording or live performance. Licensing tends to be more flexible than an assignment as it is possible to license multiple copyrights to many people simultaneously, such as multiple music publishers. This is known as a non-exclusive licence. Usually licences permit sub-licences but generally the 'head licensee' cannot grant more rights to any sub-licensee than were granted to him.

See also
Chapter 9.3.1

A licence granted by a copyright owner is binding on every successor in title to his interest in the copyright, except a purchaser in good faith for valuable consideration and without notice (actual or constructive) of the licence or a person deriving title from such a purchaser. The licensor can then do anything with the work as he sees fit.[203] This practically means that a music publisher, for example, may do anything with a composer's script, such as issue an abridged or electronic version, subject of course to non-assignable moral rights, though these may be waived by the author. The same is true of book manuscripts.

Licensing schemes for public performances of sound recordings are firmly grounded in conventional contract law, particularly in relation to 'related rights'. A recording company does not need to ask the artist's opinion on the cover sleeve of the CD, for instance, unless this is specifically recorded in the terms of the licence agreement. Famous recording artists who have exclusive licences with, for example, Warner Brothers (Warners) will insist as part of their contract deal that they receive special treatment, such as a specific photographer or hairdresser for the cover sleeve of the album (now including downloads and merchandise). Universal artist, German-born chanson singer, Ute Lemper (*Chicago* and *Cabaret*) was adamant that her album sleeve cover photo could only be taken by Helmut Newton using the pose of Marlene Dietrich.

A principle of *de minimis* will be presumed in respect of licensing requirements and that an entitlement would be intended for such an arrangement. The scope of the licence ought to be limited in respect of those opportunities as envisaged by the parties at the time of the agreement. New exploitation and/or unexpected opportunities will not be considered to be included within such scope.

What about implied assignments and licences? Given the often hurly burly world of real commercial practice, parties do not always enter into the appropriate statutory written assignment, which can cause injustice later and frustrate the real intentions of the parties. In certain circumstances

---

203 Section 90(4) CDPA.

English law recognizes an implied assignment or licence. Nowadays, record labels try to persuade recording artists to sign '360°' licence deals so that they can exploit the artists' recordings commercially, including touring and merchandise. Record labels traditionally pay for the recording and mixing of albums and tend to underwrite new acts' touring costs to help raise their profile and sales. In addition they fund the manufacturing, packaging and distribution of the recordings.

The complexities of licence assignments were highlighted in the **Golden Eye** case (2012) (below). The issue in this case was whether to grant *Norwich Pharmacal* orders, requiring the internet service provider (ISP) to disclose the contact details of customers suspected of illegal file-sharing, so that **Golden Eye** could demand compensation and threaten to sue for infringing copyright in adult films, and the other claimants, the copyright proprietors, could share proceeds under a recovery-sharing agreement. The Court of Appeal (Chancery Division) considered whether such agreements were just a money-making exercise or a genuine attempt to protect copyright.

❖ KEY CASE — *Golden Eye v Telefónica UK Ltd* [2012] EWCA Civ 1740[204]

Precedent

❖ *Norwich Pharmacal*[205] relief is a powerful remedy available to claimants in order to obtain information for the purposes of seeking legal redress.

❖ A copyright owner may seek to compel disclosure of the identity of a wrongdoer by seeking to rely on the discretionary jurisdiction of the court which was established in *Norwich Pharmacal*.

❖ Before granting a *Norwich Pharmacal* order, the court has to balance the privacy and data protection rights of the individuals against whom disclosure order is made (of names and addresses) and the interest of justice (in relation to possible tortious or criminal actions).

Facts

In this case the original judge, Mr Justice Arnold, had been asked to order *Norwich Pharmacal* relief in circumstances where the data subjects – customers of an ISP (Teléfonica – 02) – had been identified as possible downloaders of copyright-protected pornography. The appellants appealed against a decision by the Court of Chancery in the earlier 2012 **Golden Eye** action,[206] where the judge had refused to grant them *Norwich Pharmacal* relief (i.e. disclosure of the names of the illegal downloaders).

The claimants in the joint action were the owners of the copyrights in pornographic films. They issued a claim seeking *Norwich Pharmacal* relief against the defendant ISP (Teléfonica, trading in the UK as 02) in the form of the disclosure of the names and addresses of customers who appeared to have infringed their copyright through peer-to-peer (P2P) file-sharing using what was known as the BitTorrent protocol.

The claimants fell into two groups. The first comprised the first and second claimants: Golden Eye (G) sought relief in respect of its own copyrights and those of its co-claimant,

---

204 Before the Master of the Rolls Lord Justice Sullivan and Lord Justice Patten on 21 December 2012.
205 See: **Norwich Pharmacal Co v Customs and Excise Commissioners** [1974] AC 133 (HL)
206 **Golden Eye (International) Ltd;** Ben Dover Productions; Celtic Broadcasting Ltd.; Easy on the Eye; DMS Telecoms Ltd; Gary Baker; Harmony Films Ltd; Justin Ribeiro Dos Santos t/a Joybear Pictures; Orchid MG Ltd.; Kudetta BVBA; RP Films Ltd.; Sweetmeats Productions t/a S.M.P.; SLL Films Ltd. Terence Stephens t/a One Eyed Jack Productions v Telefonica UK Ltd and Consumer Focus [2012] EWHC 723 (Ch).

Ben Dover Productions (BDP), of which it was the exclusive licensee. The second group comprised 14 other claimants (C). C had entered into agreements with G under which G was authorized to act for them in relation to any alleged breaches of copyright. Among other things, the agreement gave G sole control over, and conduct of, all claims and proceedings. In consideration of the rights granted by C, G agreed to pay them a percentage, varying between 25 and 37.5 per cent, of the sums recovered.

The original trial judge, Arnold J, was asked to consider whether the agreements between G and C were *champertous* (vexatious claims by a stranger in return for a share of the proceeds); in that respect, the judge stated that he did feel able to conclude that the agreements were likely to jeopardize the proper administration of justice. Mr Justice Arnold had also been required to consider whether it was proportionate to make the *Norwich Pharmacal* order; that required him to balance the need to protect the IP rights of the claimants and the rights and freedoms of the internet users in relation to privacy and data protection. In that respect, the judge made a distinction between G and B, on the one hand, and C, on the other.

Decision
Allowing the appeal, the CA held that it would be proportionate to grant *Norwich Pharmacal* relief in favour of G and B but not in favour of C. Lord Justice Sullivan MR stated that he should not make an order which 'endorses an arrangement under which [C] surrender total control of the litigation to [G] and [G] receives about 75 per cent of the revenues in return . . . that would be tantamount to the court sanctioning the sale of the Intended Defendants' privacy and data-protection rights to the highest bidder'.

Their Lordships held that the original judge had been wrong to make a distinction between the two groups of claimants. He had summarized the specific factors which weighed in favour of preserving the data protection rights of the intended defendants over the enforcement of the claimants' copyrights, referring to the vulnerability of the users, their inability to afford specialist legal advice and the propensity in a case such as this for even innocent subscribers to pay up rather than face the embarrassment of being accused of illegally downloading pornography.

However, those were common features which had to be taken into account in relation to the relief sought by all the claimants. They were as relevant to the enforcement of the copyrights of G and B as they were to those of C. If *Norwich Pharmacal* relief was to be denied to C simply on account of the litigation arrangements entered into with G, it was necessary to identify some additional impact which those arrangements had on the position of the intended defendants over and above the factors referred to by the judge.

The only such factor identified by the judge was what he described as C's surrender of total control of the litigation to G in return for a substantial share of the recoveries, but he did not suggest that that would of itself increase the likelihood of innocent or vulnerable defendants being unfairly coerced into making some unjustified payment. It had to follow that the judge's refusal to grant relief to C was based on his disapproval of the recovery-sharing arrangements with G, which was confirmed by his statement that to make the order would be tantamount to the court sanctioning the sale of the intended defendants' rights to the highest bidder.

But the court was not sanctioning the sale of anything. Indeed, its ability to control the process and ultimately to refuse relief was the primary reason why the judge rejected the submission that the litigation arrangements made with G did not jeopardize the proper administration of justice. If the arrangements were not therefore unlawful and were not simply a money-making exercise designed to take advantage of the vulnerability of the subscribers rather than a genuine attempt to protect the rights of C, there was no justification for refusing relief based on a disapproval of those arrangements. Indeed, it was difficult to articulate what that disapproval could be based on.[207]

Analysis

The English courts have a discretionary jurisdiction to provide relief to a prospective claimant to enable that person to obtain information in order to seek redress for an arguable wrong. This is called a *Norwich Pharmacal* order. In the **Norwich Pharmacal** case (1974)[208] the HL stated that if a person through no fault of his own gets involved in tortious acts of others so as to facilitate their wrong-doing, he may come under a duty to assist the person who has been wronged by giving him full information and disclosing the identity of the wrongdoers.

Norwich Pharmacal orders have been increasingly used to reveal people's identities and addresses who have hidden behind anonymous identities on the internet (e.g. when using social networking sites such as Twitter or Facebook). While anonymity allows users to engage in online activities they would not otherwise engage in for fear of prosecution when engaging in illegal online activity (such as possession of extreme pornography or child pornography), anonymity can also mask other illegal behaviour such as defamation, harassment or contempt of court. *Norwich Pharmacal* relief has been successfully used in many different copyright cases in order to obtain disclosure. This relief has also been successfully used by claimants who seek the disclosure of someone's identity who has posted defamatory comments on a website. *Norwich Pharmacal* orders are also used to reveal the identity of those who have made music available for download and those involved in peer-to-peer (P2P) file-sharing. Disclosure will be ordered by the High Court only if it is a 'necessary' and 'proportionate' response in all the circumstances.

The budget airline Ryanair,[209] for instance, brought a *Norwich Pharmacal* action, seeking to identify the users behind comments which were alleged to have been threatening and abusive. At the trial, however, the High Court found that the comments were not wrongful or actionable and the court also looked to the motive behind the action, finding that the real purpose was to break the resolve of pilots who were in dispute with the claimant at the time. In **Maguire v Gill**[210] an order for third-party discovery was made against an ISP requiring it to identify a user but without giving the ISP an opportunity to be heard, without considering whether or not the balance lay in favour of disclosure and without explicitly ordering safeguards in respect of the use of this information.

The Court of Appeal – Chancery Division in **Golden Eye** considered the use of *Norwich Pharmacal* orders in relation to copyright infringement via P2P file-sharing of pornography. Their Lordships decided that the original judge had been wrong to make a distinction

---

207 See paras 26–28 of the judgment.
208 **Norwich Pharmacal Co v Customs and Excise Commissioners** [1974] AC 133.
209 **Ryanair v Johnston** (2006) Unreported 12 July 2006 (High Court Smyth J).
210 **Maguire v Gill** (2006) Unreported 5 October 2006 (High Court, Hannah J).

between the two groups of claimants (Golden Eye, its co-claimant Ben Dover Productions (BDP) and the second group being the 14 other claimants (C)). The original judge, Arnold J, had refused *Norwich Pharmacal* relief to those in the second group (C), being copyright owners who had allowed the first claimant to pursue the claim under recovery-sharing arrangements. The CA now allowed the appeal, granting the *Norwich Pharmacal* relief in favour of G and B but not in favour of C. (see also: **Media CAT Ltd v Adams** (2011)[211]).[212]

 FOR THOUGHT

What happens if it can be proved that a company is guilty of copyright infringement? What do you need to prove in relation to the company's director/s or secretary?

8.9 Copyright infringements

In April 2006, after a three-week hearing in the High Court, Peter Smith J rejected claims that Dan Brown's best-selling novel *The DaVinci Code* (published in 2003) breached the copyright of an earlier book by authors Michael Baigent and Richard Leigh. Their non-fiction book, *The Holy Blood and the Holy Grail* (published in 1982), explores in detail many hypotheses, myths and legends relating to Christianity, particularly Catharism in medieval times. The book also considers in depth the hypothesis of Jesus Christ having a child and it marrying into the Merovingian dynasty.

The Da Vinci Code is a murder thriller with a historical-religious theme, based on the idea that Jesus Christ was of noble birth, had a child by Mary Magdalene and his descendants emigrated to France where they intermarried into the Merovingian royal dynasty. The novel suggests that his descendants survive to the modern day and are protected by an entity known as the Priory of Sion.

In early 2006, Baigent and Leigh filed a copyright law suit against Dan Brown's publishers, Random House. In **Baigent and Leigh v The Random House Group Ltd** (2007),[213] the claimants (two of three authors) alleged that significant portions of *The DaVinci Code* were plagiarized from *The Holy Blood and the Holy Grail*, violating their copyright. Brown confirmed during the court hearing that he named the principal Grail expert of his story Leigh Teabing as an anagram of 'Baigent Leigh' – the two claimants. Whilst Brown admitted that he had referred to *The Holy Blood and the Holy Grail* in the course of his research, he denied copyright infringement. At first instance Mr Justice Peter Smith found that six chapters of *The DaVinci Code* were largely derived from the claimants' text but rejected the claim of copying. The claimants' appeal was dismissed. Lloyd LJ in the CA agreed with the trial judge's decision on the issue of 'substantiality' in that there had been no 'central theme' to copy and accordingly no breach of copyright was found.[214] The claimants were ordered to pay 85 per cent of Random House's legal costs, estimated at £1.3m.[215]

---

211 [2011] EWPCC 6; [2011] FSR 28 (PCC).
212 For further discussion see: Stephens, Fuller and Atherton (2013).
213 [2007] EWCA Civ 247 (CA) ('The *DaVinci Code* case').
214 For further discussion see: Kirk (2006).
215 Source: 'Brown wins Da Vinci Code case', *Guardian*, 7 April 2006.

If a person carries out any of the 'restricted acts' without the authorization of the copyright owner, this constitutes copyright infringement, an act of strict liability where *mens rea* is not an issue.[216] Restricted acts include:

- to issue copies of the work to the public (including rental rights);
- to perform, show or play the work in public;
- to communicate the work (which includes broadcasts);
- to make an adaptation of the work, which includes translations, or do any work or do any of the above in relation to an adaptation.[217]

Court actions offer relief in the form of civil and criminal remedies sufficient to deter P2P file-sharing, film piracy or copying of MP3 music files. Possible defences include permitted acts, fair dealing (reviews, news reporting, criticism, etc.) and research and private study.

If the owner of the copyright in an original work believes that his work has been copied or pirated, he can enforce these rights in the Patents County Court or the Chancery Division.[218] The court usually uses equitable remedies such as 'specific performance' or injunctions to remedy IP infringement. In addition the High Court can issue a warrant for an inspection of the copiers' premises for evidence of production or possession of the copied or 'pirated' goods (see glossary: '*Anton Piller* order'). There could be an interim injunction (or interdict in Scotland) to stop the illegal activities. The copyright owner's rights are not limited by the amount of work used. If he believes that a 'substantial part' of his work is being copied or broadcast, this will still constitute an infringement of the work. A 'substantial part' is assessed qualitatively and could be a very small part of the work if that part was distinctive and thus substantial.

See also
s 8.11.4

8.9.1 Secondary infringement of copyright

The copyright owner is also able to take action against persons who subsequently deal with an infringing copy or who facilitated the infringement itself. These acts are known as acts of secondary liability (or infringement) and are covered by ss 22 to 26 CDPA. Section 23 CDPA includes the copyright in a work which is infringed by a person who, without the licence of the copyright owner:

(a)   possesses it in the course of a business;
(b)   sells or lets it for hire, or offers or exposes it for sale or hire;
(c)   in the course of a business exhibits it in public or distributes it; or
(d)   distributes it otherwise than in the course of a business to such an extent as to affect prejudicially the owner of the copyright, an article which is, and which he knows or has reason to believe is, an infringing copy of the work.

In relation to secondary liability, it must also be shown that the person who conducted those restricted acts knew or had reason to believe that he was infringing copyright. This may become an issue when, for instance, counterfeit DVDs are sold at car boot sales by third parties.

European Union legislation has amended the CDPA in this respect. The Copyright Regulations[219] introduced the ability for copyright owners (and certain licensees) to take infringement proceedings

---

216 Chapter II of the CDPA.
217 Section 16 CDPA.
218 The Chancery Division is based at the Rolls Building (off Chancery Lane/Fetter Lane). The Head of Division, The Chancellor of the High Court, is the Right Honourable Sir Andrew Morritt CVO (2013).
219 See: EU Regulation 2003/2498 on Copyright and Related Rights Regulations and EU Regulation 2003/2426 on Privacy and Electronic Communications Regulations.

against anyone who circumvents technological measures – such as copy control devices which have been applied to a work – or who removes or alters electronic rights management information associated with a work or imports or sells devices for these acts to be done.

It is worth noting that Digital Rights Management (DRM)[220] has a chequered history. Originally advocated as a means to prevent illegal copies, there has been controversy about it preventing legal copies from running on some platforms and more recently about proposals in the gaming market to prevent legal second-hand copies from being used without payment of an additional fee. In the e-book market it has by and large proven problematic and a high proportion of eBooks are published without DRM.

In the **Karen Murphy (Pub Landlady)** case (CJEU decision in two joined cases),[221] the European Court of Justice (Court of Justice of the European Union – CJEU) ruled that the FA Premier League cannot stop individuals from seeking better deals for TV sports subscriptions than that offered by BSkyB, which paid more than £1bn for the UK broadcast rights for Premier League matches from foreign broadcasters. Karen Murphy, the landlady of the Red, White and Blue pub in Portsmouth, spent six years fighting a prosecution for showing live football at the pub without a Sky subscription. Instead of using Sky, on which it costs £700 a month to see Premier League matches, she used the Greek TV station Nova, which has the rights to screen the games in Greece, and which cost her £800 a year. Karen Murphy was convicted of an offence under s 297(1) CDPA ('Offence of fraudulently receiving programmes'[222]). She paid nearly £8,000 in fines and costs in her legal action and eventually took her case to the CJEU, which found in her favour in October 2011. In February 2012 the High Court also found in her favour.

The CJEU ruled that attempting to prohibit the 'import, sale or use of foreign decoder cards is contrary to the freedom to provide services and cannot be justified either in light of the objective of protecting intellectual property rights or by the objective of encouraging the public to attend football stadiums'. However, the court ruled against the bid by Karen Murphy to be allowed to use a Greek decoder card to show live Premier League matches to pub goers at much cheaper rates than BSkyB charges commercial premises in the UK on copyright grounds.

Section 72(1) CDPA 1988 provides that where someone plays or shows a broadcast in public, to an audience which has not paid for admission to his premises, he does not infringe any copyright in the broadcast or any film included in the broadcast. The CJEU found that the pubs in the conjoined action could rely on the s 72(1) defence in relation to the broadcast and to the films included in it (however, this defence does not apply in relation to other protectable works incorporated in it, such as the rights holders' logo and anthem).

The CJEU said the transmission in a pub is a 'communication to the public', which means that without the permission of the Premier League Murphy would be in breach of the EU Copyright Directive (Directive 93/83/EEC). But this Directive does not stop individuals from buying foreign decoder cards for domestic use.

The European Court of Justice ruled that live match coverage itself was not covered by copyright protection, although the Premier League could claim ownership of FAPL-branded opening

---

220 Digital Rights Management (DRM) is a class of controversial technologies that are used by hardware manufacturers and publishers with the intent to control the use of digital content and devices *after* sale. The idea is to control copying, while second-generation DRM schemes seek to control viewing, copying, printing, and altering of works or devices. The term is also sometimes referred to as *copy protection, copy prevention* or *copy control*. DRM is a set of access control technologies, used by companies such as Amazon, AOL, Apple Inc., Google, Microsoft, Sony and the BBC.

221 **Karen Murphy v Media Protection Services Ltd** (C-429/08) and **Football Association Premier League Ltd and Others v QC Leisure and Others** (C–403/08) Judgment of the European Court of Justice – Grand Chamber of 4 October 2011. The cases related to pubs in the UK which, in order to screen Football Association Premier League (FAPL) football matches, were purchasing foreign decoder cards rather than buying the more expensive authorised BSkyB subscription. The foreign decoder cards also enabled the pubs to show the Saturday 3pm matches, which no UK broadcaster is permitted to show live.

222 This establishes an offence where a person dishonestly receives a programme included in a broadcasting service provided from a place in the UK with intent to avoid payment of any charge applicable to the reception of the programme.

video sequences, theme music, on-screen graphics and highlights of previous matches. This means that as long as the FAPL and BSkyB ensure that match coverage includes enough copyright elements pubs will not be allowed to show foreign broadcasts.

The *Karen Murphy* ruling is complex and it is worth reading the full judgment in order to fully understand the applicability of the s 72(1) CDPA defence to acts of communication to the public. Clearly, the Premier League was disappointed with the outcome of the case. There is, however, a positive outcome for the FAPL in that there is no defence available to pubs who communicate FAPL's logos, anthems or any other copyright works to the public (part 2 of the CJEU judgment).

 FOR THOUGHT

How would you advise a client – the copyright owner – who wants to take action in relation to acts of secondary liability against a person who conducts restricted acts within the provision of the UK Copyright Act (CDPA – as amended)? How realistic is it to trace the person who conducted the original infringement (the acts of primary liability), and how would you go about it?

8.9.2 Trademark infringements

L'Oréal v Bellure (2010)[223] marked two landmark rulings, first in 2007 and then in 2010, concerning counterfeit 'smell-alike' perfumes. This complex litigation – involving other brands, such as Lancôme and Laboratoire Garnier products – was heard in the Chancery Division, first before Lewison J in 2006 and concluding before the Court of Appeal in 2010 before the Rt Hon Lord Justice Jacob, the Rt Hon Lord Justice Wall and the Rt Hon Lord Justice Rimer. The courts had to determine whether the Belgian defendants Bellure had contravened the Trademark Directive, in that it was alleged by the claimants that the defendants had used comparison lists for retailers, indicating which smell-alike product corresponds with which luxury brand.[224] Bellure was trading in three ranges of products called Stitch, Création Lamis and Dorrall. Each member of the range smelt like a famous, luxury branded perfume known by a well-known registered trademark. L'Oréal alleged that the defendants' use of comparison lists for each of the defendants' ranges of product, showing which products correspond to which L'Oréal (and others) perfume, infringed its registered trademarks for those perfumes. Originally it also contended that some of the packaging used for the Création Lamis and Dorrall ranges also infringed other registered trademarks. No complaint was made about the packaging of the Stitch range. All counterfeit products were manufactured in Dubai by the Belgian company Bellure, who, in turn, claimed that the articles were not imitations in the sense of being counterfeits.

The use of trademarks in this case was used for 'comparative advertising', which the trademark holder, L'Oréal, opposed. They had to show that there was detriment to *any* of the functions of their trademark. L'Oréal and the other brands claimed that Bellure took unfair advantage of their own product names, packaging and brand image. Lewison J (Chancery Division) found Bellure to have infringed L'Oréal's and others' trademarks, and that Bellure had taken unfair advantage of L'Oréal

---

223 *L'Oréal SA; Lancôme Parfums et Beauté & CIE; Laboratoire Garnier & CIE v Bellure NV Malaika Investments Ltd (t/a Honeypot Cosmetic & Perfumery Sales); Starion International Ltd* [2010] EWCA Civ 535; See also: *L'Oréal SA; Lancôme Parfums et Beauté & CIE; Laboratoire Garnier & CIE v Bellure NV; North West Cosmetics Ltd., HMC Cosmetics Ltd; Malaika Investments Ltd., Sveonmakeup.co.uk; Starion International Ltd* [2007] EWCA Civ 968 (Ch).

224 Contrary to Article 5(1)(a) Trademarks Directive (use of an identical sign for identical goods) (Directive 2008/95/EC: to approximate the laws of the Member States relating to trademarks).

et al.'s reputation in the UK; that is, trying to pass off its own brand as that of L'Oréal (see also: *L'Oréal SA v eBay France SA* (2009);[225] also: *L'Oréal SA v eBay International AG* (2009)[226]).

However, the case did not end there. The case was referred to the European Court of Justice for a preliminary ruling on trademark offences.[227] In its decision the ECJ gave guidance on many issues regarding trademark law, providing a synthesis of several earlier decisions. The decision stresses the wide-reaching protection under Article 5(2) of the Trademarks Directive. The Directive protects trademarks which have a reputation and protects the brand against the use of unfair advantage and detriment to the brand which is of distinctive character (including its trademark). The Court of Justice stressed that *any* comparative advertising which would not meet the requirements of the Directive, while using the trademark, would constitute a trademark infringement; for example, if the goods in question are presented as an imitation or replica (which had been the case in *L'Oréal v Bellure*). The Court of Justice stressed that actual detriment or actual unfair advantage need not be shown, but that it suffices that the use *would* take unfair advantage of, or *would* be detrimental to the distinctive character or the trademark reputation.

Helpfully, the ECJ supplemented the term 'trademark infringement' with alternative terms, such as 'tarnishment' and 'degradation' to a brand. And the term 'gaining of unfair advantage' was broadly defined with alternative terms such as 'parasitism' and 'free-riding'. These concepts relate not only to the detriment caused to the trademark but to the unfair advantage taken by the infringer as a result of the use of the identical or similar signs.

It is fair to say that companies which specialize in copied goods have experienced lawyers who advise them on a daily basis on how close to the copyright infringement line they can get without crossing it. However, the *L'Oréal v Bellure* ruling (both in the UK Court of Appeal and the ECJ) is seen by the fashion and cosmetics industries as ground-breaking in deterring future copying and trademark infringements of genuine brands.

8.9.3 Criminal offences

Some acts of copyright infringement can constitute a criminal offence and therefore criminal proceedings can be brought by the copyright owner, Trading Standards or HM Revenue and Customs. European Union Copyright law now allows for criminal prosecution where there is deliberate intent or passing off in a commercial context. A person commits an intellectual property offence if he knew or had reason to believe that he was conducting any of the acts (defined by statute – CDPA and Regulations) with an infringing article or that his actions would cause an infringement. Criminal liability for making or dealing with infringing articles is covered by s 107 CDPA, which states that a person commits an offence who, without the licence of the copyright owner:

(a)   makes for sale or hire; or
(b)   imports into the UK otherwise than for his private and domestic use; or
(c)   possesses in the course of a business with a view to committing any act infringing the copyright; or
(d)   in the course of a business –

    (i)   sells or lets for hire; or
    (ii)   offers or exposes for sale or hire; or
    (iii) exhibits in public; or
    (iv)   distributes; or

---

225 (2009) (RG 07/11365) Tribunal de grande instance, Paris, judgment of 13 May 2009 (unreported).
226 [2009] EWHC 1094 (Ch).
227 *L'Oréal SA v Bellure NV* (2010) European Court of Justice (First Chamber) Case C-487/07 10 February 2009 [2010] RPC 1.

(e)   distributes otherwise than in the course of a business to such an extent as to affect prejudi-
        cially the owner of the copyright,

an article which is, and which he knows or has reason to believe is, an infringing copy of a copyright work.[228]

The courts can also order damages for loss of financial rewards (e.g. royalties) and recognition
of the work.[229] Criminal copyright prosecution allows for imprisonment and fines and infringing
goods may be seized.

It is important to understand that even if a criminal prosecution succeeds, a separate civil case
will be necessary to recover financial losses caused by the infringement. However, the difficulty of
proving intent and the higher standard of proof ('beyond reasonable doubt') required for a criminal prosecution means that copyright infringement is almost always dealt with as a civil procedure
with the aim of recovering damages.

8.10 General defences

The CDPA allows a number of uses of copyright works without the permission of the copyright
owner in certain specific circumstances. There are two distinct types of permitted acts: fair dealing
and exceptions. It is an offence to perform any of the following acts without the consent of the
owner:

* copy the work;
* rent, lend or issue copies of the work to the public;
* perform, broadcast or show the work in public;
* adapt the work.

As stated previously, the author of a work or a director of a film may also have certain moral rights:

* the right to be identified as the author.
* the right to object to derogatory treatment.

8.10.1 Fair dealing

Fair dealing acts (or 'fair use', 'free use' or 'fair practice') differ from other exceptions to copyright
in that these involve an assessment as to whether the dealing is fair. In determining this issue the
courts have considered the following questions. In certain circumstances, some works may be used
if that use is considered to be 'fair dealing'. Regrettably, the CDPA provides no strict definition of
what this means but it has been interpreted by the courts on a number of occasions by looking at
the economic impact of the use on the copyright owner. Where the economic impact is not significant, the use may count as fair dealing. The courts usually ask these questions: first, is the person
really using the work for the stated purpose? For example, if an entire work has been used and it is
followed by two lines of vague review, this will not constitute criticism and review. If the use has
not been for one of the stated purposes, it will not fall within 'fair dealing' and as such any use
without permission will be an infringement. If the work has been used for one of the stated
purposes, the court will then consider whether the use of the work was fair in all the circumstances.

---

228 Section 107(1)(a)–(e) CDPA.
229 Sections 17–21 CDPA.

Such an assessment will involve a number of factors and will depend upon the particular circumstances of each case. Second, has the (alleged) copyright infringer availed himself of the 'fair dealing' exception? And if so, has he provided a sufficient acknowledgement alongside his work? Has he demonstrated a visible and prominent notice which amounts to a sufficient acknowledgement to the copyright owner? So, it could well be within the scope of 'fair dealing' to make single photocopies of short extracts of a copyrighted work for non-commercial research or private study, criticism or review, or reporting current events.

Fair dealing sets out certain actions that may be carried out, but would not normally be regarded as copyright infringement. The fair dealing exceptions are fairly limited, covered by ss 30 and 171(3) CDPA 1988. The idea behind this is that if copyright laws are too restrictive, it may stifle free speech and news reporting, or result in disproportionate penalties for inconsequential or accidental inclusion. Fair dealing describes acts which are permitted to a certain degree without infringing the work. These acts are:

- private and research study purposes;
- performance, copies or lending for educational purposes;
- reviews and news reporting (see: *Time Warner v Channel 4* (1994)[230]);
- incidental inclusion;
- copies and lending by librarians;
- acts for the purposes of royal commissions, statutory enquiries, judicial proceedings and parliamentary purposes;
- recording of broadcasts for the purposes of listening to or viewing at a more convenient time ('time-shifting'), including podcasts and BBC iPlayer;
- producing a back-up copy for personal use of a computer program;
- playing a sound recording for a non-profit-making organization, club or society.

In **Fraser-Woodward Limited v (1) British Broadcasting Corporation (2) Brighter Pictures Ltd** (2005),[231] the High Court (Chancery Division) provided further guidance on the application of the fair dealing defence for review and criticism.

 KEY CASE

Fraser-Woodward Limited v (1) British Broadcasting Corporation (2) Brighter Pictures Ltd [2005] EWHC 472 (Ch) (sub nom 'The Jason Fraser case')

Precedent

- ❖ Fair dealing for the purpose of criticism or review is an established exclusion in the Copyright Designs and Patents Act of 1988[232] – providing only a *reasonable* amount of the work is used.
- ❖ The defence is relied on for day-to-day journalistic practices by all media organizations.
- ❖ The key requirement for the defence of fair dealing to apply is that the author/s of the allegedly infringing material must demonstrate a genuine intention to criticize or

230 [1994] EMLR 1 of 22 October 1993 (CA).
231 [2005] EWHC 472 (Ch).
232 Fair Dealing – ss 30 and 171(3) CDPA 1988.

review, rather than a desire to compete with the copyright work or to reproduce the copyright work simply to advance or promote their own product or service.

Facts
The case concerned the use by the BBC and Brighter Pictures of 14 'off-guard' photos of the Beckham family, taken by celebrity photographer Jason Fraser, during the making of a TV programme, *Tabloid Tales*, presented by Piers Morgan. Fraser-Woodward Ltd and its owner Jason Fraser sued for copyright infringement seeking flagrancy damages. The BBC and Brighter Pictures (the division of *Big Brother* creator Endemol that made *Tabloid Tales*) argued that the photos fell within the 'fair dealing' defence (s 30 CDPA 1988). The defendants argued that the programme included criticism of the photos and the tabloid press in general. Mr Fraser argued that there was no fair dealing and that there was no sufficient acknowledgement.

Decision
Mr Fraser's appeal was dismissed. The CA held that all but one of the photographs had been used for the purposes of criticism and review (in the tabloid press and magazines). This meant that the BBC could use his photographs of the Beckhams without his permission and without paying for them because the programme *Tabloid Tales* amounted to a review of the press coverage of the high-profile couple.

Mann J referred to Walker LJ's judgment in the **Pro Sieben** case,[233] that the defence of fair dealing should be interpreted liberally. Mann J also confirmed **Hubbard v Vosper** (1972),[234] that there could be no limitations on the extent of commentary capable of amounting to 'criticism' for the purpose of the defence.

Analysis
Fair dealing for the purpose of criticism or reviews is an established exclusion in the CDPA 1988. It is relied on for day-to-day journalistic practices by all media organizations, not just the BBC. The important outcome of the **Jason Fraser** case was that any review or criticism should be considered in its context. Mr Justice Mann held that the programme did include criticism of the photographs themselves and therefore amounted to 'fair dealing' and that the programme was a legitimate review of tabloid journalism. Importantly, the court found that the reproduction of the photographs did not prejudice the legitimate interests of Mr Fraser. The fact that Mr Frazer on occasion licenses his photographs for use in television programmes, and without apparently significantly undermining his ability to license the pictures elsewhere, contradicted his evidence that undue damage to their value was inevitable from their use in the BBC show. Overall, Mr Justice Mann held that there was not 'excessive use' of the material in question.

Some lawyers have argued that the fair dealing provisions in UK copyright law are too restrictive and that they are asphyxiating the copyright system, calling into question both its credibility and efficacy. A number of cases, cited in the **Jason Fraser** case, demonstrate these current restrictions, such as **Ashdown v Telegraph Group Ltd** (2001).[235] The *Sunday Telegraph* had published verbatim extracts from a

---

233 See: **Pro Sieben Media AG v Carlton UK TV Ltd** [1999] FSR 160 at p. 162 (Walker LJ) (CA).
234 [1972] 2 Q.B. 84; concerning a Scientology case where Lord Denning defined the defence of fair dealing under s 6(2)*Copyright Act 1956*.
235 [2001] Ch 685 (Ch).

lengthy minute of a meeting between Lord Ashdown, the Prime Minister and other political figures. The extracts contradicted denials emanating from Downing Street of stories in other newspapers concerning the extent of planned co-operation between New Labour and the Liberal Democrats. Lord Ashdown was intending to publish the diaries of which the minute formed part. Although the newspaper did not pay to publish the extracts, the editor of the *Sunday Telegraph* had clearly understood that the minute was confidential. The claimant brought proceedings for breach of copyright and breach of confidence. The Vice Chancellor granted the application and ordered disclosure so that the claimant could elect between an account of profits or damages. The defendants' appeal was dismissed in that they could not avail themselves of a s 30 defence ('fair dealing') because they could not bring themselves within any of its parameters. The court did say that it might have considered a separate public interest defence (but not in this case).

The **Ashdown** case is an authority for the proposition that the criticism must be of a work or another work; it was held not sufficient in this case to criticize anything to invoke 'fair dealing'; there was no requirement that the criticism and review contain specific reference to the work in question. In addition the **Jason Fraser** case also provides guidance as to the meaning of sufficient acknowledgement, in respect of which there is very little case law. The ruling in respect of 'fair dealing' in the **Jason Fraser** case extended the scope of the defence, which now stretches not only to criticism and review of other copyrighted works, but will also cover criticism of works that may not be protected by copyright at all or are unpublished or identified with any specificity, such as the tabloid press in general (see also: **IPC Media Ltd v News Group Newspapers Ltd** (2005)[236]).

8.10.2 Exceptions and permitted acts in relation to copyrighted works

There are a number of general exceptions in relation to copyrighted works (known as 'permitted acts'), covered by Chapter III CDPA. Figure 8.1 opposite shows the broad exceptions.

8.10.3 The 'three steps' test

Is UK copyright law compliant in relation to defences or permitted acts? How 'harmonized' are EU copyright laws really? In her speech at a forum in Avignon, France, in November 2010, the then EU Commissioner for the Digital Agenda, Neelie Kroes, said:

> Today our fragmented copyright system is ill-adapted to the real essence of art, which has no frontiers . . . [W]e must look beyond national and corporatist self-interest to establish a new approach to copyright. We want *'une Europe des cultures'* and for this we need a debate at European level.[237]

Since TRIPS incorporated the test, it regulates all exceptions to IP rights.

Article 9(2) of the Berne Convention introduced the 'three steps test', which imposes on signatories to the treaty constraints on the possible limitations and exceptions to exclusive rights under national copyright laws. The 'three steps' clause was subsequently included in several international copyright treaties such as the TRIPS Agreement,[238] the WIPO Copyright Treaty (WCT), the EU Copyright Directive, the WIPO Performances and Phonograms Treaty and by Article 5(5) Directive 2001/29/EC

---

236 [2005] EWHC 317 (Ch).
237 Source: N. Kroes, 'A digital world of opportunities', Speech at the Forum d'Avignon, 'Les rencontres internationales de la culture, de l'économie et des medias', Avignon (France), 5 November 5 2010.
238 The World Trade Organization (WTO) Agreement on Trade Related Aspects of Intellectual Property Rights 1994 (WTO-TRIPS or TRIPS).

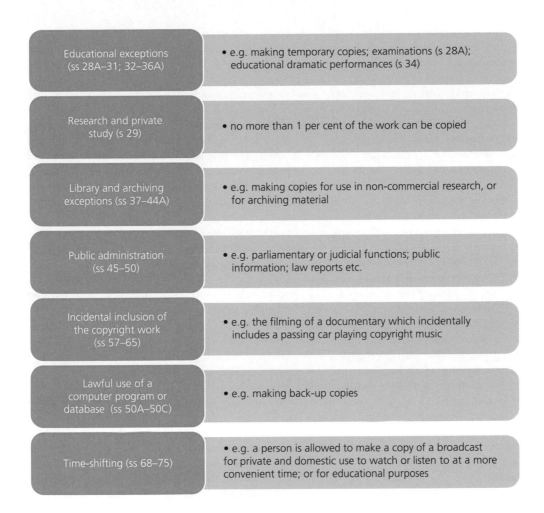

Educational exceptions (ss 28A–31; 32–36A)	• e.g. making temporary copies; examinations (s 28A); educational dramatic performances (s 34)
Research and private study (s 29)	• no more than 1 per cent of the work can be copied
Library and archiving exceptions (ss 37–44A)	• e.g. making copies for use in non-commercial research, or for archiving material
Public administration (ss 45–50)	• e.g. parliamentary or judicial functions; public information; law reports etc.
Incidental inclusion of the copyright work (ss 57–65)	• e.g. the filming of a documentary which incidentally includes a passing car playing copyright music
Lawful use of a computer program or database (ss 50A–50C)	• e.g. making back-up copies
Time-shifting (ss 68–75)	• e.g. a person is allowed to make a copy of a broadcast for private and domestic use to watch or listen to at a more convenient time; or for educational purposes

Figure 8.1 Permitted acts in relation to copyrighted works (Chapter III Copyright, Designs and Patents Act 1988)

('The Information Society Directive' – 'InfoSoc Directive'), which has extended the importance of the 'three steps' test. The test also exists in Article 10 WCT (WIPO Copyright Treaty), Article 16 WPPT (WIPO Performances and Phonograms Treaty), Article 6(3) Directive 91/250 ('Software Directive'), Article 10(3) Directive 2006/115 ('Rental Right Directive'), Article 6(3) Directive 96/9 ('Database Directive') and Article 5(5) Directive 2001/29 ('Information Society Directive').

'Three steps' is defined by Article 13 TRIPS:

> . . . members shall confine limitations and exceptions to exclusive rights to certain special cases which do not conflict with a normal exploitation of the work and do not unreasonably prejudice the legitimate interests of the rights holder.

The 'three steps test' curbs state discretion, setting 'limitations' and 'exceptions' – an ultimately political tool. The test remains ambiguous for states to promote and interpret the legislation as they see fit to suit their domestic interests.[239] The Berne Convention[240] further contains specific discretionary areas for signatory member states to determine conditions to exercise certain rights inherent in their own domestic legislation (such as the CDPA in the UK). Ultimately Berne, WIPO and TRIPS convert or default into national legislation. However, a narrow interpretation of Article13 TRIPS ('three steps') reduces state sovereignty to balance the right-holder against the public needs as they 'shall confine limitations' to those satisfying the test.

By signing up to the international copyright treaties countries aim to strike a balance between rights holders' rights and the 'fair use' or 'fair dealing' in limited circumstances of authorized reproductions or communications of copyrighted works. This usually centres on educational[241] or non-commercial purposes. At the 'Revision Conference (2003),[242] Ricketson suggested a specific, non-exhaustive list of exceptions that countries could choose from, to construct national policy in respect of the safeguarding of authors', songwriters etc. copyright. Suggested exceptions include:

- regulated reprography of copyright works without licence or with free licences from the right-holder to be provided exclusively for educational institutions;
- translation of educational materials into native language(s);
- format changes to Braille and other accessibility formats to benefit those with disabilities;
- private use by pupils of reproduced copyright works at home, to facilitate continuous learning outside of the classroom (for example, to complete homework);
- use by public libraries, or third parties on their behalf, to reproduce additional copies of essential works using reprography of to build their collections;
- using and downloading digitized works;
- digitization of works for ease of transfer where the technology is available.
- circumvention of TPMs[243] on educational works;
- teaching resources, such that where possible, teachers may use media, including songs and films, for demonstrations in lessons.[244]

However, it soon became clear that signatory countries to the treaties were either ignoring the complex legislation or simply did not understand it. The European Court of Justice's decision in the **Infopaq**[245] case therefore presented such problems and the further need to harmonize copyright legislation. In this case a reference for a preliminary ruling was made by the Danish Supreme Court (Højesteret) in the context of proceedings between Infopaq and Danske Dagblades Forening (DDF),[246] concerning the dismissal of Infopaq's application for a declaration that it was not required to obtain the consent of the copyright owners for acts of reproduction of newspaper articles obtained by collective licensing. The ECJ considered whether reproduction of extracts from newspaper articles infringed copyright.

Infopaq is an organization, operating in the Nordic countries such as Sweden, Denmark and Norway, that monitors everything in the media. Their main work includes business analyses and the drawing up of summaries of selected articles from daily newspapers, magazines, broadcasting and

239 For further discussion see: Senftleben (2004).
240 Berne Convention Articles 10bis and 11bis.
241 For further discussion on the 'Right to education, national poverty and international copyright restrictions', see: Thomas (2012).
242 See: WIPO (World Intellectual Property Organization) (2003) at: www.wipo.int/edocs/mdocs/copyright/en/sccr_9/sccr_9_7.pdf.
243 In computing a Trusted Platform Module (TPM) is both the name of a published specification detailing a secure cryptoprocessor that can store cryptographic keys that protect information, and the general name of implementations of that specification, often called the 'TPM chip' or 'TPM Security Device'.
244 See also: Ricketson (2003).
245 See: **Infopaq International A/S v Danske Dagblades Forening** (C-5/08) [2009] ECR I-6569 (ECJ (4th Chamber)).
246 The professional association of Danish daily newspapers; its function is, inter alia, to offer advice on copyright issues.

social networking. The print press article selection follows certain subject criteria agreed with customers and is carried out by means of a data capture process.

In 2005 the Danish DDF informed Infopaq that it required authorization from the copyright owners in order to carry out its activities. Eventually Infopaq brought an action against DDF before the High Court of Eastern Denmark (Østre Landsret) to obtain a declaration that it had the right to apply the data capture process without the consent of DDF or its members (i.e. to avoid copyright breaches). The court dismissed the action as unfounded and Infopaq appealed the decision before the Højesteret. The Danish Supreme Court held that it was not disputed that consent from copyright owners was not required in press monitoring activities. The writing up of summaries consisted of manual reading of each publication, selection of relevant articles on the basis of predetermined search words and production of a manually prepared cover sheet for the summary writers, providing an identified search word in an article and its position in the newspaper. The Danish court further held that there was no dispute on the fact that the data capture process involved two acts of reproduction, these being the creation of the image file, when the printed articles were scanned, and its consequent conversion into a text file.

The Højesteret noticed that there was disagreement between the parties as to whether this amounted to 'reproduction' within the meaning of Article 2 of Directive 2001/29 ('InfoSoc Directive'). The parties further disagreed as to whether, if there was reproduction, the acts in question, taken as a whole, were covered by the exemption envisaged by Article 5(1) of the InfoSoc Directive. For these reasons the Højesteret referred the proceedings to the ECJ.

Part of the ECJ's ruling revealed weakness in the InfoSoc Directive as copyright law had moved on considerably: the Directive did not define either the meaning of 'reproduction' or of 'reproduction in part'. Part of the preliminary ruling included that authors have the exclusive right to authorize or prohibit reproduction, in whole or in part, of their works under Article 2(a) of the InfoSoc Directive. Further, that copyright within the meaning of Article 2(a) of the Directive is liable to apply only in relation to a subject matter which is *original* in the sense that it is its author's own intellectual creation.

Applying the 'three steps' test to reach a decision, the ECJ held that Infopaq's data capture process did come within the concept of 'reproduction' as set out in Article 2 of the Copyright Directive, if the elements reproduced were the 'expression of the intellectual creation of their author'. The ECJ also ruled that the act of printing out an extract of 11 words, during such a data capture process, was not transient in nature as required by Article 5(1) of the Copyright Directive. Therefore, that process could not be carried out without the relevant right-holders' consent.[247]

'Three steps' then imposes limitations on exclusive copyrights which are confined to certain special cases that do not conflict with a normal exploitation of the work and do not unreasonably prejudice the legitimate interests of the author. The 'three steps' test is seen as the most enduring of standards affecting copyright limitations. Its application outlines the delicate balance between exclusive rights and sufficient breathing space for the free flow of ideas and information.

The problem is that at no point is this mentioned in the CDPA 1988, though the UK argues that the defences are balanced in such a way as to satisfy the general requirement. Lucas (2010) argues that this is not the case. The battleground in copyright disputes and in copyright litigation will be over the question of whether the reproduction in question will constitute an 'expression of the intellectual creation of their author'. This question is then left to the national courts to decide on this very issue.

English courts have dealt with copyright infringement matters since the **Infopaq** case by assessing whether a 'substantial part' of the copyright work has been reproduced. The substantial part of the new test (taking in the 'three steps' test) is whether the reproduced text alone is the

---

247 For further discussion see: Rosati (2011).

expression of the intellectual creation of the author. This is not an easy test and provides for lengthy litigation proceedings.

Generally, national courts now rely on the **Infopaq** judgment, where the ECJ provided some useful guidance on Article 5(1) of the Copyright Directive in respect of what amounts to a 'transient' act for the purposes of that provision. In order to fall within this condition the process has to be automated so that the copy created will be automatically deleted without human intervention.

8.11 Remedies

For much of the time, copyright infringements go undetected and many creative people and organizations complain that there is little point in their endeavours if they go unrewarded. The massive scale on which copyright is ignored means that to prosecute every infringement is just not practical. It is argued that only a series of high-profile successful cases will dissuade the copiers.

The court will order remedies for infringement of copyright depending on the circumstances, such as how flagrant the infringement was and what benefit the defendant gained from the infringement. Did that person carry out one of the restricted acts without the copyright owner's permission?

Most commonly, damages are awarded for loss of royalties or loss of profit. The calculation is usually based on the licence fee, or alternatively on the equitable remedy of an account for profits which focuses on the illegal gains of the defendant as opposed to the damages suffered by the claimant. Exemplary (or punitive) damages can be made, though they are rarely awarded in the UK. These are compensation awards in excess of actual damages – a form of punishment awarded in cases of malicious or wilful misconduct or breach of copyright. Section 97(2) CDPA provides some forms of damages in copyright infringement actions:

> . . . the court may in an action for infringement of copyright having regard to all the circumstances, and in particular to –
>
> (a) the flagrancy of the infringement, and
> (b) any benefit accruing to the defendant by reason of the infringement, award such additional damages as the justice of the case may require.

8.11.1 Injunctions

Injunctions (or Scottish *interdicts*) are granted to enforce a legal or equitable right. Accordingly, a grant presupposes the existence of such a right. Injunctions are made by a court and usually require a person to do or refrain from doing specified acts, although they may also require a person to positively do something to prevent what would be unlawful conduct leading to damage to the claimant, such as 'delivery up' of a plagiarized manuscript or music score. Injunctions (born out of equity) are discretionary remedies, which can be positive or negative. If the loss or damage sustained by the claimant was to be satisfactorily compensated by an award of money, then it is said that damages are an adequate remedy, and an injunction will not be available unless the case presents exceptional circumstances. Injunctions may be granted only within the awarding legal jurisdiction and they can be on an interim, perpetual or permanent basis.

A Master[248] or district judge has the power to vary or discharge an injunction granted by any judge with the consent of all the parties. An order for an injunction for breach of copyright must

---

248 Masters are the procedural judges for the majority of the civil business in the Chancery and Queen's Bench Divisions.

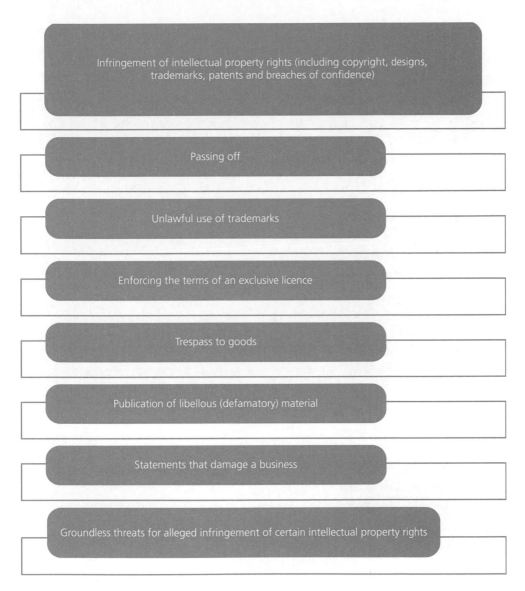

Figure 8.2 Key areas in intellectual property law

be made in the presence of all parties to ensure that they are bound by it. Other court orders may include those shown in Figure 8.4.

8.11.2 Scottish interdicts

An injunction in Scots law is referred to as an 'interdict'. Similar to the English injunction, the interdict is a judicial prohibition or court order preventing someone from doing something. In an emergency, an interim interdict can be obtained in the absence of the person against whom the order is sought (i.e. *ex parte*). Scottish actions in the form of interdicts will usually follow this procedure, as

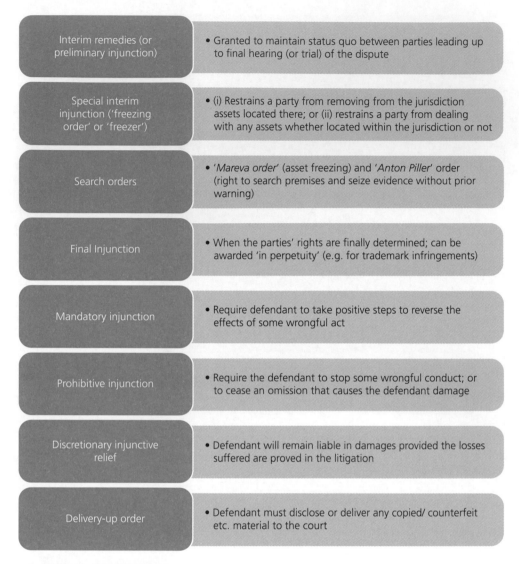

Interim remedies (or preliminary injunction)	• Granted to maintain status quo between parties leading up to final hearing (or trial) of the dispute
Special interim injunction ('freezing order' or 'freezer')	• (i) Restrains a party from removing from the jurisdiction assets located there; or (ii) restrains a party from dealing with any assets whether located within the jurisdiction or not
Search orders	• 'Mareva order' (asset freezing) and 'Anton Piller' order (right to search premises and seize evidence without prior warning)
Final Injunction	• When the parties' rights are finally determined; can be awarded 'in perpetuity' (e.g. for trademark infringements)
Mandatory injunction	• Require defendant to take positive steps to reverse the effects of some wrongful act
Prohibitive injunction	• Require the defendant to stop some wrongful conduct; or to cease an omission that causes the defendant damage
Discretionary injunctive relief	• Defendant will remain liable in damages provided the losses suffered are proved in the litigation
Delivery-up order	• Defendant must disclose or deliver any copied/ counterfeit etc. material to the court

Figure 8.3 Types of injunctions[249]

highlighted in the **Gleneagles** case.[250] This concerned an intellectual property action and trademark infringement. Lord Nimmo Smith granted the following interim interdicts on 11 February 2003 on behalf of the pursuers, Gleneagles Hotels:

> For interdict against the defenders or either of them, their employees or agents or anyone on
> their behalf or acting under their instruction from infringing or continuing to infringe the

---

249 See: Civil Procedure Rules, 60th update, 1 April 2013. Particular attention should be paid to changes in civil legal aid, Part 48 Civil Procedure Rules and Part 2 of the Legal Aid, Sentencing and Punishment of Offenders Act 2012, relating to civil litigation funding and costs: Transitional provisions in relation to pre-commencement funding arrangements.
250 **Gleneagles Hotels Ltd against Quillco 100 Ltd and Toni Antioniou** (2003) Outer House, Court of Sessions (Case No: A 372/03) 1 April 2003 (unreported).

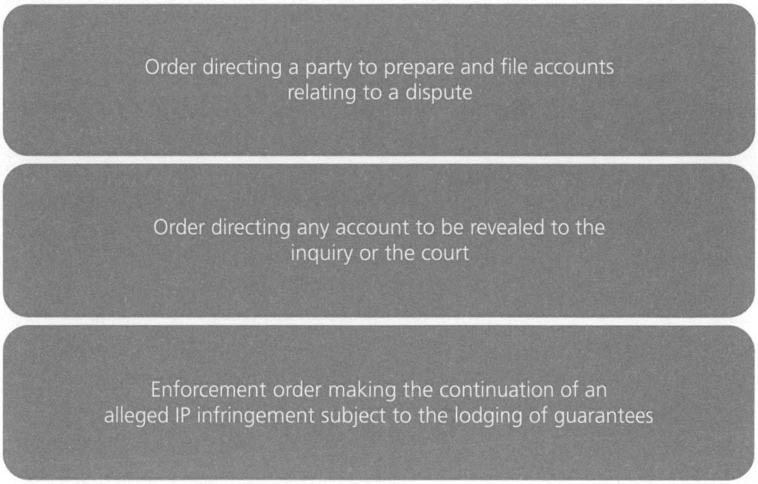

Figure 8.4 Court Orders

pursuer's rights in United Kingdom trademarks in the word 'GLENEAGLES' ... and that by using the name 'GLENEAGLES FILM STUDIOS' and/or the Gleneagles Film Studios (GFS) sign comprising the words 'GLENEAGLES FILM STUDIOS' and depicting a glen and an eagle in substantially similar form (a) in the course of developing and/or marketing a hotel, conference facilities, timeshare lodges, golf courses, club house and restaurant facilities at Aberuthven, Perthshire or any of the foregoing, and (b) in the course of developing and/or marketing a film studio complex and/or housing at Aberuthven, Perthshire aforesaid and (c) causing, directing, procuring, assisting or enabling others to do any of the above acts; and for interdict *ad interim*;

. . . For interdict against the defenders or either of them, their employees or agents or anyone on their behalf from passing off as those of the pursuer the services provided by, and the business operated by, the defenders, and that by promoting or advertising the 'Gleneagles Film Studios' development at Aberuthven, Perthshire under the GFS name or GFS sign similar to the said GFS sign in the Appendix hereto; and for interim interdict.

(See also: *Alan Mackie T / A 197 Aerial Photography against Nicola Askew, Largsholidaylets.co.uk* (2009)[251] for copyright infringement of a website).

8.11.3 Delivery up

As previously stated, the copyright owner is able to take civil as well as criminal action for copyright infringement. There are a number of remedies available.[252] An order for 'delivery up' is made under s 99 CDPA, where a person has an infringing copy of a work in his possession, has made copies of

---

251 (2009) Sheriffdom of South Strathclyde, Dumfries and Galloway, 11 August 2009 (Case No: SA1251/08) (unreported).
252 Sections 96–100 CDPA 'Rights and remedies of the copyright owner'.

the particular design or copyright work or has adapted the work for making copies, knowing or having reason to believe that the work was an original by the right-holder.

The owner of the copyright in the work may apply to the court for an order that the infringing copy or article be 'delivered up' to him.[253] The infringing articles may also be seized and destroyed.[254] Delivery up is usually part of a default judgment (i.e. without a trial or where a defendant has failed to file either an acknowledgement of service or a defence). On an application for judgment for delivery up of goods where the defendant will not be given the alternative of paying their value, the evidence must identify the goods and state where the claimant believes the goods to be situated and why their specific delivery up is sought.

8.11.4 Search orders

The 'right to seize' enables the police and other agencies such as trading standards, collecting agencies and anti-piracy units to enter a property in order to seize the infringing articles. Trading Standards (or the police) usually apply to the magistrates' court to obtain a search warrant in order to seize infringing articles.[255]

One of the most important search orders in IP infringement is the 'Anton Piller' order. It is a court order obtained *ex parte*, and allows the requesting party to access the premises of the other party to gather evidence that the court fears may be destroyed if the search is not conducted immediately. The 'Anton Piller' order was established in **Anton Piller KG v Manufacturing Processes Ltd and Others** (1975)[256] (see below), which involved an action for copyright infringement and misuse of confidential information. Until that time there was no such court order. No constable or bailiff could knock at the door and demand entry to inspect papers or documents. The householder could simply shut the door and refuse entry; a principle established in the leading case of **Entick v Carrington** (1765).[257]

The *Anton Piller* order is not simply a search warrant (conducted by the police) – it is an order which is made without the permission of the defendant. In the past, if permission was not granted, the claimant would be guilty of contempt of court.[258] *Anton Piller* is an order without notice to the defendant (*ex parte*). *Anton Piller* orders play an increasingly important role in protecting businesses from disgruntled or departing employees, who may well take intellectual property with them upon 'clearing their desks'. Some liken *Anton Piller* orders to a search warrant though Lord Denning was at pains to deny this characterization in the **Anton Piller** case itself (see below). Rather, Denning LJ found that it was an exercise of the court's inherent jurisdiction to protect its own process. The order does not authorize entry. Rather, it commands the defendant to permit entry. The defendant may deny entry, and thereafter face contempt proceedings and possible adverse inferences. However, the claimants' agents may not use force to effect entry in the face of the defendant's denial of permission. These 'search orders' are nowadays applied for where the claimant alleges that important documents have been stolen, copied or counterfeited ('piracy'). The same goes for freezing orders. If the court grants such an order, it will usually order a close examination of company accounts alongside the search (and asset-freezing) order.

---

253 Section 99 (1) CDPA.
254 Section 100 (1) CDPA.
255 Section 109 CDPA.
256 [1975] EWCA 12 (Civ Div).
257 (1765) 2 Wils 275.
258 Ibid., as per Lord Denning MR.

 **KEY CASE** **Anton Piller KG v Manufacturing Processes Ltd [1975] EWCA 12 (Civ Div)**

Precedent

❖ To apply for and be granted an *Anton Piller* (search) order, a court will look at three preconditions to be satisfied prior to the making the order. These are:

(i)   there must be a strong prima facie case;

(ii) The potential or actual damage to the claimant must be serious;

(iii) there must be clear evidence that the defendant has documents or articles in their possession that would give rise to liability, and there must be a real possibility that these would be destroyed prior to the hearing of application by notice.

❖ An *Anton Piller* order is applied for to the court without notice (*ex parte*) to the defendant.

Facts

Since 1972, German manufacturers of high repute, Anton Piller KG (part of the Piller Group GmbH in Osterode Harz) (the claimants) made electric motors and generators and increasingly played an important part in the growing computer industry, by designing frequency converters. They used as their agents in the UK a company called Manufacturing Processes Ltd (MPL) (the defendants), run by Mr A. H. S. Baker and Mr B. P. Wallace, the two directors. These agents acted as dealers who would obtain machines from Pillers in Germany and sell them to customers in the UK. Pillers supplied MPL with much confidential information about the machines, including a manual showing how they work, and drawings which were the subject of copyright.

Pillers claimed that the defendants were in secret communication with other German manufacturers called Ferrostaal and Lechmotoren and that MPL was also secretly negotiating with Canadian and United States firms, each time disclosing confidential and copyrighted information about Pillers' power units and details of a new converter ('Silent Block'), the disclosure of which could be most damaging to the claimants.

In order to prevent the disposal by the defendants, before discovery in an action, of documents in their possession relating to Pillers' machines or designs, the claimants applied *ex parte* for an interim injunction to restrain the defendants from infringing Pillers' copyrights and disclosing confidential information and for an order to enter the defendants' premises to inspect all such documents and to remove them into the claimants' solicitors' custody. They told the court that there was strong prima facie evidence that the defendant company was by now engaged in seeking to copy the Piller components for MPL's own financial profit to the great detriment of the claimants and in breach of their rights. Mr Justice Brightman of the Chancery Division granted the interim injunction but refused to order inspection or removal of documents. The claimants appealed.

Decision

The appeal was allowed and the search order granted on the evidence before the court (i.e. infringement of copyright and breach of confidential information). The interim order stated that the defendants must permit the claimants and their solicitors to enter the defendants' premises for the purpose of inspecting documents and files, and removing those which belonged to the claimants. Lord Denning MR stated that the granting of such a search and confiscation order was extremely rare and should be made only when there was no alternative way of ensuring that justice was done. The court made this interim order on the claimants' *ex parte* application.

Analysis

Nowadays *Anton Piller* search orders are granted only in the most exceptional circumstances, where claimants have a very strong prima facie case, that actual or potential damage to them is very serious and there is clear evidence that defendants possess vital material which they might destroy or dispose of so as to defeat the ends of justice before any application *inter partes* can be made.

Anton Piller orders are not without criticism because therein lies an underlying suggestion that a person (the defendant) cannot be trusted and is likely to destroy evidence, and that is a very serious thing. The argument against *Anton Piller* orders (and *Mareva*[259] injunctions[260]) was highlighted by Hoffmann J in **Lock International**[261] where such an order was wrongfully granted, implying dishonesty of the defendant, which, in turn can be costly for him and damage his reputation.

When making decisions about *Anton Piller* orders and deciding liability courts might look at alterative (interim) remedies, such as cross-undertakings in the presence of both parties. Hoffman J in **Lock International** gave examples of alternative orders (such as 'delivery up') when he said:

> . . . not everyone who is misusing confidential information will destroy documents in the face of a court order requiring him to preserve them. In many cases it will therefore be sufficient to make an order for delivery up of the plaintiff's documents to his solicitor or, in cases in which documents belong to the defendant but may provide evidence against him, an order that he preserve the documents pending further order, or allow the solicitor to make copies. The more intrusive orders, allowing searches of premises or vehicles, require a careful balancing of, on the one hand, the plaintiff's right to recover his property or to preserve important evidence against, on the other hand, violation of the privacy of a defendant who has had no opportunity to put his side of the case.[262]

8.12 The future of copyright in the digital age: analysis and discussion

As more and more authors choose to go it alone by self-publishing their book on the internet, the issue of copyright in relation to online publishing has come to the fore, especially given the rise in 'fan art' and 'fan fiction' on sites such as Tumblr[263] and other user-generated content websites. Aubrey Rose, whose *Me, Cinderella?* was self-published in the US on Amazon.com, was put off by the small sum offered by the online book giant and by the lack of control she would have over her own

---

259 See: **Mareva Compania Naviera SA v International Bulkcarriers SA** [1975] 2 Lloyd's Rep. 509 (sub nom 'The Mareva' or 'asset freezing orders').
260 *Mareva* injunctions (also known as 'freezing orders') are court orders that negate the banker's duty to pay or transfer funds as per the instructions of the customer. A *Mareva* order is an interlocutory order (injunction), granted ancillary to a substantive claim involving money, that seeks to prevent a defendant from rendering a decree against him worthless by removing his assets from the jurisdiction of the court.
261 **Lock International plc v Beswick** [1989] 1 WLR 1268 (Hoffman J).
262 Ibid., at 1279 (Hoffman J).
263 See: www.tumblr.com.

copyright, book layout and book cover. Rose wrote in her blog: 'As a writer of BBW (big beautiful women) romantic fiction, I'm acutely aware of the limited amount of cover material available to us and I DO NOT want a thin girl on my cover.' Rose was offered $5,000, with 35 per cent royalties.[264]

The multi-million pound (Euro, dollar etc.) best-seller, *Fifty Shades of Grey* by E. L. James, started life as *Twilight* fan fiction.[265] James began writing erotic fiction in 2009 and submitted her stories to the website www.fanfiction.net. '50shades.com' was taken up by the initial publisher 'The Writer's Coffee Shop', and then resold to Vintage. However the 'fan fiction' version (known as 'Masters of the Universe') was subsequently taken down by the author herself. including deleting those pages from internet archives such as 'The Wayback Machine'. Subsequently, *Fifty Shades* topped the printed best-seller lists around the world. Foreign rights alone were sold to 54 different countries and the film release was scheduled for August 2014 starring Jamie Dornan.[266]

Fan fiction and vanity publications online (e.g. Tumblr) are increasing and there are millions of devoted readers downloading such fiction on their iPad, Kindle, tablet or smartphone – in preference to the printed novel. Some serious British literary talent is migrating to online publishing, joining the colony of fantasy authors and amateur fan fiction writers. In the vanguard are authors such as Iain Pears and Will Self. Pears's best-selling historical novels, *An Instance of the Fingerpost* and *Stone's Fall*, have sold millions as e-fiction. Additionally, Pears offers his readers the chance to go back to check detailed elements of his narrative by way of an interactive readers' website, so that they can flag up suggestions for possible alternative endings to his novels.[267]

See also
Chapter 9.2.1

How can these websites be controlled and policed not only in terms of copyright but also of content? How do we know that this kind of 'grey' publication does not infringe copyright by passing off on a daily basis by unknown (or known) authors? At what point is there a crossover between the fine line of 'fandom' to 'copyright theft'?

Some online publishers now include interactive features in their eBooks (e.g. Mobipocket.com – owned by Amazon), such as sound, where the novelist can create a virtual world (similar to a computer game), giving the reader a chance to engage in the active process of publishing. This new literary interactivity brings with it copyright issues, especially for those authors who are desperate to get published.

Widespread online and offline copyright infringement (whether wilful or unwitting) underlines the need for media companies to better explain to consumers what they can and cannot do with the products they bought or 'illegally' downloaded. Maybe there should be more copyright guidance for rights holders rather than just issuing a list of 'don'ts'. However, it is a fair bet that many infringers know perfectly well that what they are doing is illegal and still continue. Law enforcement is about as effective in some areas as it was in the old Wild West.

8.12.1 EU copyright legislation

The UK Government and Ofcom, the EU Commission and international organizations such as WIPO have been analysing and measuring the various legislative measures in relation to intellectual property. But from an economic perspective, it is unclear whether the current levels of legal protection of IP rights are sufficient to protect authors, artists and musicians. Protectionism may also come into play, resulting from import and export control regulations (e.g. via HM Revenue and Customs), which may not affect the music trade within the EU, but could be excessively restrictive

264 Source: 'Erotic romance author turned down Amazon publishing deal', by Liz Bury, *Guardian*, 8 August 2013.
265 See: www.fanfiction.net/book/Twilight.
266 Sources: 'Q&A: EL James "How would I like to be remembered? As someone who could tell a rollicking good love story"', by Rosanna Greenstreet, *Guardian*, 28 December 2012; *Glamour* Magazine, 25 October 2013 at: www.glamourmagazine.co.uk/news/celebrity/2012/06/21/50-shades-of-grey-cast-rumours-news-trailers.
267 Source: 'Top novelists look to ebooks to challenge the rules of fiction', by Vanessa Thorpe, *Observer*, 10 March 2013.

on trade to and from other countries, depending on political decisions and multilateral negotiations and agreements.

France and to a certain extent the UK have adopted a punishing 'three strikes' approach to online copyright infringement: the UK with the Digital Economy Act 2010 and France with its 'HADOPI' legislation. In April 2009, the French upper legislative house, le Sénat, passed new copyright legislation in the form of *la loi HADOPI* (*haute autorité pour la diffusion des oeuvres et la protection des droits sur l'internet*). The HADOPI law forms a progressive yet graduated response strategy to combat and punish internet piracy. It requires ISPs to monitor their subscribers' use of copyrighted works on their networks and implement progressively more severe punishments to repeat offenders, culminating in suspension or termination of their internet accounts. The HADOPI legislation also established an agency for monitoring compliance and addressing disputes. The agency has the powers to send warning letters to file sharers and ultimately cut them off. Though welcomed by the then EU Commissioner Viviane Reding, France's HADOPI has not found overall support from other EU Member States.[268]

See Chapter
9.8.1

The Gowers Review (2006)[269] rejected the proposals that copyright of recorded music should extend from 50 to 70 or even 95 years (as the EU Commission suggests). Gowers's recommendations were taken up by the Intellectual Property Office, resulting in the consultation document *Taking Forward the Gowers Review of Intellectual Property: Proposed Changes to Copyright Exceptions* in 2009.[270]

The Gowers consultation report provoked an overwhelming response from the music industry, demanding 'fair play for musicians'. Among the most famous respondents were Robbie Williams, Robert Plant and Roger Daltrey. This was soon followed by the EU Parliament's passing the new 70-year copyright term for sound recordings and performers in 2011. One of the most fervent lobbyists, Feargal Sharkey, formerly of the punk group The Undertones and head of the industry group UK Music until 2012, declared, 'I am especially pleased that the announcement focuses on the "invisible" members of our industry . . . who could derive real benefits from this move at a time in life when their earning power would be severely diminished.'[271]

In November 2010, Prime Minister David Cameron commissioned Professor Ian Hargreaves to undertake a review into the impact the intellectual property system has on growth and innovation. *The Review of Intellectual Property and Growth* (the 'Hargreaves Review')[272] and its consultation report were published in June 2012.[273] There was some support for the view that, although creators should continue to be protected and rewarded, reforms were necessary to increase access to information, knowledge and cultural resources, and to make full use of the opportunities created by new technologies. Some respondents to the Hargreaves Review even commented that there are presently substantial quantities of knowledge which are inaccessible, and that creating more opportunities for reusing works and sharing information would foster numerous socially and economically beneficial activities, as well as promoting freedom of expression and enabling research. Some rights holders argued that the existing copyright framework did not impede growth and innovation; and that it was only through strengthening the framework that further growth and innovation could be delivered. At the same time there were respondents who argued that stronger IP rights would give creators greater legal certainty, which in turn would incentivise innovation.

Over the past decade, there have been revolutionary changes in technology. The internet sits alongside devices ranging from MP3 players and e-readers to vast online electronic music and

---

268 For further discussion see: Senftleben (2004).
269 Source: HM Treasury (2006).
270 See: HM Treasury (2009).
271 Source: Feargal Sharkey speech at Music Week Conference, 4 June 2009.
272 See: Hargreaves (2011) at: www.ipo.gov.uk/ipreview-finalreport.pdf.
273 See: HM Government (2012) at: www.ipo.gov.uk/copyright-summaryofresponses-pdf.

literature libraries, all made possible by inexpensive ultra-fast broadband, allowing for the sending or receiving of 200 MP3 music files, an entire *Star Wars* DVD or the complete digitized works of Charles Dickens in a matter of minutes. This technology has meant that P2P file-sharing is now an almost insurmountable problem in protecting the IP rights of authors and artists. Will the world of recorded music and literature be destroyed by piracy and illegal downloads or can new sources of revenue and funding be found to punish illegal downloaders? Or should one take an educational (rather than a punishing) approach, as has been advanced by Ofcom, consulting on online infringement of copyright and cost-sharing orders?[274]

There are different views on policy in this respect. One is that legal regimes of IP protection are ineffective and users expect the basic product (e.g. a music MP3 file) for free, but are prepared to pay for added content (e.g. add-ons such as outtakes, samples, or videos of the actual recording) and to attend concerts and music gigs. How add-ons could be protected is of course still an issue, but it does begin to address the issue of what consumers are actually prepared to pay for. Several new bands (such as H.U.M.A.N.W.I.N.E[275]) have moved towards a route of publishing songs for free on YouTube, but asking for donations and using 'Kickstarter'[276] to raise funds for recording new material. Another is that for most artists the key problem is no longer being pirated; it is all about being noticed in the first place. Some artists would say that file-sharing has been the route to certain bands becoming well known and attempts to prevent it only start once they *are* well known. One such 'beneficiary' is Blackpool pop diva Victoria Christina Hesketh, better known by her stage name 'Little Boots', an English electropop singer-songwriter and DJ. She launched her own career by uploading her songs on to YouTube and MySpace in 2007.

Promoting the cross-border exchange of intellectual assets – such as music or literary manuscripts – is not only about adopting, implementing and enforcing copyright (IP) laws. There needs to be a coherent and multidisciplinary policy setting which promotes the safe creation, exchange and transfer of intellectual assets. There is no detailed survey available of UK, EU or international data as to the scale of illegal downloads and copyright piracy. Estimates of the scale of illegal digital downloads in the UK ranges between 13 and 65 per cent. Most affected are the creative and music industries, which are experiencing great economic instability from digital copyright infringement.

It has become clear that IP laws have to be clarified so that they can be widely understood, especially where new technology and markets create ever-increasing uncertainties, particularly in the design sector (e.g. 3D printing). It will be interesting to see whether the implementations or and secondary legislation to the Digital Economy Act 2010 (effective from 2013) will make an impact, enforced by Ofcom – to support rights holders in enforcing their rights in the Patents County Court and Chancery Division.

See also
Chapter 9.8.2

 FOR THOUGHT

How can copyright be upheld, maintained, claimed and protected in the constantly evolving digital world? Is current legislation creaking at the seams and are attempts by legislators to update current legislation working or simply confusing matters?

---

274 Office of Communications (Ofcom) (2012c) at: http://stakeholders.ofcom.org.uk/binaries/consultations/onlinecopyright/summary/condoc.pdf.
275 H.U.M.A.N.W.I.N.E. is a band based in Boston, Massachusetts, United States. Their name is an acronym of the phrase 'Humans Underground Making Anagrams Nightly While Imperialistic Not-Mes Enslave'.
276 Kickstarter is an American-based private for-profit company founded in 2009 that provides tools to raise funds for creative projects via crowd funding through its website: www.kickstarter.com.

8.12.2 The Intellectual Property Bill 2013–14

As the law stands at the moment, businesses must obtain separate patents covering individual EU countries and enforce them in the national courts of each country. Decades-long negotiations have resulted in EU Regulations being adopted (December 2012) to create a single unitary patent which can be enforced in a Unified Patent Court. In May 2011, Professor Ian Hargreaves published an independent review of UK copyright legislation. The Hargreaves Review, *Digital Opportunity*,[277] made 10 recommendations which were broadly accepted by the UK Government. The main thrust of the Review was that the Government should pursue an integrated approach based on enforcement, education and measures to strengthen and grow legitimate markets in copyright and other IP protected fields.[278] Hargreaves concluded that the present copyright regime 'cannot be considered fit for the digital age when millions of citizens are in daily breach of copyright, simply for shifting a piece of music or video from one device to another'. He further said that people are confused about what is allowed and what is not in relation to 'copyright', with the risk that the law falls into disrepute.

The Intellectual Property Bill 2013–14 (IP Bill) was introduced in May 2013 by Lord Younger in the House of Lords. The Bill has largely taken on the Hargreaves recommendations and had its first reading in the House of Commons after the parliamentary recess in October 2013. The Bill aims to reform the law on the meaning of 'design' (and its infringements) and 'patents' (and their infringements). The Bill proposes changes that will help businesses to better understand what is protected under IP law and thereby reduce the need for costly litigation, and provide greater certainty for investors in new designs and technologies.[279]

Key elements of the Bill include:

- New powers to enable the UK to implement the Unitary Patent Court Agreement. The Court is a central part in introducing a single patent across almost all EU countries. It is estimated that this would lead to direct benefits to business of up to £40 million per year. It is also anticipated that the London Court, which will adjudicate on pharmaceutical and life sciences patent disputes, will benefit the economy by an estimated £200 million per annum.
- The introduction of criminal penalties for copying UK registered designs and the strengthening of design protection. This is already the case for copyright and trademark disputes and brings parity to this area of IP law.
- Proposals for a designs opinion service and an expanded patents opinions service. This would allow design or patent rights holders, or anyone else, to ask the Intellectual Property Office to provide an expert opinion on whether a UK design or patent is valid or being infringed. This will help businesses assess the strength of their case before embarking on more formal and costly legal proceedings, and may help avoid litigation altogether.

The contents of the Bill includes the following:

Part 1

Design – Unregistered design right

1. Meaning of 'design' and 'original'
2. Ownership of design

---

277 See: Hargreaves (2011) at pp. 4–5.
278 Ibid., at p. 9.
279 Source: Press Release by the Intellectual Property Office of 10 May 2013.

3.   Qualification criteria
4.   Infringement: exceptions

Registered Community design

1.   Infringement exception

Registered designs

1.   Ownership of design and application for registration
2.   Right of prior use
3.   Accession to the Hague Agreement
4.   The register: changes of ownership and inspection of documents
5.   Legal proceedings and appeals
6.   Opinions service
7.   Use of directions by the registrar
8.   Offence of unauthorized copying etc. of design in course of business
9.   Offences committed by partnerships

Part 2

Patents

1.   Infringement: marking product with internet link
2.   Opinions service
3.   Unified Patent Court
4.   Sharing information with overseas patent offices
5.   Minor amendments to the Patents Act 1977

Part 3

Miscellaneous

1.   Freedom of information: exemption for research
2.   Reporting duty
3.   Recognition of foreign copyright work and performances

Part 4

General

1.   Power to make consequential or transitional provisions etc.
2.   Commencement, extent and short title.

8.12.3 The Unified Patent Court

The introduction of a European Unitary Patent and associated Unified Patent Court (UPC) has been an EU-wide legal topic for over 40 years. In December 2012, an agreement was reached by the EU Commission to legislate on the so-called 'patent package', a legislative initiative consisting of two Regulations:

1.   The Unified Patent Regulations, and
2.   The Unified Patent Court Agreement (or 'UPC Agreement').

The proposed regulation creates the 'Unitary Patent Protection' in the European Union.[280] The Intellectual Property Bill is an essential first step in bringing the UPC and the unitary patent into effect.[281] The UPC is a proposed patent court common to several Member States of the European Union. The Court would hear cases regarding copyright infringement and revocation proceedings of European patents valid in the territories of participating states. The Court is to be established by the Agreement on a Unified Patent Court, which was signed in 2013 by 25 states (i.e. all EU Member States except Croatia, Poland and Spain). If established, the UPC would eliminate the need for separate litigation of infringement of European patents in each state in which the patent court is applicable. The court will consist of a Court of First Instance, a Court of Appeal (in Luxembourg) and a common Registry. The Court of First Instance consists of a central division with its seat in Paris and sections in London and Munich, as well as local and regional divisions.

This means that the Unitary Patent and Unified Patent Court place a further layer of complexity on top of the current IP regime, which will exist alongside the new legislation, in addition to current EU legislation on copyright.

 ## 8.13 Further reading

Baden-Powell, E. and Anthony, L. (2012) 'Digital Economy Act 2'. *Entertainment Law Review*, 23(5), 130–133.
The article discusses whether the Digital Economy Act 2010 (DEA) is working in tackling online piracy in the United Kingdom. The authors note that the UK legislation can only work alongside educational initiatives by regulators (e.g. Ofcom) and through co-operation with ISPs. They examine the French 'three strikes' authority, HADOPI and how it is working in practice, resulting in a 26 per cent overall reduction in unauthorised peer-to-peer network activity since October 2010.

Barron, A. (2012) 'Kant, copyright and communicative freedom'. *Law & Philosophy*, 31(1), 1–48.
Anne Barron discusses the rapid expansion of copyright worldwide which has sparked numerous efforts to defend the 'public domain' in relation to defending a free IP culture. But what are the authors' rights in such a free culture? Barron's article argues that such a conception – of what a free culture is – emerges from a direct engagement with the philosophy of Immanuel Kant (liberal individualism). Although the idea of freedom is at the heart of Kant's philosophy, his understanding of freedom is not at all reducible to the ideas of individual liberty or personal autonomy at play in contemporary liberal IP thought (see Kant's essay 'An Answer to the Question: "What is Enlightenment?" ' of 1784). The article's main claim is that when Kant's rather less famous essay 'On the Wrongfulness of Unauthorized Publication' (1785) is read in relation to the arguments for publicity, he advances a necessary connection between authors' rights (as distinct from copyrights) and what Jürgen Habermas has named the 'public sphere'. Barron argues that from a Kantian perspective, it is the public sphere of open, inclusive and principled criticism – not the public domain as such – that should serve as the regulative idea for any evaluation of copyright law's role in relation to the possibility of a free culture.

---

280 See: European Commission (2013).
281 See: Regulation 2013/0268 (COD) amending Regulation 1215/2012 on jurisdiction and the recognition and enforcement of judgments in civil and commercial matters (see also: Council Regulation 44/2001 On jurisdiction and the recognition and enforcement of judgments in civil and commercial matters (the 'Brussels I Regulation')).

Carty, H. (2008) 'An analysis of the modern action for breach of commercial confidence: when is protection merited?' *Intellectual Property Quarterly*, 4, 416–455.
Hazel Carty revisits the *Coco Engineers* test in breach of confidence and identifies it as being too limited. She compares *Coco* with *Douglas v Hello Ltd* (2007),[282] arguing that there is a need for a new formulation which must in particular reflect the modern judicial approach as to what is protectable information and when an obligation of confidence arises in protecting 'ideas'. She argues that protection can only be granted when it is 'merited'.

Cornish, W., Llewelyn, D. and Aplin, T. (2013) *Intellectual Property: Patents, Copyrights, Trademarks & Allied Rights*. 8th edn. London: Sweet & Maxwell.
This is the classic textbook by William ('Bill') Cornish and other excellent specialist and reputable authors in the IP field, if you want to read more in depth about intellectual property (IP) law. Since the text is written by practising lawyers, it is up to date, accurate and straight to the point. Additionally, the text provides thoughtful analysis of every area of IP law and guides the reader through complex legislation, particularly recent EU law. There are questions and issues for the reader to develop further. This is a 'flip and find' practitioner reference work, aimed at IP professionals.

Daly, M. (2013) 'Is there an entitlement to anonymity? A European and international analysis'. *European Intellectual Property Review*, 35(4), 198–211.
Maureen Daly asks whether there can be true anonymity on the internet. She argues that, with the advancements in technology, it is now difficult to remain anonymous online. This article examines how the battle of balancing the right of privacy against the right to identify an anonymous user involved in illegal activity in order to defend and enforce intellectual property rights is addressed at European and international level.

Harding, T. (2013) 'BitTorrent tracking as a means of detecting illegal file-sharing'. *E-Commerce Law & Policy*, 15(2), 8–9.
The article discusses the legal issues for copyright proprietors who use specialized software to track users of the BitTorrent file-sharing system, detect copyright infringement and apply to the court for disclosure of the names and addresses of the alleged infringers. Harding discusses two cases in this area of copyright infringement and licensing: *Golden Eye v Telefonica* (2012) and *Media CAT Ltd v Adams* (2011). He also considers, *inter alia*, the study by Chothia and Cova, 'The Unbearable Lightness of Monitoring', on the technical aspects of monitoring BitTorrent. An examination of (complex) case law suggests that there are problems with this sort of evidence and its probative value.

Kerly, Sir Duncan Mackenzie (Keeling, D. T, Llewelyn, D. and Mellor, J., eds) (2009) *Kerly's Law of Trade Marks and Trade Names*. 15th edn. London: Sweet & Maxwell.
If you wanted to become an expert in trademarks, this is the seminal reference text. The hardback edition, compiled by specialist lawyers in the IP and trademark field, provides a full explanation of the UK law of trademarks and trade names, covering, *inter alia*, UK and EU registration, different types of marks, enforcement and infringement. The text also goes through licensing, merchandizing and franchising and deals with available remedies, such as mediation and arbitration in the context of trademarks.

Larusson, H. K. (2009) 'Uncertainty in the scope of copyright: the case of illegal file-sharing in the UK'. *European Intellectual Property Review*, 31(3), 124–134.
Haflidi Kristjan Larusson discusses the way digital technology and its use on the internet have revolutionized the way in which various copyright material is captured, stored, copied and distributed. He argues that technology reduces production and transaction costs and provides

---

282 OBG Ltd and others v Allan and others; Douglas and another and others v Hello! Ltd and others; Mainstream Properties Ltd v Young and others and another [2007] UKHL 21 (sub nom 'Douglas v Hello! No 7').

authors, right holders and users with a wide range of new means to create, market and share content, means which 'old' media (such as books, vinyl records and video tapes) do not offer. It further allows for the making of exact copies of the digital original in a fast and cheap way, thereby enabling individuals to copy and distribute copyright material on a quantitative and qualitative scale previously only available to commercial operators. This has brought with it legal uncertainty in relation to copyright laws in the music business. The author of this article discusses the lack of clear legislative policy and yet the growth of both black-letter law and case law. Larusson argues that copyright law has had more than its fair share of imprecise legislation and confusing case-law, both of which make it difficult to find clear answers to concrete legal questions.

Price, M. E., Verhulst, S. G. and Morgan, L. (eds) (2013) *Routledge Handbook of Media Law.* **Abingdon and New York: Routledge.**
The contributors to this mighty tome, mostly academics and legal theorists from international universities, have written a collection of serious theoretical essays and research papers on media policy, free speech, media governance, technological development and comparative aspects of media law. Some of the chapters deal with media regulation and global media governance of social media (e.g. Michael Latzer, Natascha Just and Florian Saurwei's 'Self- and co-regulation' in Part IV). Some essays crystallize the EU regulatory and treaties framework, including the Audiovisual Media Services Directive (AVMS) and the Television without Frontiers Directive (TWF) (e.g. Jan Loisen, Caroline Pauwels and Karen Donders, 'Mainstreaming EU cultural policies internally and externally' in Chapter 4). Bernd Holznagel in Chapter 8 on 'internet freedom' compares UK and German constitutional law in relation to the protection of the individual from privacy invasion (*Schutzpflicht* – duty of protection). He discusses EU law in relation to privacy as well as protection under the European Charter of Fundamental Rights. Holznagel also mentions the French HADOPI legislation, comparing this to the UK Digital Economy Act 2010 and how the two countries have implemented 'three strikes' legislation in relation to online copyright infringement.

Richardson, M. and Thomas, J. (2012) *Fashioning Intellectual Property: Exhibition, advertising and the press 1789–1918.* **Cambridge, New York and Melbourne Cambridge University Press.**
Megan Richardson and Julian Thomas provide an enthusiastic historical overview of the development of intellectual property law in Europe, covering the emergence of the print press and advertising during the French nouvelle epoch of the late eighteenth and early nineteenth centuries, leading up to the great exhibitions in Vienna and Paris. Linked to technological advancement and inventions, the authors discuss the fears of creators and inventors of having their works copied without any backing of copyright legislation at the time. How could patents for knitting machines be protected without an international patent office? How could new Parisian fashion creations by either Chanel or Dior be protected from being copied or passed off by cheaper labels even in those days? Richardson and Thomas provide an insight into these answers based on archive material and illustrated case law, such as *Prince Albert v Strange* (1849) and *Walter v Lane* (1900). A fascinating and very readable book which charts the history of how IP law came about, demonstrating the socio-legal aspects of UK common law, later adopted in the United States and other common law countries.

Sellars, S. (2011) 'Online privacy: do we have it and do we want it? A review of the risks and UK case law'. *European Intellectual Property Review,* **33(1), 9–17.**
This article discusses the increase in social networking and blogging and the amount of personal data which is thereby being made available online. Simon Sellars discusses the potential risks to individuals who are sharing personal opinions and various other personal information via the internet. The author examines the scale of the infrastructure upon which today's technology is built, which brings increased levels of risk of data disclosure. He argues that, while enforcement of privacy rights used to be the domain of the celebrity, the courts are increasingly entertaining issues of individual privacy. This article reviews some of the potential online privacy risks, and how these have been addressed in the UK courts. The clear impression that emerges is that the standard of what amounts to a reasonable expectation of privacy is not the same as it once was.

Wei, W. (2009) 'ISP indirect copyright liability: conflicts of rights on the internet'. *Computer and Telecommunications Law Review,* **15(8), 181–185.**
This article examines the impact of ISP copyright liability on other aspects of life, such as personal and private life. Weixiao Wei contemplates how the law should be modified to ensure a proper balance between different interests, such as freedom of information and a right to privacy. The discussion suggests that effective copyright enforcement over the internet need not come at the expense of internet users' privacy and denial of public access to information, nor result in a retreat of technology. The author argues that a better balance needs to be struck among all stakeholders by employing legislative means to ensure copyright works and other rights of the public can be simultaneously protected over the internet. Finally, it concludes that, even though a developing ISP copyright liability system may, in the short term, bring negative effects to certain parts of society, if effort by legislators are made to advance this liability system, society as a whole will eventually benefit.

Chapter 9

Copyright II: Entertainment Law

Chapter Contents

9.1 Overview

This chapter picks up from the previous chapter, discussing the development and advancement of online technology and the impact on authors' and creators' intellectual property (IP) rights. The main focus will be on the music and entertainment industry and how copyright legislation is protecting artists' and performers' economic rights in the form of royalty payments. Copyright in relation to a piece of music may involve copyright over the musical work itself and, in addition to this, there can be copyright over the lyrics. There may also be a copyright over the sound recording.

See 9.4 and 9.5 below.

Some performance artists, such as Lily Allen, have argued that their royalties have been dramatically reduced since music downloads via peer-to-peer (P2P) file-sharing have become increasingly easy. In the form of some case studies, this chapter will focus on the development of the phonogram (recording) industry and the technological developments which have led to some industrial copyright infringements, such as internet piracy, P2P file-sharing and sampling. The chapter also touches on other IP violations in the book publishing, film and games industries.

The emergence of online music distribution services – such as Amazon's Cloud Player and MP3 Store – and internet radio services and free digital services such as Spotify has created challenges for the music industry and the various royalty-collecting and performance rights societies. The complex issue of music piracy will also be discussed using the **Pirate Bay** case, the first P2P file-sharing site charged with facilitating illegal downloading of copyrighted material.

See also Chapter 8.7

This chapter also discusses the UK Digital Economy Act 2010 as well as actions taken at international and European Commission level. The chapter aslo discusses book publishing and the ebook industries. They are generally exclusive rights – subject to a number of limitations and exceptions – aimed at fine-tuning the balance between legitimate interests of right holders and of users. The legislation has been enhanced by the Enterprise and Regulatory Reform Act 2013 and will no doubt be further amended by the Intellectual Property Bill 2013.

See also Chapter 8.5.4

9.2 Artists in revolt: what price piracy?

From 2009 onwards, a number of pop stars declared war on peer-to-peer (P2P) file-sharing, including Gary Barlow of Take That and Queen's Diamond Jubilee concert fame[1] in April 2012, and prominent music promoter and *X Factor* creator Simon Cowell.[2] Singer Lily Allen voiced strong concerns via her blog about internet piracy, calling all file-sharing illegal and claiming that her number one enemies are millions of people all over the world who download her music without paying for it.[3]

Some artists, however, thought differently, such as Radiohead, Pink Floyd and Blur. They believed that free releases of their new singles on YouTube would help artists attract a new generation of fans and promote them on a wider platform; and, moreover, that ultimately greater revenue would be generated by live acts and artist-related merchandise. It is difficult to establish at what point music downloads become illegal and the international debate surrounding music downloads, encouraged by famous pop stars, continues.

UK Music[4] is an umbrella organization representing the UK music industry. The pressure group has regularly lobbied Parliament and was instrumental in advising on the Digital Economy Act 2010 and subsequent secondary legislation, including the EU Commission. UK Music notes that the British music industry generates around £4 billion per annum, contributing significantly to exports and providing more than 130,000 UK jobs. The enormous value created by the UK music and creative industry was fully recognized by Government when Prime Minister David Cameron said at a convention:

> . . . so government must get out of the way where it is inhibiting enterprise and it's got to get active in those areas where it is needed. And there's a third, crucial part of our coalition strategy for growth – which is to rebalance our economy.

> . . . we are determined that should change. That doesn't mean picking winners but it does mean supporting growing industries – aerospace, pharmaceuticals, high-value manufacturing, hi-tech engineering, low-carbon technology. And all the knowledge-based businesses including the creative industries.[5]

9.2.1 Piracy: music downloads and e-books

One of the main factors which eventually killed off the UK music store HMV and high-street video rental giant Blockbuster was piracy. Increasingly people, particularly young people, listen to music online which they do not want to pay for. As a result CD and online album sales dropped dramatically from 2008 onwards. Blockbuster could no longer compete in its traditional business of lending DVDs and games. Online businesses such as LoveFilm and Netflix had destroyed the rental market for physical media, forcing the high street video rental store into administration.[6]

At the same time HMV shops in China, Hong King and Singapore continued to thrive after a subsequent Asian buy-out by 'AID Partners', headed by Kelvin Wu. Unlike its sickly British business, the eight HMV Hong Kong and Singapore stores were debt-free by March 2013. Mr Wu reasoned

---

1 See: 'Diamond Jubilee: Gary Barlow album tops chart', BBC News Online, 3 June 2012 at: www.bbc.co.uk/news/entertainment-arts-18318304.
2 See: 'Simon Cowell has called in cops after Leona Lewis' new track was leaked on to the Internet,' Sun, 19 August 2009.
3 Source: 'Lily Allen campaigns against music piracy', Daily Telegraph, 21 September 2009.
4 For more information see: www.ukmusic.org/about-us.
5 Source: A transcript of a speech given by Prime Minister David Cameron on 28 May 2010 on the economy at: www.number10.gov.uk/news/transforming-the-british-economy-coalition-strategy-for-economic-growth.
6 Source: 'HMV calls in the administrators', by Andrea Felsted and Robert Budden, Financial Times, 15 January 2012.

that Chinese music lovers would still pay full price for CDs and DVDs in addition to music downloads; he planned to open more stores in Shenzhen and Guangzhou before expanding to Taiwan and Macau. Mr Wu also denied that there were difficulties because of piracy, stating that the attitude to buying fakes in China had changed: 'if you buy an 84-inch LG television for HK$180,000 [£15,000], why would it bother you to buy a HK$200 [£15] DVD?'[7]

The book publishing industry also suffered in the same way with e-readers such as Kindle,[8] iPads and tablets, often with free publication downloads, making reading easier while travelling and commuting. The titillating sex publication market grew rapidly during 2012, and digital fiction sales showed an increase of 188 per cent on the same period in 2011. At Christmas 2012, some 640,000 tablets were unwrapped in the UK, and by the beginning of 2013, there were 1.22m e-readers, according to YouGov. The Publishers Association (PA) reported that Britain's consumer sales of e-books increased by 366 per cent in 2011 (compared with the previous year), bringing the figure to £92m sales in December 2012.

In 2010, Amazon released its Digital Text Platform for its online authors (the platform's name was changed to Kindle Direct Publishing (KDP) in 2011). Using KDP, anybody with a 'literary work' was now able to pop it straight into the Kindle online store. KDP became a roaring success, though it raises the question: where does copyright lie in this venture and with whom? Amazon offers its KDP authors one of two royalty percentages, depending on the price the writers choose to charge for their books. If an author chooses to sell the book for up to £1.48, he gets a 35 per cent royalty share; at £1.49 or more, the royalty becomes 70 per cent. If one compares this with the typical royalties for academic textbook publishing (such as this one), the author is lucky if she receives between 8 and 10 per cent of royalties on net sales of the published edition.

Amazon's KDP agreement states that the person who uploads his e-book is the publisher and that copyright is retained by the author, which makes the KDP publication a licence to distribute. The reason for the higher royalty rates (35 to 70 per cent) is generally considered to be a fair reflection of the fact that Amazon as 'publisher' has no print costs and no setting costs, as conventional book publishers have. In 'self-publishing' on the internet, the uploading process, plus any necessary file formatting, is done by the author; additionally e-books support the online content that have increased Kindle sales (owned by Amazon).

The Kindle Million Club – an unofficial society for writers who have sold a million e-books – includes some self-published stars, such as American writers John Locke and Amanda Hocking, who specialize in crime adventures and paranormal romances. The British author E. L. James (aka Erika Leonard) began her *Fifty Shades of Grey* series in 2009 as internet 'fanfic' (fan fiction), based on the characters of the *Twilight* vamps-and-vampires series; she has since written more 'mummy porn', uploaded via KDP. E. L. James's standard weekly earnings were more than £640,000 in 2012.[9] 'Fanfic' stories and novels, written by fans of existing characters (such as J. K. Rowling's Harry Potter), are then shared mainly on the internet. This kind of fiction remains a nearly invisible form of outsider 'art' and has grown exponentially in volume and in legal importance over the past two or three years. Because of its nature, authorship and underground status, fan fiction stands at an intersection of key issues regarding intellectual property.[10] One of the youngest British 'fanfic' writers is Ben Galley (aged 27 at the time of writing), who is selling tens of thousands of his fantasy novels, set in the magical realm of Emaneska. His first novel, *The Written*, was completed on his iPhone between serving hot snacks at the West Cornwall Pasty Company at Guildford station.

When Penguin merged with Random House (an Anglo-German merger) in October 2012, the deal included high-end investment in the fast-moving world of digital books and digital readers.

---

7 Source: 'Asia promises new records for HMV as music lovers pump up the volume,' by Emily Ford, *The Times*, 21 March 2013.
8 Amazon first launched the Kindle electronic reader in 2007 and it has become an international phenomenon.
9 Source: 'Ebook Revolution', *Sunday Times Magazine*, 11 November 2012, pp. 44–47.
10 For a detailed discussion see: Schwabach (2011).

Amazon appears to have a rather laissez-faire approach to online publishing, especially where erotic fiction under pseudonyms is concerned. A *Sunday Times Magazine* feature on e-book and vanity publishing found that authors writing under false names, such as Amy Valenti or Sidonic Spice, were making between £700 and £1,000 per month from self-publishing on themes such as 'lesbian babysitters' and 'threesome books'. However, Amazon reader power triumphed when pro-paedophilia titles, such as *The Paedophile's Guide to Love and Pleasure*, were discovered in the Kindle Store in 2010. Customers threatened to boycott the company unless it got rid of these titles. Though Amazon initially fought this kind of online 'censorship', it eventually wiped the titles from the online store.[11]

See also
Chapter 8.12

How can one be sure, though, as a self-publisher on Amazon or via a blog, that one's e-book or article is not plagiarized or 'stolen'? It is relatively easy now to purchase a .mobi file from Amazon and convert the online text with this file converter to a Word document. It is then equally possible to change the title and author of the publication and then republish the stolen book on a website, or even on Amazon under the KDP agreement. Amazon say they have a plagiarism checker but it is relatively easy to fool the programme (as it is with other software, such as Turnitin or Torrentsradar.com).

What is piracy? The Office of Fair Trading (OFT) and Trading Standards commonly use the term 'piracy' to describe the deliberate infringement of copyright on a commercial scale, including activities that cause commercial harm. In relation to the music industry it refers to unauthorized copying. Piracy falls into four categories, namely physical piracy, counterfeits, bootlegs and internet piracy. Physical music piracy is the making or distribution of copies of sound recordings on physical carriers without the permission of the rights owner whereby the packaging of pirate copies may or may not be different from the original. Pirate copies are often compilations, such as the 'Greatest Hits' or 'Best Of' a specific artist or group, or a compilation of a specific genre, such as dance tracks or hip hop, and can extend to music videos, films and games.[12]

See below 9.4

 FOR THOUGHT

What advice would you give on copyright to someone who publishes his book online via a 'fan fiction' website? What if someone steals his e-book by copying it and passing it off as their own? By publishing your book via the Amazon KDP platform, for instance, who then becomes the publisher? Advise your client accordingly.

9.2.2 The 'Napster' case

Napster became the first online song-swapping file-share service, based in the USA, attracting more than 60 million users by 2000. Created by Shawn Fanning, while he was studying at Northeastern University in Boston, the service was named after Fanning's unusual hairstyle. Napster's technology allowed people to share their MP3 music files with other internet users, thereby bypassing the commercial music licensing market and avoiding buying CDs. The service operated between June 1999 and July 2000, when Napster was accused of violating US copyright legislation, namely the Digital Millennium Copyright Act of 1998 (DMCA).[13]

---

11 Ibid. p. 47.
12 For further discussion see: Parsons (2000).
13 Pub. L. No. 105–304, 112 Stat. 2860 (28 October 1998). The DMCA was signed into law by President Clinton on 28 October 1998. The legislation implements two 1996 World Intellectual Property Organization (WIPO) treaties: the WIPO Copyright Treaty and the WIPO Performances and Phonograms Treaty.

In 1999, Shawn Fanning initially worked on a borrowed PC in his uncle's office in Massachusetts and slept in a nearby utility cupboard during day-long programming sessions. During early 2000, the founders of Napster moved to an office above a bank in San Mateo, California. Figures scrawled on a whiteboard told how many people around the world had installed their file-sharing application and were using Napster to download music from each other's computers. There were some 20 million users at the time.[14]

A lawsuit was subsequently filed jointly by the Recording Industry Association of America (RIAA), AOL, Time Warner, Bertelsmann, EMI, Vivendi Universal and Sony. Heavy metal band Metallica and rap artist Dr Dre sued in separate legal actions, demanding, *inter alia*, that some 60,000 pages be removed from Napster containing the artists' names. In May 2000, San Francisco Judge Marilyn Hall Patel ruled that Napster was guilty of online copyright infringement and trading copyrighted music without permission. Napster was not entitled to claim protection under the DMCA, because the company did not transmit, route or provide connections for infringing material through its system. Napster was ordered to pay damages and the service was shut down in July 2000.[15] While appealing against the court's decision, Napster's chief executive, Konrad Hilbers, tried to reach an amicable settlement with the companies concerned, involving various licensing agreements.

See Chapter
8.8.1

In January 2002, Napster's brand and logo were registered as trademarks. Napster then launched a legal file-swapping service as a free beta test version to a selected 20,000 users with more than 100,000 music files on a subscription basis. Shawn Fanning assured the courts that 98 per cent of the code behind the program had been rewritten, adding a music player, chat rooms and instant messaging to the service.[16] There is no doubt that Napster paved the way for decentralized P2P file-sharing and distribution programs. These have become increasingly difficult to control, making internet piracy still relatively easy.

9.2.3 The *Pirate Bay* case

The event that took the issue of music piracy and copyright infringement one step further was the **Pirate Bay** case. By 2003, Sweden had the highest penetration of high-speed broadband fibre-optic connections in Europe and the Pirate Bay (TPB) website, founded in Sweden, was offering 'BitTorrent protocol' and 'magnet links' to facilitate peer-to-peer (P2P) file-sharing of music, films and TV shows at the time.[17]

On 17 April 2009, the Stockholm district court (Tingsrätt) found the four men behind TPB guilty of internet piracy, i.e. facilitating illegal downloading of copyrighted material. After a 13-day trial, judge Tomas Norström and three *namndeman* (a jury with extended powers) found Peter Sunde, Gottfrid Svartholm Warg, Fredrik Neij and Carl Lundström guilty of 'assisting in making copyright content available', that is, having made 33 copyright-protected files accessible for illegal file-sharing via the TPB website. The Pirate Bay's founders and owners were imprisoned for one year.[18]

---

14 In an online special feature, Tom Lamont recalls the incredible sense of liberation he felt as a young music fan, the day he found Napster online as a teenager in 1999, *Guardian Online* 24 February 2013 at: www.guardian.co.uk/music/2013/feb/24/napster-music-free-file-sharing.
15 The movie documentary *Downloaded* (2013) tells the story of Napster.
16 The new service offered standard MP3 music files and 'nap' files, which are MP3s with the addition of a protective layer that prevented them being copied off the host computer or burned onto CDs. There was also a 'buy' button, linking the service to the music retail site CDNow, owned by Bertelsmann.
17 Prosecutor's charges against the four defendants in Swedish: Internationella åklagarkammaren Stockholm, 31 January 2008, available at www.idg.se/polopoly_fs/1.143041!stamningsansokanpb.pdf.
18 Source: 'Artist hoppar av Pirate bay-åtalet', *Svenska Dagbladet*, publicerad Tobias Brandel, 17 April 2009.

The Stockholm court found that by providing a website with search functions, upload and storing capabilities and contacts between file-sharers, TPB had made it very easy to commit illegal 'copyright' acts. The four accused used as a defence the fact that the platform did not actually 'host' any files, but this was not acceptable to the Stockholm court.

Resulting from a parallel civil legal action, the four TPB defendants were fined SEK 30 million (€2.7m or £3m) in damages to copyright holders for lost sales, including 17 media and record companies such as Warners, MGM Pictures, Columbia Pictures, Twentieth Century Fox Film, Sony BMG, Universal and EMI. The Pirate Bay website was shut down by a court order. The TPB appellants demanded a retrial on the grounds that the Stockholm Tingsrätt judge had been biased in that he was a member of several copyright protection agencies in Sweden, but their appeal was dismissed by the Swedish Court of Appeal.[19]

By March 2013, The Pirate Bay had regrouped and set up shop in North Korea. In a post on its website, TPB said Pyongyang had invited the online file-sharing service to use its network and the site had reportedly altered its ship logo to bear the North Korean flag.[20] In June 2013, a founder of the Pirate Bay, Gottfrid Svartholm Warg, was sentenced to two years' imprisonment for his part in one of the biggest hacking attacks to take place in Sweden. The attacks were carried out against the Nordea banking group and services firm Logica. Personal data about thousands of Swedes were stolen in the attacks and was subsequently published online.[21]

In August 2013 – to coincide with celebrations of its tenth anniversary – the Pirate Bay released the 'PirateBrowser', a bundle of Firefox add-ons that helps users 'dodge' ISP filters.[22] This browser is intended to circumvent censorship, to remove limits on accessing sites which government 'spies' such as Ofcom or the Internet Watch Foundation (IWF) do not want you to know about.[23]

Internet pirates now tend to move away from EU Member States to new 'cyber' territories, such as China or Ukraine, or to work via drone satellites, to avoid prosecution for illegal file-sharing. This change has come about via 'bulletproof hosting' by websites which are apparently impervious to legal threats and blocks using non-EU countries (or space) with less stringent IP legislation. 'Bulletproof' services are generally linked to illegal activities, such as extreme or child pornography, which are very popular with criminal groups, spammers and illegal file-sharing services (see also: **Hit Bit Software GmbH v AOL Bertelsmann Online GmbH & Co KG** (2001)[24]).

In January 2012, Megaupload, one of the internet's largest file-sharing sites, was shut down by officials in the United States. The site's founders were charged with violating US piracy laws. Federal prosecutors accused it of costing copyright holders more than $500m (£320m) in lost revenue. The US Justice Department said that Megaupload's two co-founders – Kim Dotcom, formerly known as Kim Schmitz, and Mathias Ortmann – were arrested in Auckland, New Zealand along with two other employees of the business at the request of US officials.[25] The law enforcement argument was that Megaupload was a file-sharing service that enabled pirated material to be shared. However, the site was also used by many new and upcoming musicians to post their own material for publicity purposes. When the site was closed down some of these artists (legal file-sharers) lost access to their own copyrighted material. There was a brief period in which they were allowed to apply to have files copied back to them but not all were able to do so in time. Mr Dotcom said on Twitter that his lawyers 'had repeatedly asked LeaseWeb not to delete Megaupload servers while court

19 Source: Reuters 'Swedish court says Pirate Bay judge not biased', 25 June 2009.
20 Source: 'Doubt cast on Pirate Bay's claim to have set up in North Korea', by Amada Holpuch, *Guardian*, 4 March 2013.
21 Source: 'Pirate Bay co-founder jailed over hacking attack', by Richard Milne, *Financial Times*, 20 June 2013.
22 PirateBrowser also supplies an index of bookmarked torrent sites including Kickass Torrents, Bitsnoop and H33T.
23 Source: 'The Pirate Bay launches its own "Pirate Browser" to dodge filters', by James Vincent, *Independent*, 12 August 2013.
24 [2001] ECDR 18 (Landgericht München).
25 Source: 'Megaupload file-sharing site shut down', BBC *News Online*, 20 January 2012.

proceedings are pending in the US'. Mr Dotcom was free on bail in New Zealand at the time (June 2013) while fighting extradition to the US to face charges of copyright fraud.[26]

9.2.4 Legal music streaming: Spotify and iTunes

One further element in the demise of high-street music giant HMV was the introduction of the online 'jukebox' Spotify (based in Sweden)[27] and digital music downloads via Apple's iTunes. The BPI (British Phonographic Industry), representing the British music recording industry, reported in early 2012 that online digital music sales had outstripped sales of physical music CDs and DVDs for the first time. Music fans had streamed more than 3.7 billion tracks and bought 30.5 million digital albums and 183.3 million digital singles online during the Christmas period of 2011. The BPI chief Geoff Taylor said that some 1.2 billion tracks had been downloaded illegally in 2008.[28] As one in five physical music buyers left the high street in 2012, internet-savvy Britons flocked to digital products such as iTunes or Spotify; both Adele and Ed Sheeran released their albums online that year before releasing physical CDs.

By 2013 Google was in talks with big music labels to launch a streaming service to compete with Spotify and Deezer (another popular online music service) as it looked to expand into the fastest growing areas of the music market. Most important for both Spotify and Google was the income from premium advertising-supported music streaming, with revenues in the region of $468m or 16 per cent of global digital music revenues, according to IFPI, which represents the global recording industry.[29]

The question is: is it legal? Seemingly so, though songwriter and producer Pete Waterman thinks that streamed music services online are 'scandalous', stating that 'these streaming business models are a disgrace, they devalue our artists, they damage this country economically, culturally and morally.'[30] All the music on Spotify has been licensed from and delivered by labels or other rights holders. If an artist asks the server how their music ended up on Spotify, it can turn out that the artist's music has been licensed and delivered by a label or aggregator without the artist knowing about this. Spotify has negotiated deals with necessary rights holders in all of their launch countries, and has agreed royalties, based on how frequently an artist's or producer's music is played. All the metadata (name of album, track, artist, etc.) is delivered by the relevant record label or aggregator.

The internet has given us access to a wide range of social networks, allowing us to share experiences and swap songs, films or books. Will the literary world or recorded music eventually be destroyed by piracy? How can new sources of revenue and therein funding for new artists be found as an alternative to punishing illegal downloaders?

See below 9.2.7

9.2.5 Counterfeiting

Counterfeits are another example of physical piracy. They are recordings made without the required permission from the artist or publisher, which are then packaged so that they resemble the original as closely as possible. The original artwork is reproduced on sophisticated copiers,

---

26 Source: 'Kim Dotcom angry after Megaupload files deleted', BBC News Online, 20 June 2013.
27 Spotify uses a piece of software that allows online users to play any of its music on demand. It keeps a secret cache on your PC and uses that to serve music to other users, known as 'legal BitTorrent' for music.
28 Source: 'The role of record labels in the digital age'. Extract from the speech by BPI Chief Executive Geoff Taylor on 20 June 2008.
29 Source: 'Google looks to beat music rivals', by Robert Budden and Robert Cookson, Financial Times, 22 February 2013.
30 Source: 'A bum note for rock 'n' roll', by Justin Stoneman, Sunday Times, Culture Supplement, 3 January 2010, p. 27.

including trademarks and logos. This is likely to mislead the consumer into believing that they are buying the real thing.

Counterfeiting is a global issue and does not only affect the music industry. Counterfeit bottles of whisky, vodka, rum and other spirits are a growing problem for global drinks companies like Diageo, forcing them into cat-and-mouse games with bootleggers as they try to expand sales in Asia and Eastern Europe. In the Czech Republic 30 people died from drinking a fake version of local rum, tainted with methanol, in September 2012, and the poisonings then spread to Poland and Slovakia, where some 50 people were eventually arrested in connection with the deadly liquor in late 2012.[31]

In August 2008 a British woman who had put a game on a file-sharing network was successfully sued at London's Patents County Court by the game's creator, Topware Interactive, and ordered to pay damages of £16,000. Isabella Barwinska from London had shared a copy of 'Dream Pinball'. Topware Interactive had started its campaign against pirates of 'Dream Pinball' in early 2007 after legal action forced 18 British internet firms to pass on details of suspected pirates that it had identified. Davenport Lyons, the law firm acting for Topware, sent out about 500 letters to identified persons in the UK who had made the game available via file-sharing networks such as 'eMule', 'eDonkey' and 'Gnutella'. In the letters the lawyers had asked for a payment of £300 as a 'settlement' figure that would head off further legal action. Some of those accused of sharing the game chose to fight the legal action and it was in one of these contested cases that Topware Interactive won its claim for damages.[32] The test case opened the floodgates for litigation against thousands of other Britons suspected of sharing games online.

See also
Chapter 8.7

9.2.6 Bootlegs

Bootlegs are unauthorized audio or video recordings of live performances, not officially released by the artist. The process of making and distributing such recordings is known as bootlegging. The first bootlegged live recording of a Bob Dylan concert, 'live at the Albert Hall', part of his first UK tour, can be traced back to 1965, with songs including 'The Times They Are a-Changin'' and 'Mr Tambourine Man'. 'Dylan Bootlegs' were then duplicated and sold without the artist's permission. A great many such recordings were then simply copied and traded among Dylan fans without any financial reward in the form of royalties to the artist. Changing technologies have had a great impact on the recording, distribution and varying profitability of the underground industry. Today, some bootlegged records are sold as rarities for profit, sometimes by adding professional-quality sound engineering and packaging to the raw material.

By the early 1980s the bootleg industry in Germany and the Netherlands was thriving. Music industry experts claim that there were about 30,000 illegal Dylan bootleg recordings in Italy alone, claiming that the bootleg industry was the most serious form of piracy.[33] It is interesting to note that Bob Dylan has released his own official edition of a 'bootleg' series in several volumes. Volume 9 (2010), for example, features the legend's studio recordings from 1962 to 1964, also known as the 'Witmark' and 'Leeds' demos in mono format, never previously released on CD; just one way to extend copyright in his recordings and thereby increase royalties. For die-hard Dylan enthusiasts there now exists a large collection of previously buried treasure brought to light in a cornucopia of unissued material, including demo recordings, outtakes and coffee-house recordings, such as the legendary 1966 'Royal Albert Hall' appearance (see also 'the **Bob Dylan** case'[34]).

31 Source: 'Drinks companies battle counterfeiters, by Alan Rappeport and Jan Cienski, *Financial Times*, 4 November 2012.
32 Source: 'Game sharers face legal crackdown', *BBC News Online*, 19 August 2008.
33 See: Heylin (1994).
34 **Sony Music Entertainment (Germany) GmbH v Falcon Neue Medien Vertrieb GmbH** (C-240/07) [2009] ECDR 12.

It could, however, be argued that in some cases bootlegging serves a useful cultural service. Some of the early recordings of the great opera singer Maria Callas, for example, in her live perform-ances at La Scala Opera House in Milan only exist – and are now sold 'officially' by record compa-nies – because of the illicit activities of members of the audience and technicians!

9.2.7 Piracy and file-sharing: is it legal?

The advent of personal computers made it easy and convenient for someone to convert media in a physical/analogue or broadcast form into a universal, digital form (also known as 'ripping'). The original may or may not be in copyright. Combined with the internet and file-sharing tools, it then became very easy to make unauthorized copies for distribution of (copyrighted) digital media and the counterfeit market of music CDs and (film) DVDs grew.

What is the law on file-sharing? File-sharing is not in itself illegal. On file-sharing or P2P networks the files being shared are held on members' computers and those who want a particular game, music track or video get bits of it from anyone else who has it via the internet. It only becomes illegal when users are sharing content, such as music or films, which are protected by copyright legislation. Can the Internet Service Providers be held to account for illegal file-sharing, P2P downloads and internet piracy? How can a fair balance be struck between allocating responsi-bilities to the end user and the (music) industry?

A Hertfordshire couple in their 60s were horrified to receive a letter from Davenport Lyons in November 2008, accusing them of downloading a hardcore gay porn movie. The 20-page 'pre-settlement letter' from the lawyers, acting on behalf of German pornographers, insisted the couple pay £503 to their clients for the 115-minute film *Army Fuckers*, which featured 'Gestapo' officers and 'Czech' farmers, or face court action. The lawyers also sent out similar demands to other individuals for a German gay porn film with an even more offensive title.[35] By March 2010, the Solicitors Regulation Authority[36] was investigating the London-based law firm Davenport Lyons (and others) for complaints received by the consumer group Which? that a number of 'online victims' had been bullied and harassed for being wrongly accused of illegal P2P file-sharing.[37]

Owners of films, music and computer games need to protect their rights and prevent illegal copying. But many of these letters are sent to people who have no idea what a download is and are innocent. If all of the recipients of these settlement letters paid up, the film producers would be raking in £12.5 million per year, which would make the porn film industry even more profitable. A German company called DigiProtect claims the users are breaking copyright law and is demanding £500 to settle out of court. A 20-page legal letter lists the name of the film involved along with the time and date of the alleged download. Michael Coyle from Southampton-based solicitors Lawdit was acting on behalf of hundreds of people who received legal papers in the post in 2010. Allegations against the Hertfordshire couple were eventually dropped.[38] Michael Coyle said: 'The cynical lawyer in me would say this is a money-making exercise. If you send out 10,000 letters and ask for £500 each time, you only have to get half to pay up and you've made a significant amount of money. Because it is porn, the person who's being accused won't want to go to court and is more likely to pay up to make the matter go away even if they are completely innocent.'

---

35 Source: 'Porn bill for couple who can't download', by Tony Levene, *Guardian*, 29 November 2008.
36 The Solicitors Regulation Authority (SRA) regulates more than 110,000 solicitors in England and Wales, as well as registered European lawyers and registered foreign lawyers. The SRA is the independent regulatory body of the Law Society for England and Wales.
37 Source: 'Law firm investigated over claims that it bullied alleged filesharers', by Bobbie Johnson, *Guardian*, 5 March 2010.
38 Source: 'Cash demand over "porn downloads" ', BBC *Newsbeat* broadcast, 5 December 2008.

In September 2010 the UK's Information Commissioner (IC), Christopher Graham, told the BBC that the firm behind a leak of thousands of Sky Broadband customers' personal data could face a fine of half a million pounds. The list, produced by ACS:Law, contained the names and addresses of more than 5,300 people alleged to be illegally sharing adult films online. Mr Graham said that ACS:Law had 'a number of questions to answer', such as: 'how secure was this information and how was it so easily accessed from outside?' The Information Commissioner has significant power to take action and can levy a fine of up to half a million pounds on companies that flout the Data Protection Act 1998.

The documents appeared online after users of the message-board '4chan' attacked ACS:Law's website in reaction to its sending thousands of letters to alleged net pirates, asking them to pay compensation of about £500 per infringement or face court. Armed with IP (internet protocol) addresses – which can identify the internet connection used in any copyright infringement – ACS lawyers were then able to apply for a court order to get the physical address of the broadband licence holder from the service provider whose network had allegedly been used for the file-sharing. The leak contained around 1,000 confidential emails, including personal correspondence between Andrew Crossley – who runs ACS:Law – and work colleagues, as well as lists of potential file-sharers and information on how much the firm had made through its anti-file-sharing activities. The leaked unencrypted document also contained personal details of more than 5,300 BSkyB Broadband subscribers alongside a list of adult videos they may have downloaded and shared online. A BBC investigation in August found a number of people saying they were wrongly accused by ACS:Law of illegal file-sharing.[39]

In December 2012, the Government announced that it would abolish the archaic laws that make it illegal for music fans to download a legally purchased CD onto a laptop, smartphone or MP3 player. In fact millions of British consumers have been format-shifting, for example uploading a CD onto an MP3 player or laptop, for years without realizing that it is actually illegal. Business Secretary Vince Cable ruled out imposing an 'iTax' on all 'music storage devices', a levy imposed across Europe. Just as well: a 'music storage device' can mean any device from computer equipment (hard drive) to a flash memory, a CD-ROM, even a printer's memory buffer, or just an iPod or MP3 player.

This move put the UK at loggerheads with EU Commissioners in Brussels, who were planning to charge users for copying (or format-shifting) music files. For example, in France a 64GB iPod has an additional tax levy (iTax) of £12.20. The proposals further include that record companies would no longer be able to block parodies of songs by their artists, such as the YouTube spoof 'Newport State of Mind' in 2010, a parody of Jay-Z's 'Empire State of Mind' which went viral on the website. The legislative move was criticized by the Chairman of the British Academy of Songwriters, Composers and Authors, Sarah Rodgers, who said: 'The government had an opportunity to help consumers and, at the same time, support creative communities, by putting a few pence on to the cost of a listening device.' However, consumer groups welcomed the move as a 'common sense reform for the digital age.'[40]

Part 6 of the Enterprise and Regulatory Reform Act 2013 (ERRA) amended certain aspects of the Copyright, Designs and Patents Act 1988 (CDPA), for example repealing s 52 CDPA. Section 75 ERRA ('Penalties under provision amending exceptions: copyright and rights in performances') ensures, for instance, that where s 2(2) of the European Communities Act 1972 (ECA) is used to narrow or remove exceptions to copyright and performance rights, the restriction to criminal penalties as detailed in paragraph 1 of Schedule 2 to the ECA 1972 does not apply

---

39 Source: 'ACS:Law could face £500,000 fine for porn list leak', by Daniel Emery, BBC News Online, 28 September 2010.
40 Source: 'UK copyright laws to be freed up and parody laws relaxed', by Mark Sweney, Guardian, 20 December 2012.

and the current level of criminal penalties can be maintained. The maximum term of imprisonment that can be applied is three months for summary offences and two years for those on indictment.

Section 78 ERRA ('Penalties under provision implementing Directive on term of protection') is used to implement EU Directive 2011/77/EU ('on the term of protection of copyright and certain related rights'). The primary function of the Directive is to extend the copyright term for sound recordings and performers' rights from 50 to 70 years. This section then criminalizes acts which under the former copyright law had been lawful. The penalties which can now be imposed are by regulations made by each Member State of the EU.

9.3 Phonograms and the recording industry

The music industry is a complicated business with a number of representative sectors and components interacting to make it work. The music industry worldwide was worth £30 billion in 2006, with the UK being Europe's largest music market (the world's third largest) with around 10.4 per cent of physical record sales worldwide in 2005.[41]

Over the past decade, there have been revolutionary changes ranging from the internet and MP3 players to e-readers and vast online electronic music and literature libraries. All have been made possible by inexpensive broadband, which allows fast, efficient and user-friendly downloads.[42] The global recorded music industry then experienced a recession due to increased illegal P2P music downloads. An estimated 95 per cent of all digital music was downloaded from 2008 onwards and research by the International Federation of the Phonographic Industry (IFPI)[43] found that around 40 billion music files were downloaded illegally (without payment) and that 70 per cent of all music consumed in the US, UK, France and Germany in 2009 came through digital channels, while revenues from digital platforms in those countries accounted for only 35 per cent of revenues.

However, the latest IFPI annual *Digital Music Report* (2013) looks more positive, reporting that the music industry is on a path to recovery, fuelled by licensed digital music services (e.g. Spotify) and rapid expansion into new markets internationally. Global recorded music industry revenues rose by an estimated 0.3 per cent to US$16.5 billion in 2012, the first year of industry growth since 1999. Digital revenues saw accelerating growth for the second year running, up 9 per cent, with most major digital revenue streams – downloads, subscription and advertising-supported – on the rise.[44]

Music video streaming services are also seeing strong growth. YouTube, the most popular digital video service, had more than 800 million active users globally in 2013 and 9 out of 10 of the most popular videos on the service are music-related. Internet radio is also soaring in popularity, with leading service Pandora accounting for 8 per cent of all radio listening in the US. Services such as Slacker and iHeartRadio are also growing in popularity. The music industry is now less reliant on income from physical format sales (CDs), with their share declining from 61 per cent in 2011 to 58 per cent in 2012, although physical formats still account for the majority of industry revenue. In Japan and China, CDs and DVD music video sales were still increasing in 2013

---

41 Source: IFPI (International Federation of the Phonographic Industry) Annual Report 2010: 'Music How, When, Where You Want It – But Not Without Addressing Piracy', by John Kennedy the then Chairman and Chief Executive, IFPI, available at www.ifpi. org/content/library/dmr2010.pdf.

42 The terms upload and download often create confusion, as their definitions depend on the exact context. Download and upload refer to the transfer of information between computers. The person/computer sending the information refers to the transfer as an upload, while the person/computer receiving the information refers to it as a download.

43 Source: IFPI Annual Report 2011.

44 Source: IFPI *Digital Music Report* 2013 at: www.ifpi.org/content/library/DMR2013.pdf.

and in South Korea sales increased for the third consecutive year, underpinned by K-Pop acts whose fans predominantly want high-quality physical formats.[45]

The UK is still the world's fourth-largest music publishing market, providing 10 per cent of worldwide revenues, and is second only to the USA as a source of repertoire. While English-language albums continue to sell well across borders, IFPI analysis of the charts in leading markets including France, Germany, Italy, Spain and Sweden reveals the vast majority of the top 10 best-selling albums of 2012 were local repertoire.

The top-selling global album artist was British singer-songwriter Adele, who achieved phenomenal success with her second album, 21, released in January 2011, selling 8.3 million units globally in 2012 and 18.1 million in 2011. The album went to number one in more than 26 countries. US artist Taylor Swift took the second spot with Red, reaching sales of 5.2 million. The album spent six non-consecutive weeks at the top of the Billboard 200, making Swift the first artist since the Beatles to achieve six weeks at the top of the US chart with three consecutive studio albums. English-Irish band One Direction also achieved phenomenal international success in 2012. Their debut album Up All Night was the third best selling title of the year and their second album Take Me Home became a best-seller in 35 countries, ranking it fourth in the global chart. On average, one in five units of the top-selling albums (21 per cent) were bought in a digital format, with One Direction's Up All Night seeing 38 per cent of its units sold digitally.[46]

Record labels are the main developers of musical talent. Today, around 23 per cent of label revenue is reinvested in 'talent spotting', that is the signing and developing of new artists through their A&R (artist and repertoire) departments. Record labels enable artists, through advances in royalties, sales and marketing support, to be able to have a musical career. If one purchases sheet music of, for instance, Elton John's 'Song for Guy', this gives the right to use each single copy purchased, but it does not grant the right to photocopy additional copies, nor to perform the work in a live public performance, nor to record the work, nor to broadcast a recording or live performance. The process is covered by mechanical copyright protection and licensing, whereby the cost of the sheet music is expected to cover approximately half of the total licensing expenses required to put on a public performance.

9.3.1 Music publishing

Does an artist or performer need to register his work or sound recording to be protected? Not really. Copyright protection is formality-free in countries party to the Berne Convention, which means that protection does not depend on compliance with any formalities such as registration or deposit of copies. It exists immediately it is created. However, the various performance rights and collecting agencies and the Musicians' Union (MU) tend to differ. Commonly, authors do insert a small 'c' in a circle (©) – sometimes with the date – to warn people that the work is in copyright, but this is a matter of practice, not a legal requirement, in the UK.

Under s 5(1) CDPA 1988, the 'author' of a sound recording ('musical work') or a film is the producer, though it is commonly accepted that the copyright owner will be the person who made the arrangements for the recording to be made – typically a record label. It is then through advances in royalties, sales, marketing support and more recently 360-degree branding that a recording artist is able to have a musical career. Can a recording artist protect his name or the song by copyright? It depends. Copyright may or may not be available for titles, slogans or logos, depending on whether they contain sufficient authorship. In most circumstances copyright does not protect names, though

45 Ibid., at p. 8.
46 Ibid., at p. 11.

a wrongful attribution of authorship or a performance may give rights under s 84 CDPA or in the tort of passing off (see: **Clark v Associated Newspapers Ltd** (1998)[47]).

The minimum protection guaranteed by the Rome Convention 1961 to performers is to sanction performances without their consent. It is important to remember that the performer of the song has rights as well as the writer of the song (note: a performer's rights ought not to be confused with the performance right in copyright law). This expression was used in order to allow IFPI countries like the UK to continue to protect performers by virtue of penal statutes, determining offences and penal sanctions under public law, such as the Copyright Acts of 1911 and 1956. Under the Rome Convention, record producers ('producers of phonograms') have the right to authorize or prohibit the direct or indirect reproduction of their recordings ('phonograms'). The Convention also provides for the payment of equitable remuneration for broadcasting and communication to the public of phonograms.[48]

Traditionally there are a number of categories of 'performers' involved in the process of music composition and exploitation. Some are direct copyright holders; others indirect. At the start of the creative process there is the person who is responsible for writing the music: the composer of the music and the lyricist of musical works (remember that there are two separate copyrights here – musical in the notes and literary in the words). Copyright law recognizes them as the 'authors'. The second stage involves the musicians or singers of the 'song', or melody and lyrics, composed by the authors. These are the 'performers', covered by a separate regime of performers' rights.[49]

In recordings, the phonogram producers ('record producers' or 'record labels') finance the performance and will normally own a sound recording copyright and a recording right in relation to the performers used, in the sense that they may provide finance and recording studio facilities.[50] Each record label will try to secure an exclusive contract with the artist or group. For example, the Beatles recorded their albums at Abbey Road Studios exclusively with EMI. Tom Jones also used to record with EMI (*What's New Pussycat?* and *Delilah*), and then left for the Island record label (*Praise and Blame*); Decca Records have their own classical, jazz and crossover artists, like Wynton Marsalis (blues trumpet), Rolando Vilazón (tenor) and the Three Tenors: José Carreras, Plácido Domingo and Luciano Pavarotti.

The reproduction of the recorded materials began on vinyl and, later, on CDs. Authors, performers and producers are each given 'performers' rights' for their creative works (related rights). The record label, by way of licence, will then be able to control the exploitation of the works. Indirect copyright holders comprise the music publishers, who are not directly involved in the creative process of the works. Their task is to support the authors and ensure that the musical works and scores are exploited by making sure that the repertoires are provided to the public and that the rights holders are granted their copyright; this includes all productions such as musicals or operettas performed by amateur societies.

See also
Chapter 8.8.1

9.3.2 Music Publishers Association (MPA)

The business of music publishing is concerned with developing, protecting and valuing music. The business is diverse and demands a variety of skills. Music publishers play a vital role in the development of new music and in taking care of the business side, allowing composers and songwriters to concentrate on their creative work.

---

47 [1998] All ER 6 (Ch D).
48 Article 10 Rome Convention.
49 See: Part III CDPA.
50 See: ss 185–188 CDPA.

Traditionally, music publishers were also responsible for the printing and selling of sheet music. Between 1868 and 1877, for example, Richard D'Oyly Carte wrote and published his own music compositions, as well as several comic operas, such as *Doctor Ambrosias – His Secret* (1868) and *Opera Comique* (1871) with his father's music publishing company.[51] Mechanical reproduction of a song or a recording (i.e. sheet music) covered the making of multiple copies and was undertaken by well-known music publishers, such as Breitkopf und Härtel (German music publishers in Leipzig),[52] Chappell Music (now the music publishing arm of Warners), Harry Fox Music Publishing (HFA) and the Hartenshield Group for choral and chamber music. Over recent years, physical music publishing activities have decreased as the revenues generated are minor compared to, say, book publishing revenues.[53]

See also
Chapter 8.2.2

The Music Publishers Association[54] has a worldwide catalogue of printed music and links to publishers (digitally and in hard copy). The MPA can act as a link between a performer seeking permission to photocopy printed music or perform it and the copyright owner; that is, the songwriter/s. The Association argues that all recordings should be licensed, even non-commercial recordings. In the UK this is also covered by the MCPS (Mechanical Copyright Protection Society).

See below 9.4.1

 FOR THOUGHT

Is it right to say 'all recordings must be licensed'? If your friends sing 'Happy Birthday' to you in a pub and video-record the 'performance' on their mobile phone, and one of the 'group members' uploads the recording on to Facebook, should she obtain a licence? At what point does someone need to obtain a music licence? Discuss.

9.4 Musical works

Copyright is the foundation upon which the music business is built. This intellectual property right gives the creator, owner or author of the work exclusive rights over how it is published, distributed and adapted. Copyright is essential in the music business to ensure that creators, artists and producers are adequately protected and compensated for the use and sale of their creative works in the form of royalties (or 'economic rights'). Civil and criminal remedies available to the UK courts have not really been sufficient to deter piracy and copying of MP3 music files and DVDs.[55] Though the original creator ('author') of a piece of work is protected by the CDPA 1988, IP legislation remains essentially weak in the UK, in spite of additional EU legislation.

See below 9.7

In order to understand the various levels of musical copyright, it is important to distinguish between the copyright in a song in terms of music publishing (mechanical rights) and copyright in the sound recording of that song, where the copyright holder is usually the (music) producer. These are two different copyrights and carry different durations. 'Sampling' is dealt with as 'third party' copyright.

---

51 Sources: 'Music and Musicians, *The Daily News*, 12 April 1895; 'Original Correspondence', *The Era*, 10 September 1871.
52 Important and prominent publishers dating back to 1725 when Bernhard Christoph Breitkopf brought out a Hebrew Bible as their first major publication. Works published subsequently included those by composers Telemann, Leopold Mozart, Haydn and Bach. 'Härtel' was added to the name when Gottfried Christoph Härtel took over the company in 1795. By the latter half of the 1700s, all major composers wanted to have 'Breitkopf' publish their works.
53 Source: Wallis *et al.* (1999).
54 The MPA had 260 music publishing members in 2013, ranging from small to large businesses, representing nearly 4,000 catalogues of every music genre. Subscriptions start from £100 per year. Source: www.mpaonline.org.uk.
55 For further details see: Harrison (2011).

9.4.1 Mechanical rights

It is important to distinguish ownership of a physical product from the ownership of the copyright embodied within it. For example, the purchase of a pop music DVD does not mean that the purchaser owns the copyright in the musical work within it or the copyright in the sound recording. Therefore purchasing a DVD alone does not entitle the purchaser to copy the work or do any other acts which are restricted to the copyright owner. The same goes for the purchase of a book – it does not mean that the purchaser owns the copyright of the manuscript.

Performing rights royalties are paid to a songwriter, composer or publisher whenever their music is played or performed in any public space or place. This includes TV, radio, online, in a shop, an office, pub or restaurant, at a concert, a sporting event and thousands of other places.

Mechanical rights royalties are different and are paid to the songwriter, composer or publisher when music is reproduced as a physical product or for broadcast or online. These royalties are collected by the MCPS (The Mechanical Copyright Protection Society – now part of the PRS).[56] The MCPS is now covered by the broader 'PRS for Music' brand, and licenses the mechanical (reproduction) rights and pays mechanical royalties to the original author (music copyright holder).

In a fast-changing digital world where music can be 'packaged' in a range of different formats, it can be difficult to identify and verify whether the use of the musical composition is licensed, by whom and for what kind of use. The record industry eventually came up with an identification system, the International Standard Recording Code (ISRC) and the Information System Work Code (ISWC), to identify composers, authors and music publishers to support the sales, licensing and tracking needs of artists and record labels, crucial to the successful operation of online commerce.

9.4.2 Joint ownership of copyright

Where two or more people collaborate in creating a work and their individual contributions are not distinct, they are 'joint authors' of that work (or joint owners of copyright). However, where two or more persons collaborate but it is possible to determine the separate parts attributable to each author, it will not be a work of joint authorship. Generally the author of the work is the first owner of copyright. If there are two or more authors of a work, they jointly have first ownership of copyright. In relation to sound recordings, this is the producer.[57] In commercial films the principal director and producer are usually joint authors. The author of a broadcast is the person who made it. The publisher of a typographical arrangement of a published edition is the author of it and so on.

In **Ray v Classic FM** (1998),[58] Robin Ray (1934–98)[59] brought an action against the radio station Classic FM, alleging infringement of his copyright in five documents containing his proposals for categorizing the tracks on the classical music radio station's recordings and in a catalogue created by him over a five-year period. Robin Ray was one of the first executives hired by the commercial classical music radio station, with which he remained associated from 1991 to 1997. He undertook the mammoth task of drawing up a list of 50,000 pieces of classical music, and rating them for popular appeal, which became the basis for the Classic FM playlist. This list proved to be extremely attractive to similar popular classical music radio stations in other countries.

Ray's legal dispute centred on the question as to who was entitled to the copyright in the playlist and ratings ('the works'). Classic FM claimed joint authorship of these works on the basis

---

56 MCPS-PRS collects royalties whenever a piece of music is reproduced for broadcast or online.
57 Section 5(1) CDPA.
58 [1998] ECC 488 (Ch D).
59 From 1965 Robin Ray was the chairman of the BBC's *Call My Bluff*; he was also a regular panel member on the BBC's classical music series *Face the Music* from 1966 onwards. Ray was able to recognize all kinds of musical pieces, including the composer, opus and Köchel number for Mozart pieces.

that Mr Ray had simply put into writing ideas initiated by the radio station's representatives at a series of meetings concerning the contents of the catalogue and its categories.

The Chancery Division upheld Mr Ray's claim, that in order to be a joint author for the purposes of s 10 CDPA, a significant creative contribution as an author had to be made to the production of the work which was not distinct from that of the other author with whom there was a collaboration. The contribution had to be something which was incorporated into the finished work and protected by copyright. Since copyright did not subsist in ideas, but in their written expression (known as 'penmanship'), a joint author had to do more than contribute ideas and had to participate in the writing or be the creator of the work. Although penmanship did not have to be exercised, a joint author had to have a direct responsibility for what ended up on paper, which was equivalent to penmanship. The court observed that Mr Ray had not merely written down the ideas of Classic FM's representatives, but was solely responsible for five documents in question (i.e. the catalogue and ideas contained in these).

The court duly awarded Mr Ray copyright in the five documents. The decision in the **Robin Ray** case set out several factors to consider when deciding upon joint ownership:

1. Commissioning in itself is not indicative of ownership;
2. The agreement may state ownership in the work;
3. A contractor is entitled to retain copyright in the absence of any terms to the contrary.

The usual contractual rules will be applied. Conditions/terms must be:

(i)   reasonable and equitable;
(ii)   necessary to effect business efficacy;
(iii) obvious;
(iv)   clearly expressed;
(v)   not contradictory to other express terms.

In the **Spandau Ballet** case,[60] the court ruled that to be a joint owner of copyright the parties must have substantially contributed to the song's creation, not just to its interpretation. As per Park J:

> There is a vital distinction between composition or creation of a musical work on the one hand and performance or interpretation of it on the other.[61]

So, if a drummer just adds a short drum loop, this would not make any material difference to the song, and would not justify the claim that the song was co-written. However, one could argue that the performable arrangement produced by a group would constitute a separate copyright for the new arrangement.

In the landmark case of **Fisher v Brooker** (2009),[62] the House of Lords asserted the joint ownership and copyright in the famous song 'A Whiter Shade of Pale' (released on 12 May 1967), eventually granted to Mathew Fisher of the 1960s group Procul Harum. Crucial in this case was that Mr Fisher made his claim some forty years after the song's release.

---

60 *Hadley v Kemp* [1999] EMLR 589.
61 Ibid., at para 589 (Park J).
62 [2009] UKHL 41 (HL).

❖ KEY CASE   *Fisher v Brooker* [2009] UKHL 41 (HL)

Precedent
- ❖ A claimant of copyright cannot be estopped from asserting his copyright interest on equitable grounds, to declare that the right existed (under the equitable doctrine of proprietary estoppel).
- ❖ A claimant cannot be denied the opportunity of exercising his right of property even after an extensive time period has passed (here nearly forty years).

Facts
On 7 March 1967, the original band members of Procul Harum, namely Gary Brooker, Bobby Harrison, Ray Royer and Dave Knight, entered into a recording contract ('the licence') with Essex Music Ltd ('Essex'). Shortly after, Matthew Fisher ('the claimant') joined the band as Hammond organist. The licence gave the label the right to manufacture, sell, lease, otherwise use or dispose of the band's performances. In other words, Essex could exploit any recording made by the band under the Copyright Act of 1956 'absolutely'.

'A Whiter Shade of Pale' ('the song') became an instant worldwide hit after the recording was released as a single by the Decca label on 12 May 1967. The song achieved sales in the millions and is still regarded as one of the greatest songs ever written. The band had registered the song with the Performing Right Society (PRS) and the Mechanical Copyright Protection Society (MCPS) on 17 March 1967.

The claimant had crucially composed the familiar organ solo at the beginning of the song and he raised the question of his having a share in the rights of the song with Brooker and the band's manager Keith Reid at the time of the recording. But he was rebuffed. Mathew Fisher left the band in 1969. In 1993 Essex Music's rights were assigned to Onward Music Ltd.

During April 2005, the claimant, Mr Fisher (then aged 61 and working as a computer programmer in Croydon) launched his claim against the lead singer of Procol Harum, Gary Brooker, and Essex and Onward Music. The main claim was that Mr Fisher wanted a share of the musical copyright in the song. After his claim was rejected, Mr Fisher began legal proceedings on 31 May 2005. At the High Court, the respondents argued that the claimant was far too late, nearly forty years, in claiming the copyright for joint owner- and authorship of the song. They asked the court for laches and to strike out the claim under the doctrines of estoppel. The judge held that the claimant was entitled to declarations (i) that he was a joint author of the work, (ii) that he was a joint owner of the copyright to the extent of 40 per cent, and (iii) that the defendants' implied licence had been revoked from the date of issue of proceedings. After a number of cross-appeals, the case reached the House of Lords in 2009.

Decision
The HL declared that Matthew Fisher was joint owner of copyright: 'Mr Fisher's instrumental introduction – the organ solo – is sufficiently different from what Mr Brooker had composed on the piano to qualify in law, and by quite a wide margin, as an original contribution to the work.'[63]

---

63 Ibid., at 42.

Their Lordships held that it did not matter that the claimant had not asserted his joint authorship and copyright for such a long time. His claim was still valid even after 40 years, and they awarded Mr Fisher a 40 per cent share in royalties, backdated to the date of his original claim in 2005. Baroness Hale (one of five Law Lords) commented: 'As one of those people who do remember the Sixties, I am glad that the author of that memorable organ part has at last achieved the recognition he deserves.'

Analysis

It might strike us as extraordinary that Matthew Fisher had waited some 38 years before he brought his co-ownership action, fully in the knowledge, and without reasonable excuse, that the other band members of Procul Harum, in particular Gary Brooker, had exploited the work for so many years.

Fisher v Brooker set the precedent for any future claims of this kind where an artist wishes to assert his (joint authorship) rights in a song or recording during his lifetime; even if the claim is more than 40 years old. The court ruling meant that Mathew Fisher (and his heirs) could receive royalties in 'A Whiter Shade of Pale' for years to come. For the various royalty-collecting societies, such as the PRS and the MCPS, it meant that they had to amend their records and backdate the royalties payable to Mr Fisher to the start of his legal action. The HL ruling in *Fisher v Brooker* has meant an ongoing music copyright headache for major artists, musicians and their lawyers, who will have all lined up for similar claims for their contributions to successful songs.

9.5 Sound recordings, performers' rights and extended copyright

Every record track has two rights: (1) a copyright in the musical and lyrical composition and (2) a separate copyright in the actual sound. The sound recording owner is usually the record company which released the original recording (or 'single') for a public performance and airplay. Live performances are often recorded or transmitted and may be sold for a profit, for example a live recording of a comedy act. It is then perfectly acceptable to make your own recording of your own performance of, say, Mozart's Piano Concerto No 21 (because the author has been dead for more than 70 years). Provided you performed and recorded the work yourself, then no infringement would have occurred. However, what if someone else wanted to copy that recording and sell it commercially? This is where the copyright in the sound recording comes into play. EU copyright law (known as the 'Copyright acquis') has recognized the problematic nature of this situation, which is unique to sound recordings and live performances. While separate copyright subsists in the recording of the performer, the performance itself is also IP protected. The performance then gives rise to performer's rights which – in turn – are covered by the term 'dramatic performances', which include dance and mime, musical performances, readings and recitations of literary works and variety acts. Circus acts can also be included as well as certain sporting events, such as ice dancing.

The duration of these has changed in recent years with EU legislation. Sound recordings and performances now have distinct protection in their own right, clearly separate from that in the underlying work. The copyright in the sound recording will run for 70 years from the year of recording, or 70 years from date of release if released in that time.

FOR THOUGHT

Many people at festivals (e.g. Glastonbury or Isle of Wight) make amateur video recordings of events at the festival, such as impromptu performances of an 'unknown' artist's original songs that do not take place on one of the main stages. If you make recordings and subsequently compile them for sale on your own website, who has copyright in what aspects of the performance and the recording?

9.5.1 Directive 2011/77/EU: extended copyright Directive for performers and sound recordings

Directive 2011/77/EU ('The Copyright in Sound Recordings Extension Directive') requires an extension of copyright term in fixations of performances in sound recordings and for sound recordings from 50 to 70 years (from the date of publication or communication to the public) provided that those works were published (or communicated to the public) during the initial 50-year term.

The main aim of the Directive was to protect performers, such as Sir Paul McCartney or Sir Cliff Richard, who would be unable to continue receiving royalties from their early recordings of their performances because the period for copyright protection would have expired after 50 years. This has now changed with the Directive to 70 years. The Directive is commonly known as 'The Cliff Richard Directive'.

See Chapter 8.5.1

The EU Commission gave Member States two years to implement Directive 2011/77/EU (i.e. until 1 November 2013) and the IPO was charged with drafting regulations and administrative provisions to comply with this Directive in the UK. The IPO consultation paper looked at very broad issues during the consultation period, including *inter alia* different aspects such as commercial reasons for entering markets, licensing practices, collection agencies and the development of inter-operable formats for e-books. Before writing the new regulations and advising the UK Parliament on the new Copyright Act, the IPO wanted to ensure that the UK copyright framework would support economic growth for the UK at a time of rapid technological change and business innovation, since legislative developments at European Commission level could potentially have a major impact on what happens in the UK in relation to copyright.[64]

As EU Member States were adopting the new measures imposed by the Copyright in Sound Recordings Extension Directive, each state was equally concerned about its own publishing and music industry, wondering whether the Directive would truly 'harmonize' EU-wide copyright law.[65] EU Commissioner Michel Barnier saw the adoption of the Directive as a personal and significant victory. Barnier, Vice President of the European People's Party, said at the time: 'Today's decision to increase the term of protection for musicians' copyright from 50 to 70 years will make a real difference for performers.'[66] Belgium, the Czech Republic, Luxembourg, the Netherlands, Romania, Slovakia, Slovenia and Sweden had been opposed to the adoption of the Directive, with Austria and Estonia abstaining.[67]

See also Chapters 8.12.1 and 8.12.2

---

64 See: Intellectual Property Office (IPO) (2013b) at: www.ipo.gov.uk/consult-2013-copyrighteurope.pdf.
65 See: Intellectual Property Office (IPO) (2013c) at: www.ipo.gov.uk/consult-2013-copyterm.pdf.
66 Source: Statement by EU Commissioner Barnier, Brussels, 12 September 2011 at: http://ec.europa.eu/commission_2010-2014/barnier/headlines/news/2011/09/20110912_en.htm.
67 For further discussion see: Hanison (2013).

What do we mean by a 'recording'? In relation to a performance, a film or sound recording, this must be made *directly*:

(a)   from the live performance;
(b)   from a broadcast of the performance; or
(c)   . . . indirectly, from another recording of the performance.

The rights conferred to the performer or recording artist are independent rights in copyright (and moral rights), relating to any work performed or any film or sound recording of, or broadcast of the performance, and therefore have independent obligations arising on behalf of third parties. All these rights include the right to carry out any of these acts with a substantial part of the work. The performance (or part thereof) is then assessed qualitatively in order to establish the economic interest (royalties) in the performance of the work. A performer's rights are infringed by a person who, without consent, makes a copy of a recording (or samples it) of the whole or any substantial part of a qualifying performance (other than for his private or domestic use).[68]

See above 9.3.1

Directive 2011/77/EU[69] ('On the term of protection of copyright and certain related rights') extended the term of protection for performers and sound recordings to 70 years. The aim of the Directive is to bring performers' protection more in line with that already given to authors – 70 years after their death.

The extended term of copyright now enables performers to earn money for a longer period of time and in any event throughout their lifetime. The Directive also contains accompanying measures which aim specifically to help performers. 'Use it or lose it' clauses will now have to be included in performers' contracts, thereby linking performers to their record companies. The Directive allows performers to get their rights back if the record producer does not market the sound recording during the extended period. In this way the performer will be able to either find another record producer willing to sell his music or do it himself, something that is possible easily via the internet. Finally, record companies are now required to set up a fund into which they will have to pay 20 per cent of their revenues earned during the extended period. The money from this fund is destined to help session musicians and start-up performers.

There has been much debate concerning Directive 2006/116/EC On the 'Term of Protection of Copyright and Certain Related Rights Enforcement Directive' of 12 December 2006 ('the EU Term Directive'). Angelopoulos (2012) argues that, in spite of a single rule applicable now across Europe, in terms of harmonizing Member States' intellectual property – namely copyright legislation – there remain 'drastically divergent terms of protection', leaving some jurisdictions clearly 'unharmonized'. Though the Directive is now in force in all 28 Member States, it has been left to the legislators in each state to 'translate' the Directive into national law. This, Angelopoulos argues, hampers the end user, specifically cultural heritage organizations, from taking full advantage of the new opportunities now technically available for the digitization and exploitation of the public domain. The author concludes that 'if the EU wishes to establish a truly harmonized term of protection for copyright and related rights, a more committed and comprehensive approach will be necessary.'[70] The **Bob Dylan** case (below) demonstrates some of the difficulties.

---

68 Sections 182A–D CDPA 1988 added by SI 1996/2967; s182A(1A) CDPA added, by SI 2003/2498.
69 Amending Directive 2006/116/EC.
70 See: Angelopoulos (2012).

❖ KEY CASE

The 'Bob Dylan' case: Sony Music Entertainment (Germany) GmbH v Falcon Neue Medien Vertrieb GmbH (2009)[71]

Precedent

❖ Directive 2006/116/EC harmonized the terms of protection of copyright and neighbouring rights; and

❖ established a total harmonization of the period of protection for each type of work and each related right in Member States.

Facts

German record label Falcon had distributed two CDs containing recordings of original US performances by Bob Dylan from 1964 to 1965, including 'Blowin' in the Wind', 'Gates of Eden' and 'The Times They Are A-Changin'. Sony (Germany) held the related rights. Article 85 of the German Copyright Act (*Urheberrechtsgesetz* 1965)[72] states that the producer of an audio recording (phonogram) has the exclusive right to reproduce and distribute the recording, meaning that companies are simply holders of the producer's rights of phonograms. In German law at the time (prior to EU harmonization Directives), these rights expired 50 years after production of the audio recording – which the Falcon label seized after expiry.

The German courts argued that under the Convention for the Protection of Producers of Phonograms against Unauthorized Duplication of their Phonograms, in force both in the USA and in Germany, protection could only be claimed in relation to work created after 1 January 1966, the date when the German Copyright Act came into force. Sony claimed that the UK's Copyright, Designs and Patents Act 1988 grants protection to phonograms created before 1 January 1966 and also extends to phonograms of US producers. For this reason, Sony claimed that Dylan's albums were also protected in Germany, relying on Article 137f German Copyright Act and Article 10(2) of the EU 'harmonization' Directive 2006/116.[73]

Sony argued that, even if copyright in the Dylan recordings expired prior to 1 July 1995, protection would still continue as long as the right existed under the law of another EU Member State or related contracting party to the agreement on the European Economic Area (EEA) on that date.

The claim to copyright proceedings between Sony and Falcon reached an impasse at final appeal at the German Federal Court of Justice (Bundesgerichtshof), which, in turn, referred the case to the ECJ for a preliminary ruling on the interpretation of the 'copyright harmonization' Directive (Directive 2006/116).

---

71 [2009] ECDR 12 (C-240/07) (ECJ).
72 *Urheberrechtsgesetz* 1965, Article 85 (1) 'The producer of an audio recording shall have the exclusive right to reproduce and distribute the recording. If the audio recording has been produced by an enterprise, the owner of the enterprise shall be deemed the producer. The right shall not subsist by reason of the reproduction of an audio recording. (2) The right shall expire 50 years after publication of the audio recording.'
73 Initially called Directive 93/98, which was later codified by Directive 2006/116 on the term of protection of copyright and certain related rights.

Decision

Referring to the ECJ's judgment in the **Phil Collins** case,[74] Advocate General Ruiz-Jarabo Colomer cited the principle of non-discrimination and equal rights among Member States on literary works, artistic works and related rights. This meant that Sony could claim protection of Dylan's albums in Germany on the basis that they were still protected under UK legislation, by way of the 'harmonization' Directive 2006/116, even though they had at no time been directly protected under the provisions of the German Copyright Act.

Analysis

The case set the precedent in the application of EU Directive 2006/116 in the harmonization of related copyright of performers and producers in EU Member States. The Court of Justice's decision in the **Bob Dylan** case was seen as a major victory for the music industry. Sony records saw this as a personal victory, for the label could thereby continue holding copyright in the sound recordings and live performances of Dylan.

There was an added complication in this case. The Dylan recordings were fast coming out of copyright (which then stood at 50 years from the time the recording or live performance was made). This meant that Falcon records could freely 'grab' the old releases and issue them under relatively cheap 'supermarket' labels to the general public as 'best of' releases and compilations. However, if under Article 7(2) Directive 2006/116 the copyright holder of a sound recording right was not an EU Community national, then without prejudice to international obligations, the term of the right could be no longer than that which was applicable in the country of which the right holder was a national. Thus, if the right holder was a national of country X and under the laws of country X protection was 30 years from 'fixation' (publication), the protection granted in the EC community could not extend beyond 30 years. The ECJ effectively said that Articles 7(2) and 10(2) of the Directive were dealing with different situations. Thus, the ECJ ruled that, provided that, as of 1 July 1995, a right holder who was a national of a non-Member State was protected in at least one Member State, then the copyright was 'revived' under Article 10(2) of Directive 2006/116.

It is worth noting that the ECJ was not ruling on the inapplicability of Article 7(2) of the Directive, but merely stating that it was irrelevant to the interpretation of Article 10(2). Thus, it may be the case that copyright is revived under Article 10(2) but disapplied under Article 7(2) if the right holder who is a national of a non-EU Member State cannot demonstrate that he has commensurate equivalent protection in the country of which he is a national.[75]

---

74 **Collins (Phil) v Imtrat Handelsgesellschaft mbH** (C-92/92); see also: **Patricia Im- und Export Verwaltungsgesellschaft mbH v EMI Electrola GmbH** (C-326/92) [1993] ECR I-5145.
75 For further discussion, see: Traub (2009).

9.6 Performing rights and collecting societies

Collective management is the practice by which organizations, which were founded by and represent creators, look after the enforcement of the authors' rights (i.e. collect royalties and make sure their music is not copied or sampled). It is fair to say that generally individual IP right holders in the music and publishing industries cannot easily enforce their economic rights on their own. For instance, the BBC uses almost 60,000 music items every week. Since the middle of the nineteenth century, composers and publishers have responded by creating collective bodies, so-called collecting societies, which monitor musical activity in a given territory and collect and distribute royalties accordingly. These societies, first established in Western Europe, operate on two principles: the principle of reciprocity, linking monopolistic national societies; and the principle of solidarity, making a collecting service available to all rights holders at roughly the same rate. Created for the administration of music rights, the societies' emergence is a consequence of the development of copyright, which in the eighteenth century had already established its legal roots under the influence of the law of nature that was flourishing throughout Europe.

Collecting societies established themselves during the mid-nineteenth century when French composers realized the benefits of operating collectively when licensing public places to use their music. The 'propriété littéraire et artistique' had already been recognized in France by two laws from the revolutionary period dated 1791 and 1793. Prussia passed its first 'copyright' law on 11 June 1837, 'Gesetz zum Schutze des Eigenthums an Werken der Wissenschaft und Kunst in Nachdruck und Nachbildung' (legislation for the protection of intellectual ownership of scientific and artistic works against reproduction and copying), one of the most comprehensive and advanced laws protecting intellectual property in central Europe at the time.[76]

In 1847, the French popular chanson composer Ernest Bourget visited the Paris Concert Café 'Ambassadeurs', whose orchestras regularly played his music. When the waiter presented the composer with the bill for the sugared water that he and his colleague had consumed as the fashionable luxury drink of the period, Bourget refused to pay, claiming that the orchestra had repeatedly played his music, without paying him anything. Bourget took the café owner to court and on 8 September 1847, the Tribunal de Commerce de la Seine prohibited the owner from playing any further works by Bourget unless the composer consented. The Ambassadeurs' owner lost his appeal on 26 April 1849 at the Cour d'appel de Paris and was sentenced to pay compensation to Monsieur Bourget, thereby establishing one of the first royalties cases.[77] During the following decades, composers and music publishers in other counties formed collective syndicates. Pierre Proudhon and Mikhail Bakunin formed the first syndicate for composers and music publishers in Spain during the 1930s.[78]

9.6.1 Collective rights management in the twenty-first century

Collecting societies act as intermediaries between right holders in the music industry but also in other art forms like books or films. They license rights, collect royalties, and redistribute revenue to the right holders in circumstances where individually negotiating licences with individual creators would be impractical and entail high transaction costs.

---

76 See: Kreile and Becker (2001).
77 For further discussion see: Gillieron (2006).
78 See: Koempel (2007).

In 2013, there were more than 250 collecting societies in the EU, managing revenues of around 6 billion euros annually. The use of rights in the music sector accounts for about 80 per cent of the total revenue collected by collecting societies.[79]

Today, the collective management of copyright (the rights of right holders) is crucially important for the licensing of online music service providers (e.g. music download services, streaming services etc.). Of particular importance are the rights of those who compose the music or write the lyrics. Online service providers (ISPs) are often cross-territorial, covering large catalogues of music, which makes online licensing ever more demanding. Many collecting societies are not ready for these challenges and as a result, ISPs face serious difficulties when trying to obtain the licences necessary to launch online music services across the EU. This results in fewer online music services available to consumers across the EU and a slower incorporation of innovative services or alternatively illegal platforms.[80]

Some users make use of a large amount of copyright material in different ownership, such as clubs, leisure centres, radio stations and funeral parlours – all playing music in public. It would be impractical and very expensive to try to identify and pay the individual owners of the copyright in all the music that is being played. Consequently, collecting societies have been formed which license a large repertoire of copyright works. These societies have often been formed in response to changes in technology and use.

Collecting societies are in charge of the repertoire of the various rights holders. They monitor the use of it, negotiate the conditions for licensing agreements and commercial use, collect royalties and distribute them to the various rights holders. Collecting societies enjoy considerable market power since their collective practice is largely standardized, such as using the same tariffs, licensing conditions and distribution rights in the repertoire. This system guarantees a certain level of solidarity among rights holders and strengthens the rights of relatively unknown or niche authors and artists, who can expect the same level of protection as popular performers or songwriters. Administrative fees are the main source of income of the collecting agencies. In general, fees are charged to the collecting societies' members for the services of collecting the income from the users (collection fee), and allocating such revenues to rights holders (allocation fee).[81]

That said, there will be those artists who prefer to manage their own conditions and royalties. In any case, certain rights generally have to be managed by right holders individually, such as the right to make an adaptation of a work or the use of music for the purposes of synchronization of films, commercials, ringtones or 'viral' marketing use on social networking sites. If anything, artists ought to ensure that the moral rights in their work are adhered to, including integrity rights of their original composition. Collecting agencies have tried to stop the practice of author-managed works.[82]

These days, collecting and performance rights societies administer a considerable proportion of composers' and music publishers' rights. Most importantly, collecting societies ensure that right holders are rewarded through licensing agreements by way of royalties for the use of their music by commercial users including radio and television broadcasters, record companies, music service providers and music retailers. They act on behalf of their individual members in the negotiation of licensing agreements with commercial users who wish to avail themselves of music by copying, broadcasting or sampling music or by making it available on the internet, such as through YouTube or Spotify.

---

79 Sources: 'Copyright: Commission proposes easier music licensing in the Single Market', EU Commission Press Release, 11 July 2012.
80 See also: European Commission (2011).
81 See: Ficsor (2003).
82 For further discussion see: Lui (2003).

Several countries have different forms of royalty collection. Some record labels and their artists have exclusive rights of reproduction ('private copying') and reprographic reproduction and therefore different rights to remuneration covered by EU legislation.[83] As well as copyright law the societies are subject to competition law to prevent them abusing their monopoly rights as there is usually only one society in relation to a particular area.[84] Many countries are subject to supervision by expert tribunals, such as the Copyright Tribunal in the UK.[85] Such courts or tribunals have the power to adjust collection schemes and the levels of licence fees, if these are regarded as unreasonable. Additionally, the Berne Convention provides harmonizing legislation in the countries of the Berne Union to determine the conditions under which certain exclusive rights may be exercised.[86] In general, the Convention provides for mandatory collective management of rights of subscribing countries to the Berne Union.

Where a right is not provided for an exclusive right of authorization but rather for a mere right to remuneration, the so-called 'Article 12 rights' of performers and producers of phonograms comes into play. Article 12 Rome Convention reads as follows:

> . . . if a phonogram published for commercial purposes, or a reproduction of such phonogram, is used directly for broadcasting or for any communication to the public, a single equitable remuneration shall be paid by the user to the performers, or to the producers of the phonograms, or to both. Domestic law may, in the absence of agreement between these parties, lay down the conditions as to the sharing of this remuneration.

Some collecting societies traditionally apply social and cultural deductions when collecting royalties. These deductions are gathered into funds and dedicated to a number of services of social or cultural benefit to their members, such as pension schemes, assurances, sponsoring of cultural events, etc. The original model was introduced by CISAC (Confédération Internationale des Sociétés d'Auteurs et de Compositeurs), the International Confederation of Societies of Authors and Composers, founded in 1926.

After the Second World War, royalty deductions were limited to a maximum of 10 per cent of all remunerations collected. This created an international solidarity among members of collecting societies and among repertoires. As deductions were applied on all royalties collected domestically (including those related to foreign repertoires), large foreign repertoires contributed to increased social and cultural revenues in favour of the domestic repertoire and CISAC and its members. CISAC has imposed complete reciprocity: if one collecting society decides to deduct, the other collecting society is also fully entitled to do so.

Today, CISAC is a powerful and influential world leader in international authors' performance rights societies, an organization that co-ordinates the protection of its member creators' rights, with its headquarters in Paris and regional offices in Budapest, Buenos Aires and Singapore. CISAC counted some 231 collective management organizations (collecting societies) in 121 countries protecting the interests of over three million creators and rights holders in 2013. CISAC

---

83 See: Directive 92/100/EEC On Rental Rights and Lending Rights and on Certain Rights Related to Copyright in the Field of Intellectual Property which introduced such a right in favour of the authors and performers – the 'unwaivable right to equitable remuneration' in respect of the rental of phonograms and audio-visual works into which their works or, respectively, performances have been incorporated.
84 See: Articles 101 and 102 TFEU (Treaty on the Functioning of the European Union 2008), preventing abuse of a dominant position.
85 See: ss116–149 CDPA.
86 Article 11bis(2) and Article 13(1) Berne Convention.

represents all kinds of artistic repertoires, including music, drama, literature, audio-visual, graphic and visual arts.[87]

Since there is now a great deal of cross-border representation of artists and performers, collecting societies have created different categories of rights (to existing copyright) under one umbrella, referred to in the industry as the GEMA categories (Gesellschaft für musikalische Aufführungs- und mechanische Vervielfältigungsrechte: Society for musical performing and mechanical reproduction rights). GEMA is the society for musical performing and mechanical reproduction rights which originated in Germany.[88] GEMA, in turn, is a member of the BIEM (Bureau International des Sociétés Gérant les Droits d'Enregistrement et de Reproduction Mécanique: International bureau of societies administering the rights of mechanical recording and reproduction). BIEM is an organization that co-ordinates statutory licence agreements and is based in Neuilly-sur-Seine, France (currently representing 44 societies from 42 countries). Virtually every international performing rights society has now entered into some form of reciprocal representation agreement with its world counterparts, and practically all GEMA countries are also members of CISAC.[89]

Importantly, fully developed collective management systems may grant 'blanket licences' for the use of the entire world repertoire of works or other protected subject matter which they manage. In practice, one collecting society would never grant an entire repertoire to the world at large. Article 18 of EC Directive 2001/29 ('The Information Society Directive' – InfoSoc) states that:

> . . . this Directive is without prejudice to the arrangements in the Member States concerning the management of rights such as extended collective licences.

Most commonly, there will be a system of bilateral reciprocal representation agreements in the case of performing rights. The 'guarantee-based system' involves the following elements:

(i)   The legality of authorizing the use of works not belonging to the organization's repertoire covered by statutory copyright law and/or common law.
(ii)   The organization guarantees that individual rights owners will not claim anything from users to whom blanket licences have been granted and, if they still try to do so, that such claims will be settled by the organization; any user will be indemnified for any prejudice and expense caused to him as a result of justified claims by individual owners of rights.
(iii) The organization guarantees that it treats rights owners who have not delegated their rights to it in a reasonable way, taking into account the nature of the right involved.

The alternative to the 'guarantee-based system' is the so-called 'extended collective management system'. The collecting agency is authorized by the various rights holders to manage their rights collectively. Rights holders have the opportunity to 'opt out' from the collecting system, in which case they will take care of their own rights and remuneration management – a model understandably not favoured by collecting agencies.

---

87 CISAC's mandate follows ISO standards and in turn delivers the ISAN system of voluntary numbering and metadata system for the identification of audio-visual content (International Standard Audiovisual Numbers – ISAN). In order to assign IPMP (Intellectual Property Management and Protection) numbers on a worldwide scale the CISAC secretariat was appointed by the ISO as Registration Authority for IPMP (MPEG-4, Part 1 – ISO/IEC 14496-1) in July 2001.
88 The reference to the GEMA categories was notably relied on by the EU Commission in its 1971 GEMA Decision. See Decision of 2 June 1971 (IV/26 760–GEMA) [2971] OJ L134/15.
89 For full and detailed discussion see: Dehin (2010).

Each collecting society relates to a specific form of exploitation of musical works and the conditions under which such exploitation is permissible. These categories result mainly from the day-to-day activities of collecting societies and are broadly used in the music industry. In particular:

1. Mechanical reproduction rights which define the author's (or creator's) right to authorize the sound recording of his work.
2. Public performance rights which authorize the public performance of the works; these reflect the fee authors and publishers are entitled to when a musical work is performed 'live', or via broadcasts, or as background music in shops, bars, hairdressers, restaurants, etc.

The two main royalty-collecting societies in the UK are the Performing Right Society (PRS) and the Mechanical Copyright Protection Society (MCPS). The PRS and MCPS represent the rights owners and obtain rights clearances. They entered into an operational alliance in 1997 and rebranded in January 2009 as 'PRS-MCPS', which is now the largest UK collecting society. The alliance became one of the founding members of UK Music,[90] an industry-wide body representing all aspects of the music business, in September 2008, headed until 2011 by Feargal Sharkey (co-founder of punk band The Undertones in 1976).

9.6.2 Public performance rights: the Performing Right Society (PRS)

The PRS regulates the public performance and communication rights in relation to music and literary copyright in musical works (but not the performance of these by singers etc.).[91] The PRS provides a performance licence for live performances and live broadcast of a musical work. Public performance rights may be licensed directly from the copyright owner by way of a direct request or from the collection society PRS directly (or the BMI in the United States[92]).

Any person or business wishing to play copyrighted music in public will require the consent by way of a licence from either the copyright owner or the collecting society to do so. If the person does not obtain the required licence, they run the risk of infringing copyright. Businesses typically applying for music licences include fitness clubs, cinemas, shopping centres, funeral parlours, providers of wedding functions and medical premises. Royalties are then distributed to the artist, creator or producer by the PRS.

9.6.3 Mechanical reproduction rights: The Mechanical Copyright Protection Society (MCPS)

The distinction between mechanical and performing rights arose at a time when the exploitation of musical works occurred mainly in the public arena – that is in live performances – from the mid-nineteenth century onwards. A mechanical licence is a broad term that refers to the reproduction for distribution or sale of musical compositions in the form of sound recordings. 'Mechanicals' are often confused with master rights (PPL); mechanicals are publishing rights. Any time an artist or producer produces a recording of a composition which they do not control, they need a mechanical licence. There are a large number of legal challenges in this area of musical copyright and piracy.

---

90 UK Music was previously known as British Music Rights, representing live music and musicians, publishing and record companies.
91 A performer can prevent someone from making a recording of their live broadcast; see: ss 181–184 CDPA.
92 Broadcast Music, Inc. (BMI) collects licence fees on behalf of songwriters, composers and music publishers and distributes them as royalties to those members whose works have been performed: www.bmi.com/licensing.

'Mechanical royalties' (to the publisher) are usually based on the amount of 'phonorecords' sold; that is, sales based on sound recordings determined by the record companies through 'Sound Scan' and other reporting systems. While US mechanical royalties are calculated on a 'penny basis' per song, other countries might base mechanical royalties on percentages. The current statutory rate for a US copyright is 9.1 cents per song.

The PRS-MCPS system grants a mechanical licence for the entire record based on a percentage of the wholesale or retail price, regardless of the number of songs. Public performance monies collected by the organization depend on their survey and consensus of how many times the song is played, when, where and at what time of day, and on what type of medium. Each collecting society has its own unique monitoring and survey systems and detection techniques based on random survey, census, sampling, or digital detection methods. The difficulty remains how the various layers of collecting organizations track all of the music and samples accurately so that royalty monies are correctly paid to songwriters and publishers, because each of the organizations uses slightly different systems and methods for calculations.

The main music publishers (known as the 'Majors') and independent record labels (known as the 'Indies') are now just a few. The Majors are now Warner Brothers Records ('Warners'), Sony and Universal Music Group ('Universal', also including Decca, Deutsche Grammophon, Island Records, Republic Records and many Indie labels).[93] EMI Music Publishing is now mainly in the business of acquiring, protecting, administering and exploiting the rights in musical compositions and holds one of the largest music publishing catalogues. The main challenge for the music industry is now to find a way to replace declining album (CD) sales. Subscription services such as Spotify have also reduced album sales and the efforts of the record labels to bundle music with mobile phone or pay TV subscriptions have failed to catch on.

That said, from May 2012 onwards the British Phonographic Industry (BPI) reported that the UK digital music revenue had overtaken sales of 'physical formats' (CDs and vinyl records) for the first time. According to figures compiled by BPI, digital accounted for 55.5 per cent of the £155.8m spent on music in the UK in the first three months of 2012. The impressive growth in digital boosted the record industry's overall market value by 2.7 per cent to £155.8m and helped to offset a decline in sales of CDs. The BPI's figures showed income from digital sales had risen by nearly a quarter year-on-year to £86.5m. BPI Chief Executive, Geoff Taylor, said the results represented a 'significant milestone in the evolution of the music business ... UK record labels have embraced digital to their core, supporting innovation and licensing more new online and mobile services than any other country'.[94]

While musical and performance copyright needs to be protected, licence fees can prove prohibitive to many musicians and may outweigh the artistic merit in using a sample or song cover. Nowadays, digital music services involve a combination of mechanical rights (storage of the digital musical work on a hard disk) and performing rights (the musical work is made available to the public on a website). So a performing artist needs to obtain several licences from several entities, each holding either the performing or the mechanical rights. The mechanical licence is usually limited to one configuration, such as a physical CD or album, as opposed to a digital download, which is different again from a mobile phone ringtone. Almost all publishers require a separate licence for each use.

In February 1971, for example, Bright Tunes Music Corporation ('Bright Tunes'), then copyright holder of the song 'He's So Fine', composed by Ronald Mack, brought a copyright infringement action in the US District Court for the Southern District of New York (SDNY) against a former

---

93 See also: 'Universal Gamble: the music business', The Economist, 21 July 2012 p. 67.
94 Source: 'Digital revenues overtake physical in UK Recorded Music Market', BPI Press Release, 31 May 2012.

member of the Beatles, George Harrison, and also against related entities, 'Harrison Interests', alleging that the Harrison composition, 'My Sweet Lord', infringed Ronald Mack's composition. In late November 1975, Allen Klein (on behalf of ABKCO[95]) offered to pay Bright Tunes $100,000 as a settlement. Bright Tunes made a counter-offer demanding $148,000 and 40 per cent of the writers' and publishers' royalties earned in the US. The parties were unable to reach an agreement and the matter proceeded to trial. After a number of cross-appeals, the US Supreme Court found copyright infringement in favour of Mr Mack[96] (applying: **Warner Brothers v American Broadcasting Companies** (1981);[97] also: **Sheldon v Metro-Goldwyn Pictures Corp**. (1936);[98] also: **Northern Music Corp. v Pacemaker Music Co.** (1965)[99]).

With the onset of the digital age, the distinction between the two rights (mechanical and performance) has become increasingly blurred and it is for economic rationalization reasons that the MCPS and PRS joined forces, now operating as one performing rights society. Mechanical rights royalties are different and are paid to the songwriter, composer or publisher when music is reproduced as a physical product (such as sheet music) or for broadcast or online downloads such as iTunes. The mechanical licence royalties are collected by the MCPS.

Under the present copyright system (both in the US and in UK/EU law) any phonogram or 'phono recording' is subject to both a copyright for the sound recording and a copyright for the written song itself. The mechanical licensing for entire repertoires involves paying the composition copyright owners for the right to re-record a song, and is mostly handled by the Harry Fox Agency in the United States, the Canadian Mechanical Rights Reproduction Agency (CMRRA) in Canada, the MCPS in the UK and the GEMA authorities Europe-wide. The rise of global media corporations combined with digital production and distribution technologies has seriously undermined the principles of collecting societies. Wallis *et al.* (1999) concluded that the current structure of music copyright is likely to collapse, skewing the distribution of revenues in favour of big corporate players and global musical producers if there is no institutional intervention.

See above 9.6.1

What are *'mechanicals'*?

The term normally means CD copies, but also includes:

- music videos
- ringtones
- MIDI files[100]
- downloaded tracks
- computer games
- musical toys etc.

---

95 Founded in 1960, ABKCO Music and Records is one of the world's leading independent entertainment companies. It owns a prestigious repertoire catalogue, including compositions and recordings by Sam Cooke, the Rolling Stones, Bobby Womack, The Animals, Herman's Hermits, Marianne Faithfull and The Kinks.
96 See: **ABKCO Music Inc. v Harrisongs Music, Ltd** [1983] US Court of Appeals, Second Circuit, 3 November 1983, 722 F.2d 988; 221 USPQ 490.
97 [1981] 654 F.2d 204; 211 USPQ 97 (2d Cir. 1981).
98 [1936] 81 F.2d 49, 54, 28 USPQ 330, 335 (2d Cir. 1936).
99 [1965] 147 USPQ 358 (SDNY 1965).
100 MIDI (Musical Instrument Digital Interface) is a technical standard, describing a protocol, digital interface and connectors, allowing a variety of electronic musical instruments, computers and other related devices to connect and communicate with one another. A single MIDI link can carry up to 16 channels of information, each of which can be routed to a separate device. MIDI technology was standardized in 1983 by a panel of music industry representatives, and is maintained by the MIDI Manufacturers Association (MMA). All official MIDI standards are jointly developed and published by the MMA in Los Angeles, and for Japan, the MIDI Committee of the Association of Musical Electronics Industry (AMEI) in Tokyo.

It covers any copyright audio composition that is rendered mechanically, i.e. without a new live performance.

9.6.4 Public performance licences

See above 9.5

'Public performance' occurs whenever sound recordings are played outside the domestic or family circle. Whenever a sound recording is played in a commercial environment, even if only one person can hear it, it becomes a public performance and a fee is payable to Phonographic Performance Ltd (PPL). If a business plays music videos, they will be required additionally to apply for a VPL licence (Video Performance Ltd). The VPL licence fees are assessed according to the number and size of the screens upon which music videos are played.

When Amazon launched its Cloud Player[101] in February 2011 without securing additional music licences it was regarded by the music industry as a bold move. For it took some guts for Amazon to simply declare that it did not need licences, in spite of the fact that the music industry thought otherwise. UK Music, the umbrella organization which represents the collective interests of the UK's commercial music industry (e.g. artists, musicians, songwriters, composers, record labels, music managers, music publishers, studio producers etc.), strongly objected to this practice.[102] Amazon argued that its Cloud Drive and Cloud Player were just services (or 'hosts') that let users upload and play back their own music. After all, Amazon argued, copyright legislation states that licences are not necessary for users to *play* their own music. But the record labels and the music licensing and collective rights management societies strongly disagreed, with Sony Music threatening to take legal action.

Meanwhile, record labels fantasize about huge revenues from online streaming services, and they fear 'digital lockers'[103] like the plague. There is an increasing requirement by content providers to obtain 'platform agnostic' content from copyright owners and producers. How can this be managed legally to preserve and recognize copyright content and protect an author's or musician's intellectual property in a constantly changing medium?

The internet is borderless, but where online markets are concerned, many layers of legislation exist. This is particularly true in Europe and is stifling competitiveness in the digital economy. It is perhaps not surprising that the EU is falling behind in markets such as media services, both in terms of what consumers can access and the business models that can create jobs. Most of the successful internet business models, such as Google, Hotmail or Facebook, originated outside Europe and therefore mostly operate outside EU law. Despite the body of key single-market legislation in Europe on e-Commerce, e-Invoicing and e-Signatures, transactions in the digital environment are still too complex, with inconsistent implementation of laws across EU Member States.

Authors and creators of works are faced with considerable uncertainty about their rights and legal protection for their intellectual property, with different duration rights. As technology continues to develop, film producers, recording companies, games manufacturers, publishers and authors will become increasingly affected by piracy. There is an urgent need for greater copyright guidance for rights holders but also for the end user. Simply cutting peer-to-peer file-sharers off

---

101 Amazon offers 'Cloud Drive' and 'Cloud Player' with free online storage to use for whatever a user may wish to store; though Amazon heavily encourages users to upload their local music libraries. All Amazon MP3 purchases are automatically synced to the user's Cloud Drive without counting against the quota. Source: 'Music Industry Will Force Licenses on Amazon Cloud Player — or Else', Jacqui Cheng, *Wired*, 4 February 2011.

102 UK Music (2012) *Response to HM Government's Consultation on Copyright* at: www.ukmusic.org/assets/media/UK%20Music%20 Submission%20-%20Consultation%20on%20Copyright%20March%202012.pdf.

103 A digital locker is file storage space on servers that are accessible over the internet. The servers are owned and managed by a company that offers hard drive space to the public to store files for a fee. Registered users can access music, movies, videos, photographs, video games and other multimedia files. This remote web access avoids the problem of localization, where files are stored at home or an office on a single physical hard drive that is only accessible by logging into the computer directly.

from the internet will not solve the problem. Many quickly reappear. Or will savvy media and entertainment lawyers make a fast buck by pursuing individual file-sharers in the courts? Will the music industry force licensing on Amazon because UK and EU copyright legislation cannot possibly keep up with such fast digital and technological changes made possible through the internet?

9.6.5 Public performance licensing: Phonographic Performance Ltd (PPL)

Phonographic Performance Ltd (PPL) was formed by EMI and Decca records in May 1934. Its formation was due to a successful action under the Copyright Act of 1911 against Stephen Carwardine & Co., restaurant proprietors, to restrain use of a recording written by Auber and played by the LSO, in its tea and coffee rooms. EMI, then called The Gramophone Company, argued it was against the law to play the recordings in public without first receiving the permission of the copyright owners. The judge agreed. The case established the principle that owners of sound recordings should be paid for the broadcasting and public performance of their works. EMI and Decca formed PPL to carry out this licensing role and opened the first office in London.

There has been much technological, social and legal advancement since PPL was formed in the 1930s. The Copyright Act 1956 led to PPL's role expanding to cover the licensing of broadcasters that played recorded music. The popularity and growth of radio in the 1960s and 1970s led to burgeoning PPL revenues. The right to receive equitable remuneration for recorded performances came into law on 1 December 1996. This meant that qualifying performers who had made a commercial recording since 1946 could now receive remuneration if their recording was broadcast or played in public in the UK or overseas. Performer organizations PAMRA (Performing Artists Media Rights Association)[104] and AURA (Association of United Recording Artists)[105] merged with PPL in 2006. PPL now collects approximately £150 million in royalties per year by managing artists' and performers' rights and granting public performance music licences.

A PPL licence is required when recorded music, including radio and TV, is played in public. There is no statutory definition of 'playing in public' (also sometimes referred to as 'public performance') but the UK courts have given guidance on its meaning and ruled that it is any playing of music outside of a domestic setting – so, for example, playing recorded music at a workplace, public event or in the course of any business activities is considered to be 'playing in public'. In contrast, any recorded music being played as part of domestic home life or when there is an audience entirely comprised of friends and/or family (such as at a private family party) does not require a PPL licence.

PPL issues different types of licences according to businesses type and size, typically including cinemas, shopping centres, funeral parlours, dental practices or gyms. If they do not obtain the required public music licence, they risk copyright infringement and prosecution. Each business must register with and pay a fee to the music licence collecting agency, PPL. The various categories comprise, for instance, educational establishments, health and fitness, holiday parks, offices and factories, shops and stores and public transport.

Until April 2013, aerobics instructors and dance teachers needed their own PPL licence, depending on the size of groups and venues. This has now changed. After four years of negotiation, PPL and the Fitness Industry Association (FIA) eventually reached an agreement to reform PPL's exercise tariff, which covers the use of recorded music in fitness classes. From 1 May 2013, the sole responsibility for holding a PPL licence for group exercise classes held in fitness centres lies with the operators of fitness and leisure centres. Independent fitness instructors are still required to hold

---

104 PAMRA collected performers' royalties from PPL and paid artists directly; the association was mainly used by session musicians.
105 AURA was mainly used by featured artists and producers but also by session musicians.

a PPL licence for any classes that they operate on premises other than fitness centres (e.g. hired halls, offices). The 'Exercise to Music' tariff varies depending on the size and number of classes operated by the establishment (ranging from 0.95 pence per class to £1.88).[106]

Examples of PPL licences for businesses playing recorded music in public

Aerobics Instructor • Airport • Amateur Dramatic Society • Amusement Arcade • Armed Service Base • Art Gallery • Arts Centre • Bed and Breakfast Establishments • Banks • Bars • Barber • Baths • Beauty Salon • Bingo Hall • Boats and Ships • Boutiques • Bus Station • Buses • Café • Caravan Park • Carvery • Casino • Cinema • Circus • College • Community Centre • Concert Venue • Country Club • Dance Studio • Dance Teachers • Dentist • Department Store • Disco • DJ • Doctor • Exhibition • Factory • Festival • Fire/Police Station • Fitness Centre • Football Club • Gallery • Guesthouse • Gym • Hairdresser • Health Club • Holiday Centre • Holiday Homes • Holiday Park • Hospital • Hotel • Ice Skating Rink • Keep Fit Instructor • Laser Space Game • Leisure Centre • Library • Lido • Live Music Venue • Lodge • Mall • Manicurist • Members' Club • Mobile DJ • Motel • Motor Race Track • Museum • Nail Studio • Nightclub • Nursing Home • Offshore Gas/ Oil Rig • Old People's Home • Operatic Society • Penny Arcade • Picture House • Political Club • Port • Production Company • Promoter • Public House • Railway Station • Residential Hotel • Resort • Restaurant • Retirement Home • Roller Skating Rink • Rugby Club • School • Shop • Shopping Centre • Social Club • Spa • Speedway Track • Sports Centre • Sports Club • Surgery • Swimming Pool • Tea Rooms • Ten Pin Bowling Centre • Theatre • Theme Park • Trade Show • University • Village Hall • Warehouse • Wine Bar • Working Men's Club • Youth Club.

What then is the difference between a PPL licence and a PRS for Music licence? PPL and PRS for Music are two separate independent companies and in most instances a licence is required from both organizations for anyone to legally play recorded music in public. While both organizations licence the use of music and collect royalties for the music industry, each represents different rights holders and has separate licences, terms and conditions. PPL collects and distributes money for the use of recorded music on behalf of record companies and performers; PRS for Music collects and distributes money for the use of the musical composition and lyrics on behalf of authors, song-writers, composers and publishers

See above 9.6.2.

As we have seen above, MCPS, PRS and PPL operate many different licences. Even people who work for these collecting societies often do not know how to distinguish between all these different licences and societies. Simply put: a music user who buys a licence can perform or duplicate relevant works under a standard set of limited conditions, set by the collecting societies. Other music applications have separate licences and some music users may need several. The best place to find complete and up-to-date lists of these licences is on the collection societies' individual websites.

9.6.6 Licensing background music and viral marketing

How many licences does a business need? It can be confusing as to whether one needs a PRS/MCPS or PPL licence in order to play music in public. This issue was addressed in **Re Phonographic Performance Ltd** (PPL) (2009),[107] where an action was brought by the British Beer and Pub Association (BBPA)

---

106 Source: PPL Exercise to Music Tariff 1 May 2013–30 April 2014 at: http://ppluk.com/Documents/Exercise%20to%20Music/Exercise%20To%20Music%20Tariff.pdf.
107 **Phonographic Performance Ltd v The British Hospitality Association** [2009] EWHC 175 (Ch).

and the British Hospitality Association (BHA) against PPL for charging additional fees for background music since 2005. PPL had demanded from the hotel and catering businesses that they needed two licences, one for public performances (PRS) and another for phonographic playback (background music) from PPL. This had brought in additional subscription fee revenue of about £20 million for PPL.

In **Re PPL**, Kitchin J held that the PPL could not charge a separate licence fee for playing background music of sound recordings because the businesses in question had already paid their PRS fees; a second music licence was therefore not necessary. Based on the Chancery Court's decision, Mr Justice Kitchin stated that there was nothing in ss 125–128 Copyright, Designs and Patents Act of 1988 to suggest that separate royalties ought to be charged for playing background music, since that was covered by 'public performances'. The case had first been decided by the Copyright Tribunal; Kitchin further ruled that the Tribunal had only limited jurisdiction in this respect, with no power under s 128(B) CDPA to order back payments in respect of users who used sound recordings not contained in a broadcast. He therefore ordered that PPL pay back all over-charged licence fees to the hoteliers and pub landlords.

Re Phonographic Performance Ltd was a landmark victory for the hospitality industry, who can now play background music with just one music licence. What about viral marketing – a new online trend to promote a particular product simply by 'word of mouth' – or a social networking site or tweets? The viral marketing trend is being defined as the utilization of pre-existing social networks to produce increases in brand awareness or to achieve other marketing objectives by identifying individuals with high social networking potential. Viral marketing has become a cheap and cost-effective online buzz to promote a particular product or idea.

In 2002 (three years before YouTube's birth), BMW launched a short internet video clip entitled *The Hire*, starring British actor Clive Owen. More than 11 million viewers initially 'tuned in', though in order to view the clip one had to register on the BMW website. More than two million registered, providing the German car manufacturer with an enormous (free) database and future clientele for marketing the new Z3 sports car. Though one cannot really tell how many of those clicks were converted into sales, an estimated 100 million viewers clicked on the video in the first four years.[108] *The Battle for Milkquarious* – a short online rock opera released on YouTube in February 2010 – was an aggressive viral marketing videospot by the California Milk Processor Board promoting the 'Got Milk' campaign.[109]

In July 2010, MJ (Morgan Jane) Delaney availed herself of the 'viral marketing' medium when she release her title 'Newport' (Ymerodraeth State of Mind)' on YouTube. Arguably, this 'spoof' unashamedly breached copyright law. MJ claims that her short video clip, promoting the Welsh city of Newport, is a 'parody' of Alicia Keys' and Jay-Z's 'Empire State Of Mind'.[110]

More than 100,000 people rushed to view the 'Newport' clip on the video-sharing website within the first 48 hours after its debut release, apparently with enthusiastic support from Twitter queen Lily Allen and retweet support from Welsh actor-comedian Rob Brydon and Radio 2's show host Claudia Winkleman. The internet sensation featured Newport rapper Alex Warren and singer Terema Wainwright. The music video was littered with witty one-liners, among them the city's twinning with Guangxi Province in China ('There's no province finer'). Instead of the Manhattan skyline as a backdrop to their video, scenes from the Welsh town were featured. MJ Delaney told Sky News that the video music clip was merely an 'in-joke' with her boyfriend and that she had not even contemplated getting a music rights licence. However, her 'joke' probably amounted to copyright infringement. YouTube was forced by EMI to take the Newport viral down.

---

108 *The Hire* can be viewed on YouTube, under 'BMW Films', available at www.youtube.com/watch?v=rIHGT8vWleQ.
109 Source: 'Battle for Milquarious', YouTube, 26 February 2010, available at www.youtube.com/whitegoldiswhitegold.
110 Source: 'Jay-Z and Keys spoof is YouTube hit', YouTube, 30 July 2010, available at www.youtube.com/watch?v=maNgAxUnJ8I.

Viral marketing is now used as a tool on all social networking sites, including Twitter, PayPal, Facebook, MySpace and Flickr, spreading brand names across the social media landscape, often accompanied by music. 'Virals' have become a powerful tool for advertisers, who are increasingly leaving TV advertising for online marketing spots made possible via streaming media such as YouTube. So does it need a music or video licence?

The cheap social marketing tool 'virals' rely on 'spreading the word' about a product or idea and hoping it continues to grow – and if it uses music video clips or brief samples, like the 'Newport' rap, it will require a music licence, because, in copyright terms, virals plagiarize existing music without paying the original artists any royalties. Artists like MJ Delaney might argue, however, that her music video clip is a 'new creation' and therefore does not breach copyright laws – alternatively, she could argue that it was a parody of the original song. That said, she should have paid a licence fee to one of the collecting societies for the song or at least asked Jay-Z and Alicia Keys for permission to 'sample' their song.

9.6.7 Regulating the collecting societies

New digital technologies have opened up great opportunities for creators, consumers and businesses alike. There is an increasing demand for online access to cultural content (e.g. music, films and books) which – in turn – does not recognize borders or national restrictions. Collecting societies have played an increasing role, particularly in the music sector, with ever-increasing music dowloads. Nowadays, they mainly manage the licensing of copyright-protected music tracks for online use on behalf of composers and lyricists and collect and redistribute to them corresponding royalties.

As already mentioned above, there are a number of collecting societies and models across Europe, the United States and Canada. Some collecting societies control only public performance rights (e.g. PPL) while others also control the reproduction rights. The Performing Right Society looks after an assignment from the composer or music publisher regarding their performing rights in musical and literary works and the Mechanical Copyright Protection Society acts on behalf of its members for the purpose of administering the 'mechanical' (music publishing) rights and distributes royalties to its members after deducting a commission fee. GEMA (Gesellschaft für musikalische Aufführungs- und mechanische Vervielfältigungsrechte) administers both the public performance and the mechanical rights based on a representative contract.

This can be confusing for the composer, artist or performer and it has long been suggested that the European Commission should establish a unified model of collective rights management for the music industry. Additionally confusing are domestic and EU legislation, and – if the recording was outside the EU – resulting legal differences in approaches to intellectual property legislation. In Germany, for instance, a composer may not assign copyright (s 29 Urheberrechtsgesetz – UrhG), while this is expressly permitted under UK law if done in writing.[111]

In April 2013, artists from some of the world's best-known bands, including Radiohead and Pink Floyd, along with famous singers such as Sandie Shaw, accused the European Commission of breaking promises over musicians' missing pay. In a letter, the group of artists said they were 'deeply disappointed' with draft legislation, designed to force collection societies to hand over royalties more quickly. They accused the societies of keeping 'substantial amounts of money' on their books. The legislation will allow societies 12 months after the financial year in which a song was played to pay royalties. If the royalty-owner remains unidentified, the funds can be kept by the collecting

---

111 Section 90 CDPA.

society for five years. 'You have broken your promises and encourage the management of collecting societies to keep the fruits of our creativity', the artists said in the letter.[112]

The European Commission had proposed measures to modernize collecting societies and put in place incentives to promote their transparency and efficiency.[113] It is fair to say that some collecting societies have struggled to adapt to the requirements of the management of rights for online use of musical works, in particular in a cross-border context. Under the proposed legislation, those collecting societies willing to engage in the multi-territorial licensing of their repertoire will have to comply with EU regulations and standards. The aim is to make it easier for ISPs to obtain the necessary licences for music to be distributed online across the EU and to ensure that revenue is correctly collected and fairly distributed to composers and lyricists.

Another more general aim is that collecting societies operating in all sectors would have to comply with new European standards providing for improved governance and greater transparency in the conduct of their activities. The need for a change in collecting societies' practices was highlighted by certain cases where royalties collected on behalf of rights holders were lost, due to poor investment policies, but also by evidence of long-delayed payments of royalties to rights holders. Commissioner for Internal Market and Services Michel Barnier said:

> . . . we need a European digital Single Market that works for creators, consumers and service providers. More efficient collecting societies would make it easier for service providers to roll out new services available across borders – something that serves both European consumers and cultural diversity . . . more generally, all collecting societies should ensure that creators are rewarded more quickly for their work and must operate with full transparency. This is paramount to sustaining investment in creativity and innovation which will in turn lead to additional growth and increased competitiveness.[114]

Key elements of the proposed Directive include:

- To promote greater transparency and improved governance of collecting societies through strengthened reporting obligations and right holders' control over their activities, so as to create incentives for more innovative and better quality services.
- Building upon this – and more specifically – to encourage and facilitate multi-territorial and multi-repertoire licensing of authors' rights in musical works for online uses in the EU/EEA.

What this would mean in practice is as follows:

- Right holders would have a direct say in the management of their rights, be remunerated more quickly and their ability to choose the most efficient collecting society for their purposes would be enshrined in law. This would bring about better protection of right holders' interests, as well as increased access to cultural content for consumers.
- The new rules would change the way in which collecting societies work across Europe, with new requirements such as improved management of repertoire, quicker payments to members, clarity in revenue streams from exploitation of rights, an annual transparency report and additional information provided directly to right holders and business partners (such as other collecting societies). Member states would need to have mechanisms for solving disputes

---

112 Sources: 'European Commission has "broken promises", say artists', by Jamie Dunkley, Daily Telegraph, 2 April 2013.
113 See: European Commission (2012).
114 Source: 'Copyright: Commission proposes easier music licensing in the Single Market', Press Release by the European Commission, Brussels, 11 July 2012.

between collecting societies and right holders. Improved standards and processes should result in better functioning collecting societies and more confidence surrounding their activities.

● The multi-territorial licensing of authors' rights for the use of music on the internet across borders would be facilitated but also subjected to the demonstration of the technical capacity to perform this task efficiently. This would benefit authors, internet service providers and citizens alike.[115]

The ongoing policy question for domestic and EU governments around collecting societies has been to develop a workable model that meets the primary objective, which is to protect authors' and creators' copyright and safeguard the economic interests of writers, composers, producers and music publishers. Koempel (2007) suggests that works should be accessible for commercial use by developing effective distribution models that protect copyright and the ability for right holders to collect accurate royalties and rewards. He argues that this model should be implemented by collecting societies supported by workable EU legislation.

9.7 Acquiring rights from third parties: who sampled whom?

A little over a decade ago, the economic income for a professional songwriter was quite straightforward. There were basically three streams: sales of records, radio play and, once in a while, possibly a movie soundtrack or an advertisement. Sales rates were a set percentage of the price, and radio play was paid as a percentage of advertising revenue with a minimum per play or, for the BBC, a per-play set rate ('needle time'). This all changed with digital music services. Today, collection societies, record labels and publishers are forced to sign non-disclosure agreements (NDAs) covering the deals they make with services such as YouTube and Spotify, and the artists and songwriters they represent are not allowed to know how much, or on what basis, they're supposed to be paid. Songwriters are paid relatively little by Google's giant YouTube; typically a British independent label would receive around £1,000 per million YouTube streams, depending on what type of 'ads' were served up with the video.

In February 2013, Baauer (aka Brooklyn-born producer Harry Bauer Rodrigues) experienced a freak success with his bass-heavy minimalist dance track 'Harlem Shake'. The sample was propelled to the top of the *Billboard* charts, creating a viral dance craze across the world on YouTube. Baauer had posted 'two pages' of Soundcloud tracks of 'Harlem Shake' on his popular 'BBC Radio One Essential Mix' in April 2012; in May, the Mad Decent label released 'Harlem Shake' as a single. Baauer had become famous for his sample-snipping and interest in rap beats (called 'trap' music), which mixes 'dubstep' drops with rap's artillery-fire drum programming.[116]

The underground club track suddenly became a worldwide phenomenon thanks to tens of thousands of people including Egyptian protesters, Manchester City football players[117] and The Simpsons, all filming themselves dancing like idiots to a 30-second excerpt. St Hilda's College, Oxford, even sacked its librarian, Calypso Nash, for taking part in the recording of their 'Harlem Shake' video, which helped raise a six-figure sum for bursaries for needy students. The college's student body appealed to the college in the 'strongest terms for Calypso to be rehired', arguing in

---

115 See: European Commission (2012).
116 Source: 'FADER Explains: Harlem Shake', by Naomi Zeichner, *Fader* magazine, 20 March 2013. Read more: www.thefader.com/2013/02/15/fader-explains-harlem-shake/#ixzz2O7WCgFkt.
117 See: *Guardian* online video 13 March 2013 at: www.guardian.co.uk/football/video/2013/feb/22/manchester-city-harlem-shake-video.

a motion that 'the Harlem Shake did not cause a disturbance coming as it did at 11:30 pm on a Sunday evening' and that the event 'only lasted roughly seven minutes'.[118]

But Baauer had failed to license the sample which had become No 1 on YouTube views, in a single week attracting 103 million hits in mid-February 2013. Digital licensing is confusing, but it can mean that a songwriter may receive on average $40 per million streams for their work.

As soon as the 'Harlem Shake' sampler became a hit, Baauer was contacted by lawyers for the retired reggae artist Hector Delgado and Philadelphia MC Jayson Musson claiming original copyright in the song sample. Musson claimed that more than a decade ago, he, then a Philadelphia art student, had written a song about a fight, which was then sampled into the new song, 'Harlem Shake'. This is how Musson's lyrics made it into Baauer's song, ending up in a million video views on YouTube. Both Delgado – who sang 'Con los terroristas' on his 2006 single 'Malades', and Musson, who rapped 'Do the Harlem Shake!' on 'Miller Time', a 2001 track by his group Plastic Little, ended up on Baauer's successful record but neither of the original performers was either approached (regarding their copyright in the song and lyrics) or paid any royalties.

When Baauer's 'Harlem Shake' was first released on an underground EP in May 2012, the sample went completely unnoticed. Only when it took off in February 2013 did Delgado and Musson become aware of the record hit; and they saw big money coming their way. Understandably they both wanted their cut, although, interestingly, they disagree on the ethics of illegal sampling. Musson responded, 'I'm cool with it. That's how artists do', while Delgado complained, 'It's almost like they came on my land and built a house.' Baauer has had to learn his lesson.[119]

But nothing is legally clear in the area of sampling law. The golden rule of music licensing for an artist and producer begins with the knowledge as to which licences exist and how to obtain them. Is the work in the public domain? Is the artist using a composition or a sound recording, or both? Is he creating a cover song? Is he sampling an existing recording? Or is the work out of copyright? Knowing the difference between compositions and sound recordings is key to determining the necessary licence and can be a headache for any budding artist, who may incur high legal costs from copyright violations. The short answer is: unless the artist or producer controls the composition or sound recording, he will need a licence to use it.

Building on past works is part of the essence of songwriting, but copyright law views songwriting as the genesis of a new song with no ties to previous lyrics or melodies. Many classical composers based their compositions on folk music and previous works. Bela Bartók's works, for instance, are based on Hungarian folk music and Dvořák's 1893 Symphony No 9 'From the New World' quotes 'Swing Low Sweet Chariot'. Yet the pop group DNA was forced to settle out of court in 1990 by paying a relatively small fine of £4,000 for a remix of Suzanne Vega's 1981 song 'Tom's Diner'.[120]

The issue of copyright, licensing and royalty payments becomes complicated when portions of music are used or reused as part of a different song, advertisement or ringtone, known as 'sampling'. In sampling the artist is creating a derivative work, which requires negotiation as there is no standard rate, and will require direct contact with all parties involved, usually by way of a collecting agency such as PRS-MCPS. But this system is far from perfect and there is a fundamental problem with data collection. The collection societies try to distribute royalties accurately and fairly, but many outlets, including radio stations as well as other broadcasting outlets such as bars or clubs, do not always report every song played or sampled. Strictly speaking, if a band or DJ wishes to sample a song, the artist should get paid by either beats per minute or be paid per second (or minute) sampled.

---

118 For comment and the video see *Guardian* online, 20 March 2013 at: www.guardian.co.uk/music/booksblog/2013/mar/20/oxford-librarian-fired-harlem-shake.

119 Source: 'Harlem Shake: could it kill sampling?' By Dorian Lynskey, *Guardian*, 13 March 2013.

120 For further discussion see: Beaujon (1999).

Michael Jackson's songs have been sampled on 95 songs by other artists and the Red Hot Chilli Peppers in eight other songs. Eminem's single 'Beautiful', for instance, used the rock band Queen and singer-songwriter Paul Rodgers' single 'Reachin' Out/Tie Your Mother Down'. Sampling is different to 'covering' (or 'covers'), where typically one artist sings the song of another artist. Samples can be a few bars of a song or a distinct sound recording, like the guitar entry to Led Zeppelin's 'Whole Lotta Love'. Sampling is typically done with a 'sampler', which could be a piece of hardware or a computer program. The technique of sampling probably dates back to the late 1970s, when a Jamaican-born DJ in the Bronx named Kool DJ Herc began playing the 'break' in a rock, soul, funk or even Latin song over and over by switching between records, while MCs[121] would 'rap' over the beat they created. From rap's inception to the present day, many rap beats contain parts of recognizable songs, such as Run DMC's 1986 hit 'Walk This Way' which borrows a guitar riff, drum beat and chorus from rock band Aerosmith.[122]

Using a sample means the use of a pre-recorded track – for example, Van Halen's 'Jump' – in a new recording or rap mix. In this case, the artist, MC or DJ needs to clear the sound recording copyright with Van Halen's record label as well as the mechanical licence from the music publisher in order to legally use the underlying composition.[123] Sampling may also fall foul of the composer's moral rights if it distorts his work in the sample.[124]

The process of sampling inherently infringes the copyright in the underlying and original composition and sound recording. Even if a rap artist or DJ wishes to use only a couple of beats, this process will involve either licensing the sample from the copyright holder(s) or asking the artist or right holder for permission (or both). The US District Court for the Southern District of New York decided in **Grand Upright Music Ltd. v Warner Bros. Records, Inc.** (1991)[125] that rapper Biz Markie had violated the copyright of Gilbert O'Sullivan's 'Alone Again (Naturally)', which Markie had sampled in his song 'Alone Again' on his album I Need A Haircut (1991). The track 'Alone Again' was subsequently not included on Markie's audio CD since, after his unsuccessful lawsuit, he was told by the court to remove it from the album. Nor could he make it available in MP3 format.

Sampling artists are at the mercy of large record labels, music publishers and collecting societies – most of whom have legal departments devoted to finding out 'who sampled whom'.[126] Cover songs have always been popular, witnessing a daily resurgence as tribute albums and 'best of' CDs or digital-only releases are issued by record labels to cash in on artists like the Beatles or Rolling Stones before copyright in their songs expires. If a sampling artist is being confronted by the legitimate copyright holder in a legal challenge, he can possibly use the de minimis defence, which means the sample used was small enough so that the rights holder cannot claim that he 'owned' the sampled section. This constitutes 'fair use' of the original. Alternatively, the defendant MC or DJ could claim that the sampling was done in parody, which also amounts to 'fair use' (see: **Twentieth Century Music Corp. v Aiken** (1975)[127]).

If a sampler is considered a musical instrument rather than a copying device, then the use of a sample will be more similar to 'covering' the sound than duplicating it. In this case, a sample would constitute covering a small segment of a song and therefore would be subject to compulsory royalty rates.[128]

---

121 MC (Master of Ceremonies) is a music artist and/or performer who usually creates and performs vocals for his own original material. This must not be confused with a DJ (Disc Jockey), who plays party music and creates music mixes.
122 See: Sanjek (1992).
123 See: McLeod (2004).
124 See: ss 79–82 CDPA.
125 [1991] 780 F. Supp. 182 (SDNY 1991).
126 To check who samples whom see: www.whosampled.com.
127 [1975] 422 US 151.
128 See: Hampel (1992).

Two early US cases imply that the size of the borrowed portion could determine whether or not IP infringement occurred. In **Boosey v Empire Music Co.** (1915),[129] the Southern District Court of New York ruled that six similar notes or more constituted copyright infringement; while in **Northern Music Corp. v King Record Distribution Co.** (1952),[130] the same court indicated that the use of more than four bars constituted an infringement.

In addition to mechanical licensing for covers, a song also has a public performance right that derives from the section of copyright that applies to performing a composition in public. Only the underlying composition copyright holders receive income from performance rights societies. Most artists who use a sample licence pay either a flat fee or a royalty calculation based on the number of copies of their new work sold. A more popular song or artist demands a higher licensing fee, as when Puff Daddy sampled The Police's 'Every Breath You Take' for his 'I'll Be Missing You'. When The Verve, a 'Britpop' rock band from Wigan, scored their first major global hit with 'Bitter Sweet Symphony' in 1997 and sold 1.8 million copies of their album *Urban Hymns* in the UK alone, the band and their record label, Virgin, were faced with a major legal challenge at the time the band had won the title of 'best British group' at the 1998 Brit Awards. In writing the song 'Bitter Sweet Symphony', Verve singer Richard Ashcroft had used a sample of the Rolling Stones' hit song 'The Last Time', originally recorded and performed by the Andrew Oldham Orchestra in the early 1960s.[131]

Andrew Loog Oldham was the Stones' original manager. Though the Stones' subsequent manager Allen Klein initially refused to license 'The Last Time' to The Verve, Verve manager Jazz Summer eventually persuaded Klein to allow the group to use the sample. One of the conditions imposed on the band was that Mick Jagger and Keith Richards receive the songwriting credit for the title. This way, Klein also received the copyright to the (new) composition in the Verve song.

When Nike used 'Bitter Sweet Symphony' in their 'I Can' commercial for the Super Bowl XXXII on 25 January 1998, The Verve's (commercial) hit also boosted album sales of *Urban Hymns* in the USA. The Verve subsequently gave $175,000 of that profit to charity.[132] But that was not all. The Verve faced another legal challenge in 1999, when Andrew Loog Oldham (by that time living in Bogotá, Columbia) served a writ on The Verve and their label Virgin. At the High Court in London, Oldham claimed that he owned the recording rights of the orchestral version of 'The Last Time', not Decca (the Stones' original record company). He sued Virgin and The Verve for using the sound recording, demanding a million pounds in royalties. In their defence, the band and Virgin said that they had paid royalties to Decca Records for the song, in the honest belief that Decca owned the recording of Mr Oldham's version of the song. But Oldham and music publishers ABKCO successfully argued that too much of 'The Last Time' had been sampled by The Verve. The Verve's songwriter and singer Richard Ashcroft had to cede authorship of 'his' song and all publishing and royalty rights to ABKCO and Mr Oldham.[133] In an interview with *New Musical Express* in 2008, Mr Loog Oldham joked about the legal battle with The Verve and how Richard Ashcroft 'should have known better' and that the band had just used too much in the sample song.[134]

Is sampling illegal? Yes, contrary to popular belief and practice, sampling of an original copyrighted song without permission from the right holder is illegal. Unauthorized sampling actually violates two potential legal rights. First, the minute when someone samples a portion of another's song, this constitutes a violation of the copyright in the song itself. Second, sampling violates the sound recording copyright, usually owned by the record label or recording artist.

---

129 [1915] 224 F 646 (SDNY 1915).
130 [1952] 105 F Supp 393 (SDNY 1952).
131 The Andrew Oldham Orchestra was a musical side project in the mid-1960s, created by Andrew Loog Oldham, the original producer/manager of the Rolling Stones. There was no actual orchestra per se. The name was applied to recordings made by Oldham using a number of session musicians, including members of the Rolling Stones.
132 Source: 'Nike deal sweetens US prospects of British band', by Alice Rawsthorn, *Financial Times*, 6 April 1998.
133 Source: 'Who's suing whom: Bitter Symphony as The Verve is sued by Oldham', by John Willcock, *Independent*, 11 January.
134 Source: 'Rolling Stones' manager derides The Verve', *NME News*, 7 October 2008.

When Baauer used the defence that he had not made 'a penny' (or 'dime') from the 'Harlem Shake' sampler, that may have kept potential litigants at bay. It was his fault for not licensing the sample before uploading it on YouTube. However, the law is clear: sampling without prior permission subjects the illegal copier to a copyright infringement of both the original author (or publisher) and the record company. It is worth noting that sampling may also infringe the moral rights of the author or creator of the work in the UK and Europe (but not the US), whereby the creator may object to derogatory treatment of their work.[135]

Many prominent performers, including LL Cool J, Biz Markie and Massive Attack, have been sued for allegedly using uncleared 'samples' by contravening 'needle time' restrictions.[136] SST records[137] charged UK sampler and record producer, DJ Norman Cook (aka 'Fatboy Slim') $1,000 for sampling California-based band Negativland's recording, called 'Michael Jackson'. Cook had used the sample on his *Better Living Through Chemistry* CD, released in the US by Astralwerks in 1996. Subsequently, Coca-Cola unwittingly used Fatboy Slim's version of the song in its advertising campaign and also breached copyright of the Negativland song. It was later established that Negativland had 'appropriated' the song from an unlicensed record of a 1966 religious church recording in Concord, California.

Negativland were themselves sued in 1991 by Island Records over a song called 'U2'. Island argued that the record was packaged so that consumers might think it was a song called 'Negativland' by the band U2, rather than the other way around. SST records agreed to delete the record, but Negativland scored a public relations success when founder member Mark Hosler called U2 guitarist The Edge and asked him to help pay the group's legal costs in the law suit. The Edge expressed his sympathies but no cheque was forthcoming. Interestingly, in 2008, Mark Hosler was invited by the Digital Freedom Campaign – a fair-use advocacy group that is dedicated to defend the rights of artists, consumers and innovators – to travel to Washington DC as a 'citizen lobbyist' to speak with various members of Congress about Negativland's work.[138]

 FOR THOUGHT

The failure of UK copyright law to acknowledge sufficiently the manner in which musical works are created has led to a large number of copyright infringements particularly in the field of P2P (peer-to-peer) file-sharing. Frequently, artists and DJs take copyrighted music, edit and remix it. Whom would you sue in copyright infringement? Those services (ISPs) that permit the uploading of such music to others? The end user?

9.8 Codifying cyberspace: towards legislation to protect authors and artists from piracy?

In July 2011, High Court judge Mr Justice Arnold ruled that British Telecom (BT) must block access to a website which provided links to pirated movies, namely 'Newzbin 2',[139] a members-only

---

135 See: Article 6bis Berne Convention 1886 (as amended).
136 See: s 135A (5) CDPA: 'Needle time' means the time in any period (whether determined as a number of hours in the period or a proportion of the period, or otherwise) in which any recordings may be included in a broadcast.
137 SST Records is an American independent record label formed in 1978 in Long Beach, California by musician Greg Ginn. The company was initially called Solid State Transmitters, through which Ginn sold electronics equipment.
138 Source: *Negativland News*, 27 October, 2008, available at www.negativland.com/news/?cat=5.
139 **Twentieth Century Fox Film Corporation; Universal City Studios Productions LLLP; Warner Bros. Entertainment Inc; Paramount Pictures Corporation; Disney Enterprises, Inc; Columbia Pictures Industries Inc. v British Telecommunications plc** [2011] EWHC 1981 (Ch) ('the *Newzbin 2 case*').

website which aggregated a large amount of the illegally copied material found on 'Usenet' discussion forums. The landmark case was the first time that an ISP was ordered to block access to such a site, which paved the way for other sites to be blocked as part of a major crackdown on piracy.

The **Newzbin 2** case concerned the legal remedies that can be obtained to combat online copyright infringement. The six applicant movie corporations and film production companies brought their action against BT, seeking an injunction under s 97A of the Copyright, Designs and Patents Act 1988 to block or impede access by BT's subscribers to the website which provided illegal downloads of films (see also: **Totalise plc v Motley Fool Ltd** (2001)[140]). In his ruling, Arnold J stated:

> . . . in my judgment it follows that BT has actual knowledge of other persons using its service to infringe copyright: it knows that the users and operators of Newzbin 2 infringe copyright on a large scale, and in particular infringe the copyrights of the studios in large numbers of their films and television programmes. . . . It knows that the users of Newzbin 2 include BT subscribers, and it knows those users use its service to receive infringing copies of copyright works made available to them by Newzbin 2.[141]

Mr Justice Arnold's ruling helps ensure that UK ISPs do not become 'copyright cops' on behalf of the music or film industries. The **Newzbin 2** judgment turned BT into an internet policeman or censor in that the company was ordered to block its customers from accessing the Newzbin website, well known at the time for streaming pirated films. The judgment meant that ISPs in the UK must now block websites that aid (and abet) copyright infringing.

The impact of the internet and digital technologies has been on national, regional and international copyright agendas for some time. For example, the European Commission's *Green Paper on Copyright in the Knowledge Economy* (2007)[142] looked at the long-term future of copyright policy in the knowledge-intensive areas. The UK Government lobbied the Commission over internet piracy, backed by a strong UK Music lobby, including U2 manager Paul McGuinness, former lead vocalist of The Undertones Feargal Sharkey, Pink Floyd drummer Nick Mason and singers Annie Lennox and Tom Jones. At the heart of the debate is who should bear the burden of policing and protecting the music industry. On the other side of the musical spectrum is a group of musicians, the Featured Artists Coalition (FAC), who claim that despite the damage that file-sharing does to sales of their records, it can also encourage people to buy concert tickets and merchandise.[143]

Lord Mandelson, championing the Digital Economy Bill in 2009 in the House of Lords, petitioned former EU Commissioner for Information Society and Media, Viviane Reding, advocating that ISPs should operate a 'three strikes' policy, whereby anyone found illegally downloading music repeatedly should be given a 'red card' and be cut off from the internet. The ISPs continued to argue that they were only 'hosting' websites and have so far refused to become the internet police.

Lord Mandelson's *Digital Britain Report* of 2009 referred to a 'guidepath' of how Britain could sustain its position as a leading digital economy and society.[144] Following Lord Mandelson's proposal to suspend the internet accounts of those who engage in persistent file-sharing, the music and film industries voiced some concern that the proposed legislation might well target the 'soft underbelly' of file-sharing, namely teenagers who are doing it because they are either apathetic or believe they can get away with it; furthermore that this drastic legislation would potentially criminalize a whole generation of music fans.

---

140 [2001] EWCA Civ 1897.
141 Ibid., at 190.
142 See: European Commission (2007).
143 Source: 'Musicians hit out at plans to cut off Internet for file sharers', The Times, 10 September 2009, by Patrick Foster, Media Correspondent: http://entertainment.timesonline.co.uk/tol/arts_and_entertainment/music/article6828262.ece
144 HM Department for Culture, Media and Sports (DCMS) and Department for Innovation, Business and Skills (BIS) (2009).

9.8.1 EU legislation on regulating performing rights societies

How has digital copyright protection been addressed across Europe? In July 2007, the Court of First Instance in Belgium issued a decision in a copyright infringement case brought by the Belgian music collecting society SABAM against an ISP, Scarlet (formerly known as Tiscali).[145] In its decision, the court ordered Scarlet to install filtering software within six months to prevent the ISP's users from accessing unauthorized music downloads via peer-to-peer (P2P) systems, and to remove copyrighted music from its network.

The Belgian decision in **SABAM v Tiscali (Scarlet)** was the first time that a European court considered whether ISPs can be required to monitor or filter the activities of their users in order to stop file-sharing on P2P networks. The Belgian decision generated a substantial amount of criticism. Was the technology available to employ such filtering systems? Who should pay for it? How should one resolve the competing claims of rights holders as to their intellectual property and intermediaries (ISPs) as to their responsibility for traffic passing across their networks and – at the same time – protect end-users' right to privacy?

In January 2008, the Swiss file-sharing service 'RapidShare' was dealt a blow by the German district court (Landgericht) in Hamburg, whereby the author-licensing association GEMA had filed a claim against RapidShare for the uploading of copyrighted content.[146] The court ruled that the site must take responsibility for copyright infringement, even when the material in question was uploaded by its members. The case sent a clear message to any German-language service providers which might gain financial benefit from unlawful uses of copyrighted works.

On 29 January 2008, the European Court of Justice handed down its decision in **Promusicae v Telefónica** (C-275/06).[147] The ECJ looked at the various European Directives currently in force on the question of copyright, the enforcement of IP rights and e-commerce plus the human rights legislation on the right to privacy under Article 8 ECHR. The Court of Justice confirmed that while Community law does not require Member States to implement in their national laws an obligation to disclose personal data in the context of civil proceedings in order to ensure the effective protection of copyright, it does not preclude it either. The Court also underlined how important it was that the authorities and courts of the Member States should not only interpret their national law in a manner consistent with the Directives, but also make sure that they do not rely on an interpretation of them which would be in conflict with fundamental rights or other general principles of Community law, such as the principle of proportionality.

On 25 August 2009, the Utrecht District Court ordered the Dutch website Mininova to remove all files on its server that point to copyrighted works, or face a fine of up to €5m. Mininova – similar to Sweden's Pirate Bay – had one of the largest indexes of 'BitTorrent' files. The action was brought by Stichting Brein, an organization funded by copyright-holder groups.[148]

The Dutch court found that Mininova was inciting users to infringe copyrights while at the same time profiting from advertising on the site. Mininova's defence was that it was impossible to find and remove bit torrents that point to copyrighted materials. Unlike The Pirate Bay, Mininova had already been in the process of removing files when it received the 'takedown' notice from copyright holders. The court said that Mininova should have known that commercially made films, games, music and TV series are copyrighted and that these works are only copyright-free in exceptional cases. Ignorance was no defence.

---

145 **SABAM (La Société Belge des Auteurs, Compositeurs et Éditeurs) v S.A. Tiscali (Scarlet)** [2007] (N° 04/8975A) Tribunal de la première instance de Bruxelles a l'audience publique du 18 May 2007; décision de 29 juin 2007.
146 Oberlandesgericht Hamburg, Urteil v. 02.07.2008 – Az.: 5 U 73/07 – Haftung von Rapidshare IV.
147 Source: Press release No 5/08 of 29 January 2008 of the European Court of Justice in the judgment of court in Case C-275/06: **Productores de Música de España (Promusicae) v Telefónica de España SAU**.
148 LJN: BJ6008, Rechtbank Utrecht, 250077 / HA ZA 08-1124, 25. 8. 2009.

There have been a number of differing legal approaches in Europe with France's HADOPI legislation presenting the most aggressive strategy, requiring its ISPs to monitor their subscribers' use of copyrighted works where repeat-downloading music pirates are either cut off or suspended from internet use. The ECJ's decision in **Promusicae v Telefónica** may be seen as striking the right balance between fundamentally competing rights.

The Belgian Court decision in **SABAM v Tiscali (Scarlet)** was appealed on 28 January 2010, following the **Promusicae** decision. The Belgian court of appeal held that there were no sufficient remedies for an existing infringement and that there was no sufficient legal guidance provided by Belgian legislation which specifically gave injunctive relief to order filtering and blocking devices, preventing future copyright infringements. This question was referred back to the ECJ.

In conclusion, there is – to date – no unified legislation across EU Member States in the form of definite 'harmonization' legislation to either discourage copyright infringement or to discourage P2P file-sharing. Clearly, common Europe-wide answers to these issues are needed. The European Court of Justice should be asked to rule on these issues as soon as possible.

9.8.2 The Digital Economy Act 2010

The Digital Economy Act 2010 gives UK ministers, court authorities and Ofcom the power to disconnect illegal file-sharers, and permits courts to block websites containing copyright-infringing material. The music and games industries have welcomed the Digital Economy Act and its 'cut-off' measures as a step in the right direction. The Internet Service Providers' Association (ISPA), on the other hand, is 'outraged' about the new legislation that grants the High Court powers to force ISPs to block websites containing 'substantial' amounts of copyrighted material; particularly if the rights holder demands redress, regardless of whether the website has any knowledge of the actions of its users. Additionally, the communications regulator Ofcom was given the power to disconnect persistent illegal file-sharers. Ofcom's duty is to secure a significant reduction in unlawful file-sharing by imposing two specific obligations: notification of unlawful activity and, for repeat infringers, a court-based process of identity release and civil action. This facility has eased the burden on ISPs.

See Chapter 10.6

The Digital Economy Act 2010 received Royal Assent during the 'wash-up' period in April 2010 before the dissolution of Parliament to make way for the General Election on 6 May 2010. The Act centres on four main objectives:

(1)   To advance and modernize the UK's competitive digital communications infrastructure.
(2)   To support the UK's creative industries by taking action to tackle online copyright infringement ('piracy') and to strengthen the framework for the creation of successful business models.
(3)   To support local and regional news in the UK and update licensing arrangements.
(4)   To improve public confidence in digital activities by providing security of the communications network.

In more detail, the 2010 Act covers the following provisions:

(i)   Ofcom – to require the sectoral regulator to carry out an assessment of the UK's communications infrastructure every three years.
(ii)   Online infringement of copyright – to tackle online copyright infringement (piracy) by placing obligations on internet service providers to work with rights holders and, if necessary, to take technical measures against infringing subscribers. It also provides a power for the Secretary of State to introduce regulations for rights holders to seek a court injunction to prevent access to specified online locations for the prevention of online copyright infringement.

(iii)   Internet domain registries – to provide reserve powers in respect of efficient and effective management and distribution of internet domain names.

(iv)   Channel 4 Television Corporation – to adjust the corporation's functions from a focus on traditional broadcast activities to include provision of public service media content on other platforms, including the internet.

(v)   Independent television services – to enable future alterations of the Channel 3 and Channel 5 licences.

(vi)   Digital radio – to provide arrangements for digital switchover by making changes to the existing radio licensing regulatory framework.

(vii)   Access to electromagnetic spectrum – to allow for the charging of periodic payments on auctioned spectrum licences, and confer more proportionate enforcement powers on Ofcom.

(viii)   Video games – to make changes to how video games should be classified in the UK; e.g. age ratings of computer games must be on the same statutory footing for ratings of 12 years and above.

(ix)   Public lending rights (PLR) – to extend PLRs to non-print books.

(x)   Copyright penalties – changes to levels of penalties for copyright infringement.

The most drastic measure in the Digital Economy Act 2010 is the disconnection of broadband customers who are deemed to be infringing[149] copyright laws without their first being given the opportunity to plead their innocence before a court. This was passed to Ofcom on the legal basis that the regulator can send out warning letters to illegal file-sharers as well as monitor online traffic.[150]

As soon as the 2010 Act came into force, media and entertainment law firms began sending out thousands of letters to suspected illegal file-sharers. Soho firm Gallant Macmillan completed a mailshot to 2,000 individuals in July 2010, claiming that they infringed dance music label The Ministry of Sound's copyright after downloading and sharing music, typically demanding around £350. It followed in the footsteps of ACS:Law, who had also sent thousands of letters demanding compensation from alleged file-sharers. The Ministry of Sound's move marks an intensification of the legal battle against file-sharers. Some recipients of the letters, concerned about forking out huge damages, actually paid up. Others complained to Which? and local trading standards authorities.[151]

The idea behind the Digital Economy Act is to make it clear that ISPs, Ofcom or rights holders have to notify users of alleged P2P file-sharing infringements and can issue 'warning letters' on a 'three strikes' basis, thereby demanding damages, takedown notices and eventually cutting the infringer off from his server. Legal critics say that the process is complicated and expensive, and that the only penalty that can be levied is a fine. Unless a user confesses to illegally downloading a file, or a court order is obtained to seize a computer and the file is then located on its hard drive, it is hard to see how such an action will succeed. ISPs have denied responsibility, stating that they are merely temporarily 'hosting' connections and services. Broadband providers like O_2 are not interested in disconnecting their users and have left it to regulator Ofcom to deal with internet pirates under the recent statutory powers to monitor, disconnect and prosecute with the support of the Culture Secretary.

There are potential grounds for appeal once the measures under the 2010 Act are enforced. First, there is a serious risk of arbitrary enforcement touching on civil liberties. Second, there is the question of proportionality and reasonableness, because suspending web access to persistent offenders is a draconian step and diminishes freedom of expression and potentially disenfranchises citizens where e-government has become the norm.

---

149   The statutory definition of an 'infringing copy' is contained in s 27(2) CDPA 1988.
150   For further discussion see: Koempel (2010).
151   Source: 'File sharers targeted with legal action over music downloads', by Miles Brignall, *Guardian*, 17 July 2010.

FOR THOUGHT

Are injunctions and takedown notices the right step towards protecting the publishing, entertainment and games industries in order to safeguard copyright? Or have these industries failed to develop services and devices that will stop file-sharing infringement or alternatively pay-to-use services? Discuss with reference to UK and EU legislation and case law.

9.8.3 The US Digital Millennium Copyright Act 1998 ('the DMCA')

The Digital Millennium Copyright Act (DMCA)[152] is probably the most important US copyright legislation, which, *inter alia*, also incorporates two 1996 WIPO treaties. The DMCA with its draconian measures criminalizes the production and dissemination of technology, devices or services intended to circumvent measures, such as digital rights management (DRM), which control access to copyrighted works.[153]

The DMCA's 'anti-circumvention provisions' changed the remedies for the circumvention of copy-prevention systems (also known as 'technical protection measures') and require that all analogue video recorders have support for a specific form of copy prevention created by 'Macrovision' (now known as 'Rovi Corporation'). The DMCA also criminalizes the act of circumventing an access control, whether or not there is actual infringement of copyright itself. Most importantly, the DMCA extended and increased the penalties for copyright infringement on the internet. Title II of the Act – the 'Online Copyright Infringement Liability Limitations Act' or 'OCILLA' – creates a safe harbour for online service providers (OSPs, including ISPs) against copyright liability. This practically means that if US ISPs (or OSPs) adhere promptly to the requirement to block access to allegedly infringing material or remove such material from their systems – after receiving notification from a copyright holder or a performing rights society – ISPs will not be liable. OCILLA then provides a safe harbour from liability to their users and service providers. However, s 1201(c) of Title II does not change the underlying substantive copyright infringement rights, remedies or defences in US law.

The DMCA is silent in relation to websites that contain hyperlinks to infringing material. There have been a few US lower-court decisions which have ruled against linking in some narrowly prescribed circumstances. One is when the owner of a website has already been issued with an injunction against posting infringing material on their website and then links to the same material in an attempt to circumvent the injunction. One such case was **Intellectual Reserve (IR) v Utah Lighthouse Ministry (ULM)** (1999),[154] a religious organization that often criticized the claimant's Mormon religion. IR won an injunction against ULM to stop them from posting its copyrighted *Mormon Church Handbook of Instructions*. ULM's response was to simply link to other websites which held a copy of the copyrighted works. These websites did not have permission to host the copyrighted book. The court found ULM's linking to be 'contributory infringement' and therefore it granted a preliminary injunction preventing ULM from linking to the copyrighted *Mormon Church Handbook of Instructions*. The court found that ULM's linking to the unauthorized material was likely to be found to be 'contributory infringement' of IR's copyright. Therefore, it granted a preliminary injunction preventing ULM from linking to the sites in question.

---

152 United States Pub. L. No. 105–304, 112 Stat. 2860 (28 October 1998).
153 Passed on 12 October 1998 by a unanimous vote in the US Senate, signed into law by President Bill Clinton, the DMCA amended Title 17 of the US Code to extend the reach of copyright, while limiting the liability of the providers of online services for copyright infringement by their users.
154 See: **Intellectual Reserve, Inc. Utah Lighthouse Ministry, Inc**. United States District Court, D. Utah, Central Division, 6 December 1999.

In **Lenz v Universal Music Corp.** (2008),[155] the US District Court for the Northern District of California ruled that copyright holders must consider fair use before issuing takedown notices for content posted on the internet. Stephanie Lenz had posted on YouTube a home video of her children dancing to Prince's song 'Let's Go Crazy'. Universal Music Corp. ('Universal') sent YouTube a take-down notice pursuant to the DMCA, claiming that Lenz's video violated their copyright in Prince's song. Lenz claimed 'fair use' of the copyrighted material and sued Universal for misrepresentation of a DMCA claim. The court held that, in violation of the DMCA, Universal had not in good faith considered fair use when filing a takedown notice.

ISPs in the United States have made it clear that they do not wish to become the 'internet police', reiterating that they merely see themselves as 'conduits' or 'wires' for internet traffic that provide content to the end user. It is not in their commercial interest to disconnect their users. For this reason ISPs are reluctant to accept content-related liability, touching on legal areas such as libel, fraud, obscenity and copyright infringement.

 FOR THOUGHT

Is it acceptable for ISPs to impose filters so that certain types of files cannot be down-loaded by specific users, such as filename suffixes, file metadata or child pornography?

9.8.4 New business models instead of 'three strikes' legislation?

The former EU Commissioner for Information and Digital Affairs, Neelie Kroes, firmly believed that more should be done to open up access to books, out of print and orphan works, and promote free online digital libraries which would influence pan-European education and political decision-making. She hailed the Google Book Project as one of the major solutions. In her report *A Digital Agenda for Europe* (2010),[156] Kroes stated that the Commission wanted to ensure a regulatory frame-work which would pave the way for a rapid roll-out of freely available online services, similar to those made possible in the United Sates by the 'Google Settlement'.[157]

While digital music sales have increased, CD sales have fallen dramatically since 2005. Record companies' profit margins have been savaged by piracy and CD burning. Labels such as Sony, Warners and Universal are desperate to earn profits elsewhere, with many successful artists such as Prince and Radiohead releasing new songs free online. Record labels are now looking for solutions that will enable them to continue being viable enterprises.

How are songwriters, artists and authors going to be protected when ISP applications such as Spotify make uploads of whole album recordings freely available as downloads? How are authors, artists and performers going to support their creativity when they are not receiving the necessary rewards for their intellectual originality in the form of royalties? Most performing artists (and authors) strongly believe they have a right to make money from their creative work and deserve payment in royalties.

---

155 *Lenz (Stephanie) v Universal Music Corp; Universal Music Publishing, Inc., and Universal Music Publishing Group* [2008] Case Number C 07-3783 JF, Filed 20 August 2008 in the United States District Court for the Northern District of California San Jose Division.
156 See: European Commission (2010).
157 The Google Settlement included that for each work claimed against, minimum rates of $60 (books), $15 (inserts) or $5 (partial inserts) apply. The money attaches to the digitized content, so multiple claims for exactly the same text appearing in multiple volumes will not attract multiple payments. If total claims are less than $45m, further payments will be made: up to $300 per book, up to $75 per insert.

For record labels, the new '360° deals' mean they can still earn revenue if album sales continue to slide, like a hedge fund against a declining CD market. For artists, the deals may mean that labels are more committed to their cause, because if an artist makes money in any of his ventures, such as tours and merchandise, the label makes money too. Aside from financial benefits, some say the changing label–artist relationship could re-energize the music industry.

The likes of Madonna and Jennifer Lopez have become recognized brands in themselves, linked to their brand is a multi-million-dollar industry involving clothing, make-up, movies and mobile phone ringtones. In a historic two-album deal, EMI Music reportedly paid the heavy metal group Korn $15 million in 2005 for a percentage of the band's touring, merchandise, publishing and licensing revenue. Warner Brothers' deal with the US rock band My Chemical Romance includes part of their merchandise sales and Interscope Records signed LA's Pussycat Dolls, launching a series of ventures with the group, including a Las Vegas nightclub and a cosmetics line.[158]

 FOR THOUGHT

You are making a video recording on your mobile phone device of a street busker. You then upload the 'performance' on to YouTube. To what extent could it be a defence in any potential copyright claim that the video was shot in a public location where there is no expectation of privacy, and that the artist knew that someone was making the video and continued the performance anyway? Discuss with reference to human rights and copyright legislation.

The Strategic Advisory Board for Intellectual Property (SABIP) looked at 'offline' copyright infringement and online piracy. Its 2009 findings and subsequent report revealed how consumers obtain films, music and games for free. Following on from the 'Gowers Report'[159] of 2006, SABIP was set up as a 'quango' by the Labour Government to partner the Intellectual Property Office. Their remit was to provide a strategic overview of the government's intellectual property and to develop a workable strategy to understand the economic value of IP.

SABIP's review concluded that policy-makers urgently needed a better understanding of how consumers behave in both the online and offline digital environment. The report also showed that consumers were more interested in factors such as price, quality and availability of material, rather than its legal status, and that the digital world needed to be looked at from a new perspective. This would include consumer choice rather than criminal behaviour, where some artists even claimed that file-sharing leads people to buy more of the legally available products. When the new Coalition Government came to power in May 2010, SABIP was dissolved and its research programme was integrated into the Intellectual Property Office's research work. The IPO is now the government office that deals with UK patent, trademark and design registration and plays a vital part of promoting the creative industry and economy in the UK. Its prime remit is to protect original artistic works through copyright in order to incentivize innovation in design.

Should ISPs be more proactive? Some of the major providers already routinely monitor traffic sent over their network – primarily for maintenance and security purposes – and it should therefore be relatively easy to keep an eye on traffic sent using file-sharing programmes. But is it technically more difficult to establish exactly what is being shared and by whom?

---

158 Source: 'Korn, MCR cut new deals to combat sinking CD sales', *Rolling Stone* magazine, 27 October 2005.
159 HM Treasury (2006).

Content rights owners often monitor websites which offer links to copyright content and then obtain the Internet Protocol address of the online computer being used to share that data. While most countries have their own national copyright law, globally they operate – as previously discussed – within an international framework established by a number of copyright agreements such as the Berne and Rome Conventions, the WTO-TRIPS Agreement and the WIPO Copyright Treaties. These multilateral treaties allow not only the protection of rights holders but also the monitoring of illegal P2P file-sharing, such as that of the UK Internet Watch Foundation.

Additionally, domestic legislation, such as the UK Copyright Act, will protect, for example, a US copyrighted work which is published or made available in the UK, provided certain basic qualifying conditions have been met. Furthermore, there is now the EU 'harmonizing' legislation in place. These international and regional instruments establish certain parameters and limits on the ability to make changes to national copyright laws. Furthermore, modern web-based technologies have global reach and are not bound by national frontiers. The management of rights on an international basis where, for example, permissions are needed to use music in a pan-European service is an emerging area requiring attention.

 FOR THOUGHT

How many people buy counterfeit DVDs, CDs or video games? How many people illegally download music without paying for it online? What information would you provide as a policy adviser to a minister in the Department for Business, Innovation and Skills to tackle piracy threats to the recording and publishing industries?

 ## 9.9 Further reading

Angelopoulos, C. (2012) 'The myth of European term harmonisation – 27 public domains for 27 Member States'. *International Review of Intellectual Property and Competition Law*, 43(5), 567–594.
Christina Angelopoulos examines European copyright law, specifically the 'intricate' provision of Directive 2006/116/EC 'On the Term of Protection of Copyright and Certain Related Rights Enforcement' of 12 December 2006 ('the EU Term Directive') which, she argues, preserves many differences between the national rules of EU Member States. In her article she identifies and analyses four main sources of legislative variability in the term of protection in Europe. Though the EU Term Directive was aimed at harmonizing Europe-wide copyright legislation, the author argues that some areas of substantive copyright law remain 'unharmonized'.

Farrand, B. (2012) 'Too much is never enough? The 2011 Copyright in Sound Recordings Extension Directive'. *European Intellectual Property Review*, 34(5), 297–304.
Benjamin Farrand questions whether the EU Directive 2011/77/EU on the term of protection of copyright and certain related rights ('The Copyright in Sound Recordings Extension Directive') actually benefits performing artists. He argues that the Directive is predominantly justified upon a combination of 'just reward' and 'incentive providing' by extending the duration of copyright for performing artists to the life of the artist (the performer) plus 70 years, thus gradually aligning authors' and performers' rights protection. Farrand argues that the Directive was mainly driven by record companies and the music industry plus famous artists' lobbying politicians in Brussels, rather than sound empirical research.

Harrison, A. (2011) *Music: The Business. The essential guide to the law and the deals* **(5th edn). Chatham: Virgin Books/Random House.**
Ann Harrison's text is the most comprehensive and user-friendly guide for anyone working in the music industry. The book is not only useful for budding music and entertainment lawyers, but also a valuable starting point for singer-songwriters and artists setting up their own showcase. Harrison cites a large number of cases, such as the *George Michael* case, when the young and inexperienced Andrew Ridgeley and George Michael from Wham! signed their first exclusive record deal. Harrison makes contract law fun with plenty of case examples from the music industry, such as the *Spice Girls* case, concerned with unauthorized branding and merchandizing. An important section of the book discusses duration of copyright, which has been extended by EU law to a period of 70 years in musical works from the end of the year in which the author (creator) dies. The book covers music piracy and peer-to-peer file-sharing with music downloads now freely available.

McEvedy, V. (2002) 'The Digital Millennium Copyright Act and the E-Commerce Directive'. *European Intellectual Property Review,* **24(2), 65–73.**
The author compares the US legislation of the Digital Millennium Copyright Act (DMCA) with EU legislation, such as the E-Commerce Directive which, she argues, closely resembles the DMCA. McEvedy discusses the 'horizontal' approach to ISP liability in the EU framework Directive on Certain Legal Aspects of Information Society Services, in particular Electronic Commerce, in the Internal Market (2000/31) ('the E-Commerce Directive'), which applies to 'copyright piracy, unfair competition practices, misleading advertising, etc.' In addition, she looks at protection provided for copyright infringement in both EU and US legislation. The two key differences are that the E-Commerce Directive does not protect information location tools and there is no notice and takedown procedure and therefore little guidance or protection for ISPs in the removal or restoration of material. However, the E-Commerce Directive was intended to remove primary barriers to cross-border commerce on the internet and not to regulate comprehensively.

Passman, D. S. (2011) *All You Need to Know about the Music Business* **(8th edn). London/New York: Viking.**
This is a 'must read' for anyone who wants to get basic and extended knowledge of the music business. No one understands the music business and the changes it has undergone in recent years better than LA lawyer Donald Passman. For 20 years his book has offered detailed advice to artists and executives, novices and experts alike on how to thrive in these volatile times. This is a completely revised edition and sets out recent developments in record deals, copyright, new technologies and film music. It also offers unique advice on how to navigate your way through the ins and outs of songwriting, music publishing, merchandizing and performing. Music and performance artists are the main concern in this book, a good start if you want to manage your own band or launch your own label. For budding music and entertainment lawyers, this is a useful start. Passman offers invaluable on-hand information, uncovering essential and hidden information about the structure and potential hazards in interpretation of contracts.

Schwabach, A. (2011) *Fan Fiction and Copyright: Outsider work and intellectual property Protection.* **Farnham: Ashgate.**
Aaron Schwabach discusses disputes between authors and their fans over the use of copyright and copyrighted characters in online fan fiction ('fan fic'), such as works which resemble closely that of authors like J. K. Rowling. 'Fan fic' stories and novels, written by fans of existing characters, and shared mainly on the internet, are a nearly invisible form of outsider art, but over the past decade this has grown exponentially in volume and in legal importance. Because of its nature, authorship and underground status, fan fiction stands at an intersection of key issues regarding intellectual property. This book examines the various types of fan-created content, most of which are to some extent derivative works, and asks whether and to what extent they can be protected as transformative uses.

Simon, I. (2006) 'The introduction of performers' moral rights: Parts 1 and 2'. *European Intellectual Property Review,* **28(12), 552–561 and 600–610.**

This is a two-part article analysing the impact of the introduction of moral rights for performers in the United Kingdom in the form of the Performances (Moral Rights, etc.) Regulations 2006, and the degree to which the new regime complies with the WIPO Performances and Phonograms Treaty. Ilanah Simon discusses the way in which the United Kingdom has implemented performers' moral rights and looks at the moral right of integrity (i.e. freedom from distortion, mutilation or other prejudicial modification), as well as various practical considerations concerning both types of moral rights, such as their duration and the conditions under which they can be waived and transmitted, before offering some general conclusions on the likely impact of the Regulations. She discusses the definition of a 'qualifying performance' within the CDPA, the meaning of paternity right, derived from s 180(2) CDPA and the ramifications of the s 180(2) definition defining a 'qualifying performance'. Simon concludes that performers' moral rights are better protected under the 2006 Regulations.

Synodinou, T. E. (2013) 'E-books, a new page in the history of copyright law?' *European Intellectual Property Review,* **35(4), 220–227.**

This article deals with the legal issues related to the creation, marketing and use of e-books. While searching for traces of the legal position of e-books in copyright law, Tatiana-Eleni Synodinou places her emphasis on the distinctive characteristics and unique features of e-books. The significant differences that exist between e-books and physical (paper) books seem to warrant the emergence of a specific legal and contractual framework for e-books. The author speculates whether the e-book format is capable of creating a new legal identity for the oldest cultural medium in our history.

Chapter 10

Regulatory Authorities

10.1 Overview

This book closes with a chapter on regulators and 'quangos'. When the present Government – a Conservative–Liberal coalition – came to power in May 2010, Prime Minister David Cameron set out to overhaul the 'quango' system. Quangos (quasi-autonomous non-Governmental organizations) are public bodies operating at arm's length from Government, but for which ministers are ultimately accountable. In the case of Ofcom it is the Department of Culture, Media and Sport (DCMS). Ministers are usually responsible for appointments, subject to scrutiny by an appointments review body under a Code of Practice, to avoid such things as conflicts of interest. For example, the Government could not appoint media mogul Rupert Murdoch unless he were to dispose of all his media interests. Major players in the UK regulatory field include London Transport, the Environment Agency and pay review bodies.

See below
10.6

In his pre-election pledge in July 2009, David Cameron chiefly declared war on Ofcom (Office of Communications), the broadcasting and communications regulator.[1] At the time, Ofcom had 873 staff, a budget of £142 million and was paying its chief executive nearly £400,000. This chapter will demonstrate that Ofcom is very much alive and its role as a statutory regulator has been given additional power under the Digital Economy Act 2010 when it comes to holding ISPs to account for online defamation and copyright infringement.

See below 10.7

Some regulators have come and gone, depending on governmental preference and policy issues. The regulation of the film, games and commercial video industry is covered by the British Board of Film Classification (BBFC), a self-regulatory body with some statutory recognition such as the Video Recordings Act 1984. The impact of new media in general, and the internet in particular, continues to dominate the thoughts of those involved in the regulation of online audio-visual material.

But how much does the ordinary member of the public actually know about regulators and government quangos? The best-known regulators in the UK have been the non-statutory Press Complaints Commission (PCC – though this is about to change), regulating the print press and their online content, and the statutory body Ofcom, which oversees broadcasters (mainly the BBC) and telecommunication providers.

---

1 Source: 'Tories pledge to cut back quangos', BBC *Breakfast*, 6 July 2009; see also: 'David Cameron plans to save millions by cutting quangos', by Nicholas Watt, *Guardian*, 6 July 2009.

How much is actually known about the self-regulators such as the Internet Watch Foundation (IWF) or the even more obscure existence of the prime-time, pre-pay phoneline regulator PhonepayPlus? PhonepayPlus regulates Premium Rate Telecoms Services (PRTS), which provide services via fixed or mobile telecoms lines, and all '118' directory enquiry services and interactive digital TV.[2] PRTS is a well-known source of fraud and scams, though one reason for its popularity is that it provides an anonymous way of making payments for goods and services purchased remotely, including pornography channels and gambling. The BBC was fined a record £400,000 by the regulator in 2008, when the *Liz Kershaw Show* on BBC 6 Music had faked competition winners, thus people paying for calls at the time of the broadcasts had no chance of winning.

The independent self-regulator the Internet Watch Foundation 9 monitors child sexual abuse and obscene and violent content hosted on websites worldwide. The IWF is funded and backed by the EU as well as major ISPs, mobile phone operators and manufacturers, content service providers, filtering companies, search providers, trade associations and the financial sector.[3] The IWF's core function is to provide an internet hotline for the public to report their accidental exposure to criminal online content.[4]

While all regulators have elaborate websites, are freely accessible and offer free advice, it is arguably not well known by ordinary citizens that these authorities exist and offer free alternative redress to going to court in areas of privacy, defamation, harassment, obscenity, violence or child pornography. This chapter discusses the merits and disadvantages of regulatory bodies and whether voluntary regulatory powers are sufficient to deal with wrongdoers or whether court action is still the most effective answer.

In summary, there are three regulatory models in the UK. These are:

- Industry self-regulation, e.g. the Independent Press Standards Organisation (IPSO) (for print media and online activities) or the Advertising Standards Authority (ASA) in relation to non-broadcast advertising.
- Co-regulation, a combination of industry self-regulation with oversight by a statutory body (e.g. PhonepayPlus and the ASA in relation to broadcast advertising).
- Statutory regulation control by a statutory body, such as Ofcom, in relation to, for example, complaints about taste and decency, privacy and unfairness in relation to broadcasters.

A substantial part of this chapter will focus on the Leveson Inquiry and its recommendations. When Lord Justice Leveson concluded his 22-minute London press conference on 29 November 2012, he was applauded by journalists. However, since the Leveson Report was published in November 2012, press plaudits have been harder to come by. This chapter will reflect on the findings of the Leveson Report, media responses and parliamentary debates leading to a Royal Charter which may well see an end of British press freedom which so many journalists and writers have fought for throughout history.

See below 10.4

See Chapter 1.2.2

---

2   Phonepayplus provides a weekly list online of services which have been banned or withdrawn from public use at: www. phonepayplus.org.uk/For-Business/Register-with-us/Check-a-providers-registration-status.aspx.
3   For companies supporting the IWF with approximately £20,000 per annum see: www.iwf.org.uk/members/current-members.
4   The Protection of Children Act 1978 (as amended by the Sexual Offences Act 2003 and Coroners and Justice Act 2009) makes it an offence to take, make, permit to be taken, distribute, show, possess with intent to distribute, and advertise indecent photographs or pseudo-photographs of children under the age of 18.

10.2 Regulators and quangos

The Nolan Committee, chaired by Lord Nolan,[5] was set up in 1994 under the then Conservative Government, at the request of Prime Minister John Major, to examine, *inter alia*, standards of public life in the wake of allegations that MPs were asking parliamentary questions for cash. The Committee concentrated on Members of Parliament, ministers and civil servants, executive quangos and NHS bodies. The Committee concluded:

> . . . we cannot say conclusively that standards of behaviour in public life have declined. We can say that conduct in public life is more rigorously scrutinised than it was in the past, that the standards which the public demands remain high, and that the great majority of people in public life meet those high standards. But there are weaknesses in the procedures for main-taining and enforcing those standards. As a result people in public life are not always as clear as they should be about where the boundaries of acceptable conduct lie. This we regard as the principal reason for public disquiet. It calls for urgent remedial action.[6]

Nolan recommended that all public appointments should be subject to independent scrutiny, that merit should be the overriding principle governing appointments and that all public bodies should follow a code of conduct. The post of Commissioner for Public Appointments was created in the wake of the Nolan Report and first held by Dame (now Baroness) Rennie Fritchie. Her role was to regulate, monitor and report on the public appointments process. However, only 12,500 of the total 35,000 public body appointments came under her remit at the time.

Once the Conservatives were back in power from May 2010 (as part of a coalition with the Liberal Democrats), Prime Minister David Cameron promised that policy work would be returned to Whitehall departments to ensure there was greater parliamentary accountability via ministers. Those quangos that would survive would carry out only purely administrative functions, with ministers taking responsibility for serious performance failures.

It could be argued that, if the advantages of regulators are generally speed and dealing with public complaints out of court, the downside of self-regulation is that these authorities tend not to have legal powers in the form of injunctions, fines or damages (apart from Ofcom). Traditionally, non-statutory regulatory authorities could not be challenged in the administrative courts by way of judicial review, though Lord Woolf stated in the **Ian Brady** case,[7] when the Moors Murderer chal-lenged an adjudication by the PCC, that any exercise of jurisdiction over the PCC 'would be reserved for cases where it would clearly be desirable for this court to intervene'. Newsreader Anna Ford also tried to seek judicial review in a PCC decision, but the courts could see no justifiable basis for inter-fering with a self-regulatory body.[8]

However, if the actions of a voluntary regulator impinge on the rights of the subjects of the decision, particularly their human rights such as freedom of expression or privacy rights, then it is likely that the courts will intervene, which could mean that the strict demarcation between non-statutory (self- or voluntary) and statutory regulators is breaking down. The regulators' ability to hand out 'informal' advice and publish decisions, commentaries and adjudications tends to alleviate

5 Michael Patrick Nolan, Baron Nolan, PC, QC, DL, KCSG (1928–2007) was a judge and chairman of the Committee on Standards in Public Life (1994 to 1997).
6 See: House of Commons (1994).
7 **R v PCC ex parte Stewart-Brady** [1997] EMLR 185.
8 See: **R v PCC, ex parte Anna Ford** [2002] EMLR 5, 31 July 2001 (unreported) (QBD).

most complaints from 'ordinary' people, leaving only a handful of complaints, which tend to be from celebrities or royalty who, mostly accompanied by their lawyers, attempt to use the regulators as a first step to gain privacy by trying to protect their reputations.

From time to time, events occur which cause questions to be asked about the methods used by journalists and press photographers to gather material for publication. In January 2007 there was persistent harassment by photographers of Kate Middleton, HRH Prince William's girlfriend at the time and future wife (as HRH The Duchess of Cambridge), amid speculation that an engagement was about to be announced.[9]

Then, in the same month, Mr Clive Goodman, a reporter employed by the *News of the World*, was jailed following his conviction for conspiracy to intercept communications, including some involving the Royal Family, without lawful authority, which led to the *Guardian*'s and PCC's (separate) investigations into clandestine recording devices and unethical undercover journalism. A further event was the release of the Information Commissioner's list of publications that employed journalists who had had dealings with a particular private investigator known to have obtained personal data by illegal means. These events gave rise to renewed doubts about whether the press was overstepping the mark in the methods used to obtain information and the question of whether press regulation was working in its present form.[10]

See below 10.4

The democratic model of freedom of expression acknowledges the pre-eminence of political speech and sees a pedagogical role for the media. Many journalists are committed to the principle of objectivity and make an effort to report news free of bias. Schudson (2003) states that one of the fundamental underpinnings of the Anglo-American model of journalism is the notion of 'objectivity', which the American sociologist describes as 'a kind of industrial discipline [for journalists]'.[11]

See Chapter 6

But does objectivity in journalism really exist? Every journalist knows when undertaking his training that the fundamental basis of journalism is based on the classic model of inquiry: 'Who, What, How, Where, When and Why?' But this seemingly simple principle, which is based on objectivity, can become extraordinarily problematic in practice. Journalists, like any other human beings, have a set of prejudices and other views that can affect their objectivity. That said, they ought to have a set of professional values and expectations which affect their daily work. The ideal scenario should be that a journalist, when going about a news story or documentary investigation, should be able to put aside his own personal beliefs, feelings, politics and prejudices and become genuinely objective in the coverage of the story. But in practice, he may well have to adhere to the editorial policy of the news organization he works for, which permeates the paper, online copy or broadcast. Additionally, the need for a pay cheque may override ethical concerns the journalist might hold.

Take the classic example of Rupert Murdoch's UK media empire, which covers not only *The Times*, the *Sun* (and formerly the now defunct *News of the World*) newspapers (and online editions) but also Sky and Fox News on TV and the *Wall Street Journal*, making the Murdoch News Corporation ('News Corp') one of the largest media conglomerates in the world. Parts of the Murdoch assets have been run by members of his family, such as his son James Murdoch and his daughter Elisabeth Murdoch, though this changed after the parliamentary phone-hacking and Leveson inquiries in 2011–12.

The way the media mogul Rupert Murdoch has influenced political decisions can be demonstrated in a number of ways too numerous to list here. Clearly Mr Murdoch has used his wealth and media muscle to promote his ideas. For example, the *Sun* switched its generally conservative stance and backed Tony Blair and the Labour Party in the 1997 UK General Election, also backing Barack

---

9 See: **Miss Kate Middleton v The Daily Mirror**. PCC adjudication 5.4.2007.
10 For further discussion see: Gaber (2009).
11 See: Schudson (2003), p. 82.

Obama in the US in 2008. In August 2010, Rupert Murdoch gave $1m to help Republicans in that year's US mid-term elections.[12]

During the summer of 2010, Rupert Murdoch announced that he would merge his main company, News Corp, with BSkyB, a UK satellite broadcaster in which it already had a minority stake. While a price had yet to be set and the acquiescence of the shareholders secured, News Corp was lobbying the EU Commissioners to win pre-clearance for the deal on competition grounds, even though the deal might well fall foul of EU competition law governing media diversity. Ofcom indicated that it would review Mr Murdoch's proposal under concurrent powers it holds with the Office of Fair Trading in relation to media competition matters under the Enterprise Act 2002 and the Communications Act 2003.

See below 10.4

Murdoch's British media empire had been at the centre of a political storm since 2009, with newly emerging allegations in September 2010 that illegal phone-hacking had taken place at his tabloid newspaper, the *News of the World* (*NoW*). Much attention focused on the role of David Cameron's former media adviser, Andy Coulson, who had been editor of the paper at the time of the alleged hacking, yet continued to deny any knowledge of it. This raised broader questions about Mr Murdoch's powerful grip on the UK media industry and laid bare the extent to which British politicians are intimidated by him, a state of affairs which some regard as profoundly unhealthy. As the 'Coulson saga' played out, Mr Murdoch continued to work on the consummation of the BSkyB deal, which would increase his power still further. Mr Coulson resigned as the Prime Minister's press chief on 21 January 2011, while Culture Secretary Jeremy Hunt referred the acquisition of BSkyB to the Competition Commission. Evidence was later provided to the Leveson Inquiry, revealing contacts between Tories and News Corp while it attempted to take ownership of BSkyB. For example, on 18 January 2006, Mr Murdoch had lunch with David Cameron and George Osborne, where 'politics and policy' were discussed (also present: Les Hinton, Rebekah Brooks and Trevor Kavanagh).

It goes without saying that any journalist who wants to work for the Murdoch empire will need to adhere to the policies and editorial line of that media corporation which, during the last General Election, for example, was anti-Labour and pro-Conservative. The *Sun*'s editor wrote shortly before the General Election in April 2010 that Gordon Brown's 'ailing Labour Party was in disarray'.[13] Following the death of Baroness Margaret Thatcher, the media mogul donated £10,000 to the Thatcher charity, the 'Chelsea Pensioners Appeal', in memory of the Prime Minister 'who changed Britain and the world for the better'.[14] However, the Leveson Report revealed that the day-to-day relationship between journalists and politicians was in 'robust good health and performing the vital public interest functions in a vigorous democracy'.

10.3 Regulating the print press

Self-regulation of the British print press began with the Press Council in 1953, a voluntary body that aimed to maintain high ethical standards of journalism and to promote press freedom. The origins of the Press Council go back to 1947 when the Labour Government established a Royal Commission under the chairmanship of Sir David Ross to review and advise Parliament on the finance, control, management and ownership of the press. When the Commission reported on its findings in 1949 it recommended the establishment of a self-regulatory press council.

---

12 Source: 'Murdoch $1m donation may not prove bias', by Mark Mardell, BBC News Online, 18 August 2010.
13 Source: 'Brown's blown it', by Tom Newton Dunn (Political Editor); further stories on the same day by Kevin Schofield and Alex West, Sun, 17 April 2010.
14 Source: 'Rupert Murdoch gives £10,000 to Thatcher charity', by Lisa O'Carroll, Guardian, 19 April 2013.

However, during the 1980s a small number of publications failed in the view of many to observe the basic ethics of journalism. This in turn reinforced a belief among many Members of Parliament that the Press Council, which had lost the confidence of some in the press, was not a sufficiently effective body. Some believed that it would be preferable to enact a law of privacy and right of reply as well as to set up a statutory press council wielding enforceable legal sanctions.[15] Given the serious implications of such a course of action, the Conservative Home Secretary Douglas Hurd appointed a Departmental Committee in 1989 under (later Sir) David Calcutt QC to consider the matter. The Committee's task was to consider what measures were needed to give further protection to individual privacy from the activities of the press and improve recourse against the press for the individual citizen.[16]

The Calcutt Report on 'Privacy and Related Matters' (1990) did not suggest new statutory controls but recommended that a 'Press Complaints Commission' ought to replace the Press Council. The new commission was given just 18 months to demonstrate 'that non-statutory self-regulation can be made to work effectively. This is a stiff test for the press. If it fails, we recommend that a statutory system for handling complaints should be introduced.'[17]

Members of the press responded with vigour to the Calcutt Report, acting with great speed to set up their own self-regulator in the form of the Press Complaints Commission (the PCC) in 1991. Five years later, in July 1995, the Conservative Secretary of State for National Heritage, Virginia Bottomley, reported the findings of the Select Committee on Privacy and Media Intrusion to the House of Commons, that a case had not been made out to enact a privacy law as a form of civil remedy for media intrusion into a person's privacy.[18] The Labour MP for Islington and Finsbury, Chris Smith, asked Mrs Bottomley why a criminal offence had not been introduced specifically designed to prevent physical intrusion from bugging devices planted by the press which seriously invaded a person's private property.[19] The Secretary of State's response was non-committal, stating that it was up to the press regulator, the PCC, to keep its journalists in check by way of adherence to their Code of Practice.

In 2003, a House of Commons Parliamentary Select Committee on 'Culture, Media and Sport' considered whether some form of statutory regulation of the print press ought to be introduced since there had been too many calls for the abolition of the PCC. Giving evidence to the Select Committee, Mr Justice Tugendhat QC had stated that 'no new laws are necessary because recent changes in the law have already cured the defect in English law. I agree with the PCC that there is no need to introduce new legislation at the present time.'[20] Tugendhat J based his views on the statutory provisions of the Human Rights Act 1998, the Data Protection Act 1998 and the Protection from Harassment Act 1997, as well as common-law decisions in **Campbell** (2002),[21] **A v B** (2002)[22] and the Strasbourg court's ruling in **Peck** (2003)[23] (see below). In other words, no new laws were necessary because recent changes in the law had already cured the defect in English privacy law.

15 For further discussion see: Rampal (1981).
16 See: House of Commons (1990).
17 Ibid.
18 House of Commons (1995).
19 Ibid., at 1326.
20 Source: House of Commons – Department of Culture, Media and Sport (2003). Supplementary memorandum submitted by Mr Michael Tugendhat QC. Comment on the Supplementary Memorandum submitted by the PCC, 16 June 2003, at para 501.
21 [2004] 2 AC 457 (HL).
22 [2002] EWCA 337 (QB).
23 **Peck v UK** (2003) 36 EHRR 719 (ECHR).

❖ KEY CASE   *Peck v UK* [2003] (ECHR)

Precedent

❖ Where a public official abuses his position by performing an administrative act maliciously, or which he knows he has no power to do, and causes foreseeable harm, then the injured person may recover damages on the basis of misfeasance in public office.

❖ Depending on the circumstances in which any film (or CCTV footage) has been taken or published, the unauthorized taking or publication of pictures might be prevented (or damages recovered) on the grounds of copyright breach or breach of contract.

❖ Alternatively, the remedy of breach of confidence is available if there has been an 'unauthorized use of that information to the detriment of the party communicating it.'[24]

❖ The remedy of defamation is also available if the claimant's reputation has suffered.

❖ A further remedy can be found in the tort of harassment causing personal injury (see: **Burnett v George** (1992)[25] and **Khorasandjin v Bush** (1993)[26]).

Facts

On the evening of 20 August 1995, Geoffrey Dennis Peck,[27] suffering from depression, attempted suicide in Brentwood High Street by cutting his wrists with a kitchen knife. The incident was caught on CCTV installed by Brentwood Borough Council. The CCTV operator alerted the police, who arrested Mr Peck for possession of a dangerous weapon. He was released without charge. On 9 October 1995, Brentwood Council issued two CCTV photographs of Mr Peck to CCTV News with an article promoting neighbourhood safety, entitled: 'Defused: the partnership between CCTV and the police prevents a potentially dangerous situation'. The *Brentwood Weekly News* front page of 12 October 1995 showed a clear photograph of Mr Peck's face; and the *Yellow Advertiser*, with a circulation of 24,000, published a similar article and photo of Mr Peck entitled 'Gotcha', publishing a follow-up article on 16 February 1996, entitled 'Eyes in the sky triumph'. A number of people recognized Mr Peck. Anglia TV showed the 'Peck' CCTV footage on 17 October 1995 though his face was pixelated; the average audience was 350,000 at the time. The same council CCTV footage – with Mr Peck's face not pixelated – was also shown on BBC TV's national *Crime Beat* on 11 March 1996, with an average of 9.2 million viewers. Friends and family recognized him.

Mr Peck objected to the media and on 25 April 1996 complained to the Broadcasting Standards Commission (BSC) about the *Crime Beat* broadcast, claiming his right to privacy had been infringed under Article 8 ECHR and that he had received unfair and unjust treatment. On 13 June 1997, the BSC upheld both complaints. On 1 May 1996, Mr Peck complained to the Independent Television Commission (ITC). The ITC found that the applicant's identity was not adequately obscured and that the ITC Code had been breached. Following an apology by Anglia TV, no further action was taken. On 17 May 1996, Mr Peck complained unsuccessfully to the PCC about the newspaper articles. Mr Peck applied to the High Court for leave to apply for judicial review on 23 May 1996, which was rejected,

---

24 See: *Coco v. A.N. Clark Engineers Ltd* [1969] RPC 41 at para 47.
25 [1992] 1 FLR 525.
26 [1993] 3 All ER 669.
27 Born 1955 in Brentwood, Essex.

as was his appeal to the Court of Appeal. He subsequently lodged an application with the European Commission of Human Rights on 22 April 1996 under Article 8 'right to privacy'.

Decision

The Human Rights Commission ruled that the disclosures by Brentwood Council of the CCTV material to CCTV News, the *Yellow Advertiser*, Anglia TV and BBC TV were not accompanied by sufficient safeguards and therefore breached the applicant's private life in violation of Article 8 ECHR. The ECtHR found that the refusal of judicial review had deprived Mr Peck of an effective remedy in relation to the violation of his right to respect for his private life and the right to proper redress. The ECtHR commented, *inter alia*, on the lack of legal power of the PCC (in addition to other regulators complained to, namely BSC and ITC) in that they were unable to award damages to the applicant or indeed punish the print press and broadcasters.

The Court also found that the facts in Mr Peck's case were rather different from those in the **Earl Spencer** case[28] in that the applicant had exhausted all actionable domestic remedies for breach of confidence at the relevant time (whereas Earl Spencer had not).

Finding that the applicant had no effective remedy in domestic legislation, the Strasbourg court awarded Mr Peck 11,800 Euros in respect of non-pecuniary damages and 218,075 Euros in costs and expenses.

Analysis

The main issue in **Peck** related to the circumstances in which the CCTV footage was taken of Mr Peck in a public place (in Brentwood High Street) and the resulting publication in various newspapers and TV broadcasts of the self-harm incident. The Strasbourg human rights court had to decide whether the publication of the pictures of the applicant constituted an interference with his right to respect for private life under Article 8 ECHR, and whether any such interference was proportionate to the legitimate aims of public safety, the prevention of disorder or crime and protection of the rights of others. Furthermore, the ECtHR had to decide whether the domestic remedies available to the applicant for an arguable breach of Article 8 were effective as required under Article 13(3) ECHR, namely judicial review.

The problem in Mr Peck's case was that the issue of CCTV and authorities invading his privacy had arisen before the HRA 1998 legislation had come into force in the UK. Otherwise he would have had a sound claim for damages, not only against the local authority but also against the various regulators, whom Mr Peck had complained to. The Strasbourg court ruled that certain incidents which take place in public can still fall within someone's private sphere, covered by Article 8 ECHR, and that Mr Peck should have had a reasonable expectation of privacy.

---

28 **Earl and Countess Spencer v the United Kingdom** (applications nos. 28851/95 and 28852/95, decision of 16 January 1998, Decisions and Reports (DR) 25, p. 56).

10.3.1 Self-regulation of the print press: the Press Complaints Commission

Following the Calcutt Report in January 1991, the Press Complaints Commission (PCC) was established as an independent self-regulatory body for the print press (including magazines and, later, online editions). The main role of the PCC was to handle readers' complaints, by administering and upholding the Editors' Code of Practice. By the time the PCC drew to a close, following the Leveson Inquiry in 2014, the Commission comprised six editorial industry representatives from across a range of newspapers and magazines, and nine lay members – including its chairman, Lord Hunt of Wirral.

The PCC included the Editors' Code of Practice Committee ('the Code Committee'), made up of regional editors of newspapers. This Code Committee produced the PCC Code of Practice ('the Code') for the Commission. The Code underwent numerous changes between 1991 and 2013. The Code included a definition of 'public interest' and set the benchmark for ethical press standards, protecting both the rights of the individual and the public's right to know. In the absence of any statutory codified definition of the 'public interest', the PCC's definition is still regarded as the most helpful today:

The public interest[29]

1. The public interest includes, but is not confined to:

    (i)   Detecting or exposing crime or serious impropriety.
    (ii) Protecting public health and safety.
    (iii) Preventing the public from being misled by an action or statement of an individual or organization.

2. There is a public interest in freedom of expression itself.
3. Whenever the public interest is invoked, the PCC will require editors to demonstrate fully that they reasonably believed that publication, or journalistic activity undertaken with a view to publication, would be in the public interest and how, and with whom, that was established at the time.
4. The PCC will consider the extent to which material is already in the public domain, or will become so.
5. In cases involving children under 16, editors must demonstrate an exceptional public interest to override the normally paramount interest of the child.

All members of the press who had signed up to the PCC and its Code had a duty to maintain the highest professional standards. In July 2013, for example, the PCC rejected privacy complaints from Chris Huhne and Carina Trimingham about five national newspapers. Mr Huhne was the disgraced politician who served a prison sentence for perverting the course of justice over a 2003 speeding charge. He had persuaded his then wife, Vicky Pryce, to 'take the points'. Mr Huhne had been a Cabinet Minister, and Member of Parliament of the Liberal Democrat Party for the Eastleigh constituency in Hampshire from 2005 until February 2012. He served his eight-month prison sentence at HMP Leyhill. Both Huhne and Pryce were convicted of the same offence.

---

29 Source: PCC Code as at 18 July 2013.

The Press Complaints Commission issued decisions on complaints by Chris Huhne and Carina Trimingham against the *Daily Mail*, *Daily Mirror*, *Daily Telegraph*, the *Sun* and *Sunday Mirror* in July 2013 regarding their complaints about the publication of photographs showing Mr Huhne and Ms Trimingham in and around the grounds of an open prison where Mr Huhne was serving his sentence. Ms Trimingham had started working for Chris Huhne in 2007 during his (ultimately unsuccessful) bid to become leader of the Liberal Democrats. They were thought to have embarked on an affair around the end of 2007 despite the fact Ms Trimingham had only entered into a civil partnership with her lesbian lover Julie Bennett earlier that year.[30]

At the time the photographs were taken, Mr Huhne was serving his prison sentence at HMP Leyhill following his conviction for perverting the course of justice. Mr Huhne and Ms Trimingham claimed the photographs had breached Clause 3 (Privacy) of the PCC's of Practice. They argued that the publication of the images was not justified by any public interest and only served to embarrass them. The pictures had been taken from public locations around the open prison. Clause 3 − Privacy − sets out that 'it is unacceptable to photograph individuals in private places without their consent', defining private spaces as 'public or private property where there is a reasonable expectation of privacy'.

The newspapers said that at all times the complainants had been standing in places where they were visible to other prisoners or visitors to the prison; they did not accept that the complainants had a reasonable expectation of privacy. Several of the newspapers also advanced a public interest defence to justify publication of the photographs.

The Commission considered in detail the evidence submitted by the complainants regarding the circumstances in which the photographs had been taken but concluded that it 'could not agree that the locations in which the complainants had been photographed were private places' for the purposes of the Editors' Code. Furthermore, the Commission noted that 'Mr Huhne's trial, conviction and imprisonment − and the indirect but central role that his relationship with Ms Trimingham had played in the crime's coming to light − had been the subject of wide publicity'. In the view of the Commission, 'neither the photographs nor the articles revealed any additional information about the complainants or their relationship which was intrinsically private'.[31] Charlotte Dewar, Director of Complaints and Pre-publication Services of the PCC, said:

> Deciding whether an individual has a reasonable expectation of privacy in a particular place can be difficult. The Commission carefully considered the circumstances in which these photographs [of Mr Huhne and Ms Trimingham] were taken − including the background to the story − and concluded that, in this instance, the area in and around the grounds of HMP Leyhill where the photographs were taken was not private.[32]

The PCC Code was regarded as the cornerstone of (print) press self-regulation, to which the industry and its editors had made a binding commitment. It was then the responsibility of editors and publishers to apply the Code to editorial material in both printed and online versions of

---

30 Source: 'Carina Trimingham: former journalist who fell for Huhne', by Martin Evans, *Daily Telegraph*, 7 March 2013.
31 Source: **Mr Chris Huhne and Ms Carina Trimingham v The Sun**, PCC adjudication 18 July 2013. See also: PCC Press Statement, 'PCC rejects privacy complaints from Chris Huhne and Carina Trimingham about five national newspapers', official press statement by the Press Complaints Commission, 18 July 2013.
32 Ibid.

See below 10.4.3

publications. Until 2013, Paul Dacre, Editor of the *Daily Mail* and Editor in Chief of Associated Newspapers, was Code Committee Chairman.

Following the Leveson Inquiry and Lord Hunt's recommendations,[33] the PCC moved into a transitional phase from March 2012, awaiting possible legislation in the form of a Royal Charter to set up a new press regulatory body.

Lord Hunt, who became Chairman of the PCC after predecessor Baroness Peta Buscombe left the post in 2011 amid mounting claims of phone-hacking by the *News of the World*, claimed he would replace the PCC with a 'robust, independent regulator with teeth'. Speaking to BBC Radio 4's *Today* programme, former Conservative Cabinet Minister Lord Hunt said Lord Justice Leveson had urged him to 'press on' with reforming the regulator. Lord Hunt said further that:

> British people deserve a press that takes its responsibilities seriously and exercises profes-
> sional standards by recognizing that the precious freedom it enjoys is a privilege, not a God-
> given right . . . I decided early on that the problem really was that the PCC was being criticized
> for not exercising powers it never had in the first place, so I recommended we start again with
> a new body with a press regulator with teeth.[34]

The PCC said of itself (on its website) that it offered a service which was both 'quick and free' and that 'it costs nothing to complain to the PCC – you do not need a solicitor or anyone else to repre-sent you', thanks to the commitment of the newspaper industry, which self-regulates through tough and effective sanctions without being a burden on the taxpayer. It was true that most disputes were resolved amicably and quickly by the PCC, averaging about 35 working days to do so.

In its last Annual Report of 2012, the PCC stated that it received over 7,300 complaints in writing during 2011, but a large number of these could not be taken forward, generally because they fell outside the PCC's remit (for example, complaints about adverts) or because the complainant did not respond to the Commission when requested to supply further information about their concerns. The PCC issued rulings, or brokered amicable resolutions, in respect of just over 1,700 cases. There were 719 complaints which the PCC judged to have merit under the terms of the Code, i.e. they raised a likely breach of the Editors' Code. Of these, 600 cases related to privacy. In 20 cases where a suitable remedy had not been offered or was not appropriate, the PCC found an outstanding breach of the Code and upheld complaints.[35]

Issues raised by complainants to the PCC (2011)

- 90.7% – accuracy and opportunity to reply (Clauses 1 & 2)
- 29.2% – privacy issues (Clauses 3–9 & 11)
- 1.6% – subterfuge (Clause 10)
- 1.1% – discrimination (Clause 12)
- 0.8% – others (Clauses 13–16)

The PCC would frequently assist those persons who found themselves at the centre of a media story, usually through no fault of their own, particularly when the individual was particularly vulnerable, for instance as the result of a bereavement. The PCC would then distribute a 'cease

---

33 Source: Lord Hunt, Chair of the PCC, speaking in a debate in the House of Lords on the Leveson Report, 11 January 2013.
34 Sources: 'Lord Hunt defends decision to scrap PCC', by Ben Glaze, *Independent*, 9 March 2012.
35 Source: PCC Annual Report and Statistics, June 2012 at: www.pcc.org.uk/assets/80/PCC_Complaints_Statistics_for_2011.pdf.

and desist' request to newspaper editors, reporters and photographers, to help to ensure that the complainant would receive privacy wherever possible. The outcome of these requests would invariably result in a reduction in physical media intrusion. The table below shows the PCC complaints statistics for June 2013.

PCC complaints summary – June 2013[36]

Adjudicated upheld	0
Adjudicated not upheld	0
Remedial action	1
Resolved	28
Sufficient remedial action	6
Sufficient response	0
No breach	88
Third party	125
Not pursued	190
Delay	0
Outside remit	35
Matter of taste	10
No finding	0
TOTAL:	**483**

10.3.2 Examples of PCC adjudications

Each year, clauses 3 ('privacy') and 15 ('accuracy') were the most challenged parts of the Code, with the PCC taking complaints lodged by members of the Royal Family particularly seriously. That meant, for example, no interviewing or photographing and no long-lens photos or harassment at the time when young princes William and Harry were under the age of 18.

In 2008, Professor Sir Roy Meadow complained that a comment piece in The Times, headlined 'A moving response to our family justice campaign', was inaccurate and misleading.[37] His complaint centred on Clause 1 ('Accuracy').[38] The journalist's point was that the complainant's submission of statistics-based evidence in the **Sally Clark**[39] case, when he was not a statistician, was an example of his going beyond his remit, and that other women had won their appeals against similar 'cot death' murder convictions, based also on the misleading statistical evidence of Sir Roy on 'Sudden Infant Death Syndrome' – simply, that he had misled the jury in the **Sally Clark** case. As a means of resolving the complaint by Sir Roy, The Times invited the Professor to submit a letter for publication outlining his concerns, but the complainant rejected the offer. The PCC did not uphold Professor Meadow's

---

36 Source: PCC Complaints Summary for the month of June 2013 at: http://www.pcc.org.uk/assets/471/Complaints_Summary_June_2013.pdf.
37 Source: 'A moving response to our family justice campaign', by Camilla Cavendish, The Times, 17 July 2008.
38 **Professor Sir Roy Meadow v The Times**. PCC adjudication of 17. 7. 2008.
39 Solicitor Mrs Sally Clark was convicted in 1999 of killing her 11-week-old son Christopher in December 1996 and 8-week-old Harry in January 1998 (the 'cot death' case). Her first appeal against the convictions failed in 2000, but the second succeeded and she was acquitted in 2003, when three Appeal Court judges ruled that Mrs Clark's conviction was 'unsafe', based on Professor Sir Roy Meadow's evidence during her trial. Expert witness Professor Meadow (for the prosecution) told the jury that the probability of two natural unexplained cot deaths in a family was 73 million to one. At appeal, the Royal Statistical Society and other medical experts disputed that figure, stating that the odds of a second cot death in a family were around 200 to one. The GMC found Sir Roy guilty of serious professional misconduct in July 2005; he was struck off the medical register. Sally Clark died on 16 March 2007, aged 42.

complaint, stating that *The Times* piece was an opinion piece and that the columnist's interpretation of the 'cot death' cases was accurately based on the appeal judgments, including those in other cases.[40] Above all, they held that the piece had been in the public interest.

Following the untimely death of 33-year-old singer Stephen Gately of pop band Boyzone on 10 October 2009 in Mallorca, the PCC received more than 23,000 complaints from the public about an opinion piece written by the *Daily Mail* columnist Jan Moir on 13 October. The article was published the day before Gately's funeral in Dublin with the original headline on the *Mail's* website: 'Why there was nothing "natural" about Stephen Gately's death'. This was later amended in the printed edition and online to: 'A strange, lonely and troubling death'. Moir told her readers that Gately's death after a drunken night out in Mallorca 'strikes another blow to the happy-ever-after myth of civil partnerships'.

The public outcry about Moir's article was fuelled by widespread discussions on social networking sites like Twitter, and resulted in the highest number of complaints the PCC had ever received about a single article. Justifying its public interest responsibility, the Commission got in touch with Gately's family. The Commission also asked the *Daily Mail* editor, Paul Dacre – a member of the PCC's editorial board – to supply a response. In a new *Daily Mail* piece on 23 October 2009, Jan Moir expressed regret over her original column, though she stood by her earlier assertion that the circumstances surrounding the pop star's sudden death were 'more than a little sleazy' and that there was 'nothing natural' about Gately's death. The PCC's decision not to uphold the public complaint against the *Daily Mail* over its publication of Jan Moir's article caused great controversy. The adjudication made the point that one of the primary functions of a self-regulatory system was to defend freedom of speech. The PCC endorsed the newspaper's view that it must allow its journalists freedom of speech, which includes offensive views by its columnists. The PCC's director at the time, Stephen Abell, said the article contained flaws, but the Commission had decided 'it would not be proportionate to rule against the columnist's right to offer freely expressed views about something that was the focus of public attention'.[41]

The PCC remained under constant criticism for performing inadequately amid claims that the search for an alternative system had become urgent. The Jan Moir decision may not have weighed in the press regulator's favour.

In **Vernon Kay v Reveal Magazine**, the PCC ruled in March 2013 that *Reveal* had breached Clause 1 (Accuracy) of the Code, following the publication of an article on 3 July 2012, headlined 'Vernon's still walking on eggshells', about the television presenter Vernon Kay. Mr Kay had complained to the regulator that the article had reported inaccurate claims about his marriage to TV show host Tess Daley. The magazine quoted an unnamed source (a 'close friend') who alleged that Mr Kay felt he was 'walking on eggshells' following his public admission in 2010 that he had sent flirtatious text messages to several women. He said that the claims contained in the article had not been put to him for comment before publication. The magazine stood by the claims.

See below
10.5

The Commission ruled that despite the provision in Clause 14 ('confidential sources') of the Code, publications cannot simply rely on referring to confidential sources as a defence against complaints about the accuracy of material. Publications should generally be able to produce on-the-record material to corroborate significant claims, or demonstrate that the individual concerned had a suitable opportunity to respond before publication. In this case, the magazine apparently accepted that it had not taken these steps, but sought to defend the piece to the PCC on the basis that the claims were not new.

---

40 Angela Cannings served 18 months after being wrongly convicted of killing her two sons. Donna Anthony served 6 years after being wrongly convicted of killing her son and daughter. Trupti Patel was cleared of killing three of her children.
41 Source: Press release by the PCC on 17 February 2010.

The Commission disagreed with the magazine's argument, saying that 'the article had contained specific, and significant, assertions about the current state of the couple's relationship, two years after the texting incidents'. The magazine had not demonstrated that it had taken care over the accuracy of the story, and the Commission therefore found a breach of Clause 1(i) of the Editors' Code.[42]

In *Rosemary MacLeod v The Scottish Sun*, the PCC upheld a complaint against the Scottish daily tabloid in April 2013, after it decided to publish photographs of grieving family members at the funeral of Sir Chris Hoy's uncle, despite mourners having made clear that the photographer's presence was unwelcome. The complaint to the PCC was made on behalf of the Hoy family by Rosemary MacLeod, who said that publication of a photograph showing the deceased's widow being comforted after the service was grossly intrusive in breach of Clause 5 ('intrusion into grief or shock') of the Code. The newspaper apologized for the distress caused to the Hoy family, but said that the attendance of Olympic cyclist, Sir Chris, at the funeral had made it newsworthy and in the public interest.

The Commission ruled that the photographer's presence at the funeral was a clear breach of Clause 5, stating the presence of a well-known individual at the funeral 'did not in any way lessen the newspaper's obligation under Clause 5', and ruled that the newspaper ought to have recognized that the family's wishes should be respected at such a difficult time. Charlotte Dewar, Head of Complaints and Pre-publication Services, said:

> . . . one of the aims of the Code is to ensure that at times of great distress, family members are protected from unnecessary concern about press intrusion. While some families welcome coverage of funerals, for many others, such services are extremely private events, as was the case here. The Commission's ruling reminds editors of the need to take account of this as part of their general obligation under Clause 5 to handle the publication of such stories with sensitivity.[43]

In the adjudication, *A Man v The Daily Mail* (2012), the journalistic activity under complaint related to a potential story involving a doctor, who was allegedly offering to donate sperm by having unprotected sex with women rather than using artificial insemination. The man complained to the PCC that the freelance reporter for the *Daily Mail* had obtained material that intruded into his private life in a manner that breached Clauses 1 (Accuracy), 3 (Privacy), 4 (Harassment) and 10 (Clandestine devices and subterfuge) of the Editors' Code of Practice. The complaint was not upheld.

The newspaper said that the journalist was not employed by the *Daily Mail*, and it had not commissioned the article from her. It emerged that the journalist had obtained the information from the complainant's personal computer and that she had contacted the women concerned. The reporter had also sent one email about the complainant to the owner of a sperm donation website trying to gather information about the doctor-donor.

The newspaper considered that there was a strong public interest in the allegations that the complainant doctor had abused his position by encouraging recipients to be 'naturally inseminated'

---

42 Source: *Vernon Kay v Reveal Magazine*, PCC adjudication of 28 March 2013.
43 Source: 'PCC Adjudication' published in the *Scottish Sun* on 30 April 2013 at: www.thescottishsun.co.uk/scotsol/homepage/news/4898669/PCC-ADJUDICATION.html.

with his sperm. Claims that he had fathered large numbers of children raised additional public interest issues. The newspaper had sought the complainant's side of the story, but he had refused to comment. Though the newspaper had no immediate intention to publish the story, in view of the public interest, it was not willing to offer an assurance requested by the complainant that it would not in any future articles identify him as a sperm donor or publish the identity of a donor recipient or child in a context that might lead to his identification. The complainant maintained that there was no public interest in the matter – the information was inherently private.

This case was an example of the difficulties that can sometimes arise when a freelance journalist publishes a story for a newspaper (or online). The question arose of where the editor's responsibility lay in relation to the conduct of his own staff. The PCC held that the newspaper was not responsible for the preceding behaviour (prior to publication) by the freelance journalist in circumstances where it had apparently been unaware of the activity, had not commissioned the activity, and had not published any story that had originated from the activity. This material was contact information for women connected to the complainant's sperm donor activity. The source of this information was a woman who had been a donor recipient and had had access to his computer.

While the newspaper had made relevant inquiries over the course of four days, following receipt of the information, the Commission noted that it had not made use of the contact details once it was made aware – in the course of its journalistic enquiries – of the manner in which they had been acquired. Nothing had then been published on the story.

Clause 10 of the PCC Code ('Clandestine devices and subterfuge') states that 'the press must not seek to obtain or publish material acquired by . . . accessing digitally-held private information without consent'. The Commission accepted that the names and contact details of a list of women connected to the complainant had been acquired from the doctor's computer. This information had been obtained by the freelance journalist's source and subsequently provided to the newspaper by that journalist. Once the manner in which the information had been obtained came to light, the newspaper had not made further use of it and had undertaken not to publish it. The Commission therefore found that there was no breach of the Code.

In terms of Clause 1 (Accuracy), the Commission found that the newspaper had taken care not to publish inaccurate or misleading information. Through the newspaper's attempts to contact the complainant for comment, questions had been raised as to the means by which certain information had been obtained. It was clear that the newspaper had made a number of attempts to contact the complainant: by telephone and email, and in person. However, the Commission did not consider that this amounted to unduly persistent questioning, given the nature of the allegations. When the complainant did not respond to enquiries, the contact ceased. In the circumstances, which included the legitimate aim of seeking to ascertain the complainant's position, the Commission did not consider that there had been harassment in breach of Clause 4 (Harassment).[44]

10.3.3 A 'toothless poodle':[45] continued criticism of the PCC

The PCC continued to face criticism for being 'toothless'. How effective was the press regulator really in dealing with serious media intrusion into people's private lives? There was relentless press coverage with extensive media intrusion into the lives of Gerry and Kate McCann following the disappearance of their daughter Madeleine while on holiday in Portugal in May 2007. There was harassment and defamation of a prime suspect, Robert Murat. Neither the McCanns nor Mr Murat were helped by the PCC, so they sought 'proper' legal redress via the High Court in the tort of

---

44 Source: *A Man v The Daily Mail*, adjudication of 15 May 2012.
45 Source: quoted from a speech in Parliament by the Labour opposition leader Ed Miliband on 7 July 2011, saying that the press self-regulatory watchdog should be replaced. Reported in the *Guardian* and *The Scotsman*, 7 July 2011.

defamation, with the result that four national newspaper groups had to apologize to Robert Murat in July 2008 for publishing false allegations about him over claims that he was involved in the abduction of Madeleine McCann. Murat received £600,000 in libel damages from News International, Mirror Group Newspapers, Express Newspapers and Associated Newspapers.[46] The Express Newspapers' titles, including the *Daily Express, Daily Star* and *Sunday Express*, were made to apologize to Kate and Gerry McCann for wrongly suggesting that the couple were responsible for Madeleine's death, by printing front-page apologies and paying a settlement of £550,000 damages.[47]

See below 10.4

When the House of Commons Department for Culture, Media and Sport launched another inquiry into the possible discontinuation of press self-regulation in 2007, its report concluded that the PCC should continue, since there were now sufficient safeguards in statutory and common law to support private individuals if they could not be granted satisfactory redress by the regulator. Citing the words by Sedley LJ in **Douglas v Hello! Ltd**,[48] chairman Mr John Whittingdale MP (Conservative, Maldon and East Chelmsford) said that there was now a 'qualified right to privacy' in English law where individuals could seek redress against the media by way of the Human Rights Act 1998.[49]

See Chapter 2.2.5

The PCC did not help the families of young suicide victims in Bridgend, Wales in 2008, in spite of numerous complaints to the regulator. The story made global news, including a feature in US magazine *Vanity Fair* which reported on a 'suicide epidemic' in a small Welsh town.[50]

The subsequent PCC report into the reporting of suicides revealed a complex web of public anxieties in Bridgend. The PCC concluded that it was a 'cumulative jigsaw effect of collective media activity, which became a problem only when the individual pieces were put together', and found that no clause of the PCC Code had been breached.[51]

Leading media lawyer Geoffrey Robertson QC had frequently attacked the existence of the PCC, saying that 'the most satisfactory reform of the PCC would be its abolition', and questioning whether its 'lay' members really are 'lay' and truly represent ordinary members of society. In a *Guardian* blog debating the continued existence of the press regulator, Mr Robertson wrote in November 2009:

> . . . the PCC tries to function as a poor person's libel court, but why should the vilified poor have to resort to an amateur set of adjudicators who can award them no compensation or damages – not even their bus fare home – and cannot direct newspapers to publish any correction prominently? The PCC's worst feature has been its propagandistic claim that it has raised standards of journalism – which it has not, other than perhaps the reporting of the Royal Family, over whom it is obsessively protective. It goes to extravagant lengths to deter people from asserting their legal rights.[52]

Mr Robertson also attacked the PCC for not stamping out bad journalistic behaviour and suggested that the self-regulator was standing in the way of suitable privacy legislation. He urged editors to follow the example set by *Private Eye* editor Ian Hislop, who had never joined the PCC and consistently refused to do so.[53]

46 Source: 'Madeleine McCann: Newspapers pay out £600,000 to Robert Murat', by Oliver Luft and John Pluckett, *Guardian*, 17 July 2008.
47 Source: 'Papers paying damages to McCanns', *BBC News Online*, 19 March 2008.
48 [2001] 2WLR 992.
49 Source: House of Commons – Department of Culture, Media and Sport (2007).
50 Source: 'The Mystery Suicides of Bridgend County', by Alex Shoumatoff, *Vanity Fair*, 27 February 2009.
51 Source: Press release by the PCC on the 'reporting on suicides' of 9 March 2009.
52 Source: 'What should be done with the PCC?', by Geoffrey Robertson QC, *Guardian*, 23 November 2009.
53 Source: Geoffrey Robertson's speech at the joint event of English PEN and Index on Censorship at the Free Word Centre, London, 10 November 2009; see: www.englishpen.org/aboutenglishpen/campaigns/reformingthelibellaws/penindexlibelreportlaunch.

Another report by the House of Commons Culture, Media and Sport Committee on 'Press Standards, Privacy and Libel' in 2010 said:

> We conclude, therefore, that for now matters relating to privacy should continue to be determined according to common law, and the flexibility that permits, rather than set down in statute.[54]

This meant that no changes were made to the possible statutory footing of the PCC. The editorial committee of the PCC ruled out making pre-notification mandatory, as this was not 'in the public interest'.[55]

See Chapter 3

During a February 2010 debate in the House of Commons on 'Press Standards, Privacy and Libel', the PCC was again criticized for being ineffective and being 'toothless' on the issue of use of phone-tapping and clandestine recording devices, particularly by the *News of the World*.[56] At the same time, Justice Secretary Jack Straw and Lord Lester proposed that the libel laws and press regulation ought to be reformed by way of the Defamation Bill and also in the light of the **Max Mosley** case at that time before the Strasbourg human rights court (see: **Mosley v UK** (2011)[57]).

One question remained: how could the PCC realistically punish its journalistic miscreants when it had no real power to sanction an editor or photographer who continued to contravene its Code? All the PCC could do was to demand that an offending publication printed an apology, published a relatively small summary of the outcome of its adjudications or present editors with 'cease and desist' notifications which were repeatedly not followed – though *Daily Mail* editor Paul Dacre strongly denied that editors took no notice of the PCC.

See below
10.4.2

In March 2012, the PCC, under the auspices of Lord Hunt, unanimously agreed to move into a transitional phase, transferring its assets, liabilities and staff to a new regulatory body once Leveson had reported and the Government had made up its mind as to whether statutory legislation would be put in place to regulate the British press.[58]

10.3.4 Self-regulation or legislation: comparison with other countries

One could argue that the PCC was the cornerstone of British press self-regulation, to which the print press had made a binding commitment in that all editors, photographers and publishers who subscribed to the PCC and therefore the Code of Practice had to ensure that it was observed by all editorial staff and external contributors. In its report 'Self-Regulation of the Press' (2007) the House of Commons Culture, Media and Sport Select Committee found that the PCC had become 'a more open body' providing 'a better service to complainants'.[59]

Others, like Alan Rusbridger, editor of the *Guardian*, and Ian Hislop, editor of *Private Eye*, said that the PCC was 'toothless', lacking in powers to impose any penalties or legislative sanctions, and that the PCC's Code had been pure window dressing.[60]

For the purpose of comparison, it is worth looking at a press regulator established by legislation, namely the Press Council of Ireland. Ireland's press-council-plus-ombudsman system now has most of the 'Fleet Street' papers (which sell copies in Ireland) as voluntary members. Even Richard Desmond, owner of Express Newspapers and founder of Northern & Shell, signed up to the Irish Press Council. Desmond left the PCC following the Madeleine McCann story.

---

54 Source: House of Commons (2010a) Culture, Media and Sport Committee. *Second Report on Press Standards, Privacy and Libel* at p. 67 of 24 February 2010: www.publications.Parliament.uk/pa/cm200910/cmselect/cmcumeds/362/36202.htm.
55 For further discussion see: Bingham (1996).
56 Source: House of Commons (2010a), at page 58.
57 (Application no. 48009/08) Judgement by the Strasbourg European Court of Human Rights of 10 May 2011 (ECTHR).
58 See PCC press release, PCC transition to a new regulatory body, 9 March 2012 at: www.pcc.org.uk/news/index.html?article–zcyNA
59 Source: House of Commons – Department of Culture, Media and Sport (2007).
60 For further discussion see: Carney (2008).

Mr Desmond, owner of the *Daily Express* and *Daily Star*, gave evidence to the Leveson Inquiry on 12 January 2012, where he launched a scathing attack on the Press Complaints Commission, describing it as a 'useless organization . . . and it was run by the people that hated our guts, that wanted us out of business'.[61]

In March 2008, Madeleine McCann's parents won a libel settlement and apology from Express Newspapers for suggesting they were responsible for their three-year-old daughter's death in May 2007. The newspaper group paid £550,000 to the 'Find Madeleine' campaign, and the *Daily Express* and *Daily Star* both carried front-page apologies under the headline: 'Kate and Gerry McCann: Sorry'.

The Irish Press Council and Ombudsman have an additional statutory underpinning in the Irish 2009 Defamation Act,[62] which means, *inter alia*, that press members qualify for lower libel damages. The Irish Republic established the statutory press regulator in 2003 – though it did not come into full force until 1 January 2008.[63] The Council's first Chairman was Professor Thomas Mitchell, former Provost of Trinity College Dublin. The Press Council is accountable to the Dáil, which means there is parliamentary scrutiny of its performance, and 'sits' within the Ministry of Justice for Ireland. Consequently, when the *Irish Daily Star* published topless pictures of the Duchess of Cambridge, the Ministry of Justice ordered an immediate review of Irish privacy laws, threatening to introduce a draconian privacy bill. On 15 September 2012, the *Irish Daily Star* broke ranks with its British rivals to publish topless pictures of the wife of Prince William, angering its British co-owners and risking legal action from the Royal Family. The tabloid published a two-page spread of 10 photographs of the Duchess of Cambridge from *Closer* magazine, sunbathing in bikini bottoms on the balcony of a chateau in France, under the headline 'Angry Kate to sue mag over snaps'. A teaser headline on the front page promised 'the magazine shots everyone wants to see'. Two days later, after investigation by the Irish Press Ombudsman, the publisher of the *Daily Star on Sunday* offered its 'deepest apologies' for publishing the topless pictures. On 24 November that year, editor Michael O'Kane resigned.

See Chapter 3.6.3

The Irish Press Council and the Office of the Press Ombudsman are joint independent regulatory statutory bodies. The Press Ombudsman (at the time of publication) is Professor John Horgan, who can be regarded as the public face of Irish press regulation. Complaints about possible breaches of the Code of Practice are made to the Press Ombudsman. The Ombudsman's Office will, in the first instance, attempt to resolve the matter by making direct contact with the publication concerned. Though it is arguably an independent office, Professor Horgan is still a journalist, and Emeritus Professor of Journalism at Dublin City University.[64]

This means the office of the Irish Press Ombudsman is not completely 'independent', as Lord Leveson would like to prescribe. Furthermore, the Irish Press Council is not in itself particularly independent by the recommended Leveson standards, since six of its nominated members represent the press in various ways (seven are not from the press). The Office of the Press Ombudsman receives complaints from members of the public, investigates and seeks a resolution wherever possible. Where dispute resolution and (re)conciliation are not possible, the Ombudsman will make a decision based on the 'Code of Practice for Newspapers and Periodicals' ('the Code').[65]

The Code sets out the professional and ethical standards expected of the Irish print press and its online editions. The fundamental principle enshrined in the Code is 'freedom to publish', based on Article 10 ECHR, which includes news and comment 'without fear or favour' – as long as the

---

61 Source: 'Desmond attacks "useless" press body', *BBC News Online*, 12 January 2012 at: www.bbc.co.uk/news/uk-16525968
62 See: clause 44 of the Defamation Act 2009; also: Schedule 2 of the Irish Defamation Act 2009 'Minimum Requirements in Relation to Press Council'.
63 For further discussion see: McGonagle and Barrett (2007).
64 See: Preliminary statement for Leveson Inquiry by Professor John Horgan, Press Ombudsman, Ireland, 13 July 2012. MOD400001549 at: www.levesoninquiry.org.uk/wp-content/uploads/2012/07/Submission-by-Professor-John-Horgan-Irish-Press-Ombudsman.pdf.
65 For a copy of the Irish Code of Practice see: www.pressombudsman.ie/code-of-practice.150.html.

article is in the public interest. The Code bears similarities to the PCC's (last) Code of Practice, but also took some aspects from the 'Statement of Principles' of the Australian Press Council, the 'Publishing Principles' of the German Press Council and the 'Ethics Code' of the US-based 'National Conference of Editorial Writers'.

Nagle (2009) comments that 'free expression' is not explicitly guaranteed in Irish law and when confronted with the tort of defamation, 'free speech has had to bow to the right to a good name.'[66] Coad (2005) argues that both the PCC and the Irish Press Council's concerted efforts of democratic independence and self-regulation bear significant shortcomings and 'alarming procedural opaqueness'.

The National Union of Journalists (NUJ) adopted Ireland's regulatory system as its preferred future model following the Leveson Report recommendations and the Westminster parliamentary recommendations for a Royal Charter on press regulation in 2013.

In New Zealand, the Law Commission issued a consultation paper in October 2011, seeking views on the extension of media regulation and the reform of civil wrongs.[67] The Minister[68] requested that the Commission's review should deal explicitly with the following matters:

- how to define 'news media' for the purposes of the law;
- whether and to what extent the jurisdiction of the New Zealand Broadcasting Standards Authority and/or the Press Council should be extended to cover currently unregulated news media and, if so, what legislative changes would be required to achieve this end; and
- whether the existing criminal and civil remedies for wrongs such as defamation, harassment, breach of confidence and privacy are effective in the new media environment and, if not, whether alternative remedies may be available.[69]

 FOR THOUGHT

Would you say that press self-regulation – as provided by the PCC until 2014 – offered sufficient protection against unwarranted invasions of privacy? Or would you agree with a statutory model like the Irish Press Council? Discuss.

10.4 The Leveson Inquiry

Lord Justice Leveson's inquiry was ordered by the UK Prime Minister in 2011 as a result of the emerging scandal of 'phone hacking' by the *News of the World* (*NoW*), which closed following the revelation that someone working for it had, in 2002, illegally accessed the mobile phone messages of a missing schoolgirl, Milly Dowler – who was later found murdered. This was the culmination of a series of claims and discoveries about the extent of phone-hacking of celebrities and others. The Right Honourable Lord Justice Leveson spent nearly 18 months gathering evidence from

---

66 See: Nagle (2009).
67 The consultant leading the project was Professor John Burrows, who has an extensive background in media law. He was assisted by senior researcher and policy adviser, and former editor, Cate Honore Brett.
68 Minister means the Minister of the Crown who acts under the authority of any warrant or with the authority of the New Zealand Prime Minister.
69 See: Law Commission of New Zealand, Review of Regulatory Gaps and the New Media' at: www.lawcom.govt.nz/project/review-regulatory-gaps-and-new-media. See also the Commission's Report on: 'The News Media Meets "New Media": Rights, Responsibilities and Regulation in the Digital Age' (NZLC R128, 2013).

editors, politicians and victims of press intrusion. The key decision for Lord Leveson was whether to try again with some beefed-up form of pure self-regulation – with the risk that nothing would really change – or argue for formal press regulation enshrined in legislation. That, as was made clear in a number of editorials and comment pieces in the run-up to the report's publication in November 2012, would be regarded by at least some sections of the UK media as tantamount to ending press freedoms that were in existence following the General Election in 2010.

The Leveson Inquiry, led by Lord Justice Leveson and set up by Prime Minister David Cameron in late August 2011 in response to the now well-known accusations of telephone hacking by journalists at NoW and subsequent, related revelations, made recommendations for a new, more effective policy and regulatory regime designed to encourage the highest ethical and professional standards, without stifling the independence or plurality of the media. The Leveson Report ('Leveson')[70] made recommendations on how future concerns about press behaviour, media policy, regulation and cross-media ownership should be dealt with and by which authorities; and, in particular, whether statutory intervention is either warranted or desirable.

10.4.1 The phone-hacking scandal

To understand the background and full impact of Leveson, we should look back to events which led up to the inquiry, namely the phone-hacking scandal and its scale which emerged during Lord Justice Leveson's Inquiry.

For many years, there had been complaints that certain parts of the tabloid press were riding roughshod over both individuals and the public at large, without any justifiable public interest. Attempts to take them to task – for example by the Press Complaints Commission – were not successful. The 'crunch' came in 2009 with the beginning of the major News of the World scandal. By that time Clive Goodman, the NoW's Royal Correspondent before 2007, and Private Investigator of 'Nine Consultancy', Glen Mulcaire, had already been dealt with as individual mavericks, but News International had been able to argue that abuses were not routine, systemic or institutionalized. Mulcaire, formerly a striker at AFC Wimbledon, had had a year's contract with NoW for 'research and information services' worth £104,988 and also received £12,300 in cash from the newspaper. But in reality he was providing the Sunday tabloid with the mobile phone details of celebrities and the Royals. He was eventually arrested in August 2006.[71]

There had been previous attempts to demonstrate the systemic nature of journalistic 'tabloid' abuse going back to the 1990s, though typically only a few individuals had been brought to account. Investigations had included the Metropolitan Police's Operation Nigeria (1999) and the Information Commissioner's Office (ICO)'s Operation Glade (2003), which were at least able to show that around 30 publications had purchased confidential information from government bodies.

Operation Nigeria was run by the Metropolitan Police's anti-corruption squad CIB3. The purpose of the enormous CIB3 bugging and surveillance was twofold: to pursue the unsolved murder of Daniel Morgan, a private detective killed in 1987, and to gather evidence about continued allegations that his detective agency, Southern Investigations, was involved with corrupt police officers and former detectives who supplied confidential information and did other favours. One of CIB3's principal targets was Jonathan Rees, Morgan's former partner, who continued to run Southern Investigations after the murder. With the backing of the Met's then Commissioner, Sir (now Lord) Paul Condon, warrants were obtained for the planting of listening devices in Southern's offices in Thornton Heath, south-west London. The police surveillance caught tabloid journalists on tape obtaining information from the private detective agency. The tabloids involved were the News of the

70 The Leveson Inquiry's terms of reference are accessible at: www.levesoninquiry.org.uk/about/terms-of-reference.
71 Source: 'Profile: Glenn Mulcaire', BBC News Online, 17 September, 2013.

World, *Daily Mirror* and *Sunday Mirror* doing business with private investigator Jonathan Rees. Twelve suspects were eventually arrested and 23 premises raided. Three men, Jonathan Rees, DC Austin Warnes and businessman Simon James, were each given long prison sentences at the Old Bailey. The tapes provided a rare picture of the covert black market in data run by private detectives and corrupt police.[72]

Operation Glade was a joint operation between the Metropolitan Police and the Information Commissioner's Office into allegations of possible corruption in the police service or civilians working in the service. Under scrutiny were the *NoW*'s alleged practices of hacking into people's mobile phones and text messages. The ICO raided the home of a Hampshire private investigator, Steve Whittamore, and seized paperwork recording 13,000 occasions on which he had been paid by newspapers and magazines to obtain confidential data from organizations including British Telecom, the DVLA and mobile phone companies. The ICO found that Whittamore had obtained information from the Police National Computer. Operation Glade discovered that Whittamore's ultimate source was a civilian worker at Wandsworth police station, South London, Paul Marshall, who was logging phoney 999 calls in order to justify accessing the computer records of public figures who were of interest to newspapers. Marshall was passing the information to a former police officer, Alan King, who then passed it to a private investigator, John Boyall, who supplied it to Whittamore. At the time nine victims were eligible for payouts by the Murdoch press: the former Glasgow MP George Galloway, the former director of the Football Association David Davies, the comic actor Steve Coogan, the former football executive Mick McGuire, the jockey Kieren Fallon, the consultant Mary-Ellen Field, the personal assistant Ben Jackson and the actor Leslie Ash.[73] When Whittamore, Boyall, King and Marshall appeared at Blackfriars Crown Court in April 2005, they pleaded guilty to trading information from the police computer. The judge, John Samuels QC, queried the fact that no one from any newspaper had been charged even though Fleet Street titles had clearly commissioned the activity.[74]

The Information Commissioner's Office had long suspected the existence of an organized trade in confidential personal information. The ICO's investigation and report 'What Price Privacy' (2006) provided a relatively early insight into the scale of this unlawful market, including Operation Glade (above) and the ICO's own Operation Motorman (2002) into data protection offences. In Motorman, the ICO had been invited to attend a search of premises in Surrey executed under warrant by the Devon and Cornwall Constabulary. The raid concerned the suspected misuse of data from the Police National Computer (PNC) by serving and former police officers. Recognizing the significance of documents listing vehicle registration numbers, the ICO investigating officer was able to link the apparently random numbers to vehicle checks carried out within the Driver and Vehicle Licensing Agency (DVLA) by two officials. Corruption was the stark conclusion in both the Motorman and Glade investigations.[75]

See also
Chapter 6.3.2

In retrospect some of those investigations along with the PCC investigations were not as rigorous as they probably could have been.

On 26 January 2007, the *News of the World* Royal Editor, Clive Goodman, was sentenced to four months in prison after pleading guilty to intercepting phone messages from Prince William's voice-mail. His co-conspirator, private investigator Glenn Mulcaire, also pleaded guilty to a further five counts of unlawful interception of communications under s 1 Regulation of Investigatory Powers Act 2000 (RIPA), which states:

---

72 Source: 'Journalists caught on tape in police bugging', by Graeme McLagan, *Guardian*, 21 September 2002.
73 See: Information Commissioner's Office (ICO) (2006a) *What Price Privacy? The unlawful trade in confidential personal information*, presented by the Information Commissioner to Parliament pursuant to s 52(2) of the Data Protection Act 1998, 10 May 2006.
74 Source: 'Phone hacking: Rebekah Brooks faces questioning. Investigation of illegal news-gathering at News of World turns to newspaper's former editor', by Nick Davies, Dan Sabbagh and Vikram Dodd, *Guardian*, 11 April 2011.
75 See: ICO (2006a) at paras 5.1–5.4.

... it shall be an offence for a person intentionally and without lawful authority to intercept, at any place in the United Kingdom, any communication in the course of its transmission by means of –

(a)   a public postal service; or

(b)   a public telecommunication system.

Those counts related to the Liberal Democrat MP Simon Hughes, supermodel Elle Macpherson, publicist Max Clifford, football agent Skylet Andrew and Gordon Taylor, Chief Executive of the Professional Footballers' Association.

Mulcaire was sentenced to six months' imprisonment. The clandestine recordings had come to light in the *NoW* 'Blackadder' column on 6 November 2005, revealing how Prince William had consulted doctors over a pulled knee tendon and had postponed a mountain rescue course. Hardly anyone from the Royal Household knew about this.

Prosecutor David Perry QC told the court that Goodman and Mulcaire had hacked into a total of 609 people's mobile phone voicemails and that the newspaper had paid Mulcaire more than £100,000 a year for his services. Goodman, in turn, had paid Mulcaire £12,300 in cash between 9 November 2005 and 7 August 2006, hiding Mulcaire's identity by using the code name 'Alexander' on his expenses claim.[76] Sentencing judge Mr Justice Gross described Goodman and Mulcaire's behaviour as 'low conduct, reprehensible in the extreme' and added that 'neither journalists nor private security consultants are above the law. This case was not about press freedom; it was about a grave, inexcusable invasion of privacy.'[77]

After the trial, the then *NoW* Editor, Andy Coulson, promised a substantial donation to the Prince's charities by way of an apology and later resigned. He was replaced by former *Sunday Mirror* editor Colin Myler (who had resigned from the Mirror Group in 2002 after an article in the *Sunday Mirror* caused the collapse of a trial against Leeds footballers Lee Bowyer and Jonathan Woodgate. The paper was fined £75,000 for contempt of court).[78]

See Chapter 4.6.2

The most controversial area of the PCC Code of Practice had been Clause 10 ('clandestine devices and subterfuge'), relating to journalistic practices of planting illegal recording devices and subterfuge – something Max Mosley fell foul of a little later when, in March 2008, the former Formula 1 boss complained of an article in the *NoW*, written by Neville Thurlbeck, under the heading 'F1 BOSS HAS SICK NAZI ORGY WITH 5 HOOKERS'. The tabloid newspaper claimed the scoop as an 'EXCLUSIVE', accompanied by the subheading 'Son of Hitler-loving fascist in sex shame'.[79] The delicate matter concerned an event which took place on 28 March 2008, described in the article as a 'party' and 'an orgy'.[80]

A report by the then Information Commissioner (IC) Richard Thomas, entitled 'What Price Privacy?', suggested that journalists were increasingly contravening s 55 of the Data Protection Act 1998 by obtaining information via illicit means, such as phone tapping or using private detectives in order to dig up stories at any price.[81]

See above 10.3.3

The IC's investigation, supported by the police, had uncovered evidence of a pervasive and widespread media industry devoted to the illegal buying and selling of information. The regulator's findings caused outrage in certain editorial circles since the Commission found 'no evidence' that it had been 'materially misled' by News International.[82]

See Chapter 6.3.2

---

76 Source: 'Clive Goodman sentenced to four months', by Chris Tryhorn, *Guardian*, 26 January 2007.

77 Source: 'Pair jailed over royal phone taps', *BBC News Online*, 26 January 2007.

78 Source: 'Media 100: Colin Myler', *Guardian*, 9 July 2007.

79 Source: *News of the World*, 30 March 2008.

80 See: **Mosley v NGN Ltd** [2008] EWHC 1777 at para 1.

81 See: Information Commissioner's Office (ICO) (2006a).

82 Source: PCC's Report on phone message tapping allegations of 9 November 2009, available at www.pcc.org.uk/news/index. html?article–jAyOA==.

Rumours and jokes about the extent to which phone-hacking was prevalent throughout the newspaper industry were rife, but the press regulator, the PCC, did nothing to investigate it or to expose the unethical conduct tolerated at News International (publishers of NoW). Complex civil proceedings were undertaken by those whose identity as victims of phone-hacking had been exposed by the prosecution of Goodman and Mulcaire.

On 9 July 2009, an article was published in the Guardian which alleged a cover-up at NoW. Investigative journalist Nick Davies had started to uncover the truth about phone-hacking and some incredible settlements that some of the (celebrity) victims had negotiated with Rupert Murdoch's News Group Newspapers (NGN). The Guardian learnt that NGN paid out more than £1m to settle legal cases out of court that threatened to reveal evidence of NoW journalists' repeated involvement in the use of criminal methods to get stories. The payments secured secrecy (some would call it 'hush money') in at least three cases in 2009 that threatened to expose evidence of Murdoch journalists using private investigators who illegally hacked into the mobile phone messages of numerous public figures as well as gaining unlawful access to confidential personal data, including tax records, social security files, bank statements and itemized phone bills. Cabinet ministers, MPs, actors, royalty and sports stars were all targets of the private investigators.[83]

Following the 'Clive Goodman' scandal, and relentlessly pressurized by the Guardian, the PCC launched its own inquiry into journalistic practices and possible breaches of Clause 10 of its Code ('clandestine practices and subterfuge'). The PCC had revised Clause 10 in 2007, accompanied by a number of recommendations to editors and publishers to ensure that phone message-tapping and other clandestine practices were strictly against the spirit of the Code and contravened human rights legislation (see: **Malone v UK** (1984)[84]).

But the problem did not go away. The Guardian continued its campaign to stamp out dirty journalistic practices. The paper reported on 9 July 2009 that phone-tapping and subterfuge was still going on at NoW, in spite of the PCC changing its Clause 10 and increased legislation in the form of data protection and the Regulation of Investigatory Powers Act 2000 (RIPA).[85] Following the Guardian allegations, the PCC launched another inquiry into phone-tapping and subterfuge. The Commission examined two issues: first, whether it had been misled by News International (publishers of NoW) in 2007 in relation to the 'Clive Goodman' phone-hacking scandal; and second, whether NoW still employed and indeed condoned clandestine practices in 2009.

In its second investigation in 2009 into phone-hacking allegations at NoW, the PCC condemned the Guardian for publishing the results of the Commission's investigation into phone-hacking at NoW. Guardian Editor Alan Rusbridger accused the PCC of not interviewing a single witness in the 'Goodman' case, nor had the PCC inspected any further documents other than those already supplied and inspected by the police in their 2005–06 investigation. Speaking on BBC Radio 4's Today programme, Rusbridger also said that questioning Colin Myler was rather pointless, since he had only been recently appointed as NoW editor.[86]

A special TV documentary, Dispatches, on Channel 4 in October 2010 examined the allegations that, during Andy Coulson's time as NoW editor, phone-hacking had been routine practice at the tabloid, allegedly carried out with his knowledge. Responding to the Guardian's and Dispatches' revelations, Andy Coulson issued a statement insisting he was unaware of any of the illegal activities that took place at the paper while he was editor: 'I took full responsibility at the time for what happened

---

83 Source: 'Murdoch papers paid £1m to gag phone-hacking victims', by Nick Davies, Guardian, 8 July 2009.
84 (1984) 7 EHRR 14; see also: **Malone v Metropolitan Police Commissioner** [1979] 1 Ch 344.
85 Source: 'Timeline: News of the World phone-hacking scandal', Guardian, 9 November 2009.
86 Source: Alan Rusbridger, comment on BBC Radio 4's Today programme, 9 November 2009.

on my watch but without my knowledge.'[87] Demands increased that Andy Coulson ought to resign his post as the Prime Minister's public relations adviser, which he did in January 2011.

In a complex court action in 2012 – known as **Re Phillips**[88] – the Court of Appeal upheld orders from the High Court requiring the notorious private investigator for *NoW*, Glenn Mulcaire, to provide information regarding his phone-hacking activities. As part of the 50 actions at that time by phone-hacking victims against Rupert Murdoch's 'News Corp', Nicola Phillips (former PA to PR guru Max Clifford) and actor-comedian Steve Coogan sought disclosure of information from Glenn Mulcaire about his intercepting their voicemails at the time. This, Phillips and Coogan argued, would help their claims against 'News Corp' for compensation. Mulcaire, who was jailed in 2007 for charges in relation to hacking of phones of members of the Royal Household, argued that disclosure could leave him open to further prosecution.

In **Re Phillips**, Glenn Mulcaire (defendant 2 – D2) argued at the High Court action that he should be able to rely on his common law right to privilege from self-incrimination (PSI) in order to negate the obligation to provide information requested from him by the claimants, Phillips and Coogan. Ms Phillips and Mr Coogan had applied for an order that D2 provide a sworn affidavit identifying: (a) the individuals who had instructed him directly or indirectly to intercept Phillips's voice messages and the voice messages of others working for Max Clifford; (b) the nature of the interception he was instructed to carry out; and (c) similar facts about the interception of voice messages of another employee of Mr Clifford.

D2 (Mulcaire) objected on the ground that such disclosure may well incriminate him, and he worried that further criminal charges would be brought against him under s 1(1) Regulation of Investigatory Powers Act ('intercepting phone messages'). Ms Phillips contended that, *inter alia*, s 72 Senior Courts Act 1981 applied to this action, which provides that PSI *cannot* be relied on. The issues at the Court of Appeal were:

1. To what extent does s 72 Senior Courts Act 1981 (SCA) apply to claims for breach of confidence?
2. What is an 'apprehended infringement' within s 72(2) SCA?
3. What is a 'relevant offence' within s 72(5) SCA?
4. Is s 72 SCA compatible with Article 6 ECHR?

Mann J held that while D2 (Mulcaire) was prima facie able to rely on PSI, s 72 SCA applied, and so he was prevented from relying on PSI. In the joint action, Vos J handed down the judgment in **Coogan**, also holding that s 72 was applicable, thereby depriving D2 of a defence of PSI. Steve Coogan had made similar information requests to D2.

The result was that, on 18 July 2012, former *NoW* private investigator Glenn Mulcaire was ordered by the High Court to hand over the information in relation to the hacking of the phone of Nicola Phillips, then PA to PR guru Max Clifford, and similarly for Steve Coogan. Lawyers acting for 50 further phone-hacking victims had argued at a previous case management conference hearing that this information was vital to their claims. Vos J agreed, citing Article 6 ECHR relating to the individuals' right to a fair trial.

In November 2011, the BBC *Newsnight* team obtained a dossier from an ex-policeman, Derek Webb, who had been hired by *NoW*. It emerged that over a period of eight years Webb had been paid to follow more than one hundred targets, including Prince William, Prince Harry's ex-girlfriend

---

87 Source: 'Tabloids, Tories and Telephone Hacking', *Dispatches*, Channel 4, 5 October 2010. Political journalist Peter Oborne investigated the *News of the World*'s working relationship with the police, claiming undue influence together with claims of intimidation against politicians, exploring the broader links between News International and the Government.

88 See: **Phillips v News Group Newspapers Ltd (1) News Group Newspapers Ltd (2) Glenn Mulcaire; Coogan v (1) News Group Newspapers Ltd (2) Glenn Mulcaire** [2012] EWCA Civ 48 (also cited as '**Steve Coogan v News Group Newspapers Ltd and Glenn Mulcaire; Nicola Phillips v News Group Newspapers Ltd and Glenn Mulcaire**).

Chelsy Davy, former Attorney General Lord Goldsmith, football manager José Mourinho, football pundit Gary Lineker, the parents of Harry Potter actor Daniel Radcliffe, London Mayor Boris Johnson, Angelina Jolie, Simon Cowell, Sir Paul McCartney, former Liberal Democrat Leader Charles Kennedy, David Miliband, Elle Macpherson and Heather Mills.[89]

The Leveson Inquiry later established that phone-hacking became rife and known at NoW from about 2003 onwards. One of the witnesses at the inquiry giving evidence[90] about the NoW phone-hacking scandal was Rebekah Brooks (née Wade), formerly the youngest newspaper editor of a British national newspaper at NoW from 2000 to 2003, and the first female editor of the Sun from 2003 to 2009. Mrs Brooks was also Chief Executive Officer (CEO) at the Murdoch empire, News International, from 2009 to 2011. Brooks became a prominent figure in the News International phone-hacking scandal, being Editor in Chief at the most crucial time during the illegal phone-hacking at NoW, resulting in her resignation as CEO of News International on 15 July 2011, following widespread criticism of her role in the controversy.

From February to August 2013 over a hundred arrests had been made by the police as part of Scotland Yard's investigation into phone-hacking ('Operation Weeting'). At the same time the 'Yard' was working on 'Operation Elveden' (investigation into alleged corrupt payments to public official by journalists) and 'Operation Tuleta' (computer hacking).

By mid-2013, the Met had 185 officers and civilian staff working on the investigations: 96 on Weeting, 70 on Elveden and 19 on Tuleta. Among the public officials arrested as part of Elveden were a member of the armed forces, a prison official and police officers.

Further arrests were made, following similar announcements by the CPS and the review of 'Operation Elveden' evidence. Charges for conspiracy to commit misconduct in public office were laid against Duncan Larcombe, formerly Chief Royal Correspondent at the Sun, John Hardy, who served as a Colour Sergeant based at the Royal Military Training Academy in Sandhurst, and Claire Hardy, his wife. It was alleged that from 10 February to 15 October 2008, 34 payments were made to either John Hardy or Claire Hardy totalling over £23,000 for stories relating mainly to the Royal Family or matters at Sandhurst. A further charge was laid against Tracy Bell, a pharmacy assistant at Sandhurst Medical Centre (whilst acting as a public official), who allegedly received £1,250 between 17 October 2005 and 7 July 2006, relating to five articles published in the Sun regarding matters at Sandhurst. The charge read that she had misconducted herself to such a degree as to amount to an abuse of the public's trust in her public office, contrary to common law.[91]

The 'phone-hacking trial' began on 28 October 2013 at the Old Bailey in London. Former News International Chief Executive Rebekah Brooks,[92] her racehorse trainer husband Charlie, Prime Minister David Cameron's former Director of Communications Andy Coulson[93] and seven other defendants faced a number of charges linked to phone-hacking at the now-defunct News of the World. The trial was to last until at least Easter 2014. The other defendants were Stuart Kuttner, former Managing Editor of NoW, Ian Edmondson, former NoW Head of News, Cheryl Carter, Rebekah Brooks's former secretary, Mark Hanna, Head of Security for News International, and Clive Goodman, former NoW Royal Correspondent before 2007. All pleaded not guilty to the charges of conspiring to pervert the course of justice.

---

89 Source: 'NoW hired ex-policeman to track hundreds of people', BBC News Online, 8 November 2011.
90 Rebekah Brooks gave evidence to the Leveson Inquiry on Friday 11 May 2012 from 9.30 am to 1 pm. She discussed and defended, inter alia, the NoW's 'Sarah's law' campaign, her friendship with Prime Minister David Cameron and how she met him on at least three occasions over Christmas 2010 (Brooks denied that Cameron texted her 12 times a day); and her 'informal role' in lobbying for News Corp's BSkyB bid and how she had discussed the News Corp Sky bid with Cameron and Chancellor George Osborne.
91 Source: CPS Press Release 'Operation Elveden: Duncan Larcombe, John Hardy, Claire Hardy and Tracy Bell to be charged', on 24 April 2013.
92 Rebekah Brooks was also Editor of the Sun between 14 January 2003 and 1 September 2009.
93 Andy Coulson was the News of the World's Deputy Editor between 2000 and 2003 and Editor between 2003 and 2007.

At the start of the trial, the jury was told that three former *NoW* employees had pleaded guilty to phone-hacking charges at an earlier hearing. These were *NoW* former news editors Neville Thurlbeck, Greg Miskiw and James Weatherup. The court heard that the Private Investigator contracted by the newspaper to undertake the alleged hacking, Glenn Mulcaire, had also pleaded guilty. Prosecuting Counsel Andrew Edis QC reminded the jury that journalism was not on trial.

> There is no justification of any kind for journalists for getting involved in phone hacking. That is an intrusion into people's privacy which is against the law . . . The Prosecution says that journalists are no more entitled to break the law than anyone else.[94]

The main media focus was on Rebekah Brooks and Andy Coulson. Brooks faced five charges spanning over a decade including one in relation to allegations of conspiracy to hack phones. Other charges included conspiracy with others to commit misconduct in public office and two charges that she conspired with others to pervert the course of justice.[95] Coulson faced charges relating to an alleged conspiracy to commit misconduct in public office, and allegations linked to a phone-hacking conspiracy on the paper.[96]

This became the first of four trials involving newspaper journalists and others linked to the Murdoch empire at the *News of the World* or the *Sun* following the Metropolitan Police's Operations Weeting and Elveden investigations into allegations of phone-hacking since July 2011. With such a large number of defendants being tried, the Old Bailey had to make special arrangements to accommodate all those entitled to have access to Court 12, which became one of the main 'ticketed' events of modern media history.

At the start of the trial in late October 2013, 25 barristers for the Crown were present, and (at least) one solicitor for each defendant. Since there was not enough room in the courtroom, the proceedings could be watched live by streamed video. Television and newspaper journalists from all over the world were attending, all of whom had to adhere to the strict contempt laws of the UK, which, unlike the US, bans any comment on active trials (*sub judice*) until the verdict has been delivered. Presiding over the trial was Mr Justice Saunders, who, together with the Attorney General, Dominic Grieve QC, had issued warnings to the media reminding them not to stray from the strict liability Contempt of Court Act 1981 reporting rules in the UK, which require fair and accurate reporting of trials as they happen ('contemporaneous reporting'). There were particular concerns that MPs might comment on the trial because of Mr Coulson's former role in Downing Street.

See Chapter 4.4

It had become clear that the phone-hacking and bribery scandals were going beyond merely the *News of the World*'s practices, extending to the *Sun*, the *Daily Mirror* and possibly other tabloids.

10.4.2 The Leveson Report 2012[97]

Sixteen months after the *Guardian* revealed that the *News of the World* had hacked into murdered victim Milly Dowler's mobile phone, Prime Minister David Cameron established the Leveson

---

94 Source: 'Phone-hacking trial: three ex-News of the World staff plead guilty', by Lisa O'Carroll, *Guardian*, 30 October 2013.

95 It was alleged that Rebekah Brooks together with Bettina Jordan-Barber, employed by the Ministry of Defence, and John Kay, Chief Reporter at the *Sun* between 1990 and 2011, conspired together (and with others charged) between 1 January 2004 and 31 January 2012, to commit misconduct in public office, contrary to s 1(1) of the Criminal Law Act 1977. Source: CPS Press Release by Alison Levitt QC, Principal Legal Advisor to the Director of Public Prosecutions, 20 November 2012.

96 It was alleged that Andy (Andrew) Coulson together with Clive Goodman, between 31 August 2002 and 31 January 2003, conspired together and with 'a person or persons unknown' to commit misconduct in public office, contrary to s 1(1) of the Criminal Law Act 1977. Source: CPS Press Release by Alison Levitt QC, Principal Legal Advisor to the Director of Public Prosecutions, 20 November 2012.

97 The Report of An Inquiry into the Culture, Practices and Ethics of the Press was presented to Parliament (HC 780) ('The Leveson Report' or 'Leveson') 29 November 2012.

Inquiry. For the sixth time in less than 70 years, a report had been commissioned by the Government which was to deal with concerns about the press.[98] From that beginning, the scope of the inquiry was expanded to cover the culture, practices and ethics of the press in its relations with the public, with the police, with politicians; and, as to the police and politicians, the conduct of each. On 29 November 2012, Lord Justice Leveson published the eagerly awaited report (hereafter 'Leveson').[99]

The report covers four volumes comprising some 1,987 pages, plus a 46-page executive summary. Leveson proposed to change British press freedom, by reintroducing statutory control of the media after hundreds of years. The Right Honourable Lord Justice Leveson recommended a new 'independent self-regulation' system for the print press that would be underpinned by legislation – though Prime Minister David Cameron had promised, when ordering the inquiry into the practices and ethics of the press, that there ought not to be statutory regulation.

Leveson delivered withering verdicts on the behaviour of many journalists and editors, 'wholly rejecting' the suggestion that these were 'aberrations and do not reflect on the culture, practices or ethics of the press as a whole'. Lord Justice Leveson concluded that parts of the press acted as if its own code simply did not exist and 'wreaked havoc' in the lives of innocent people. Ordinary members of the public, caught up in tragic events, had their experiences 'made much much worse by press behaviour that, at times, can only be called outrageous'. Leveson stated that:

> . . . there has been a recklessness in prioritising sensational stories, almost irrespective of the harm that the stories may cause and the rights of those who would be affected, like the Dowlers, the McCanns and Abigail Witchalls.[100]

Lord Justice Leveson was particularly critical of the publishers of the *News of the World* over their response to the conviction of the paper's Royal Correspondent for hacking into phone messages.

Leveson: main findings

- **Phone-hacking** – Lord Leveson made no findings on any individual but stated that he was not convinced hacking was confined to one or two people. 'The evidence drives me to conclude that this was far more than a covert, secret activity, known to nobody save one or two practitioners of the "dark arts".'
- **Newspapers recklessly pursued sensational stories** – 'There has been a recklessness in prioritising sensational stories, almost irrespective of the harm the stories may cause and the rights of those who would be affected.'
- **Families of actors and footballers also have rights to privacy** – Leveson said that families of famous people had some of their lives destroyed by the relentless pursuit of the press. Parts of the press decided that actors, footballers, writers and pop stars were 'fair game, public property with little if any entitlement to any sort of private life or respect for dignity . . . Their families, including their children, are pursued and important personal moments are destroyed.'

---

98 There were Royal Commissions in 1947, 1962 and 1973, the Younger Commission on Privacy and the Calcutt Report.
99 See also: Wragg (2013a).
100 Source: *An Inquiry into the Culture, Practices and Ethics of the Press*. The Leveson Report, Executive Summary, 29 November 2012, at paras 5–7.

- **Covert surveillance** – Leveson condemned covert surveillance. He found that there was a 'willingness to deploy covert surveillance, blagging and deception in circumstances where it is extremely difficult to see any public interest justification'.
- **Complainants were not taken seriously** – Leveson found that there was a 'cultural tendency within parts of the press vigorously to resist or dismiss complaints almost as a matter of course'.
- **The Dowlers** – The *Guardian*'s revelation that messages had been deleted from 13-year-old Milly Dowler's phone when it was hacked turned out to be an error that 'was significant enough'. But Leveson said that the fact remains that the *NoW* hacked the phone of a dead schoolgirl. 'The revelation of that story rightly shocked the public conscience in a way that other stories of phone hacking may not have, but it also gave momentum to growing calls for light to be shed on an unethical and unlawful practice of which there were literally thousands of victims. In that context, whether or not NoW journalists had caused the "false hope" moment is almost irrelevant.'
- **The McCanns** – Leveson devotes almost 12 pages to the McCann family. Some of the reporting of the disappearance of three-year-old Madeleine McCann from Praia da Luz in Portugal in May 2007 was, Leveson states, 'outrageous'. A number of newspapers were 'guilty of gross libels', with the *Daily Star* singled out for its headline claiming the McCanns sold their child: 'Maddie sold by hard up McCanns'.
- **The police** – Leveson perceives that senior Met officers were 'too close' to News International, which was 'entirely understandable' given police actions and decision-making. 'Poor decisions, poorly executed, all came together to contribute to the perception.' The hospitality police received from the media, including lavish restaurant meals and champagne, did not enhance the Met's reputation. The Met's decision not to reopen the criminal inquiry into hacking was 'incredibly swift' and resulted in a 'defensive mindset'.

The Leveson Report: key recommendations

- **An independent self-regulatory body** underpinned by statute, independent of MPs and newspapers ('free of any influence from industry and government').
- **A First Amendment-style law**
- **Powers, remedies and sanctions of the regulator** with fines of 1 per cent of turnover, with a maximum of £1m. The watchdog should have 'sufficient powers to carry out investigations both into suspected serious or systemic breaches of the code'.
- **A libel resolution unit** – the new regulator should have an arbitration process in relation to civil legal claims against subscribers.
- **Membership** – though this would not be legally obligatory, and editors could opt out of the regulatory body.

The Tories' initial response to *Leveson* (which called for a statutory underpinning of press regulation) was dismissive, though they were later willing to contemplate and recognize an absolute minimum of press regulation, following more vociferous campaigning by Hacked

Off[101] victims (of press intrusion), prompted by the *Leveson* recommendations (see Crime and Courts Act 2013 below).

The Leveson Report was debated in Parliament on 30 November 2012, with an immediate response from Labour opposition leader, Ed Miliband, who told the Commons that they should trust Leveson's recommendations and that the report's proposals should be 'accepted in full'. Mr Miliband also said that Ofcom was the 'right body to oversee the establishment of a new press regulator'.[102] The Prime Minister's Liberal Democrat coalition partner, Deputy Prime Minister Nick Clegg, and the Labour opposition, made it clear in Parliament that they preferred statutory press regulation, as recommended by *Leveson*. But David Cameron was unwilling to bear the odium for breaking the centuries-old tradition of British press freedom. Lord Hunt, the then chairman of the PCC, and Lord Black, chairman of the Press Standards Board of Finance, additionally recommended a 'beefed-up' version of the PCC based on five-year rolling contracts in the House of Lords.

Following the fall-out over the Leveson Report, Liberty Director Shami Chakrabarti – a prominent member of Lord Justice Leveson's panel – sided with the Prime Minister. In an interview with the *Independent on Sunday*, Ms Chakrabarti rejected legislation to regulate the press. She was effectively throwing a lifeline to the Prime Minister, David Cameron, who was – at that time – at odds with not only Lord Justice Leveson but with the Deputy Prime Minister Nick Clegg, most Members of Parliament and the Hacked Off victims.[103] Ms Chakrabarti's dissent had been buried in the small print of the Leveson Report on page 1,775, where *Leveson* recommends that the statutory communications regulator, Ofcom, is given new powers to oversee a new press regulator. A further footnote revealed that the Liberty director was opposed to this key principle.

The Rt Hon. Lord Justice Leveson made a range of recommendations to reform the regulatory framework for the press, creating a new framework for press regulation, with the principle of industry self-regulation at its heart. The new framework proposed a system of voluntary self-regulation, overseen by a recognition body established by Royal Charter and strengthened by a series of incentives for members of the press in the application of costs and exemplary damages, encouraging them to join a recognized regulator.

Leveson essentially recommended statutory regulation of the press, similar to the Irish Press Council model. The newspaper industry considered this an unacceptable violation of the freedom of the press – and if a statutory press regulator was to be set up, they would not join. *The Spectator* magazine's Editor, Fraser Nelson, was the first to vow that they would not take part in such a scheme.[104]

10.4.3 What does Lord Leveson mean by 'freedom of the press'?

See Chapters 1.2 and 1.2.2

This book began with a brief history of freedom of speech fighters, such as Immanuel Kant, Voltaire, Jean-Jacques Rousseau, John Milton, John Locke and Aleksandr Solzhenitsyn. What would John Milton have made of the Leveson Report that was published on 29 November 2012? In 1644, Milton had appealed to Parliament in the *Areopagitica* to rescind its order to bring publishing under government control by creating official censors.

Leveson marked a turning point in British constitutional history. In a country governed by the rule of law the independence of the press is a constitutional necessity and the UK does not have a

101 Hacked Off represented most of the victims of press abuse who gave evidence at the Leveson Inquiry, including Gerry and Kate McCann, Christopher Jefferies and actor Hugh Grant as well as non-celebrities. 'We're campaigning with victims of press abuse to ensure that the Leveson Inquiry leads to a free and fair press, promoting world-class public interest journalism' – source at: https://twitter.com/hackinginquiry.

102 Source: 'Leveson proposals should be accepted in full, says Ed Miliband – video', *Guardian*, Parliamentary debate on 30 November 2012 at: www.guardian.co.uk/media/video/2012/nov/29/leveson-ed-miliband-video.

103 Source: 'Chakrabarti backs Cameron as Leveson panel splits', by Jane Merrick and James Cusick, *Independent on Sunday*, 2 December 2012.

104 Source: 'Why The Spectator won't sign the Royal Charter', by Fraser Nelson, *The Spectator*, 23 March 2013.

written constitution (or at least there is no one document that is wholly in writing). There is no statute which states expressly that the independence of the press is a constitutional principle – and the 'freedom of expression' in Article 10 of the European Convention might only be seen as persuasive in UK jurisprudence. Arguably, after *Leveson*, the UK was well on the way to returning to the days of state licensing of the print press which was abolished in 1695. While the United States adopted the First Amendment in 1791[105] to its Constitution, barring Congress from limiting free speech or press freedom, the United Kingdom does not have this enshrined in its (unwritten) constitution.

The Leveson Report in Part 2[106] discusses media freedom and democracy in great detail. Lord Leveson begins this section with a quote from Churchill's take on press freedom taken from a speech in 1949 that the press must be 'vigilant guardians of the rights of the ordinary citizen', followed by Lord Bingham, who said:

> The proper functioning of a modern participatory democracy requires that the media be free, active, professional and inquiring. For this reason the courts, here and elsewhere, have recognised the cardinal importance of press freedom and the need for any restriction on that freedom to be proportionate and no more than necessary to promote the legitimate object of the restriction.[107]

Whilst Lord Bingham stressed the importance of a free press in a democratic society, he also made clear that the quality of that freedom requires consideration. Lord Leveson agrees with Lord Bingham, indicating that 'press freedom' has many components and is rarely absolute or paramount in a democracy. Democracy, according to Leveson, 'may itself be thought of as a system for reconciling competing freedoms'.[108] Equally, a press that is free and nothing else will not necessarily enhance democracy.

10.4.4 A Royal Charter for press regulation

As the parliamentary session drew to a close in spring of 2013, Lord McNally's Defamation Bill (originally Lord Lester's) was about to be sabotaged by incorporating some of the *Leveson* recommendations, as suggested by the opposition Labour Party.[109]

See Chapter 3.7.2

Cabinet Office Minister Oliver Letwin had been leading all-party talks on the *Leveson* recommendations which proposed a Royal Charter to introduce a new press regulatory body. A Royal Charter is a way of incorporating a body that turns it from a collection of individuals into a single legal entity. A body incorporated by Royal Charter has all the powers of a natural person, including the power to sue and be sued in its own right. Royal Charters were at one time the only means of incorporating a body, but there are now other means (becoming a registered company, for example), so the grant of new Charters is comparatively rare and is reserved for eminent professional bodies or charities, such as the BBC or the Red Cross. To receive Charter status, granted by the Privy Council, the professional body in question should represent a field of activity which is unique and not covered by any other professional body. Once incorporated by Royal Charter a body surrenders significant aspects of the control of its internal affairs to the Privy Council. Amendments to Charters can be made only with the agreement of the Sovereign in Council, and amendments to the body's by-laws require the approval of the Council (though not normally the Monarch). This effectively

---

105 The First Amendment (Amendment I) to the United States Constitution prohibits the making of any law respecting an establishment of religion, impeding the free exercise of religion, abridging freedom of speech, infringing on the freedom of the press, interfering with the right to peaceably assemble or prohibiting the petitioning for a governmental redress of grievances. It was adopted on 15 December 1791 as one of the 10 amendments that comprise the Bill of Rights.
106 See: Leveson Report (2012), Volume I, Part B ('the freedom of the press and democracy'), at paras 1.1–1.7.
107 Lord Bingham of Cornhill in **R (on the application of Laporte) v Chief Constable of Gloucestershire** [2006] UKHL 55 at para 35).
108 Leveson Report (2012), Volume I, Part B at para 1.1 p. 56.
109 See also: Chamberlain (2013) at pp. 21–24.

means a significant degree of Government regulation of the affairs of the body. Therefore, the Privy Council needs to be satisfied that such regulation accords with public policy.

Monday 18 March 2013 saw a heavily whipped vote in the House of Commons for a billed debate on 'freedom of expression' and press freedom which was to decide the policy on press regulation and the Royal Charter following *Leveson*. Prime Minister, David Cameron, was facing a double defeat in the Commons, following the Clegg–Miliband proposals presented as a basis for the Charter. Tory whips spent the weekend preceding the debate putting the squeeze on their back-benchers to back a still radically reformed system of press regulation, which stopped short of the demands being made by Labour and the Liberal Democrats as well as the Hacked Off campaigners. Confusingly for Parliament, rival Royal Charters were proposed by the newspaper industry and Hacked Off, setting out new systems of press regulation (see below). Eventually, the Government agreed a Draft Royal Charter,[110] which proposed a new system of 'exemplary damages' for non-licensed publications (though this may yet prove to be against EU law).

Following the Government's draft Royal Charter the newspaper industry counter-proposed a different system of self-regulation, also backed by Royal Charter. Lord Justice Leveson had foreseen that some newspaper groups would be reluctant to participate in a system that was actually effective. In a lengthy televised statement which followed the publication of his report into media standards, Lord Leveson had said that 'press freedom in Britain, hard won over 300 years ago', should not be jeopardized. The High Court judge said the press had caused 'real hardship' to members of the public as it chased stories and had been guilty of 'outrageous' behaviour at times. Speaking at the Queen Elizabeth II Conference Centre in Westminster, on 29 November 2012, Lord Justice Leveson stressed that a free press 'is one of the true safeguards of our democracy'.[111]

From July 2013, the newspaper and magazine industry pushed ahead with the establishment of a new press regulator and its own version of a Royal Charter, despite Lord Leveson's warnings. Leading publishers and editors included Rupert Murchoch's News UK, the *Daily Mail* publishers Associated Newspapers and the Telegraph Media Group. They announced that the new regulator replacing the PCC is the Independent Press Standards Organisation (Ipso). The announcement of the establishment of Ipso came shortly after Lord Prescott resigned from the Privy Council in protest against the delays in implementing the Government's Royal Charter for a press regulator, which was agreed by the three main parties and Hacked Off in the early hours of 18 March 2013.

In a joint statement, the publishers said: 'The Independent Press Standards Organisation will be a complete break with the past, and will deliver all the key Leveson recommendations.' The statement was signed by the Newspaper Society (representing regional and local papers), Newspaper Publishers Association (national papers), the Scottish Newspaper Society and PPA (magazine publishers).[112] Ipso's Charter ('The Newspaper Industry Charter') includes:

- The removal of Parliament's power to block or approve future changes to regulation. Instead the regulator, trade bodies and a newly created 'recognition panel' would have to agree to changes;

110 See: 'Draft operative provisions for a Royal Charter', 12 February 2013 at: https://www.gov.uk/government/uploads/system/uploads/attachment_data/file/136347/RC_Draft_Royal_Charter_12_February_2013.pdf.

111 Source: 'Leveson Report: the Press has wreaked havoc with innocent people's lives', *Daily Telegraph* video coverage, 29 November 2012 at: www.telegraph.co.uk/news/uknews/leveson-inquiry/9712767/Leveson-Report-the-Press-has-wreaked-havoc-with-innocent-peoples-lives.html.

112 Source: 'Press industry pushes ahead with new regulator despite political deadlock', by Lisa O'Carroll, *Guardian*, 8 July 2013.

- An appointments committee to select the new regulatory panel, chaired by Sir Hayden Phillips was set up in January 2014 IPSO was to commence on 1 May 2014, including one representative of the industry's interests, one member representing the public interest and one public appointments assessor nominated by the Commissioner for Public Appointments for England and Wales, chaired by a Supreme Court judge;
- The removal of the ban on former editors sitting on the panel;
- Giving newspaper and magazine readers a say on the industry's proposals for regulation;
- Making it more difficult to bring group complaints;
- Changing the power of the regulator to 'direct' the nature, extent and placement of corrections and apologies, saying it should 'require' not 'direct'.

IPSO's Charter was supported by some politicians, including London Mayor Boris Johnson and the House of Commons Culture Media and Sport Committee Chairman John Whittingdale.[113] *Guardian* publisher Guardian News and Media, and the publishers of the *Financial Times, Independent* and *Evening Standard* did not (at that stage) sign up to the newspaper industry-proposed regulator.

Confusingly, Hacked Off also published its own proposals for (another) alternative Royal Charter, drafted largely by Hugh Tomlinson QC and parliamentary counsel Daniel Greenberg. The draft 'Hacked-Off Bill' included:

- To enshrine the freedom of the press in statute, making attempted ministerial or other state interference in the media explicitly illegal;
- To specify the standards that the voluntary independent press self-regulator would have to meet to satisfy public demand for a system that is effective and independent of government, Parliament and the newspaper industry;
- To set out a transparent, democratic system to appoint a recognition commission to verify on behalf of the public that the press self-regulator is doing its job properly.

Actor Hugh Grant, a director of the Hacked Off campaign, told the BBC's *Andrew Marr Show* that the draft 'Hacked-Off Bill' proposed to set up an appointments commission mainly involving the judiciary which, in turn, would appoint a recognition body that in turn would oversee the body established by the press to regulate itself.[114]

At the close of the parliamentary session in early May 2013, the Crime and Courts Bill was amended to include clauses on three key points arising from *Leveson*, granting exemption to single-author blogs, community newsletters, hobby magazines such as *Angling Times* or the *Decanter* and scientific journals (see below). Both the Crime and Courts Bill and the Defamation Bill received Royal Assent by Queen Elizabeth II on 8 May 2013.[115] The Government's draft Royal Charter Bill went before the Privy Council[116] at the start of the new parliamentary session on 15 May 2013, meaning that the Council was faced with new constitutional territory.

Sections 34 to 42 and Schedule 15 of the Crime and Courts Act 2013 now cover 'Publishers of news-related material: damages and costs' and incorporate the recommendations of *Leveson*. These sections set out the new system for 'exemplary damages and costs', as well as defining those who meet the definition of a 'relevant publisher' to whom the new system of exemplary damages will apply.

---

113 See: www.ipso.co.uk.
114 Source:' Leveson: Hugh Grant slams Cameron's press reform plan', *The Andrew Marr Show*, BBC TV, 17 March 2013 at: www.bbc.co.uk/news/uk-21822040.
115 The Fixed Term Parliament Act 2011 sets out new rules on the timing of general elections. This means that the next general election will be on 7 May 2015.
116 Deputy Prime Minister Nick Clegg MP became Lord President of the Privy Council in May 2010.

Section 41 of the Crime and Courts Act 2013 explains what is meant by a 'relevant publisher':

(1) . . . 'relevant publisher' means a person who, in the course of a business (whether or not carried on with a view to profit), publishes news-related material –

(a)   which is written by different authors, and
(b)   which is to any extent subject to editorial control.

. . . (2) News-related material is 'subject to editorial control' if there is a person (whether or not the publisher of the material) who has editorial or equivalent responsibility for –

(a)   the content of the material,
(b)   how the material is to be presented, and
(c)   the decision to publish it.

(3) A person who is the operator of a website is not to be taken as having editorial or equivalent responsibility for the decision to publish any material on the site, or for content of the material, if the person did not post the material on the site.

Schedule 15 of the Crime and Courts Act 2013 further explains s 41 of the 2013 Act, detailing the exclusions for the definition of 'relevant publisher'. These exclusions include:

Broadcasters

1.   The British Broadcasting Corporation.
2.   Sianel Pedwar Cymru (S4C).
3.   Any holder of a licence under the Broadcasting Act 1990 or 1996 who publishes news-related material in connection with the broadcasting activities authorized under the licence.

Special interest titles

1.   relating to a particular pastime, hobby, trade, business, industry or profession.
2.   containing only news-related material on an incidental basis that is relevant to the main content of the title.

Scientific or academic journals

Public bodies and charities

1.   A public body or charity that publishes news-related material in connection with the carrying out of its functions.
2.   Company news publications.
3.   A newsletter, circular or other document which –

    (a)   relates to a business carried on by the person, and
    (b)   only contains news-related material on an incidental basis that is relevant to the person's business.

Micro-businesses

1.   A person who, in carrying on a micro-business, publishes news-related material where either condition A or condition B is met.
2.   Condition A is that the news-related material is contained in a multi-author blog.
3.   Condition B is that the news-related material is published on an incidental basis that is relevant to the main activities of the business.
4.   'Micro-business' means a business which –

   (a)   has fewer than ten employees, and
   (b)   has an annual turnover not exceeding £2,000,000.

5.   'Multi-author blog' means a blog that contains contributions from different authors.

Book publishers

1.   A person who is the publisher of a book.
2.   'Book' does not include any title published on a periodic basis with substantially different content.

In a last-minute attempt to stop the Privy Council introducing a Royal Charter on press regulation, a group of newspaper and magazine publishers tried to seek a High Court injunction. Industry bodies representing the publishers were granted an emergency High Court hearing on 30 October 2013, just hours before the Government's Press Regulation Royal Charter – backed by the three main parties and Hacked Off campaigners – was set to go before the Privy Council for sealing by the Queen at 5.30pm that Wednesday afternoon. However, the injunction was not granted by Lord Justice Richards and Mr Justice Sales. The applicant newspaper publishers immediately declared their intention to take their case to the Court of Appeal. They were also seeking a legal ruling that any decision to seal the cross-party charter could be overturned by way of Judicial Review.[117] The Queen gave her royal consent to the Charter on the evening of 30 October 2013.

10.4.5 Do we need a law to rein in the press? Analysis of the Leveson Inquiry

The response to the Leveson Report has been plagued with confusion, not only in policy terms, but also in terms of the possible ensuing legislation (i.e. three Royal Charters). It is now well known that the Leveson Inquiry was set up by Prime Minister David Cameron in a knee-jerk response to the phone-hacking crimes and intrusion into people's grief and shock, committed by journalists with a press self-regulator – the PCC – who could and would not put a stop to such crimes. The Rt Hon. Lord Justice Leveson was hesitant in his comments on relations between the press, the police and those in power – though he acknowledged that press freedom is a virtue.

But is the media not already surrounded by a wall of statute and common law, such as contempt of court, libel, surveillance (RIPA), harassment (Harassment Act 1997), data projection, forgery and fraud (Fraud Act 2006)? Even if the PCC was not able to investigate malpractice at the *News of the World*, there were other statutory regulatory bodies who could have done so. The police watchdog,

---

117   Source: '"Newspaper" bid for injunction against press regulation royal charter fails', by Mark Sweney, *Guardian*, 30 October 2013.

the Independent Police Complaints Commission (IPCC) found, for instance, that former senior officers at Surrey Police failed to act on evidence of the alleged hacking of schoolgirl Milly Dowler's phone during their 2002 investigation of her murder. The IPCC investigation found that police officers at all levels of the investigation knew an allegation of hacking had been made against the *NoW* but they did nothing, despite suggestions a crime had been committed. The IPCC Report of April 2013 stated that senior officers appeared to be suffering from a 'form of collective amnesia'. The IPCC investigation found that there was knowledge of the phone-hacking allegation in 2002 at all levels in 'Operation Ruby', Surrey Police's investigation into the abduction and murder of Milly Dowler, but that no action was taken to investigate it despite an indication that a crime had potentially been committed.[118]

The Information Commissioner's Office also had strong evidence that many journalists had broken the law but failed to act because it did not dare take on the press. This was alleged by a former senior Met detective, Alex Owens, when giving evidence to the Leveson Inquiry in December 2012. Mr Owens told the inquiry that phone-hacking could have been identified two or three years earlier if the ICO had investigated the evidence properly. He told the inquiry that he became the senior investigator for the ICO, but that he was prevented from pursuing newspapers by the Information Commissioner, then Richard Thomas, who had ordered that no journalist should be contacted. Mr Owens alleged that the ICO had tried to cover up its failure.

See Chapter 6.3.2

The ICO had published a report in May 2006, 'What Price Privacy?',[119] because it had become aware that the police were investigating phone-hacking at the *NoW*.[120] The ICO's investigations in 2002 and 2003 had disclosed the names of thousands of victims, many of whom later had their phones hacked by the *NoW*, but only about sixty were told that they had been targeted. The first arrests for phone hacking were not made until August 2006.

Arguably, what took place at News International was not a breach of press ethics but sustained criminality against which there had been laws under which the police could have prosecuted the wrongdoers. Additionally, the Bribery Act 2010 could have stopped journalists paying police for information; and the Regulation of Investigatory Powers Act 2000 could have easily been used to pursue and investigate all those journalists and editors who carried out surveillance, illegal phone tapping or clandestine recordings of celebrities. This meant there were already legal avenues open to those who could have stopped the press from getting anywhere close to publishing the story. The fact also remains that the PCC did not investigate the phone-hacking properly, and possibly could not do so, since it had no statutory powers to do so. Following the publication of the Leveson Report, Sir Max Hastings[121] – who had served as editor on the PCC for 15 years – stated in the *Financial Times* that 'no regulatory body past, present or future, could investigate and punish such wrongdoing. It was plain to some of us years ago that the police had disgracefully failed in their duty to investigate News International.'[122]

Will the Royal Charter solve the problems that have dogged the British press and appalled the public with dreadful examples of press intrusion? *Leveson* revealed horrendous press practices of

118 Source: Independent Police Complaints Commission (IPCC) (2013).
119 See: Information Commissioner's Office (ICO) (2006a).
120 Source: Access to evidence submitted by Mr Alexander Owens, pursuant to Section 21 of the Inquiries Act 2005. A requirement was made that Mr Alex Owens (formerly a senior investigator employed by the Information Commissioner) produce the documents which were in his custody, which reflected spreadsheets of the materials seized from the private detective, Steven Whittamore, during the course of Operation Motorman and which were contained on a USB stick. The Information Commissioner has not raised any concerns that the Inquiry should have copies of those documents and in particular, has not suggested that Section 59 of the Data Protection Act 1998 should prevent the Inquiry from seeing and analysing the material. Witness statement at the Leveson Inquiry. Order of 2 December 2011.
121 Max Hastings was BBC foreign correspondent during the Falklands War in 1982. He was editor of the London *Evening Standard* until 1996 and for 10 years editor and then editor-in-chief of the *Daily Telegraph*.
122 Source: 'Press misconduct was criminal, not a breach of ethics', by Max Hastings, *Financial Times*, 1 December 2012.

voicemail hacking, the theft of Kate McCann's diary, allegations of police officers' taking bribes from tabloid journalists, amounting to sickening abuses of press power. But they were all violations of existing laws, resulting eventually in scores of journalists being arrested – facing trial. Would any of the proposals from the draft Royal Charter have helped the McCanns, Hugh Grant, Max Mosley, Sienna Miller or the other celebrities who were represented by the Hacked Off campaign? Labour leader Ed Miliband rightly pointed out in Parliament, following *Leveson*, that there had been a 'pattern of decades and decades where politicians promised to act on wrongdoing by the press, and failed to do so'.

The report does not make it quite clear whether Lord Justice Leveson broadly endorses a kind of 'PCC Plus' regime, involving proper investigatory powers and tough fines (now enshrined in s 34 Crime and Courts Act 2013) – also advanced by Lord Hunt (of the PCC) and Lord Black. Statutory restrictions may well mean a slow, unremarked death of vital information and the end to investigative journalism (coupled with the new Defamation Act 2013).

See Chapter 3.2.7

In his 13th Annual Justice Lecture (2011),[123] the most senior member of the judiciary, Lord Chief Justice Igor Judge, made an argument against new laws that would specifically govern the press. He said:

> . . . an independent press, or one or other of its constituents, will from time to time behave appallingly, or employ individuals who in order to pursue a story will commit criminal offences. No editors, I think, have ever advocated that they are entitled to some special journalistic privilege if they do so, immunising them or their employees from criminal prosecution. Of course not. So that is not the issue . . .
>
> The conundrum which faces us, and Leveson LJ in particular, is how best to avoid dilution of the essential constitutional principles. It would be easy, on the basis of a number of disturbing instances in recent times to say that self-regulation has failed. Let me examine this, recognising that some very sad examples of press misbehaviour have happened.
>
> First, crime is crime. If and when crime is committed by reporters with or without the support and encouragement of an editor, it should be investigated, and if on the available evidence there is a reasonable prospect of a successful prosecution, he or they are prosecuted. We do not say that the General Medical Council and self-regulation have failed when, as sometimes happens, a doctor sexually molests one or more of his patients, or like Dr Shipman murders them.[124]

When drawing up the draft Royal Charter on press regulation, it is understandable that many MPs may very well have rubbed their hands with glee as they drafted new statutory legislation to regulate the press. For they can surely never forgive the *Daily Telegraph* for its exposé of the abuse of the parliamentary expenses system, which now means that Parliamentarians have to submit their expenses to an independent scrutineer. With the Royal Charter in place, one thing is clear: the press will henceforth be regulated more heavily and investigative journalism underpinned by freedom of expression will become more complicated.

One issue which has not been specified by the new legislation is that presently there is no effective enforcement of a code (e.g. by the former PCC) or costs awarded to victims of media intrusion. With current membership of the regulatory body IPSO being voluntary, this means that

123 See: Judge, Lord LCJ (2011) 13th Annual Justice Lecture: Press Regulation, 19 October 2011 at: www.judiciary.gov.uk/
Resources/JCO/Documents/Speeches/lcj-speech-annual-justice-lecture-2011.pdf.
124 Ibid.

there is no likely enforcement by the courts. What then is to be done for the Dowlers or McCanns of this world, if any future compensatory vindication is to be payable via the courts? It could be that media organizations are encouraged to settle matters early out of court ('offers to settle').[125]

From 1 April 2013, the Jackson reforms to civil litigation funding and costs ('no win – no fee') were introduced in England and Wales. This concerns the way that civil cases are funded, and the costs involved in bringing those cases.[126] 'No win no fee' Conditional Fee Agreements (CFAs) remain available in civil cases, but the additional costs involved (success fee and insurance premiums) are no longer payable by the losing side.[127]

10.5 What happens to the whistleblowers? Protection of journalistic sources

Following the revelations of the phone-hacking and police corruption scandals which emerged from the Leveson Inquiry, *The Times* reported in February 2012 that its Management and Standards Committee (MSC) had handed to a police team (ensconced in News International's own offices) emails and documents identifying sources of journalists working for the *Sun*. In short, the MSC was accused of throwing the company's own journalists to the wolves. The MSC was set up by News Corporation to root out criminality and malpractice. Thereafter, about a hundred MSC personnel – a mixture of lawyers, forensic accountants, police officers and specialist computer analysts – would arrive via a security system to trawl through emails and phone calls to look for informants and journalistic sources. Among the companies represented were Linklaters, PricewaterhouseCoopers, the forensic IT consultants Stroz Friedberg and Scotland Yard. Some 300 million emails, taken from News International (NI) computers, were scrutinized for possible criminal offences. Subsequently nine *Sun* journalists were arrested and their property searched in dawn raids, on suspicion of breaching the Prevention of Corruption Act 1906. The committee's test for identifying sources was: 'if there is evidence that the source was a public official who may have been paid'. Arguably, not all payments to public officials for information are regarded, in practice or in law, as contrary to the 1906 Act, especially now that Article 10 ECHR requires the public interest of disclosure to be taken into account in the light of freedom of expression.[128]

The Prevention of Corruption Act 1906 is directed at bribery, but there will always be cases where sources for stories of genuine public interest require expenses payments. A number of reports followed the MSC-inspired dawn raids, revealing, for example, that one *Sun* journalist was questioned by police about a £50 restaurant bill for taking two police officers to lunch, after his expenses claim was handed over by the committee. Geoffrey Robertson QC took issue, and commented on the MSC investigations with some criticism:

> If *The Sun* did pay a prison officer for private information, that might warrant a prosecution, whereas payment made to expose mistakes that put the lives of British troops at risk might not.

---

125 The sanctions under Part 36 of the Civil Procedure Rules (offers to settle) were reformed to encourage early settlement. This will encourage claimants to make, and defendants to accept, reasonable early offers. This will help to reduce the time taken for cases to settle and consequently help to lower overall costs.

126 These reforms are in part as a result of changes in legislation: under Part 2 of the Legal Aid, Sentencing and Punishment of Offenders Act 2012 (LASPO).

127 The arrangements for 'no win no fee' cases have changed under LASPO. There are two types of no win no fee cases: conditional fee agreements (CFAs) and damages-based agreements (DBAs – sometimes called contingency fees). For both types of no win no fee cases, the lawyer's payment is conditional on the case being successful. If the case is lost, the lawyer is not paid. If the case is won, the lawyer is paid: the normal fee plus an uplift or success fee (CFAs); or a percentage of the damages recovered (DBAs). See s 44 LAPSO.

128 Source: 'NI's standards committee once looked like a fig leaf. Now some say it's the enemy within', by Ian Burrell, *Independent*, 13 February 2012.

Nor would it stop our current *deus ex machina*, the Director of Public Prosecutions, Keir Starmer – who produced acceptable guidelines for the right to die – doing the same for the media's right to make necessary payments to expose malfeasance.[129]

There have been a number of events in the UK revealing the potential for conflict between a judicial order either prohibiting the publication of details relating to a matter before the courts in form of superinjunctions, or ordering a journalist to reveal his sources of information.[130]

Wainwright v The Home Office (2003)[131] confirmed that the UK does not have an established law of privacy (see also: **Kaye v Robertson** (1991)[132]). Individuals seeking to protect their private lives from media intrusion have instead brought their grievances to the courts via a number of creative means such as the law of confidence, defamation, Article 8 ECHR, breach of copyright and under the Data Protection Act 1998. In the absence of any privacy legislation, the UK courts have been left to develop this area to such an extent that Sedley LJ said in **Douglas v Hello! Ltd** (2001)[133] that 'we have reached a point at which it can be said with confidence that the law recognizes and will appropriately protect the right of personal privacy'.[134]

The conflict between an individual's right to privacy and the media's claim to freedom of expression have been discussed at length in Chapters 1 and 2 of this book. Do we really have the right to share someone's private life in public? Recent case law from both the UK and the Strasbourg human rights courts seems to suggest otherwise. There was Naomi Campbell's victory in the House of Lords against the *Daily Mirror*[135] and Princess Caroline's victory in the Strasbourg court.[136]

See Chapter 2.2.4.

Since the **Campbell**, **Princess Caroline von Hannover** and **Max Mosley** cases, journalists have become more astute about protecting genuinely private matters, such as medical information or rehabilitative treatment details, which – though said by some to be in the public interest – should be kept totally private.

Then there were the applications for superinjunctions applied for by ingenious lawyers on behalf of famous individuals and public figures, such as footballer John Terry, who tried to 'gag' the media in early 2010 by attempting to prevent news about his illicit affair with his best friend's girlfriend.[137] In this area of law, the courts became more astute and generally followed the ruling in **Campbell**, saying that the Naomi Campbell privacy case meant that the law must not be misused.

The head of Britain's 2012 Olympic bid, Lord Sebastian Coe, tried to bar two Sunday papers from reporting details of his affair with Vanessa Lander around the same time in 2004 that Naomi Campbell's case was heard before the Law Lords. He pleaded with the courts by way of a superinjunction to be left alone, but the courts denied him the right to privacy and details of his private life and his 10-year affair with Ms Lander became public. Ms Lander revealed that she had an abortion after falling pregnant by the Olympic gold medallist in May 1996. At the time, the papers said, Lord Coe's then wife Nicola was expecting their third child. Lord Coe was unable to persuade the High Court to grant him an injunction to prevent the publication of an article about his extra-marital affair with Vanessa Lander and her terminated pregnancy. The *Sunday Mirror* claimed to have taken 'no pleasure in exposing the failures of one of our greatest living athletes'.[138]

---

129 Source: Comment by Geoffrey Robertson QC, *The Times*, 16 February 2012.
130 For further discussion see: Geddis (2010).
131 [2003] UKHL 53 (HL).
132 [1991] FSR 62.
133 [2001] QB 967.
134 Ibid., at 134 (Sedley LJ).
135 *Campbell v Mirror Group Newspapers Ltd* [2004] 2 AC 457 (HL).
136 *von Hannover v Germany (No 1)* (2005) 40 EHRR 1 (ECHR).
137 **John Terry (previously referred to as LNS) v Persons Unknown** [2010] EWHC 119 (QB).
138 Source: 'My 10 year affair with Lord Sebastian Coe', by Suzanne Kerins, *Sunday Mirror*, 30 May 2004.

Nevertheless, as unhappy as the Mirror may have been with the unintended consequences of its 'kiss-and-tell' feature, the newspaper's revelations about the peer's love life and the alleged abortion of Lord Coe's love-child sat uncomfortably with the Law Lords' decision in **Campbell**. By using the successful Campbell appeal, Lord Coe seemed to misunderstand the significance of that judgment: Naomi Campbell's right to seek drug treatment privately is rather different from Lord Coe's requesting a superinjunction to avoid loss of reputation. Mr Justice Fulford could not agree to Lord Coe's request for an injunction, stating that Ms Lander's right to free speech, and the Sunday Mirror's right to tell its readers about the habits of those in the public eye, outweighed Lord Coe's right to privacy. Had Lord Coe and John Terry succeeded in their requests for an injunction, this could have been a celebratory day for adulterers[139] (see: **Coe v Mirror Group Newspapers** (2004)[140]).

It is in areas such as these, where most claimants lack the financial resources of the likes of John Terry or Lord Sebastian Coe, that the scope of the law is out of reach for many. It is at this point that the ordinary citizen should be able to turn to the free advice of self-regulatory bodies, like the (now defunct) PCC, which may be of more use in spite of their limitations and lack of compensatory powers.

The cultivation of sources is essential for journalists. It is a basic tool of their trade, the means by which newsworthy and investigative information is brought to the public's attention. Should journalists reveal their sources of information if ordered by a court? The short answer is 'no'. The most fundamental tenet of journalism was set out in Clause 14 of the PCC's Code of Practice. Drafted originally by Les Hinton, former chairman of News International, it reads:

> Journalists have a moral obligation to protect confidential sources of information.

Nevertheless, there are no 'laws' that define whether or not a journalist should reveal his sources, but the various codes of journalism appear to be very clear: journalists do not reveal their sources. The UK National Union of Journalists (NUJ) drew up a Code of Ethics in 1936 which became the bedrock of the language of the Code of Practice for the PCC. In addition to Clause 14 of the PCC Code, Article 7 of the NUJ rulebook states: 'A journalist shall protect confidential sources of information.' But these codes express moral and ethical standards, not legal ones, meaning that not protecting the source is *always* wrong.

How then does this sit with 'contempt' legislation, where s 10 of the Contempt of Court Act 1981 states:

> No court may require a person to disclose, nor is any person guilty of contempt of court for refusing to disclose, the source of information contained in a publication for which he is responsible unless it is established to the satisfaction of the court that it is necessary in the interests of justice or national security or for the prevention of disorder or crime.

Neither the law of confidence nor the Contempt of Court Act 1981 explain how 'necessity' and 'in the interests of justice' are to be applied in practice. Additionally, the NUJ code permits transgressions on the basis of the public interest. This includes 'preventing the public from being misled by some statement or action of an individual or organisation' and 'exposing hypocritical behaviour by those holding high office'. While there is no law which covers the fact that journalists *must* reveal their sources, a court can nevertheless order a journalist to do so.

---

139 See also: 'The complete history of the Love Rat; Rod Liddle's extra-marital antics have kept the public entertained of late, but has he really taken brazen philandering to its limits?', by Adrian Turpin, Independent, 17 July 2004.
140 (2004) 29 May 2004 (unreported) (QBD).

There have been British journalists who chose to go to prison for 'contempt of court' rather than reveal their sources when ordered by a court to do so. Reg Foster of the *Daily Sketch* and Brendan Mulholland of the *Daily Mail* refused to disclose their sources in stories about the 'Vassall sex and spy scandal' to the Radcliffe Inquiry in 1962. The 'Vassal spy scandal' revealed the outrageously inappropriate lifestyle of aristocratic ministers and government mandarins who felt no need to justify themselves to the public. Foster and Mulholland exposed John Vassall, an assistant private secretary to an Admiralty junior minister, as a Soviet spy, who was subsequently sentenced to 18 years' imprisonment. After the trial, held largely in *camera*, the opposition, led by George Brown, succeeded in persuading a reluctant Harold Macmillan to set up the Radcliffe Tribunal of Inquiry, which turned out to be more censorious of the press than of the British security services. The Vassall affair turned out to be the central link in a chain of events culminating in the Profumo scandal and Prime Minister Harold Macmillan's resignation. Investigative journalism managed to tumble the old order, by exposing the Vassall affair of 1962 and the Profumo and Christine Keeler affair of 1963. Both these rather tasteless affairs became synonymous with a crusade for press freedom and journalistic martyrdom. Since Foster and Mulholland did not reveal their sources to the inquiry, they were ordered to go to prison for six months for contempt of court in 1963.

In 1971, BBC *Tonight* reporter Bernard Falk served two and a half days in a prison of his own choice, namely Belfast's Crumlin Road Jail, for contempt of court rather than reveal his source, a member of the IRA.[141]

On 22 October 1983, the *Guardian* published an electrifying front-page exclusive which led to a court battle with the Government.[142] Documents about cruise missile arrivals at Greenham Common had been anonymously leaked to the newspaper. Peter Preston, then editor of the *Guardian*, was drawn into a legal battle with the Government to reveal his source of information and to hand over all leaked documents – which, in turn, would identify the whistleblower. The *Guardian* lost the battle and Peter Preston was forced to hand over the evidence – one of the great regrets of his time at the *Guardian*. The whistleblower was identified as young civil servant and Foreign Office clerk, Sarah Tisdall, and on 23 March 1984 she was sentenced to six months in prison for leaking government secrets. Peter Preston learnt a horrible lesson and was shunned by his fellow journalists for years to come for revealing his source. Preston defended his action later, strongly believing that s 10 of the Contempt of Court Act 1981 and the various journalistic and PCC codes would provide him with legal protection;[143] he found out, however, that these did not provide any definite guidelines on the obligation not to disclose journalistic sources for sensitive documents and information.

Does present contempt law contravene human rights' freedom of expression? In **Goodwin v UK** (2002),[144] the applicant, Bill Goodwin, a trainee journalist with *The Engineer* magazine, complained of a violation of Article 10 of the Convention. Goodwin had received information regarding the financial status of a company. The information, leaked from a confidential corporate plan, was provided over the telephone from a source who wished to remain anonymous. The company obtained orders preventing Mr Goodwin from disclosing the confidential information and for delivery up under s 10 Contempt of Court Act 1981. The order compelled the applicant to divulge the identity of his source. The applicant appealed unsuccessfully to the Court of Appeal and House of Lords. He refused to disclose his source and was convicted of contempt and fined £5,000. Bill Goodwin learnt that he had no legal right to protect the source of his story.

---

141 See: Briggs (1995) Vol 5, at pp. 911–912.

142 Source: 'Whitehall sets November 1 Cruise Arrival: Troops stand by for the Greenham Missile Date', by David Fairhall, *Guardian*, 22 October 1983.

143 See: 'A source of great regret', by Peter Preston, *Guardian*, 5 September 2005.

144 (2002) 35 EHRR 18 (ECTHR).

When Mr Goodwin sought redress at the ECtHR, the Strasbourg court commented that it would be difficult to frame the law in this area with absolute clarity and that s 10 CCA 1981 was sufficiently clear ('*acte clair*') to satisfy the requirement of foreseeability. The ECtHR ruled that the order for disclosure of the source was not necessary (bearing in mind that publication of the confidential information was already prohibited by an injunction) and thus no breach of Article 10. This meant that the company's legitimate expectation for disclosure of the source (presumably an employee) and dissemination of the confidential information were outweighed by the interest of a free press in a democratic society.

See also
Chapter 2.3.1

The **Goodwin** judgment is a significant decision on the protection of journalists' sources. However, the s 10 CCA balancing test still leaves the courts to decide whether or not to make an order requiring a journalist to identify his sources. If journalists are forced to reveal their sources the role of the press as public watchdog could be seriously undermined because of the chilling effect that such disclosure would have on the free flow of information (see also: **Ashworth Hospital v MGN Ltd** (2001)[145] and **Interbrew SA v Financial Times** (2002)[146]).

So what can be done? The DPP may have to produce guidelines setting out when journalists are allowed to pay for information and when they must reveal their sources.[147]

 FOR THOUGHT

Is a court order for journalistic source disclosure necessary in a democratic society for the protection of the rights of an individual or a company? Discuss with reference to s 10 Contempt of Court Act 1981 (CCA) and relevant human rights legislation.

10.6 Regulating the communications industry

Despite the controlling commercial interests of politicians in the media in a few Western democratic states, leading to accusations of some interference, most countries now enjoy independent broadcasting and regulation, free from overt political manipulation and with relatively inexpensive licensing regimes that encourage diversity, equality and freedom of expression. In most countries the internet, radio and television are the main sources of news and information; yet there are still plenty of state-controlled media outlets, such as in China, which has banned Google and YouTube.

However, in July 2013 the UK Information Commissioner's Office took action against Google's updated privacy policy, together with all 28 EU Member States, demanding greater privacy protection across the EU. The ICO's statement read:

> We have today written to Google to confirm our findings relating to the update of the company's privacy policy. In our letter we confirm that its updated privacy policy raises serious questions about its compliance with the UK Data Protection Act. In particular, we believe that the updated policy does not provide sufficient information to enable UK users of Google's services to understand how their data will be used across all of the company's products. Google must now amend their privacy policy to make it more informative for individual service users. Failure to

---

145 [2001] 1 WLR 515 (CA Civ Div).
146 [2002] EWCA Civ 274.
147 For further discussion see: Costigan (2007).

take the necessary action to improve the policies compliance with the Data Protection Act by 20 September 2013 will leave the company open to the possibility of formal enforcement action.[148]

France, Germany and Spain wrote similar letters to the company, with France's Information Commissioner (Commission nationale de l'informatique et des libertés – CNIL) threatening fines if Google did not comply. Google responded:

Our privacy policy respects European law and allows us to create simpler, more effective services. We have engaged fully with the authorities involved throughout this process, and we'll continue to do so going forward.[149]

Google said in January 2012 that it would rewrite its privacy policies to unite them across its disparate sites such as YouTube, Maps, Shopping, Mail and Search so that people's data use would be unified. Despite warnings from the ICO and CNIL and others that the change might not be lawful, it implemented the change in March 2012.

Democracy demands a plurality of service providers to enable access by viewers, listeners or internet users to a wide range of sources and views. Equally accepted in most countries is an independent regulatory system that supervises an independent broadcasting industry which is also in charge of licensing the system. Arguably, proper delegation of responsibilities to an independent regulatory body set up by statute not only creates faith in the fairness of the licensing process but also removes governments from the potential political controversy which can be associated with the grant of broadcasting and broadband licences. In the European Member States, there exists additional legislation which regulates the broadcasting media in the form of the Audiovisual Media Services Directive (AVMSD),[150] now called the Television without Frontiers Directive. The AVMSD modernized TV advertising rules to better finance audio-visual content.

See below 10.8

In October 2011, the European Commission established a high-level group on media freedom and pluralism. The then European Commission Vice-President Neelie Kroes convened the first meeting of the High Level Group on Media Freedom and Pluralism to advise and provide recommendations for the respect, protection, support and promotion of media freedom and pluralism in Europe.[151] The Group examined whether legal frameworks and their application in Europe were adequate to ensure respect for media freedom and pluralism and recommended to the Commission how any new threats to media freedom and invasion of privacy should best be addressed.

Sometimes, broadcasting-related intellectual property issues, defamation disputes or trademark infringements also come under the auspices of a broadcasting regulator, although in most industrialized democratic countries such disputes are generally dealt with by law and the relevant courts. It would be unlikely and very costly for a broadcasting regulator to develop and retain the necessary in-house expertise to deal with such disputes, though greater power in this respect has been granted to Ofcom under the Digital Economy Act 2010.

See below 10.6.3

148 Source: ICO Press Statement of 4 July 2013.
149 Source: 'European watchdogs order Google to rewrite privacy policy or face legal action', by Charles Arthur, *Guardian*, 5 July 2013.
150 EC Directive 2007/65 'Audiovisual Media Services Directive' (AVMSD) of 11 December 2007.
151 Source: European Commission Press Release, 'Digital Agenda: high-level group to discuss freedom and pluralism of the media across the EU', 11 October 2011 at: http://europa.eu/rapid/press-release_IP-11-1173_en.htm?locale=en.

> 👁 **FOR THOUGHT**
>
> Does self-regulation by an organization like the Internet Watch Foundation (IWF) pose a threat to civil liberties? Should one not be able to view any material on the internet in the privacy of one's own home?

10.6.1 Broadcasting regulations

Until the early 1980s, Western European broadcasting was largely state-controlled. For example, advertising 'spots' were either not permitted or strictly controlled by state regulation, and increasingly by EU Treaty provision and EU Regulations.[152] This special regulatory framework still exists to a certain extent today, though it has been frequently challenged by independent broadcasting providers in recent times. The UK was one of the first European countries to dismantle this monopoly by the introduction of commercial broadcasting in 1954 via ITV, now legally known as Channel 3 or more commonly as ITV1.[153]

The broadcasting and communications sector broadly comprises the following areas of regulation:

- Broadcasting equipment, such as cameras and recording transmission equipment.
- Data transmission networks and associated cables and ducts; transmission networks, including masts and other large, fixed equipment.
- Equipment and software that supports fixed and mobile communications, such as telephone lines, video and satellite communications.
- Services, such as communications network providers and ISPs, systems integration, communications software, research and development.

A range of factors play a significant role in shaping this sector with key drivers in the telecommunications ('telecoms'), radio-communications ('radiocomms') and broadcasting equipment sector, including:

- globalization of the market for the manufacture and design of components, leading to major international players buying smaller, innovative businesses;
- new markets opening up as more countries develop a taste for technology;
- consumers and businesses viewing interaction with telecoms, radiocomms and broadcasting as an everyday experience;
- advances in the mainstream use of technology, such as digital technology, broadband and high definition;
- technology convergence bringing new innovative products to market along with improved performance.

---

152 See: **Commission v Kingdom of Spain (supported by United Kingdom of Great Britain and Northern Ireland)** (2011) (Case C-281/09) Judgment of the Court (First Chamber) of 24 November 2011. The case concerned 'advertising spots' and transmission times on Spanish national TV and the state's failure to fulfil obligations under Directive 89/552/EEC.

153 For further discussion see: Scherer (2013), Part 3 'Telecommunications laws in EU Member States', pp. 213–285.

The UK communications watchdog, Ofcom, has concurrent powers with the new regulator the Competition and Markets Authority (CMA).[154] The CMA investigates where there may be breaches of UK or EU prohibitions against anti-competitive agreements and abuses of dominant positions bringing criminal proceedings against individuals who commit the cartels offence under the Enterprise Act 2002 (EA02). Commission to create a new, powerful single competition authority, the Competition and Markets Authority (CMA). The new regulator, the CMA, has jurisdiction to carry out all reviews under UK merger control laws and all market investigations. It is now the primary enforcer of both civil and criminal competition laws, although the Serious Fraud Office (SFA) retains its concurrent power to bring criminal proceedings. Most of the OFT's existing consumer protection powers were transferred to other bodies, such as Trading Standards authorities.

See below 10.6.3.

10.6.2 Statutory powers: the Ofcom Broadcasting Code

Areas covered by any broadcasting or regulatory standards normally include the following guidelines:

- protection of minors;
- offence to human dignity;
- protection against harm, e.g. flashing lights; on-air hypnosis;
- no encouragement of behaviour which is harmful to health or safety;
- no incitement to crime and disorder;
- no incitement to hatred, contempt, racial hatred or on grounds of national or ethnic origin, colour, religion, sex, sexual orientation, age or mental or physical disability;
- rules on advertising and programming.

 FOR THOUGHT

You have been asked to set up an independent broadcasting regulator in a newly democratized state. What, on a practical level, are the considerations and practical obstacles to setting up such a regulator? Draft a code of standards for the new regulator.

10.6.3 Ofcom

The creation of Ofcom (the Office of Communications) in 2003 replaced the Broadcasting Standards Commission (BSC), the Independent Television Commission (ITC) and the Radio Authority, the regulators that previously dealt with complaints against broadcasters. From 25 July 2005, Ofcom operated under a single Broadcasting Code applicable across the UK communications industry. The Ofcom Broadcasting Code for TV and Radio provides a framework for standards of content, such as protection of the public from offensive or harmful material,[155] in line with EU legislation.[156] Two code regulations, for example, are that children under the age of 18 must be

---

154 As from April 2014, when CMA took over many of the functions and responsibilities of the Competition Commission and the Office of Fair Trading (OFT), The Enterprise and Regulatory Reform Act 2013 merged the OFT and the Competition Commission to create a new, powerful single competition authority, the Competition and Markets Authority (CMA). The new regulator, the CMA, has jurisdiction to carry out all reviews under UK merger control laws and all market investigations. It is now the primary enforcer of both civil and criminal competition laws, although the Serious Fraud Office (SFA) retains its concurrent power to bring criminal proceedings. Most of the OFT's existing consumer protection powers were transferred to other bodies, such as Trading Standards authorities.
155 Section 319(2)(f) Communications Act 2003 ('Ofcom's Standards Code').
156 The 2005 Code gave effect to a number of EC Directives relating to television: including Directive 89/552/EEC, as amended by EC Directive 97/36/EC ('sans frontières').

protected[157] and that the inclusion of advertising which may be misleading, harmful or offensive on TV or radio is prevented.[158]

Ofcom – also known as the 'media watchdog' – operates in the UK under statute, set up under the Communications Act 2003, which outlines the regulator's general responsibilities, further enhanced by the Digital Economy Act 2010 (DEA) which extended Ofcom's role to enforce copyright infringement. Section 2 DEA inserted new ss 124A to 124N into the Communications Act 2003 and put in place obligations on internet service providers (ISPs) to meet the criteria set out in the Broadcasting Code. Sections 17 and 18 DEA enable regulations to be made about the granting by a court of injunctions requiring service providers to block access to websites that are used, or are likely to be used, to infringe copyright.

Every time Ofcom receives a complaint from a viewer or listener, the regulator assesses it under the Broadcasting Code[159] to see if it needs further investigation. The Code sets standards for television and radio shows and all broadcasters have to follow these rules.

As has been shown, Ofcom's remit is now much wider than 'simply' broadcasting. For example, s 134C Communications Act 2003 requires Ofcom to report on matters specified by the Secretary of State (for Culture, Media and Sport) relating to internet domain names when requested to do so. These matters might include the management and distribution of internet domain names by registries and the misuse of domain names or the use of unfair practices by registries, end-users of domain names or their agents (known as registrars).

The Communications Act 2003 specifically highlights the furtherance of citizens' interests and the advancement of modern technology in line with consumers' needs. The Act is a considerable piece of legislation with 411 sections and 19 schedules. Many sections involve the incorporation of EU legislation relating to telecommunications and 'borderless' broadcasting.[160] Ofcom's principal duties are listed in section 3(1) of the Act, which reads:

> it shall be the principal duty of Ofcom, in carrying out their functions;
>
> (a) to further the interests of citizens in relation to communications matters; and
>
> (b) to further the interests of consumers in relevant markets, where appropriate by promoting competition.

Ofcom describes its responsibilities as falling into six main areas. These are:

1. Ensuring the optimal use of the electro-magnetic spectrum.
2. Ensuring that a wide range of electronic communications services are available throughout the UK, including high-speed data services.
3. Ensuring a wide range of TV and radio services of high quality and wide appeal.
4. Maintaining plurality in the provision of broadcasting.
5. Applying adequate protection for audiences against offensive or harmful material.
6. Applying adequate protection for audiences against unfairness or the infringement of privacy.

---

157 Section 319(2)(a) Communications Act 2003.
158 Section 319(2)(h) Communications Act 2003.
159 The Ofcom Broadcasting Code ('the Code'), the most recent version of which took effect on 21 March 2013, covers all programmes broadcast on or after 21 March 2013.
160 Anything in the Act which is inconsistent with EU legislation has been overridden by s 4 of the Act, such as s 4(4), which requires the regulator to pay attention to 'the desirability of encouraging the availability and use of high-speed data transfer services throughout the United Kingdom'.

Ofcom is also responsible for the specification of the procedural and enforcement aspects of these obligations through the approval or adoption of legally binding codes of practice. For example, ss 3 to 16 Communications Act 2003 require Ofcom to report on media content, such as infringement of copyright. Additionally, the Digital Economy Act 2010 covers online infringement of copyright, particularly in music, film and video games.

Section 355 of the Communications Act 2003 obliges the regulator to carry out periodic reviews and reallocation of (local) radio licences. Part of the remit involves the character of the service, the quality and range of programming and the amount of local content. Ofcom has other responsibilities, such as shaping public policy in the future of broadcasting and new media. Apart from watching over correct allocation of broadband width and ISP compliance, Ofcom also allocates and administers radio frequencies and bandwidths under its periodic 'spectrum trading process', the relevant legislation being the Wireless Telegraphy Act 2006.

Section 264 of the 2003 Act requires Ofcom to report at least every five years on the fulfilment of the public service remit for television by public service broadcasters, namely television services provided by the British Broadcasting Corporation (the BBC), Channel 4, Sianel Pedwar Cymru (S4C), Channel 3 services, and Channel 5 and 6. The public service remit involves the provision of a balanced diversity of high-quality content, which meets the needs and interests of different audiences in the UK.[161] Under the new s 264A of the 2003 Act, Ofcom is required to consider the wider delivery of public service media content on other platforms, such as the internet and video-on-demand programme services, and review the extent to which such content contributes towards the fulfilment of the public service objectives defined in s 264(6)(b) to (j).

See also Chapter 6.4.2

10.6.4 Ofcom enforcement and secondary legislation

As a statutory regulator, Ofcom takes enforcement action across a number of industry sectors and is able to use a range of statutory powers granted by:

- The Broadcasting Act 1996
- The Broadcasting Act 1990
- The Competition Act 1998
- The Enterprise Act 2002
- The Communications Act 2003
- The Wireless Telegraphy Act 2006
- The Digital Economy Act 2010
- Enterprise and Regulatory Reform Act 2013
- EU Regulations

Its main enforcement actions on behalf of citizens and consumers include the following aims and objectives to:

- encourage competition;
- resolve regulatory disputes between communications providers;
- enforce consumer protection law;
- enforce copyright law;
- encourage compliance;

---

161 Paragraphs (b) to (j) of s 264(6) of the 2003 Act provide detailed public service objectives underpinning this remit.

- protect members of the public from the inclusion of offensive and harmful material, from unfair treatment and from unwarranted infringements of privacy in television and radio programmes;
- protect and manage the radio spectrum.

In practical terms, this means that broadcasting enforcement continues to be the main aim, namely to secure public protection under the Broadcasting Code – in particular, paying close attention to participation television and the use of premium rate phone services (e.g. for competitions on TV or radio). There have been a number of investigations into dishonest competition practices, and Ofcom wants to ensure the market provides clear, honest and transparent value. In spectrum enforcement, the communications regulator principally targets the most persistent and harmful illegal equipment manufacturers and retailers and illegal users of the radio spectrum including illegal (pirate) broadcasters.

Ofcom became the regulator for postal services under the Postal Services Act 2011 (abolishing the then existing regulator, Postcomm).[162] This means that Ofcom has the power to:

- designate a universal service provider;
- approve a consumer redress scheme and require postal operators to be a member of that scheme;
- authorize appropriate consumer protection conditions;
- publish a statement of policy on information-gathering of postal services.

In March 2012, Ofcom's Review of postal users' needs concluded. The consultation document and Ofcom's research findings on the future of consumer and business needs of postal services in the UK found that people did not generally rely solely on postal services, namely the Royal Mail. From 2010, users were increasingly substituting post with electronic methods of communication such as email, telephone or text, online document-sharing and video-calling. Residential users in particular sent little mail: the volume of items they reported sending by post was on average 1.5 items per week (per user) compared with 3.5 items in 2006. Businesses sent more mail than residential users: 45 per cent of businesses spent under £10 per month on post, while 5 per cent sent over £450 per month. The mean average spent for businesses was around £245 a month in 2010. While letter volumes decreased, there has been a trend towards ordering more goods over the internet to be delivered by post: 35 per cent of residential users received packets at least once a month in 2012, a figure which has increased from 27 per cent in 2010.[163]

10.6.5 Measures to tackle online copyright infringement

Copyright plays a critical role in the creative industries, fostering innovation, entrepreneurialism and growth. As part of an effective copyright framework, Ofcom welcomed the Hargreaves Review[164] on copyright recommendation of an 'integrated approach' to addressing infringement, which emphasizes the development of legitimate services, alongside education and enforcement.

---

162 The Royal Mail and The Post Office are separate companies with independent Boards. Royal Mail – privatised in September 2013 – is the company that delivers parcels and letters: the provider of the universal postal service. The Post Office is the nationwide network of branches offering a range of postal, government and financial services and was not privatised. Under the Communications Act 2003, Ofcom is required to carry out an 'Impact Assessment' and annual regulatory financial controls via an independent auditor of the postal services. The universal postal service is protected in statute under the Postal Services Act 2011 and Ofcom has a duty to secure the provision of a six-day-a-week, uniform price service.
163 See: Office of Communications (Ofcom) (2012d).
164 Hargreaves (2011).

See Chapter 8.12.1

Work by the creative industries to increase the variety of attractive content available legitimately online has been furthered by copyright reform to modernize the licensing process.

The Digital Economy Act 2010 created new responsibilities for Ofcom to adopt measures aimed at significantly reducing levels of unlawful file-sharing via peer-to-peer (P2P) networks. The DEA set out two initial obligations on internet service providers in order to secure a co-ordinated approach, involving both copyright owners and ISPs. The act also provides powers to the Secretary of State (for Culture, Media and Sport) to require that ISPs implement technical measures against serious repeat infringers (see also: the Enterprise and Regulatory Reform Act 2013 (ERRA)).[165]

When British Telecom (BT) and TalkTalk lost their appeal against the judicial review of the government's controversial anti-piracy legislation (The Digital Economy Act 2010) in March 2012, the Government was finally given the green light to implement the DEA fully after the final legal challenge by the two ISPs.[166] Three Court of Appeal judges ruled that the DEA does not contravene EU law (Lady Justice Arden, Lord Justice Richards and Lord Justice Patten). This meant that the Government (via Ofcom) can now compel ISPs to send out warning letters to subscribers accused of illegal file-sharing. The ruling found that the DEA is compatible with EU law.

The DEA now requires ISPs to notify subscribers of allegations made by copyright owners that their account has been used for unlawful file-sharing and to maintain a list of the subscribers who receive multiple unchallenged notifications.[167] Subscribers who have allegedly breached online copyright – e.g. by illegal P2P downloading of music or films – must be provided with sufficient information, once Ofcom's notification of copyright breach (piracy) has been sent, so that they can challenge the basis under which the notification has been sent. Subscribers on Ofcom's 'blacklists' may have their details passed to relevant copyright owners, who may pursue legal action. Such disclosure of names to the copyright owner requires a court order. It goes without saying that any processing and disclosure of copyright infringers' data (subscriber) must adhere to relevant data protection laws.

In June 2012, Ofcom issued a consultation document on 'cost-sharing' for online copyright infringement (with a working title of the 'Initial Obligations Code' (IOC)). The Code then compels an individual copyright owner to share the costs of prosecution (and other civil legal actions) of online copyright infringement with the ISP. The order proposes that the copyright owner, together with the ISP, 'share' Ofcom's enforcement costs of pursuing the claim against the 'subscriber' (copyright infringer).[168] The secondary legislation in the form of the 'Cost Sharing Order' ('the Code') received Royal Assent in April 2013 and now provides the opportunity for efficient cost recovery by ISPs. As much as 75 per cent of the costs will be met by rights holders.

---

165 The Enterprise and Regulatory Reform Act received Royal Assent on 25 April 2013. The competition provisions came into force in April 2014. The biggest change is the merger of the Office of Fair Trading and the Competition Commission to create a new, powerful single competition authority. The new Competition and Markets Authority (CMA) has jurisdiction to carry out all reviews under UK merger control laws and all market investigations. The CMA is the primary enforcer of both civil and criminal competition laws, although the Serious Fraud Office (SFA) retains its concurrent power to bring criminal proceedings. Sections 74–78 Enterprise and Regulatory Reform Act 2013 deal with Copyright and rights in performances and exploitation of design derived from artistic work.

166 See: *R (on the application of (1) British Telecommunications, (2) TalkTalk Telecom Group plc v Secretary of State for Culture, Olympics, Media and Sport and (1) BPI (British Recorded Music Industry) Ltd, (2) British Video Association Ltd, (3) Broadcasting Entertainment Cinematograph and Theatre Union, (4) Equity, (5) Film Distributors' Association Ltd, (6) Football Association Premier League Ltd, (7) Motion Picture Association Inc, (8) The Musicians' Union, (9) Producers' Alliance for Cinema and Television Ltd, (10) Unite* [2012] EWCA Civ 232.

167 Under s 124D of the Communications Act 2003 (as inserted by the DEA 2010), Ofcom was given the duty to make a Code for the purpose of regulating the initial obligations of ISPs to send notifications and provide copyright infringement lists to copyright owners on request. Under s 403 of the Communications Act 2003, Ofcom must give notice of an order it is proposing to make, giving at least one month for representations to be made.

168 Official title of the SI 'Online Infringement of Copyright: Implementation of the Online Infringement of Copyright (Initial Obligations) (Sharing of Costs) Order 2012'. Ofcom's Consultation on the order was published on 26 June 2012.

Illegal downloaders started to receive warning letters from ISPs, such as BT, 0_2, TalkTalk, Virgin Media or Everything Everywhere (EE) from 1 March 2014 under the Code, warning them when there is an allegation from a film, TV or music company that there has been illegal downloading from their computer. Illegal copyright-infringing web users who receive three warning letters in a year will face having anonymous information of their downloading and file-sharing history provided to copyright owners, which could then be used to gain a court order to reveal the customer's identity and take legal action against piracy.

Internet users will be able to appeal against a report on their alleged infringement, at a cost of £20, which will be refunded if they are successful. Ofcom was establishing an appeals body and other elements necessary to police the Code (which implements anti-piracy provisions under the Digital Economy Act 2010) at the time of this book going to print. While copyright owners can already seek court orders against digital pirates, the new (Ofcom) Code is designed to enable them to take legal action against the most persistent alleged infringers.

Ofcom's Director of Internet Policy, Campbell Cowie, stated:

> . . . we must ensure our creative industries can protect their investment. They have the right to charge people to access their content if they wish, whether in the physical world or on the internet. . . . We are putting in place a system to educate people about copyright to ensure they know what legitimate content is and where to find it. The Digital Economy Act is an important part of protecting our creative industries against unlawful activity.[169]

Ofcom also has the duty to provide quarterly reports to the Secretary of State estimating levels of unlawful file-sharing and assessing the extent of legal action by copyright owners.

10.6.6 Ofcom adjudications and decisions

An important role arising from Ofcom's remit is to consider and adjudicate on, inter alia, fairness and privacy complaints, whereby recent case law has confirmed and recognized Ofcom's role in privacy issues.[170] Section 392 of the Communications Act 2003 gives Ofcom the power to punish breaches of the Code and impose penalties as it sees fit. Before determining how to publish, the regulator must consult the Secretary of State.[171]

There have been a number of prominent Ofcom adjudications in recent regulatory broadcasting history. One concerned the 'Shilpa Shetty' incident on Channel 4's Celebrity Big Brother in January 2007. The broadcast had been created and produced by Brighter Pictures, part of Endemol UK, and was broadcast by the Channel Four TV corporation on its Channel 4 service. The fifth instalment in the series of Celebrity Big Brother was broadcast in January 2007. Disagreements between the 'housemates' had developed, in particular, between Indian film actress and model Shilpa Shetty and the late Jade Goody, famous for being one of the first Big Brother contestants, as well as Jo O'Meara, former lead singer of the pop group S Club 7, and Playboy model and former Miss Great Britain, Danielle Lloyd. During the 26-week series, which ran until 28 January 2007, Ofcom received over 44,500 complaints about alleged racist bullying of Ms Shetty.

---

169 The author interviewed Campbell Cowie in August 2012 at Ofcom's Head Office, 2a Southwark Bridge Road, London, SE1 9HA.
170 For further discussion see: Epworth (2005).
171 Section 392(6) Communications Act 2003.

Following Ofcom's investigation into the 'Shilpa Shetty' affair, the regulator found that there were three events that had breached the Broadcasting Code, where Channel 4 had failed to handle the material appropriately and had not adequately protected members of the public from offensive material. These were:

1. Remarks about cooking in India by the housemates (transmitted 15 January 2007);
2. Danielle Lloyd's comment: 'I think she should fuck off home' (transmitted 17 January 2007);
3. Jade Goody's comment: 'I couldn't think of her surname. Why would I be talking to someone like that, I don't know what her surname is. What is it? Shilpa Cookamada, Shilpa whatever Rockamada, Shilpa Poppadom?' (transmitted 18 and 19 January 2007).

In particular, Ofcom found that Channel 4 had breached Rule 1.3 ('protection of children from offensive and unsuitable material') and Rule 2.3 ('offensive material') of the Code. Channel 4 was subsequently fined £1.5 million, which was 5 per cent of the broadcaster's qualifying revenue at that time.[172]

Another important investigation concerned the 'prank' played by Russell Brand and Jonathan Ross on their BBC Radio 2 shows on 18 and 25 October 2008 involving a series of messages left on the answerphone of the former *Fawlty Towers* star Andrew Sachs, who had played 'Manuel' in the 1970s sitcom series. When Mr Sachs cancelled a scheduled broadcast appearance on the late-night Ross–Brand radio show, Russell Brand and Jonathan Ross swore on air and left lewd messages on the actor's answering machine, telling him that Brand had had sex with his granddaughter. Immediately after the radio broadcast, the BBC received only two complaints. But Mr Sachs's agent, Meg Pool, enraged about the contents of the broadcast, contacted BBC Radio 2's controller, Lesley Douglas, on 23 October 2008, asking for an unreserved apology to Mr Sachs and his family. Ms Pool was also contacted by the *Mail on Sunday* for comment. On 26 October, the *Mail on Sunday* reported that 'the BBC could face prosecution over obscene phone calls to Andrew Sachs', which resulted in more than 27,000 public complaints to the BBC and Ofcom.

On 28 October 2008 Ofcom began its inquiry into the 'Ross–Brand affair' and on 3 April 2009 found the BBC to be in breach of the Broadcasting Code, namely Rule 2.1 ('generally accepted standards must be applied in all programmes'); that there had been a lack of clarity about the exact role in the programme of a senior figure at the agency that represented Russell Brand, such as the executive producer who represented the independent production company. Additionally, there had been a failure by the Controller of BBC Radio 2, Lesley Douglas, who had given the go-ahead for the transmission of the programme which included the offensive telephone recordings. Ofcom also ruled that there had been a general compliance failure by the Executive Producer to sign off the necessary compliance forms for the said programmes on 18 and 25 October 2008. Furthermore, that there had been a general lack of clarity about who had editorial oversight of the series. Ofcom also ruled that Rule 2.3 of the Broadcasting Code had been breached ('offensive material must be justified by the context') in that the radio broadcast had been gratuitously offensive, humiliating and demeaning. Rule 8.1 had also been breached (the standard requiring 'adequate protection for members of the public from unwarranted infringements of privacy'), in that the offensive broadcast had seriously infringed Mr Sachs's privacy and that of his family. For the Rules 2.1 and 2.3 breaches Ofcom imposed a fine of £70,000 on the BBC, and for Rule 8.1 an additional £80,000 was ordered for the contraventions.[173]

---

172 See: Adjudication of Ofcom Content Sanctions Committee – Channel Four Television Corporation in respect of its service Channel 4 of 24 May 2007.

173 Source: 'The Russell Brand Show', Ofcom Broadcast Bulletin Issue number 131, 6 April 2009.

Following Ofcom's findings, Russell Brand resigned from the BBC on 29 October 2008. Lesley Douglas, Radio 2's controller, resigned on 25 November. Mark Thompson, the then Director-General of the BBC, made a public apology for the serious breach of editorial compliance that had allowed grossly offensive material to be broadcast; he also apologized personally to Andrew Sachs and his family. Clearly, Ofcom's investigation into the 'Ross–Brand affair' had identified a general weakness in managerial control and compliance within the public sector broadcaster with the Broadcasting Code.

In July 2010, radio presenter Jon Gaunt lost his High Court 'freedom of expression' challenge against Ofcom. Gaunt was represented by the human rights group Liberty. Mr Gaunt challenged Ofcom's decision, which upheld complaints about a talkSPORT radio interview in which he described a local councillor as a 'Nazi' and an 'ignorant pig' (see: *Gaunt and Liberty v Ofcom* (2010)[174]). The radio interview on 7 November 2008 was with Michael Stark, the then Cabinet Member for Children's Services for Redbridge London Borough Council, about the council's controversial proposal to ban smokers from becoming foster parents on the ground that passive smoking has a propensity for harming foster children. The radio show host Jon Gaunt, who had himself been in care as a child and had then had foster parents, strongly opposed this proposal. He wrote a highly critical newspaper article published in the Sun on 7 November 2008 on this topic under the headline 'Fags didn't stop my foster mum caring for me'. The article was expressed in forceful and colourful language. It expressed great appreciation for foster parents generally, and Mr Gaunt criticized Redbridge Council as 'health and safety Nazis', referring to a 'master race philosophy' by Redbridge Social Services, whom he called 'The SS'. But the High Court did not hold this article to be unduly offensive.[175]

On the same day, 7 November, at around 11am, Jon Gaunt conducted a live interview with Mr Stark on talkSPORT radio. After carefully reviewing the transcript of the interview, the High Court stated that the first part of the radio interview had been reasonably controlled. Mr Gaunt had then asked Mr Stark about existing foster parents who only ever smoke in the open air. Mr Stark explained that the council would not drag children away from existing foster parents, but that smoker parents would not be used in the future, the trouble being that 'such people do smoke in the house', to which Mr Gaunt responded, 'So you are a Nazi, then?' After Mr Stark protested, Mr Gaunt reiterated, 'No you are, you're a Nazi', with the interview degenerating into an unseemly slanging match. When Mr Stark protested that the insult, as he saw it, was probably actionable, the claimant, Jon Gaunt, replied, 'Take action if you wish', adding, 'You're a health Nazi.' Mr Stark asked him just to shut up for a moment, and said in effect that the conditions of those in care were better than they had been. Jon Gaunt regarded this as an offensive insult to his own upbringing and called Mr Stark 'you ignorant pig' and, a little later, a 'health fascist' and an 'ignorant idiot'. About an hour after the broadcast, Jon Gaunt broadcast an apology, saying, 'The councillor wants me to apologize for calling him a Nazi. I'm sorry for calling you a Nazi.' Jon Gaunt was immediately suspended and the radio station terminated his contract without notice by letter, dated 17 November 2008.

Ofcom was asked to investigate the matter under the Broadcasting Code, after the regulator received 53 complaints from listeners. Ofcom issued its finding on 8 June 2009, stating that Mr Gaunt had breached rules 2.1 and 2.3 of the Code.[176] The regulator also expressed concern that talkSPORT's compliance procedures did not appear robust enough to deal with problematic

---

174 [2010] EWHC 1756 (QBD); see also: **R (on the application of Gaunt) v Ofcom** [2011] EWCA Civ 692.
175 [2010] EWHC 1756 judgment at para 3 (Blair J).
176 Rule 2.1 of the Code provides that generally accepted standards must be applied to the contents of television and radio services so as to provide adequate protection for members of the public from the inclusion in such services of harmful and/or offensive materials. Rule 2.3 provides that, in applying generally accepted standards, broadcasters must ensure that material which may cause offence is justified by the context. Such material may include, among other material, offensive language.

material being broadcast live. They recommended that the broadcaster should retain control over all output to ensure that presenters apply generally accepted standards and protect members of the public adequately from the inclusion of material which is offensive or harmful.

Mr Gaunt took legal action against Ofcom, claiming that its decision breached Article 10 ECHR; that is, it was an unlawful interference with his freedom of expression. Mr Millar QC, on behalf of the claimant, submitted that Ofcom's findings were a 'disproportionate interference with the claimant's freedom of expression' for which there was no pressing social need and that Ofcom's reasons were insufficient to justify the interference under Article 10(2) ECHR[177] (see for this approach: **R v Shayler** (2003)[178]). As to 'offensive expression', Mr Millar drew attention to **Handyside v UK** (1976),[179] where the Strasbourg court said that freedom of expression was not applicable only to inoffensive material, but also to that which offends, shocks or disturbs the state or any sector of the population. He argued that without pluralism, tolerance and broadmindedness there is no democratic society. Restrictions must therefore be proportionate to the legitimate aim pursued.

Mr Anderson QC, for Ofcom, submitted that the regulator's ruling did not interfere with the claimant's human rights since his employers had allowed the broadcaster a rather robust freedom of expression where Jon Gaunt had been able to express his own views on live radio. Mr Anderson referred to the judgment of Collins J in the **Ken Livingstone** case,[180] where the judge said that Mr Livingstone was not to be regarded as expressing a political opinion, attracting a high level of protection, when he indulged in offensive abuse of an *Evening Standard* journalist outside a City Hall reception. The facts of that case were different, but the general point made was that gratuitous offensive abuse cannot be regarded as the expression of political opinion.

In the judicial review action (**R (on the application of Gaunt) v Ofcom** (2011)[181]) – the High Court agreed. It did not see Ofcom's finding as an interference with Mr Gaunt's freedom of speech but ruled that the 'ignorant pig' comment and the continued bullying and insulting of the Redbridge councillor had amounted to gratuitous and offensive abuse and therefore breached the Broadcasting Code.

Ofcom also investigates unwanted and nuisance calls, such as silent calls. These are caused by automated systems known as 'diallers', which are used in call centres to generate and attempt to connect calls. If there are not enough call centre agents available to handle all of the successfully connected calls the person on the receiving end of the line will be greeted with a silent call. In April 2013, Ofcom fined telecoms giant TalkTalk £750,000 for making an excessive number of abandoned and silent calls to potential customers during the months of February and March 2011. Ofcom has clear guidelines on silent and abandoned calls, whereby the abandoned call rate should be no more than 3 per cent of live calls over a 24-hour period. The regulator's investigations found that during one of TalkTalk's telemarketing campaigns, the company exceeded this limit by a substantial amount, and during a separate marketing campaign it failed to check its technology's accuracy or to keep adequate records of calls.[182]

10.7 Film, video and games censorship

Deciding where to draw the line when regulating sexually explicit and violent material relates to the degree of control exercised by a society. Film and games regulators in each country have to

---

177 [2010] EWHC 1756 at para 17.
178 [2003] 1 AC 247 at para 23 (Lord Bingham) and paragraph 61 (Lord Hope).
179 (1976) 1 EHRR 737 at para 59 (ECHR).
180 *Livingstone v Adjudication Panel for England* [2006] HRLR 45.
181 [2011] EWCA Civ 692.
182 Source: Ofcom website on nuisance and silent calls at: http://consumers.ofcom.org.uk/files/2012/09/silent-calls.pdf.

See Chapter
7.4.1

decide where to place restrictions on access to these images, who can watch them and what is appropriate for adults. They can then decide for themselves what is appropriate. The means of regulating sexually explicit and violent material has been debated for decades. Arguments over what denotes a masterpiece or an obscenity in film, image or literature abound. Are the controversial images by Robert Mapplethorpe photographic masterpieces or obscene and explicit homoerotic images which must be banned from university libraries? Should J.D. Salinger's *The Catcher in the Rye* and D. H. Lawrence's *Lady Chatterley's Lover* be boycotted in school libraries?

That said, censorship of a film, song, play or book can draw attention to the material at issue, thereby making it even more popular. The BBC has frequently banned songs with 'naughty' lyrics or films with either raunchy or defamatory themes. In 1969, for example, 'Auntie Beeb' banned 'Je t'aime . . . moi non plus' by Serge Gainsbourg and Jane Birkin because of the song's heavy breathing (rather than its licentious lyrics which could only be understood by fluent French speakers), which was deemed far too inflammatory for *Top of the Pops* during the Woodstock era. 'Je t'aime' was also banned on national radio stations in Spain, Brazil, Italy, Poland and Portugal, was not played by many radio stations in the United States because it was deemed too risqué, and was denounced by the Vatican.

See also
Chapter
8.7.2

Frankie Goes to Hollywood also had their knuckles rapped by Radio 1 DJ Mike Read, who declared their single 'Relax' 'overtly obscene' and banned the single from his radio show in 1984 for its 'unwelcome' sexual overtones: 'Relax don't do it, when you want to go to it. Relax don't do it, when you want to come . . .' Predictably, both records were huge hits.

The British Board of Film Classification (BBFC – originally the British Board of Film Censors) has, from time to time, rejected foreign films even though they were openly released in their countries of origin, with sexual topics generally being the norm for rejection, such as *The Best of the New York Erotic Film Festival*, rejected in April 1975, or *Confessions of a Blue Movie Star*, a 1978 West German documentary by Wes Craven and Andrzej Kostenko. The 1969 film *99 Women* (Der Heiße Tod/99 donne/ 99 mujeres) by Jess Franco, released in Liechtenstein, Spain, Italy and West Germany, was rejected for its 'soft-core' women-in-prison lesbian nature with 'nasty torture sequences'. *The Awakening of Emily*, an Ann Summers production of 1976 featuring Koo Stark, was rejected by the BBFC for its sex scene of two women in a shower in 1983. Prince Andrew was dating the actress at that time but the relationship ended after it emerged that Ms Stark had appeared in the soft-porn film.

The BBFC has habitually banned prison films that feature women, such as *Deported Women of the SS* (*Le deportate della sezione speciale SS*), a 1976 Italian prison film by Rino Di Silvestro, or *Barbed Wire Dolls* (*Frauengefängnis*), a 1975 Swiss prison drama by Jess Franco, featuring 'caged women'. *Bamboo House Dolls* (Nu ji zhong ying), a 1974 Hong Kong film by Chin Hung Kuei, was banned by the BBFC because of its sensitive topic featuring a Japanese women's POW camp.

Prior to the 1990s it was not an uncommon occurrence that local authorities would ban films in their local cinemas, such as Ken Russell's *The Devils* and Stanley Kubrick's *A Clockwork Orange* in 1971, and Monty Python's *Life of Brian* in 1988. Even as late as 1996, Westminster Council banned *Crash* by David Cronenberg, a film first premiered at the 1996 London Film Festival and initially permitted by the BBFC. When Westminster Council demanded cuts to certain parts of this sexually violent film – solely for screenings in Westminster – the distributors declined, and the film was therefore banned from screens in the West End, including Leicester Square. However, cinemagoers could easily see the film in neighbouring Camden, where that council allowed the film to play uncut with its BBFC certificate. This meant that local councils were effectively reclassifying films.

Hally (2012) found that liberal councils, such as Manchester, were frequently ahead of BBFC policy and practice during the 1950s and 1960s, first in having an adults-only category before the 'X' certificate, then in relaxing the strictures against screen nudity (the naturist films) and over artistic sex and 'bad language' (e.g. *Ulysses*). More conservative councils such as Sale continued trying to hold back the tide of 'X' films. Manchester tended to be more liberal than the British Board of Film Censorship (as it was known then) on matters of nudity, sex and language but less so on issues of violence and disorder.[183]

10.7.1 *The Mary Whitehouse Experience* and *The Exorcist*

The Mary Whitehouse Experience was a topical comedy show devised by Bill Dare, starring young Cambridge graduates David Baddiel, Robert Newman, Hugh Dennis and Steve Punt. It began on BBC Radio 1 in 1988 and was moved from its Friday lunchtime slot to a late-night slot in 1989 because of its 'raunchiness'. It then moved to BBC TV in 1990, produced by the same company as *Spitting Image*, running for 13 episodes. The show mixed stand-up comedy monologues with sketches and impressions. The show was named after Mary Whitehouse, the prominent campaigner for public morality who made it her life's quest to highlight public decency and the moral decline of television standards – particularly at the BBC. Mrs Whitehouse became the first General Secretary of the National Viewers' and Listeners' Association in 1965. The first chairman of the subsequent BSC (Broadcasting Standards Council), Lord Rees-Mogg, credited Mrs Whitehouse for her influence on the setting-up of the Council in 1988 and for ensuring that the public view was always taken into account.

See Chapter 7.2.1

Mrs Whitehouse threatened legal action a number of times, including against famous BBC titles such as *Monty Python's Flying Circus*, *The Kenny Everett Television Show* – with its skimpily-clad dance troupe, Hot Gossip, run by Arlene Phillips – and *Doctor Who*. Not surprisingly, she also threatened to take the BBC to court over the 'Whitehouse Experience', demanding an alternative title, such as 'The William Rees-Mogg Experience' (see also: ***Whitehouse v Lemon*** (1979)[184]). But the BBC staunchly kept the title and the show became a massive hit, particularly with its famous sketch 'History Today', where Newman and Baddiel played two old historians who discussed an important historical issue in a very childish fashion.

When the film *The Exorcist* opened in America on 26 December 1973, the response was immediate and extraordinary. It is based on a book by William Peter Blatty, published in 1971, and depicts a riveting demonic possession and subsequent exorcism of a young girl in Washington DC. Despite much press attention in advance of the film's release, the 'Classification and Ratings Administration' of the Motion Picture Academy of America (MPAA) granted *The Exorcist* an uncut 'R' rating ('for strong language and disturbing images'), allowing minors to view the film if accompanied by an adult. MPAA President Jack Valenti pointed out that *The Exorcist* contained 'no overt sex' and 'no excessive violence', a conclusion echoed by the generally cautious Catholic Conference, which rated the film 'A-IV', an adult classification meaning that the film was 'moral, but may offend some [adult] viewers'. Yet Washington police barred persons under the age of 17 from showings of the movie in spite of the MPAA's 'R' rating. Eventually, Marvin Goldman, head of the KB Theatre chain, which owned the Cinema Theatre in DC where the movie was first shown, told the *Washington Post* that he would comply with the [MPAA] ruling, stating that the movie should have been rated X (no one under 17 admitted) in the first place.[185] Walter Cronkite devoted a full 10 minutes of his legendary CBS news programme to 'The Exorcist Phenomenon' and the history of demonic possession.

The film struck a unique chord with audiences around the world. In Milan, the crowd at a packed news conference refused to leave a museum where the film's Director, William Friedkin, and technical adviser Father Thomas Bermingham were answering questions about *The Exorcist*. In Rome, the film made the national news when a sixteenth-century church across the street from a cinema

---

183 See: Hally (2012).
184 [1979] AC 617.
185 Source: 'Exorcist: No one under 17 admitted', by Tom Shales, *Washington Post*, 4 January 1974.

where the film premiered was struck by lightning, causing an ancient cross to plummet from its roof onto the pavement below. At a preview screening in New York, one audience member had to be helped out after becoming dizzy, provoking a wave of press reports of fainting, vomiting and other hysterical reactions. By the time The Exorcist came to the UK, rumours of its traumatizing power had grown to such proportions that the St John Ambulance Brigade were standing by for the first showings around London.

But The Exorcist was immediately banned by the BBFC, due to Mrs Whitehouse's urging them to prohibit it. She called the film 'outright nasty – blasphemous and evil', despite the fact she had never seen a frame of it. She relied purely on adverse media coverage such as Stanley Kaufmann's comment in New Republic: 'This is the most scary film I've seen in years – the only scary film I've seen in years . . . If you want to be shaken – and I found out, while the picture was going, that that's what I wanted – then The Exorcist will scare the hell out of you.'[186] The British film board eventually granted an 'X' certificate to The Exorcist in January 1974, which allowed over-18s to view it without cuts or alterations. At the Golden Globe awards of 1974, The Exorcist picked up awards for Best Film, Best Director (William Friedkin), Best Screenplay (William Peter Blatty) and Best Supporting Actress (Linda Blair), while the Oscars that year generated 10 nominations including Best Picture, Best Screenplay (Blatty) and Best Sound. In box-office terms, the movie became the biggest-grossing hit in Warner Brothers' history, nearly trebling the $34m gross of the studio's previous record holder, My Fair Lady.[187]

Even after Mrs Whitehouse officially retired in 1994, she continued to vent her spleen well into her nineties from her nursing home, against the 'crassness' of the BBC in particular. Tainted with an image as a blue-rinse reactionary, Mrs Whitehouse endured years of mockery. In her book Whatever Happened to Sex, she explained that as a happy family woman she had nothing against sex, but only against its exploitation in the media.[188] After Mrs Whitehouse's death in 2001, complaints to the Independent Television Commission (ITC)[189] about taste and decency rose by 50 per cent. In 1999, Mrs Whitehouse's crusade was taken up by Tory frontbencher Ann Widdecombe. More than 10 years later, in October 2010, Miss Widdecombe emerged as an unexpected star when she appeared in the popular BBC TV series Strictly Come Dancing. As she took to the dance floor with partner Anton du Beke, bookmakers slashed her odds of winning the show from 100:1 to 12:1, placing her ahead of Felicity Kendal at 14:1.

10.7.2 The British Board of Film Classification

The British Board of Film Classification (BBFC) is an independent regulator and censor of film, video,[190] DVDs and video games.[191] The board was set up in 1912, then known as the British Board of Film Censors, with the aim of bringing a degree of uniformity to nationally acceptable film standards. From the mid-1920s on, it became general practice for local authorities to accept the decisions of the board.

---

186 Kaufmann's quote in New Republic, as quoted in Travers and Reiff (1974), pp. 152–154.
187 Source: 'Entertainment: The Exorcist – hype or horror?', Mark Kermode, BBC Radio 1 Online, 2 November 1998.
188 Source: 'Mary Whitehouse: Moral crusader or spoilsport?' BBC News Online, 23 November 2001, available at http://news.bbc.co.uk/1/hi/uk/763998.stm.
189 The ITC ceased to exist on 18 December 2003 and its duties were assumed by Ofcom (the Office of Communications), the new communications sector regulator. Ofcom inherited the duties of the then five existing regulators, namely The Broadcasting Standards Commission (BSC), the Independent Television Commission (ITC), Oftel, the Radio Authority and the Radiocommunications Agency.
190 In addition there are the Video Packaging Regulations 1985 and the Statutory Instruments SI No. 911 that brought the Video Recordings (Labelling) Regulations 1985 into UK law on 12 June 1985.
191 Computer games are generally exempt from legal classification in the UK but under the Video Recordings Act 1984 (as amended) some games can lose this exemption and are required to be classified by the BBFC. Exemption is usually lost because of grossly violent or sexual content or because the game disc contains video footage that is not part of the game.

When T. P. O'Connor was appointed President of the BBFC in 1916,[192] one of his first tasks was to give evidence to the Cinema Commission of Inquiry, set up by the National Council for Public Morals of the time.[193] He summarized the board's policy by listing 43 grounds for a film's exclusion or rejection. Some of the topics included:

- the irreverent treatment of sacred subjects;
- drunken scenes carried to excess;
- vulgar accessories;
- the *modus operandi* of criminals;
- nude figures;
- indecorous dancing;
- excessively passionate love scenes;
- realistic horrors of warfare including scenes and incidents calculated to afford information to the enemy;
- subjects dealing with India in which British Officers are seen in an odious light;
- scenes laid in disorderly houses.

The BBFC is widely regarded as one of the most trusted and highly regarded non-governmental organizations in the UK, funded by the film, DVD and games industries. Generally, the BBFC rejects, bans or passes films (as well as DVDs and some video games). It may alter film categories under its own licensing jurisdiction, even though the film may have been given a different category in another country (see *The Exorcist* above). Trading Standards and law enforcement officers have the power to seize illegal video works including, but not limited to, DVDs, Blu-rays and video games. The BBFC is designated by the Government (the Department of Culture, Media and Sport) to provide evidence to help secure convictions under the terms of the Video Recordings Act (VRA) 1984. The BBFC will issue a Certificate of Evidence under the VRA 1984 or the Criminal Procedure (Scotland) Act 1995. This evidence is admissible in court as 'standalone' evidence and does not require anyone from the BBFC to attend as a witness.

The 'film censor' keeps a fascinatingly accurate statistical record, dating back to 1931, showing detailed descriptions of each film, DVD etc., with censorship comments (this can be viewed online). Since 2000, the BBFC has operated under a series of published guidelines, which regulate the basis of its work and include public consultation exercises, the last being in 2004. As the board has developed different sections of its classification process, standards and censorship have changed with evolving pieces of legislation in line with public opinion and changing morality.

The BBFC rates about 10,000 pieces a year. Local authorities have the power to decide under what circumstances films are shown in cinemas, but they nearly always choose to follow the advice of the regulator. Looking at the statistics over the past 20 years, the board has rejected fewer films; for example, *Murder-Set-Pieces* in 2008 and *Terrorists, Killers and other Wackos* in 2005, that is, films which generally include clips of real torture and execution. In 2010, for example, of 407 films censored, five had to be cut (1.2 per cent), compared with 1983, when the board cut 123 of the 514 submitted films (24 per cent) – the highest censorship rate in 20 years.

With increasing online film and video the BBFC is now working a 'traffic light' censoring system that warns users about the film footage they are about to access online. The regulator has

---

192 President from 11 December 1916 to 18 November 1929. Thomas Power O'Connor (1848–1929), known as T. P. O'Connor, was a journalist and Irish nationalist, as well as a Member of Parliament at Westminster for nearly 50 years.

193 Source: National Council for Public Morals (1917).

developed this new classification system ('Watch & Rate') which allows the public to rate online film content. The regulator works with the Dutch media regulator NICAM (Netherlands Institute for the Classification of Audiovisual Media) on this system to rate user-generated content that might ordinarily slip through the net and go unclassified. The system involves the viewer uploading the material and providing details about its content. This online film censoring system already exists as in Italy, provided by the commercial broadcaster Mediaset. Although the BBFC has no specific powers to rate online material, a number of companies have been keen to seek their classifications on a voluntary basis, including video-on-demand service Netflix, which sought a certificate for online-only series such as *House Of Cards*.[194]

10.7.3 Film classification and censorship

The BBFC is governed by several pieces of legislation, the most significant being the Video Recordings Acts (VRA) of 1984 and 2010, which particularly affect classification standards. The 1984 Act requires all 'video works' (films, TV programmes, video games, etc.) which are supplied on a disc, tape or any other device capable of storing data electronically, to be classified by the BBFC, unless they fall within the definition of an exempted work. Section 4A of the 1984 VRA requires 'special regard' to be given to the likelihood of video works being viewed in the home and to any harm that may be caused to potential viewers or, through their behaviour, to society by the manner in which the work deals with criminal behaviour, illegal drugs, violent behaviour or incidents, horrific behaviour or incidents, and human sexual activity, particularly when video works deal with:

(i)   criminal behaviour;
(ii) illegal drugs;
(iii) violent behaviour or incidents;
(iv) horrific behaviour or incidents; or
(v)   human sexual activity.

The Video Recordings Act 2010 repealed and then brought back into force parts of the Video Recordings Act 1984.[195] The reintroduction of the 1984 act was deemed necessary after Parliament forgot to notify the European Commission in August 2009 of the (original) existence of the 1984 act.[196] This meant neither the 1984 nor the 2010 VRA were initially in accordance with Directive 98/34/EC.[197] The Digital Economy Act 2010 additionally passed responsibility for games ratings to the Video Standards Council, particularly for those video games that include violence or encourage criminal activity. Video games with specific themes or content – such as the *Grand Theft Auto* series – must also be submitted to the BBFC to receive a legally binding rating in the same way as videos. In considering all these issues, the BBFC needs to be mindful of the possible effect not only on children but also on other vulnerable groups.

The Obscene Publications Acts 1959 and 1964 made it illegal to publish a work in the UK which is regarded as 'obscene' in content (as a whole). The film, DVD, game, etc. must have the tendency to 'deprave and corrupt', unless the 'publication' can be justified as being for the 'public

---

194 Source: British Board of Film Classification announcement, 11 July 2013 at: www.bbfc.co.uk/industry-services/digital-video-ratings.

195 Section 1 VRA 2010 ('Repeal and revival of provisions of the Video Recordings Act 1984'): ss 1 to 17, 19, 21 and 22 of the VRA 1984 ceased to be in force.

196 See: House of Commons, Parliamentary debate of 6 January 2010, Hansard, column 181–209.

197 EC Directive 98/34/EC laying down a procedure for the provision of information in the field of technical standards and regulations and of rules on Information Society services of 22 June 1998.

good' on the grounds that it is in the interests of science, art, literature or learning or other objects of general concern.

The Public Order Act 1986 makes it illegal to distribute or play to the public a recording of images or sounds which are threatening, abusive or insulting if the intention is to stir up racial hatred or hatred on the grounds of sexual orientation.[198]

See Chapter 7.3

There are two acts which cover animal welfare issues in films. The Cinematograph Films (Animals) Act 1937 renders it illegal to show any scene 'organised or directed' for the purposes of a film that involves the cruel treatment of any animal. Section 1 ('production of films involving cruelty to animals') reads:

> No person shall exhibit to the public, or supply to any person for public exhibition (whether by him or by another person), any cinematograph film (whether produced in Great Britain or else-where) if in connection with the production of the film any scene represented in the film was organised or directed in such a way as to involve the cruel infliction of pain or terror on any animal or the cruel goading of any animal to fury.

The Animal Welfare Act 2006 makes it illegal to show or publish a recording of an animal fight which has taken place in the UK since 6 April 2007. This is to combat illegal dog fighting (and the breeding of dangerous dogs for fights), habitually filmed and uploaded by criminals on to YouTube.

In May 2013, a controversial new video featuring the latest single by David Bowie, 'The Next Day' was streamed on YouTube. It was immediately banned by the movie regulator for its blasphemous and obscene content under the Obscene Publications Act 1959. The BBFC asked YouTube to take the video down from its UK site. However, a day later, the video was once again up on the site, with a YouTube spokesperson telling *Billboard* magazine: 'With the massive volume of videos on our site, sometimes we make the wrong call. When it's brought to our attention that a video has been removed mistakenly, we act quickly to reinstate it.' Alongside Bowie, the promotional video features actors Gary Oldman and Marion Cotillard in a pub with a cast and crew of religious characters. Bowie plays a Christ-like figure, Oldman portrays a priest and Cotillard plays a saint-like character while a cardinal hands out cash with a nun praying.[199]

BBFC examiners normally view video and DVD submissions on their own ('solo viewing'). Films for cinema release, video games and pornography submissions are classified in teams of two. Controversial works, such as extreme reality material, are viewed in teams of three. Games are measured by the regulator's IT department, who assess how long examiners will need to play the game by viewing all its video elements. Many films and videos are submitted in foreign languages – most notably Hindi and Cantonese – and examiners with linguistic skills then view these works. Where the work is in a language not spoken by any of the examiners and there are no subtitles, the Board will use an interpreter, who will sit alongside the examiner or team. BBFC examiners log the following details:

- general context: plot, characters, outline of individual scenes;
- timings of classification moments, including camera angles, type of shots, on- and off-screen moments;
- bad language, sex and drug references, etc.

---

198 Section 22 Public Order Act 1986.
199 Source: 'New David Bowie video reinstated after YouTube ban. The religious themed promo for "The Next Day" had "contravened"' the site's terms of use.' *New Musical Express*, 9 May 2013 at: www.nme.com/news/david-bowie/70180 gpDs1RIt MyO2t8.99.

The BBFC then examines the overall tone of a film, DVD or video game and assesses how these may affect the classification of each. A 'U' ('Universal') film should be suitable for audiences aged four years and over, allowing very mild bad language, such as 'damn' and 'hell'; for example, the 1964 Walt Disney film, *Mary Poppins*, featuring Julie Andrews and Dick van Dyke.

A 'PG' (Parental Guidance) film should not disturb a child aged around eight. There may be mild bad language, such as 'shit' or 'son of a bitch', and violence is only acceptable in a historical or fantasy setting. An example would be the 2007 film, *Mr Bean's Holiday*, starring Rowan Atkinson, or Michael Jackson's *This Is It*,[200] released following the legendary pop singer's death in June 2009.

No one under 15 is legally allowed to see, buy or rent a certificate '15'-rated film, DVD or video game. This classification generally includes strong violence, frequent strong language such as 'fuck', and brief scenes of sexual activity or violence are permitted – so are discriminatory language and drug-taking. A games example would be *Castlevania: Lords of Shadow* (2010), which contains 'strong bloody violence'.

See below
10.7.4

No one under 18 is legally allowed to see a certificate '18'-rated film in the cinema, or to rent or buy the DVD or video game. Films or games rated '18' are essentially adult works, and generally include very strong violence and/or sexual activity with frequently strong language such as 'cunt'. The regulator occasionally orders cuts to '18' films or games, particularly where the material is in breach of criminal law, such as portraying extremely violent or dangerous acts or illegal drug use, causing potential harm to public health or morals. Examples include the games series, *Grand Theft Auto* (GTA) or the film *A Clockwork Orange*.

As the internet has provided greater choice and freedom to download films and games, the BBFC has recognized that such online content also needs to be classified before a film can be downloaded. The regulator's own research found that the majority of viewers still consider it important to be able to check the suitability of films they download from trusted sources and particularly for parental guidance.[201] Some recent online classification decisions include:

WHO NEEDS ENEMIES (Certificate 18)

A British crime drama about a strip club owner who takes revenge on an old friend when he discovers his club is being used to entertain wealthy paedophiles. It is rated 18 for very strong language. There are repeated and often aggressive uses of very strong language ('c**t') and multiple uses of strong language ('f**k' and 'motherf***er'), as well as some racist language. The film also contains strong violence with occasional glimpses of blood, and brief scenes of suffocation. There are also oblique and discreet references to child sex abuse and infrequent scenes of hard drug use.[202]

BASTARDS (Certificate 12A)

A documentary that follows a young village woman as she fights to have her daughter legitimised in Morocco. There are three uses of moderate language ('bitch'). A man tells another 'why would I want to see that bitch?' referring to his niece who is sitting inside a car. Standing

---

200 Feature film directed by Kenny Ortega. The cast includes: Michael Jackson, Kenny Ortega, Orianthi. Columbia Pictures Corporation Ltd. Classified 27 October, 2009 as PG.
201 See: British Board of Film Classification (BBFC) (2011).
202 BBFC release date 16 August 2013. Director: Peter Stylianou. Cast includes: Michael McKell, Ian Pirie, Emma Barton, Kris Johnson, Glen Fox.

directly outside her as she remains seated, he shouts 'You bitch, go and look for the real father.' In another scene, a woman retells a story about her lover who was forced to have a DNA test by the court, recalling him saying to her, 'Celebrate all you like, you bitch'. Other language includes 'bastard' and 'slut'. There are also references to domestic violence as a woman talks about her married life, saying there was 'nothing but beatings' and that she was forced to sleep with him every night. She adds that her husband's parents also told him to beat her, making reference to bruises and being hit with a belt. In court, a man talks about his niece being suicidal and there is reference to a woman being too young to be touched. A woman says 'he took my virginity, he raped me' and then is made to swear an oath that 'he took my virginity legally'.[203]

10.7.4 Screen and internet violence

Can screen violence really lead to actual violence? This has been the question that legislators and regulators have asked themselves for years. Dr Guy Cumberbatch, Chartered Psychologist and Director of The Communications Research Group, undertook extensive research in this field. In a report to the Video Standards Council (2004), Cumberbatch established that screen violence does influence children's behaviour, particularly their style of play, which changed in line with the programmes they watched on TV, or DVD or the video games they played. He gave the examples of *Power Rangers*, *Ninja Turtles* and *Spiderman*.[204]

The American film director Stanley Kubrick had moved to England in 1962 to film *Lolita*, his motivation being that the UK would prove to have laxer censorship laws than the USA. But he fell foul of the Obscene Publications Act 1959. He subsequently made a large number of films including *Dr Strangelove* (with Peter Sellers), *2001: A Space Odyssey* and *Eyes Wide Shut*.

See Chapter 7.3

Kubrick's 1971 film *A Clockwork Orange*, based on an adaptation of Anthony Burgess's novel of 1962, proved to be a controversial film. It worried the Government to such an extent that before the film's general release in January 1972, Home Secretary Reginald Maudling arranged a private viewing of the film. *A Clockwork Orange* is a dark satirical film depicting Alex (Malcolm McDowell), a charismatic delinquent who engages in 'ultra-violence', including rape, performed to Beethoven's music. The BBFC had passed the film with an 'X' rating, requiring no cuts (the age bar for an 'X'-rated film had just been raised from 16 to 18). With the film's general release, the BBFC had advised the distributors, Warner Brothers, that the film portrayed 'an unrelieved diet of vicious violence and hooliganism'.

Kubrick became a target for hate mail and abusive phone calls in the UK after a number of rapes and murders in the early 1970s were linked to the film, including a sex attack in Lancashire carried out by a gang chanting the Gene Kelly song 'Singin' in the Rain'. This resulted in Kubrick secretly withdrawing the film by arranging with Warners that the film would just be allowed to die off quietly, after further allegations that *A Clockwork Orange* was inspiring young people to copy its scenes of violence. Stanley Kubrick died on 7 March 1999, aged 70, and the director's widow, German-born actress and painter Christiane, retained all consultation rights on the re-released *A Clockwork Orange* in the same year. In the film a large floral oil painting by Christiane can be seen during the famous 'Singin' in the Rain' scene.

Since the arrival of internet-based audio-visual services it has been difficult for a succession of governments to create statutory provisions for movie downloads and interactive internet-based games, particularly those that display an extraordinary amount of screen violence. There is a fine line between privacy – what can be viewed or played in one's own home – and the continuation of freedom of expression.

---

203 BBFC release date 2 September 2013. Director: Deborah Perkin. Cast includes: Rabha El Haymar and Deborah Perkin.
204 See: Cumberbatch (2004).

FOR THOUGHT

How far should film and games censorship go – given the fact that anything can now be viewed in private on the internet?

10.8 Advertising and online censorship

In July 2013, a TV advertisement for the (Scottish) soft drink Irn-Bru, created by Edinburgh's Leith Agency, attracted 176 complaints from viewers. The TV 'ad' featured a mother showing off her cleavage to her son's teenage friends as she is cleaning the kitchen table. One of her teenage son's friends looks at her cleavage and she says: 'New push-up bra. Amazing eh?'

The son is initially appalled while his friends gawp, but after a sip of Irn-Bru, he says: 'Looking good mum'. She then leans forward to clean the table again, with the boys watching, then says, 'C'mere you', before embracing her son against her chest. He looks uncomfortable, then drinks more Irn-Bru and smiles. The mother says, 'group hug?' and the friends jump from their chairs. The ad's catch line, 'Irn-Bru – gets you through' is written on two balloons balanced behind two cans of the soft drink.[205]

Most of the complainants said that the Irn-Bru advertisement was offensive and irresponsible, as the scene between the mother and the young men was sexual and inappropriate. Some claimed the ad was sexist and demeaning to women, while some said it was scheduled at an inappropriate time when children could have been viewing.

In its ruling, the Advertising Standards Authority (ASA) noted that the interaction between the mother and the two boys did not constitute irresponsible behaviour and cleared the advertisement for general viewing. A spokesman for the ASA said:

> Although we noted that some complainants had interpreted the action in the ad as portraying an inappropriate relationship between the mum and the son's friends, we did not consider that their interaction was a portrayal of irresponsible behaviour. We considered that the action relied on the mum being confident and attractive, but not consciously or overtly behaving in a sexualised or flirtatious way. We also considered that the focus of the ads was the son's embarrassment at the effect his mum's appearance was having on his friends. Therefore, and particularly in the context of ads intended to portray a surreal and light-hearted comedic approach, we did not consider that the action or depiction of the female protagonist was sexist or demeaning and concluded that the ads were not in breach of the code.[206]

In October 2012, Natalie Portman's eyelashes were the subject of intense scrutiny after a Christian Dior advert for mascara featuring the actress and the 'miracle effects' of the make-up was banned for misleading consumers. The magazine advertisement for the 'Dior Show New Look' mascara showed an image of the actress and model, Natalie Portman, with accompanying text stating: 'Lash-multiplying effect volume and care mascara. The miracle of a nano brush for an unrivalled lash creator effect. It delivers spectacular volume-multiplying effect, lash by lash.'

Cosmetics rival L'Oreal UK had challenged the Dior advertisement, complaining to the Advertising Standards Authority that it had misleadingly exaggerated the likely effects of the

---

205 Source: 'Irn-Bru "push-up bra" ad cleared despite more than 170 complaints', by John Reynolds, *Guardian*, 10 July 2013 (including the Irn-Bru video clip) at: www.theguardian.com/media/2013/jul/10/irn-bru-push-up-bra-ad.
206 ASA Ruling of 10 July 2013.

product. The ASA investigated and subsequently banned the Dior mascara advert, stating in its ruling that Dior had exaggerated the effect of the product on Portman's eyelashes. In its defence, Dior said that it had received no complaints and that the advert was 'stylised' and 'aspirational', which demonstrated that the ad did not go beyond likely consumer expectations.[207]

10.8.1 Dealing with non-compliant advertisers

Each year, the UK public sees millions of advertisements ('ads'), direct marketing and sales promotions about products, services, causes and awareness campaigns. The vast majority of ads comply with the advertising rules. The UK advertising regulatory system is a mixture of self-regulation and co-regulation for the publication and broadcast industries. There are a number of bodies which make the system work, including the Advertising Standards Authority, Committees of Advertising Practice (CAP), the Advertising Standards Board of Finance (Asbof), which raises the funds for the self-regulation for all non-broadcast advertising, and the Broadcast Advertising Standards Board of Finance (Basbof), which raises the funds for the self-regulation for all broadcast advertising.

The Committee of Advertising Practice is the self-regulatory body that creates, revises and enforces the CAP Code (for non-broadcast advertisers). CAP's members include organizations that represent the advertising, sales promotion, direct marketing and media businesses. Through their membership of CAP member organizations, or through contractual agreements with media publishers and carriers, those businesses agree to comply with the CAP Code so that marketing communications are legal, decent, honest and truthful and consumer confidence is maintained. CAP writes and maintains the UK Advertising Codes, which are administered by the ASA; the committee also offers the industry authoritative advice and guidance on how to create campaigns that comply with the advertising code and its rules.

The background to this self-regulatory system goes back to the 1970s, when the UK Government recognized that the standards of advertising were becoming increasingly misleading, particularly in non-broadcast advertising (broadcast advertising was then controlled under statute by the Independent Television Companies' Association – ITCA).[208]

Asbof was formed in January 1975 in order to enhance the funding of the ASA, and introduced the levy scheme which continues to the present. Asbof was deliberately constructed as a separate company, to handle the funding of the ASA at arm's length, thus ensuring the ASA's operational independence. Under this, advertisers pay a levy of £1 per £1,000 on display advertising in the press and magazines, and on cinema, outdoor and, since August 2004, internet advertising. The leading advertising industry bodies therefore agreed to raise funds for an enhanced system of non-broadcast self-regulation, to be provided by the ASA.

Since 1992, Asbof has also collected the Mailing Standards levy. This funds the self-regulation of direct mail, including the work of the Mailing Preference Service (MPS) and the ASA. This levy is £2 per £1,000 on the cost of direct mail postage, and is collected in the main by Royal Mail, which includes this on their postage mailing invoices. The Mailing Preference Service is a free service to enable consumers to have their names and home addresses in the UK removed from lists and databases used by the industry. It is actively supported by Royal Mail and all directly involved trade associations and fully supported by the Information Commissioner's Office.

---

207 Source: ASA Adjudication on Parfums Christian Dior (UK) / Ltd Parfums Christian Dior (UK) Ltd t/a Complaint Ref: A12-196932, Dior, 24 October 2012.

208 Now the United Kingdom Independent Broadcasting (or UKIB), an affiliation of three British independent TV production companies and broadcasters. The primary function of its predecessor (ITCA) was to represent independent British television interests as a member of the European Broadcast Union. The members of UKIB are the ITV Network Centre, the 17 ITV Companies, Channel 4 and S4C.

Basbof was formed in January 2004 to fund the ASA's broadcast remit. Like Asbof, it was deliberately constructed as a separate company to handle the funding of the ASA at arm's length, thus ensuring the ASA's operational independence necessary to gain acceptance by Government. Under this set-up, advertisers pay a levy of £1 per £1,000 on display advertising in press, magazines, cinema, outdoor, and since August 2004, on TV, radio and internet advertising.

The ASA (and the other joint bodies mentioned above) exists as an independent regulator to take action against those advertisements that do not comply with the Advertising Standards Code. Each year the ASA deals with about 30,000 complaints. The 2012 Annual Report particularly highlights the 'big five' misleading advertising priorities – free trials, pricing, daily deals, testimonials and health claims – and what the ASA and CAP have done to tackle these so that consumers and businesses not only obtain a fair deal but also regain confidence in certain brands.[209]

The advertising codes are the responsibility of two industry committees – the Committee of Advertising Practice (CAP) and the Broadcast Committee of Advertising Practice (BCAP) – and are independently administered by the ASA. The ASA's self-regulation is accepted by the Competition and Markets Authority (CMA) (formerly by the Department of Business, Innovation and Skills and the (former) Office of Fair Trading (OFT)), and from September 2010 the ASA was designated by Ofcom as the co-regulator for advertising appearing on video-on-demand (VOD) services.

Ofcom acts as a backstop regulator, which means the ASA can refer cases to Ofcom if advertising continues to appear despite an ASA adjudication against it. Ofcom can then take immediate action on serious breaches of the ASA rules, for instance by using its legal powers to order the immediate suspension of an advertisement accompanied by a fine. Not all VOD advertising is subject to the ASA's regulation, however. Only advertisements on services that are subject to statutory regulation will be affected. Services as defined by the Communications Act 2003 are required to notify the Association for Television on Demand (ATVOD) that they are operating.[210]

The regulation of video-on-demand services and product placement on commercial radio and TV is shared by the ASA and Ofcom. While product placement is the '*dernier cri*' in advertising during the programming for films, drama, sports and light entertainment, the embedded marketing of branded goods will be banned from children's, religious, current affairs and consumer affairs programmes.

Product placement is when a company pays a TV channel or a programme-maker to include its products or brands in a programme. So, for example, a fashion company might pay for a presenter to wear its clothes during a programme, or a car manufacturer might pay for a character to mention one of its cars in a scene in a drama. Ofcom is responsible for the rules governing product placement, including what can and cannot be shown on TV screens.[211] Generally banned products include cigarettes and other tobacco products, medicinal products, alcoholic drinks, salty foods and gambling services.

10.8.2 Gaming and betting: online gambling

Online gambling has become an emotive subject and one that can polarize public opinion. For some it is a sophisticated and glamorous pastime where vast sums of money can be won and lost. For many it is a mainstream leisure activity, seen as a bit of harmless fun, such as bingo or roulette. There are those, however, who suffer from a gambling addiction which can ruin lives.

---

209 Source: Advertising Standards Authority (ASA) and Committee of Advertising Practice (CAP) (2012) Annual Report.
210 Section 368A Communications Act 2003.
211 See: The Ofcom Broadcasting Code, the most recent version of which took effect on 21 March 2013. The Code covers all programmes broadcast on or after 21 March 2013.

Since September 2007, betting and gaming companies have been permitted to advertise across all media, but the introduction of strict content rules has ensured that they can do so only in a socially responsible way. Gaming and betting is strictly regulated by legislation, the main statute being the Gambling Act 2005, which removed licensing from the magistrates and placed it with the local authority. Section 4(1) of the Gambling Act covers 'remote' gambling, including the internet, the telephone, radio and 'any other kind of electronic communication' (s 4(1)(e)).

Gaming and betting advertising rules place an emphasis on the importance of protecting children and vulnerable persons (also covered by Part 4 of the Gambling Act 2005). Among the key clauses, the rules state that advertisements for gambling must not:

- portray, condone or encourage gambling behaviour that is socially irresponsible or could lead to financial, social or emotional harm;
- be likely to be of particular appeal to under 18s, especially by reflecting or being associated with youth culture;
- suggest that gambling can be a solution to financial concerns, an alternative to employment or a way to achieve financial security;
- exploit the susceptibilities, aspirations, credulity, inexperience or lack of knowledge of children, young persons or other vulnerable persons;
- link gambling to seduction, sexual success or enhanced attractiveness.

For those advertisers who breach the regulations, they face referral by the ASA to Ofcom or the Gambling Commission for potential additional sanctions.

How has gambling changed? Before 2007, licensed casinos were only allowed to advertise in classified ads. However, following the change in the rules and legislation,[212] companies based in the UK or in certain approved jurisdictions (known as the 'White List') in the European Economic Area or holding a Gambling Commission licence are now legally permitted to advertise across all media.

Unless a lottery is licensed by the Gambling Commission, is part of the National Lottery or is a small or private lottery, it is likely to be illegal.[213] Before September 2007, marketing communications for bingo halls could advertise the game of bingo, but were not allowed to refer to other gambling facilities such as gaming machines. The Gambling Act 2005 allows bingo halls to refer to the other gambling facilities found on their premises.[214]

 FOR THOUGHT

How do you judge someone as vulnerable? Gambling ads should not be directed to under 18s or vulnerable adults. Study the relevant gambling legislation and the CAP (Committee of Advertising Practice) Code of standards on the definition of 'vulnerable' (e.g. mentally, socially or emotionally immature, or those suffering from an alcohol or drug addiction). Draft a letter of complaint to the ASA objecting to the following Facebook advertisement (a Facebook banner ad for a gambling website). The text reads: 'Addicted to slots?'. The ad features a picture of a fruit machine. Further text states: 'Register now on .666casino & spin. You get a whole year ABSOLUTELY FREE! Get the chance to win every day. No deposit necessary.'

212 See: s 7 Gambling Act 2005 ('casinos').
213 See: ss 14 and 15 Gambling Act 2005 ('lotteries and National Lottery').
214 See: s 91 Gambling Act 2005 ('bingo operating license').

10.8.3 Advertising codes and standards

The ASA codes lay down rules for advertisers and media owners. The main aim of the codes states that advertisements must be responsible and must not mislead or offend. There are specific rules that cover advertising to children, and adverts for alcohol, gambling, motoring, health and financial products. The essential rulebook for the advertising industry is the so-called CAP Code (The UK Code of Non-broadcast Advertising, Sales Promotion and Direct Marketing).[215] Non-compliance with the CAP Code can result in Competition and Markets Authority action (formerly the Office of Fair Trading), under the Consumer Protection from Unfair Trading Regulations 2008[216] or the Business Protection from Misleading Marketing Regulations 2008 (BPR).[217]

Advertising campaigns increasingly cross national boundaries. The European Advertising Standards Alliance (EASA), founded in 1992 and based in Brussels, brings together national advertising self-regulatory bodies and organizations representing the advertising industry in Europe. The EASA comprises around 130 representatives from all sectors of the advertising industry under one charter, based on a 'Statement of Common Principles and Operating Standards of Best Practice', and represents more than 20 countries. The Alliance operates a cross-border complaints procedure, known as the *Blue Book*.[218]

The self-regulatory levy system in advertising appears to work well. Significantly, the ASA/ Asbof/Basbof set-up has been hailed by successive governments and regulatory bodies around the world as a model method of ensuring consumer confidence in advertising, and it has become a template for many similar systems in other countries.

10.8.4 Examples of ASA rulings

Each year, the UK public sees many millions of ads, direct marketing programmes and sales promotions about products, services, causes and awareness campaigns. The vast majority of ads comply with the advertising rules. The ASA's activities include investigating and adjudicating on complaints. Anyone can complain to the ASA free of charge and its self-regulatory value is founded on EC Directives, including those on misleading and comparative advertising.[219] The regulator also watches over product placement in TV productions, sales promotions, direct marketing and online advertisements in the UK. Its powers include stopping misleading, harmful or offensive advertising, ensuring that sales promotions are run fairly, and reducing unwanted commercial mail (by post, email or SMS) in conjunction with the Information Commissioner's Office. The advertising watchdog also resolves problems with mail-order purchases.

In 2012, the ASA dealt with 31,298 complaints. As a result of their investigation, some 3,700 ads were changed or withdrawn and it is fair to say that the vast majority of advertisers, promoters and direct marketers comply with the CAP or broadcasting codes. Those that do not may be subject to sanctions. The regulator's Broadcast Committee of Advertising Practice (BCAP) can additionally investigate a challenge with the licence holder if it finds a potential breach. If a complaint is upheld, the commercial is usually immediately withdrawn, or in rarer cases amended. In more serious cases, Ofcom can apply sanctions to licensees who frequently break the rules, by issuing a formal

215 See: The CAP Code (2010) at: www.cap.org.uk/Advertising-Codes/~/media/Files/CAP/Codes%20CAP%20pdf/CAP%20 Code%200712.ashx.
216 The Consumer Protection from Unfair Trading Regulations 2008 of 26 May 2008 (No. 1277) ('The Unfair Trading Regulations'); see also: EC Directive on Directive 2005/29/EC concerning unfair business-to-consumer commercial practices in the internal market of 11 May 2005 ('The Unfair Commercial Practices Directive').
217 The Business Protection from Misleading Marketing Regulations 2008 (BPR) of 26 May 2008 ('Trade Descriptions') which prohibit businesses from advertising products in a way that misleads traders and set out conditions under which comparative advertising to consumers and business is permitted.
218 See: European Advertising Standards Alliance (EASA) *Blue Book*. 6th ed.
219 Directives 2005/29/EC and 2006/114/EC.

warning. They can also request a broadcast correction or statement of findings or impose a penalty which may include a fine or the shortening, suspending or taking-away of a station's licence to broadcast.

The ASA publishes weekly rulings on its website. Decisions are subject to independent review by the Administrative Division of the High Court.

See above
10.6.1

❖ **KEY CASE**   *Adjudication on Iceland Foods Ltd*, 21 August 2013 (Complaint Ref: A13-223122)

Advertisement

A national press ad, published in the '*i*' newspaper, was headed 'FOOD YOU CAN TRUST ... Iceland has always led the way in developing Food You Can Trust'. Further text included, 'No horsemeat has ever been found in an Iceland product.* All our burgers are made in the UK from British beef'. Text underneath stated. '*Recent testing by the Food Safety Authority of Ireland (FSAI) found traces of equine DNA at one tenth of one per cent in two Iceland Quarter Pounder burgers. The testing method used by the FSAI was not an accredited test and the current accepted threshold level is 1% (10 times the level reported in the Iceland product). Two subsequent tests of the same batch of burgers carried out by two accredited independent laboratories found no evidence of contamination.'

Issue

The complainant challenged whether:

1.   the ad was misleading, because the claim 'No horsemeat has ever been found in an Iceland product' was contradicted by text which stated that two Iceland burgers had been found to contain 0.1 per cent equine DNA; and
2.   the ad denigrated the FSAI.[220]

Response

1.   Iceland Foods Ltd (Iceland) said the ad had been published in response to an FSAI report relating to tests which had found horse DNA in beef products sold by a range of retailers. Samples from two Iceland own-label burger ranges had been found to contain traces of horse DNA. One sample had tested positive at 0.1 per cent horse DNA, and the other had tested positive at less than 0.1 per cent horse DNA.

     Iceland said the main claim and explanatory text in the ad made a distinction between horsemeat and horse DNA. They considered that this distinction was important and was not contradictory. They said it was widely understood that traces of DNA could be found after only brief contact, and therefore the fact that traces of horse DNA had been detected in the two samples did not necessarily indicate that horsemeat was present. They considered that horse DNA in levels as low as those found in the FSAI tests could have occurred for many reasons, including minor cross-contamination during processing or in the testing laboratories. They highlighted that they had arranged for the remainder of the samples tested

---

220   CAP Code (Edition 12) 3.13.133.33.423.73.9.

by the FSAI to be tested at an independent, accredited laboratory which specialized in testing for horse DNA. The lab reported that no equine DNA could be detected in the samples. Iceland said that in response to the FSAI's report, retailers had agreed with the UK Food Standards Agency (FSA) that they would carry out comprehensive testing of their beef products.

2. Iceland said that after publication of their ad, the FSAI had contacted them with concerns about the ad. Iceland said that in order to preserve their good working relationship with the FSAI, they amended the ad and published a statement on their website which acknowledged that the FSAI's test results were valid and that their testing method was widely used in the burger industry elsewhere in the world. Iceland said the FSAI had informed them they were satisfied with that action.

Assessment

1. Not upheld
The ASA noted Iceland's assertion that although the FSAI's tests had found a maximum of 0.1 per cent horse DNA in two samples from their burgers, further tests commissioned by Iceland on the remainder of those samples were negative for horse DNA (the additional tests). The additional tests could not call into question the FSAI's test results, because it was not possible for them to detect horse DNA at the levels found by the FSAI's tests. Samples from the original production runs of the burger ranges had been found to have no horse DNA present in tests that were capable of detecting horse DNA at less than 1 per cent. The ASA concluded the ad was not contradictory or misleading.

There was no breach under CAP Code (Edition 12) rules 3.1 and 3.3 ('misleading advertising'), 3.7 ('substantiation'), 3.9 ('qualification') and 3.13 ('exaggeration').

2. Upheld
The ASA expressed concern about the way in which the ad described the FSAI's tests and further tests commissioned by Iceland. The ad did not make clear that the test methodology used in the initial FSAI tests was an established methodology commonly used in North America. The ASA also noted the ad referred to the tests commissioned by Iceland as having been 'carried out by two accredited independent laboratories'. Whilst the ASA acknowledged that the statement was accurate, they understood that both of the FSAI's sets of tests were also carried out at independent accredited laboratories. By omitting any reference to the second set of accredited tests carried out by the FSAI, by not making clear that the test methodology used in the FSAI's initial tests was an established methodology commonly used in North America, and by highlighting that Iceland's tests were carried out by an accredited independent laboratory whilst omitting that information in relation to the FSAI's tests, the overall impression created by the ad was that the FSAI had not taken due care to ensure the accuracy or validity of the tests used, and therefore that its findings were questionable. It was understood that this was not the case. The ASA concluded the ad discredited the FSAI and therefore breached the Code. The ad breached CAP Code (Edition 12) rule 3.42 ('imitation and denigration').

Action
The ad must not appear again in its current form. Iceland was told to ensure their advertising did not discredit or denigrate organizations in future.

> ### ❖ KEY CASE
>
> ### *ASA Adjudication on LA Fitness Ltd* 1 May 2013 (Complaint Ref: A13-222803)

Advertisement

A text message and website for a gym membership with LA Fitness:

(a) The text message stated 'Online Exclusive: Join today from only £16.00 per month + get Feb free! Ends Thurs 28th Feb! Visit lafitness.co.uk/hurry. T&Cs apply.'

(b) Claims on the website, www.lafitness.co.uk, stated 'Join the revolution and start achieving your fitness goals this February with our 50% off membership offer . . . Sign up today and you can get 50% off membership.' Text below that stated 'Select your club . . . Join' linked to a sign-up page, which provided the membership options for the selected club. One of the options stated 'Anytime from £15 per month'.

Issue

1. Two complainants challenged whether ad (a) was misleading, because it did not make clear that the 'from' price only applied to the first month of a 12-month contract and that a joining fee was payable.

2. Four complainants challenged whether ad (b) was misleading, because it did not make clear that the 50 per cent discount and 'from' price only applied to the first month of a 15-month contract.

***Response: Breach of the Code upheld*[221]**

Ad (a) stated 'from only £16.00 per month' and the ASA considered that, in the absence of qualification, recipients would understand from this that £16 referred to the ongoing price at which membership was available from each month. The ad did not make clear that the stated price referred only to the first month of a 12-month contract and also did not state that a joining fee was payable. It was considered that this was information consumers needed to make an informed decision about whether or not to take advantage of the offer and therefore concluded that the ad was misleading. On this point ad (a) breached CAP Code (Edition 12) rules 3.1 and 3.3 (misleading advertising) and 3.9 (qualification).

Assessment

The LA Fitness website stated '. . . our 50% off membership offer . . . get '50% off membership' and one of the options for a selected club stated 'Anytime from £15 per month'. The '50% off membership offer' applied only to the first 12 months of their 'Freedom' membership, and not to any other membership options, and the ASA considered that this should have been stated in the headline claim. The regulator also understood that there was another offer running simultaneously that offered 50 per cent off the first month only, in relation to various membership options. However, the website did not indicate that there were two '50% off' offers running and that the 'Anytime from £15 per month' claim related to the offer that provided a 50 per cent discount off the first month only. The ASA considered that the details of both offers and the membership options they applied to should have been stated clearly on the website. Because they were not, it was concluded that the ad was misleading. On this point ad (b) breached CAP Code (Edition 12) rules 3.1 and 3.3 (misleading advertising), 3.17 and 3.22 (prices).

---

221 CAP Code (Edition 12) 3.13.173.223.3.

Action

The ASA ruled that the advertisements must not appear again in their current form. LA Fitness Ltd was told that they had to ensure that price statements and discounts relating to their memberships were clear and that, if they applied to the first month only, this was stated in the headline claim. Furthermore, LA Fitness was asked to ensure that any other fees were prominently stated in the body copy.

❖ **KEY CASE**

ASA Adjudication on Starwhite Ltd, The Lodge Gentleman's Club, Pitt Street, Barnsley, 14 August 2013 (Complaint Ref: A13-232945)

Advertisement

A poster for a gentlemen's club showed an image of a woman wearing a bra lying on her back, looking towards the camera. With her right hand she was playing with her hair; the left side of her body was obscured by shadow.

Issue

The complainant stated that the poster had been placed within 100 metres of a nursery and directly opposite a youth hostel, and challenged whether the advertisement:

1. was offensive, sexist and degrading to women; and
2. was irresponsible, because it appeared where it could be seen by children.[222]

Response to the breach of the Code

Starwhite Ltd, The Lodge Gentleman's Club ('The Lodge') stated that they did not wish to offend anyone, but felt that the image was not of an offensive nature and that the text was innocuous. They said the poster was located almost opposite a youth hostel, but not within 100 metres of a nursery. They also said that before the poster had been put up, the ad had been submitted to the CAP Copy Advice team, who had advised that it was suitable. Primesight Ltd, the site owner, said the imagery in the ad was in their opinion not overtly sexual and they had deemed it appropriate. They acknowledged that the poster was displayed within 25 metres of a youth hostel, but said that was not a restricted location. They provided information about the youth hostel, including that the average age of hostel guests was 16–18 years. They said the poster was 350 to 400 metres away from the nursery and they could not find any record of other schools in that area.

Assessment

1. Breach not upheld

The ASA acknowledged that advertising for gentlemen's clubs would often contain images of women, many of which were likely to be seen as at least mildly sexual because of the nature of the service promoted. However, the fact that a product was offensive to some people was not grounds for finding a marketing communication in breach of the Code. It was therefore necessary to consider the overall impression given by the ad. The ASA Code

---

222 CAP Code (Edition 12) 1.34.1.

Committee noted that the image showed a woman lying on her back, looking towards the camera. The complainant had described this as a sexually submissive position. Much of the woman's body was shrouded in darkness, but she was shown alone and did not look distressed or coerced in any way, and given that she was wearing a bra and most of the lower part of her body was not visible it was considered that the image was only mildly sexual in nature. Whilst acknowledging that the ad would be distasteful to some, it was not considered that it would be generally seen as objectifying or being sexist or degrading to women, and it was concluded that it was therefore unlikely to cause serious or wide-spread offence.

The ASA also found that CAP Code rule 4.1 ('harm and offence') was not breached.

2. Not upheld

The CAP Code Advice committee had viewed the ad before it appeared, and had advised that it should not be placed within 100 metres of a school or places that children frequented. The committee considered that, given the sexually suggestive nature of the ad, this restriction was appropriate and would reduce the risk of its being seen by children. The complainant had believed that the poster was located within that distance of a nursery. However, the ASA found that the poster was in fact about 350 metres away from the nursery school. The youth hostel referred to by the complainant was generally used by those aged 16–18 years, who were not classed as children under the Code. Because the ad had been placed away from schools or businesses that provided child-based services, the ASA concluded that it was not irresponsible.

The ASA found that the ad did not breach CAP Code rule 1.3 ('responsible advertising').

Action

No further action was necessary.

10.9 Media regulation 'sans frontières': codifying cyberspace or self-regulation in the digital age?

Since 1989 the European Union has issued legislation which governs the audio-visual sector across all EU Member States. Linked in rationale to restrictions on overseas ownership are rules which set quotas for domestic programme production. Where trade areas have been established, these quotas are often extended. All signatory states to the 'Television Without Frontiers Directive' (TVWF)[223] have agreed to European production quotas providing minimum broadcasting standards. In 1997, the TVWF Directive was updated,[224] covering media access to major sporting events, teleshopping and promoting EU products.[225] The EU is also tasked with encouraging its member countries to co-operate in conserving and safeguarding cultural heritage of European significance, including TV, cinema and film.[226]

---

223 EU Directive 89/552 EEC on Transfrontier Television 'Television without Frontiers Directive' (TVWF).
224 Directive 97/36/EC amended Council Directive 89/552/EEC 'Television without Frontiers' (above) concerning the pursuit of television broadcasting activities.
225 The Commission ordered that Directive 2007/65 be transposed into domestic legislation by the end of 2009.
226 Article 151(2) EC Treaty.

Since the TVWF Directive came into force in 1989, the international audio-visual landscape has changed significantly with the impact of technological developments in the information society. New players and platforms have emerged, boosting or requiring more content production for emerging markets. The important 'sans frontières' Directive has now largely been replaced by the 'Audio Visual Media Services Directive' (AVMSD),[227] additionally covering public service broadcasters such as the BBC.[228]

The AVMSD covers all services with audio-visual content irrespective of the technology used to deliver the content. The rules of the Directive apply irrespective of whether one watches news or other audio-visual content on TV, on the internet or on one's mobile phone. However, taking into account the degree of choice and user control over services, the AVMSD makes a distinction between linear (television broadcasts) and non-linear (on-demand) services. The AVMSD also modernized TV advertising rules to better finance audio-visual content, including teleshopping, product placement and sponsorship.[229]

As has already been explained in Chapter 8, EU law has been further modified to cover services delivered over the internet in order to combat internet piracy, copyright infringement and to monitor mass-market advertising on TV and the internet in the 'pay per click' society.

See Chapter 8.6

While the AVMSD created a level playing field in Europe for emerging audio-visual media, it also sought to safeguard and preserve cultural diversity, protect children, consumers and media pluralism, and combat racial and religious hatred.[230]

10.9.1 Does regulation infringe freedom of expression? Analysis and discussion

While the internet has brought global freedom to communicate and exchange ideas, its growth has introduced difficulties too – for instance, the expression on social networking sites and blogs of personal opinions, with the risk therein of misinformation, defamation and harassment. There is also the ability to search the World Wide Web for content of pretty well any extreme nature, ranging from the sexual to the political. Anderson and Rainie (2006 – 'The Pew Report) believed, based on a survey of technology thinkers and stakeholders conducted in 2005, that the internet would continue to spread in a 'flattening' and improving world, and furthermore, that the internet would provide 'low-cost networks of billions of devices' by 2020.[231]

That said, the number of free web access providers has declined sharply in recent years, as the industry has seen a number of players consolidate or go out of business, due to increased regulation of the industry. Much reliable content is now only available via paid-for services, such as The Times, Reuters Business News, The Wall Street Journal or smartphone applications ('apps'). What regulation there is must reflect that the internet is widely used and extremely beneficial. Over-regulation can impair and limit the growth of the information society. Judicial review of regulation can potentially restrict free speech. If regulators are put in place by governments, they should be left to conduct their own standard of strict scrutiny.

---

227 EC Directive 2007/65 'Audiovisual Media Services Directive' (AVMSD) amended EU Directive 89/552/EEC 'Television without Frontiers Directive' (TVWF) and includes the pursuit of television broadcasting activities including on-demand services of 11 December 2007.
228 Ibid.
229 Article 3e AVMSD.
230 Source: 2009/C 257/01 Communication from the Commission on the application of State aid rules to public service broadcasting. Official Journal of the European Union, C 257, Vol 52, 27 October 2009.
231 See: Anderson and Rainie (2006).

Article 10 ECHR protects not only the substance of ideas and information expressed, but also the form in which they are conveyed. Journalistic freedom covers possible recourses to a degree of exaggeration, or even provocation. However, even where a statement amounts to a value judgement, the proportionality of an interference may depend on whether there exists a sufficient factual basis for the impugned statement, since even a value judgement without any factual basis to support it may be excessive (see: **Dichand v Austria** (2002);[232] also: **Monnat v Switzerland** (2006)[233]). Freedom of expression is fundamental to the functioning of democracy. This applies especially to the communication of opinions and argument about policies which all levels of government pursue, including those made in radio and TV broadcasts (see: **R (Animal Defenders International v Secretary of State for Culture, Media and Sport** (2008)[234]).

In December 2008, the European Court of Human Rights handed down its judgment in the case of **TV Vest & Rogaland Pensjonistparti v Norway**.[235] The Court found that the application of a blanket ban on advertising for political parties violated Article 10 ECHR. The Norwegian TV channel, TV Vest – located in Stavanger in the county of Rogaland – had been fined in September 2003 by the Norwegian Media Authority NOK 35,000 under s 10(3) of the Norwegian Broadcasting Act 1992 and s 10(2) of the Broadcasting Regulations, for violating the prohibition on political advertising in TV broadcasts. The broadcast concerned three advertising slots for the Norwegian Pensioners Party during the run-up to the local and regional elections in 2003. TV Vest appealed against the decision to Oslo City Court (Oslo tingrett), stating that the prohibition in the Broadcasting Act was incompatible with the right to freedom of expression under Article 10 ECHR. The City Court upheld the Media Authority's decision in February 2004, supported by the Norwegian Supreme Court in November of that year. However, Christos Rozakis, President of the (First Section) of the European Court of Human Rights, held that there had been a violation of Article 10, stating that there had not been a:

> reasonable relationship of proportionality between the legitimate aim pursued by the prohibition on political advertising and the means deployed to achieve that aim. The restriction which the prohibition and the imposition of the fine entailed on the applicants' exercise of their freedom of expression cannot therefore be regarded as having been necessary in a democratic society, within the meaning of paragraph 2 of Article 10, for the protection of the rights of others, notwithstanding the margin of appreciation available to the national authorities.[236]

The judgment in the **Norwegian Pensioner** case caused great controversy and subsequently had great consequences for political advertising in other signature countries to the Convention.

Freedom of political expression includes not only the inoffensive, but also the irritating, the contentious, the eccentric, the heretical, the unwelcome and the provocative, provided it does not tend to provoke violence (see: **Redmond-Bate v DPP** (1999)[237]). But in **Otto-Preminger-Institut v Austria** (1994),[238] the ECtHR included as an obligation under Article 10.2 ECHR to avoid – as far as possible – expressions that are gratuitously offensive to others.

In human rights adjudications, the Strasbourg jurisdiction has primarily been concerned with whether the claimant's human rights have been infringed (for example 'freedom of speech' under

---

232 (2002) (Application no. 29271/95) of 26 February 2002 (ECHR).
233 (2006) (Application no. 73604/01) of 21 September 2006 (ECHR).
234 [2008] 1 AC 1312 at para 27 (Lord Bingham).
235 See: **TV Vest AS & Rogaland Pensjonistparti v Norway** (2008) (Application no. 21132/05) Judgment of the 11 December 2008 (ECtHR) ('the Norwegian Pensioner case').
236 Ibid., at para 78 (Christos Rozakis, President, ECHR).
237 (1999) 163 JP 789.
238 [1994] ECHR 26 at para 49 (ECHR).

See Chapter 3

Article 10 ECHR). The ECtHR is not concerned with domestic administrative matters, such as whether a broadcasting or press regulator took human rights law properly into account in its adjudication. It is a domestic court's role to assess for itself the proportionality of the democratic principle of freedom of speech versus other areas of the Convention, such as a person's right to privacy or whether a person has been defamed.

It is accepted that Strasbourg jurisprudence does not protect gratuitous abuse unrelated to a topic being discussed (on the radio for example), but this is a very limited exception to the broad protection of political expression. For this reason, the regulatory body's decision in the **Jon Gaunt**[239] case may well be incompatible with Convention Article 10 if tested in the ECtHR.

The existence of a discretionary area of judgement means that such decisions can only be made by a domestic court of law, rather than a regulator which may not have full statutory powers. In this context, it is submitted that the courts should not regard a regulatory authority as better able than jurisprudence to assess what are 'generally accepted standards', such as the Broadcasting Code or the (former) PCC's Editors' Code (or subsequent Royal Charter legislation) for the print press (see: **R (SB) v Governors of Denbigh High School** (2007);[240] also: **Belfast City Council v Miss Behavin' Ltd** (2007);[241] also: **R (Nasseri) v SSHD** (2010)[242]). It is then up to regulators to introduce safeguards into their codes of practice which express responsibilities. As Lord Walker said in the **ProLife case**,[243] in practice the obligation to avoid offensive material is interpreted as limited to what is needlessly or gratuitously shocking or offensive (see also: **Murphy v Ireland** (2000)[244]).

A regulator ought to strike a fine balance between the parameters of indecent, obscene and violent material and sensitive issues such as ethics and morals, existing legislation and the effective monitoring of the service, without being too prohibitive. Regulation of the internet, the games and film industries, telecommunications and media pose ongoing challenges to governments. Where should the line be drawn between regulating indecency and obscenity, freedom of expression and, ultimately, the autonomy of end-users? If an adult signs up to an adult pornographic website or views a 'porn movie' streamed in the comfort of his own home, should there be only minimal control over what he chooses to view? The EU has developed guidelines in that respect by trying to provide adequate protection for the young and vulnerable in society in the form of regulatory standards by meeting a multicultural definition of indecency on the one hand and upholding fundamental freedom of expression principles and the right to privacy on the other.

While the international community is fast promoting the transfer of technology and information, there appear to be a number of different policies and laws in place across Europe and the United States,[245] each attempting to regulate, control and curtail the internet and fast-advancing new media technology. Has legislation been passed too late? Is internet governance now dominated by the private sector? The internet is highly robust, dynamic and geographically diverse and can be seen as a positive as well as negative tool. It remains to be seen whether the World Wide Web can really be legally controlled and regulated.

Because the UK Government believes that a balance needs to be struck between media harassment and the need for a free press, especially investigative journalism, it has consistently refused to

---

239 See: **R (on the application of Gaunt) v Ofcom** [2011] EWCA Civ 692.
240 [2007] 1 AC 100.
241 [2007] 1 WLR 1420.
242 [2010] 1 AC 1 (HL).
243 **R (ProLife Alliance) v BBC** [2004] 1 AC 185 at 121 (Lord Walker).
244 (2000) 38 EHRR 13 (ECtHR).
245 See: the Digital Millennium Copyright Act ('the Copyright Act') (Title 17 of the US Code) to provide in part certain limitations on the liability of online service providers (OSPs) for copyright infringement. Section 512(c) of the Copyright Act provides limitations on service provider liability for storage, at the direction of a user, of copyrighted material residing on a system or network controlled or operated by or for the service provider, if, among other things, the service provider has designated an agent to receive notifications of claimed infringement by providing contact information to the Copyright Office and by posting such information on the service provider's website in a location accessible to the public.

set in stone a privacy law, preferring to rely on media regulations and common law. The House of Lords said as much in the **Naomi Campbell**[246] case.

10.10 Further reading

Carney, D. (2008) 'Self regulation of unlawful newsgathering techniques'. *Communications Law,* **13(3), 76–81.**
This article examines the evolution of the PCC's Code of Practice in relation to forms of newsgathering prior to 2006. Damian Carney provides a context in which he examines both data trading and the Clive Goodman (phone-hacking at the *News of the World*) case. The author explains why the press regulator felt it necessary to strengthen its Code and make the recommendations it did in the aftermath of these events. The article ends with an analysis of these changes and a discussion of how the tripartite system of controlling newsgathering can be used successfully to minimise widespread and unjustified illegal actions by journalists.

Chamberlain, P. (2013) 'Where now? The Leveson Report and what to do with it'. *Communications Law* **, 18(1), 21–24.**
This article looks at the events leading up to the Leveson Inquiry into the culture, practices and ethics of the press. Sparked by public outrage about the phone-hacking by the *News of the World*, in particular of the mobile phone of murdered teenager Milly Dowler, Paul Chamberlain looks beyond the scope of the Leveson Report which covered the culture, practices and ethics of the print press but also the police and politicians. The article focuses primarily on the Leveson recommendations in relation to the future of press regulation and the practical consequences.

Costigan, R. (2007) 'Protection of journalists' sources'. *Public Law* **, Autumn, 464–487.**
This article critiques the jurisprudence of s 10 of the Contempt of Court Act 1981, which affords journalists a qualified immunity from compulsory revelation of sources. Ruth Costigan contends that the courts have failed to appreciate sufficiently the change in the nature of the decision-making exercise required by s 10 and examines relevant case law, such as **Ashworth Hospital v MGN** (2001) and **X Ltd v Morgan Grampian** (1991). The author further argues that the Human Rights Act (HRA) 1998 insufficiently protects journalistic sources, contrasting the judicial decision-making process at common law and under s 10 (pre and post the HRA) with the problems in judicial conception of these processes, and considers the HRA's impact in these cases. Costigan examines disclosure of sources 'in the public interest' and the journalist's conduct and standing. The piece ends with the argument that the Convention requirement of proportionality is not implemented in an appropriate and sufficiently demanding manner.

European Advertising Standards Alliance (EASA) *Blue Book.* **6th edn. Brussels: EASA.**
Published tri-annually, the *Blue Book* is a 'must' for those wanting to work in the advertising industry. It is a comprehensive guide to the self-regulatory and legislative rules governing advertising across Europe, written with both the practitioner and researcher in mind. The sixth edition was fully revised and contains detailed overviews of the advertising self-regulatory systems both in Europe and beyond, including the composition and activities of each self-regulatory organization, statutory structures for advertising and national advertising codes. There is also an in-depth analysis of the key issues facing the advertising industry today, including advertising to children, food and alcohol advertising and the new media challenge online and cross-border complaints handling.

---

246 See: *Campbell v Mirror Group Newspapers Ltd* [2004] 2 AC 457.

Geddis, A. (2010) 'What we cannot talk about we must pass over in silence: judicial orders and reporting Parliamentary speech'. *Public Law*, **July, 443–451.**
This article discusses the conflict between judicial orders – such as superinjunctions – and the media's freedom to discuss and publish. Andrew Geddis examines the *Trafigura* case and the injunction (obtained by the law firm Carter-Ruck) which tried to suppress parliamentary proceedings. Geddis doubts whether existing law would have provided the *Guardian* with a defence to a contempt of court action had it printed Paul Farrelly MP's parliamentary question about Trafigura and the Minton Report. The author draws attention not only to the fact that there is no general right to report on parliamentary proceedings, but also to broader concerns about the place of freedom of expression in the United Kingdom's law, compared with the jurisdiction in New Zealand.

Higgins, A. (2012) 'Legal lessons from the *News of the World* phone hacking scandal'. *Civil Justice Quarterly*, **31(3), 274–284.**
Andrew Higgins discusses the phone-hacking scandal at the *News of the World* (from 2003) which emerged in 2010 and 2011. The largest British tabloid had hacked the phones of thousands of people, including politicians, celebrities and ordinary citizens. The author argues that the phone-hacking and corruption scandal provides a salutary reminder of the limitations of public law enforcement and the value of an effective and accessible civil justice system in exposing unlawful conduct and providing redress for victims. He further examines the limitations of the PCC and looks at self-regulation of the print press and the corruption scandals surrounding the arrests related to phone-hacking, payments to police and attempts to pervert the course of justice.

Jordan, B. (2011) 'Self-regulation and the British press'. *Entertainment Law Review*, **22(8), 242–243.**
Brid Jordan reflects in this article on the intention and purpose behind the establishment of the print press regulator, the Press Complaints Commission (PCC). The author discusses the history of self-regulation of the British media, which appeared to work for successive governments until the phone-hacking revelations. Jordan reflects on the resignation of the Chairman of the PCC, Baroness Buscombe, and the ensuing Leveson Inquiry and wonders where the future lies for British press regulation.

Khan, A. (2012) 'A "right not to be offended" under Article 10(2) ECHR? Concerns in the construction of the "rights of others" '. *European Human Rights Law Review* , **2, 191–204.**
This article evaluates the courts' approach to unpopular political speech, focusing on six cases which reveal a similar problem: the restriction of speech by way of the 'rights of others to be free from offence' exception under Article 10(2) ECHR. Aatifa Khan considers this development from both a black-letter and jurisprudential point of view, concluding that it is unsupported in law and in principle. Rather, the author suggests, there should be greater regard to underlying free-speech principles, and a separation between the speech's popularity and the level of legal protection given to it. This involves taking a 'transformative view' (or normative approach) to public attitudes. Khan evaluates the English courts' approach to unpopular political speech, focusing on the method of restricting speech under Article 10(2) in six cases, including *Gaunt v Ofcom*, and the way the courts deal with unpopular speech. Khan argues that the cases discussed demonstrate a troubling trend of restricting unpopular speech based on the 'right of others' not to be offended.

Scherer, J. (ed) (2013) *Telecommunication Laws in Europe: Law and regulation of electronic communications in Europe.* **6th edn. Haywards Heath: Bloomsbury Professional.**
Joachim Scherer's 'bumper' edition of *Telecommunication Laws* offers a 'one-stop' legal reference guide for practising lawyers in the telecoms industry. The text covers the most important EU legal frameworks and regulatory 'packages' for some of the major EU and non-EU players in the

telecommunications marketplace. The well-structured text covers, *inter alia*, the Access[247] and Data Retention[248] Directives, regulatory frameworks in each country, the way that non-compliance with legislation is enforced and penalized, and how data subjects (individuals) are protected under domestic privacy and data protection legislation.

Wragg, P. (2013) 'Time to end the tyranny: Leveson and the failure of the fourth estate'. *Communications Law* **, 18(1), 11–20.**
Paul Wragg discusses and comments on the Leveson Report and its recommendations for the creation of a press regulator which would hold the press to account for its treatment of people, following the phone-hacking scandals. The author argues that these recommendations by Lord Justice Leveson have generated specific issues about the practicability of implementation as well as the wider issue of whether this form of press regulation would be compatible with free speech principles, in theory and in practice. Wragg rightly argues that too much seems to hang on whether the print media itself is prepared to fundamentally shift its perspective on privacy.

---

247 Directive 2002/19/EC On access to, and interconnection of, electronic communications networks and associated facilities.
248 Directive 2006/24/EC On the retention of data generated or processed in connection with the provision of publicly available electronic communications services or of public communications networks and amending Directive 2002/58/EC (E-Privacy Directive).

Bibliography

Advertising Standards Authority (ASA) and Committee of Advertising Practice (CAP) (2012) *Annual Report 2012: Keeping Ads Honest: A fair deal for consumers and competitors.* London: ASA/CAP.

Ainger, M. (2002). *Gilbert and Sullivan: A dual biography.* Oxford: Oxford University Press.

Akdeniz, Y. (2008) *Internet Child Pornography and the Law: National and international responses.* Aldershot: Ashgate.

Allen, T. F. W. (2002) 'Scandalising the court: the impact of Bills of Rights', (2002) 10 *Asia Pacific Law Review* 1.

Allen, T. and Seaton, J. (1999) *The Media of Conflict: War reporting and representations of ethnic violence.* London: Zed Books Ltd.

Anderson, J. Q. and Rainie, L. (2006) *The Future of the Internet.* Washington DC: Pew Internet & American Life Project ('The Pew Report').

Andrew, C. (2009) *The Defence of the Realm: The authorized history of MI5.* London: Allen Lane.

Angelopoulos, C. (2012) 'The myth of European term harmonisation – 27 public domains for 27 Member States', *International Review of Intellectual Property and Competition Law*, 43(5), 567–594.

Archbold, *Criminal Pleading, Evidence and Practice*, see Richardson (2014).

Atkin, W. R. (2001) 'Defamation law in New Zealand "refined" and "amplified" ', 30 *Common Law World Review* 237.

Aubrey, W. H. S. (orig. 1895 – reprint 2007) *The Rise and Growth of the English Nation, with Special Reference to Epochs and Crises: A history of, and for, the people.* Whitefish, MT: Kessinger Publishing.

Baden-Powell, E. and Anthony, L. (2012) 'Digital Economy Act 2', *Entertainment Law Review*, 23(5), 130–133.

Bainham, A. and Cretney, S. (1993) 'Children', *The Modern Law*, 409–413.

Balin, R., Handman, L. and Reid, E. (2009) 'Libel tourism and the Duke's manservant: an American perspective,' *European Human Rights Law Review*, 3, 303–331.

Baloch, T. A. (2007) 'Law booksellers and printers as agents of unchange', *Cambridge Law Journal*, 66(2), 389–421.

Bar Council, The (2011) 'Jackson: The Next Chapter'. Peter Lodder QC Chairman's Report. May 2011.

Barber, N.W. (2003) 'A right to privacy?' *Public Law*, Winter, 602–610.

Barendt, E. (1989) 'Spycatcher and freedom of speech', *Public Law*, PO 204.

Barendt, E. (1990) 'Broadcasting censorship', *Law Quarterly Review*, 106 (July), 354–361.

Barendt, E. (2007) *Freedom of Speech* (2nd edn). Oxford: Oxford University Press.

Barendt, E. (2009) *Media Freedom and Contempt of Court: Library of essays in media law.* London: Ashgate.

Barendt, E., Lustgarten, L, Norrie, K. and Stephenson, H. (1997) *Libel and the Media: The chilling effect.* Oxford: Clarendon Press, p.1032 (referred to in Reynolds [2001] 2 AC 127).

Barnum, D. G. (2006) 'Indirect incitement and freedom of speech in Anglo-American law', *European Human Rights Law Review*, 3, 258–280.

Barron, A. (2012) 'Kant, copyright and communicative freedom', *Law & Philosophy*, 31(1), 1–48.

Barsby, C. and Ashworth, A. J. (2004) 'Juries: Contempt of Court Act 1981, s. 8. Case comment', *Criminal Law Review*, Dec, 1041–1044.

BBC Trust (2012) *Findings of the Editorial Standards Committee of the BBC Trust* (The 'MacQuarrie Report'), 14 December 2012, at: http://downloads.bbc.co.uk/bbctrust/assets/files/pdf/appeals/esc_bulletins/2012/newsnight_2nov.pdf.

Beaujon, A. (1999) 'It's not the beat, it's the Mocean', *CMJ New Music Monthly*, April, 25.

Bennett, T. D. C. (2010) 'Horizontality's new horizons – re-examining horizontal effect: privacy defamation and the Human Rights Act (Part 2)', *Entertainment Law Review*, 21(4), 145–149.

Bentham, J. (1843a) 'Draft of the Organization of Judicial Establishments', *The Works of Jeremy Bentham, Published under the Supervision of His Executor, John Bowring*, 11 volumes, 1838–1843. Edinburgh: W. Tait.

Bentham, J. (1843b, reprinted 2001) 'The anarchical fallacies', *The Works of Jeremy Bentham, Published under the Supervision of His Executor, John Bowring*, 11 volumes, 1838–1843. Boston, MA: Adamant Media Corporation.

Bernard, N. (1996) 'Discrimination and Free Movement in EC Law', *International and Comparative Law Quarterly*, 45, 82–108.

Bilton, M. (2003) *Wicked Beyond Belief: The hunt for the Yorkshire Ripper*. London: HarperCollins.

Bindman, G. (1989) 'Spycatcher: judging the judges', *New Law Journal*, 139, 94.

Bingham, T. (1996) 'Should there be a law to protect rights of personal privacy?', *European Human Rights Law Review*, 5, 455–462.

Blackstone, Sir W. (1765) *Commentaries on the Laws of England* (16th edn – revised in 1825). London: University of Cambridge.

Blair, A. (2010) *A Journey*. London: Hutchinson/Random House.

Blom-Cooper, L. (2008) 'Press freedom: constitutional right or cultural assumption?', *Public Law*, Summer, 260–276.

Bonnington, A. J. and McInnes, R. (2010) *Scots Law for Journalists* (8th edn). Edinburgh: W. Green/Sweet & Maxwell Ltd.

Bower, T. (2006) *Conrad and Lady Black: Dancing on the edge*. London: Harper Collins.

Brems, E. (1996) 'The margin of appreciation in the case law of the European Court of Human Rights', *Zeitschrift für ausländisches öffentliches Recht und Völkerrecht (Heidelberg Journal of International Law)*, 56, 240–314.

Briggs, A. (ed) (1995) *The History of Broadcasting* (5 vols). Oxford: Oxford University Press.

Brisby, P. (2006) 'The regulation of telecommunications networks and services in the United Kingdom', *Computer and Telecommunications Law Review*, 12(4), 114–139.

Britton, D. (1989) *Lord Horror*. London: Savoy Books.

British Board of Film Classification (BBFC) (2011) *On-line Media Regulation Research Findings* by Bernice Hardie at: www.bbfc.co.uk/sites/default/files/attachments/Media%20Regulation%20Research_0.pdf.

Brimsted, K. (2003) 'Commission reports uneven playing field for data protection', *Privacy Laws & Business International Newsletter*, 68 (May/June), 22–23.

Broadway, J. (2008) 'Aberrant accounts: William Dugdale's handling of two Tudor murders in the antiquities of Warwickshire', *Midland History* 33(1) (Spring), 2–20.

Brooke, H. (2010) *The Silent State. Secrets, surveillance and the myth of British democracy*. London: William Heinemann.

Brooks, T. (2004) 'A defence of jury nullification', *Res Publica*, 10(4), 401–423.

Burchill, R., White, N. D. and Morris, J. (eds) (2005) *International Conflict and Security Law: Essays in memory of Hilaire McCoubrey*. Cambridge: Cambridge University Press.

Burke, E. (1790) *Reflections on the Revolution in France and on the Proceedings in Certain Societies in London Relevant to the Event in a Letter Intended to Have Been Sent to a Gentleman in Paris* (10th edn). London: Printed for J. Dodsley in Pall Mall.

Burns Coleman, E. and White, K. (2006) *Negotiating the Sacred in Multicultural Societies: Blasphemy and sacrilege in a multicultural society*. Canberra: University of Australia National University Press.

Busch, D. and MacGregor, L. (2009) *The Unauthorised Agent: Perspectives from European and Comparative Law*. Cambridge: Cambridge University Press.

Callery, C. (2010) 'John Terry: reflections on public image, sponsorship, and employment', *International Sports Law Review*, 2, 48–52.

Campbell, A. (2012) *The Burden of Power: Countdown to Iraq – The Alastair Campbell Diaries*. London: Hutchinson/ Random House.

Campbell, W. J. (2001) *Yellow Journalism: Puncturing the myths, defining the legacies*. Opa-Locka, FL: Praeger.

CAP Code, The (2010) *The UK Code of Non-broadcast Advertising, Sales Promotion and Direct Marketing*. Edition 12. London: The Stationery Office.

Capp, B. (2004) 'The Potter Almanacs', *Electronic British Library Journal*, 1–2: www.bl.uk/eblj/2004articles/pdf/article4.pdf.

Carey Miller, D. L. and Irvine, D. (2005) *Corporeal Moveables in Scots Law* (2nd rev. edn). Edinburgh: W. Green Publishers.

Carney, D. (2008) 'Self regulation of unlawful newsgathering techniques', *Communications Law*, 13(3), 76–81.

Carter-Ruck, P. F. (1990) *Memoirs of a Libel Lawyer*. London: Weidenfeld & Nicolson.

Carter-Silk, A. and Cartwright-Hignett, C. (2009) 'A child's right to privacy: "Out of a parent's hands"', *Entertainment Law Review*, 20(6), 212–217.

Carty, H. (2007) 'The common law and the quest for the IP effect'. *Intellectual Property Quarterly*, 3, 237–266.

Carty, H. (2008) 'An analysis of the modern action for breach of commercial confidence: when is protection merited?' *Intellectual Property Quarterly*, 4, 416–455.

Chamberlain, P. (2013) 'Where now? The Leveson Report and what to do with it', *Communications Law*, 18(1), 21–24.

Christie, A. and Gare, S. (2008) *Blackstone's Statutes on Intellectual Property* (9th edn). Oxford: Oxford University Press.

Clark, A. (1993) *Diaries*. London: Weidenfeld & Nicolson.

Clark, B. (2009) 'Princess Caroline: German Federal Supreme Court again considers the lawfulness of the publication of a celebrity photograph', *Entertainment Law Review*, 20(3), 107–111.

Clayton, R. and Tomlinson, H. (2009) *The Law of Human Rights* (2nd edn). Oxford: Oxford University Press.

Clegg, C. S. (2001) *Censorship in Jacobean England*. Cambridge: Cambridge University Press.

Clutterbuck, R. (1981) *The Media and Political Violence*. London: Macmillan.

Coad, J. (2005) 'The Press Complaints Commission: Are we safe in its hands?', *Entertainment Law Review*, 16(7), 167–73.

Cobbett, W. (1806) *Cobbett's Parliamentary History of England*, Vol. 6, col. 1063. London: House of Commons. Oxford University Digital Library.

Colligan, C. (2003) 'Race of born pederasts: Homosexuality, and the Arabs', *Nineteenth Century Contexts*, 25(1) (March), 1–20.

Colston, C. and Galloway, J. (2010) *Modern Intellectual Property Law* (3rd edn). London: Routledge.

Cook, T. (2010) *EU Intellectual Property Law*. Oxford: Oxford University Press.

Cornish, W. (2009) 'Conserving culture and copyright: A partial history', *Edinburgh Law Review*, 13(1), 8–26.

Cornish, W., Llewelyn, D. and Aplin, T. (2013) *Intellectual Property: Patents, Copyrights, Trademarks & Allied Rights* (8th edn). London: Sweet & Maxwell.

Costigan, R. (2007) 'Protection of journalists' sources', *Public Law*, Autumn, 464–487.

Council of Europe (1996) 'The European Convention on Human Rights in the New Architecture of Europe'. General Report presented by Lord Lester of Herne Hill, QC, in Proceedings of the 8th International Colloquy on the European Convention on Human Rights, pp. 227–240.

Council of Europe (2009) *International Justice for Children*. Brussels: Council of Europe Publication.

Council of Europe (2010) 'Blasphemy, insult and hatred: Finding answers in a democratic society', *Science and Technique of Democracy 47*. Brussels: Council of Europe Publication.

Coutts, J. A. (1999) 'Contempt by scandalising the court', *Journal of Criminal Law*, 63, 472.

Craig, R. (2009) 'Non-jury courts in Northern Ireland', *Criminal Law and Justice Weekly*, 5 June: www.criminallawandjustice.co.uk/features/Non-Jury-Courts-Northern-Ireland.

Criminal Law Revision Committee (1984) *Fifteenth Report of the Criminal Law Revision Committee, Sexual Offences*. Cmnd 9213, April 1984.

Crossan, S. J. and Wylie, A. B. (2010) *Introduction to Scots Law: Theory and practice* (2nd edn). London: Hodder Gibson.

Crossman, R. H. S. (1976a) *The Diaries of a Cabinet Minister, 1964–1966*. Volume I. New York: Holt, Rinehart & Winston.

Crossman, R. H. S. (1976b) *The Diaries of a Cabinet Minister: Lord President of the Council, 1966–68*. Volume II. London: Hamish Hamilton.

Crossman, R. H. S. (1977) *The Diaries of a Cabinet Minister: Secretary of State for Social Services, 1968–70*. Volume III. London: Penguin.

Crown Prosecution Service (2012) 'Interim guidelines on prosecuting cases involving communications sent via social media', issued by the Director of Public Prosecutions on 19 December 2012.

Cumberbatch, G. (2004) 'Villain or victim? A review of the research evidence concerning media violence and its effects in the real world with additional reference to video games', A report prepared for The Video Standards Council.

Currie, E. (2002) Diaries, 1987–1992. London: Times Warner Books UK.

Daly, M. (2013) 'Is there an entitlement to anonymity? A European and international analysis', European Intellectual Property Review, 35(4), 198–211.

Darnton, R. (1990) What was Revolutionary about the French Revolution? Waco, TX: Baylor University Press.

Davies, M. (2010) 'The demise of professional self-regulation? Evidence from the "ideal type" professions of medicine and law', Professional Negligence, 26(1), 3–38.

De Waele, H. (2012) 'Implications of replacing the Data Protection Directive with a Regulation – a legal perspective', Privacy & Data Protection, 12(4), 3–5.

Deazley, R. (2008) Rethinking Copyright: History, theory, language. Northampton, MA: Edward Elgar Publishing Ltd.

Dehin, V. (2010) 'The future of legal online music services in the European Union: A review of the EU Commission's recent initiatives in cross-border copyright management', European Intellectual Property Review, 32(5), 220–237.

Denham, E. (2009) 'Report Of Findings into the Complaint Filed by the Canadian Internet Policy and Public Interest Clinic (CIPPIC) against Facebook Inc'. Office of the Privacy Commissioner of Canada, 16 July 2009: www.priv.gc.ca/cf-dc/2009/2009_008_0716_e.pdf.

Denning, Lord (1949) 'Freedom under the Law'. The Hamlyn Lectures, First Series. London.

Deringer, K. F. (2003) 'Privacy and the Press: The convergence of British and French Law in accordance with the European Convention of Human Rights', Penn State International Law Review, 22 (Summer). Carlisle, PA: Dickinson School of Law.

Descheemaeker, E. (2009) 'Protecting reputation: defamation and negligence', Oxford Journal of Legal Studies, 29(4), 603–641.

Devlin, Sir Patrick (1956, reprinted 1966) Trial by Jury. London: Methuen.

Doley, C., Starte, H., Addy, C., Helme, I., Griffiths, J., Scott, A. and Mullis, A. (eds) (2009) Carter-Ruck on Libel and Slander. London: Butterworths.

Downie, J. A. (1979) Robert Harley and the Press: Propaganda and public opinion in the age of Swift and Defoe. Cambridge: Cambridge University Press.

Duncan, A. G. M., Gordon, W. M., Gamble, A. J. and Reid, K. G. C. (1996) The Law of Property in Scotland. Edinburgh: Butterworths.

Dunlop, R. (2006) 'Article 10, the Reynolds test and the rule in the Duke of Brunswick's case – the decision in Times Newspapers Ltd v United Kingdom', European Human Rights Law Review, 3, 327–339.

Dupré, C. (2000) 'The protection of private life against freedom of expression in French law', European Human Rights Law Review, 6, 627–649.

Edwards, S.M. (1997) 'A safe haven for hardest core', Entertainment Law Review, 8(4), 137–42.

Edwards, S. M. (1998) 'On the contemporary application of the Obscene Publications Act 1959', Criminal Law Review, December, 843–853.

Edwards, S.M. (2000) 'The failure of British obscenity law in the regulation of pornography', Journal of Sexual Aggression: An international, interdisciplinary forum for research, theory and practice, 6(1), 111–127.

Elliott, D. W. (1993) 'Blasphemy and other expressions of offensive opinion', Ecclesiastical Law Journal, 3(13), 70–85.

Epworth, J. (2005) 'Protecting your private life: The future of OFCOM privacy complaints', Communications Law, 10(6), 191–196.

Ericson, E. E. and Mahoney, D. J. (eds) (2009) The Solzhenitsyn Reader: New and essential writings, 1947–2005. Wilmington, NC: ISI Books (Intercollegiate Studies Institute).

European Advertising Standards Alliance (EASA) Blue Book (6th edn). Brussels: EASA.

European Commission (2007) Green Paper on Copyright in the Knowledge Economy. COM (2007) 724 final, Brussels, 20 November.

European Commission (2010) *A Digital Agenda for Europe.* COM (2010) 245 final, Brussels, 19 May.

European Commission (2011) *A Single Market for Intellectual Property Rights. Boosting creativity and innovation to provide economic growth, high quality jobs and first class products and services in Europe.* COM (2011) 287. Brussels, 24 May.

European Commission (2012) *Proposal for a Directive of the European Parliament and the Council on collective management of copyright and related rights and multi-territorial licensing of rights in musical works for online uses in the internal market.* COM (2012) 372 final 2012/0180 (COD), Brussels, 11 July.

European Commission (2013) *Proposal for a Regulation of the European Parliament and of the Council amending Regulation (EU) No 1215/2012 on jurisdiction and the recognition and enforcement of judgments in civil and commercial matters.* COM (2013) 554. 2013/0268 (COD), Brussels, 26 July.

Evans, H. (1983) *Good Times, Bad Times.* London: Weidenfeld & Nicolson.

Farrand, B. (2012) 'Too much is never enough? The 2011 Copyright in Sound Recordings Extension Directive', *European Intellectual Property Review,* 34(5), 297–304.

Fenwick, H. and Phillipson, G. (2006) *Media Freedom under the Human Rights Act.* Oxford: Oxford University Press.

Ficsor, M. (2003) 'Collective management of copyright and related rights at a triple crossroads: Should it remain voluntary or may it be "extended" or made mandatory?' Copyright Bulletin 3. United Nations, Educational, Scientific and Cultural Organization (online publication): http://portal.unesco.org/culture/en/ev.php-URL_ID=14935&URL_DO=DO_TOPIC&URL_SECTION=201.html.

Fohl, K. (2009) 'Which factors leading to decreasing sales in the music industry can be influenced by online marketing tools?' Budapest Business School. Faculty of International management and Business: http://elib.kkf.hu/edip/D_15267.pdf.

Foster, S. (2010) 'Possession of extreme pornographic images, public protection and human rights', *Coventry Law Journal,* 15(1), 21–27.

Foster, S. (2011) 'The public interest in press intrusion into the private lives of celebrities: the decision in *Ferdinand v MGN Ltd'*, Communications Law, 16(4), 201, 127–131.

Fox, Sir John C. (1927) *The History of Contempt of Court. The form of trial and the mode of punishment.* Oxford: The Clarendon Press.

Foxon, D. (1965) *Libertine Literature in England 1660–1745.* New York: New Hyde Park Publishing, pp. 19–30.

Freud, S. (1976) *The Interpretation of Dreams.* London: Penguin Books. (1900, 1st edn, *Über den Traum.* Wiesbaden: Verlag J. F. Bergmann).

Fritscher, J. (2002) 'What happened when? Censorship, gay history and Robert Mapplethorpe', in D. Jones (ed.) *Censorship: A world encyclopaedia.* New York: Fitzroy Dearborn Publishers, pp. 67–98.

Frost, C. (2011) *Journalism, Ethics and Regulation* (3rd edn). Harlow: Longman.

Gaber, I. (2009) 'Three cheers for subjectivity: Or the crumbling of the seven pillars of traditional journalistic wisdom', *Communications Law,* 14(5), 150–156.

Garzaniti, L. (2009) *Telecommunications, Broadcasting and the Internet: EU competition law and regulation* (3rd edn). London: Sweet & Maxwell.

Gatley, J. C. C. (2013) *Gatley on Libel and Slander* (12th edn) (eds Milmo, P., Rogers, W. V. H., Parkes, R., Walker, C. and Busuttil, G.). London: Sweet & Maxwell.

Geddis, A. (2010) 'What we cannot talk about we must pass over in silence: judicial orders and reporting Parliamentary speech', *Public Law,* July, 443–451.

Gibbons, T. (1996) 'Defamation reconsidered', *Oxford Journal of Legal Studies,* 16(4), 587–615.

Giles, P. (2000) 'Virtual Eden: Lolita, pornography, and the perversions of American studies', *Cambridge Journal of American Studies,* 34(1), 41–66.

Gillieron, P. (2006) 'Performing Rights Societies in the Digital Environment', unpublished thesis, Stanford Law School: www.law.stanford.edu/sites/default/files/biblio/108/143082/doc/slspublic/GilliieronPhilippe-tft2006.pdf.

Gilvarry, E. (1990) 'Mapplethorpe retrospective sparks pornography debate', *Law Society Gazette,* 87(33), 10–11.

Goldberg, D. (2009) 'Freedom of information in the 21st century: bringing clarity to transparency', *Communications,* 14(2), 50–56.

Goldsmith, J. and Wu, T. (2008) *Who Controls the Internet?: Illusions of a borderless world*. London/ New York: Oxford University Press.

Gordon, S. (2008) *The Future of the Music Business. How to succeed with the new digital technologies. A guide for artists and entrepreneurs* (2nd edn). San Francisco, CA: Backbeat Books (Hal Leonard Corporation).

Grant, H. and Round, N. (2012) 'Recent decisions of the Commissioner and Tribunal', *Freedom of Information*, 9(2), 8–12.

Gravells, N. P. (2007) 'Authorship and originality: The persistent influence of *Walter v Lane*', *Intellectual Property Quarterly*, 3, 267–293.

Griffiths, J. (2010) 'Rhetoric and the "Three-Step Test": Copyright reform in the United Kingdom', *European Intellectual Property Review*, 32(7), 309–312.

Groll, L. (1980) *Freedom and Self Discipline of the Swedish Press*. Stockholm: The Swedish Institute.

Habermas, J. (1962, translation 1989) *The Structural Transformation of the Public Sphere: An inquiry into a category of bourgeois society* (original in German *Strukturwandel der Öffentlichkeit. Untersuchungen zu einer Kategorie der bürgerlichen Gesellschaft*). Cambridge: Polity Press.

Habermas, J. (1992, translation 1996) *Between Facts and Norms: Contributions to a discourse theory of law and democracy* (original in German *Faktizität und Geltung*). Cambridge: Polity Press.

Habermas, J. (1994) 'Three normative models of democracy', *Constellations: An International Journal of Critical and Democratic Theory*, 1(1) (December), 10.

Haig, S. (2013) 'The Defamation Act 2013 and what it means for the Internet', *E-Commerce Law & Policy*, 15(6), 14–15.

Hain, P. (2012) *Outside In*. London: Biteback Publishing.

Hally, M. (2012) 'Local authorities and film censorship: a historical account of the "Naughty Pictures Committees" in Sale and Manchester'. *Entertainment and Sportw Law Journal*, 11 (ISSN 1748–944X): www2.warwick.ac.uk/fac/soc/law/elj/eslj/issues/volume11/hally/hally.pdf.

Hanison, D. (2013) 'Performers, session musicians and record producers set to have their rights extended from November 2013', *Entertainment Law Review*, 24(3), 73–77.

Hayman, A. and Gilmore, M. (2009) *The Terrorist Hunters: The ultimate inside story of Britain's fight against terror*. London: Bantam Press.

Hampel, S. (1992) 'Note: Are Samplers Getting a Bum Rap? Copyright infringement of technological creativity?', *University of Illinois Law Review*, 559.

Harding, T. (2013) 'BitTorrent tracking as a means of detecting illegal file-sharing', *E-Commerce Law & Policy*, 15(2), 8–9.

Hargreaves, I. (2011) *Digital Opportunity. A Review of Intellectual Property and Growth* ('The Hargreaves Review'). Newport: Intellectual Property Office: http://www.ipo.gov.uk/ipreview-finalreport.pdf.

Harris, D., O'Boyle, M., Warbrick, C., Bates, E. and Buckley, C. (2009) *Law of the European Convention on Human Rights* (2nd edn). Oxford: Oxford University Press.

Harrison, A. (2011) *Music: The Business. The essential guide to the law and the deals* (5th edn). Chatham: Virgin Books/Random House.

Hauch, J. M (1994) 'Protecting private facts in France: The Warren and Brandeis tort is alive and well and flourishing in Paris', *Tulane Law Review*, 68, 1219.

Hedley, S. and Aplin, T. (2008) *Blackstone's Statutes on IT and e-Commerce* (4th edn). Oxford: Oxford University Press.

Henderson, G. (2009) 'A new form of libel tourist? *Ewing v Times Newspapers Ltd*. Case Comment', *Scots Law Times*, 20, 116–118.

Herzfeld, P. (2005) 'Corporations, defamation and general damages: back to first principles', *Media and Arts Law Review*, 10, 135.

Herring, J. (2011) *Family Law* (5th edn). Harlow: Longman.

Hewitt, S. (2010) *Snitch! A history of the modern intelligence informer*. London: Continuum.

Heylin, C. (1994) *The Great White Wonders: A history of rock bootlegs*. London: Viking.

Higgins, A. (2012) 'Legal lessons from the *News of the World* phone hacking scandal', *Civil Justice Quarterly*, 31(3), 274–284.

Hildebrand, L. (2009) *Inherent Vice: Bootleg histories of videotape and copyright*. Durham, NC: Duke University Press.

Hirst, M. (2002) 'Cyberobscenity and the Ambit of English Criminal Law', Computers and Law, 13, 25.

Hixson, R. (1987) Privacy in a Public Society: Human rights in conflict. Oxford: Oxford University Press.

HM Department for Culture, Media and Sports (DCMS) and Department for Innovation, Business and Skills (BIS) (2009) Digital Britain. Presented to Parliament by The Secretary of State for Culture, Media and Sport and the Minister for Communications, Technology and Broadcasting. June 2009. London: The Stationery Office, Cm 7650.

HM Government (2012) Consultation on Copyright. Summary of Responses. June 2012 ('The Hargreaves Review') at: www.ipo.gov.uk/copyright-summaryofresponses-pdf.

HM Treasury (2006) Gowers Review of Intellectual Property. London: HMSO.

HM Treasury (2009) Taking Forward the Gowers Review of Intellectual Property: Proposed Changes to Copyright Exceptions. Second stage consultation on copyright. London: HMSO.

Hoffmann, Lord (2009) 'The universality of human rights', Law Quarterly Review, 125 (July), 416–432.

Holdsworth, W., Sir (1920) 'Press control and copyright in the 16th and 17th Centuries', Yale Law Journal, 29, 841.

Holdsworth, W., Sir (1942) A History of English Law (5th edn). London: Methuen & Co.

Hollingsworth, M. and Fielding, N. (1999) Defending the Realm: MI5 and the David Shayler affair. London: Andre Deutsch Ltd.

Home Office (1975) Report of the Advisory Group on the Law of Rape ('the Heilbron Report'). Cmnd 6352, December. London: HMSO.

Home Office (1987) The Byford Report. Home Office papers 1981–86. London: HMSO.

Home Office (1997) No More Excuses: A new approach to tackling youth crime in England and Wales. A White Paper presented to Parliament by the Secretary of State for the Home Department, Mr Jack Straw MP. November. Cm 3809. London: HMSO.

Home Office (2002) The Criminal Justice Bill: Justice for All. Cm 5563, July. London: Stationery Office.

Home Office and The Scottish Executive (2005) Consultation: On the Possession of Extreme Pornographic Material. August. London and Edinburgh.

Hooper, D., Waite, K. and Murphy, O. (2013) 'Defamation Act 2013 – what difference will it really make?', Entertainment Law Review, 24(6), 199–206.

House of Commons (1973) 'Privacy: Younger Committee's report', HC Debate 6 June 1973. Hansard, vol. 343: cc 104–178.

House of Commons (1974) Report of the Committee on Contempt of Court. Cmnd 5794. London: HMSO.

House of Commons (1980) Contempt of Court. A discussion paper. Cmnd 7145. London: HMSO.

House of Commons (1981) Report of the Committee on Contempt of Court. Cmnd. 5794. London: HMSO.

House of Commons (1990) 'The Calcutt Report'. HC Debate 21 June 1990. Hansard, vol. 174: cc 1125–1134.

House of Commons (1994) First Report of the Committee on Standards in Public Life: The Nolan Report. Volume 1: Report, Cm 2850–I; Volume 2: Transcripts of Oral Evidence, Cm 2850–II. London: HMSO.

House of Commons (1995) 'Privacy and media intrusion'. HC Debate 17 July 1995, Hansard, vol. 263: cc 132–139.

House of Commons (2003) Fifth Annual Report. 24 June: www.publications.parliament.uk/pa/cm200203/cmselect/cmhaff/639/63902.htm.

House of Commons – Department of Culture, Media and Sport (2003) Privacy and Media Intrusion. Select Committee Report. Session 2003–03. 16 June. HC 458-I. London: The Stationery Office.

House of Commons (2004) Report of the Inquiry into the Circumstances Surrounding the Death of Dr David Kelly C.M.G. by Lord Hutton ('The Hutton Report'). HC 247 London: The Stationery Office.

House of Commons – Department of Culture, Media and Sport (2007) Report by the Select Committee on 'Self-Regulation of the Press', 7th Report, 3 July. Session 2006–07, HC 375. London: The Stationery Office.

House of Commons (2009) Intelligence and Security Committee Report: 'Could 7/7 have been prevented? Review of the intelligence on the London terrorist attacks on 7 July 2005. Cm 7617. London: The Stationery Office.

House of Commons – Department of Culture, Media and Sport Select Committee (2010a) Second Report on 'Press standards, privacy and libel', 9 February. London: The Stationery Office: www.publications.parliament.uk/pa/cm200910/cmselect/cmcumeds/362/36202.htm.

House of Commons (2010b) *The Government's Response to the Culture, Media and Sport Select Committee on Press Standards, Privacy and Libel*. April. Cm 7851: London: The Stationery Office: www.official-documents.gov.uk/document/cm78/7851/7851.pdf.

House of Commons – Department of Culture, Media and Sport Select Committee (2010c) *Press Standards, Privacy and Libel*, Session 2009–10, HC 362. London: The Stationery Office.

House of Commons – Department of Culture, Media and Sport Committee (2012a) *News International and Phone-hacking*. Eleventh Report of Session 2010–12 Volume I: Report, together with formal minutes; Volume II: Oral and written evidence. 1 May 2012 HC 903-I. London: The Stationery Office: www.publications.parliament.uk/pa/cm201012/cmselect/cmcumeds/903/903i.pdf.

House of Commons (2012b) *The Report of the Hillsborough Independent Panel*. September. HC 581 London: The Stationery Office: http://hillsborough.independent.gov.uk/repository/report/HIP_report.pdf.

House of Lords (1983) Press Council Report. House of Lords Debate', Hansard: HL Deb 20 July 1983, Vol. 443: cc 1159–1170 (see also: Press Council 1983).

House of Lords and House of Commons (2010) *Human Rights Joint Committee. Counter-Terrorism Policy and Human Rights*. 16th Report. Annual Renewal of Control Orders Legislation 2010. Internet publication: www.publications.parliament.uk/pa/jt200910/jtselect/jtrights/64/6402.htm.

Independent Police Complaints Commission (IPCC) (2013) *Commissioner's report IPCC independent investigation into Surrey Police's knowledge of the alleged illegal accessing of Amanda (Milly) Dowler's mobile phone in 2002* by Deborah Glass, IPCC Deputy Chair, April 2013.

Information Commissioner's Office (ICO) (2006a) *What Price Privacy? The unlawful trade in confidential personal information*, presented by the Information Commissioner to Parliament pursuant to section 52(2) of the Data Protection Act 1998. 10 May 2006. HC 1056. London: The Stationery Office.

Information Commissioner's Office (ICO) (2006b) *A Report on the Surveillance Society, for the Information Commissioner by the Surveillance Studies Network*. September 2006. Online report: http://www.ico.org.uk/ /media/documents/library/Data_Protection/Practical_application/SURVEILLANCE_SOCIETY_FULL_REPORT_2006.ashx.

Information Commissioner's Office (2013) *Implications of the European Commission's proposal for a general data protection regulation for business. Final report to the Information Commissioner's Office*. May 2013 at: http://www.ico.org.uk/about_us/research/ /media/documents/library/Data_Protection/Research_and_reports/implications-european-commissions-proposal-general-data-protection-regulation-for-business.ashx.

Intellectual Property Office (IPO) (2013a) *Intellectual Property Rights in India*. Newport: Intellectual Property Office, April: http://www.ipo.gov.uk/ipindia.pdf.

Intellectual Property Office (IPO) (2013b) *Copyright in Europe. Call for views*. Consultation Paper. Newport: Intellectual Property Office: www.ipo.gov.uk/consult–2013-copyrighteurope.pdf.

Intellectual Property Office (IPO) (2013c) *Consultation on the Implementation of Directive 2011/77/EU Amending Directive 2006/116/EC on the Term of Protection of Copyright and Certain Related rights*. Newport: Intellectual Property Office: www.ipo.gov.uk/consult–2013-copyterm.pdf.

Internet Watch Foundation (2011) *Annual and Charity Report*. Cambridge: Internet Watch Foundation: www.iwf.org.uk/assets/media/annual-reports/annual%20med%20res.pdf.

Isocrates (1980) *Isocrates: with an English Translation in three volumes*, by George Norlin, PhD, LLD. Cambridge, MA, Harvard University Press; London, William Heinemann Ltd.

Iyer, V. (2009) 'The Media and Scandalising: Time for a Fresh Look', *Northern Ireland Legal Quarterly*, 60, 245 . Jackson, R. M. (1903) *Jackson's Machinery of Justice*: see Spencer, J. R. (1989).

Jackson, R. M. (1937) 'Common law misdemeanours', *Cambridge Law Journal*, 6, 193–201.

Jaconelli, J. (2002) *Open Justice: A critique of the public trial*. Oxford: Oxford University Press.

Jaconelli, J. (2007) 'Defences to speech crimes', *European Human Rights Law Review*, 1, 27–46.

James, J. and Ghandi, S. (1998) 'The English law of blasphemy and the European Convention on Human Rights', *European Human Rights Law Review*, 4, 430–451.

Jerrold, C. (1913) *The Married Life of Queen Victoria*. London: G. Bell & Sons Ltd.

Johnson, H. (2006) 'Family justice: open justice'. *Communications Law*, 11(5), 171–174.

Johnson, H. (2008a) 'Freedom of information – confidence and journalism exemptions from Disclosure', *Communications Law*, 13(5), 174–176.

Johnson, H. (2008b) 'Defamation: The media on the defensive?', *Communications Law*, 13(4), 126–131.

Johnson, H. (2013a) 'Leveson and feelings of anti-climax', *Communications Law*, 18(1), 1–2.

Johnson, H. (2013b) Loss of sensitive health data – challenging a monetary penalty: *Central London Community Healthcare Trust v Information Commissioner* (EA/2012/00111). Case Comment'. *Communications Law*, 18(1), 25–28.

Jordan, B. (2010a) 'Existing defamation law needs to be updated so that it is fit for the modern age. The Government's consultation on the multiple publication rule', *Entertainment Law Review*, 21(2), 41–47.

Jordan, B. (2010b) 'Reputation and Article 8: *Karako v Hungary*. Case Comment', *Entertainment Law Review*, 21(3), 109–111.

Jordan, B. (2011) 'Self-regulation and the British press', *Entertainment Law Review*, 22(8), 242–243.

Jordan, B. and Hurst, I. (2012) 'Privacy and the Princess – a review of the Grand Chamber's decisions in *Von Hannover* and *Axel Springer*', *Entertainment Law Review*, 23(4), 108–113.

Judge, Lord LCJ (2008) 'Time of change: The criminal justice system in England and Wales'. Speech to the University of Hertfordshire, 4 November: www.judiciary.gov.uk/Resources/JCO/Documents/Speeches/lcj-speech-uni-hertfordshire–041108.pdf.

Judge, Lord LCJ (2011) 13th Annual Justice Lecture: Press Regulation, 19 October 2011: www.judiciary.gov.uk/Resources/JCO/Documents/Speeches/lcj-speech-annual-justice-lecture–2011.pdf.

Kearns, P. (2000) 'Obscene and blasphemous libel: Misunderstanding art', *Criminal Law Review*, Aug, 652–660.

Keeling, D. T., Llewelyn, D. and Mellor, J. (2010) *Kerly's Law of Trade Marks and Trade Names* (15th edn). London: Sweet & Maxwell.

Kendrick, W. (1997) *The Secret Museum: Pornography in modern culture*. Ewing, NJ: University of California Press.

Kennedy, J. (2010) *Music How, When, Where You Want It – but not without addressing piracy*. London: International Federation of the Phonographic Industry (IFPI).

Kerly, Sir D. M., Keeling, D. T., Llewelyn, D. and Mellor, J. (eds) (2009) *Kerly's Law of Trade Marks and Trade Names* (15th edn). London: Sweet & Maxwell.

Khan, A. (2012) 'A "right not to be offended" under article 10(2) ECHR? Concerns in the construction of the "rights of others" ', *European Human Rights Law Review*, 2, 191–204.

Kilbrandon, Lord (1964) *Report of the Committee on Children and Young Persons, Scotland* ('The Kilbrandon Report'). Cmnd 2306, London: HMSO.

Kilbrandon, Lord (1971) 'The Law of Privacy in Scotland', 2 *Cambrian Law Review*, 35, 128.

Kirk, E. (2006) 'The *DaVinci Code* case – *Baigent & Leigh v Random House*: ideas v expression revisited', *Intellectual Property & Information Law*, 11(3), 4–6.

Klang, M. and Murray, A. (2004) *Human Rights in the Digital Age*. Oxford: Routledge-Cavendish.

Klazmer, E. (2012) 'The uncertainties of libel tourism, is diplomacy the answer?', *Entertainment Law Review*, 23(6), 164–168.

Kleinwachter, W. (2012) 'Internet governance outlook 2012: cold war or constructive dialogue?', *Communications Law*, 17(1), 14–18.

Koempel, F. (2005) 'Data protection and intellectual property', *Computer and Telecommunications Law Review*, 11(6), 185–187.

Koempel, F. (2007) 'If the kids are united', *Journal of Intellectual Property Law & Practice*, 2(6), 371–376.

Koempel, F. (2010) 'The Digital Economy Bill', *Computer and Telecommunications Law Review*, 16(2), 39–43.

Kreile, R. and Becker, J. (2001) 'Rechtedurchsetzung und Rechteverwaltung durch Verwertungsgesellschaften in der Informationsgesellschaft' ('Rights enforcement and management by collecting societies in the information society'), *GEMA Yearbook* 2000/2001, pp. 85, 89. Berlin: GEMA.

Ky Chan, G. (2013) 'Corporate defamation: reputation, rights and remedies', *Legal Studies*, 33(2) (June), 264–288.

Laddie, H., Prescott, P. and Vitoria, M. (2011) (Vioria, M., Speck, A., Lane, L., Alexander, D., Tappin, M., Clark, F., Onslow, R., May, C., Berkeley, I. and Whyte, J. eds) *The Modern Law of Copyright and Designs* (4th edn). London: Butterworths.

Larusson, H. K. (2009) 'Uncertainty in the scope of copyright: the case of illegal file-sharing in the UK', *European Intellectual Property Review*, 31(3), 124–134.

Law Commission (1982) *Criminal Libel*. Working Paper No. 84. London: HMSO.

Law Commission, The (2002) *Defamation and the Internet: A preliminary investigation, Scoping Study No 2*, December 2002. London: HMSO.

Law Commission (2011) *Eleventh Programme of Law Reform*. Presented to Parliament pursuant to section 3(2) of the Law Commissions Act 1965. (LAW COM No 330) HC 1407. 19 July 2011. London: The Stationery Office.

Law Commission, The (2012a) *Contempt of Court: Scandalising the Court*. Consultation Paper No 207. London: The Stationery Office. ID P002506634 08/12 22941 19585: http://lawcommission.justice.gov.uk/docs/cp207_Scandalising_the_Court_for_web.pdf.

Law Commission (2012b) *Contempt of Court*. Consultation Paper No 209. November 2012. London: The Stationery Office: http://lawcommission.justice.gov.uk/docs/cp209_contempt_of_court.pdf. Law Commission of New Zealand (2011) *The News Media meets 'New media': Rights, responsibilities and Regulation in the Digital Age*, December 2011: www.lawcom.govt.nz/project/review-regulatory-gaps-and-new-media.

Lawrence, D. H. (1928; first UK publication 1960) *Lady Chatterley's Lover*. London: Penguin Classics.

Lee, S. (1987) 'Spycatcher', *The Law Quarterly Review* 103, 506.

Leigh, I. (1992) 'Spycatcher in Strasbourg', *Public Law*, 200.

Lennon, C. (2005) *John*. London: Hodder & Stoughton.

Lester, Lord of Herne Hill (1993) 'Freedom of expression', in Macdonald, R. J., Matscher, F. and Petzold, H. (eds) *The European System for the Protection of Human Rights*. Dordrecht: Martinus Nijhoff, pp. 465–481.

Lester; Lord Lester of Herne Hill, Panick, Lord David and Herberg, Javan (eds) (2009) *Human Rights Law and Practice* (3rd rev. edn). London: LexisNexis.

Leveson, Lord LJ (2012) *An Inquiry into the Culture, Practices and Ethics of the Press. Report by The Right Honourable Lord Justice Leveson in 4 Volumes*. Volume I 'The Inquiry', Volume II 'The Culture, Practices and Ethics of the Press', Volume III 'The Press and Data Protection', Volume IV 'Aspects of regulation: the law and the Press Complaints Commission'. November 2012. London: The Stationery Office. ID P002525215 11/12 22930 19585. (also cited as: The Report of An Inquiry into the Culture, Practices and Ethics of the Press as presented to Parliament (HC 780) ('The Leveson Report' or 'Leveson'). 29 November: http://www.official-documents.gov.uk/document/hc1213/hc07/0780/0780.asp.

Lewis, T. (2002) 'Human Earrings, Human Rights and Public Decency', *Entertainment Law*, 1(2), Summer, 50–71.

Lindon, M. (1998) *Le Procès de Jean-Marie Le Pen*. Paris: POL.

Lipstadt, D. E. (1994) *Denying the Holocaust: The growing assault on truth and memory*. London: Penguin.

Lipstadt, D. E. (2006) *History on Trial: My day in court with David Irving*. New York: Harper Collins.

Lloyd-Bostock, S. (2007) 'The Jubilee Line jurors: Does their experience strengthen the argument for judge-only trial in long and complex fraud cases?', *Criminal Law Review*, Apr, 255–273.

Loveland, I. (1998) 'The constitutionalisation of political libels in English Common Law?', *Public Law*, 633.

Loveland, I. (2000) *Political Libels: A comparative study*. Oxford: Hart Publishing.

Lovelace, L. (Linda Susan Boreman) (1976) *Inside Linda Lovelace*. London: Pinnacle Books.

Lucas, A. (2010) 'For a reasonable interpretation of the three-step test', *European Intellectual Property Review*, 32(6), 277–282.

Lui, E. (2003) 'The Eurovision Song Contest: a proposal for reconciling the national regulation of music collecting societies and the Single European Market', *Entertainment Law Review*, 14(4), 67–84.

Macmillan, K. (2009) 'Internet publication rule survives', *Communications Law*, 14(3), 80–2.

MacQueen, H. (2012) *Studying Scots Law* (4th edn). Edinburgh: Bloomsbury Professional.

Mahoney, P. (1997) 'Universality versus subsidiarity in the Strasbourg case law on free speech: Explaining some recent judgments', *European Human Rights Law Review*, 4, 364–379.

Manchester, C. (1988) 'Lord Campbell's Act: England's first obscenity statute', *Journal of Legal History*, 9(2), 223–241.

Mansfield, M. (2010) *Memoirs of a Radical Lawyer*. London: Bloomsbury.

Markesinis, B. S. (1990) *The German Law of Torts: A comparative introduction* (2nd edn). Oxford: Clarendon Press.

Markesinis, B. S. and Unberath, H. (2002) *The German Law of Torts: A comparative treatise*. London: Hart.

Marsh, K. (2012) *Stumbling over Truth*. London: Biteback Publishing.

Master of the Rolls (2011) *Report of the Committee on Super-Injunctions: Super-Injunctions, Anonymised Injunctions and Open Justice* ('the Neuberger Report'): www.judiciary.gov.uk/Resources/JCO/ Documents/Reports/super-injunction-report–20052011.pdf.

Matthews, R., Hancock, L. and Briggs, D. (2004) *Jurors' Perceptions, Understanding, Confidence and Satisfaction in the Jury System: A study in six courts*. Research Development and Statistics Directorate. Home Office Report No. 05/04: http://library.npia.police.uk/docs/hordsolr/ rdsolr0504.pdf.

McEvedy, V. (2002) 'The Digital Millennium Copyright Act and the E-Commerce Directive', *European Intellectual Property Review*, 24(2),65–73.

McEvedy, V. (2013) 'Defamation and intermediaries: ISP defences', *Computer and Telecommunications Law Review* 19(4), 108–112.

McGlynn, C. and Rackley, E. (2007) 'Striking a balance: arguments for the criminal regulation of extreme pornography', *Criminal Law Review*, Sep, 677–690.

McGlynn, C. and Rackley, E. (2009) 'Criminalising extreme pornography: a lost opportunity', *Criminal Law Review*, 4, 245–260.

McGonagle, M. and Barrett, N. (2007) 'Reforming media law in Ireland: Broadcasting', *Communications Law*, 12(1), 11–17.

McInnes, R. (2009a) 'Footballers' faces: Photographs, identification and publication contempt', *Scots Law Times*, 21, 123–126.

McInnes, R. (2009b) 'The ones which got away? Reporting of criminal trials', *Scots Law Times*, 25, 149–152.

McInnes, R. (2010) *Scots Law for Journalists* (8th edn). Edinburgh: W Green/ Sweet & Maxwell.

McKittrick, D. and McVea, D. (2001) *Making Sense of the Troubles*. London: Penguin.

McLagan, G (2004) *Bent Coppers: The inside story of Scotland Yard's battle against police corruption*. London: Orion.

McLeod, K. (2004) 'How Copyright Law Changed Hip Hop', *Stay Free* magazine, 20, 23 June: www.stayfreemagazine.org/archives/20/public_enemy.html.

McLuhan, M. (1962) *The Gutenberg Galaxy*. Toronto: University of Toronto Press.

McLuhan, M. (1964; reprint 2013) *Understanding Media: The extensions of man*. Berkeley, CA: Gingko Press.

McLuhan, M. (1967) *The Medium is the Message*. London: Penguin.

Mill, J. S. (1859) *On Liberty* (4th edn). London: Longmans, Green, Reader and Dyer.

Miller, F. P., Vandome, A. F and McBrewster, J. (eds) (2009) *Intellectual Property: Government-granted monopoly, exclusive right, copyright, trademark, patent, industrial design right, trade secret, history of patent law, history of copyright law*. Beau Bassin, Mauritius: Alphascript Publishing/VDM Publishing House Ltd.

Milmo, P., Rogers, W. V. H., Parkes, R., Walker, C. and Busuttil, G. (eds) (2010) *Gatley on Libel and Slander* (12th edn). London: Sweet & Maxwell.

Milo, D. (2008) *Defamation and Freedom of Speech*. Oxford: Oxford University Press.

Milton, J. (1644) *Areopagitica: A Speech for the Liberty of Unlicensed Printing to the Parliament of England*. London: printed in the Year 1644. (Reprinted edn 1915. London: MacMillan and Co. Limited).

Mindell, R. (2012) 'Rewriting privacy: the impact of online social networks', *Entertainment Law Review*, 23(3), 52–58.

Ministry of Justice (Home Office) (1965) *Report of the Departmental Committee on Jury Service* ('The Morris Report'), Cmnd 2627. London: HMSO.

Ministry of Justice (2001) *A Review of the Criminal Courts of England and Wales by The Right Honourable Lord Justice Auld* ('The Auld Review'). London: HMSO.

Ministry of Justice (2007) *Diversity and Fairness in the Jury System*, Research Analysis by Thomas, C. and Balmer, N., Ministry of Justice Research Series 2/07 June 2007. London: HMSO.

Ministry of Justice (2009a) *Sensitive Reporting in Coroners' Courts – Response to Comments 2006–2008*, Coroners and Burials Division, January 2009. London: Ministry of Justice.

Ministry of Justice (2009b) *Defamation and the Internet: The Multiple Publication Rule*, Consultation Paper, CP20/09, 16 September 2009. London: Ministry of Justice.

Ministry of Justice (2009c) *Defamation and the Internet: The Multiple Publication Rule*, Response to Consultation, CP(R) 20/09, 23 March 2010. London: Ministry of Justice.

Ministry of Justice (2009d) 'Possession of Extreme Pornographic Images and increase in the maximum sentence for offences under the Obscene Publications Act 1959: Implementation of Sections 63–67 and Section 71 of the Criminal Justice and Immigration Act 2008'. Circular No. 2009/01, 19 January 2009. London: Ministry of Justice.

Ministry of Justice (2010a) *Are Juries Fair?* Research conducted by Professor Cheryl Thomas of the Centre for Empirical Legal Studies, University College London. Ministry of Justice Bulletin Number 39, March 2010.

Ministry of Justice (2010b) *Review of Civil Litigation Costs*. Final Report by Rupert Jackson J, December 2009. P002341871 c7 01/10 860 19585 ('The Jackson Report') London: HMSO: www.judiciary.gov.uk/NR/rdonlyres/8EB9F3F3–9C4A–4139–8A93–56F09672EB6A/0/jacksonfinalreport140110.pdf.

Ministry of Justice (2010c) *Providing Anonymity to those Accused of Rape: An assessment of evidence*. Ministry of Justice Research Series 20/10, November 2010.

Ministry of Justice (2011a) *Draft Defamation Bill*: Consultation Paper CP3/11, March 2011. Cm 8020. London: HMSO.

Ministry of Justice (2011b) *Family Justice Review*. Final Report. November 2011: www.justice.gov.uk/downloads/publications/moj/2011/family-justice-review-final-report.pdf.

Ministry of Justice (2012a) *Swift and Sure Justice: The Government's Plans for Reform of the Criminal Justice System*. White Paper. July 2012. Cm 8388: www.justice.gov.uk/downloads/publications/policy/moj/swift-and-sure-justice.pdf.

Ministry of Justice (2012b) *Putting Victims First: More effective responses to anti-social behaviour*. White Papter, 22 May 2012: www.official-documents.gov.uk/document/cm83/8367/8367.pdf.

Ministry of Justice (2013) *Implementing the Coroner Reforms in Part 1 of the Coroners and Justice Act 2009. Consultation on Rules, Regulations, Coroner Areas and Statutory Guidance*. Consultation Paper CP2/ 2013, 12 April 2013.

Mitchell, P. (1999) 'Malice in qualified privilege', *Public Law*, Summer, 328–340.

Mitchell, P. (2005) *The Making of the Modern Law of Defamation*. Oxford and Oregon, OR: Hart Publishing.

Mommsen, T. (1954) *The History of Rome*, Volumes I–V. (orig. *Römische Geschichte* 1854–1856). New York: Appleton & Co.

Moore, B. (1984) *Privacy: Studies in social and cultural history*. Armonk, NY: M. E. Sharpe Publishing.

Moreham, N. A. (2001) '*Douglas and Others v. Hello! Ltd*: The protection of privacy in English private law', *The Modern Law Review*, 767.

Moreham, N. A. (2008) 'The right to respect for private life in the European Convention on Human Rights: A re-examination', *European Human Rights Law Review*, 1, 44–79.

Morgan P. (2005) *The Insider: The private diaries of a scandalous decade*. London: Ebury Press.

Mullis, A. and Scott, A. (2009) 'Something rotten in the state of English Libel Law? A rejoinder to the clamour for reform of defamation', *Communications Law*, 14(6), 173–183.

Mullis, A. and Scott, A. (2012) 'The swing of the pendulum: reputation, expression and the re-centring of English libel law', *Northern Ireland Legal Quarterly*, 63(1), 27–58.

Munro, V. (2006) 'Sex, laws and videotape: the R18 category', *Criminal Law Review*, Nov, 957–968.

Munro, V. (2007) 'Dev'l-in Disguise? Harm, Privacy and the Sexual Offences Act 2003' in Munro, V and Stychin. C. (eds) *Sexuality and the Law – feminist engagements*. Abingdon. Routledge.

Music Managers Forum (2003) *The Music Management Bible* (2nd edn). London: Sanctuary Publishing Ltd.

Nabokov, V. V. (1958) *Lolita*. New York: Berkley Publishing Group (first published 1955 in French, Paris: Olympia Press; first British edition 1959, published by Weidenfeld and Nicolson, London).

Nagle, E. (2009) 'Keeping its own counsel: The Irish Press Council, self-regulation and media freedom', *Entertainment Law Review*, 20(3), 93–99.

National Audit Office (2009) *The Procurement of Criminal Legal Aid in England and Wales by the Legal Services Commission*. Report by the Comptroller and Auditor General. Session 2009–10. HC 29. London: HMSO.

National Council for Public Morals (1917) 'The Cinema: Its present position and future possibilities', Report of Chief Evidence. London: Williams and Norgate.

Neethling, J., Potgieter, J. M. and Scott, T. J. (1995) *Casebook on the Law of Delict /Vonnisbundel oor die Deliktereg* (2nd edn). Cape Town: Juta Legal and Academic Publishers.

Neethling, J., Potgieter, J. M. and Visser, P. J. (1996) *Neethling's Law of Personality*. Cape Town: Juta Legal and Academic Publishers.

New York Times (2001) *Political Censorship. 20th Century Review*. Chicago, IL: Fitzroy Dearbourn Publishers.

Nokes, G. D. (1928) *A History of the Crime of Blasphemy*. London: Sweet & Maxwell.

Normand, the Right Hon Lord (1938) 'The Law of Defamation in Scotland', *The Cambridge Law Journal*, 6, 327–338.

Norrie, K. (1995) *Defamation and Related Actions in Scots law*. London: Butterworths.

Oats, L. and Sadler, P. (2002) ' "This great crisis in the republick of letters" – the introduction in 1712 of stamp duties on newspapers and pamphlets', *British Tax Review*, 4, 353–366.

Oberholzer-Gee, F. and Strumpf, K. (2005) 'The effect of file sharing on record sales. an empirical analysis.' Harvard Business School UNC Chapel Hill: www.unc.edu/ cigar/papers/ FileSharing_June2005_final.pdf.

Office of Communications (Ofcom) (2012a) *Annual Report and Accounts*. For the period 1 April 2011 to 31 March 2012. HC 237. London: The Stationery Office.

Office of Communications (Ofcom) (2012b) *Communications Market Report 2012*. Research Document of 18 July 2012: http://stakeholders.ofcom.org.uk/binaries/research/cmr/cmr12/ CMR_UK_2012.pdf.

Office of Communications (Ofcom) (2012c) *Online Infringement of Copyright: Implementation of the Online Infringement of Copyright (Initial Obligations) (Sharing of Costs) Order 2012*. Consultation document. June 2012: http://stakeholders.ofcom.org.uk/binaries/consultations/onlinecopyright/ summary/condoc.pdf.

Office of Communications (Ofcom) (2012d) *Review of Postal Users' Needs. A consultation document on the reasonable needs of users in relation to the market for the provision of postal services in the United Kingdom*. December 2012: http://stakeholders.ofcom.org.uk/binaries/consultations/review-of-user- needs/summary/condoc.pdf.

Ormerod, D. (1995) 'Publicity and children cases', *Family Law*, 25, 686.

Ormerod, D. and Williams, D. H. (2007) *Smith's The Law of Theft* (9th edn). Oxford: Oxford University Press.

Orwell, G. (1941) 'The Art of Donald McGill', in *Critical Essays*. London: Horizon (also in *Critical Essays* (1946). London: Secker and Warburg).

Oswald, J. F. (2010) *Contempt of Court, Committal, and Attachment and Arrest Upon Civil Process*. London: Lightning Source UK Ltd.

Owen, L. (ed.) (2007) *Clark's Publishing Agreements: A book of precedents* (7th edn). Haywards Heath: Tottel Publishing.

Oxford Economics (2009) 'Respect for Film: Economic impact of legislative reform to reduce audio-visual piracy'. March 2009, Final Report. Oxford: Oxford Economics.

Page, W. (2007) 'Economics: It's time to face the music', *The Report*, 178 (18 October), 7–8.

Palmer, H. (1997) 'Queen Victoria's not so "Victorian" writings: About pregnancy, children, marriage and men', *Victoriana Magazine*. Online publication: www.victoriana.com/doors/ queenvictoria.htm.

Palmer, T. (1971) *Trials of Oz*. London: Blond & Briggs.

Parsons, K. (2000) 'Pirates' web', *European Lawyer*, 1(1), 38–39, 41–42.

Passman, D. S. (2011) *AllYou Need to Know about the Music Business* (8th edn). London/New York: Viking.

Pedley, P. (2008) *Copyright Compliance: Practical steps to stay within the law*. London: Facet Publishing.

Pfeifer, K-N. (2008) 'The return of the commons: Copyright history as a helpful source?', *International Review of Intellectual Property and Competition Law*, 39(6), 679–688.

Phillips, J. (2009) *Copyright in the UK and the European Community*. London: Butterworths.

Phillipson, G. (2003) 'Breach of confidence, celebrities, freedom of expression, legal reasoning, newspapers, privacy, public interest, right to respect for private and family life', *European Human Rights Law Review* (Special Issue 'Privacy'), 54–72.

Pike, L. O. (1894) *A Constitutional History of the House of Lords*. London: Macmillan.

Pila, J. (2010) 'Copyright and its categories of original works', *Oxford Journal of Legal Studies*, 30(2), 229–254.

Pillans, B. (2012) 'Private lives in St Moritz: *von Hannover v Germany* (no 2). Case Comment', *Communications Law*, 17(2), 63–67.

Pimlot, N. (2007) 'ICSTIS – 20 years on', *Entertainment Law Review*, 18(4), 135–137.

Politkovskaya, A. (2001) *A DirtyWar: A Russian reporter in Chechnya*. London. Harvill Press.

Poole, T. and Shah, S. (2009) 'The impact of the Human Rights Act on the House of Lords', *Public Law*, April, 347–371.

Press Complaints Commission (2009) *The Editor's Code Book* (2nd edn). London: Press Complaints Commission.

Press Council (1983) 'Fair trial and the presumption of innocence', Report on Media Events Surrounding the Peter Sutcliffe Trial. London: The Press Council (as reported in House of Lords Debates, Hansard – see House of Lords (1983) above).

Price, D., Cain, N. and Duodu, K. (2009) *Defamation: Law, procedure and practice*. London: Sweet & Maxwell.

Price, M. E., Verhulst, S. G. and Morgan, L. (eds) (2013) *Routledge Handbook of Media Law*. Abingdon and New York: Routledge.

Rachels, J. (1975) 'Why privacy is important', 4 *Philosophy and Public Affairs*, 323.

Rampal, K. R. (1981) 'The concept of the Press Council', *International Communication Gazette*, 28, 91–103.

Rana, I. S. (1990) *Law of Obscenity in India, USA and UK*. London: Mittal Publications.

Raphael, A. (1989) *My Learned Friends: An insider's view of the Jeffrey Archer Case and other notorious libel actions*. London: W.H. Allen/Virgin Books.

Rawls, J. (1971; 1999 reprinted edn) *A Theory of Justice*. Oxford: Oxford University Press.

Raymond, J. (1998) 'The newspaper, public opinion, and the public sphere in the seventeenth century', *Prose Studies*, 21(2) (August), 109–136.

Reid, E. (2010) *Personality, Confidentiality and Privacy in Scots Law*. Edinburgh: W. Green.

Reid, K. G. C. (1993) *The Laws of Scotland*, Stair Memorial Encyclopaedia, Vol. 18. Edinburgh: Butterworths.

Reid, K. G. C. and Zimmermann, R. (2000) *A History of Private Law in Scotland*. Oxford: Oxford University Press.

Richardson, J. (ed.) (2014) *Archbold: Criminal Pleading, Evidence and Practice 2014*. London: Sweet & Maxwell.

Richardson, M. and Thomas, J. (2012) *Fashioning Intellectual Property: Exhibition, advertising and the press 1789–1918*. Cambridge: Cambridge University Press.

Ricketson, S. (2003) 'The three-step test, deemed quantities, libraries and closed exceptions,' Advice prepared for the Centre for Copyright Studies, Sydney.

Rimington, S. (2002) *Open Secret: The autobiography of the former Director-General of MI5*. London: Arrow Books Ltd.

Roberts, A. and Guelff, R. (2000) *Documents on the Laws of War* (3rd edn). Oxford: Oxford University Press.

Robertson, G. and Nicol, A. (2007) *Media Law* (5th edn). London: Penguin.

Rogers, W. V. H. and Parkes, R. (eds) (2010) *Gatley on Libel and Slander* (11th edn). London: Sweet & Maxwell.

Rogerson, P. (2010) 'Conflict of laws – foreign copyright jurisdiction', *Cambridge Law Journal*, 69(2), 245–247.

Rosati, E. (2011) 'Originality in a work, or a work of originality: the effects of the Infopaq decision', *European Intellectual Property Review*, 33(12), 746–755.

Rösler, H. (2008) 'Dignitarian posthumous personality rights – An analysis of U.S. and German constitutional and tort law', *Berkeley Journal of International Law*, 26 (9 December), 153–205.

Routledge, G. (1989) 'Blasphemy – The Report of the Archbishop of Canterbury's Working Paper on Offences against Religion and Public Worship', *Ecclesiastical Law Review*, 4, 27–31.

Rowbottom, J. (2006) 'Obscenity laws and the internet: targeting the supply and demand', *Criminal Law Review*, February, 97–109.

Rowbottom, J. (2012) 'To rant, vent and converse: protecting low level digital speech', *Cambridge Law Review*, 71(2), 355–383.

Royal Commission (1993) *Report of the Royal Commission on Criminal Justice* ('The Runciman Commission'). London: Stationery Office Books.

Rushdie, S. (1989; new edition 1998) *The Satanic Verses*. Minneapolis, MI and London: Consortium Press.

Rushdie, S. (2012) *Joseph Anton*. London: Jonathan Cape/Random House.

Samuels, A. (2009) 'Obscenity and pornography', *Criminal Law and Justice Weekly*, 173(12), 187–189.

Samuels, E. (2001) *The Illustrated Story of Copyright*. New York: Palgrave Macmillan.

Sanders, K (2003) *Ethics and Journalism*. London: Sage.

Sanjek, D. (1992) ' "Don't have to DJ no more": Sampling and the "autonomous" creator', *Cardozo Arts and Entertainment Law Journal*, 10(2), 612–615.

Schauer, F. (1991) 'Reflections on the value of truth', *Case Western Reserve Law Review*, 41, 699.

Scherer, J. (ed) (2013) *Telecommunication Laws in Europe: Law and regulation of electronic communications in Europe* (6th edn). Haywards Heath: Bloomsbury Professional.

Schilling, K. (1991) 'Privacy and the press: Breach of confidence – the nemesis of the tabloids?', *Entertainment Law Review*, 2(6), 169–176.

Schudson, M. (2003) 'The sociology of news media', in Alexander, G.C. (ed.), *Contemporary Societies*. New York: W.W. Norton & Co.

Schwabach, A. (2011) *Fan Fiction and Copyright: Outsider work and intellectual property protection*. Farnham: Ashgate.

Scottish Children's Reporter Administration (2012) *Reforming Scots Criminal Law and Practice: The Carloway Report*. 5 October 2012: http://www.scra.gov.uk/cms_resources/Reforming%20Scots%20Criminal%20Law%20and%20Practice%20The%20Carloway%20Report%20response.pdf.

Scottish Executive; Northern Ireland Office; Home Office (2006) *Making Sure That Crime Doesn't Pay: Proposals for a new measure to prevent convicted criminals profiting from published accounts of their crimes*. November: http://www.scotland.gov.uk/Resource/Doc/154027/0041420.pdf.

Scottish Government (2009) 'The Modern Scottish Jury in Criminal Trials – Next Steps'. Criminal Justice Directorate. 22 December: www.scotland.gov.uk/Resource/Doc/254431/0092629.pdf

Scottish Government (2011) *Death of a Good Name: Defamation and the Deceased. A Consultation Paper*. Produced for the Scottish Government by APS Group Scotland. DPPAS11019 (01/11). Edinburgh: Scottish Government.

Sellars, S. (2011) 'Online privacy: do we have it and do we want it? A review of the risks and UK case law', *European Intellectual Property Review*, 33(1), 9–17.

Senftleben, M. (2004) *Copyright, Limitations and The Three-Step Test: An analysis of the three-step test in international and EC Copyright Law*. The Hague: Kluwer Law International.

Sentencing Guidelines Council (2009) *Overarching Principles: Sentencing youths*. London: Sentencing Guidelines Council (November).

Sereny, G. (1998) *Cries Unheard: The story of Mary Bell*. London: Macmillan.

Shannon, R. (2001) *A Press Free and Responsible: Self regulation and the press complaints commission, 1991–2001*. London: John Murray Publications.

Simon, I. (2006a) 'The introduction of performers' moral rights: Part 1', *European Intellectual Property Review*, 28, 552–561.

Simon, I. (2006b) 'The introduction of performers' moral rights: Part 2', *European Intellectual Property Review*, 28(12), 600–610.

Simpson, A. W. B. (2004) *Human Rights and the End of Empire. Britain and the genesis of the European Convention.* Oxford: Oxford University Press.

Singh, S. and Ernst, E. (2009) *Trick or Treatment: Alternative medicine on trial.* London: Transworld Publishing.

Smartt, U. (1999) 'Constitutionalism in the British Overseas Territories', *European Journal of Crime, Criminal Law and Criminal Justice*, 3 (June), 300–314.

Smartt, U. (2004) 'Stay out of jail: Performance, multimedia and copyright laws', in L. Hill and H. Paris, *Guerrilla Performance and Multimedia* (2nd edn). London/New York: Continuum Press.

Smartt, U. (2006) *Media Law for Journalists.* London: Sage Publications.

Smartt, U. (2007) 'Who still observes the law of contempt?', *Justice of the Peace Journal*, 171 (3 February), 76–83.

Smartt, U. (2008) 'Crime and punishment in the Turks and Caicos Islands', *Justice of the Peace Journal*, 172 (April), 200–203.

Smartt, U. (2010a) 'Criminal actions – copyright in the digital age', *Criminal Law & Justice Weekly*, 174(42), 645–647.

Smartt, U. (2010b) 'Crime and punishment in the Turks and Caicos Islands', in J. P. Stamatel and H.-E. Sung (vol. eds); G. R. Newman (ed.) *Crime and Punishment Around the World. The Americas*, Vol. 2, pp. 322–328. Santa Barbara, CA, Denver, CO and Oxford, UK: ABC-CLIO, LLC-Greenwood Press.

Smartt, U. (2011) 'Twitter undermines superinjunctions', *Communications Law*, 16(4), 135–140.

Smartt, U. (2012) 'Safety first: the Ryan Giggs superinjunction Part 2 of March 2012', *Communications Law*, 17(2), 50–52.

Smartt, U. (2014) *Optimize Public Law.* Oxford: Routledge.

Smith, J. C. *The Law of Theft*; see Ormerod and Williams (2007).

Smith, T. B. (1964) 'Civil jury trial: A Scottish assessment', *Virginia Law Review*, 1.

Solzhenitsyn, A. (1962) *One Day in the Life of Ivan Denisovich.* London: Penguin. (reprinted in 1996. London: Bantam Press).

Spencer, J. R. (1977) 'Criminal libel: A skeleton in the cupboard', *Criminal Law Review*, 383.

Spencer, J. R. (1989) *Jackson's Machinery of Justice.* (8th edn of the original publication by Professor R. M. Jackson in 1903). Cambridge: Cambridge University Press.

Spencer, J. R. (2000) 'Naming and shaming young offenders', *Cambridge Law Journal*, 59(3), 466–8.

Spencer, J. R. (2006) 'Can juvenile offenders be "named and shamed" when they are adults?' *Justice of the Peace & Local Government Law*, 170(34), 644–647.

Spurrier, M. (2012) '*Gillberg v Sweden*: towards a right of access to information under Article 10?' *European Human Rights Law Review*, 5, 551–558.

Stahl, J. M (1997) 'CDA is DOA: Zoning the information superhighway to exclude adult motels and community service organisations', *Entertainment Law Review*, 8(5), 166–175.

Stair, Viscount (The Stair Society, 1981) *The Tercentenary of the First Publication of Viscount Stair's Institutions of the Laws of Scotland.* Papers delivered at a Conference held in the University of Glasgow. The Stair Society. Edinburgh: W. Green & Son.

Stein, E. (2000) *Thoughts from a Bridge. A retrospective of writings on new Europe and American federalism.* Michigan, MI: University of Michigan Press.

Stephen, J. F. (1883) *A History of the Criminal Law of England.* London: Macmillan and Co.

Stephens, K., Fuller, Z. and Atherton, H. (2013) 'Copyright: *Norwich Pharmacal* orders against ISPs', *Chartered Institute of Patent Agents Journal*, 42(1), 45.

Sterling, A. L. (2008) *World Copyright Law* (3rd edn). London: Sweet & Maxwell.

Strachan, J. F., Lord (1959) *Civil Jury Trial in Scotland*, The Scotland Committee on Civil Jury Trial. Edinburgh: HMSO.

Strachan, J. and Singh, R. (2002) 'The right to privacy in English law', *European Human Rights Law Review*, 2, 129–161.

Synodinou, T. E. (2013) 'E-books, a new page in the history of copyright law?', *European Intellectual Property Review*, 35(4), 220–227.

Thomas, N. M. (2012) 'An education: the three-step test for development', *European Intellectual Property Review*, 34(4), 244–260.

Thompson, B. (ed.) (2012) *Ban This Filth! Letters from the Mary Whitehouse Archive*. London: Faber & Faber (Kindle edition).

Thornton, S. (2009) *Seven Days in the Art World*. London: Granta Books.

Tomkinson, M. and Gillard, M. (1980) *Nothing to Declare: Political corruptions of John Poulson*. Richmond, Surrey: Calder Publications.

Traub, F. (2009) 'Bob Dylan's Albums Protected in Germany', *Entertainment Law Review*, 20(4), 144–146.

Travers, P. and Reiff, S. (1974) *The Story Behind 'The Exorcist'*. New York: Signet Books.

Tugendhat and Christie (2011) *The Law of Privacy and The Media* (Warby, M., Mareham, N. and Christie. I., eds) (2nd edn). Oxford: Oxford University Press.

UK Music (2012) *Response to HM Government's Consultation on Copyright*. March 2012: www.ukmusic. org/assets/media/UK%20Music%20Submission%20-%20Consultation%20on%20 Copyright%20March%202012.pdf.

Van Vechten., V. (1903) 'The History and Theory of the Law of Defamation I', *Columbia Law Review*, 3, 546.

Van Vechten, V. (1904) 'The History and Theory of the Law of Defamation II', *Columbia Law Review*, 4, 33.

Wacks, R. (2013) *Privacy and Media Freedom*. Oxford: Oxford University Press.

Walker, C. and Starmer, K. (1999) *Miscarriages of Justice: A review of justice in error*. London: Blackstone Press.

Wall, L. J. (1995) 'Publicity in Children Cases – a Personal View', *Family Law*, 25, 136.

Wallis, R., Baden-Fuller, C., Kretschmer, M. and Klimis, G.M (1999) 'Contested collective administration of Intellectual Property Rights in music: The challenge to the principles of reciprocity and solidarity', *European Journal of Communication*, 14(1), 5–35.

Ward, J. (1993) *Ambushed*. London: Vermillion.

Warren, S. D. and Brandeis, L. D. (1890) 'The right to privacy', *Harvard Law Review*, 4(5) (15 December 1890), 193–220.

Weber, R. H. (in collaboration with M. Grosz and R. Weber) (2010) *Shaping Internet Governance: Regulatory challenges*. Zürich: Springer.

Wei, W. (2009) 'ISP indirect copyright liability: conflicts of rights on the internet', *Computer and Telecommunications Law Review*, 15(8), 181–185.

Whitty, N. R. (2005) 'Rights of personality, property rights and the human body in Scots law', *Edinburgh Law Review*, 9(2), 194–237.

Whitty, N. R. and Zimmermann, R. (eds) (2009) *Rights of Personality in Scots Law: A Comparative Perspective*. Dundee: Dundee University Press.

Williams, A. T. (2012) *A Very British Killing: The death of Baha Mousa*. London: Jonathan Cape.

Williams, D. G. T. (1972) 'Oz and obscenity', *Cambridge Law Journal*, 30(1).

Wilmshurst P. (2011) 'The regulation of medical devices', *British Medical Journal*, 342, 1093–4.

Wilmshurst P. (2012) 'CLOSURE 1 seen through the MIST', *British Medical Journal*, 344, 51.

Winfield, P. H. (1937) *A Textbook of the Law of Tort*. London: Sweet & Maxwell.

WIPO (World Intellectual Property Organization) (2003) *WIPO Study on Limitations and Exceptions of Copyright and Related Rights in the Digital Environment*. Study by the Standing Committee on Copyright and Related Rights. 9th Session, Geneva, June 23 to 27, 2003: www.wipo.int/ edocs/mdocs/copyright/en/sccr_9/sccr_9_7.pdf.

Witzleb, N. (2009) 'Justifying gain-based remedies for invasions of privacy', *Oxford Journal of Legal Studies*, 29, 325.

Wragg, P. (2013a) 'Time to end the tyranny: Leveson and the failure of the fourth estate', *Communications Law*, 18(1), 11–20.

Wragg, P. (2013b) 'Mill's dead dogma: the value of truth to free speech jurisprudence', *Public Law*, April, 363–385.

Wulff, B. and Maibaum, N. (2012) Jenseits des Protokolls. München: Riva Verlag.

Wright, P. (1987) *Spycatcher: The candid autobiography of a secret intelligence officer*. Australia: William Heinemann and Viking Press.

Wylie, A. B. and Crossan, S. J. (2010) *Introductory Scots Law: Theory and practice* (2nd edn). London: Hodder Gibson.

Young, J. (1981) 'The Contempt of Court Act 1981', *British Journal of Law & Society*, 8(2), 243ff.

Zimmermann, R. (1996) *The Law of Obligations: Roman foundations of the civilian tradition*. Oxford: Clarendon Press.

Zuckerman, A. (2010) 'Super injunctions – curiosity-suppressant orders undermine the rule of law', *Civil Justice Quarterly*, 29, 131.

Internet Sources and Useful Websites

Access Info Europe: www.access-info.org
Advertising Standards Authority (ASA): www.asa.org.uk
Association of American Publishers: www.publishers.org
Association of Independent Music (AIM): www.musicindie.com
Associated Press (AP) (Global News Network): www.ap.org
Association for Journalism Education (AJE): www.ajeuk.org
Association for Television on Demand (ATVOD): http://atvod.co.uk
Attorney General's Office (England & Wales): www.attorneygeneral.gov.uk
Authors Guild: www.authorsguild.org
Authors' Licensing and Collecting Society (ALCS): www.alcs.co.uk
BBC News Online: www.bbc.co.uk/news
BBC Northern Ireland Service online: www.bbc.co.uk/northernireland
BMI – Broadcast Music, Inc: www.bmi.com
British Board of Film Classification (BBFC): www.bbfc.co.uk
British Phonographic Industry (BPI): www.bpi.co.uk
CISAC (Confédération Internationale des Sociétés d'Auteurs et Compositeurs – the International Confederation of Societies of Authors and Composers: www.cisac.org
CNN International: http://edition.cnn.com
Court martial results: https://www.gov.uk/government/publications/court-martial-results-from-the-military-court-centres
Creative Scotland: www.creativescotland.com
Department for Business, Innovation and Skills: www.bis.gov.uk
Department for Culture, Media and Sport: www.culture.gov.uk
Deutsche Presseagentur (German News Agency): www.dpa.de/en/unternehmenswelt/index.html
English PEN: www.englishpen.org
European Advertising Standards Alliance (EASA): www.easa-alliance.org
European Commission: http://ec.europa.eu
European Court of Human Rights: www.echr.coe.int
European Court of Justice (ECJ): www.curia.eu
European Parliament: www.europarl.eu
European Patent Office: www.european-patent-office.org
Featured Artists Coalition (FAC): www.featuredartistscoalition.com
Federation Against Copyright Theft (FACT): www.fact-uk.org.uk
Freedom of Information Advocates: www.freedominfo.org
GEMA (Gesellschaft für musikalische Aufführungs- und mechanische Vervielfältigungsrechte – Musical copyright association): www.gema.de
Hansard: www.parliament.the-stationery-office.co.uk/pa/cm/cmhansrd.htm
HUDOC (database for case-law of the European Court of Human Rights): http://hudoc.echr.coe.int/sites/eng
Index on Censorship: www.indexoncensorship.org
Independent Press Standards Organisation (IPSO): www.ipso.co.uk
Intellectual Property Office UK: www.ipo.gov.uk
International Federation of Journalists: www.ifj.org/en
International Federation of the Phonographic Industry (IFPI): www.ifpi.org

Information Commissioner's Office (ICO): www.ico.gov.uk
International Confederation of Societies of Authors and Composers (Confèdération Internationale des Sociétés d'Auteurs et Compositeurs): www.cisac.org
International Press Institute (IPI): www.freemedia.at
Internet Corporation for Assigned Names and Numbers (ICANN): www.icann.org
Internet Watch Foundation (IWF): www.iwf.org.uk
Irish Department of Justice and Law Reform: www.justice.ie
Irish Parliament for the Dáil – Houses of the Oireachtas: www.oireachtas.ie
Irish Patent Office: www.patentsoffice.ie
Mechanical Copyright Protection Society (MCPS) – see: PRS
Music Managers Forum (MMF): www.musicmanagersforum.co.uk
Music Publishers Association (for sheet/printed music): www.mpaonline.org.uk
Musicians' Union (MU): www.musiciansunion.org.uk
National Archives: www.nationalarchives.gov.uk
National Union of Journalists (NUJ): www.nuj.org.uk
Northern Ireland Assembly: www.niassembly.gov.uk
Northern Ireland Courts and Tribunal Service: www.courtsni.gov.uk
Ofcom (Office of Communications): www.ofcom.org.uk
Office for Harmonization in the Internal Market (OHIM) (EU Trademark Office): http://oami.europa.eu
Office of Fair Trading (OFT): www.oft.gov.uk
Office of National Statistics (UK): www.statistics.gov.uk
Office of Public Sector Information: www.opsi.gov.uk/psi
Parliament, UK: www.parliament.uk
Performing Right Society (PRS): www.prsformusic.com
Phonographic Performance Ltd (PPL): www.ppluk.com
PhonepayPlus (regulates phone-paid services in the UK): www.phonepayplus.org.uk
Press Association: www.pressassociation.com
Scots Law Online: www.scottishlaw.org.uk
Scottish Court Service: www.scotcourts.gov.uk
Scottish Information Commissioner: www.itspublicknowledge.info/home/ScottishInformationCommissioner.asp
Scottish Law Commission: www.scotlawcom.gov.uk
Scottish Parliament: www.scottish.parliament.uk
Service Prosecuting Authority (SPA) (Court Martial): http://spa.independent.gov.uk
Society of Authors: www.societyofauthors.net
Society of Editors: www.societyofeditors.co.uk
Trading Standards Institute (TSI): www.tradingstandards.gov.uk
UK Copyright Service: www.copyrightservice.co.uk
US Patent Office (Patents & Trademarks): www.uspto.gov
Video Standards Council (VSC): www.videostandards.org.uk
Welsh Music Foundation: www.welshmusicfoundation.com
WIPO Phonogram Treaties: www.wipo.int/treaties/en/ip/phonograms
World Intellectual Property Organization (WIPO): www.wipo.int
World Summit on the Information Society (WSIS): www.itu.int/wsis
World Trade Organization (WTO): www.wto.org

Index